Presented to Minnie
by B. M. T.
Jan 1st / 59

"Should auld acquaintance be forgot
And never brought to mind
Should auld acquaintance be forgot
And days of auld lang syne?

Robert Burns.

THE

Poetical and Prose Works

OF

ROBERT BURNS.

WITH LIFE, NOTES AND CORRESPONDENCE BY

A. C. CUNNINGHAM, ESQ:

AND ILLUSTRATIONS.

But á the pleasures eer I saw,
Though three times doubled fairly.

HARTFORD
WILLIAM J. HAMERSLEY.

THE

Poetical and Prose Works

OF

ROBERT BURNS:

WITH

LIFE, NOTES AND CORRESPONDENCE:

BY

A. CUNNINGHAM, ESQ.

WITH

Original Pieces from the Collection of Sir Egerton Brydges, Bart.

AND

Illustrations.

HARTFORD:
PUBLISHED BY WM. JAS. HAMERSLEY.
1855.

Illustrations.

Contents.

Life of Robert Burns.

Poetical Works of Robert Burns.

Correspondence of Burns.

Life of Burns.

Life of Robert Burns.

Initiatory Remarks.

THOUGH the dialect in which many of the happiest effusions of ROBERT BURNS are composed be peculiar to Scotland, yet his reputation has extended itself beyond the limits of that country, and his poetry has been admired as the offspring of original genius, by persons of taste in every part of the sister islands. It seems proper, therefore, to write the memoirs of his life, not with the view of their being read by Scotchmen only, but also by natives of England, and of other countries where the English language is spoken or understood.

Robert Burns was, in reality, what he has been represented to be, a Scottish peasant. To render the incidents of his humble story generally intelligible, it seems, therefore, advisable to prefix some observations on the character and situation of the order to which he belonged—a class of men distinguished by many peculiarities: by this means we shall form a more correct notion of the advantages with which he started, and of the obstacles which he surmounted. A few observations on the Scottish peasantry will not, perhaps, be found unworthy of attention in other respects—and the subject is, in a great measure, new. Scotland has produced persons of high distinction in every branch of philosophy and literature; and her history, while a separate and independent nation, has been successfully explored. But the present character of the people was not then formed, the nation then presented features similar to those which the feudal system and the Catholic religion had diffused over Europe, modified, indeed, by the peculiar nature of her territory and climate. The Reformation, by which such important changes were produced on the national character, was speedily followed by the accession of the Scottish monarchs to the English throne; and the period which elapsed from that accession to the Union, has been rendered memorable, chiefly, by those bloody convulsions in which both divisions of the island were involved, and which, in a considerable degree, concealed from the eye of the historian the domestic history of the people, and the gradual variations in their condition and manners. Since the Union, Scotland, though the seat of two unsuccessful attempts to restore the house of Stuart to the throne, has enjoyed a comparative tranquillity; and it is since this period that the present character of her peasantry has been in a great measure formed, though the political causes affecting it are to be traced to the previous acts of her separate legislature.

A slight acquaintance with the peasantry of Scotland will serve to convince an unprejudiced observer, that they possess a degree of intelligence not generally found among the same class of men in the other countries of Europe. In the very humblest condition of the Scottish peasants, every one can read, and most persons are more or less skilled in writing and arithmetic; and, under the disguise of their uncouth appearance, and of their peculiar manners and dialect, a stranger will discover that they possess a curiosity, and have obtained a degree of information, corresponding to these acquirements.

These advantages they owe to the legal provision made by the Parliament of Scotland in 1646, for the establishment of a school in every parish throughout the kingdom, for the express purpose of educating the poor—a law which may challenge comparison with any act of legislation to be found in the records of history, whether we consider the wisdom of the ends in view, the simplicity of the means employed, or the provisions—made to render these means effectual to their purpose. This excellent statute was repealed on the accession of Charles II. in 1660, together with all the other laws passed during the Commonwealth, as not being sanctioned by the Royal assent. It slept during the reigns of Charles and James II., but was re-enacted precisely in the same terms, by the Scottish Parliament, in 1696, after the Revolution; and this is the last provision on the subject. Its effects on the national character may be considered to have commenced about the period of the Union, and doubtless it cooperated with the peace and security arising from that happy event, in producing the extraordinary change in favour of industry and good morals, which the character of the common people of Scotland has since undergone.

The church establishment of Scotland happily coincides with the institution just mentioned, which may be called its school establishment. The clergyman, being everywhere resident in his particular parish, becomes the natural patron and superintendant of the parish school, and is enabled in various ways to promote the comfort of the teacher, and the proficiency of the scholars. The teacher himself is often a candidate for holy orders, who, during the long course of study and probation required in the Scottish church, renders the time which can be spared from his professional studies useful to others as well as to himself, by assuming the respectable character of a schoolmaster. It is common for the established schools, even in the country parishes of Scotland, to enjoy the means of classical instruction; and many of the farmers, and some even of the cottagers, submit to much privation, that they may obtain, for one of their sons at least, the precarious advantage of a learned education. The difficulty to be surmounted arises indeed, not from the expense of instructing their children, but from the charge of supporting them. In the country parish schools, the English language, writing and accounts, are generally taught at the rate of six shillings, and Latin at the rate of ten or twelve shillings, per annum. In the towns the prices are somewhat higher.

It would be improper in this place to inquire minutely into the degree of instruction received at these seminaries, or to attempt any precise estimate of its effects, either on the individuals who are the subjects of this instrnction, or on the community to which they belong. That it is, on the whole, favourable to industry and morals, though doubtless with some individual exceptions, seems to be proved by the most striking and decisive experience; and it is equally clear, that it is the cause of that spirit of emigration and of adventure so prevalent among the Scotch. Knowledge has, by Lord Verulam, been denominated power; by others it has, with less propriety, been denominated virtue or happiness: we may with confidence consider it as motion. A human being, in proportion as he is informed, has his wishes enlarged, as well as the means of gratifying those wishes. He may be considered as taking within the sphere of his vision a large portion of the globe on which we tread, and discovering advantage at a greater distance on its surface. His desires or ambition, once excited. are stimulated by his imagination; and distant and uncertain objects, giving freer scope to the operation of this faculty, often acquire, in the mind of the youthful adventurer, an attraction from their very distance and uncertainty. If, therefore, a greater degree of instruction be given to the peasantry of a country comparatively poor, in the neighbourhood of other countries rich in natural and acquired advantages, and if the barriers be removed that kept them separate, emigration from the former to the latter will take place to a certain extent, by laws nearly as uniform as those by which heat diffuses itself among surrounding bodies, or water finds its level when left to its natural course. By the articles of the Union, the barrier was broken down which divided the two British nations, and knowledge and poverty poured the adventurous natives of the north over the fertile plains of England; and more especially, over the colonies which she had settled in the east and in the west. The stream of population continues to flow from the north to the south, for the causes that originally impelled it continue to operate; and the richer country is constantly invigorated by the accession of an informed and hardy race of men, educated in poverty, and prepared for hardship and danger; patient of labour and prodigal of life.

The preachers of the Reformation in Scotland were disciples of Calvin, and brought with them the temper as well as the tenets of that celebrated heresiarch. The Presbyterian form of worship and of church government was endeared to the people, from its being established by themselves. It was endeared to them, also, by the struggle it had to maintain with the Catholic and Protestant episcopal churches; over both of which, after a hundred years of fierce, and sometimes bloody contention, it finally triumphed, receiving the countenance of government and the sanction of law. During this long period of contention and of suffering, the temper of the people became more and more obstinate and bigoted; and the nation received that deep tinge of fanaticism which coloured their public transactions, as well as their private virtues, and of which evident traces may be found in our own times. When the public schools were established, the instruction communicated in them partook of the religious character of the people. The Catechism of the Westminster Divines was the universal school-book, and was put into the hands of the young peasant as soon as he had acquired a knowledge of his alphabet; and his first exercise in the art of reading, introduced him to the most mysterious doctrines of the Christian faith. This practice is continued in our own times. After the Assembly's Catechism, the Proverbs of Solomon, and the New and Old Testament follow in regular succession; and the scholar departs, gifted with the knowledge of the sacred writings, and receiving their doctrines according to the interpretation of the Westminster Confession of Faith. Thus, with the instruction of infancy in the schools of Scotland, are blended the dogmas of the national church; and hence the first and most constant exercise of ingenuity among the peasantry of Scotland, is displayed in religious disputation. With a strong attachment to the national creed, is conjoined a bigoted preference for certain forms of worship; the source of which would be often altogether obscure, if we did not recollect that the ceremonies of the Scottish Church were framed in direct opposition, in every point, to those of the Church of Rome.

The eccentricities of conduct, and singularities of opinion and manners, which characterised the English sectaries in the last century, afforded a subject for the comic muse of Butler, whose pictures lose their interest since their archetypes are lost. Some of the peculiarities common among the more rigid disciples of Calvinism in Scotland, in the present times, have given scope to the ridicule of Burns, whose humour is equal to Butler's, and whose drawings from living manners are singularly expressive and exact. Unfortunately, the correctness of his taste did not always correspond with the strength of his genius.

The information and the religious education of the peasantry of Scotland, promote sedateness of conduct, and habits of thought and reflection. These good qualities are not counteracted by the establishment of poor laws. Happily, in Scotland, the same legislature which established a system of instruction for the poor, resisted the introduction of a legal provision for the support of poverty; hence it will not appear surprising, if the Scottish peasantry have a more than usual share of prudence and reflection, if they approach nearer than persons of their order usually do to the definition of a man—that of "a being that looks before and after." These observations must indeed be taken with many exceptions; the favourable operation of the causes just mentioned is counteracted by others of an opposite tendency; and the subject, if fully examined, would lead to discussions of great extent.

When the Reformation was established in Scotland, instrumental music was banished from the churches, as savouring too much of "profane minstrelsy." Instead of being regulated by an instrument, the voices of the congregation are led and directed by a person under the name of a precentor, and the people are all expected to join in the tune which he chooses for the psalm which is to be sung. Church music is therefore a part of the education of the peasantry of Scotland, in which they are usually instructed in the long winter nights by the parish schoolmaster, who is generally the precentor, or by itinerant teachers, more celebrated for their powers of voice. This branch of education had, in the last reign, fallen into some neglect, but was revived about thirty or forty years ago, when the music itself was reformed and improved. The Scottish system of psalmody is, however, radically bad. Destitute of taste or harmony, it forms a striking contrast with the delicacy and pathos of the profane airs. Our poet, it will be found, was taught church music, in which, however he attained little proficiency.

That dancing should also be very generally a part of the education of the Scottish peasantry, will surprise those who have only seen this description of men; and still more those who reflect on the rigid spirit of Calvinism, with which the nation is so deeply affected, and to which this recreation is so strongly abhorrent. The winter is also the season when they acquire dancing, and, indeed, almost all their other instruction. They are taught to dance by persons generally of their own number, many of whom work at daily labour during the summer months. The school is usually a barn, and the arena for the performers is generally a clay floor. The dome is lighted by candles stuck in one end of a cloven stick, the other end of which is thrust into the wall. Reels, strathspeys, contra-dances, and hornpipes, are here practised. The jig, so much in favour among the English peasantry, has no place among them. The attachment of the people of Scotland of every rank, and particularly of the peasantry, to this amusement, is very great. After the labours of the day are over, young men and women walk many miles, in the cold and dreary nights of winter, to these country dancing-schools; and the instant that the violin sounds a Scottish air, fatigue seems to vanish, the toil-bent rustic becomes erect, his features brighten with sympathy, every nerve seems to thrill with sensation, and every artery to vibrate with life. These rustic performers are indeed less to be admired for grace than for agility and animation, and for their accurate observance of time. Their modes of dancing, as well as their tunes, are common to every rank in Scotland, and are now generally known. In our own day they have penetrated into England, and have established themselves even in the circle of royalty. In another generation they will be naturalised in every part of the island.

The prevalence of this taste, or rather passion, for dancing, among a people so deeply tinctured with the spirit and doctrines of Calvin, is one of those contradictions which the philosophic observer so often finds in national character and manners. It is probably to be ascribed to the Scottish music, which, throughout all its varieties, is so full of sensibility, and which, in its livelier strains, awakes those vivid emotions that find in dancing their natural solace and relief.

This triumph of the music of Scotland over the spirit of the established religion, has not however, been obtained, without long-continued and obstinate struggles. The numerous sectaries who dissent from the Establishment on account of the relaxation which they perceive, or think they perceive, in the Church, from her original doctrines and discipline, universally condemn the practice of dancing, and the schools where it is taught; and the more elderly and serious part of the people, of every persuasion, tolerate rather than approve these meetings of the young of both sexes, where dancing is practised to their spirit-stirring music, where care is dispelled, toil is forgotten, and prudence itself is sometimes lulled to sleep. (1)

The Reformation, which proved fatal to the rise of the other fine arts in Scotland, probably impeded, but could not obstruct, the progress of its music—a circumstance that will convince the impartial inquirer, that this music not only existed previously to that era, but had taken a firm hold of the nation, thus affording a proof of its antiquity stronger than any produced by the researches of our antiquaries. (2)

The impression which the Scottish music has made on the people, is deepened by its union with the national songs, of which various collections of unequal merit are before the public. These songs, like those of other nations, are many of them humorous, but they chiefly treat of love, war, and drinking. Love is the subject of the greater proportion. Without displaying the higher powers of the imagination, they exhibit a perfect knowledge of the human heart, and breathe a spirit of affection, and sometimes of delicate and romantic tenderness, not to be surpassed in modern poetry, and which the more polished strains of antiquity have seldom possessed.

The origin of this amatory character in the rustic muse of Scotland, or of the greater number of these love-songs themselves, it would be difficult to trace; they have accumulated in the silent lapse of time, and it is now perhaps impossible to give an arrangement of them in the order of their date, valuable as such a record of taste and manners would be. Their present influence on the character of the nation is, however, great and striking. To them we must attribute, in a great measure, the romantic passion which so often characterises the attachments of the humblest of the people of Scotland, to a degree that, if we mistake not, is seldom found in the same rank of society in other countries. The pictures of love and happiness exhibited in their rural songs, are early impressed on the mind of the peasant, and are rendered more attractive from the music with which they are united. They associate themselves with his own youthful emotions; they elevate the object as well as the nature of his attachment; and give to the impressions of sense the beautiful colours of imagination. Hence, in the course of his passion, a Scottish peasant often exerts a spirit of adventure, of which a Spanish cavalier need not be ashamed. After the labours of the day are over, he sets out for the habitation of his mistress, perhaps at many miles' distance, regardless of the length or the dreariness of the way. He approaches her in secrecy, under the disguise of night. A signal at the door or window, perhaps agreed on, and understood by none but her, gives information of his arrival; and sometimes it is repeated again and again, before the capricious fair-one will obey the summons. But if she favours his addresses, she escapes unobserved, and receives the vows of her lover under the gloom of twilight or the deeper shade of night. Interviews of this kind are the subjects of many of the Scottish songs, some of the most beautiful of which Burns has imitated or improved. In the art which they celebrate he was perfectly skilled; he knew and had practised all its mysteries. Intercourse of this sort is indeed universal, even in the humblest condition of man in every region of the earth. But it is not unnatural to suppose that it may exist in a greater degree, and in a more romantic form, among the peasantry of a country who are supposed to be more than commonly instructed;—who find in their rural songs expressions for their youthful emotions;—and in whom the embers of passion are continually fanned by the breathings of a music full of tenderness and sensibility. The direct influence of physical causes on the attachment between the sexes is comparatively small, but it is modified by moral causes beyond any other affection of the mind. Of these, music and poetry are the chief. Among the snows of Lapland, and under the burning sun of Angola, the savage is seen hastening to his mistress, and everywhere he beguiles the weariness of his journey with poetry and song. (3)

In appreciating the happiness and virtue of a community, there is perhaps no single criterion on which so much dependence may be placed, as the state of the intercourse between the sexes. Where this displays ardour of attachment, accompanied by purity of conduct, the character and the influence of women rise in society, our imperfect nature mounts in the scale of moral excellence; and, from the source of this single affection, a stream of felicity descends, which branches into a thousand rivulets that enrich and adorn the field of life. Where the attachment between the sexes sinks into an appetite, the heritage of our species is comparatively poor, and man approaches the condition of *the brutes that perish.* "If we could with safety indulge the pleasing supposition that Fingal lived and that Ossian sung" (4), Scotland, judging from this criterion, might be considered as ranking high in happiness and virtue in very remote ages. To appreciate her situation by the same criterion in our own times, would be a delicate and a difficult undertaking. After considering the probable influence of her popular songs and her national music, and examining how far the effects to be expected from these are supported by facts, the inquirer would also have to examine the influence of other causes, and particularly of her civil and ecclesiastical institutions, by which the character, and even the manners of a people, though silently and slowly, are often powerfully controlled. In the point of view in which we are considering the subject, the ecclesiastical establishments of Scotland may be supposed peculiarly favourable to purity of conduct. The dissoluteness of manners among the Catholic clergy, which preceded, and in some measure produced the Reformation, led to an extraordinary strictness on the part of the reformers, and especially in that particular in which the licentiousness of the clergy had been carried to its greatest height—the intercourse between the sexes. On this point, as on all others connected with austerity of manners, the disciples of Calvin assumed a greater severity than those of the Protestant Episcopal church. The punishment of illicit connection between the sexes was, throughout all Europe, a province which the clergy assumed to themselves; and the church of Scotland, which at the Reformation renounced so many powers and privileges, at that period took this crime under her more especial jurisdiction. Where pregnancy takes place without marriage, the condition of the female causes the discovery; and it is on her, therefore, in the first instance, that the clergy and elders exercise their zeal. After examination before the kirk-session, touching the circumstance of her guilt, she must endure a public penance and sustain a public rebuke from the pulpit, for three Sabbaths successively, in the face of the congregation to which she belongs, and thus have her weakness exposed, and her shame blazoned. The sentence is the same with respect to the male, but how much lighter the punishment! It is well known that this dreadful law, worthy of the iron minds of Calvin and of Knox, has often led to consequences, at the very mention of which human nature recoils. (5)

While the punishment of incontinence prescribed by the institutions of Scotland is severe, the culprits have an obvious method of avoiding it, afforded them by the law respecting marriage, the validity of which requires neither the ceremonies of the church, nor any other ceremonies, but simply the deliberate acknowledgement of each other as husband and wife, made by the parties before witnesses, or in any other way that gives legal evidence of such an acknowledgement having taken place. And as the parties themselves fix the date of their marriage, an opportunity is thus given to avoid the punishment, and repair the consequences, of illicit gratification. Such a degree of laxity respecting so serious a contract might produce much confusion in the descent of property without a still farther indulgence; but the law of Scotland, legitimating all children born before wedlock, on the subsequent marriage of their parents, renders the actual date of the marriage itself of little consequence. Marriages contracted in Scotland without the ceremonies of the church, are considered as *irregular*, and the parties usually submit to a *rebuke* for their conduct, in the face of their respective congregations, which is not however necessary to render the marriage valid. Burns, whose marriage, it will appear, was *irregular*, does not seem to have undergone this part of the discipline of the church.

Thus, though the institutions of Scotland are in many particulars favourable to a conduct among the peasantry founded upon foresight and reflection, on the subject of marriage the reverse of this is true. Irregular marriages, it may be naturally supposed, are often improvident ones, in whatever rank of society they occur. The children of such marriages, poorly endowed by their parents, find a certain degree of instruction of easy acquisition, but the comforts of life, and the gratifications of ambition, they find of more difficult attainment in their native soil; and thus the marriage laws of Scotland conspire, with other circumstances, to produce that habit of emigration, and spirit of adventure, for which the people are so remarkable.

The manners and appearance of the Scottish peasantry do not bespeak to a stranger the degree of their cultivation. In their own country, their industry is inferior to that of the same description of men in the southern division of the island. Industry and the useful arts reached Scotland later than England; and though their advance has been rapid there, the effects produced are as yet far inferior both in reality and in appearance. The Scottish farmers have in general neither the opulence nor the comforts of those of England, neither vest the same capital in the soil, nor receive from it the same return. Their clothing, their food, and their habitations, are almost everywhere inferior. (6) Their appearance in these respects corresponds with the appearance of their country; and under the operation of patient industry, both are improving. Industry and the useful arts came later into Scotland than into England, because the security of property came later. With causes of internal agitation and warfare, similar to those which occurred to the more southern nation, the people of Scotland were exposed to more imminent hazards and to more extensive and destructive spoliation, from external war. Occupied in the maintenance of their independence against their more powerful neighbours, to this purpose were necessarily sacrificed the arts of peace, and, at certain periods, the flower of their population. And when the union of the crowns produced a security from national wars with England, for the century succeeding, the civil wars common to both divisions of the island, and the dependence, perhaps the necessary dependence, of the Scottish councils on those of the more powerful kingdom, counteracted this disadvantage. Even the union of the British nations was not, from obvious causes, immediately followed by all the benefits which it was ultimately destined to produce. At length, however, these benefits are distinctly felt, and generally acknowledged. Property is secure; manufactures and commerce increasing; and agriculture is rapidly improving in Scotland. As yet indeed, the farmers are not, in general, enabled to make improvements out of their own capitals, as in England; but the landholders who have seen and felt the advantages resulting from them, contribute towards them with a liberal hand. Hence property, as well as population, is accumulating rapidly on the Scottish soil; and the nation, enjoying a great part of the blessings of Englishmen, and retaining several of their own happy institutions, might be considered, if confidence could be placed in human foresight, to be as yet only in an early stage of their progress. Yet there are obstructions in their way. To the cultivation of the soil are opposed the extent and the strictness of the entails; to the improvement of the people, the rapidly increasing use of spirituous liquors, a detestable practice, which includes in its consequences almost every evil, physical and moral. (7) The peculiarly social disposition of the Scottish peasantry exposes them to this practice. This disposition, which is fostered by their national songs and music, is perhaps characteristic of the nation at large. Though the source of many pleasures, it counteracts, by its consequences, the effects of their patience, industry, and frugality, both at home and abroad, of which those especially who have witnessed the progress of Scotsmen in other countries must have known many striking instances.

Since the Union, the manners and language of the people of Scotland have no longer a standard among themselves, but are tried by the standard of the nation to which they are united. Though their habits are far from being flexible, yet it is evident that their manners and dialect are undergoing a rapid change. Even the farmers of the present day appear to have less of the peculiarities of their country in their speech than the men of letters of the last generation. Burns, who never left the island, nor penetrated farther into England than Carlisle on the one hand, or Newcastle on the other, had less of the Scottish dialect than Hume, who lived for many years in the best society of England and France—or perhaps than Robertson, who wrote the English language in a style of such purity; and if he had been in other respects fitted to take a lead in the British House of Commons, his pronunciation would neither have fettered his eloquence, nor deprived it of its due effect.

A striking particular in the character of the Scottish peasantry, is one which it is hoped will not be lost—the strength of their domestic attachments. The privations to which many parents submit for the good of their children, and particularly to obtain for them instruction, which they consider as the chief good, has already been noticed. If their children live and prosper, they have their certain reward, not merely as witnessing, but as sharing of their prosperity. Even in the humblest ranks of the peasantry, the earnings of the children may generally be considered as at the disposal of their parents: perhaps in no country is so large a portion of the wages of labour applied to the support and comfort of those whose days of labour are past. A similar strength of attachment extends through all the domestic relations. Our poet partook largely of this amiable characteristic of his humble compeers: he was also strongly tinctured with another striking feature which belongs to them—a partiality for his native country, of which many proofs may be found in his writings. This, it must be confessed, is a very strong and general sentiment among the natives of Scotland, differing, however, in its character, according to the character of the different minds in which it is found—in some appearing a selfish prejudice, in others a generous affection.

An attachment to the land of their birth is, indeed, common to all men. It is found among the inhabitants of every region of the earth, from the arctic to the ant-arctic circle, in all the vast variety of climate, of surface, and of civilisation. To analyse this general sentiment, to trace it through the mazes of association up to the primary affection in which it has its source, would neither be a difficult nor an unpleasing labour. On the first consideration of the subject, we should perhaps expect to find this attachment strong in proportion to the physical advantages of the soil; but inquiry, far from confirming this supposition, seems rather to lead to an opposite conclusion. In those fertile regions where beneficent nature yields almost spontaneously whatever is necessary to human wants, patriotism, as well as every other generous sentiment, seems weak and languid. In countries less richly endowed, where the comforts, and even necessaries of life, must be purchased by patient toil, the affections of the mind, as well as the faculties of the understanding, improve under exertion, and patriotism flourishes amidst its kindred virtues. Where it is necessary to combine for mutual defence, as well as for the supply of common wants, mutual good-will springs from mutual difficulties and labours, the social affections unfold themselves, and extend from the men with whom we live to the soil on which we tread. It will perhaps be found, indeed, that our affections cannot be originally called forth, but by objects capable, or supposed capable, of feeling our sentiments, and of returning them; but when once excited, they are strengthened by exercise; they are expanded by the powers of imagination, and seize more especially on those inanimate parts of creation, which form the theatre on which we have first felt the alternations of joy and sorrow, and first tasted the sweets of sympathy and regard. If this reasoning be just, the love of our country, although modified, and even extinguished in individuals by the chances and changes of life, may be presumed, in our general reasonings, to be strong among a people, in proportion to their social, and more especially to their domestic affections. Under free governments it is found more active than under despotic ones, because, as the individual becomes of more consequence in the community, the community becomes of more consequence to him. In small states it is generally more active than in large ones, for the same reason, and also because the independence of a small community being maintained with difficulty, and frequently endangered, sentiments of patriotism are more frequently excited. In mountainous countries it is generally found more active than in plains, because there the necessities of life often require a closer union of the inhabitants; and more especially, because in such countries, though less populous than plains, the inhabitants, instead of being scattered equally over the whole, are usually divided into small communities on the sides of their separate vallies, and on the banks of their respective streams—situations well calculated to call forth and to concentrate the social affections, amidst scenery that acts most powerfully on the sight, and makes a lasting impression on the memory. It may also be remarked, that mountainous countries are often peculiarly calculated to nourish sentiments of national pride and independence, from the influence of history on the affections of the mind. In such countries from their natural strength, inferior nations have maintained their independence against their more powerful neighbours, and valour, in all ages, has made its most successful efforts against oppression. Such countries present the fields of battle where the tide of invasion was rolled back, and whereon the ashes rest of those who have died in defence of their nation!

The operation of the various causes we have mentioned is doubtless more general and more permanent, where the scenery of a country, the peculiar manners of its inhabitants, and the martial achievements of their ancestors, are embodied in national songs, and united to national music. By this combination, the ties that attach men to the land of their birth are multiplied and strengthened, and the images of infancy, strongly associating with the generous affections, resist the influence of time, and of new impressions; they often survive in countries far distant, and amidst far different scenes, to the latest period of life, to soothe the heart with the pleasures of memory, when those of hope die away.

If this reasoning be just, it will explain to us why among the natives of Scotland, even of cultivated minds, we so generally find a partial attachment to the land of their birth, and why this is so strongly discoverable in the writings of Burns, who joined to the higher powers of the understanding the most ardent affections. Let not men of reflection think it a superfluous labour to trace the rise and progress of a character like his. Born in the condition of a peasant, he rose, by the force of his mind, into distinction and influence, and in his works has exhibited what are so rarely found, the charms of original genius. With a deep insight into the human heart, his poetry exhibits high powers of imagination—it displays, and as it were embalms, the peculiar manners of his country; and it may be considered as a monument, not to his own name only, but to the expiring genius of an ancient and once independent nation. In relating the incidents of his life, candour will prevent us from dwelling invidiously on those failings which justice forbids us to conceal; we will tread lightly over his yet warm ashes, and respect the laurels that shelter his untimely grave.

ROBERT BURNS was, as is well known, the son of a farmer in Ayrshire, and afterwards himself a farmer there; but, having been unsuccessful, he was about to emigrate to Jamaica. He had previously, however, attracted some notice by his poetical talents in the vicinity where he lived; and having published a small volume of his poems at

Kilmarnock, this drew upon him more general attention. In consequence of the encouragement he received, he repaired to Edinburgh, and there published, by subscription, an improved and enlarged edition of his poems, which met with extraordinary success. By the profits arising from the sale of this edition, he was enabled to enter on a farm in Dumfries-shire; and having married a person to whom he had been long attached, he retired to devote the remainder of his life to agriculture. He was again, however, unsuccessful; and, abandoning his farm, he removed into the town of Dumfries, where he filled an inferior office in the Excise, and where he terminated his life in July 1796, in his thirty-eighth year.

The strength and originality of his genius procured him the notice of many persons distinguished in the republic of letters, and, among others, that of Dr. Moore, well known for his Views of Society and Manners on the Continent of Europe, for his Zeluco, and various other works. To this gentleman our poet addressed a letter, after his first visit to Edinburgh, giving a history of his life, up to the period of his writing. In a composition never intended to see the light, elegance, or perfect correctness of composition, will not be expected. These, however, will be compensated by the opportunity of seeing our poet, as he gives the incidents of his life, unfold the peculiarities of his character with all the careless vigour and open sincerity of his mind.

"*Mauchline, 2nd August*, 1787.

"Sir.— For some months past I have been rambling over the country, but I am now confined with some lingering complaints, originating, as I take it, in the stomach. To divert my spirits a little in this miserable fog of *ennui*, I have taken a whim to give you a history of myself. My name has made some little noise in this country —you have done me the honour to interest yourself very warmly in my behalf; and I think a faithful account of what character of a man I am, and how I came by that character, may perhaps amuse you in an idle moment. I will give you an honest narrative, though I know it will be often at my own expense; for I assure you sir, I have, like Solomon, whose character, excepting in the trifling affair of *wisdom*, I sometimes think I resemble—I have, I say, like him *turned my eyes to behold madness and folly*, and, like him, too frequently shaken hands with their intoxicating friendship. * * * After you have perused these pages, should you think them trifling and impertinent, I only beg leave to tell you, that the poor author wrote them under some twitching qualms of conscience, arising from suspicion that he was doing what he ought not to do—a predicament he has more than once been in before."

"I have not the most distant pretensions to assume that character which the pye-coated guardians of escutcheons call a gentleman. When at Edinburgh last winter I got acquainted in the Herald's Office; and, looking through that granary of honours, I there found almost every name in the kingdom! but for me,

'My ancient but ignoble blood
Has crept thro' scoundrels ever since the flood.'

Gules, Purpure, Argent, &c., quite disowned me."

My father was of the north of Scotland, the son of a farmer, and was thrown by early misfortunes on the world at large, where, after many years' wanderings and sojournings, he picked up a pretty large quantity of observation and experience, to which I am indebted for most of my little pretensions to wisdom. I have met with few who understood *men, their manners, and their ways*, equal to him; but stubborn, ungainly integrity, and headlong ungovernable irascibility, are disqualifying circumstances, consequently I was born a very poor man's son. For the first six or seven years of my life, my father was gardener to a worthy gentleman of small estate in the neighbourhood of Ayr. Had he continued in that station, I must have marched off to be one of the little underlings about a farm-house; but it was his dearest wish and prayer to have it in his power to keep his children under his own eye till they could discern between good and evil; so, with with the assistance of his generous master, my father ventured on a small farm on his estate. At those years I was by no means a favourite with any body. I was a good deal noted for a retentive memory, a stubborn sturdy something in my disposition, and an enthusiastic idiotic piety. I say *idiotic* piety, because I was then but a child. Though it cost the schoolmaster some thrashings, I made an excellent English scholar, and by the time I was ten or eleven years of age, I was a critic in substantives, verbs, and particles. In my infant and boyish days, too, I owed much to an old woman who resided in the family, remarkable for her ignorance, credulity, and superstition. She had, I suppose, the largest collection in the country of tales and songs concerning devils, ghosts, fairies, brownies, witches, warlocks, spunkies, kelpies, elf-candles, dead-lights, wraiths, apparitions, cantraips, giants, enchanted towers, dragons, and other trumpery. This cultivated the latent seeds of poetry, but had so strong an effect on my imagination, that to this hour, in my nocturnal rambles, I sometimes keep a sharp look-out in suspicious places; and though nobody can be more sceptical than I am in such matters, yet it often takes an effort of philosophy to shake off these idle terrors. The earliest composition that I recollect taking pleasure in was The Vision of Mirza, and a hymn of Addison's, beginning, "How are thy servants blest, oh Lord!" I particularly remember one half-stanza, which was music to my boyish ear:—

'For though on dreadful whirls we hung
High on the broken wave.'

I met with these pieces in Mason's English Collection, one of my school-books. The two first books I ever read in private, and which gave me more pleasure than any two books I ever read since, were the Life of Hannibal, and The History of Sir William Wallace. Hannibal gave my young ideas such a turn, that I used to strut in raptures up and down after the recruiting drum and bagpipe, and wish myself tall enough to be a soldier; while the story of Wallace poured a Scottish prejudice into my veins, which will boil along there till the flood-gates of life shut in eternal rest."

"Polemical divinity about this time was putting the country half mad; and I, ambitious of shining in conversation parties on Sundays, between sermons, at funerals, &c., used, a few years afterwards, to puzzle Calvinism with so much heat and indiscretion, that I raised a hue and cry of heresy against me, which has not ceased to this hour."

"My vicinity to Ayr was of some advantage to me. My social disposition, when not checked by some modifications of spirited pride, was, like our Catechism definition of infinitude, *without bounds or limits.* I formed several connections with other younkers who possessed superior advantages, the *youngling* actors, who were busy in the rehearsal of parts in which they were shortly to appear on the stage of life, where, alas! I was destined to drudge behind the scenes. It is not commonly at this green age that our young gentry have a just sense of the immense distance between them and their ragged playfellows. It takes a few dashes into the world, to give the young great man that proper, decent, unnoticing disregard for the poor insignificant, stupid devils, the mechanics and peasantry around him, who were perhaps born in the same village. My young superiors never insulted the *clouterly* appearance of my plough-boy carcase, the two extremes of which were often exposed to all the inclemencies of all seasons. They would give me stray volumes of books: among them, even then, I could pick up some observations; and one, whose heart I am sure not even the *Munny Begum* scenes have tainted, helped me to a little French. Parting with these my young friends and benefactors, as they occasionally went off for the East or West Indies, was often to me a sore affliction; but I was soon called to more serious evils. My father's generous master died; the farm proved a ruinous bargain; and to clench the misfortune, we fell into the hands of a factor, who sat for the picture I have drawn of one in my tale of Twa Dogs. My father was advanced in life when he married; I was the eldest of seven children; and he, worn out by early hardships, was unfit for labour. My father's spirit was soon irritated, but not easily broken. There was a freedom in his lease in two years more; and to weather these two years, we retrenched our expenses. We lived very poorly. I was a dexterous ploughman, for my age; and the next eldest to me was a brother (Gilbert) who could drive the plough very well, and help me to thrash the corn. A novel-writer might perhaps have viewed these scenes with some satisfaction, but so did not I; my indignation yet boils at the recollection of the scoundrel factor's insolent, threatening letters, which used to set us all in tears."

"This kind of life—the cheerless gloom of hermit, with the unceasing toil of a galley-slave, brought me to my sixteenth year; a little before which period I first committed the sin of rhyme. You know our country custom of coupling a man and woman together as partners in the labours of harvest. In my fifteenth autumn my partner was a bewitching creature a year younger than myself. My scarcity of English denies me the power of doing her justice in that language; but you know the Scottish idiom—she was a *bonnie, sweet, sonsie lass.* In short, she altogether unwittingly to herself, initiated me in that delicious passion which, in spite of acid disappointment, gin-horse prudence, and book-worm philosophy, I hold to be the first of human joys, our dearest blessing here below! How she caught the contagion, I cannot tell; you medical people talk much of infection from breathing the same air, the touch, &c., but I never expressly said I loved her. Indeed I did not know myself why I liked so much to loiter behind with her when returning in the evening from our labours; why the tones of her voice made my heart-strings thrill like an Æolian harp; and particularly, why my pulse beat such a furious ratan when I looked and fingered over her little hand to pick out the cruel nettle-stings and thistles. Among her other love-inspiring qualities, she sang sweetly; and it was her favourite reel to which I attempted giving an embodied vehicle in rhyme. (8) I was not so presumptuous as to imagine that I could make verses like printed ones, composed by men who had Greek and Latin; but my girl sang a song, which was said to be composed by a small country laird's son, on one of his father's maids, with whom he was in love, and I saw no reason why I might not rhyme as well as he; for, excepting that he could smear sheep, and cast peats, his father living in the moor-lands, he had no more scholar-craft than myself."

"Thus with me began love and poetry; which at times have been my only, and till within the last twelve months, have been my highest enjoyment. My father struggled on till he reached the freedom in his lease, when he entered on a larger farm, about ten miles farther in the country. The nature of the bargain he made was such as to throw a little ready money into his hands at the commencement of his lease; otherwise the affair would have been impracticable. For four years we lived comfortably here; but a difference commencing between him and his landlord as to terms, after three years' tossing and whirling in the vortex of litigation, my father was just saved from the horrors of a jail by a consumption, which, after two years' promises, kindly stepped in, and carried him away, to *where the wicked cease from troubling, and the weary are at rest.*"

"It is during the time that we lived on this farm that my little story is most eventful. I was, at the beginning of this period, perhaps the most ungainly, awkward boy in the parish—no *solitaire* was less acquainted with the ways of the world. What I knew of ancient story was gathered from Salmon's and Guthrie's geographical grammars; and the ideas I had formed of modern manners, of literature and criticism, I got from the Spectator. These, with Pope's Works, some plays of Shakspeare, Tull and Dickson on Agriculture, the Pantheon, Locke's Essay on the Human Understanding, Stackhouse's History of the Bible, Justice's British Gardener's Directory, Bayle's Lectures, Allan Ramsay's Works, Taylor's Scripture Doctrine of Original Sin, A Select Collection of English Songs, and Hervey's Meditations, had formed the whole of my reading. The collection of songs was my *vade mecum.* I pored over them driving my cart, or walking to labour, song by song, verse by verse—carefully noting the true, tender or sublime, from affectation and fustian. I am convinced I owe to this practice much of my critic craft, such as it is."

"In my seventeenth year, to give my manners a brush, I went to a country dancing school. My father had an unaccountable antipathy against these meetings, and my going was, what to this moment I repent, in opposition to his wishes. My father, as I said before, was subject to strong passions; from that instance of disobedience in me he took a sort of dislike to me, which I believe was one cause of the dissipation which marked my succeeding years. I say dissipation, comparatively with the strictness, and sobriety, and regularity, of Presbyterian country life; for though the Will o' Wisp meteors of thoughtless whim were almost the sole lights of my path, yet early ingrained piety and virtue kept me for several years afterwards within the line of innocence. The great misfortune of my life was to want an aim. I had felt early some stirrings of ambition, but they were the blind gropings of Homer's Cyclops round the walls of his cave. I saw my father's situation entailed on me perpetual labour. The only two openings by which I could enter the temple of fortune, was the gate of niggardly economy, or the path of little, chicaning bargain-making. The first is so contracted an aperture, I never could squeeze myself into it; the last I always hated—there was contamination in the very entrance! Thus abandoned of aim or view in life, with a strong appetite for sociability, as well from native hilarity as from a pride of observation and remark—a constitutional melancholy or hypochondriasm that made me fly to solitude; add to these incentives to social life, my reputation for bookish knowledge, a certain wild logical talent, and a strength of thought, something like the rudiments of good sense, and it will not seem surprising that I was generally a welcome guest where I visited, or any great wonder that, always where two or three met together, there was I among them. But far beyond all other impulses of my heart, was *un penchant à l' adorable moitié du genre humain.* My heart was completely tinder, and was eternally lighted up by some goddess or other; and as in every other warfare in this world, my fortune was various, sometimes I was received with favour, and sometimes I was mortified with a repulse. At the plough, scythe, or reaphook, I feared no competitor, and thus I set absolute want at defiance; and as I never cared farther for my labours than while I was in actual exercise, I spent the evenings in the way after my own heart. A country lad seldom carries on a love-adventure without an assisting confidant. I possessed a curiosity, zeal, and intrepid dexterity, that recommended me as a proper second on these occasions; and, I dare say, I felt as much pleasure in being in the secret of half the loves of the parish of Tarbolton, as ever did statesman in knowing the intrigues of half the courts of Europe. (9) The very goose-feather in my hand seems to know instinctively the well-worn path of my imagination, the favourite theme of my song, and is with difficulty restrained from giving you a couple of paragraphs on the love-adventures of my compeers, the humble inmates of the farm-house and cottage; but the grave sons of science, ambition, or avarice, baptise these things by the name of follies. (10) To the sons and daughters of labour and poverty, they are matters of the most serious nature; to them, the ardent hope, the stolen interview, the tender farewell, are the greatest and most delicious parts of their enjoyments."

"Another circumstance in my life which made some alteration in my mind and manners was, that I spent my nineteenth summer on a smuggling coast, a good distance from home, at a noted school, to learn mensuration, surveying, dialling, &c., in which I made a pretty good progress. But I made a greater progress in the knowledge of mankind. The contraband trade was at that time very successful, and it sometimes happened to me to fall in with those who carried it on. Scenes of swaggering riot and roaring dissipation were till this time new to me; but I was no enemy to social life. Here, though I learnt to fill my glass, and to mix without fear in a drunken squabble, yet I went on with a high hand with my geometry, till the sun entered Virgo, a month which is always a carnival in my bosom, when a charming *filette*, who lived next door to the school, overset my trigonometry, and set me off at a tangent from the sphere of my studies. I, however, struggled on with my *sines* and *co-sines* for a few days more; but, stepping into the garden one charming noon to take the sun's altitude, there I met my angel,

'Like Proserpine, gathering flowers,
Herself a fairer flower——'

It was in vain to think of doing any more good at school. The remaining week I staid I did nothing but craze the faculties of my soul about her, or steal out to meet her; and the two last nights of my stay in the country, had sleep been a mortal sin, the image of this modest and innocent girl had kept me guiltless."

"I returned home very considerably improved. My reading was enlarged with the very important addition of Thomson's and Shenstone's Works. I had seen human nature in a new phasis; and I engaged several of my school-fellows to keep up a literary correspondence with me. This improved me in composition. I had met with a collection of letters by the wits of Queen Anne's reign, and I pored over them most devoutly; I kept copies of any of my own letters that pleased me; and a comparison between them and the composition of most of my correspondents, flattered my vanity. I carried this whim so far, that though I had not three farthings' worth of business in the world, yet almost every post brought me as many letters as if I had been a broad plodding son of day-book and ledger."

"My life flowed on much in the same course till my twenty-third year. *Vive l'amour, et vive la bagatelle*, were my sole principles of action. The addition of two more authors to my library gave me great pleasure; Sterne and M'Kenzie—Tristram Shandy and The Man of Feeling—were my bosom favourites. Poesy was still a darling walk for my mind, but it was only indulged in according to the humour of the hour."

"I had usually half a dozen or more pieces on hand; I took up one or other, as it suited the momentary tone of the mind, and dismissed the work as it bordered on fatigue. My passions, when once lighted up, raged like so many devils, till they got vent in rhyme; and then the conning over my verses, like a spell, soothed all into quiet! None of the rhymes of those days are in print, except Winter, a Dirge, the eldest of my printed pieces; The Death of Poor Mailie, John Barleycorn, and songs first, second, and third. (11) Song second was the ebullition of that passion which ended the fore-mentioned school-business."

"My twenty-third year was to me an important era. Partly through whim, and partly that I wished to set about doing something in life, I joined a flax-dresser in a neighbouring town (Irvine) to learn his trade. This was an unlucky affair. My * * *; and, to finish the whole, as we were giving a welcome carousal to the new-year, the shop took fire, and burnt to ashes,and I was left, like a true poet, not worth a sixpence."

"I was obliged to give up this scheme: the clouds of misfortune were gathering thick round my father's head; and, what was worst of all, he was visibly far gone in a consumption; and, to crown my distresses, a *belle fille* whom I adored, and who had pledged her soul to meet me in the field of matrimony, jilted me, with peculiar circumstances of mortification. The finishing evil that brought up the rear of this infernal file, was my constitutional melancholy being increased to such a degree, that for three months I was in a state of mind scarcely to be envied by the hopeless wretches who have got their mittimus—*Depart from me, ye accursed!*"

"From this adventure I learned something of a town life; but the principal thing which gave my mind a turn, was a friendship I formed with a young fellow, a very noble character, but a hapless son of misfortune. He was the son of a simple mechanic; but a great man in the neighbourhood taking him under his patronage, gave him a genteel education, with a view of bettering his situation in life. The patron dying just as he was ready to launch out into the world, the poor fellow in despair went to sea, where, after a variety of good and ill fortune, a little before I was acquainted with him, he had been set on shore by an American privateer, on the wild coast of Connaught, stripped of everything. I cannot quit this poor fellow's story without adding, that he is at this time master of a large West-Indiaman belonging to the Thames."

"His mind was fraught with independence, magnanimity, and every manly virtue. I loved and admired him to a degree of enthusiasm, and of course strove to imitate him. In some measure I succeeded—I had pride before, but he taught it to flow in proper channels. His knowledge of the world was vastly superior to mine, and I was all attention to learn. He was the only man I ever saw who was a greater fool than myself, where woman was the presiding star; but he spoke of illicit love with the levity of a sailor, which hitherto I had regarded with horror. (12) Here his friendship did me a mischief; and the consequence was that, soon after I resumed the plough, I wrote the Poet's Welcome. (13) My reading only increased, while in this town, by two stray volumes of Pamela, and one of Ferdinand Count Fathom, which gave me some idea of novels. Rhyme, except some religious pieces that are in print, I had given up; but meeting with Fergusson's Scottish Poems, I strung anew my wildly-sounding lyre with emulating vigour. When my father died, his all went among the hell-hounds that prowl in the kennel of justice; but we made a shift to collect a little money in the family amongst us, with which to keep us together; my brother and I took a neighbouring farm. My brother wanted my hair-brained imagination, as well as my social and amorous madness; but, in good sense, and every sober qualification, he was far my superior."

"I entered on this farm with a full resolution, *Come, go to, I will be wise!* I read farming books—I calculated crops—I attended markets—and, in short, in spite of *the devil, and the world, and the flesh,* I believe I should have been a wise man; but the first year, from unfortunately buying bad seed, the second, from a late harvest, we lost half our crops. This overset all my wisdom, and I returned, *like the dog to his vomit, and the sow that was washed, to her wallowing in the mire.*"

"I now began to be known in the neighbourhood as a maker of rhymes. The first of my poetic offspring that saw the light, was a burlesque lamentation on a quarrel between two reverend Calvinists, both of them *dramatis personæ* in my Holy Fair. I had a notion myself that the piece had some merit; but to prevent the worst, I gave a copy of it to a friend who was very fond of such things, and told him that I could not guess who was the author of it, but that I thought it pretty clever. With a certain description of the clergy, as well as laity, it met with a roar of applause. (14) Holy Willie's Prayer next made its appearance, and alarmed the kirk-session so much, that they held several meetings to look over their spiritual artillery, if haply any of it might be pointed against profane writers. Unluckily for me, my wanderings led me on another side, within point-blankshot of their heaviest metal. This is the unfortunate story that gave rise to my printed poem—The Lament. This was a most melancholy affair, which I cannot yet bear to reflect on, and had very nearly given me one or two of the principal qualifications for a place among those who have lost the chart, and mistaken the reckoning, of rationality. I gave up my part of the farm to my brother—in truth it was only nominally mine—and made what little preparation was in my power for Jamaica. But, before leaving my native country for ever, I resolved to publish my poems. I weighed my productions as impartially as was in my power: I thought they had merit, and it was a delicious idea that I should be called a clever fellow even though it should never reach my ears—a poor negro-driver; or perhaps a victim to that inhospitable clime, and gone to the world of spirits! I can truly say, that *pauvre inconnu* as I then was, I had pretty nearly as high an idea of myself and of my works as I have at this moment, when the public has decided in their favour. It ever was my opinion, that the mistakes and blunders, both in a rational and religious point of view, of which we see thousands daily guilty, are owing to their ignorance of themselves. To know myself had been all along my constant study. I weighed myself alone—I balanced myself with others—I watched every means of information, to see how much ground I occupied as a man and as a poet;—I studied assiduously Nature's design in my formation—where the lights and shades in my character were intended. I was pretty confident my poems would meet with some applause (15); but, at the worst, the roar of the Atlantic would deafen the voice of censure, and the novelty of West-Indian scenes make me forget neglect. I threw off six hundred copies, of which I had got subscriptions for about three hundred and fifty. My vanity was highly gratified by the reception I met with from the public; and, besides, I pocketed, all expenses deducted, nearly twenty pounds. This sum came very seasonably, as I was thinking of indenting myself, for want of money to procure my passage. As soon as I was master of nine guineas, the price of wafting me to the torrid zone, I took a steerage-passage in the first ship that was to sail from the Clyde; for

'Hungry ruin had me in the wind.'

"I had been for some days skulking from covert to covert, under all the terrors of a jail; as some ill-advised people had uncoupled the merciless pack of the law at my heels. I had taken the last farewell of my few friends; my chest was on the road to Greenock; I had composed the last song I should ever measure in Caledonia—The Gloomy Night is Gathering Fast—when a letter from Dr. Blacklock to a friend of mine overthrew all my schemes, by opening new prospects to my poetic ambition. The doctor belonged to a set of critics for whose applause I had not dared to hope. His opinion, that I would meet with encouragement in Edinburgh for a second edition, fired me so much, that away I posted for that city, without a single acquaintance, or a single letter of introduction. The baneful star that had so long shed its blasting influence in my zenith, for once made a revolution to the nadir; and a kind Providence placed me under the patronage of one of the noblest of men, the Earl of Glencairn. *Oublie moi, Grand Dieu, si jamais je l'oublie!*"

"I need relate no farther. At Edinburgh I was in a new world; I mingled among many classes of men, but all of them new to me, and I was all attention to *catch* the characters and *the manners living as they rise*. Whether I have profited, time will show. * * *"

"My most respectful compliments to Miss W. (16) Her very elegant and friendly letter I cannot answer at present, as my presence is requisite in Edinburgh, and I set out to-morrow." (17)

At the period of our poet's death, his brother, Gilbert Burns, was ignorant that he had himself written the forgoing narrative of his life while in Ayrshire; and having been applied to by Mrs. Dunlop for some memoirs of his brother, he complied with her request in a letter, from which the following narrative is chiefly extracted. When Gilbert Burns afterwards saw the letter of our poet to Dr. Moore, he made some annotations upon it, which shall be noticed as we proceed.

Robert Burns was born on the 25th day of January 1759, in a small house about two miles from the town of Ayr, and within a few hundred yards of Alloway church, which his poem of Tam o' Shanter has rendered immortal. (18) The name, which the poet and his brother modernised into Burns, was originally Burnes or Burness. Their father, William Burnes, was the son of a farmer in Kincardineshire, and had received the education common in Scotland to persons in his condition of life; he could read and write, and had some knowledge of arithmetic. His family having fallen into reduced circumstances, he was compelled to leave his home in his nineteenth year, and turned his steps towards the south, in quest of a livelihood. The same necessity attended his elder brother Robert. "I have often heard my father" (says Gilbert Burns, in his letter to Mrs. Dunlop) "describe the anguish of mind he felt when they parted on the top of a hill on the confines of their native place, each going off his several way in search of new adventures, and scarcely knowing whither he went. My father undertook to act as a gardener, and shaped his course to Edinburgh, where he wrought hard when he could get work, passing through a variety of difficulties. Still, however, he endeavoured to spare something for the support of his aged parent; and I recollect hearing him mention his having sent a bank-note for this purpose, when money of that kind was so scarce in Kincardineshire, that they scarcely knew how to employ it when it arrived." From Edinburgh, William Burnes passed westward into the county of Ayr, where he engaged himself as a gardener to the laird of Fairly, with whom he lived two years; then changing his service for that of Crawford of Doonside. At length, being desirous of settling in life, he took a perpetual lease of seven acres of land from Dr. Campbell, physician in Ayr, with the view of commencing nurseryman and public gardener; and, having built a house upon it with his own hands, married, in December, 1757, Agnes Brown, the mother of our poet, who still survives. (19) The first fruit of this marriage was Robert, the subject of these memoirs, born on the 25th of January, 1759, as has already been mentioned. Before William Burnes had made much progress in preparing his nursery, he was withdrawn from that undertaking by Mr. Ferguson, who purchased the estate of Doonholm, in the immediate neighbourhood, and engaged him as his gardener and overseer; and this was his situation when our poet was born. Though in the service of Mr. Ferguson, he lived in his own house, his wife managing her family and her little dairy, which consisted sometimes of two, sometimes of three milch-cows; and this state of unambitious content continued till the year 1766. His son Robert was sent by him in his sixth year to a school at Alloway Miln, about a mile distant, taught by a person of the name of Campbell; but this teacher being in a few months appointed master of the workhouse at Ayr, William Burnes, in conjunction with some other heads of families, engaged John Murdoch in his stead. The education of our poet, and of his brother Gilbert, was in common; and of their proficiency under Mr. Murdoch, we have the following account:— "With him we learnt to read English tolerably well (20), and to write a little. He taught, us, too, the English grammar. I was too young to profit much from his lessons in grammar, but Robert made some proficiency in it—a circumstance of consisiderable weight in the unfolding of his genius and character; as he soon became remarkable for the fluency and correctness of his expression, and read the few books that came in his way with much pleasure and improvement: for even then he was a reader when he could get a book. Murdoch, whose library at that time had no great variety in it, lent him The Life of Hannibal, which was the first book he read (the school-books excepted), and almost the only one he had an opportunity of reading while he was at school; for The Life of Wallace, which he classes with it in one of his letters to you, he did not see for some years after wards, when he borrowed it from the blacksmith who shod our horses."

It appears that William Burnes approved himself greatly in the service of Mr. Ferguson, by his intelligence, industry, and integrity. In consequence of this, with a view of promoting his interest, Mr. Ferguson leased him a farm, of which we have the following account:—

"The farm was upwards of seventy acres (21) (between eighty and ninety, English statute measure), the rent of which was to be forty pounds annually for the first six years, and afterwards forty-five pounds. My father endeavoured to sell his leasehold property, for the purpose of stocking this farm, but at that time was unable, and Mr. Ferguson lent him a hundred pounds for that purpose. He removed to his new situation at Whitsuntide, 1766. It was, I think, not above two years after this, that Murdoch, our tutor and friend, left this part of the country; and there being no school near us, and our little services being useful on the farm, my father undertook to teach us arithmetic in the winter evenings, by candle-light; and in this way my two eldest sisters got all the education they received. I remember a circumstance that happened at this time, which, though trifling in itself, is fresh in my memory, and may serve to illustrate the early character of my brother. Murdoch came to spend a night with us, and to take his leave when he was about to go into Carrick. He brought us, as a present and memorial of him, a small compendium of English Grammar, and the tragedy of Titus Andronicus, and, by way of passing the evening, he began to read the play aloud. We were all attention for some time, till presently the whole party was dissolved in tears. A female in the play (I have but a confused remembrance of it) had her hands chopt off, and her tongue cut out, and then was insultingly desired to call for water to wash her hands. At this, in an agony of distress, we with one voice desired he would read no more. My father observed, that if we would not hear it out, it would be needless to leave the play with us, Robert replied, that if it was left he would burn it. My father was going to chide him for this ungrateful return to his tutor's kindness; but Murdoch interfered, declaring that he liked to see so much sensibility; and he left the School for Love, a comedy, translated I think from the French, in its place." (22)

"Nothing," continues Gilbert Burns, "could be more retired than our general manner of living at Mount Oliphant; we rarely saw any body but the members of our own family. There were no boys of our own age, or near it, in the neighbourhood. Indeed, the greatest part of the land in the vicinity was at that time possessed by shopkeepers, and people of that stamp, who had retired from business, or who kept their farm in the country, at the same time that they followed business in town. My father was for some time almost the only companion we had. He conversed familiarly on all subjects with us, as if we had been men; and was at great pains, while we accompanied him in the labours of the farm, to lead the conversation to such subjects as might tend to increase our knowledge, or confirm us in virtuous habits. He borrowed Salomon's Geographical Grammar for us, and endeavoured to make us acquainted with the situation and history of the different countries of the world; while, from a book-society in Ayr, he procured for us the reading of Durham's Physico and Astro-Theology, and Ray's Wisdom of God in the Creation, to give us some idea of astronomy and natural history. Robert read all these books with an avidity and industry scarcely to be equalled. My father had been a subscriber to Stackhouse's History of the Bible, then lately published by James Meuros in Kilmarnock: from this Robert collected a competent knowledge of ancient history; for no book was so voluminous as to slacken his industry, or so antiquated as to damp his researches. A brother of my mother, who had lived with us some time, and had learned some arithmetic by our winter evening's candle, went into a bookseller's shop in Ayr, to purchase The Ready Reckoner, or Tradesman's Sure Guide, and a book to teach him to write letters. Luckily, in place of The Complete Letter-Writer, he got by mistake a small collection of letters by the most eminent writers, with a few sensible directions for attaining an easy epistolary style. This book was to Robert of the greatest consequence. It inspired him with a strong desire to excel in letter-writing, while it furnished him with models by some of the first writers in our language."

"My brother was about thirteen or fourteen, when my father, regretting that we wrote so ill, sent us, week about, during a summer quarter, to the parish school of Dalrymple, which, though between two or three miles distant, was the nearest to us, that we might have an opportunity of remedying this defect. About this time a bookish acquaintance of my father's procured us a reading of two volumes of Richardson's Pamela, which was the first novel we read, and the only part of Richardson's works my brother was acquainted with till towards the period of his commencing author. Till that time, too, he remained unacquainted with Fielding, with Smollett (two volumes of Ferdinand Count Fathom, and two volumes of Peregrine Pickle, excepted), with Hume, with Robertson, and almost all our authors of eminence of the later times. I recollect, indeed, my father borrowed a volume of English history from Mr. Hamilton of Bourtreehill's gardener. It treated of the reign of James I., and his unfortunate son Charles, but I do not know who was the author; all that I remember of it is something of Charles's conversation with his children. About this time, Murdoch, our former teacher, after having been in different places in the country, and having taught a school some time in Dumfries, came to be the established teacher of the English language in Ayr, a circumstance of considerable consequence to us. The remembrance of my father's former friendship, and his attachment to my brother, made him do every thing in his power for our improvement. He sent us Pope's works, and some other poetry, the first that we had an opportunity of reading, excepting what is contained in the English Collection, and in the volume of the Edinburgh Magazine for 1772; excepting also *those excellent new songs* that are hawked about the country in baskets, or exposed on stalls in the streets."

"The summer after we had been at

Dalrymple school, my father sent Robert to Ayr, to revise his English grammar, with his former teacher. He had been there only one week, when he was obliged to return to assist at the harvest. When the harvest was over, he went back to school, where he remained two weeks; and this completes the account of his school education, excepting one summer quarter, some time afterwards, that he attended the parish school of Kirkoswald (where he lived with a brother of my mother's), to learn surveying."

"During the two last weeks that he was with Murdoch, he himself was engaged in learning French (23), and he communicated the instructions he received to my brother, who, when he returned, brought home with him a French dictionary and grammar, and the Adventures of Telemachus in the original. In a little while, by the assistance of these books, he had acquired such a knowledge of the language, as to read and understand any French author in prose. This was considered as a sort of prodigy, and through the medium of Murdoch, procured him the acquaintance of several lads in Ayr, who were at that time gabbling French, and the notice of some families, particularly that of Dr. Malcolm, where a knowledge of French was a recommendation."

"Observing the facility with which he had acquired the French language, Mr. Robinson, the established writing-master in Ayr, and Mr. Murdoch's particular friend, having himself acquired a considerable knowledge of the Latin language, by his own industry, without ever having learned it at school, advised Robert to make the same attempt, promising him every assistance in his power. Agreeably to this advice, he purchased the Rudiments of the Latin Tongue, but finding this study dry and uninteresting, it was quickly laid aside. He frequently returned to his Rudiments on any little chagrin or disappointment, particularly in his love affairs; but the Latin seldom predominated more than a day or two at a time, or a week at most. Observing, himself, the ridicule that would attach to this sort of conduct if it were known, he made two or three humorous stanzas on the subject, which I cannot now recollect, but they all ended,

'So I'll to my Latin again.'

"Thus you see Mr. Murdoch was a principal means of my brother's improvement. Worthy man! though foreign to my present purpose, I cannot take leave of him without tracing his future history. He continued for some years a respected and useful teacher at Ayr, till one evening that he had been overtaken in liquor, he happened to speak somewhat disrespectfully of Dr. Dalrymple, the parish minister, who had not paid him that attention to which he thought himself entitled. In Ayr he might as well have spoken blasphemy. He found it proper to give up his appointment. He went to London, where he still lives, a private teacher of French. He has been a considerable time married, and keeps a shop of stationery wares." (24)

"The father of Dr. Paterson, now physician at Ayr, was, I believe, a native of Aberdeenshire, and was one of the established teachers in Ayr when my father settled in the neighbourhood. He early recognised my father as a fellow native of the north of Scotland, and a certain degree of intimacy subsisted between them during Mr. Paterson's life. After his death, his widow, who is a very genteel woman, and of great worth, delighted in doing what she thought her husband would have wished to have done, and assiduously kept up her attentions to all his acquaintances. She kept alive the intimacy with our family, by frequently inviting my father and mother to her house on Sundays, when she met them at church."

"When she came to know my brother's passion for books she kindly offered us the use of her husband's library, and from her we got the Spectator, Pope's Translation of Homer, and several other books that were of use to us. Mount Oliphant, the farm my father possessed in the parish of Ayr, is almost the very poorest soil I know of in a state of cultivation. A stronger proof of this I cannot give, than that, notwithstanding the extraordinary rise in the value of lands in Scotland, it was let, after a considerable sum laid out in improving it by the proprietor, a few years ago, five pounds per annum lower than the rent paid for it by my father, thirty years ago. My father, in consequence of this, soon came into difficulties, which were increased by the loss of several of his cattle by accidents and disease. To the buffetings of misfortune, we could only oppose hard labour and the most rigid economy. We lived very sparingly. For several years butcher's meat was a stranger in the house, while all the members of the family exerted themselves to the utmost of their strength, and rather beyond it, in the labours of the farm. My brother, at the age of thirteen assisted in thrashing the crop of corn, and at fifteen was the principal labourer on the farm, for we had no hired servant, male or female. The anguish of mind we felt at our tender years, under these straits and difficulties, was very great. To think of our father growing old (for he was now above fifty), broken down with the long-continued fatigues of his life, with a wife and five other children, and in a declining state of circumstances—these reflections produced in my brother's mind and mine sensations of the deepest distress. I doubt not but the hard labour and sorrow of this period of his life, was in a great measure the cause of that depression of spirits with which Robert was so often afflicted through his whole life afterwards. At this time he was almost constantly afflicted in the evenings with a dull headache, which, at a future period of his life, was exchanged for a palpitation of the heart, and a threatening of fainting and suffocation in his bed in the night-time.

"By a stipulation in my father's lease, he had a right to throw it up, if he thought proper, at the end of every sixth year. He attempted to fix himself in a better farm at the end of the first six years, but failing in that attempt, he continued where he was for six years more. He then took the farm of Lochlea, of 130 acres, at the rent of twenty shillings an acre, in the parish of Tarbolton, of Mr. ——, then a merchant in Ayr, and now (1797) a merchant in Liverpool. He removed to this farm on Whitsunday, 1777, and possessed it only seven years. No writing had ever been made out of the conditions of the lease; a misunderstanding took place respecting them; the subjects in dispute were submitted to arbitration, and the decision involved my father's affairs in ruin. He lived to know of this decision, but not to see any execution in consequence of it. He died on the 13th of February, 1784."

"The seven years we lived in Tarbolton parish (extending from the 19th to the 26th of my brother's age), were not marked by much literary improvement; but during this time, the foundation was laid of certain habits in my brother's character, which afterwards became but too prominent, and which malice and envy have taken delight to enlarge on. Though when young he was bashful and awkward in his intercourse with women, yet, when he approached manhood, his attachment to their society became very strong, and he was constantly the victim of some fair enslaver. The symptoms of his passion were often such as nearly to equal those of the celebrated Sappho. I never indeed knew that he *fainted, sunk, and died away;* but the agitations of his mind and body exceeded anything of the kind I ever knew in real life. He had always a particular jealousy of people who were richer than himself, or who had more consequence in life. His love, therefore, rarely settled on persons of this description. When he selected any one out of the sovereignty of his good pleasure, to whom he should pay his particular attention, she was instantly invested with a sufficient stock of charms, out of the plentiful stores of his own imagination; and there was often a great dissimilitude between his fair captivator, as she appeared to others, and as she seemed when invested in the attributes he gave her. One generally reigned paramount in his affections; but as Yorick's affections flowed out toward Madame de L— at the remise door, while the eternal vows of Eliza were upon him, so Robert was frequently encountering other attractions, which formed so many underplots in the drama of his love. As these connections were governed by the strictest rules of virtue and modesty (from which he never deviated till he reached his 23rd year), he became anxious to be in a situation to marry. This was not likely soon to be the case while he remained a farmer, as the stocking of the farm required a sum of money he had no probability of being master of for a great while. He began, therefore, to think of trying some other line of life. He and I had for several years taken land of my father for the purpose of raising flax on our own account. In the course of selling it, Robert began to think of turning flax-dresser, both as being suitable to his grand view of settling in life, and as subservient to the flax raising. He accordingly wrought at the business of a flax-dresser in Irvine for six months, but abandoned it at that period, as neither agreeing with his health nor inclination. In Irvine he had contracted some acquaintance of a freer manner of thinking and living than he had been used to, whose society prepared him for overleaping the bounds of rigid virtue which had hitherto restrained him. Towards the end of the period under review (in his 26th year), and soon after his father's death, he was furnished with the subject of his epistle to John Rankin. During this period also he became a freemason, which was his first introduction to the life of a boon companion. Yet, notwithstanding the circumstances and the praise he has bestowed on Scotch drink (which seems to have misled his historians), I do not recollect, during these seven years, nor till towards the end of his commencing author (when his growing celebrity occasioned his being often in company), to have ever seen him intoxicated; nor was he at all given to drinking. A stronger proof of the general sobriety of his conduct need not be required than what I am about to give. During the whole of the time we lived in the farm of Lochlea with my father, he allowed my brother and me such wages for our labour as he gave to other labourers, as a part of which, every article of our clothing manufactured in the family, was regularly accounted for. When my father's affairs drew near a crisis, Robert and I took the farm of Mossgiel, consisting of 118 acres, at the rent of £90 per annum (the farm on which I live at present), from Mr. Gavin Hamilton, as an asylum for the family in case of the worst. It was stocked by the property and individual savings of the whole family, and was a joint concern among us. (25) Every member of the family was allowed ordinary wages for the labour he performed on the farm. (26) My brother's allowance and mine was seven pounds per annum each. And during the whole time this family concern lasted, which was for four years, as well as during the preceding period at Lochlea, his expenses never in any one year exceeded his slender income. As I was entrusted with the keeping of the family accounts, it is not possible that there can be any fallacy in this statement in my brother's favour. His temperance and frugality were every thing that could be wished."

"The farm of Mossgiel lies very high, and mostly on a cold wet bottom. The first four years that we were on the farm were very frosty, and the spring was very late. Our crops in consequence were very unprofitable; and, notwithstanding our utmost diligence and economy, we found ourselves obliged to give up our bargain, with the loss of a considerable part of our original stock. It was during these four years that Robert formed his connexion with Jean Armour, afterwards Mrs. Burns. This connexion *could no longer be concealed* about the time we came to a final determination to quit the farm. Robert durst not engage with a family in his poor unsettled state, but was anxious to shield his partner, by every means in his power, from the consequences of their imprudence. It was agreed, therefore, between them, that they should make a legal acknowledgment of an irregular and private marriage; that he should go to Jamaica to *push his fortune;* and that she should remain with her father till it might please Providence to put the means of supporting a family in his power."

"Mrs. Burns was a great favourite of her father's. The intimation of a marriage was the first suggestion he received of her real situation. He was in the greatest distress, and fainted away. The marriage did not appear to him to make the matter better. A husband in Jamaica appeared to him and his wife little better than none, and an effectual bar to any other prospects of a settlement in life that their daughter might have. They therefore expressed a wish to her, that the written papers which respected the marriage should be cancelled, and thus the marriage rendered void. In her melancholy state, she felt the deepest remorse at having brought such heavy affliction on parents that loved her so tenderly, and submitted to their entreaties. Their wish was mentioned to Robert. He felt the deepest anguish of mind. He offered to stay at home and provide for his wife and family in the best manner that his daily labours could provide for them, that being the only means in his power. Even this offer they did not approve of; for humble as Miss Armour's station was, and though great her imprudence had been, she still, in the eyes of her partial parents, might look to a better connection than that with my friendless and unhappy brother, at that time without house or biding-place. Robert at length consented to their wishes; but his feelings on this occasion were of the most distracting nature; and the impression of sorrow was not effaced, till by a regular marriage they were indissolubly united. In the state of mind which this separation produced, he wished to leave the country as soon as possible, and agreed with Dr. Douglas to go out to Jamaica as an assistant overseer, or, as I believe it is called, a bookkeeper on his estate. As he had not sufficient money to pay his passage, and the vessel in which Dr. Douglas was to procure a passage for him was not expected to sail for some time, Mr. Hamilton advised him to publish his poems in the mean time by subscription, as a likely way of getting a little money, to provide him more liberally in necessaries for Jamaica. Agreably to this advice, subscription-bills were printed immediately, and the printing was commenced at Kilmarnock, his preparations going on at the same time for his voyage. (27) The reception, however, which his poems met with in the world, and the friends they procured him, made him change his resolution of going to Jamaica, and he was advised to go to Edinburgh to publish a second edition. On his return, in happier circumstances, he renewed his connection with Mrs. Burns, and rendered it permanent by a union for life."

Thus, madam, have I endeavoured to give you a simple narrative of the leading circumstances in my brother's early life. The remaining part he spent in Edinburgh, or in Dumfries-shire, and its incidents are as well known to you as to me. His genius having procured him your patronage and friendship, this gave rise to the correspondence between you, in which, I believe, his sentiments were delivered with the most respectful, but most unreserved confidence, and which only terminated with the last days of his life."

This narrative of Gilbert Burns may serve as a commentary on the preceding sketch of our poet's life by himself. It will be seen that the distraction of mind which he mentions arose from the distress and sorrow in which he had involved his future wife. The whole circumstances attending this connexion are certainly of a very singular nature. (28)

The reader will perceive, from the foregoing narrative, how much the children of William Burnes were indebted to their father, who was certainly a man of uncommon talents, though it does not appear that he possessed any portion of that vivid imagination for which the subject of these memoirs was distinguished. In page 13, it is observed by our poet, that his father had an unaccountable antipathy to dancing-schools, and that his attending one of these brought on him his displeasure and even dislike. On this observation Gilbert has made the following remark, which seems entitled to implicit credit:—"I wonder how Robert could attribute to our father that lasting resentment of his going to a dancing-school against his will, of which he was incapable. I believe the truth was, that he, about this time, began to see the dangerous impetuosity of my brother's passions, as well as his not being amenable to counsel, which often irritated my father, and which he would naturally think a dancing-school was not likely to correct. But he was proud of Robert's genius, which he bestowed more expense in cultivating than on the rest of the family, in the instances of sending him to Ayr and Kirkoswald schools; and he was greatly delighted with his warmth of heart and his conversational powers. He had, indeed, that dislike of dancing-schools which Robert mentions, but so far overcame it during Robert's first month of attendance, that he allowed all the rest of the family that were fit for it to accompany him during the second month. Robert excelled in dancing, and was for some time distractedly fond of it."

"In the original letters to Dr. Moore, our poet described his ancestors as "renting lands of the noble Keiths of Marischal, and having had the honour of sharing their fate." "I do not," continues he, "use the word *honour* with any reference to political principles; *loyal* and *disloyal*, I take to be merely relative terms, in that ancient and formidable court, known in this country by the name of Club-law, where the right is always with the strongest. But those who dare welcome ruin, and shake hands with infamy, for what they scarcely believe to be the cause of their God, or their king, are, as Mark Antony says in Shakspeare of Brutus and Cassius, *honourable men*. I mention this circumstance, because it threw my father on the world at large."

This paragraph has been omitted in printing the letter, at the desire of Gilbert Burns; and it would have been unnecessary to have noticed it on the present occasion, had not several manuscript copies of that letter been in circulation. "I do not know," observed Gilbert Burns, "how my brother could be misled in the account he has given of the Jacobitism of his ancestors. I believe the Earl Marischal forfeited his title and estate in 1715, before my father was born; and, among a collection of parish-certificates in his posession, I have read one, stating that the bearer had no concern in the *late wicked rebellion*." On the information of one, who knew William Burnes soon after he arrived in the country of Ayr, it may be mentioned, that a report did prevail that he had taken the field with the young Chevalier—a report which the certificate mentioned by his son was, perhaps, intended to counteract. Strangers from the north, in the low country of Scotland, were in those days liable to suspicions of having been, in the familiar phrase of the country, "Out in the forty-five" (1745), especially when they had any stateliness or reserve about them, as was the case with William Burnes. It may easily be conceived, that our poet would cherish the belief of his father's having been engaged in the daring enterprise of Prince Charles Edward. The generous attachment, the heroic valour, and the final misfortunes of the adherents of the house of Stuart, touched with sympathy his youthful and ardent mind, and influenced his original political opinions. (29)

The father of our poet is described by one who knew him towards the latter end of his life, as above the common stature, thin, and bent with labour. His countenance was serious and expressive, and the scanty locks on his head were grey. He was of a religious turn of mind, and, as is usual among the Scottish peasantry, a good deal conversant in speculative theology. There is, in Gilbert's hands, a little manual of religious belief, in the form of a dialogue between a father and his son, composed by him for the use of his children, in which the benevolence of his heart seems to have led him to soften the rigid Calvinism of the Scotch church, into something approaching to Arminianism. He was a devout man, and in the practice of calling his family together to join in prayer. It is known that the following exquisite picture, in the Cotter's Saturday Night, represents William Burnes and his family at their evening devotions:—

"The cheerful supper done, with serious face, [wide ;
They, round the ingle (30), form a circle
The sire turns o'er, with patriarchal grace,
The big *hall*-Bible, once his father's pride:
His bonnet rev'rently is laid aside, [bare ;
His lyart haffets (31) wearing thin and
Those strains that once did sweet in Zion glide, [care ;
He wales (32) a portion with judicious
And 'Let us worship God!' he says with solemn air.

They chant their artless notes in simple guise ; [aim :
They tune their hearts, by far the noblest
Perhaps *Dundee's* (33) wild warbling measures rise, [name ;
Or plaintive *Martyrs* (34), worthy of the
Or noble *Elgin* (35) beets (36) the heavenly flame,
The sweetest far of Scotia's holy lays ;
Compar'd with these Italian trills are tame,
The tickled ears no heart-felt raptures raise ; [praise.
No unison have they with our Creator's

The priest-like father reads the sacred page, (37)
How Abram was the friend of God on high:
Or Moses bade eternal welfare wage
With Amalek's ungracious progeny ;
Or how the royal bard did groaning lie, [ire;
Beneath the stroke of Heaven's avenging
Or Job's pathetic plaint, and wailing cry ;
Or rapt Isaiah wild seraphic fire ;
Or other holy seers that tune the sacred lyre.

Perhaps the Christian volume is the theme,
How guiltless blood for guilty man was shed ; [name,
How he who bore in heaven the second
Had not on earth whereon to lay his head,
How his first followers and servants sped ;
The precepts sage they wrote to many a land ;
How he, who lone in Patmos banished,
Saw in the sun a mighty angel stand,
And heard great Babylon's doom pronounced, by Heaven's command!

Then kneeling down to heaven's eternal King, [prays ;
The saint, the father, and the husband,
'Hope springs exulting on triumphant wing,' [days ;
That thus they all shall meet in future
There ever bask in uncreated rays,
No more to sigh, or shed the bitter tear,
Together hymning their Creator's praise,
In such society, yet still more dear ;
While circling time moves round in an eternal sphere.

* * * * *

Then homeward all take off their several way ;
The youngling cottagers retire to rest :
The parent pair their secret homage pay,
And offer up to Heaven the warm request:
That He who stills the raven's clam'rous nest,
And decks the lily fair in flowery pride,
Would, in the way his wisdom sees the best,
For them and for their little ones provide ;
But, chiefly, in their hearts with grace divine preside!"

Of a family so interesting as that which inhabited the cottage of William Burnes, and particularly of the father of the family, the reader will perhaps be willing to listen to some farther account. What follows is given by one already mentioned with so much honour in the narrative of Gilbert Burns, Mr. Murdoch, the preceptor of our poet, who, in a letter to Joseph Cooper Walker, Esq., of Dublin, author of the Historical Memoirs of the Irish Bards, and of the Historical Memoir of the Italian Tragedy, thus expresses himself:—

"SIR.—I was lately favoured with a letter from our worthy friend, the Rev. Wm. Adair, in which he requested me to communicate to you whatever particulars I could recollect concerning Robert Burns, the Ayrshire poet. My business being at present multifarious and harassing, my attention is consequently so much divided, and I am so little in the habit of expressing my thoughts on paper, that at this distance of time I can give but a very imperfect sketch of the early part of the life of that extraordinary genius, with which alone I am acquainted.

William Burnes, the father of the poet,

was born in the shire of Kincardine, and bred a gardener. He had been settled in Ayrshire ten or twelve years before I knew him, and had been in the service of Mr. Crawford of Doonside. He was afterwards employed as a gardener and overseer by Provost Ferguson of Doonholm, in the parish of Alloway, which is now united with that of Ayr. In this parish, on the roadside, a Scotch mile and a half from the town of Ayr, and half a mile from the bridge of Doon, Willian Burnes took a piece of land, consisting of about seven acres; part of which he laid out in garden ground, and part of which he kept to graze a cow, &c., still continuing in the employ of Provost Ferguson. Upon this little farm was erected a humble dwelling, of which William Burnes was the architect. It was, with the exception of a little straw, literally a tabernacle of clay. In this mean cottage, of which I myself was at times an inhabitant, I really believe there dwelt a larger portion of content than in any palace in Europe. The Cotter's Saturday Night will give some idea of the temper and manners that prevailed there."

"In 1765, about the middle of March, Mr. W. Burnes came to Ayr, and sent to the school where I was improving in writing, under my good friend Mr. Robinson, desiring that I would come and speak to him at a certain inn, and bring my writing book with me. This was immediately complied with. Having examined my writing, he was pleased with it—you will readily allow he was not difficult—and told me that he had received very satisfactory information of Mr. Tennant, the master of the English school, concerning my improvement in English, and in his method of teaching. In the month of May following, I was engaged by Mr. Burnes, and four of his neighbours, to teach, and accordingly began to teach the school at Alloway, which was situated a few yards from the argillaceous fabric above-mentioned. My five employers undertook to board me by turns, and to make up a certain salary, at the end of the year, provided my quarterly payments from the different pupils did not amount to that sum."

"My pupil, Robert Burns, was then between six and seven years of age; his preceptor about eighteen. Robert, and his younger brother, Gilbert, had been grounded a little in English before they were put under my care. They both made a rapid progress in reading, and a tolerable progress in writing. In reading, dividing words into syllables by rule, spelling without book, passing sentence, &c., Robert and Gilbert were generally at the upper end of the class, even when ranged with boys by far their seniors. The books most commonly used in the school were the Spelling Book, the New Testament, the Bible, Mason's Collection of Prose and Verse, and Fisher's English Grammar. They committed to memory the hymns, and other poems of that collection, with uncommon facility. This facility was partly owing to the method pursued by their father and me in instructing them, which was, to make them thoroughly acquainted with the meaning of every word in each sentence that was be committed to memory. By the bye, this may be easier done, and at an earlier period, than is generally thought. As soon as they were capable of it, I taught them to turn verse into its natural prose order; sometimes to substitute synonymous expressions for poetical words, and to supply all the ellipses. These, you know, are the means of knowing that the pupil understands his author. These are excellent helps to the arrangement of words in sentences, as well as to a variety of expression."

"Gilbert always appeared to me to possess a more lively imagination, and to be more of the wit, than Robert. I attempted to teach them a little church-music. Here they were left far behind by all the rest of the school. Robert's ear, in particular, was remarkably dull, and his voice untunable. It was long before I could get them to distinguish one tune from another. Robert's countenance was generally grave, and expressive of a serious, contemplative, and thoughtful mind. Gilbert's face said, *Mirth, with thee I mean to live;* and certainly, if any person who knew the two boys had been asked which of them was the most likely to court the muses, he would surely never have guessed that Robert had a propensity of that kind."

"In the year 1767, Mr. Burnes quitted his mud edifice, and took possession of a farm (Mount Oliphant), of his own improving, while in the service of Provost Ferguson. This farm being at a considerable distance from the school, the boys could not attend regularly; and some changes taking place among the other supporters of the school, I left it, having continued to conduct it for nearly two years and a half."

"In the year 1772, I was appointed (being one of five candidates who were examined) to teach the English school at Ayr; and in 1773, Robert Burns came to board and lodge with me, for the purpose of revising English grammar, &c., that he might be better qualified to instruct his brothers and sisters at home. He was now with me day and night, in school, at all meals, and in all my walks. At the end of one week, I told him, that, as he was now pretty much master of the parts of speech, &c., I should like to teach him something of French pronunciation; that when he should meet with the name of a French town, ship officer, or the like, in the newspapers, he might be able to pronounce it something like a French word. Robert was glad to hear this proposal, and immediately we attacked the French with good courage."

"Now there was little else to be heard but the declension of nouns, the conjugation of verbs, &c. When walking together, and even at meals, I was constantly telling him the names of different objects, as they presented themselves, in French; so that he was hourly laying in a stock of words, and sometimes little phrases. In short, he took such pleasure in learning, and I in teaching, that it is difficult to say which of the two was most zealous in the business; and about the end of the second week ofour study of the French, we began to read a little of the Adventures of Telemachus, in Fenelon's own words."

"But now the plains of Mount Oliphant began to whiten, and Robert was summoned to relinquish the pleasing scenes that surround the grotto of Calypso, and, armed with a sickle, to seek glory by signalising himself in the field of Ceres—and so he did; for, although but about fifteen, I was told that he performed the work of a man."

"Thus was I deprived of my very apt pupil, and consequently agreeable companion, at the end of three weeks, one of which was spent entirely in the study of English, and the other two chiefly in that of French. I did not, however, lose sight of him, but was a frequent visitant at his father's house, when I had my half holiday; and very often went, accompanied with one or two persons more intelligent than myself, that good William Burnes might enjoy a mental feast. Then the labouring oar was shifted to some other hand. The father and the son sat down with us, when we enjoyed a conversation, wherein solid reasoning, sensible remark, and a moderate seasoning of jocularity, were so nicely blended, as to render it palatable to all parties. Robert had a hundred questions to ask me about the French, &c.; and the father, who had always rational information in view, had still some questions to propose to my more learned friends, upon moral or natural philosophy, or some such interesting subject. Mrs. Burnes, too, was of the party as much as possible;

'But still the house affairs would draw her thence,
Which ever as she could with haste dispatch,
She'd come again, and with a greedy ear,
Devour up their discourse'—

and particularly that of her husband. At all times, and in all companies, she listened to him with a more marked attention than to any body else. When under the necessity of being absent while he was speaking, she seemed to regret, as a real loss, that she had missed what the good man had said. This worthy woman, Agnes Brown, had the most thorough esteem for her husband of any woman I ever knew. I can by no means wonder that she highly esteemed him; for I myself have always considered William Burnes as by far the best of the human race that ever I had the pleasure of being acquainted with—and many a worthy character I have known. I can cheerfully join with Robert in the last line of his epitaph (borrowed from Goldsmith),

'And ev'n his failings lean'd to virtue's side.'

"He was an excellent husband, if I may judge from his assiduous attention to the ease and comfort of his worthy partner, and from her affectionate behaviour to him, as well as her unwearied attention to the duties of a mother."

"He was a tender and affectionate father; he took pleasure in leading his children in the path of virtue, not in driving them, as some parents do, to the performance of duties to which they themselves are averse. He took care to find fault but very seldom; and therefore, when he did rebuke, he was listened to with a kind of reverential awe. A look of disapprobation was felt; a reproof was severely so; and a strip with the *tawz*, even on the skirt of the coat, gave heart-felt pain, produced a loud lamentation, and brought forth a flood of tears."

"He had the art of gaining the esteem and goodwill of those that were labourers under him. I think I never saw him angry but twice; the one time, it was with the foreman of the band, for not reaping the field as he was desired; and the other time, it was with an old man, for using smutty inuendoes and *double entendres*. Were every foul-mouthed old man to receive a reasonable check in this way, it would be to the advantage of the rising generation. As he was at no time overbearing to inferiors, he was equally incapable of that passive, pitiful, paltry spirit, that induces some people to *keep booing and booing* in the presence of a great man. He always treated superiors with a becoming respect; but he never gave the smallest encouragement to aristocratical arrogance. But I must not pretend to give you a description of all the manly qualities, the rational and Christian virtues, of the venerable William Burnes. Time would fail me. I shall only add that he carefully practised every known duty, and avoided every thing that was criminal; or, in the apostle's words, *Herein did he exercise himself, in living a life void of offence towards God and towards men.* Oh for a world of men of such dispositions! We should then have no wars. I have often wished, for the good of mankind, that it were as customary to honour and perpetuate the memory of those who excel in moral rectitude as it is to extol what are called heroic actions: then would the mausoleum of the friend of my youth overtop and surpass most of the monuments I see in Westminster Abbey."

"Although I cannot do justice to the character of this worthy man, yet you will perceive, from these few particulars, what kind of person had the principal hand in the education of our poet. He spoke the English language with more propriety (both with respect to diction and pronunciation) than any man I ever knew with no greater advantages. This had a very good effect on the boys, who began to talk, and reason like men, much sooner than their neighbours. I do not recollect any of their contemporaries, at my little seminary, who afterwards made any great degree as literary characters, except Dr. Tennant, who was chaplain to Colonel Fullarton's regiment, and who is now in the East Indies. He is a man of genius and learning; yet affable, and free from pedantry."

"Mr. Burnes, in a short time, found that he had overrated Mount Oliphant, and that he could not rear his numerous family upon it. After being there some years, he removed to Lochlea, in the parish of Tarbolton, where, I believe, Robert wrote most of his poems."

"But here, sir, you will permit me to pause. I can tell you but little more relative to our poet. I shall, however, in my next, send you a copy of one of his letters to me, about the year 1783. I received one since, but it is mislaid. Please remember me, in the best manner, to my worthy friend Mr. Adair, when you see him, or write to him."

"*Hart Street, Bloomsbury Square,*
London, Feb. 22, 1799."

As the narrative of Gilbert Burns was written at a time when he was ignorant of the existence of the preceding narrative of his brother, so this letter of Mr. Murdoch was written without his having any knowledge that either of his pupils had been employed on the same subject. The three relations serve, therefore, not merely to illustrate, but to authenticate each other. Though the information they convey might have been presented within a shorter compass, by reducing the whole into one unbroken narrative, it is scarcely to be doubted, that the intelligent reader will be far more gratified by a sight of these original documents themselves.

[The poet mentions in his own narrative his visit in his nineteenth summer to Kirkoswald parish, and his mingling in scenes of dissipation there amongst the Carrick smugglers. The following additional particulars respecting this period of his life will probably be interesting: they were collected by the present editor, but appeared originally in *Chambers Edinburgh Journal.*

If Burns be correct in stating that it was his nineteenth summer which he spent in Kirkoswald parish, the date of his residence there must be 1777. What seems to have suggested his going to Kirkoswald school, was the connection of his mother with that parish. She was the daughter of Gilbert Brown, farmer of Craigenton, in this parochial division of Carrick, in which she had many friends still living, particularly a brother, Samuel Brown, who resided, in the miscellaneous capacity of farm-labourer, fisherman, and dealer in wool, at the farm-house of Ballochneil, above a mile from the village of Kirkoswald. This Brown, though not the farmer or guidman of the place, was a person held to be in creditable circumstances in a district where the distinction between master and servant was, and still is, by no means great. His wife was the sister of Niven, the tenant; and he lived in the "chamber" or better portion of the farm-house, but was now a widower. It was with Brown that Burns lived during his attendance at Kirkoswald school, walking every morning to the village where the little seminary of learning was situated, and returning at night.

The district into which the young poet of Kyle was thus thrown, has many features of a remarkable kind. Though situated on the shore of the Firth of Clyde, where steamers are every hour to be seen on their passage between enlightened and busy cities, it is to this day the seat of simple and patriarchal usages. Its land, composed of bleak green uplands, partly cultivated and partly pastoral, was, at the time alluded to, occupied by a generation of primitive small farmers, many of whom, while preserving their native simplicity, had superadded to it some of the irregular habits arising from a concern in the trade of introducing contraband goods on the Carrick coast. (38) Such dealings did not prevent superstition from flourishing amongst them in a degree of vigour of which no district of Scotland now presents any example. The parish has six miles of sea coast; and the village, where the church and school are situated, is in a sheltered situation about a couple of miles inland.

The parish schoolmaster, Hugh Rodger, enjoyed great local fame as a teacher of mensuration and geometry, and was much employed as a practical land surveyor. On the day when Burns entered at the school, another youth, a little younger than himself, also entered. This was a native of the neighbouring town of Maybole, who having there completed a course of classical study, was now sent by his father, a respectable shopkeeper, to acquire arithmetic and mensuration under the famed mathematician of Kirkoswald. It was then the custom, when pupils of their age entered at a school, to take the master to a tavern, and implement the engagement by treating him to some liquor. Burns and the Maybole youth, accordingly united to regale Rodger with a potation of ale, at a public house in the village, kept by two gentlewomanly sort of persons named Kennedy—Jean and Anne Kennedy—the former of whom was destined to be afterwards married to immortal verse, under the appellation of *Kirkton Jean*, and whose house, in consideration of some pretensions to birth or style above the common, was always called "the Leddies' House." From that time, Burns and the Maybole youth became intimate friends, insomuch, that, during this summer, neither had any companion with whom he was more frequently in company than with the other. Burns was only at the village during school hours; but when his friend Willie returned to the paternal dome on Saturday nights, the poet would accompany him, and stay till it was time for both to come back to school on Monday morning. There was also an interval between the morning and afternoon meetings of the school, which the two youths used to spend together. Instead of amusing themselves with ball or any other sport, like the rest of the scholars, they would take a walk by themselves in the outskirts of the village, and converse on subjects calculated to improve their minds. By and bye, they fell upon a plan of holding disputations or arguments on speculative questions, one taking one side, and the other the other, without much regard to their respective opinions on the point, whatever it might be, the whole object being to sharpen their intellects. They asked several of their companions to come and take a side in these debates, but not one would do so; they only laughed at the young philosophers. The matter at length reached the ears of the master, who, however skilled in mathematics, possessed but a narrow understanding and little general knowledge. With all the bigotry of the old school, he conceived that this supererogatory employment of his pupils was a piece of absurdity, and he resolved to correct them in it. One day, therefore, when the school was fully met, and in the midst of its usual business, he went up to the desk where Burns and Willie were sitting opposite to each other, and began to advert in sarcastic terms to what he had heard of them. They had become great debaters, he understood, and conceived themselves fit to settle affairs of importance, which wiser heads usually let alone. He hoped their disputations would not ultimately become quarrels, and that they would never think of coming from words to blows; and so forth. The jokes of schoolmasters always succeed amongst the boys, who are too glad to find the awful man in any thing like good humour, to question either the moral aim or the point of his wit. They therefore, on this occasion, hailed the master's remarks with hearty peals of laughter. Nettled at this, Willie resolved he would "speak up" to Rodger; but first he asked Burns in a whisper if he would support him, which Burns promised to do. He then said that he was sorry to find that Robert and he had given offence; it had not been intended. And indeed he had expected that the master would have been rather pleased to know of their endeavours to improve their minds. He could assure him that such improvement was the sole object they had in view. Rodger sneered at the idea of their improving their minds by nonsensical discussions, and contemptuously asked what it was they disputed about. Willie replied, that generally there was a new subject every day; that he could not recollect all that had come under their attention; but the question of to-day had been—"Whether is a great general or a respectable merchant the most valuable member of society?" The dominie laughed outrageously at what he called the silliness of such a question, seeing there could be no doubt for a moment about it. "Well," said Burns, "if you think so, I will be glad if you take any side you please, and allow me to take the other, and let us discuss it before the school." Rodger most unwisely assented, and commenced the argument by a flourish in favour of the general. Burns answered by a pointed advocacy of the pretensions of the merchant, and soon had an evident superiority over his preceptor. The latter replied, but without success. His hand was observed to shake; then his voice trembled; and he dissolved the house in a state of vexation pitiable to behold. In this anecdote, who can fail to read a prognostication of future eminence to the two disputants? The one became the most illustrious poet of his country; and it is not unworthy of being mentioned in the same sentence, that the other advanced, through a career of successful industry in his native town, to the possession of a large estate in its neighbourhood, and some share of the honours usually reserved in this country for birth and aristocratic connection.

The coast in the neighbourhood of Burns's residence at Ballochneil presented a range of rustic characters upon whom his genius was destined to confer an extraordinary interest. At the farm of Shanter, on a slope overlooking the shore, not far from Turnberry Castle, lived Douglas Graham, a stout hearty specimen of the Carrick farmer, a little addicted to smuggling, but withal a worthy and upright member of society, and a kind-natured man. He had a wife named Helen M'Taggart, who was unusually addicted to superstitious beliefs and fears. The *steading* where this good couple lived is now no more, for the farm has been divided for the increase of two others in its neighbourhood; but genius has given them a perennial existence in the tale of Tam o'Shanter, where their characters are exactly delineated under the respective appellations of Tam and Kate. * * * *

At Ballochneil, Burns engaged heartily in the sports of leaping, dancing, wrestling, *putting* (throwing) the stone, and others of the like kind. His innate thirst for distinction and superiority was manifested in these as in more important affairs; but though he was possessed of great strength, as well as skill, he could never match his young bedfellow, John Niven. Obliged at last to acknowledge himself beat by this person in bodily warfare, he had recourse for amends to a spiritual mode of contention, and would engage young Niven in an argument about some speculative question, when, of course, he invariably floored his antagonist. His satisfaction on these occasions is said to have been extreme. One day, as he was walking slowly along the street of the village in a manner customary to him, with his eyes bent on the ground, he was met by the Misses Biggar, the daughters of the parish pastor. He would have passed without noticing them, if one of the young ladies had not called him by name. She then rallied him on his inattention to the fair sex, in preferring to look towards the inanimate ground, instead of seizing the opportunity afforded him of indulging in the most invaluable privilege of man, that of beholding and conversing with the ladies. "Madam," said he, "it is a natural and right thing for man to contemplate the ground, from whence *he* was taken, and for woman to look upon and observe man, from whom she was taken." This was a conceit, but it was the conceit of "no vulgar boy."

There is a great fair at Kirkoswald in the beginning of August—on the same day, we believe, with a like fair at Kirkoswald in Northumberland, both places having taken their rise from the piety of one person, Oswald, a Saxon king of the heptarchy, whose memory is probably honoured in these observances. During the week preceding this fair in the year 1777, Burns made overtures to his Maybole friend, Willie, for their getting up a dance, on the evening of the approaching festival, in one of the public-houses of the village, and inviting their sweethearts to it. Willie knew little at that time of dances or sweethearts; but he liked Burns, and was no enemy to amusement. He therefore consented, and it was agreed that some other young men should be requested to join in the undertaking. The dance took place, as designed, the requisite music being supplied by a hired band; and about a dozen couples partook of the fun. When it was proposed to part, the reckoning was called, and found to amount to eighteen shillings and fourpence. It was then discovered that almost every one present had looked to his neighbours for the means of settling this claim. Burns, the originator of the scheme, was in the poetical condition of not being master of a single penny. The rest were in the like condition, all except one, whose resources amounted to a groat, and Maybole Willie, who possessed about half-a-crown. The last individual, who alone boasted any worldly wisdom or experience, took it upon him to extricate the company from its difficulties. By virtue of a candid and sensible narration to the landlord, he induced that individual to take what they had, and give credit for the remainder. The payment of the debt is not the worst part of the story. Seeing no chance from begging or borrowing, Willie resolved to gain it, if possible, by merchandise. Observing that stationery articles for the school were procured at Kirkoswald with difficulty, he supplied himself with a stock from his father's warehouse at Maypole, and for some weeks sold pens and paper to his companions, with so much advantage, that at length he realised a sufficient amount of profit to liquidate the expense of the dance. Burns and he then went in triumph to the inn, and not only settled the claim to the last penny, but gave the kind-hearted host a bowl of thanks into the bargain. Willie, however, took care from that time forth to engage in no schemes for country dances without looking carefully to the probable state of the pockets of his fellow adventurers.

Burns, according to his own account, concluded his residence at Kirkoswald in a blaze of passion for a fair *filette* who lived next door to the school. At this time, owing to the destruction of the proper school of Kirkoswald, a chamber at the end of the old church, the business of parochial instruction was conducted in an apartment on the ground floor of a house in the main street of the village, opposite the churchyard. From behind this house, as from behind each of its neighbours in the same row, a small stripe of kail-yard (*Anglice*, kitchen garden) runs back about fifty yards, along a rapidly ascending slope. When Burns went into the particular patch behind the school to take the sun's altitude, he had only to look over a low enclosure to see the similar patch connected with the next house. Here, it seems, Peggy Thomson, the daughter of the rustic occupant of that house, was walking at the time, though more probably engaged in the business of cutting a cabbage for the family dinner, than imitating the flower-gathering Proserpine, or her prototype Eve. Hence the bewildering passion of the poet. Peggy was the theme of his "Song composed in August," beginning,

"Now westlin winds and slaughtering guns
Brings Autumn's pleasant weather."

She afterwards became Mrs. Neilson, and lived to a good age in the town of Ayr, where her children still reside.

At his departure from Kirkoswald, he engaged his Maybole friend and some other lads to keep up a correspondence with him. His object in doing so, as we may gather from his own narrative, was to improve himself in composition. "I carried this whim so far," says he, "that, though I had not three farthings' worth of business in the world, yet almost every post brought me as many letters as if I had been a broad plodding son of day-book and ledger." To Willie, in particular, he wrote often, and in the most friendly and confidential terms. When that individual was commencing business in his native town, the poet addressed him a poetical epistle of appropriate advice, headed with the well-known lines from Blair's Grave, beginning—

"Friendship! mysterious cement of the soul,
Sweetener of life and solder of society."

This correspondence continued till the period of the publication of the poems, when Burns wrote to request his friend's good offices in increasing his list of subscribers. The young man was then possessed of little influence; but what little he had, he exerted with all the zeal of friendship, and with considerable success. A considerable number of copies was accordingly transmitted in proper time to his care, and soon after the poet came to Maybole to receive the money. His friend collected a few choice spirits to meet him at the King's Arms Inn, and they spent a happy night together. Burns was on this occasion particularly elated, for Willie, in the midst of their conviviality, handed over to him above seven pounds, being the first considerable sum of money the poor bard had ever possessed. In the pride of his heart, next morning, he determined that he should not walk home, and accordingly he hired from his host a certain poor hack mare, well known along the whole road from Glasgow to Portpatrick—in all probability the first hired conveyance that Poet Burns had ever enjoyed, for even his subsequent journey to Edinburgh, aspicious as were the prospects under which it was undertaken, was performed on foot. Willie and a few other youths who had been in his company on the preceding night, walked out of town before him, for the purpose of taking leave at a particular spot; and before he came up, they had prepared a few mock-heroic verses in which to express their farewell. When Burns rode up, accordingly, they saluted him in this formal manner, a little to his surprise. He thanked them, however, and instantly added, "What need of all this fine parade of verse? It would have been quite enough if you had said—

Here comes Burns,
  On Rosinante;
She's d —— poor,
  But he's d ——canty."

The company then allowed Burns to go on his way rejoicing. (39.)

Under the humble roof of his parents, it appears that our poet had great advantages; but his opportunities of information at school were more limited as to time than they usually are among his countrymen in his condition of life; and the acquisitions which he made, and the poetical talent which he exerted, under the pressure of early and incessant toil, and of inferior, and perhaps scanty nutriment, testify at once the extraordinary force and activity of his mind. In his frame of body he rose nearly to five feet ten inches, and assumed the proportions that indicate agility as well as strength. In the various labours of the farm he excelled all his competitors. Gilbert Burns declares that in mowing, the exercise that tries all the muscles most severely, Robert was the only man that, at the end of a summer's day, he was ever obliged to acknowledge as his master. But though our poet gave the powers of his body to the labours of the farm, he refused to bestow on them his thoughts or his care. While the ploughshare under his guidance passed through the sward, or the grass fell under the sweep of his scythe, he was humming the songs of his country, musing on the deeds of ancient valour, or wrapt in the illusion of fancy, as her enchantments rose on his view. Happily the Sunday is yet a sabbath, on which man and beast rest from their labours. On this day, therefore, Burns could indulge in a free intercourse with the charms of nature. It was his delight to wander alone on the banks of the Ayr, whose stream is now immortal, and to listen to the song of the blackbird at the close of the summer's day. But still greater was his pleasure, as he himself informs us, in walking on the sheltered side of a wood, in a cloudy winter day, and hearing the storm rave among the trees; and more elevated still his delight, to ascend some eminence during the agitations of nature; to stride along its summit, while the lightning flashed around him; and, amidst the howlings of the tempest, to apostrophise the spirit of the storm. Such situations he declares most favourable to devotion:—"Rapt in enthusiasm, I seem to ascend towards Him *who walks on the wings of the winds!*" If other proofs were wanting of the character of his genius, this might determine it. The heart of the poet is peculiarly awake to every impression of beauty and sublimity; but with the higher order of poets, the beautiful is less attractive than the sublime.

The gaiety of many of Burns's writings, and the lively and even cheerful colouring with which he has portrayed his own character, may lead some persons to suppose, that the melancholy which hung over him towards the end of his days was not an original part of his constitution. It is not to be doubted, indeed, that this melancholy acquired a darker hue in the progress of his life; but, independent of his own and of his brother's testimony, evidence is to be found among his papers, that he was subject very early to those depressions of mind, which are perhaps not wholly separable from the sensibility of genius, but which in him arose to an uncommon degree. The following letter, addressed to his father, will serve as a proof of this observation. It was written at the time when he was learning the business of a flax dresser, and is dated

"*Irvine, December* 27, 1781.

"HONOURED SIR.—I have purposely delayed writing, in the hope that I should have the pleasure of seeing you on New-year's-day; but work comes so hard upon us, that I do not choose to be absent on that account, as well as for some other little reasons, which I shall tell you at meeting. My health is nearly the same as when you were here, only my sleep is a little sounder; and, on the whole, I am rather better than otherwise, though I mend by very slow degrees. The weakness of my nerves has so debilitated my mind, that I dare neither review past events, nor look forward into futurity; for the least anxiety or perturbation in my breast, produces most unhappy effects on my whole frame. Sometimes, indeed, when for an hour or two my spirits are a little lightened, I *glimmer* a little into futurity; but my principal, and indeed my only pleasurable employment, is looking backwards and forwards in a moral and religious way. I am quite transported at the thought, that ere long, very soon, I shall bid an eternal adieu to all the pains and uneasinesses, and disquietudes of this weary life, for I assure you I am heartily tired of it; and, if I do not very much deceive myself, I could contentedly and gladly resign it.

'The soul, uneasy and confin'd at home,
Rests and expatiates in a life to come.'

"It is for this reason I am more pleased with the 15th, 16th, and 17th verses of the 7th chapter of Revelations, than with any ten times as many verses in the whole Bible, and would not exchange the noble enthusiasm with which they inspire me, for all that this world has to offer. (40) As for this world, I despair of ever making a figure in it. I am not formed for the bustle of the busy, nor the flutter of the gay. I shall never again be capable of entering into such scenes. Indeed, I am altogether unconcerned at the thoughts of this life. I foresee that poverty and obscurity probably await me; I am in some measure prepared, and daily preparing, to meet them. I have but just time and paper to return you my grateful thanks for the lessons of virtue and piety you have given me, which were too much neglected at the time of giving them, but which, I hope, have been remembered ere it is yet too late. Present my dutiful respects to my mother, and my compliments to Mr. and Mrs. Muir; and with wishing you a merry New-year's-day, I shall conclude. I am, honoured sir, your dutiful son, "ROBERT BURNS.

"P. S.—My meal is nearly out; but I am going to borrow, till I get more."

This letter, written several years before the publication of his poems, when his name was as obscure as his condition was humble, displays the philosophic melancholy which so generally forms the poetical temperament, and that buoyant and ambitious spirit which indicates a mind conscious of its strength. At Irvine, Burns at this time possessed a single room for his lodging, rented perhaps at the rate of a shilling a-week. He passed his days in constant labour as a flax-dresser, and his food consisted chiefly of oatmeal, sent to him from his father's family. The store of this humble, though wholesome nutriment, it appears was nearly exhausted, and he was about to borrow till he should obtain a supply. (41) Yet even in this situation, his active imagination had formed to itself pictures of eminence and distinction. His despair of making a figure in the world, shows how ardently he wished for honourable fame; and his contempt of life, founded on this despair, is the genuine expression of a youthful and generous mind. In such a state of reflection, and of suffering, the imagination of Burns naturally passed the dark boundaries of our earthly horizon, and rested on those beautiful representations of a better world, where there is neither thirst, nor hunger, nor sorrow; and where happiness shall be in proportion to the capacity of happiness.

Such a disposition is far from being at variance with social enjoyments. Those who have studied the affinities of mind, know that a melancholy of this description, after a while, seeks relief in the endearments of society, and that it has no distant connection with the flow of cheerfulness, or even the extravagance of mirth. It was a few days after the writing of this letter that our poet, "in giving a welcome carousal to the new year, with his gay companions," suffered his flax to catch fire, and his shop to be consumed to ashes. (42)

The energy of Burns's mind was not exhausted by his daily labours, the effusion of his muse, his social pleasures, or his solitary meditations. Some time previous to his engagement as a flax-dresser, having heard that a debating club had been established in Ayr, he resolved to try how such a meeting would succeed in the village of Tarbolton. About the end of the year 1780, our poet, his brother, and five other young peasants of the neighbourhood, formed themselves into a society of this sort, the declared objects of which were to relax themselves after toil, to promote sociality and friendship, and to improve the mind. The laws and regulations were furnished by Burns. The members were to meet after the labours of the day were over, once a week, in a small public-house in the village, where each should offer his opinion on a given question or subject, supporting it by such arguments as he thought proper. The debate was to be conducted with order and decorum; and after it was finished, the members were to choose a subject for discussion at the ensuing meeting. The sum expended by each was not to exceed threepence; and, with the humble potation that this could procure, they were to toast their mistresses, and to cultivate friendship with each other. This society continued its meetings regularly for some time; and in the autumn of 1782, wishing to preserve some account of their proceedings, they purchased a book, into which their laws and regulations were copied, with a preamble, containing a short history of their transactions down to that period. This curious document, which is evidently the work of our poet, has been discovered, and it deserves a place in his memoirs.

"HISTORY OF THE RISE, PROCEEDINGS, AND REGULATIONS OF THE BACHELORS' CLUB.

'Of birth or blood we do not boast,
Nor gentry does our club afford;
But ploughman and mechanics we
In Nature's simple dress record.'

"As the great end of human society is to become wiser and better, this ought therefore to be the principal view of every man in every station of life. But as experience has taught us, that such studies as inform the head and mend the heart, when long continued, are apt to exhaust the faculties of the mind, it has been found proper to relieve and unbend the mind by some employment or another, that may be agreeable enough to keep its powers in exercise, but at the same time not so serious as to exhaust them. But superadded to this, by far the greater part of mankind are under the necessity *of earning the sustenance of human life by the labour of their bodies*, whereby, not only the faculties of mind, but the nerves and sinews of the body, are so fatigued, that it is absolutely necessary to have recourse to some amusement or diversion, to relieve the wearied man, worn down with the necessary labours of life.

"As the best of things, however, have been perverted to the worst of purposes, so, under the pretence of amusement and diversion, men have plunged into all the madness of riot and dissipation; and, instead of attending to the grand design of human life, they have begun with extravagance and folly, and ended with guilt and wretchedness. Impressed with these considerations, we, the following lads in the parish of Tarbolton, viz. Hugh Reid, Robert Burns, Gilbert Burns, Alexander Brown, Walter Mitchell, Thomas Wright, and William M'Gavin, resolved, for our mutual entertainment, to unite ourselves into a club, or society, under such rules and regulations, that while we should forget our cares and labours in mirth and diversion, we might not transgress the bounds of innocence and decorum; and after agreeing on these, and some other regulations, we held our first meeting at Tarbolton, in the house of John Richard, upon the evening of the 11th November, 1780, commonly called Hallowe'en, and after choosing Robert Burns president for the night, we proceeded to debate on this question: 'Suppose a young man, bred a farmer, but without any fortune, has it in his power to marry either of two women, the one a girl of large fortune, but neither handsome in person nor agreeable in conversation, but who can manage the household affairs of a farm well enough; the other of them a girl every way agreeable in person conversation, and behaviour, but without any fortune: which of them shall he choose?' Finding ourselves very happy in our society, we resolved to continue to meet once a month in the same house, in the way and manner proposed, and shortly thereafter we chose Robert Ritchie for another member. In May, 1781, we brought in David Sillar, (43) and in June, Adam Jamaison, as members. About the beginning of the year 1782, we admitted Matthew Patterson and John Orr, and in June following we choose James Patterson as a proper brother for such a society. The club being thus increased, we resolved to meet at Tarbolton on the race night, the July following, and have a dance in honour of our society. Accordingly, we did meet, each one with a partner, and spent the evening in such innocence and merriment, such cheerfulness and good humour, that every brother will long remember it with pleasure and delight." To this preamble are subjoined the rules and regulations.

The philosophical mind will dwell with interest and pleasure on an institution that combined so skilfully the means of instruction and of happiness; and if grandeur looks down with a smile on these simple annals, let us trust that it will be a smile of benevolence and approbation. It is with regret that the sequel of the history of the Bachelors' Club of Tarbolton must be told. It survived several years after our poet removed from Ayrshire, but no longer sustained by his talents, or cemented by his social affections, its meetings lost much of their attraction; and at length, in an evil hour, dissension arising amongst its members, the institution was given up, and the records committed to the flames. Happily, the preamble and the regulations were spared; and, as matter of instruction and of example, they are transmitted to posterity.

After the family of our bard removed from Tarbolton to the neighbourhood of Mauchline, he and his brother were requested to assist in forming a similar institution there. The regulations of the club at Mauchline were nearly the same as those of the club at Tarbolton; but one laudable alteration was made. The fines for non-attendance had at Tarbolton been spent in enlarging their scanty potations: at Mauchline it was fixed, that the money so arising should be set apart for the purchase of books, and the first work procured in this manner was the Mirror, the separate numbers of which were at that time recently collected and published in volumes. After it, followed a number of other works, chiefly of the same nature, and among these the Lounger. The society of Mauchline still [1800] subsists, and appeared in the list of subscribers to the first edition of the works of its celebrated associate.

The members of these two societies were originally all young men from the country, and chiefly sons of farmers—a description of persons, in the opinion of our poet, more agreeable in their manners, more virtuous in their conduct, and more susceptible of improvement, than the self-sufficient mechanics of country towns. With deference to the Conversation Society of Mauchline, it may be doubted, whether the books which they purchased were of a kind best adapted to promote the interest and happiness of persons in this situation of life. The Mirror and the Lounger, though works of great merit, may be said, on a general view of their contents, to be less calculated to increase the knowledge than to refine the taste of those who read them; and to this last object their morality itself, which is, however, always perfectly pure, may be considered as subordinate. As works of taste, they deserve great praise. They are, indeed, refined to a high degree of delicacy; and to this circumstance it is perhaps owing, that they exhibit little or nothing of the peculiar manners of the age or country in which they were produced. But delicacy of taste, though the source of many pleasures, is not without some disadvantages; and, to render it desirable, the possessor should, perhaps, in all cases, be raised above the necessity of bodily labour, unless, indeed, we should include under this term the exercise of the imitative arts, over which taste immediately presides. Delicacy of taste may be a blessing to him who has the disposal of his own time, and who can choose what book he shall read, of what diversion he shall partake, and what company he shall keep. To men so situated, the cultivation of taste affords a grateful occupation in itself, and opens a path to many other gratifications. To men of genius, in the possession of opulence and leisure, the cultivation of the taste may be said to be essential; since it affords employment to those faculties, which without employment would destroy the happiness of the possessor, and corrects that morbid sensibility, or, to use the expressions of Mr. Hume, that delicacy of passion, which is the bane of the temperament of genius. Happy had it been for our bard, after he emerged from the condition of a peasant, had the delicacy of his taste equalled the sensibility of his passions, regulating all the effusions of his muse, and presiding over all his social enjoyments. But to the thousands who share the original condition of Burns, and who are doomed to pass their lives in the station in which they were born, delicacy of taste, were it even of easy attainment, would, if not a positive evil, be at least a doubtful blessing. Delicacy of taste may make many necessary labours irksome or disgusting; and should it render the cultivator of the soil unhappy in his situation, it presents no means by which that situation may be improved. Taste and literature, which diffuse so many charms throughout society, which sometimes secure to their votaries distinction while living, and which still more frequently obtain for them posthumous fame, seldom procure opulence, or even independence, when cultivated with the utmost attention, and can scarcely be pursued with advantage by the peasant in the short intervals of leisure which his occupations allow. Those who raise themselves from the condition of daily labour, are usually men who excel in the practice of some useful art, or who join habits of industry and sobriety to an acquaintance with some of the more common branches of knowledge. The penmanship of Butterworth, and the arithmetic of Cocker, may be studied by men in the humblest walks of life; and they will assist the peasant more in the pursuit of independence than the study of Homer or of Shakespeare, though he could comprehend, and even imitate, the beauties of those immortal bards.

These observations are not offered without some portion of doubt and hesitation. The subject has many relations, and would justify an ample discussion. It may be observed, on the other hand, that the first step to improvement is, to awaken the desire of improvement, and that this will be most effectually done by such reading as interests the heart and excites the imagination. The greater part of the sacred writings themselves, which in Scotland are more especially the manual of the poor, come under this description. It may be further observed, that every human being is the proper judge of his own happiness, and, within the path of innocence, ought to be permitted to pursue it. Since it is the taste of the Scottish peasantry to give a preference to works of taste and of fancy (44), it may be presumed they find a superior gratification in the perusal of such works; and it may be added, that it is of more consequence they should be made happy in their original condition, than furnished with the means, or with the desire, of rising above it. Such considerations are, doubtless, of much weight; nevertheless, the previous reflections may deserve to be examined, and here we shall leave the subject.

Though the records of the society at Tarbolton are lost, and those of the society at Mauchline have not been transmitted, yet we may safely affirm, that our poet was a distinguished member of both these associations, which were well calculated to excite and to develope the powers of his mind. From seven to twelve persons constituted the society of Tarbolton, and such a number is best suited to the purposes of information. Where this is the object of these societies, the number should be such, that each person may have an opportunity of imparting his sentiments, as well as of receiving those of others; and the powers of private conversation are to be employed, not those of public debate. A limited society of this kind, where the subject of conversation is fixed beforehand, so that each member may revolve it previously in his mind, is perhaps one of the happiest contrivances hitherto discovered for shortening the acquisition of knowledge, and hastening the evolution of talents. Such an association requires indeed somewhat more of regulation than the rules of politeness, established in common conversation, or rather, perhaps, it requires that the rules of politeness, which in animated conversation are liable to perpetual violation, should be vigorously enforced. The order of speech established in the club at Tarbolton, appears to have been more regular than was required in so small a society; where all that is necessary seems to be the fixing on a member to whom every speaker shall address himself, and who shall in return secure the speaker from interruption. Conversation, which among men whom intimacy and friendship have relieved from reserve and restraint, is liable, when left to itself, to so many inequalities, and which, as it becomes rapid, so often diverges into separate and collateral branches, in which it is dissipated and lost, being kept within its channel by a simple limitation of this kind, which practice renders easy and familiar, flows along in one full stream, and becomes smoother, and clearer, and deeper, as it flows. It may also be observed, that in this way the acquisition of knowledge becomes more pleasant and more easy, from the gradual improvement of the faculty employed to convey it. Though some attention has been paid to the eloquence of the senate and the bar, which in this, as in all other free governments, is productive of so much influence to the few who excel in it, yet little regard has been paid to the humbler exercise of speech in private conversation—an art that is of consequence to every description of persons under every form of government, and on which eloquence of every kind ought perhaps to be founded.

The first requisite of every kind of elocution, a distinct utterance, is the offspring of much time and of long practice. Children are always defective in clear articulation, and so are young people, though in a less degree. What is called slurring in speech, prevails with some persons through life, especially in those who are taciturn. Articulation does not seem to reach its utmost degree of distinctness in men before the age of twenty, or upwards; in women it reaches this point somewhat earlier. Female occupations require much use of speech, because they are duties in detail. Besides, their occupations being generally sedentary, the respiration is left at liberty. Their nerves being more delicate, their sensibility as well as fancy is more lively; the natural consequence of which is, a more frequent utterance of thought, a greater fluency of speech, and a distinct articulation at an earlier age. But in men who have not mingled early and familiarly with the world, though rich perhaps in knowledge, and clear in apprehension, it is often painful to observe the difficulty with which their ideas are communicated by speech, through the want of those habits that connect thoughts, words, and sounds together; which, when established, seem as if they had arisen spontaneously, but which, in truth, are the result of long and painful practice; and when analysed, exhibit the phenomena of most curious and complicated association.

Societies then, such as we have been describing, while they may be said to put each member in possession of the knowledge of all the rest, improve the powers of utterance; and by the collision of opinion, excite the faculties of reason and reflection. To those who wish to improve their minds in such intervals of labour as the condition of a peasant allows, this method of abbreviating instruction, may, under proper regulations, be highly useful. To the student, whose opinions, springing out of solitary observation and meditation, are seldom in the first instance correct, and which have, notwithstanding, while confined to himself, an increasing tendency to assume in his own eye the character of demonstrations, an association of this kind, where they may be examined as they arise, is of the utmost importance; since it may prevent those illusions of imagination, by which genius being bewildered, science is often debased, and error propagated through successive generations. And to men who having cultivated letters, or general science, in the course of their education, are engaged in the active occupations of life, and no longer able to devote to study or to books the time requisite for improving or preserving their acquisitions, associations of this kind, where the mind may unbend from its usual cares in discussions of literature or science, afford the most pleasing, the most useful, and the most rational of gratifications.

Whether in the humble societies of which he was a member, Burns acquired much direct information, may perhaps be questioned. It cannot, however, be doubted, that by collision the faculties of his mind would be excited; that by practice his habits of enunciation would be established; and thus we have some explanation of that early command of words and of expression which enabled him to pour forth his thoughts in language not unworthy of his genius, and which, of all his endowments, seemed, on his appearance in Edinburgh, the most extraordinary. For associations of a literary nature, our poet acquired a considerable relish; and happy had it been for him, after he emerged from the condition of a peasant, if fortune had permitted him to enjoy them in the degree of which he was capable, so as to have fortified his principles of virtue by the purification of his taste; and given to the energies of his mind, habits of exertion that might have excluded other associations, in which it must be acknowledged they were too often wasted, as well as debased.

[The allusions in Burns's letter, and that of his brother, to his connection with Jean Armour, afford but a vague account of that affair; and it seems necessary that some farther and clearer particulars should now be given.

John Blane reports the following interesting circumstances respecting the attachment of the poet to Miss Armour:—There was a singing school at Mauchline, which Blane attended. Jean Armour was also a pupil, and he soon became aware of her talents as a vocalist. He even contracted a kind of attachment to this young woman, though only such as a country lad of his degree might entertain for the daughter of a substantial country mason. One night, there was a *rocking* at Mossgiel, where a lad named Ralph Sillar sang a number of songs in what was considered a superior style. When Burns and Blane were retired to their usual sleeping place in the stable-loft, the former asked the latter what he thought of Sillar's singing, to which Blane answered that the lad thought so much of it himself, and had so many airs about it, that there was no occasion for others expressing a favourable opinion—yet, he added, "I would not give Jean Armour for a score of him." "You are always talking of this Jean Armour," said Burns; "I wish you could contrive to bring me to see her." Blane readily consented to do so, and next evening, after the plough was loosed, the two proceeded to Mauchline for that purpose. Burns went into a public-house, and Blane went into the singing-school, which chanced to be kept in the floor above. When the school was dismissing, Blane asked Jean Armour if she would come to see Robert Burns, who was below, and anxious to speak to her. Having heard of his poetical talents, she said she would like much to see him, but was afraid to go without a female companion. This difficulty being overcome by the frankness of a Miss Morton—the Miss Morton of the Six Mauchline Belles—Jean went down to the room where Burns was sitting. "From that time," Blane adds very naïvely, "I had little of the company of Jean Armour."

Here for the present ends the story of Blane. The results of Burns's acquaintance with Jean have been already in part detailed. When her pregnancy could be no longer concealed, the poet, under the influence of honourable feeling, gave her a written paper, in which he acknowledged his being her husband—a document sufficient to constitute a marriage in Scotland, if not in the eye of decency, at least in that of law. But her father, from a dislike to Burns, whose theological satires had greatly shocked him, and from hopelessness of his being able to support her as a husband, insisted that she should destroy this paper, and remain as an unmarried woman.

Some violent scenes ensued. The parents were enraged at the imprudence of their daughter, and at Burns. The daughter, trembling beneath their indignation, could ill resist the command to forget and abandon her lover. He, in his turn, was filled with the extremest anguish when informed that she had given him up. Another event occurred to add to the torments of the unhappy poet. Jean, to avoid the immediate pressure of her father's displeasure, went about the month of May (1786) to Paisley, and took refuge with a relation of her mother, one Andrew Purdie, a wright. There was at Paisley a certain Robert Wilson, a good-looking young weaver, a native of Mauchline, and who was realising wages to the amount of perhaps three pounds a-week by his then flourishing profession. Jean Armour had danced with this "gallant weaver" at the Mauchline dancing-school balls, and, besides her relative Purdie, she knew no other person in Paisley. Being in much need of a small supply of money, she found it necessary to apply to Mr. Wilson, who received her kindly, although he did not conceal that he had a suspicion of the reason of her visit to Paisley. When the reader is reminded that village life is not the sphere in which high-wrought and romantic feelings are most apt to flourish, he will be prepared in some measure to learn that Robert Wilson not only relieved the necessities of the fair applicant, but formed the wish to possess himself of her hand. He called for her several times at Purdie's, and informed her, that, if she should not become the wife of Burns, he would engage himself to none while she remained unmarried. Mrs. Burns long after assured a female friend that she never gave the least encouragement to Wilson; but, nevertheless, his visits occasioned some gossip, which soon found its way to Mauchline, and entered the soul of the poet like a demoniac possession. He now seems to have regarded her as lost to him for ever, and that not purely through the objections of her relations, but by her own cruel and perjured desertion of one whom she had acknowledged as her husband. It requires these particulars, little as there may be of pleasing about them, to make us fully understand much of what Burns wrote at this time, both in verse and prose. Long afterwards, he became convinced that Jean, by no part of her conduct with respect to Wilson, had given him just cause for jealousy: it is not improbable that he learned in time to make it the subject of sport, and wrote the song, "Where Cart rins rowing to the sea," in jocular allusion to it. But for months—and it is distressing to think that these were the months during which he was putting his matchless poems for the first time to press —he conceived himself the victim of a faithless woman, and life was to him, as he himself describes it,

——— "a weary dream,
The dream of ane that never wauks."

In a letter dated June 12, 1786, he says "Poor ill-advised ungrateful Armour came home on Friday last. You have heard all the particulars of that affair, and a black affair it is. What she thinks of her conduct now, I don't know; one thing I do know, she has made me completely miserable. Never man loved, or rather adored, a woman more than I did her; and, to confess a truth between you and me, I do love her still to distraction, after all, though I won't tell her so if I were to see her, which I don't want to do. * * May Almighty God forgive her ingratitude and perjury to me, as I from my very soul forgive her." On the 9th July he writes—"I have waited on Armour since her return home, not from the least view of reconciliation, but merely to ask for her health, and—to you I will confess it—from a foolish hankering fondness—very ill-placed indeed. The mother forbade me the house, nor did Jean show the penitence that might have been expected. However, the priest, I am informed, will give me a certificate as a single man, if I comply with the rules of the church, which, for that very reason, I intend to do. I am going to put on sackcloth and ashes this day. I am indulged so far as to appear in my own seat. *Peccavi, pater, miserere mei.*"

In a letter of July 17, to Mr. David Brice of Glasgow, the poet thus continues his story:—I have already appeared publicly in church, and was indulged in the liberty of standing in my own seat. Jean and her friends insisted much that she should stand along with me in the kirk, but the minister would not allow it, which bred a great trouble, I assure you, and I am blamed as the cause of it, though I am sure I am innocent; but I am very much pleased, for all that, not to have had her company," And again, July 30—"Armour has got a warrant to throw me in jail till I find security for an enormous sum. This they keep an entire secret, but I got it by a channel they little dream of; and I am wandering from one friend's house to another, and, like a true son of the gospel, 'have no where to lay my head.' I know you will pour an execration on her head, but spare the poor ill-advised girl, for my sake; though may all the furies that rend the injured, enraged lover's bosom, await her mother until her latest hour! I write in a moment of rage, reflecting on my miserable situation—exiled, abandoned, forlorn,"

In this dark period, or immediately before it (July 22), the poet signed an instrument, in anticipation of his immediately leaving the kingdom, by which he devised all property of whatever kind he might leave behind, including the copyright of his poems, to his brother Gilbert, in considera-tion of the latter having undertaken to support his daughter Elizabeth, the issue of "Elizabeth Paton in Largieside." Intima-tion of this instrument was publicly made at the Cross of Ayr, two days after, by William Chalmers, writer. If he had been upon better terms with the Armours, it seems unlikely that he would have thus devised his property without a respect for the claims of his offspring by Jean.

After this we hear no more of the legal severities of Mr. Armour—the object of which was, not to abridge the liberty of the unfortunate Burns, but to drive him away from the country, so as to leave Jean more effectually disengaged. The POEMS now appeared, and probably had some effect in allaying the hostility of the old man to-wards their author. It would at least appear that, at the time of Jean's accouche-ment, September 3, the "skulking" had ceased, and the parents of the young woman were not so cruel as to forbid his seeing her. We now resume the story of John Blane.

At this time, Blane had removed from Mossgiel to Mauchline, and become servant to Mr. Gavin Hamilton; but Burns still remembered their old acquaintance. When, in consequence of information sent by the Armours as to Jean's situation, the poet came from Mossgiel to visit her, he called in passing at Mr. Hamilton's, and asked John to accompany him to the house. Blane went with him to Mr. Armour's, where, according to his recollection, the bard was received with all desirable civility. Jean held up a pretty female infant to Burns, who took it affectionately in his arms, and, after keeping it a little while. returned it to the mother, asking the bless-ing of God Almighty upon her and her infant. He was turning away to converse with the other people in the room, when Jean said, archly, "But this is not all—here is another baby," and handed him a male child, which had been born at the same time. He was greatly surprised, but took that child too for a little into his arms, and repeated his blessing upon it. (This child was afterwards named Robert, and still lives: the girl was named Jean, but only lived fourteen months.) The mood of the melancholy poet then changed to the mirth-ful, and the scene was concluded by his giving the ailing lady a hearty caress, and rallying her on this promising beginning of her history as a mother.

It would appear, from the words used by the poet on this occasion, that he was not without hope of yet making good his matri-monial alliance with Jean. This is rendered the more likely by the evidence which exists of his having, for some time during Sep-tember, entertained a hope of obtaining an excise appointment, through his friends Hamilton and Aiken; in which case he would have been able to present a respect-able claim upon the countenance of the Armours. But this prospect ended in dis-appointment; and there is reason to con-clude, that, in a very short time after the accouchement, he was once more forbidden to visit the house in which his children and *all but wife* resided. There was at this time a person named John Kennedy, who tra-velled the district on horseback as mercan-tile agent, and was on intimate terms with Burns. One day, as he was passing Moss-giel, Burns stopped him, and made the request that he would return to Mauchline with a present for "his poor wife." Kennedy consented, and the poet hoisted upon the pommel of the saddle a bag filled with the delicacies of the farm. He proceeded to Mr. Armour's house, and requested per-mission to see Jean, as the bearer of a message and a present from Robert Burns. Mrs. Armour violently protested against his being admitted to an interview, and be-stowed upon him sundry unceremonious appellations for being the friend of such a man; she was, however, overruled in this instance by her husband, and Kennedy was permitted to enter the apartment where Jean was lying. He had not been there many minutes, when he heard a rushing and screaming in the stair, and, immediately after, Burns burst into the room, followed closely by the Armours, who seemed to have exhausted their strength in endeavouring to repel his intrusion. Burns flew to the bed, and putting his cheek to Jean's, and then in succession to those of the slumbering infants, wept bitterly. The Armours, it is added by Kennedy, who has himself re-ported the circumstances (45), remained un-affected by his distress; but whether he was allowed to remain for a short time, or immediately after expelled, is not mentioned. After hearing this affecting anecdote of Burns, the Lament may verily appear to us as arising from

"No idly feigned poetic pains." (46)

The whole course of the Ayr is fine; but the banks of that river, as it bends to the eastward above Mauchline, are singularly beautiful, and they were frequented, as may be imagined, by our poet in his solitary walks. Here the muse often visited him. In one of these wanderings, he met among the woods, a celebrated beauty of the west of Scotland—a lady, of whom it is said that the charms of her person correspond with the character of her mind. (47) This incident gave rise, as might be expected, to a poem, of which an account will be found in the following letter, in which he enclosed it to the object of his inspiration:—

"To Miss ———

"*Mossgiel, 18th November,* 1786.

"MADAM.—Poets are such outré beings, so much the the children of wayward fancy and capricious whim, that I believe the world generally allows them a larger latitude in the laws of propriety, than the sober sons of judgment and prudence. I mention this as an apology for the liberties that a nameless stranger has taken with you in the enclosed poem, which he begs leave to present you with. Whether it has poetical merit any way worthy of the theme, I am not the proper judge, but it is the best my abilities can produce: and what to a good heart will perhaps be a superior grace, it is equally sincere as fervent.

"The scenery was nearly taken from real life, though I dare say, madam, you do not recollect it, as I believe you scarcely noticed the poetic *reveur* as he wandered by you. I had roved out as chance directed, in the favourite haunts of my muse, on the banks of the Ayr, to view nature in all the gaiety of the vernal year. The evening sun was flaming over the distant western hills; not a breath stirred the crimson opening blossom, or the verdant spreading leaf. It was a golden moment for a poetic heart. I listened to the feathered warblers, pouring their harmony on every hand, with a congenial kindred regard, and frequently turned out of my path, lest I should disturb their little songs, or frighten them to another station. Surely, said I to myself, he must be a wretch indeed, who, regardless of your harmonious endeavours to please him, can eye your elusive flights to discover your secret recesses, and to rob you of all the property nature gives you, your dearest comforts, your helpless nestlings. Even the hoary hawthorn twig that shot across the way, what heart at such a time but must have been interested in its welfare, and wished it preserved from the rudely-browsing cattle, or the withering eastern blast? Such was the scene, and such the hour, when, in a corner of my prospect, I spied one of the fairest pieces of nature's workmanship that ever crowned a poetic landscape, or met a poet's eye; those visionary bards excepted who hold commerce with aërial beings! Had calumny and villany taken my walk, they had at that moment sworn eternal peace with such an object.

"What an hour of inspiration for a poet! It would have raised plain, dull, historic prose into metaphor and measure.

"The enclosed song was the work of my return home; and perhaps it but poorly answers what might have been expected from such a scene. (48) * * *

"I have the honour to be, madam, your most obedient, and very humble servant,

"ROBERT BURNS."

'Twas even—the dewy fields were green,
  On every blade the pearls hang: (49)
The Zephyr wanton'd round the bean,
  And bore its fragrant sweets alang;
In every glen the mavis sang,
  All nature listening seemed the while,
Except where greenwood echoes rang,
  Amang the braes o' Ballochmyle.

With careless step I onward strayed,
  My heart rejoiced in nature's joy,
When, musing in a lonely glade,
  A maiden fair I chanced to spy;
Her look was like the morning's eye,
  Her hair like nature's vernal smile,
Perfection whispered passing by,
  Behold the lass o' Ballochmyle! (50)

Fair is the morn in flowery May,
  And sweet is night in Autumn mild;
When roving through the garden gay,
  Or wandering in the lonely wild:
But woman, Nature's darling child!
  There all her charms she does compile;
Even there her other works are foil'd
  By the bony lass o' Ballochmyle.

Oh had she been a country maid,
  And I the happy country swain!
Though sheltered in the lowest shed
  That ever rose on Scotland's plain,
Through weary winter's wind and rain,
  With joy, with rapture I would toil;
And nightly to my bosom strain
  The bonny lass o' Ballochmyle.

Then pride might climb the slippery steep,
  Where fame and honours lofty shine;
And thirst of gold might tempt the deep,
  Or downward seek the Indian mine;
Give me the cot below the pine,
  To tend the flocks, or till the soil,
And every day have joys divine
  With the bony lass o' Ballochmyle."

In the manuscript book in which our poet has recounted this incident, and into which the letter and poem are copied, he complains that the lady made no reply to his effusions, and this appears to have wounded his self-love. It is not, however, difficult to find an excuse for her silence. Burns was at this time little known; and, where known at all, noted rather for the wild strength of his humour, than for those strains of tenderness in which he afterwards so much excelled. To the lady herself his name had, perhaps, never been mentioned, and of such a poem she might not consider herself as the proper judge. Her modesty might prevent her from perceiving that the muse of Tibullus breathed in this nameless poet, and that her beauty was awakening strains destined to immortality on the banks of the Ayr. It may be conceived, also, that supposing the verse duly appreciated, delicacy might find it difficult to express its acknowledgments. The fervent imagination of the rustic bard possessed more of tenderness than of respect. Instead of raising himself to the condition of the object of his admiration, he presumed to reduce her to his own, and to strain this high-born beauty to his daring bosom. It is true, Burns might have found precedents for such freedoms among the poets of Greece and Rome, and, indeed, of every country. And it is not to be denied, that lovely women have generally submitted to this sort of profanation with patience, and even with good humour. To what purpose is it to repine at a misfortune which is the necessary consequence of their own charms, or to remonstrate with a description of men who are incapable of control?

"The lunatic, the lover, and the poet,
Are of imagination all compact."

It may be easily presumed, that the beautiful nymph of Ballochmyle, whoever she may have been, did not reject with scorn the adorations of our poet, though she received them with silent modesty and dignified reserve.

The sensibility of our bard's temper, and the force of his imagination, exposed him, in a particular manner, to the impressions of beauty; and these qualities, united to his impassioned eloquence, gave him in turn a powerful influence over the female heart. The banks of the Ayr formed the scene of youthful passions of a still tenderer nature, the history of which it would be improper to reveal, were it even in our power; and the traces of which will soon be discoverable only in those strains of nature and sensibility to which they gave birth. The song entitled Highland Mary is known to relate to one of these attachments. "It was written," says our bard, "on one of the most interesting passages of my youthful days." The object of this passion died early in life, and the impression left on the mind of Burns seems to have been deep and lasting. (51) Several years afterwards, when he was removed to Nithsdale, he gave vent to the sensibility of his recollections in the following impassioned lines. In the manuscript book from which we extract them, they are addressed To Mary in Heaven!

"Thou lingering star, with less'ning ray,
That lov'st to greet the early morn,
Again thou usher'st in the day
My Mary from my soul was torn.
Oh, Mary! dear departed shade!
Where is thy place of blissful rest?
Seest thou thy lover lowly laid?
Hear'st thou the groans that rend his breast?

That sacred hour can I forget,
Can I forget the hallowed grove,
Where by the winding Ayr we met
To live one day of parting love?
Eternity will not efface
Those records dear of transports past;
Thy image at our last embrace;
Ah! little thought we 'twas our last!

Ayr gurgling kissed his pebbled shore,
O'erhung with wild woods, thick'ning, green;
The fragrant birch, and hawthorn hoar,
Twin'd amorous round the raptured scene.
The flowers sprang wanton to be prest,
The birds sang love on every spray,
Till too, too soon, the glowing west
Proclaim'd the speed of winged day.

Still o'er these scenes my mem'ry wakes,
And fondly broods with miser care;
Time but the impression stronger makes,
As streams their channels deeper wear.
My Mary, dear departed shade!
Where is thy place of blissful rest?
Seest thou thy lover lowly laid?
Hear'st thou the groans that rend his breast?"

To the delineations of the poet by himself, by his brother, and by his tutor, these additions are necessary, in order that the reader may see his character in its various aspects, and may have an opportunity of forming a just notion of the variety, as well as of the power of his original genius. (52)

We have dwelt the longer on the early part of his life, because it is the least known, and because, as has already been mentioned, this part of his history is connected with some views of the condition and manners of the humblest ranks of society, hitherto little observed, and which will perhaps be found neither useless nor uninteresting.

About the time of his leaving his native county, his correspondence commences; and in the series of letters given to the world, the chief incidents of the remaining part of his life will be found. This authentic, though melancholy record, will supersede in future the necessity of any extended narrative.

Burns set out for Edinburgh in the month of November, 1786. He was furnished with a letter of introduction to Dr. Blacklock (53), from the gentleman to whom the doctor had addressed the letter which is represented by our bard as the immediate cause of his visiting the Scottish metropolis. He was acquainted with Mr. Stewart, Professor of Moral Philosophy in the university, and had been entertained by that gentleman at Catrine, his estate in Ayrshire. He had been introduced by Mr. Alexander Dalzeil (54) to the Earl of Glencairn, who had expressed his high approbation of his poetical talents. He had friends, therefore, who could introduce him into the circles of literature as well as of fashion, and his own manners and appearance exceeding every expectation that could have been formed of them, he soon became an object of general curiosity and admiration. (55) The following circumstance contributed to this in a considerable degree:—At the time when Burns arrived in Edinburgh, the periodical paper, entitled The Lounger, was publishing, every Saturday producing a successive number. His poems had attracted the notice of the gentlemen engaged in that undertaking, and the ninety-seventh number of those unequal, though frequently beautiful essays, is devoted to An Account of Robert Burns, the Ayrshire Ploughman, with extracts from his Poems, written by the elegant pen of Mr. Mackenzie. The Lounger had an extensive circulation among persons of taste and literature, not in Scotland only, but in various parts of England, to whose acquaintance, therefore, our bard was immediately introduced. The paper of Mr. Mackenzie was calculated to introduce him advantageously. The extracts are well selected; the criticisms and reflections are judicious as well as generous; and in the style and sentiments there is that happy delicacy, by which the writings of the author are so eminently distinguished. The extracts from Burns's poems in the ninety-seventh number of The Lounger, were copied into the London as well as into many of the provincial papers, and the fame of our bard spread throughout the island. Of the manners, character, and conduct of Burns at this period, the following account has been given by Mr. Stewart, Professor of Moral Philosophy in the University of Edinburgh, in a letter to the editor, which he is particularly happy to have obtained permission to insert in these memoirs:—

"The first time I saw Robert Burns was on the 23rd of October, 1786, when he dined at my house in Ayrshire, together with our common friend Mr. John Mackenzie, surgeon in Mauchline, to whom I am indebted for the pleasure of his acquaintance. I am enabled to mention the date particularly, by some verses which Burns wrote after he returned home, and in which the day of our meeting is recorded. My excellent and much lamented friend, the late Basil, Lord Daer, happened to arrive at Catrine the same day, and by the kindness and frankness of his manners, left an impression on the mind of the poet which was never effaced. (56) The verses I allude to are among the most imperfect of his pieces; but a few stanzas may perhaps be an object of curiosity to you, both on account of the character to which they relate, and of the light which they throw on the situation and feelings of the writer, before his name was known to the public.

I cannot positively say, at this distance of time, whether, at the period of our first acquaintance, the Kilmarnock edition of his poems had been just published, or was yet in the press. I suspect that the latter was the case, as I have still in my possession copies in his own handwriting of some of his favourite performances; particularly of his verses On Turning up a Mouse with his Plough; on the Mountain Daisy; and The Lament. On my return to Edinburgh, I showed the volume, and mentioned what I knew of the author's history to several of my friends; and among others to Mr. Henry Mackenzie, who first recommended him to public notice in the 97th number of The Lounger.

"At this time Burns's prospects in life were so extremely gloomy, that he had seriously formed a plan of going out to Jamaica in a very humble situation, not however without lamenting that his want of patronage should force him to think of a project so repugnant to his feelings, when his ambition aimed at no higher an object than the station of an exciseman or gauger in his own country.

"His manners were then, as they continued ever afterwards, simple, manly, and independent; strongly expressive of conscious genius and worth, but without any thing that indicated forwardness, arrogance, or vanity. He took his share in conversation, but not more than belonged to him; and listened with apparent attention and deference on subjects where his want of education deprived him of the means of information. If there had been a little more of gentleness and accommodation in his temper, he would,

I think, have been still more interesting; but he had been accustomed to give law in the circle of his ordinary acquaintance; and his dread of any thing approaching to meanness or servility, rendered his manner somewhat decided and hard. Nothing, perhaps, was more remarkable among his various attainments, than the fluency, and precision, and originality of his language, when he spoke in company; more particularly as he aimed at purity in his turn of expression, and avoided more successfully than most Scotchmen the peculiarities of Scottish phraseology.

"He came to Edinburgh early in the winter following, and remained there for several months. By whose advice he took this step, I am unable to say. Perhaps it was suggested only by his own curiosity to see a little more of the world; but, I confess, I dreaded the consequences from the first, and always wished that his pursuits and habits should continue the same as in the former part of life—with the addition of, what I considered as then completely within his reach, a good farm on moderate terms, in a part of the country agreeable to his taste.

"The attentions he received during his stay in town from all ranks and descriptions of persons, were such as would have turned any head but his own. I cannot say that I could perceive any unfavourable effect which they left on his mind. He retained the same simplicity of manners and appearance which had struck me so forcibly when I first saw him in the country; nor did he seem to feel any additional self-importance from the number and rank of his new acquaintance. His dress was perfectly suited to his station, plain and unpretending, with a sufficient attention to neatness. If I recollect right, he always wore boots; and, when on more than usual ceremony, buckskin breeches.

"The variety of his engagements, while in Edinburgh, prevented me from seeing him so often as I could have wished. In the course of the spring, he called on me once or twice, at my request, early in the morning, and walked with me to Braid Hills, in the neighbourhood of the town, when he charmed me still more by his private conversation than he had ever done in company. He was passionately fond of the beauties of nature; and I recollect once he told me, when I was admiring a distant prospect in one of our morning walks, that the sight of so many smoking cottages gave a pleasure to his mind, which none could understand who had not witnessed, like himself, the happiness and the worth which they contained.

"In his political principles he was then a Jacobite; which was perhaps owing partly to this, that his father was originally from the estate of Lord Mareschal. Indeed, he did not appear to have thought much on such subjects, nor very consistently. He had a very strong sense of religion, and expressed deep regret at the levity with which he had heard it treated occasionally in some convivial meetings which he frequented. I speak of him as he was in the winter of 1786-7; for afterwards we met but seldom, and our conversations turned chiefly on his literary projects, or his private affairs.

"I do not recollect whether it appears or not from any of your letters to me, that you had ever seen Burns. (57) If you have, it is superfluous for me to add, that the idea which his conversation conveyed of the powers of his mind, exceeded, if possible, that which is suggested by his writings. Among the poets whom I have happened to know, I have been struck, in more than one instance, with the unaccountable disparity between their general talents, and the occasional inspirations of their more favoured moments. But all the faculties of Burns's mind, were, as far as I could judge, equally vigorous; and his predilection for poetry was rather the result of his own enthusiastic and impassioned temper, than of a genius exclusively adapted to that species of composition. From his conversation I should have pronounced him to be fitted to excel in whatever walk of ambition he had chosen to exert his abilities.

"Among the subjects on which he was accustomed to dwell, the characters of the individuals with whom he happened to meet, was plainly a favourite one. The remarks he made on them were always shrewd and pointed, though frequently inclining too much to sarcasm. His praise of those he loved was sometimes indiscriminate and extravagant; but this, I suspect, proceeded rather rather from the caprice and humour of the moment, than from the effects of attachment in blinding his judgment. His wit was ready, and always impressed with the marks of a vigorous understanding; but, to my taste, not often pleasing or happy. His attempts at epigram, in his printed works, are the only performances, perhaps, that he has produced totally unworthy of his genius.

"In summer 1787, I passed some weeks in Ayrshire, and saw Burns occasionally. I think that he made a pretty long excursion that season to the Highlands, and that he also visited what Beattie calls the Arcadian ground of Scotland, upon the banks of the Teviot and the Tweed.

"I should have mentioned before, that, notwithstanding various reports I heard during the preceding winter, of Burns's predilection for convivial, and not very select society, I should have concluded in favour of his habits of sobriety, from all of him that ever fell under my own observation. He told me indeed himself, that the weakness of his stomach was such as to deprive him entirely of any merit in his temperance. I was, however, somewhat alarmed about the effect of his now comparatively sedentary and luxurious life, when he confessed to me, the first night he spent in my house after his winter's campaign in town, that he had been much disturbed when in bed, by a palpitation at his heart, which, he said, was a complaint to which he had of late become subject.

"In the course of the same season, I was led by curiosity to attend for an hour or two a Mason Lodge in Mauchline, where Burns presided. He had occasion to make some short unpremeditated compliments to different individuals from whom he had no reason to expect a visit, and everything he said was happily conceived, and forcibly as well as fluently expressed. If I am not mistaken, he told me, that in that village, before going to Edinburgh, he had belonged to a small club of such of the inhabitants as had a taste for books, when they used to converse and debate on any interesting questions that occurred to them in the course of their reading. His manner of speaking in public had evidently the marks of some practice in extempore elocution.

"I must not omit to mention, what I have always considered as characteristical in a high degree of true genius, the extreme facility and good-nature of his taste, in judging of the compositions of others where there was any real ground for praise. I repeated to him many passages of English poetry with which he was unacquainted, and have more than once witnessed the tears of admiration and rapture with which he heard them. The collection of songs by Dr. Aikin, which I first put into his hands, he read with unmixed delight, notwithstanding his former efforts in that very difficult species of writing; and I have little doubt that it had some effect in polishing his subsequent compositions.

"In judging of prose, I do not think his taste was equally sound. I once read to him a passage or two in Franklin's works, which I thought very happily executed, upon the model of Addison; but he did not appear to relish, or to perceive the beauty which they derived from their exquisite simplicity, and spoke of them with indifference, when compared with the point, and antithesis, and quaintness of Junius. The influence of this taste is very perceptible in his own prose compositions, although their great and various excellences render some of them scarcely less objects of wonder than his poetical performances. The late Dr. Robertson used to say, that considering his education, the former seemed to him the more extraordinary of the two.

"His memory was uncommonly retentive, at least for poetry, of which he recited to me, frequently long compositions with the most minute accuracy. They were chiefly ballads, and other pieces in our Scottish dialect; great part of them, he told me, he had learned in his childhood from his mother, who delighted in such recitations, and whose poetical taste, rude as it probably was, gave, it is presumable, the first direction to her son's genius.

"Of the more polished verses which accidentally fell into his hands in his early years, he mentioned particularly the recommendatory poems by different authors, prefixed to Hervey's Meditations; a book which has always had a very wide circulation among such of the country people of Scotland as affect to unite some degree of taste with their religious studies. And these poems (although they are certainly below mediocrity) he continued to read with a degree of rapture beyond expression. He took notice of this fact himself, as a proof how much the taste is liable to be influenced by accidental circumstances.

"His father appeared to me, from the account he gave of him, to have been a respectable and worthy character, possessed of a mind superior to what might have been expected from his station in life. He ascribed much of his own principles and feelings to the early impressions he had received from his instructions and example. I recollect that he once applied to *him* (and, he added, that the passage was a literal statement of the fact) the two last lines of the following passage in the Minstrel, the whole of which he repeated with great enthusiasm:

'Shall I be left forgotten in the dust,
When fate, relenting, lets the flower revive;
Shall nature's voice, to man alone unjust,
Bid him, though doom'd to perish, hope to live?

Is it for this fair virtue oft must strive
With disappointment, penury, and pain?
No! Heaven's immortal spring shall yet arrive;
And man's majestic beauty bloom again,
Bright thro' th' eternal year of love's triumphant reign. [taught:
This truth sublime his simple sire had
In sooth, 'twas almost all the shepherd knew.'

"With respect to Burns's early education, I cannot say anything with certainty. He always spoke with respect and gratitude of the schoolmaster who had taught him to read English, and who, finding in his scholar a more than ordinary ardour for knowledge, had been at pains to instruct him in the grammatical principles of the language. He began the study of Latin, but dropt it before he had finished the verbs. I have sometimes heard him quote a few Latin words, such as *omnia vincit amor*, &c., but they seemed to be such as he had caught from conversation, and which he repeated by *rote*. I think he had a project, after he came to Edinburgh, of prosecuting the study under his intimate friend, the late Mr. Nicol, one of the masters of the grammar-school here; but I do not know that he ever proceeded so far as to make the attempt.

"He certainly possessed a smattering of French; and if he had an affectation in anything, it was in introducing occasionally a word or phrase from that language. It is possible that his knowledge in this respect might be more extensive than I suppose it to be; but this you can learn from his more intimate acquaintance. It would be worth while to inquire, whether he was able to read the French authors with such facility as to receive from them any improvement to his taste. For my own part, I doubt it much; nor would I believe it, but on very strong and pointed evidence.

"If my memory does not fail me, he was well instructed in arithmetic, and knew something of practical geometry, particularly of surveying. All his other attainments were entirely his own.

"The last time I saw him was during the winter 1788-89, (59) when he passed an evening with me at Drumseugh, in the neighbourhood of Edinburgh, where I was then living. My friend, Mr. Alison, was the only other person in company. I never saw him more agreeable or interesting. A present which Mr. Alison sent him afterwards of his Essays on Taste, drew from Burns a letter of acknowledgment, which I remember to have read with some degree of surprise, at the distinct conception he appeared from it to have formed of the general principles of the doctrine of *association*." (60)

The scene that opened on our bard in Edinburgh was altogether new, and in a variety of other respects highly interesting, especially to one of his disposition of mind. To use an expression of his own, he found himself "suddenly translated from the veriest shades of life," into the presence, and, indeed, into the society, of a number of persons, previously known to him by report as of the highest distinction in his country, and whose characters it was natural for him to examine with no common curiosity. (61)

From the men of letters, in general, his reception was particularly flattering. The late Dr. Robertson, Dr. Blair, Dr. Gregory, Mr. Stewart, Mr. Mackenzie, and Mr. Fraser Tytler, may be mentioned in the list of those who perceived his uncommon talents, who acknowledged more especially his powers in conversation, and who interested themselves in the cultivation of his genius. (62) In Edinburgh literary and fashionable society are a good deal mixed. Our bard was an acceptable guest in the gayest and most elevated circles, and frequently received from female beauty and elegance those attentions above all others most grateful to him. (63) At the table of Lord Monboddo he was a frequent guest; and while he enjoyed the society, and partook of the hospitalities of the venerable judge, he experienced the kindness and condescension of his lovely and accomplished daughter. The singular beauty of this young lady was illuminated by that happy expression of countenance which results from the union of cultivated taste and superior understanding with the finest affections of the mind. The influence of such attractions was not unfelt by our poet. "There has not been anything like Miss Burnet," said he in a letter to a friend, "in all the combination of beauty, grace, and goodness, the Creator has formed since Milton's Eve on the first day of her existence." In his Address to Edinburgh, she is celebrated in a strain of still greater elevation:—

"Fair Burnet strikes th' adorning eye,
Heaven's beauties on my fancy shine!
I see the Sire of Love on high,
And own his work indeed divine!"

This lovely woman died a few years afterwards in the flower of youth. Our bard expressed his sensibility on that occasion, in verses addressed to her memory.

Among the men of rank and fashion, Burns was particularly distinguished by James, Earl of Glencairn. (64) On the motion of this nobleman, the *Caledonian Hunt*, an association of the principal of the nobility and gentry of Scotland, extended their patronage to our bard, and admitted him to their gay orgies. He repaid their notice by a dedication of the enlarged and improved edition of his poems, in which he has celebrated their patriotism and independence in very animated terms.

"I congratulate my country that the blood of her ancient heroes runs uncontaminated, and that, from your courage, knowledge, and public spirit, she may expect protection, wealth, and liberty. * * * * * * * May corruption shrink at your kindling indignant glance; and may tyranny in the ruler, and licentiousness in the people, equally find in you an inexorable foe."

It is to be presumed that these generous sentiments, uttered at an era singularly propitious to independence of character and conduct, were favourably received by the persons to whom they were addressed, and that they were echoed from every bosom, as well as from that of the Earl of Glencairn. This accomplished nobleman, a scholar, a man of taste and sensibility, died soon afterwards. Had he lived, and had his power equalled his wishes, Scotland might still have exulted in the genius, instead of lamenting the early fate of her favourite bard.

A taste for letters is not always conjoined with habits of temperance and regularity; and Edinburgh, at the period of which we speak, contained, perhaps, an uncommon proportion of men of considerable talents, devoted to social excesses, in which their talents were wasted and debased.

Burns entered into several parties of this description, with the usual vehemence of his character. His generous affections, his ardent eloquence, his brilliant and daring imagination, fitted him to be the idol of such associations; and accustoming himself to conversation of unlimited range, and to festive indulgences that scorned restraint, he gradually lost some portion of his relish for the more pure, but less poignant pleasures, to be found in the circles of taste, elegance, and literature. This sudden alteration in his habits of life operated on him physically as well as morally. The humble fare of an Ayrshire peasant he had exchanged for the luxuries of the Scottish metropolis, and the effects of this change on his ardent constitution could not be inconsiderable. But whatever influence might be produced on his conduct, his excellent understanding suffered no corresponding debasement. He estimated his friends and associates of every description at their proper value, and appreciated his own conduct with a precision that might give scope to much curious and melancholy reflection. He saw his danger, and at times formed resolutions to guard against it; but he had embarked on the tide of dissipation, and was borne along its stream.

Of the state of his mind at this time, an authentic, though imperfect, document remains, in a book which he procured in the spring of 1787, for the purpose, as he himself informs us, of recording in it whatever seemed worthy of observation. The following extracts may serve as a specimen:—

"*Edinburgh, April* 9, 1787.

"As I have seen a good deal of human life in Edinburgh, a great many characters which are new to one bred up in the shades of life as I have been, I am determined to take down my remarks on the spot. Gray observes, in a letter to Mr. Palgrave, that 'half a word fixed upon, or near the spot, is worth a cart-load of recollection.' I don't know how it is with the world in general, but with me, making my remarks is by no means a solitary pleasure. I want some one to laugh with me, some one to be grave with me, some one to please me and help my discrimination, with his or her own remark, and at times, no doubt, to admire my acuteness and penetration. The world are so busied with selfish pursuits, ambition, vanity, interest, or pleasure, that very few think it worth their while to make any observation on what passes around them, except where that observation is a sucker, or branch of the darling plant they are rearing in their fancy. Nor am I sure, notwithstanding all the sentimental flights of novel-writers, and the sage philosophy of moralists, whether we are capable of so intimate and cordial a coalition of friendship, as that one man may pour out his bosom, his every thought and floating fancy, his very inmost soul, with unreserved confidence to another, without hazard of losing part of that respect which man deserves from man; or, from the unavoidable imperfections attending human nature, of one day repenting his confidence.

"For these reasons I am determined to make these pages my confidant. I will sketch every character that any way strikes me, to the best of my power, with unshrinking justice. I will insert anecdotes, and take down remarks, in the old law phrase, *without feud or favour.* Where I hit on any thing clever, my own applause will in some measure feast my vanity; and, begging Patroclus' and Achates' pardon, I think a lock and key a security, at least equal to the bosom of any friend whatever.

"My own private story likewise, my love adventures, my rambles; the frowns and smiles of fortune on my bardship; my poems and fragments, that must never see the light, shall be occasionally inserted. In short, never did four shillings purchase so much friendship, since confidence went first to market, or honesty was set up to sale.

"To these seemingly invidious, but too just ideas of human friendship, I would cheerfully make one exception—the connection between two persons of different sexes, when their interests are united and absorbed by the tie of love—

'When thought meets thought, ere from the lips it part,
And each warm wish springs mutual from the heart.'

There confidence, confidence that exalts them the more in one another's opinion, that endears them the more to each other's hearts, unreservedly 'reigns and revels.' But this is not my lot; and, in my situation, if I am wise (which, by the bye, I have no great chance of being), my fate should be cast with the Psalmist's sparrow, 'to watch alone on the house tops.' Oh the pity!

* * * * * *

"There are few of the sore evils under the sun give me more uneasiness and chagrin than the comparison how a man of genius, nay of avowed worth, is received every where, with the reception which a mere ordinary character, decorated with the trappings and futile distinctions of fortune, meets. I imagine a man of abilities, his breast glowing with honest pride, conscious that men are born equal, still giving *honour to whom honour is due;* he meets at a great man's table, a Squire something, or a Sir somebody; he knows the *noble* landlord, at heart, gives the bard or whatever he is, a share of his good wishes, beyond, perhaps, any one at table; yet how will it mortify him to see a fellow whose abilities would scarcely have made an *eightpenny tailor,* and whose heart is not worth three farthings, meet with attention and notice, that are withheld from the son of genius and poverty!

"The noble Glencairn has wounded me to the soul here, because I dearly esteem, respect, and love him. He showed so much attention, engrossing attention, one day, to the only blockhead at table (the whole company consisted of his lordship, dunderpate, and myself), that I was within half a point of throwing down my gage of contemptuous defiance; but he shook my hand, and looked so benevolently good at parting. God bless him! though I should never see him more, I shall love him until my dying day! I am pleased to think I am so capable of the throes of gratitude, as I am miserably deficient in some other virtues.

"With Dr. Blair I am more at my ease. I never respect him with humble veneration; but when he kindly interests himself in my welfare, or still more, when he descends from his pinnacle, and meets me on equal ground in conversation, my heart overflows with what is called *liking.* When he neglects me for the mere carcase of greatness, or when his eye measures the difference of our points of elevation, I say to myself, with scarcely any emotion, what do I care for him or his pomp either?"

The intentions of the poet in procuring this book, so fully described by himself, were very imperfectly executed. He has inserted in it few or no incidents, but several observations and reflections, of which the greater part that are proper for the public eye will be found interwoven in his letters. The most curious particulars in the book are the delineations of the characters he met with. These are not numerous; but they are chiefly of persons of distinction in the republic of letters, and nothing but the delicacy and respect due to living characters prevents us from committing them to the press. Though it appears that in his conversation he was sometimes disposed to sarcastic remarks on the men with whom he lived, nothing of this kind is discoverable in these more deliberate efforts of his understanding, which, while they exhibit great clearness of discrimination, manifest also the wish, as well as the power, to bestow high and generous praise.

As a specimen of these delineations, we give the character of Dr. Blair, who has now paid the debt of nature, in the full confidence that this freedom will not be found inconsistent with the respect and veneration due to that excellent man, the last stir in the literary constellation, by which the metropolis of Scotland was, in the earlier part of the present reign, so beautifully illuminated.

"It is not easy forming an exact judgment of any one; but, in my opinion, Dr. Blair is merely an astonishing proof of what industry and application can do. Natural parts like his are frequently to be met with; his vanity is proverbially known among his acquaintance; but he is justly at the head of what may be called fine writing; and a critic of the first, the very first, rank in prose; even in poetry, a bard of Nature's making can only take the *pas* of his. He has a heart not of the very finest water, but far from being an ordinary one. In short, he is truly a worthy and most respectable character."

[Mr. Cromek informs us that one of the poet's remarks, when he first came to Edinburgh, was, that between the men of rustic life and the polite world, he observed little difference; that in the former, though unpolished by fashion and unenlightened by science, he had found much observation, and much intelligence; but a refined and accomplished woman was a thing almost new to him, and of which he had formed but a very inadequate idea. Mr. Lockhart adds, that there is reason to believe that Burns was much more a favourite amongst the female than the male part of elevated Edinburgh society to which he was introduced, and that in consequence, in all probability, of the greater deference he paid to the gentler sex. "It is sufficiently apparent," adds Mr. L., "that there were many points in Burns's conversational habits, which men, accustomed to the delicate observances of refined society, might be more willing to tolerate under the first excitement of personal curiosity, than from any very deliberate estimate of the claims of such a genius, under such circumstances developed. He by no means restricted his sarcastic observations on those whom he encountered in the world to the confidence of his note-book, but startled ears polite with the utterance of audacious epigrams, far too witty not to obtain general circulation in so small a society as that of the northern capital, far too bitter not to produce deep resentment, far too numerous not to spread fear almost as widely as admiration." An example of his unscrupulousness is thus given by Mr. Cromek. "At a private breakfast, in a literary circle of Edinburgh, the conversation turned on the poetical merit and pathos of Gray's Elegy, a poem of which he was enthusiastically fond. A clergyman present, remarkable for his love of paradox, and for his eccentric notions upon every subject, distinguished himself by an injudicious and ill-timed attack on this exquisite poem, which Burns, with generous warmth for the reputation of Gray, manfully defended. As the gentleman's remarks were rather general than specific, Burns urged him to bring forward the passages which he thought exceptionable. He made several attempts to quote the poem, but always in a blundering, inaccurate manner. Burns bore all this for a good while with his usual good-natured forbearance, till at length, goaded by the fastidious criticisms and wretched quibblings of his opponent, he roused himself, and with an eye flashing contempt and indignation, and with great vehemence of gesticulation, he thus addressed the cold critic: 'Sir, I now perceive a man may be an excellent judge of poetry by square and rule, and after all, be a d—d blockhead.'" "To pass from these trifles," says Mr. Lockart, "it needs no effort of imagination to conceive what the sensations of an isolated set of scholars (almost all either clergymen or professors) must have been in the presence of this big-boned, black-browed, brawny stranger, with his great flashing eyes, who having forced his way among them from the plough-tail, at a single stride, manifested, in the whole strain of his bearing and conversation, a most thorough conviction, that, in the society of the most eminent men of his nation, he was exactly where he was entitled to be; hardly deigned to flatter them by exhibiting even an occasional symptom of being flattered by their notice; by turns calmly measured himself against the most cultivated understandings of his time in discussion; overpowered the *bon mots* of the most celebrated convivialists by broad floods of merriment, impregnated with all the burning life of genius; astounded bosoms habitually enveloped in the thrice-plied folds of social reserve, by compelling them to tremble, nay, to tremble visibly, beneath the fearless touch of natural pathos; and all this without indicating the smallest willingness to be ranked among those professional ministers of excitement, who are content to be paid in money and smiles for doing what the spectators and auditors would be ashamed of doing in their own persons, even if they had the power of doing it; and, last, and probably worst of all, who was known to be in the habit of enlivening societies which they would have scorned to approach, still more frequently than their own, with eloquence no less magnificent; with wit in all likelihood still more daring; often enough, as the superiors whom he fronted without alarm, might have guessed from the beginning, and had, ere long, no occasion to guess, with wit pointed at themselves."]

"By the new edition of his poems, (65)

Burns acquired a sum of money that enabled him not only to partake of the pleasures of Edinburgh, but to gratify a desire he had long entertained, of visiting those parts of his native country most attractive by their beauty or their grandeur; a desire which the return of summer naturally revived. The scenery on the banks of the Tweed, and of its tributary streams, strongly interested his fancy; and accordingly he left Edinburgh on the 6th of May, 1787, on a tour through a country so much celebrated in the rural songs of Scotland. He travelled on horseback, and was accompanied, during some part of his journey, by Mr. Ainslie, now writer to the signet, a gentleman who enjoyed much of his friendship and of his confidence. Of this tour a journal remains, which, however, contains only occasional remarks on the scenery, and which is chiefly occupied with an account of the author's different stages, and with his observations on the various characters to whom he was introduced. In the course of this tour he visited Mr. Ainslie of Berrywell, the father of his companion; Mr. Brydone, the celebrated traveller, to whom he carried a letter of introduction from Mr. Mackenzie; the Rev. Dr. Somerville of Jedburgh, the historian; Mr. and Mrs. Scott of Wauchope; Dr. Elliott, a physician, retired to a romantic spot on the banks of the Roole; Sir Alexander Don; Sir James Hall of Dunglass; and a great variety of other respectable characters. Every where the fame of the poet had spread before him, and every where he received the most hospitable and flattering attentions. At Jedburgh he continued several days, and was honoured by the magistrates with the freedom of their borough. The following may serve as a specimen of this tour, which the perpetual reference to living characters prevents our giving at large:—

"*Saturday, May 6th.* Left Edinburgh—Lammer-muir-hills, miserably dreary in general, but at times very picturesque.

"Lanson-edge, a glorious view of the Merse. Reach Berrywell. * * * The family meeting with my *compagnon de voyage*, very charming; particularly the sister. * * *

"*Sunday.* Went to Church at Dunse. Heard Dr. Bowmaker.

"*Monday.* Coldstream—glorious river Tweed—clear and majestic—fine bridge—dine at Coldstream with Mr. Ainslie and Mr. Foreman. Beat Mr. Foreman in a dispute about Voltaire. Drink tea at Lenel-House with Mr. and Mrs. Brydone. * * * Reception extremely flattering. Sleep at Coldstream.

"*Tuesday.* Breakfast at Kelso—charming situation of the town—fine bridge over the Tweed. Enchanting views and prospects on both sides of the river, especially on the Scotch side. * * * Visit Roxburgh Palace—fine situation of it. Ruins of Roxburgh Castle—a holly-bush growing where James II. was accidentally killed by the bursting of a cannon. A small old religious ruin, and a fine old garden planted by the religious, rooted out and destroyed by a Hottentot, *a maitre d'hotel* of the duke's—climate and soil of Berwickshire, and even Roxburghshire, superior to Ayrshire—bad roads—turnip and sheep husbandry, their great improvements. * * * Low markets, consequently low lands—magnificence of farmers and farm-houses. Come up the Teviot, and up the Jed to Jedburgh to lie, and so wish myself good-night.

"*Wednesday.* Breakfast with Mr. Fair. * * * * Charming romantic situation of Jedburgh, with gardens and orchards, intermingled among the houses and the ruins of a once magnificicent cathedral. All the towns here have the appearance of old rude grandeur, but extremely idle. Jed, a fine romantic little river. Dined with Captain Rutherford, * * * return to Jedburgh. Walk up the Jed with some ladies to be shown Love-lane, and Blackburn, two fairy-scenes. Introduced to Mr. Potts, writer, and to Mr. Somerville, the clergyman of the parish, a man and a gentleman, but sadly addicted to punning. (66). * * * * *

"*Jedburgh Saturday.* Was presented by the magistrates with the freedom of the town.

"Took farewell of Jedburgh with some melancholy sensations.

"*Monday, May 14th, Kelso.* Dine with the farmers' club—all gentlemen talking of high matters—each of them keeps a hunter from £30 to £50 value, and attends the fox-hunting club in the county. Go out with Mr. Ker, one of the club, and a friend of Mr. Ainslie's, to sleep. In his mind and manners, Mr. Ker is astonishingly like my dear old friend Robert Muir—every thing in his house elegant. He offers to accompany me in my English tour.

"*Tuesday.* Dine with Sir Alexander Don—a very wet day. * * * Sleep at Mr. Ker's again, and set out next day for Melrose—visit Dryburgh, a fine old ruined abbey, by the way. Cross the Leader, and come up the Tweed to Melrose. Dine there, and visit that far-famed glorious ruin—come to Selkirk up the banks of Ettrick. The whole country hereabouts, both on Tweed and Ettrick, remarkably stony."

Having spent three weeks in exploring this interesting scenery, Burns crossed over into Northumberland. Mr. Ker, and Mr. Hood, two gentlemen with whom he had become acquainted in the course of his tour, accompanied him. He visited Alnwick Castle, the princely seat of the Duke of Northumberland; the Hermitage and Old Castle of Warkworth; Morpeth and Newcastle. In this last town he spent two days, and then proceeded to the south-west by Hexam and Wardrue, to Carlisle. After spending a day at Carlisle with his friend Mr. Mitchel, he returned into Scotland, and at Annan his journal terminates abruptly.

Of the various persons with whom he became acquainted in the course of this journey, he has, in general, given some account, and almost always a favourable one. That on the banks of the Tweed, and of the Teviot, our bard should find nymphs that were beautiful, is what might be confidently presumed. Two of these are particularly described in his journal. But it does not appear that the scenery, or its inhabitants, produced any effort of his muse, as was to have been wished and expected. From Annan, Burns proceeded to Dumfries, and thence through Sanquhar, to Mossgiel, near Mauchline, in Ayrshire, where he arrived about the 8th of June, 1787, after a long absence of six busy and eventful months. It will easily be conceived with what pleasure and pride he was received by his mother, his brothers, and sisters. He had left them poor, and comparatively friendless; he returned to them high in public estimation, and easy in his circumstances He returned to them unchanged in his ardent affections, and ready to share with them to the uttermost farthing, the pittance that fortune had bestowed. (67)

Having remained with them a few days, he proceeded again to Edinburgh, and immediately set out on a journey to the Highlands. Of this tour no particulars have been found among his manuscripts. A letter to his friend Mr. Ainslie, dated *Arrochar, by Lochlong, June 28*, 1787, commences as follows:—

"I write you this on my tour through a country where savage streams tumble over savage mountains, thinly overspread with savage flocks, which starvingly support as savage inhabitants. My last stage was Inverary—to-morrow night's stage, Dumbarton. I ought sooner to have answered your kind letter, but you know I am a man of many sins."

Part of a letter from our bard to a friend (68), giving some account of his journey, has been communicated to the editor. The reader will be amused with the following extract:—

"On our return, at a Highland gentleman's hospitable mansion, we fell in with a merry party, and danced till the ladies left us, at three in the morning. Our dancing was none of the French or English insipid formal movements; the ladies sang Scotch songs like angels, at intervals: then we flew at *Bab at the bewster, Tullochgorum, Loch Erroch side* (69), &c., like midges sporting in the mottie sun, or craws prognosticating a storm in a hairst day. When the dear lasses left us, we ranged round the bowl till the good-fellow hour of six; except a few minutes that we went out to pay our devotions to the glorious lamp of day peering over the towering top of Benlomond. We all kneeled; our worthy landlord's son held the bowl, each man a full glass in his hand; and I, as priest, repeated some rhyming nonsense, like Thomas-a-Rhymer's prophecies I suppose. After a small refreshment of the gifts of Somnus, we proceeded to spend the day on Lochlomond, and reached Dumbarton in the evening. We dined at another good fellow's house, and consequently push'd the bottle; when we went out to mount our horses, we found ourselves 'No vera fou but gaylie yet.' My two friends and I rode soberly down the Loch side, till by came a Highlandman at the gallop, on a tolerably good horse, but which had never known the ornaments of iron or leather. We scorned to be out-galloped by a Highlandman, so off we started, whip and spur. My companions, though seemingly gaily mounted, fell sadly astern; but my old mare, Jenny Geddes, one of the Rosinante family, she strained past the Highlandman in spite of all his efforts, with the hair-halter: just as I was passing him, Donald wheeled his horse, as if to cross before me to mar my progress, when down came his horse, and threw his breekless rider in a clipt hedge; and down came Jenny Geddes over all, and my bardship between her and the Highlandman's horse. Jenny Geddes trode over me with such cautious reverence, that matters were not so bad as might well have been expected; so I came off with a few cuts and bruises, and a thorough resolution to be a pattern of sobriety for the future.

"I have yet fixed on nothing with respect to the serious business of life. I am, just as usual, a rhyming, mason-making, raking, aimless, idle fellow. However, I shall somewhere have a farm soon. I was going to say, a wife too; but that must never be my blessed lot. I am but a younger son of the house of Parnassus, and, like other younger sons of great families, I may intrigue, if I choose to run all risks, but must not marry.

"I am afraid I have almost ruined one source, the principal one, indeed, of my former happiness—that eternal propensity I always had to fall in love. My heart no more glows with feverish rapture. I have no paradisiacal evening interviews stolen from the restless cares and prying inhabitants of this weary world. I have only * * * *. This last is one of your distant acquaintance, has a fine figure, and elegant manners, and, in the train of some great folks whom you know, has seen the politest quarters in Europe. I do like her a good deal; but what piques me is her conduct at the commencement of our acquaintance. I frequently visited her when I was in———, and after passing regularly the intermediate degrees between the distant formal bow and the familiar grasp round the waist, I ventured, in my careless way, to talk of friendship in rather ambiguous terms; and, after her return to ———, I wrote to her in the same style. Miss, construing my words farther I suppose than I intended, flew off in a tangent of female dignity and reserve, like a mountain-lark in an April morning; and wrote me an answer which measured me out very completely what an immense way I had to travel before I could reach the climate of her favour. But I am an old hawk at the sport; and wrote her such a cool, deliberate, prudent reply, as brought my bird from her aërial towerings, pop down at my foot like corporal Trim's hat. (70)

"As for the rest of my acts, and my wars, and all my wise sayings, and why my mare was called Jenny Geddes, they shall be recorded in a few weeks hence, at Linlithgow, in the chronicles of your memory, by

"ROBERT BURNS."

From this journey Burns returned to his friends in Ayrshire, with whom he spent the month of July, renewing his friendships, and extending his acquaintance throughout the country, where he was now very generally known and admired. In August he again visited Edinburgh, whence he undertook another journey towards the middle of this month, in company with Mr. M. Adair, now Dr. Adair, of Harrowgate (71), of which this gentleman has favoured us with the following account:—

"Burns and I left Edinburgh together in August, 1787. We rode by Linglithgow and Carron, to Stirling. We visited the iron works at Carron, with which the poet was forcibly struck. The resemblance between that place and its inhabitants, to the cave of the Cyclops, which must have occurred to every classical reader, presented itself to Burns. At Stirling the prospects from the castle strongly interested him; in a former visit to which, his national feelings had been powerfully excited by the ruinous and roofless state of the hall in which the Scottish parliaments had frequently been held. His indignation had vented itself in some imprudent, but not unpoetical lines, which had given much offence, and which he took this opportunity of erasing, by breaking the pane of the window at the inn on which they were written.

"At Stirling we met with a company of travellers from Edinburgh, among whom was a character in many respects congenial with that of Burns. This was Nicol, one of th teachers of the High Grammar School at Edinburgh—the same wit and power of conversation, the same fondness for convivial society, and thoughtlessness of to-morrow, characterised both. Jacobitical principles in politics were common to both of them; and these have been suspected, since the revolution of France, to have given place in each to opinions apparently opposite. (72) I regret that I have preserved no *memorabilia* of their conversation, either on this or on other occasions, when I happened to meet them together. Many songs were sung; which I mention for the sake of observing, that when Burns was called on in his turn, he was accustomed, instead of singing, to recite one or other of his own shorter poems, with a tone and emphasis which, though not correct or harmonious, were impressive and pathetic. This he did on the present occasion.

"From Stirling we went next morning through the romantic and fertile vale of Devon to Harvieston, in Clackmannanshire, then inhabited by Mrs. Hamilton (73), with the younger part of whose family Burns had been previously acquainted. He introduced me to the family, and there was formed my first acquaintance with Mrs. Hamilton's eldest daughter, to whom I have been married for nine years. Thus was I indebted to Burns for a connection from which I have derived, and expect farther to derive, much happiness.

"During a residence of about ten days at Harvieston, we made excursions to visit various parts of the surrounding scenery, inferior to none in Scotland in beauty, sublimity, and romantic interest; particularly Castle Campbell, the ancient seat of the family of Argyle; and the famous cataract of the Devon, called the Caldron Linn; and the Rumbling Bridge, a single broad arch, thrown by the devil, if tradition is to be believed, across the river, at about the height of a hundred feet above its bed. I am surprised that none of these scenes should have called forth an exertion of Burns's muse. But I doubt if he had much taste for the picturesque. I well remember, that the ladies at Harvieston, who accompanied us on this jaunt, expressed their disappointment at his not expressing, in more glowing and fervid language, his impressions of the Caldron Linn scene, certainly highly sublime, and somewhat horrible.

"A visit to Mrs. Bruce of Clackmannan, a lady above ninety, the lineal descendant of that race which gave the Scottish throne its brightest ornament, interested his feelings more powerfully. This venerable dame, with characteristical dignity, informed me, on my observing that I believed she was descended from the family of Robert Bruce, that Robert Bruce was sprung from her family. Though almost deprived of speech by a paralytic affection, she preserved her hospitality and urbanity. She was in possession of the hero's helmet and two-handed sword, with which she conferred on Burns and myself the honour of knighthood, remarking, that she had a better right to confer that title than *some people*. * * You will, of course, conclude, that the old lady's political tenets were as Jacobitical as the poet's, a conformity which contributed not a little to the cordiality of our reception and entertainment. She gave, as her first toast after dinner, *Awa' Uncos*, or Away with the Strangers. Who these strangers were, you will readily understand. Mrs. A. corrects me by saying it should be *Hooi*, or *Hooi Uncos*, a sound used by shepherds to direct their dogs to drive away the sheep. (74)

"We returned to Edinburgh by Kinross (on the shore of Lochleven) and Queensferry. I am inclined to think Burns knew nothing of poor Michael Bruce, who was then alive at Kinross, or had died there a short while before. A meeting between the bards, or a visit to the deserted cottage and early grave of poor Bruce, would have been highly interesting. (75)

"At Dunfermline we visited the ruined abbey, and the abbey-church, now consecrated to Presbyterian worship. Here I mounted the *cutty stool*, or stool of repentance, assuming the character of a penitent for fornication; while Burns, from the pulpit, addressed to me a ludicrous reproof and exhortation parodied from that which had been delivered to himself in Ayrshire, where he had, as he assured me, once been one of seven who mounted the *seat of shame* together.

"In the church-yard two broad flag-stones marked the grave of Robert Bruce, for whose memory Burns had more than common veneration. He knelt and kissed the stone with sacred fervour, and heartily *(suus ut mos erat)* execrated the worse than Gothic neglect of the first of Scottish heroes." (76)

The surprise expressed by Dr. Adair, in his excellent letter, that the romantic scenery of the Devon should have failed to call forth any exertion of the poet's muse, is not in its nature singular; and the disappointment felt at his not expressing in more glowing language his emotions on the sight of the famous cataract of that river, is similar to what was felt by the friends of Burns on other occasions of the same nature. Yet the inference that Dr. Adair seems inclined to draw from it, that he had little taste for the picturesque might be questioned, even if it stood uncontroverted by other evidence. The muse of Burns was in a high degree capricious; she came uncalled, and often refused to attend at his bidding. Of all the numerous subjects suggested to him by his friends and correspondents, there is scarcely one that he adopted. The very expectation that a particular occasion would excite the energies of fancy, if communicated to Burns, seemed in him, as in other poets, destructive of the effect expected. Hence perhaps may be explained, why the banks of the Devon and of the Tweed form no part of the subjects of his song.

A similar train of reasoning may perhaps explain the want of emotion with which he viewed the Caldron Linn. Certainly there are no affections of the mind more deadened by the influence of previous expectation, than those arising from the sight of natural objects, and more especially of objects of grandeur. Minute descriptions of scenes, of a sublime nature, should never be given to those who are about to view them, particularly if they are persons of great strength and sensibility of imagination. Language seldom or never conveys an adequate idea of such objects, but in the mind of a great poet it may excite a picture that far transcends them. The imagination of Burns might form a cataract, in comparison with which the Caldron Linn should seem the purling of a rill, and even the mighty falls of Niagara a humble cascade. (77)

Whether these suggestions may assist in explaining our bard's deficiency of impression on the occasion referred to, or whether it ought rather to be imputed to some pre-occupation, or indisposition of mind, we presume not to decide: but that he was in general feelingly alive to the beautiful or sublime in scenery, may be supported by irresistible evidence. It is true this pleasure was greatly heightened in his mind, as might be expected, when combined with moral emotions of a kind with which it happily unites. That under this association Burns contemplated the scenery of the Devon with the eye of a genuine poet, the following lines written at this very period may bear witness :—

"ON A YOUNG LADY, (78) RESIDING ON THE BANKS OF THE SMALL RIVER DEVON, IN CLACKMANNANSHIRE, BUT WHOSE INFANT YEARS WERE SPENT IN AYRSHIRE.

How pleasant the banks of the clear-winding Devon, [blooming fair;
With green-spreading bushes, and flowers
But the bonniest flower on the Banks of the Devon [Ayr.
Was once a sweet bud on the braes of the

Mild be the sun on this sweet-blushing flower [dew!
In the gay rosy morn as it bathes in the
And gentle the fall of the soft vernal shower,
That steals on the evening each leaf to renew.

Oh spare the dear blossom, ye orient breezes,
With chill hoary wing as ye usher the dawn!
And far be thou distant, thou reptile that seizes
The verdure and pride of the garden and lawn!

Let Bourbon exult in his gay gilded lilies,
And England triumphant display her proud rose;
A fairer than either adorns the green vallies
Where Devon, sweet Devon, meandering flows."

The different journies already mentioned did not satisfy the curiosity of Burns. About the beginning of September, he again set out from Edinburgh on a more extended tour to the highlands, in company with Mr. Nicol, with whom he had now contracted a particular intimacy, which lasted during the remainder of his life. Mr. Nicol was of Dumfries-shire, of a descent equally humble with our poet. Like him he rose by the strength of his talents, and fell by the strength of his passions. He died in the summer of 1797. Having received the elements of a classical instruction at his parish-school, Mr. Nicol made a very rapid and singular proficiency; and by early undertaking the office of an instructor himself, he acquired the means of entering himself at the University of Edinburgh. There he was first a student of theology, then a student of medicine, and was afterwards employed in the assistance and instruction of graduates in medicine, in those parts of their exercises in which the Latin language is employed. In this situation he was the contemporary and rival of the celebrated Dr. Brown, whom he resembled in the particulars of his history, as well as in the leading features of his character. The office of assistant-teacher in the High School being vacant, it was as usual filled up by competition; and in the face of some prejudices, and perhaps of some well-founded objections, Mr. Nicol, by superior learning, carried it from all the other candidates. This office he filled at the period of which we speak.

It is to be lamented, that an acquaintance with the writers of Greece and Rome does not always supply an original want of taste and correctness in manners and conduct; and where it fails of this effect, it sometimes inflames the native pride of temper, which treats with disdain those delicacies in which it has not learnt to excel. It was thus with the fellow-traveller of Burns. Formed by nature in a model of great strength, neither his person nor his manners had any tincture of taste or elegance; and his coarseness was not compensated by that romantic sensibility, and those towering flights of imagination, which distinguished the conversation of Burns, in the blaze of whose genius all the deficiencies of his manners were absorbed and disappeared.

Mr. Nicol and our poet travelled in a post-chaise, which they engaged for the journey, and passing through the heart of the Highlands, stretched northwards, about ten miles beyond Inverness. There they bent their course eastward, across the island, and returned by the shore of the German sea to Edinburgh. In the course of this tour, some particulars of which will be found in a letter of our bard, they visited a number of remarkable scenes, and the imagination of Burns was constantly excited by the wild and sublime scenery through which he passed. Of this several proofs may be found in the poems formerly printed. (79) Of the history of one of these poems, the Humble

Petition of Bruar Water, and of the bard's visit to Athole-house, some particulars will be found in his correspondence; and by the favour of Mr. Walker, of Perth, then residing in the family of the Duke of Athole, we are enabled to give the following additional account:—

"On reaching Blair, he sent me notice of his arrival (as I had been previously acquainted with him), and I hastened to meet him at the inn. The Duke, to whom he brought a letter of introduction, was from home; but the Duchess, being informed of his arrival, gave him an invitation to sup and sleep at Athole-house. He accepted the invitation; but as the hour of supper was at some distance, begged I would in the interval be his guide through the grounds. It was already growing dark; yet the softened though faint and uncertain view of their beauties, which the moonlight afforded us, seemed exactly suited to the state of his feelings at the time. I had often, like others, experienced the pleasures which arise from the sublime or elegant landscape, but I never saw those feelings so intense as in Burns. When we reached a rustic hut on the river Tilt, where it is overhung by a woody precipice, from which there is a noble waterfall, he threw himself on the heathy seat, and gave himself up to a tender, abstracted, and voluptuous enthusiasm of imagination. I cannot help thinking it might have been here that he conceived the idea of the following lines, which he afterwards introduced into his poem on Bruar Water, when only fancying such a combination of objects as were now present to his eye.

'Or by the reaper's nightly beam,
Mild, chequering through the trees,
Rave to my darkly-dashing stream,
Hoarse-swelling on the breeze.'

It was with much difficulty I prevailed on him to quit this spot, and to be introduced in proper time to supper.

"My curiosity was great to see how he would conduct himself in company so different from what he had been accustomed to. (80) His manner was unembarrassed, plain, and firm. He appeared to have complete reliance on his own native good sense for directing his behaviour. He seemed at once to perceive and to appreciate what was due to the company and to himself, and never to forget a proper respect for the separate species of dignity belonging to each. He did not arrogate conversation, but, when led into it, he spoke with ease, propriety, and manliness. He tried to exert his abilities, because he knew it was ability alone gave him a title to be there. The Duke's fine young family attracted much of his admiration; he drank their healths as *honest men and bonnie lasses*, an idea which was much applauded by the company, and with which he has very felicitously closed his poem. (81)

"Next day I took a ride with him through some of the most romantic part of that neighbourhood, and was highly gratified by his conversation. As a specimen of his happiness of conception and strength of expression, I will mention a remark which he made on his fellow-traveller, who was walking at the time a few paces before us. He was a man of a robust but clumsy person; and while Burns was expressing to me the value he entertained for him, on account of his vigorous talents, although they were clouded at times by coarseness of manners; 'in short,' he added, 'his mind is like his body—he has a confounded strong in-knee'd sort of a soul.'

"Much attention was paid to Burns both before and after the Duke's return, of which he was perfectly sensible, without being vain; and at his departure I recommended to him, as the most appropriate return he could make, to write some descriptive verses on any of the scenes with which he had been so much delighted. After leaving Blair, he, by the Duke's advice, visited the Falls of Bruar, and in a few days I received a letter from Inverness, with the verses enclosed." (82)

It appears that the impression made by our poet on the noble family of Athole, was in a high degree favourable; it is certain he was charmed with the reception he received from them, and he often mentioned the two days he spent at Athole-house as among the happiest of his life. He was warmly invited to prolong his stay, but sacrificed his inclinations to his engagement with Mr. Nicol; which is the more to be regretted, as he would otherwise have been introduced to Mr. Dundas (83) (then daily expected on a visit to the Duke), a circumstance that might have had a favourable influence on Burns's future fortunes. At Athole-house he met, for the first time, Mr. Graham of Fintry, to whom he was afterwards indebted for his office in the Excise.

The letters and poems which he addressed to Mr. Graham, bear testimony of his sensibility, and justify the supposition, that he would not have been deficient in gratitude had he been elevated to a situation better suited to his disposition and to his talents.

A few days after leaving Blair of Athole, our poet and his fellow-traveller arrived at Fochabers. In the course of the preceding winter Burns had been introduced to the Duchess of Gordon at Edinburgh, and presuming on this acquaintance, he proceeded to Gordon Castle, leaving Mr. Nicol at the inn in the village. At the castle our poet was received with the utmost hospitality and kindness, and the family being about to sit down to dinner, he was invited to take his place at table as a matter of course. This invitation he accepted, and after drinking a few glasses of wine, he rose up, and proposed to withdraw. On being pressed to stay, he mentioned, for the first time, his engagement with his fellow-traveller; and his noble host offering to send a servant to conduct Mr. Nicol to the castle, Burns insisted on undertaking that office himself. He was, however, accompanied by a gentleman, a particular acquaintance of the duke, by whom the invitation was delivered in all the forms of politeness. The invitation came too late; the pride of Nicol was inflamed into a high degree of passion, by the neglect which he had already suffered. He had ordered the horses to be put to the carriage, being determined to proceed on his journey alone; and they found him parading the streets of Fochabers, before the door of the inn, venting his anger on the postilion, for the slowness with which he obeyed his commands. As no explanation nor entreaty could change the purpose of his fellow-traveller, our poet was reduced to the necessity of separating from him entirely, or of instantly proceeding with him on their journey. He chose the last of these alternatives; and seating himself beside Nicol in the post-chaise, with mortification and regret, he turned his back on Gordon Castle, where he had promised himself some happy days. Sensible, however, of the great kindness of the noble family, he made the best return in his power, by the following poem:—(84)

"Streams that glide in orient plains,
Never bound by winter's chains;
Glowing here on golden sands,
There commix'd with foulest stains
From tyranny's empurpled bands;
These, their richly-gleaming waves,
I leave to tyrants and their slaves;
Give me the stream that sweetly laves
The banks by Castle-Gordon.

Spicy forests, ever gay,
Shading from the burning ray
Helpless wretches sold to toil,
Or the ruthless native's way,
Bent on slaughter, blood, and spoil:
Woods that ever verdant wave,
I leave the tyrant and the slave;
Give me the groves that lofty brave
The storms by Castle-Gordon.

Wildly here, without control,
Nature reigns and rules the whole;
In that sober pensive mood
Dearest to the feeling soul,
She plants the forest, pours the flood;
Life's poor day I'll musing rave,
And find at night a sheltering cave,
Where waters flow and wild woods wave,
By bonnie Castle-Gordon." (85)

Burns remained at Edinburgh during the greater part of the winter, 1787-8, (86) and again entered into the society and dissipation of that metropolis. (87) It appears that on the 31st December he attended a meeting to celebrate the birth-day of the lineal descendant of the Scottish race of kings, the late unfortunate Prince Charles Edward. Whatever might have been the wish or purpose of the original institutors of this annual meeting, there is no reason to suppose that the gentlemen of whom it was at this time composed, were not perfectly loyal to the king on the throne. It is not to be conceived that they entertained any hope of, any wish for, the restoration of the House of Stuart; but, over their sparkling wine, they indulged the generous feelings which the recollection of fallen greatness is calculated to inspire, and commemorated the heroic valour which strove to sustain it in vain—valour worthy of a nobler cause, and a happier fortune. On this occasion our bard took upon himself the office of a poet-laureate, and produced an ode, which, though deficient in the complicated rhythm and polished versification that such compositions require, might on a fair competition, where energy of feelings and of expression were alone in question, have won the butt of Malmsey from the real laureate of that day.

The following extracts may serve as a specimen:—

* * * *

"False flatterer, Hope, away!
Nor think to lure us as in days of yore:
We solemnise this sorrowing natal day,
To prove our loyal truth—we can no more;
And, owning heaven's mysterious sway,
Submissive low, adore.

Ye honoured mighty dead!
Who nobly perished in the glorious cause,
Your king, your country, and her laws!
From great Dundee, who smiling victory led,

And fell a martyr in her arms,
(What breast of northern ice but warms?)
To bold Balmerino's undying name, [flame,
Whose soul of fire, lighted at heaven's high
Deserves the proudest wreath departed heroes
claim. (88)

Nor unreveng'd your fate shall be,
It only lags the fatal hour:
Your blood shall with incessant cry
Awake at last th' unsparing power.
As from the cliff, with thundering course,
The snowy ruin smokes along,
With doubling speed and gathering force,
Till deep it crashing whelms the cottage in
So vengeance" * * * [the vale!

In relating the incidents of our poet's life in Edinburgh, we ought to have mentioned the sentiments of respect and sympathy with which he traced out the grave of his predecessor Fergusson, over whose ashes, in the Canongate churchyard, he obtained leave to erect a humble monument, which will be viewed by reflecting minds with no common interest, and which will awake in the bosom of kindred genius many a high emotion. Neither should we pass over the continued friendship he experienced from a poet then living, the amiable and accomplished Blacklock. To his encouraging advice it was owing (as has already appeared) that Burns, instead of emigrating to the West Indies, repaired to Edinburgh. He received him there with all the ardour of affectionate admiration—he eagerly introduced him to the respectable circle of his friends—he consulted his interest—he blazoned his fame—he lavished upon him all the kindness of a generous and feeling heart, into which nothing selfish or envious ever found admittance. Among the friends to whom he introduced Burns, was Mr. Ramsay of Ochtertyre (89), to whom our poet paid a visit in the autumn of 1787 [October], at his delightful retirement in the neighbourhood of Stirling, and on the banks of the Teith. Of this visit we have the following particulars:—

"I have been in the company of many men of genius" says Mr. Ramsay, "some of them poets; but never witnessed such flashes of intellectual brightness as from him, the impulse of the moment, sparks of celestial fire! I never was more delighted, therefore, than with his company for two days, tête-a-tête. In a mixed company I should have made little of him; for, in the gamester's phrase, he did not always know when to play off and when to play on. * * * I not only proposed to him the writing of a play similar to the Gentle Shepherd, *qualem decet esse sororem,* but Scottish Georgics, a subject which Thomson has by no means exhausted in his Seasons. What beautiful landscapes of rural life and manners might not have been expected from a pencil so faithful and forcible as his, which could have exhibited scenes as familiar and interesting as those in the Gentle Shepherd, which every one who knows our swains in their unadulterated state, instantly recognises as true to nature. But to have executed either of these plans, steadiness and abstraction from company were wanting, not talents. When I asked him whether the Edinburgh literati had mended his poems by their criticisms. 'Sir,' said he, 'these gentlemen remind me of some spinsters in my country, who spin their thread so fine that it is neither fit for weft nor woof.' He said he had not changed a word except one, to please Dr. Blair." (90)

Having settled with his publisher, Mr. Creech, in February 1788, Burns found himself master of nearly five hundred pounds, after discharging all his expenses. Two hundred pounds he immediately advanced to his brother Gilbert, who had taken upon himself the support of their aged mother, and was struggling with many difficulties in the farm of Mossgiel. With the remainder of this sum, and some farther eventual profits from his poems, he determined on settling himself for life in the occupation of agriculture, and took from Mr. Miller of Dalswinton (91), the farm of Ellisland, on the banks of the river Nith, six miles above Dumfries, on which he entered at Whitsunday, 1788. Having been previously recommended to the Board of Excise, his name had been put on the list of candidates for the humble office of a gauger or exciseman (92); and he immediately applied to acquiring the information necessary for filling that office, when the honourable board might judge it proper to employ him. He expected to be called into service in the district in which his farm was situated, and vainly hoped to unite with success the labours of the farmer with the duties of the exciseman.

When Burns had in this manner arranged his plans for futurity, his generous heart turned to the object of his most ardent attachment, and, listening to no considerations but those of honour and affection, he joined with her in a public declaration of marriage, thus legalising their union, and rendering it permanent for life.

Before Burns was known in Edinburgh, a specimen of his poetry had recommended him to Mr. Miller of Dalswinton. Understanding that he intended to resume the life of a farmer, Mr. Miller had invited him, in the spring of 1787, to view his estate in Nithsdale, offering him at the same time the choice of any of his farms out of lease, at such a rent as Burns and his friends might judge proper. It was not in the nature of Burns to take an undue advantage of the liberality of Mr. Miller. He proceeded in this business, however, with more than usual deliberation. Having made choice of the farm of Ellisland, he employed two of his friends skilled in the value of land, to examine it, and, with their approbation, offered a rent to Mr. Miller, which was immediately accepted. (93) It was not convenient for Mrs. Burns to remove immediately from Ayrshire, and our poet therefore took up his residence alone at Ellisland, to prepare for the reception of his wife and children, who joined him towards the end of the year.

[Dr. Currie omits all allusion to the circumstances which led to a permanent union between Burns and his Jean. That the mind of the poet, notwithstanding all past irritation, and various entanglements with other beauties, was never altogether alienated from her, is evident; but up to June 1787, when he first returned from Edinburgh to Mauchline, he certainly did not entertain any self-avowed notion of ever again renewing his acquaintance with her. It was in this state of his feelings, that, one day, soon after his return from Edinburgh, when meeting some friends over a glass at John Dow's tavern, close to the residence of his once fondly loved mistress, he chanced to encounter her in the court behind the inn, and was immediately inflamed with all his former affection. Their correspondence was renewed—was attended with its former results—and, towards the end of the year, when the poet was fixed helplessly in Edinburgh by a bruised limb, her shame becoming apparent to her parents, she was turned out of doors, and would have been utterly destitute, if she had not obtained shelter from a relation in the village of Ardrossan. Jean was once more delivered of twins—girls—on the 3rd of March, 1788: the infants died a few days after their birth. In a letter of that date to Mr. R. Ainslie, written from Mauchline, Burns says—"I found Jean banished, forlorn, destitute, and friendless: I have reconciled her to her fate, and I have reconciled her to her mother." Soon after, he seems to have formed the resolution of overlooking all dishonouring circumstances, in her past history, and making her really his own for life. On the 7th of April, we find him writing to Miss Chalmers, evidently with allusion to this resolution:—"I have lately made some sacrifices, for which, were I *viva voce* with you to paint the situation and recount the circumstances, you would applaud me." And then, on the 28th, in a letter to Smith, we see the resolution has been virtually acted upon. "To let you a little into the secrets of my pericranium, there is, you must know, a certain clean-limbed, handsome, bewitching young hussy of your acquaintance, to whom I have lately given a matrimonial title to my corpus. * * I intend to present Mrs. Burns with a printed shawl, an article of which I dare say you have variety: 'tis my first present to her since I irrevocably called her mine. * * Mrs. Burns ('tis only her private designation) presents her best compliments to you." He tells Ainslie, May 26, that the title is now avowed to the world—a sufficient legal proof of marriage in Scotland. Ultimately, on the 3rd of August, as we learn from the session books, the poet and Jean were openly married; when Burns, being informed that it was customary for the bridegroom, in such cases, to bestow something on the poor of the parish, gave a guinea for that purpose. The ceremony took place in Dow's tavern, unsanctioned by the lady's father, who never, to the day of the poet's death, would treat him as a friend; even Gavin Hamilton, from respect for the feelings of Armour, declined being present. It was not till the ensuing winter that Mrs. Burns joined her husband at Ellisland—their only child Robert following her in the subsequent spring.]

The situation in which Burns now found himself was calculated to awaken reflection. The different steps he had of late taken were in their nature highly important, and might be said to have, in some measure, fixed his destiny. He had become a husband and a father; he had engaged in the management of a considerable farm, a difficult and laborious undertaking; in his success the happiness of his family was involved. It was time, therefore, to abandon the gaiety and dissipation of which he had been too much enamoured; to ponder seriously on the past, and to form virtuous resolutions respecting the future. That such was actually the state of his mind, the following extract from his common-place book may bear witness:—

"*Ellisland, Sunday*, 14*th June*, 1788.

"This is now the third day that I have been in this country. 'Lord, what is man!'

What a bustling little bundle of passions, appetites, ideas, and fancies! And what a capricious kind of existence he has here! * * There is indeed an elsewhere, where, as Thomson says, *virtue sole survives.*

'Tell us, ye dead;
Will none of you in pity disclose the secret,
What 'tis you are, and we must shortly be;
——————A little time
Will make us wise as you are, and as close.'

"I am such a coward in life, so tired of the service, that I would almost at any time, with Milton's Adam, 'gladly lay me in my mother's lap, and be at peace.' But a wife and children bind me to struggle with the stream, till some sudden squall shall overset the silly vessel, or, in the listless return of years, its own craziness reduce it to a wreck. Farewell now to those giddy follies, those varnished vices, which, though half sanctified by the bewitching levity of wit and humour, are at best but thriftless idling with the precious current of existence; nay, often poisoning the whole, that, like the plains of Jericho, *the water is naught and the ground barren*, and nothing short of a supernaturally gifted Elisha can ever after heal the evils.

"Wedlock, the circumstance that buckles me hardest to care, if virtue and religion were to be any thing with me but names, was what in a few seasons I must have resolved on; in my present situation it was absolutely necessary. Humanity, generosity, honest pride of character, justice to my own happiness for after-life, so far as it could depend (which it surely will a great deal) on internal peace; all these joined their warmest suffrages, their most powerful solicitations, with a rooted attachment, to urge the step I have taken. Nor have I any reason on her part to repent it. I can fancy how, but have never seen where, I could have made a better choice. Come then, let me act up to my favourite motto, that glorious passage in Young—

'On reason build resolve,
That column of true majesty in man!'"

Under the impulse of these reflections, Burns immediately engaged in rebuilding the dwelling-house on his farm, which, in the state he found it, was inadequate to the accommodation of his family. On this occasion he himself resumed at times the occupation of a labourer, and found neither his strength nor his skill impaired. Pleased with surveying the grounds he was about to cultivate, and with the rearing of a building that should give shelter to his wife and children, and, as he fondly hoped, to his own grey hairs, sentiments of independence buoyed up his mind, pictures of domestic content and peace rose on his imagination; and a few days passed away, as he himself informs us, the most tranquil, if not the happiest, which he had ever experienced. (94.)

It is to be lamented that at this critical period of his life, our poet was without the society of his wife and children. A great change had taken place in his situation; his old habits were broken, and the new circumstances in which he was placed were calculated to give a new direction to his thoughts and conduct. But his application to the cares and labours of his farm was interrupted by several visits to his family in Ayrshire; and as the distance was too great for a single day's journey, he generally spent a night at an inn on the road. On such occasions he sometimes fell into company, and forgot the resolutions he had formed. In a little while, temptation assailed him nearer home.

His fame naturally drew upon him the attention of his neighbours, and he soon formed a general acquaintance in the district in which he lived. The public voice had now pronounced on the subject of his talents; the reception he had met with in Edinburgh had given him the currency which fashion bestows; he had surmounted the prejudices arising from his humble birth, and he was received at the table of the gentlemen of Nithsdale with welcome, with kindness, and even with respect. Their social parties too often seduced him from his rustic labours and his rustic fare, overthrew the unsteady fabric of his resolutions, and inflamed those propensities which temperance might have weakened, and prudence ultimately suppressed. (95) It was not long, therefore, before Burns began to view his farm with dislike and despondence, if not with disgust.

Unfortunately, he had for several years looked to an office in the Excise as a certain means of livelihood, should his other expectations fail. As has already been mentioned, he had been recommended to the Board of Excise, and had received the instruction necessary for such a situation. He now applied to be employed; and by the interest of Mr. Graham of Fintry, was appointed exciseman, or, as it is vulgarly called, gauger, of the district in which he lived. (96.) His farm was after this in a great measure abandoned to servants, while he betook himself to the duties of his new appointment.

He might, indeed, still be seen in the spring directing his plough, a labour in which he excelled; or with a white sheet, containing his seed-corn, slung across his shoulders, striding with measured steps along his turned-up furrows, and scattering the grain in the earth. But his farm no longer occupied the principal part of his care or his thoughts. (97) It was not at Ellisland that he was now in general to be found. Mounted on horseback, this high-minded poet was pursuing the defaulters of the revenue among the hills and vales of Nithsdale, his roving eye wandering over the charms of nature, and *muttering his wayward fancies* as he moved along.

"I had an adventure with him in the year 1790," says Mr. Ramsay of Ochtertyre, in a letter to the editor, "when passing through Dumfries-shire, on a tour to the south, with Dr. Stewart of Luss. Seeing him pass quickly, near Closeburn, I said to my companion, 'that is Burns.' On coming to the inn, the hostler told us he would be back in a few hours to grant permits; that where he met with anything seizable he was no better than any other gauger; in everything else, that he was perfectly a gentleman. After leaving a note to be delivered to him on his return, I proceeded to his house, being curious to see his Jean, &c. I was much pleased with his *uxor Sabina qualis*, and the poet's modest mansion, so unlike the habitation of ordinary rustics. In the evening he suddenly bounced in upon us, and said, as he entered, 'I come, to use the words of Shakspeare, *stewed in haste*.' In fact, he had ridden incredibly fast after receiving my note We fell into conversation directly, and soon got into the *mare magnum* of poetry. He told me that he had now gotten a story for a drama, which he was to call Rob Macquechan's Elshon, from a popular story of Robert Bruce being defeated on the water of Caern, when the heel of his boot having loosened in his flight, he applied to Robert Macquechan to fit it; who, to make sure, ran his awl nine inches up the king's heel. We were now going on at a great rate, when Mr. S—— popped in his head; which put a stop to our discourse, which had become very interesting. Yet in a little while it was resumed; and such was the force and versatility of the bard's genius, that he made the tears run down Mr. S——'s cheeks, albeit unused to the poetic strain. * * * From that time we met no more, and I was grieved at the reports of him afterwards. Poor Burns! we shall hardly ever see his like again. He was, in truth, a sort of comet in literature, irregular in its motions, which did not do good proportioned to the blaze of light it displayed."

In the summer of 1791, two English gentlemen, who had before met with him in Edinburgh, paid a visit to him at Ellisland. On calling at the house, they were informed that he had walked out on the banks of the river; and dismounting from their horses, they proceeded in search of him. On a rock that projected into the stream, they saw a man employed in angling, of a singular appearance. He had a cap made of a fox's skin on his head, a loose great-coat fixed round him by a belt, from which depended an enormous Highland broad-sword. It was Burns. He received them with great cordiality, and asked them to share his humble dinner—an invitation which they accepted. On the table they found boiled beef, with vegetables, and barley-broth, after the manner of Scotland, of which they partook heartily. After dinner, the bard told them ingenuously that he had no wine to offer them, nothing better than Highland whisky, a bottle of which Mrs. Burns set on the board. He produced at the same time his punch-bowl made of Inverary marble; and, mixing the spirit with water and sugar, filled their glasses, and invited them to drink. (98) The travellers were in haste, and, besides, the flavour of the whisky to their *suthron* palates was scarcely tolerable; but the generous poet offered them his best, and his ardent hospitality they found it impossible to resist. Burns was in his happiest mood, and the charms of his conversation were altogether fascinating. He ranged over a great variety of topics, illuminating whatever he touched. He related the tales of his infancy and of his youth; he recited some of the gayest and some of the tenderest of his poems; in the wildest of his strains of mirth, he threw in some touches of melancholy, and spread around him the electric emotions of his powerful mind. The Highland whisky improved in its flavour; the marble bowl was again and again emptied and replenished; the guests of our poet forgot the flight of time, and the dictates of prudence: at the hour of midnight they lost their way in returning to Dumfries, and could scarcely distinguish it when assisted by the morning's dawn.

Besides his duties in the excise, and his social pleasures, other circumstances interfered with the attention of Burns to his farm. He engaged in the formation of a society for purchasing and circulating books among the farmers of his neighbourhood, of which he undertook the management; and he occupied himself occasionally in composing songs for the musical work of Mr.

Johnson, then in the course of publication. These engagements, useful and honourable in themselves, contributed, no doubt, to the abstraction of his thoughts from the business of agriculture.

The consequences may be easily imagined. Notwithstanding the uniform prudence and good management of Mrs, Burns, and though his rent was moderate and reasonable, our poet found it convenient, if not necessary, to resign his farm to Mr. Miller, after having occupied it three years and a half. His office in the excise had originally produced about fifty pounds per annum. Having acquitted himself to the satisfaction of the board, he had been appointed to a new district, the emoluments of which rose to about seventy pounds per annum. Hoping to support himself and his family on this humble income till promotion should reach him, he disposed of his stock and of his crop on Ellisland by public auction, and removed to a small house which he had taken in Dumfries, about the end of the year 1791.

Hitherto Burns, though addicted to excess in social parties, had abstained from the habitual use of strong liquors, and his constitution had not suffered any permanent injury from the irregularities of his conduct. In Dumfries, temptations to *the sin that so easily beset him* continually presented themselves; and his irregularities grew by degrees into habits. These temptations unhappily occurred during his engagements in the business of his office, as well as during his hours of relaxation; and though he clearly foresaw the consequences of yielding to them, his appetites and sensations, which could not prevent the dictates of his judgment, finally triumphed over the powers of his will. Yet this victory was not obtained without many obstinate struggles, and at times temperance and virtue seemed to have obtained the mastery. Besides his engagements in the excise, and the society into which they led, many circumstances contributed to the melancholy fate of Burns. His great celebrity made him an object of interest and curiosity to strangers, and few persons of cultivated minds passed through Dumfries without attempting to see our poet, and to enjoy the pleasure of his conversation. As he could not receive them under his own humble roof, these interviews passed at the inns of the town, and often terminated in those excesses which Burns sometimes provoked, and was seldom able to resist. And among the inhabitants of Dumfries and its vicinity, there were never wanting persons to share his social pleasures; to lead or accompany him to the tavern; to partake in the wildest sallies of his wit; to witness the strength and the degradation of his genius.

Still, however, he cultivated the society of persons of taste and of respectability. and in their company could impose on himself the restraints of temperance and decorum. Nor was his muse dormant. In the four years which he lived in Dumfries, he produced many of his beautiful lyrics, though it does not appear that he attempted any poem of considerable length. During this time he made several excursions into the neighbouring country, of one of which, through Galloway, an account is preserved in a letter of Mr. Syme, written soon after; which, as it gives an animated picture of him by a correct and masterly hand, we shall present to the reader.

"I got Burns a grey Highland shelty to ride on." We dined the first day, 27th July, 1793, at Glendenwynes of Parton! a beautiful situation on the banks of the Dee. In the evening we walked out, and ascended a gentle eminence, from which we had as fine a view of Alpine scenery as can well be imagined. A delightful soft evening showed all its wilder as well as its grander graces. Immediately opposite, and within a mile of us, we saw Airds, a charming romantic place, where dwelt Low, the author of *Mary weep no more for me.* (99) This was classical ground for Burns. He viewed 'the highest hill which rises o'er the source of Dee;' and would have staid till 'the passing spirit' had appeared, had we not resolved to reach Kenmure that night. We arrived as Mr. and Mrs. Gordon (100) were sitting down to supper.

"Here is a genuine baron's seat. The castle, an old building, stands on a large natural moat. In front, the river Ken winds for several miles through the most fertile and beautiful *holm* (101), till it expands into a lake twelve miles long, the banks of which, on the south, present a fine and soft landscape of green knolls, natural wood, and here and there a grey rock. On the north, the aspect is great, wild, and, I may say, tremendous. In short, I can scarcely conceive a scene more terribly romantic than the castle of Kenmure. Burns thinks so highly of it, that he meditates a description of it in poetry. Indeed, I believe he has begun the work. We spent three days with Mr. Gordon, whose polished hospitality is of an original and endearing kind. Mrs. Gordon's lap-dog, *Echo*, was dead. She would have an epitaph for him. Several had been made. Burns was asked for one. This was setting Hercules to his distaff. He disliked the subject; but, to please the lady, he would try. Here is what he produced:—

'In wood and wild, ye warbling throng,
Your heavy loss deplore!
Now half extinct your powers of song,
Sweet Echo is no more.

Ye jarring screeching things around,
Scream your discordant joys!
Now half your din of tuneless song
With Echo silent lies.'

"We left Kenmure, and went to Gatehouse. I took him the moor-road, where savage and desolate regions extended wide around. The sky was sympathetic with the wretchedness of the soil; it became lowering and dark. The hollow winds sighed, the lightnings gleamed, the thunder rolled. The poet enjoyed the awful scene; he spoke not a word, but seemed rapt in meditation. In a little while the rain began to fall; it poured in floods upon us. For three hours did the wild elements *rumble their belly full* upon our defenceless heads. *Oh! oh! 'twas foul.* We got utterly wet; and, to revenge ourselves, Burns insisted at Gatehouse on our getting utterly drunk.

"From Gatehouse, we went next day to Kirkcudbright, through a fine country. But here I must tell you that Burns had got a pair of *jemmy* boots for the journey, which had been thoroughly wet, and which had been dried in such manner that it was not possible to get them on again. The brawny poet tried force, and tore them to shreds. A whiffling vexation of this sort is more trying to the temper than a serious calamity. We were going to Saint Mary's Isle, the seat of the Earl of Selkirk, and the forlorn Burns was discomfited at the thought of his ruined boots. A sick stomach, and a headache, lent their aid, and the man of verse was quite *accablé*. I attempted to reason with him. Mercy on us, how he did fume and rage! Nothing could reinstate him in temper. I tried various expedients, and at last hit on one that succeeded. I showed him the house of * * * *, across the bay of Wigton. Against * * * *, with whom he was offended, he expectorated his spleen, and regained a most agreeable temper. He was in a most epigrammatic humour indeed! He afterwards fell on humbler game. There is one * * * * * whom he does not love. He had a passing blow at him.

'When ———, deceased to the devil went down,
'Twas nothing would serve him but Satan's own crown;
Thy fool's head, quoth Satan, that crown shall wear never,
I grant thou'rt as wicked, but not quite so clever.'

"Well, I am to bring you to Kirkcudbright along with our poet, without boots. I carried the torn ruins across my saddle in spite of his fulminations, and in contempt of appearances; and what is more, Lord Selkirk (102) carried them in his coach to Dumfries. He insisted they were worth mending.

"We reached Kirkcudbright about one o'clock. I had promised that we should dine with one of the first men in our country, J. Dalzell. But Burns was in a wild and obstreperous humour, and swore he would not dine where he should be under the smallest restraint. We prevailed, therefore, on Mr. Dalzell to dine with us in the inn, and had a very agreeable party. In the evening we set out for St. Mary's Isle. Robert had not absolutely regained the milkiness of good temper, and it occurred once or twice to him, as he rode along, that St. Mary's Isle was the seat of a Lord; yet that Lord was not an aristocrat, at least in his sense of the word. We arrived about eight o'clock, as the family were at tea and coffee. St. Mary's Isle is one of the most delightful places that can, in my opinion be formed by the assemblage of every soft, but not tame object, which constitutes natural and cultivated beauty. But not to dwell on its external graces, let me tell you that we found all the ladies of the family (all beautiful) at home, and some strangers; and, among others, who but Urbani! The Italian sang us many Scottish songs, accompanied with instrumental music. The two young ladies of Selkirk sang also. We had the song of Lord Gregory, which I asked for, to have an opportunity of calling on Burns to recite *his* ballad to that tune. He did recite it; and such was the effect, that a dead silence ensued. It was such a silence as a mind of feeling naturally preserves when it is touched with that enthusiasm which banishes every other thought but the contemplation and indulgence of the sympathy produced. Burns's Lord Gregory is, in my opinion, a most beautiful and affecting ballad. The fastidious critic may perhaps say, some of the sentiments and imagery are of too elevated a kind for such a style of composition; for instance, 'Thou bolt of Heaven that passest by;' and, 'Ye mustering thunder,' &c.; but this is a cold-blooded objection, which will be *said* rather than *felt*.

"We enjoyed a most happy evening at Lord Selkirk's. We had, in every sense of the word, a feast, in which our minds and our senses were equally gratified. The poet was delighted with his company, and acquitted himself to admiration. The lion that had raged so violently in the morning, was now as mild and gentle as a lamb. Next day we returned to Dumfries, and so ends our peregrination. I told you that, in the midst of the storm, on the wilds of Kenmure, Burns was wrapt in meditation. What do you think he was about? He was charging the English army, along with Bruce, at Bannockburn. He was engaged in the same manner on our ride home from St. Mary's Isle, and I did not disturb him. Next day he produced me the following address of Bruce to his troops, and gave me a copy for Dalzell:—

'Scots wha hae wi' Wallace bled,' &c. (103)"

Burns had entertained hopes of promotion in the Excise; but circumstances occurred which retarded their fulfilment, and which, in his own mind, destroyed all expectation of their being ever fulfilled. The extraordinary events which ushered in the revolution of France, interested the feelings, and excited the hopes of men in every corner of Europe. Prejudice and tyranny seemed about to disappear from among men, and the day-star of reason to rise upon a benighted world. In the dawn of this beautiful morning, the genius of French freedom appeared on our southern horizon with the countenance of an angel, but speedily assumed the features of a demon, and vanished in a shower of blood.

Though previously a Jacobite and a cavalier, Burns had shared in the original hopes entertained of this astonishing revolution by ardent and benevolent minds. The novelty and the hazard of the attempt meditated by the First, or Constituent Assembly, served rather, it is probable, to recommend it to his daring temper; and the unfettered scope proposed to be given to every kind of talent, was doubtless gratifying to the feelings of conscious but indignant genius. Burns foresaw not the mighty ruin that was to be the immediate consequence of an enterprise, which, on its commencement, promised so much happiness to the human race. And even after the career of guilt and of blood commenced, he could not immediately, it may be presumed, withdraw his partial gaze from a people who had so lately breathed the sentiments of universal peace and benignity, or obliterate in his bosom the pictures of hope and of happiness to which those sentiments had given birth. Under these impressions, he did not always conduct himself with the circumspection and prudence which his dependent situation seemed to demand. He engaged, indeed, in no popular associations, so common at the time of which we speak; but in company he did not conceal his opinions of public measures, or of the reforms required in the practice of our government; and sometimes, in his social and unguarded moments, he uttered them with a wild and unjustifiable vehemence. Information of this was given to the Board of Excise, with the exaggerations so general in such cases. A superior officer in that department was authorized to inquire into his conduct. Burns defended himself in a letter addressed to one of the board [Mr. Graham of Fintry], written with great independence of spirit, and with more than his accustomed eloquence. The officer appointed to inquire into his conduct gave a favourable report. (104) His steady friend, Mr. Graham of Fintry, interposed his good offices in his behalf; and the imprudent gauger was suffered to retain his situation, but given to understand that his promotion was deferred, and must depend on his future behaviour.

This circumstance made a deep impression on the mind of Burns. Fame exaggerated his misconduct, and represented him as actually dismissed from his office; and this report induced a gentleman of much respectability [Mr. Erskine of Marr] to propose a subscription in his favour. The offer was refused by our poet in a letter of great elevation of sentiment, in which he gives an account of the whole of this transaction, and defends himself from the imputation of disloyal sentiments on the one hand, and on the other, from the charge of having made submissions for the sake of his office unworthy of his character.

"The partiality of my countrymen," he observes, "has brought me forward as a man of genius, and has given me a character to support. In the poet I have avowed manly and independent sentiments, which I hope have been found in the man. Reasons of no less weight than the support of a wife and children, have pointed out my present occupation as the only eligible line of life within my reach. Still my honest fame is my dearest concern, and a thousand times have I trembled at the idea of the degrading epithets that malice or misrepresentation may affix to my name. Often in blasting anticipation have I listened to some future hackney scribbler, with the heavy malice of savage stupidity, exultingly asserting that Burns, notwithstanding the *fanfaronade* of independence to be found in his works, and after having been held up to public view, and to public estimation, as a man of some genius, yet, quite destitute of resources within himself to support his borrowed dignity, dwindled into a paltry exciseman, and slunk out the rest of his insignificant existence in the meanest of pursuits, and among the lowest of mankind.

"In your illustrious hands, Sir, permit me to lodge my strong disavowal and defiance of such slanderous falsehoods. Burns was a poor man from his birth, and an exciseman by necessity; but—I *will* say it! the sterling of his honest worth poverty could not debase, and his independent British spirit oppression might bend, but could not subdue."

It was one of the last acts of his life to copy this letter into his book of manuscripts, accompanied by some additional remarks on the same subject. It is not surprising, that at a season of universal alarm for the safety of the constitution, the indiscreet expressions of a man so powerful as Burns should have attracted notice. The times certainly required extraordinary vigilance in those entrusted with the administration of the government, and to ensure the safety of the constitution was doubtless their first duty. Yet generous minds will lament that their measures of precaution should have robbed the imagination of our poet of the last prop on which his hopes of independence rested; and by embittering his peace, have aggravated those excesses which were soon to conduct him to an untimely grave. (105)

Though the vehemence of Burns's temper, increased as it often was by stimulating liquors, might lead him into many improper and unguarded expressions, there seems no reason to doubt of his attachment to our mixed form of government. In his common-place book, where he could have no temptation to disguise, are the following sentiments:—"Whatever might be my sentiments of republics, ancient or modern, as to Britain, I ever abjured the idea. A constitution, which, in its original principles, experience has proved to be every way fitted for our happiness, it would be insanity to abandon for an untried visionary theory." In conformity to these sentiments, when the pressing nature of public affairs called, in 1795, for a general arming of the people, Burns appeared in the ranks of the Dumfries volunteers, and employed his poetical talents in stimulating their patriotism (106); and at this season of alarm, he brought forward the following hymn, worthy of the Grecian Muse, when Greece was most conspicuous for genius and valour:—

Scene—A field of battle—Time of the day, evening—The wounded and dying of the victorious army are supposed to join in the following song:—

Farewell, thou fair day, thou green earth and ye skies,
Now gay with the bright setting sun!
Farewell loves and friendships, ye dear tender ties,
Our race of existence is run!

Thou grim king of terrors, thou life's gloomy foe,
Go, frighten the coward and slave;
Go, teach them to tremble, fell tyrant! but know,
No terrors hast thou to the brave!

Thou strik'st the dull peasant, he sinks in the dark,
Nor saves e'en the wreck of a name;
Thou strik'st the young hero—a glorious mark!
He falls in the blaze of his fame!

In the field of proud honour—our swords in our hands,
Our king and our country to save—
While victory shines on life's last ebbing sands,
Oh! who would not rest with the brave! (107)

Though by nature of an athletic form, Burns had in his constitution the peculiarities and the delicacies that belong to the temperament of genius. He was liable, from a very early period of life, to that interruption in the process of digestion, which arises from deep and anxious thought, and which is sometimes the effect, and sometimes the cause, of depression of spirits. Connected with this disorder of the stomach, there was a disposition to head-ache, affecting more especially the temples and eye-balls, and frequently accompanied by violent and irregular movements of the heart. Endowed by nature with great sensibility of nerves, Burns was, in his corporeal, as well as in his mental system, liable to inordinate impressions—to fever of body as well as of mind. This predisposition to disease, which strict temperance in diet, regular exercise, and sound sleep, might have subdued, habits of a very different nature strengthened and inflamed. Perpetually stimulated by alcohol in one or other of its various forms, the inordinate actions of the circulating system became at length habitual; the process of nutrition was unable to supply the waste, and the powers of life began to fail. Upwards of a year before his death, there was an evident decline in our poet's personal appearance, and though his appetite continued unimpaired, he was himself sensible that his constitution was sinking. In his moments of thought he reflected with the deepest regret on his fatal progress, clearly foreseeing the goal towards which he was hastening, without the strength of mind necessary to stop, or even to slacken his course. His temper now became more irritable and gloomy; he fled from himself into society, often of the lowest kind. And in such company, that part of the convivial scene in which wine increases sensibility and excites benevolence, was hurried over, to reach the succeeding part, over which uncontrolled passion generally presided. He who suffers the pollution of inebriation, how shall he escape other pollution? But let us refrain from the mention of errors over which delicacy and humanity draw the veil.

[A similar view of the latter days of Burns is taken by his biographers, Heron, Irving, Walker, and, in general, by all who wrote soon after his death. Mr. Lockhart, supported by attestations from Gilbert Burns, James Gray, then rector of the grammar-school of Dumfries, and Mr. Findlater, the poet's superior officer, gives a more favourable representation. The letter of Gray presents so interesting a picture of Burns in all respects, that we cannot resist the temptation to connect it with the text of Currie:—

"I love Dr. Currie, but I love the memory of Burns more, and no consideration shall deter me from a bold declaration of the truth. The poet of the Cotter's Saturday Night, who felt all the charms of the humble piety and virtue which he sang, is charged (in Dr. Currie's narrative) with vices which would reduce him to a level with the most degraded of his species. As I knew him during that period of his life emphatically called his evil days, *I am enabled to speak from my own observation.* It is not my intention to extenuate his errors, because they were combined with genius; on that account, they were only the more dangerous, because the more seductive, and deserve the more severe reprehension; but I shall likewise claim that nothing may be said in malice even against him. . . . . It came under my own view professionally, that he superintended the education of his children with a degree of care that I have never seen surpassed by any parent in any rank of life whatever. In the bosom of his family he spent many a delightful hour in directing the studies of his eldest son, a boy of uncommon talents. I have frequently found him explaining to this youth, then not more than nine years of age, the English poets, from Shakspeare to Gray, or storing his mind with examples of heroic virtue, as they live in the pages of our most celebrated English historians. I would ask any person of common candour, if employments like these are consistent with *habitual drunkenness?* It is not denied that he sometimes mingled with society unworthy of him. He was of a social and convivial nature. He was courted by all classes of men for the fascinating powers of his conversation, but over his social scene uncontrolled passion never presided. Over the social bowl, his wit flashed for hours together, penetrating whatever it struck, like the fire from heaven; but even in the hour of thoughtless gaiety and merriment, I never knew it tainted by indecency. It was playful or caustic by turns, following an allusion through all its windings; astonishing by its rapidity, or amusing by its wild originality, and grotesque, yet natural combinations, but never, within my observation, disgusting by its grossness. In his morning hours, I never saw him like one suffering from the effects of last night's intemperance. He appeared then clear and unclouded. He was the eloquent advocate of humanity, justice, and political freedom. From his paintings, virtue appeared more lovely, and piety assumed a more celestial mien. While his keen eye was pregnant with fancy and feeling, and his voice attuned to the very passion which he wished to communicate, it would hardly have been possible to conceive any being more interesting and delightful. I may likewise add, that, to the very end of his life, reading was his favourite amusement. I have never known any man so intimately acquainted with the elegant English authors. He seemed to have the poets by heart. The prose authors he could quote either in their own words, or clothe their ideas in language more beautiful than their own. Nor was there ever any decay in any of the powers of his mind. To the last day of his life, his judgment, his memory, his imagination, were fresh and vigorous as when he composed the Cotter's Saturday Night. The truth is, that Burns was seldom *intoxicated.* The drunkard soon becomes besotted, and is shunned even by the convivial. Had he been so, he could not long have continued the idol of every party. It will be freely confessed, that the hour of enjoyment was often prolonged beyond the limit marked by prudence; but what man will venture to affirm, that in situations where he was conscious of giving so much pleasure, he could at all times have listened to her voice?

"The men with whom he generally associated were not of the lowest order, He numbered among his intimate friends many of the most respectable inhabitants of Dumfries and the vicinity. Several of those were attached to him by ties that the hand of the calumny, busy as it was, could never snap asunder. They admired the poet for his genius, and loved the man for the candour, generosity, and kindness of his nature. His early friends clung to him through good and bad report, with a zeal and fidelity that prove their disbelief of the malicious stories circulated to his disadvantage. Among them were some of the most distinguished characters in this country, and not a few females eminent for delicacy, taste, and genius. They were proud of his friendship, and cherished him to the last moment of his existence. He was endeared to them even by his misfortunes, and they still retain for his memory that affectionate veneration which virtue alone inspires."

In the midst of all his wanderings, Burns met nothing in his domestic circle but gentleness and forgiveness, except in the gnawings of his own remorse. He acknowledged his transgressions to the wife of his bosom, promised amendment, and again and again received pardon for his offences. But as the strength of his body decayed, his resolution became feebler, and habit acquired predominating strength.

From October 1795 to the January following, an accidental complaint confined him to the house. A few days after he began to go abroad, he dined at a tavern, and returned home about three o'clock in a very cold morning, benumbed and intoxicated. (108) This was followed by an attack of rheumatism, which confined him about a week. His appetite now began to fail; his hand shook, and his voice faltered on any exertion or emotion. His pulse became weaker and more rapid, and pain in the larger joints, and in the hands and feet, deprived him of the enjoyment of refreshing sleep. Too much dejected in his spirits, and too well aware of his real situation to entertain hopes of recovery, he was ever musing on the approaching desolation of his family, and his spirits sank into a uniform gloom.

It was hoped by some of his friends, that if he could live through the months of spring, the succeeding season might restore him. But they were disappointed. The genial beams of the sun infused no vigour into his languid frame; the summer wind blew upon him, but produced no refreshment. About the latter end of June he was advised to go into the country; and impatient of medical advice, as well as of every species of control, he determined for himself to try the effects of bathing in the sea. For this purpose he took up his residence at Brow, in Annandale, about ten miles east of Dumfries, on the shore of the Solway Firth.

It happened that at that time a lady with whom he had been connected in friendship by the sympathies of kindred genius, was residing in the immediate neighbourhood. (109) Being informed of his arrival, she invited him to dinner, and sent her carriage for him to the cottage where he lodged, as he was unable to walk. "I was struck," says this lady (in a confidential letter to a friend written soon after), "with his appearance on entering the room. The stamp of death was imprinted on his features. He seemed already touching the brink of eternity. His first salutation was, 'Well, madam, have you any commands for the other world?' I replied, that it seemed a doubtful case which of us should be there soonest, and that I hoped he would yet live to write my epitaph. (I was then in a bad state of health.) He looked in my face with an air of great kindness, and expressed his concern at seeing me look so ill, with his accustomed sensibility. At table he ate little or nothing, and he complained of having entirely lost the tone of his stomach. We had a long and serious conversation about his present situation, and the approaching termination of all his earthly prospects. He spoke of his death without any of the ostentation of philosophy, but with firmness as well as feeling, as an event likely to happen very soon, and which gave him concern chiefly from leaving his four children so young and unprotected, and his wife in so interesting a situation—in hourly expectation of lying in of a fifth. He mentioned, with seeming pride and satisfaction, the promising genius of his eldest son, and the flattering marks of approbation he had received from his teachers, and dwelt particularly on his hopes of that boy's future conduct and merit. His anxiety for his family seemed to hang heavy upon him, and the more perhaps from the reflection that he had not done them all the justice he was so well qualified to do. Passing from this subject, he showed great concern about the care of his literary fame, and particularly the publication of his posthumous works. He said he was well aware that his death would occasion some noise, and that every scrap of his writing would be revived against him to the injury of his future reputation; that letters and verses written with unguarded and improper freedom, and which he earnestly wished to have buried in oblivion, would be handed about by idle vanity or malevolence, when no dread of his resentment would restrain them, or prevent the censures of shrill-tongued malice, or the insidious sarcasms of envy, from pouring forth all their venom to blast his fame.

"He lamented that he had written many epigrams on persons against whom he entertained no enmity, and whose characters he should be sorry to wound; and many indifferent poetical pieces, which he feared would now, with all their imperfections on their head, be thrust upon the world. On this account he deeply regretted having deferred to put his papers in a state of arrangement, as he was now quite incapable of the exertion." The lady goes on to mention many other topics of a private nature on which he spoke. "The conversation," she adds, "was kept up with great evenness and animation on his side. I had seldom seen his mind greater or more collected. There was frequently a considerable degree of vivacity in his sallies, and they would probably have had a greater share, had not the concern and dejection I could not disguise damped the spirit of pleasantry he seemed not unwilling to indulge.

"We parted about sunset on the evening of that day (the 5th of July 1796): the next day I saw him again, and we parted to meet no more!"

At first Burns imagined bathing in the sea had been of benefit to him: the pains in his limbs were relieved; but this was immediately followed by a new attack of fever. When brought back to his own house in Dumfries, on the 18th of July, he was no longer able to stand upright. At this time a tremor pervaded his frame: his tongue was parched, and his mind sank into delirium, when not roused by conversation. On the second and third day the fever increased, and his strength diminished. On the fourth, the sufferings of this great, but ill-fated genius, were terminated; and a life was closed in which virtue and passion had been in perpetual variance. (110)

The death of Burns made a strong and general impression on all who had interested themselves in his character, and especially on the inhabitants of the town and county in which he had spent the latter years of his life. Flagrant as his follies and errors had been, they had not deprived him of the respect and regard entertained for the extraordinary powers of his genius, and the generous qualities of his heart. The Gentlemen-Volunteers of Dumfries determined to bury their illustrious associate with military honours, and every preparation was made to render this last service solemn and impressive. The Fencible Infantry of Angus-shire, and the regiment of cavalry of the Cinque Ports, at that time quartered in Dumfries, offered their assistance on this occasion; the principal inhabitants of the town and neighbourhood determined to walk in the funeral procession; and a vast concourse of persons assembled, some of them from a considerable distance, to witness the obsequies of the Scottish Bard. On the evening of the 25th of July, the remains of Burns were removed from his house to the Town Hall, and the funeral took place on the succeeding day. A party of the volunteers, selected to perform the military duty in the churchyard, stationed themselves in the front of the procession, with their arms reversed; the main body of the corps surrounded and supported the coffin, on which were placed the hat and sword of their friend and fellow-soldier; the numerous body of attendants ranged themselves in the rear; while the Fencible regiments of infantry and cavalry lined the streets from the Town Hall to the burial ground in the southern churchyard, a distance of more than half a mile. The whole procession moved forward to that sublime and affecting strain of music, the Dead March in Saul; and three vollies fired over his grave marked the return of Burns to his parent earth! The spectacle was in a high degree grand and solemn, and accorded with the general sentiments of sympathy and sorrow which the occasion had called forth.

It was an affecting circumstance, that, on the morning of the day of her husband's funeral, Mrs. Burns was undergoing the pains of labour; and that during the solemn service we have just been describing, the posthumous son of our poet was born. This infant boy, who received the name of Maxwell, was not destined to a long life. He has already become an inhabitant of the same grave with his celebrated father. The four other children of our poet, all sons (the eldest at that time about ten years of age), yet survive, and give every promise of prudence and virtue that can be expected from their tender years. They remain under the care of their affectionate mother in Dumfries, and are enjoying the means of education which the excellent schools of that town afford; the teachers of which, in their conduct to the children of Burns, do themselves great honour. On this occasion the name of Mr. Whyte deserves to be particularly mentioned, himself a poet as well as a man of science. (111)

Burns died in great poverty; but the independence of his spirit, and the exemplary prudence of his wife, had preserved him from debt. (112) He had received from his poems a clear profit of about nine hundred pounds. Of this sum, the part expended on his library (which was far from extensive) and in the humble furniture of his house, remained; and obligations were found for two hundred pounds advanced by him to the assistance of those to whom he was united by the ties of blood, and still more by those of esteem and affection. When it is considered, that his expenses in Edinburgh, and on his various journies, could not be inconsiderable; that his agricultural undertaking was unsuccessful; that his income from the Excise was for some time as low as fifty, and never rose to above seventy pounds a-year; that his family was large, and his spirit liberal—no one will be surprised that his circumstances were so poor, or that, as his health decayed, his proud and feeling heart sank under the secret consciousness of indigence, and the apprehensions of absolute want. Yet poverty never bent the spirit of Burns to any pecuniary meanness. Neither chicanery nor sordidness ever appeared in his conduct. He carried his disregard of money to a blameable excess. Even in the midst of distress he bore himself loftily to the world, and received with a jealous reluctance every offer of friendly assistance. His printed poems had procured him great celebrity, and a just and fair recompense for the latter offsprings of his pen might have produced him considerable emolument. In the year 1795, the editor of a London newspaper, high in its character for literature and independence of sentiment, made a proposal to him that he should furnish them, once a-week, with an article for their poetical department, and receive from them a recompense of fifty-two guineas per annum; an offer which the pride of genius disdained to accept. Yet he had for several years furnished, and was at that time furnishing, the Museum of Johnson with his beautiful lyrics, without fee or reward, and was obstinately refusing all recompense for his assistance to the greater work of Mr. Thomson, which the justice and generosity of that gentleman was pressing upon him.

The sense of his poverty, and of the approaching distress of his infant family, pressed heavily on Burns as he lay on the bed of death. Yet he alluded to his indigence, at times, with something approaching to his wonted gaiety. "What business," said he to Dr. Maxwell, who attended him with the utmost zeal, "has a physician to waste his time on me? I am a poor pigeon not worth plucking. Alas! I have not feathers enough upon me to carry me to my grave." And when his reason was lost in delirium, his ideas ran in the same melancholy train; the horrors of a jail were continually present to his troubled imagination, and produced the most affecting exclamations.

As for some months previous to his death he had been incapable of the duties of his office, Burns dreaded that his salary should be reduced one half, as is usual in such cases. His full emoluments were, however, continued to him by the kindness of Mr. Stobie (113), a young expectant in the Excise, who performed the duties of his office without fee or reward; and Mr. Graham of Fintry, hearing of his illness, though unacquainted with its dangerous nature, made an offer of his assistance towards procuring him the means of preserving his health. Whatever might be the faults of Burns, ingratitude was not of the number. Amongst his manuscripts, various proofs are found of the sense he entertained of Mr. Graham's friendship, which delicacy towards that gentleman has induced us to suppress; and on this last occasion there is no doubt that his heart overflowed towards him, though he had no longer the power of expressing his feelings. (114)

On the death of Burns, the inhabitants of Dumfries and its neighbourhood opened a subscription for the support of his wife and family; and Mr. Miller, Mr. M'Murdo, Dr. Maxwell, Mr. Syne, and Mr. Cunningham, gentlemen of the first respectability, became trustees for the application of the money to its proper objects. The subscription was extended to other parts of Scotland, and of England also, particularly London and Liverpool. By this means a sum was raised amounting to seven hundred pounds; and thus the widow and children were rescued from immediate distress, and the most melancholy of the forebodings of Burns happily disappointed. It is true, this sum, though equal to their present support, is insufficient to secure them from future penury.

Their hope in regard to futurity depends on the favourable reception of these volumes from the public at large, in the promoting of which the candour and humanity of the reader may induce him to lend his assistance.

Burns, as has already been mentioned, was nearly five feet ten inches in height, and of a form that indicated agility as well as strength. His well-raised forehead, shaded with black curling hair, indicated extensive capacity. His eyes were large, dark, full of ardour and intelligence. His face was well formed; and his countenance uncommonly interesting and expressive. His mode of dressing, which was often slovenly, and a certain fulness and bend in his shoulders, characteristic of his original profession, disguised in some degree the natural symmetry and elegance of his form. The external appearance of Burns was most strikingly indicative of the character of his mind. On a first view, his physiognomy had a certain air of coarseness, mingled, however, with an expression of deep penetration, and of calm thoughtfulness, approaching to melancholy. There appeared in his first manner and address, perfect ease and self-possession, but a stern and almost supercilious elevation, not, indeed, incompatible with openness and affability, which, however, bespoke a mind conscious of superior talents. Strangers that supposed themselves approaching an Ayrshire peasant who could make rhymes, and to whom their notice was an honour, found themselves speedily overawed by the presence of a man who bore himself with dignity, and who possessed a singular power of correcting forwardness and of repelling intrusion. (115) But though jealous of the respect due to himself, Burns never enforced it where he saw it was willingly paid; and, though inaccessible to the approaches of pride, he was open to every advance of kindness and of benevolence. His dark and haughty countenance easily relaxed into a look of good will, of pity, or of tenderness; and, as the various emotions succeeded each other in his mind, assumed with equal ease the expression of the broadest humour, of the most extravagant mirth, of the deepest melancholy, or of the most sublime emotion. The tones of his voice happily corresponded with the expression of his features, and with the feelings of his mind. When to these endowments are added a rapid and distinct apprehension, a most powerful understanding, and a happy command of language—of strength as well as brilliancy of expression—we shall be able to account for the extraordinary attractions of his conversation—for the sorcery which in his social parties he seemed to exert on all around him. In the company of women this sorcery was more especially apparent. Their presence charmed the fiend of melancholy in his bosom, and awoke his happiest feelings; it excited the powers of his fancy, as well as the tenderness of his heart; and, by restraining the vehemence and exuberance of his language, at times gave to his manners the impression of taste, and even of elegance, which in the company of men they seldom possessed. This influence was doubtless reciprocal. A Scottish lady accustomed to the best society, declared with characteristic *näiveté*, that no man's conversation ever *carried her so completely off her feet* as that of Burns; and an English lady, familiarly acquainted with several of the most distinguished characters of the present times, assured the editor, that in the happiest of his social hours, there was a charm about Burns which she had never seen equalled. This charm arose not more from the power than the versatility of his genius. No languor could be felt in the society of a man who passed at pleasure from *grave to gay*, from the ludicrous to the pathetic, from the simple to the sublime; who wielded all his faculties with equal strength and ease, and never failed to impress the offspring of his fancy with the stamp of his understanding.

This, indeed, is to represent Burns in his happiest phasis. In large and mixed parties he was often silent and dark, sometimes fierce and overbearing; he was jealous of the proud man's scorn, jealous to an extreme of the insolence of wealth, and prone to avenge, even on its innocent possessor, the partiality of fortune. By nature kind, brave, sincere, and in a singular degree compassionate, he was on the other hand proud, irascible, and vindictive. His virtues and his failings had their origin in the extraordinary sensibility of his mind, and equally partook of the chills and glows of sentiment. His friendships were liable to interruption from jealousy or disgust, and his enmities died away under the influence of pity or self-accusation. His understanding was equal to the other powers of his mind, and his deliberate opinions were singularly candid and just; but, like other men of great and irregular genius, the opinions which he delivered in conversation were often the offspring of temporary feelings, and widely different from the calm decisions of his judgment. This was not merely true respecting the characters of others, but in regard to some of the most important points of human speculation.

On no subject did he give a more striking proof of the strength of his understanding, than in the correct estimate he formed of himself. He knew his own failings; he predicted their consequence; the melancholy foreboding was never long absent from his mind; yet his passions carried him down the stream of error, and swept him over the precipice he saw directly in his course. The fatal defect in his character lay in the comparative weakness of his volition, that superior faculty of the mind, which, governing the conduct according to the dictates of the understanding, alone entitles it to be denominated rational; which is the parent of fortitude, patience, and self-denial; which, by regulating and combining human exertions, may be said to have effected all that is great in the works of man, in literature, in science, or on the face of nature. The occupations of a poet are not calculated to strengthen the governing powers of the mind, or to weaken that sensibility which requires perpetual control, since it gives birth to the vehemence of passion as well as to the higher powers of imagination. Unfortunately, the favourite occupations of genius are calculated to increase all its peculiarities; to nourish that lofty pride which disdains the littleness of prudence, and the restrictions of order: and, by indulgence, to increase that sensibility which, in the present form of our existence, is scarcely compatible with peace or happiness, even when accompanied with the choicest gifts of fortune!

It is observed by one who was a friend and associate of Burns (116), and who has contemplated and explained the system of animated nature, that no sentient being with mental powers greatly superior to those of men, could possibly live and be happy in this world. "If such a being really existed," continues he, "his misery would be extreme. With senses more delicate and refined; with perceptions more acute and penetrating; with a taste so exquisite that the objects around him would by no means gratify it; obliged to feed on nourishment too gross for his frame—he must be born only to be miserable, and the continuation of his existence would be utterly impossible. Even in our present condition, the sameness and the insipidity of objects and pursuits, the futility of pleasure, and the infinite sources of excruciating pain, are supported with great difficulty by cultivated and refined minds. Increase our sensibilities, continue the same objects and situation, and no man could bear to live."

Thus it appears, that our powers of sensation, as well as all our other powers, are adapted to the scene of our existence; that they are limited in mercy, as well as in wisdom.

The speculations of Mr. Smellie are not to be considered as the dreams of a theorist; they were probably founded on sad experience. The being he supposes "with senses more delicate and refined, with perceptions more acute and penetrating," is to be found in real life. He is of the temperament of genius, and perhaps a poet. Is there, then, no remedy for this inordinate sensibility? Are there no means by which the happiness of one so constituted by nature may be consulted? Perhaps it will be found, that regular and constant occupation, irksome though at first it may be, is the true remedy. Occupation in which the powers of the understanding are exercised, will diminish the force of external impressions, and keep the imagination under restraint.

That the bent of every man's mind should be followed in his education and in his destination in life, is a maxim which has been often repeated, but which cannot be admitted without many restrictions. It may be generally true when applied to weak minds, which being capable of little, must be encouraged and strengthened in the feeble impulses by which that little is produced. But where indulgent nature has bestowed her gifts with a liberal hand, the very reverse of this maxim ought frequently to be the rule of conduct. In minds of a higher order, the object of instruction and of discipline is very often to restrain, rather than to impel; to curb the impulses of imagination, so that the passions also may be kept under control. (117)

Hence the advantages, even in a moral point of view, of studies of a severer nature, which, while they inform the understanding, employ the volition, that regulating power of the mind, which, like all our other faculties, is strengthened by exercise, and on the superiority of which virtue, happiness, and honourable fame, are wholly dependent. Hence also the advantage of regular and constant application, which aids the voluntary power by the production of habits so necessary to the support of order and virtue, and so difficult to be formed in the temperament of genius. The man who is so endowed and so regulated, may pursue his course with confidence in almost any of the various walks of life which choice or accident shall open to him; and, provided he employ the talents he has cultivated, may hope for such imperfect happiness, and such limited success, as are reasonably to be expected from human exertions.

The pre-eminence among men, which procures personal respect, and which terminates in lasting reputation, is seldom or never obtained by the excellence of a single faculty of mind. Experience teaches us, that it has been acquired by those only who have possessed the comprehension and the energy of general talents, and who have regulated their application in the line which choice, or perhaps accident, may have determined, by the dictates of their judgment. Imagination is supposed, and with justice, to be the leading faculty of the poet. But what poet has stood the test of time by the force of this single faculty? Who does not see that Homer and Shakspeare excelled the rest of their species in understanding as well as in imagination; that they were pre-eminent in the highest species of knowledge—the knowledge of the nature and character of man? On the other hand, the talent of ratiocination is more especially requisite to the orator; but no man ever obtained the palm of oratory, even by the highest excellence in this single talent. Who does not perceive that Demosthenes and Cicero were not more happy in their addresses to the reason than in their appeals to the passions? They knew, that to excite, to agitate, and to delight, are among the most potent arts of persuasion; and they enforced their impression on the understanding, by their command of all the sympathies of the heart. These observations might be extended to other walks of life. He who has the faculties fitted to excel in poetry, has the faculties which, duly governed, and differently directed, might lead to pre-eminence in other, and, as far as respects himself, perhaps in happier destinations. The talents necessary to the construction of an Iliad, under different discipline and application, might have led armies to victory, or kingdoms to prosperity; might have wielded the thunder of eloquence, or discovered and enlarged the sciences that constitute the power and improve the condition of our species. (118) Such talents are, indeed, rare among the productions of nature, and occasions of bringing them into full exertion are rarer still. But safe and salutary occupations may be found for men of genius in every direction, while the useful and ornamental arts remain to be cultivated, while the sciences remain to be studied and to be extended, and principles of science to be applied to the correction and improvement of art. In the temperament of sensibility, which is, in truth, the temperament of general talents, the principal object of discipline and instruction is, as has already been mentioned, to strengthen the self-command; and this may be promoted by the direction of the studies, more effectually, perhaps, than has been generally understood.

If these observations be founded in truth, they may lead to practical consequences of some importance. It has been too much the custom to consider the possession of poetical talents as excluding the possibility of application to the severer branches of study, and as, in some degree, incapacitating the possessor from attaining those habits, and from bestowing that attention, which are necessary to success in the details of business, and in the engagements of active life. It has been common for persons conscious of such talents, to look with a sort of disdain on other kinds of intellectual excellence, and to consider themselves as in some degree absolved from those rules of prudence by which humbler minds are restricted. They are too much disposed to abandon themselves to their own sensations, and to suffer life to pass away without regular exertion or settled purpose.

But though men of genius are gênerally prone to indolence, with them indolence and unhappiness are in a more especial manner allied. The unbidden splendours of imagination may, indeed, at times irradiate the gloom which inactivity produces; but such visions, though bright, are transient, and serve to cast the realities of life into deeper shade. In bestowing great talents, Nature seems very generally to have imposed on the possessor the necessity of exertion, if he would escape wretchedness. Better for him than sloth, toils the most painful, or adventures the most hazardous. Happier to him than idleness were the condition of the peasant, earning with incessant labour his scanty food; or that of the sailor, though hanging on the yard-arm, and wrestling with the hurricane.

These observations might be amply illustrated by the biography of men of genius of every denomination, and more especially by the biography of the poets. Of this last description of men, few seem to have enjoyed the usual portion of happiness that falls to the lot of humanity, those excepted who have cultivated poetry as an elegant amusement in the hours of relaxation from other occupations, or the small number who have engaged with success in the greater or more arduous attempts of the muse, in which all the faculties of the mind have been fully and permanently employed. Even taste, virtue, and comparative independence, do not seem capable of bestowing on men of genius peace and tranquillity, without such occupation as may give regular and healthful exercise to the faculties of body and mind. The amiable Shenstone has left us the records of his imprudence, of his indolence, and of his unhappiness, amidst the shades of the Leasowes; and the virtues, the learning, and the genius of Gray, equal to the loftiest attempts of the epic muse, failed to procure him in the academic bowers of Cambridge that tranquillity and that respect which less fastidiousness of taste, and greater constancy and vigour of exertion, would have doubtless obtained.

It is more necessary that men of genius should be aware of the importance of self-command, and of exertion, because their indolence is peculiarly exposed, not merely to unhappiness, but to diseases of mind, and to errors of conduct, which are generally fatal. This interesting subject deserves a particular investigation; but we must content ourselves with one or two cursory remarks. Relief is sometimes sought from the melancholy of indolence in practices which, for a time, soothe and gratify the sensations, but which, in the end, involve the sufferer in darker gloom. To command the external circumstances by which happiness is affected, is not in human power; but there are various substances in nature which operate on the system of the nerves, so as to give a fictitious gaiety to the ideas of imagination, and to alter the effect of the external impressions which we receive. Opium is chiefly employed for this purpose by the disciples of Mahomet and the inhabitants of Asia; but alcohol, the principle of intoxication in vinous and spirituous liquors, is preferred in Europe, and is universally used in the Christian world. (119) Under the various wounds to which indolent insensibility is exposed, and under the gloomy apprehensions respecting futurity to which it is so often a prey, how strong is the temptation to have recourse to an antidote by which the pain of these wounds is suspended, by which the heart is exhilirated, visions of happiness are excited in the mind, and the forms of external nature clothed with new beauty!

"Elysium opens round,
A pleasing phrenzy buoys the lighten'd soul,
And sanguine hopes dispel your fleeting care;
And what was difficult, and what was dire,
Yields to your prowess, and superior stars:
The happiest you of all that e'er were mad,
Or are, or shall be, could this folly last.
But soon your heaven is gone; a heavier gloom
Shuts o'er your head ——
* * * *
—— Morning comes; your cares return
With tenfold rage. An anxious stomach well
May be endured—so may the throbbing head:
But such a dim delirium, such a dream
Involves you; such a dastardly despair
Unmans your soul, as madd'ning Pentheus felt,
When, baited round Cithæron's cruel sides.
He saw two suns and double Thebes ascend."
—*Armstrong's Art of Preserving Health*, b. iv. l. 163.

Such are the pleasures and pains of intoxication, as they occur in the temperament of sensibility, described by a genuine poet, with a degree of truth and energy which nothing but experience could have dictated. There are, indeed, some individuals of this temperament on whom wine produces no cheering influence. On some, even in very moderate quantities, its effects are painfully irritating; in large draughts it excites dark and melancholy ideas; and in draughts still larger, the fierceness of insanity itself. Such men are happily exempted from a temptation to which experience teaches us the finest dispositions often yield, and the influence of which, when strengthened by habit, it is a humiliating truth, that the most powerful minds have not been able to resist.

It is the more necessary for men of genius to be on their guard against the habitual use of wine, because it is apt to steal on them insensibly, and because the temptation to excess usually presents itself to them in their social hours, when they are alive only to warm and generous emotions, and when prudence and moderation are often contemned as selfishness and timidity.

It is the more necessary for them to guard against excess in the use of wine, because on them its effects are, physically and morally, in an especial manner injurious. In proportion to its stimulating influence on the system (on which the pleasurable sensations depend, is the debility that ensues—a debility that destroys digestion, and terminates in habitual fever, dropsy, jaundice, paralysis, or insanity. As the strength of the body decays, the volition fails; in proportion as the sensations are soothed and gratified, the sensibility increases; and morbid sensibility is the parent of indolence, because, while it impairs the regulating power of the mind, it exaggerates all the obstacles to exertion. Activity, perseverance, and self-command, become more and more difficult, and the great purposes of utility, patriotism, or of honourable ambition, which had occupied the imagination, die away in fruitless resolutions, or in feeble efforts.

To apply these observations to the subject of our memoirs, would be a useless as well as a painful task. It is, indeed, a duty we owe to the living, not to allow our admiration of great genius, or even our pity for its unhappy destiny, to conceal or disguise its errors. But there are sentiments of respect, and even of tenderness, with which this duty should be performed; there is an awful sanctity which invests the mansions of the dead; and let those who moralise over the graves of their contemporaries, reflect with humility on their own errors, nor forget how soon they may themselves require the candour and the sympathy they are called upon to bestow.

Soon after the death of Burns, the following article appeared in the Dumfries Journal, from which it was copied into the Edinburgh newspapers, and into various other periodical publications. It is from the elegant pen of a lady, already alluded to in the course of these memoirs (120), whose exertions for the family of our bard, in the circles of literature and fashion in which she moves, have done her so much honour.

"The attention of the public seems to be much occupied at present with the loss it has recently sustained in the death of the Caledonian poet, Robert Burns; a loss calculated to be severely felt throughout the literary world, as well as lamented in the narrower sphere of private friendship. It was not, therefore, probable that such an event should be long unattended with the accustomed profusion of posthumous anecdotes and memoirs which are usually circulated immediately after the death of every rare and celebrated personage: I had, however, conceived no intention of appropriating to myself the privilege of criticising Burns's writings and character, or of anticipating on the province of a biographer.

"Conscious, indeed, of my own inability to do justice to such a subject, I should have continued wholly silent, had misrepresentation and calumny been less industrious; but a regard to truth, no less than affection for the memory of a friend, must now justify my offering to the public a few at least of those observations which an intimate acquaintance with Burns, and the frequent opportunities I have had of observing equally his happy qualities and his failings for several years past, have enabled me to communicate.

"It will actually be an injustice done to Burns's character, not only by future generations and foreign countries, but even by his native Scotland, and perhaps a number of his contemporaries, that he is generally talked of, and considered, with reference to his poetical talents *only*; for the fact is, even allowing his great and original genius its due tribute of admiration, that poetry (I appeal to all who have had the advantage of being personally acquainted with him) was actually not his *forte*. Many others, perhaps, may have ascended to prouder heights in the region of Parnassus, but none certainly ever outshone Burns in the charms, the sorcery, I would almost call it, of fascinating conversation, the spontaneous eloquence of social argument, or the unstudied poignancy of brilliant repartee; nor was any man, I believe, ever gifted with a larger portion of the '*vivida vis animi*.' His personal endowments were perfectly correspondent to the qualifications of his mind—his form was manly—his action, energy itself—devoid in a great measure perhaps of those graces, of that polish, acquired only in the refinement of societies where in early life he could have no opportunities of mixing; but where such was the irresistible power of attraction that encircled him, though his appearance and manners were always peculiar, he never failed to delight and to excel. His figure seemed to bear testimony to his earlier destination and employments. It seemed rather moulded by nature for the rough exercises of agriculture, than the gentler cultivation of the Belles Lettres. His features were stamped with the hardy character of independence, and the firmness of conscious, though not arrogant, pre-eminence; the animated expressions of countenance were almost peculiar to himself; the rapid lightnings of his eye were always the harbingers of some flash of genius, whether they darted the fiery glances of insulted and indignant superiority, or beamed with the impassioned sentiment of fervent and impetuous affections. His voice alone could improve upon the magic of his eye: sonorous, replete with the finest modulations, it alternately captivated the ear with the melody of poetic numbers, the perspicuity of nervous reasoning, or the ardent sallies of enthusiastic patriotism. The keenness of satire was, I am almost at a loss whether to say, his *forte* or his foible; for though nature had endowed him with a portion of the most pointed excellence in that dangerous talent, he suffered it too often to be the vehicle of personal, and sometimes unfounded, animosities. It was not always that sportiveness of humour, that 'unwary pleasantry,' which Sterne has depicted with touches so conciliatory, but the darts of ridicule were frequently directed as the caprice of the instant suggested, or as the altercations of parties and of persons happened to kindle the restlessness of his spirit into interest or aversion. This, however, was not invariably the case; his wit (which is no unusual matter indeed) had always the start of his judgment, and would lead him to the indulgence of raillery uniformly acute, but often accompanied with the least desire to wound. The suppression of an arch and full-pointed *bon-mot*, from a dread of offending its object, the sage of Zurich very properly classes as a virtue *only to be sought for in the calendar of saints;* if so, Burns must not be too severely dealt with for being rather deficient in it. He paid for his mischievous wit as dearly as any one could do. ''Twas no extravagant arithmetic,' to say of him, as was said of Yorick, that 'for every ten jokes he got a hundred enemies;' but much allowance will be made by a candid mind for the splenetic warmth of a spirit whom 'distress had spited with the world,' and which, unbounded in its intellectual sallies and pursuits, continually experienced the curbs imposed by the waywardness of his fortune. The vivacity of his wishes and temper was indeed checked by almost habitual disappointments, which sat heavy on a heart that acknowledged the ruling passion of independence, without having ever been placed beyond the grasp of penury. His soul was never languid or inactive, and his genius was extinguished only with the last spark of retreating life. His passions rendered him, according as they disclosed themselves in affection or antipathy, an object of enthusiastic attachment, or of decided enmity; for *he* possessed none of that negative insipidity of character, whose love might be regarded with indifference, or whose resentment could be considered with contempt. In this, it should seem, the temper of his associates took the tincture from his own; for *he* acknowledged in the universe but two classes of objects, those of adoration the most fervent, or of aversion the most uncontrollable; and it has been frequently a reproach to him, that, unsusceptible of indifference, often hating where he ought only to have despised, he alternately opened his heart and poured forth the treasures of his understanding to such as were incapable of appreciating the homage; and elevated to the privileges of an adversary some who were unqualified in all respects for the honour of a contest so distinguished.

"It is said that the celebrated Dr. Johnson professed to 'love a good hater'—a temperament that would have singularly adapted him to cherish a prepossession in favour of our bard, who perhaps fell but little short even of the surly doctor in this qualification, as long as the disposition to ill-will continued; but the warmth of his passions was fortunately corrected by their versatility. He was seldom, indeed never, implacable in his resentments, and sometimes, it has been alleged, not inviolably faithful in his engagements of friendship. Much, indeed, has been said about his inconstancy and caprice; but I am inclined to believe, that they originated less in a levity of sentiment, than from an extreme impetuosity of feeling, which rendered him prompt to take umbrage; and his sensations of pique, where he fancied he had discovered the traces of neglect, scorn, or unkindness, took their measure of asperity from the overflowings of the opposite sentiment which preceded them, and which seldom failed to regain its ascendancy in his bosom on the return of calmer reflection. He was candid and manly in the avowal of his errors, and *his avowal* was a *reparation*. His native *fierté* never forsaking him for a moment, the value of a frank acknowledgment was enhanced tenfold towards a generous mind, from its never being attended with servility. His mind, organised only for the stronger and more acute operations of the passions, was impracticable to the efforts of superciliousness that would have depressed it into humility, and equally superior to the encroachments of venal suggestions that might have led him into the mazes of hypocrisy.

"It has been observed that he was far from averse to the incense of flattery, and could receive it tempered with less delicacy than might have been expected, as he seldom transgressed extravagantly in that way himself; where he paid a compliment, it might indeed claim the power of intoxication, as approbation from him was always an honest tribute from the warmth and sincerity of his heart. It has been sometimes represented by those who, it should seem, had a view to depreciate, though they could not hope wholly to obscure, that native brilliancy which the powers of this extraordinary man had invariably bestowed on every thing that came from his lips or pen, that the history of the Ayrshire ploughboy was an ingenious fiction, fabricated for the purposes of obtaining the interests of the great, and enhancing the merits of what in reality required no foil. The Cotter's Saturday Night, Tam o' Shanter, and The Mountain Daisy, besides a number of later productions, where the maturity of his genius will be readily traced, and which will be given to the public as soon as his friends have collected and arranged them, speak sufficiently for themselves; and had they fallen from a hand more dignified in the ranks of society than that of a peasant, they had perhaps bestowed as unusual a grace there, as even in the humbler shade of rustic inspiration from whence they really sprang.

"To the obscure scene of Burns's education, and to the laborious, though honourable station of rural industry in which his parentage enrolled him, almost every inhabitant of the south of Scotland can give testimony. His only surviving brother, Gilbert Burns, now guides the ploughshare of his forefathers in Ayrshire, at a farm near Mauchline; and our poet's eldest son, a lad of nine years of age, whose early dispositions already prove him to be in some measure the inheritor of his father's talents as well as indigence, has been destined by his family to the humble employments of the loom.

"That Burns had received no classical education, and was acquainted with the Greek and Roman authors only through the medium of translations, is a fact of which all who were in the habit of conversing with him might readily be convinced. I have, indeed, seldom observed him to be at a loss in conversation, unless where the dead languages and their writers have been the subjects of discussion. When I have pressed him to tell me why he never applied himself to acquire the Latin, in particular, a language which his happy memory would have so soon enabled him to be master of, he used only to reply with a smile, that he had already learnt all the Latin he desired to know, and that was *omnia vincit amor*—a sentence, that from his writings and most favourite pursuits, it should undoubtedly seem that he was most thoroughly versed in; but I really believe his classic erudition extended little, if any, farther.

"The penchant Burns had uniformly acknowledged for the festive pleasures of the table, and towards the fairer and softer objects of nature's creation, has been the rallying point whence the attacks of his censors have been uniformly directed; and to these, it must be confessed, he showed himself no stoic. His poetical pieces blend with alternate happiness of description, the frolic spirit of the flowing bowl, or melt the heart to the tender and impassioned sentiments in which beauty always taught him to pour forth his own. But who would wish to reprove the feelings he has consecrated with such lively touches of nature? And where is the rugged moralist who will persuade us so far to 'chill the genial current of the soul,' as to regret that Ovid ever celebrated his Corinna, or that Anacreon sang beneath his vine?

"I will not, however, undertake to be the apologist of the irregularities even of a man of genius, though I believe it is as certain that genius never was free from irregularities, as that their absolution may, in great measure, be justly claimed, since it is perfectly evident that the world had continued very stationary in its intellectual acquirements, had it never given birth to any but men of plain sense. Evenness of conduct, and a due regard to the decorums of the world, have been so rarely seen to move hand in hand with genius, that some have gone as far as to say, though there I cannot wholly acquiesce, that they are even incompatible; besides, the frailties that cast their shade over the splendour of superior merit, are more conspicuously glaring than where they are the attendants of mere mediocrity. It is only on the gem we are disturbed to see the dust; the pebble may be soiled, and we never regard it. The eccentric intuitions of genius too often yield the soul to the wild effervescence of desires, always unbounded, and sometimes equally dangerous to the repose of others as fatal to its own. No wonder, then, if virtue herself be sometimes lost in the blaze of kindling animation, or that the calm monitions of reason are not invariably found sufficient to fetter an imagination, which scorns the narrow limits and restrictions that would chain it to the level of ordinary minds. The child of nature, the child of sensibility, unschooled in the rigid precepts of philosophy, too often unable to control the passions which proved a source of frequent errors and misfortunes to him, Burns made his own artless apology in language more impressive than all the argumentatory vindications in the world could do, in one of his own poems, where he delineates the gradual expansion of his mind to the lessons of the 'tutelary muse,' who concludes an address to her pupil, almost unique for simplicity and beautiful poetry, with these lines:—

'I saw thy pulse's madd'ning play
Wild send thee pleasure's devious way;
Misled by Fancy's meteor ray,
By passion driven;
But yet the light that led astray:
Was *light from heaven.*'

"I have already transgressed beyond the bounds I had proposed to myself on first committing this sketch to paper, which comprehends what at least I have been led to deem the leading features of Burns's mind and character. A literary critique I do not aim at—mine is wholly fulfilled if, in these pages, I have been able to delineate any of those strong traits that distinguished him, of those talents which raised him from the plough, where he passed the bleak morning of his life, weaving his rude wreaths of poesy with the wild field-flowers that sprang around his cottage, to that enviable eminence of literary fame, where Scotland will long cherish his memory with delight and gratitude; and proudly remember that, beneath her cold sky, a genius was ripened, without care or culture, that would have done honour to climes more favourable to those luxuriances—that warmth of colouring and fancy in which he so eminently excelled.

"From several paragraphs I have noticed in the public prints, ever since the idea of sending this sketch to some one of them was formed, I find private animosities have not yet subsided, and that envy has not yet exhausted all her shafts. I still trust, however, that honest fame will be permanently affixed to Burns's character, which I think it will be found he *has* merited, by the candid and impartial among his countrymen. And where a recollection of the imprudences that sullied his brighter qualifications interpose, let the imperfection of all human excellence be remembered at the same time, leaving those inconsistencies, which alternately exalted his nature into the seraph, and sank it again into the man, to the tribunal which *alone* can investigate the labyrinths of the human heart—

'Where they alike in trembling hope *repose*,
—The bosom of his father and his *God*.'

GRAY'S *Elegy*.

"*Annandale, August* 7, 1796."

After this account of the life and personal character of Burns, it may be expected that some inquiry should be made into his literary merits. It will not, however, be necessary to enter very minutely into this investigation. If fiction be, as some suppose, the soul of poetry, no one had ever less pretensions to the name of poet than Burns. Though he has displayed great powers of imagination, yet the subjects on which he has written are seldom, if ever, imaginary; his poems, as well as his letters, may be considered as the effusions of his sensibility, and the transcript of his own musings on the real incidents of his humble life. If we add, that they also contain most happy delineations of the characters, manners, and scenery, that presented themselves to his observation, we shall include almost all the subjects of his muse. His writings may, therefore, be regarded as affording a great part of the data on which our account of his personal character has been founded; and most of the observations we have applied to the man, are applicable, with little variation, to the poet.

The impression of his birth, and of his original station in life, was not more evident on his form and manners, than on his poetical productions. The incidents which form the subjects of his poems, though some of them highly interesting, and susceptible of poetical imagery, are incidents in the life of a peasant who takes no pains to disguise the lowliness of his condition, or to throw into shade the circumstances attending it, which more feeble or more artificial minds would have endeavoured to conceal. The same rudeness and inattention appears in the formation of his rhymes, which are frequently incorrect, while the measure in which many of the poems are written has little of the pomp or harmony of modern versification, and is, indeed, to an English ear strange and uncouth. The greater part of his earlier poems are written in the dialect of his country, which is obscure, if not unintelligible, to Englishmen; and which, though it still adheres more or less to the speech of almost every Scotsman, all the polite and the ambitious are now endeavouring to banish from their tongues as well as their writings. The use of it in composition naturally, therefore, calls up ideas of vulgarity in the mind. These singularities are increased by the character of the poet, who delights to express himself with a simplicity that approaches to nakedness, and with an unmeasured energy that often alarms delicacy, and sometimes offends taste. Hence, in approaching him, the first impression is, perhaps, repulsive: there is an air of coarseness about him, which is difficultly reconciled with our established notions of poetical excellence.

As the reader, however, becomes better acquainted with the poet, the effects of his peculiarities lessen. He perceives in his poems, even on the lowest subjects, expressions of sentiment, and delineations of manners, which are highly interesting. The scenery he describes is evidently taken from real life; the characters he introduces, and the incidents he relates, have the impression of nature and truth. His humour, though wild and unbridled, is irresistibly amusing, and is sometimes heightened in its effects by the introduction of emotions of tenderness, with which genuine humour so happily unites. Nor is this the extent of his power. The reader, as he examines farther, discovers that the poet is not confined to the descriptive, the humorous, or the pathetic; he is found, as occasion offers, to rise with ease into the terrible and the sublime. Everywhere he appears devoid of artifice, performing what he attempts with little apparent effort, and impressing on the offspring of *his fancy the stamp of his understanding*. The reader, capable of forming a just estimate of poetical talents, discovers in these circumstances marks of uncommon genius, and is willing to investigate more minutely its nature and its claims to originality. This last point we shall examine first.

That Burns had not the advantages of a classical education, or of any degree of acquaintance with the Greek or Roman writers in their original dress, has appeared in the history of his life. He acquired, indeed, some knowledge of the French language, but it does not appear that he was ever much conversant in French literature, nor is there any evidence of his having derived any of his poetical stores from that source. With the English classics he became well acquainted in the course of his life, and the effect of this acquaintance are observable in his later productions; but the character and style of his poetry were formed very early, and the model which he followed, in as far as he can be said to have had one, is to be sought for in the works of the poets who have written in the Scottish dialect—in the works of such of them more especially, as are familiar to the peasantry of Scotland. Some observations on these may form a proper introduction to a more particular examination of the poetry of Burns. The studies of the editor in this direction are indeed very recent and very imperfect. It would have been imprudent for him to have entered on this subject at all, but for the kindness of Mr. Ramsay of Ochtertyre, whose assistance he is proud to acknowledge, and to whom the reader must ascribe whatever is of any value in the following imperfect sketch of literary compositions in the Scottish idiom.

It is a circumstance not a little curious, and which does not seem to be satisfactorily explained, that in the thirteenth century, the language of the two British nations, if at all different, differed only in dialect, the Gaelic in the one, like the Welsh and Armoric in the other, being confined to the mountainous districts. The English under the Edwards, and the Scots under Wallace and Bruce, spoke the same language. We may observe also, that in Scotland, the history of poetry ascends to a period nearly as remote as in England. Barber, and Blind Harry, James the First, Dunbar, Douglas, and Lindsay, who lived in the fourteenth, fifteenth, and sixteenth centuries, were coeval with the fathers of poetry in England; and, in the opinion of Mr. Warton, not inferior to them in genius or in composition. Though the language of the two countries gradually deviated from each other during this period, yet the difference on the whole was not considerable; not perhaps, greater than between the different dialects of the different parts of England in our own time.

At the death of James V. in 1542, the language of Scotland was in a flourishing condition, wanting only writers in prose equal to those in verse. Two circumstances, propitious on the whole, operated to prevent this. The first was the passion of the Scots for composition in Latin, and the second, the accession of James VI. to the English throne. It may easily be imagined, that if Buchanan had devoted his admirable talents, even in part, to the cultivation of his native tongue, as was done by the revivers of letters in Italy, he would have left compositions in that language which might have incited other men of genius to have followed his example (121), and given duration to the language itself. The union of the two crowns in the person of James, overthrew all reasonable expectation of this kind. That monarch, seated on the English throne, would no longer suffer himself to be addressed in the rude dialect in which the Scottish clergy had so often insulted his dignity. He encouraged Latin or English only, both of which he prided himself on writing with purity, though he himself never could acquire the English pronunciation, but spoke with a Scottish idiom and intonation to the last. Scotsmen of talents declined writing in their native language, which they knew was not acceptable to their learned and pedantic monarch; and at a time when national prejudice and enmity prevailed to a great degree, they disdained to study the niceties of the English tongue, though of so much easier acquisition than a dead language. Lord Stirling, and Drummond of Hawthornden, the only Scotsmen who wrote poetry in those times, were exceptions. They studied the language of England, and composed in it with precision and elegance. They were, however, the last of their countrymen who deserved to be considered as poets in that century. The muses of Scotland sank into silence, and did not again raise their voices for a period of eighty years.

To what causes are we to attribute this extreme depression among a people comparatively learned, enterprising, and ingenious? Shall we impute it to the fanaticism of the Covenanters, or to the tyranny of the house of Stuart after their restoration to the throne? Doubtless these causes operated, but they seem unequal to account for the effect. In England, similar distractions and oppression took place, yet poetry flourished there in a remarkable degree. During this period, Cowley, and Waller, and Dryden, sang, and Milton raised his strain of unparalleled grandeur. To the causes already mentioned, another must be added, in accounting for the torpor of Scottish literature—the want of a proper vehicle for men of genius to employ. The civil wars had frightened away the Latin Muses, and no standard had been established of the Scottish tongue, which was deviating still farther from the pure English idiom.

The revival of literature in Scotland may be dated from the establishment of the Union, or rather from the extinction of the rebellion in 1715. The nations being finally incorporated, it was clearly seen that their tongues must be in the end incorporate also; or rather, indeed, that the Scottish language must degenerate into a provincial idiom, to be avoided by those who would aim at distinction in letters, or rise to eminence in the united legislature.

Soon after this, a band of men of genius appeared, who studied the English classics, and imitated their beauties, in the same manner as they studied the classics of Greece and Rome. They had admirable models of composition lately presented to them by the writers of the reign of Queen Anne; particularly in the periodical papers published by Steele, Addison, and their associated friends, which circulated widely through Scotland, and diffused everywhere a taste for purity of style and sentiment, and for critical disquisition. At length, the Scottish writers succeeded in English composition, and an union was formed of the literary talents, as well as of the legislatures of the two nations. On this occasion the poets took the lead. While Henry Home (122), Dr. Wallace, and their learned associates, were only laying in their intellectual stores, and studying to clear themselves of their Scottish idioms, Thomson, Mallett, and Hamilton of Bangour, had made their appearance before the public, and been enrolled on the list of English poets. The writers in prose followed—a numerous and powerful band—and poured their ample stores into the general stream of British literature. Scotland possessed her four universities before the accession of James to the English throne. Immediately before the Union, she acquired her parochial schools. These establishments combining happily together, made the elements of knowledge of easy acquisition, and presented a direct path by which the ardent student might be carried along into the recesses of science or learning. As civil broils ceased, and faction and prejudice gradually died away, a wider field was opened to literary ambition, and the influence of the Scottish institutions for instruction, on the productions of the press, became more and more apparent.

It seems, indeed, probable, that the establishment of the parochial schools produced effects on the rural muse of Scotland also, which have not hitherto been suspected, and which, though less splendid in their nature, are not, however, to be regarded as trivial, whether we consider the happiness or the morals of the people.

There is some reason to believe, that the original inhabitants of the British isles possessed a peculiar and an interesting species of music, which being banished from the plains by the successive invasions of the Saxons, Danes, and Normans, was preserved with the native race, in the wilds of Ireland and in the mountains of Scotland and Wales. The Irish, the Scottish, and the Welsh music, differ indeed from each other, but the difference may be considered as in dialect only, and probably produced by the influence of time, and like the different dialects of their common language. If this conjecture be true, the Scottish music must be more immediately of a Highland origin, and the Lowland tunes, though now of a character somewhat distinct, must have descended from the mountains in remote ages. Whatever credit may be given to conjectures, evidently involved in great uncertainty, there can be no doubt that the Scottish peasantry have been long in possession of a number of songs and ballads composed in their native dialect, and sung to their native music. The subjects of these compositions were such as most interested the simple inhabitants, and in the succession of time varied probably as the condition of society varied. During the separation and the hostility of the two nations, these songs and ballads, as far as our imperfect documents enable us to judge, were chiefly warlike; such as the Huntis of Cheviot, and the Battle of Harlaw. After the union of the two crowns, when a certain degree of peace and of tranquillity took place, the rural muse of Scotland breathed in softer accents. "In the want of real evidence respecting the history of our songs," says Mr. Ramsay of Ochtertyre, "recourse may be had to conjecture. One would be disposed to think, that the most beautiful of the Scottish tunes were clothed with new words after the union of the crowns. The inhabitants of the borders, who had formerly been warriors from choice, and husbandmen from necessity, either quitted the country, or were transformed into real shepherds, easy in their circumstances, and satisfied with their lot. Some sparks of that spirit of chivalry for which they are celebrated by Froissart, remained, sufficient to inspire elevation of sentiment and gallantry towards the fair sex. The familiarity and kindness which had long subsisted between the gentry and the peasantry, could not all at once be obliterated, and this connexion tended to sweeten rural life. In this state of innocence, ease, and tranquillity of mind, the love of poetry and music would still maintain its ground, though it would naturally assume a form congenial to the more peaceful state of society. The minstrels, whose metrical tales used once to rouse the borderers like the trumpet's sound, had been, by an order of the legislature (in 1579), classed with rogues and vagabonds, and attempted to be suppressed. Knox and his disciples influenced the Scottish parliament, but contended in vain with her rural muse. Amidst our Arcadian vales, probably on the banks of the Tweed, or some of its tributary streams, one or more original geniuses may have arisen, who were destined to give a new turn to the taste of their countrymen. They would see that the events and pursuits which chequer private life were the proper subjects for popular poetry. Love, which had formerly held a divided sway with glory and ambition, became now the master passion of the soul. To portray in lively and delicate colours, though with a hasty hand, the hopes and fears that agitate the breast of the love-sick swain, or forlorn maiden, affords ample scope to the rural poet. Love-songs of which Tibullus himself would not have been ashamed, might be composed by an uneducated rustic with a slight tincture of letters; or if in these songs the character of the rustic be sometimes assumed, the truth of character, and the language of nature, are preserved. With unaffected simplicity and tenderness, topics are urged most likely to soften the heart of a cruel and coy mistress, or to regain a fickle lover. Even in such as are of a melancholy cast, a ray of hope breaks through, and dispels the deep and settled gloom which characterises the sweetest of the Highland *luenigs*, or vocal airs. Nor are these songs all plaintive; many of them are lively and humorous, and some appear to us coarse and indelicate. They seem, however, genuine descriptions of the manners of an energetic and sequestered people in their hours of mirth and festivity, though in their portraits some objects are brought into open view, which more fastidious painters would have thrown into shade.

As those rural poets sang for amusement, not for gain, their effusions seldom exceeded a love-song, or a ballad of satire or humour, which, like the works of the elder minstrels, were seldom committed to writing, but treasured up in the memory of their friends and neighbours. Neither known to the learned nor patronised by the great, these rustic bards lived and died in obscurity; and by a strange fatality, their story, and even their very names, have been forgotten. (123) When proper models for pastoral songs were produced, there would be no want of imitators. To succeed in this species of composition, soundness of understanding, and sensibility of heart, were more requisite than flights of imagination or pomp of numbers. Great changes have certainly taken place in Scottish song-writing, though we cannot trace the steps of this change; and few of the pieces admired in Queen Mary's time are now to be discovered in modern collections. It is possible, though not probable, that the music may have remained nearly the same, though the words to the tunes were entirely new-modelled." (124)

These conjectures are highly ingenious. It cannot, however, be presumed, that the state of ease and tranquillity described by Mr. Ramsay, took place among the Scottish peasantry immediately on the union of the crowns, or indeed during the greater part of the seventeenth century. The Scottish nation, through all its ranks, was deeply agitated by the civil wars, and the religious persecutions which succeeded each other in that disastrous period; it was not till after the revolution in 1688, and the subsequent establishment of their beloved form of church government, that the peasantry of the Lowlands enjoyed comparative repose; and it is since that period that a great number of the most admired Scottish songs have been produced, though the tunes to which they are sung are in general of much greater antiquity. It is not unreasonable to suppose that the peace and security derived from the Revolution and the Union, produced a favourable change on the rustic poetry of Scotland; and it can scarcely be doubted, that the institution of parish schools in 1696, by which a certain degree of instruction was diffused universally among the peasantry, contributed to this happy effect.

Soon after this appeared Allan Ramsay, the Scottish Theocritus. He was born on the high mountains that divide Clydesdale and Annandale, in a small hamlet by the banks of Glengonar, a stream which descends into the Clyde. The ruins of this hamlet are still shown to the inquiring traveller. He was the son of a peasant, and probably received such instruction as his parish-school bestowed, and the poverty of his parents admitted. (125) Ramsay made his appearance in Edinburgh in the beginning of the present century, in the humble character of an apprentice to a barber, or peruke-maker; he was then fourteen or fifteen years of age. By degrees he acquired notice for his social disposition, and his talent for the composition of verses in the Scottish idiom; and, changing his profession for that of a bookseller, he became intimate with many of the literary, as well as the gay and fashionable characters of his time. (126) Having published a volume of poems of his own in 1721, which was favourably received, he undertook to make a collection of ancient Scottish poems, under the title of The Evergreen, and was afterwards encouraged to present to the world a collection of Scottish songs. "From what sources he procured them," says Mr. Ramsay of Ochtertyre, "whether from tradition or manuscript, is uncertain. As in the Evergreen, he made some rash attempts to improve on the originals of his ancient poems, he probably used still greater freedom with the songs and ballads. The truth cannot, however, be known on this point, till manuscripts of the songs printed by him more ancient than the present century, shall be produced, or access be obtained to his own papers, if they are still in existence. To several tunes which either wanted words, or had words that were improper or imperfect, he, or his friends, adapted verses worthy of the melodies they accompanied, worthy indeed of the golden age. These verses were perfectly intelligible to every rustic, yet justly admired by persons of taste, who regarded them as the genuine offspring of the pastoral muse. In some respects, Ramsay had advantages not possessed by poets writing in the Scottish dialect in our days. Songs in the dialect of Cumberland or Lancashire could never be popular, because these dialects have never been spoken by persons of fashion. But till the middle of the present century, every Scotsman, from the peer to the peasant, spoke a truly Doric language. It is true, the English moralists and poets were by this time read by every person of condition, and considered as the standards for polite composition. But as national prejudices were still strong, the busy, the learned, the gay, and the fair, continued to speak their native dialect, and that with an elegance and poignancy, of which Scotsmen of the present day can have no just notion. I am old enough to have conversed with Mr. Spittal, of Leuchat, a scholar and a man of fashion, who survived all the members of the Union Parliament, in which he had a seat. His pronunciation and phraseology differed as much from the common dialect, as the language of St. James's from that of Thames Street. Had we retained a court and parliament of our own, the tongues of the two sister-kingdoms would indeed have differed like the Castilian and Portuguese; but each would have had its own classics, not in a single branch, but in the whole circle of literature.

"Ramsay associated with the men of wit and fashion of his day, and several of them attempted to write poetry in his manner. Persons too idle or too dissipated to think of compositions that required much exertion, succeeded very happily in making tender sonnets to favourite tunes in compliment to their mistresses, and, transforming themselves into impassioned shepherds, caught the language of the characters they assumed. Thus, about the year 1731, Robert Crawford of Auchinames wrote the modern song of Tweed Side (127), which has been so much admired. In 1743, Sir Gilbert Elliot, the first of our lawyers who both spoke and wrote English elegantly, composed, in the character of a love-sick swain, a beautiful song, beginning, 'My sheep I neglected, I lost my sheep-hook,' on the marriage of his mistress, Miss Forbes, with Ronald Crawford. And about twelve years afterwards, the sister of Sir Gilbert wrote the *ancient* words to the tune of the Flowers of the Forest (128), and supposed to allude to the battle of Flowden. In spite of the double rhyme, it is a sweet, and, though in some parts allegorical, a natural expression of national sorrow. The more *modern* words to the same tune, beginning, 'I have seen the smiling of fortune beguiling,' were written long before by Mrs. Cockburn, a woman of great wit, who outlived all the first group of *literati* of the present century, all of whom were very fond of her. (129) I was delighted with her company, though, when I saw her, she was very old. Much did she know that is now lost."

In addition to these instances of Scottish songs produced in the earlier part of the present century, may be mentioned the ballad of Hardiknute, by Lady Wardlaw; the ballad of William and Margaret; and the song entitled the Birks of Endermay, by Mallett; the love-song, beginning. "For ever fortune, wilt thou prove," produced by the youthful muse of Thomson; and the exquisite pathetic ballad, the Braes of Yarrow, by Hamilton of Bangour. On the revival of letters in Scotland, subsequent to the Union, a very general taste seems to have prevailed for the national songs and music. "For many years," says Mr. Ramsay, "the singing of songs was the great delight of the higher and middle order of the people, as well as of the peasantry; and though a taste for Italian music has interfered with this amusement, it is still very prevalent. Between forty and fifty years ago, the common people were not only exceedingly fond of songs and ballads, but of metrical history. Often have I, in my cheerful morn of youth, listened to them with delight, when reading or reciting the exploits of Wallace and Bruce against the southrons. Lord Hailes was wont to call Blind Harry their *bible*, he being their great favourite next to the Scriptures. When, therefore, one in the vale of life felt the first emotions of genius, he wanted not models *sui generis*. But though the seeds of poetry were scattered with a plentiful hand among the Scottish peasantry, the product was probably like that of pears and apples—of a thousand that spring up, nine hundred and fifty are so bad as to set the teeth on edge; forty-five or more are passable and useful; and the rest of an exquisite flavour. Allan Ramsay and Burns are wildings of this last description. They had the example of the elder Scottish poets; they were not without the aid of the best English writers; and, what was still of more importance, they were no strangers to the book of nature, and to the book of God."

"From this general view, it is apparent that Allan Ramsay may be considered as in a great measure the reviver of the rural poetry of his country. His collection of ancient Scottish poems, under the name of The Evergreen, his collection of Scottish songs, and his own poems, the principal of which is the Gentle Shepherd, have been universally read among the peasantry of his country, and have in some degree superseded the adventures of Bruce and Wallace, as recorded by Barbour and Blind Harry. Burns was well acquainted with all these. He had also before him the poems of Fergusson in the Scottish dialect, which have been produced in our own times, and of which it will be necessary to give a short account.

"Fergusson was born of parents who had it in their power to procure him a liberal education—a circumstance, however, which in Scotland implies no very high rank in society. From a well-written and apparently authentic account of his life (130), we learn that he spent six years at the schools of Edinburgh and Dundee, and several years at the universities of Edinburgh and St. Andrews. It appears that he was at one time destined for the Scottish church; but, as he advanced towards manhood, he renounced that intention, and at Edinburgh entered the office of a writer to the signet—a title which designates a separate and higher order of Scottish attornies. Fergusson had sensibility of mind, a warm and generous heart, and talents for society of the most attractive kind. To such a man no situation could be more dangerous than that in which he was placed. The excesses into which he was led impaired his feeble constitution, and he sank under them in the month of October, 1774 in his twenty-third or twenty-fourth year. Burns was not acquainted with the poems of this youthful genius when he himself began to write poetry; and when he first saw them, he had renounced the muses. But while he resided in the town of Irvine, meeting with Fergusson's Scottish Poems, he informs us that he "strung his lyre anew with emulating vigour." Touched by the sympathy originating in kindred genius, and in the forebodings of similar fortune, Burns regarded Fergusson with a partial and an affectionate admiration. Over his grave he erected a monument, as has already been mentioned; and his poems he has, in several instances, made the subjects of his imitation.

From this account of the Scottish poems known to Burns, those who are acquainted with them will see that they are chiefly humorous or pathetic, and under one or other of these descriptions most of his own poems will class. Let us compare him with his predecessors under each of these points of view, and close our examination with a few general observations.

It has frequently been observed, that Scotland has produced, comparatively speaking, few writers who have excelled in humour. But this observation is true only when applied to those who have continued to reside in their own country, and have confined themselves to composition in pure English; and, in these circumstances, it admits of an easy explanation. The Scottish poets who have written in the dialect of Scotland, have been at all times remarkable for dwelling on subjects of humour, in which, indeed, many of them have excelled. It would be easy to show, that the dialect of Scotland having become provincial, is now scarcely suited to the more elevated kinds of poetry. If we may believe that the poem of Christis Kirk of the Grene was written by James I. of Scotland (131), this accomplished monarch, who had received an English education under the direction of Henry IV., and who bore arms under his gallant successor, gave the model on which the greater part of the humorous productions of the rustic muse of Scotland has been formed. Christis Kirk of the Grene was reprinted by Ramsay somewhat modernised in the orthography, and two cantos were added by him, in which he attempts to carry on the design. Hence the poem of King James is usually printed in Ramsay's works. The royal bard describes, in the first canto, a rustic dance, and afterwards a contention in archery, ending in an affray. Ramsay relates the restoration of concord, and the renewal of the rural sports, with the humours of a country wedding. Though each of the poets describes the manners of his respective age, yet in the whole piece there is a very sufficient uniformity—a striking proof of the identity of character in the Scottish peasantry at the two periods, distant from each other three hundred years. It is an honourable distinction to this body of men, that their character and manners, very little embellished, have been found to be susceptible of an amusing and interesting species of poetry; and it must appear not a little curious, that the single nation of modern Europe which possesses an original rural poetry, should have received the model, followed by their rustic bards, from the monarch on the throne.

The two additional cantos to Christis Kirk of the Grene, written by Ramsay, though objectionable in point of delicacy, are among the happiest of his productions. His chief excellence, indeed, lay in the description of rural characters, incidents, and scenery; for he did not possess any very high powers either of imagination or of understanding. He was well acquainted with the peasantry of Scotland, their lives and opinions. The subject was in a great measure new; his talents were equal to the subject; and he has shown that it may be happily adapted to pastoral poetry. In his Gentle Shepherd, the characters are delineations from nature, the descriptive parts are in the genuine style of beautiful simplicity, the passions and affections of rural life are finely pourtrayed, and the heart is pleasingly interested in the happiness that is bestowed on innocence and virtue. Throughout the whole there is an air of reality which the most careless reader cannot but perceive; and, in fact, no poem ever perhaps acquired so high a reputation, in which truth received so little embellishment from the imagination. In his pastoral songs, and in his rural tales, Ramsay appears to less advantage indeed, but still with considerable attraction. The story of the Monk and the Miller's Wife, though somewhat licentious, may rank with the happiest productions of Prior, or La Fontaine. But when he attempts subjects from higher life, and aims at pure English composition, he is feeble and uninteresting, and seldom ever reaches mediocrity. Neither are his familiar epistles and elegies in the Scottish dialect entitled to much approbation. Though Fergusson had higher powers of imagination than Ramsay, his genius was not of the highest order; nor did his learning, which was considerable, improve his genius. His poems written in pure English, in which he often follows classical models, though superior to the English poems of Ramsay, seldom rise above mediocrity; but in those composed in the Scottish dialect he is often very successful. He was in general, however, less happy than Ramsay in the subjects of his muse. As he spent the greater part of his life in Edinburgh, and wrote for his amusement in the intervals of business or dissipation, his Scottish poems are chiefly founded on the incidents of a town life, which, though they are susceptible of humour, do not admit of those delineations of scenery and manners, which vivify the rural poetry of Ramsay, and which so agreeably amuse the fancy and interest the heart. The town-eclogues of Fergusson, if we may so denominate them, are, however, faithful to nature, and often distinguished by a very happy vein of humour. His poems entitled The Daft Days, The King's Birth-day in Edinburgh, Leith Races, and the Hallow Fair, will justify this character. In these, particularly in the last, he imitated Christis Kirk of the Grene, as Ramsay had done before him. His Address to the Tron Kirk Bell is an exquisite piece of humour, which Burns has scarcely excelled. In appreciating the genius of Fergusson, it ought to be recollected, that his poems are the careless effusions of an irregular though amiable young man, who wrote for the periodical papers of the day, and who died in early youth. Had his life been prolonged under happier circumstances of fortune, he would probably have risen to much higher reputation. He might have excelled in rural poetry; for though his professed pastorals, on the established Sicilian model, are stale and uninteresting, The Farmer's Ingle (132), which may be considered as a Scottish pastoral, is the happiest of all his productions, and certainly was the prototype of the Cotter's Saturday Night. Fergusson, and more especially Burns, have shown that the character and manners of the peasantry of Scotland of the present times, are as well adapted to poetry as in the days of Ramsay, or of the author of Christis Kirk of the Grene.

The humour of Burns is of a richer vein than that of Ramsay or Fergusson, both of whom, as he himself informs us, he had "frequently in his eye, but rather with a view to kindle at their flame, than to servile imitation." His descriptive powers, whether the objects on which they are employed be comic or serious, animate or inanimate, are of the highest order. A superiority of this kind is essential to every species of poetical excellence. In one of his earlier poems, his plan seems to be to inculcate a lesson of contentment on the lower classes of society, by showing that their superiors are neither much better nor happier than themselves; and this he chooses to execute in the form of a dialogue between two dogs. He introduces this dialogue by an account of the persons and characters of the speakers. The first, whom he has named Cæsar, is a dog of condition:—

"His locked, letter'd, braw brass collar,
Show'd him the gentleman and scholar."

High-bred though he is, he is, however, full of condescension:—

"At kirk or market, mill or smiddie,
Nae tawted tyke, tho' e'er so duddie,
But he wad stan't, as glad to see him,
And stroan't on stanes and hillocks wi' him."

The other, Luath, is a "ploughman's collie," but a cur of a good heart and a sound understanding.

"His honest, sonsie, baws'nt face,
Aye gat him friends in ilka place.
His breast was white, his towsie back
Weel clad wi' coat o' glossy black;
His gaucie tail, wi' upward curl,
Hung o'er his hurdies wi' a swirl."

Never were *twa dogs* so exquisitely delineated. Their gambols before they sit down to moralise are described with an equal degree of happiness; and through the whole dialogue, the character, as well as the different condition of the two speakers, is kept in view. The speech of Luath, in which he enumerates the comforts of the poor, gives the following account of their merriment on the first day of the year:—

"That merry day the year begins,
They bar the door on frosty win's;
The nappy reeks wi' mantling ream,
And sheds a heart-inspiring steam;
The luntin pipe, and sneeshinmill,
Are handed round wi' right guid will;
The canty auld folks crackin crouse,
The young anes rantin thro' the house—
My heart has been sae fain to see them,
That I for joy hae barkit wi' them."

Of all the animals who have moralised on human affairs since the days of Æsop, the dog seems best entitled to this privilege, as well from his superior sagacity as from his being, more than any other, the friend and associate of man. The dogs of Burns, excepting in their talent for moralising, are downright dogs; and not like the horses of Swift, or the Hind and Panther of Dryden, men in the shape of brutes. It is this circumstance that heightens the humour of the dialogue. The "twa dogs" are constantly kept before our eyes, and the contrast between their form and character as dogs, and the sagacity of their conversation, heightens the humour, and deepens the impression of the poet's satire. Though in this poem the chief excellence may be considered as humour, yet great talents are displayed in its composition; the happiest powers of description, and the deepest insight into the human heart. (133) It is seldom, however, that the humour of Burns appears in so simple a form. The liveliness of his sensibility frequently impels him to introduce into subjects of humour emotions of tenderness or of pity; and, where occasion admits, he is sometimes carried on to exert the higher powers of imagination. In such instances, he leaves the society of Ramsay and of Fergusson, and associates himself with the masters of English poetry, whose language he frequently assumes.

Of the union of tenderness and humour, examples may be found in The Death and Dying Words of poor Mailie, in The Auld Farmer's New-Year's Morning Salutation to his Mare Maggie, and in many of his other poems. The praise of whisky is a favourite subject with Burns. To this he dedicates his poem of Scotch Drink. After mentioning its cheering influence in a variety of situations, he describes, with singular liveliness and power of fancy, its stimulating effects on the blacksmith working at his forge:—

"Nae mercy, then, for airn and steel;
The brawnie, bainie, plougman chiel,
Brings hard owre-hip, wi' sturdy wheel,
The strong fore-hammer,
Till block and studdie ring and reel
Wi' dinsome clamour."

On another occasion (134), choosing to exalt whisky above wine, he introduces a comparison between the natives of more genial climes, to whom the vine furnishes their beverage, and his own countrymen who drink the spirit of malt. The description of the Scotsman is humorous:—

"But bring a Scotsman frae his hill,
Clap in his cheek a Highland gill (135),
Say such is royal George's will,
And there's the foe,
He has nae thought but how to kill
Twa at a blow."

Here the notion of danger rouses the imagination of the poet. He goes on thus:—

"Nae cauld, faint-hearted doubtings teaze him;
Death comes—wi' fearless eye he sees him,
Wi' bluidy hand a welcome gies him;
And when he fa's,
His latest draught o' breathing lea'es him
In faint huzzas."

Again, however, he sinks into humour, and concludes the poem with the following most laughable but most irreverent apostrephe:—

"Scotland, my auld, respected mither!
Tho' whyles ye moistify your leather,
Till whare ye sit, on craps o' heather,
Ye tine your dam:
Freedom and *whiskey* gang thegither—
Tak aff your dram!"

Of this union of humour with the higher powers of imagination, instances may be found in the poem entitled Death and Dr. Hornbook, and in almost every stanza of the Address to the Deil, one of the happiest of his productions. After reproaching this terrible being with all his "doings" and misdeeds, in the course of which he passes through a series of Scottish superstitions, and rises at times into a high strain of poetry, he concludes this address, delivered in a tone of great familiarity, not altogether unmixed with apprehension, in the following words:—

"But, fare-ye-well, auld Nickie-ben!
Oh wad you tak a thought and men'!
Ye aiblins might—I dinna ken—
Sill hae a stake—
I'm wae to think upon yon den
E'en for your sake!"

Humour and tenderness are here so happily intermixed, that it is impossible to say which preponderates.

Fergusson wrote a dialogue between the Causeway and the Plainstones (136) of Edinburgh. This probably suggested to Burns his dialogue between the Old and the New Bridge over the river Ayr. (137) The nature of such subjects requires that they shall be treated humorously, and Fergusson has attempted nothing beyond this. Though the Causeway and the Plainstones talk together, no attempt is made to personify the speakers. A "cadie" (138) heard the conversation, and reported it to the poet.

In the dialogues between the Brigs of Ayr, Burns himself is the auditor, and the time and occasion on which it occurred is related with great circumstantiality. The poet, "pressed by care," or "inspired by whim," had left his bed in the town of Ayr, and wandered out alone in the darkness and solitude of a winter-night, to the mouth of the river, where the stillness was interrupted only by the rushing sound of the influx of the tide. It was after midnight. The dungeon-clock (139) had struck two, and the sound had been repeated by Wallace Tower. (140) All else was hushed. The moon shone brightly, and

"The chilly frost, beneath the silver beam,
Crept gently crusting, o'er the glittering stream."

In this situation the listening bard hears the "clanging sugh" of wings moving through the air, and speedily he perceives two beings reared, the one on the Old, the other on the New Bridge, whose form and attire he describes, and whose conversation with each other he rehearses. These genii enter into a comparison of the respective edifices over which they preside, and afterwards, as is usual between the old and young, compare modern characters and manners with those of past times. They differ, as may be expected, and taunt and scold each other in broad Scotch. This conversation, which is certainly humorous, may be considered as the proper business of the poem. As the debate runs high, and threatens serious consequences, all at once it is interrupted by a new scene of wonders:—

> ——————"all before their sight
> A fairy train appear'd in order bright;
> Adown the glittering stream they featly danc'd; [glanc'd;
> Bright to the moon their various dresses
> They footed o'er the wat'ry glass so neat,
> The infant ice scarce bent beneath their feet;
> While arts of Minstrelsy among them rung,
> And soul-enobling Bards heroic ditties sung."
> * * * *
> "The Genius of the Stream in front appears—
> A venerable chief, advanc'd in years;
> His hoary head with water-lilies crown'd,
> His manly leg with garter-tangle bound."

Next follow a number of other allegorical beings, among whom are the four seasons, Rural Joy, Plenty, Hospitality, and Courage.

> "Benevolence, with mild benignant air,
> A female form, came from the tow'rs of Stair;
> Learning and wealth in equal measures trode,
> From simple Catrine, their long-lov'd abode;
> Last, white-rob'd Peace, crown'd with a hazel-wreath,
> To rustic Agriculture did bequeath
> The broken iron instruments of Death;
> At sight of whom our Sprites forgat their kind'ling wrath."

This poem, irregular and imperfect as it is, displays various and powerful talents, and may serve to illustrate the genius of Burns. In particular, it affords a striking instance of his being carried beyond his original purpose by the powers of imagination.

In Fergusson's poem, the Plainstones and Causeway contrast the characters of the different persons who walked upon them. Burns probably conceived, that by a dialogue between the Old and New Bridge, he might form a humorous contrast between ancient and modern manners in the town of Ayr. Such a dialogue could only be supposed to pass in the stillness of night; and this led our poet into a description of a midnight scene, which excited in a high degree the powers of his imagination. During the whole dialogue the scenery is present to his fancy, and at length it suggests to him a fairy dance of aërial beings, under the beams of the moon, by which the wrath of the Genii of the Brigs of Ayr is appeased.

Incongruous as the different parts of this poem are, it is not an incongruity that displeases; and we have only to regret that the poet did not bestow a little pains in making the figures more correct, and in smoothing the versification.

The epistles of Burns, in which may be included his Dedication to G. H., Esq., discover, like his other writings, the powers of a superior understanding. They display deep insight into human nature, a gay and happy strain of reflection, great independence of sentiment and generosity of heart. It is to be regretted, that, in his Holy Fair, and in some of his other poems, his humour degenerates into personal satire, and that it is not sufficiently guarded in other respects. The Halloween of Burns is free from every objection of this sort. It is interesting, not merely from its humorous description of manners, but as it records the spells and charms used on the celebration of a festival, now even in Scotland, falling into neglect, but which was once observed over the greater part of Britain and Ireland. (141) These charms are supposed to afford an insight into futurity, especially on the subject of marriage, the most interesting event of rural life. In the Halloween, a female, in performing one of the spells, has occasion to go out by moonlight to dip her shift-sleeve into a stream *running towards the south.* It was not necessary for Burns to give a description of this stream. But it was the character of his ardent mind to pour forth not merely what the occasion required, but what is admitted; and the temptation to describe so beautiful a natural object by moonlight, was not to be resisted—

> "Whyles owre a linn the burnie plays,
> As through the glen it wimpl't;
> Whyles round a rocky scaur it strays;
> Whyles in a wiel it dimpl't;
> Whyles glitter'd to the nightly rays,
> Wi' bickering, dancing dazzle;
> Whyles cookit underneath the braes,
> Below the spreading hazel,
> Unseen that night."

Those who understand the Scottish dialect will allow this to be one of the finest instances of description which the records of poetry afford. (142) Though of a very different nature, it may be compared, in point of excellence, with Thomson's description of a river swoollen by the rains of winter, bursting through the streights that confine its torrent, "boiling, wheeling, foaming, and thundering along."

In pastoral, or, to speak more correctly, in rural poetry of a serious nature, Burns excelled equally as in that of a humorous kind; and, using less of the Scottish dialect in his serious poems, he becomes more generally intelligible. It is difficult to decide whether the Address to a Mouse, whose nest was turned up with the plough, should be considered as serious or comic. Be this as it may, the poem is one of the happiest and most finished of his productions. If we smile at the "bickering brattle" of this little flying animal, it is a smile of tenderness and pity. The descriptive part is admirable; the moral reflections beautiful, and arising directly out of the occasion; and in the conclusion there is a deep melancholy, a sentiment of doubt and dread, that rises to the sublime. The address to a Mountain Daisy, turned down with the plough, is a poem of the same nature, though somewhat inferior in point of originality, as well as in the interest produced. To extract out of incidents so common, and seemingly so trivial as these, so fine a train of sentiment and imagery, is the surest proof, as well as the most brilliant triumph, of original genius. The vision, in two cantos, from which a beautiful extract is taken by Mr. Mackenzie, in the 97th number of The Lounger, is a poem of great and various excellence. The opening, in which the poet describes his own state of mind, retiring in the evening, wearied from the labours of the day, to moralise on his conduct and prospects, is truly interesting. The chamber, if we may so term it, in which he sits down to muse, is an exquisite painting:

"There, lanely, by the ingle cheek
I sat and ey'd the spewing reek,
That filled wi' hoast-provoking smeek
The auld clay biggin;
And heard the restless rattons squeak
About the riggin."

To reconcile to our imagination the entrance of an aërial being into a mansion of this kind, required the powers of Burns—he however succeeds. Coila enters, and her countenance, attitude, and dress, unlike those of other spiritual beings, are distinctly pourtrayed. To the painting on her mantle, on which is depicted the most striking scenery, as well as the most distinguished characters, of his native countrry, some exceptions may be made. The mantle of Coila, like the cup of Thyrsis, and the shield of Achilles, is too much crowded with figures, and some of the objects represented upon it are scarcely admissible, according to the principles of design. The generous temperament of Burns led him into these exuberances. In his second edition he enlarged the number of figures originally introduced, that he might include objects to which he was attached by sentiments of affection, gratitude, or patriotism. The second duan, or canto, of this poem, in which Coila describes her own nature and occupations, particularly her superintendence of his infant genius, and in which she reconciles him to the character of a bard, is an elevated and solemn strain of poetry, ranking in all respects, excepting the harmony of numbers, with the higher productions of the English muse. The concluding stanza, compared with that already quoted, will show to what a height Burns rises in this poem, from the point at which he set out:—

"*And wear thou this*—she solemn said,
And bound the *holly* round my head;
The polished leaves, and berries red,
Did rustling play:
And, like a passing thought, she fled
In light away."

In various poems, Burns has exhibited the picture of a mind under the deep impressions of real sorrow. The Lament, the Ode to Ruin, Despondency, and Winter, a Dirge, are of this character. In the first of these poems, the 8th stanza, which describes a sleepless night from anguish of mind, is particularly striking. Burns often indulged in those melancholy views of the nature and condition of man, which are so congenial to the temperament of sensibility. The poem entitled Man was Made to Mourn, affords an instance of this kind, and the Winter Night is of the same description. The last is highly characteristic, both of the temper of mind, and of the condition of Burns. It begins with a description of a dreadful storm on a night in winter. The poet represents himself as lying in bed, and listening to its howling. In this situation he naturally turns his thoughts to the *owrie* (143) *cattle*, and *silly* (144) *sheep*, exposed to all the violence of the tempest. Having lamented their fate, he proceeds in the following manner:—

"Ilk happing bird—wee, helpless thing!
That, in the merry months o' spring,
Delighted me to hear thee sing,
What comes o' thee?
Whare wilt thou cow'r thy chittering wing,
And close thy ee?"

Other reflections of the same nature occur to his mind; and as the midnight moon "muffled with clouds" casts her dreary light on his window, thoughts of a darker and more melancholy nature crowd upon him. In this state of mind, he hears a voice pouring through the gloom a solemn and plaintive strain of reflection. The mourner compares the fury of the elements with that of man to his brother man, and finds the former light in the balance.

"See stern Oppression's iron grip,
Or mad Ambition's gory hand,
Sending, like bloodhounds from the slip,
Woe, want, and murder, o'er the land."

He pursues this train of reflection through a variety of particulars, in the course of which he introduces the following animated apostrophe :—

"Oh, ye! who, sunk in beds of down,
Feel not a want but what yourselves create,
Think, for a moment, on his wretched fate,
Whom friends and fortune quite disown!
Ill-satisfied keen nature's clam'rous call,
Stretch'd on his straw he lays him down to sleep,
While thro' the ragged roof and chinky wall,
Chill o'er his slumbers piles the drifty heap."

The strain of sentiment which runs through this poem is noble, though the execution is unequal, and the versification is defective.

Among the serious poems of Burns, The Cotter's Saturday Night is perhaps entitled to the first rank. The Farmer's Ingle of Fergusson evidently suggested the plan of this poem, as has been already mentioned; but after the plan was formed, Burns trusted entirely to his own powers for the execution. Fergusson's poem is certainly very beautiful. It has all the charms which depend on rural characters and manners happily pourtrayed, and exhibited under circumstances highly grateful to the imagination. The Farmer's Ingle begins with describing the return of evening. The toils of the day are over, and the farmer retires to his comfortable fireside. The reception which he and his men-servants receive from the careful housewife, is pleasingly described. After their supper is over, they begin to talk on the rural events of the day.

"'Bout kirk and market eke their tales gae on,
How *Jock* woo'd *Jenny* here to be his bride;
And there how *Marion* for a bastard son,
Upo' the cutty-stool was forced to ride,
The waefu' scauld o' our *Mess John* to bide."

The "guidame" is next introduced as forming a circle round the fire, in the midst of her grandchildren, and while she spins from the rock, and the spindle plays on her "russet lap," she is relating to the young ones tales of witches and ghosts. The poet exclaims,

"Oh, mock na this, my friends! but rather mourn,
Ye in life's brawest spring wi' reason clear,
Wi' eild our idle fancies a' return,
And dim our dolefu' days wi' bairnly fear;
The mind's aye *cradled* when the *grave* is near."

In the meantime, the farmer, wearied with the fatigues of the day, stretches himself at length on the *settle*, a sort of rustic couch which extends on one side of the fire, and the cat and house-dog leap upon it to receive his caresses. Here resting at his ease, he gives his directions to his men-servants for the succeeding day. The housewife follows his example, and gives her orders to the maidens. By degrees the oil in the cruise begins to fail, the fire runs low, sleep steals on this rustic group, and they move off to enjoy their peaceful slumbers. The poet concludes by bestowing his blessings on the "husbandman and all his tribe."

This is an original and truly interesting pastoral. It possesses every thing required in this species of composition. We might have perhaps said every thing that it admits, had not Burns written his Cotter's Saturday Night.

The cottager returning from his labours, has no servants to accompany him, to partake of his fare, or to receive his instructions. The circle which he joins, is composed of his wife and children only; and if it admits of less variety, it affords an opportunity for representing scenes that more strongly interest the affections. The younger children running to meet him, and clambering round his knee—the elder, returning from their weekly labours with the neighbouring farmers, dutifully depositing their little gains with their parents, and receiving their father's blessing and instructions—the incidents of the courtship of Jenny, their eldest daughter, "woman grown"—are circumstances of the most interesting kind, which are most happily delineated; and after their frugal supper, the representation of these humble cottagers forming a wider circle round their hearth, and uniting in the worship of God, is a picture the most deeply affecting of any which the rural muse has ever presented to the view. Burns was admirably adapted to this delineation. Like all men of genius, he was of the temperament of devotion, and the powers of memory co-operated in this instance with the sensibility of his heart, and the fervour of his imagination. (145) The Cotter's Saturday Night is tender and moral, it is solemn and devotional, and rises at length into a strain of grandeur and sublimity, which modern poetry has not surpassed. The noble sentiments of patriotism with which it concludes, correspond with the rest of the poem. In no age or country have the pastoral muses breathed such elevated accents, if the Messiah of Pope be excepted, which is indeed a pastoral in form only. It is to be regretted that Burns did not employ his genius on other subjects of the same nature, which the manners and customs of the Scottish peasantry would have amply supplied. Such poetry is not to be estimated by the degree of pleasure which it bestows; it sinks deeply into the heart, and is calculated, far beyond any other human means, for giving permanence to the scenes and characters it so exquisitely describes.

Before we conclude, it will be proper to offer a few observations on the lyric productions of Burns. His compositions of this kind are chiefly songs, generally in the Scottish dialect, and always after the model of the Scottish songs, on the general character and moral influence of which some observations have already been offered. We may hazard a few more particular remarks.

Of the historic or heroic ballads of Scotland, it is unnecessary to speak. Burns has nowhere imitated them, a circumstance to be regretted, since in this species of composition, from its admitting the more terrible as well as the softer graces of poetry, he was eminently qualified to have excelled The Scottish songs which served as a model to Burns, are, almost without exception, pastoral, or rather rural. Such of them as are comic, frequently treat of a rustic courtship or a country wedding; or they describe the differences of opinion which arise in married life. Burns has imitated this species, and surpassed his models. The song, beginning, "Husband, husband, cease your strife," may be cited in support of this observation. (146) His other comic songs are of equal merit. In the rural songs of Scotland, whether humorous or tender, the sentiments are given to particular characters, and very generally, the incidents are referred to particular scenery. This last circumstance may be considered as the distinguishing feature of the Scottish songs, and on it a considerable part of their attraction depends. On all occasions the sentiments, of whatever nature, are delivered in the character of the person principally interested. If love be described, it is not as it is observed, but as it is felt; and the passion is delineated under a particular aspect. Neither is it the fiercer impulses of desire that are expressed, as in the celebrated ode of Sappho, the model of so many modern songs. but those gentler emotions of tenderness and affection, which do not entirely absorb the lover, but permit him to associate his emotions with the charms of external nature, and breathe the accents of purity and innocence, as well as of love. In these respects, the love-songs of Scotland are honorably distinguished from the most admired classical compositions of the same kind; and by such associations, a variety, as well as liveliness, is given to the representation of this passion, which are not to be found in the poetry of Greece or Rome, or perhaps of any other nation. Many of the love-songs of Scotland describe scenes of rural courtship; many may be considered as invocations from lovers to their mistresses. On such occasions a degree of interest and reality is given to the sentiments, by the spot destined to these happy interviews being particularized. The lovers perhaps meet at the Bush aboon Traquair, or on the banks of Ettrick; the nymphs are invoked to wander among the wilds of Roslin, or the woods of Invermay. Nor is the spot merely pointed out; the scenery is often described as well as the characters, so as to present a complete picture to the fancy. (147) Thus the maxim of Horace *ut pictura poesis*, is faithfully observed by these rustic bards, who are guided by the same impulse of nature and sensibility which influenced the father of epic poetry, on whose example the precept of the Roman poet was perhaps founded. By this means the imagination is employed to interest the feelings. When we do not conceive distinctly, we do not sympathise deeply in any human affection; and we conceive nothing in the abstract. Abstraction, so useful in morals, and so essential in science, must be abandoned when the heart is to be subdued by the powers of poetry or of eloquence. The bards of a ruder condition of society paint individual objects; and hence, among other causes, the easy access they obtain to the heart. Generalization is the vice of poets whose learning overpowers their genius; of poets of a refined and scientific age.

The dramatic style which prevails so much in the Scottish songs, while it contributes greatly to the interest they excite, also shows that they have originated among a people in the earlier stages of society. Where this form of composition appears in songs of a modern date, it indicates that they have been written after the ancient model. (148)

The Scottish songs are of very unequal poetical merit, and this inequality often extends to the different parts of the same song. Those that are humorous, or characteristic of manners, have in general the merit of copying nature; those that are serious, are tender, and often sweetly interesting, but seldom exhibit high powers of imagination, which indeed do not easily find a place in this species of composition. The alliance of the words of the Scottish songs with the music, has in some instance given to the former a popularity, which otherwise they would not have obtained.

The association of the words and the music of these songs, with the more beautiful parts of the scenery of Scotland, contributes to the same effect. It has given them not merely popularity, but permanence; it has imparted to the works of man some portion of the durability of the works of nature. If, from our imperfect experience of the past, we may judge with any confidence respecting the future, songs of this description are of all others least likely to die. In the changes of language they may no doubt suffer change; but the associated strain of sentiment and of music will perhaps survive, while the clear stream sweeps down the vale of Yarrow, or the yellow broom waves on Cowden-Knowes.

The first attempts of Burns in song-writing were not very successful. His habitual inattention to the exactness of rhymes, and to the harmony of numbers, arising probably from the models on which his versification was formed, were faults likely to appear to more disadvantage in this species of composition than in any other; and we may also remark, that the strength of his imagination, and the exuberance of his sensibility, were with difficulty restrained within the limits of gentleness, delicacy, and tenderness, which seemed to be assigned to the love-songs of his nation. Burns was better adapted by nature for following, in such compositions, the model of the Grecian than of the Scottish muse. By study and practice, he however surmounted all these obstacles. In his earlier songs, there is some ruggedness, but this gradually disappears in his successive efforts; and some of his later compositions of this kind may be compared, in polished delicacy, with the finest songs in our language, while in the eloquence of sensibility they surpass them all.

The songs of Burns, like the models he followed and excelled, are often dramatic, and for the greater part amatory; and the beauties of rural nature are everywhere associated with the passions and emotions of the mind. Disdaining to copy the works of others, he has not, like some poets of great name, admitted into his descriptions exotic imagery. The landscapes he has painted, and the objects with which they are embellished, are, in every single instance, such as are to be found in his own country. In a mountainous region, especially when it is comparatively rude and naked, the most beautiful scenery will always be found in the vallies, and on the banks of the wooded streams. Such scenery is peculiarly interesting at the close of a summer-day. As we advance northwards, the number of the days of summer, indeed diminishes; but from this cause, as well as from the mildness of the temperature, the attraction of the season increases, and the summer night becomes still more beautiful. The greater obliquity of the sun's path on the ecliptic, prolongs the grateful season of twilight to the midnight hours; and the shades of the evening seem to mingle with the morning's dawn. The rural poets of Scotland, as may be expected, associate in their songs the expressions of passion with the most beautiful of their scenery, in the fairest season of the year, and generally in those hours of the evening when the beauties of nature are most interesting. (149.)

To all these adventitious circumstances, on which so much of the effect of poetry depends, great attention is paid by Burns. There is scarcely a single song of his, in which particular scenery is not described, or allusions made to natural objects, remarkable for beauty or interest; and though his descriptions are not so full as are sometimes met with in the older Scottish songs, they are in the highest degree appropriate and interesting. Instances in proof of this might be quoted from the Lea Rig, Highland Mary, the Soldier's Return, Logan Water; from that beautiful pastoral, Bonnie Jean, and a great number of others. Occasionally the force of his genius carries him beyond the usual boundaries of Scottish song, and the natural objects introduced have more of the character of sublimity. An instance of this kind is noticed by Mr. Syme, and many others might be adduced:

"Had I a cave on some wild distant shore,
Where the winds howl to the wave's dashing roar;
There would I weep my woes,
There seek my lost repose,
Till grief my eyes should close,
Ne'er to wake more."

In one song, the scene of which is laid in a winter night, the "wan moon" is described as "setting behind the white waves;"

in another, the "storms" are apostrophised, and commanded to "rest in the cave of their slumbers." On several occasions, the genius of Burns lost sight entirely of his archetypes, and rises into a strain of uniform sublimity. Instances of this kind appear in Libertie, a Vision; and in his two war-songs, Bruce to his Troops, and the Song of Death. These last are of a description of which we have no other in our language. The martial songs of our nation are not military, but naval. If we were to seek a comparison of these songs of Burns with others of a similar nature, we must have recourse to the poetry of ancient Greece, or of modern Gaul.

Burns has made an important addition to the songs of Scotland. In his compositions, the poetry equals and sometimes surpasses the music. He has enlarged the poetical scenery of his country, Many of her rivers and mountains, formerly unknown to the muse, are now consecrated by his immortal verse. The Doon, the Lugar, the Ayr, the Nith, and the Cluden, will in future, like the Yarrow, the Tweed, and the Tay, be considered as classical streams, and their borders will be trodden with new and superior emotions.

The greater part of the songs of Burns were written after he removed into the county of Dumfries. Influenced, perhaps, by habits formed in early life, he usually composed while walking in the open air. When engaged in writing these songs, his favourite walks were on the banks of the Nith, or of the Cluden, particularly near the ruins of Lincluden Abbey; and this beautiful scenery he has very happily described under various aspects, as it appears during the softness and serenity of evening, and during the stillness and solemnity of the moonlight night.

There is no species of poetry, the productions of the drama not excepted, so much calculated to influence the morals, as well as the happiness of a people, as those popular verses which are associated with national airs: and which being learnt in the years of infancy, make a deep impression on the heart before the evolution of the powers of the understanding. The compositions of Burns of this kind, now presented in a collected form to the world, make a most important addition to the popular songs of his nation. Like all his other writings, they exhibit independence of sentiment; they are peculiarly calculated to increase those ties which bind generous hearts to their native soil, and to the domestic circle of their infancy; and to cherish those sensibilities which, under due restriction, form the purest happiness of our nature. If in his unguarded moments he composed some songs on which this praise cannot be bestowed, let us hope that they will speedily be forgotten. In several instances where Scottish airs were allied to words objectionable in point of delicacy, Burns has substituted others of a purer character. On such occasions, without changing the subject, he has changed the sentiments. A proof of this may be seen in the air of John Anderson my Joe, which is now united to words that breathe a strain of conjugal tenderness, that is as highly moral as it is exquisitely affecting.

Few circumstances could afford a more striking proof of the strength of Burns's genius, than the general circulation of his poems in England, notwithstanding the dialect in which the greater part are written, and which might be supposed to render them here uncouth or obscure. In some instances he has used this dialect on subjects of a sublime nature; but in general he confines it to sentiments or description of a tender or humorous kind; and, where he rises into elevation of thought, he assumes a purer English style. The singular faculty he possessed of mingling in the same poem humorous sentiments and descriptions with imagery of a sublime and terrific nature, enabled him to use this variety of dialect on some occasions with striking effect. His poem of Tam o' Shanter affords an instance of this. There he passes from a scene of the lowest humour to situations of the most awful and terrible kind. He is a musician that runs from the lowest to the highest of his keys; and the use of the Scottish dialect enables him to add two additional notes to the bottom of his scale.

Great efforts have been made by the inhabitants of Scotland, of the superior ranks, to approximate in their speech to the pure English standard. Yet an Englishman who understands the meaning of the Scottish words, is not offended, nay, on certain subjects, he is, perhaps, pleased with the rustic dialect.

But a Scotchman inhabiting his own country, if a man of education, and more especially if a literary character, has banished such words from his writings, and has attempted to banish them from his speech. A dislike of this kind is, however, accidental, not natural. It is of the species of disgust which we feel at seeing a female of high birth in the dress of a rustic; which, if she be really young and beautiful, a little habit will enable us to overcome. A lady who assumes such a dress puts her beauty, indeed, to a severer trial. She rejects—she, indeed, opposes the influence of fashion; she, possibly, abandons the grace of elegant and flowing drapery; but her native charms remain, the more striking, perhaps, because the less adorned, and to these she trusts for fixing her empire on those affections over which fashion has no sway. If she succeeds, a new association arises. The dress of the beautiful rustic becomes itself beautiful, and establishes a new fashion for the young and the gay. And when, in after ages, the contemplative observer shall view her picture in the gallery that contains the portraits of the beauties of successive centuries, each in the dress of her respective day, her drapery will not deviate, more than that of her rivals, from the standard of his taste, and he will give the palm to her who excels in the lineaments of nature.

Burns wrote professedly for the peasantry of his country, and by them their native dialect is universally relished. To a numerous class of the natives of Scotland of another description, it may also be considered as attractive in a different point of view. Estranged from their native soil, and spread over foreign lands, the idiom of their country unites with the sentiments and the descriptions on which it is employed, to recal to their minds the interesting scenes of infancy and youth—to awaken many pleasing, many tender recollections. Literary men, residing at Edinburgh or Aberdeen, cannot judge on this point for one hundred and fifty thousand of their expatriated countrymen. (150)

To the use of the Scottish dialect in one species of poetry, the composition of songs, the taste of the public has been for some time reconciled. The dialect in question excels, as has already been observed, in the copiousness and exactness of its terms for natural objects; and in pastoral or rural songs, it gives a Doric simplicity which is very generally approved. Neither does the regret seem well founded which some persons of taste have expressed, that Burns used this dialect in so many other of his compositions. His declared purpose was to paint the manners of rustic life among his "humble compeers," and it is not easy to conceive, that this could have been done with equal humour and effect, if he had not adopted their idiom. There are some, indeed, who will think the subject too low for poetry. Persons of this sickly taste will find their delicacies consulted in many a polite and learned author; let them not seek for gratification in the rough and vigorous lines, in the unbridled humour, or in the overpowering sensibility of this bard of nature.

To determine the comparative merit of Burns would be no easy task. Many persons, afterwards distinguished in literature, have been born in as humble a situation of life; but it would be difficult to find any other, who, while earning his subsistence by daily labour, has written verses which have attracted and retained universal attention, and which are likely to give the author a permanent and distinguished place among the followers of the muses. If he is deficient in grace, he is distinguished for ease as well as energy; and these are indications of the higher order of genius. The father of epic poetry exhibits one of his heroes as excelling in strength, another in swiftness—to form his perfect warrior, these attributes are combined. Every species of intellectual superiority admits, perhaps, of a similar arrangement. One writer excels in force—another in ease; he is superior to them both, in whom both these qualities are united. Of Homer himself it may be said, that, like his own Achilles, he surpasses his competitors in mobility as well as strength.

The force of Burns lay in the powers of his understanding and in the sensibility of his heart; and these will be found to infuse the living principle into all the works of genius which seem destined to immortality. His sensibility had an uncommon range. He was alive to every species of emotion. He is one of the few poets that can be mentioned, who have at once excelled in humour, in tenderness, and in sublimity; a praise unknown to the ancients, and which in modern times is only due to Ariosto, to Shakspeare, and perhaps to Voltaire. To compare the writings of the Scottish peasants with the works of these giants in literature, might appear presumptuous; yet it may be asserted that he has displayed the *foot of Hercules*. How near he might have approached them by proper culture, with lengthened years, and under happier auspices, it is not for us to calculate. But while we run over the melancholy story of his life, it is impossible not to heave a sigh at the asperity of his fortune; and as we survey the records of his mind, it is easy to see, that out of such materials have been reared the fairest and the most durable of the monuments of genius.

Addenda.

Extracts from Letters.

FROM GILBERT BURNS TO DR. CURRIE, RESPECTING THE COMPOSITION OF HIS BROTHER'S POEMS.

"*Mossgiel, 2nd April*, 1798.

"I CANNOT pretend to be very accurate in respect to the dates of the poems, but none of them, excepting Winter, a Dirge (which was a juvenile production), The Death and Dying Words of poor Mailie, and some of the songs, were composed before the year 1784. The circumstances of the poor sheep were pretty much as he has described them.

"Among the earliest of his poems was the Epistle to Davie. Robert often composed without any regular plan. When anything made a strong impression on his mind, so as to rouse it to poetic exertion, he would give way to the impulse, and embody the thought in rhyme. If he hit on two or three stanzas to please him, he would then think of proper introductory, connecting, and concluding stanzas; hence the middle of a poem was often first produced. It was, I think, in summer 1784, when, in the interval of harder labour, he and I were weeding in the garden (kail-yard), that he repeated to me the principal part of this epistle. I believe the first idea of Robert's becoming an author was started on this occasion. I was much pleased with the epistle, and said to him I was of opinion it would bear being printed, and that it would be well received by people of taste; that I thought it at least equal, if not superior, to many of Allan Ramsay's epistles; and that the merit of these, and much other Scotch poetry, seemed to consist principally in the knack of the expression, but here there was a train of interesting sentiment, and the Scotticism of the language scarcely seemed affected, but appeared to be the natural language of the poet: that, besides, there was certainly some novelty in a poet pointing out the consolations that were in store for him when he should go a-begging. Robert seemed very well pleased with my criticism, and we talked of sending it to some magazine; but as this plan afforded no opportunity of knowing how it would take, the idea was dropped.

"It was, I think, in the winter following, as we were going together with carts for coal to the family fire (and I could yet point out the particular spot), that the author first repeated to me the Address to the Deil. The curious idea of such an address was suggested to him by running over in his mind the many ludicrous accounts and representations we have from various quarters of this august personage. Death and Doctor Hornbook, though not published in the Kilmarnock edition, was produced early in the year 1785. The schoolmaster of Tarbolton parish, to eke out the scanty subsistence allowed to that useful class of men, had set up a shop of grocery goods. Having accidentally fallen in with some medical books, and become most hobby-horsically attached to the study of medicine, he had added the sale of a few medicines to his little trade. He had got a shop-bill printed, at the bottom of which, overlooking his own incapacity, he had advertised that 'Advice would be given in common disorders at the shop gratis.' Robert was at a mason meeting in Tarbolton, when the *dominie* unfortunately made too ostentatious a display of his medical skill. As he parted in the evening from this mixture of pedantry and physic, at the place where he describes his meeting with Death, one of those floating ideas of apparitions he mentions in his letter to Dr. Moore, crossed his mind; this set him to work for the rest of the way home. These circumstances he related when he repeated the verses to me next afternoon, as I was holding the plough, and he was letting the water off the field beside me. The Epistle to John Lapraik was produced exactly on the occasion described by the author. He says in that poem, 'On Fasten e'en we had a rockin.' I believe he has omitted the word *rocking* in the glossary. It is a term derived from those primitive times, when the countrywomen employed their spare hours in spinning on the rock, or distaff. The simple implement is a very portable one, and well fitted to the social inclination of meeting in a neighbour's house; hence the phrase of *going a-rocking*, or *with the rock*. As the connection the phrase had with the implement was forgotten, when the rock gave place to the spinning-wheel, the phrase came to be used by both sexes on social occasions, and men talk of going with their rocks as well as women.

"It was at one of these *rockings* at our

house, when we had twelve or fifteen young people with their *rocks*, that Lapraik's song, beginning—'When I upon thy bosom lean,' was sung, and we were informed who was the author. Upon this, Robert wrote his first epistle to Laipraik, and his second in reply to his answer. The verses to the Mouse and Mountain Daisy were composed on the occasions mentioned, and while the author was holding the plough; I could point out the particular spot where each was composed. Holding the plough was a favourite situation with Robert for poetic composition, and some of his best verses were produced while he was at that exercise. Several of the poems were produced for the purpose of bringing forward some favourite sentiment of the author. Robert had frequently remarked to me that he thought there was something peculiarly venerable in the phrase, 'Let us worship God,' used by a decent, sober head of a family, introducing family worship. To this sentiment of the author the world is indebted for the Cotter's Saturday Night. When my brother had some pleasure in view, in which I was thought fit to participate, we used frequently to walk together, when the weather was favourable, on the Sunday afternoons (those precious breathing times to the labouring part of the community), and enjoyed such Sundays as would make one regret to see their number abridged. It was in one of these walks that I first had the pleasure of hearing the author repeat the Cotter's Saturday Night. I do not recollect to have read or heard anything by which I was more highly *electrified*. The fifth and sixth stanzas, and the eighteenth, thrilled with peculiar ecstacy through my soul. I mention this to you, that you may see what hit the taste of unlettered criticism. I should be glad to know, if the enlightened mind and refined taste of Mr. Roscoe, who has borne such honourable testimony to this poem, agrees with me in the selection. Fergusson, in his Hallow Fair of Edinburgh, I believe, likewise furnished a hint of the title and plan of the Holy Fair. The farcical scene the poet there describes was often a favourite field of his observation, and the most of the incidents he mentions had actually passed before his eyes. It is scarcely necessary to mention, that The Lament was composed on that unfortunate passage in his matrimonial history which I have mentioned in my letter to Mrs. Dunlop, after the first distraction of his feelings had a little subsided. The Twa Dogs was composed after the resolution of publishing was nearly taken. Robert had had a dog, which he called Luath, that was a great favourite. The dog had been killed by the wanton cruelty of some person the night before my father's death. Robert said to me, that he should like to confer such immortality as he could bestow upon his old friend Luath, and that he had a great mind to introduce something into the book, under the title of Stanzas to the Memory of a Quadruped Friend; but this plan was given up for the tale as it now stands. Cæsar was merely the creature of the poet's imagination, created for the purpose of holding chat with his favourite Luath. The first time Robert heard the spinnet played upon, was at the house of Dr. Lawrie, then minister of the parish of Loudon, now in Glasgow, having given up the parish in favour of his son. Dr. Lawrie has several daughters; one of them played; the father and mother led down the dance; the rest of the sisters, the brother, the poet, and the other guests, mixed in it. It was a delightful family scene for our poet, then lately introduced to the world. His mind was roused to a poetic enthusiasm, and the stanzas [which he wrote on the occasion] were left in the room where he slept. It was to Dr. Lawrie that Dr. Blacklock's letter was addressed, which my brother, in his letter to Dr. Moore, mentions as the reason of his going to Edinburgh. * * *"

LETTER OF GILBERT BURNS.

(First inserted in the Second Edition.)

The editor [Dr. Currie] has particular pleasure in presenting to the public the following letter, to the due understanding of which a few previous observations are necessary.

The biographer of Burns was naturally desirous of hearing the opinion of the friend and brother of the poet, on the manner in which he had executed his task, before a second edition should be committed to the press. He had the satisfaction of receiving this opinion, in a letter dated the 24th of August, approving of the Life in very obliging terms, and offering one or two trivial corrections as to names and dates chiefly, which are made in this edition. One or two observations were offered of a different kind. In the 319th page [corresponding to the 66th page of the present reprint of Dr. Currie's memoir], a quotation is made from the pastoral song, Ettrick Banks, and an explanation given of the phrase "mony feck," which occurs in this quotation. Supposing the sense to be complete after "mony," the editor had considered "feck" a rustic oath which confirmed the assertion. The words were, therefore, separated by a comma. Mr. Burns considered this an error. "Feck," he presumes, is the Scottish word for quantity, and "mony feck" to mean simply, very many. The editor, in yielding to this authority, expressed some hesitation, and hinted that the phrase "mony feck" was, in Mr. Burns's sense, a pleonasm, or barbarism, which deformed this beautiful song. His reply to this observation makes the first clause of the following letter.

In the same communication he informed me, that the Mirror and the Lounger were proposed by him to the Conversation Club of Mauchline, and that he had thoughts of giving me his sentiments on the remarks I had made respecting the fitness of such works for such societies. The observations of such a man on such a subject, the editor conceived, would be received with particular interest by the public, and, having pressed earnestly for them, they will be found in the following letter. Of the value of this communication, delicacy towards his very respectable correspondent prevents him from expressing his opinion. The original letter is in the hands of Messrs. Cadell and Davies.

"*Dinning, Dumfries-shire,* 24*th Oct.*, 1800.

"DEAR SIR.—Yours of the 17th instant came to my hand yesterday, and I sit down this afternoon to write you in return; but when I shall be able to finish all I wish to say to you, I cannot tell. I am sorry your conviction is not complete respecting *feck*. There is no doubt, that if you take two English words which appear synonymous to *mony feck*, and judge by the rules of English construction, it will appear a barbarism. I believe, if you take this mode of translating from any language, the effect will frequently be the same. But if you take the expression *mony feck* to have, as I have stated it, the same meaning with the English expression *very many* (and such licence every translator must be allowed, especially when he translates from a simple dialect which has never been subjected to rule, and where the precise meaning of words is, of consequence, not minutely attended to), it will be well enough. One thing I am certain of, that ours is the sense universally understood in this country; and I believe no Scotsman who has lived contented at home, pleased with the simple manners, the simple melodies, and the simple dialect of his native country, unvitiated by foreign intercourse, 'whose soul-proud science never taught to stray,' ever discovered barbarism in the song of Ettrick Banks.

"The story you have heard of the gable of my father's house falling down, is simply as follows (151):—When my father built his 'clay biggin,' he put in two stone-jambs, as they are called, and a lintel, carrying up a chimney in his clay-gable. The consequence was, that as the gable subsided, the jambs, remaining firm, threw it off its centre; and one very stormy morning, when my brother was nine or ten days old, a little before daylight, a part of the gable fell out, and the rest appeared so shattered, that my mother, with the young poet, had to be carried through the storm to a neighbour's house, where they remained a week till their own dwelling was adjusted. That you may not think too meanly of this house, or of my father's taste in building, by supposing the poet's description in the Vision (which is entirely a fancy picture) applicable to it, allow me to take notice to you, that the house consisted of a kitchen in one end, and a room in the other, with a fire-place and chimney; that my father had constructed a concealed bed in the kitchen, with a small closet at the end, of the same materials with the house; and when altogether cast over, outside and in, with lime, it had a neat, comfortable appearance, such as no family of the same rank, in the present improved style of living, would think themselves ill-lodged in. I wish likewise to take notice in passing, that although the 'Cotter' in the Saturday Night, is an exact copy of my father in his manners, his family-devotion, and exhortations, yet the other parts of the description do not apply to our family. None of us were ever 'at service out amang the neibors roun'.' Instead of our depositing our 'sair-won penny fee' with our parents, my father laboured hard, and lived with the most rigid economy, that he might be able to keep his children at home, thereby having an opportunity of watching the progress of our young minds, and forming in them early habits of piety and virtue; and from this motive alone did he engage in farming—the source of all his difficulties and distresses.

"When I threatened you in my last with a long letter on the subject of the books I recommended to the Mauchline Club, and the effects of refinement of taste on the labouring classes of men, I meant merely to write you on that subject, with the view that, in some future communication to the public, you might take up the subject more at large; that by means of your happy manner of writing, the attention of people of power and influence might be fixed on it. I had little expectation, however, that I should overcome my indolence, and the difficulty of arranging my thoughts so far as to put my threat in execution; till some time ago, before I had finished my harvest, having a call from Mr. Ewart (152), with a message from you, pressing me to the performance of this task, I thought myself no longer at liberty to decline it, and resolved to set about it with my first leisure. I will now, therefore, endeavour to lay before you what has occurred to my mind, on a subject where people capable of observation, and of placing their remarks in a proper point of view, have seldom an opportunity of making their remarks on real life. In doing this, I may perhaps be led sometimes to write more in the manner of a person communicating information to you which you did not know before, and at other times more in the style of egotism, than I would choose to do to any person, in whose candour, and even personal good will, I had less confidence.

"There are two several lines of study that open to every man as he enters life: the one, the general science of life, of duty, and of happiness; the other, the particular arts of his employment or situation in society, and the several branches of knowledge therewith connected. This last is certainly indispensable, as nothing can be more disgraceful than ignorance in the way of one's own profession; and whatever a man's speculative knowledge may be, if he is ill-informed there, he can neither be a useful nor a respectable member of society. It is, nevertheless, true, that 'the proper study of mankind is man;' to consider what duties are incumbent on him as a rational creature, and a member of society; how he may increase or secure his happiness; and how he may prevent or soften the many miseries incident to human life. I think the pursuit of happiness is too frequently confined to the endeavour after the acquisition of wealth. I do not wish to be considered as an idle declaimer against riches, which, after all that can be said against them, will still be considered by men of common sense as objects of importance, and poverty will be felt as a sore evil, after all the fine things that can be said of its advantages; on the contrary, I am of opinion, that a great proportion of the miseries of life arise from the want of economy, and a prudent attention to money, or the ill-directed or intemperate pursuit of it. But however valuable riches may be as the means of comfort, independence, and the pleasure of doing good to others, yet I am of opinion that they may be, and frequently are, purchased at too great a cost, and that sacrifices are made in the pursuit, which the acquisition cannot compensate. I remember hearing my worthy teacher, Mr. Murdoch, relate an anecdote to my father, which I think sets this matter in a strong light, and perhaps was the origin, or at least tended to promote this way of thinking in me. When Mr. Murdoch left Alloway, he went to teach and reside in the family of an opulent farmer who had a number of sons. A neighbour coming on a visit, in the course of conversation, asked the father how he meant to dispose of his sons. The father replied that he had not determined. The visitor said that, were he in his place, he would give them all good education and send them abroad, without, perhaps, having a precise idea where. The father objected, that many young men lost their health in foreign countries, and many their lives. True, replied the visitor, but as you have a number of sons, it will be strange if some one of them does not live and make a fortune.

"Let any person who has the feelings of a father, comment on this story; but though few will avow, even to themselves, that such views govern their conduct, yet do we not daily see people shipping off their sons (and who would do so by their daughters also, if there were any demand for them), that they may be rich or perish?

"The education of the lower classes is seldom considered in any other point of view than as the means of raising them from that station to which they were born, and of making a fortune. I am ignorant of the mysteries of the art of acquiring a fortune without any thing to begin with, and cannot calculate, with any degree of exactness, the difficulties to be surmounted, the mortifications to be suffered, and the degradation of character to be submitted to, in lending one's self to be the minister of other people's vices, or in the practice of rapine, fraud, oppression, or dissimulation, in the progress; but even when the wished-for end is attained, it may be questioned whether happiness be much increased by the change. When I have seen a fortunate adventurer of the lower ranks of life returned from the East or West Indies, with all the hauteur of a vulgar mind accustomed to be served by slaves, assuming a character, which, from early habits of life, he is ill fitted to support—displaying magnificence which raises the envy of some, and the contempt of others—claiming an equality with the great, which they are unwilling to allow—inly pining at the precedence of the hereditary gentry—maddened by the polished insolence of some of the unworthy part of them—seeking pleasure in the society of men who can condescend to flatter him, and listen to his absurdity for the sake of a good dinner and good wine—I cannot avoid concluding, that his brother, or companion, who, by a diligent application to the labours of agriculture, or some useful mechanic employment, and the careful husbanding of his gains, has acquired a competence in his station, is a much happier, and, in the eye of a person who can take an enlarged view of mankind, a much more respectable man.

"But the votaries of wealth may be considered as a great number of candidates striving for a few prizes: and whatever addition the successful may make to their pleasure or happiness, the disappointed will always have more to suffer, I am afraid, than those who abide contented in the station to which they were born. I wish, therefore, the education of the lower classes to be promoted and directed to their improvement as men, as the means of increasing their virtue, and opening to them new and dignified sources of pleasure and happiness. I have heard some people object to the education of the lower classes of men, as rendering them less useful, by abstracting them from their proper business; others, as tending to make them saucy to their superiors, impatient of their condition, and turbulent subjects; while you, with more humanity, have your fears alarmed, lest the delicacy of mind, induced by that sort of education and reading I recommended, should render the evils of their situation insupportable to them. I wish to examine the validity of each of these objections, beginning with the one you have mentioned.

"I do not mean to controvert your criticism of my favourite books, the Mirror and Lounger, although I understand there are people who think themselves judges, who do not agree with you. The acquisition of knowledge, except what is connected with human life and conduct, or the particular business of his employment, does not appear to me to be the fittest pursuit for a peasant. I would say with the poet,

'How empty learning, and how vain is art,
Save where it guides the life, or mends the heart!'

"There seems to be a considerable latitude in the use of the word taste. I understand it to be the perception and relish of beauty, order, or any other thing, the contemplation of which gives pleasure and delight to the mind. I suppose it is in this sense you wish it to be understood. If I am right, the taste which these books are calculated to cultivate (besides the taste for fine writing, which many of the papers tend to improve and to gratify), is what is proper, consistent, and becoming in human character and conduct, as almost every paper relates to these subjects.

"I am sorry I have not these books by me, that I might point out some instances. I remember two; one, the beautiful story of La Roche, where, besides the pleasure one derives from a beautiful simple story, told in M'Kenzie's happiest manner, the mind is led to taste, with heartfelt rapture, the consolation to be derived in deep affliction, from habitual devotion and trust in Almighty God. The other, the story of General W——, where the reader is led to have a high relish for that firmness of mind which disregards appearances, the common forms and vanities of life, for the sake of doing justice in a case which was out of the reach of human laws.

"Allow me then to remark, that if the morality of these books is subordinate to the cultivation of taste; that taste, that refinement of mind and delicacy of sentiment which they are intended to give, are the strongest guard and surest foundation of morality and virtue. Other moralists guard, as it were, the overt act; these papers, by exalting duty into sentiment, are calculated to make every deviation from rectitude and propriety of conduct, painful to the mind

'Whose temper'd powers,
Refine at length, and every passion wears
A chaster, milder, more attractive mien.'

"I readily grant you, that the refinement of mind which I contend for increases our sensibility to the evils of life; but what station of life is without its evils? There seems to be no such thing as perfect happiness in this world, and we must balance the pleasure and the pain which we derive from taste, before we can properly appreciate it in the case before us. I apprehend, that on a minute examination it will appear, that the evils peculiar to the lower ranks of life derive their power to wound us, more from the suggestions of false pride, and the 'contagion of luxury, weak and vile,' than the refinement of our taste. It was a favourite remark of my brother's, that there was no part of the constitution of our nature to which we were more indebted, than that by which *'custom makes things familiar and easy'* (a copy Mr. Murdoch used to set us to write); and there is little labour which custom will not make easy to a man in health, if he is not ashamed of his employment, or does not begin to compare his situation with those he may see going about at their ease.

"But the man of enlarged mind feels the respect due to him as a man; he has learned that no employment is dishonourable in itself; that while he performs aright the duties of that station in which God has placed him, he is as great as a king in the eyes of Him whom he is principally desirous to please; for the man of taste, who is constantly obliged to labour, must of necessity be religious. If you teach him only to reason, you may make him an atheist, a demagogue, or any vile thing; but if you teach him to feel, his feelings can only find their proper and natural relief in devotion and religious resignation. He knows that those people who are to appearance at ease, are not without their share of evils, and that even toil itself is not destitute of advantages. He listens to the words of his favourite poet:

'Oh, mortal man, that livest here by toil,
Cease to repine and grudge thy hard estate!
That like an emmet thou must ever moil,
Is a sad sentence of an ancient date;
And, certes, there is for it reason great;
Although sometimes it makes thee weep and wail, [late;
And curse thy star, and early drudge, and
Withouten that would come an heavier bale,
Loose life, unruly passions, and diseases pale!'

"And while he repeats the words, the grateful recollection comes across his mind, how often he has derived ineffable pleasure from the sweet song of 'nature's darling child.' I can say, from my own experience, that there is no sort of farm-labour inconsistent with the most refined and pleasurable state of the mind that I am acquainted with, thrashing alone excepted. That, indeed, I have always considered as insupportable drudgery, and think the ingenious mechanic who invented the thrashing-machine, ought to have a statue among the benefactors of his country, and should be placed in the niche next to the person who introduced the culture of potatoes into this island.

"Perhaps the thing of most importance in the education of the common people is, to prevent the intrusion of artificial wants. I bless the memory of my worthy father for almost every thing in the dispositions of my mind, and my habits of life, which I can approve of; and for none more than the pains he took to impress my mind with the sentiment, that nothing was more unworthy the character of a man, that that his happiness should in the least depend on what he should eat or drink. So early did he impress my mind with this, that although I was as fond of sweetmeats as children generally are, yet I seldom laid out any of the half-pence which relations or neighbours gave me at fairs, in the purchase of them; and if I did, every mouthful I swallowed was accompanied with shame and remorse; and to this hour I never indulge in the use of any delicacy, but I feel a considerable degree of self-reproach and alarm for the degradation of the human character. Such a habit of thinking I consider as of great consequence, both to the virtue and happiness of men in the lower ranks of life. And thus, Sir, I am of opinion, that if their minds are early and deeply impressed with a sense of the dignity of man, as such; with the love of independence and of industry, economy and temperance, as the most obvious means of making themselves independent, and the virtues most becoming their situation, and necessary to their happiness; men in the lower ranks of life may partake of the pleasures to be derived from the perusal of books calculated to improve the mind and refine the taste, without any danger of becoming more unhappy in their situation, or discontented with it. Nor do I think there is any danger of their becoming less useful. There are some hours every day that the most constant labourer is neither at work nor asleep. These hours are either appropriated to amusement or to sloth. If a taste for employing these hours in reading were cultivated, I do not suppose that the return to labour would be more difficult. Every one will allow, that the attachment to idle amusements, or even to sloth, has as powerful a tendency to abstract men from their proper business, as the attachment to books; while the one dissipates the mind, and the other tends to increase its powers of self-government. To those who are afraid that the improvement of the minds of the common people might be dangerous to the state, or the established order of society, I would remark, that turbulence and commotion are certainly very inimical to the feelings of a refined mind. Let the matter be brought to the test of experience and observation. Of what description of people are mobs and insurrections composed? Are they not universally owing to the want of enlargement and improvement of mind among the common people? Nay, let any one recollect the characters of those who formed the calmer and more deliberate associations, which lately gave so much alarm to the government of this country. I suppose few of the common people who were to be found in such societies, had the education and turn of mind I have been endeavouring to recommend. Allow me to suggest one reason for endeavouring to enlighten the minds of the common people. Their morals have hitherto been guarded bv a sort of dim religious awe, which, from a variety of causes, seems wearing off. I think the alteration in this respect considerable, in the short period of my observation. I have already given my opinion of the effects of refinement of mind on morals and virtue. Whenever vulgar minds begin to shake off the dogmas of the religion in which they have been educated, the progress is quick and immediate to downright infidelity; and nothing but refinement of mind can enable them to distinguish between the pure essence of religion, and the gross systems which men have been perpetually connecting it with. In addition to what has already been done for the education of the common people of this country, in the establishment of parish schools, I wish to see the salaries augmented in some proportion to the present expense of living, and the earnings of people of similar rank, endowments, and usefulness, in society; and I hope that the liberality of the present age will be no longer disgraced by refusing, to so useful a class of men, such encouragement as may make parish schools worth the attention of men fitted for the important duties of that office. In filling up the vacancies, I would have more attention paid to the candidate's capacity of reading the English language with grace and propriety—to his understanding thoroughly, and having a high relish for, the beauties of English authors, both in poetry and prose—to that good sense and knowledge of human nature which would enable him to acquire some influence on the minds and affections of his scholars—to the general worth of his character, and the love of his king and his country—than to his proficiency in the knowledge of Latin and Greek. I would then have a sort of high English class established, not only for the purpose of teaching the pupils to read in that graceful and agreeable manner that might make them fond of reading, but to make them understand what they read, and discover the beauties of the author, in composition and sentiment. I would have established in every parish a small circulating library, consisting of the books which the young people had read extracts from in the collections they had read at school, and any other books well calculated to refine the mind, improve the moral feelings, recommend the practice of virtue, and communicate such knowledge as might he useful and suitable to the labouring classes of men. I would have the schoolmaster act as librarian; and in recommending books to his young friends, formerly his pupils, and letting in the light of them upon their young minds, he should have the assistance of the minister. If once such education were become general, the low delights of the public-house, and other scenes of riot and depravity, would be contemned and neglected; while industry, order, cleanliness, and every virtue which taste and independence of mind could recommend, would prevail and flourish. Thus possessed of a virtuous and enlightened populace, with high delight I should consider my native country as at the head of all the nations of the earth, ancient or modern.

"Thus, Sir, have I executed my threat to the fullest extent, in regard to the length of my letter. If I had not presumed on doing it more to my liking, I should not have undertaken it; but I have not time to attempt it anew; nor, if I would, am I certain that I should succeed any better. I have learned to have less confidence in my capacity of writing on such subjects.

"I am much obliged by your kind inquiries about my situation and prospects. I am much pleased with the soil of this farm, and with the terms on which I possess it. I receive great encouragement likewise in building, enclosing, and other conveniences, from my landlord, Mr. G. S. Monteith, whose general character and conduct, as a landlord and country-gentleman, I am highly pleased with. But the land is in such a state as to require a considerable immediate outlay of money in the purchase of manure, the grubbing of brush-wood, removing of stones, &c., which twelve years' struggle with a farm of a cold ungrateful soil has but ill-prepared me for. If I can get these things done, however, to my mind, I think there is next to a certainty that in five or six years I shall be in a hopeful way of attaining a situation which I think as eligible for happiness as any one I know; for I have always been of opinion, that if a man bred to the habits of a farming life, who possesses a farm of good soil, on such terms as enables him easily to pay all demands, is not happy, he ought to look somewhere else than to his situation for the causes of his uneasiness.

"I beg you will present my most respectful compliments to Mrs. Currie, and remember me to Mr. and Mrs. Roscoe, and Mr Roscoe, Junior, the worth of whose kind attentions to me, when in Liverpool, I shall never forget. I am, dear sir, your most obedient, and much obliged humble servant,

"GILBERT BURNS.

"*To James Currie, M.D., F.R.S.*
Liverpool."

The Widow, Children, and Brother of Burns.

AT the time of Burn's decease, his family consisted of his wife and four sons—Robert, born at Mauchline, in 1786; Francis Wallace, born at Ellisland, April 9, 1791; William Nicol, born at Dumfries, November 21, 1792; and James Glencairn. On the day of the poet's funeral, Mrs. Burns produced a fifth son, who received the name of Maxwell, but did not long survive. Francis Wallace, a child of uncommon vivacity, died at the age of fourteen. The three other sons yet (1838) survive. Robert received a good education at the academy of Dumfries, was two sessions at the university of Edinburgh, and one at the university of Glasgow; and in 1804 obtained a situation in the Stamp Office, London, where he continued for twenty-nine years, improving a narrow income by teaching the classics and mathematics. It is remarkable, that during that long time he and his mother, though on the best terms, never once met. In 1833, having obtained a superannuation allowance, he retired to Dumfries, where he now lives. He has the dark eyes, large head, and swarthy complexion of his father, and possesses much more than the average of mental capacity. He has written many verses far above mediocrity; but the bent of his mind is towards geometry—a study in which his father was much more accomplished than his biographers seem to have been aware of. William and James went out to India on cadetships, and have each risen to the rank of major in the Company's service. "Wherever these men wander, at home or abroad, they are regarded as the scions of a noble stock, and receive the cordial greetings of hundreds who never saw their faces before, but who account it a happiness to grasp, in friendly pressure, the hand in which circulates the blood of Burns."—*M'Diarmid's Picture of Dumfries.*

The only dependence of Mrs. Burns, after her husband's death, was on an annuity of ten pounds, arising from a benefit society connected with the Excise, the books and other moveable property left to her, and the generosity of the public. The subscription, as we are informed by Dr. Currie, produced seven hundred pounds; and the works of the poet, as edited with singular taste and judgment by that gentleman, brought nearly two thousand more. One half of the latter sum was lent on a bond to a Galloway gentleman, who continued to pay five per cent. for it till a late period. Mrs. Burns was thus enabled to support and educate her family in a manner creditable to the memory of her husband. She continued to reside in the house which had been occupied by her husband and herself, and

——"never changed, nor wished to change her place."

For many years after her sons had left her to pursue their fortunes in the world, she lived in a decent and respectable manner, on an income which never amounted to more than £62 per annum. At length, in 1817, at a festival held in Edinburgh to celebrate the birth-day of the bard, Mr. Henry, (now Lord) Cockburn acting as president, it was proposed by Mr. Maule of Panmure (now Lord Panmure), that some permanent addition should be made to the income of the poet's widow. The idea appeared to be favourably received, but the subscription did not fill rapidly. Mr. Maule then said that the burden of the provision should fall upon himself, and immediately executed a bond, entitling Mrs. Burns to an annuity of £50 as long as she lived. This act, together with the generosity of the same gentleman to Nathaniel Gow, in his latter and evil days, must ever endear the name of Lord Panmure to all who feel warmly on the subjects of Scottish poetry and Scottish music.

Mr. Maule's pension had not been enjoyed by the widow more than a year and a half, when her youngest son James attained the rank of Captain with a situation in the commissariat, and was thus enabled to relieve her from the necessity of being beholden to a stranger's hand for any share of her support. She accordingly resigned the pension. Mr. M'Diarmid, who records these circumstances, adds in another place, that, during her subsequent years, Mrs. Burns enjoyed an income of about two hundred a-year, great part of which, as not needed by her, she dispensed in charities. Her whole conduct in widowhood was such as to secure universal esteem in the town where she resided. She died, March 26, 1834, in the 68th year of her age, and was buried beside her illustrious husband, in the mausoleum at Dumfries. (153)

Mr. Gilbert Burns, the early companion and at all times the steadfast friend of the poet, continued to struggle with the miserable glebe of Mossgiel till about the year 1797, when he removed to the farm of Dinning, on the estate of Mr. Monteith of Closeburn, in Nithsdale. The poet had lent him £200 out of the profits of the Edinburgh edition of his works, in order that he might overcome some of his difficulties; and he, some years after, united himself to a Miss Breckonridge, by whom he had a family of six sons and five daughters. In consideration of the support he extended to his widowed mother, the poet seems never to have thought of a reckoning with him for the above sum. He was a man of sterling sense and sagacity, pious without asceticism or bigotry, and entertaining liberal and enlightened views, without being the least of an enthusiast. His letter to Dr. Currie, dated from Dinning, October 24, 1800, shows no mean powers of composition, and embodies nearly all the philanthropic views of human improvement which have been so broadly realised in our own day. We are scarcely more affected by the consideration of the penury under which some of his brother's noblest compositions were penned, than by the reflection that this beautiful letter was the effusion of a man who, with his family, daily wrought long and laboriously under all those circumstances of parsimony which characterise Scottish rural life. Some years after, Mr. Gilbert Burns was appointed by Lady Blantyre to be land-steward or factor upon her estate of Lethington in East-Lothian, to which place he accordingly removed. His conduct in this capacity, during near twenty-five years, was marked by great fidelity and prudence, and gave the most perfect satisfaction to his titled employer. It was not till 1820, that he was enabled to repay the money borrowed from his brother in 1788 Being then invited by Messrs. Cadell and Davies to superintend, and improve as much as possible, a new edition of the poet's works, he received as much in remuneration of his labour, as enabled him to perform this act of duty.

The mother of Robert and Gilbert Burns lived in the household of the latter at Grant's Braes, near Lethington, till 1820, when she died at the age of eighty-eight, and was buried in the churchyard of Bolton. In personal aspect, Robert Burns resembled his mother; Gilbert had the more aquiline features of his father. The portrait of Robert Burns, painted by a Mr. Taylor, and published in an engraved form by Messrs. Constable and Company a few years ago, bore a striking resemblance to Gilbert. This excellent man died at Grant's Braes, November 8, 1827, aged about sixty-seven years. His sons, having received an excellent education. occupy respectable stations in society. One is factor to Lord Blantyre, and another is minister of the parish of Monkton, near Ayr.

Two sisters of Burns, one of whom is by marriage Mrs. Begg, yet survive. They reside in the village of Tranent, East-Lothian.

Phrenological Development of Burns.

At the opening of the Mausoleum, March 1834, for the interment of Mrs. Burns, it was resolved by some citizens of Dumfries, with the concurrence of the nearest relative of the widow, to raise the cranium of the poet from the grave, and have a cast moulded from it, with a view to gratifying the interest likely to be felt by the students of phrenology respecting its peculiar development. This purpose was carried into effect during the night between the 31st March and the 1st April, and the following is the description of the cranium, drawn up at the time by Mr. A. Blacklock, surgeon, one of the individuals present:—

"The craniel bones were perfect in every respect, if we except a little erosion of their external table, and firmly held together by their sutures; even the delicate bones of the orbits, with the trifling exception of the *os unguis* in the left, were sound, and uninjured by death and the grave. The superior maxillary bones still retained the four most posterior teeth on each side, including the dentes sapientiæ, and all without spot or blemish; the incisores, cuspidati, &c., had, in all probability, recently dropped from the jaw, for the alveoli were but little decayed. The bones of the face and palate were also sound. Some small portions of black hair, with a very few grey hairs intermixed, were observed while detaching some extraneous matter from the occiput. Indeed, nothing could exceed the high state of preservation in which we found the bones of the cranium, or offer a fairer opportunity of supplying what has so long been desiderated by phrenologists — a correct model of our immortal poet's head: and in order to accomplish this in the most accurate and satisfactory manner, every particle of sand, or other foreign body, was carefully washed off, and the plaster of Paris applied with all the tact and accuracy of an experienced artist. The cast is admirably taken, and cannot fail to prove highly interesting to phrenologists and others.

"Having completed our intention, the skull, securely enclosed in a leaden case, was again committed to the earth, precisely where we found it.

ARCHD. BLACKLOCK."

A cast from the skull having been transmitted to the Phrenological Society of Edinburgh, the following view of the cerebral development of Burns was drawn up by Mr. George Combe, and published in connection with four views of the cranium. (*W. and A. K. Johnston, Edinburgh*):—

"I. DIMENSIONS OF THE SKULL.

	Inches.
Greatest circumference	22¼
From Occipital Spine to Individuality, over the top of the head . .	14
„ Ear to Ear vertically over the top of the head	13
„ Philoprogenitiveness to Individuality, (greatest length) . . .	8
„ Concentrativeness to Comparison	7¼
„ Ear to Philoprogenitiveness . .	4⅞
„ „ Individuality	4¾
„ „ Benevolence	5½
„ „ Firmness	6½
„ Destructiveness to Destructiveness	5¾
„ Secretiveness to Secretiveness .	5⅞
„ Cautiousness to Cautiousness .	5½
„ Ideality to Ideality	4⅝
„ Constructiveness to Constructiveness	4½
„ Mastoid process to Mastoid Process	4¾

"II. DEVELOPEMENT OF THE ORGANS.

	Scale
1. Amativeness, rather large . . .	16
2. Philoprogenitiveness, very large .	20
3. Concentrativeness, large	18
4. Adhesiveness, very large . . .	20
5. Combativeness, very large . . .	20
6. Destructiveness, large	18
7. Secretiveness, large	19
8. Acquisitiveness, rather large . .	16
9. Constructiveness, full	15
10. Self-Esteem, large	18
11. Love of Approbation, very large .	20
12. Cautiousness, large	19
13. Benevolence, very large	20
14. Veneration, large	18
15. Firmness, full	15
16. Conscientiousness, full	15
17. Hope, full	14
18. Wonder, large	18
19. Ideality, large	18
20. Wit, or Mirthfulness, full . . .	15
21. Imitation, large	19
22. Individuality, large	19
23. Form, rather large	16
24. Size, rather large	17
25. Weight, rather large	16
26. Colouring, rather large	16
27. Locality, large	18
28. Number, rather full	12
29. Order, full	14
30. Eventuality, large	18
31. Time, rather large	16
32. Tune, full	15
33. Language, uncertain	
34. Comparison, rather large . . .	17
35. Causality, large	18

"*The scale of the organs indicates their relative proportions to each other; 2 is idiotcy—10 moderate—14 full—18 large; and 20 very large.*

"The cast of a skull does not show the temperament of the individual, but the portraits of Burns indicate the bilious and nervous temperaments, the sources of strength, activity, and susceptibility; and the descriptions given by his contemporaries of his beaming and energetic eye, and the rapidity and impetuosity of his manifestations, establish the inference that his brain was active and susceptible.

"Size in the brain, other conditions being equal, is the measure of mental power. The skull of Burns indicates a large brain. The length is eight, and the greatest breadth nearly six inches. The circumference is 22¼ inches. These measurements exceed the average of Scotch living heads, *including the integuments*, for which four-eighths of an inch may be allowed.

"The brain of Burns, therefore, possessed the two elements of power and activity.

"The portions of the brain which manifest the animal propensities, are uncommonly large, indicating strong passions, and great energy in action under their influence. The group of organs manifesting the domestic affections (Amativeness, Philoprogenitiveness, and Adhesiveness), is large; Philoprogenitiveness uncommonly so for a male head. The organs of Combativeness and Destructiveness are large, bespeaking great heat of temper, impatience, and liability to irritation.

"Secretiveness and Cautiousness are both large, and would confer considerable power of restraint, where he felt restraint to be necessary.

"Acquisitiveness, Self-Esteem, and Love of Approbation, are also in ample endowment, although the first is less than the other two; these feelings give the love of property, a high consideration of self, and desire of the esteem of others. The first quality will not be so readily conceded to Burns as the second and third, which, indeed, were much stronger; but the phrenologist records what is presented by nature, in full confidence that the manifestations, when the character is correctly understood, will be found to correspond with the developement, and he states that the brain indicates considerable love of property.

"The organs of the moral sentiments are also largely developed. Ideality, Wonder, Imitation, and Benevolence, are the largest in size. Veneration also is large. Conscientiousness, Firmness, and Hope, are full.

"The Knowing organs, or those of perceptive intellect, are large; and the organs of Reflection are also considerable, but less than the former. Causality is larger than Comparison, and Wit is less than either.

"The skull indicates the combination of strong animal passions with equally powerful moral emotions. If the natural morality had been less, the endowment of the propensities is sufficient to have constituted a character of the most desperate description. The combination as it exists, bespeaks a mind extremely subject to contending emotions—capable of great good, or great evil—and encompassed with vast difficulties in preserving a steady, even, onward course of practical morality.

"In the combination of very large Philoprogenitiveness and Adhesiveness, with very large Benevolence and large Ideality, we find the elements of that exquisite tenderness and refinement, which Burns so frequently manifested, even when at the worst stage of his career. In the combination of great Combativeness, Destructiveness, and Self-Esteem, we find the fundamental qualities which inspired 'Scots wha hae wi' Wallace bled,' and similar productions.

"The combination of large Secretiveness, Imitation, and the perceptive organs, gives the elements of his dramatic talent and humour. The skull indicates a decided talent for Humour, but less for Wit. The public are apt to confound the talents for Wit and Humour. The metaphysicians, however, have distinguished them, and in the phrenological works their different elements are pointed out. Burns possessed the talent for satire; Destructiveness, added to the combination which gives Humour, produces it.

"An unskilful observer looking at the forehead, might suppose it to be moderate in size; but when the dimensions of the anterior lobe, in both length and breadth, are attended to, the Intellectual organs will be recognised to have been large. The anterior lobe projects so much, that it gives an appearance of narrowness to the forehead which is not real. This is the cause, also, why Benevolence appears to lie farther back than usual. An anterior lobe of this magnitude indicates great Intellectual power. The combination of large Perceptive and Reflecting organs (Causality predominant), with large Concentrativeness and large organs of the feelings, gives that sagacity and vigorous common sense, for which Burns was distinguished.

"The skull rises high above Causality, and spreads wide in the region of Ideality; the strength of his moral feelings lay in that region.

"The combination of large organs of the Animal Propensities, with large Cautiousness, and only full Hope, together with the unfavourable circumstances in which he was placed, accounts for the melancholy and internal unhappiness with which Burns was so frequently afflicted. This melancholy was rendered still deeper by bad health.

"The combination of Acquisitiveness, Cautiousness, Love of Approbation, and Conscientiousness, is the source of his keen feelings in regard to pecuniary independence. The great power of his Animal Propensities would give him strong temptations to waste; but the combination just mentioned would impose a powerful restraint. The head indicates the elements of an economical character, and it is known that he died free from debt, notwithstanding the smallness of his salary.

"No phrenologist can look upon this head, and consider the circumstances in which Burns was placed, without vivid feelings of regret. Burns must have walked the earth with a consciousness of great superiority over his associates in the station in which he was placed—of powers calculated for a far higher sphere than that which he was able to reach, and of passions which he could with difficulty restrain, and which it was fatal to indulge. If he had been placed from infancy in the higher ranks of life, liberally educated, and employed in pursuits corresponding to his powers, the inferior portion of his nature would have lost part of its energy, while his better qualities would have assumed a decided and permanent superiority."

A more elaborate paper on the skull of Burns appeared in the Phrenological Journal, No. XLI., from the pen of Mr. Robert Cox. This gentleman endeavours to show that the character of Burns was in conformity with the full development of Acquisitiveness. "According to his own description," says Mr. Cox, "he was a man who 'had little art in making money, and still less in keeping it.' That his art in making money was sufficiently moderate, there can be no doubt, for he was engaged in occupations which his soul loathed, and thought it below his dignity to accept of pecuniary remuneration for some of his most laborious literary performances. He was, however, by no means insensible to the value of money, and never threw it away. On the contrary, he was remarkably frugal, except when feelings stronger than Acquisitiveness came into play—such as Benevolence, Adhesiveness, and Love of Approbation; the organs of all which are very large, while Acquisitiveness is only rather large. During his residence at Mossgiel, where his revenue was not more than £7, his expenses, as Gilbert mentions, 'never in any one year exceeded his slender income.' It is also well known that he did not leave behind him a shilling of debt; and I have learned from good authority that his household was much more frugally managed at Dumfries than at Ellisland—as in the former place, but not in the latter, he had it in his power to exercise a personal control over the expenditure. I have been told also, that, after his death, the domestic expenses were greater than when he was alive. These facts are all consistent with a considerable development of Acquisitiveness, for, when that organ is small, there is habitual inattention to pecuniary concerns, even although the love of independence and dislike to ask a favour be strong. The indifference with respect to money, which Burns occasionally ascribes to himself, appears therefore to savour of affectation—a failing into which he was not unfrequently led by Love of Approbation and Secretiveness. Indeed, in one of his letters to Miss Chalmers, he expressly intimates a wish to be rich." The whole of this essay is highly worthy of perusal by all who take an interest in the character of the Ayrshire bard.

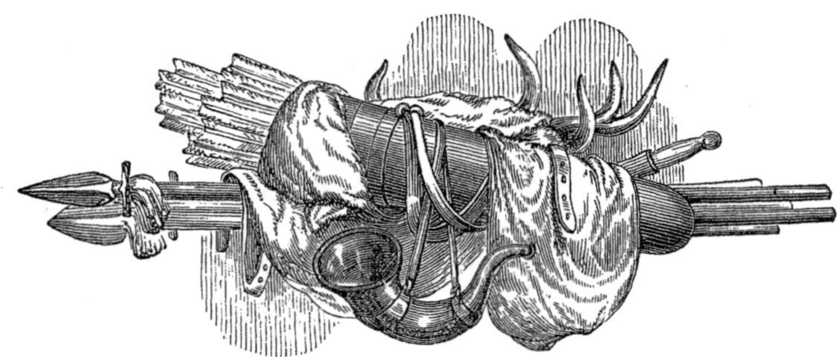

The
Poetical Works of Robert Burns.

POOR MAILIE.

He gaped wide, but naething spak;
At length poor Mailie silence brak:

Burns's Poetical Works.

The Death and Dying Words of Poor Mailie.

THE AUTHOR'S ONLY PET YOWE.

AN UNCO MOURNFU' TALE. (1)

As Mailie, and her lambs thegither,
Were ae day nibbling on the tether,
Upon her cloot she coost a hitch,
And owre she warsled in the ditch:
There, groaning, dying, she did lie,
When Hughoc he cam doytin by.

Wi' glowering een and lifted han's,
Poor Hughoc like a statue stands;
He saw her days were near-hand ended,
But, waes my heart! he could na mend it.
He gaped wide but naething spak—
At length poor Mailie silence brak.

"Oh thou, whose lamentable face
Appears to mourn my woefu' case!
My dying words attentive hear,
And bear them to my master dear.

"Tell him, if e'er again he keep
As muckle gear as buy a sheep,
Oh bid him never tie them mair
Wi' wicked strings o' hemp or hair!
But ca' them out to park or hill,
And let them wander at their will;
So may his flock increase, and grow
To scores o' lambs, and packs o' woo'!

"Tell him he was a master kin',
And aye was guid to me and mine;
And now my dying charge I gie him—
My helpless lambs I trust them wi' him.

"Oh bid him save their harmless lives
Frae dogs, and tods, and butchers' knives!
But gie them guid cow-milk their fill,
Till they be fit to fend themsel;
And tent them duly, e'en and morn,
Wi' teats o' hay, and ripps o' corn.

"And may they never learn the gaets
Of other vile wanrestfu' pets;
To slink through slaps, and reave and steal
At stacks o' peas, or stocks o' kail.
So may they, like their great forbears,
For many a year come through the shears:
So wives will gie them bits o' bread,
And bairns greet for them when they're dead.

"My poor toop-lamb, my son and heir,
Oh, bid him breed him up wi' care;
And if he live to be a beast,
To pit some havins in his breast!

"And warn him, what I winna name,
To stay content wi' yowes at hame;
And no to rin and wear his cloots,
Like ither menseless, graceless brutes.

"And neist my yowie, silly thing,
Gude keep thee frae a tether string;
Oh, may thou ne'er forgather up
Wi' ony blastit, moorland toop,
But aye keep mind to moop and mell
Wi' sheep o' credit like thysel.

"And now, my bairns, wi' my last breath,
I lea'e my blessin' wi' you baith:
And when you think upo' your mither,
Mind to be kin' to ane anither.

"Now, honest Hughoc, dinna fail
To tell my master a' my tale;
And bid him burn this cursed tether,
And, for thy pains, thou's get my blether."
This said, poor Mailie turn'd her head,
And clos'd her een amang the dead.

Poor Mailie's Elegy.

LAMENT in rhyme, lament in prose,
Wi' saut tears trickling down your nose;
Our bardie's fate is at a close,
Past a' remead;
The last sad cape-stane of his woes—
Poor Mailie's dead!

It's no the loss o' warl's gear,
That could sae bitter draw the tear,
Or mak our bardie, dowie, wear
The mourning weed:
He's lost a friend and neibor dear,
In Mailie dead.

Thro' a' the toun she trotted by him;
A lang half-mile she could descry him;
Wi' kindly bleat, when she did spy him,
She ran wi' speed:
A friend mair faithfu' ne'er cam nigh him
Than Mailie dead.

I wat she was a sheep o' sense,
And could behave hersel' wi' mense:
I'll say't she never brak a fence,
Thro' thievish greed.
Our bardie, lanely, keeps the spence
Sin' Mailie's dead.

Or, if he wanders up the howe,
Her living image in her yowe,
Comes bleating to him, owre the knowe,
For bits o' bread;
And down the briny pearls rowe
For Mailie dead.

She was nae get o' moorland tips,
Wi' tawted ket, and hairy hips,
For her forbears were brought in ships
Frae yont the Tweed:
A bonnier fleesh ne'er cross'd the clips
Than Mailie dead.

Wae worth the man wha first did shape
That vile, wanchancie thing—a rape!
It maks guid fellows girn and gape,
Wi' chokin' dread;
And Robin's bonnet wave wi' crape
For Mailie dead.

Oh, a' ye bards on bonnie Doon!
And wha on Ayr your chanters tune!
Come, join, the melancholious croon
O' Robin's reed!
His heart will never get aboon—
His Mailie's dead!

Epistle to Davie.

A BROTHER POET. (2)

January, 1784.

WHILE winds frae aff Ben Lomond blaw,
And bar the doors with driving snaw,
And hing us owre the ingle,
I set me down to pass the time,
And spin a verse or twa o' rhyme,
In hamely westlin jingle.
While frosty winds blaw in the drift,
Ben to the chimla lug,
I grudge a wee the great folk's gift,
That live sa bien and snug:
I tent less, and want less
Their roomy fire-side;
But hanker and canker
To see their cursed pride.

It's hardly in a body's power
To keep, at times, frae being sour,
To see how things are shar'd;
How best o' chiels are whiles in want,
While coofs on countless thousands rant,
And ken na how to wair't;
But Davie, lad, ne'er fash your head,
Tho' we hae little gear,
We're fit to win our daily bread,
As lan's we're hale and fier:
"Mair spier na, no fear na" (3),
Auld age ne'er mind a feg,
The last o't, the warst o't.
Is only but to beg. (4)

To lie in kilns and barns at e'en
When banes are craz'd, and bluid is thin,
Is, doubtless, great distress!
Yet then content could make us blest;
Ev'n then, sometimes we'd snatch a taste
Of truest happiness.
The honest heart that's free frae a'
Intended fraud or guile,
However fortune kick the ba',
Has aye some cause to smile:
And mind still, you'll find still,
A comfort this nae sma';
Na mair then, we'll care then,
Nae farther we can fa'.

What though, like commoners of air,
We wander out we know not where,
But either house or hal'?
Yet nature's charms, the hills and woods,
The sweeping vales, and foaming floods,
Are free alike to all.
In days when daisies deck the ground,
And blackbirds whistle clear,
With honest joy our hearts will bound
To see the coming year:

On braes when we please, then,
We'll sit and sowth a tune;
Syne rhyme till't, we'll time till't,
And sing't when we hae dune.

It's no in titles nor in rank;
It's no in wealth like Lon'on bank,
To purchase peace and rest;
It's no in makin' muckle mair;
It's no in books; it's no in lear,
To mak us truly blest;
If happiness hae not her seat
And centre in the breast,
We may be wise, or rich, or great,
But never can be blest:
Nae treasures nor pleasures
Could make us happy lang;
The heart aye's the part aye
That makes us right or wrang.

Think ye, that sic as you and I,
Wha drudge and drive through wet and dry,
Wi' never-ceasing toil;
Think ye, are we less blest than they,
Wha scarcely tent us in their way,
As hardly worth their while?
Alas! how aft, in haughty mood,
God's creatures they oppress!
Or else neglecting a' that's guid,
They riot in excess!
Baith careless and fearless
Of either heaven or hell!
Esteeming and deeming
It's a' an idle tale!

Then let us cheerfu' acquiesce;
Nor make our scanty pleasures less,
By pining at our state;
And, even should misfortunes come,
I, here wha sit, hae met wi' some,
An's thankfu' for them yet,
They gie the wit of age to youth;
They let us ken oursel;
They make us see the naked truth,
The real guid and ill.
Though losses and crosses
Be lessons right severe,
There's wit there, ye'll get there,
Ye'll find nae other where.

But tent me, Davie, ace o' hearts!
(To say aught less wad wrang the cartes,
And flatt'ry I detest)
This life has joys for you and I;
And joys that riches ne'er could buy:
And joys the very best.
There's a' the pleasures o' the heart,
The lover and the frien';
Ye hae your Meg (5), your dearest part,
And I my darling Jean!
It warms me, it charms me,
To mention but her name:
It heats me, it beets me,
And sets me a' on flame!

Oh, all ye pow'rs who rule above!
Oh, Thou, whose very self art love!
Thou know'st my words sincere!
The life-blood streaming thro' my heart,
Or my more dear immortal part,
Is not more fondly dear!
When heart-corroding care and grief
Deprive my soul of rest,
Her dear idea brings relief
And solace to my breast,
Thou Being, all-seeing,
Oh hear my fervent pray'r!
Still take her, and make her
Thy most peculiar care!

All hail, ye tender feelings dear!
The smile of love, the friendly tear,
The sympathetic glow!
Long since, this world's thorny ways
Had number'd out my weary days,
Had it not been for you!
Fate still has blest me with a friend,
In every care and ill;
And oft a more endearing band,
A tie more tender still.
It lightens, it brightens
The tenebrific scene,
To meet with, and greet with
My Davie or my Jean!

Oh, how that name inspires my style!
The words come skelpin', rank and file,
Amaist before I ken!
The ready measure rins as fine
As Phœbus and the famous Nine
Were glowrin' owre my pen.
My spaviet Pegasus will limp,
Till ance he's fairly het;
And then he'll hilch, and stilt, and jimp,
And rin an unco fit:
But lest then, the beast then
Should rue this hasty ride,
I'll light now, and dight now,
His sweaty, wizen'd hide.

Address to the Deil. (6)

Oh Prince! Oh chief of many throned pow'rs,
That led th' embattled seraphim to war.—
MILTON.

OH thou! whatever title suit thee,
Auld Hornie, Satan, Nick, or Clootie,
Wha in yon cavern grim and sootie,
Closed under hatches,
Spairges about the brunstane cootie,
To scaud poor wretches!

Hear me, auld Hangie, for a wee,
And let poor damned bodies be;
I'm sure sma' pleasure it can gie,
E'en to a deil,
To skelp and scaud poor dogs like me,
And hear us squeel!

Great is thy pow'r, and great thy fame;
Far ken'd and noted is thy name;
And tho' yon lowin' heugh's thy hame,
Thou travels far;
And, faith! thou's neither lag nor lame,
Nor blate nor scaur.

Whyles, ranging like a roaring lion,
For prey a' holes and corners tryin';
Whyles on the strong-wing'd tempest flyin',
Tirlin' the kirks;
Whyles, in the human bosom pryin',
Unseen thou lurks.

I've heard my reverend granny say,
In lanely glens ye like to stray;
Or where auld ruin'd castles, gray,
Nod to the moon,
Ye fright the nightly wand'rer's way
Wi' eldritch croon.

When twilight did my granny summon,
To say her prayers, douce honest woman!
Aft yont the dyke she's heard you bummin',
Wi' eerie drone;
Or, rustlin', thro' the boortries comin',
Wi' heavy groan.

Ae dreary, windy, winter night,
The stars shot down wi' sklentin' light,
Wi' you, mysel, I gat a fright
Ayont the lough;
Ye, like a rash-bush, stood in sight
Wi' waving sough.

The cudgel in my nieve did shake,
Each bristl'd hair stood like a stake,
When wi' an eldritch, stoor quaick—quaick—
Amang the springs,
Awa ye squatter'd, like a drake,
On whistling wings.

Let warlocks grim, and wither'd hags,
Tell how wi' you, on ragweed nags,
They skim the muirs and dizzy crags,
Wi wicked speed;
And in kirk-yards renew their leagues
Owre howkit dead.

Thence countra wives, wi' toil and pain,
May plunge and plunge the kirn in vain;
For, oh! the yellow treasure's taen
By witching skill;
And dawtit, twal-pint hawkie's gaen
As yell's the bill.

When thowes dissolve the snawy hooord,
And float the jinglin' icy boord,
Then water kelpies haunt the foord,
By your direction;
And 'nighted trav'llers are allur'd
To their destruction.

And aft your moss-traversing spunkies
Decoy the wight that late and drunk is:
The bleezin', curst, mischievous monkies
Delude his eyes,
Till in some miry slough he sunk is,
Ne'er mair to rise.

When masons' mystic word and grip
In storms and tempests raise you up,
Some cock or cat your rage maun stop
Or, strange to tell!
The youngest brother ye wad whip
Aff straught to hell!

Lang syne, in Eden's bonny yard,
When youthfu' lovers first were pair'd,
And all the soul of love they shar'd,
The raptur'd hour,
Sweet on the fragrant flow'ry sward,
In shady bow'r (7):

Then you, ye auld snec-drawing dog!
Ye came to Paradise incog,
And played on man a cursed brogue,
(Black be your fa!)
And gied the infant warld a shog,
'Maist ruin'd a'.

D'ye mind that day, when in a bizz,
Wi' reekit duds, and reestit gizz,
Ye did present your smoutie phiz
'Mang better folk,
And sklented on the man of Uzz
Your spitefu' joke?

And how ne gat him i' your thrall,
And brak him out o' house and hall,
While scabs and botches did him gall,
Wi' bitter claw,
And lows'd his ill-tongued, wicked scawl,
Was warst ava?

But a' your doings to rehearse,
Your wily snares and fetchin' fierce,
Sin' that day Michael did you pierce,
Down to this time,
Wad ding a Lallan tongue, or Earse,
In prose or rhyme.

And now, auld Cloots, I ken ye're thinkin',
A certain bardie's rantin', drinkin',
Some luckless hour will send him linkin'
To your black pit;
But, faith! he'll turn a corner jinkin',
And cheat you yet.

But, fare you weel, auld Nickie-ben!
Oh wad ye tak a thought and men'!
Ye aiblins might—I dinna ken—
Still hae a stake—
I'm wae to think upo' yon den,
Ev'n for your sake!

The Auld Farmer's New-Year Morning Salutation to his Auld Mare Maggie,

ON GIVING HER THE ACCUSTOMED RIPP OF CORN TO HANSEL IN THE NEW YEAR.

A GUID New-year I wish thee, Maggie!
Hae, there's a ripp to thy auld baggie;
Tho' thou's howe-backit, now, and knaggie,
I've seen the day
Thou could hae gaen like onie staggie
Out-owre the lay.

Tho' now thou's dowie, stiff, and crazy,
And thy auld hide's as white's a daisy,
I've seen thee dappl't, sleek, and glaizie,
A bonny gray:
He should been tight that daur't to raise thee
Ance in a day.

Thou ance was i' the foremost rank,
A filly, buirdly, steeve, and swank,
And set weel down a shapely shank
As e'er tread yird;
And could hae flown out-owre a stank,
Like ony bird.

It's now some nine-and-twenty year,
Sin' thou was my guid-father's mere;
He gied me thee, o' tocher clear
And fifty mark;
Tho' it was sma', 'twas weel-won gear,
And thou was stark.

When first I gaed to woo my Jenny,
Ye then was trottin' wi' your minnie:
Tho' ye was trickie, slee, and funnie,
Ye ne'er was donsie;
But hamely, tawie, quiet, and cannie,
And unco sonsie.

That day ye pranc'd wi' muckle pride,
When ye bure hame my bonny bride:
And sweet and gracefu' she did ride,
Wi' maiden air!
Kyle Stewart I could bragged wide,
For sic a pair.

Tho' now ye dow but hoyte and hoble,
And wintle like a saumont-coble,
That day ye was a jinker noble,
For heels and win'!
And ran them till they a' did wauble,
Far, far behin'!

When thou and I were young and skeigh,
And stable-meals at fairs were dreigh,
How thou wad prance, and snore, and skreigh
And tak the road!
Town's bodies ran, and stood abeigh,
And ca't thee mad.

When thou was corn't, and I was mellow,
We took the road aye like a swallow:
At brooses thou had ne'er a fellow
For pith and speed;
But ev'ry tail thou pay't them hollow,
Whare'er thou gaed.

The sma' droop-rumpl't, hunter, cattle,
Might aiblins waur't thee for a brattle;
But sax Scotch miles thou try't their mettle,
And gar't them whaizle:
Nae whip nor spur, but just a wattle
O' saugh or hazle.

Thou was a noble fittie-lan',
As e'er in tug or tow was drawn!
Aft thee and I, in aucht hours' gaun,
In guid March weather,
Hae turn'd sax rood beside our han'
For days thegither.

Thou never braindg't, and fech't, and fliskit,
But thy auld tail thou wad hae whiskit,
And spread abreed thy well-fill'd brisket,
Wi' pith and pow'r,
Till spritty knowes wad rair't and risket,
And slypet owre.

When frosts lay lang, and snaws were deep,
And threaten'd labour back to keep,
I gied thy cog a wee-bit heap
Aboon the timmer;
I ken'd my Maggie wad na sleep
For that, or simmer.

In cart or car thou never reestit;
The steyest brae thou wad hae fac't it;
Thou never lap, and sten't, and breastit,
Then stood to blaw;
But just thy step a wee thing hastit,
Thou snoov't awa.

My pleugh is now thy bairn-time a';
Four gallant brutes as e'er did draw;
Forbye sax mae I've sell't awa,
That thou hast nurst:
They drew me thretteen pund and twa,
The vera warst.

Monie a sair daurk we twa hae wrought,
And wi' the weary warl' fought!
And monie an anxious day I thought
We wad be beat!
Yet here to crazy age we're brought,
Wi' something yet.

And think na, my auld trusty servan',
That now perhaps thou's less deservin',
And thy auld days may end in starvin',
For my last fou,
A heapit stimpart, I'll reserve ane
Laid by for you.

We've worn to crazy years thegither;
We'll toyte about wi' ane anither;
Wi' tentie care I'll flit thy tether,
To some hain'd rig,
Whare ye may nobly rax your leather,
Wi' sma' fatigue.

Halloween. (8)

Upon that night, when fairies light,
On Cassilis Downans (9) dance,
Or owre the lays, in splendid blaze,
On sprightly coursiers prance;
Or for Coleon the route is ta'en,
Beneath the moon's pale beams;
There, up the cove (10), to stray and rove
Amang the rocks and streams
To sport that night.

Amang the bonny, winding banks,
Where Doon rins, wimplin', clear,
Where Bruce (11) ance rul'd the martial ranks,
And shook his Carrick spear,
Some merry, friendly, countra folks,
Together did convene,
To burn their nits, and pou their stocks,
And haud their Halloween
Fu' blythe that night.

The lasses feat, and cleanly neat,
Mair braw than when they're fine;
heir faces blythe, fu' sweetly kythe,
Hearts leal, and warm, and kin':
The lads sae trig, wi' wooer-babs,
Weel knotted on their garten,
Some unco blate, and some wi' gabs,
Gar lasses' hearts gang startin'
Whiles fast at night.

Then, first and foremost, thro' the kail,
Their stocks (12) maun a' be sought ance;
They steek their een, and graip, and wale,
For mucklè anes and straught anes.
Poor hav'rel Will fell aff the drift,
And wander'd thro' the bow-kail,
And pou't, for want o' better shift,
A runt was like a sow-tail,
Sae bow't that night.

Then, straught or crooked, yird or nane,
They roar and cry a' throu'ther;
The vera wee-things, todlin', rin
Wi' stocks out-owre their shouther:
And gif the custoc's sweet or sour,
Wi' joctelegs they taste them;
Syne coziely, aboon the door,
Wi' cannie care, they've placed them
To lie that night.

The lasses straw frae 'mang them a'
To pou their stalks o' corn (13);
But Rab slips out, and jinks about,
Behint the muckle thorn:
He grippet Nelly hard and fast;
Loud skirl'd a' the lasses;
But her tap-pickle maist was lost,
When kuittlin' in the fause-house (14)
Wi' him that night.

The auld guidwife's weel-hoordet nits (15)
Are round and round divided,
And mony lads' and lasses' fates
Are there that night decided:
Some kindle, couthie, side by side,
And burn thegither trimly;
Some start awa wi' saucy pride,
And jump out-owre the chimlie
Fu' high that night.

Jean slips in twa wi' tentie e'e;
Wha 'twas, she wadna tell;
But this is Jock, and this is me,
She says in to hersel':
He bleez'd owre her, and she owre him,
As they waud never mair part;
Till, fuff! he started up the lum,
And Jean had e'en a sair heart
To see't that night.

Poor Willie, wi' his bow-kail runt,
Was brunt wi' primsie Mallie;
And Mary, nae doubt, took the drunt,
To be compared to Willie.
Mall's nit lap out wi' pridefu' fling,
And her ain fit it burnt it;
While Willie lap, and swoor, by jing,
'Twas just the way he wanted
To be that night.

Nell had the fause-house in her min,'
She pits hersel and Rob in;
In loving bleeze they sweetly join,
Till white in ase they're sobbin'.
Nell's heart was dancin' at the view,
She whisper'd Rob to leuk for't:
Rob, stowlins, prie'd her bonny mou'
Fu' cozie in the neux for't,
Unseen that night.

But Merran sat behint their backs,
Her thoughts on Andrew Bell;
She lea'es them gashin' at their cracks,
And slips out by hersel':
She through the yard the nearest taks,
And to the kiln she goes then,
And darklins graipit for the bauks,
And in the blue-clue (16) throws then
Right fear't that night.

And aye she win't, and aye she swat,
I wat she made nae jaukin';
Till something held within the pat,
Guid L—d! but she was quakin'!
But whether 'twas the deil himsel,
Or whether 'twas a bauk-en',
Or whether it was Andrew Bell,
She did na wait on talkin'
To spier that night.

Wee Jenny to her granny says,
"Will ye go wi' me, granny?
I'll eat the apple (17) at the glass,
I gat frae uncle Johnny:"

She fuff't her pipe wi' sic a lunt,
In wrath she was sae vap'rin',
She notic't na, aizle brunt
Her braw new worset apron
Out thro' that night.
"Ye little skelpie-limmer's face!
I daur you try sic sportin',
As seek the foul thief onie place,
For him to spae your fortune:
Nae doubt but ye may get a sight!
Great cause ye hae to fear it;
For monie a ane has gotten a fright,
And lived and died deleeret.
On sic a night.
Ae hairst afore the Sherra-moor—
I mind't as well's yestreen,
was a gilpey, then I'm sure
I was na past fyfteen:
The simmer had been cauld and wat,
And stuff was unco' green;
And aye a rantin' kirn we gat,
And just on Halloween
It fell that night.
Our stibble rig was Rab M'Graen,
A clever, sturdy fallow:
He's sin' gat Eppie Sim w' wean,
That lived in Achmacalla:
He gat hemp-seed (18), I mind it weel,
And he made unco light o't;
But mony a day was by himsel',
He was sae sairly frighted
That very night."
Then up gat fechtin' Jamie Fleck,
And he swoor by his conscience,
That he could sow hemp-seed a peck;
For it was a' but nonsense.
The auld guidman raught down the pock,
And out a handfu' gied him;
Syne bade him slip frae 'mang the folk,
Sometime when nae ane see'd him,
And try'd that night.
He marches through amang the stacks,
Tho' he was something sturtin:
The graip he for a harrow taks,
And hauls at his curpin;
And every now and then he says,
"Hemp-seed I saw thee,
And her that is to be my lass,
Come after me, and draw thee
As fast this night."
He whistl'd up Lord Leonox' march,
To keep his courage cheery;
Altho' his hair began to arch,
He was sae fley'd and eerie:
Till presently he hears a squeak,
And then a grane and gruntle;
He by his shouther gae a keek,
And tumbl'd wi' o wintle
Out-owre that night.
He roar'd a horrid murder-shout,
In dreadfu' desperation!
And young and auld cam rinnin' out,
And hear the sad narration:
He swoor 'twas hilchin Jean M'Craw,
Or crouchie Merran Humphie,
Till, stop—she trotted through them a'—
And wha was it but grumphie
Asteer that night!

Meg fain wad to the barn hae gaen,
To win three wechts o' naething (19);
But for to meet the deil her lane,
She pat cut little faith in:
She gies the herd a pickle nits,
And twa red-cheekit apples,
To watch, while for the barn she sets,
In hopes to see Tam Kipples
That vera night.

She turns the key wi' cannie thraw,
And owre the threshold venturs;
But first on Sawny gies a ca',
Syne bauldly in she enters:
A ratton rattled up the wa',
And she cried, "L—d, preserve her!"
And ran thro' midden hole and a',
And pray'd with zeal and fervour,
Fu' fast that night.

They hoy't out Will, wi' sair advice;
They hecht him some fine braw ane;
It chanc'd the stack he faddom't thrice (20),
Was timmer-propt for thrawin';
He taks a surly auld moss oak
For some black, grousome carlin;
And loot a winze, and drew a stroke,
Till skin in blypes cam haurlin'
Aff's nieves that night.

A wanton widow Leezie was,
As canty as a kittlin;
But, och! that night, amang the shaws,
She got a fearfu' settlin'!
She thro' the whins, and by the cairn,
And owre the hill gaed scrievin,
Where three lairds' lands met at a burn (21),
To dip her left sark-sleeve in,
Was bent that night.

Whyles owre a linn the burnie plays,
As through the glen it whimpl't;
Whyles round a rocky scaur it strays;
Whyles in a wiel it dimpl't;
Whyles glitter'd to the nightly rays,
Wi' bickering, dancing dazzle;
Whyles cooyit underneath the braes,
Below the spreading hazel,
Unseen that night.

Amang the brackens, on the brae,
Between her and the moon,
The deil, or else an outler quey,
Gat up and gae a croon:

Poor Leezy's heart maist lap the hool;
Near lav'rock height she jumpit,
But mist a fit, and in the pool
Out-owre the lugs she plumpit,
Wi' a plunge that night.

In order, on the clean hearth-stane,
The luggies three (22) are ranged,
And every time great care is ta'en,
To see them duly changed:
Auld uncle John, wha' wedlock's joys
Sin' Mars' year did desire,
Because he gat the toom-dish thrice,
He heav'd them on the fire
In wrath that night.

Wi' merry sangs, and friendly cracks,
I wat they did nae weary:
And unco tales, and funny jokes,
Their sports were cheap and cheery;
Till butter'd so'ns (23), wi' fragrant lunt,
Set a' their gabs a-steerin';
Syne, wi' a social glass o' strunt,
They parted aff careerin'
Fu' blythe that night. (24)

A Winter Night.

Poor naked wretches, wheresoe'er you are,
That bide the pelting of the pitiless storm!
How shall your houseless heads and unfed sides, [defend you
Your looped and windowed raggedness,
From seasons such as these?—SHAKSPEARE.

When biting Boreas, fell and doure,
Sharp shivers thro' the leafless bow'r;
When Phœbus gies a short-lived glow'r
Far south the lift,
Dim-darkening thro' the flaky show'r,
Or whirling drift:

Ae night the storm the steeples rocked,
Poor labour sweet in sleep was locked,
While burns, wi' snawy wreaths up-choked,
Wild eddying swirl,
Or thro' the mining outlet bocked,
Down headlong hurl.

Listening, the doors and winnocks rattle,
I thought me on the ourie cattle,
Or silly sheep, wha bide this brattle
O' winter war, [sprattle,
And through the drift, deep-lairing
Beneath a scaur.

Ilk happing bird, wee, helpless thing,
That in the merry months o' spring,
Delighted me to hear thee sing,
What comes o' thee!
Whare wilt thou cow'r thy chittering wing,
And close thy e'e?

Ev'n you on murd'ring errands toil'd,
Lone from your savage homes exil'd,
The blood-stain'd roost and sheep-cot spoil'd
My heart forgets,
While pitiless the tempest wild
Sore on you beats.

Now Phœbe, in her midnight reign,
Dark muffled, view'd the dreary plain;

Still crowding thoughts, a pensive train,
Rose in my soul,
When on my ear this plaintive strain
Slow, solemn, stole:—

"Blow, blow, ye winds, with heavier gust!
And freeze, thou bitter-biting frost!
Descend ye chilly, smothering snows!
Not all your rage, as now united, shows
More hard unkindness, unrelenting,
Vengeful malice unrepenting,
Than heaven-illumined man on brother man bestows!
See stern oppression's iron grip,
Or mad ambition's gory hand,
Sending, like blood-hounds from the slip
Woe, want, and murder o'er a land!
E'en in the peaceful rural vale,
Truth, weeping, tells the mournful tale,
How pamper'd Luxury, Flattery by her side,
The parasite empoisoning her ear,
With all the servile wretches in the rear,
Looks o'er proud property, extended wide;
And eyes the simple rustic hind,
Whose toil upholds the glittering show,
A creature of another kind,
Some coarser substance, unrefined,
Placed for her lordly use thus far, thus vile below.
Where, where is Love's fond, tender throe,
With lordly Honour's lofty brow,
The powers you proudly own?
Is there beneath Love's noble name,
Can harbour dark the selfish aim,
To bless himself alone!
Mark maiden innocence a prey
To love-pretending snares,
This boasted Honour turns away,
Shunning soft Pity's rising sway, [ers!
Regardless of the tears and unavailing pray-
Perhaps this hour in misery's squalid nest,
She strains your infant to her joyless breast, [rocking blast!
And with a mother's fears shrinks at the
Oh ye! who, sunk in beds of down,
Feel not a want but what yourselves create,

Think for a moment on his wretched fate,
Whom friends and fortune quite disown!
Ill satisfied keen nature's clamorous call,
Stretched on his straw he lays himself to sleep, [wall,
While through the ragged roof and chinky
Chill o'er his slumbers piles the drifty heap;
Think on the dungeon's grim confine,
Where guilt and poor misfortune pine!
Guilt, erring man, relenting view!
But shall thy legal rage pursue
The wretch, already crushed low
By cruel fortune's undeserved blow?
Affliction's sons are brothers in distress;
A brother to relieve, how exquisite the bliss!"

I hear nae mair, for chanticleer
Shook off the poutheray snaw,
And hailed the morning with a chee—
A cottage-rousing craw.

But deep this truth impressed my mind—
Through all his works abroad,
The heart benevolent and kind
The most resembles GOD.

Epistle to J. Lapraik.

AN OLD SCOTTISH BARD. (25.)

April 1, 1785.

WHILE briers and woodbines budding green,
And paitricks scraichin' loud at e'en,
And morning poussie whiddin seen,
Inspire my muse,
This freedom in an unknown frien'
I pray excuse.

On Fasten-e'en we had a rockin',
To ca' the crack and weave our stockin';
And there was muckle fun and jokin',
Ye need na' doubt;
At length we had a hearty yokin'
At sang about.

There was ae sang, amang the rest,
Aboon them a' it pleas'd me best,
That some kind husband had addrest
To some sweet wife:
It thirl'd the heart-strings thro' the breast,
A' to the life.

I've scarce heard ought described sae weel,
What gen'rous manly bosoms feel;
Thought I, "Can this be Pope, or Steele,
Or Beattie's wark?"
They tauld me 'twas an odd kind chiel
About Muirkirk.

It pat me fidgin-fain to hear't,
And sae about him there I spier't,
Then a' that ken't him round declar'd
He had ingine,
That nane excell'd it, few cam near't,
It was sae fine.

That, set him to a pint of ale,
And either douce or merry tale,
Or rhymes and sangs he'd made himsel',
Or witty catches,
'Tween Inverness and Teviotdale,
He had a few matches.

Then up I gat, and swoor an aith,
Tho' I should pawn my pleugh and graith,
Or die a cadger pownie's death
At some dyke back
A pint and gill I'd gie them baith
To hear your crack.

But, first and foremost, I should tell,
Amaist as soon as I could spell,
I to the crambo-jingle fell;
Tho' rude and rough,
Yet crooning to a body's sell,
Does weel eneugh.

I am nae poet, in a sense,
But just a rhymer, like by chance,
And hae to learning nae pretence,
Yet, what the matter!
Whene'er my muse does on me glance,
I jingle at her.

Your critic folk may cock their nose,
And say, "How can you e'er propose,
You, wha ken hardly verse frae prose,
To mak a sang?"
But, by your leaves, my learned foes,
Ye're may be wrang.

What's a' your jargon o' your schools,
Your Latin names for horns and stools;
If honest nature made you fools,
What sairs your grammars?
Ye'd better taen up spades and shools,
Or knappin-hammers.

A set o' dull, conceited hashes,
Confuse their brains in college classes!
They gang in stirks, and come out asses,
Plain truth to speak;
And syne they think to climb Parnassus
By dint o' Greek!

Gie me ae spark o' nature's fire!
That's a' the learning I desire;
Then tho' I drudge thro' dub and mire
At pleugh or cart,
My muse, tho' hamely in attire,
May touch the heart.

Oh for a spunk o' Allan's glee,
Or Fergusson's the bauld and slee,
Or bright Lapraik's, my friend to be,
If I can hit it!
That would be lear eneugh for me,
If I could get it!

Now, sir, if ye hae friends enow,
Tho' real friends I believe are few,
Yet, if your catalogue be fou,
I'se no insist,
But gif ye want ae friend that's true,
I'm on your list.

I winna blaw about mysel;
As ill I like my faults to tell;
But friends and folk that wish me well,
They sometimes roose me;
Tho' I maun own, as monie still
As far abuse me.

But Mauchline race (26), or Mauchline fair,
I should be proud to meet you there;
We'se gie ae night's discharge to care,
If we forgather,
And hae a swap o' rhymin'-ware
Wi' ane anither.

The four-gill chap, we'se gar him clatter,
And kirsen him wi' reekin' water;
Syne we'll sit down and tak our whitter,
To cheer our heart;
And, faith, we'se be acquainted better
Before we part.

Awa ye selfish war'ly race,
Wha think that havins, sense, and grace,
Ev'n love and friendship, should give place
To catch the plack!
I dinna like to see your face,
Nor hear your crack.

But ye whom social pleasure charms,
Whose hearts the tide of kindness warms,
Who hold your being on the terms,
"Each aid the others."
Come to my bowl, come to my arms,
My friends, my brothers!

But, to conclude my lang epistle,
As my auld pen's worn to the grissle;
Twa lines frae you wad gar me fissle,
Who am, most fervent,
While I can either sing or whissle,
Your friend and servant.

To the Same.

April 21, 1785.

While new-ca'd kye rowte at the stake,
And pownies reek in pleugh or braik,
This hour on e'enin's edge I take,
To own I'm debtor,
To honest-hearted, auld Lapraik,
For his kind letter.

Forjesket sair, wi' weary legs,
Rattlin' the corn out-owre the rigs,
Or dealing thro' amang the naigs
Their ten hours' bite,
My awkwart muse sair pleads and begs
I would na write.

The tapetless ramfeezl'd hizzie,
She's saft at best, and something lazy,
Quo' she, "Ye ken, we've been sae busy,
This month and mair,
That trouth, my head is grown right dizzie,
And something sair."

Her dowff excuses pat me mad:
"Conscience," says I, "ye thowless jad!
I'll write, and that a hearty blaud,
This vera night;
So dinna ye affront your trade,
But rhyme it right.

Shall bauld Lapraik, the king o' hearts,
Tho' mankind were a pack o' cartes,
Roose you sae weel for your deserts,
In terms sae friendly,
Yet ye'll neglect to shaw your parts,
And thank him kindly?"

Sae I gat paper in a blink,
And down gaed stumpie in the ink:
Quoth I, "before I sleep a wink,
I vow I'll close it;
And if ye winna mak it clink,
By Jove I'll prose it!"

Sae I've begun to scrawl, but whether
In rhyme, or prose, or baith thegither,
Or some hotch-potch that's rightly neither,
Let time mak proof;
But I shall scribble down some blether
Just clean aff-loof.

My worthy friend, ne'er grudge and carp,
Tho' fortune use you hard and sharp;
Come, kittle up your moorland-harp
Wi' gleesome touch;
Ne'er mind how fortune waft and warp—
She's but a b-tch!

She's gien me monie a jirt and fleg,
Sin' I could striddle owre a rig;
But, by the L—d, tho' I should beg
Wi' lyart pow,
I'll laugh, and sing, and shake my leg,
As lang's I dow!

Now comes the sax and twentieth simmer,
I've seen the bud upo' the timmer,
Still persecuted by the limmer
Frae year to year;
But yet, despite the kittle kimmer,
I, Rob, am here.

Do ye envy the city gent,
Behint a kist to lie and sklent,
Or purse-proud, big wi' cent. per cent.
And muckle wame,
In some bit brugh to represent
A bailie's name?

Or is't the paughty, feudal Thane,
Wi' ruffl'd sark and glancing cane,
Wha thinks himsel nae sheep-shank bane,
But lordly stalks,
While caps and bonnets aff are taen,
As by he walks?

Oh Thou wha gies us each guid gift!
Gie me o' wit and sense a lift,
Then turn me, if Thou please, adrift,
Thro' Scotland wide;
Wi' cits nor lairds I wadna shift,
In a' their pride!

Were this the charter of our state,
"On pain' o' hell be rich and great,"
Damnation then would be our fate,
Beyond remead;
But, thanks to Heav'n, that's no the gate
We learn our creed.

For thus the royal mandate ran,
When first the human race began,
"The social, friendly, honest man,
Whate'er he be,
'Tis he fulfils great Nature's plan,
And none but he!"

Oh mandate glorious and divine!
The followers o' the ragged Nine,
Poor thoughtless devils yet may shine
In glorious light,
While sordid sons o' Mammon's line
Are dark as night.

Tho' here they scrape, and squeeze, and growl,
Their worthless nievfu' of a soul
May in some future carcase howl,
The forest's fright;
Or in some day-detesting owl
May shun the light.

Then may Lapraik and Burns arise,
To reach their native kindred skies,
And sing their pleasures, hopes, and joys,
In some mild sphere,
Still closer knit in friendship's ties
Each passing year!

To William S[impson],

OCHILTREE. (27)

May, 1785,

I GAT your letter, winsome Willie;
Wi' gratefu' heart I thank you brawlie;
Tho' I maun say't, I wad be silly,
And unco vain,
Should I believe, my coaxin' billie,
Your flatterin' strain.

But I'se believe ye kindly meant it,
I sud be laith to think ye hinted
Ironic satire, sidelins sklented
On my poor Musie;
Tho' in sic phraisin' terms ye've penn'd it
I scarcely excuse ye.

My senses wad be in a creel,
Should I but dare a hope to speel,
Wi' Allan, or wi Gilbertfield,
The braes o' fame;
Or Fergusson, the writer chiel,
A deathless name.

(Oh Fergusson! thy glorious parts
Ill suited law's dry musty arts!
My curse upon your whunstane hearts,
Ye E'nbrugh gentry;
The tythe o' what ye waste at cartes
Wad stow'd his pantry!)

Yet when a tale comes i' my head,
Or lassies gie my heart a screed,
As whiles they're like to be my dead,
(Oh sad disease!)
I kittle up my rustic reed;
It gies me ease.

Auld Coila, now, may fidge fu' fain,
She's gotten poets o' her ain,
Chiels wha their chanters winna hain,
But tune their lays,
Till echoes a' resound again
Her weel-sung praise

Nae poet thought her worth his while,
To set her name in measur'd style;
She lay like some unken'd-of-isle
Beside New Holland,
Or whare wild-meeting oceans boil
Besouth Magellan.
Ramsay and famous Fergusson
Gied Forth and Tay a lift aboon
Yarrow and Tweed, to monie a tune,
Owre Scotland rings,
While Irwin, Lugar, Ayr, and Doon,
Naebody sings.

Th' Illissus, Tiber, Thames, and Seine,
Glide sweet in monie a tunefu' line;
But, Willie, set your fit to mine,
And cock your crest,
We'll gar our streams and burnies shine
Up wi' the best!

We'll sing auld Coila's plains and fells,
Her moors red-brown wi' heather bells,
Her banks and braes, her dens and dells,
Where glorious Wallace
Aft bure the gree, as story tell,
Frae southron billies.

At Wallace' name what Scottish blood
But boils up in spring-tide flood!
Oft have our fearless fathers strode
By Wallace' side,
Still pressing onward, red-wat shod,
Or glorious died!

Oh sweet are Coila's haughs and woods,
When lintwhites chant amang the buds,
And jinkin' hares, in amorous whids,
Their loves enjoy,
While thro' the braes the crushat croods
With wailfu' cry!

Ev'n winter bleak has charms to me
When winds rave thro' the naked tree;
Or frosts on hills of Ochiltree
Are hoary gray:
Or blinding drifts wild furious flee,
Dark'ning the day!

Oh nature! a' thy shows and forms
To feeling, pensive hearts hae charms!
Whether the summer kindly warms,
Wi' life and light,
Or winter howls, in gusty storms,
The lang, dark night!

The muse, nae poet ever fand her,
Till by himsel he learn'd to wander,
Adown some trotting burn's meander,
And no think lang;
Oh sweet, to stray and pensive ponder,
A heart-felt sang!

The war'ly race may drudge and drive,
Hog-shouther, jundie, stretch and strive;
Let me fair nature's face descrive,
And I, wi' pleasure,
Shall let the busy grumbling hive
Bum owre their treasure.

Fareweel, "my rhyme-composing brither!"
We've been owre lang unkenn'd to ither:
Now let us lay our heads thegither,
In love fraternal;
May envy wallop in a tether,
Black fiend, infernal!

While highlandmen hate tolls and taxes:
While moorlan' heads like guid fat braxies;
While terra firma on her axis
Diurnal turns,
Count on a friend, in faith and practice,
In ROBERT BURNS.

POSTSCRIPT.

My memory's no worth a preen;
I had amaist forgotten clean,
Ye bade me write you what they mean,
By this New Light,
'Bout which our herds sae aft hae been
Maist like to fight.

In days when mankind were but callans
At grammar, logic, and sic talents,
They took nae pains their speech to balance,
Or rules to gie,
But spak their thoughts in plain braid lallans.
Like you or me.

In thae auld times, they thought the moon,
Just like a sark, or pair o' shoon,
Wore by degrees, till her last roon
Gaed past their viewing,
And shortly after she was done,
They gat a new one.

This past for certain—undisputed;
It ne'er cam i' their heads to doubt it,
Till chiels gat up and wad confute it,
And ca'd it wrang;
And muckle din there was about it,
Baith loud and lang.

Some herds, well learn'd upo' the beuk,
Wad threap auld folk the think misteuk;
For 'twas the auld moon turned a neuk,
And out o' sight,
And backlins-comin', to the leuk
She grew mair bright.

This was denied—it was affirmed;
The herds and hirsels were alarmed:
The rev'rend grey-beards rav'd and storm'd
That beardless laddies
Should think they better were inform'd
Than their auld daddies.

Frae less to mair it gaed to sticks;
Frae words and aiths to clours and nicks,
And mony a fallow gat his licks,
Wi' hearty crunt;
And some, to learn them for their tricks,
Were hang'd and brunt.

This game was play'd in monie lands,
And Auld Light caddies bure sic hands,
That, faith, the youngsters took the sands
Wi' nimble shanks,
Till lairds forbade, by strict commands,
Sic bluidy pranks.

But New Light herds gat sic a cowe,
Folk thought them ruin'd stick-and-stowe,
Till now amaist on every knowe,
Ye'll find ane plac'd;
And some their New-Light fair avow,
Just quite barefac'd.

Nae doubt the Auld Light flocks are bleatin';
Their zealous herds are vex'd and sweatin';
Mysel' I've even seen them greetin'
Wi' girnin' spite,
To hear the moon sae sadly lied on
By word and write.

But shortly they will cowe the loons!
Some Auld Light herds in neebor towns
Are mind't in thinns they ca' balloons,
To tak a flight,
And stay ae month among the moons
And see them right.

Guid observation they will gie them;
And when the auld moon's gaun to lea'e them.
The hindmost shair'd, they'll fetch it wi' them,
Just i' their pouch,
And when the New Light billies see them,
I think they'll crouch!

Sae, ye observe that a' this clatter
Is naething but a "moonshine matter;"
But tho' dull prose-folk Latin splatter
In logic tulzie,
I hope we bardies ken some better
Than mind sic brulzie.

Death and Dr. Hornbook.

A TRUE STORY. (28)

SOME books are lies frae end to end,
And some great lies were never penn'd;
E'en ministers they hae been kenn'd,
In holy rapture,
A rousing whid at times to vend.
And nail't wi' Scripture.

But this that I am gaun to tell,
Which lately on a night befell,
Is just as true's the deil's in hell
Or Dublin city:
That e'er he ne nearer comes oursel
's a muckle pity.

The clachan yill had made me canty—
I was na fou, but just had plenty;
I stacher'd whyles, but yet took tent aye
To free the ditches;
And hillocks, stanes, and bushes kenned aye
Frae ghaists and witches.

The rising moon began to glow'r
The distant Cumnock hills out-owre:
To count her horns, wi' a' my pow'r,
I set mysel;
But whether sha had three or four,
I could na tell.

I was come round about the hill,
And todlin' down on Willie's mill (29),
Setting my staff wi' all my skill,
To keep me sicker;
Tho' leeward whyles, against my will,
I took a bicker.

I there wi' something did forgather,
That put me in an eerie swither;
An awfu' scythe, out-owre ae shouther,
Clear-dangling, hang;
A three-taed leister on the ither
Lay, large and lang.

Its stature seem'd lang Scotch ells twa,
The queerest shape that e'er I saw,
For fient a wame it had ava;
And then, its shanks,
They were as thin, as sharp and sma',
As cheeks o' branks.

"Guid e'en," quo' I; "Friend, hae ye been mawin',
When other folk are busy sawin'?"
It seem'd to mak a kind o' stan',
But naething spak;
At length says I, "Friend, whare ye gaun,
Will ye go back?"

It spake right howe—"My name is Death,
But be na fley'd." Quoth I, "Guid faith,
Ye're maybe come to stap my breath;
But tent me, billie—
I red ye weel, tak care o' skaith.
See, there's a gully!"

"Guidman," quo' he, "put up your whittle,
I'm no designed to try its mettle;
But if I did, I wad be kittle
To be mislear'd;
I wad na mind it, no, that spittle
Out-owre my beard."

"Weel, weel!" says I, "a bargain be't;
Come, gies your hand, and sae we're gree't;
We'll ease our shanks and tak a seat—
Come, gies your news;
This while ye hae been mony a gate,
At mony a house."

"Ay, ay!" quo' he, and shook his head,
"It's e en a lang time indeed
Sin' I began to nick the thread,
And choke the breath:
Folk maun do something for their bread,
And sae maun Death.

"Sax thousand years are near hand fled
Sin' I was to the butching bred,
And mony a scheme in vain's been laid,
To stap or scaur me;
Till ane Hornbook's taen up the trade,
And faith he'll waur me.

"Ye ken Jock Hornbook i' the clachan,
Deil mak his king's-hood in a spleuchan!
He's grown sae well acquaint wi' Buchan (30),
And ither chaps,
The weans haud out their fingers laughin',
And pouk my hips.

"See, here's a scythe, and there's a dart,
They hae pierc'd mony a gallant heart;
But Doctor Hornbook wi' his art
And cursed skill,
Has made them both no worth a f—t;
Damn'd haet they'll kill.

"'Twas but yestreen, nae farther gaen,
I threw a noble throw at ane;
Wi' less, I'm sure, I've hundreds slain;
But deil-ma-care,
It just play'd dirl on the bane,
But did nae mair.

"Hornbrook was by wi' ready art,
And had sae fortified the part,
That when I looked to my dart,
It was sae blunt,
Fient haet o't wad hae pierc'd the heart
Of a kail-runt.

"I drew my scythe in sic a fury,
I nearhand cowpit wi' my hurry,
But yet the bauld apothecary
Withstood the shock;
I might as weel hae tried a quarry
O' hard whin rock.

"And then a' doctor's saws and whittles,
Of a' dimensions, shapes, and metals,
A' kinds o' boxes, mugs, and bottles,
He's sure to hae;
Their Latin names as fast he rattles
As A B C.

"Calces o' fossils, earths, and trees;
True sal-marinum o' the seas;
The farina of beans and peas,
He has't in plenty;
Aqua-fontis, what you please,
He can content ye.

"Forbye some new, uncommon weapons,
Urinus spiritus of capons;
Or mite-horn shavings, filings, scrapings,
Distill'd *per se;*
Sal-alkali o' midge-tail clippings,
And mony mae."

"Waes me for Johnny Ged's Hole (31) now,"
Quo' I; "if that thae news be true,
His braw calf-ward whare gowans grew,
Sae white and bonny,
Nae doubt they'll rive it wi' the plew;
They'll ruin Johnny!"

The creature grain'd an eldritch laugh,
And says, "Ye need na yoke the pleugh,
Kirkyards will soon be till'd eneugh,
Tak ye nae fear:
They'll a' be trench'd wi' mony a sheugh
In twa-three year.

"Whare I kill'd ane a fair strae death,
By loss o' blood or want o' breath,
This night I'm free to tak my aith,
That Hornbook's skill
Has clad a score i' their last claith,
By drap and pill.

"An honest wabster to his trade,
Whase wife's twa nieves were scarce well-bred,
Gat tippence worth to mend her head,
When it was sair;
The wife slade cannie to her bed,
But ne'er spak mair.

"A countra laird had taen the batts,
Or rome curmurring in his guts;
His only son for Hornbook sets,
And pays him well—
The lad, for twa guid gimmer-pets,
Was laird himsel.

"That's just a swatch o' Hornbook's way;
Thus goes he on from day to day,
Thus does he poison, kill, and slay,
An's weel paid for't;
Yet stops me o' my lawfu' prey
Wi' his curs'd dirt:

"But hark! I'll tell you of a plot,
Though dinna ye be speaking o't;
I'll nail the self-conceited sot
As dead's a herrin':
Neist time we meet, I'll wad a groat,
He gets his fairin'!"

But just as he began to tell,
The auld kirk-hammer strak the bell
Some wee short hour ayont the twal,
Which rais'd us baith:
I took the way that pleas'd mysel',
And sae did Death.

The Holy Fair.

A robe of seeming truth and trust
Hid crafty observation;
And secret hung, with poison'd crust,
The dirk of Defamation:
A mask that like the gorget show'd,
Dye-varying on the pigeon;
And for a mantle large and broad,
He wrapt him in Religion.

HYPOCRISY A-LA-MODE. (11.)

UPON a simmer Sunday morn,
When Nature's face is fair,
I walked forth to view the corn,
And snuff the cauler air,
The rising sun owre Galston muirs,
Wi' glorious light was glintin';
The hares were hirplin' down the furs,
The lav'rocks they were chantin'
Fu' sweet that day.

As lightsomely I glowr'd abroad,
To see a scene sae gay,
Three hizzies, early at the road,
Cam skelpin' up the way;
Twa had manteeles o' dolefu' black,
But ane wi' lyart lining;
The third, that gaed a-wee a-back,
Was in the fashion shining,
Fu' gay that day.

HALLOWEEN.

Poor Leezie's heart maist lap the hool;
Near lav'rock-height she jumpit;

The twa appear'd like sisters twin,
  In feature, form, and claes;
Their visage wither'd, lang, and thin,
  And sour as ony slaes:
The third cam up, hap-step-an'-lowp,
  As light as ony lambie,
And wi' a curchie low did stoop,
  As soon as e'er she saw me,
    Fu' kind that day.

Wi' bonnet aff, quoth I, "Sweet lass,
  I think ye seem to ken me;
I'm sure I've seen that bonny face,
  But yet I canna name ye."
Quo' she, and laughin' as she spak,
  And taks me by the hands,
"Ye, for my sake, hae gien the feek,
  Of a' the ten commands
    A screed some day.

"My name is Fun—your cronie dear,
  The nearest friend ye hae;
And this is Superstition here,
  And that's Hypocrisy.
I'm gaun to Mauchline holy fair,
  To spend an hour in daffin':
Gin ye'll go there, yon runkl'd pair,
  We will get famous laughin'
    At them this day."

Quoth I "With a' my heart, I'll do't;
  I'll get my Sunday's sark on,
And meet you on the holy spot—
  Faith, we'se hae fine remarkin'!"
Then I gaed hame at crowdie-time,
  And soon I made me ready;
For roads were clad, from side to side,
  Wi' monie a wearie body,
    In droves that day.

Here farmers gash, in ridin' graith
  Gaed hoddin by their cottars;
There, swankies young, in braw braid-claith,
  Are springin' o'er the gutters.
The lasses, skelpin' barefit, thrang,
  In silks and scarlets glitter;
Wi' sweet-milk cheese, in mony a whang,
  And farls bak'd wi' butter,
    Fu' crump that day.

When by the plate we set our nose,
  Weel heaped up wi' ha'pence,
A greedy glow'r black bonnet throws,
  And we maun draw our tippence,
Then in we go to see the show;
  On ev'ry side they're gath'rin',
Some carrying dails, some chairs, and stools,
  And some are busy blethrin'
    Right loud that day.

Here stands a shed to fend the show'rs,
  And screen our country gentry,
There, racer, Jess (33), and twa-three wh-res,
  Are blinkin' at the entry.
Here sits a raw of tittlin' jauds,
  Wi' heaving breast and bare neck,
And there a batch o' wabster lads,
  Blackguarding frae Kilmarnock
    For fun this day.

Here sum are thinkin' on their sins,
  And some upo' their claes;
Ane curses feet that fyi'd his shins,
  Anither sighs and prays:
On this hand sits a chosen swatch,
  Wi' screw'd-up grace-proud faces;
On that a set o'chaps at watch,
  Thrang winkin' on the lasses
    To chairs that day.

Oh happy is that man and blest!
  (Nae wonder that it pride him!)
Wha's ain dear lass that he likes best,
  Comes clinkin' down beside him!
Wi' arm repos'd on the chair back,
  He sweetly does compose him;
Which, by degrees, slips round her neck,
  An's loof upon her bosom,
    Unkenn'd that day.

Now a' the congregation o'er
  Is silent expectation:
For Moodie speels the holy door,
  Wi' tidings o' d-mn-tion. (34)
Should Hornie, as in ancient days,
  'Mang sons o' God present him,
The vera sight o' Moodie's face,
  To's ain het hame had sent him
    Wi' fright that day.

Hear how he clears the points o' faith
  Wi rattlin' and wi' thumpin'!
Now meekly calm, now wild in wrath,
  He's stampin' and he's jumpin'!
His lengthened chin, his turn'd-up snout,
  His eldritch squeal and gestures,
Oh, how they fire the heart devout,
  Like cantharidian plasters,
    On sic a day!

But hark! the tent has chang'd its voice:
  There's peace and rest nae langer;
For a' the real judges rise,
  They canna sit for anger.
Smith opens out his cauld harangues (35),
  On practice and on morals;
And aff the godly pour in thrangs,
  To gie the jars and barrels
    A lift that day.

What signifies his barren shine,
  Of moral powr's and reason?
His English style and gesture fine
  Are a' clean out o' season.

Like Socrates or Antonine,
 Or some auld pagan heathen,
The moral man he does define,
 But ne'er a word o' faith in
  That's right that day.

In guid time comes an antidote
 Against sic poison'd nostrum;
For Peebles, frae the water-fit (36),
 Ascends the holy rostrum:
See, up he's got the word o' God,
 And meek and mim has view'd it,
While Common Sense (37) has ta'en the road,
 And aff, and up the Cowgate (38),
  Fast, fast, that day.

Wee Miller (39) neist the guard relieves,
 And orthodoxy raibles,
Tho' in his heart he weel believes,
 And thinks it auld wives' fables;
But, faith! the birkie wants a manse,
 So, cannily he hums them;
Altho' his carnal wit and sense
 Like hafflins-ways o'ercomes him
  At times that day.

Now butt and ben the change-house fills,
 Wi' yill-caup commentators;
Here's crying out for bakes and gills,
 And there the pint-stoup clatters;
While thick and thrang, and loud and lang,
 Wi' logic and wi' Scripture,
They raise a din, that, in the end,
 Is like to breed a rupture
  O' wrath that day.

Leeze me on drink! it gies us mair
 Than either school or college:
It kindles wit, it waukens lair,
 It pangs us fou o' knowledge.
Be't whisky gill, or penny wheep,
 Or ony stronger potion,
It never fails, on drinking deep,
 To pittle up our notion
  By night or day.

The lads and lasses, blythely bent
 To mind baith saul and body,
Sit round the table weel content,
 And steer about the toddy.
On this ane's dress, and that ane's leuk,
 They're making observations;
While some are cozie i' the neuk,
 And formin' assignations
  To meet some day.

But now the L—d's ain trumpet touts,
 Till a' the hills are rairin',
And echoes back return the shouts—
 Black Russell (40) is na sparin':
His piercing words, like Highlan' swords,
 Divide the joints and marrow;
His talk o' hell, whare devils dwell,
 Our vera sauls does harrow (41)
  Wi' fright that day.

A vast, unbottom'd, boundless pit,
 Fill'd fou o' lowin' brunstane,
Wha's ragin' flame, and scorchin' heat,
 Wad melt the hardest whun-stane!
The half asleep start up wi' fear,
 And think they hear it roarin',
When presently it does appear
 'Twas but some neebor snorin'
  Asleep that day.

'Twad be owre long a tale, to tell
 How monie stories past,
And how they crowded to the yill
 When they were a' dismist:
How drink gaed round, in cogs and caups,
 Amang the furms and benches:
And cheese and bread, frae women's laps,
 Was dealt about in lunches,
  And dauds that day.

In comes a gaucie, gash guidwife,
 And sits down by the fire,
Syne draws her kebbuck and her knife;
 The lasses they are shyer.
The auld guidmen, about the grace,
 Frae side to side they bother,
Till some ane by his bonnet lays,
 And gi'es them't like a tether,
  Fu' lang that day.

Waesuck! for him that gets nae lass,
 Or lasses that hae nathing!
Sma' need has he to say a grace,
 Or melvie his braw claithing!
Oh wives be mindfu' ance yoursel
 How bonny lads ye wanted,
 And dinna, for a kebbuck-heel,
 Let lasses be affronted
  On sic a day!

Now Clinkumbell, wi' rattlin' tow,
 Begins to jow and croon;
Some swagger hame the best they dow,
 Some wait the afternoon.
At slaps the billies halt a blink,
 Till lassess trip their shoon:
Wi' faith and hope, and love and drink,
 They're a' in famous tune
  For crack that day.

How monie hearts this day converts
 O' sinners and o' lasses!
Their hearts o' stane, gin night, are gane,
 As saft as ony flesh is.
There's some are fou o' love divine;
 There's some are fou' o' brandy;
And many jobs that day begin
 May end in houghmagandy,
  Some ither day.

The Ordination.

"For sense they little owe to frugal Heav'n—
To please the mob they hide the little giv'n."
(42)

KILMARNOCK wabsters fidge and claw,
And pour your creeshie nations;
And ye wha leather rax and draw,
Of a' denominations, (43)
Swith to the Laigh Kirk, ane and a',
And there tak up your stations;
Then aff to Begbie's (44) in a raw,
And pour divine libations.
For joy this day.

Curst Common Sense, that imp o' hell,
Cam in wi' Maggie Lauder (45);
But Oliphant aft made her yell,
And Russell sair misca'd her;
This day M——— taks the flail,
And he's the boy will blaud her!
He'll clap a shangan on her fail,
And set the bairns to daud her.
Wi' dirt this day.

Mak haste and turn king David owre,
And lilt wi' holy clangor;
O' double verse come gie us four,
And skirl up the Bangor:
This day the Kirk kicks up a stoure,
Nae mair the knaves shall wrang her,
For Heresy is in her pow'r,
And gloriously she'll whang her
Wi' pith this day.

Come, let a proper text be read.
And touch it aff wi' vigour,
How graceless Ham (46) leugh at his dad,
Which made Canaan a nigger;
Or Phineas (47) drove the murdering blade,
Wi' wh-re-abhorring rigour;
Or Zipporah (48), the scauldin' jad,
Was like a bluidy tiger
I' th' inn that day.

There, try his mettle on the creed,
And bind him down wi' caution,
That stipend is a carnal weed
He taks but for the fashion;
And gie him o'er the flock, to feed,
And punish each transgression;
Especial, rams that cross the breed,
Gie them sufficient threshin',
Spare them nae day.

Now, auld Kilmarnock, cock thy tail.
And toss thy horns fu' canty;
Nae mair thou'lt rowte out-owre the dale,
Because thy pasture's scanty;
For lapfu's large o' gospel kail
Shall fill thy crib in plenty,
And runts o' grace the pick and wale,
No gi'en by way o' dainty,
But ilka day.

Nae mair by Babel's streams we'll weep,
To think upon our Zion;
And hing our nddles up to sleep,
Like baby-clouts a-dryin';
Come, screw the pegs, wi' tunefu' cheap
And o'er the thairms be tryin';
Oh, rare! to see our elbucks wheep,
And a' like lamb-tails flyin'
Fu' fast this day;

Lang Patronage, wi' rod o' airn,
Has shor'd the Kirk's undoin',
As lately Fenwick, sair forfairn,
Has proven to its ruin:
Our patron, honest man! Glencairn,
He saw mischief was brewin';
And like a godly elect bairn
He's wal'd us out a true ane,
And sound this day.

Now, Robertson (49), harangue nae mair
But steek your gab for ever:
Or try the wicked town of Ayr,
For there they'll think you clever;
Or, nae reflection on your lear,
Ye may commence a shaver;
Or to the Netherton (50) repair,
And turn a carpet-weaver
Aff-hand this day.

Mutrie (51) and you were just a match,
We never had sic twa drones:
Auld Hornie did the Laigh Kirk watch,
Just like a winkin' baudrons:
And aye he catched the tither wretch,
To fry them in his caudrons:
But now his honour maun detach,
Wi' a' his brimstone squadrons,
Fast, fast this day.

See, see auld Orthodoxy's faes
She's swingein through the city;
Hark, how the nine-tail'd cat she plays!
I vow it's unco pretty:
There, Learning, with his Greekish face,
Grunts out some Latin ditty,
And Common Sense is gaun, she says,
To mak to Jamie Beattie (52)
Her plant this day.

But there's Morality himsel',
Embracing all opinions;
Hear, how he gies the tither yell,
Between his twa companions;
See, how she peels the skin and fell,
As ane were peelin' onions!
Now there—they're packed aff to hell,
And banish'd our dominions,
Henceforth this day.

Oh, happy day! rejoice, rejoice!
Come bouse about the porter!
Morality's demure decoys
Shall here nae mair find quarter:

M———, Russell, are the boys,
That Heresy can torture:
They'll gie her on a rape a hoyse,
And cowe her measure shorter
By th' head some day.

Come, bring the tither mutchkin in,
And here's, for a conclusion,
To every New Light (53) mother's son,
From this time forth, Confusion:
If mair they deave us wi' their din,
Or Patronage intrusion,
We'll light a spunk, and every skin
We'll rin them aff in fusion,
Like oil some day.

To James Smith. (54)

"Friendship! mysterious cement of the soul!
Sweet'ner of life, and solder of society!
I owe thee much!"—Blair.

Dear Smith, the slee'est, paukie thief,
That e'er attempted stealth or rief,
Ye surely hae some warlock-breef
Owre human hearts;
For ne'er a bosom yet was prief
Against your arts.

For me, I swear by sun and moon,
And ev'ry star that blinks aboon,
Ye've cost me twenty pair o' shoon
Just gaun to see you;
And ev'ry ither pair that's done,
Mair ta'en I'm wi' you.

That auld capricious carlin, Nature,
To mak amends for scrimpit stature,
She's turn'd you aff, a human Creature
On her first plan;
And in her freaks, on every feature
She's wrote, the Man.

Just now I've ta'en the fit o' ryhme,
My barmie noddle's working prime,
My fancy yerkit up sublime
Wi' hasty summon:
Hae ye a leisure-moment's time,
To hear what's comin'!

Some rhyme a neighbour's name to lash;
Some rhyme (vain thought) for needfu' cash;
Some rhyme to court the country clash,
And raise a din;
For me, an aim I never fash—
I rhyme for fun.

The star that rules my luckless lot,
Has fated me the russet coat,
And damn'd my fortune to the groat;
But in requit,
Has blest me wi' a random shot
O' countra wit.

This while my notion's ta'en a sklent,
To try my fate in guid black prent;
But still the mair I'm that way bent,
Something cries "Hoolie!
I red you, honest man, tak tent!
Ye'll shaw your folly.

There's ither poets much your betters,
Far seen in Greek, deep men o' letters,
Hae thought they had ensur'd their debtors
A' future ages;
Now moths deform in shapeless tatters,
Their unknown pages."

Then farewell hopes o' laurel-boughs,
To garland my poetic brows!
Henceforth I'll rove where busy ploughs
Are whistling thrang,
And teach the lanely heights and howes
My rustic sang.

I'll wander on, with tentless heed
How never-halting moments speed,
Till fate shall snap the brittle thread;
Then, all unknown,
I'll lay me with th' inglorious dead,
Forgot and gone!

But why o' death begin a tale?
Just now we're living sound and hale,
Then top and maintop crowd the sail,
Heave care o'er side!
And large before enjoyment's gale,
Let's tak the tide.

This life, sae far's I understand,
Is a' enchanted fairy land,
Where pleasure is the magic wand,
That, wielded right,
Maks hours like minutes, hand in hand,
Dance by fu' light.

The magic wand then let us wield;
For, ance that five-and-forty's speel'd,
See, crazy, weary, joyless eild,
Wi' wrinkl'd face,
Comes hostin', hirplin' owre the field,
Wi' creepin' pace.

When ance life's day draws near the gloamin',
Then fareweel vacant careless roamin';
And fareweel cheerfu' tankards foamin',
And social noise;
And fareweel dear, deluding woman!
The joy of joys!

Oh life! how pleasant in thy morning,
Young Fancy's rays the hills adorning!
Cold-pausing caution's lesson scorning,
We frisk away,
Like school-boys, at th' expected warning,
To joy and play.

We wander there, we wander here,
We eye the rose upon the brier,
Unmindful that the thorn is near,
Among the leaves!
And tho' the puny wound appear,
Short while it grieves.

Some, lucky, find a flow'ry spot,
For which they never toil'd or swat;
They drink the sweet and eat the fat,
But care or pain;
And, haply, eye the barren hut
With high disdain.

With steady aim some Fortune chase;
Keen hope does ev'ry sinew brace;
Thro' fair, thro' foul, they urge the race,
And seize the prey:
Then cannie, in some cozie place,
They close the day.

And others', like your humble servan',
Poor wights! nae rules nor roads observin';
To right or left, eternal swervin',
They zig-zag on;
Till curst with age, obscure and starvin,'
They aften groan.

Alas! what bitter toil and straining—
But truce with peevish, poor complaining!
Is fortune's fickle Luna waning?
E'en let her gang!
Beneath what light she has remaining,
Let's sing our sang.

My pen I here fling to the door,
And kneel, "Ye Pow'rs," and warm implore,
"Tho' I should wander terra o'er,
In all her climes,
Grant me but this, I ask no more,
Aye rowth o' rhymes.

Gie dreeping roasts to countra lairds,
Till icicles hing frae their beards;
Gie' fine braw claes to fine life guards,
And maids of honour!
And yill and whisky gie to cairds,
Until they sconner.

A title, Dempster merits it;
A garter gie to Willie Pitt;
Gie wealth to some be-ledger'd cit,
In cent. per cent.
But give me real, sterling wit,
And I'm content.

While ye are pleased to keep me hale,
I'll sit down o'er my scanty meal,
Be't water-brose, or muslin-kail,
Wi' cheerfu' face,
As lang's the muses dinna fail
To say the grace."

An anxious e'e I never throws
Behint my lug or by my nose;
I jouk beneath misfortune's blows
As weel's I may:
Sworn foe to sorrow, care, and prose,
I rhyme away.

Oh ye douce folk, that live by rule,
Grave, tideless-blooded, calm and cool,
Compar'd wi' you—oh fool! fool! fool!
How much unlike;
Your heart's are just a standing pool,
Your lives a dyke!

Nae hair-brain'd, sentimental traces,
In your unletter'd nameless faces!
In arioso trills and graces
Ye never stray,
But gravissimo, solemn basses
Ye hum away.

Ye are sae grave, nae doubt ye're wise;
Nae ferly tho' ye do despise
The hairum-scairum, ram-stam boys,
The rattling squad:
I see you upward cast your eyes—
—Ye ken the road.

Whilst I—but I shall haud me there—
Wi' you I'll scarce gang ony where—
Then, Jamie, I shall say nae mair,
But quat my sang,
Content wi' you to mak a pair,
Whare'er I gang.

The Jolly Beggars.—A Cantata. (55)

RECITATIVO.

When lyart leaves bestrew the yird,
Or wavering like the bauckie-bird,
Bedim cauld Boreas' blast;
When hailstanes drive wi' bitter skyte
And infant frosts begin to bite,
In hoary cranreuch drest;
Ae night at e'en a merry core
O' randie, gangrel bodies,
In Poosie Nancy's held the splore,
To drink their orra duddies:
Wi' quaffing and laughing,
They ranted and they sang;
Wi' jumping and thumping,
The vera girdle rang.

First, neist the fire, in auld red rags,
Ane sait weel brac'd wi' mealy bags,
And knapsack a' in order;
His doxy lay within his arm,
Wi' usquebae and blankets warm—
She blinket on her sodger:
And aye he gies the tozie drab
The tither skelpin' kiss,
While she held up her greedy gab
Just like an aumos dish. (56)

Ilk smack still, did crack still,
Just like a cadger's whip,
Then staggering and swaggering
He roared this ditty up.

AIR.

TUNE—*Soldiers' Joy.*

I am a son of Mars, who have been in many
wars, [come;
And show my cuts and scars wherever I
This here was for a wench, and that other in
a trench, [the drum.
When welcoming the French at the sound of
Lal de daudle, &c.

My 'prenticeship I past where my leader
breath'd his last, [of Abram (57);
When the bloody die was cast on the heights
I served out my trade when the gallant game
was play'd, [sound of the drum.
And the Morro (58) low was laid at the
Lal, de daudle, &c.

I lastly was with Curtis, among the floating
batt'ries (59), [limb;
And there I left for witness an arm and a
Yet let my country need me, with Elliot (60)
to head me, [drum.
I'd clatter on my stumps at the sound of a
Lal de daudle, &c.

And now tho' I must beg with a wooden arm
and leg, [bum.
And many a tatter'd rag hanging over my
I'm as happy with my wallet, my bottle and
my callet,
As when I us'd in scarlet to follow a drum.
Lal de daudle, &c.

What tho' with hoary locks, I must stand the
winter shocks, [a home,
Beneath the woods and rocks oftentimes for
When the tother bag I sell, and the tother
bottle tell, [a drum.
I could meet a troop of hell at the sound of
Lal de daudle, &c.

RECITATIVO.

He ended; and the kebars sheuk,
Aboon the chorus roar;
While frighted rattons backward leuk,
And seek the benmost bore;
A fairy fiddler frae the neuk,
He skirl d out "Encore!"
But up arose the martial chuck,
And laid the loud uproar.

AIR.

TUNE—*Soldier Laddie.*

I once was a maid, tho' I cannot tell when,
And still my delight is in proper young men;
Some one of a troop of dragoons was my
daddie,
No wonder I'm fond of a sodger laddie.
Sing, Lal de lal, &c.

The first of my loves was a swaggering blade,
To rattle the thundering drum was his trade;
His leg was so tight, and his cheek was so
ruddy,
Transported I was with my sodger laddie.
Sing, Lal de lal, &c.

But the godly old chaplain left him in the
lurch, [church;
The sword I forsook for the sake of the
He ventur'd the soul, and I risk'd the body—
'Twas then I prov'd false to my sodger laddie.
Sing, Lal, de lal, &c.

Full soon I grew sick of my sanctified sot,
The regiment at large for a husband I got;
From the gilded spontoon to the fife I was
ready,
I asked no more but a sodger laddie
Sing, Lal, de lal, &c.

But the peace it reduc'd me to beg in despair,
Till I met my old boy at Cunningham fair;
His rags regimental they flutter'd so gaudy,
My heart it rejoic'd at a sodger laddie.
Sing, Lal de lal, &c.

And now I have liv'd—I know not how long
And still I can join in a cup and a song;
But whilst with both hands I can hold the
glass steady,
Here's to thee, my hero, my sodger laddie.
Sing, Lal de lal, &c.

RECITATIVO.

Poor Merry Andrew in the neuk,
Sat guzzling wi' a tinkler hizzie;
They mind't na wha the chorus teuk,
Between themselves they were sae busy:
At length wi' drink and courting dizzy,
He stoiter'd up and made a face;
Then turn'd, and laid a smack on Grizzie,
Syne tuned his pipes wi' grave grimace.

AIR.

TUNE—*Auld Sir Symon.*

Sir Wisdom's a fool when he's fou,
Sir Knave is a fool in a session:
He's there but a 'prentice I trow,
But I am a fool by profession.

My grannie she bought me a beuk,
And I held awa to the school;
I fear I my talent misteuk,
But what will ye hae of a fool?

For drink I would venture my neck,
A hizzie's the half o' my craft,
But what could ye other expect,
Of ane that's avowedly daft?

I ance was tied up like a stirk;
For civilly swearing and quaffin';
I ance was abus'd in the kirk,
For touzling a lass i' my daffin.

Poor Andrew that tumbles for sport,
Let n'aebody name wi' a jeer;
There's ev'n, I'm taught, i' the court
A tumbler ca'd the premier.

Observ'd ye, yon reverend lad
Maks faces to tickle the mob;
He rails at our mountebank squad—
It's rivalship just i' the job.

And now my conclusion I'll tell,
For faith I'm confoundedly dry;
The chiel that's a fool for himsel',
Gude L—d! he's far dafter than I.

RECITATIVO.

Then neist outspak a raucle carlin,
Wha keut fu' weel to cleek the sterling,
For monie a pursie she had hooked,
And had in mony a well been ducked.
Her dove had been a Highland laddie,
But weary fa' the waefu' woodie!
Wi' sighs and sobs she thus began
To wail her braw John Highlandman.

AIR.

TUNE—*O an ye were dead Guidman.*

A Highland lad my love was born,
The Lawland laws he held in scorn
But he still was faithfu' to his clan,
My gallant braw John Highlandman.

CHORUS.

Sing, hey my braw John Highlandman!
Sing, ho, my braw John Highlandman!
There's not a lad in a' the lan'
Was match for my John Highlandman.

With his philabeg and tartan plaid,
And guid claymore down by his side,
The ladies' hearts he did trepan,
My gallant braw John Highlandman.
Sing, hey, &c.

We ranged a' from Tweed to Spey,
And liv'd like lords and ladies gay;
For a Lawland face he feared none,
My gallant braw John Highlandman.
Sing, hey, &c.

They banish'd him beyond the sea,
But ere the bud was on the tree,
Adown my cheeks the pearls ran,
Embracing my John Highlandman.
Sing, hey, &c.

But, oh! they catch'd him at the last,
And bound him in a dungeon fast:
My curse upon them every one,
They've hang'd my braw John Highlandman.
Sing, hey, &c.

And now a widow, I must mourn,
The pleasure's that will ne'er return;
No comfort but a hearty can,
When I think on John Highlandman.
Sing, hey, &c.

RECITATIVO.

A pigmy scraper, wi' his fiddle,
Wha us'd at trysts and fairs to driddle,
Her strappin' limb, and gaucy middle
(He reach'd na higher)
Had hol'd his heartie like a riddle,
And blawn't on fire.

Wi' hand on haunch, and upward e'e
He croon'd his gamut, one, two, three,
Then in an arioso key,
The wee Apollo
Set off wi' allegretto glee
His giga solo.

AIR.

TUNE—*Whistle oe'r the lave o't.*

Let me ryke up to dight that tear,
And go wi' me and be my dear,
And then you every care and fear
May whistle owre the lave o't.

CHORUS.

I am a fiddler to my trade,
And a' the tunes that e'er I play'd,
The sweetest still to wife or maid,
Was whistle owre the lave o't.

At kirns and weddings we'se be there,
And oh! sae nicely's we will fare;
We'll bouse about till Daddie Care
Sings whistle owre the lave o't.
I am, &c.

Sae merrily the banes we'll pyke,
And sun oursells about the dyke,
And at our leisure, when ye like,
We'll whistle ow're the lave o't.
I am, &c.

But bless me wi' your heav'n o' charms,
And while I kittle hair on thairms,
Hunger, cauld, and a sic harms.
May whistle ow're the lave o't.
I am, &c.

RECITATIVO.

Her charms had struck a sturdy cair'd.
As weel as poor gut-scraper;
He taks the fiddler by the beard,
And draws a roosty rapier—

He swoor by a' was swearing worth,
  To speet him like a pliver,
Unless he wad from that time forth
  Relinquish her for ever.

Wi' ghastly e'e, poor tweedle-dee
  Upon his hunkers bended,
And pray'd for grace wi' ruefu' face,
  And sae the quarrel ended.

But tho' his little heart did grieve
  When round the tinkler prest her,
He feign'd to snirtle in his sleeve,
  When thus the caird address'd her:

AIR.

TUNE—*Clout the Caudron.*

My bonny lass, I work in brass,
  A tinkler is my station:
I've travell'd round all Christian ground
  In this my occupation:
I've ta'en the gold, I've been enroll'd
  In many a noble squadron:
But vain they search'd, when off I march'd
  To go and clout the caudron,
          I've tae'n the gold, &c.

Despise that shrimp, that wither'd imp,
  Wi' a' his noise and caprin,'
And tak a share wi' those that bear
  The budget and the apron.
And by that stoup, my faith and houp,
  And by that dear Kilbagie (61),
If e'er ye want, or meet wi' scant,
  May I ne'er weet my craigie.
          And by that stoup, &c.

RECITATIVO.

The caird prevail'd—the unblushing fair
  In his embraces sunk,
Partly wi' love o'ercome sae sair,
  And partly she was drunk.
Sir Violino, with an air
  That show'd a man of spunk,
Wish'd unison between the pair,
  And made the bottle clunk
          To their health that night.

But hurchin Cupid shot a shaft,
  That play'd a dame a shavie,
The fiddler raked her fore and aft,
  Ahint the chicken cavie.
Her lord, a wight o' Homer's craft,
  Tho' limping wi' the spavie,
He hirpl'd up, and lap like daft,
  And shor'd them Dainty Davie
          O' boot that night

He was a care-defying blade
  As ever Bacchus listed,
Tho' Fortune sair upon him laid,
  His heart she ever miss'd it.

He had nae wish but—to be glad,
  Nor want but—when he thirsted;
He had nought but—to be sad,
  And thus the Muse suggested
          His sang that night.

AIR.

TUNE—*For a' that, and a' that.*

I am a bard of no regard,
  Wi' gentle folks, and a' that:
But Homer-like, the glowrin' byke,
  Frae town to town I draw that.

CHORUS.

For a' that, and a' that,
  And twice as muckle's a' that;
I've lost but ane, I've twa behin,'
  I've wife eneugh for a' that.

I never drank the Muses' stank,
  Castalia's burn and a' that;
But there it streams, and richly reams,
  My Helicon I ca' that,
          For a' that, &c.

Great love I bear to a' the fair,
  Their humble slave, and a' that;
But lordly will, I hold it still
  A mortal sin to thraw that.
          For a' that, &c.

In raptures sweet, this hour we meet,
  Wi' mutual love and a' that:
But for how lang the flee may stang,
  Let inclination law that.
          For a' that, &c.

Their tricks and craft have put me daft,
  They've ta'en me in, and a' that;
But clear your decks, and here's the sex
  I like the jads for a' that.

CHORUS.

For a' that, and a' that,
  And twice as muckle's a' that;
My dearest bluid, to do them guid,
  They're welcome till't for a' that.

RECITATIVO.

So sang the bard—and Nansie's wa's
Shook with a wonder of applause,
  Re-echo'd from each mouth:
They toom'd their pocks, and pawn'd their
  duds.
They scarcely left to co'er their fuds,
  To quench their lowin' drougth.
Then owre again, the jovial thrang,
  The poet did request,
To loose his pack and wale a sang,
  A ballad o' the best;
    He rising, rejoicing,
      Between his twa Deborahs,
    Looks round him, and found them
      Impatient for the chorus.

AIR.

TUNE—*Jolly Mortals, fill your Glasses.*

See! the smoking bowl before us,
  Mark our jovial ragged ring!
Round and round take up the chorus,
  And in raptures let us sing.

CHORUS.

A fig for those by law protected!
  Liberty's a glorious feast!
Courts for cowards were erected,
  Churches built to please the priest.

What is title? what is treasure?
  What is reputation's care?
If we lead a life of pleasure,
  'Tis no matter how or where!
    A fig, &c.

With the ready trick and fable,
  Round we wander all the day;
And at night in barn or stable,
  Hug our doxies on the hay.
    A fig, &c.

Does the train-attended carriage
  Through the country lighter rove?
Does the sober bed of marriage
  Witness brighter scenes of love!
    A fig, &c.

Life is all a variorum,
  We regard not how it goes;
Let them cant about decorum
  Who have characters to lose.
    A fig, &c.

Here's to budgets, bags, and wallets!
  Here's to all the wandering train!
Here's our ragged brats and callets!
  One and all cry out—Amen!

A fig for those by law protected!
  Liberty's a glarious feast!
Courts for cowards were erected,
  Churches built to please the priest.

Man was Made to Mourn. (62)

A DIRGE.

WHEN chill November's surly blast
  Made fields and forests bare,
One ev'ning, as I wandered forth
  Along the banks of Ayr,
I spied a man whose aged step
  Seem'd weary, worn with care;
His face was furrow'd o'er with years,
  And hoary was his hair.

"Young stranger, whither wand'rest thou?"
  Began the rev'rend sage:
"Does thirst of wealth thy step constrain,
  Or youthful pleasure's rage?
Or haply, prest with cares and woes,
  Too soon thou hast began
To wander forth, with me, to mourn
  The miseries of man.

The sun that overhangs yon moors,
  Out-spreading far and wide,
Where hundreds labour to support
  A haughty lordling's pride:
I've seen yon weary winter-sun
  Twice forty times return,
And ev'ry time has added proofs
  That man was made to mourn.

Oh man, while in thy early years,
  How prodigal of time!
Misspending all thy precious hours,
  Thy glorious youthful prime!
Alternate follies take the sway;
  Licentious passions burn;
Which tenfold force gives nature's law,
  That man was made to mourn.

Look not alone on youthful prime,
  Or manhood's active might;
Man then is useful to his kind,
  Supported is his right;
But see him on the edge of life,
  With cares and sorrows worn;
Then age and want—oh! ill-match'd pair!—
  Show man was made to mourn.

A few seem favourites of fate,
  In pleasure's lap carest;
Yet, think not all the rich and great
  Are likewise truly blest.
But, oh! what crowds in every land,
  All wretched and forlorn!
Thro' weary life this lesson learn—
  That man was made to mourn.

Many and sharp the num'rous ills
  Inwoven with our frame!
More pointed still we make ourselves
  Regret, remorse, and shame;
And man, whose heaven-erected face
  The smiles of love adorn,
Man's inhumanity to man
  Makes countless thousands mourn!

See yonder poor, o'erlabour'd wight,
  So abject, mean, and vile,
Who begs a brother of the earth
  To give him leave to toil;
And see his lordly fellow-worm
  The poor petition spurn,
Unmindful, though a weeping wife
  And helpless offspring mourn.

If I'm design'd yon lordling's slave—
  By Nature's law designed—
Why was an independent wish
  E'er planted in my mind?

If not, why am I subject to
  His cruelty or scorn?
Or why has man the will and power
  To make his fellow mourn?

Yet, let not this too much, my son,
  Disturb thy youthful breast;
This partial view of human-kind
  Is surely not the last!
The poor, oppressed, honest man
  Had never, sure, been born,
Had there not been some recompense
  To comfort those that mourn!

Oh Death! the poor man's dearest friend—
  The kindest and the best!
Welcome the hour, my aged limbs
  Are laid with thee at rest!
The great, the wealthy, fear thy blow,
  From pomp and pleasure torn!
But, oh! a blest relief to those
  That weary-laden mourn!"

To a Mouse,

ON TURNING UP HER NEST WITH THE PLOUGH,

November 1785. (63.)

WEE, sleekit, cow'rin', tim'rous beastie,
Oh, what a panic's in thy breastie!
Thou need na start awa sae hasty,
    Wi' bickering brattle!
I wad be laith to rin and chase thee,
    Wi' murd'ring pattle!

I'm truly sorrow man's dominion
Has broken nature's social union,
And justifies that ill opinion,
    Which makes thee startle
At me, thy poor earth-born companion,
    And fellow-mortal!

I doubt na, whyles, but thou may thieve;
What then? poor beastie, thou maun live!
A daimen icker in a thrave
    's a sma' request:
I'll get a blessin' wi' the laive,
    And never miss't!

Thy wee bit housie, too, in ruin!
Its silly wa's the win's are strewin'!
And naething, now, to big a new ane,
    O' foggage green
And bleak December's winds ensuin',
    Baith snell and keen!

Thou saw the fields laid bare and waste,
And weary winter comin' fast,
And cozie here, beneath the blast,
    Thou thought to dwell,
'Till, crash! the cruel coulter past
    Out thro' thy cell.

That wee bit heap o' leaves and stibble,
Has cost thee mony a weary nibble!
Now thou's turn'd out for a' thy trouble,
    But house or hald,
To thole the winter's sleety dribble,
    And cranreuch cauld!

But, Mousie, thou art no thy lane,
In proving foresight may be vain:
The best laid schemes o' mice and men,
    Gang aft a-gley,
And lea'e us nought but grief and pain,
    For promis'd joy.

Still thou art blest, compar'd wi' me!
The present only toucheth thee:
But, och! I backward cast my e'e,
    On prospects drear!
And forward, tho' I canna see,
    I guess and fear.

The Vision.

DUAN FIRST. (64)

THE sun had clos'd the winter day,
The curlers quat their roaring play (65),
And hunger'd maukin ta'en her way
    To kail-yards green,
While faithless snaws ilk step betray
    Whare she has been.

The thresher's weary flingin'-tree
The lee-lang day had tired me;
And when the day had clos'd his e'e,
    Far i' the west,
Ben i' the spence (66), right pensivelie,
    I gaed to rest.

There, lanely, by the ingle-cheek,
I sat and ey'd the spewing reek,
That fill'd wi' hoast-provoking smeek,
    The auld clay biggin';
And heard the restless rattons squeak
    About the riggin'.

All in this mottie, misty clime,
I backward mus'd on wasted time,
How I had spent my youthfu' prime,
    And done nae thing,
But stringin' blethers up in rhyme,
    For fools to sing.

Had I to guid advice but harkit,
I might, by this, hae led a market,
Or strutted in a bank, and clarkit
    My cash-account:
While here, half-mad, half-fed, half-sarkit,
    Is a' th' amount.

I started, mutt'ring, blockhead! coof!
And heav'd on high my waukit loof,
To swear by a' yon starry roof,
Or some rash aith,
That I henceforth would be rhyme-proof
Till my last breath—

When, click! the string the snick did draw;
And, jee! the door gaed to the wa';
And by my ingle-lowe I saw,
Now bleezin' bright,
A tight, outlandish hizzie, braw,
Come full in sight.

Ye needna doubt, I held my whisht;
The infant aith, half-form'd, was crusht;
I glowr'd as eerie's I'd been dusht
In some wild glen;
When sweet, like modest worth, she blusht,
And stepped ben.

Green, slender, leaf-clad holly-boughs
Were twisted graceful' round her brows;
I took her for some Scottish Muse,
By that same token,
And come to stop those reckless vows,
Wou'd soon been broken.

A "hair-brain'd, sentimental trace"
Was strongly marked in her face;
A wildly-witty, rustic grace
Shone full upon her;
Her eye, ev'n turn'd on empty space,
Beam'd keen with honour.

Down flow'd her robe a tartan sheen,
Till half a leg was scrimply seen;
And such a leg! my bonnie Jean
Could only peer it;
Sae thought, sae taper, tight and clean,
Nane else came near it.

Her mantle large, of greenish hue,
My gazing wonder chiefly drew;
Deep lights and shades, bold-mingling, threw
A lustre grand;
And seem'd, to my astonish'd view,
A well-known land.

Here, rivers in the sea were lost;
There, mountains to the skies were tost:
Here, tumbling billows mark'd the coast
With surging foam
There, distant shone Art's lofty boast,
The lordly dome.

Here, Doon pour'd down his far-fetch'd floods;
There, well-fed Irwine stately thuds:
Auld hermit Ayr staw thro' his woods,
On to the shore,
And many a lesser torrent scuds,
With seeming roar.

Low in a sandy valley spread,
An ancient borough rear'd her head (67);
Still, as in Scottish story read,
She boasts a race,
To ev'ry nobler virtue bred,
And polish'd grace.

By stately tow'r or palace fair,
Or ruins pendent in the air,
Bold stems of heroes, here and there,
I could discern;
Some seem'd to muse, some seem'd to dare,
With feature stern,

My heart did glowing transport feel,
To see a race (68) heroic wheel,
And brandish round the deep-dy'd steel
In sturdy blows;
While back-recoiling seem'd to reel
Their suthron foes.

His Country's Saviour (69), mark him well!
Bold Richardton's (70) heroic swell;
The chief on Sark (71) who glorious fell
In high command;
And he whom ruthless fates expel
His native land.

There, where a sceptr'd Pictish shade (72)
Stalk'd round his ashes lowly laid,
I mark'd a martial race, portray'd
In colours strong;
Bold, soldier-featur'd, undismayed
They strode along.

Thro' many a wild romantic grove (73),
Near many a hermit-fancy'd cove
(Fit haunts for friendship or for love),
In musing mood.
An aged judge, I saw him rove,
Dispensing good.

With deep-struck reverential awe (74),
The learned sire and son I saw (75),
To Nature's God and Nature's law
They gave their lore,
This, all its source and end to draw;
That, to adore.

Brydone's brave ward (76) I well could spy
Beneath old Scotia's smiling eye;
Who call'd on Fame, low standing by,
To hand him on,
Where many a patriot-name on high
And hero shone.

DUAN SECOND.

With musing-deep, astonish'd stare,
I view'd the heav'nly-seeming fair;
A whisp'ring throb did witness bear
Of kindred sweet,
When with an elder sisters's air
She did me greet.

"All hail! my own inspired bard!
In me thy native Muse regard!
Nor longer mourn thy fate is hard,
Thus poorly low!
I come to give thee such regard
As we bestow.

Know, the great genius of this land
Has many a light, aërial band,
Who, all beneath his high command,
Harmoniously,
As arts or arms they understand,
Their labours ply.

They Scotia's race among them share;
Some fire the soldier on to dare;
Some raise the patriot on to bare
Corruption's heart:
Some teach the bard, a darling care,
The tuneful art.

'Mong swelling floods of reeking gore,
They, ardent, kindling spirits, pour;
Or, 'mid the venal senate's roar,
They, sightless, stand,
To mend the honest patriot-lore,
And grace the hand.

And when the bard, or hoary sage,
Charm or instruct the future age,
They bind the wild, poetic rage
In energy,
Or point the inconclusive page
Full on the eye.

Hence Fullarton, the brave and young;
Hence Dempster's zeal-inspired tongue;
Hence sweet harmonious Beattie sung
His 'Minstrel lays;'
Or tore, with nobler ardour stung,
The sceptic's bays.

To lower orders are assign'd
The humbler ranks of human-kind,
The rustic bard, the lab'ring hind,
The artizan;
All choose, as various they're inclin'd,
The various man.

When yellow waves the heavy grain,
The threat'ning storm some, strongly, rein:
Some teach to meliorate the plain,
With tillage-skill;
And some instruct the shepherd-train,
Blythe o'er the hill.

Some hint the lover's harmless wile;
Some grace the maiden's artless smile;
Some soothe the lab'rer's weary toil,
For humble gains,
And make his cottage-scenes beguile
His cares and pains.

Some, bounded to a district-space,
Explore at large man's infant race,
To mark the embryotic trace
Of rustic bard;
And careful note each op'ning grace,
A guide and guard.

Of these am I—Coila my name (77);
And this district as mine I claim.
Where once the Campbells (78), chiefs of fame,
Held ruling pow'r:
I mark'd thy embryo tuneful flame,
Thy natal hour.

With future hope, I oft would gaze,
Fond, on thy little early ways,
Thy rudely caroll'd, chiming phrase,
In uncouth rhymes,
Fir'd at the simple, artless lays,
Of other times.

I saw thee seek the sounding shore,
Delighted with the dashing roar;
Or when the north his fleecy store
Drove through the sky,
I saw grim nature's visage hoar
Struck thy young eye.

Or when the deep green-mantled earth
Warm cherish'd ev'ry flow'ret's birth,
And joy and music pouring forth
In ev'ry grove,
I saw thee eye the general mirth
With boundless love.

When ripen'd fields, and azure skies,
Called forth the reaper's rustling noise,
I saw thee leave their evening joys,
And lonely stalk,
To vent thy bosom's swelling rise
In pensive walk.

When youthful love, warm-blushing, strong,
Keen-shivering shot thy nerves along,
Those accents, grateful to thy tongue,
Th' adored Name,
I taught thee how to pour in song,
To soothe thy flame.

I saw thy pulse's maddening play,
Wild send thee pleasure's devious way,
Misled by Fancy's meteor-ray,
By passion driven;
But yet the light that led astray
Was light from Heaven.

I taught thy manners-painting strains,
The loves, the ways of simple swains,
Till now, o'er all my wide domains
Thy fame extends;
And some, the pride of Coila's plains,
Become thy friends.

Thou canst not learn, nor can I show,
To paint with Thomson's landscape glow;
Or wake the bosom-melting throe,
With Shenstone's art;
Or pour, with Gray, the moving flow
Warm on the heart.

Yet, all beneath the unrivall'd rose,
The lowly daisy sweetly blows;
Tho' large the forest's monarch throws
His army shade,
Yet green the juicy hawthorn grows,
Adown the glade.

Then never murmur nor repine;
Strive in thy humble sphere to shine;
And, trust me, not Potosi's mine,
Nor king's regard,
Can give a bliss o'ermatching thine,
A rustic bard.

To give my counsels all in one—
Thy tuneful flame still careful fan;
Preserve the dignity of man,
With soul erect;
And trust, the universal plan
Will all protect.

And wear thou this"—she solemn said,
And bound the holly round my head:
The polish'd leaves, and berries red,
Did rustling play;
And, like a passing thought, she fled
In light away.

The Author's Earnest Cry and Prayer

TO THE SCOTCH REPRESENTATIVES IN THE HOUSE OF COMMONS. (79)

"Dearest of distillation! last and best!
How art thou lost!"—PARODY ON MILTON.

YE Irish lords, ye knights and squires,
Wha represent our brughs and shires,
And doucely manage our affairs
In parliament,
To you a simple Bardie's prayers
Are humbly sent.

Alas! my roopit Muse is hearse!
Your honour's heart wi' grief 'twad pierce'
To see her sittin' on her a—
Low i' the dust,
And scriechin' out prosaic verse,
And like to brust!

Tell them wha hae the chief direction,
Scotland and me's in great affliction,
E'er sin' they laid that curst restriction
On aqua vitæ;
And rouse them up to strong conviction,
And move their pity.

Stand forth, and tell yon Premier youth (80),
The honest, open, naked truth:
Tell him o' mine and Scotland's drouth,
His servants humble:
The muckle devil blaw ye south,
If ye dissemble!

Does ony great man glunch and gloom?
Speak out, and never fas your thoom!
Let posts and pensions sink or soom
W' them wha grant 'em:
If honestly they canna come,
Far better want 'em.

In gathrin' votes you were na slack;
Now stand as tightly by your tack;
Ne'er claw your lug, and fidge your back,
And hum and haw;
But raise your arm, and tell your crack
Before them a'.

Paint Scotland greeting ower her thrissle,
Her mutchkin stoup as toom's a whissle;
And d-mn'd excisemen in a bussle,
Seizin' a stell,
Triumphant crushin't like a mussel
Or lampit shell.

Then on the tither hand present her,
A blackguard smuggler, right behint her,
And cheek-for-chow, a chuffie vintner,
Colleaguing join,
Picking her pouch as bare as winter
Of a' kind coin.

Is there, that bears the name o' Scot,
But feels his heart's bluid rising hot,
To see his poor auld mither's pot
Thus dung in staves,
And plundered o' her hindmost groat
By gallows knaves?

Alas! I'm but a nameless wight,
Trod i' the mire out o' sight!
But could I like Montgomeries fight (81),
Or gab like Boswell (82),
There's some sark-necks I wad draw tight,
And tie some hose well.

God bless your honours, can ye see't,
The kind, auld, cantie carlin greet,
And no get warmly to your feet,
And gar them hear it,
And tell them, with a patriot heat,
Ye winna bear it?

Some o' you nicely ken the laws,
To round the period and pause,
And wi' rhetoric clause on clause
To mak harangues;
Then echo thro' Saint Stephen's wa's
Auld Scotland's wrangs.

Dempster (83), a true blue Scot I'se warran',
Thee, aith-detesting, chaste Kilkerran (84);
And that glib-gabbet Highland baron,
The Laird o' Graham (85);
And ane, a chap that's d-mn'd auldfarran,
Dundas his name. (86)

Erskine (87), a spunkie Norland billie;
True Campbells, Frederick (88) and Ilay (89);
And Livingstone, the bauld Sir Willie;
And monie ithers,
Whom auld Demosthenes or Tully
May'n own for brithers.

See' sodger Hugh, my watchmen stented,
If bardies e'er are represented;
I ken if that your sword were wanted,
Ye'd lend a hand,
But when there's ought to say anent it,
Ye're at a stand. (90)

Arouse, my boys! exert your mettle,
To get auld Scotland back her kettle;
Or faith! I'll wad my now pleugh-pettle,
Ye'll see't ere lang,
She'll teach you wi' a reekin' whittle,
Anither sang.

This while she's been in crankus mood,
Her lost militia fir'd her bluid;
(Deil na they never mair do guid,
Play'd her that pliskie!)
And now she's like to run red-wud
About her whisky.

And L—d! if ance they pit her till't,
Her tartan petticoat she'll kilt,
And durk and pistol at her belt,
She'll tak the streets,
And rin her whittle to the hilt,
I' th' first she meets!

For G-d sake, sirs! then speak her fair,
And straik her cannie wi' the hair,
And to the muckle house repair,
Wi' instant speed,
And strive, wi' a' your wit and lear,
To get remead.

Yon ill-tongu'd tinkler, Charlie Fox,
May taunt you wi' his jeers and mocks;
But gie him't het, my hearty cocks!
E'en cowe the cadie!
An send him to his dicing box
And sportin' lady.

Tell yon guid bluid o' auld Boconnock's (91),
I'll be his debt twa mashlum bonnocks (92),
And drink his health in auld Nanse Tinnock's (93)
Nine times a-week,
If he some scheme, like tea and winnocks (94),
Wad kindly seek.

Could he some commutation broach,
I'll pledge my aith in guid braid Scotch,
He'll need na fear their foul reproach,
Nor erudition,
Yon mixtie-maxtie queer hotch-potch,
The Coalition.

Auld Scotland has a raucle tongue;
She's just a devil wi' a rung;
And if she promise auld or young
To tak their part,
Tho' by the neck she should be strung,
She'll no desert.

And now, ye chosen Five-and-Forty,
May still your mither's heart support ye;
Then, though a minister grow dorty,
And kick your place,
Ye'll snap your fingers poor and hearty,
Before his face.

God bless your honours a' your days,
Wi' sowps o' kail and brats o' claise,
In spite o' a' the thievish kaes,
That haunt St. Jamies!
Your humble Poet sings and prays,
While Rab his name is.

POSTCRIPT.

Let half-starv'd slaves in warmer skies
See future wines, rich clust'ring, rise;
Their lot auld Scotland ne'er envies,
But blythe and frisky,
She eyes her freeborn, martial boys
Tak aff their whisky.

What tho' their Phœbus kinder warms,
While fragrance blooms and beauty charms!
When wretches range, in famish'd swarms,
The scented groves,
Or hounded forth, dishonour arms
In hungry droves.

Their gun's a burthen on their shoulther;
They downa bide the stink o' powther;
Their bauldest thought's a hank'ring swither
To stan' or rin,
Till skelp—a shot—they're aff, a'throwther,
To save their skin.

But bring a Scotsman frae his hill,
Clap in his cheek a Highland gill,
Say such is royal George's will,
And there's the foe,
He has nae thought but how to kill
Twa at a blow.

Nae cauld, faint-hearted doubtings tease him;
Death comes—wi' fearless eye he sees him;
Wi' bluidy han' a welcome gies him;
And when he fa's,
His latest draught o' breathin' lea's him
In faint huzzas!

Sages their solemn een may steek,
And raise a philosophic reek,
And physically causes seek,
In clime and season;
But tell me whisky's name in Greek,
I'll tell the reason.

Scotland, my auld, respected mither!
Tho' whiles ye moistify your leather,

THE JOLLY BEGGARS.

I lastly was with Curtis, among the floating batt'ries,
And there I left for witness an arm and a limb;

Till whare ye sit, on craps o' heather
Ye tine your dam;
Freedom and whisky gang thegither!—
Take aff your dram!

Scotch Drink.

"Gie him strong drink, until he wink,
That's sinking in despair;
And liquor guid to fire his bluid,
That's prest w' grief and care;
There let him bouse, and deep carouse,
Wi' bumpers flowing o'er,
Till he forgets his loves or debts.
And minds his griefs no more." (95.)
SOLOMON'S PROVERB, xxxi, 6, 7.

LET other poets raise a fracas,
'Bout vines, and wines, and dru'ken Bacchus,
And crabbit names and stories wrack us,
And grate our lug,
I sing the juice Scotch beer can mak us,
In glass or jug.

Oh thou, my Muse! guid auld Scotch drink;
Whether thro' wimplin' worms thou jink,
Or, richly brown, ream o'er the brink,
In glorious faem,
Inspire me, till I lisp and wink,
To sing thy name!

Let husky wheat the haughs adorn,
And aits set up their awnie horn,
And peas and beans, at e'en or morn,
Perfume the plain,
Leeze me on thee, John Barleycorn,
Thou king o' grain!

On thee aft Scotland chows her cood,
In souple scones, the wale o' food!
Or tumblin' in the boilin' flood
Wi' kail and beef;
But when thou pours thy strong heart's blood,
There thou shines chief,

Food fills the wame, and keeps us livin';
Tho' life's a gift no worth receivin',
When heavy dragg'd wi' pine and grievin';
But, oil'd by thee,
The wheels o' life gae down-hill scrievin',
Wi' rattlin' glee,

Thou clears the head o' doited Lear:
Thou cheers the heart o' drooping Care;
Thou strings the nerves o' Labour sair,
At's weary toil;
Thou even brightens dark Despair
Wi' gloomy smile.

Aft clad in massy, siller weed,
Wi' gentles thou erects thy head (96);
Yet humbly kind in time o' need,
The poor man's wine,
His wee drap parritch, or his bread,
Thou kitchens fine. (97)

K

Thou art the life o' public haunts;
But thee, what were our fairs and rants?
Ev'n godly meetings o' the saunts,
By thee inspir'd,
When gaping they besiege the tents (98),
Are doubly fir'd.

That merry night we get the corn in,
Oh sweetly then thou reams the horn in!
Or reekin' on a new-year morning
In cog or bicker,
And just a wee drap sp'ritual burn in,
And gusty sucker!

When Vulcan gies his bellows breath,
And ploughmen gather wi' their graith,
Oh rare! to see thee fizz and freath
I' th' lugget caup!
Then Burnewin comes on like death
At ev'ry chap.

Nae mercy, then, for air or steel;
The brawnie, bainie, ploughman chiel,
Brings hard owrehip, wi' sturdy wheel,
The strong forehammer,
Till block and studdie ring and reel
Wi' dinsome clamour.

When skirlin' weanies see the light,
Thou maks the gossips clatter bright,
How fumblin' cuifs their dearies slight;
Wae worth the name!
Nae howdie gets a social night,
Or plack frae them.

When neebors anger at a plea,
And just as wud as wud can be,
How easy can the barley-bree
Cement the quarrel!
Its aye the cheapest lawyer's fee,
To taste the barrel.

Alake! that e'er my Muse has reason
To wyte her countrymen wi' treason!
But monie daily weet their weason
Wi' liquors nice,
And hardly, in a winter's season,
E'er spier her price.

Wae worth that brandy, burning trash!
Fell source o' monie a pain and brash!
Twins monie a poor, doylt, drucken hash,
O' half his days;
And sends, beside, auld Scotland's cash
To her warst faes.

Ye Scots, wha wish auld Scotland well,
Ye chief, to you my tale I tell,
Poor plackless devils like mysel,
It sets you ill,
Wi' bitter, dearthfu' wines to mell,
Or foreign gill.

May gravels round his blather wrench,
And gouts torment him inch by inch,

Wha twists his gruntle wi' a glunch
O' sour disdain,
Out owre a glass o' whisky punch
Wi' honest men!

Oh whisky! soul o' plays and pranks!
Accept a Bardie's gratefu' thanks!
When wanting thee, what tuneless cranks
Are my poor verses!
Thou comes——they rattle i' their ranks
At ither's a—!

Thee, Ferintosh! oh sadly lost! (99)
Scotland lament frae coast to coast!
Now colic grips, and barkin' hoast,
May kill us a';
For loyal Forbes' charter'd boast,
Is ta'en awa!

Thae curst horse-leeches o' th' Excise,
Wha mak the whisky stells their prize!
Haud up thy han', Deil! ance, twice, thrice!
There, seize the blinkers!
And bake them up in brunstane pies
For poor d—nd drinkers,

Fortune! if thou'll but gie me still
Hale breeks, a scone, and whisky gill,
And rowth o' rhyme to rave at will,
Tak a' the rest,
And deal't about as thy blind skill
Directs thee best.

Address to the Unco Guid,

OR THE RIGIDLY RIGHTEOUS.

"My son, these maxims make a rule,
And lump them aye thegither;
The Rigid Righteous is a fool,
The Rigid Wise anither;
The cleanest corn that e'er was dight
May hae some pyles o' caff in;
So ne'er a fellow-creature slight
For random fits o' daffin."
SOLOMON—Eccles. vii, 16.

OH ye wha are sae guid yoursel,
Sae pious and sae holy,
Ye've nought to do but mark and tell
Your neebour's fauts and folly!
Whase life is like a weel-gaun mill,
Supplied wi' store o' water,
The heaped happer's ebbing still,
And still the clap plays clatter.

Hear me, ye venerable core,
As counsel for poor mortals,
That frequent pass douce Wisdom's door
For glaiket Folly's portals;
I, for their thoughtless, careless sakes,
Would here propone defences,
Their donsie tricks, their black mistakes,
Their failings and mischances.

Ye see your state wi' theirs compar'd,
And shudder at the niffer,
But cast a moment's fair regard,
What maks the mighty differ?
Discount what scant occasion gave
That purity ye pride in,
And (what's aft mair than a' the lave)
Your better art o' hiding.

Think, when your castigated pulse
Gies now and then a wallop,
What ragings must his veins convulse,
That still eternal gallop:
Wi' wind and tide fair i' your tail,
Right on ye scud your sea-way;
But in the teeth o' baith to sail,
It maks an unco lee-way.

See social life and glee sit down,
All joyous and unthinking,
Till, quite transmugrified, they're grown
Debauchery and drinking:
Oh would they stay to calculate
Th' eternal consequences;
Or your more dreaded hell to state,
D-mnation of expenses!

Ye high, exalted, virtuous dames,
Tied up in godly laces,
Before ye gie poor frailty names,
Suppose a change o' cases;
A dear lov'd lad, convenience snug,
A treacherous inclination—
But, let me whisper i' your lug,
Ye're aiblins nae temptation.

Then gently scan your brother man,
Still gentler sister woman;
Though they may gang a kennin' wrang,
To step aside is human:
One point must still be greatly dark,
The moving why they do it:
And just as lamely can ye mark,
How far perhaps they rue it.

Who made the heart, 'tis He alone
Decidedly can try us,
He knows each chord—its various tone,
Each spring—its various bias:
Then at the balance let's be mute,
We never can adjust it;
What's done we partly may compute,
But know not what's resisted.

Tam Samson's Elegy.

"An honest man's the noblest work of God."
POPE.

HAS auld Kilmarnock seen the deil?
Or great M'Kinlay (100) thrawn his heel?
Or Robertson (101) again grown weel,
To preach and read?

"Na, waur than a'!" cries ilka chiel—
Tam Samson's dead!

Kilmarnock lang may grunt and grane,
And sigh, and sob, and greet her lane,
And cleed her bairns, man, wife, and wean,
In mourning weed;
To death, she's dearly paid the kane—
Tam Samson's dead!

The brethren o' the mystic level
May hing their head in woefu' bevel,
While by their nose the tears will revel,
Like ony head;
Death's gi'en the lodge an unco devel—
Tam Samson's dead!

When winter muffles up his cloak,
And binds the mire like a rock;
When to the lochs the curlers flock
Wi' gleesome speed,
Wha will they station at the cock?—
Tam Samson's dead?

He was the king o' a' the core,
To guard, or draw, or wick a bore,
Or up the rink like Jehu roar
In time o' need;
But now he lags on death's hog-score—
Tam Samson's dead!

Now safe the stately sawmont sail,
And trouts be-dropp'd wi' crimson hail,—
And eels weel kenn'd for souple tail,
And geds for creed,
Since dark in death's fish-creel we wail
Tam Samson dead!

Rejoice, ye birring paitricks a';
Ye cootie moorcocks, crousely craw;
Ye maukins, cock your fud fu' braw,
Withouten dread;
Your mortal fae is now awa'—
Tam Samson's dead!

That woefu mourn be ever mourn'd
Saw him in shootin' graith adorn'd,
While pointers round impatient burn'd,
Frae couples freed;
But, och! he gaed and ne'er return'd!—
Tam Samson's dead!

In vain auld age his body batters;
In vain the gout his ancles fetters;
In vain the burns cam' down like waters,
An acre braid!
Now ev'ry auld wife, greetin', clatters,
Tam Samson's dead!

Owre many a weary hag he limpit,
And aye the tither shot he thumpit,
Till coward death behind him jumpit,
Wi' deadly feide;
Now he proclaims, wi' tout o' trumpet,
Tam Samson's dead!

When at his heart he felt the dagger,
He reel'd his wonted bottle-swagger,
But yet he drew the mortal trigger
Wi' weel-aim'd heed;
"L—d, five!" he cried, and owre did stagger—
Tam Samson's dead!

Ilk hoary hunter mourn'd a brither;
Ilk sportsman youth bemoan'd a father;
Yon auld grey stane, amang the heather,
Marks out his head,
Whare Burns has wrote, in rhyming blether,
Tam Samson's dead!

There now he lies, in lasting rest;
Perhaps upon his mould'ring breast
Some spitefu' muirfowl bigs her nest,
To hatch and breed;
Alas! nae mair he'll them molest!—
Tam Samson's dead!

When August winds the heather wave,
And sportsmen wander by yon grave,
Three volleys let his mem'ry crave
O' pouther and lead,
Till echoe answer frae her cave,
Tam Samson's dead!

Heav'n rest his saul, whare'er he be!
Is th' wish o' mony mae than me;
He had twa fauts, or maybe three,
Yet what remead?
Ae social, honest man want we:
Tam Samson's dead!

EPITAPH.

Tam Samson's weel worn clay here lies,
Ye canting zealots spare him!
If honest worth in heaven rise,
Ye'll mend or ye win near him.

PER CONTRA.

Go, Fame, and canter like a filly
Thro' e the streets and neuks o' Killie (102),
Tell ev'ry social, honest billy
To cease his grievin',
For yet, unskaith'd by death's gleg gullie,
Tam Samson's livin' (103)!

Despondency.

AN ODE.

Oppress'd with grief, oppress'd with care,
A burden more than I can bear,
I set me down and sigh;
Oh life! thou art a galling load.
Along a rough, a weary road,
To wretches such as I!
Dim-backward as I cast my view,
What sick'ning scenes appear!
What sorrows yet may pierce me thro',
Too justly I may fear!

Still caring, despairing,
Must be my bitter doom;
My woes here shall close ne'er
But with the closing tomb!
Happy, ye sons of busy life,
Who, equal to the bustling strife,
No other view regard!
Ev'n when the wished end's denied,
Yet while the busy means are plied,
They bring their own reward:
Whilst I, a hope-abandon'd wight,
Unfitted with an aim,
Meet ev'ry sad returning night
And joyless morn the same;
You, bustling, and justling,
Forget each grief and pain;
I listless, yet restless,
Find every prospect vain.
How blest the solitary's lot,
Who, all-forgetting, all-forgot,
Within his humble cell,
The cavern wild with tangling roots,
Sits o'er his newly-gather'd fruits,
Beside his crystal well!
Or haply to his ev'ning thought,
By unfrequented stream,
The ways of men are distant brought,
A faint collected dream;
While praising and raising
His thoughts to heav'n on high,
As wand'ring, meand'ring,
He views the solemn sky.
Than I, no lonely hermit plac'd
Where never human footstep trac'd,
Less fit to play the part;
The lucky moment to improve,
And just to stop, and just to move,
With self-respecting art:
But, ah! those pleasures, loves, and joys,
Which I too keenly taste,
The solitary can despise,
Can want, and yet be blest!
He needs not, he heeds not,
Or human love or hate,
Whilst I here, must cry here
At perfidy ingrate!
Oh! enviable, early days,
When dancing thoughtless pleasure's maze,
To care, to guilt unknown!
How ill exchang'd for riper times,
To feel the follies, or the crimes,
Of others or my own!
Ye tiny elves that guiltless sport,
Like linnets in the bush,
Ye little know the ills ye court,
When manhood is your wish!
The losses, the crosses,
That active man engage!
The fears all, the tears all,
Of dim declining age!

The Cotter's Saturday Night.

INSCRIBED TO ROBERT AIKIN, ESQ. (104)

"Let not ambition mock their useful toil,
Their homely joys and destiny obscure;
Nor grandeur hear, with a disdainful smile,
The short and simple annals of the poor."
(105)—GRAY.

MY loved, my honour'd, much respected friend,
No mercenary bard his homage pays:
With honest pride I scorn each selfish end:
My dearest meed, a friend's esteem and praise:
To you I sing, in simple Scottish lays,
The lowly train in life's sequester'd scene;
The native feelings strong, the guileless ways;
What Aitken in a cottage would have been;
Ah! tho' his worth unknown, far happier there, I ween.

November chill blaws loud wi' angry sough;
The short'ning winter-day is near a close;
The miry beasts retreating frae the pleugh;
The black'ning trains o' craws to their repose:
The toil-worn Cotter frae his labour goes,
This night his weekly moil is at an end,
Collects his spades, his mattocks, and his hoes,
Hoping the morn in ease and rest to spend,
And weary, o'er the moor, his course does hameward bend.

At length his lonely cot appears in view,
Beneath the shelter of an aged tree;
Th' expectant wee things toddlin, stacher thro'
To meet their dad, wi' flichterin' noise and glee.
His wee bit ingle, blinkin' bonnily,
His clean hearth-stane, his thriftie wifie's smile,
The lisping infant prattling on his knee,
Does a' his weary kiaugh and care beguile,
And makes him quite forget his labour and his toil.

Belyve, the elder bairns come drapping in,
At service out amang the farmers roun',
Some ca' the pleugh, some herd, some tentie rin
A cannie errand to a neibor town;
Their eldest hope, their Jenny, woman grown,
In youthfu' bloom, love sparklin' in her e'e,
Comes hame, perhaps, to show a bra' new gown,
Or deposit her sair-won penny fee,
To help her parents dear, if they in hardship be.

With joy unfeign'd brothers and sisters
meet, [spiers:
And each for other's weelfare kindly
The social hours, swift-wing'd, unnotic'd
fleet; [hears;
Each tells the uncos that he sees or
The parents, partial, eye their hopeful
years;
Anticipation forward points the view,
The mother, wi' her needle and her shears,
Gars auld claes look amaist as weel's
the new;
The father mixes a' wi' admonition due.

Their master's and their mistress's com-
mand,
The younkers a' are warned to obey;
And mind their labours wi' an eydent
hand, [play;
And ne'er, tho' out o' sight, to jauk or
"And oh! be sure to fear the Lord alway!
And mind your duty, duly, morn and
night!
Lest in temptation's path ye gang astray,
Implore His counsel and assisting
might: Lord aright!"
They never sought in vain that sought the

But, hark! a rap comes gently to the
door, [same,
Jenny wha kens the meaning o' the
Tells how a neibor lad cam o'er the moor,
To do some errands, and convoy her
hame.
The wily mother sees the conscious flame
Sparkle in Jenny's e'e, and flush her
cheek, [name,
Wi' heart-struck anxious care, inquires his
While Jenny hafflins is afraid to speak;
eel pleas'd the mother hears it's nae wild
worthless rake.

Wi' kindly welcome, Jenny brings him
ben; [e'e;
A strappin youth; he taks the mether's
Blithe Jenny sees the visit's no ill ta'en;
The father cracks of horses, pleughs,
and kye. [joy,
The youngster's artless heart o'erflows wi'
But blate and lathefu', scarce can weel
behave; [spy
The mother, wi' a woman's wiles, can
What makes the youth sae bashfu' an'
sae grave;
Weel pleas'd to think her bairn's respected
like the lave.

Oh happy love!—where love like this is
found! [compare!
Oh heart-felt raptures! bliss beyond
I've paced much this weary, mortal round,
And sage experience bids me this de-
clare— [spare,
"If Heaven a draught of heavenly pleasure
One cordial in this melancholy vale,
'Tis when a youthful, loving, modest pair
In other's arms breathe out the tender
tale, [the ev'ning gale."
Beneath the milk-white thorn that scents

Is there, in human form, that bears a heart,
A wretch! a villain! lost to love and
truth!—
That can, with studied, sly, ensnaring art,
Betray sweet Jenny's unsuspecting
youth? [smooth!
Curse on his perjur'd arts! dissembling
Are honour, virtue, conscience, all exil'd?
Is there no pity, no relenting ruth,
Points to the parents fondling o'er their
child? [traction wild?
Then paints the ruin'd maid, and their dis-

But now the supper crowns their simple
board, [food;
The halesome parritch, chief of Scotia's
The soupe their only hawkie does afford,
That 'yont the hallan snugly chows her
cood: [mood,
The dame brings forth, in complimental
To grace the lad, her weel-hain'd keb-
luck, fell,
And aft he's prest, and aft he ca's it guid;
The frugal wifie, garrulous, will tell,
How 'twas a towmond auld, sin' lint was
i' the bell.

The cheerfu' supper done, wi' serious face,
They, round the ingle, form a circle wide;
The sire turns o'er, with patriarchal grace,
The big ha'-bible, ance his father's pride;
His bonnet rev'rently is laid aside,
His lyart haffets wearing thin and bare;
Those strains that once did sweet in Zion
glide,
He wales a portion with judicious care;
And "Let us worship God!" he says, with
solemn air.

They chant their artless notes in simple
guise; [aim:
They tune their hearts, by far the noblest
Perhaps Dundee's wild-warbling measures
rise, [name,
Or plaintive Martyrs, worthy of the
Or noble Elgin beets the heaven-ward
flame,
The sweetest far of Scotia's holy lays:
Compar'd with these, Italian trills are
tame; [raise;
The tickl'd ear no heart-felt raptures
Nae unison hae they with our Creator's
praise.

The priest-like father reads the sacred page—
How Abram was the friend of GOD on [high;
Or, Moses bade eternal warfare wage
With Amalek's ungracious progeny;
Or how the royal bard did groaning lie
Beneath the stroke of Heaven's avenging ire;
Or Job's pathetic plaint, and wailing cry;
Or rapt Isaiah's wild, seraphic fire;
Or other holy seers that tune the sacred lyre.

Perhaps the Christian volume is the theme—
How guiltless blood for guilty man was [shed;
How He, who bore in Heaven the second name,
Had not on earth whereon to lay his [head:
How his first followers and servants sped,
The precepts sage they wrote to many a land:
How he, who lone in Patmos banished,
Saw in the sun a mighty angel stand;
And heard great Bab'lon's doom pronounced by Heaven's command.

Then kneeling down to HEAVEN'S ETERNAL KING,
The saint, the father, and the husband [prays:
Hope "springs exulting on triumphant wing," (106)
That thus they all shall meet in future [days:
There ever bask in uncreated rays,
No more to sigh, or shed the bitter tear,
Together hymning their Creator's praise,
In such society, yet still more dear;
While circling time moves round in an eternal sphere.

Compar'd with this, how poor Religion's pride,
In all the pomp of method, and of art,
When men display to congregations wide,
Devotion's ev'ry grace, except the heart!
The pow'r, incens'd, the pageant will desert,
The pompous strain, the sacerdotal stole;
But, haply, in some cottage far apart,
May hear, well pleas'd, the language of the soul;
And in his book of life the inmates poor [enrol.

Then homeward all take off their sev'ral way;
The youngling cottagers retire to rest:
The parent-pair their secret homage pay,
And proffer up to Heaven the warm request,
That HE, who stills the raven's clam'rous [nest,
And decks the lily fair in flow'ry pride,
Would, in the way his wisdom sees the best,
For them and for their little ones provide;
But, chiefly, in their hearts with grace divine preside.

From scenes like these old Scotia's grandeur springs,
That makes her lov'd at home, rever'd [abroad:
Princes and lords are but the breath of kings,
"An honest man's the noblest work of [GOD!"
And certes, in fair virtue's heav'nly road,
The cottage leaves the palace far behind;
What is a lordling's pomp?—a cumbrous load,
Disguising oft the wretch of human [kind
Studied in arts of hell, in wickedness refin'd!

Oh Scotia! my dear, my native soil!
For whom my warmest wish to Heaven is sent!
Long may thy hardy sons of rustic toil,
Be blest with health, and peace, and sweet content!
And oh! may Heaven their simple lives [prevent
From luxury's contagion, weak and vile!
Then, howe'er crowns and coronets be rent,
A virtuous populace may rise the while,
And stand a wall of fire around their much-lov'd isle.

Oh Thou! who pour'd the patriotic tide
That stream'd through Wallace's undaunted heart,
Who dar'd to nobly stem tyrannic pride,
Or nobly die the second glorious part,
(The patriot's God, peculiarly thou art,
His friend, inspirer, guardian, and reward!)
Oh never, never, Scotia's realm desert;
But still the patriot, and the patriot bard,
In bright succession raise, her ornament and [guard!

To a Mountain Daisy.

IN TURNING ONE DOWN WITH THE PLOUGH IN APRIL, 1786. (107)

WEE, modest, crimson-tipped flow'r,
Thou's met me in an evil hour;
For I maun crush amang the stoure
Thy slender stem:
To spare thee now is past my pow'r,
Thou bonnie gem.

Alas! it's no thy neibor sweet,
The bonnie lark, companion meet,
Bending thee 'mang the dewy weet!
Wi' speckl'd breast,
When up-ward-springing, blythe, to greet
The purpling east.

Cauld blew the bitter-biting north
Upon thy early, humble birth;
Yet cheerfully thou glinted forth
Amid the storm,
Scarce rear'd above the parent earth
Thy tender form.

The flaunting flowers our gardens yield,
High shelt'ring woods and wa's maun shield:
But thou, beneath the random bield
O' clod or stane,
Adorn the histie stibble-field,
Unseen, alane.

There, in thy scanty mantle clad,
Thy snawie bosom sun-ward spread,
Thou lifts thy unassuming head,
In humble guise;
But now the share uptears thy bed
And low thou lies!

Such is the fate of artless maid,
Sweet flow'ret of the rural shade!
By love's simplicity betray'd,
And guileless trust,
Till she, like thee, all soil'd, is laid
Low i' the dust.

Such is the fate of simple bard,
On life's rough ocean luckless starr'd!
Unskilful he to note the card
Of prudent lore,
Till billows rage, and gales blow hard,
And whelm him o'er!

Such fate to suffering worth is giv'n,
Who long with wants and woes has striv'n,
By human pride or cunning driv'n
To mis'ry's brink,
Till wrench'd of ev'ry stay but Heav'n,
He, ruin'd, sink!

Ev'n thou who mourn'st the Daisy's fate,
That fate is thine—no distant date;
Stern Ruin's ploughshare drives, elate,
Full on thy bloom,
Till crush'd beneath the furrow's weight,
Shall be thy doom.

Epistle to a Young Friend.

MAY, 1796. (108)

I LANG hae thought, my youthfu' friend,
A something to have sent you,
Though it should serve nae other end
Than just a kind momento;
But how the subject-theme may gang,
Let time and chance determine;
Perhaps it may turn out a sang,
Perhaps turn out a sermon.

Ye'll try the world fu' soon, my lad,
And, Andrew dear, believe me,
Ye'll find mankind an unco squad,
And muckle they may grieve ye:
For care and trouble set your thought,
Ev'n when your end's attained;
And a' your views may come to nought,
Where ev'ry nerve is strained.

I'll no say men are villains a':
The real, harden'd wicked,
Wha hae nae check but human law,
Are to a few restricked
But, och! mankind are unco weak,
And little to be trusted;
If self the wavering balance shake,
It's rarely right adjusted!

Yet they wha fa' in fortune's strife,
Their fate we should na censure,
For still th' important end of life,
They equally may answer;
A man may hae an honest heart,
Tho' poortith hourly stare him;
A man may tak a neibor's part.
Yet hae no cash to spare him.

Aye free, aff han, your story tell,
When wi' a bosom crony;
But still keep something to yoursel
Ye scarcely tell to ony.
Conceal yoursel as weel's ye can
Frae critical dissection;
But keek through ev'ry other man,
Wi' sharpen'd, sly inspection.

The sacred lowe o' weel-plac'd love,
Luxuriantly indulge it;
But never tempt th' illicit rove,
Tho' naething should divulge it:
I waive the quantum o' the sin,
The hazard of concealing;
But, och! it hardens a' within,
And petrifies the feeling!

To catch dame Fortune's golden smile,
Assiduous wait upon her;
And gather gear by ev'ry wile
That's justified by honour;
Not for to hide it in a hedge,
Nor for a train-attendant,
But for the glorious privilege
Of being independent.

The fear o' hell's a hangman's whip
To haud the wretch in order;
But where ye feel your honour grip,
Let that aye be your border:
Its slightest touches, instant pause—
Debar a' side pretences;
And resolutely keeps its laws,
Uncaring consequences.

The great Creator to revere
  Must sure become the creature,
But still the preaching can forbear,
  And e'en the rigid feature:
Yet ne'er with wits profane to range,
  Be complaisance extended;
An Atheist laugh's a poor exchange
  For Deity offended!

When ranting round in pleasure's ring,
  Religion may be blinded;
Or if she gie a random sting,
  It may be little minded;
But when on life we're tempest driv'n,
  A conscience but a canker,
A correspondence fix'd wi' Heav'n
  Is sure a noble anchor!

Adieu! dear, amiable youth
  Your heart can ne'er be wanting!
May prudence, fortitude, and truth
  Erect your brow undaunting!
In ploughman phrase, "God send you speed,"
  Still daily to grow wiser:
And may you better reck the rede
  Than ever did th' adviser!

A Dedication to Gavin Hamilton, Esq.

(109)

Expect na, sir, in this narration,
A fleeching, fleth'rin dedication,
To roose you up, and ca' you guid,
And sprung o' great and noble bluid,
Because ye're surnam'd like his grace;
Perhaps related to the race;
Then when I'm tir'd, and sae are ye,
Wi' mony a fulsome, sinfu' lie,
Set up a face, how I stop short,
For fear your modesty be hurt.

This may do—maun do, sir, wi' them wha
Maun please the great folk for a wamefou;
For me!—sae laigh I needna bow,
For, lord be thankit, I can plough;
And when I downa yoke a naig,
Then, Lord be thankit, I can beg;
Sae I shall say, and that's nae flatt'rin',
It's just sic poet, and sic patron.
The Poet, some guid angel help him,
Or else, I fear some ill ane skelp him,
He may do weel for a' he's done yet,
But only he's no just begun yet.

The Patron (sir, ye maun forgive me,
I winna lie, come what will o' me),
On ev'ry hand it will allowed be,
He's just—nae better than he should be.

I readily and freely grant,
He downa see a poor man want;
What's no his aim he winna tak it,
What ance he says he winna break it;
Ought he can lend he'll no refus't
Till aft his goodness is abus'd;
And rascals whyles that do him wrang,
Ev'n that, he does na mind it lang:
As master, landlord, husband, father,
He does na fail his part in either.

But then, nae thanks to him for a' that;
Nae godly symptom ye can ca' that;
It's naething but a milder feature,
Of our poor sinfu', corrupt nature:
Ye'll get the best o' moral works,
'Mang black Gentoos and pagan Turks,
Or hunter's wild on Ponotaxi,
Wha never heard of orthodoxy.
That he's the poor man's friend in need,
The gentleman in word and deed,
It's no thro' terror of d-mn-tion;
It's just a carnal inclination.

Morality, thou deadly bane,
Thy tens o' thousands thou hast slain!
Vain is his hope, whose stay and trust is
In moral mercy, truth, and justice!

No—stretch a point to catch a plack;
Abuse a brother to his back;
Seal thro' a winnock frae a wh-re,
But point the rake that taks the door;
Be to the poor like ony whunstane,
And haud their noses to the grunstane,
Ply ev'ry art o' legal thieving!
No matter—stick to sound believing!

Learn three-mile pray'rs, and half-mile graces,
Wi' weel-spread looves, and lang wry faces;
Grunt up a solemn, lengthen'd groan,
And damn a' parties but your own;
I'll warrant then, ye're nae deceiver,
A steady, sturdy, staunch believer.

Oh ye wha leaves the springs o' Calvin,
For gumlie dubs of your ain delvin'!
Ye sons of heresy and error,
Ye'll some day squeel in quaking terror
When Vengeance draws the sword in wrath,
And in the fire throws the sheath;
When Ruin, with his sweeping besom,
Just frets, till heav'n commission gies him:
While o'er the harp pale Mis'ry moans,
And strikes the ever-deep'ning tones,
Still louder shrieks, and heavier groans!

Your pardon, Sir, for this digression,
I maist forgat my dedication;
But when divinity comes cross me,
My readers still are sure to loss me.

So, Sir, ye see 'twas nae daft vapour,
But I maturely thought it proper,
When a' my woaks I did review,
To dedicate them, Sir, to you:
Because (ye need na tak it ill)
I thought them something lik yoursel.

Then patronise them wi' your favour,
And your petitioner shall ever——
I had amaist said, ever pray,
But that's a word I need na say:
For prayin' I hae little skill o't;
I'm baith dead sweer, and wretched ill o't;
But I'se repeat each poor man's pray'r,
That kens or hears about you, Sir—

"May ne'er misfortune's growling bark,
Howl thro' the dwelling o' the clerk!
May ne'er his gen'rous, honest heart,
For that same gen'rous spirit smart!
May Kennedy's far-honour'd name
Lang beet his hymeneal flame,
Till Hamiltons, at least a dizen,
Are by their canty fireside risen:
Five bonnie lasses round their table,
And seven braw fellows, stout and able
To serve their king and country weel,
By word, or pen, or pointed steel!
May health and peace, with mutual rays,
Shine on the ev'ning o' his days,
Till his wee curlie John's ier-oe,
When ebbing life nae mair shall flow,
The last, sad, mournful rites bestow."

I will not wind a lang conclusion,
With complimentary effusion:
But whilst your wishes and endeavours
Are blest with fortune's smiles and favours,
I am, dear Sir, with zeal most fervent,
Your much indebted, humble servant.
But if (which pow'rs above prevent)
That iron-hearted carl, Want,

Attended in his grim advances,
By sad mistakes and black mischances,
While hopes, and joys, and pleasures fly him,
Make you as poor a dog as I am,
Your humble servant then no more;
For who would humbly serve the poor!
But, by a poor man's hopes in Heav'n!
While recollection's power is giv'n,
If, in the vale of humble life,
The victim sad of fortune's strife,
I, thro' the tender gushing tear,
Should recognise my master dear,
If friendless, low, we meet together,
Then, Sir, your hand—my friend and broter.

A Dream.

"Thoughts, words, and deeds, the statute blames with reason:
But surely dreams were ne'er indicted treason." (110)

Guid-mornin' to your Majesty!
May Heaven augment your blisses,
On ev'ry new birth-day ye see,
A humble poet wishes!
My bardship here, at your levee,
On sic a day as this is,
Is sure an uncouth sight to see,
Amang thae birth-day dresses
Sae fine this day.

I see ye're complimented thrang,
By many a lord and lady;
"God save the king!" 's a cuckoo sang
That's unco easy said aye;
The poets, too, a venal gang,
Wi' rhymes weel-turn'd and ready,
Wad gar you trow ye ne'er do wrang,
But aye unerring steady,
On sic a day.

For me! before a monarch's face,
Ev'n there I winna flatter;
For neither pension, post, nor place,
Am I your humble debtor:
So, nae reflection on your grace,
Your kingship to bespatter;
There's mony waur been o' the race,
And aiblins ane been better
Than you this day.

'Tis very true, my sov'reign king,
My skill may weel be doubted:
But facts are chiels that winna ding,
And downa be disputed:
Your royal nest, beneath your wing,
Is e'en right reft and clouted,
And now the third part of the string,
And less, will gang about it
Than did ae day.

Far be't frae me that I aspire
To blame your legislation,
Or say, ye wisdom want, or fire,
To rule this mighty nation!
But faith! I muckle doubt, my sire,
Ye've trusted ministration
To chaps, wha, in a barn or byre,
Wad better fill'd their station
Than courts yon day.

And now ye've gien auld Britain peace;
Her broken shins to plaister;
Your sair taxation does her fleece,
Till she has scarce a tester;
For me, thank God, my life's a lease,
Nae bargain wearing faster,
Or, faith! I fear, that, wi' the geese,
I shortly boost to pasture
I' the craft some day.

I'm no mistrusting Willie Pitt,
  When taxes he enlarges,
(And Will's a true guid fallow's get (111)
  A name not envy spairges),
That he intends to pay your debt,
  And lessen a' your charges;
But, G-d-sake! let nae saving-fit
  Abridge your bonnie barges (112)
      And boats this day.

Adieu, my liege! may freedom geck
  Beneath your high protection;
And may ye rax corruption's neck,
  And gie her for dissection!
But since I'm here, I'll no neglect,
  In loyal, true affection,
To pay your Queen, with due respect,
  My fealty and subjection
      This great birth-day.

Hail, Majesty Most Excellent!
  While nobles strive to please ye,
Will ye accept a compliment
  A simple poet gies you?
Thae bonnie bairntime, Heav'n has lent,
  Still higher may they heeze ye
In bliss, till fate some day is sent,
  For ever to release ye
      Frae care that day.

For you, young potentate o' Wales,
  I tell your Highness fairly,
Down pleasure's stream, wi' swelling sails,
  I'm tauld ye're driving rarely;
But some day ye may gnaw your nails,
  And curse your folly sairly,
That e'er ye brak Diana's pales,
  Or rattl'd dice wi' Charlie (113),
      By night or day.

Yet aft a ragged cowte's been known
  To mak a noble aiver;
So, ye may doucely fill a throne,
  For a' their clish-ma-claver:
There, him at Agincourt wha shone,
  Few better were or braver;
And yet, wi' funny, queer Sir John,
  He was an unco shaver
      For monie a day (114.)

For you, right rev'rend Osnaburg (115),
  Nane sets the lawn-sleeve sweeter,
Altho' a ribbon at your lug,
  Wad been a dress completer:
As ye disown yon paughty dog
  That bears the keys of Peter,
Then, swith! and get awife to hug,
  Or, trouth! ye'll stain the mitre,
      Some luckless day.

Young, royal Tarry Breeks (116), I learn,
  Ye've lately come athrawt her;
A glorious galley (117), stem and stern,
  Weel rigg'd for Venus' barter;
But first hang out, that she'll discern
  Your hymeneal charter,
Then heave aboard your grapple airn,
  And, large upon her quarter,
      Come full that day.

Ye, lastly, bonnie blossoms a',
  Ye royal lasses dainty,
Heav'n mak ye guid as well as braw,
  And gie you lads a-plenty:
But sneer na British boys awa',
  For kings are unco scant eye;
And German gentles are but sma',
  They're better just than want aye
      On onie day.

God bless you a'! consider now,
  Ye're unco muckle dautet;
But ere the course o' life be thro',
  It may be bitter sautet:
And I hae seen their coggie fou,
  That yet hae tarrow't at it;
But or the day was done, I trow,
  The luggen they hae clautet
      Fu' clean that day.

A Bard's Epitaph.

Is there a whim-inspired fool,
Owre fast for thought, owre hot for rule,
Owre blate to seek, owre proud to snool,
      Let him draw near;
And owre this grassy heap sing dool,
      And drap a tear.

Is there a bard of rustic song,
Who, noteless, steals the crowds among,
That weekly this area throng,
      Oh, pass not by!
But, with a frater-feeling strong,
      Here, heave a sigh.

Is there a man, whose judgment clear,
Can others teach the course to steer,
Yet runs, himself, life's mad career,
      Wild as the wave;
Here pause—and, through the starting tear,
      Survey this grave.

The poor inhabitant below,
Was quick to learn, and wise to know,
And keenly felt the friendly glow,
      And softer flame;
But thoughtless follies laid him low,
      And stain'd his name!

Reader, attend—whether thy soul
Soar's fancy's flights beyond the pole,
Or darkling grubs this earthly hole,
      In low pursuit;
Know, prudent, cautious self-control
      Is wisdom's root.

The Twa Dogs,

A TALE. (118)

'TWAS in that place o' Scotland's isle
That bears the name o' Auld King Coil (119),
Upon a bonnie day in June,
When wearing through the afternoon,
Twa dogs that were na thrang at hame,
Forgather'd ance upon a time.

The first I'll name, they ca'd him Cæsar,
Was keepit for his honour's pleasure;
His hair, his size, his mouth, his lugs,
Show'd he was nane o' Scotland's dogs;
But whalpit some place far abroad,
Whare sailor's gang to fish for cod.

His locked, letter'd, braw brass collar
Show'd him the gentleman and scholar;
But though he was o' high degree,
The fient a pride—nae pride had he;
But wad hae spent an hour caressin',
E'en wi' a tinkler-gipsy's messin'.
At kirk or market, mill or smiddie,
Nae tawted tyke, though ere sae duddie,
But he wad stan't, as glad to see him,
And stroan't on stanes and hillocks wi' him.
The tither was a ploughman's collie,
A rhyming, ranting, raving billie,
Wha for his friend and comrade had him,
And in his freaks had Luath ca'd him,
After some dog in Highland sang (120),
Was made lang syne—Lord knows how lang.
He was a gash and faithful tyke,
As ever lap or sheugh or dyke.
His honest, sonsie, baws'nt face,
Aye gat him friends in ilka place,
His breast was white, his touzie back
Weel clad wi' coat o' glossy black;
His gaucie tale, wi' upward curl,
Hung o'er his hurdies wi' a swirl.

Nae doubt but they were fain o' ither,
And unco pack and thick thegither:
Wi' social nose whyles snuff'd and snowkit.
Whyles mice and moudieworts they howkit;
Whyles scour'd awa in lang excursion,
And worried ither in diversion;
Until wi' daffin' weary grown,
Upon a knowe they sat them down,
And there began a lang digression
About the lords o' the creation.

CÆSAR.

I've aften wonder'd, honest Luath,
What sort o' life poor dogs like you have;
And when the gentry's life I saw,
What way poor bodies liv'd ava.

Our laird gets in his racked rents,
His coals, his kain, and a' his stents;
He rises when he likes himsel;
His flunkies answer at the bell;
He ca's his coach, he ca's his horse;
He draws a bonnie silken purse
As lang's my tail, whare, through the steeks,
The yellow letter'd Geordie keeks.

Frae morn to e'en its nought but toiling,
At baking, roasting, frying, boiling;
And though the gentry first are stechin,
Yet e'en the ha' folk fill their pechan
Wi' sauce, ragouts, and sic like trashtrie:
That's little short o' downright wastrie.
Our whipper-in, wee blastit wonner,
Poor worthless elf, it eats a dinner,
Better than ony tenant man
His hanour has in a' the lan';
And what poor cot-folk pit their painch in,
I own its past my comprehension.

LUATH.

Trowth, Cæsar, whyles they're fash't enough;
A cotter howkin' in a sheugh,
Wi' dirty stanes biggin' a dyke,
Baring a quarry, and sic like;
Himself, a wife, he thus sustains,
A smytrie o' wee duddie weans,
And nought but his han' dark, to keep
Them right and tight in thack and rape.

And when they meet wi' sair disasters,
Like loss o' health, or want o' masters,
Ye maist wad think, a wee touch langer,
And they maun starve o' cauld or hunger;
But, how it comes, I never kenn'd yet,
Theyre' maistly wonderfu' contented:
And buirdly chiels, and clever hizzies,
Are bred in sic a way as this is.

CÆSAR.

But then to see how ye're neglecit,
How huff'd, and cuff'd, and disrespeckit!
L—d, man, our gentry care as little
For delvers, ditchers, and sic cattle;
They gang as saucy by poor folk,
As I wad by a stinkin' brock.
I've notic'd, on our Laird's court-day,
And mony a time my heart's been wae,
Poor tenant bodies, scant o' cash,
How they maun thole a factor's snash;
He'll stamp and threaten, curse and swear,
He'll apprehend them, poind their gear;
While they maun stan', wi' aspect humble,
And hear it a', and fear and tremble!
I see how folk live that hae riches;
But surely poor folk maun be wretches!

LUATH.

They're no sae wretched's ane wad think;
Tho' constantly on poortith's brink:
They're sae accustom'd wi' the sight,
The view o't gies them little fright.

Then chance and fortune are sae guided,
They're aye in less or mair provided;
And tho' fatigu'd wi' close employment,
A blink o' rest's sweet enjoyment.

The dearest comfort o' their lives,
Their grushie weans and faithfu' wives;
The prattling things are just their pride,
That sweetens a' their fire-side;
And whyles twalpennie worth o' nappy
Can make the bodies unco happy;
They lay aside their private cares,
To mind the Kirk and State affairs:
They'll talk o' patronage and priests,
Wi' kindling fury in their breasts.
Or tell what new taxation's comin',
And ferlie at the folk in Lon'on.

As bleak-fac'd Hallowmas returns,
They get the jovial, ranting kirns,
When rural life, o' ev'ry station,
Unite in common recreation;
Love blinks, Wit slaps, and social Mirth
Forgets there's Care upo' the earth.

That merry day the year begins,
They bar the door on frosty win's;
The nappy reeks wi' mantling ream,
And sheds a heart-inspiring steam;
The luntin pipe, and sneeshin mill,
Are handed round wi' right guid will;
The cantie auld folks crackin' crouse,
The young anes rantin' thro' the house—
My heart has been sae fain to see them,
That I for joy hae barkit wit' them.

Still it's owre true that ye hae said,
Sic game is now owre aften play'd.
There's monie a creditable stock
O' decent, honest, fawsont fo'k,
Are riven out baith root and branch,
Some rascal's pridefu' greed to quench,
Wha thinks to knit himsel the faster
In favour wi' some gentle master,
Wha' aiblins thrang a parliamentin',
For Britain's guid his saul indentin'——

CÆSAR.

Haith, lad, ye little ken about it;
For Britain's guid! guid faith, I doubt it.
Say rather, gaun as Premiers lead him,
And saying ay or no's they bid him:
At operas and plays parading,
Mortgaging, gambling, masquerading:
Or may be, in a frolic daft,
To Hague or Calais takes a waft,
To mak a tour and tak a whirl,
To learn *bon ton*, and see the worl'.

There' at Vienna or Versailles,
He rives his father's auld entails;
Or by Madrid he takes the route,
To thrum guitars, and fecht wi' nowte;
Or down Italian vista startles,
W-re hunting amang groves o' myrtles;
Then bouses drumly German water,
To mak himsel' look fair and fatter,
And clear the consequential sorrows,
Love-gifts of Carnival signoras.
For Britain's guid!—for her destruction!
Wi' dissipation, feud, and faction.

LUATH.

Hech man! dear sirs! is that the gate
They waste sae mony a braw estate!
Are we sae foughten and harass'd
For gear to gang that gate at last!

Oh would they stay aback frae courts,
And please themselves wi' countra sports,
It wad for ev'ry ane be better,
The Laird, the Tenant, and the Cotter!
For thae frank, rantin', ramblin' billies,
Fient haet o' them's ill-hearted fellows;
Except for breakin' o' their timmer,
Or speakin' lightly o' their limmer,
Or shootin' o' a hare or moor-cock,
The ne'er a bit they're ill to poor folk.

But will ye tell me, Master Cæsar,
Sure great folk's life's a life o' pleasure?
Nae cauld or hunger e'er can steer them,
The vera thought o't need na fear them,

CÆSAR.

L—d, man, were ye but whyles whare I am,
The gentles ye wad ne'er envy 'em.
It's true, they needna starve or sweat,
Thro' winter's cauld, or simmer's heat;
They've nae sair wark to craze their banes,
And fill auld age wi' grips and granes;
But human bodies are sic fools,
For a' their colleges and schools,
That when nae real ills perplex them,
They mak enow themselves to vex them;
And aye the less they hae to sturt them,
In like proportion less will hurt them.

A country fellow at the pleugh,
His acre's till'd, he's right eneugh;
A country girl at her wheel,
Her dizzen's done, she's unco weel:
But Gentlemen, and Ladies warst,
Wi' ev'n down want o' wark are curst,
They loiter, lounging, lank, and lazy;
Tho' deil haet ails them, yet uneasy;
Their days insipid, dull, and tasteless;
Their nights unquiet, lang, and restless;
And e'en their sports, their balls and races,
Their gallopping thro' public places,
There's sic parade, sic pomp, and art,
The joy can scarcely reach the heart.
The men cast out in party matches,
Then sawther a' in deep debauches;

THE COTTER'S SATURDAY NIGHT.

The sire turns o'er, wi' patriarchal grace,
The big ha'-Bible, ance his father's pride:

Ae night they're mad wi' drink and wh-ring,
Niest day their life is past enduring.
The Ladies arm-in-arm in clusters,
As great and gracious a' as sisters;
But hear their absent thoughts o' ither,
They're a' run deils and jads thegither.
Whyles, o'er the wee bit cup and platie,
They sip the scandal potion pretty;
Or lee-lang nights, wi' crabbit leuks,
Pore owre the devil's pictur'd beuks;
Stake on a chance a farmer's stackyard,
And cheat like onie unhang'd blackguard.
There's some exception, man and woman;
But this is Gentry's life in common.

By this, the sun was out o' sight
And darker gloaming brought the night:
The bum-clock humm'd wi' lazy drone;
The kye stood rowtin' i' the loan;
When up they gat, and shook their lugs,
Rejoic'd they were na men, but dogs;
And each took off his several way,
Resolv'd to meet some ither day.

Lament,

OCCASIONED BY THE UNFORTUNATE ISSUE OF A FRIEND'S AMOUR. (121)

"Alas! how oft does goodness wound itself!
And sweet affection prove the spring of woe!"
HOME!

OH thou pale orb, that silent shines,
While care-untroubled mortals sleep!
Thou seest a wretch who inly pines,
And wanders here to wail and weep!
With woe I nightly vigils keep,
Beneath thy wan, unwarming beam;
And mourn, in lamentation deep,
How life and love are all a dream.

I joyless view thy rays adorn
The faintly marked distant hill:
I joyless view thy trembling horn,
Reflected in the gurgling rill:
My fondly-fluttering heart, be still!
Thou busy pow'r, remembrance, cease!
Ah! must the agonizing thrill
For ever bar returning peace!

No idly-feign'd poetic pains,
My sad, love-lorn lamentings claim;
No shepherd's pipe—Arcadian strains;
No fabled tortures, quaint and tame:
The plighted faith; the mutual flame;
The oft-attested Pow'rs above;
The promis'd father's tender name;
These were the pledges of my love!

Encircled in her clasping arms,
How have the raptur'd moments flown
How have I wish'd for fortune's charms,
For her dear sake, and her's alone!
And must I think it—is she gone,
My secret heart's exulting boast?
And does she heedless hear my groan?
And is she ever, ever lost?

Oh! can she bear so base a heart,
So lost to honour, lost to truth,
As from the fondest lover part,
The plighted husband of her youth!
Alas! life's path may be unsmooth!
Her way may lie thro' rough distress!
Then, who her pangs and pains will soothe,
Her sorrows share, and make them less?

Ye winged hours that o'er us past,
Enraptur'd more, the more enjoy'd,
Your dear remembrance in my breast,
My fondly treasur'd thoughts employ'd.
That breast, how dreary now, and void,
For her too scanty once of room!
Ev'n ev'ry ray of hope destroy'd,
And not a wish to guild the gloom!

The morn that warns th' approaching day,
Awakes me up to toil and woe:
I see the hours in long array,
That I must suffer, lingering, slow.
Full many a pang, and many a throe,
Keen recollection's direful train,
Must wring my soul, ere Phœbus, low,
Shall kiss the distant, western main.

And when my nightly couch I try,
Sore-harass'd out with care and grief,
My toil-beat nerves, and tear-worn eye,
Keep watchings with the nightly thief:
Or if I slumber, fancy, chief,
Reigns haggard-wild, in sore affright:
Ev'n day, all-bitter, brings relief,
From such a horror-breathing night.

Oh! thou bright queen, who, o'er th' expause,
Now highest reign'st, with boundless sway!
Oft has thy silent-marking glance
Observ'd us, fondly-wand'ring, stray!
The time, unheeded, sped away,
While love's luxurious pulse beat high,
Beneath thy silver-gleaming ray,
To mark the mutual kindling eye.

Oh! scenes in strong remembrance set!
Scenes never, never to return!
Scenes, if in stupor I forget,
Again I feel, again I burn!
From ev'ry joy and pleasure torn,
Life's weary vale I'll wander thro';
And hopeless, comfortless, I'll mourn
A faithless woman's broken vow.

Address to Edinburgh.

EDINA! Scotia's darling seat!
All hail thy palaces and towr'rs.
Where once beneath a monarch's feet
Sat Legislation's sov'reign pow'rs!
From marking wildly-scatter'd flow'rs,
As on the banks of Ayr I stray'd,
And singing, lone, the ling'ring hours,
I shelter in thy honour'd shade.

Here wealth still swells the golden tide,
As busy Trade his labour plies;
There Architecture's noble pride
Bids elegance and splendour rise;
Here Justice, from her native skies,
High wields her balance and her rod;
There learning, with his eagle eyes,
Seeks Science in her coy abode.

Thy sons, Edina! social, kind,
With open arms the stranger hail;
Their views enlarg'd, their lib'ral mind,
Above the narrow, rural vale;
Attentive still to sorrow's wail,
Or modest merit's silent claim;
And never may their sources fail!
And never envy blot their name!

Thy daughters bright thy walks adorn,
Gay as the gilded summer sky,
Sweet as the dewy milk-white thorn,
Dear as the raptur'd thrill of joy!
Fair Burnet strikes th' adoring eye,
Heav'n's beauties on my fancy shine;
I see the Sire of Love on high,
And own his work indeed divine (122)!

There, watching high the least alarms.
Thy rough, rude fortress gleams afar:
Like some bold vet'ran, grey in arms,
And mark'd with many a seaming scar:
The pond'rous wall and massy bar,
Grim-rising o'er the rugged rock;
Have oft withstood assailing war,
And oft repell'd th' invader's shock,

With awe-struck thought, and pitying tears,
I view that noble, stately dome,
Where Scotia's kings of other years,
Fam'd heroes! had their royal home:
Alas, how chang'd the times to come!
Their royal name low in the dust!
Their hapless race wild-wand'ring roam,
Tho' rigid law cries out, 'twas just!

Wild beats my heart to trace your steps,
Whose ancestors, in days of yore,
Thro' hostile ranks and ruin'd gaps
Old Scotia's bloody lion bore:
Ev'n I who sing in rustic lore,
Haply, my sires have left their shed,
And fac'd grim danger's loudest roar,
Bold-following where your fathers led!

Edina! Scotia's darling seat!
All hail thy palaces and tow'rs,
Where once beneath a monarch's feet
Sat Legislation's sov'reign pow'rs!
From marking wildly-scatter'd flow'rs,
As on the banks of Ayr I stray'd,
And singing, lone, the ling'ring hours,
I shelter in thy honour'd shade.

The Brigs of Ayr.

INSCRIBED TO JOHN BALLANTYNE, ESQ., AYR.

THE simple Bard, rough at the rustic plough,
Learning his tuneful trade from ev'ry bough;
The chanting linnet, or the mellow thrush,
Hailing the setting sun, sweet, in the green thorn bush;
The soaring lark, the perching red-breast shrill,
Or deep-ton'd plovers, grey, wild-whistling o'er the hill;
Shall he, nurst in the peasant's lowly shed,
To hardy independence bravely bred,
By early poverty to hardship steel'd,
And train'd to arms in stern misfortune's field—
Shall he be guilty of their hireling crimes,
The servile, mercenary Swiss of rhymes?
Or labour hard the panegyric close,
With all the venal soul of dedicating prose?
No! though his artless strains he rudely sings,
And throws his hand uncouthly o'er the strings,
He glows with all the spirit of the Bard,
Fame, honest fame, his great, his dear reward!
Still, if some patron's gen'rous care he trace,
Skill'd in the secret to bestow with grace;
When Ballantyne befriends his humble name,
And hands the rustic stranger up to fame,
With heartfelt throes his grateful bosom swells,
The god-like bliss, to give, alone excels.

'Twas when the stacks get on their winter-hap,
And thack and rape secure the toil-won crap;
Potato-bings are snugged up frae skaith
Of coming Winter's biting, frosty breath;
The bees, rejoicing o'er their summer toils,
Unnumber'd buds and flow'rs' delicious spoils,
Seal'd up with frugal care in massive waxen piles,
Are doom'd by man, that tyrant o'er the weak,
The death o' devils smoor'd wi' brimstone reek:

The thundering guns are heard on ev'ry
side,
The wounded conveys, reeling, scatter wide;
The feather'd field-mates, bound by Nature's
tie,
Sires, mothers, children, in one carnage lie:
(What warm, poetic heart, but inly bleeds,
And execrates man's savage, ruthless deeds!)
Nae mair the flow'r in field or meadow
springs;
Nae mair the grove with airy concert rings,
Except, perhaps, the robin's whistling glee,
Proud o' the height o' some bit half-lang
tree:
The hoary morns precede the sunny days,
Mild, calm, serene, wide-spreads the noon-
tide blaze, [the rays.
While thick the gossamour waves wanton in

'Twas in that season, when a simple bard,
Unknown and poor, simplicity's reward,
Ae night, within the ancient brugh of Ayr,
By whim inspired, or haply prest wi' care,
He left his bed, and took his wayward route,
And down by Simpson's (123) wheel'd the
left about:
(Whether impell'd by all-directing Fate
To witness what I after shall narrate;
Or whether, rapt in meditation high,
He wander'd out he knew not where or why)
The drowsy Dungeon-clock (124) had num-
ber'd two, [was true:
And Wallace Tower (125) had sworn the fact
The tide-swoln Firth, with sullen sounding
roar, [the shore.
Through the still night dash'd hoarse along
All else was hush'd as Nature's closed e'e:
The silent moon shone high o'er tow'r and
tree:
The chilly frost, beneath the silver beam,
Crept, gently-crusting, o'er the glittering
stream. [Bard,
When, lo! on either hand the list'ning
The clanging sugh of whistling wings is
heard;
Two dusky forms dart thro' the midnight air,
Swift as the gos (126) drives on the wheel-
ing hare;

Ane on the Auld Brig his airy shape uprears,
The ither flutters o'er the rising piers:
Our warlock Rhymer instantly descry'd
The Sprites that owre the Brigs of Ayr pre-
side.
(That Bards are second-sighted is nae joke,
And ken the lingo of the sp'ritual folk;
Fays, Spunkies, Kelpies, a', they can explain
them, [them.)
And ev'n the vera deils they brawly ken
Auld Brig appear'd of ancient Pictish race,
The very wrinkles Gothic in his face;
He seem'd as he wi' Time had warstl'd lang,
Yet, teughly doure, he bade an unco bang.
New Brig was buskit in a braw new coat,
That he at Lon'on, frae ane Adams, got;
In's hand five taper staves as smooth's a
bead,
Wi' virls and whirlygigums at the head.
The Goth was stalking round with anxious
search,
Spying the time-worn flaws in ev'ry arch;—
It chanc'd his new-come neebor took his e'e,
And e'en a vex'd and angry heart had he!
Wi' thieveless sneer to see his modish mien,
He, down the water, gies him this guid-
e'en:—

AULD BRIG.

I doubt na', frien', ye'll think ye're nae
sheepshank,
Ance ye were streekit o'er frae bank to bank!
But gin ye be a brig as auld as me,
Tho', faith, that day I doubt ye'll never see;
There'll be, if that date come, I'll wad a
boddle,
Some fewer whigmaleeries in your noddle.

NEW BRIG.

Auld Vandal, ye but show your little
mense,
Just much about it wi' your scanty sense;
Will your poor, narrow foot-path of a street,
Whare twa wheel-barrows tremble when they
meet— [lime,
Your ruin'd, formless bulk o' stane and
Compare wi' bonnie Brigs o' modern time?
There's men o' taste wou'd tak the Ducat-
stream (127), [swim,
Tho' they should cast the vera sark and
Ere they would grate their feelings wi' the
view
Of sic an ugly, Gothic hulk as you.

AULD BRIG.

Conceited gowk! puff'd up wi' windy
pride— [tide;
This mony a year I've stood the flood and
And tho' wi' crazy eild I'm sair forfairn,
I'll be a Brig, when ye'se a shapeless cairn!
As yet ye little ken about the matter,
But twa-three winters will inform ye better.
When heavy, dark, continued a'-day rains,
Wi' deepening deluges o'erflow the plains;
When from the hills where springs the
brawling Coil,
Or stately Lugar's mossy fountains boil,
Or where the Greenock winds his moorland
course, [source,
Or haunted Garpal (128) draws his feeble
Arous'd by blust'ring winds and spotting
thowes, [rowes;
In mony a torrent down his snaw-broo

While crashing ice, borne on the roaring speat, [gate;
Sweeps dams and mills, and brigs, a' to the
And from Glenbuck (129), down to the Ratton-key (130), [sea—
Auld Ayr is just one lengthen'd tumbling
Then down ye'll hurl, deil nor ye never rise!
And dash the gumlie jaups up to the pouring skies.
A lesson sadly teaching, to your cost,
That Archietcture's noble art is lost!

NEW BRIG.

Fine Architecture, trowth, I needs must say't o't! [gate o't!
The L—d be thankit that we've tint the
Gaunt, ghastly, ghaist-alluring edifices,
Hanging with threat'ning jut like precipices;
O'er-arching, mouldy, gloom-inspiring coves,
Supporting roofs fantastic, stony groves:
Windows, and doors in nameless sculpture drest,
With order, symmetry, or taste unblest;
Forms like some bedlam Statuary's dream,
The craz'd creations of misguided whim;
Forms might be worshipp'd on the bended knee,
And still the second dread command be free,
Their likeness is not found on earth, in air, or sea. [taste
Mansions that would disgrace the building
Of any mason reptile, bird or beast;
Fit only for a doited monkish race,
Or frosty maids forsworn the dear embrace;
Or cuifs of latter times wha held the notion
That sullen gloom was sterling true devotion;
Fancies that our good Brugh denies protection! [resurrection!
And soon may they expire, unblest with

AULD BRIG.

Oh ye, my dear-remember'd ancient yealings, [ings!
Were ye but here to share my wounded feel-
Ye worthy Proveses, and mony a Bailie,
Wha in the paths o'righteousness did toil aye;
Ye dainty Deacons and ye douce Conveneers,
To whom our moderns are but causey-cleaners;
Ye godly Councils wha hae blest this town;
Ye godly brethren o' the sacred gown,
Wha meekly ga'e your hurdies to the smiters; [writers;
And (what would now be strange) ye godly
A' ye douce folk I've borne aboon the broo,
Were ye but here, what would ye say or do!
How would your spirits groan in deep vexation,
To see each melancholy alteration;
And agonising, curse the time and place
When ye begat the base, degen'rate race!
Nae langer rev'rend men, their country's glory. [braid story!
In plain braid Scots hold forth a plain
Nae longer thrifty citizens and douce,
Meet owre a pint, or in the council-house;
But staumrel, corky-headed, graceless gentry,
The herryment and ruin of the country;
Men, three parts made by tailors and by barbers, [new Brigs and Harbours!
Wha waste your weel-hain'd gear on d—d

NEW BRIG.

Now haud you there! for faith you've said enough, [through;
And muckle mair than ye can mak to
As for your Priesthood, I shall say but little,
Corbies and Clergy are a shot right kittle:
But, under favour o' your langer beard,
Abuse o' Magistrates might weel be spar'd:
To liken them to your auld-warld squad,
I needs must say, comparisons are odd.
In Ayr, wag-wits nae mair can have a handle
To mouth "a citizen," a term o' scandal;
Nae mair the Council waddles down the street,
In all the pomp of ignorant conceit;
Men wha grew wise priggin' owre hops and raisins,
Or gather'd lib'ral views in bonds and seisins,
If haply Knowledge, on a random tramp,
Had shor'd them with a glimmer of his lamp,
And would to Common-sense for once betray'd them, [them.
Plain, dull Stupidity stept kindly in to aid

What further clish-ma-claver might been said, [shed,
What bloody wars, if Spirites had blood to
No man can tell; but all before their sight,
A fairy train appear'd in order bright:
Adown the glitt'ring stream they featly danc'd: [glanc'd:
Bright to the moon their various dresses
They footed o'er the wat'ry glass so neat,
The infant ice scarce bent beneath their feet:
While arts of minstrelsy among them rung,
And soul-ennobling bards heroic ditties sung.
Oh, had M'Lauchlan (131), thairm-inspiring Sage,
Been there to hear this heavenly band engage,
When thro' his dear strathspeys they bore with highland rage;
Or when they struck old Scotia's melting air,
The lover's raptur'd joys or bleeding cares;

How would his highland lug been nobler fir'd,
And ev'n his matchless hand with finer touch
inspir'd!
No guess could tell what instrument appear'd,
But all the soul of Music's self was heard;
Harmonious concert rung in every part,
While simple melody pour'd moving on the
heart.

The Genius of the stream in front appears,
A venerable Chief advanc'd in years;
His hoary head with water-lilies crown'd,
His manly leg with garter tangle bound:
Next came the loveliest pair in all the ring,
Sweet Female Beauty hand in hand with
Spring; [Joy,
Then, crown'd with flow'ry hay, came Rural
And Summer, with his fervid-beaming eye:
All-cheering Plenty, with her flowing horn,
Led yellow Autumn, wreath'd with nodding
corn; [show,
Then Winter's time-bleach'd locks did hoary
By Hospitality with cloudless brow.
Next follow'd Courage, with his martial
stride; [hide (132);
From where the Feal wild woody coverts
Benevolence, with mild, benignant air.
A female form, came from the tow'rs of
Stair (133);
Learning and Worth in equal measures trode,
From simple Catrine, their long-lov'd abode
(134); [wreath,
Last, white-rob'd Peace, crown'd with a hazel
To rustic Agriculture did bequeath
The broken iron instruments of death;
At sight of whom our Sprites forgat their
kindling wrath.

On Captain Matthew Henderson,

A GENTLEMAN WHO HELD THE PATENT FOR HIS HONOURS IMMEDIATELY FROM ALMIGHTY GOD. (135)

"Should the poor be flattered?"—SHAKSPEARE.

But now his radiant course is run,
For Matthew's course was bright;
His soul was like the glorious sun,
A matchless heavenly light!

OH Death! thou tyrant fell and bloody!
The meikle devil wi' a woodie
Haurl thee hame to his black smiddie,
O'er hurcheon hides,
And like stock-fish come o'er his studdie
Wi' thy auld sides!

He's gane! he's gane! he's frae us torn,
The ae best fellow e'er was born!

L

Thee Matthew, Nature's sel' shall mourn
By wood and wild,
Where, haply, Pity stray's forlorn,
Frae man exil'd!

Ye hills! near neighbours o' the starns,
That proudly cock your cresting cairns!
Ye cliffs, the haunts of sailing yearns (136),
Where echo slumbers!
Come join, ye Nature's sturdiest bairns,
My wailing numbers!

Mourn, ilka grove the cushat kens!
Ye haz'ly shaws and briary dens!
Ye burnies, wimplin' down your glens,
Wi' toddlin' din,
Or foaming strang, wi' hasty stens,
Frae lin to lin!

Mourn, little harebells o'er the lea;
Ye stately foxgloves fair to see;
Ye woodbines, hanging bonnilie,
In scented bow'rs;
Ye roses on your thorny tree,
The first o' flow'rs.

At dawn, when ev'ry grassy blade
Droops with a diamond at its head,
At ev'n, when beans their fragrance shed,
I' th' rustling gale,
Ye maukins whiddin thro' the glade,
Came join my wail.

Mourn ye wee songsters o' the wood;
Ye grouse that crap the heather bud;
Ye curlews calling thro' a clud;
Ye whistling plover;
And mourn, ye whirring paitrick brood!—
He's gane for ever!

Mourn, sooty coots, and speckled teals
Ye fisher herons, watching eels;
Ye duck and drake, wi' airy wheels
Circling the lake;
Ye bitterns, till the quagmire reels,
Rair for his sake.

Mourn, clam'ring craiks at close o' day,
'Mang fields o' flow'ring clover gay;
And when ye wing your annual way
Frae our cauld shore,
Tell the far warlds, wha lies in clay
Wham we deplore.

Ye owlets, frae your ivy bow'r,
In some auld tree, or eldritch tow'r,
What time the moon, wi' silent glow'r
Sets up her horn,
Wail thro' the dreary midnight hour
Till waukrife morn!

Oh, rivers, forests, hills, and plains!
Oft have ye heard my canty strains:

But, now, what else for me remains
But tales of woe?
And frae my een the drapping rains
Maun ever flow.

Mourn, spring, thou darling of the year!
Ilk cowslip cup shall kep a tear:
Thou, simmer, while each corny spear
Shoots up its head,
Thy gay, green, flow'ry tresses shear
For him that's dead.

Thou, autumn, wi' thy yellow hair,
In grief thy sallow mantle tear!
Thou, winter, hurling thro' the air
The roaring blast,
Wide o'er the naked world declare
The worth we've lost!

Mourn him, thou sun, great source of light;
Mourn, empress of the silent night!
And you, ye twinkling starries bright,
My Matthew mourn!
For through your orbs he's ta'en his flight,
Ne'er to return.

Oh, Henderson! the man—the brother!
And art thou gone, and gone for ever?
And hast thou cross'd that unknown river,
Life's dreary bound?
Like thee, where shall I find another,
The world around?

Go to your sculptur'd tombs, ye great,
In a' the tinsel trash o' state!
But by thy honest turf I'll wait,
Thou man of worth!
And weep the ae best fellow's fate
E'er lay in earth.

THE EPITAPH.

Stop, passenger!—my story's brief
And truth I shall relate, man;
I tell nae common tale o' grief—
For Matthew was a great man.

If thou uncommon merit hast,
Yet spurn'd at fortune's door, man,
A look of pity hither cast—
For Matthew was a poor man.

If thou a noble sodger art,
That passest by this grave, man,
There moulders here a gallant heart—
For Matthew was a brave man.

If thou on men, their works and ways,
Canst throw uncommon light, man,
Here lies wha weal had won thy praise—
For Matthew was a bright man.

If thou at friendship's sacred ca'
Wad life itself resign, man,
Thy sympathetic tear maun fa'—
For Matthew was a kind man!

If thou art staunch without a stain,
Like the unchanging blue, man,
This was a kinsman o' thine ain—
For Matthew was a true man.

If thou hast wit, and fun, and fire,
And ne'er guid wine did fear, man,
This was thy billie, dam, and sire—
For Matthew was a queer man.

If ony whiggish whingin' sot,
To blame poor Matthew dare, man,
May dool and sorrow be his lot!
For Matthew was a rare man.

Tam O' Shanter,

A TALE. (137)

"Of brownysis and of bogilis full is this buke."
GAWIN DOUGLAS.

WHEN chapman billies leave the street,
And drouthy neighbours, neighbours meet,
As market-days are wearing late,
And folk begin to tak the gate;
While we sit bousing at the nappy,
And gettin' fou and unco happy,
We think na on the lang Scots miles,
The mosses, waters, slaps, and stiles,
That lie between us and our hame,
Where sits our sulky sullen dame,
Gathering her brows like gathering storm,
Nursing her wrath to keep it warm.

This truth fand honest Tam o' Shanter,
As he frae Ayr ae night did canter,
(Auld Ayr, wham ne'er a town surpasses,
For honest men and bonnie lasses).

Oh Tam! had'st thou but been sae wise,
As ta'en thy ain wife Kate's advice!
She tauld thee weel thou was a skellum,
A blethering, blustering, drunken blellum;

That frae November till October:
Ae market-day thou was nae sober;
That ilka melder, wi' the miller,
Thou sat as lang as thou had siller;
That ev'ry naig was ca'd a shoe on,
The smith and thee gat roaring fou on;
That at the Lord's house, ev'n on Sunday,
Thou drank wi' Kirton Jean till Monday. (138)
She prophesied, that, late or soon,
Thou would be found deep drown'd in Doon,
Or catch'd wi' warlocks in the mirk,
By Alloway's auld haunted kirk.

Ah, gentle dames! it gars me greet,
To think how mony counsels sweet,
How mony lengthen'd sage advices,
The husband frae the wife despises;
But to our tale:—Ae market night,
Tam had got planted unco right,

Fast by an ingle, bleezing finely,
Wi' reaming swats, that drank divinely;
And at his elbow, Souter Johnny,
His ancient, trusty, drouthy crony;
Tam lo'ed him like a vera brither—
They had been fou' for weeks thegither!
The night drave on wi' sangs and clatter,
And aye the ale was growing better:
The landlady and Tam grew gracious,
Wi' favours secret, sweet, and precious,
The Souter tauld his queerest stories.
The landlord's laugh was ready chorus:
The storm without might rair and rustle—
Tam did na mind the storm a whistle.

Care, mad to see a man sae happy,
E'en drown'd himself amang the nappy;
As bees flee hame wi' lades o' treasure,
The minutes wing'd their way wi' pleasure:
Kings may be blest, but Tam was glorious,
O'er a' the ills o' life victorious.

But pleasures are like poppies spread,
You seize the flower, its bloom is shed;
Or like the snowfall in the river,
A moment white—then melts for ever;
Or like the borealis race,
That flit ere you can point their place;
Or like the rainbow's lovely form
Evanishing amid the storm.

Nae man can tether time or tide,
The hour approaches Tam maun ride;
That hour, o' night's black arch the key-
stane,
That dreary hour he mounts his beast on;
And sic a night he taks the road in
As ne'er poor sinner was abroad in.

The wind blew as 'twad blawn its last;
The rattling show'rs rose on the blast;
The speedy gleams the darkness swallow'd,
Loud, deep, and lang the thunder bellow'd:
That night, a child might understand,
The deil had business on his hand.

Weal mounted on his grey mare, Meg,
A better never lifted leg,
Tam skelpit on thro' dub and mire,
Despising wind, and rain, and fire;
Whiles holding fast his guid blue bonnet,
Whiles crooning o'er some auld Scot's son-
net;
Whiles glow'ring round wi prudent cares,
Lest bogles catch him unawares.
Kirk-Alloway was drawing nigh (139),
Where ghaists and owlets nightly cry.

By this time he was cross the ford,
Where in the snaw the chapman smoor'd;
And past the birks and meikle stane,
Where drunken Charlie brak's neck bane;
And thro' the whins, and by the cairn,
Where hunters fand the murder'd bairn;
And near the thorn, aboon the well,
Where Mungo's mither hang'd hersel.
Before him Doon pours all his floods;
The doubling storm roars thro' the woods;
The lightnings flash from pole to pole,
Near and more near the thunders roll;
When glimmering thro' the groaning trees,
Kirk-Alloway seem'd in a bleeze;
Thro' ilka bore the beams were glancing,
And loud resounded mirth and dancing.

Inspiring bold John Barleycorn!
What dangers thou can'st make us scorn!
Wi' tippenny, we fear nae evil;
Wi' usquebae we'll face the devil!—
The swats sae ream'd in Tammie's noddle,
Fair play, he car'd nae deils a boddle.
But Maggie stood right sair astonish'd,
Till, by the heel and hand admonish'd,
She ventur'd forward on the light;
And, wow! Tam saw an unco sight!
Warlocks and witches in a dance;
Nae cotillon brent new frae France,
But hornpipes, jigs, strathspeys, and reels,
Put life and mettle in their heels:
A winnock-bunker in the east,
There sat auld Nick, in shape o' beast;
A towzie tyke, black, grim and large,
To gie them music was his charge;
He screw'd the pipes and garb them skirl,
Till roof and rafters a' did dirl.
Coffins stood round, like open presses,
That shaw'd the dead in their last dresses;
And by some devilish cantrip slight
Each in its cauld hand held a light—
By which heroic Tam was able
To note upon the haly table,
A murderer's banes in gibbet airns;
Twa span-lang, wee unchristen'd bairns;
A thief, new-cutted frae a rape,
Wi' his last gasp his gab did gape;
Five tomahawks, wi' bluid red-rusted;
Five scimitars, wi' murder crusted;
A garter, which a babe had strangled,
A knife, a father's throat had mangled,
Whom his ain son o' life bereft,
The grey hairs yet stack to the heft:
Wi' mair o' horrible and awfu',
Which ev'n to name wad be unlawfu'.

As Tammie glowr'd, amaz'd and curious,
The mirth and fun grew fast and furious:
The piper loud and louder blew;
The dancers quick and quicker flew;
They reel'd, they set, they cross'd, they
cleckit,
Till ilka carline swat and reckit,
And coost her duddies to the wark,
And linket at it in her sark;

Now Tam, oh Tam! had thae been queans
A' plump and strapping, in their teens;

Their sarks, instead o' creeshie flannen,
Been snaw-white seventeen-hunder linen!
Their breeks o' mine, my only pair,
That ance were plush o' guid blue hair,
I wad hae gi'en them off my hurdies,
For ae blink o' the bonnie burdies!

But wither'd beldams, auld and droll,
Rigwoodie hags, wad spean a foal,
Louping and flinging on a cummock,
I wonder didna turn thy stomach.
But Tam kenn'd what was what fu' brawlie;
There was a winsome wench and walie,
That night enlisted in the core,
(Lang after kenn'd on Carrick shore;
For mony a beast to dead she shot,
And perish'd mony a bonnie boat,
And shook baith meikle corn and beer,
And kept the country-side in fear.)
Her cutty sark, o' Paisley harn,
That while a lassie she had worn,
In longitude tho' sorely scanty,
It was her best, and she was vauntie—
Ah! little kenn'd thy reverend grannie,
That sark she coft for her wee Nannie,
Wi' twa pund Scots ('twas a' her riches),
Wad ever grac'd a dance o' witches!
But here my muse her wing maun cour,
Sic flights are far beyond her pow'r;
To sing how Nannie lap and flang,
(A souple jade she was and strang,)
And how Tam stood like ane bewitch'd,
And thought his very een enrich'd;
Even Satan glowr'd and fidg'd fu' fain,
And hotch'd and blew wi' might and main:
Till first ae caper, syne anither,
Tam tint his reason a' thegither,
And roars out, "Weel done, Cutty-sark!"
And in an instant all was dark:
And scarcely had he Maggie rallied,
When out the hellish legion sallied.

As bees bizz out wi' angry fyke,
When plundering herds assail their byke;
As open pussie's mortal foes,
When, pop! she starts before their nose;
As eager runs the market-crowd,
When "Catch the thief!" resounds aloud;
So Maggie runs, the witches follow,
Wi' mony an eldritch screech and hollow.
Ah, Tam! ah, Tam! thou'll get thy fairin'!
In hell they'll roast thee like a herrin'!
In vain thy Kate awaits thy comin'!
Kate soon will be a woefu' woman!
Now, do thy speedy utmost, Meg,
And win the key-stane (140) o' the brig;
There at them thou thy tail may toss,
A running stream they darena cross!
But ere the key-stane she could make,
The fient a tail she had to shake!
For Nannie, far before the rest,
Hard upon noble Maggie prest,
And flew at Tam wi' furious ettle,
But little wist she Maggie's mettle—
Ae spring brought off her master hale,
But left behind her ain grey tail;
The carline caught her by the rump,
And left poor Maggie scarce a stump.

Now, wha this tale o' truth shall read,
Ilk man and mother's son take heed:
Whene'er to drink you are inclin'd,
Or cutty-sarks run in your mind,
Think! ye may buy the joys over dear—
Remember Tam o' Shanter's mare.

Tragic Fragment. (141)

All devil as I am, a damned wretch,
A harden'd, stubborn, unrepenting villain,
Still my heart melts at human wretchedness;
And with sincere tho' unavailing sighs,
I view the helpless children of distress.
With tears indignant I behold th' oppressor
Rejoicing in the honest man's destruction,
Whose unsubmitting heart was all his crime.
Even you, ye helpless crew, I pity you;
Ye whom the seeming good think sin to pity;
Ye poor, despis'd, abandon'd vagabonds,
Whom vice, as usual, has turn'd o'er to ruin.
—Oh, but for kind, tho' ill-requited friends,
I had been driven forth like you forlorn,
The most detested, worthless wretch among
you!

Winter, a Dirge. (142)

The wintry west extends his blast,
And hail and rain does blaw;
Or the stormy north sends driving forth
The blinding sleet and snaw:
While tumbling brown, the burn comes down,
And roars frae bank to brae;
And bird and beast in covert rest,
And pass the heartless day.

"The sweeping blast, the sky o'ercast" (143),
The joyless winter day
Let others fear, to me more dear
Than all the pride of May:
The tempest's howl, it soothes my soul,
My griefs it seems to join;
The leafless trees my fancy please,
Their fate resembles mine!

Thou Power Supreme, whose mighty scheme
These woes of mine fulfil,
Here, firm, I rest, they must be best,
Because they are thy will!

Then all I want (oh, do thou grant
This one request of mine!)
Since to enjoy thou dost deny,
Assist me to resign.

A Prayer,

UNDER THE PRESSURE OF VIOLENT ANGUISH. (144)

OH thou great Being! what thou art
Surpasses me to know:
Yet sure I am, that known to Thee
Are all thy works below.

Thy creature here before Thee stands,
All wretched and distrest;
Yet sure those ills that wring my soul
Obey Thy high behest.

Sure Thou, Almighty, canst not act
From cruelty or wrath!
Oh, free my weary eyes from tears,
Or close them fast in death!

But if I must afflicted be,
To suit some wise design;
Then man my soul with firm resolves,
To bear and not repine!

A Prayer,

ON THE PROSPECT OF DEATH.

OH thou unknown, Almighty Cause
Of all my hope and fear!
In whose dread presence, ere an hour,
Perhaps I must appear!

If I have wander'd in those paths
Of life I ought to shun;
As something, loudly, in my breast,
Remonstrates I have done.

Thou know'st that Thou hast formed me,
With passions wild and strong;
And list'ning to their witching voice
Has often led me wrong.

Where human weakness has come short,
Or frailty stept aside,
Do Thou, All-good! for such thou art,
In shades of darkness hide.

Where with intention I have err'd,
No other plea I have,
But, Thou art good; and goodness still
Delighteth to forgive.

Stanzas

ON THE SAME OCCASION. (145)

WHY am I loth to leave this earthly scene?
Have I so found it full of pleasing charms?
Some drops of joy with draughts of ill between:
Some gleams of sunshine 'mid renewing storms:
Is it departing pangs my soul alarms?
Or death's unlovely, dreary, dark abode?
For guilt, for guilt, my terrors are in arms;
I tremble to approach an angry God,
And justly smart beneath his sin-avenging rod.

Fain would I say, "Forgive my foul offence!"
Fain promise never more to disobey;
But should my Author health again dispense,
Again I might desert fair virtue's way:
Again in folly's path might go astray;
Again exalt the brute and sink the man;
Then how should I for heavenly mercy pray,
Who act so counter heavenly mercy's plan?
Who sin so oft have mourn'd, yet to temptation ran?

Oh Thou, great Governor of all below!
If I may dare a lifted eye to Thee,
Thy nod can make the tempest cease to blow,
Or still the tumult of the raging sea:
With that controlling pow'r assist ev'n me,
Those headlong furious passions to confine;
For all unfit I feel my pow'rs to be,
To rule their torrent in the hallowed line;
Oh, aid me with Thy help, Omnipotence Divine!

Elegy on the Death of Robert Ruisseaux.

(146.)

Now Robin lies in his last lair,
He'll gabble rhyme, nor sing nae mair,
Cauld poverty, wi' hungry stare,
Nae mair shall fear him;
Nor anxious fear, nor cankert care,
E'er mair come near him.

To tell the truth, they seldom fash't him,
Except the moment that they crush't him;
For sune as chance or fate had hush't 'em,
Tho' e'er sae short,
Then wi' a rhyme or song he lash't 'em,
And thought it sport.

Tho' he was bred to kintra wark,
And counted was baith wight and stark,
Yet that was never Robin's mark
To mak a man;
But tell him, he was learned and clark,
Ye roos'd him than!

The Calf.

TO THE REV. MR. JAMES STEVEN. (147)

On his Text, MAL. iv. 2.—"And they shall go forth, and grow up, like CALVES of the stall."

RIGHT, Sir! your text I'll prove it true,
Though Heretics may laugh;
For instance, there's yoursel' just now,
God knows, an unco calf!

And should some patron be so kind,
As bless you wi' a kirk,
I doubt na, Sir, but then we'll find,
Ye're still as great a stirk.

But, if the lover's raptur'd hour
Shall ever be your lot,
Forbid it, ev'ry heavenly power
You e'er should be a Scot!

Tho', when some kind, connubial dear,
Your but-and-ben adorns,
The like has been that you may wear
A noble head of horns.

And in your lug, most reverend James,
To hear you roar and rowte,
Few men o' sense will doubt your claims
To rank amang the nowte.

And when ye're number'd wi' the dead,
Below a grassy hillock,
Wi' justice they may mark your head—
"Here lies a famous bullock!"

The Twa Herds,

OR THE HOLY TULZIE. (148)

OH a' ye pious godly flocks,
Weel fed on pastures orthodox,
Wha now will keep you frae the fox,
Or worrying tykes,
Or wha will tent the waifs and crocks,
About the dykes?

The twa best herds in a' the wast,
That e'er gae gospel horn a blast,
These five and twenty simmers past,
Oh! dool to tell,
Ha'e had a bitter black out-cast
Atween themsel.

Oh, Moodie, man, and wordy Russell,
How could you raise so vile a bustle,
Ye'll see how New-Light herds will whistle,
And think it fine:
The L—'s cause ne'er got sic a twistle
Sin' I ha'e mine.

O, Sirs! whae'er wad ha'e expeckit
Your duty ye wad sae negleckit,
Ye wha were ne'er by lairds respeckit,
To wear the plaid,
But by the brutes themselves eleckit,
To be their guide.

What flock wi' Moodie's flock could rank,
Sae hale and hearty every shank!
Nae poison'd sour Arminian stank,
He let them taste,
Frae Calvin's well, aye clear, they drank—
Oh sic a feast!

The thummart, wil'-cat, brock, and tod,
Well kenn'd his voice through a' the wood,
He smelt their ilka hale and rod,
Baith out and in,
And weel he lik'd to shed their bluid,
And sell their skin.

What herd like Russell (149) tell'd his tale,
His voice was heard thro' muir and dale,
He kenn'd the Lord's sheep, ilka tail,
O'er a' the height,
And saw gin they were sick or hale,
At the first sight.

He fine a mangy sheep could scrub,
Or nobly fling the gospel club,
And New-Light herds could nicely drub,
Or pay their skin;
Could shake them o'er the burning dub,
Or heave them in.

Sic twa—Oh! do I live to see't,
Sic famous twa should disagreet,
And names like villain, hypocrite,
Ilk ither gi'en,
While New-Light herds, wi' laughin' spite,
Say neither's lyin'!

A' ye wha tent the gospel fauld,
There's Duncan (150), deep, and Peebles, shaul (151),
But chiefly thou, apostle Auld (152),
We trust in thee,
That thou wilt work them, het and cauld,
Till they agree.

Consider, Sirs, how we're beset;
There's scarce a new herd that we get
But comes frae 'mang that cursed set
I winna name;
I hope frae heav'n to see them yet
In fiery flame.

Dalrymple (153) has been lang our fae,
M'Gill (154) has wrought us meikle wae,
And that curs'd rascal ca'd M'Quhae (155),
And baith the Shaws (156),
That aft ha'e made us black and blae,
Wi' vengefu' paws.

Auld Wodrow (157) lang has hatch'd mischief,
We thought aye death wad bring relief,
But he has gotten, to our grief,
Ane to succeed him,
A chield wha'll soundly buff our beef;
I meikle dread him.

And mony a ane that I could tell,
Wha fain would openly rebel,
Forbye turn-coats amang oursel.
There's Smith for ane,
I doubt he's but a grey-nick quill,
And that ye'll fin'.

Oh ! a' ye flocks o'er a' the hills,
By mosses, meadows, moors and fells,
Come, join your counsel and your skills
To cowe the lairds,
And get the brutes the powers themsels
To choose their herds.

Then Orthodoxy yet may prance,
And Learning in a woody dance,
And that fell cur ca'd Common Sense,
That bites sae sair,
Be banish'd o'er the sea to France:
Let him bark there.

Then Shaw's and Dalrymple's eloquence,
M'Gill's close nervous excellence,
Quhae's pathetic manly sense,
And guid M'Math, [158
Wi' Smith, wha thro' the heart can glance,
May a' pack aff.

Holy Willie's Prayer. (159)

Oh Thou, wha in the heavens dost dwelt,
Wha, as it pleases best thysel',
Sends ane to heaven, and ten to hell,
A' for thy glory,
And no for ony giude or ill
They've done afore thee!

I bless and praise thy matchless might,
When thousands thou hast left in night,
That I am here afore thy sight,
For gifts and grace,
A burnin' and a shinin' light
To a' this place.

What was I, or my generation,
That I should get sic exaltation,
I wha deserve sic just damnation,
For broken laws,
Five thousand years 'fore my creation,
Thro' Adam's cause.

When frae my mither's womb I fell,
Thou might hae plunged me into hell,
To gnash my gums, to weep and wail,
In burnin' lake,
Where damned devils roar and yell,
Chain'd to a stake.

Yet I am here a chosen sample;
To show thy grace is great and ample;
I'm here a pillar in thy temple,
Strong as a rock,
A guide, a buckler, an example,
To a' thy flock.

But yet, oh Lord! confess I must,
At times I'm fash'd wi' fleshly lust;
And sometimes, too, wi' wardly trust,
Vile self gets in;
But thou remembers we are dust,
Defil'd in sin.

* * * *

Maybe thou lets't this fleshly thorn,
Beset thy servant e'en and morn,
Lest he owre high and proud should turn,
'Cause he's sae gifted;
If sae, thy han' maun e'en be borne,
Until thou lift it.

Lord, bless thy chosen in this place,
For here thou hast a chosen race:
But God confound their stubborn face,
And blast their name,
Wha bring thy elders to disgrace
And public shame.

Lord, mind Gaw'n Hamilton's deserts,
He drinks, and swears, and plays at cartes,
Yet has sae mony takin' arts,
Wi' grat and sma',
Frae God's ain priests the people's hearts
He steals awa'.

And when we chasten'd him therefore,
Thou kens how he bred sic a splore,
As set the warld in a roar
O' laughin' at us;—
Curse thou his basket and his store,
Kail and potatoes,

Lord, hear my earnest cry and pray'r,
Against the presbyt'ry of Ayr;
Thy strong right hand, Lord, mak it bare
Upo' their heads,
Lord, weigh it down, and dinna spare,
For their misdeeds.

Oh Lord my God, that glib-tongu'd Aikin,
My very heart and saul are quakin',
To think how we stood groanin', shakin'
And swat wi' dread,
While he wi' hingin' lips and snakin',
Held up his head.

Lord, in the day of vengeance try him,
Lord, visit them wha did employ him,
And pass not in thy mercy by 'em,
Nor hear their pray'r;
But for thy people's sake destroy 'em,
And dinna spare.

But, Lord, remember me and mine,
Wi' mercies temp'ral and divine,
That I for gear and grace may shine,
Excell'd by nane,
And a' the glory shall be thine,
Amen, Amen!

Epitaph on Holy Willie.

HERE Holy Willie's sair-worn clay
 Taks up its last abode;
His soul has ta'en some other way,
 I fear the left-hand road.

Stop! there he is, as sure's a gun,
 Poor, silly body, see him;
Nae wonder he's as black's the grun',
 Observe wha's standing wi' him.

Your brunstane devilship, I see,
 Has got him there before ye;
But haud your nine-tail cat a wee,
 Till ance you've heard my story.

Your pity I will not implore,
 For pity ye hae nane;
Justice, alas! has gi'en him o'er,
 And mercy's day is gaen.

But hear me, sir, deil as ye are,
 Look something to your credit;
A coof like him wad stain your name,
 If it were kent ye did it.

Epistle to John Goudie of Kilmarnock.

ON THE PUBLICATION OF HIS ESSAYS. (160)

OH Goudie! terror of the Whigs,
Dread of black coats and rev'rend wigs,
Sour Bigotry, on her last legs,
 Girnin', looks back,
Wishin' the ten Egyptian plagues
 Wad seize you quick.

Poor gapin', glowrin' Superstition,
Waes me! she's in a sad condition;
Fie! bring Black Jock, her state physician,
 To see her water.
Alas! there's ground o' great suspicion
 She'll ne'er get better.

Auld Orthodoxy lang did grapple,
But now she's g t an unco ripple;
Haste, gie' her name up i' the chapel,
 Nigh unto death;
See, how she fetches at the thrapple,
 And gasps for breath.

Enthusiasm's past redemption,
Gane in a galloping consumption,
Not a' the quacks, wi' a' their gumption,
 Will ever mend her.
Her feeble pulse gies strong presumption,
 Death soon will end her.

'Tis you and Taylor (161) are the chief,
Wha are to blame for this mischief,
But gin the Lord's ain fouk gat leave,
 A toom tar-barrel
And twa red peats wad send relief,
 And end the quarrel.

Epistle to John Rankine,

ENCLOSING SOME POEMS. (162)

OH rough, rude, ready-witted Rankine,
The wale o' cocks for fun and drinkin'!
There's mony godly folks are thinkin',
 Your dreams (163) and tricks
Will send you, Korah-like, a-sinkin',
 Straught to Auld Nick's.

Ye hae sae mony cracks and cants,
And in your wicked, drunken rants,
Ye mak a devil o' the saunts,
 And fill them fou (164);
And then their failings, flaws, and wants,
 Are a' seen through.

Hypocrisy, in mercy spare it!
That holy robe, oh dinna tear it!
Spare't for their sakes wha aften wear it,
 The lads in black!
But your curst wit, when it comes near it,
 Rives't aff their back.

Think, wicked sinner, wha ye're skaithing,
It's just the blue-gown badge and claithing
O' saunts; tak that, ye lea'e them naething
 To ken them by,
Frae ony unregenerate heathen
 Like you or I.

I've sent you here some rhyming ware,
A' that I bargain'd for, and mair;
Sae, when you hae an hour to spare,
 I will expect
Yon sang (165), ye'll sen't wi' canny care,
 And no neglect.

* * * *

Third Epistle to John Lapraik. (166)

September 13, 1785.

GOOD speed and furder to you, Johnny,
Guide health, hale han's, and weather bonny;
Now when ye're nickan down fu' canny
 The staff o' bread,
May ye ne'er want a stoup o' bran'y
 To clear your head.

May Boreas never thresh your rigs,
Nor kick your rickles aff their legs,
Sendin' the stuff o'er muirs and haggs
 Like drivin' wrack;
But may the tapmast grain that wags
 Come to the sack.

I'm bizzie too, and skelpin' at it,
But bitter, daudin' showers hae wat it,
Sae my auld stumpie pen I gat it
 Wi' muckle wark,
And took my jotteleg and whatt' it,
 Like ony clark.

TAM O' SHANTER.

The piper loud and louder blew;
The dancers quick and quicker flew;

It's now twa month that I'm your debtor,
For your braw, nameless, dateless letter,
Abusin' me for harsh ill nature
On holy men,
While deil a hair yoursel' ye're better,
But mair profane.

But let the kirk-folk ring their bells,
Let's sing about our noble sel's;
We'el cry nae jads frae heathen hills
To help, or roose us,
But browster wives and whiskey stills,
They are the muses.

Your friendship, Sir, I winna quat it,
And if ye mak objections at it,
Then han' in nieve some day we'll knot it,
And witness take,
And when wi' usquebæ we've wat it,
It winna break.

But if the beast and branks be spar'd
Till kye be gaun without the herd,
And a' the vittel in the yard,
And theekit right,
I mean your ingle-side to guard
Ae winter night.

Then muse-inspirin' aqua vitæ
Shall make us baith sae blythe and witty
Till ye forget ye're auld and gatty,
And be as canty
As ye were nine year less than thretty,
Sweet ane and twenty!

But stooks are cowpet wi' the blast,
And now the sinn keeks in the west,
Then I maun rin amang the rest
And quat my chanter;
Sae I subscribe myself in haste
Your's Rab the Ranter.

Epistle to the Rev. John M'Math. (167)

September 17, 1785.

While at the stook the shearers cow'r
To shun the bitter blaudin' show'r,
Or in gulravage rinnin' scow'r
To pass the time,
To you I dedicate the hour
In idle rhyme.

My musie, tir'd wi' mony a sonnet
On gown, and ban', and douse black bonnet,
Is grown right eerie now she's done it,
Lest they should blame her,
And rouse their holy thunder on it,
And anathem her.

I own 'twas rash, and rather hardy,
That I, a simple, countra bardie,
Shou'd meddle wi' a pack sae sturdy,
Wha, if they ken me,
Can easy, wi' a single wordie,
Louse h-ll upon me.

But I gae mad at their grimaces,
Their sighin', cantin', grace-proud faces,
Their three-mile prayers, and hauf-mile graces,
Their raxin' conscience,
Whase greed, revenge, and pride disgraces,
Waur nor their nonsense.

There's Gawn (168), misca't waur than a beast,
Wha has mair honour in his breast
Than mony scores as guid's the priest
Wha sae abus't him.
And may a bard no crack his jest
What way they've use't him?

See him, the poor man's friend in need,
The gentleman in word and deed,
And shall his fame and honour bleed
By worthless skellums,
And not a muse erect her head
To cowe the blellums?

Oh, Pope, had I thy satire's darts
To gie the rascals their deserts,
I'd rip their rotten, hollow hearts,
And tell aloud
Their jugglin' hocus-pocus arts
To cheat the crowd.

God knows, I'm no the thing I shou'd be,
Nor am I even the thing I cou'd be,
But twenty times I rather wou'd be
An atheist clean,
Then under gospel colours hid be
Just for a screen.

An honest man may like a glass,
An honest man may like a lass,
But mean revenge, and malice fause,
He'll still disdain,
And then cry zeal for gospel laws,
Like some we ken.

They take religion in their mouth;
They talk o' mercy, grace, and truth,
For what?—to gie their malice skouth
On some puir wight,
And hunt him down, o'er right and ruth,
To ruin straight.

All hail, Religion! maid divine!
Pardon a muse sae mean as mine,
Who in her rough imperfect line,
Thus daurs to name thee;
To stigmatise false friends of thine
Can ne'er defame thee.

Tho' blotch't and foul wi' mony a stain,
And far unworthy of thy train,
With trembling voice I tune my strain
To join with those
Who boldly daur thy cause maintain
In spite o' foes:

In spite o' crowds, in spite o' mobs,
In spite o' undermining jobs,

In spite o' dark banditti stabs
At worth andrit
By scoundrels, even wi' holy robes,
But hellish spite.

Oh Ayr! my dear, my native ground,
Within thy presbyterial bound
A candid lib'ral band is found
Of public teachers,
As men, as Christians too, renown'd,
And manly preachers.

Sir, in that circle you are nam'd;
Sir, in that circle you are fam'd;
And some, by whom your doctrine's blam'd
(Which gies you honour),
Ev'n Sir, by them your heart's esteem'd,
And winning manner.

Pardon this freedom I have ta'en,
And if impertinent I've been,
Impute it not, good Sir, in ane
Whase heart ne'er wrang'd ye,
But to his utmost would befriend
Ought that belang'd ye.

The American War,

A FRAGMENT. (169)

When Guildford good our pilot stood,
And did our helm thraw, man,
Ae night, at tea, began a plea,
Within America, man:
Then up they gat the maskin'-pat,
And in the sea did jaw, man;
And did nae less, in full Congress,
Than quite refuse our law, man.

Then thro' the lakes Montgomery takes,
I wat he was na slaw, man;
Down Lowrie's burn he took a turn,
And Carleton did ca' man;
But yet, what-reck, he, at Quebec,
Montgomery-like did fa', man,
Wi' sword in hand, before his band,
Amang his en'mies a', man.

Poor Tammy Gage, within a cage,
Was kept at Boston ha', man;
Till Willie Howe took o'er the knowe
For Philadelphia, man:
Wi' sword and gun he thought a sin
Guid Christian blood to draw, man:
But at New York, wi' knife and fork,
Sir-loin he hacked sma', man.

Burgoyne gaed up, like spur and whip,
Till Fraser brave did fa', man;
Then lost his way, ae misty day,
In Saratoga shaw, man.
Cornwallis fought as lang's he dought,
And did the buckskins claw, man;
But Clinton's glaive frae rust to save,
He hung it to the wa', man.

Then Montague, and Guildford, too,
Began to fear a fa', man;
And Sackville dour, wha stood the stoure,
The German Chief to thraw, man:
For Paddy Burke, like ony Turk,
Nae mercy had at a', man;
And Charlie Fox threw by the box,
And lows'd his tinkler jaw, man.

Then Rockingham took up the game,
Till death did on him ca', man;
When Shelburne meek held up his cheek,
Conform to gospel law, man;
Saint Stephen's boys, wi' jarring noise,
They did his measures thraw, man,
For North and Fox united stocks,
And bore him to the wa', man.

Then clubs and hearts were Charlie's cartes,
He swept the stakes awa', man,
Till the diamond's ace, of Indian race,
Led him a sair *faux pas*, man;
The Saxon lads, wi' loud placads,
On Chatham's boy did ca', man;
And Scotland drew her pipe, and blew,
"Up, Willie, waur them a', man!"

Behind the throne then Grenville's gon
A secret word or twa, man;
While slee Dundas arous'd the class,
Be-north the Roman wa', man;
And Chatham's wraith, in heavenly graith,
(Inspired Bardies saw, man)
Wi' kindling eyes cry'd, "Willie, rise!
Would I hae fear'd them a', man?"

But, word and blow, North, Fox, and Co.,
Gowff'd Willie like a ba', man,
Till Suthron raise, and coost their claise
Behind him in a raw, man;
And Caledon threw by the drone,
And did her whittle draw, man;
And swoor fu' rude, thro' dirt and blood,
To make it guid in law, man. (170)

* * * *

Second Epistle to Davie,

A BROTHER POET.

AULD NEIBOR,
I'm three times doubly o'er your debtor,
For your auld-farrant, frien'ly letter;
Tho' I maun say't, I doubt ye flatter,
Ye speak sae fair,
For my puir, silly, rhymin' clatter
Some less maun sair.

Hale be your heart, hale be your fiddle:
Lang may your elbock jink and diddle,
To cheer you thro' the weary widdle
O' war'ly cares,
Till bairns' bairns kindly cuddle
Your auld, gray hairs.

But, Davie lad, I'm red ye're glaikit;
I'm tauld the muse ye hae negleckit;
And gif it's sae, ye sud be licket
Until ye fyke;
Sic hauns as you sud ne'er be faiket,
Be hain't wha like.

For me, I'm on Parnassus' brink,
Rivin' the words to gar them clink;
Whyles daez't wi' love, whyles daez't wi' drink,
Wi' jads or masons;
And whyles, but aye owre late, I think
Braw sober lessons.

Of a' the thoughtless sons o' man,
Commen' me to the bardie clan;
Except it be some idle plan
O' rhymin' clink,
The devil-haet, that I sud ban,
They ever think.

Nae thought, nae view, nae scheme o'livin'
Nae cares to gie us joy or grievin';
But just the pouchie put the nieve in,
And while ought's there,
Then hiltie skiltie, we gae scrievin',
And fash nae mair.

Leeze me on rhyme! it's aye a treasure,
My chief, amaist my only pleasure,
At hame, a-fiel', at wark, or leisure,
The Muse, poor hizzie!
Tho' rough and raploch be her measure,
She's seldom lazy.

Haud to the Muse, my dainty Davie:
The warl' may play you monie a shavie;
But for the Muse, she'll never leave ye,
Tho' e'er sae puir,
Na, even tho' limpin' wi' the spavie
Frae door to door.

To Ruin.

All hail! inexorable lord!
At whose destruction-breathing word
The mightiest empires fall!
Thy cruel, woe-delighted train,
The ministers of grief and pain,
A sullen welcome, all!
With stern-resolv'd, despairing eye,
I see each aimed dart!
For one has cut my dearest tie,
And quivers in my heart.
Then low'ring and pouring,
The storm no more I dread;
Though thick'ning and black'ning,
Round my devoted head.

And thou grim pow'r, by life abhorr'd,
While life a pleasure can afford,
Oh hear a wretch's prayer!
No more I shrink appall'd, afraid;
I court, I beg thy friendly aid,
To close this scene of care!
When shall my soul, in silent peace,
Resign life's joyless day;
My weary heart its throbbings cease,
Cold mould'ring in the clay?
No fear more, no tear more,
To stain my lifeless face;
Enclasped, and grasped
Within thy cold embrace!

The First Six Verses of the Ninetieth Psalm.

Oh Thou, the first, the greatest friend
Of all the human race!
Whose strong right hand has ever been
Their stay and dwelling place!

Before the mountains heav'd their heads,
Beneath Thy forming hand,
Before this ponderous globe itself
Arose at Thy command;

That Pow'r which raised and still upholds
This universal frame,
From countless, unbeginning time
Was ever still the same.

Those mighty periods of years
Which seem to us so vast,
Appear no more before Thy sight
Than yesterday that's past.

Thou giv'st the word: Thy creature, man,
Is to existence brought;
Again Thou say'st, "Ye sons of men,
Return ye into nought!"

Thou layest them with all their cares
In everlasting sleep;
As with a flood Thou tak'st them off
With overwhelming sweep,

They flourish like the morning flow'r,
In beauty's pride array'd;
But long here night, cut down, it lies
All wither'd and decay'd.

The First Psalm.

The man, in life wherever plac'd,
Hath happiness in store,
Who walks not in the wicked's way,
Nor learns their guilty lore!

Nor from the seat of scornful pride
  Casts forth his eyes abroad,
But with humility and awe
  Still walks before his God.

That man shall flourish like the trees
  Which by the streamlets grow;
The fruitful top is spread on high,
  And firm the root below.

But he whose blossom buds in guilt,
  Shall to the ground be cast,
And, like the rootless stubble, tost
  Before the sleeping blast.

For why? that God the good adore
  Hath giv'n them peace and rest,
But hath decreed that wicked men
  Shall ne'er be truly blest.

To a Louse,

ON SEEING ONE ON A LADY'S BONNET, AT CHURCH. (171)

HA! whare ye gaun, ye crowlin' ferlie!
Your impudence protects you sairly:
I canna say but ye strunt rarely,
    Owre gauze and lace;
Tho', faith, I fear ye dine but sparely
    On sic a place.

Ye ugly, creepin', blastit wonner,
Detested, shunn'd, by saunt and sinner,
How dare you set your feet upon her,
    Sae fine a lady!
Gae somewhere else, and seek your dinner
    On some poor body.

Swith, in some beggar's haffet squattle;
There ye may creep, and sprawl and sprattle
Wi' ither kindred, jumping cattle,
    In shoals and nations;
Whare horn nor bane ne'er daur unsettle
    Your thick plantations.

Now haud you there, ye're out o' sight,
Below the fatt'rells, snug and tight;
Na, faith ye yet! ye'll no be right
    Till ye've got on it,
The vera tapmost, tow'ring height
    O' Miss's bonnet.

My sooth! right bauld ye set your nose out,
As plump and grey as ony grozet;
Oh for some rank, mercurial rozet,
    Or fell, red smeddum,
I'd gie you sic a hearty dose o't,
    Wad dress your droddum!

I wad na been surpris'd to spy
You on an auld wife's flannen toy;
Or aiblins some bit duddie boy,
    On's wyliecoat;
But Miss's fine Lunardi! fie! (172)
    How daur ye do't?

Oh, Jenny, dinna toss your head,
And set your beauties a' abread!
Ye little ken what cursed speed
    The blastie's makin'!
Thae winks and finger-ends, I dread,
    Are notice takin'!

Oh wad some power the giftie gie us
To see oursels as others see us!
It wad frae mony a blunder free us
    And foolish notion:
What airs in dress and gait wad lea'e us,
    And ev'n devotion!

The Inventory.

IN ANSWER TO A MANDATE BY THE SURVEYOR OF THE TAXES, (173.)

SIR, as your mandate did request,
I send you here a faithfu' list
O' gudes and gear, and a' my graith,
To which I'm clear to gie my aith.

Imprimis, then, for carriage cattle,
I have four brutes o' gallant mettle,
As ever drew afore a pettle.
My han' afore's (174) a gude auld has been
And wight and wilfu' a' his days been.
My han' ahin's (175) a weel gaun filly,
That aft has borne me hame frae Killie (176),
And your auld burro' mony a time,
In days when riding was nae crime—
But ance, whan in my wooing pride,
I like a blockhead boost to ride,
The wilfu' creature sae I pat to,
(L— pardon a' my sins and that too!)
I play'd my filly sic a shavie,
She's a' bedevil'd with the spavie.
My fur ahin's (177) a wordy beast,
As e'er in tug or tow was trac'd.
The fourth's a Highland Donald hastie,
A d—n'd red wud Kilburnie blastie!
Forbye a cowte o' cowtes the wale,
As ever ran afore a tail.
If he be spar'd to be a beast,
He'll draw me fifteen pun' at least—
Wheel carriages I hae but few,
Three carts, and twa a feckly new;
Ae auld wheelbarrow, mair for token,
Ae leg and baith the trams are broken;
I made a poker o' the spin'le,
And my auld mither brunt the trin'le.

For men, I've three mischievous boys,
Run de'ils for rantin' and for noise;
A gaudsman ane, a thrasher t'other,
Wee Davock hauds the nowt in fother.
I rule them, as I ought, discreetly,
And aften labour them completely;
And aye on Sundays duly, nightly,
I on the Questions targe them tightly;
Till, faith, wee Davock's turn'd sae gleg,
Tho' scarcely langer than your leg,
He'll screed you aff Effectual Calling (178),
As fast as ony in the dwalling.
I've nane in female servan' station,
(L— keep me aye frae a' temptation!)
I hae nae wife—and that my bliss is,
And ye have laid nae tax on misses;
And then, if kirk folks dinna clutch me,
I ken the devils dare na touch me.
Wi' weans I'm mair than weel contented,
Heav'n sent me ane mae than I wanted.
My sonsie smirking dear-bought Bess (179),
She stares the daddy in her face,
Enough of ought ye like but grace;
But her, my bonny sweet wee lady,
I've paid enough for her already,
And gin ye tax her or her mither,
B' the L—! ye'se get them a' thegither.

And now, remember, Mr. Aiken,
Nae kind of licence out I'm takin';
Thro' dirt and dub for life I'll paidle,
Ere I sae dear pay for a saddle;
My travel ao n foot I'll shank it,
I've sturdy bearers, Gude be thankit.
Sae dinna put me in your buke,
Nor for my ten white shillings luke.

This list wi' my ain hand I've wrote it,
The day and date as under noted;
Then know all ye whom it concerns,
Subscripsi huic,
ROBERT BURNS

Mossgiel, February 22, 1786.

A Note to Gavin Hamilton, Esq.,
MAUCHLINE.

(RECOMMENDING A BOY.)

Mossgiel, May 3, 1786.

I HOLD it, Sir, my bounden duty,
To warn you how that Master Tootie,
Alias, Laird M'Gaun,
Was here to hire yon lad away
'Bout whom ye spak the tither day,
And wad hae don't aff han':
But lest he learn the callan tricks,
As, faith, I muckle doubt him,
Like scrapin' out auld Crummie's nicks (180),
And tellin' lies about them:
As lieve then, I'd have then,
Your clerkship he should sair,
If sae be ye may be
Not fitted other where.

Altho' I say't, he's gleg enough,
And 'bout a house that's rude and rough,
The boy might learn to swear;
But then wi' you he'll be sae taught,
A get sic fair example straught,
I havena ony fear.
Ye'll catechise him every quirk,
And shore him weel wi' hell;
And gar him follow to the kirk—
—Aye when ye gang yoursel.
If ye then maun be then
Frae hame this comin' Friday;
Then please, Sir, to lea'e, Sir,
The orders wi' your lady.

My word of honour I hae gien,
In Paisley John's, that night at e'en,
To meet the warld's worm;
To try to get the twa to gree,
And name the airless (181) and the fee,
In legal mode and form:
I ken he weel a snick can draw,
When simple bodies let him;
And if a devil be at a',
In faith he's sure to get him.
To phrase you, and praise you,
Ye ken your Laureat scorns:
The pray'r still, you share still,
Of grateful MINSTREL BURNS.

Willie Chalmers. (182)

WI' braw new branks in mickle pride,
And eke a braw new brechan,
My Pegasus I'm got astride,
And up Parnassus pechin;
Whiles owre a bush wi' downward crush,
The doited beastie stammers;
Then up he gets and off he sets
For sake o' Willie Chalmers.

I doubt na, lass, that weel kenn'd name
May cost a pair o' blushes;
I am nae stranger to your fame,
Nor his warm urged wishes.
Your bonnie face sae mild and sweet,
His honest heart enamours,
And faith ye'll no be lost a whit,
Tho' waired on Willie Chalmers.

Auld truth hersel' might swear ye're fair,
And honour safely back her,
And modesty assume your air,
And ne'er a ane mistak' her:
And sic twa love inspiring een
Might fire even holy Palmers;
Nae wonder then they've fatal been
To honest Willie Chalmers.

I doubt na fortune may you shore
Some mim-mou'd pouther'd priestie,
Fu' lifted up wi' Hebrew lore,
And band upon his breastie:
But oh! what signifies to you
His lexicons and grammars;
The feeling heart's the royal blue,
And that's wi' Willie Chalmers.

Some gapin' glowrin' countra laird,
May warsle for your favour;
May claw his lug, and straik his beard,
And hoast up some palaver.
My bonnie maid, before ye wed
Sic clumsy-witted hammers,
Seek Heaven for help, and barefit skelp
Awa' wi' Willie Chalmers.

Forgive the Bard! my fond regard
For ane that shares my bosom,
Inspires my muse to gie'm his dues,
For deil a hair I roose him.
May powers aboon unite you soon,
And fructify your amours,
And every year come in mair dear
To you and Willie Chalmers.

Lines Written on a Bank Note. (183)

Wae worth thy power, thou cursed leaf,
Fell source o' a' my woe and grief:
For lack o' thee I've lost my lass,
For lack o' thee I scrimp my glass.
I see the children of affliction
Unaided, through thy cursed restriction.
I've seen the oppressor's cruel smile
Amid his hapless victim's spoil,
And, for thy potence, vainly wish'd
To crush the villain in the dust.
For lack o' thee I leave this much loved shore,
Never, perhaps, to greet old Scotland more.

R. B.—Kyle.

To a Kiss. (184)

Humid seal of soft affections,
Tend'rest pledge of future bliss,
Dearest tie of young connections,
Love's first snow-drop, virgin kiss.

Speaking silence, dumb confession,
Passion's birth, and infants' play,
Dove-like fondness, chaste concession,
Glowing dawn of brighter day.

Sorrowing joy, adieu's last action,
When ling'ring lips no more must join;
What words can ever speak affection,
So thrilling and sincere as thine!

Verses Written under Violent Grief.
(185)

Accept the gift a friend sincere
Wad on thy worth be pressin';
Remembrance oft may start a tear,
But oh! that tenderness forbear,
Though 'twad my sorrows lessen.

My 'morning raise sae clear and fair,
I thought sair storms wad never
Bedew the scene; but grief and care
In wildest fury hae made bare
My peace, my hope, for ever!

You think I'm glad; oh, I pay weel,
For a' the joy I borrow,
In solitude—then, then I feel
I canna to mysel' conceal
My deeply ranklin' sorrow.

Farewell! within thy bosom free
A sigh may whiles awaken;
A tear may wet thy laughin' ee,
For Scotia's son—ance gay like thee—
Now hopeless, comfortless, forsaken!

LYING AT A FRIEND'S HOUSE ONE NIGHT, THE AUTHOR LEFT THE FOLLOWING

Verses

IN THE ROOM WHERE HE SLEPT. (186)

Oh thou dread Power, who reign'st above,
I know thou wilt me hear,
When for this scene of peace and love
I make my prayer sincere!

The hoary sire—the mortal stroke,
Long, long, be pleased to spare,
To bless his filial little flock
And show what good men are.

She, who her lovely offspring eyes
With tender hopes and fears,
Oh, bless her with a mother's joys,
But spare a mother's tears!

Their hope, their stay, their darling youth,
In manhood's dawning blush—
Bless him, thou God of love and truth,
Up to a parent's wish!

The beauteous, seraph sister-band,
  With earnest tears I pray,
Thou know'st the snares on every hand—
  Guide Thou their steps alway.

When soon or late they reach that coast,
  O'er life's rough ocean driven,
May they rejoice, no wanderer lost,
  A family in heaven!

To Mr. M'Adam,

OF CRAIGEN-GILLAN.

SIR, o'er a gill I gat your card,
  I trow it made me proud;
"See wha taks notice o' the bard!"
  I lap and cried fu' loud.

Now deil-ma-care about their jaw,
  The senseless, gawky million:
I'll cock my nose aboon them a'—
  I'm roos'd by Craigen-Gillan!

'Twas noble, Sir; 'twas like yoursel,
  To grant your high protection:
A great man's smile, ye ken fu' well,
  Is aye a blest infection.

Tho' by his (187) banes who in a tub
  Match'd Macedonian Sandy!
On my ain legs thro' dirt and dub,
  I independent stand aye.

And when those legs to guid, warm kail,
  Wi' welcome canna bear me;
A lee dyke-side, a sybow-tail,
  A barley-scone shall cheer me.

Heaven spare you lang to kiss the breath
  O' many flow'ry simmers!
And bless your bonnie lasses baith—
  I'm tauld they're loosome kimmers!

And God bless young Dunaskin's laird,
  The blossom of our gentry!
And may he wear an auld man's beard,
  A credit to his country.

Lines on Meeting with Basil, Lord Daer.

(188)

THIS wot ye all whom it concerns,
I, Rhymer Robin, alias Burns,
    October twenty-third,
A ne'er-to-be-forgotten day,
Sae far I sprachled up the brae,
    I dinner'd wi' a Lord.

I've been at drucken writers' feasts,
Nay, been bitch-fou 'mang godly priests,
    Wi' rev'rence be it spoken;
I've ev'n join'd the honour'd jorum,
When mighty squireships of the quorum,
    Their hydra drouth did sloken.

But wi' a Lord!—stand out my shin,
A Lord—a Peer—an Earl's son!
    Up higher yet my bonnet!
And sic a Lord!—lang Scotch ells twa,
Our Peerage he o'erlooks them a',
    As I look o'er my sonnet.

But, oh! for Hogarth's magic pow'r!
To show Sir Bardie's willyart glow'r,
    And how he star'd and stammer'd,
When goavan, as if led wi' branks,
And stumpin' on his ploughman shanks,
    He in the parlour hammer'd.

I sidling shelter'd in a nook,
And at his Lordship steal't a look,
    Like some portentous omen;
Except good sense and social glee,
And (what surprised me) modesty,
    I marked nought uncommon.

I watch'd the symptoms o' the great,
The gentle pride, the lordly state,
    The arrogant assuming;
The fient a pride, nae pride had he,
Nor sauce, nor state, that I could see,
    Mair than an honest ploughman.

Then from his Lordship I shall learn,
Henceforth to meet with unconcern
    One rank as weel's another;
Nae honest worthy man need care
To meet with noble youthful Daer,
    For he but meets a brother.

Epistle to Major Logan. (189)

HAIL, thairm-inspirin', rattlin' Willie!
Though fortune's road be rough and hilly
To every fiddling, rhyming billie,
    We never heed,
But take it like the unback'd filly,
    Proud o' her speed.

When idly goavan whyles we saunter
Yirr, fancy barks, awa we canter
Uphill, down brae, till some mishanter,
    Some black bog-hole,
Arrests us, then the scathe and banter
    We're forced to thole.

Hale be your heart!—hale be your fiddle!
Lang may your elbock jink and diddle,
To cheer you through the weary widdle
    O this wild warl',
Until you on a crummock driddle
    A grey-hair'd carle.

Come wealth, come poortith, late or soon
Heaven send your heart-strings aye in tune,
And screw your temper pins aboon
    A fifth or mair,
The melancholious, lazy croon
    O' cankrie care.

May still your life from day to day
Nae "lente largo" in the play,
But "allegretto forte" gay
Harmonious flow
A sweeping, kindling, bauld strathspey—
Encore! Bravo!

A blessing on the cheery gang
Wha dearly like a jig or sang,
And never think o' right and wrang
By square and rule,
But as the clegs o' feeling stang
Are wise or fool.

My hand-waled curse keep hard in chase
The harpy, hoodock, purse-proud race,
Wha count on poortith as disgrace—
Their tuneless hearts!
May fireside discords jar a base
To a' their parts!

But come, your hand, my careless brither,
I'th' ither warl', if there's anither—
And that there is I've little swither
About the matter—
We cheek for chow shall jog thegither;
I'se ne'er bid better.

We've faults and failings—granted clearly,
We're frail backsliding mortals merely,
Eve's bonnie squad priests wyte them sheerly
For our grand fa';
But still, but still, I like them dearly—
God bless them a'!

Ochon for poor Castalian drinkers,
When they fa' foul o' earthly jinkers,
The witching curs'd delicious blinkers
Hae put me hyte,
And gart me weet my waukrife winkers,
Wi' girnin' spite.

But by yon moon!—and that's high swearin'
And every star within my hearin'!
And by her een wha was a dear ane!
I'll ne'er forget;
I hope to gie the jads a clearin'
In fair play yet.

My loss I mourn, but not repent it,
I'll seek my pursie whare I tint it,
Ance to the Indies I were wonted,
Some cantrip hour,
By some sweet elf I'll yet be dinted,
Then, *vive l'amour!*

Faites mes baissemains respectueuses,
To sentimental sister Susie,
And honest Lucky; no to roose you,
Ye may be proud,
That sic a couple fate allows ye
To grace your blood.

Nae mair at present can I measure
And trowth, my rhymin' ware's nae treasure;
But when in Ayr, some half-hour's leisure,
Be't light, be't dark,
Sir bard will do himself the pleasure
To call at Park.

ROBERT BURNS.

Mossgiel, 30th October 1786.

Lament,

WRITTEN WHEN THE POET WAS ABOUT TO LEAVE SCOTLAND.

O'ER the mist-shrouded cliffs of the lone mountain straying,
Where the wild winds of winter incessantly rave,
What woes wring my heart while intently surveying
The storm's gloomy path on the breast of the wave.

Ye foam-crested billows, allow me to wail,
Ere ye toss me afar from my lov'd native shore;
Where the flower which bloom'd sweetest in Coila's green vale,
The pride of my bosom, my Mary's no more.

No more by the banks of the streamlet we'll wander,
And smile at the moon's rimpled face in the wave;
No more shall my arms cling with fondness around her,
For the dew-drops of morning fall cold on her grave.

No more shall the soft thrill of love warm my breast,
I haste with the storm to a far distant shore;
Where unknown, unlamented, my ashes shall rest,
And joy shall revisit my bosom no more.

On a Scotch Bard,

GONE TO THE WEST INDIES. (190)

A' YE wha live by sowps o' drink,
A' ye wha live by crambo-clink,
A' ye wha live and never think,
Come, mourn wi' me!
Our billie's gien us a' jink,
And owre the sea.

Lament him a' ye rantin' core,
Wha dearly like a random-splore,
Nae mair he'll join the merry roar
In social key;
For now he's taen anither shore,
And owre the sea!

The bonny lasses weel may miss him,
And in their dear petitions place him:

The widows, wives, and a' may bless him,
Wi tearfu' e'e;
For weel I wat they'll sairly miss him
That's owre the sea!

Oh fortune, they ha'e room to grumble!
Had'st thou taen aff some drowsy bumble,
Wha can do nought but fyke and fumble,
'Twad been nae plea;
But he was gleg as ony wumble,
That's owre the sea!

Auld cantie Kyle may weepers wear
And stain them wi' the saut, saut tear;
'Twill mak her poor auld heart, I fear,
In flinders flee;
He was her laureat mony a year,
That's owre the sea!

He saw misfortune's cauld nor-west;
Lang mustering up a bitter blast;
A jillet brak his heart at last,
Ill may she be!
So, took a berth afore the mast,
And owre the sea.

To tremble under fortune's cummock,
On scarce a bellyfu' o' drummock,
Wi' his proud, independent stomach,
Could ill agree;
So row't his hurdies in a hammock,
And owre the sea.

He ne'er was gien to great misguiding,
Yet coin his pouches wad na bide in;
Wi' him it ne'er was under hiding—
He dealt it free:
The muse was a' that he took pride in,
That's owre the sea.

Jamaica bodies, use him weel,
And hap him in a cozie biel:
Ye'll find him aye a dainty chiel,
And fou' o' glee;
He wad na wrang'd the vera deil,
That's owre the sea.

Fareweel, my rhyme-composing billie!
Your native soil was right ill-willie;
But may ye flourish like a lily,
Now bonnilie!
I'll toast ye in my hindmost gillie,
Tho' owre the sea!

Written

ON THE BLANK LEAF OF A COPY OF THE POEMS, PRESENTED TO AN OLD SWEETHEART, THEN MARRIED.

ONCE fondly lov'd and still remembered dear;
Sweet early object of my youthful vows!
Accept this mark of friendship, warm, sincere,
Friendship! 'tis all cold duty now allows.

M

And when you read the simple artless rhymes,
One friendly sigh for him—he asks no more,
Who distant burns in flaming torrid climes,
Or haply lies beneath th' Atlantic roar.

The Farewell.

"The valiant, in himself, what can he suffer
Or what does he regard his single woes?
But when, alas! he multiplies himself,
To dearer selves, to the lov'd tender fair,
To those whose bliss, whose beings hang upon him,
To helpless children!—then, oh then! he feels
The point of misery fest'ring in his heart,
And weakly weeps his fortune like a coward.
Such, such am I! undone!"
THOMSON'S *Edward and Eleanora.*

FAREWELL, old Scotia's bleak domains,
Far dearer than the torrid plains
Where rich ananas blow!
Farewell, a mother's blessing dear!
A brother's sigh! a sister's tear!
My Jean's heart-rending throe!
Farewell, my Bess! tho' thou'rt bereft
Of my parental care;
A faithful brother I have left,
My part in him thou'lt share!
Adieu too, to you too,
My Smith, my bosom frien';
When kindly you mind me,
Oh then befriend my Jean!

What bursting anguish tears my heart!
From thee, my Jeany, must I part!
Thou, weeping, answ'rest "No!"
Alas! misfortune stares my face,
And points to ruin and disgrace,
I for thy sake must go!
Thee, Hamilton, and Aiken dear,
A grateful, warm adieu!
I, with a much indebted tear,
Shall still remember you?
All-hail then, the gale then,
Wafts me from thee, dear shore!
It rustles, and whistles—
I'll never see thee more!

To a Haggis. (191)

FAIR fa' your honest, sonsie face,
Great chieftain o' the puddin'-race!
Aboon them a' ye tak your place,
Painch, tripe, or thairm
Weel are ye wordy of a grace
As lang's my arm.

The groaning trencher there ye fill,
Your hurdies like a distant hill,

Your pin wad help to mend a mill
In time o' need,
While thro' your pores the dews distil
Like amber bead.

His knife see rustic labour dight,
And cut you up wi' ready slight,
Trenching your gushing entrails bright
Like ony ditch;
And then, oh what a glorious sight,
Warm-reekin', rich!

Then horn for horn they stretch and strive,
Deil tak the hindmost, on they drive,
Till a' their weel-swall'd kytes belyve
Are bent like drums;
Then auld guid man, maist like to rive,
Bethankit hums.

Is there that o'er his French ragout
Or Olio that wad staw a sow,
Or fricassee wad make her spew
Wi' perfect scunner,
Looks down wi' sneering, scornfu' view
On sic a dinner!

Poor devil! see him owre his trash,
As feckless as a wither'd rash,
His spindle shank a guid whip-lash,
His nieve a nit;
Thro' bloody flood or field to dash,
Oh how unfit!

But mark the rustic, haggis-fed,
The trembling earth resounds his tread,
Clap in his walie nieve a blade,
He'll mak it whissle;
And legs, and arms, and heads will sned,
Like taps o' thrissle.

Ye pow'rs wha mak mankind your care,
And dish them out their bill o' fare,
Auld Scotland wants nae skinking ware
That jaups in luggies;
But, if ye wish her grateful pray'r,
Gie her a Haggis!

To Miss Logan, with Beattie's Poems,

AS A NEW YEAR'S GIFT, JAN. 1. 1787.

(192)

AGAIN the silent wheels of time
Their annual round have driv'n,
And you, tho' scarce in maiden prime,
Are so much nearer Heav'n.

No gifts have I from Indian coasts
The infant year to hail;
I send you more than India boasts
In Edwin's simple tale.

Our sex with guile and faithless love
Is charg'd, perhaps, too true;
But may, dear maid, each lover prove
An Edwin still to you!

Extempore in the Court of Session.

TUNE—*Cillicrankie.*

LORD ADVOCATE. (193)

HE clench'd his pamphlets in his fist,
He quoted and he hinted,
Till in a declamation-mist,
His argument he tint it:
He gaped for't, he graiped for't,
He fand it was awa, man;
But what his common sense came short,
He eked out wi' law, man.

MR. ERSKINE. (194)

Collected Harry stood a wee,
Then open'd out his arm, man:
His lordship sat wi' ruefu' e'e,
And ey'd the gathering storm, man;
Like wind-driv'n hail, it did assail,
Or torrents owre a linn, man;
The bench sae wise lift up their eyes,
Half-wauken'd wi' the din, man.

To the Guidwife of Wauchope House.

(195)

"My cantie, witty, rhyming ploughman,
I hafflins doubt it is na' true, man,
That ye between the stilts was bred,
Wi' ploughmen schooled, wi' ploughmen fed
I doubt it sair, ye've drawn your knowledge
Either frae grammar-school or college.
Guid troth, your saul and body baith
War better fed, I'd gie my aith,
Than theirs who sup sour milk and parritch,
And bummil through the single Carritch.
Whaever heard the ploughman speak,
Could tell gif Homer was a Greek?
He'd flee as soon upon a cudgel,
As get a single line of Virgil.
And then sae slee ye crack your jokes
O' Willie Pitt and Charlie Fox:
Our great men a' sae weel descrive,
And how to gar the nation thrive,
Ane maist wad swear ye dwelt amang them.
And as ye saw them sae ye sang them.
But be ye ploughman, be ye peer,
Ye are a funny blade, I swear;
And though the cauld I ill can bide,
Yet twenty miles and mair I'd ride
O'er moss and moor, and never grumble,
Though my auld yad should gie a stumble,
To crack a winter night wi' thee,
And hear thy sangs and sonnets slee.
Oh gif I kenn'd but where ye baide,
I'd send to you a marled plaid;
'Twad houd your shouthers warm and braw,
And douce at kirk or market shaw;
Fra' south as weel as north, my lad,
A' honest Scotsmen loe the maud."

I MIND it weel in early date,
When I was beardless young, and blate,
And first could thresh the barn;
Or haud a yokin' at the pleugh;
And tho' forfoughten sair eneug
Yet unco proud to learn:

When first amang the yellow corn
 A man I reckon'd was,
And wi' the lave ilk merry morn
 Could rank my rig and lass,
 Still shearing, and clearing,
 The tither stooked raw,
 Wi' claivers, and haivers,
 Wearing the day awa.

E'en then, a wish, I mind its pow'r—
A wish that to my latest hour
 Shall strongly heave my breast—
That I, for poor auld Scotland's sake,
Some usefu' plan or beuk could make
 Or sing a sang at least
The rough burr-thissle, spreading wide
 Amang the bearded bear,
I turn'd the weeder-clips aside,
 And spar'd the symbol dear:
 No nation, no station,
 My envy e'er could raise,
 A Scot still, but blot still,
 I knew nae higher praise.

But still the elements o' sang
In formless jumble, right and wrang,
 Wild floated in my brain;
Till on that hur'st I said before,
My partner in the merry core,
 She rous'd the forming strain:
I see her yet, the sonsie quean,
 That lighted up her jingle,
Her witching smile, her pauky een
 That gart my heart-strings tingle:
 I fired, inspired,
 At every kindling keek,
 But bashing and dashing
 I feared aye to speak.

Health to the sex, ilk guid chiel says,
Wi' merry dance in winter days,
 And we to share in common:
The gust o' joy, the balm of woe,
The saul o' life, the heaven below,
 Is rapture-giving woman.
Ye surly sumphs, who hate the name,
 Be mindfu' o' your mither:
She, honest woman, may think shame
 That ye're connected with her.
 Ye're wae men, ye're nae men
 That slight the lovely dears;
 To shame ye, disclaim ye,
 Ilk honest birkie swears.

For you, no bred to barn and byre,
Wha sweetly tune the Scottish lyre,
 Thanks to you for your line:
The marled plaid ye kindly spare,
By me should gratefully be ware;
 'Twad please me to the nine.

I'd be mair vauntie o' my hap,
 Douce hingin' owre my curple,
Than ony ermine ever lap,
 Or proud imperial purple.
 Fareweel then, lang heal then,
 And plenty be your fa',
 May losses and crosses
 Ne'er at your hallan ca'.

Verses

WRITTEN UNDER THE PORTRAIT OF FERGUSSON, THE POET, IN A COPY OF THAT AUTHOR'S WORKS PRESENTED TO A YOUNG LADY IN EDINBURGH, MARCH 19, 1787.

CURSE on ungrateful man, that can be pleas'd,
And yet can starve the author of the pleasure!
Oh thou, my elder brother in misfortune,
By far my elder brother in the muses,
With tears I pity thy unhappy fate!
Why is the bard unpitied by the world,
Yet has so keen a relish of its pleasures?

Inscription

ON THE HEADSTONE OF FERGUSSON.

Here lies
ROBERT FERGUSSON, Poet,
Born, Sept. 5, 1751.
Died, Oct. 15, 1774.

No sculptured marble here, nor pompous lay,
 "No storied urn nor animated bust;"
This simple stone directs pale Scotia's way
 To pour her sorrows o'er her poet's dust.

Prologue,

SPOKEN BY MR. WOODS ON HIS BENEFIT NIGHT.

Monday, 16th April, 1787. (196)

WHEN by a generous Public's kind acclaim,
That dearest meed is granted—honest fame:
When here your favour is the actor's lot,
Nor even the man in private life forgot;
What breast so dead to heav'nly Virtue's glow,
But heaves impassion'd with the grateful throe.

Poor is the task to please a barb'rous throng,
It needs no Siddons' powers in Southern's song,
But here an ancient nation fam'd afar,
For genius, learning high, as great in war—
Hail, CALEDONIA, name for ever dear!
Before whose sons I'm honour'd to appear!

Where every science—every nobler art—
That can inform the mind, or mend the heart,
Is known; as grateful nations oft have found
Far as the rude barbarian marks the bound.
Philosophy, no idle pedant dream,
Here holds her search by heaven-taught Reason's beam;
Here history paints with elegance and force,
The tide of Empire's fluctuating course;
Here Douglas forms wild Shakespeare into plan,
And Harley (197) rouses all the god in man,
When well-form'd taste and sparkling wit unite
With manly lore, or female beauty bright
(Beauty, where faultless symmetry and grace,
Can only charm us in the second place),
Witness my heart, how oft with panting fear
As on this night, I've met these judges here!
But still the hope Experience taught to live,
Equal to judge—you're candid to forgive.
No hundred-headed Riot here we meet,
With decency and law beneath his feet;
Nor Insolence assumes fair Freedom's name;
Like CALEDONIANS, you applaud or blame.

Oh thou dread Power; whose empire-giving hand
Has oft been stretch'd to shield the honour'd land!
Strong may she glow with all her ancient fire!
May every son be worthy of his sire!
Firm may she rise with generous disdain
At Tyranny's, or direr Pleasure's chain!
Still self-dependent in her native shore,
Bold may she brave grim Danger's loudest roar,
Till fate the curtain drop on world's to be no more.

Epistle to William Creech.

(198)

AULD chuckie Reekie's (199) sair distrest,
Down droops her ance weel-burnish'd crest,
Nae joy her bonnie buskit nest,
Can yield awa,
Her darling bird that she lo'es best,
Willie's ava!

Oh Willie was a witty wight,
And had o' things an unco slight;
Auld Reekie aye he keepit tight,
And trig and braw:
But now they'll busk her like a fright—
Willie's awa!

The stiffest o' them a' he bow'd;
The bauldest o' them a' he cow'd;
They durst nae mair than he allow'd,
That was a law:
We've lost a birkie weel worth gowd—
Willie's awa!

Now gawkies, tawpies, gowks, and fools,
Frae colleges and boarding-schools,
May sprout like simmer puddock-stools
In glen or shaw;
He wha could brush them down to mools,
Willie's awa!

The brethren o' the Commerce-Chaumer (200)
May morn their loss wi' doolfu' clamour;
He was a dictionar and grammar
Amang them a';
I fear they'll now mak mony a stammer—
Willie's awa!

Nae mair we see his levee door
Philosophers and poets pour,
And toothy critics by the score,
In bloody raw!
The adjutant o' a' the core,
Willie's awa!

Now worthy Gregory's Latin face,
Tytler's and Greenfield's modest grace;
Mackenzie, Stewart, sic a brace
As Rome ne'er saw;
They a' maun meet some ither place,
Willie's awa!

Poor Burns — e'en Scotch drink canna quicken,
He cheeps like some bewilder'd chicken,
Scar'd frae its minnie and the cleckin
By hoodie-craw!
Grief's gien his heart an unco kickin'—
Willie's awa!

Now ev'ry sour-mou'd girnin' blellum,
And Calvin's folk, are fit to fell him;
And self-conceited critic skellum
His quill may draw;
He wha could brawlie ward their bellum,
Willie's awa!

Up wimpling stately Tweed I've sped,
And Eden scenes on crystal Jed,
And Ettrick banks now roaring red,
While tempests blaw;
But every joy and pleasure's fled—
Willie's awa!

May I be slander's common speech;
A text for infamy to preach;
And lastly, streekit out to bleach
In winter snaw;
When I forget thee, Willie Creech,
Tho' far awa!

JOHN ANDERSON MY JO.

But now your head's turned bald, John, your locks are like the snaw,
Yet blessings on your frosty pow, John Anderson, my jo.

May never wicked fortune touzle him!
May never wicked men bamboozle him!
Until a pow as auld's Methusalem
He canty claw!
Then to the blessed New Jerusalem,
Fleet wing awa!

On the Death of Sir James Hunter Blair.

(201)

THE lamp of day, with ill-presaging glare,
Dim, cloudy, sank beneath the western wave.
Th' inconstant blast howl'd through the dark'ning air,
And hollow whistled in the rocky cave.

Lone as I wander'd by each cliff and dell,
Once the lov'd haunts of Scotia's royal train (202);
Or mus'd where limpid streams once hallow'd well (203),
Or mould'ring ruins mark the sacred fane. (204)

Th' increasing blast roared round the beetling rocks,
The clouds, swift-wing'd, flew o'er the starry sky,
The groaning trees untimely shed their locks,
And shooting meteors caught the startled eye.

The paly moon rose in the livid east,
And 'mong the cliffs disclos'd a stately form,
In weeds of woe, that frantic beat her breast,
And mix'd her wailings with the raving storm.

Wild to my heart the filial pulses glow,
'Twas Caledonia's trophied shield I view'd:
Her form majestic-droop'd in pensive woe,
The lightning of her eye in tears imbued.

Revers'd that spear, redoubtable in war,
Reclin'd that banner, erst in fields unfurl'd,
That like a deathful meteor gleam'd afar,
And brav'd the mighty monarchs of the world.

"My patriot son fills an untimely grave!"
With accents wild and lifted arms—she cried;
"Low lies the hand that oft was stretch'd to save,
Low lies the heart that swell'd with honest pride.

A weeping country joins a widow's tear;
The helpless poor mix with the orphan's cry;
The drooping arts surround their patron's bier;
And grateful science heaves the heart-felt sigh!

I saw my sons resume their ancient fire;
I saw fair freedom's blossoms richly blow:
But ah! how hope is born but to expire!
Relentless fate has laid their guardian low.

My patriot falls, but shall he lie unsung,
While empty greatness saves a worthless name?
No; every muse shall join her tuneful tongue,
And future ages hear his growing fame.

And I will join a mother's tender cares.
Thro' future times to make his virtue last;
That distant years may boast of other Blairs!"—
She said, and vanish'd with the sweeping blast.

On Scaring some Water-Fowl in Loch-Turit.

A WILD SCENE AMONG THE HILLS OF OCHTERTYRE.

WHY ye tenants of the lake,
For me your wat'ry haunt forsake?
Tell me, fellow-creatures, why
At my presence thus you fly?
Why disturb your social joys,
Parent, filial, kindred ties?—
Common friend to you and me,
Nature's gifts to all are free:
Peaceful keep your dimpling wave,
Busy feed, or wanton lave;
Or beneath the sheltering rock,
Bide the surging billows shock.

Conscious, blushing for our race.
Soon, too soon, your fears I trace.
Man, your proud usurping foe,
Would be lord of all below:
Plumes himself in Freedom's pride,
Tyrant stern to all beside.
The eagle, from yon cliffy brow,
Marking you his prey below,
In his breast no pity dwells,
Strong necessity compels:
But man, to whom alone is giv'n
A ray direct from pitying Heav'n
Glories in his heart humane—
And creatures for his pleasure slain.
In these savage, liquid plains,
Only known to wand'ring swains,
Where the mossy riv'let strays,
Far from human haunts and ways;
All on Nature you depend,
And life's poor season peaceful spend.

Or, if man's superior might
Dare invade your native right.
On the lofty ether borne,
Man with all his pow'rs you scorn;
Swiftly seek, on clanging wings,
Other lakes and other springs;
And the foe you cannot brave,
Scorn, at least, to be his slave.

The Humble Petition of Bruar Water.

TO THE NOBLE DUKE OF ATHOLE. (205)

My Lord, I know your noble ear
  Woe ne'er assails in vain;
Embolden'd thus, I beg you'll hear
  Your humble slave complain,
How saucy Phœbus' scorching beams,
  In flaming summer-pride,
Dry-withering, waste my foamy streams,
  And drink my crystal tide.

The lightly-jumpin' glowrin' trouts,
  That thro' my waters play,
If, in their random, wanton spouts,
  They near the margin stray;
If, hapless chance! they linger lang,
  I'm scorching up so shallow,
They're left the whitening stanes amang,
  In gasping death to wallow.

Last day I grat wi' spite and teen,
  As poet Burns came by,
That to a bard I should be seen
  Wi' half my channel dry:
A panegyric rhyme, I ween,
  Even as I was he shor'd me;
But had I in my glory been,
  He, kneeling, wad ador'd me.

Here, foaming down the shelvy rocks,
  In twisting strength I rin;
There, high my boiling torrent smokes,
  Wild roaring o'er a linn:
Enjoying large each spring and well,
  As nature gave them me,
I am, altho' I say't mysel'
  Worth gaun a mile to see.

Would then my noble master please
  To grant my highest wishes,
He'll shade my banks wi' tow'ring trees,
  And bonnie spreading bushes.
Delighted doubly then, my Lord,
  You'll wander on my banks,
And listen mony a grateful bird
  Return you tuneful thanks.

The sober laverock, warbling wild,
  Shall to the skies aspire;
The gowdspink, music's gayest child,
  Shall sweetly join the choir.
The blackbird strong, the lintwhite clear.
  The mavis mild and mellow;
The robin pensive autumn cheer,
  In all her locks of yellow.

This, too, a covert shall insure
  To shield them from the storm;
And coward maukin sleep secure,
  Low in her grassy form:
Here shall the shepherd make his seat,
  To weave his crown of flow'rs:
Or find a shelt'ring safe retreat
  From prone descending show'rs.

And here, by sweet endearing stealth,
  Shall meet the loving pair,
Despising worlds with all their wealth
  As empty idle care.
The flow'rs shall vie in all their charms
  The hour of heav'n to grace,
And birks extend their fragrant arms
  To screen the dear embrace.

Here, haply too, at vernal dawn,
  Some musing bard may stray,
And eye the smoking, dewy lawn,
  And misty mountain gray;
Or, by the reaper's nightly beam,
  Mild-chequering thro' the trees,
Rave to my darkly-dashing stream,
  Hoarse swelling on the breeze.

Let lofty firs, and ashes cool,
  My lowly banks o'erspread,
And view, deep-bending in the pool,
  Their shadows' water'y bed!
Let fragrant birks in woodbines drest
  My craggy cliffs adorn;
And, for the little songsters nest,
  The close embow'ring thorn.

So may old Scotia's darling hope,
  Your little angel band,
Spring, like their fathers, up to prop
  Their honour'd native land!
So may, thro' Albion's farthest ken,
  To social flowing glasses,
The grace be—"Athole's honest men,
  And Athole's bonnie lasses!"

The Hermit.

WRITTEN ON A MARBLE SIDEBOARD, IN THE HERMITAGE BELONGING TO THE DUKE OF ATHOLE, IN THE WOOD OF ABERFELDY.

Whoe'er thou art, these lines now reading,
Think not, though from the world receding,
I joy my lonely days to lead in
    This desert drear;
That fell remorse a conscience bleeding
    Hath led me here.

No thought of guilt my bosom sours;
Free-will'd I fled from courtly bowers;
For well I saw in halls and towers
    That lust and pride,
The arch-fiend's dearest, darkest powers,
    In state preside.

I saw mankind with vice encrusted;
I saw that honour's sword was rusted;
That few for aught but folly lusted;
That he was still deceiv'd who trusted
To love or friend;
And hither came, with men disgusted,
My life to end.

In this lone cave, in garments lowly,
Alike a foe to noisy folly,
And brow-bent gloomy melancholy,
I wear away
My life, and in my office holy
Consume the day.

This rock my shield; when storms are blowing,
The limpid streamlet yonder flowing
Supplying drink, the earth bestowing
My simple food;
But few enjoy the calm I know in
This desert wood.

Content and comfort bless me more in
This grot, than e'er I felt before in
A palace—and with thoughts still soaring
To God on high,
Each night and morn with voice imploring,
This wish I sigh.

"Let me, oh Lord! from life retire,
Unknown each guilty worldly fire,
Remorse's throb, or loose desire;
And when I die,
Let me in this belief expire—
To God I fly."

Stranger, if full of youth and riot,
And yet no grief has marr'd thy quiet,
Thou haply throw'st a scornful eye at
The hermit's prayer—
But if thou hast good cause to sigh at
Thy fault or care;

If thou hast known false love's vexation,
Or hast been exiled from thy nation,
Or guilt affrights thy contemplation,
And makes thee pine,
Oh! how must thou lament thy station,
And envy mine!

Verses

WRITTEN WITH A PENCIL OVER THE CHIMNEY-PIECE, IN THE PARLOUR OF THE INN AT KENMORE, TAYMOUTH.

Admiring Nature in her wildest grace,
These northern scenes with weary feet I trace;
O'er many a winding dale and painful steep,
Th' abodes of covied grouse and timid sheep,
My savage journey, curious, I pursue,
Till fam'd Breadelbane opens to my view.
The meeting cliffs each deep-sunk glen divides,
The woods, wild scatter'd, clothe their ample sides;
Th' outstretching lake, embosom'd 'mong the hills,
The eye with wonder and amazement fills;
The Tay, meand'ring sweet in infant pride,
The palace, rising on its verdant side;
The lawns, wood-fring'd in Nature's native taste;
The hillocks, dropt in Nature's careless haste;
The arches, striding o'er the new-born stream;
The village, glittering in the noontide beam—

* * * *

Poetic ardours in my bosom swell,
Lone wand'ring by the hermit's mossy cell:
The sweeping theatre of hanging woods;
Th' incessant roar of headlong tumbling floods—

* * * *

Here Poesy might wake her heav'n-taught lyre,
And look through nature with creative fire;
Here, to the wrongs of fate half reconcil'd
Misfortune's lighten'd steps might wander wild;
And disappointment, in these lonely bounds,
Find balm to soothe her bitter, rankling wounds:
Here heart-struck Grief might heav'nward stretch her scan,
And injur'd Worth forget and pardon man.

* * * *

Elegy on the Death of Lord President Dundas. (206)

Lone on the bleaky hills the straying flocks
Shun the fierce storms among the sheltering rocks;
Down from the rivulets, red with dashing rains,
The gathering floods burst o'er the distant plains;
Beneath the blasts the leafless forests groan;
The hollow caves return a sullen moan.

Ye hills, ye plains, ye forests, and ye caves,
Ye howling winds, and wintry swelling waves!
Unheard, unseen, by human ear or eye,
Sad to your sympathetic scenes I fly;
Where to the whistling blast and waters' roar
Pale Scotia's recent wound I may deplore.
Oh heavy loss, thy country ill could bear!
A loss these evil days can ne'er repair!
Justice, the high vicegerent of her God,
Her doubtful balance ey'd, and sway'd her rod;
Hearing the tidings of the fatal blow
She sank, abandon'd to the wildest woe.
Wrongs, injuries, from many a darksome den,
Now gay in hope explore the paths of men:

See from his cavern grim Oppression rise,
And throw on poverty his cruel eyes;
Keen on the helpless victim see him fly,
And stifle, dark, the feebly-bursting cry.

Mark ruffian Violence, distained with crimes
Rousing elate in these degenerate times;
View unsuspecting Innocence a prey,
As guileful Fraud points out the erring way:
While subtile Litigation's pliant tongue
The life-blood equal sucks of Right and Wrong:
Hark, injur'd Want recounts th' unlisten'd tale,
And much-wrong'd mis'ry pours th' unpitied Wail!

Ye dark waste hills, and brown unsightly plains,
To you I sing my grief-inspired strains:
Ye tempests, rage! ye turbid torrents, roll!
Ye suit the joyless tenor of my soul.
Life's social haunts and pleasures I resign,
Be nameless wilds and lonely wanderings mine,
To mourn the woes my country must endure,
That wound degenerate ages cannot cure.

Verses

WRITTEN WHILE STANDING BY THE FALL OF FYERS, NEAR LOCH-NESS.

AMONG the heathy hills and ragged woods;
The foaming Fyers pours his mossy floods,
Till full he dashes on the rocky mounds,
Where, thro' a shapeless beach, his stream resounds,
As high in air the bursting torrents flow,
As deep-recoiling surges foam below,
Prone down the rock the whitening sheet descends,
And viewless Echo's ear, astonished, rends.
Dim seen, through rising mists and ceaseless show'rs,
The hoary cavern, wide surrounding low'rs;
Still thro' the gap the struggling river toils,
And still below, the horrid cauldron boils—

* * * *

ON READING IN A NEWSPAPER

The Death of John M'Leod, Esq.,

BROTHER TO A YOUNG LADY, A PARTICULAR FRIEND OF THE AUTHOR'S.

SAD thy tale, thou idle page,
And rueful thy alarms—
Death tears the brother of her love
From Isabella's arms.

Sweetly deck'd with pearly dew
The morning rose may blow,
But cold successive noontide blasts
May lay its beauties low.

Fair on Isabella's morn
The sun propitious smil'd,
But, long ere noon, succeeding clouds
Succeeding hopes beguil'd.

Fate oft tears the bosom cords
That Nature finest strung;
So Isabella's heart was form'd,
And so that heart was wrung.

Were it in the poet's power,
Strong as he shares the grief.
That pierces Isabella's heart,
To give that heart relief.

Dread Omnipotence, alone,
Can heal the wound he gave—
Can point the brimful grief-worn eyes
To scenes beyond the grave.

Virtue's blossoms there shall blow,
And fear no with'ring blast;
There Isabella's spotless worth
Shall happy be at last.

On William Smellie. (207)

SHREW'D Willie Smellie to Crochallan (208) came,
The old cock'd hat, the grey surtout, the same;
His bristling beard just rising in its might,
'Twas four long nights and days to shaving night;
His uncomb'd grizzly locks wild staring, thatch'd
A head for thought profound and clear unmatch'd;
Yet tho' his caustic wit was biting, rude,
His heart was warm, benevolent, and good.

Address to Mr. William Tytler.

WITH THE PRESENT OF THE BARD'S PICTURE. (209)

REVERED defender of beauteous Stuart,
Of Stuart a name once respected—
A name which to love was the mark of a true heart,
But now 'tis despised and neglected.

Tho' something like moisture conglobes in my eye,
Let no one misdeem me disloyal;
A poor friendless wand'rer may well claim a sigh,
Still more, if that wand'rer were royal.

My fathers that name have rever'd on a throne;
My fathers have fallen to right it;
Those fathers would spurn their degenerate son,
That name should he scoffingly slight it.

Still in prayers for King George I most heartily join,
  The Queen, and the rest of the gentry,
Be they wise, be they foolish, is nothing of mine;
  Their title's avowed by my country,

But why of that epocha make such a fuss,
  That gave us the Hanover stem;
If bringing them over was lucky for us,
  I'm sure 'twas as lucky for them.

But loyalty, truce! we're on dangerous ground,
  Who knows how the fashions may alter?
The doctrine, to-day, that is loyalty sound,
  To-morrow may bring us a halter!

I send you a trifle, a head of a bard,
  A trifle scarce worthy your care;
But accept it, good Sir, as a mark of regard,
  Sincere as a saint's dying prayer,

Now life's chilly evening dim shades on your eye,
  And ushers the long dreary night;
But you like the star that athwart gilds the sky,
  Your course to the latest is bright.

A Sketch. (210)

A LITTLE, upright, pert, tart tripping wight,
And still his precious self his dear delight:
Who loves his own smart shadow in the streets,
Better than e'er the fairest she he meets,
A man of fashion too, he made his tour,
Learn'd *vive la bagatelle, et vive l'amour*
So travelled monkies their grimace improve,
Polish their grin, nay, sigh for ladies love.
Much specious lore, but little understood;
Veneering oft outshines the solid wood:
His solid sense—by inches you must tell,
But mete his cunning by the old Scots ell!
His meddling vanity, a busy fiend
Still making work his selfish craft must mend.

To Miss Cruikshanks.

A VERY YOUNG LADY. (211)

WRITTEN ON THE BLANK LEAF OF A BOOK PRESENTED TO HER BY THE AUTHOR.

BEAUTEOUS rose-bud, young and gay,
Blooming in thy early May,
Never may'st thou, lovely flow'r,
Chilly shrink in sleety show'r;
Never Boreas' hoary path,
Never Eurus' poisonous breath,
Never baleful stellar lights,
Taint thee with untimely blights!
Never, never reptile thief
Riot on thy virgin leaf!
Nor even Sol too fiercely view
Thy bosom blushing still with dew!

May'st thou long, sweet crimson gem,
Richly deck thy native stem:
'Till some evening, sober, calm,
Dropping dews and breathing balm,
While all around the woodland rings,
And every bird thy requiem sings;
Thou, amid the dirgeful sound,
Shed thy dying honours round,
And resign to parent earth
The loveliest form she e'er gave birth.

An Extempore Effusion,

ON BEING APPOINTED TO THE EXCISE.

SEARCHING auld wives barrels,
  Och, hon! the day!
That clarty barm should stain my laurels;
  But—what'll ye say!
These muvin' things ca'd wives and weans,
Wad muve the very hearts o' stanes!

To Clarinda,

WITH A PRESENT OF A PAIR OF DRINKING GLASSES. (212)

FAIR Empress of the Poet's soul,
  And Queen of Poetesses!
Clarinda, take this little boon,
  This humble pair of glasses.

And fill them high with generous juice,
  As generous as your mind;
And pledge me in the generous toast—
  "The whole of human kind!"

"To those who love us!"—second fill;
  But not to those whom we love;
Lest us love those who love not us!—
  A third—"To thee and me, love!"

To Clarinda,

ON HIS LEAVING EDINBURGH.

CLARINDA, mistress of my soul,
  The measur'd time is run!
The wretch beneath the dreary pole
  So marks his latest sun.

To what dark cave of frozen night
  Shall poor Sylvander hie;
Depriv'd of thee, his life and light,
  The sun of all his joy.

We part—but, by these precious drops
  That fill thy lovely eyes!
No other light shall guide my steps
  Till thy bright beams arise.

She, the fair sun of all her sex,
  Has blest my glorious day;
And shall a glimmering planet fix
  My worship to its ray?

Epistle to Hugh Parker. (213)

In this strange land, this uncouth clime,
A land unknown to prose or rhyme;
Where words ne'er crossed the muse's [heckles,
Nor limpet in poetic shackles;
A land that prose did never view it,
Except when drunk he stacher't thro' it;
Here, ambush'd by the chimla cheek,
Hid in an atmosphere of reek,
I hear a wheel thrum i' the neuk,
I hear it—for in vain I leuk.
The red peat gleams, a fiery kernel,
Enhusked by a fog infernal:
Here for my wonted rhyming raptures,
I sit and count my sins by chapters,
For life and spunk like ither Christians,
I'm dwindled down to mere existence,
Wi' nae converse but Gallowa' bodies,
Wi' nae-kenn'd face but Jenny Geddes.
Jenny, my Pegasean pride!
Dowie she saunters down Nithside,
And aye a westlin heuk she throws,
While tears hap o'er her auld brown nose!
Was it for this, wi' canny care,
Thou bure the Bard through many a shire?
At howes or hillocks never stumbled,
And late or early never grumbled?
Oh, had I power like inclination,
I'd heeze thee up a constellation,
To canter with the Sagitarre,
Or loup the ecliptic like a bar!
Or turn the pole like any arrow;
Or, when auld Phœbus bids good-morrow,
Down the zodiac urge the race,
And cast dirt on his godship's face;
For I could lay my bread and kail
He'd ne'er cast salt upo' thy tail.
Wi' a' this care and a' this grief,
And sma', sma' prospect of relief,
And nought but peat-reek i' my head
How can I write what ye can read?
Tarbolton, twenty-fourth o' June,
Ye'll find me in a better tune;
But till we meet and weet our whistle,
Tak this excuse for nae epistle.

Robert Burns.

Written

IN FRIARS' CARSE HERMITAGE, ON THE BANKS OF NITH. (214).

Thou whom chance may hither lead,
Be thou clad in russet weed,
Be thou deckt in silken stole,
Grave these maxims on thy soul.

Life is but a day at most,
Sprung from night; in darkness lost;
Day, how rapid in its flight—
Day, how few must see the night;
Hope not sunshine every hour,
Fear not clouds will always lower.
Happiness is but a name,
Make content and ease thy aim.
Ambition is a meteor gleam;
Fame a restless idle dream:
Pleasures, insects on the wing
Round Peace, the tend'rest flower of Spring;
Those that sip the dew alone,
Make the butterflies thy own;
Those that would the bloom devour,
Crush the locusts—save the flower.
For the future be prepar'd,
Guard wherever thou can'st guard;
But thy utmost duly done,
Welcome what thou can'st not shun.
Follies past, give thou to air,
Make their consequence thy care:
Keep the name of man in mind,
And dishonour not thy kind.
Reverence with lowly heart,
Him whose wondrous work thou art;
Keep his goodness still in view,
Thy trust—and thy example, too.
Stranger, go; Heaven be thy guide!
Quoth, the Beadsman on Nithside

Thou whom chance may hither lead.
Be thou clad in russet weed,
Be thou deckt in silken stole,
Grave these counsels on thy soul.

Life is but a day at most,
Sprung from night, in darkness lost;
Hope not sunshine ev'ry hour,
Fear not clouds will always lower.

As youth and love with sprightly dance,
Beneath thy morning star advance,
Pleasure with her siren air
May delude the thoughtless pair;
Let Prudence bless Enjoyment's cup,
Then raptur'd sip, and sip it up,
As thy day grows warm and high,
Life's meridian flaming nigh,
Dost thou spurn the humble vale?
Life's proud summits would'st thou scale?
Check thy climbing step elate,
Evils lurk in felon wait:
Dangers, eagle-pinion'd, bold,
Soar around each cliffy hold,
While cheerful peace, with linnet song,
Chants the lowly dells among.
As the shades of ev'ning close,
Beck'ning thee to long repose.
As life itself becomes disease,
Seek the chimney-neuk of ease;
There ruminate with sober thought,
On all thou'st seen, and heard, and wrought;
And teach the sportive younkers round,
Saws of experience, sage and sound.

Say, man's true, genuine estimate,
The grand criterion of his fate,
Is not—art thou high or low?
Did thy fortune ebb or flow?
Wast thou cottager or king?
Peer or peasant?—no such thing!
Did many talents gild thy span?
Or frugal nature grudge thee one?
Tell them, and press it on their mind,
As thou thyself must shortly find,
The smile or frown of awful Heav'n,
To virtue or to vice is giv'n.
Say, to be just, and kind, and wise,
There solid self-enjoyment lies;
That foolish, selfish, faithless ways
Lead to the wretched, vile and base.

Thus resign'd and quiet, creep
To the bed of lasting sleep;
Sleep, whence thou shalt ne'er awake,
Night, where dawn shall never break.
Till future life, future no more,
To light and joy the good restore,
To light and joy unknown before.

Stranger, go! Heav'n be thy guide!
Quoth, the Beadsman of Nith-side.

Extempore to Captain Riddel,

OF GLENRIDDLE, ON RETURNING A NEWSPAPER. (215)

Ellisland, Monday Evening.

YOUR news and review, Sir, I've read through and through, Sir,
With little admiring or blaming;
The papers are barren of home-news or foreign,
No murders or rapes worth the naming.

Our friends, the reviewers, those chippers and hewers,
Are judges of mortar and stone, Sir;
But of *meet* or *unmeet*, in a *fabric complete*,
I'll boldly pronounce they are none, Sir.

My goose-quill too rude is to tell all your goodness
Bestowed on your servant, the Poet;
Would to God I had one like a beam of the sun,
And then all the world, Sir, should know it!

A Mother's Lament.

FOR THE DEATH OF HER SON. (216)

FATE gave the word, the arrow sped,
And pierc'd my darling's heart!
And with him all the joys are fled
Life can to me impart.

By cruel hands the sapling drops,
In dust dishonour'd laid:
So fell the pride of all my hopes,
My age's future shade.

The mother linnet in the brake
Bewails her ravish'd young;
So I, for my lost darling's sake,
Lament the live-day long.
Death, oft I've fear'd thy fatal blow,
Now, fond I bare my breast,
Oh, do thou kindly lay me low
With him I love, at rest!

Elegy

ON THE YEAR 1788.

FOR Lords or Kings I dinna mourn,
E'en let them die—for that they're born:
But oh! prodigious to reflec'!
A towmont, Sirs, is gane to wreck!
Oh Eighty-eight, in thy sma' space
What dire events ha'e taken place!
Of what enjoyments thou hast reft us!
In what a pickle thou hast left us!

The Spanish empire's tint a head,
And my auld teethless Bawtie's dead;
The tulzie's sair 'tween Pitt and Fox,
And our guidwife's wee birdie cocks;
The tane is game, a bluidie devil,
But to the hen-birds unco civil:
The tither's something dear o' treadin',
But better stuff ne'er claw'd a midden.
Ye ministers, come mount the pu'pit'
And cry till ye be hoarse or roupit,
For Eighty-eight he wish'd you weel,
And gied you a' baith gear and meal;
E'en mony a plack, and mony a peck,
Ye ken yoursels, for little feck!

Ye bonnie lasses' dight your e'en,
For some o' you ha'e tint a frien';
In Eighty-eight, ye ken, was ta'en,
What ye'll ne'er hae to gie again.
Observe the very nowte and sheep,
How dowf and dowie now they creep;
Nay, even the yirth itsel' does cry,
For Embro' wells are grutten dry.

Oh Eighty-nine, thou's but a bairn,
And no owre auld, I hope, to learn!
Thou beardless boy, I pray tak' care,
Thou now has got thy daddy's chair,
Nae hand-cuff'd, muzzl'd, hap-shackl'd Regent,
But like himsel', a full free agent,
Be sure ye follow out the plan
Nae waur than he did, honest man!
As muckle better as you can.

Address to the Tooth-Ache.

MY curse upon thy venom'd stang,
That shoots my tortur'd gums alang;
And thro' my lugs gies mony a twang,
Wi' gnawing vengeance;
Tearing my nerves wi' bitter pang,
Like racking engines!

When fevers burn, or ague freezes,
Rheumatics gnaw, or cholic squeezes;
Our neighbour's sympathy may ease us,
Wi' pitying moan;
But thee—thou hell o' a' diseases,
Aye mocks our groan!

Adown my beard the slavers trickle!
I kick the wee stools o'er the mickle,
As round the fire the giglets keckle,
To see me loup;
While, raving mad, I wish a heckle
Were in their doup.

O' a' the num'rous human dools,
Ill har'sts, daft bargains, cutty-stools,
Or worthy friends rak'd i' the mools,
Sad sight to see!
The tricks o' knaves, or fash o' fools—
Thou bear'st the gree.

Where'er that place be priests ca' hell,
Whence a' the tones o' mis'ry yell,
And ranked plagues their numbers tell,
In dreadfu' raw,
Thou, Toothache, surely bear'st the bell
Amang them a'!

Oh thou grim mischief-making chiel,
That gars the notes of discord squeel,
Till daft mankind aft dance a reel
In gore a shoe-thick!—
Gie a' the faes o' Scotland's weal
A towmond's Toothache!

Ode,

SACRED TO THE MEMORY OF MRS. OSWALD. (217)

DWELLER in yon dungeon dark,
Hangman of creation, mark!
Who in widow-weeds appears,
Laden with unhonoured years,
Noosing with care a bursting purse,
Baited with many a deadly curse!

STROPHE.

View the wither'd beldam's face—
Can thy keen inspection trace
Aught of humanity's sweet melting grace?
Note that eye, 'tis rheum o'erflows,
Pity's flood there never rose.
See these hands, ne'er stretch'd to save,
Hands that took—but never gave.
Keeper of Mammon's iron chest,
Lo, there she goes, unpitied and unblest
She goes, but not to realms of everlasting rest!

ANTISTROPHE.

Plunderer of armies, lift thine eyes,
(Awhile forbear, ye tort'ring fiends;)
Seest thou whose step, unwilling, hither bends?
No fallen angel, hurl'd from upper skies;
'Tis thy trusty quondam mate,
Doom'd to share thy fiery fate,
She, tardy, hell-ward plies,

EPODE.

And are they of no more avail,
Ten thousand glitt'ring pounds a-year?
In other words, can Mammon fail,
Omnipotent as he is here?
Oh, bitter mock'ry of the pompous bier,
While down the wretched vital part is driv'n!
The cave-lodg'd beggar, with a conscience clear,
Expires in rags, unknown, and goes to Heav'n.

Letter to James Tennant,

OF GLENCONNER. (218)

AULD comrade dear, and brither sinner,
How's a' the folk about Glenconner?
How do you this blae, eastlin wind,
That's like to blaw a body blind?
For me, my faculties are frozen,
And ilka member nearly dozen'd.

I've sent you here, by Johnnie Simson,
Twa sage philosophers to glimpse on:—
Smith, wi' his sympathetic feeling,
And Reid, to common sense appealing.
Philosophers have fought and wrangled,
And meikle Greek and Latin mangled,
Till wi' their logic-jargon tir'd,
And in the depth of science mir'd,
To common sense they now appeal,
What wives and wabsters see and feel.
But, hark ye, friend! I charge you strictly,
Peruse them, and return them quickly,
For now I'm grown sae cursed douce
I pray and ponder butt the house;
My shins, my lane, I there sit roastin',
Perusing Bunyan, Brown, and Boston;
Till bye and bye, if I haud on,
I'll grunt a blouset gospel groan:
Already I begin to try it,
To cast my e'en up like a pyet,
When by the gun she tumbles o'er,
Flutt'ring and gasping in her gore:
Sae shortly you shall see me bright,
A burning and a shining light.

My heart-warm love to guid auld Glen,
The ace and wale o' honest men:
When bending down wi' auld grey hairs,
Beneath the load of years and cares,
May He who made him still support him,
And views beyond the grave comfort him.
His worthy fam'ly, far and near
God bless them a' wi' grace and gear!
My auld schoolfellow, preacher Willie,
The manly tar, my mason Billie,
And Auchenbay, I wish him joy;
If he's a parent, lass or boy,
May he be dad, and Meg the mither,
Just five-and-forty years thegither!
And no forgetting wabster Charlie,
I'm told he offers very fairly.
And, Lord remember singing Sannock,
Wi' hale breeks, sexpence, and a bannock;
And next my auld acquaintance Nancy,
Since she is fitted to her fancy;
And her kind stars hae airted till her
A good chiel wi' a pickle siller.
My kindest, best respects I sen' it,
To cousin Kate and sister Janet;
Tell them, frae me, wi' chiels be cautious,
For, faith, they'll aiblins fin' them fashious.
And lastly, Jamie, for yoursel,
May guardian angels tak a spell,
And steer you seven miles south o' hell.
But first, before you see heaven's glory,
May ye get mony a merry story,
Mony a laugh, and mony a drink,
And aye enough o' needfu' clink.

Now fare ye weel, and joy be wi' you,
For my sake this I beg it o' you,
Assist poor Simson a' ye can,
Ye'll fin' him just an honest man:
Sae I conclude, and quat my chanter,
Your's, saint or sinner,

ROB THE RANTER.

A Fragment.

INSCRIBED TO THE RIGHT HON. C. J. FOX.

How wisdom and folly meet, mix and unite;
How virtue and vice blend their black and their white;
How genius, th' illustrious father of fiction,
Confounds rule and law, reconciles contradiction—
I sing: if these mortals, the critics, should bustle,
I care not, not I—let the critics go whistle!

But now for a patron, whose name and whose glory
At once may illustrate and honour my story.

Thou first of our orators, first of our wits;
Yet whose parts and acquirements seem mere lucky hits;
With knowledge so vast, and with judgment so strong,
No man with the half of 'em e'er went far wrong;
With passions so potent, and fancies so bright,
No man with the half of 'em e'er went quite right;—
A sorry, poor misbegot son of the muses,
For using thy name offers fifty excuses.

Good L—d, what is man? for as simple he looks;
Do but try to develope his hooks and his crooks,
With his depths and his shallows, his good and his evil,
All in all he's a problem must puzzle the devil.

On his one ruling passion Sir Pope hugely labours,
That, like th' Hebrew walking-switch, eats up its neighbours;
Mankind are his show-box—a friend, would you know him?
Pull the string, ruling passion the picture will show him.
What pity, in rearing so beauteous a system,
One trifling, particular truth should have miss'd him;
For, spite of his fine theoretic positions,
Mankind is a science defies definitions.

Some sort all our qualities, each to its tribe,
And think human nature they truly describe;
Have you found this, or t'other! there's more in the wind,
As by one drunken fellow his comrades you'll find.
But such is the flaw, or the depth of the plan,
In the make of that wonderful creature call'd man,
No two virtues, whatever relation they claim,
Nor even two different shades of the same,
Though like as was ever twin brother to brother,
Possessing the one shall imply you've the other.

On Seeing a Wounded Hare

LIMP BY ME, WHICH A FELLOW HAD JUST SHOT. (219)

INHUMAN man! curse on thy barb'rous art,
And blasted be thy murder-aiming eye;
May never pity soothe thee with a sigh
Nor ever pleasure glad thy cruel heart.

Go live, poor wanderer of the wood and field!
The bitter little that of life remains;
No more the thickening brakes and verdant plains
To thee shall home, or food, or pastime yield.

Seek, mangled wretch, some place of wonted rest.
No more of rest, but now thy dying bed!
The sheltering rushes whistling o'er thy head,
The cold earth with thy bloody bosom prest.

Oft as by winding Nith, I, musing, wait
The sober eve, or hail the cheerful dawn;
I'll miss thee sporting o'er the dewy lawn,
And curse the ruffian's aim, and mourn thy hapless fate.

The Kirk's Alarm.

A SATIRE. (220)

ORTHODOX, orthodox,
Wha believe in John Knox,
Let me sound an alarm to your conscience;
There's a heretic blast
Has been blawn in the wast,
That what is no sense must be nonsense.

Dr. Mac (221), Dr. Mac,
You should stretch on a rack,
To strike evil doers wi' terror;
To join faith and sense
Upon ony pretence,
Is heretic, damnable error.

Town of Ayr (222), town of Ayr,
It was mad, I declare,
To meddle wi' mischief a-brewing;
Provost John (223) is still deaf
To the church's relief,
And orator Bob (224) is its ruin.

D'rymple mild (225), D'rymple mild,
Tho' your heart's like a child,
And your life like the new-driven snaw,
Yet that winna save ye,
Auld Satan must have ye,
For preaching that three's ane and twa.

Rumble John (226), Rumble John,
Mount the steps wi' a groan,
Cry the book is wi' heresy cramm'd;
Then lug out your ladle,
Deal brimstone like adle,
And roar every note of the damn'd.

Simper James (227), Simper James,
Leave the fair Killie dames,
There's a holier chase in your view;
I'll lay on your head,
That the pack ye'll soon lead,
For puppies like you, there's but few.

Singet Sawney (228), Singet Sawney,
Are ye huirding the penny,
Unconscious what evil await;
Wi, a jump, yell, and howl,
Alarm every soul,
For the foul thief is just at your gate.

Daddy Auld (229), Daddy Auld,
There's a tod in the fauld,
A tod meikle waur than the clerk (230):
Though ye do na skaith,
Ye'll be in at the death,
And if ye canna bite, ye may bark.

Davie Bluster (231), Davie Bluster,
If for a saint ye do muster,
The corps is no nice of recruits;
Yet to worth let's be just.
Royal blood ye might boast,
If the ass was the king of the brutes.

Jamy Goose (232), Jamy Goose,
Ye ha'e made but toom roose,
In hunting the wicked lieutenant;
But the Doctor's your mark,
For the L—d's haly ark;
He has cooper'd and cawt a wrong pin in't.

Poet Willie (233), Poet Willie,
Gie the Doctor a volley,
Wi' your Liberty's Chain and your wit;
O'er Pegasus' side
Ye ne'er laid a stride,
Ye but smelt, man, the place where he * *

Andro Gouk (234), Andro Gouk,
Ye may slander the book,
And the book not the waur, let me tell ye;
Ye are rich, and look big,
But lay by hat and wig,
And ye'll hae a calf's head o' sma' value.

Barr Steenie (235), Barr Steenie,
What mean ye, what mean ye?
If ye'll meddle nae mair wi' the matter,
Ye may hae some pretence
To havins and sense,
Wi' people wha ken ye know better.

Irvine side (236), Irvine side,
Wi' your turkey-cock pride,
Of manhood but sma' is your share;
Ye've the figure, 'tis true,
Even your faes will allow,
And your friends they dare grant you nae mair.

Muirland Jock (237), Muirland Jock,
When the Lord makes a rock
To crush Common Sense for her sins,
If ill manners were wit,
There's no mortal so fit
To confound the poor Doctor at ance.

Holy Will (238), Holy Will,
There was wit i' your skull,
When ye pilfer'd the alms o' the poor;
The timmer is scant,
When ye're ta'en for a saunt,
Wha should swing in a rape for an hour,

Calvin's sons, Calvin's sons,
Seize your spir'tual guns,
Ammunition you never can need;
Your hearts are the stuff,
Will be powther enough,
And your skulls are storehouses o' lead.

Poet Burns, Poet Burns,
Wi' your priest-skelping turns,
Why desert ye your auld native shire?
Your muse is a gipsie:
E'en though she were tipsie,
She could ca' us nae waur than we are.

To Dr. Blacklock,

IN ANSWER TO A LETTER.

Ellisland, 21st Oct. 1789.

Wow, but your letter made me vauntie!
And are ye hale, and weel, and cantie?
I kenn'd it still your wee bit jauntie,
Wad bring ye to:
Lord send you aye as weel's I want ye,
And then ye'll do.

The ill-thief blaw the Heron south! (239)
And never drink be near his drouth!
He tauld mysel by word o' mouth,
He'd tak my letter;
I lippen'd to the chield in trouth,
And bade (240) nae better,

But aiblins honest Master Heron
Had at the time some dainty fair one
To ware his theologic care on,
And holy study;
And tir'd o' sauls to waste his lear on,
E'en tried the body.

But what d'ye think, my trusty fier,
I'm turned a gauger—Peace be here!
Parnassian queans, I fear, I fear,
Ye'll now disdain me!
And then my fifty pounds a-year
Will little gain me.

Ye glaiket, gleesome, dainty damies,
Wha, by Castalia's wimplin' streamies,
Lowp, sing, and lave your pretty limbies,
Ye ken, ye ken,
That strang necessity supreme is
'Mang sons o' men.

I hae a wife and twa wee laddies,
They maun hae brose and brats o' duddies;
Ye ken yoursels my heart right proud is—
I need na vaunt,
But I'll sned besoms—thraw saugh woodies,
Before they want.

Lord help me thro' this warld o' care!
I'm weary sick o't late and air!
Not but I hae a richer share
Than mony ithers;
But why should ae man better fare,
And a' men brithers?

Come, firm Resolve, take thou the van,
Thou stalk o' carl hemp in man!
And let us mind, faint heart ne'er wan
A lady fair:
Wha does the utmost that he can,
Will whyles do mair.

But to conclude my silly rhyme,
(I'm scant o' verse, and scant o' time,)
To make a happy fire-side clime
To weans and wife,
That's the true pathos and sublime
Of human life.

My compliments to sister Beckie;
And eke the same to honest Lucky,
I wat she is a dainty chuckie,
As e'er tread clay!
And gratefully, my guid auld cockie,
I'm yours for aye.

ROBERT BURNS.

Delia. (241)

FAIR the face of orient day,
Fair the tints of op'ning rose;
But fairer still my Delia dawns,
More lovely far her beauty shows.

Sweet the lark's wild warbled lay,
Sweet the tinkling rill to hear;
But, Delia, more delightful still,
Steal thine accents on mine ear.

The flower-enamoured busy bee,
The rosy banquet loves to sip;
Sweet the streamlet's limpid lapse
To the sun-brown'd Arab's lip.

But, Delia, on thy balmy lips
Let me, no vagrant insect, rove;
Oh, let me steal one liquid kiss,
For, oh! my soul is parched with love.

Sketch—New-Year's Day.

TO MRS DUNLOP. (242)

THIS day, Time winds th' exhausted chain,
To run the twelvemonth's length again:
I see the old, bald-pated fellow,
With ardent eyes, complexion sallow,
Adjust the unimpair'd machine,
To wheel the equal, full routine.

The absent lover, minor heir,
In vain assail him with their prayer;
Deaf as my friend, he sees them press,
Nor makes the hour one moment less.
Will you (the Major's (243) with the hounds,
The happy tenants share his rounds;
Coila's fare Rachel's (244) care to-day,
And blooming Keith's engaged with Gray)
From housewife cares a minute borrow—
—That grandchild's cap will do to-morrow—
And join with me a-moralizing:
This day's propitious to be wise in.
First, what did yesternight deliver?
"Another year is gone for ever."
And what is this day's strong suggestion?
"The passing moment's all we rest on!"
Rest on—for what? what do we here?
Or why regard the passing year?
Will time, amus'd with proverb'd lore,
Add to our date one minute more?
A few days may—a few years must—
Repose us in the silent dust.
Then is it wise to damp our bliss?
Yes—all such reasonings are amiss!
The voice of Nature loudly cries,
And many a message from the skies,
That something in us never dies:
That on this frail, uncertain state,
Hang matters of eternal weight:
That future life in worlds unknown
Must take its hue from this alone;
Whether as heavenly glory bright,
Or dark as misery's woeful night,
Since, then, my honour'd, first of friends,
On this poor being all depends.
Let us th' important *now* employ,
And live as those who never die.
Tho' you, with days and honours crown'd,
Witness that filial circle round,
(A sight, life's sorrows to repulse,
A sight, pale envy to convulse,)
Others now claim your chief regard;
Yourself, you wait your bright reward.

Prologue,

SPOKEN AT THE THEATRE, DUMFRIES, ON NEW-YEAR'S-DAY EVENING. [1790]

No song nor dance I bring from yon great city
That queens it o'er our taste—the more's the pity:
Tho', by-the-bye, abroad why will you roam?
Good sense and taste are natives here at home:
But not for panegyric I appear,
I come to wish you all a good new year!
Old Father Time deputes me here before ye,
Not for to preach, but tell his simple story:
The sage grave ancient cough'd, and bade me say,
"You're one year older this important day."
If wiser, too—he hinted some suggestion,
But 'twould be rude, you know, to ask the question;
And with a would-be roguish leer and wink,
He bade me on you press this one word—"think!"

Ye sprightly youths quite flushed with hope and spirit,
Who think to storm the world by dint of merit,
To you the dotard has a deal to say,
In his sly, dry, sententious, proverb way;
He bids you mind, amid your thoughtless rattle,
That the first blow is ever half the battle;
That tho' some by the skirt may try to snatch him,
Yet by the forelock is the hold to catch him,
That whether doing, suffering, or forbearing,
You may do miracles by persevering.

Last, tho' not least in love, ye youthful fair,
Angelic forms, high Heaven's peculiar care!
To you old Bald-pate smooths his wrinkled brow,
And humbly begs you'll mind the important Now!
To crown your happiness he asks your leave,
And offers bliss to give and to receive.

For our sincere, tho' haply weak endeavours,
With grateful pride we own your many favours;
And howsoe'er our tongues may ill reveal it,
Believe our glowing bosoms truly feel it.

Prologue,

FOR MR. SUTHERLAND'S BENEFIT NIGHT, DUMFRIES.

What needs this din about the town o' Lon'on,
How this new play and that new sang is comin'?
Why is outlandish stuff sae meikle courted?
Does nonsense mend like whiskey, when imported?
Is there nae poet, burning keen for fame,
Will try to gie us songs and plays at hame?
For comedy abroad he needna toil,
A fool and knave are plants of every soil;
Nor need he hunt as far as Rome and Greece
To gather matter for a serious piece;

WILLIE BREW'D A PECK O'MAUT

It is the moon, I ken her horn,
That's blinking in the lift sae high

There's themes enough in Caledonian story,
Would show the tragic muse in a' her glory.

Is there no daring bard will rise, and tell
How glorious Wallace stood, how hapless fell?
Where are the muses fled that could produce
A drama worthy o' the name o' Bruce;
How here, even here, he first unsheath'd the sword,
'Gainst mighty England and her guilty lord;
And after mony a bloody, deathless doing,
Wrench'd his dear country from the jaws of ruin?
Oh for a Shakspeare or an Otway scene
To draw the lovely, hapless Scottish Queen!
Vain all th' omnipotence of female charms
'Gainst headlong, ruthless, mad Rebellion's arms.
She fell, but fell with spirit truly Roman,
To glut the vengeance of a rival woman:
A woman—tho' the phrase may seem uncivil—
As able and as cruel as the Devil!
One Douglas lives in Home's immortal page,
But Douglasses were heroes every age:
And tho' your fathers, prodigal of life,
A Douglas followed to the martial strife,
Perhaps if bowls row right, and Right succeeds,
Ye yet may follow where a Douglas leads!

As ye hae generous done, if a' the land
Would take the muses' servants by the hand;
Not only hear, but patronise, befriend them,
And where ye justly can commend, commend them;
And aiblins when they winna stand the test,
Wink hard and say the folks hae done their best!
Would a' the land do this, then I'll be caution
Ye'll soon hae poets o' the Scottish nation,
Will gar fame blaw until her trumpet crack,
And warsle Time, and lay him on his back!
For us and for our stage should ony spier,
"Wha's aught thae chiels maks a' this bustle here?"
My best leg foremost, I'll set up my brow,
We have the honour to belong to you!
We're your ain bairns, e'en guide us as ye like,
But like gude mithers, shore before you strike.
And gratefu' still I hope ye'll ever find us,
For a' the patronage and meikle kindness
We've got frae a' professions, sets and ranks;
God help us! we're but poor—ye'se get but thanks.

Written

TO A GENTLEMAN WHO HAD SENT THE POET A NEWSPAPER, AND OFFERED TO CONTINUE IT FREE OF EXPENSE.

KIND Sir, I've read your paper through,
And, faith, to me 'twas really new!
How guessed ye, Sir, what maist I wanted?
This mony a day I've grain'd and gaunted,
To ken what French mischief was brewin',
Or what the drumlie Dutch were doin';
That vile doup-skelper, Emperor Joseph,
If Venus yet had got his nose off;
Or how the collieshangie works
Atween the Russians and the Turks;
Or if the Swede, before he halt,
Would play anither Charles the Twalt:
If Denmark, ony body spak o't;
Or Poland, wha had now the tack o't;
How cut-throat Prussian blades were hingin;
How libbet Italy was singin';
If Spaniard, Portuguese, or Swiss,
Were sayin' or takin' aught amiss;
Or how our merry lads at hame,
In Britain's court, kept up the game:
How royal George, the Lord leuk o'er him!
Was managing St Stephen's quorum;
If sleekit Chatham Will was livin',
Or glaikit Charlie got his nieve in;
How daddie Burke the plea was cookin',
If Warren Hastings' neck was yeukin';
How cesses, stents, and fees were rax'd,
Or if bare —— yet were tax'd;
The news o' princes, dukes, and earls,
Pimps, sharpers, bawds, and opera girls;
If that daft buckie, Geordie Wales,
Was threshin' still at hizzies' tails;
Or if he was grown oughtlins douser,
And na o' perfect kintra cooser.
A' this and mair I never heard of,
And but for you I might despair'd of.
So gratefu', back your news I send you,
And pray, a' guid things may attend you!

Ellisland, Monday Morning.

Peg Nicholson. (245)

PEG Nicholson was a good bay mare,
As ever trod on airn;
But now she's floating down the Nith,
And past the mouth o' Cairn.

Peg Nicholson was a good bay mare,
And rode thro' thick and thin;
But now she's floating down the Nith,
Aud wanting e'en the skin.

Peg Nicholson was a good bay mare,
  And ance she bore a priest;
But now she's floating down the Nith,
  For Solway fish a feast.

Peg Nicholson was a good bay mare,
  And the priest he rode her sair;
And much oppressed and bruis'd she was,
  As priest-rid cattle are—

* *

To My Bed. (246)

Thou bed, in which I first began
To be that various creature—*Man!*
And when again the Fates decree,
The place where I must cease to be;—
When sickness comes, to whom I fly,
To soothe my pain, or close mine eye;—
When cares surround me, where I weep,
Or lose them all in balmy sleep;—
When sore with labour, whom I court,
And to thy downy breast resort—
Where, too ecstatic joys I find,
When deigns my Delia to be kind—
And full of love, in all her charms,
Thou giv'st the fair one to my arms.
The centre thou—where grief and pain,
Disease and rest, alternate reign.
Oh, since within thy little space,
So many various scenes take place;
Lessons as useful shalt thou teach,
As sages dictate—churchmen preach;
And man, convinced by thee alone,
This great important truth shall own:
"*That thin partitions do divide*
The bounds where good and ill reside;
That nought is perfect here below;
But BLISS *still bordering upon* WOE." (247)

First Epistle to Mr. Graham
OF FINTRY.

When Nature her great masterpiece designed,
And fram'd her last best work, the human
  mind,
Her eye intent on all the mazy plan,
She formed of various parts the various man.

Then first she calls the useful many forth;
Plain plodding industry, and sober worth:
Thence peasants, farmers, native sons of
  earth, [birth:
And merchandise' whole genus take their
Each prudent cit a warm existence finds,
And all mechanics' many-apron'd kinds.
Some other rarer sorts are wanted yet,
The lead and buoy are needful to the net;
The *caput mortuum* of gross desires [squires;
Makes a material for mere knights and
The martial phosphorus is taught to flow,
She kneads the lumpish philosophic dough,
Then marks th' unyielding mass with grave
  designs,
Law, physic, politics, and deep divines:
Last, she sublimes th' Aurora of the poles,
The flashing elements of female souls.
The order'd system fair before her stood,
Nature, well-pleas'd, pronounc'd it very good;
But ere she gave creating labour o'er,
Half-jest, she cried one curious labour more.
Some spumy, fiery, *ignis fatuus* matter,
Such as the slightest breath of air might
  scatter;
With arch alacrity and conscious glee
(Nature may have her whim as well as we,
Her Hogarth-art perhaps she meant to show it)
She forms the thing, and christens it—a poet,
Creature, tho' oft the prey of care and sorrow,
When blest to-day, unmindful of to-morrow,
A being form'd t'amuse his graver friends,
Admir'd and prais'd—and there the homage
  ends:
A mortal quite unfit for fortune's strife,
Yet oft the sport of all the ills of life;
Prone to enjoy each pleasure riches give,
Yet haply wanting wherewithal to live;
Longing to wipe each tear, to heal each groan,
Yet frequently unheeded in his own.

But honest Nature is not quite a Turk,
She laugh'd at first, then felt for her poor work.
Pitying the propless climber of mankind,
She cast about a standard tree to find;
And, to support his helpless woodbine state,
Attach'd him to the generous truly great,
A title, and the only one I claim,
To lay strong hold for help on bounteous
  Graham.

Pity the tuneful muses' hapless train,
Weak, timid landsmen on life's stormy main!
Their hearts no selfish stern absorbent stuff,
That never gives—tho' humbly takes enough;
The little fate allows, they share as soon,
Unlike sage proverb'd wisdom's hard-wrung
  boon.
The world were blest did bliss on them depend,
Ah, that "the friendly e'er should want a
  friend!"
Let prudence number o'er each sturdy son,
Who life and wisdom at one race begun,
Who feel by reason and who give by rule,
(Instinct's a brute, and sentiment a fool!)
Who make poor *will do* wait upon *I should*—
We own they're prudent, but who feels
  they're good!
Ye wise ones, hence! ye hurt the social eye!
God's image rudely etch'd on base alloy!
But, come, ye who the godlike pleasure know,
Heaven's attribute distinguished—to bestow!

Whose arms of love would grasp the human race: [grace;
Come thou who giv'st with all a courtier's
Friend of my life, true patron of my rhymes!
Prop of my dearest hopes for future times.
Why shrinks my soul half blushing, half afraid,
Backward, abash'd, to ask thy friendly aid?
I know my need, I know thy giving hand,
I crave thy friendship at thy kind command;
But there are such who court the tuneful nine—
Heavens! should the branded character be mine! [flows,
Whose verse in manhood's pride sublimely
Yet vilest reptiles in their begging prose.
Mark, how their lofty independent spirit
Soars on the spurning wing of injur'd merit!
Seek not the proofs in private life to find;
Pity the best of words should be but wind!
So to heaven's gates the lark's shrill song ascends,
But grovelling on the earth the carol ends.
In all the clam'rous cry of starving want,
They dun benevolence with shameless front;
Oblige them, patronise their tinsel lays,
They persecute you all your future days!
Ere my poor soul such deep damnation stain!
My horny fist assume the plough again;
The pie-bald jacket let me patch once more;
On eighteen-pence a-week I've liv'd before.
Tho', thanks to Heaven, I dare even that last shift!
I trust, meantime, my boon is in thy gift:
That, plac'd by thee upon the wish'd-for height,
Where, man and nature fairer in her sight,
My muse may imp her wing for some sublimer flight.

The Five Carlines. (248)

THERE were five carlines in the south,
They fell upon a scheme,
To send a lad to Lon'on town,
To bring them tidings hame.

Nor only bring them tidings hame,
But do their errands there,
And aiblins gowd and honour baith
Might be that laddie's share.

There was Maggy by the banks o' Nith,
A dame with pride eneugh,
And Marjory o' the Monylochs,
A carline auld and teugh.

And blinkin' Bess o' Annandale,
That dwelt near Solwayside,
And whisky Jean, that took her gill,
In Galloway sae wide.

And black Joan, frae Crichton Peel,
O' gipsy kith and kin—
Five wighter carlines warna foun'
The south countra within.

To send a lad to Lon'on town,
They met upon a day,
And mony a knight, and mony a laird,
Their errand fain would gae.

O mony a knight and many a laird,
This errand fain would gae;
But nae ane could their fancy please,
O ne'er a ane but twae.

The first he was a belted knight (249),
Bred o' a border clan,
And he wad gae to Lon'on town,
Might nae man him withstan'.

And he wad do their errands weel,
And meikle he wad say,
And ilka ane at Lon'on court
Would bid to him guid day.

Then next came in a sodger youth (250),
And spak wi' modest grace,
And he wad gae to Lon'on town,
If sae their pleasure was.

He wadna hecht them courtly gifts,
Nor meikle speech pretend,
But he wad hecht an honest heart,
Wad ne'er desert a friend,

Now, wham to choose, and wham refuse,
At strife their carlines fell!
For some had gentle folks to please,
And some would please themsel.

Then out spak mim-mou'd Meg o' Nith,
And she spak up wi' pride,
And she wad send the sodger youth,
Whatever might betide.

For the auld guidman o' Lon'on court (251)
She didna care a pin;
But she wad send the sodger youth
To greet his eldest son. (252)

Then up sprang Bess o' Annandale,
And a deadly aith she's ta'en,
That she wad vote the border knight,
Though she should vote her lane.

For far-aff fowls hae feathers fair,
And fools o' change are fain;
But I hae tried the border knight,
And I'll try him yet again.

Says black Joan frae Crichton Peel,
A carline stoor and grim,
The auld guidman, and the young guidman,
For me may sink or swim;

For fools will freat o' right or wrang,
While knaves laugh them to scorn;
But the sodger's friends hae blawn the best,
So he shall bear the horn.

Then whisky Jean spak owre her drink,
Ye weel ken, kimmers a',
The auld guidman o' Lon'on court,
His back's been at the wa';

And mony a friend that kiss'd his cup,
Is now a fremit wight:
But it's ne'er be said o' whisky Jean—
I'll send the border knight.

Then slow raise Marjory o' the Loch,
And wrinkled was her brow,
Her ancient weed was russet grey,
Her auld Scots bluid was true;

There's some great folks set light by me—
I set as light by them;
But I will send to Lon'on town
Wham I like best at hame.

Sae how this weighty plea may end,
Nae mortal wight can tell:
God grant the king and ilka man
May look weel to himsel.

Second Epistle to Mr. Graham,

OF FINTRY. (253).

FINTRY, my stay in worldly strife,
Friend o' my muse, friend o' my life,
Are ye as idle's I am?
Come then, wi' uncouth, kintra fleg,
O'er Pegasus I'll fling my leg,
And ye shall see me try him.

I'll sing the zeal Drumlanrig bears,
Who left the all-important cares
Of princes and their darlings;
And bent on winning borough towns,
Came shaking hands wi' wabster louns,
And kissing barefit carlins.

Combustion through our boroughs rode
Whistling his roaring pack abroad,
Of mad, unmuzzled lions;
As Queensberry buff and blue unfurl'd,
And Westerha' and Hopeton hurl'd
To every Whig defiance.

But Queensberry, cautious, left the war,
The unmanner'd dust might soil his star,
Besides, he hated bleeding;
But left behind him heroes bright,
Heroes in Cæsarean fight
Or Ciceronian pleading.

O for a throat like huge Mons-meg (254),
To muster o'er each ardent Whig
Beneath Drumlanrig's banners;
Heroes and heroines commix
All in the field of politics,
To win immortal honours.

M'Murdo and his lovely spouse,
(Th' enamour'd laurels kiss her brows,)
Led on the loves and graces;
She won each gaping burgess' heart
While he, all conquering, play'd his part
Among their wives and lasses.

Craigdarroch led a light-arm'd corps;
Tropes, metaphors, and figures pour,
Like Hecla streaming thunder;
Glenriddel, skill'd in rusty coins,
Blew up each Tory's dark designs,
And bar'd the treason under.

In either wing two champions fought,
Redoubted Staig, who set at nought
The wildest savage Tory.
And Welsh, who ne'er yet flinch'd his ground,
High wav'd his magnum bonum round
With Cyclopean fury.

Miller brought up the artillery ranks,
The many pounders of the Banks,
Resistless desolation;
While Maxwelton, that baron bold,
Mid Lawson's port entrench'd his hold,
And threaten'd worse damnation.

To these, what Tory hosts oppos'd;
With these, what Tory warriors clos'd,
Surpasses my descriving:
Squadrons extended long and large,
With furious speed rush'd to the charge,
Like raging devils driving.

What verse can sing, what prose narrate,
The butcher deeds of bloody fate
Amid this mighty tulzie?
Grim horror grinn'd; pale terror roar'd
As murther at his thrapple shor'd;
And hell mixt in the brulzie!

As Highland crags, by thunder cleft,
When lightnings fire the stormy lift,
Hurl down wi' crashing rattle;
As flames amang a hundred woods;
As headlong foam a hundred floods;
Such is the rage of battle.

The stubborn Tories dare to die;
As soon the rooted oaks would fly,
Before th' approaching fellers;
The Whigs come on like ocean's roar
When all his wintry billows pour
Against the Buchan Bullers. (255)

Lo, from the shades of death's deep night,
Departed Whigs enjoy the fight,
And think on former daring;
The muffled murtherer of Charles (256),
The Magna Charta flag unfurls,
All deadly gules its bearing.

Nor wanting ghosts of Tory fame;
Bold Scrimgeour (257) follows gallant Grahame—(258)
Auld Covenanters shiver—
(Forgive, forgive, much-wrong'd Montrose!
While death and hell engulf thy foes,
Thou liv'st on high for ever!)

Still o'er the field the combat burns;
The Tories, Whigs, give way by turns;
But fate the word has spoken—
For woman's wit, or strength of man,
Alas! can do but what they can—
The Tory ranks are broken!

Oh that my e'en were flowing burns!
My voice a lioness that mourns
Her darling cub's undoing!
That I might greet, that I might cry,
While Tories fall, while Tories fly,
And furious Whigs pursuing!

What Whig but wails the good Sir James;
Dear to his country by the names
Friend, Patron, Benefactor?
Not Pulteny's wealth can Pulteny save!
And Hopeton falls, the generous brave!
And Stuart bold as Hector!

Thou, Pitt, shall rue this overthrow,
And Thurlow growl a curse of woe,
And Melville melt in wailing!
Now Fox and Sheridan rejoice!
And Burke shall sing, "Oh prince, arise!
Thy power is all-prevailing!"

For your poor friend, the Bard afar,
He hears, and only hears the war,
A cool spectator purely;
So when the storm the forest rends,
The robin in the hedge descends
And sober chirps securely.

On Captain Grose's Peregrinations

THROUGH SCOTLAND, COLLECTING THE ANTIQUITIES OF THAT KINGDOM. (259)

HEAR, land o' Cakes, and brither Scots,
Frae Maidenkirk (260) to Johnny Groats;
If there's a hole in a' your coats,
I rede you tent it:
A chield's amang you taking notes,
And, faith, he'll prent it.

If in your bounds ye chance to light
Upon a fine, fat fodgel wight,
O' stature short, but genius bright,
That's he, mark weel—
And wow! he has an unco slight
O' cauk and keel.

By some auld houlet-haunted biggin,
Or kirk deserted by its riggin,
It's ten to ane ye'll find him snug in
Some eldritch part,
Wi' deils, they say, Lord save's! colleaguin'
At some black art.

Ilk ghaist that haunts auld ha' or chaumer,
Ye gipsey-gang that deal in glamour,
And you, deep-read in hell's black grammar,
Warlocks and witches;
Ye'll quake at his conjuring hammer,
Ye midnight bitches.

It's tauld he was a sodger bred,
And ane wad rather fa'n than fled;
But now he's quat the spurtle blade,
And dog skin wallet,
And ta'en the—Antiquarian trade,
I think they call it.

He has a fouth o' auld nick-nackets,
Rusty aird caps and jinglin' jackets,
Wad haud the Lothians three in tackets,
A towmont guid;
And parritch-pats, and auld saut-backets,
Before the Flood.

Of Eve's first fire he has a cinder;
Auld Tubalcain's fire-shool and fender;
That which distinguished the gender
O' Balaam's ass;
A broom-stick o' the witch of Endor,
Weel shod wi' brass.

Forbye, he'll shape you aff, fu' gleg,
The cut of Adam's philabeg;
The knife that nicket Abel's craig,
He'll prove you fully,
It was a faulding jocteleg,
Or lang-kail gully.

But wad ye see him in his glee,
For meikle glee and fun has he,
Then set him down, and twa or threo
Guid fellows wi' him.
And port, Oh port! shine thou a wee,
And then ye'll see him;

Now, by the pow'rs o' verse and prose!
Thou art a dainty chiel, oh Grose!—
Whae'er o' thee shall ill suppose,
They sair misca' thee;
I'd take the rascal by the nose,
Wad say, shame fa' thee.

Written in an Envelope,

ENCLOSING A LETTER TO CAPTAIN GROSE. (261)

KEN ye ought o' Captain Grose?
Igo and ago,
If he's amang his friends or foes?
Iram, coram, dago.
Is he south or is he north?
Igo and ago,
Or drowned in the river Forth?
Iram, coram, dago.
Is he slain by Highlan' bodies?
Igo and ago,
And eaten like a wether haggis?
Iram, coram, dago.
Is he to Abram's bosom gane?
Igo and ago,
Or haudin Sarah by the wame?
Iram, coram, dago.
Where'er he be, the Lord be near him;
Igo and ago,
As for the deil, he daurna steer him.
Iram, coram, dago.
But please transmit the enclosed letter,
Igo and ago,
Which will oblige your humble debtor,
Iram, coram, dago.
So may ye hae auld stanes in store,
Igo and ago,
The very stanes that Adam bore,
Iram, coram, dago.
So may ye get in glad possession,
Igo and ago,
The coins o' Satan's coronation!
Iram, coram, dago.

Address of Beelzebub

TO THE PRESIDENT OF THE HIGHLAND SOCIETY. (262)

LONG life, my Lord, and health be yours,
Unscaith'd by hunger'd Highland boors;
Lord grant nae duddie desperate beggar,
Wi' dirk, claymore, or rusty trigger,
May twin auld Scotland o' a life
She likes—as lambkins like a knife.
Faith, you and A——s were right
To keep the Highland hounds in sight;
I doubt na! they wad bid nae better
Than let them ance out owre the water;
Then up amang thrae lakes and seas
They'll mak what rules and laws they please;
Some daring Hancock, or a Franklin,
May set their Highland bluid a-ranklin';
Some Washington again may head them,
Or some Montgomery, fearless, lead them,
Till God knows what may be effected
When by such heads and hearts directed—
Poor dunghill sons of dirt and mire
May to Patrician rights aspire!
Nae sage North, now, nor sager Sackville,
To watch and premier o'er the pack vile,
And whare will ye get Howes and Clintons
To bring them to a right repentance,
To cowe the rebel generation,
And save the honour o' the nation?
They and be d——d! what right hae they
To meat or sleep, or light o' day?
Far less to riches, pow'r or freedom.
But what your lordship likes to gie them?

But hear, my lord! Glengarry, hear!
Your hand's owre light on them, I fear;
Your factors, grieves, trustees, and bailies,
I canna say but they do gaylies;
They lay aside a' tender mercies,
And tirl the hallions to the birses;
Yet while they're only poind't and herriet,
They'll keep their stubborn Highland spirit;
But smash them! crash them a' to spails!
And rot the dyvors i' the jails!
The young dogs, swinge them to the labour;
Let wark and hunger mak them sober!
The hizzies, if they're aughtlins fawsont,
Let them in Drury-lane be lesson'd!
And if the wives and dirty brats
E'en thigger at your doors and yetts
Flaffan wi' duds and grey wi' beas',
Frightin' awa your deucks and geese,
Get out a horsewhip or a jowler,
The langest thong, the fiercest growler,
And gar the tatter'd gypsies' pack
Wi' a' their bastards on their back!
Go on, my Lord! I lang to meet you,
And in my house at hame to greet you;
Wi' common lords ye shanna mingle,
The benmost neuk beside the ingle,
At my right han' assigned your seat
'Tween Herod's hip and Polycrate—
Or if you on your station tarrow,
Between Almagro and Pizarro,
A seat, I'm sure ye're weel deservin't;
And till ye come—Your humble servant,
BEELZEBUB.

June 1st, Anno Mundi, 5790.

Lament of Mary Queen of Scots,

ON THE APPROACH OF SPRING.

NOW Nature hangs her mantle green
On every blooming tree,
And spreads her sheet o' daises white
Out o'er the grassy lee:
Now Phœbus cheers the crystal streams,
And glads the azure skies;
But nought can glad the weary wight
That fast in durance lies.

Now lav'rocks wake the merry morn,
  Aloft on dewy wing;
The merle, in his noontide bow'r
  Makes woodland echoes ring:
The mavis wild wi' mony a note,
  Sings drowsy day to rest:
In love and freedom they rejoice,
  Wi' care nor thrall opprest.

Now blooms the lily by the bank,
  The primrose down the brae;
The hawthorn's budding in the glen,
  And milk-white is the slae;
The meanest hind in fair Scotland
  May rove their sweets amang;
But I, the Queen of a' Scotland,
  Maun lie in prison strang!

I was the Queen o' bonnie France.
  Where happy I hae been;
Fu' lightly rase I in the morn,
  As blythe lay down at e'en:
And I'm the sov'reign of Scotland,
  And mony a traitor there;
Yet here I lie in foreign bands,
  And never-ending care.

But as for thee, thou false woman!
  My sister and my fae,
Grim vengeance yet shall whet a sword
  That thro' thy soul shall gae!
The weeping blood in woman's breast
  Was never known to thee;
Nor th' balm that draps on wounds of woe
  Frae woman's pitying e'e.

My son! my son! may kinder stars
  Upon thy fortune shine!
And may those pleasures gild thy reign,
  That ne'er wad blink on mine!
God keep thee frae thy mother's faes,
  Or turn their hearts to thee:
And where thou meet'st thy mother's friend,
  Remember him for me!

Oh soon, to me, may summer-suns
  Nae mair light up the morn!
Nae mair, to me, the autumn winds
  Wave o'er the yellow corn!
And in the narrow house o' death
  Let winter round me rave:
And the next flow'rs that deck the spring
  Bloom on my peaceful grave!

The Whistle. (263).

I SING of a whistle, a whistle of worth,
I sing of a whistle, the pride of the North,
Was brought to the court of our good
  Scottish king, [shall ring.
And long with this whistle all Scotland

Old Loda, (264) still rueing the arm of
  Fingal, [hall—
The god of the bottle sends down from his
"This whistle's your challenge—to Scotland
  get o'er, [me more!"
And drink them to hell, Sir! or ne'er see

Old poets have sung, and old chronicles
  tell, [fell;
What champions ventur'd, what champions
The son of great Loda was conqueror still,
And blew on the whistle his requiem shrill.

Till Robert, the lord of the Cairn and the
  Scaur, [war,
Unmatch'd at the bottle, unconquer'd in
He drank his poor godship as deep as the
  sea.
No tide of the Baltic e'er drunker than he.

Thus Robert, victorious, the trophy has
  gain'd, [remained;
Which now in his house has for ages
Till three noble chieftains, and all of his
  blood,
The jovial contest again have renew'd.

Three joyous good fellows, with hearts clear
  as flaw; [law;
Craigdarroch, so famous for wit, worth, and
And trusty Glenriddel, so skill'd in old
  coins; [wines.
And gallant Sir Robert, deep-read in old

Craigdarroch began, with a tongue smooth
  as oil,
Desiring Glenriddle to yield up the spoil;
Or else he would muster the heads of the
  clan, [the man.
And once more, in claret, try which was

"By the gods of the ancients!" Glenriddel
  replies,
"Before I surrender so glorious a prize,
I'll conjure the ghost of the great Rorie
  More (265), [times o'er."
And bumper his horn with him twenty

Sir Robert, a soldier, no speech would
  pretend, [or his friend,
But he ne'er turned his back on his foe—
Said, toss down the whistle, the prize of the
  field, [yield.
And knee-deep in claret, he'd die, or he'd

To the board of Glenriddel our heroes
  repair, [care;
So noted for drowning of sorrow and
But for wine and for welcome not more
  known to fame [lovely dame.
Than the sense, wit, and taste, of a sweet

A bard was selected to witness the fray,
And tell future ages the feats of the day;

A bard who detested all sadness and spleen,
And wish'd that Parnassus a vineyard had been.

The dinner being o'er the claret they ply,
And ev'ry new cork is a new spring of joy;
In the bands of old friendship and kindred so set,
And the bands grew the tighter the more they were wet.

Gay pleasure ran riot as bumpers ran o'er;
Bright Phœbus ne'er witness'd so joyous a core,
And vow'd that to leave them he was quite forlorn,
Till Cynthia hinted he'd see them next morn.

Six bottles a-piece had well wore out the night,
When gallant Sir Robert, to finish the fight,
Turn'd o'er in one bumper a bottle of red,
And swore 'twas the way that their ancestor did.

Then worthy Glenriddel, so cautious and sage.
No longer the warfare, ungodly, would wage;
A high ruling Elder to wallow in wine!
He left the foul business to folks less divine.

The gallant Sir Robert fought hard to the end;
But who can with fate and quart-bumpers contend?
Though fate said—a hero shall perish in light;
So up rose bright Phœbus—and down fell the knight.

Next up rose our bard, like a prophet in drink:—
"Craigdarroch, thou'lt soar when creation shall sink;
But if thou would flourish immortal in rhyme,
Come—one bottle more—and have at the sublime!

Thy line, that have struggled for freedom with Bruce,
Shall heroes and patriots ever produce:
So thine be the laurel and mine be the bay;
The field thou hast won, by yon bright god of day!"

Elegy

ON MISS BURNET OF MONBODDO.

Life ne'er exulted in so rich a prize
As Burnet, lovely from her native skies;
Nor envious death so triumph'd in a blow,
As that which laid th' accomplished Burnet low.

Thy form and mind, sweet maid, can I forget?
In richest ore the brightest jewel set!
In thee, high Heaven above was truest shown,
As by his noblest work the Godhead best is known.

In vain ye flaunt in summer's pride, ye groves;
Thou crystal streamlet with thy flowery shore,
Ye woodland choir that chant your idle loves,
Ye cease to charm—Eliza is no more!

Ye heathy wastes, immix'd with reedy fens;
Ye mossy streams, with sedge and rushes stor'd;
Ye rugged cliffs, o'erhanging dreary glens,
To you I fly, ye with my soul accord.

Princes, whose cumb'rous pride was all their worth,
Shall venal lays their pompous exit hail?
And thou, sweet excellence! forsake our earth,
And not a muse in honest grief bewail?

We saw thee shine in youth and beauty's pride,
And virtue's light, that beams beyond the spheres;
But, like the sun eclips'd at morning tide,
Thou left'st us darkling in a world of tears.

The parent's heart that nestled fond in thee,
That heart how sunk, a prey to grief and care;
So deck'd the woodbine sweet yon aged tree;
So from it ravish'd, leaves it bleak and bare.

Lament

FOR JAMES, EARL OF GLENCAIRN (266.)

The wind blew hollow frae the hills,
By fits the sun's departing beam
Look'd on the fading yellow woods
That wav'd o'er Lugar's winding stream:
Beneath a craigy steep, a bard,
Laden with years and meikle pain,
In loud lament bewail'd his lord,
Whom death had all untimely ta'en.

He lean'd him to an ancient aik,
Whose trunk was mould'ring down with years;
His locks were bleached white with time,
His hoary cheek was wet wi' tears;
And as he touch'd his trembling harp,
And as he tun'd his doleful sang,
The winds, lamenting thro' their caves,
To echo bore the notes alang.

"Ye scatter'd birds that faintly sing
The reliques of the vernal quire!
Ye woods that shed on a' the winds
The honours of the aged year!
A few short months, and glad and gay,
Again ye'll charm the ear and e'e;
But nought in all revolving time
Can gladness bring again to me.

I am a bending aged tree,
That long has stood the wind and rain;

But now has come a cruel blast,
And my last hold of earth is gane:
Nae leaf o' mine shall greet the spring,
Nae simmer sun exalt my bloom;
But I maun lie before the storm,
And ithers plant them in my room.

I've seen sae mony changefu' years,
On earth I am a stranger grown;
I wander in the ways of men,
Alike unknowing and unknown:
Unheard, unpitied, unrelieved,
I bear alane my lade o' care,
For silent, low, on beds of dust,
Lie a' that would my sorrows share.

And last (the sum of a' my griefs!)
My noble master lies in clay;
The flow'r amang our barons bold,
His country's pride! his country's stay—
In weary being now I pine,
For a' the life of life is dead,
And hope has left my aged ken,
On forward wing for ever fled.

Awake thy last sad voice, my harp!
The voice of woe and wild despair;
Awake! resound thy latest lay—
Then sleep in silence evermair!
And thou, my last, best, only friend,
That fillest an untimely tomb,
Accept this tribute from the bard
Thou brought'st from fortune's mirkest gloom.

In poverty's low barren vale
Thick mists, obscure, involv'd me round;
Though oft I turn'd the wistful eye,
Nae ray of fame was to be found:
Thou found'st me like the morning sun,
That melts the fogs in limpid air,
The friendless bard and rustic song
Became alike thy fostering care.

Oh! why has worth so short a date?
While villains ripen grey with time;
Must thou, the noble, gen'rous, great,
Fall in bold manhood's hardy prime!
Why did I live to see that day?
A day to me so full of woe!—
Oh! had I met the mortal shaft
Which laid my benefactor low!

The bridegroom may forget the bride,
Was made his wedded wife yestreen:
The monarch may forget the crown
That on his head an hour has been;
The mother may forget the child
That smiles sae sweetly on her knee;
But I'll remember thee, Glencairn,
And a' that thou hast done for me!"

Lines

SENT TO SIR JOHN WHITEFORD, BART., OF WHITEFORD, WITH THE FOREGOING POEM.

Thou, who thy honour as thy God rever'st,
Who, save thy mind's reproach, nought earthly fear'st,
To thee this votive offering I impart,
The tearful tribute of a broken heart.
The friend thou valued'st, I, the patron, lov'd:
His worth, his honour, all the world approv'd;
We'll mourn till we too go as he has gone,
And tread the dreary path to that dark world unknown.

Third Epistle to Mr. Graham,

OF FINTRY.

Late crippl'd of an arm, and now a leg,
About to beg a pass for leave to beg:
Dull, listless, teas'd, dejected, and deprest,
(Nature is adverse to a cripple's rest);
Will generous Graham list to his Poet's wail?
(It soothes poor misery, hearkening to her tale),
And hear him curse the light he first survey'd,
And doubly curse the luckless rhyming trade?

Thou, Nature, partial Nature! I arraign;
Of thy caprice maternal I complain.
The lion and the bull thy care have found,
One shakes the forests, and one spurns the ground:
Thou givs't the ass his hide, the snail his shell,
Th' envenom'd wasp, victorious, guards his cell;
Thy minion, kings, defend, control, devour,
In all th' omnipotence of rule and power;
Foxes and statesmen, subtile wiles insure;
The cit and polecat stink, and are secure;
Toads with their poison, doctors with their drug,
The priest and hedgehog in their robes are snug;
Ev'n silly woman has her warlike arts,
Her tongue and eyes, her dreaded spear and darts;—
But, oh! thou bitter stepmother and hard,
To thy poor, fenceless, naked child—the Bard!
A thing unteachable in world's skill,
And half an idiot, too, more helpless still;
No heels to bear him from the op'ning dun;
No claws to dig, his hated sight to shun;
No horns, but those by luckless Hymen worn,
And those, alas! not Amalthea's horn:
No nerves olfact'ry, Mammon's trusty cur,
Clad in rich dulness' comfortable fur;—

In naked feeling, and in aching pride,
He bears the unbroken blast from ev'ry side:
Vampyre booksellers drain him to the heart,
And scorpion critics cureless venom dart.

Critics!—appall'd I venture on the name,
Those cut-throat bandits in the paths of fame: [(267)
Bloody dissectors, worse than ten Monroes!
He hacks to teach, they mangle to expose.

His heart by causeless wanton malice wrung,
By blockhead's daring into madness stung;
His well-won bays, than life itself more dear,
By miscreants torn, who ne'er one sprig must wear: [strife,
Foil'd, bleeding, tortur'd, in the unequal
The hapless poet flounders on through life;
Till fled each hope that once his bosom fir'd,
And fled each muse that glorious once inspired,
Low sunk in squalid, unprotected age,
Dead, even resentment, for his injur'd page,
He heeds or feels no more the ruthless critic's rage!

So, by some hedge, the generous steed deceased,
For half-starv'd snarling curs a dainty feast:
By toil and famine worn to skin and bone,
Lies senseless of each tugging bitch's son,

Oh dulness! portion of the truly blest!
Calm shelter'd haven of eternal rest!
Thy sons ne'er madden in the fierce extremes
Of fortune's polar frost or torrid beams.
If mantling high she fills the golden cup,
With sober selfish ease they sip it up:
Conscious the bounteous meed they well deserve,
They only wonder "some folks" do not starve.
The grave sage hern thus easy picks his frog,
And thinks the mallard a sad worthless dog.
When disappointment snaps the clue of hope,
And thro' disast'rous night they darkling grope,
With deaf endurance sluggishly they bear,
And just conclude that "fools are fortune's care."
So, heavy, passive to the tempest's shocks,
Strong on the sign-post stands the stupid ox.
Not so the idle muses' mad-cap train,
Not such the workings of their moon-struck brain;
In equanimity they never dwell,
By turns in soaring heav'n, or vaulted hell.

I dread thee fate, relentless and severe,
With all a poet's, husband's father's fear!
Already one strong hold of hope is lost,
Glencairn, the truly noble, lies in dust;
(Fled, like the sun eclips'd as noon appears,
And left us darkling in a world of tears):
Oh! hear my ardent, grateful, selfish, pray'r!—
Fintry, my other stay, long bless and spare!
Thro' a long life his hopes and wishes crown;
And bright in cloudless skies his sun go down;
May bliss domestic smooth his private path,
Give energy to life, and soothe his latest breath,
With many a filial tear circling the bed [death!

Fourth Epistle to Mr. Graham,

OF FINTRY ON RECEIVING A FAVOUR. (268)

I CALL no goddess to inspire my strains,
A fabled muse may suit a bard that feigns;
Friend of my life! my ardent spirit burns,
And all the tribute of my heart returns,
For boons accorded, goodness ever new,
The gift still dearer, as the giver, you.

Thou orb of day! thou other paler light!
And all ye many sparkling stars of night;
If aught that giver from my mind efface,
If I that giver's bounty e'er disgrace;
Then roll to me, along your wandering spheres,
Only to number out a villain's years!

The Rights of Woman,

AN OCCASIONAL ADDRESS SPOKEN BY MISS FONTENELLE ON HER BENEFIT NIGHT.
[NOV. 26, 1792.]

WHILE Europe's eye is fix'd on mighty things,
The fate of empires and the fall of kings;
While quacks of state must each produce his plan,
And even children lisp the Rights of Man;
Amid this mighty fuss just let me mention,
The Rights of Woman merit some attention.

First, in the sexes' intermixed connection,
One sacred Right of Woman is protection.
The tender flower that lifts its head, elate,
Helpless, must fall before the blasts of fate,
Sunk on the earth, defac'd its lovely form,
Unless your shelter ward th' impending storm.

Our second right—but needless here, is caution,
To keep that right inviolate's the fashion;
Each man of sense has it so full before him,
He'd die before he'd wrong it—'tis decorum.
There was, indeed, in far less polish'd days,
A time, when rough rude man had naughty ways;
Would swagger, swear, get drunk, kick up a riot,
Nay even thus invade a lady's quiet.

Now, thank our **stars!** these Gothic times
are fled; [bred—
Now, well-bred men—and you are all well
Most justly think (and we are much the
gainers) [ners. (269)
Such conduct neither spirit, wit, nor man-

For Right the third, our last, our best, our
dearest, [nearest,
That right to fluttering female hearts the
Which even the Rights of Kings in low
prostration [tion!
Most humbly own—'tis dear, dear admira-
In that blest sphere alone we live and move:
There taste that life of life—immortal love.
Smiles, glances, sighs, tears, fits, flirtations,
airs,
'Gains't such an host what flinty savage
dares?— [charms,
When awful Beauty joins with all her
Who is so rash as rise in rebel arms?

But truce with kings and truce with consti-
tutions,
With bloody armaments and revolutions,
Let majesty your first attention summon,
Ah! ca ira! THE MAJESTY OF WOMAN.

A Vision.

As I stood by yon roofless tower (270),
Where the wa'-flower scents the dewy air,
Where th' owlet mourns in her ivy bower,
And tells the midnight moon her care;

The winds were laid, the air was still,
The stars they shot alang the sky;
The fox was howling on the hill,
To the distant-echoing glens reply.

The stream, adown its hazelly path,
Was rushing by the ruin'd wa's,
Hasting to join the sweeping Nith,
Whose distant roaring swells and fa's.

The cauld blue north was streaming forth
Her lights, wi' hissing eerie din;
Athwart the lift they start and shift,
Like fortune's favours, tint as win.

By heedless chance I turn'd mine eyes,
And, by the moonbeam, shook to see
A stern and stalwart ghaist arise,
Attir'd as minstrels wont to be.

Had I a statue been o' stane,
His darin' look had daunted me;
And on his bonnet grav'd was plain,
The sacred motto—"Libertie!"

And frae his harp sic strains did flow,
Might rous'd the slumb'ring dead to hear;
But oh! it was a tale of woe,
As ever met a Briton's ear.

He sang wi' joy the former day,
He weeping wail'd his latter times;
But what he said it was nae play—
I winna ventur't in my rhymes.

Liberty—A Fragment.

THEE, Caledonia, thy wild heaths among,
Thee, famed for martial deed and sacred song
To thee I turn with swimming eyes!
Where is that soul of freedom fled?
Immingled with the mighty dead! [lies!
Beneath the hallow'd turf where Wallace
Hear it not, Wallace, in thy bed of death!
Ye babbling winds, in silence sweep;
Disturb not ye the hero's sleep,
Nor give the coward secret breath.
Is this the power in freedom's war,
That wont to bid the battle rage?
Behold that eye which shot immortal hate,
Crushing the despot's proudest bearing
Behold e'en grizzly death's majestic state
When Freedom's sacred glance e'en death
is wearing.

To Mr. Maxwell,

OF TERRAUGHTY, ON HIS BIRTH-DAY,

HEALTH to the Maxwell's vet'ran chief!
Health, aye unsour'd by care or grief:
Inspir'd, I turn'd Fate's sybil leaf
This natal morn;
I see thy life is stuff o' prief,
Scarce quite half worn.

This day thou metes'st three score eleven,
And I can tell that bounteous Heaven
(The second sight, ye ken, is given
To ilka poet)
On thee a tack o' seven times seven
Will yet bestow it.

If envious buckies view wi' sorrow
Thy lengthen'd days on this blest morrow,
May desolation's lang teeth'd harrow,
Nine miles an hour,
Rake them like Sodom and Gomorrah,
In brimstane shoure—

But for thy friends, and they are mony,
Baith honest men and lasses bonnie,
May couthie fortune, kind and cannie,
In social glee,
Wi' mornings blythe and e'enings funny,
Bless them and thee!

Fareweel, auld birkie! Lord be near ye,
And then the deil he daurna steer ye:
Your friends aye love, your faes aye fear ye,
For me, shame fa' me,
If near'st my heart I dinna wear ye
While BURNS they ca' me!

On Pastoral Poetry. (271)

HAIL Poesie! thou Nymph reserv'd!
In chase o' thee, what crowds hae swerv'd
Frae common sense, or sunk unnerv'd
'Mang heaps o' clavers;
And och! owre aft thy joes hae starv'd,
Mid a' thy favours!

Say, Lassie, why thy train amang,
While loud, the trump's heroic clang,
And sock or buskin skelp alang
To death or marriage;
Scarce ane has tried the shepherd-sang
But wi' miscarriage?

In Homer's craft Jock Milton thrives;
Eschylus' pen Will Shakspeare drives;
Wee Pope, the knurlin, 'till him rives
Horatian fame;
In thy sweet sang, Barbauld, survives
Ev'n Sappho's flame.

But thee, Theocritus, wha matches?
They're no herd's ballats, Maro's catches;
Squire Pope but busks his skinklin patches
O' heathen tatters:
I pass by hundred, nameless wretches,
That ape their betters.

In this braw age o' wit and lear,
Will nane the Shepherd's whistle mair
Blaw sweetly in its native air
And rural grace;
And wi' the far fam'd Grecian share
A rival place?

Yes! there is ane; a Scottish callan—
There's ane; come forrit, honest Allan!
Thou need na jouk behint the hallan,
A chiel sae clever;
The teeth o' time may gnaw Tantallan,
But thou's for ever!

Thou paints auld nature to the nines,
In thy sweet Caledonian lines;
Nae gowden stream thro' myrtles twines,
Where Philomel,
While nightly breezes sweep the vines,
Her griefs will tell!

In goweny glens thy burnie strays,
Where bonnie lasses bleach their claes;
Or trots by hazelly shaws and braes,
Wi' hawthorns grey,
Where blackbirds join the shepherd's lays
At close o' day.

Thy rural loves are nature's sel';
Nae bombast spates o' nonsense swell;
Nae snap conceits, but that sweet spell
O' witchin' love;
That charm that can the strongest quell,
The sternest move.

Sonnet,

WRITTEN ON THE 25TH JANUARY 1793, THE BIRTHDAY OF THE AUTHOR, ON HEARING A THRUSH SING IN A MORNING WALK.

SING on, sweet thrush, upon the leafless bough,
Sing on, sweet bird, I listen to thy strain,
See aged Winter, 'mid his surly reign,
At thy blythe carol clears his furrow'd brow.

So in lone Poverty's dominion drear,
Sits meek Content with light unanxious heart,
Welcomes the rapid moments, bids them part,
Nor asks if they bring ought to hope or fear.

I thank thee, Author of this opening day!
Thou whose bright sun now gilds yon orient skies!
Riches denied, thy boon was purer joys,
What wealth could never give nor take away!

Yet come, thou child of poverty and care,
The mite high Heaven bestowed, that mite with thee I'll share.

The Tree of Liberty. (272)

HEARD ye o' the tree o' France,
I watna what's the name o't;
Around it a' the patriots dance,
Weel Europe kens the fame o't.
It stands where ance the Bastile stood,
A prison built by kings, man,
When Superstition's hellish brood
Kept France in leading strings, man.

Upo' this tree there grows sic fruit,
Its virtue's a' can tell, man;
It raises man aboon the brute,
It maks him ken himself, man.
If ance the peasant taste a bit
He's greater than a lord, man,
And wi' the beggar shares a mite
O' a' he can afford, man.

This fruit is worth a' Afric's wealth,
To comfort us 'twas sent, man:
To gie the sweetest blush o' health,
And mak us a' content, man.
It clears the een, it cheers the heart,
Maks high and low guid friends, man;
And he wha acts the traitor's part,
It to perdition sends, man.

My blessings aye attend the chiel,
Wha pitied Gallia's slaves, man,
And staw'd a branch, spite o' the deil,
Frae yon't the western waves, man.

DUNCAN GRAY.

Duncan fleech'd, and Duncan pray'd;
Meg was deaf as Ailsa cray.

Fair Virtue water'd it wi' care,
And now she sees wi' pride, man
How weel it buds and blossoms there.
Its branches spreading wide, man,

But vicious folk aye hate to see
The works o' Virtue thrive, man;
The courtly vermin's banned the tree,
And grat to see it thrive, man,
King Loui' thought to cut it down,
When it was unco' sma', man;
For this the watchman cracked his crown,
Cut aff his head and a', man.

A wicked crew syne, on a time,
Did tak a solemn aith, man,
It ne'er should flourish to its prime,
I wat they pledged their faith, man;
Awa, they gaed wi' mock parade,
Like beagles hunting game, man,
But soon grew weary o' the trade,
And wished they'd been at hame, man,

For Freedom, standing by the tree,
Her sons did loudly ca', man;
She sang a song o' liberty,
Which pleased them ane and a', man.
By her inspired, the new-born race
Soon drew the avenging steel, man;
The hirelings ran—her foes gied chase,
And banged the despot weel, man.

Let Britain boast her hardy oak,
Her poplar and her pine, man,
Auld Britain ance could crack her joke,
And o'er her neighbours shine, man.
But seek the forest round and round,
And soon 'twill be agreed, man,
That sic a tree can not be found,
'Twixt London and the Tweed, man.

Without this tree, alack this life
Is but a vale o' woe man;
A scene o' sorrow mixed wi' strife,
Nae real joys we know, man.
We labour soon, we labour late,
To feed the titled knave, man;
And a' the comfort we're to get,
Is that ayont the grave, man.

Wi' plenty o' sic trees, I trow,
The warld would live in peace, man;
The sword would help to mak a plough,
The din o' war wad cease, man.
Like brethren in a common cause,
We'd on each other smile, man;
And equal rights and equal laws
Wad gladden every isle, man.

Wae worth the loon wha wadna eat
Sic whalesome, dainty cheer, man;
I'd gie my shoon frae aff my feet,
To taste sic fruit, I swear, man.

Syne let us pray, auld England may
Sure plant this far-famed tree, man;
And blythe we'll sing, and hail the day
That gave us liberty, man.

To General Dumourier.

A PARODY ON ROBIN ADAIR. (273)

You're welcome to Despots, Dumourier;
You're welcome to Despots, Dumourier.
How does Dampiere do?
Ay and Bournonville too?
Why did they not come along with you,
Dumourier?

I will fight France with you, Dumourier;
I will fight France with you, Dumourier
I will fight France with you;
I will take my chance with you;
By my soul I'll dance a dance with you,
Dumourier.

Then let us fight about, Dumourier;
Then let us fight about, Dumourier;
Then let us fight about,
Till freedom's spark is out,
Then we'll be damn'd, no doubt—Dumourier.

Lines

SENT TO A GENTLEMAN WHOM HE HAD OFFENDED.

(274)

The friend whom wild from wisdom's way,
The fumes of wine infuriate send
(Not moony madness more astray)—
Who but deplores that hapless friend?

Mine was th' insensate frenzied part,
Ah, why should I such scenes outlive!—
Scenes so abhorrent to my heart!
'Tis thine to pity and forgive.

Monody

ON A LADY FAMED FOR HER CAPRICE. (275)

How cold is that bosom which folly once fir'd,
How pale is that cheek where the rouge lately glisten'd:
How silent that tongue which the echoes oft tired,
How dull is that ear which to flattery so listen'd!

If sorrow and anguish their exit await,
From friendship and dearest affection remov'd;
How doubly severer. Eliza, thy fate,
Thou diedst unwept, as thou lived'st unlov'd.

Loves, graces, and virtues, I call not on you!
 So shy, grave, and distant, ye shed not a tear:
But come, all ye offspring of folly so true,
 And flowers let us cull for Eliza's cold bier.

We'll search through the garden for each silly flower,
 We'll roam through the forest for each idle weed;
But chiefly the nettle, so typical, shower,
 For none e'er approached her but rued the rash deed.

We'll sculpture the marble, we'll measure the lay;
 Here Vanity strums on her idiot lyre;
There keen indignation shall dart on her prey,
 Which spurning contempt shall redeem from his ire.

THE EPITAPH.

Here lies, now a prey to insulting neglect,
 What once was a butterfly gay in life's beam:
Want only of wisdom denied her respect,
 Want only of goodness denied her esteem.

Epistle from Esopus to Maria.

(276)

From those drear solitudes and frowsy cells,
Where infamy with sad repentance dwells;
Where turnkeys make the jealous portal fast,
And deal from iron hands the spare repast,
Where truant 'prentices, yet young in sin,
Blush at the curious stranger peeping in;
Where strumpets, relics of the drunken roar,
Resolve to drink, nay, half to whore no more:
Where tiny thieves not destin'd yet to swing,
Beat hemp for others, riper for the string:
From these dire scenes my wretched lines I date,
To tell Maria her Esopus' fate.

"Alas! I feel I am no actor here!"
'Tis real hangmen, real scourges bear
Prepare, Maria, for a horrid tale
Will turn thy very rouge to deadly pale;
Will make thy hair, tho' erst from gipsy poll'd,
By barber woven, and by barber sold,
Though twisted smooth with Harry's nicest care,
Like hoary bristles to erect and stare.
The hero of the mimic scene, no more,
I start in Hamlet, in Othello roar;
Or haughty chieftain, mid the din of arms,
In Highland bonnet woo Malvina's charms;
While sans culottes stoop up the mountain high,
And steal from me Maria's eye.
Blest Highland bonnet! once my proudest dress,
Now prouder still, Maria's temples press,
I see her wave thy towering plumes afar,
And call each coxcomb to the wordy war;
I see her face the first of Ireland's sons (277),
And even out-Irish his Hibernian bronze;
The crafty colonel (278) leaves the tartaned lines
For other wars, where he a hero shines;
The hopeful youth, in Scottish senate bred,
Who owns a Bushby's heart without the head,
Comes mid a string of coxcombs to display,
That *veni, vidi, vici*, is his way;
The shrinking bard adown an alley skulks,
And dreads a meeting worse than Woolwich hulks;
Though there, his heresies in church and state
Might well award him Muir and Palmer's fate:
Still she undaunted reels and rattles on,
And dares the public like a noontide sun.
(What scandal call'd Maria's jaunty stagger,
The ricket reeling of a crooked swagger;
Whose spleen e'en worse than Burn's venom, when
He dips in gall unmix'd his eager pen,
And pours his vengeance in the burning line,
Who christen'd thus Maria's lyre divine,
The idiot strum of vanity bemused,
And even th' abuse of poesy abused:
Who call'd her verse a parish Workhouse, made
For motley, foundling fancies, stolen or stray'd?)

A Workhouse! ah, that sound awakes my woes,
And pillows on the thorn my rack'd repose!
In durance vile here must I wake and weep,
And all my frowsy couch in sorrow steep!
That straw where many a rogue has lain of yore,
And vermin'd Gipsies litter'd heretofore.
Why Lonsdale thus, thy wrath on vagrants pour;
Must earth no rascal save thyself endure?
Must thou alone in guilt immortal swell,
And make a vast monopoly of hell?
Thou know'st the virtues cannot hate thee worse;
The vices also, must they club their curse?
Or must no tiny sin to others fall,
Because thy guilt's supreme enough for all?

Maria, send me too thy griefs and cares;
In all of thee sure thy Esopus shares.

As thou at all mankind the flag unfurls,
Who on my fair one satire's vengeance hurls?
Who calls thee, pert, affected, vain coquette,
A wit in folly, and a fool in wit?
Who says that fool alone is not thy due,
And quotes thy treacheries to prove it true?
Our force united on thy foes we'll turn
And dare the war with all of woman born:
For who can write and speak as thou and I?
My periods that decyphering defy,
And thy still matchless tongue that conquers all reply.

Sonnet,

ON THE DEATH OF CAPTAIN RIDDEL OF GLENRIDDEL, APRIL, 1794. (279)

No more, ye warblers of the wood—no more!
Nor pour your descant, grating, on my soul:
Thou young-eyed Spring, gay in thy verdant stole,
More welcome were to me grim Winter's wildest roar.

How can ye charm, ye flow'rs, with all your dyes?
Ye blow upon the sod that wraps my friend!
How can I to the tuneful strain attend?
That strain flows round th' untimely tomb where Riddel lies!

Yes, pour, ye warblers, pour the notes of woe!
And soothe the Virtues weeping on his bier:
The Man of Worth, who has not left his peer,
Is in his "narrow house" for ever darkly low.

Thee, Spring, again with joy shall others greet,
Me, mem'ry of my loss will only meet.

Impromptu

ON MRS RIDDEL'S BIRTH-DAY. (280)

Old Winter, with his frosty beard,
Thus once to Jove his prayer preferr'd—
"What have I done of all the year,
To bear this hated doom severe?
My cheerless suns no pleasure know;
Night's horrid car drags, dreary slow;
My dismal months no joys are crowning,
But spleeny English, hanging, drowning.

Now, Jove, for once be mighty civil,
To counterbalance all this evil;
Give me, and I've no more to say,
Give me Maria's natal day!
That brilliant gift shall so enrich me,
Spring, summer, autumn, cannot match me."
"'Tis done!" says Jove; so ends my story,
And Winter once rejoic'd in glory.

Verses to Miss Graham

OF FINTRY. (281)

Here, where the Scottish muse immortal lives,
In sacred strains and tuneful numbers join'd,
Accept the gift;—tho' humble he who gives,
Rich is the tribute of the grateful mind.

So may no ruffian-feeling in thy breast,
Discordant jar thy bosom-chords among;
But peace attune thy gentle soul to rest,
Or love ecstatic wake his seraph song.

Or pity's notes in luxury of tears,
As modest want the tale of woe reveals;
While conscious virtue all the strain endears,
And heaven-born piety her sanction seals.

The Vowels,

A TALE.

'Twas where the birch and sounding thong are plied,
The noisy domicile of pedant pride;
Where ignorance her dark'ning vapour throws,
And cruelty directs the thick'ning blows;
Upon a time, Sir A-be-ce the great,
In all his pedagogic powers elate,
His awful chair of state resolves to mount,
And call the trembling vowels to account.

First enter'd A, a grave, broad, solemn wight,
But, ah! deform'd, dishonest to the sight!
His twisted head look'd backward on his way,
And flagrant from the scourge he grunted, *ai!*

Reluctant, E stalk'd in; with piteous race
The jostling tears ran down his honest face!
That name, that well-worn name, and all his own,
Pale he surrenders at the tyrant's throne;
The Pedant stifles keen the Roman sound
Not all his mongrel diphthongs can compound;
And next the title following close behind,
He to the nameless, ghastly wretch assign'd

The cobweb'd Gothic dome resounded, Y?
In sullen vengeance, I, disdain'd reply:
The pedant swung his felon cudgel round,
And knock'd the groaning vowel to the ground!

In rueful apprehension enter'd O,
The wailing minstrel of despairing woe;

Th' Inquisitor of Spain the most expert,
Might there have learnt new mysteries of his art;
So grim, deform'd, with horrors entering U,
His dearest friend and brother scarcely knew!

As trembling U stood staring all aghast,
The pedant in his left hand clutch'd him fast,
In helpless infants' tears he dipp'd his right,
Baptiz'd him *eu*, and kick'd him from his sight.

Verses to John Rankine.

Ane day, as Death, that grusome carle,
Was driving to the tither warl'
A mixtie-maxtie, motley squad,
And mony a guilt-bespotted lad;
Black gowns of each denomination,
And thieves of every rank and station,
From him that wears the star and garter,
To him that wintles in a halter:
Ashamed himsel' to see the wretches,
He mutters, glowrin' at the bitches,
"By G—, I'll not be seen behint them,
Nor 'mang the sp'ritual core present them,
Without, at least, ane honest man,
To grace this d—d infernal clan."
By Adamhill a glance he threw,
"L— God!" quoth he, "I have it now,
There's just the man I want, i' faith!"
And quickly stoppit Rankine's breath.

On Sensibility.

TO MY DEAR AND MUCH HONOURED FRIEND, MRS. DUNLOP, OF DUNLOP.

Sensibility how charming,
Thou, my friend, canst truly tell:
But distress with horrors arming,
Thou hast also known too well!

Fairest flower, behold the lily,
Blooming in the sunny ray:
Let the blast sweep o'er the valley,
See it prostrate on the clay.

Hear the wood-lark charm the forest,
Telling o'er his little joys:
Hapless bird! a prey the surest,
To each pirate of the skies.

Dearly bought, the hidden treasure,
Finer feelings can bestow;
Chords that vibrate sweetest pleasure.
Thrill the deepest notes of woe.

Address

SPOKEN BY MISS FONTENELLE ON HER BENEFIT NIGHT (282).

Still anxious to secure your partial favour,
And not less anxious, sure, this night, than ever,
A Prologue, Epilogue, or some such matter,
'Twould vamp my bill, said I, if nothing better;
So sought a Poet, roosted near the skies,
Told him I came to feast my curious eyes;
Said, nothing like his works was ever printed;
And last, my Prologue-business slily hinted.
"Ma'am, let me tell you," quoth my man of rhymes,
"I know your bent—these are no laughing times:
Can you—but Miss, I own I have my fears—
Dissolve in sighs—and sentimental tears,
With laden breath, and solemn-rounded sentence,
Rouse from his sluggish slumbers, fell Repentance;
Paint Vengeance as he takes his horrid stand,
Waving on high the desolating brand,
Calling the storms to bear him o'er a guilty land?"

I could no more—askance the creature eyeing,
D'ye think, said I, this face was made for crying?
I'll laugh, that's poz—nay more, the world shall know it;
And so, your servant! gloomy Master Poet!
Firm as my creed, Sirs, 'tis my fix'd belief,
That Misery's another word for Grief;
I also think—so may I be a bride!—
That so much laughter, so much life enjoy'd.

Thou man of crazy care and ceaseless sigh,
Still under bleak Misfortune's blasting eye;
Doom'd to that sorest task of man alive—
To make three guineas do the work of five:
Laugh in Misfortune's face—the beldam witch!—
Say, you'll be merry, tho' you can't be rich.

Thou other man of care, the wretch in love
Who long with jiltish arts and airs hast strove;
Who, as the boughs all temptingly project,
Measur'st in desperate thought—a rope—thy neck—
Or, where the beetling cliff o'erhangs the deep,
Peerest to meditate the healing leap:
Would'st thou be cur'd, thou silly, moping elf!
Laugh at her follies—laugh e'en at thyself:
Learn to despise those frowns now so terrific,
And love a kinder—that's your grand specific.

To sum up all, be merry, I advise;
And as we're merry, may we still be wise.

To Chloris. (283)

'Tis Friendship's pledge, my young, fair
  Nor thou the gift refuse, [friend,
Nor with unwilling ear attend
  The moralising muse.

Since thou, in all thy youth and charms,
  Must bid the world adieu,
(A world 'gainst peace in constant arms)
  To join the friendly few.

Since thy gay morn of life o'ercast,
  Chill came the tempest's lower;
(And ne'er misfortune's eastern blast
  Did nip a fairer flower.)

Since life's gay scenes must charm no more,
  Still much is left behind;
Still nobler wealth hast thou in store—
  The comforts of the mind!

Thine is the self-approving glow,
  On conscious honour's part;
And, dearest gift of heaven below,
  Thine friendship's truest heart.

The joys refin'd of sense and taste,
  With every muse to rove:
And doubly were the poet blest,
  These joys could he improve.

Address to the Shade of Thomson,

ON CROWNING HIS BUST AT EDNAM, ROXBURGHSHIRE, WITH BAYS.

While virgin spring, by Eden's flood,
  Unfolds her tender mantle green,
Or pranks the sod in frolic mood,
  Or tunes Eolian strains between:

While Summer with a matron grace
  Retreats to Dryburgh's cooling shade,
Yet oft, delighted, stops to trace
  The progress of the spiky blade:

While Autumn, benefactor kind,
  By Tweed erects his aged head,
And sees, with self-approving mind,
  Each creature on his bounty fed:

While maniac Winter rages o'er
  The hills whence classic Yarrow flows,
Rousing the turbid torrent's roar,
  Or sweeping, wild, a waste of snows:

So long, sweet Poet of the year!
  Shall bloom that wreath thou well hast won;
While Scotia, with exulting tear,
  Proclaims that Thomson was her son.

O

Ballads on Mr. Heron's Elections.

[BALLAD FIRST] (284.)

Whom will you send to London town,
  To Parliament and a' that?
Or wha in a' the country round
  The best deserves to fa' that?
    For a' that, and a' that,
    Thro' Galloway and a' that;
    Where is the laird or belted knight
    That best deserves to fa' that?

Wha sees Kerroughtree's open yett,
  And wha is't never saw that?
Wha ever wi' Kerroughtree met
  And has a doubt of a' that?
    For a' that, and a' that,
    Here's Heron yet for a' that!
    The independent patriot,
    The honest man, and a' that.

Tho' wit and worth in either sex,
  St. Mary's Isle can shaw that;
Wi' dukes and lords let Selkirk mix,
  And weel does Selkirk fa' that.
    For a' that, and a' that,
    Here's Heron yet for a' that!
    The independent commoner
    Shall be the man for a' that.

But why should we to nobles jouk?
  And is't against the law that?
For why, a lord may be a gouk,
  Wi' ribbon, star, and a' that.
    For a' that, and a' that,
    Here's Heron yet for a' that!
    A lord may be a lousy loun,
    Wi' ribbon, star, and a' that.

A beardless boy comes o'er the hills,
  Wi' uncle's purse and a' that;
But we'll hae ane frae 'mang oursels,
  A man we ken, and a' that,
    For a' that, and a' that,
    Here's Heron yet for a' that!
    For we're not to be bought and sold
    Like naigs, and nowt, and a' that.

Then let us drink the Stewartry,
  Kerroughtree's laird, and a' that,
Our representative to be,
  For weel he's worthy a' that.
    For a' that, and a' that,
    Here's Heron yet for a' that!
    A House of Commons such as he,
    They would be blest that saw that.

[BALLAD SECOND.]

The Election.

Fy, let us a' to Kirkcudbright,
  For there will be bickerin' there;
For Murray's light-horse are to muster,
  And oh, how the heroes will swear!

And there will be Murray commander,
And Gordon the battle to win;
Like brothers they'll stand by each other,
Sae knit in alliance an' sin.

And there will be black-lippit Johnnie (285),
The tongue o' the trump to them a';
An' he get na hell for his haddin',
The deil gets na justice ava';
And there will be Kempleton's birkie,
A boy no sae black at the bane,
But, as for his fine nabob fortune,
We'll e'en let the subject alane. (286)

And there will be Wigton's new sheriff;
Dame Justice fu' brawlie has sped,
She's gotten the heart of a Busby,
But, Lord, what's become o' the head?
And there will be Cardoness (287), Esquire,
Sae mighty in Cardoness' eyes;
A wight that will weather damnation,
For the devil the prey will despise.

And there will be Douglasses doughty (288),
New christ'ning towns far and near;
Abjuring their democrat doings,
By kissing the — o' a peer;
And there will be Kenmure sae gen'rous,
Whose honour is proof to the storm,
To save them from stark reprobation,
He lent then his name to the firm.

But we winna mention Redcastle,
The body, e'en let him escape!
He'd venture the gallows for siller,
An' 'twere na the cost o' the rape.
And where is our king's lord lieutenant,
Sae fam'd for his gratefu' return?
The billie is gettin' his questions,
To say in St. Stephen's the morn.

And there will be lads o' the gospel,
Muirhead wha's as guid as he's true:
And there will be Buittle's apostle,
Wha's more o' the black than the blue;
And there will be folk from St. Mary's,
A house o' great merit and note,
The deil ane but honours them highly—
The deil ane will gie them his vote!

And there will be wealthy young Richard,
Dame fortune should hing by the neck;
For prodigal, thriftless, bestowing,
His merit had won him respect:
And there will be rich brother nabobs,
Tho' nabobs yet men of the first,
And there will be Collieston's whiskers,
And Quintin, o' lads not the warst.

And there will be stamp-office Johnnie,
Tak tent how ye purchase a dram; [(289)
And there will be gay Cassencarrie,
And there will be gleg Colonel Tam;

And there will be trusty Kerroughtree,
Whose honour was ever his law,
If the virtues were packed in a parcel,
His worth might be sample for a'.

And can we forget the auld major,
Wha'll ne'er be forgot in the Greys,
Our flatt'ry we'll keep for some other,
Him only 'tis justice to praise.
And there will be maiden Kilkerran,
And also Barskimming's guid knight,
And there will be roarin' Birtwhistle,
Wha, luckily, roars in the right.

And there frae the Niddesdale borders,
Will mingle the Maxwells in droves;
Teugh Johnnie, staunch Geordie, and Walie,
That griens for the fishes and loaves;
And there will be Logan Mac Douall,
Sculdudd'ry and he will be there,
And also the wild Scot of Galloway,
Sodgerin' gunpowder Blair.

Then hey the chaste interest o' Broughton,
And hey for the blessings 'twill bring!
It may send Balmaghie to the Commons,
In Sodom 'twould make him a king;
And hey for the sanctified Murray,
Our land who wi' chapels has stor'd;
He founder'd his horse among harlots,
But gied the auld naig to the Lord.

[BALLAD THIRD.]

An Excellent New Song,

TUNE—*Buy broom besoms,*

WHA will buy my troggin (290),
Fine election ware;
Broken trade o' Broughton,
A' in high repair.
Buy braw troggin,
Frae the banks o' Dee;
Who wants troggin
Let him come to me.

There's a noble Earl's
Fame and high renown (291),
For an auld sang—
It's thought the gudes were strown
Buy braw troggin, &c.

Here's the worth o' Broughton (292),
In a needle's ee:
Here's a reputation
Tint by Balmaghie. (293)
Buy braw troggin, &c.

Here's an honest conscience
Might a prince adorn;
Frae the downs o' Tinwald—
So was never worn. (294)
Buy braw troggin, &c.

Here its stuff and lining,
Cardoness's head;
Fine for a sodger
A' the wale o' lead.
Buy braw troggin, &c.

Here's a little wadset
Buittle's scrap o' truth,
Pawn'd in a gin shop
Quenching holy drouth.
Buy braw troggin, &c.

Here's armorial bearings,
Frae the manse o' Urr;
The crest, an auld crab-apple (295)
Rotten at the core.
Buy braw troggin, &c.

Here is Satan's picture,
Like a bizzard gled,
Pouncing poor Redcastle
Sprawlin' as a taed.
Buy braw troggin, &c.

Here's the worth and wisdom
Collieston can boast;
By a thievish midge
They had been nearly lost.
Buy braw troggin, &c.

Here is Murray's fragments
O' the ten commands;
Gifted by black Jock
To get them aff his hands.
Buy braw troggin, &c.

Saw ye e'er sic troggin?
If to buy ye're slack,
Hornie's turnin' chapman—
He'll buy a' the pack.
Buy braw troggin
Frae the banks o' Dee;
Wha wants troggin
Let him come to me.

On Life,

ADDRESSED TO COLONEL DE PEYSTER. (296) DUMFRIES, 1796.

My honoured colonel, deep I feel
Your interest in the poet's weal:
Ah! now sma' heart hae I to speel
The steep Parnassus,
Surrounded thus by bolus pill,
And potion glasses.

Oh what a canty warld were it,
Would pain and care and sickness spare it;
And fortune favour worth and merit,
As they deserve!
(And aye a rowth roast beef and claret;
Syne wha wad starve?)

Dame Life, tho' fiction out may trick her,
And in paste gems and frippery deck her;
Oh! flickering, feeble, and unsicker
I've found her still
Aye wavering like the willow-wicker,
'Tween good and ill.

Then that curst carmagnole, auld Satan,
Watches like baudrons by a rattan,
Our sinfu' saul to get a claut on
Wi' felon ire;
Syne, whip! his tail ye'll ne'er cast saut on—
He's aff like fire.

Auld Nick! auld Nick! it is na fair,
First showing us the tempting ware,
Bright wines and bonnie lasses rare,
To put us daft;
Syne weave, unseen, thy spider snare
O' hell's damn'd waft.

Poor man, the flie, aft bizzes by,
And aft as chance he comes thee nigh,
Thy auld damn'd elbow yeuks wi' joy,
And hellish pleasure;
Already in thy fancy's eye,
Thy sicker treasure!

Soon heel's-o'er-gowdie! in he gangs,
And like a sheep-head on a tangs,
Thy girning laugh enjoys his pangs
And murd'ring wrestle,
As, dangling in the wind, he hangs
A gibbet's tassel.

But lest you think I am uncivil,
To plague you with this draunting drivel,
Abjuring a' intentions evil,
I quat my pen:
The Lord preserve us a' frae the devil!
Amen! Amen!

Inscription

FOR AN ALTAR TO INDEPENDENCE. (297)

Thou of an independent mind,
With soul resolv'd, with soul resign'd;
Prepar'd Powers proudest frown to brave,
Who wilt not be, nor have a slave;
Virtue alone who dost revere,
Thy own reproach alone dost fear,
Approach this shrine, and worship here,

On the Death of a Favourite Child.

(298)

Oh sweet be thy sleep in the land of the grave,
My dear little angel, for ever;
For ever—oh no! let not man be a slave,
His hopes from existence to sever.

Though cold be the clay where thou pillow'st thy head,
In the dark silent mansions of sorrow,
The spring shall return to thy low narrow bed,
Like the beam of the day-star to-morrow.

The flower stem shall bloom like thy sweet seraph form,
Ere the spoiler had nipt thee in blossom,
When thou shrunk'st frae the scowl of the loud winter storm,
And nestled thee close to that bosom

Oh still I behold thee, all lovely in death,
Reclined on the lap of thy mother;
When the tear trickled bright, when the short stifled breath.
Told how dear ye were aye to each other.

My child, thou art gone to the home of thy rest,
Where suffering no longer can harm ye,
Where the songs of the good, where the hymns of the blest,
Through an endless existence shall charm thee.

While he, thy fond parent, must sighing sojourn,
Through the dire desert regions of sorrow,
O'er the hope and misfortune of being to mourn,
And sigh for this life's latest morrow.

To Mr. Mitchell,

COLLECTOR OF EXCISE, DUMFRIES, 1796.

Friend of the Poet, tried and leal,
Wha, wanting thee, might beg or steal;
Alack! alack! the meikle diel
Wi' a' his witches
Are at it, skelpin' jig and reel,
In my poor pouches!

I modestly fu' fain wad hint it,
That one pound one, I sairly want it;
If wi' the hizzie down ye sent it,
It would be kind;
And while my heart wi' lif-blood daunted,
I'd bear't in mind.

So may the auld year gang out moaning
To see the new come laden, groaning,
Wi' double plenty o'er the loanin
To thee and thine;
Domestic peace and comforts crowning
The hale design.

POSTCRIPT.

Ye've heard this while how I've been licket,
And by fell death was nearly nicket;
Grim loan! he got me by the fecket,
And sair me sheuk;
But by guid luck I lap a wicket,
And turn'd a neuk.

But by that health, I've got a shore o't,
And by that life, I'm promised mair o't
My hale and weel, I'll tak a care o't,
A tentier way;
Then farewell folly, hide and hair o't,
For ance and aye!

The Ruined Maid's Lament.

Oh, meikle do I rue, fause love,
Oh sairly do I rue,
That e'er I heard your flattering tongue,
That e'er your face I knew.

Oh, I hae tent my rosy cheeks,
Likewise my waist sae sma';
And I hae lost my lightsome heart,
That little wist a fa'.

Now I maun thole the scornfu' sneer
O' mony a saucy quean;
When, gin the truth were a' but kent,
Her life's been warse than mine.

Whene'er my father thinks on me,
He stares into the wa';
My mither, she has taen the bed
Wi' thinking on my fa'.

Whene'er I hear my father's foot,
My heart wad burst wi' pain;
Whene'er I meet my mither's ee,
My tears rin down like rain,

Alas! sae sweet a tree as love
Sic bitter fruit should bear!
Alas! that e'er a bonnie face
Should draw a sauty tear!
* * * *

The Dean of the Faculty.

A NEW BALLAD. (299)

Dire was the hate at old Harlaw,
That Scot to Scot did carry;
And dire the discord Langside saw,
For beauteous hapless Mary:
But Scot with Scot ne'er met so hot,
Or were more in fury seen, Sir,
Than 'twixt Hal and Bob for the famous job—
Who should be Faculty's Dean, Sir.

This Hal for genus, wit, and lore,
  Among the first was number'd;
But pious Bob, 'mid learning's store,
  Commandment ten remember'd.
Yet simple Bob the victory got,
  And won his heart's desire;
Which shows that Heaven can boil the pot,
  Though the devil's —— in the fire.

Squire Hal besides had in this case
  Pretensions rather brassy,
For talents to deserve a place
  Are qualifications saucy;
So their worships of the "Faculty"
  Quite sick of merit's rudeness,
Chose one who should owe it all, d'ye see,
  To their gratis grace and goodness.

As once on Pisgah purg'd was the sight
  Of a son of Circumcision,
So may be, on this Pisgah height,
  Bob's purblind, mental vision:
Nay, Bobby's mouth may be open'd yet
  Till for eloquence you hail him,
And swear he has the Angel met
  That met the Ass of Balaam.

Verses

ON THE DESTRUCTION OF THE WOODS NEAR DRUMLANRIG. (300)

As on the banks o' wandering Nith,
  Ane smiling simmer-morn I strayed,
And traced its bonnie howes and haughs,
  Where linties sang and lambkins play'd,
I sat me down upon a craig,
  And drank my fill o' fancy's dream,
When, from the eddying deep below,
  Uprose the genius of the stream.

Dark, like the frowning rock, his brow,
  And troubled, like his wintry wave,
And deep, as sighs the boding wind
  Amang his eaves, the sigh he gave—
"And came ye here, my son," he cried,
  "To wander in my birken shade?
To muse some favourite Scottish theme,
  Or sing some favourite Scottish maid.

"There was a time, it's nae lang syne,
  Ye might hae seen me in my pride,
When a' my banks sae bravely saw
  Their woody pictures in my tide;
When hanging beech and spreading elm
  Shaded my stream sae clear and cool;
And stately oaks their twisted arms
  Threw broad and dark across the pool!

"When glinting, through the trees, appeared
  The wee white cot aboon the mill,
And peacefu' rose its ingle reek,
  That slowly curled up the hill.
But now the cot is bare and cauld,
  Its branchy shelter's lost and gane,
And scarce a stinted birk is left
  To shiver in the blast is lane."

"Alas!" said I, "what ruefu' chance
  Has twin'd ye o' your stately trees?
Has laid your rocky bosom bare?
  Has stripp'd the cleeding o' your braes?
Was it the bitter eastern blast,
  That scatters blight in early spring?
Or was't the wil'fire scorched their boughs,
  Or canker-worm wi' secret sting?"

"Nae eastlin blast," the sprite replied:
  "It blew na here sae fierce and fell,
And on my dry and whalesome banks
  Nae canker-worms get leave to dwell:
Man! cruel man!" the genius sigh'd—
  As through the cliffs he sank him down—
"The worm that gnaw'd my bonnie trees,
  That reptile wears a ducal crown."

On the Duke of Queensberry. (301)

How shall I sing Drumlanrig's Grace—
Discarded remnant of a race
    Once great in martial story?
His forbears' virtues all contrasted—
The very name of Douglas blasted—
    His that inverted glory.

Hate, envy, oft the Douglas bore;
But he has superadded more,
    And sunk them in contempt;
Follies and crimes have stain'd the name,
But, Queensberry, thine the virgin claim,
    From ought that's good exempt.

Verses to John M'Murdo, Esq.

[WITH A PRESENT OF BOOKS.] (302.)

Oh, could I give thee India's wealth
  As I this trifle send,
Because thy joy in both would be
  To share them with a friend.

But golden sands did never grace
  The Heliconian stream;
Then take what gold could never buy—
  An honest Bard's esteem.

On Mr. M'Murdo.

INSCRIBED ON A PANE OF GLASS IN HIS HOUSE.

Blest be M'Murdo to his latest day!
No envious cloud o'ercast his evening ray;
No wrinkle furrowed by the hand of care,
Nor ever sorrow add one silver hair!
Oh, may no son the father's honour stain,
Nor ever daughter give the mother pain!

Impromptu on Willie Stewart. (303)

YOU'RE welcome, Willie Stewart,
You're welcome, Willie Stewart,
There's ne'er a flower that blooms in May,
That's half sae welcome's thou art.

Come, bumpers high, express your joy,
The bowl we maun renew it;
The tappit-hen gae bring her ben,
To welcome Willie Stewart.

May foes be strang, and friends be slack,
Ilk action may he rue it;
May woman on him turn her back,
That wrangs thee, Willie Stewart.

To Miss Jessy Lewars.

[WITH A PRESENT OF BOOKS.]

THINE be the volumes, Jessy fair,
And with them take the Poet's prayer—
That Fate may in her fairest page,
With ev'ry kindliest, best presage
Of future bliss enrol thy name:
With native worth, and spotless fame,
And wakeful caution still aware
Of ill—but chief, man's felon snare;
All blameless joys on earth we find,
And all the treasures of the mind—
These be thy guardian and reward;
So prays thy faithful friend the Bard.

Tibbie, I hae seen the Day. (304)

TUNE—*Invercauld's Reel.*

OH Tibbie, I hae seen the day
Ye wad na been sae shy;
For lack o' gear ye slighted me,
But, trowth, I care na by.

Yestreen I met you on the moor,
Ye spak na, but gaed by like stoure;
Ye geck at me because I'm poor,
But fient a hair care I.

I doubt na, lass, but ye may think,
Because ye hae the name o'clink,
That ye can please me at a wink,
Whene'er ye like to try.

But sorrow tak him that's sae mean,
Altho' his pouch o' coin were clean,
Wha follows ony saucy quean,
That looks sae proud and high.

Altho' a lad were e'er sae smart,
If that he want the yellow dirt,
Ye'll cast your head another airt,
And answer him fu' dry.

But if he hae the name o' gear,
Ye'll fasten to him like a brier,
Tho' hardly he, for sense or lear,
Be better than the kye.

But, Tibbie, lass, tak my advice,
Your daddie's gear maks you sae nice;
The deil a ane wad spier your price,
Were ye as poor as I.

There lives a lass in yonder park,
I would na gie her in her sark,
For thee, wi' a' thy thousan' mark;
Ye need na look sae high.

Montgomery's Peggy. (305)

TUNE—*Galla-Water.*

ALTHO' my bed were in yon muir
Amang the heather, in my plaidie,
Yet happy, happy would I be,
Had I my dear Montgomery's Peggy.

When o'er the hill beat surly storms,
And winter nights were dark and rainy;
I'd seek some dell, and in my arms
I'd shelter dear Montgomery's Peggy.

Were I a baron proud and high,
And horse and servants waiting ready,
Then a' 'twad gie o' joy to me,
The sharin't with Montgomery's Peggy.

Bonny Peggy Alison. (306)

TUNE—*Braes o' Balquhidder.*

CHORUS,

I'll kiss thee yet, yet,
And I'll kiss thee o'er again;
And I'll kiss thee, yet, yet,
My bonnie Peggy Alison;

Ilk care and fear, when thou art near,
I ever mair defy them, O;
Young kings upon their hansel throne
Are no sae blest as I am, O!

When in my arms, wi' a' thy charms,
I clasp my countless treasure, O,
I seek nae mair o' Heaven to share,
Than sic a moment's pleasure, O!

And by thy een, sae bonnie blue,
I swear I'm thine for ever, O!
And on thy lips I seal my vow,
And break it shall I never, O!

Here's to thy Health, my Bonny Lass.

TUNE—*Laggan Burn.*

HERE's to thy health, my bonnie lass,
Guid night, and joy be wi' thee;
I'll come nae mair to thy bower-door,
To tell thee that I loe thee:

Oh dinna think, my pretty pink,
But I can live without thee:
I vow and swear I dinna care
How lang ye look about ye.

Thou'rt aye sae free informing me
Thou hast nae mind to marry;
I'll be as free informing thee
Nae time hae I to tarry.
I ken thy friends try ilka means,
Frae wedlock to delay thee;
Depending on some higher chance—
But fortune may betray thee.

I ken they scorn my low estate,
But that does never grieve me;
But I'm as free as any he,
Sma' siller will relieve me.
I count my health my greatest wealth,
Sae long as I'll enjoy it:
I'll fear nae scant, I'll bode nae want,
As lang's I get employment.

But far off fowls hae feathers fair,
And aye until ye try them:
Tho' they seem fair, still have a care,
They may prove worse than I am.
But at twilit night, when the moon shines bright,
My dear, I'll come and see thee;
For the man that loes his mistress weel,
Nae travel makes him weary.

Young Peggy. (307)

TUNE—*Last time I came o'er the Muir.*

Young Peggy blooms our bonniest lass,
Her blush is like the morning,
The rosy dawn, the springing grass,
With early gems adorning:
Her eyes outshine the radiant beams
That gild the passing shower,
And glitter o'er the crystal streams,
And cheer each fresh'ning flower.

Her lips, more than the cherries bright,
A richer dye has graced them;
They charm th' admiring gazer's sight,
And sweetly tempt to taste them:
Her smile is, as the evening mild,
When feather'd tribes are courting,
And little lambkins wanton wild,
In playful bands disporting.

Were fortune lovely Peggy's foe,
Such sweetness would relent her
As blooming spring unbends the brow
Of surly, savage winter.
Detraction's eye no aim can gain,
Her winning powers to lessen;
And fretful envy grins in vain
The poison'd tooth to fasten.

Ye pow'rs of honour, love and truth,
From ev'ry ill defend her;
Inspire the highly-favour'd youth,
The destinies intend her:
Still fan the sweet connubial flame
Responsive in each bosom,
And bless the dear parental name
With many a filial blossom.

John Barleycorn.

A BALLAD. (308)

There were three kings into the east,
Three kings both great and high;
And they hae sworn a solemn oath
John Barleycorn should die.

They took a plough and plough'd him down,
Put clods upon his head;
And they hae sworn a solemn oath
John Barleycorn was dead.

But the cheerful spring came kindly on
And show'rs began to fall;
John Barleycorn got up again,
And sore surpris'd them all.

The sultry suns of summer came,
And he grew thick and strong;
His head weel arm'd wi' pointed spears,
That no one should him wrong.

The sober autumn enter'd mild,
When he grew wan and pale;
His bending joints and drooping head
Show'd he began to fail.

His colour sicken'd more and more,
He faded into age;
And then his enemies began
To show their deadly rage.

They've taen a weapon, long and sharp,
And cut him by the knee!
They tied him fast upon a cart,
Like a rogue for forgerie.

They laid him down upon his back,
And cudgell'd him full sore;
They hung him up before the storm,
And turn'd him o'er and o'er.

They filled up a darksome pit
With water to the brim;
They heaved in John Barleycorn,
There let him sink or swim.

They laid him out upon the floor
To work him farther woe;
And still, as signs of life appear'd,
They toss'd him to and fro.

They wasted o'er a scorching flame
The marrow of his bones;
But a miller us'd him worst of all,
For he crush'd him 'tween two stones.

And they hae taen his very heart's blood,
And drunk it round and round;
And still the more and more they drank,
Their joy did more abound.

John Barleycorn was a hero bold,
Of noble enterprise;
For if you do but taste his blood,
'Twill make your courage rise.

'Twill make a man forget his woe;
'Twill heighten all his joy:
'Twill make the widow's heart to sing,
Tho' the tear were in her eye.

Then let us toast John Barleycorn.
Each man a glass in hand;
And may his great posterity
Ne'er fail in old Scotland!

The Rigs o' Barley. (309)

TUNE—*Corn Rigs are bonnie.*

IT was upon a Lammas night,
When corn rigs are bonnie,
Beneath the moon's unclouded light,
I heft awa to Annie:
The time flew by wi' tentless heed,
Till 'tween the late and early,
Wi' sma' persuasion she agreed
To see me thro' the barley.

The sky was blue, the wind was still,
The moon was shining clearly;
I set her down wi' right good will
Amang the rigs o' barley;
I ken't her heart was a' my ain;
I lov'd her most sincerely;
I kiss'd her owre and owre again,
Amang the rigs o' barley.

I lock'd her in my fond embrace;
Her heart was beating rarely:
My blessings on that happy place,
Amang the rigs o' barley!
But by the moon and stars so bright,
That shone that hour so clearly!
She aye shall bless that happy night,
Amang the rigs o' barley.

I hae been blythe wi' comrades dear;
I hae been merry drinkin';
I hae been joyfu' gath'rin' gear;
I hae been happy thinkin';
But a' the pleasures e'er I saw,
Tho' three times doubl'd fairly,
That happy night was worth them a',
Amang the rigs o' barley.

CHORUS.

Corn rigs, and barley rigs,
And corn rigs are bonnie:
I'll ne'er forget that happy night
Amang the rigs wi' Annie.

The Ploughman.

TUNE—*Up wi' the Ploughman.*

THE ploughman he's a bonnie lad,
His mind is ever true, jo;
His garters knit below his knee,
His bonnet it is blue, jo.
Then up wi' my ploughman lad,
And hey my merry ploughman!
Of a' the trades that I do ken,
Commend me to the ploughman.

My ploughman he comes hame at e'en,
He's aften wat and weary;
Cast off the wat, put on the dry,
And gae to bed, my dearie!

I will wash my ploughman's hose,
And I will dress his o'erlay;
I will mak my ploughman's bed,
And cheer him late and early.

I hae been east, I hae been west,
I hae been at Saint Johnston;
The bonniest sight that e'er I saw
Was the ploughman laddie dancin'.

Snaw-white stockins on his legs,
And siller buckles glancin';
A guid blue bonnet on his head—
And oh, but he was handsome!

Commend me to the barn-yard,
And at the corn-mou, man;
I never gat my coggie fou,
Till I meet wi' the ploughman.

Song composed in August. (310)

TUNE— *I had a horse, I had nae mair.*

NOW westling winds and slaught'ring guns
Bring autumn's pleasant weather;
The moorcock springs, on whirring wings,
Amang the blooming heather:

WHEN WILD WAR'S DEADLY BLAST WAS BLAWN.

She sank within my arms, and cried,
Art thou my ain dear Willie?

Now waving grain, wide o'er the plain,
  Delights the weary farmer; [night
And the moon shines bright, when I rove at
  To muse upon my charmer.

The partridge loves the fruitful fells;
  The plover loves the mountains;
The woodcock haunts the lonely dells;
  The soaring hern the fountains;
Thro' lofty groves the cushat roves,
  The path of man to shun it;
The hazel bush o'erhangs the thrush,
  The spreading thorn the linnet.

Thus ev'ry kind their pleasure find,
  The savage and the tender;
Some social join, and leagues combine:
  Some solitary wander:
Avaunt, away! the cruel sway,
  Tyrannic man's dominion;
The sportsman's joy, the murd'ring cry,
  The flutt'ring gory pinion.

But Peggy, dear, the ev'ning's clear,
  Thick flies the skimming swallow;
The sky is blue, the fields in view,
  All fading-green and yellow;
Come, let us stray our gladsome way,
  And view the charms of nature;
The rustling corn, the fruited thorn,
  And every happy creature.

We'll gently walk, and sweetly talk,
  Till the silent moon shine clearly;
I'll grasp thy waist, and, fondly prest,
  Swear how I love thee dearly:
Not vernal show'rs to budding flow'rs,
  Not autumn to the farmer.
So dear can be as thou to me,
  My fair, my lovely charmer!

Yon Wild Mossy Mountains. (311)

TUNE—*Yon wild mossy Mountains.*

ON wild mossy mountains sae lofty and wide, [Clyde,
That nurse in their bosom the youth o' the
Where the grouse lead their coveys thro' the heather to feed,
And the shepherd tents his flock as he pipes on his reed.
  Where the grouse lead their coveys thro' the heather to feed,
  And the shepherd tents his flock as he pipes on his reed.

Not Gowrie's rich vallies, nor Forth's sunny shores,
To me hae the charms o' yon wild, mossy moors;
For there, by a lanely and sequester'd stream,
Resides a sweet lassie, my thought and my dream. [stream,
  For there, by a lanely and sequester'd
  Resides a sweet lassie, my thought and my dream.

Amang thae wild mountains shall still be my path, [strath:
'Ilk stream foaming down its ain green, narrow
For there wi' my lassie, the day lang I rove,
While o'er us unheeded flee the swift hours o' love. [rove,
  For there, wi' my lassie, the day lang I
  While o'er us unheeded flee the swift hours o' love.

She is not the fairest, altho' she is fair;
O' nice education but sma, is her share;
Her parentage humble as humble can be;
But I loe the dear lassie because she loes me.
  Her parentage humble as humble can be:
  But I loe the dear lassie because she loes me.

To beauty what man but maun yield him a prize, [sighs!
In her armour of glances, and blushes, and
And when wit and refinement hae polish'd her darts,
They dazzle our een, as they flee to our hearts.
  And when wit and refinement hae polish'd her darts, [hearts.
  They dazzle our een, as they flee to our

But kindness, sweet kindness, in the fond sparkling e'e,
Has lustre outshining the diamond to me;
And the heart beating love as I'm clasp'd in her arms, [charms!
Oh, these, are my lassie's all-conquering
  And the heart beating love as I'm clasp'd in her arms,
  Oh, these are my lassie's all-conquering charms!

My Nannie, O. (312)

TUNE—*My Nannie, O.*

BEHIND yon hills where Lugar flows,
  'Mang moors and mosses many, O,
The wintry sun the day has clos'd,
  And I'll awa to Nannie, O.

The westlin wind blaws loud and shrill;
  The night's baith mirk and rainy, O;
But I'll get my plaid, and out I'll steal,
  And owre the hills to Nannie, O.

My Nannie's charming, sweet, and young;
Nae artfu' wiles to win ye, O:
May ill befa' the flattering tongue
That wad beguile my Nannie, O.

Her face is fair, her heart is true,
As spotless as she's bonnie, O:
The op'ning gowan, wet wi dew,
Nae purer is than Nannie, O.

A country lad is my degree,
And few there be that ken me, O;
But what care I how few they be?
I'm welcome aye to Nannie, O.

My riches a's my penny-fee,
And I maun guide it cannie, O;
But warl's gear ne'er troubles me,
My thoughts are a' my Nannie, O.

Our auld guidman delights to view
His sheep and kye thrive bonnie, O;
But I'm as blythe that hauds his pleugh,
And has nae care but Nannie, O.

Come weel, come woe, I care nae by,
I'll tak what Heav'n will sen' me, O;
Nae ither care in life have I,
But live, and love my Nannie, O.

Green Grow the Rashes. (313)

TUNE—*Green grow the Rashes.*

CHORUS.

Green grow the rashes, O!
Green grow the rashes, O!
The sweetest hours that e'er I spend
Are spent amang the lasses, O.

There's nought but care on ev'ry han',
In every hour that passes, O:
What signifies the life o' man,
An 'twere na for the lasses, O.

The warlly race may riches chase,
And riches still may fly them, O;
And tho' at last they catch them fast,
Their hearts can ne'er enjoy them, O.

But gie me a canny hour at e'en,
My arms about my dearie, O;
And warl'ly cares, and warl'ly men,
May a' gae tapsalteerie, O.

For you sae douce, ye sneer at this,
Ye're nought but senseless asses, O:
The wisest man the warl' e'er saw,
He dearly lov'd the lasses, O.

Auld Nature swears, the lovely dears
Her noblest work she classes, O:
Her 'prentice han' she tried on man,
And then she made the lasses, O.

The Cure for all Care.

TUNE—*Prepare, my dear Brethren, to the Tavern let's fly.*

No churchman am I for to rail and to write,
No statesman nor soldier to plot or to fight,
No sly man of business contriving a snare—
For a big-bellied bottle's the whole of my care.

The peer I don't envy, I give him his bow;
I scorn not the peasant, tho' ever so low;
But a club of good fellows, like those that are here,
And a bottle like this, are my glory and care.

Here passes the squire on his brother—his horse;
There centum per centum, the cit with his purse;
But see you The Crown, how it waves in the air!
There a big-bellied bottle still eases my care.

The wife of my bosom, alas! she did die;
For sweet consolation to church I did fly;
I found that old Solomon proved it fair,
That a big-bellied bottle's a cure for all care.

I once was persuaded a venture to make;
A letter inform'd me that all was to wreck;—
But the pursy old landlord just waddled up stairs,
With a glorious bottle that ended my cares.

"Life's cares they are comforts" (314)—a maxim laid down
By the bard, what d'ye call him, that wore the black gown;
And, faith, I agree with th' old prig to a hair;
For a big-bellied bottle's a heav'n of care.

ADDED IN A MASON LODGE.

Then fill up a bumper and make it o'erflow,
And honours masonic prepare for to throw;
May every true brother of the compass and square
Have a big-bellied bottle when harass'd with care!

On Cessnock Banks.

TUNE—*If he be a Butcher neat and trim.*

On Cessnock banks there lives a lass,
Could I describe her shape and mien;
The graces of her weel-faur'd face,
And the glancin' of her sparklin' een!

She's fresher than the morning dawn
When rising Phœbus first is seen,
When dew-drops twinkle o'er the lawn;
And she's twa glancin' sparklin' een.

She's stately like yon youthful ash,
That grows the cowslip braes between,
And shoots its head above each bush;
And she's twa glancin' sparklin' een.

She's spotless as the flow'ring thorn,
With flow'rs so white, and leaves so green,
When purest in the dewy morn;
And she's twa glancin' sparklin' een.

Her looks are like the sportive lamb
When flow'ry May adorns the scene,
That wantons round its bleating dam;
And she's twa glancin' sparklin een.

Her hair is like the curling mist
That shades the mountain-side at e'en,
When flow'r-reviving rains are past;
And she's twa glancin' sparklin' een.

Her forehead's like the show'ry bow,
When shining sunbeams intervene,
And gild the distant mountain's brow;
And she's twa glancin' sparklin' een.

Her voice is like the evening thrush
That sings in Cessnock banks unseen,
While his mate sits nestling in the bush;
And she's twa glancin' sparklin' een.

Her lips are like the cherries ripe
That sunny walls from Boreas screen—
They tempt the taste and charm the sight;
And she's twa glancin' sparklin' een.

Her teeth are like a flock of sheep,
With fleeces newly washen clean,
That slowly mount the rising steep;
And she's twa glancin' sparklin' een.

Her breath is like the fragrant breeze
That gently stirs the blossom'd bean,
When Phœbus sinks beneath the seas;
And she's twa glancin' sparklin' een.

But it's not her air, her form, her face,
Tho' matching beauty's fabled queen,
But the mind that shines in ev'ry grace,
And chiefly in her sparklin' een.

The Highland Lassie. (315)

TUNE—*The Deuks dang o'er my Daddy!*

NAE gentle dames, tho' e'er sae fair,
Shall ever be my muse's care:
Their titles a' are empty show:
Gie me my highland lassie, O.
Within the glen sae bushy, O,
Aboon the plains sae rushy, O,
I set me down wi' right good will,
To sing my highland lassie, O.

Oh, were yon hills and vallies mine,
Yon palace and yon gardens fine!
The world then the love should know
I bear my highland lassie, O.

But fickle fortune frowns on me,
And I maun cross the raging sea;
But while my crimson currents flow,
I'll love my highland lassie, O.

Altho' thro' foreign climes I range,
I know her heart will never change,
For her bosom burns with honour's glow,
My faithful highland lassie, O.

For her I'll dare the billows' roar,
For her I'll trace a distant shore,
That Indian wealth may lustre throw
Around my highland lassie, O.

She has my heart, she has my hand,
By sacred truth and honour's band!
'Till the mortal stroke shall lay me low
I'm thine, my highland lassie, O.

Farewell the glen sae bushy, O!
Farewell the plain sae rushy, O!
To other lands I now must go,
To sing my highland lassie, O.

Powers Celestial.

TUNE—*Blue Bonnets.*

POWERS celestial! whose protection
Ever guards the virtuous fair,
While in distant climes I wander,
Let my Mary be your care:
Let her form sae fair and faultless,
Fair and faultless as your own,
Let my Mary's kindred spirit
Draw your choicest influence down.

Make the gales you waft around her
Soft and peaceful as her breast,
Breathing in the breeze that fans her,
Soothe her bosom into rest:
Guardian angel! oh protect her,
When in distant lands I roam;
To realms unknown while fate exiles me,
Make her bosom still my home.

From thee, Eliza.

TUNE—*Gilderoy,* or *Donald.*

FROM thee, Eliza, I must go,
And from my native shore,
The cruel Fates between us throw
A boundless ocean's roar:

But boundless oceans roaring wide,
  Between my love and me,
They never, never can divide
  My heart and soul from thee,

Farewell, farewell, Eliza dear,
  The maid that I adore!
A boding voice is in mine ear,
  We part to meet no more!
The latest throb that leaves my heart,
  While death stands victor by,
That throb, Eliza, is thy part,
  And thine that latest sigh!

Menie.

TUNE—*Johnny's grey Breeks.*

AGAIN rejoicing nature sees
  Her robe assume its vernal hues,
Her leafy locks wave in the breeze,
  All freshly steep'd in morning dews.
    And maun I still on Menie doat
      And bear the scorn that's in her ee?
    For it's jet, jet black, and like a hawk,
      And winna let a body be.

In vain to me the cowslips blaw,
  In vain to me the vi'lets spring;
In vain to me, in glen or shaw,
  The mavis and the lintwhite sing.

The merry ploughboy cheers his team,
  Wi' joy the tentie seedsman stalks;
But life to me's a weary dream,
  A dream of ane that never wauks.

The wanton coot the water skims,
  Amang the reeds the ducklings cry,
The stately swan majestic swims,
  And everything is blest but I.

The shepherd steeks his faulding slap,
  And owre the moorland whistles shrill;
Wi' wild, unequal, wand'ring step,
  I meet him on the dewy hill.

And when the lark, 'tween light and dark,
  Blythe waukens by the daisy's side,
And mounts and sings on flittering wings,
  A woe-worn ghaist I hameward glide.

Come, Winter, with thine angry howl,
  And raging bend the naked tree:
Thy gloom will soothe my cheerless soul,
  When nature all is sad like me!

The Farewell.

TO THE BRETHREN OF ST. JAMES'S LODGE, TARBOLTON.

TUNE—*Good-night, and joy be wi' you a'!*

ADIEU! a heart-warm, fond adieu!
  Dear brothers of the mystic tie!
Ye favour'd, ye enlighten'd few,
  Companions of my social joy;
Tho' I to foreign lands must hie,
  Pursuing Fortune's slipp'ry ba',
With melting heart and brimful eye,
  I'll mind you still, tho' far awa'.

Oft have I met your social band,
  And spent the cheerful, festive night;
Oft honour'd with supreme command,
  Presided o'er the sons of light;
And by that hieroglyphic bright,
  Which none but craftsmen ever saw!
Strong mem'ry on my heart shall write
  Those happy scenes when far awa.'

May freedom, harmony, and love
  Unite you in the grand design,
Beneath th' Omniscient eye above,
  The glorious Architect divine!
That you may keep th' unerring line,
  Still rising by the plummet's law,
Till order bright completely shine,
  Shall be my pray'r when far awa'.

And you, farewell! whose merits claim,
  Justly, that highest badge to wear!
Heav'n bless your honour'd, noble name,
  To masonry and Scotia dear;
A last request permit me here,
  When yearly ye assemble a',
One round—I ask it with a tear—
  To him, the Bard that's far awa'.

The Braes o' Ballochmyle. (316)

TUNE—*The Braes o' Ballochmyle.*

THE Catrine woods were yellow seen,
  The flowers decay'd on Catrine lea,
Nae lav'rock sang on hillock green,
  But nature sicken'd on the ee.
Thro' faded groves Maria sang,
  Hersel in beauty's bloom the while,
And aye the wild-wood echoes rang,
  Fareweel the Braes o' Ballochmyle!

Low in your wintry beds, ye flowers,
  Again ye'll flourish fresh and fair;
Ye birdies dumb, in with'ring bowers,
  Again ye'll charm the vocal air.
But, here, alas! for me nae mair
  Shall birdie charm, or flow'ret smile;
Fareweel the bonnie banks of Ayr,
  Fareweel, fareweel! sweet Ballochmyle!

The Lass o' Ballochmyle. (317)

TUNE—*Miss Forbes's Farewell to Banff.*

'TWAS even—the dewy fields were green,
On every blade the pearlies hang,
The zephyr wanton'd round the bean,
And bore its fragrant sweets alang:
In ev'ry glen the mavis sang,
All nature list'ning seem'd the while,
Except where greenwood echoes rang,
Amang the braes o' Ballochmyle.

With careless step I onward stray'd,
My heart rejoiced in nature's joy,
When, musing in a lonely glade,
A maiden fair I chanc'd to spy;
Her look was like the morning's eye,
Her air like nature's vernal smile,
Perfection whisper'd passing by,
Behold the lass o' Ballochmyle!

Fair is the morn in flow'ry May,
And sweet is night in autumn mild;
When roving thro' the garden gay,
Or wand'ring in the lonely wild:
But woman, nature's darling child!
There all her charms she does compile;
Ev'n there her other works are foil'd
By the bonnie lass o' Ballochmyle.

Oh, had she been a country maid,
And I the happy country swain,
Tho' shelter'd in the lowest shed
That ever rose on Scotland's plain,
Thro' weary winter's wind and rain,
With joy, with rapture, I would toil;
And nightly to my bosom strain
The bonnie lass o' Ballochmyle!

Then pride might climb the slipp'ry steep,
Where fame and honours lofty shine;
And thirst of gold might tempt the deep,
Or downward seek the Indian mine;
Give me the cot below the pine,
To tend the flocks, or till the soil,
And ev'ry day have joys divine
With the bonnie lass o' Ballochmyle.

The Gloomy Night is Gathering Fast. (318)

TUNE—*Roslin Castle.*

THE gloomy night is gath'ring fast,
Loud roars the wild inconstant blast;
Yon murky cloud is foul with rain,
I see it driving o'er the plain;
The hunter now has left the moor,
The scatter'd coveys meet secure;
While here I wander, prest with care,
Along the lonely banks of Ayr.

The autumn mourns her rip'ning corn,
By early winter's ravage torn;
Across her placid, azure sky,
She sees the scowling tempest fly:
Chill runs my blood to hear it rave—
I think upon the stormy wave,
Where many a danger I must dare,
Far from the bonnie banks of Ayr

'Tis not the surging billow's roar,
'Tis not that fatal deadly shore;
Tho' death in every shape appear,
The wretched have no more to fear!
But round my heart the ties are bound,
That heart transpierc'd with many a wound;
These bleed afresh, those ties I tear,
To leave the bonny banks of Ayr.

Farewell old Coila's hills and dales,
Her heathy moors and winding vales;
The scenes where wretched fancy roves,
Pursuing past, unhappy loves!
Farewell, my friends! farewell, my foes!
My peace with these, my love with those—
The bursting tears my heart declare;
Farewell the bonnie banks of Ayr!

The Banks o' Doon. (319)

TUNE—*Caledonian Hunt's Delight.*

YE banks and braes o' bonnie Doon,
How can ye bloom sae fresh and fair;
How can ye chant, ye little birds,
And I sae weary fu' o' care?
Thou'lt break my heart, thou warbling bird,
That wanton'st thro' the flowering thorn:
Thou minds'st me o' departed joys,
Departed—never to return!

Aft hae I roved by bonnie Doon,
To see the the rose and woodbine twine;
And ilka bird sang o' its luve,
And fondly sae did I o' mine.
Wi' lightsome heart I pu'd a rose,
Fu' sweet upon its thorny tree;
And my fuse luver stole my rose,
But, ah! he left the thorn wi' me.

The Birks of Aberfeldy. (320)

TUNE—*The Birks of Abergeldy.*

CHORUS.

BONNIE lassie, will ye go,
Will ye go, will ye go;
Bonnie lassie, will ye go,
To the birks of Aberfeldy?

Now simmer blinks on flowry braes,
And o'er the crystal streamlet plays;
Come, let us spend the lightsome days
In the birks of Aberfeldy.

The little birdies blythely sing,
While o'er their heads the hazels hing,
Or lightly flit on wanton wing
In the birks of Aberfeldy.

The braes ascend, like lofty wa's,
The foamy stream deep-roaring fa's,
O'erhung wi' fragrant spreading shaws,
The birks of Aberfeldy.

The hoary cliffs are crown'd wi' flowers,
White o'er the linns the burnie pours,
And rising, weets wi' misty showers
The birks of Aberfeldy.

Let fortune's gifts at random flee,
They ne'er shall draw a wish frae me
Supremely blest wi' love and thee,
In the birks of Aberfeldy.

I'm owre Young to Marry Yet.

TUNE—*I'm owre young to marry yet.*

I AM my mammy's ae bairn,
Wi' unco folk I weary, Sir;
And if I gang to your house,
I'm fley'd 'twill make me eerie, Sir.

I'm owre young to marry yet·
I'm owre young to marry yet;
I'm owre young—'twad be a sin
To take me frae my mammy yet.

Hallowmas is come and gane,
The nights are lang in winter, Sir;
And you and I in wedlock's bands,
In troth, I dare not venture, Sir.
I'm owre young, &c.

Fu' loud and shrill the frosty wind
Blaws through the leafless timmer, Sir;
But if ye come this gate again,
I'll aulder be gin simmer, Sir.
I'm owre young, &c.

M'Pherson's Farewell. (321)

TUNE—*M'Pherson's Rant.*

FAREWELL, ye dungeons dark and strong,
The wretch's destinie:
Macpherson's time will not be long
On yonder gallows-tree.
Sae rantingly, sae wantonly,
Sae dauntingly gaed he;
He play'd a spring, and danc'd it round,
Below the gallows-tree.

Oh, what is death but parting breath?—
On many a bloody plain
I've dar'd his face, and in this place
I scorn him yet again;

Untie these bands from off my hands,
And bring to me my sword;
And there's no man in all Scotland,
But I'll brave him at a word.

I've liv'd a life of sturt and strife;
I die by treacherie:
It burns my heart I must depart,
And not avenged be.

Now farewell light—thou sunshine bright,
And all beneath the sky!
May coward shame distain his name,
The wretch that dares not die!

How Long and Dreary is the Night.

How long and dreary is the night
When I am frae my dearie!
I sleepless lie frae e'en to morn,
Tho' I were ne'er sae weary.
I sleepless lie frae e'en to morn,
Tho' I were ne'er sae weary.

When I think on the happy days
I spent wi' you, my dearie,
And now what lands between us lie,
How can I be but eerie!
And now what lands between us lie,
How can I be but eerie!

How slow ye move, ye heavy hours,
As ye were wae and weary!
It was na sae ye glinted by,
When I was wi' my dearie.
It was na sae ye glinted by,
When I was wi' my dearie.

Here's a Health to them that's awa.

TUNE—*Here's a health to them that's awa.*

HERE's a health to them that's awa,
Here's a health to them that's awa;
And wha winna wish guid luck to our cause,
May never guid luck be their fa'!
It's guid to be merry and wise,
It's guid to be honest and true,
It's guid to support Caledonia's cause,
And bide by the buff and the blue.

Here's a health to them that's awa,
Here's a health to them that's awa;
Here's a health to Charlie, the chief o' the clan,
Altho' that his band be sma'.
May liberty meet wi' success!
May prudence protect her frae evil!
May tyrants and tyranny tine in the mist,
And wander their way to the devil!

Here's a health to them that's awa,
Here's a health to them that's awa; [laddie,
Here's a health to Tammie, the Norland
That lives at the lug o' the law;
Here's freedom to him that wad read!
Here's freedom to him that wad write!
There's nane ever fear'd that the truth should
be heard,
But they wham the truth wad indite.

Here's a health to them that's awa,
Here's a health to them that's awa;
Here's Chieftain M'Leod, a Chieftain worth
gow'd,
Tho' bred amang mountains o' snaw!
Here's friends on both sides of the Forth,
And friends on both sides of the Tweed;
And wha wad betray old Albion's rights,
May they never eat of her bread.

Strathallan's Lament. (322)

THICKEST night, o'erhang my dwelling!
Howling tempests, o'er me rave!
Turbid torrents, wintry swelling,
Still surround my lonely cave!

Crystal streamlets gently flowing,
. Busy haunts of base mankind,
Western breezes softly blowing,
Suit not my distracted mind.

In the cause of right engaged,
Wrongs injurious to redress,
Honour's war we strongly waged,
But the heavens denied success.

Ruin's wheel has driven o'er us,
Not a hope that dare attend:
The wide world is all before us—
But a world without a friend.

The Banks of the Devon. (323)

TUNE—*Bhannerach dhon na chri.*

How pleasant the banks of the clear winding
Devon, [blooming fair!
With green spreading bushes, and flowers
But the bonniest flower on the banks of the
Devon [Ayr.
Was once a sweet bud on the braes of the
Mild be the sun on this sweet blushing flower,
In the gay rosy morn, as it bathes in the
dew;
And gentle the fall of the soft vernal shower,
That steals on the evening each leaf to
renew.

Oh spare the dear blossom, ye orient breezes,
With chill hoary wing, as ye usher the
dawn; [seizes
And far be thou distant, thou reptile that
The verdure and pride of the garden and
lawn!
Let Bourbon exult in his gay gilded Lilies,
And England, triumphant, display her
proud Rose:
A fairer than either adorns the green vallies,
Where Devon, sweet Devon, meandering
flows.

Braving Angry Winter's Storms. (324)

TUNE—*Neil Gow's Lamentation for Abercairny.*

WHERE, braving angry winter's storms,
The lofty Ochils rise,
Far in their shade my Peggy's charms
First blest my wondering eyes;

As one, who by some savage stream,
A lonely gem surveys,
Astonish'd, doubly marks its beam,
With art's most polish'd blaze.

Blest be the wild sequester'd shade,
And blest the day and hour,
Where Peggy's charms I first survey'd,
When first I felt their pow'r!

The tyrant death, with grim control,
May seize my fleeting breath;
But tearing Peggy from my soul
Must be a stronger death.

My Peggy's Face.

TUNE—*My Peggy's Face.*

MY Peggy's face, my Peggy's form,
The frost of hermit age might warm;
My Peggy's worth, my Peggy's mind,
Might charm the first of human kind.
I love my Peggy's angel air,
Her face so truly, heavenly fair,
Her native grace so void of art,
But I adore my Peggy's heart.
The lily's hue, the rose's dye,
The kindling lustre of an eye:
Who but owns their magic sway!
Who but knows they all decay!
The tender thrill, the pitying tear,
The gen'rous purpose, nobly dear,
The gentle look, that rage disarms—
These are all immortal charms.

Raving Winds around her Blowing.

(325)

TUNE—*Macgregor of Ruara's Lament.*

RAVING winds around her blowing,
Yellow leaves the woodlands strowing,
By a river hoarsely roaring,
Isabella stray'd deploring—
"Farewell hours that late did measure
Sunshine days of joy and pleasure;
Hail, thou gloomy night of sorrow,
Cheerless night that knows no morrow!

O'er the past too fondly wandering,
On the hopeless future pondering;
Chilly grief my life-blood freezes,
Fell despair my fancy seizes.
Life, thou soul of every blessing,
Load to misery most distressing,
Gladly how would I resign thee,
And to dark oblivion join thee!"

Highland Harry. (326)

MY Harry was a gallant gay,
Fu' stately strode he on the plain:
But now he's banish'd far away,
I'll never see him back again.
Oh for him back again;
Oh for him back again!
I wad gie a' Knockhaspie's land
For Highland Harry back again.

When a' the lave gae to their bed,
I wander dowie up the glen:
I sit me down and greet my fill,
And aye I wish him back again.
Oh were some villians hangit high,
And ilka body had their ain!
Then I might see the joyfu' sight,
My Highland Harry back again.

Musing on the Roaring Ocean. (327)

TUNE—*Druimion Dubh.*

MUSING on the roaring ocean
Which divides my love and me;
Wearying Heaven in warm devotion,
For his weal where'er he be.

Hope and fear's alternate billow
Yielding late to nature's law,
Whisp'ring spirits round my pillow
Talk of him that's far awa.

Ye whom sorrow never wounded,
Ye who never shed a tear,
Care-untroubled, joy surrounded,
Gaudy day to you is dear.

Gentle night, do thou befriend me:
Downy sleep, the curtain draw;
Spirits kind, again attend me,
Talk of him that's far awa!

Blythe was She. (328)

TUNE—*Andro and his Cutty Gun.*

CHORUS.

Blythe, blythe and merry was she,
Blythe was she butt and ben:
Blythe by the banks of Ern,
And blythe in Glentwrit glen.

By Auchtertyre grows the aik,
On Yarrow banks the birken shaw;
But Phemie was a bonnier lass
Than braes o' Yarrow ever saw.

Her looks were like a flower in May,
Her smile was like a simmer morn;
She tripped by the banks o' Ern,
As light's a bird upon a thorn.

Her bonnie face it was as meek
As ony lamb upon a lea;
The evening sun was ne'er sae sweet
As was the blink o' Phemie's ee.

The Highland hills I've wander'd wide,
And o'er the lowlands I hae been;
But Phemie was the blythest lass
That ever trod the dewy green.

The Gallant Weaver.

TUNE—*The Weaver's March.*

Where Cart rins rowin' to the sea,
By mony a flow'r and spreading tree,
There lives a lad, the lad for me,
He is a gallant weaver.

Oh, I had wooers aucht or nine,
They gied me rings and ribbons fine;
And I was fear'd my heart would tine,
And I gied it to the weaver.

My daddie sign'd my tocher-band,
To gie the lad that has the land;
But to my heart I'll add my hand,
And gie it to the weaver.

While birds rejoice in leafy bowers;
While bees delight in op'ning flowers!
While corn grows green in simmer showers,
I'll love my gallant weaver.

The Blude-red Rose at Yule may Blaw.

TUNE—*To daunton me.*

THE blude-red rose at Yule may blaw,
The simmer lillies bloom in snaw,
The frost may freeze the deepest sea;
But an auld man shall never daunton me.

To daunton me, and me so young,
Wi' his fause heart and flatt'ring tongue
That is the thing you ne'er shall see:
For an old man shall never daunton me.

For a' his meal and a'his maut,
For a' his fresh beef and his saut,
For a' his gold and white monie,
An auld man shall never daunton me.

His gear may buy him kye and yowes,
His gear may buy him glens and knowes;
But me he shall not buy nor fee,
For an auld man shall never daunton me.

He hirples twa-fauld as he dow,
Wi' his teethless gab and his auld beld pow,
And the rain rains down from his red bleer'd ee—
That auld man shall never daunton me.

A Rose-bud by my Early Walk. (329)

TUNE—*The Rose-bud.*

A ROSE-BUD by my early walk,
Adown a corn-enclosed bawk,
Sae gently bent its thorny stalk,
All on a dewy morning.
Ere twice the shades o' dawn are fled,
In a' its crimson glory spread,
And drooping rich the dewy head,
It scents the early morning.

Within the bush, her covert nest,
A little linnet fondly prest,
The dew sat chilly on her breast
Sae early in the morning.
She soon shall see her tender brood,
The pride, the pleasure o' the wood,
Amang the fresh green leaves bedew'd,
Awake the early morning.

So thou, dear bird, young Jeany fair!
On trembling string or vocal air,
Shall sweetly pay the tender care
That tends thy early morning.
So thou, sweet rose-bud, young and gay,
Shalt beauteous blaze upon the day,
And bless the parent's evening ray
That watch'd thy early morning.

Bonnie Castle Gordon.

TUNE—*Morag.*

STREAMS that glide in orient plains,
Never bound by winter's chains;
Glowing here on golden sands,
There commix'd with foulest stains
From tyranny's empurpled bands;
These, their richly gleaming waves,
I leave to tyrants and their slaves;
Give me the stream that sweetly laves
The banks by Castle-Gordon.

Spicy forests, ever gay,
Shading from the burning ray
Hapless wretches sold to toil,
Or the ruthless native's way,
Bent on slaughter, blood, and spoil;
Woods that ever verdant wave,
I leave the tyrant and the slave:
Give me the groves that lofty brave
The storms by Castle-Gordon.

Wildly here without control,
Nature reigns and rules the whole;
In that sober pensive mood,
Dearest to the feeling soul,
She plants the forest, pours the flood:
Life's poor day I'll musing rave,
And find at night a sheltering cave,
Where waters flow and wild woods wave,
By bonnie Castle-Gordon.

When Januar' Wind. (330)

TUNE—*The Lass that made the Bed to Me.*

WHEN Januar' wind was blawing cauld,
As to the north I took my way,
The mirksome night did me enfauld,
I knew na where to lodge till day,

By my good luck a maid I met,
Just in the middle o' my care;
And kindly she did me invite
To walk into a chamber fair.

I bow'd fu' low unto this maid,
And thank'd her for her courtesie,
I bow'd fu' low unto this maid,
And bade her mak a bed to me.

She made the bed baith large and wide,
Wi' twa white hands she spread it down;
She put the cup to her rosy lips,
And drank, "Young man, now sleep ye soun'."

She snatch'd the candle in her hand,
And frae my chamber went wi' speed;
But I call'd her quickly back again
To lay some mair below my head.

A cod she laid below my head,
  And served me wi' due respect;
And to salute her wi' a kiss,
  I put my arms about her neck.

"Haud aff your hands, young man," she says,
  "And dinna sae uncivil be:
If ye hae ony love for me,
  Oh wrang na my virginitie!"

Her hair was like the links o' gowd,
  Her teeth were like the ivorie;
Her cheeks like lilies dipt in wine,
  The lass that made the bed to me.

Her bosom was the driven snaw,
  Twa drifted heaps sae fair to see;
Her limbs the polish'd marble stane,
  The lass that made the bed to me.

I kiss'd her owre and owre again,
  And aye she wist na what to say;
I laid her 'tween me and the wa'—
  The lassie thought na lang till day.

Upon the morrow when we rose,
  I thank'd her for her courtesie;
But aye she blush'd, and aye she sigh'd,
  And said, "Alas! ye've ruin'd me."

I clasp'd her waist, and kiss'd her syne,
  While the tear stood twinklin' in her ee;
I said, "My lassie, dinna cry,
  For ye aye shall mak the bed to me."

She took her mither's Holland sheets,
  And made them a' in sarks to me:
Blythe and merry may she be,
  The lass that made the bed to me.

The bonnie lass made the bed to me,
  The braw lass made the bed to me:
I'll ne'er forget till the day I die,
  The lass that made the bed to me!

The Young Highland Rover.

TUNE—*Morag.*

LOUD blaw the frosty breezes,
  The snaws the mountains cover;
Like winter on me seizes,
  Since my young Highland Rover
  Far wanders nations over.
Where'er he go, where'er he stray,
  May Heaven be his warden,
Return him safe to fair Strathspey,
  And bonnie Castle-Gordon!

The trees now naked groaning,
  Shall soon wi' leaves be hinging,
The birdies dowie moaning,
  Shall a' be blythely singing,
  And every flower be springing.
Sae I'll rejoice the lee-lang day,
  When by his mighty warden
My youth's returned to fair Strathspey,
  And bonnie Castle-Gordon.

Bonnie Ann. (331)

AIR—*Ye gallants bright.*

YE gallants bright, I red ye right,
  Beware o' bonnie Ann;
Her comely face sae fu' of grace,
  Your heart she will trepan.
Her een sae bright, like stars by night,
  Her skin is like the swan;
Sae jimply lac'd her genty waist,
  That sweetly ye might span.

Youth, grace, and love attendant move,
  And pleasure leads the van:
In a' their charms, and conquering arms,
  They wait on bonnie Ann.
The captive bands may chain the hands,
  But love enslaves the man;
Ye gallants braw, I red you a',
  Beware o' bonnie Ann!

Blooming Nelly.

TUNE—*On a Bank of Flowers.*

ON a bank of flowers, in a summer day,
  For summer lightly drest,
The youthful blooming Nelly lay,
  With love and sleep opprest;
When Willie, wand'ring thro' the wood,
  Who for her favour oft had sued,
He gaz'd, he wish'd, he fear'd, he blush'd,
  And trembled where he stood.

Her closed eyes like weapons sheath'd,
  Were seal'd in soft repose;
Her lips still as she fragrant breath'd,
  It richer dy'd the rose.
The springing lilies sweetly prest,
  Wild—wanton, kiss'd her rival breast;
He gaz'd, he wish'd, he fear'd, he blush'd—
  His bosom ill at rest.

Her robes light waving in the breeze,
  Her tender limbs embrace;
Her lovely form, her native ease,
  All harmony and grace:
Tumultuous tides his pulses roll,
  A faltering, ardent kiss he stole;
He gaz'd, he wish'd, he fear'd, he blush'd—
  And sigh'd his very soul.

As flies the partridge from the brake,
  On fear-inspired wings,
So Nelly starting, half awake,
  Away affrighted springs:

But Willie follow'd, as he should,
He overtook her in the wood;
He vow'd, he pray'd, he found the maid
Forgiving all and good.

My Bonnie Mary. (332)

TUNE—*Go fetch to me a Pint o' Wine.*

Go fetch to me a pint o' wine,
And fill it in a silver tassie;
That I may drink, before I go,
A service to my bonny lassie:
The boat rocks at the pier o' Leith,
Fu' loud the wind blaws frae the Ferry;
The ship rides by the Berwick-law,
And I maun leave my bonnie Mary.

The trumpets sound, the banners fly,
The glittering spears are ranked ready;
The shouts o' war are heard afar,
The battle closes thick and bloody;
But it's not the roar o' sea or shore
Wad make me langer wish to tarry;
Nor shouts o' war that's heard afar—
It's leaving thee, my bonnie Mary.

Ane Fond Kiss. (333)

TUNE—*Rory Dall's Port.*

ANE fond kiss and then we sever;
Ane fareweel, alas, for ever!
Deep in heart-wrung tears I'll pledge thee,
Warring sighs and groans I'll wage thee.
Who shall say that fortune grieves him,
While the star of hope she leaves him?
Me, nae cheerfu' twinkle lights me;
Dark despair around benights me.

I'll ne'er blame my partial fancy,
Naething could resist my Nancy
But to see her was to love her·
Love but her, and love for ever.
Had we never lov'd sae kindly,
Had we never lov'd sae blindly,
Never met—or never parted,
We had ne'er been broken-hearted.

Fare thee weel, thou first and fairest!
Fare the weel, thou best and dearest!
Thine be ilka joy and treasure,
Peace, enjoyment, love, and pleasure!
Ane fond kiss, and then we sever;
Ane fareweel, alas! for ever!
Deep in heart-wrung tears I'll pledge thee,
Warring sighs and groans I'll wage thee!

The Smiling Spring.

TUNE—*The Bonny Bell.*

THE smiling Spring comes in rejoicing,
And surly winter grimly flies;
Now crystal clear are the falling waters,
And bonnie blue are the sunny skies.
Fresh o'er the mountains breaks forth the morning,
The ev'ning gilds the ocean's swell;
All creatures joy in the sun's returning,
And I rejoice in my bonnie Bell.

The flowery spring leads sunny summer,
And yellow autumn presses near,
Then in his turn comes gloomy winter,
Till smiling spring again appear.
Thus seasons dancing, life advancing,
Old Time and Nature their changes tell,
But never ranging, still unchanging,
I adore my bonnie Bell.

The Lazy Mist.

TUNE—*The Lazy Mist.*

THE lazy mist hangs from the brow of the hill,
Concealing the course of the dark winding rill;
How languid the scenes, late so sprightly, appear!
As autumn to winter resigns the pale year.
The forests are leafless, the meadows are brown,
And all the gay foppery of summer is flown:
Apart let me wander, apart let me muse,
How quick time is flying, how keen fate pursues!
How long I have liv'd—but how much liv'd in vain!
How little of life's scanty span may remain!
What aspects old Time, in his progress, has worn!
What ties cruel fate in my bosom has torn!
How foolish, or worse, till our summit is gain'd!
And downward, how weaken'd, how darken'd, how pain'd!
This life's not worth having with all it can give—
For something beyond it poor man sure must live.

Of a' the Airts the Wind can Blaw.

(334)

OF a' the airts the wind can blaw,
I dearly like the west,
For there the bonnie lassie lives,
The lassie I loe best:

There wild woods grow, and rivers row,
And mony a hill between;
But day and night my fancy's flight
Is ever wi' my Jean.

I see her in the dewy flowers,
I see her sweet and fair:
I hear her in the tunefu' birds,
I hear her charm the air:
There's not a bonnie flower that springs
By fountain, shaw, or green,
There's not a bonnie bird that sings,
But minds me o' my Jean.

Oh blaw ye westlin winds, blaw saft
Amang the leafy trees,
Wi' balmy gale, frae hill and dale
Bring hame the laden bees;
And bring the lassie back to me
That's aye sae neat and clean;
Ane smile o' her wad banish care,
Sae charming is my Jean!

What sighs and vows amang the knowes
Hae passed atween us twa!
How fond to meet, how wae to part,
That night she gaed awa!
The powers aboon can only ken,
To whom the heart is seen,
That nane can be sae dear to me
As my sweet lovely Jean!

Oh, were I on Parnassus' Hill. (335)

TUNE.—*My Love is lost to me.*

OH, were I on Parnassus' hill!
Or had of Helicon my fill;
That I might catch poetic skill,
To sing how dear I love thee.
But Nith maun be my muse's well,
My muse maun be thy bonnie sel';
On Corsincon I'll glow'r and spell,
And write how dear I love thee.

Then come, sweet muse, inspire my lay!
For a' the lee-lang simmer's day
I couldna sing, I couldna say,
How much, how dear, I love thee.
I see thee dancing o'er the green,
Thy waist sae jimp, thy limbs sae clean,
Thy tempting lips, thy roguish een—
By heaven and earth I love thee!

By night, by day, a-field, at hame,
The thoughts o' thee my breast inflame;
And aye I muse and sing thy name—
I only live to love thee.
Tho' I were doom'd to wander on
Beyond the sea, beyond the sun,
Till my last weary sand was run;
Till then—and then I love thee.

The Chevallier's Lament. (336)

TUNE—*Captain O'Kean.*

THE small birds rejoice in the green leaves returning, [the vale;
The murm'ring streamlet winds clear thro'
The hawthorn trees blow in the dew of the morning, [green dale:
And wild scattered cowslips bedeck the
But what can give pleasure, or what can seem fair, [by care?
While the lingering moments are numbered
No flowers gaily springing, nor birds sweetly singing,
Can soothe the sad bosom of joyless despair.

The deed that I dared, could it merit their malice,
A king and a father to place on his throne?
His right are these hills, and his right are these vallies,
Where the wild beasts find shelter, but I can find none. [forlorn;
But 'tis not my sufferings thus wretched,
My brave gallant friends! 'tis your ruin I mourn! [trial—
Your deeds proved so loyal in hot bloody
Alas! I can make you no sweeter return!

My Heart's in the Highlands.

TUNE—*Failte na Miosg.*

MY heart's in the Highlands, my heart is not here, [deer;
My heart's in the Highlands a-chasing the
Chasing the wild deer, and following the roe—
My heart's in the Highlands wherever I go.

Farewell to the Highlands, farewell to the North, [worth;
The birth-place of valour, the country of
Wherever I wander, wherever I rove,
The hills of the Highlands for ever I love.

Farewell to the mountains high covered with snow; [below:
Farewell to the straths and green vallies
Farewell to the forests and wild-hanging woods; [floods.
Farewell to the torrents and loud-pouring

My heart's in the Highlands, my heart is not here, [deer:
My heart's in the Highlands a-chasing the
Chasing the wild deer, and following the roe—
My heart's in the Highlands wherever I go.

AULD LANG SYNE.

Should auld acquaintance be forgot,
And never brought to min'?

John Anderson.

TUNE—*John Anderson my jo.*

JOHN Anderson my jo, John,
When we first acquent,
Your locks were like the raven,
Your bonnie brow was brent;
But now your brow is bald, John,
Your locks are like the snaw;
But blessings on your frosty pow,
John Anderson my jo.

John Anderson my jo, John,
We clamb the hill thegither,
And mony a canty day, John,
We've had wi' ane anither:
Now we maun totter down, John,
But hand in hand we'll go,
And sleep thegither at the foot,
John Anderson my jo.

To Mary in Heaven. (337)

TUNE—*Death of Captain Cook.*

THOU ling'ring star, with less'ning ray,
That lov'st to greet the early morn,
Again thou usher'st in the day
My Mary from my soul was torn.
Oh Mary! dear departed shade!
Where is thy place of blissful rest?
See'st thou thy lover lowly laid?
Hear'st thou the groans that rend his breast?

That sacred hour can I forget,
Can I forget the hallowed grove,
Where by the winding Ayr we met,
To live one day of parting love!
Eternity will not efface
Those records dear of transports past;
Thy image at our last embrace,
Ah! little thought we 'twas our last!

Ayr, gurgling, kiss'd his pebbled shore,
O'erhung with wild woods, thick'ning green;
The fragrant birch, and hawthorn hoar,
Twin'd am'rous round the raptur'd scene;
The flow'rs sprang wanton to be prest,
The birds sang love on every spray—
Till too, too soon, the glowing west
Proclaim'd the speed of winged day.

Still o'er these scenes my mem'ry wakes,
And fondly broods with miser care!
Time but th' impression stronger makes,
As streams their channels deeper wear,
My Mary, dear departed shade!
Where is thy place of blissful rest?
See'st thou thy lover lowly laid?
Hear'st thou the groans that rend his breast?

Young Jockey.

TUNE—*Yonng Jockey.*

YOUNG Jockey was the blythest lad
In a' our town or here awa:
Fu' blythe he whistled at the gaud,
Fu' lightly danced he in the ha'.
He roosed my een, sae bonnie blue,
He roosed my waist sae genty sma',
And aye my heart came to my mou'
When ne'er a body heard or saw.

My Jockey toils upon the plain,
Thro' wind and weet, thro' frost and snaw·
And o'er the lea I leuk fu' fain,
When Jockey's owsen hameward ca'
And aye the night comes round again,
When in his arms he takes me a',
And aye he vows he'll be my ain,
As lang's he has a breath to draw.

The Day Returns. (338)

TUNE—*Seventh of November.*

THE day returns, my bosom burns,
The blissful day we twa did meet,
Tho' winter wild in tempest toil'd,
Ne'er summer-sun was half sae sweet.
Than a' the pride that loads the tide,
And crosses o'er the sultry line;
Than kingly robes, than crowns and globes,
Heav'n gave me more—it made thee mine

While day and night can bring delight,
Or nature aught of pleasure give,
While joys above my mind can move,
For thee, and thee alone, I live.
When that grim foe of life below
Comes in between to make us part,
The iron hand that breaks our band,
It breaks my bliss—it breaks mv heart!

Oh, Willie Brew'd. (339)

TUNE.—*Willie brew'd a Peck o' Mult.*

OH, Willie brew'd a peck o' maut,
And Rob and Allan cam to pree:
Three blyther hearts, that lee-lang night,
Ye wad na find in Christendie.
We are nae fou', we're no that fou',
But just a drappie in our ee;
The cock may craw, the day may daw,
And aye we'll taste the barley bree.

Here are we met, three merry boys,
Three merry boys, I trow, are we;
And mony a night we've merry been,
And mony mae we hope to be!

It is the moon, I ken her horn,
That's blinkin' in the lift sae hie;
She shines sae bright to wile us hame,
But, by my sooth, she'll wait a wee!

Wha first shall rise to gang awa',
A cuckold, coward loon is he!
Wha last beside his chair shall fa',
He is the king amang us three!

I gaed a Waefu' Gate Yestreen. (340)

TUNE—*The Blue-eyed Lass.*

I GAED a waefu' gate yestreen,
A gate, I fear, I'll dearly rue;
I gat my death frae twa sweet een,
Twa lovely een o' bonnie blue.
'Twas not her golden ringlets bright;
Her lips like roses wet wi' dew,
Her heaving bosom, lily-white—
It was her een sae bonnie blue.

She talk'd, she smil'd, my heart she wil'd;
She charm'd my soul—I wist na how;
And aye the stound, the deadly wound,
Cam frae her een sae bonnie blue.
But spare to speak, and spare to speed;
She'll aiblins listen to my vow:
Should she refuse, I'll lay my dead
To her twa een sae bonnie blue

The Banks of Nith.

TUNE—*Robie donna Gorach.*

THE Thames flows proudly to the sea,
Where royal cities stately stand;
But sweeter flows the Nith, to me,
Where Cummins ance had high command;
When shall I see that honour'd land,
That winding stream I love so dear!
Must wayward fortune's adverse hand
For ever, ever keep me here?

How lovely, Nith, thy fruitful vales,
Where spreading hawthorns gaily bloom!
How sweetly wind thy sloping dales,
Where lambkins, wanton thro' the broom!
Tho' wandering, now, must be my doom,
Far from thy bonnie banks and braes,
May there my latest hours consume,
Amang the friends of early days!

My heart is a-breaking, Dear Tittie!

TUNE—*Tam Glen.*

MY heart is a-breaking, dear Tittie!
Some counsel unto me come len',
To anger them a' is the pity,
But what will I do wi' Tam Glen?

I'm thinking wi' sic a braw fellow
In poortith I might make a fen';
What care I in riches to wallow,
If I maunna marry Tam Glen?

There's Lowrie, the laird o' Drumeller,
"Guid day to you, brute!" he comes ben;
He brags and he blaws o' his siller,
But when will he dance like Tam Glen?

My minnie does constantly deave me,
And bids me beware o' young men;
They flatter, she says, to deceive me,
But wha can think sae o' Tam Glen?

My daddie says, gin I'll forsake him,
He'll gie me guid hunder marks ten:
But if it's ordain'd I maun take him,
Oh wha will I get but Tam Glen?

Yestreen at the valentine's dealing,
My heart to my mou' gied a sten;
For thrice I drew ane without failing,
And thrice it was written—Tam Glen.

The last Halloween I was waukin
My droukit sark-sleeve, as ye ken;
His likeness cam up the house staukin,
And the very grey breeks o' Tam Glen!

Come counsel, dear Tittie! don't tarry—
I'll gie you my bonnie black hen,
Gif ye will advise me to marry
The lad I loe dearly, Tam Glen

There'll never be Peace.

TUNE—*There are few guid fellows when Willie's awa.*

BY yon castle wa', at the close of the day,
I heard a man sing, though his head it was grey;
And as he was singing, the tears down came,
There'll never be peace till Jamie comes hame.
The church is in ruins, the state is in jars;
Delusions, oppressions, and murderous wars;
We darena weel say't, though we ken wha's to blame,
There'll never be peace till Jamie comes hame.

My seven braw sons for Jamie drew sword,
And now I greet round their green beds in the yerd.
It brak the sweet heart of my faithfu' auld dame—
There'll never be peace till Jamie comes hame.
Now life is a burthen that bows me down,
Since I tint my bairns, and he tint his crown;
But till my last moments my words are the same—
There'll never be peace till Jamie comes hame!

Meikle thinks my Luve.

TUNE—*My Tocher's the Jewel.*

OH meikle thinks my luve o' my beauty,
  And meikle thinks my luve o' my kin;
But little thinks my luve I ken brawlie
  My tocher's the jewel has charms for him.
It's a' for the apple he'll nourish the tree;
  It's a' for the hiney he'll cherish the bee;
My laddie's sae meikle in luve wi' the siller,
  He canna hae luve to spare for me.

Your proffer o' luve's an arle-penny,
  My tocher's the bargain ye wad buy;
But an' ye be crafty, I am cunnin',
  Sae ye wi' another your fortune maun try.
Ye're like to the timmer o' yon rotten wood,
  Ye're like to the bark o' yon rotten tree,
Ye'll slip frae me like a knotless thread,
  And ye'll crack your credit wi' mae nor me.

How can I be Blythe and Glad.

TUNE—*The bonnie Lad that's far awa.*

OH how can I be blythe and glad,
  Or how can I gang brisk and braw,
When the bonnie lad that I loe best
  Is owre the hills and far awa?
    When the bonnie lad that I loe best
      Is owre the hills and far awa?

It's no the frosty winter wind,
  It's no the driving drift and snaw;
But aye the tear comes in my ee,
  To think on him that's far awa.
    But aye the tear comes in my ee,
      To think on him that's far awa.

My father pat me frae his door,
  My friends they hae disown'd me a',
But I hae ane will tak my part,
  The bonnie lad that's far awa.
    But I hae ane will tak my part,
      The bonnie lad that's far awa.

A pair o' gloves he gae to me,
  And silken snoods he gae me twa;
And I will wear them for his sake,
  The bonnie lad that's far awa.
    And I will wear them for his sake,
      The bonnie lad that's far awa.

I do confess thou art sae Fair. (341)

I DO confess thou art sae fair,
  I wad been owre the lugs in love,
Had I na found the slightest prayer
  That lips could speak thy heart could move.

I do confess thee sweet, but find
  Thou art sae thriftless o' thy sweets,
Thy favours are the silly wind,
  That kisses ilka thing it meets.

See yonder rose-bud, rich in dew,
  Amang its native briers sae coy;
How sune it tines its scent and hue
  When pou'd and worn a common toy!
Sic fate, ere lang, shall thee betide,
  Tho' thou may gaily bloom awhile!
Yet sune thou shalt be thrown aside
  Like ony common weed and vile.

Hunting Song.

TUNE—*I red you beware at the hunting.*

THE heather was blooming, the meadows were mawn,
Our lads gaed a-hunting ane day at the dawn.
Owre moors and owre mosses and mony a glen,
At length they discover'd a bonnie moor-hen.
  I red you beware at the hunting, young men;
  I red you beware at the hunting young men;
  Tak some on the wing, and some as they spring,
  But cannily steal on a bonnie moor-hen.

Sweet brushing the dew from the brown heather bells,
Her colours betray'd her on yon mossy fells;
Her plumage out-lustred the pride o' the spring,
And oh! as she wantoned gay on the wing.
  I red you beware, &c.

Auld Phœbus himsel, as he peep'd o'er the hill,
In spite at her plumage he tried his skill;
He levell'd his rays where she bask'd on the brae—
His rays were outshone, and but mark'd where she lay.
  I red you beware, &c.

They hunted the valley, they hunted the hill;
The best of our lads wi' the best o' their skill;
But still as the fairest she sat in their sight,
Then, whirr! she was over, a mile at a flight.
  I red you beware, &c.

* * * *

What can a Young Lassie.

TUNE—*What can a young lassie do wi' an auld man.*

WHAT can a young lassie, what shall a young lassie,
  What can a young lassie do wi' an auld man?

Bad luck on the penny that tempted my minnie
To sell her poor Jenny for siller and lan'!
Bad luck on the penny that tempted my minnie
To sell her poor Jenny for siller and lan'!

He's always compleenin' frae mornin to e'enin',
He hoasts and he hirples the weary day lang;
He's doyl't and he's dozin', his bluid it is frozen,
Oh, dreary's the night wi' a crazy auld man!
He's doyl't and he's dozin', his bluid it is frozen,
Oh, dreary's the night wi' a crazy auld man!

He hums and he hankers, he frets and he cankers,
I never can please him, do a' that I can;
He's peevish and jealous of a the young fellows:
Oh, dool on the day I met wi' an old man;
He's peevish and jealous of a' the young fellows:
Oh, dool on the day I met wi' an auld man!

My auld auntie Katie upon me takes pity,
I'll do my endeavour to follow her plan;
I'll cross him, and wrack him, until I heart-break him,
And then his auld brass will buy me a new pan.
I'll cross him, and wrack him, until I heart-break him,
And then his auld brass will buy me a new pan.

The Bonnie Wee Thing.

TUNE—*Bonnie wee thing.*

BONNIE wee thing, cannie wee thing,
Lovely wee thing, wert thou mine,
I wad wear thee in my bosom,
Lest my jewel I should tine.
Wishfully I look and languish,
In that bonnie face o' thine;
And my heart it stounds wi' anguish,
Lest my wee thing be na mine.

Wit, and grace, and love, and beauty,
In ane constellation shine;
To adore thee is my duty,
Goddess o' this soul o' mine!
Bonnie wee thing, cannie wee thing,
Lovely wee thing, wert thou mine,
I wad wear thee in my bosom,
Lest my jewel I should tine!

Lovely Davies.

TUNE—*Miss Muir.*

O HOW shall I, unskilfu', try
The poet's occupation,
The tunefu' powers, in happy hours,
That whispers inspiration?
Even they maun dare an effort mair
Than aught they ever gave us,
Or they rehearse, in equal verse,
The charms o' lovely Davies.

Each eye it cheers, when she appears,
Like Phœbus in the morning,
When past the shower, and ev'ry flower
The garden is adorning.
As the wretch looks o'er Siberia's shore,
When winter-bound the wave is;
Sae droops our heart when we maun part
Frae charming lovely Davies.

Her smile's a gift, frae 'boon the lift,
That maks us mair than princes;
A scepter'd hand, a king's command,
Is in her darting glances;
The man in arms, 'gainst female charms,
Even he her willing slave is;
He hugs his chain, and owns the reign
Of conquering, lovely Davies.

My muse to dream of such a theme,
Her feeblé powers surrender;
The eagle's gaze alone surveys
The sun's meridian splendour:
I wad in vain essay the strain,
The deed too daring brave is;
I'll drap the lyre, and mute admire
The charms o' lovely Davies.

Oh, for ane-and-twenty, Tam.

TUNE—*The Moudiewort.*

CHORUS.

AND oh, for ane-and-twenty, Tam,
And hey, sweet ane-and-twenty, Tam,
I'll learn my kin a rattlin' sang
An' I saw ane-and-twenty, Tam.

They snool me sair, and haud me down,
And gar me look like bluntie, Tam!
But three short years will soon wheel roun'—
And then comes ane-and-twenty, Tam.

A gleib o' lan', a claut o' gear,
Was left me by my auntie, Tam;
At kith or kin I need na spier,
An' I saw ane-and-twenty, Tam.

They'll hae me wed a wealthy coof,
Tho' I mysel' hae plenty, Tam;
But hear'st thou, laddie—there's my loof—
I'm thine at ane-and-twenty, Tam.

Kenmure's on and Awa. (342)

TUNE—*Oh Kenmure's on and awa, Willie.*

OH Kenmure's on and awa, Willie!
Oh Kenmure's on and awa!
And Kenmure's lord's the bravest lord,
That ever Galloway saw.

Success to Kenmure's band, Willie!
Success to Kenmure's band;
There's na a heart that fears a Whig,
That rides by Kenmure's hand.

Here's Kenmure's health in wine;
Here's Kenmure's health in wine; [blude,
There ne'er was a coward o' Kenmure's
Nor yet o' Gordon's line.

Oh Kenmure's lads are men, Willie!
Oh Kenmure's lads are men;
Their hearts and swords are metal true—
And that their faes shall ken.

They'll live or die wi' fame, Willie!
They'll live or die wi' fame;
But soon, wi' sounding victorie,
May Kenmure's lord come hame.

Here's him that's far awa, Willie!
Here's him that's far awa!
And here's the flower that I love best—
The rose that's like the snaw!

Bess and her Spinning Wheel.

TUNE—*The sweet lass that loes me.*

OH leeze me on my spinning-wheel,
Oh leeze me on my rock and reel;
Frae tap to tae that cleeds me bien,
And haps me fiel and warm at e'en!
I'll set me down and sing and spin,
While laigh descends the simmer sun,
Blest wi' content, and milk and meal—
Oh leeze me on my spinning-wheel!

On ilka hand the burnies trot,
And meet below my theekit cot;
The scented birk and hawthorn white,
Across the pool their arms unite,
Alike to screen the birdies nest,
And little fishes' caller rest:
The sun blinks kindly in the biel',
Where blythe I turn my spinning-wheel.

On lofty aiks the cushats wail,
And echo cons the doolfu' tale;
The lintwhites in the hazel braes,
Delighted, rival ither's lays:
The craik amang the clover hay,
The paitrick whirrin' o'er the ley,
The swallow jinkin' round my shiel,
Amuse me at my spinning-wheel.

Wi' sma' to sell, and less to buy,
Aboon distress, below envy,
Oh wha wad leave this humble state,
For a' the pride of a' the great?
Amid their flaring, idle toys,
Amid their cumbrous, dinsome joys,
Can they the peace and pleasure feel
Of Bessy at her spinning-wheel?

Oh Luve will Venture in.

TUNE—*The Posie.*

OH luve will venture in where it daurna well be seen; [has been;
Oh luve will venture in where wisdom ance
But I will down yon river rove, among the wood sae green—
And a' to pu' a posie to my ain dear May.

The primrose I will pu', the firstling o' the year, [dear,
And I will pu' the pink, the emblem o' my
For she's the pink o' womankind, and blooms without a peer—
And a' to be a posie to my ain dear May.

I'll pu' the budding rose, when Phœbus peeps in view, [mou';
For it's like a baumy kiss o' her sweet bonnie
The hyacinth for constancy, wi' its unchanging blue—
And a' to be a posie to my ain dear May.

The lily it is pure, and the lily it is fair,
And in her lovely bosom I'll place the lily there; [air—
The daisy's for simplicity, and unaffected
And a' to be a posie to my ain dear May.

The hawthorn I will pu' wi' its locks o' siller grey, [day.
Where, like an aged man, it stands at break of
But the songster's nest within the bush I winna tak away—
And a' to be a posie to my ain dear May.

In Simmer, when the Hay was Mawn.

TUNE—*The Country Lass.*

IN simmer, when the hay was mawn,
And corn wav'd green in ilka field,
While claver blooms white o'er the lea,
And roses blaw in ilka bield;
Blythe Bessie in the milking shiel,
Says—"I'll be wed, come o't what will."
Out spak a dame in wrinkled eild—
"O' guid advisement comes nae ill.

It's ye hae wooers mony ane,
  And, lassie, ye're but young, ye ken;
Then wait a wee, and cannie wale
  A routhie butt, a routhie ben:
There's Johnnie o' the Buskie-glen,
  Fu' is his barn, fu' is his byre;
Tak this frae me, my bonnie hen,
  It's plenty feeds the luver's fire."

"For Johnnie o' the Buskie-glen,
  I dinna care a single flie;
He loes sae weel his craps and kye,
  He has nae luve to spare for me:
But blythe's the blink o' Robie's ee,
  And, weel I wat, he loes me dear:
Ane blink o' him I wad na gie
  For Buskie-glen and a' his gear."

"Oh thoughtless lassie, life's a faught;
  The canniest gate, the strife is sair;
But aye fou han't is fechtin best,
  And hungry care's an unco care:
But some will spend, and some will spare,
  And wilfu' folk maun hae their will;
Syne as ye brew, my maiden fair,
  Keep mind that ye maun drink the yill."

"Oh, gear will buy me rigs o' land,
  And gear will buy me sheep and kye;
But the tender heart o' leesome luve
  The gowd and siller canna buy;
We may be poor—Robie and I,
  Light is the burden luve lays on;
Content and luve brings peace and joy—
  What mair hae queens upon a throne?"

Turn again thou Fair Eliza. (343)

Turn again, thou fair Eliza,
  Ane kind blink before we part,
Rue on thy despairing lover!
  Canst thou break his faithfu' heart?
Turn again, thou fair Eliza;
  If to love thy heart denies,
For pity hide the cruel sentence
  Under friendship's kind disguise!

Thee, dear maid, hae I offended?
  The offence is loving thee:
Canst thou wreck his peace for ever,
  Wha for thine wad gladly die?
While the life beats in my bosom,
  Thou shalt mix in ilka throe;
Turn again, thou lovely maiden,
  Ane sweet smile on me bestow.

Not the bee upon the blossom,
  In the pride o' sunny noon;
Not the little sporting fairy,
  All beneath the simmer moon;
Not the poet in the moment
  Fancy lightens on his ee,
Kens the pleasure, feels the rapture
  That thy presence gies to me.

Willie Wastle. (344)

Tune—*The Eight Men of Moidart.*

Willie Wastle dwalt on Tweed,
  The spot they called it Linkum-doddie:
Willie was a wabster guid,
  Cou'd stown a clew wi' ony bodie.
He had a wife was dour and din,
  Oh Tinkler Madgie was her mither.
Sic a wife as Willie had,
  I wad na gie a button for her.

She has an ee—she has but ane,
  The cat has twa the very colour:
Five rusty teeth, forbye a stump,
  A clapper tongue wad deave a miller;
A whiskin' beard about her mou',
  Her nose and chin they threaten ither.—
Sic a wife as Willie had,
  I wad na gie a button for her.

She's bough-hough'd, she's hein-shinn'd,
  Ane limpin' leg a hand-breed shorter;
She's twisted right, she's twisted left,
  To balance fair in ilka quarter:
She has a hump upon her breast,
  The twin o' that upon her shouther.
Sic a wife as Willie had,
  I wad na gie a button for her,

Auld baudrons by the ingle sits,
  And wi' her loof her face a-washin';
But Willie's wife is nae sae trig,
  She dights her grunzie wi' a hushion;
Her walie nieves like midden-creels,
  Her face wad fyle the Logan-Water.
Sic a wife as Willie had,
  I wad na gie a button for her.

Such a parcel of Rogues in a Nation.

Tune—*A parcel of rogues in a nation.*

Fareweel to a' our Scottish fame,
  Fareweel our ancient glory,
Fareweel even to the Scottish name,
  Sae fam'd in martial story.
Now Sark rins o'er the Solway sands,
  And Tweed rins to the ocean,
To mark where England's province stands:—
  Such a parcel of rogues in a nation!

What force or guile could not subdue,
  Thro' many warlike ages,
Is wrought now by a coward few,
  For hireling traitors' wages.

The English steel we could disdain,
  Secure in valour's station;
But English gold has been our bane:—
  Such a parcel of rogues in a nation!

Oh would I had not seen the day
  That treason thus could fell us,
My auld grey head had lien in clay,
  Wi' Bruce and loyal Wallace!
But pith and power, till my last hour,
  I'll mak this declaration;
We're bought and sold for English gold:—
  Such a parcel of rogues in a nation!

Song of Death. (345)

TUNE—*Oran an Diog.*

Scene—A field of battle.—Time of the day, evening.—The wounded and dying of the victorious army are supposed to join in the following song:—

FAREWELL, thou fair day, thou green earth, and ye skies,
  Now gay with the bright setting sun;
Farewell loves and friendships, ye dear tender ties—
  Our race of existence is run!

Thou grim king of terrors, thou life's gloomy foe!
  Go, frighten the coward and slave;
Go, teach them to tremble, fell tyrant! but know,
  No terrors hast thou to the brave!

Thou strik'st the dull peasant—he sinks in the dark,
  Nor saves e'en the wreck of a name;
Thou strik'st the young hero—a glorious mark!
  He falls in the blaze of his fame!

In the field of proud honour—our swords in our hands,
  Our king and our country to save—
While victory shines on life's last ebbing sands,
  Oh! who would not die with the brave!

She's Fair and Fause.

TUNE—*She's fair and fause.*

SHE's fair and fause that causes my smart,
  I loed her meikle and lang;
She's broken her vow, she's broken my heart,
  And I may e'en gae hang.

A coof cam in wi' routh o' gear,
  And I hae tint my dearest dear;
But woman is but warld's gear,
  Sae let the bonnie lassie gang.

Whae'er ye be that woman love,
  To this be never blind,
Nae ferlie 'tis tho' fickle she prove,
  A woman has't by kind.

Oh woman, lovely woman fair!
  An angel form's fa'n to thy share,
'Twad been owre meikle to gien thee mair—
  I mean an angel mind.

Flow Gently, Sweet Afton. (346)

TUNE—*The yellow-haired Laddie.*

FLOW gently, sweet Afton, among thy green braes,
Flow gently, I'll sing thee a song in thy praise;
My Mary's asleep by thy murmuring stream,
Flow gently, sweet Afton, disturb not her dream.

Thou stock-dove whose echo resounds thro' the glen,
Ye wild whistling blackbirds in yon thorny den,
Thou green-crested lapwing thy screaming forbear,
I charge you disturb not my slumbering fair.

How lofty, sweet Afton, thy neighbouring hills,
Far mark'd with the courses of clear winding rills;
There daily I wander as noon rises high,
My flocks and my Mary's sweet cot in my eye.

How pleasant thy banks and green vallies below;
Where wild in the woodlands the primroses blow;
There oft as mild evening weeps over the lea,
The sweet-scented birk shades my Mary and me.

Thy crystal stream, Afton, how lovely it glides,
And winds by the cot where my Mary resides;
How wanton thy waters her snowy feet lave,
As gathering sweet flow'rets she stems thy clear wave.

Flow gently, sweet Afton, among thy green braes,
Flow gently, sweet river, the theme of my lays;
My Mary's asleep by thy murmuring stream,
Flow gently, sweet Afton, disturb not her dream.

The Lovely Lass of Inverness.

TUNE—*Lass of Inverness.*

THE lovely lass o' Inverness,
  Nae joy nor pleasure can she see:
For e'en and morn she cries, alas!
  And aye the saut tear blin's her ee:

Drumossie moor—Drumossie day—
  A waefu' day it was to me!
For there I lost my father dear,
  My father dear, and brethren three.

Their winding sheet the bluidy clay,
  Their graves are growing green to see:
And by them lies the dearest lad
  That ever blest a woman's ee!
Now wae to thee, thou cruel lord,
  A bluidy man I trow thou be;
For mony a heart thou hast made sair,
  That ne'er did wrong to thine or thee.

A red, red Rose. (347)

TUNE—*Graham's Strathspey.*

OH, my luve's like a red, red rose
  That's newly sprung in June:
Oh, my luve's like the melodie,
  That's sweetly play'd in tune.
As fair art thou, my bonnie lass,
  So deep in luve am I:
And I will luve thee still, my dear,
  Till a' the seas gang dry.

Till a' the seas gang dry, my dear,
  And the rocks melt wi' the sun;
I will luve thee still, my dear,
  While the sands o' life shall run.
And fare thee weel, my only luve!
  And fare thee weel a while!
And I will come again my luve,
  Tho' it were ten thousand mile.

Louis what reck I by thee.

TUNE—*Louis, what reck I by thee.*

LOUIS, what reck I by thee,
  Or Geordie on his ocean?
Dyvor, beggar louns to me—
  I reign in Jeanie's bosom.

Let her crown my love her law,
  And in her breast enthrone me:
Kings and nations— swith, awa!
  Reif randies, I disown ye!

The Exciseman. (348)

TUNE—*The deil cam fiddling through the town.*

THE deil cam fiddling through the town,
  And danced awa wi' the Exciseman,
And ilka wife cries—"Auld Mahoun,
  I wish you luck o' the prize man!"
    The deil's awa, the deil's awa,
      The deil's awa wi' the Exciseman;
    He's danc'd awa, he's danc'd awa,
      He's danc'd awa wi' the Exciseman!

We'll mak our maut, we'll brew our drink,
  We'll dance, and sing, and rejoice, man;
And mony braw thanks to the meikle black deil
  That danc'd awa wi' the Exciseman.
    The deil's awa, the deil's awa,
      The deil's awa wi' the Exciseman;
    He's danc'd awa, he's danc'd awa,
      He's danc'd awa wi' the Exciseman.

There's threesome reels, there's foursome reels,
  There's hornpipes and strathspeys, man;
But the ae best dance e'er cam to the land
  Was—the deil's awa wi' the Exciseman.
    The deil's awa, the deil's awa,
      The deil's awa wi' the Exciseman;
    He's danc'd awa, he's danc'd awa,
      He's danc'd awa wi' the Exciseman.

Somebody!

TUNE—*For the sake of somebody.*

MY heart is sair—I dare na tell—
  My heart is sair for somebody;
I could wake a winter night
  For the sake of somebody.
    Oh-ho, for somebody!
    Oh-hey, for somebody!
I could range the world around,
  For the sake o' somebody!

Ye powers that smile on virtuous love,
  Oh, sweetly smile on somebody!
Frae ilka danger keep him free,
  And send me safe my somebody.
    Oh-ho, for somebody!
    Oh-hey, for somebody!
I wad do—what wad I not!
  For the sake o' somebody!

I'll aye ca' in by yon Town.

TUNE—*I'll gae nae mair to yon town.*

I'LL aye ca' in by yon town,
  And by yon garden green, again;
I'll aye ca' in by yon town,
  And see my bonnie Jean again.
There's nane sall ken, there's nane sall guess,
  What brings me back the gate again,
But she, my fairest faithfu' lass,
  And stownlins we sall meet again;

She'll wander by the aiken tree,
  When trystin-time draws near again;
And when her lovely form I see,
  Oh haith, she's doubly dear again!
I'll aye ca' in by yon town,
  And by yon garden green, again;
I'll aye ca' in by yon town,
  And see my bonnie Jean again.

Wilt thou be my Dearie? (349)

AIR—*The Sutor's Dochter.*

WILT thou be my dearie?
When sorrow wrings thy gentle heart,
Wilt thou let me cheer thee?
By the treasure of my soul,
That's the love I bear thee!
I swear and vow that only thou
Shall ever be my dearie.
Only thou, I swear and vow,
Shall ever be my dearie.

Lassie, say thou loes me;
Or if thou wilt nae be my ain.
Say na thou'lt refuse me:
If it winna, canna be,
Thou, for thine may choose me,
Let me, lassie, quickly die,
Trusting that thou loes me.
Lassie, let me quickly die,
Trusting that thou loes me.

Oh, Wat ye Wha's in yon Town. (350)

TUNE—*I'll gae nae mair to yon town.*

OH, wat ye wha's in yon town,
  Ye see the e'enin' sun upon?
The fairest dame's in yon town,
  The e'enin' sun is shining on.

Now haply down yon gay green shaw,
  She wanders by yon spreading tree;
How blest ye flow'rs that round her blaw,
  Ye catch the glances o' her ee!

How blest ye birds that round her sing,
  And welcome in the blooming year!
And doubly welcome be the spring,
  The season to my Lucy dear.

The sun blinks blythe on yon town,
  And on yon bonnie braes of Ayr;
But my delight in yon town,
  And dearest bliss, is Lucy fair.

Without my love, not a' the charms
  O' Paradise could yield me joy;
But gie me Lucy in my arms,
  And welcome Lapland's dreary sky!

My cave wad be a lover's bower,
  Tho' raging winter rent the air;
And she a lovely little flower,
  That I wad tent and shelter there.

Oh sweet is she in yon town,
  Yon sinkin' sun's gane down upon;
A fairer than's in yon town
  His setting beam ne'er shone upon.

If angry fate is sworn my foe,
  And suffering I am doom'd to bear;
I careless quit ought else below,
  But spare me—spare me, Lucy dear!

For while life's dearest blood is warm,
  Ae thought frae her shall ne'er depart,
And she—as fairest is her form!
  She has the truest, kindest heart!

But lately Seen.

TUNE—*The Winter of Life.*

BUT lately seen in gladsome green,
  The woods rejoiced the day;
Thro' gentle showers the laughing flowers,
  In double pride were gay;
But now our joys are fled
  On winter blasts awa!
Yet maiden May, in rich array,
  Again shall bring them a'.

But my white pow, nae kindly thowe
  Shall melt the snaws of age;
My trunk of eild, but buss or beild,
  Sinks in Time's wintry rage.
Oh! age has weary days,
  And nights o' sleepless pain!
Thou golden time o' youthfu' prime,
  Why comes thou not again?

Could ought of Song.

TUNE—*Could ought of song.*

COULD ought of song declare my pains,
  Could artful numbers move thee,
The muse should tell, in labour'd strains,
  Oh Mary, how I love thee!
They who but feign a wounded heart
  May teach the lyre to languish;
But what avails the pride of art,
  When wastes the soul with anguish?

Then let the sudden bursting sigh
  The heart-felt pang discover;
And in the keen, yet tender eye,
  Oh read th' imploring lover!

For well I know thy gentle mind
  Disdains art's gay disguising;
Beyond what fancy e'er refin'd,
  The voice of nature prizing.

Oh, Steer her up.

TUNE—*Oh steer her up, and haud her gaun.*

OH steer her up and haud her gaun—
  Her mother's at the mill, jo;
And gif she winna take a man,
  E'en let her take her will, jo;
First shore her wi' a kindly kiss,
  And ca' another gill, jo,
And gif she take the thing amiss,
  E'ven let her flyte her fill, jo.

Oh steer her up, and be na blate,
  And gif she take it ill, jo,
Then lea'e the lassie till her fate,
  And time nae langer spill, jo:
Ne'er break your heart for ane rebute,
  But think upon it still, jo;
Then gif the lassie winna do't,
  Ye'll find anither will, jo.

It was a' for our Rightfu' King. (351)

TUNE—*It was a' for our rightfu' king.*

IT was a' for our rightfu' king
  We left fair Scotland's strand;
It was a' for our rightfu' king
  We e'er saw Irish land,
    My dear;
  We e'er saw Irish land.

Now a' is done that men can do,
  And a' is done in vain;
My love and native land farewell,
  For I maun cross the main,
    My dear;
  For I maun cross the main.

He turned him right, and round about
  Upon the Irish shore;
And gie his bridle-reins a shake,
  With adieu for evermore,
    My dear;
  With adieu for evermore.

The sodger from the wars returns,
  The sailor frae the main;
But I hae parted frae my love,
  Never to meet again,
    My dear;
  Never to meet again.

When day is gane, and night is come,
  And a' folk bound to sleep;
I think on him that's far awa',
  The lee-lang night and weep,
    My dear;
  The lee-lang night and weep.

Oh Wha is She that Loes me.

TUNE—*Morag.*

OH wha is she that loes me,
  And has my heart a-keeping?
Oh sweet is she that loes me,
  As dews o' simmer weeping,
  In tears the rose-buds steeping!
    Oh that's the lassie o' my heart
      My lassie ever dearer;
    Oh that's the queen o' womankind,
      And ne'er a ane to peer her.

If thou shalt meet a lassie
  In grace and beauty charming,
That e'en thy chosen lassie,
  Erewhile thy breast sae warming,
  Had ne'er sic powers alarming.

If thou hadst heard her talking,
  And thy attentions plighted,
That ilka body talking,
  But her by thee is slighted,
  And thou art all delighted.

If thou hast met this fair one;
  When frae her thou hast parted,
If every other fair one,
  But her, thou hast deserted,
  And thou art broken-hearted;
    Oh that's the lassie o' my heart,
      My lassie ever dearer;
    Oh that's the queen o' womankind,
      And ne'er a ane to peer her.

Caledonia.

TUNE—*Caledonian Hunt's Delight.*

THERE was once a day—but old Time then was young—
  That brave Caledonia, the chief of her line,
From some of your northern deities sprung,
  (Who knows not that brave Caledonia's divine?)
From Tweed to the Orcades was her domain,
  To hunt, or to pasture, or do what she would:
Her heav'nly relations there fixed her reign,
  And pledg'd her their godheads to warrant it good.

A lambkin in peace, but a lion in war,
The pride of her kindred the heroine grew:
Her grandsire old Odin, triumphantly swore
"Whoe'er shall provoke thee, th' encounter shall rue!" [sport,
With tillage or pasture at times she would
To feed her fair flocks by her green rustling corn; [resort,
But chiefly the woods were her fav'rite resort, [the horn.
Her darling amusement the hounds and

Long quiet she reign'd; till thitherward steers
A flight of bold eagles from Adria's strand:
Repeated, successive, for many long years,
They darken'd the air, and they plunder'd the land; [cry,
Their pounces were murder, and terror their
They conquer'd and ruin'd a world beside;
She took to her hills, and her arrows let fly— [died.
The daring invaders they fled or they

The fell harpy-raven took wing from the north, [the shore;
The scourge of the seas, and the dread of
The wild Scandinavian boar issu'd forth
To wanton in carnage, and wallow in gore: [prevail'd,
O'er countries and kingdoms their fury
No arts could appease them, no arms could repel;
But brave Caledonia in vain they assailed,
As Largs well can witness and Loncartie tell.

The Cameleon-savage disturb'd her repose,
With tumult, disquiet, rebellion, and strife;
Provok'd beyond bearing, at last she arose,
And robb'd him at once of his hopes and his life:
The Anglian lion, the terror of France,
Oft prowling, ensanguin'd the Tweed's silver flood:
But, taught by the bright Caledonian lance,
He learned to fear in his own native wood.

Thus bold, independent, unconquer'd, and free, [run:
Her bright course of glory for ever shall
For brave Caledonia immortal must be;
I'll prove it from Euclid as clear as the sun:
Rectangle-triangle the figure we'll choose,
The upright is Chance, and old Time is the base;
But brave Caledonia's the hypothenuse;
Then ergo, she'll match them, and match them always.

Oh, lay thy Loof in Mine, Lass.

TUNE—*Cordwainer's March.*

OH lay thy loof in mine, lass,
In mine, lass, in mine, lass;
And swear on thy white hand, lass,
That thou wilt be my ain.

A slave to love's unbounded sway,
He aft has wrought me meikle wae;
But now he is my deadly fae,
Unless thou be my ain.

There's mony a lass has broke my rest,
That for a blink I hae lo'ed best;
But thou art queen within my breast,
For ever to remain.
Oh lay thy loof in mine, lass,
In mine, lass, in mine, lass:
And swear on thy white hand, lass,
That thou wilt be my ain.

Anna, thy Charms.

TUNE—*Bonnie Mary.*

ANNA, thy charms my bosom fire,
And waste my soul with care;
But, ah! how bootless to admire,
When fated to despair!
Yet in thy presence, lovely fair,
To hope may be forgiv'n;
For sure 'twere impious to despair,
So much in sight of Heav'n.

Gloomy December.

TUNE—*Wandering Willie.*

ANCE mair I hail thee, thou gloomy December!
Ance mair I hail thee, wi' sorrow and care;
Sad was the parting thou makes me remember,
Parting wi' Nancy, oh! ne'er to meet mair.
Fond lovers' parting is sweet painful pleasure, [hour;
Hope beaming mild on the soft parting
But the dire feeling, oh farewell for ever,
Is anguish unmingled and agony pure.

Wild as the winter now tearing the forest,
Till the last leaf o' the summer is flown,
Such is the tempest has shaken my bosom,
Since my last hope and last comfort is gone.

Still as I hail thee, thou gloomy December,
 Still shall I hail thee wi' sorrow and care;
For sad was the parting thou makest me remember,
 Parting wi' Nancy, oh! ne'er to meet mair.

Oh Mally's meek, Mally's sweet.

Oh Mally's meek, Mally's sweet,
 Mally's modest and discreet,
Mally's rare, Mally's fair,
 Mally's every way complete.

As I was walking up the street,
 A barefit maid I chanc'd to meet;
But oh the road was very hard
 For that fair maiden's tender feet.

It were mair meet that those fine feet
 Were weel lac'd up in silken shoon,
And 'twere more fit that she should sit
 Within yon chariot gilt aboon.

Her yellow hair, beyond compare,
 Comes trinkling down her swan-white neck;
And her two eyes, like stars in skies,
 Would keep a sinking ship frae wreck.

Cassillis' Banks.

Now bank and brae are claith'd in green,
 And scatter'd cowslips sweetly spring;
By Girvan's fairy-haunted stream
 The birdies flit on wanton wing.
To Cassillis' banks when e'ening fa's,
 There wi' my Mary let me flee,
There catch her ilka glance of love,
 The bonnie blink o' Mary's ee!

The child wha boasts o' warld's wealth
 Is aften laird o' meikle care;
But Mary she is a' my ain—
 Ah! fortune cannie gie me mair.
Then let me range by Cassillis' banks,
 Wi' her, the lassie dear to me,
And catch her ilka glance o' love,
 The bonnie blink o' Mary's ee!

My Lady's Gown, there's Gairs upon't.

Tune—*Gregg's Pipes.*

My Lady's gown, there's gairs upon't,
And gowden flowers sae rare upon't;
But Jenny's jimps and jirkinet,
My lord thinks mickle mair upon't.

My lord a-hunting he is gane,
But hounds or hawks wi' him are nane;
By Colin's cottage lies his game,
If Colin's Jenny be at hame.

My lady's white, my lady's red,
And kith and kin o' Cassillis' bluid;
But her ten-pund lands o' tocher guid
Were a' the charms his lordship loed.

Out owre yon muir, out owre yon moss,
Whare gor-cocks thro' the heather pass,
There wons auld Colin's bonnie lass,
A lily in a wilderness.

Sae sweetly move her gentle limbs,
Like music notes o' lovers' hymns:
The diamond dew is her een sae blue,
Where laughing love sae wanton swims.

My lady's dink, my lady's drest,
The flower and fancy o' the west;
But the lassie that a man loes best,
Oh that's the lass to make him blest.

The Fete Champetre. (352)

Tune—*Killicrankie.*

Oh wha will to Saint Stephen's house,
 To do our errands there, man?
Oh wha will to Saint Stephen's house,
 O' th' merry lads of Ayr, man?
Or will we send a man-o'-law?
 Or will we send a sodger?
Or him wha led o'er Scotland a'
 The meikle Ursa-Major?

Come, will ye court a noble lord,
 Or buy a score o' lairds, man?
For worth and honour pawn their word,
 Their vote shall be Glencaird's, man?
Ane gies them coin, ane gies them wine,
 Anither gies them clatter;
Anbank, wha guess'd the ladies' taste,
 He gies a Fête Champetre.

When Love and Beauty heard the news,
 The gay green-woods amang, man;
Where, gathering flowers and busking bowers,
 They heard the blackbird's sang, man:
A vow, they seal'd it with a kiss
 Sir Politics to fetter,
As theirs alone, the patent-bliss,
 To hold a Fête Champetre.

Then mounted Mirth, on gleesome wing,
 Owre hill and dale she flew, man;
Ilk wimpling burn, ilk crystal spring,
 Ilk glen and shaw she knew, man:

O LET ME IN THIS AE NIGHT.

O let me in this ae night,
This ae ae, ae night,

She summon'd every social sprite,
  That sports by wood or water,
On th' bonnie banks of Ayr to meet,
  And keep this Fête Champetre.

Cauld Boreas, wi' his boisterous crew,
  Were bound to stakes like kye, man:
And Cynthia's car, o' silver fu',
  Clamb up the starry sky, man:
Reflected beams dwell in the streams,
  Or down the current shatter;
The western breeze steals through the trees
  To view this Fête Champetre.

How many a robe sae gaily floats!
  What sparkling jewels glance, man!
To Harmony's enchanting notes,
  As moves the mazy dance, man.
The echoing wood, the winding flood,
  Like Paradise did glitter,
When angels met, at Adam's yett,
  To hold their Fête Champetre.

When Politics came there to mix
  And make his ether-stane, man:
He circled round the magic ground,
  But entrance found he nane, man: (353)
He blushed for shame, he quat his name,
  Forswore it, every letter,
Wi' humble prayer to join and share
  This festive Fête Champetre.

The Dumfries Volunteers.

TUNE—*Push about the Jorum.*

DOES haughty Gaul invasion threat?
  Then let the loons beware, Sir;
There's wooden walls upon our seas,
  And volunteers on shore, Sir.
The Nith shall run to Corsicon,
  And Criffel sink in Solway,
Ere we permit a foreign foe
  On British ground to rally!
    Fal de ral, &c.

Oh, let us not like snarling tykes
  In wrangling be divided;
Till, slap, come in an unco loon,
  And wi' a rung decide it.
Be Britain still to Britain true,
  Among oursels united;
For never but by British hands
  Maun British wrangs be righted
    Fal de ral, &c.

The kettle o' the kirk and state,
  Perhaps a claut may fail in't:
But deil a foreign tinkler loon
  Shall ever ca' a nail in't.

Q

Our father's bluid the kettle bought,
  And wha wad dare to spoil it;
By heaven, the sacrilegious dog
  Shall fuel be to boil it.
    Fal de ral, &c.

The wretch that wad a tyrant own,
  And the wretch his true-born brother,
Who would set the *mob* aboon the *throne*,
  May they be damned together!
Who will not sing "God save the King,"
  Shall hang as high's the steeple;
But while we sing "God save the King,"
  We'll ne'er forget the People.
    Fal de ral, &c.

Oh, wert Thou in the Cauld Blast. (354)

TUNE—*Lass o' Livistone.*

OH, wert thou in the cauld blast
  On yonder lea, on yonder lea,
My plaidie to the angry airt,
  I'd shelter thee, I'd shelter thee:
Or did misfortune's bitter storms
  Around the blaw, around thee blaw,
Thy bield should be my bosom,
  To share it a', to share it a'.

Or were I in the wildest waste,
  Sae black and bare, sae black and bare,
The desert were a Paradise,
  If thou wert there, if thou wert there:
Or were I monarch o' the globe,
  Wi' thee to reign, wi' thee to reign,
The brightest jewel in my crown
  Wad be my queen, wad be my queen.

Lovely Polly Stewart.

TUNE—*Ye're welcome, Charlie Stewart.*

OH lovely Polly Stewart!
  Oh charming Polly Stewart!
There's not a flower that blooms in May
  That's half so fair as thou art.
The flower it blaws, it fades and fa's,
  And art can ne'er renew it;
But worth and truth eternal youth
  Will give to Polly Stewart.

May he whose arms shall fauld thy charms
  Possess a leal and true heart;
To him be given to ken the heaven
  He grasps in Polly Stewart.
Oh lovely Polly Stewart!
  Oh charming Polly Stewart!
There's ne'er a flower that blooms in May
  That's half so sweet as thou art.

Yestreen I had a Pint o' Wine.

TUNE—*Banks of Banna.*

YESTREEN I had a pint o' wine,
  A place where body saw na';
Yestreen lay on this breast o' mine
  The gowden locks of Anna.
The hungry Jew in wilderness
  Rejoicing o'er his manna,
Was naething to my hinny bliss
  Upon the lips of Anna.

Ye monarchs tak the east and west,
  Frae Indus to Savannah!
Gie me within my straining grasp
  The melting form of Anna.
There I'll despise imperial charms,
  An empress or sultana,
While dying raptures in her arms
  I give and take with Anna!

Awa, thou flaunting god o' day!
  Awa, thou pale Diana!
Ilk star gae hide thy twinkling ray,
  When I'm to meet my Anna.
Come, in thy raven plumage, night!
  Sun, moon, and stars withdrawn a';
And bring an angel pen to write
  My transports wi' my Anna!

The Lea Rig.

TUNE—*The Lea rig.*

WHEN o'er the hill the eastern star
  Tells bughtin time is near, my jo;
And owsen frae the furrow'd field,
  Return sae dowf and weary O;
Down by the burn, where scented birks
  Wi' dew are hanging clear, my jo,
I'll meet thee on the lea-rig,
  My ain kind dearie O.

In mirkest glen, at midnight hour,
  I'd rove, and ne'er be eerie O,
If thro' that glen I gaed to thee,
  My ain kind dearie O.
Altho' the night were ne'er sae wild,
  And I were ne'er sae wearie O,
I'd meet thee on the lea-rig,
  My ain kind dearie O.

The hunter loes the morning sun,
  To rouse the mountain deer, my jo;
At noon the fisher seeks the glen,
  Along the burn to steer, my jo;
Gie me the hour o' gloamin grey,
  It maks my heart sae cheery O,
To meet thee on the lea-rig,
  My ain kind dearie O.

Bonnie Lesley. (355)

TUNE—*The Collier's Bonnie Lassie.*

OH saw ye bonnie Lesley,
  As she gaed owre the border?
She's gane, like Alexander,
  To spread her conquests farther.

To see her is to love her,
  And love but her for ever;
For nature made her what she is,
  And never made anither!

Thou art a queen, fair Lesley,
  Thy subjects we, before thee;
Thou art divine, fair Lesley,
  The hearts o' men adore thee.

The deil he could na scaith thee,
  Or aught that wad belang thee;
He'd look into thy bonnie face,
  And say "I canna wrang thee."

The powers aboon will tent thee;
  Misfortune sha' na steer thee;
Thou'rt like themselves sae lovely,
  That ill they'll ne'er let near thee.

Return again, fair Lesley,
  Return to Caledonie!
That we may brag, we hae a lass
  There's nane again sae bonnie.

Will ye Go to the Indies, my Mary. (356)

TUNE—*The Ewe-buchts.*

WILL ye go to the Indies, my Mary,
  And leave auld Scotia's shore?
Will ye go to the Indies, my Mary,
  Across the Atlantic's roar?

Oh sweet grow the lime and the orange,
  And the apple on the pine;
But a' the charms o' the Indies
  Can never equal thine.

I hae sworn by the Heavens to my Mary,
  I hae sworn by the Heavens to be true;
And sae may the Heavens forget me,
  When I forget my vow!

Oh plight me your faith, my Mary,
  And plight me your lily-white hand;
Oh plight me your faith, my Mary,
  Before I leave Scotia's strand.

We hae plighted our troth, my Mary,
  In mutual affection to join;
And curst be the cause that shall part us!
  The hour and the moment o' time!

My Wife's a Winsome Wee Thing.

SHE is a winsome wee thing,
She is a handsome wee thing,
She is a bonnie wee thing,
This sweet wee wife o' mine.

I never saw a fairer,
I never loe'd a dearer;
And neist my heart I'll wear her
For fear my jewel tine.

On leeze me on my wee thing,
My bonnie blythesome wee thing;
Sae lang's I hae my wee thing,
I'll think my lot divine.

Tho' warld's care we share o't,
And may see meikle mair o't;
Wi' her I'll blythely bear it,
And ne'er a word repine.

Highland Mary. (357)

TUNE—*Katharine Ogie.*

YE banks, and braes, and streams around
The castle o' Montgomery,
Green be your woods, and fair your flowers,
Your waters never drumlie!
There simmer first unfauld her robes,
And there the langest tarry;
For there I took the last fareweel
O' my sweet Highland Mary.

How sweetly bloomed the gay green birk,
How rich the hawthorn's blossom,
As underneath their fragrant shade,
I clasp'd her to my bosom!
The golden hours, on angel wings,
Flew o'er me and my dearie;
For dear to me as light and life,
Was my sweet Highland Mary.

Wi' mony a vow, and lock'd embrace,
Our parting was fu' tender;
And, pledging aft to meet again,
We tore oursels asunder;
But oh! fell death's untimely frost,
That nipt my flower sae early!
Now green's the sod, and cauld's the clay,
That wraps my Highland Mary!

Oh pale, pale now, those rosy lips,
I aft hae kiss'd sae fondly!
And clos'd for aye the sparkling glance
That dwelt on me sae kindly;
And mouldering now in silent dust
That heart that loe'd me dearly!
But still within my bosom's core
Shall live my Highland Mary.

Auld Rob Morris.

THERE'S auld Rob Morris that wons in yon glen,
He's the king o' guid fellows and wale o' auld men;
He has goud in his coffers, he has owsen and kine,
And ane bonnie lassie, his darling and mine.

She's fresh as the morning, the fairest in May;
She's sweet as the ev'ning amang the new hay:
As blythe and as artless as the lambs on the lea,
And dear to my heart as the light to my ee.

But, oh! she's an heiress, auld Robin's a laird,
And my daddie has naught but a cot-house and yard;
A wooer like me maunna hope to come speed,
The wounds I must hide that will soon be my dead.

The day comes to me, but delight brings me nane;
The night comes to me, but my rest it is gane:
I wander my lane like a night-troubled ghaist,
And I sigh as my heart it wad burst in my breast.

Oh had she but been of a lower degree,
I then might hae hop'd she wad smil'd upon me!
Oh, how past describing had then been my bliss,
As now my distraction no words can express!

Duncan Gray.

DUNCAN GRAY came here to woo,
Ha, ha, the wooing o't,
On blythe Yule night when we were fu',
Ha, ha, the wooing o't.
Maggie coost her head fu' high,
Look'd asklent and unco skeigh,
Gart poor Duncan stand abeigh;
Ha, ha, the wooing o't.

Duncan fleech'd, and Duncan pray'd;
Ha, ha, &c.
Meg was deaf as Ailsa Craig,
Ha, ha, &c.
Duncan sigh'd baith out and in,
Grat his een baith bleert and blin',
Spake o' lowpin' owre a linn;
Ha, ha, &c.

Time and chance are but a tide,
Ha, ha, &c.
Slighted love is sair to bide,
Ha, ha, &c.

Shall I, like a fool, quoth he,
For a haughty hizzie die?
She may gae to—France for me!
Ha, ha, &c.

How it comes let doctors tell,
Ha, ha, &c.
Meg grew sick—as he grew heal,
Ha, ha, &c.
Something in her bosom wrings,
For relief a sigh she brings;
And oh, her een, they speak sic things
Ha, ha, &c.

Duncan was a lad o' grace,
Ha, ha, &c.
Maggie's was a piteous case,
Ha, ha, &c.
Duncan could na be her death,
Swelling pity smoor'd his wrath;
Now they're crouse and canty baith;
Ha, ha, &c.

Poortith Cauld.

TUNE—*I had a Horse.*

OH poortith cauld, and restless love,
Ye wreck my peace between ye;
Yet poortith a' I could forgive,
An 'twere na for my Jeanie.
Oh why should fate sic pleasure have,
Life's dearest bands untwining?
Or why sae sweet a flower as love,
Depend on Fortune's shining?

This warld's wealth when I think on,
Its pride, and a' the lave o't;
Fie, fie on silly coward man,
That he should be the slave o't.
Oh why, &c.

Her een sae bonnie blue betray
How she repays my passion;
But prudence is her o'erword aye,
She talks of rank and fashion.
Oh why, &c,

Oh wha can prudence think upon,
And sic a lassie by him?
Oh wha can prudence think upon,
And sae in love as I am?
Oh why, &c.

How blest the humble cotter's fate!
He wooes his simple dearie;
The silly bogles, wealth and state,
Can never make them eerie.
Oh why, &c.

Gala Water. (358)

THERE's braw, braw lads on Yarrow braes,
That wander thro' the blooming heather;
But Yarrow braes, nor Ettrick shaws,
Can match the lads o' Gala Water.

But there is ane, a secret ane,
Aboon them a' I loe him better;
And I'll be his and he'll be mine,
The bonnie lad o' Gala Water.

Altho' his daddie was nae laird,
And tho' I hae na meikle tocher;
Yet rich in kindness, truest love,
We'll tent our flocks by Gala Water.

It ne'er was wealth, it ne'er was wealth,
That coft contentment, peace, or pleasure;
The bands and bliss o' mutual love,
Oh, that's the chiefest warld's treasure!

Lord Gregory.

OH mirk, mirk is this midnight hour,
And loud the tempests roar;
A waefu' wanderer seeks thy tower,
Lord Gregory, ope thy door.

An exile frae her father's ha',
And a' for loving thee;
At least some *pity* on me shaw,
If *love* it may na be.

Lord Gregory, mind'st thou not the grove
By bonnie Irwine side,
Where first I own'd that virgin-love
I lang, lang had denied?

How aften didst thou pledge and vow
Thou wad for aye be mine;
And my fond heart, itsel sae true,
It ne'er mistrusted thine.

Hard is thy heart, Lord Gregory,
And flinty is thy breast:
Thou dart of heaven that flashest by,
Oh wilt thou give me rest!

Ye mustering thunders from above
Your willing victim see;
But spare and pardon my fause love,
His wrangs to Heaven and me!

Mary Morison. (359)

TUNE—*Bide ye yet.*

OH Mary, at thy window be
It is the wish'd, the trysted hour!
Those smiles and glances let me see,
That make the miser's treasure poor:

How blythely wad I bide the stoure,
  A weary slave frae sun to sun,
Could I the rich reward secure,
  The lovely Mary Morison.

Yestreen when to the trembling string,
  The dance gaed thro' the lighted ha',
To thee my fancy took its wing,
  I sat, but neither heard nor saw.
Tho' this was fair, and that was braw,
  And yon the toast of a' the town,
I sigh'd, and said amang them a'
  "Ye are na Mary Morison."

Oh Mary, canst thou wreck his peace,
  Wha for thy sake wad gladly die?
Or canst thou break that heart of his,
  Whase only faut is loving thee?
If love for love thou wilt na gie,
  At least be pity to me shown;
A thought ungentle canna be
  The thought o' Mary Morison.

Wandering Willie.

HERE awa, there awa, wandering Willie,
Here awa, there awa, haud awa hame;
Come to my bosom, my ain only dearie,
Tell me thou bring'st me my Willie the same.

Winter-winds blew loud and cauld at our parting,
Fears for my Willie brought tears in my ee;
Welcome now simmer and welcome my Willie,
The simmer to nature, my Willie to me.

Rest, ye wild storms, in the cave of your slumbers,
How your dread howling a lover alarms!
Wauken, ye breezes! row gently, ye billows!
And waft my dear laddie ance mair to my arms!

But oh, if he's faithless, and minds na his Nannie,
Flow still between us thou wide-roaring main!
May I never see it, may I never trow it,
But, dying, believe that my Willie's my ain!

The Soldier's Return. (360)

AIR—*The mill, mill O.*

WHEN wild war's deadly blast was blawn,
  And gentle peace returning,
Wi' mony a sweet babe fatherless,
  And mony a widow mourning:
I left the lines and tented field,
  Where lang I'd been a lodger,
My humble knapsack a' my wealth,
  A poor but honest sodger.

A leal, light heart was in my breast,
  My hand unstain'd wi' plunder:
And for fair Scotia, hame again,
  I cheery on did wander.
I thought upon the banks o' Coil,
  I thought upon my Nancy;
I thought upon the witching smile
  That caught my youthful fancy.

At length I reach'd the bonnie glen
  Where early life I sported;
I pass'd the mill, and trysting thorn,
  Where Nancy aft I courted:
Wha spied I but my ain dear maid
  Down by her mother's dwelling!
And turn'd me round to hide the flood
  That in my een was swelling.

Wi' alter'd voice, quoth I, "Sweet lass,
  Sweet as yon hawthorn's blossom,
Oh! happy, happy may he be,
  That's dearest to thy bosom!
My purse is light, I've far to gang,
  And fain would be thy lodger;
I've served my king and country lang—
  Take pity on a sodger!"

Sae wistfully she gaz'd on me,
  And lovelier was than ever;
Quo' she, "A sodger ance I loe'd,
  Forget him shall I never:
Our humble cot and hamely fare
  Ye freely shall partake o't;
That gallant badge, the dear cockade,
  Ye're welcome for the sake o't.

She gaz'd—she redden'd like a rose—
  Syne pale like ony lily;
She sank within my arms, and cried,
  "Art thou my ain dear Willie?"
"By Him who made yon sun and sky,
  By whom true love's regarded,
I am the man; and thus may still
  True lovers be rewarded.

The wars are o'er, and I'm come hame,
  And find thee still true-hearted!
Tho' poor in gear, we're rich in love,
  And mair we're ne'er be parted."
Quo' she, "My grandsire left me gowd,
  A mailen plenish'd fairly;
And come, my faithfu' sodger lad,
  Thou'rt welcome to it dearly."

For gold the merchant ploughs the main,
  The farmer ploughs the manor;
But glory is the sodger's prize,
  The sodger's wealth is honour.

The brave poor sodger ne'er despise,
  Nor count him as a stranger:
Remember he's his country's stay
  In day and hour of danger.

Blythe hae I been on yon Hill.

TUNE—*Liggeram Cosh.*

BLYTHE hae I been on yon hill,
  As the lambs before me;
Careless ilka thought and free,
  As the breeze flew o'er me:
Now nae longer sport and play,
  Mirth or sang can please me;
Lesley is sae fair and coy,
  Care and anguish seize me.

Heavy, heavy is the task,
  Hopeless love declaring:
Trembling, I dow nocht but glow'r,
  Sighing, dumb, despairing!
If she winna ease the thraws
  In my bosom swelling,
Underneath the grass-green sod,
  Soon maun be my dwelling.

Logan Braes. (361)

TUNE—*Logan Water.*

OH Logan, sweetly didst thou glide
That day I was my Willie's bride;
And years sinsyne hae o'er us run,
Like Logan to the simmer sun.
But now thy flow'ry banks appear
Like drumlie winter, dark and drear,
While my dear lad maun face his faes,
Far, far frae me and Logan braes.

Again the merry month o' May
Has made our hills and vallies gay;
The birds rejoice in leafy bowers,
The bees hum round the breathing flowers:
Blythe morning lifts his rosy eye,
And evening's tears are tears of joy:
My soul, delightless, a' surveys,
While Willie's far frae Logan braes.

Within yon milk-white hawthorn bush,
Amang her nestlings sits the thrush;
Her faithfu' mate will share her toil,
Or wi' his songs her cares beguile:
But I wi' my sweet nurslings here,
Nae mate to help, nae mate to cheer,
Pass widow'd nights and joyless days,
While Willie's far frae Logan braes.

Oh, wae upon you, men o' state,
That brethren rouse to deadly hate!
As ye make many a fond heart mourn,
Sae may it on your heads return!
How can your flinty hearts enjoy
The widow's tear, the orphan's cry?
But soon may peace bring happy days,
And Willie hame to Logan braes!

Oh, gin my Love were yon Red Rose! (362)

AIR—*Hughie Graham.*

OH, gin my love were yon red rose
  That grows upon the castle wa';
And I mysel a drap o' dew,
  Into her bonnie breast to fa'!

Oh there, beyond expression blest,
  I'd feast on beauty a' the night!
Seal'd on her silk-saft faulds to rest,
  Till fley'd awa by Phœbus' light.

Oh, were my love yon lilach fair,
  Wi' purple blossoms to the spring,
And I, a bird to shelter there,
  When wearied on my little wing—

How I wad mourn, when it was torn
  By autumn wild, and winter rude!
But I wad sing on wanton wing,
  When youthfu' May its bloom renew'd.

Bonnie Jean. (363)

THERE was a lass, and she was fair,
  At kirk and market to be seen;
When a' the fairest maids were met,
  The fairest maid was bonnie Jean.

And aye she wrought her mammie's wark,
  And aye she sang sae merrilie:
The blythest bird upon the bush
  Had ne'er a lighter heart than she,

But hawks will rob the tender joys
  That bless the little lintwhite's nest;
And frost will blight the fairest flowers;
  And love will break the soundest rest.

Young Robie was the brawest lad,
  The flower and pride of a' the glen;
And he had owsen, sheep, and kye,
  And wanton naigies nine or ten.

He gaed wi' Jeanie to the tryste,
  He danc'd wi Jeanie on the down;
And lang ere witless Jeanie wist,
  Her heart was tint, her peace was stown.

As in the bosom o' the stream
  The moonbeam dwells at dewy e'en;
So trembling, pure, was tender love
  Within the breast o' bonnie Jean.

And now she works her mammie's wark,
  And aye she sighs wi' care and pain;
Yet wist na what her ail might be,
  Or what wad mak her weel again.

But did na Jeanie's heart loup light,
  And did na joy blink in her ee,
As Robie tauld a tale o' love
  Ae e'enin on the lily lea?

The sun was sinking in the west,
  The birds sang sweet in ilka grove;
His cheek to hers he fondly prest,
  And whisper'd thus his tale o' love:

"Oh Jeanie fair, I loe thee dear;
  Oh, canst thou think to fancy me;
Or wilt thou leave thy mammie's cot,
  And learn to tent the farms wi' me?

At barn or byre thou shalt na drudge,
  Or naething else to trouble thee;
But stray amang the heather-bells,
  And tent the waving corn wi' me."

Now what could artless Jeanie do?
  She had nae will to say him na;
At length she blush'd a sweet consent,
  And love was aye between them twa.

Meg o' the Mill.

AIR—*Oh Bonnie Lass will you lie in a Barrack?*

OH ken ye wha Meg o' the Mill has gotten?
And ken ye what Meg o' the Mill has gotten?
She has gotten a coof wi' a claut o' siller,
And broken the heart o' the barley Miller.

The Miller was strappin', the Miller was ruddy;
A heart like a lord, and a hue like a lady:
The Laird was a widdiefu', bleerit knurl;—
She's left the guidfellow and taen the churl.

The Miller he hecht her a heart leal and loving;
The Laird did address her wi' matter more moving,
A fine pacing horse wi' a clear chained bridle,
A whip by her side, and a bonnie side-saddle.

Oh wae on the siller, it is sae prevailing!
And wae on the love that is fixed on a mailen!
A tocher's nae word in a true lover's parle,
But gie me my love, and a fig for the warl!

Open the Door to Me, oh!

"OH! open the door, some pity to show,
  Oh! open the door to me, oh!
Tho' thou hast been false, I'll ever prove true,
  Oh! open the door to me, oh!

Cauld is the blast upon my pale cheek,
  But caulder thy love for me, oh;
The frost that freezes the life at my heart,
  Is nought to my pains frae thee, oh!

The wan moon is setting behind the white wave,
  And time is setting with me, oh!
False friends, false love, farewell! for mair
  I'll ne'er trouble them, nor thee, oh!"

She has open'd the door, she has open'd it wide;
  She sees his pale corse on the plain, oh!
"My true love!" she cried, and sank down by his side,
  Never to rise again, oh!

Young Jessie.

TUNE—*Bonnie Dundee.*

TRUE hearted was he, the sad swain o' the Yarrow,
  And fair are the maids on the banks o' the Ayr,
But by the sweet side o' the Nith's winding river,
  Are lovers as faithful, and maidens as fair:
To equal young Jessie seek Scotland all over;
  To equal young Jessie you seek it in vain:
Grace, beauty, and elegance fetter her lover,
  And maidenly modesty fixes the chain.

Oh, fresh is the rose in the gay dewy morning,
  And sweet is the lily at evening close;
But in the fair presence o' lovely young Jessie
  Unseen is the lily, unheeded the rose.
Love sits in her smile, a wizard ensnaring:
  Enthron'd in her een he delivers his law;
And still to her charms she alone is a stranger—
  Her modest demeanour's the jewel of a'!

Adown winding Nith I did Wander.

TUNE—*The Mucking o' Geordie's Byre.*

ADOWN winding Nith I did wander,
  To mark the sweet flowers as they spring
Adown winding Nith I did wander,
  Of Phillis to muse and to sing.

CHORUS.

Awa wi' your belles and your beauties,
  They never wi' her can compare;
Whaever has met wi' my Phillis,
  Has met wi' the queen o' the fair.

The daisy amus'd my fond fancy,
So artless, so simple, so wild;
Thou emblem, said I, o' my Phillis,
For she is simplicity's child.

The rose-bud's the blush o' my charmer,
Her sweet balmy lip when 'tis prest:
How fair and how pure is the lily,
But fairer and purer her breast.

Yon knot of gay flowers in the arbour,
They ne'er wi' my Phillis can vie:
Her breath is the breath o' the woodbine,
It's dew-drop o' diamond her eye.

Her voice is the song of the morning,
That wakes thro' the green-spreading grove,
When Phœbus peeps over the mountains,
On music, and pleasure, and love.

But, beauty, how frail and how fleeting—
The bloom of a fine summer's day!
While worth in the mind o' my Phillis
Will flourish without a decay.

Had I a Cave. (364)

TUNE—*Robin Adair.*

HAD I a cave on some wild distant shore,
Where the winds howl to the waves' dashing roar;
There would I weep my woes,
There seek my lost repose,
Till grief my eyes should close,
Ne'er to wake more!

Falsest of womankind, canst thou declare,
All thy fond-plighted vows—fleeting as air!
To thy new lover hie,
Laugh o'er thy perjury;
Then in thy bosom try
What peace is there!

Phillis the Fair. (365)

TUNE—*Robin Adair.*

WHILE larks with the wing,
Fann'd the pure air,
Tasting the breathing spring,
Forth I did fare;
Gay the sun's golden eye,
Peep'd o'er the mountains high;
Such thy morn! did I cry,
Phillis the fair.

In each bird's careless song,
Glad did I share;
While yon wild flowers among,
Chance led me there;
Sweet to the opening day,
Rosebuds bent the dewy spray;
Such thy bloom! did I say,
Phillis the fair.

Down in a shady walk,
Doves cooing were;
I mark'd the cruel hawk
Caught in a snare;
So kind may fortune be,
Such make his destiny,
He who would injure thee,
Phillis the fair.

By Allan Stream I chanc'd to Rove.

TUNE—*Allan Water.*

By Allan stream I chanc'd to rove,
While Phœbus sank beyond Benleddi; (366)
The winds were whispering thro' the grove,
The yellow corn was waving ready:
I listen'd to a lover's sang,
And thought on youthfu' pleasures mony;
And aye the wild-wood echoes rang—
Oh, dearly do I love thee, Annie!

Oh, happy be the woodbine bower,
Nae nightly bogle make it eerie;
Nor ever sorrow stain the hour,
The place and time I met my dearie!
Her head upon my throbbing breast,
She, sinking, said, "I'm thine for ever!"
While mony a kiss the seal imprest,
The sacred vow, we ne'er should sever.

The haunt o' spring's the primrose brae,
The simmer joys the flocks to follow;
How cheery thro' her shortening day,
Is autumn in her weeds o' yellow!
But can they melt the glowing heart,
Or chain the soul in speechless pleasure?
Or thro' each nerve the rapture dart,
Like meeting her, our bosom's treasure?

Come let me take Thee to my Breast.

AIR—*Cauld Kail.*

COME, let me take thee to my breast,
And pledge we ne'er shall sunder;
And I shall spurn as vilest dust
The warld's wealth and grandeur:
And do I hear my Jeanie own
That equal transports move her?
I ask for dearest life alone
That I may live to love her.

Thus in my arms, wi' all thy charms,
I clasp my countless treasure;
I'll seek nae mair o' heaven to share,
Than sic a moment's pleasure:
And by thy een sae bonnie blue,
I swear I'm thine for ever!
And on thy lips I seal my vow,
And break it shall I never!

Whistle and I'll Come to you, my Lad.

TUNE—*Whistle and I'll come to you, my lad.*

OH whistle and I'll come to you, my lad,
Oh whistle and I'll come to you, my lad;
Tho' father and mither and a' should gae mad,
Oh whistle and I'll come to you, my lad.

But warily tent, when ye come to court me,
And come na unless the back-yett be a-jee;
Syne up the back-stile, and let naebody see,
And come as ye were na comin' to me.
And come, &c.

At kirk, or at market, whene'er ye meet me,
Gang by me as tho' that ye car'd nae a flie;
But steal me a blink o' your bonnie black ee,
Yet look as ye were na lookin' at me.
Yet look, &c.

Aye vow and protest that ye care na for me,
And whiles ye may lightly my beauty a wee;
But court nae anither, tho' jokin' ye be,
For fear that she wile your fancy frae me.
For fear, &c.

Dainty Davie. (367)

TUNE—*Dainty Davie.*

NOW rosy May comes in wi' flowers,
To deck her gay, green spreading bowers;
And now come in my happy hours,
To wander wi' my Davie.

CHORUS.

Meet me on the warlock knowe,
Dainty Davie, dainty Davie;
There I'll spend the day wi' you,
My ain dear dainty Davie.

The crystal waters round us fa',
The merry birds are lovers a',
The scented breezes round us blaw.
A-wandering wi' my Davie.

When purple morning starts the hare,
To steal upon her early fare,
Then thro' the dews I will repair,
To meet my faithfu' Davie.

When day, expiring in the west,
The curtain draws o' nature's rest,
I flee to his arms I loe best,
And that's my ain dear Davie.

Bruce's Address. (368)

TUNE—*Hey Tuttie Taittie.*

SCOTS, wha hae wi' Wallace bled,
Scots, wham Bruce has aften led;
Welcome to your gory bed,
Or to victorie!

Now's the day, and now's the hour;
See the front o' battle lour;
See approach proud Edward's power—
Chains and slavery!

Wha will be a traitor knave?
Wha can fill a coward's grave?
Wha sae base as be a slave?
Let him turn and flee!

Wha for Scotland's king and law
Freedom's sword will strongly draw,
Freeman stand, or Freeman fa',
Let him follow me!

By oppression's woes and pains!
By your sons in servile chains!
We will drain our dearest veins,
But they shall be free!

Lay the proud usurpers low!
Tyrants fall in every foe!
Liberty's in every blow!—
Let us do, or die!

Behold the Hour. (369)

TUNE—*Oran Gaoil.*

BEHOLD the hour, the boat arrive;
Thou goest, thou darling of my heart!
Sever'd from thee, can I survive?
But fate has will'd, and we must part.
I'll often greet this surging swell,
Yon distant isle will often hail:
"E'en here I took the last farewell;
There latest mark'd her vanish'd sail."

Along the solitary shore,
While flitting sea-fowl round me cry,
Across the rolling, dashing roar,
I'll westward turn my wistful eye;
Happy thou Indian grove, I'll say,
Where now my Nancy's path may be!
While thro' thy sweets she loves to stray,
Oh, tell me, does she muse on me!

Auld Lang Syne.

SHOULD auld acquaintance be forgot,
And never brought to mind?
Should auld acquaintance be forgot,
And days o' lang syne?

CHORUS.

For auld lang syne, my dear,
For auld lang syne,
We'll tak a cup o' kindness yet,
For auld lang syne.

We twa hae run about the braes,
And pu'd the gowans fine;
But we've wandered mony a weary foot,
Sin auld lang syne.

We twa hae paidl't i' the burn,
Frae mornin' sun till dine;
But seas between us braid hae roar'd,
Sin auld lang syne.

And here's a hand, my trusty fiere,
And gie's a hand o' thine;
And we'll tak a right guid willie-waught,
For auld lang syne.

And surely ye'll be your pint stoup,
And surely I'll be mine;
And we'll tak a cup o' kindness yet
For auld lang syne,

Where are the Joys?

TUNE—*Saw ye my father?*

WHERE are the joys I have met in the morning,
That danc'd to the lark's early song?
Where is the peace that awaited my wand'ring,
At evening the wild woods among?

No more a-winding the course of yon river,
And marking sweet flow'rets so fair:
No more I trace the light footsteps of pleasure,
But sorrow and sad sighing care.

Is it that summer's forsaken our vallies,
And grim surly winter is near?
No, no! the bees humming round the gay roses,
Proclaim it the pride of the year.

Fain would I hide what I fear to discover,
Yet long, long too well have I known,
All that has caused this wreck in my bosom,
Is Jenny, fair Jenny alone.

Time cannot aid me, my griefs are immortal,
Nor hope dare a comfort bestow:
Come then, enamour'd and fond of my anguish,
Enjoyment I'll seek in my woe.

Thou hast Left me Ever.

TUNE—*Fee him, Father.*

THOU hast left me ever, Jamie, thou hast left me ever,
Thou hast left me ever, Jamie, thou hast left [me ever;
Aften hast thou vow'd that death only should us sever,
Now thou'st left thy lass for aye—I maun see thee never, Jamie,
I'll see thee never.

Thou hast me forsaken, Jamie, thou hast me forsaken,
Thou hast me forsaken, Jamie, thou hast me [forsaken;
Thou canst love anither jo, while my heart is breaking:
Soon my weary een I'll close—never mair to waken, Jamie,
Ne'er mair to waken.

Deluded Swain, the Pleasure.

TUNE—*The Collier's Bonnie Lassie.*

DELUDED swain, the pleasure
The fickle Fair can give thee,
Is but a fairy treasure—
Thy hopes will soon deceive thee.

The billows on the ocean,
The breezes idly roaming,
The clouds' uncertain motion,
They are but types of woman.

Oh! art thou not ashamed
To doat upon a feature?
If man thou would'st be named,
Despise the silly creature.

Go, find an honest fellow!
Good claret set before thee:
Hold on till thou art mellow,
And then to bed in glory.

Thine I am, my Faithful Fair.

TUNE—*Liggeram Cosh* [*the Quaker's wife*].

THINE am I, my faithful fair,
Thine, my lovely Nancy;
Ev'ry pulse along my veins,
Ev'ry roving fancy.

To thy bosom lay my heart,
There to throb and languish:
Tho' despair had wrung its core,
That would heal its anguish.

Take away these rosy lips,
Rich with balmy treasure:
Turn away thine eyes of love,
Lest I die with pleasure.

What is life when wanting love?
Night without a morning:
Love's the cloudless summer sun,
Nature gay adorning.

My Spouse, Nancy.

TUNE—*My Jo Janet.*

"HUSBAND, husband, cease your strife,
Nor longer idly rave, sir;
Tho' I am your wedded wife,
Yet I am not your slave, sir."

"One of two must still obey,
Nancy, Nancy;
Is it man, or woman, say,
My spouse, Nancy?"

"If 'tis still the lordly word,
Service and obedience;
I'll desert my sov'reign lord,
And so good-bye allegiance!"

"Sad will I be, so bereft,
Nancy, Nancy,
Yet I'll try to make a shift,
My spouse, Nancy."

"My poor heart then break it must,
My last hour I'm near it:
When you lay me in the dust,
Think, think how you will bear it."

"I will hope and trust in heaven,
Nancy, Nancy,
Strength to bear it will be given,
My spouse, Nancy."

"Well, sir, from the silent dead,
Still I'll try to daunt you;
Ever round your midnight bed
Horrid sprites shall haunt you."

"I'll wed another like my dear,
Nancy, Nancy;
Then all hell will fly for fear,
My spouse, Nancy."

The Banks of Cree.

TUNE—*The Banks of Cree.*

HERE is the glen, and here the bower,
All underneath the birchen shade;
The village-bell has toll'd the hour,
Oh, what can stay my lovely maid?

'Tis not Maria's whispering call;
'Tis but the balmy-breathing gale,
Mix'd with some warbler's dying fall,
The dewy stars of eve to hail.

It is Maria's voice I hear!—
So calls the woodlark in the grove,
His little faithful mate to cheer!
At once 'tis music and 'tis love.

And art thou come?—and art thou true?
Oh welcome, dear to love and me
And let us all our vows renew,
Along the flowery banks of Cree.

On the Seas and Far Away.

TUNE—*O'er the hills, &c.*

How can my poor heart be glad,
When absent from my sailor lad?
How can I the thought forego,
He's on the seas to meet the foe?
Let me wander, let me rove,
Still my heart is with my love;
Nightly dreams and thoughts by day
Are with him that's far away.

CHORUS.

On the seas and far away,
On stormy seas and far away;
Nightly dreams and thoughts by day
Are aye with him that's far away.

When in summer's noon I faint,
As weary flocks around me pant,
Haply in the scorching sun
My sailor's thund'ring at his gun;
Bullets spare my only joy!
Bullets, spare my darling boy!
Fate, do with me what you may,
Spare but him that's far away!

At the starless midnight hour,
When winter rules with boundless power;
As the storms the forest tear,
And thunders rend the howling air,
Listening to the doubling roar,
Surging on the rocky shore,
All I can—I weep and pray,
For his weal that's far away.

Peace, thy olive wand extend,
And bid wild war his ravage end,
Man with brother man to meet,
And as a brother kindly greet:
Then may Heaven with prosperous gales,
Fill my sailor's welcome sails,
To my arms their charge convey,
My dear lad that's far away.

Ca' the Yowes to the Knowes.

CHORUS.

Ca' the yowes to the knowes,
Ca' them where the heather grows,
Ca' them where the burnie rows,
My bonnie dearie.

Hark the mavis' evening sang
Sounding Clouden's woods amang;
Then a-faulding let us gang,
My bonnie dearie.

We'll gae down by Clouden side
Thro' the hazels spreading wide,
O'er the waves that sweetly glide
To the moon sae clearly.

Yonder Clouden's silent towers,
Where at moonshine, midnight hours,
O'er the dewy bending flowers,
Fairies dance sae cheery.

Ghaist nor bogle shalt thou fear;
Thou'rt to love and heaven sae dear,
Nocht of ill may come thee near,
My bonnie dearie.

Fair and lovely as thou art,
Thou hast stown my very heart;
I can die—but canna part,
My bonnie dearie.

While waters wimple to the sea;
While day blinks in the lift sae hie;
Till clay-cauld death shall blin' my ee,
Ye shall be my dearie.

She says she Loes me Best of A'.

TUNE—*Onagh's Lock.*

Sae flaxen were her ringlets,
Her eyebrows of a darker hue,
Bewitchingly o'er-arching
Twa laughing een o' bonnie blue.
Her smiling, sae wiling,
Would make a wretch forget his woe:
What pleasure, what treasure,
Unto these rosy lips to grow:
Such was my Chloris' bonnie face,
When first her bonnie face I saw,
And aye my Chloris' dearest charm,
She says she loes me best of a'.

Like harmony her motion;
Her pretty ancle is a spy
Betraying fair proportion,
Wad make a saint forget the sky.
Sae warming, sae charming,
Her faultless form and graceful air;
Ilk feature—auld nature
Declared that she could do nae mair.
Hers are the willing chains o' love,
By conquering beauty's sovereign law;
And aye my Chloris' dearest charm,
She says she loes me best of a'.

Let others love the city,
And gaudy show at sunny noon;
Gie me the lonely valley,
The dewy eve, and rising moon
Fair beaming, and streaming,
Her silver light the boughs amang;
While falling, recalling,
The amorous thrush concludes his sang
There, dearest Chloris, wilt thou rove
By wimpling burn and leafy shaw,
And hear my vows o' truth and love,
And say thou loes me best of a'!

Saw ye my Philly?

TUNE—*When she cam ben she bobbit.*

Oh, saw ye my dear, my Philly?
Oh, saw ye my dear, my Philly?
She's down i' the grove, she's wi' a new love
She winna come hame to her Willie.

What says she, my dearest, my Philly?
What says she, my dearest, my Philly?
She lets thee to wit that she has thee forgot
And for ever disowns thee, her Willy.

Oh, had I ne'er seen thee, my Philly!
Oh, had I ne'er seen thee, my Philly!
As light as the air, and fause as thou's fair,
Thou's broken the heart o' thy Willy.

How Long and Dreary is the Night?

(370)

TUNE—*Cauld kail in Aberdeen.*

How long and dreary is the night
When I am frae my dearie?
I restless lie frae e'en to morn,
Tho' I we're ne'er sae weary.

CHORUS.

For oh! her lanely nights are lang,
And oh! her dreams are eerie,
And oh! her widow'd heart is sair,
That's absent frae her dearie.

When I think on the lightsome days
I spent wi' thee, my dearie,
And now what seas between us roar,
How can I be but eerie?
For oh! &c.

How slow ye move, ye heavy hours!
The joyless day, how dreary!
It was na sae ye glinted by,
When I was wi' my dearie.
For oh! &c.

AULD ROBIN GRAY.

My father cou'dna work—my mother cou'dna spin;
I toil'd day and night, but their bread I cou'dna win,

Let not Woman e'er Complain.

TUNE—*Duncan Gray.*

LET not woman e'er complain
Of inconstancy in love;
Let not woman e'er complain
Fickle man is apt to rove.

Look abroad through Nature's range,
Nature's mighty law is change;
Ladies, would it not be strange,
Man should then a monster prove?

Mark the winds, and mark the skies;
Ocean's ebb, and ocean's flow:
Sun and moon but set to rise,
Round and round the seasons go.

Why then ask of silly man
To oppose great Nature's plan?
We'll be constant while we can—
You can be no more, you know.

Sleep'st Thou, or Wak'st Thou? (371)

TUNE—*Deil tak the wars.*

SLEEP'ST thou, or wak'st thou, fairest crea-
Rosy morn now lifts his eye, [ture?
Numbering ilka bud, which Nature
Waters wi' the tears o' joy:
Now thro' the leafy woods,
And by the reeking floods,
Wild Nature's tenants, freely, gladly stray:
The lintwhite in his bower
Chants o'er the breathing flower,
The lav'rock to the sky
Ascends wi' sangs o' joy,
While the sun and thou arise to bless the day.
Phœbus gilding the brow o' morning,
Banishes ilk darksome shade,
Nature gladd'ning and adorning;
Such to me my lovely maid.
When absent from my fair,
The murky shades o' care
With starless gloom o'ercast my sullen sky;
But when in beauty's light,
She meets my ravish'd sight,
When through my very heart
Her beaming glories dart,
'Tis then I wake to life, to light, and joy.

My Chloris, mark how Green the Groves.

TUNE—*My lodging is on the cold ground.*

MY Chloris, mark how green the groves,
The primrose banks how fair;
The balmy gales awake the flowers,
And wave thy flaxen hair.

The lav'rock shuns the palace gay,
And o'er the cottage sings:
For nature smiles as sweet, I ween,
To shepherds as to kings.

Let minstrels sweep the skilfu' string
In lordly lighted ha':
The shepherd stops his simple reed,
Blythe, in the birken shaw.

The princely revel may survey
Our rustic dance wi' scorn;
But are their hearts as light as ours
Beneath the milk-white thorn?

The shepherd, in the flowery glen,
In shepherd's phrase will woo:
The courtier tells a finer tale,
But is his heart as true?

These wild-wood flowers I've pu'd, to deck
That spotless breast o' thine:
The courtier's gems may witness love—
But 'tis na love like mine.

It was the Charming Month of May. (372)

TUNE—*Dainty Davie.*

IT was the charming month of May,
When all the flow'rs were fresh and gay,
One morning, by the break of day,
The youthful, charming Chloe,—
From peaceful slumber she arose,
Girt on her mantle and her hose,
And o'er the flow'ry mead she goes,—
The youthful, charming Chloe.

CHORUS.

Lovely was she by the dawn,
Youthful Chloe, charming Chloe.
Tripping o'er the pearly lawn,
The youthful, charming Chloe.

The feather'd people, you might see
Perch'd all around on every tree,
In notes of sweetest melody,
They hail the charming Chloe;
Till, painting gay the eastern skies,
The glorious sun began to rise,
Out-rivall'd by the radiant eyes
Of youthful, charming Chloe.
Lovely was she, &c.

Farewell, thou Stream that Winding Flows.

TUNE—*Nancy's to the greenwood gane.*

FAREWELL, thou stream that winding flows
Around Eliza's dwelling!
Oh mem'ry! spare the cruel throes
Within my bosom swelling:

Condemn'd to drag a hopeless chain,
  And yet in secret languish,
To feel a fire in ev'ry vein,
  Nor dare disclose my anguish.

Love's veriest wretch, unseen, unknown,
  I fain my griefs would cover:
The bursting sigh, th' unweeting groan,
  Betray the hapless lover.
I know thou doom'st me to despair,
  Nor wilt, nor canst relieve me;
But, oh! Eliza, hear one prayer,
  For pity's sake, forgive me!

The music of thy voice I heard,
  Nor wist while it enslaved me;
I saw thine eyes, yet nothing fear'd,
  Till fears no more had sav'd me.
Th' unwary sailor thus aghast,
  The wheeling torrent viewing,
'Mid circling horrors sinks at last
  In overwhelming ruin.

Lassie wi' the lint-white Locks.

TUNE—*Rothiemurche's Rant.*

CHORUS.

  LASSIE wi' the lint-white locks,
    Bonnie lassie, artless lassie,
  Wilt thou wi' me tent the flocks,
    Wilt thou be my dearie O?

Now Nature cleeds the flowery lea,
And a' is young and sweet like thee:
Oh, wilt thou share its joy wi' me,
  And say thou'lt be my dearie O?
    Lassie wi' the lint-white locks, &c.

And when the welcome simmer-shower
Has cheer'd ilk drooping little flower,
We'll to the breathing woodbine bower
  At sultry noon, my dearie O.
    Lassie wi' the lint-white locks, &c.

When Cynthia lights, wi' silver ray,
The weary shearer's hameward way,
Thro' yellow waving fields we'll stray,
  And talk o' love, my dearie O.
    Lassie wi' the lint-white locks, &c.

And when the howling wintry blast
Disturbs my lassie's midnight rest,
Enclasped to my faithful breast,
  I'll comfort thee, my dearie O.
    Lassie wi' the lint-white locks, &c.

Philly and Willy.

TUNE—*The Sow's Tail.*

WILLY.

OH Philly, happy be that day
When roving through the gather'd hay,
My youthfu' heart was stown away,
  And by thy charms, my Philly.

PHILLY.

Oh Willy, aye I bless the grove
Where first I own'd my maiden love,
Whilst thou didst pledge the powers above
  To be my ain dear Willy.

WILLY.

As songsters of the early year
Are ilka day mair sweet to hear,
So ilka day to me mair dear
  And charming is my Philly.

PHILLY.

As on the briar the budding rose
Still richer breathes and fairer blows,
So in my tender bosom grows
  The love I bear my Willy.

WILLY.

The milder sun and bluer sky,
That crown my harvest cares wi' joy,
Were ne'er sae welcome to my eye
  As is a sight o' Philly.

PHILLY.

The little swallow's wanton wing,
Tho' wafting o'er the flowery spring,
Did ne'er to me sic tidings bring,
  As meeting o' my Willy.

WILLY.

The bee that thro' the sunny hour
Sips nectar in the opening flower,
Compar'd wi' my delight is poor,
  Upon the lips o' Philly.

PHILLY.

The woodbine in the dewy weet,
When evening shades in silence meet,
Is nocht sae fragrant or sae sweet
  As is a kiss o' Willy.

WILLY.

Let fortune's wheel at random rin,
And fools may tyne, and knaves may win;
My thoughts are a' bound up in ane,
  And that's my ane dear Philly.

PHILLY.

What's a' the joys that gowd can gie?
I care nae wealth a single flie;
The lad I love's the lad for me,
  And that's my ain dear Willy.

Contented wi' Little.

TUNE—*Lumps o' Pudding.*

CONTENTED wi' little, and cantie wi' mair,
Whene'er I forgather wi' sorrow and care,
I gie them a skelp as they're creepin' alang,
Wi' a cog o' guid swats, and an auld Scottish
    sang.

I whiles claw the elbow o' troublesom thought;
But man is a sodger, and life is a faught:
My mirth and good humour are coin in my pouch,
And my freedom's my lairdship nae monarch dare touch.

A townmond o' trouble, should that be my fa',
A night o' guid fellowship sowthers it a':
When at the blythe end of our journey at last,
Wha the deil ever thinks o' the road he has past?

Blind chance, let her snapper and stoyte on her way:
Be't to me, be't frae me, e'en let the jade gae:
Come ease, or come travail: come pleasure, or pain,
My warst word is—"Welcome, and welcome again!"

Can'st thou Leave me Thus, my Katy.

(373)

TUNE—*Roy's Wife.*

CHORUS.

CANST thou leave me thus, my Katy?
Canst thou leave me thus, my Katy?
Well thou know'st my aching heart,
And canst thou leave me thus for pity?

Is this thy plighted, fond regard,
Thus cruelly to part, my Katy?
Is this thy faithful swain's reward—
An aching, broken heart, my Katy?

Farewell! and ne'er such sorrows tear
That fickle heart of thine, my Katy!
Thou may'st find those will love thee dear—
But not a love like mine, my Katy.

For a' That, and a' That.

Is there, for honest poverty,
That hangs his head, and a' that?
The coward slave we pass him by,
We dare be poor for a' that!
For a' that, and a' that,
Our toil's obscure, and a' that,
The rank is but the guinea's stamp, (374)
The man's the goud for a' that.

What tho' on hamely fare we dine,
Wear hoddin grey, and a' that;
Gie fools their silks, and knaves their wine,
A man's a man for a' that;
For a' that, and a' that,
Their tinsel show, and a' that;
The honest man, though e'er sae poor,
Is king o' men for a' that.

Ye see yon birkie, ca'd a lord,
Wha struts, and stares, and a' that;
Tho' hundreds worship at his word,
He's but a coof for a' that:
For a' that, and a' that,
His riband, star, and a' that,
The man of independent mind,
He looks and laughs at a' that.

A prince can mak a belted knight,
A marquis, duke, and a' that:
But an honest man's aboon his might,
Guid faith he maunna fa' that.
For a' that, and a' that,
Their dignities, and a' that,
The pith o' sense, and pride o' worth,
Are higher ranks than a' that.

Then let us pray that come it may,
As come it will for a' that,
That sense and worth, o'er a' the earth,
May bear the gree, and a' that.
For a' that, and a' that,
It's coming yet, for a' that,
That man to man, the warld o'er,
Shall brothers be for a' that.

My Nannie's Awa.

TUNE—*There'll never be peace, &c.*

Now in her green mantle blythe nature arrays,
And listens the lambkins that bleat o'er the braes,
While birds warble welcome in ilka green shaw;
But to me it's delightless—my Nannie's awa.

The snaw-drap and primrose our woodlands adorn,
And violets bathe in the weet o' the morn;
They pain my sad bosom, sae sweetly they blaw,
They mind me o' Nannie—and Nannie's awa.

Thou lav'rock that springs frae the dews of the lawn,
The shepherd to warn o' the grey-breaking dawn,
And thou mellow mavis that hails the night-fa',
Give over for pity—my Nannie's awa.

Come, autumn, sae pensive, in yellow and grey,
And soothe me wi' tidings o' nature's decay;
The dark, dreary winter, and wild-driving snaw,
Alane can delight me—now Nannie's awa.

Craigieburn Wood. (375)

TUNE—*Craigieburn wood.*

SWEET fa's the eve on Craigieburn,
  And blythe awakes the morrow;
But a' the pride o' spring's return
  Can yield me nocht but sorrow.

I see the flowers and spreading trees,
  I hear the wild birds singing;
But what a weary wight can please,
  And care his bosom wringing?

Fain, fain would I my griefs impart,
  Yet dare na for your anger;
But secret love will break my heart,
  If I conceal it langer.

If thou refuse to pity me,
  If thou shalt love anither,
When yon green leaves fade frae the tree,
  Around my grave they'll wither. (376)

Oh Lassie art thou Sleeping yet?

TUNE—*Let me in this ane Night.*

OH lassie art thou sleeping yet?
Or art thou wakin', I would wit?
For love has bound me hand and foot,
  And I would fain be in, jo.

CHORUS.

Oh let me in this ane night,
  This ane, ane, ane night;
For pity's sake this ane night,
  Oh rise and let me in, jo!

Thou hear'st the winter wind and weet,
Nae star blinks thro' the driving sleet;
Tak pity on my weary feet,
  And shield me frae the rain, jo.

The bitter blast that round me blaws
Unheeded howls, unheeded fa's;
The cauldness o' thy heart's the cause
  Of a' my grief and pain, jo.

Reply to the Foregoing.

OH tell na me o' wind and rain,
Upbraid na me wi' cauld disdain;
Gae back the gait ye cam again,
  I winna let you in, jo!

CHORUS.

I tell you now this ane night,
  This ane, ane, ane night;
And ance for a' this ane night,
  I winna let you in, jo.

The snellest blast, at mirkest hours,
That round the pathless wand'rer pours,
Is nocht to what poor she endures,
  That's trusted faithless man, jo.

The sweetest flower that deck'd the mead,
Now trodden like the vilest weed;
Let simple maid the lesson read,
  The weird may be her ain, jo.

The bird that charm'd his summer- day,
Is now the cruel fowler's prey;
Let witless, trusting, woman say
  How aft her fate's the same, jo.

Address to the Woodlark.

TUNE—*Where'll bonnie Ann lie?* or, *Loch-Eroch Side.*

OH stay, sweet warbling wood-lark, stay,
Nor quit for me the trembling spray,
A hapless lover courts thy lay,
  Thy soothing, fond complaining.

Again, again that tender part,
That I may catch thy melting art:
For surely that wad touch her heart,
  Wha kills me wi' disdaining.

Say, was thy little mate unkind,
And heard thee as the careless wind?
Oh! nocht but love and sorrow join'd,
  Sic notes o' woe could wauken.

Thou tells o' never-ending care:
O' speechless grief, and dark despair;
For pity's sake, sweet bird, nae mair,
  Or my poor heart is broken!

On Chloris being Ill.

TUNE—*Aye wakin O.*

CHORUS.

LONG, long the night,
  Heavy comes the morrow,
While my soul's delight
  Is on her bed of sorrow.

Can I cease to care,
  Can I cease to languish,
While my darling fair
  Is on the couch of anguish?

Every hope is fled,
  Every fear is terror;
Slumber even I dread,
  Every dream is horror,

Hear me, Pow'rs divine!
Oh! in pity hear me!
Take aught else of mine,
But my Chloris spare me!

Their Groves o' Sweet Myrtle.

TUNE—*Humours of Glen.*

THEIR groves o' sweet myrtle let foreign lands reckon, [perfume;
Where bright-beaming summers exalt the
Far dearer to me yon lone glen o' green breckan, [broom.
Wi' the burn stealing under the lang yellow

Far dearer to me are yon humble broom bowers, [unseen:
Where the blue-bell and gowan lurk lowly
For there, lightly tripping amang the wild flowers, [Jean.
A-listening the linnet, aft wanders my

Tho' rich is the breeze in their gay sunny vallies,
And cauld Caledonia's blast on the wave;
Their sweet-scented woodlands that skirt the proud palace, [and slave!
What are they?—the haunt of the tyrant

The slave's spicy forests, and gold-bubbling fountains,
The brave Caledonian views wi' disdain;
He wanders as free as the winds of his mountains, [his Jean!
Save love's willing fetters—the chains o'

How Cruel are the Parents.

ALTERED FROM AN OLD ENGLISH SONG.

TUNE—*John Anderson my Jo.*

How cruel are the parents,
Who riches only prize:
And to the wealthy booby,
Poor woman sacrifice!
Meanwhile the hapless daughter
Has but a choice of strife;—
To shun a tyrant father's hate,
Become a wretched wife.

The rav'ning hawk pursuing,
The trembling dove thus flies,
To shun impelling ruin
Awhile her pinion tries:
Till of escape despairing,
No shelter or retreat,
She trusts the ruthless falconer,
And drops beneath his feet.

'Twas na her Bonnie Blue Ee was my Ruin.

TUNE—*Laddie, lie near me.*

'TWAS na her bonnie blue ee was my ruin;
Fair tho' she be, that was ne'er my undoing:
'Twas the dear smile when naebody did mind us, [o' kindness.
'Twas the bewitching, sweet, stown glance

Sair do I fear that to hope is denied me,
Sair do I fear that despair maun abide me;
But tho' fell fortune should fate us to sever,
Queen shall she be in my bosom for ever.

Mary, I'm thine wi' a passion sincerest,
And thou hast plighted me love the dearest!
And thou'rt the angel that never can alter,
Sooner the sun in his motion would falter.

Mark yon Pomp of Costly Fashion.

TUNE—*Deil tak the Wars.*

MARK yonder pomp of costly fashion,
Round the wealthy, titled bride:
But when compar'd with real passion,
Poor is all that princely pride.
What are the showy treasures?
What are the noisy pleasures?
The gay gaudy glare of vanity and art:
The polish'd jewel's blaze
May draw the wond'ring gaze,
And courtly grandeur bright
The fancy may delight,
But never, never can come near the heart.

But did you see my dearest Chloris,
In simplicity's array;
Lovely as yonder sweet op'ning flower is,
Shrinking from the gaze of day.
Oh then the heart alarming,
And all resistless charming,
In Love's delightful fetters she chains the willing soul!
Ambition would disown
The world's imperial crown,
Even Avarice would deny
His worshipp'd deity,
And feel thro' ev'ry vein Love's raptures roll.

Oh this is no my Ain Lassie.

TUNE—*This is no my ain House.*

CHORUS.

OH this is no my ain lassie,
Fair tho' the lassie be!
Oh weel ken I my ain lassie,
Kind love is in her ee.

I see a form, I see a face,
Ye weel may wi' the fairest place:
It wants, to me, the witching grace,
  The kind love that's in her ee.

She's bonnie, blooming, straight, and tall,
And lang has had my heart in thrall;
And aye it charms my very saul,
  The kind love that's in her ee.

A thief sae pawkie is my Jean,
To steal a blink, by a' unseen;
But gleg as light are lovers' een,
  When kind love is in the ee.

It may escape the courtly sparks,
It may escape the learned clerks;
But weel the watching lover marks
  The kind love that's in her ee.

Now Spring has Clad the Grove in Green.

(377)

Now spring has clad the grove in green,
  And strew'd the lea wi' flowers:
The furrow'd, waving corn is seen
  Rejoice in fostering showers;
While ilka thing in nature join
  Their sorrows to forego,
Oh why thus all alone are mine
  The weary steps of woe!

The trout within yon wimpling burn
  Glides swift—a silver dart;
And safe beneath the shady thorn
  Defies the angler's art.
My life was ance that careless stream,
  That wanton trout was I;
But love, wi' unrelenting beam,
  Has scorch'd my fountains dry.

The little flow'ret's peaceful lot,
  In yonder cliff that grows,
Which, save the linnet's flight, I wot,
  Nae ruder visit knows,
Was mine; till love has o'er me past,
  And blighted a' my bloom,
And now beneath the with'ring blast
  My youth and joy consume.

The waken'd lav'rock warbling springs,
  And climbs the early sky,
Winnowing blythe her dewy wings
  In morning's rosy eye.
As little reck'd I sorrow's power,
  Until the flowery snare
O' witching love, in luckless hour,
  Made me the thrall o' care.

Oh, had my fate been Greenland snows,
  Or Afric's burning zone,
Wi' man and nature leagu'd my foes,
  So Peggy ne'er I'd known!
The wretch whase doom is, "hope nae mair,"
  What tongue his woes can tell!
Within whase bosom, save despair,
  Nae kinder spirits dwell.

Oh Bonnie was yon Rosy Brier.

Oh bonnie was yon rosy brier,
  That blooms so far frae haunt o' man;
And bonnie she, and ah! how dear!
  It shaded frae the e'enin' sun.

Yon rosebuds in the morning dew,
  How pure amang the leaves sae green;
But purer was the lover's vow
  They witnessed in their shade yestreen.

All in its rude and prickly bower,
  That crimson rose, how sweet and fair;
But love is far a sweeter flower
  Amid life's thorny path o' care.

The pathless wild and wimpling burn,
  Wi' Chloris in my arms, be mine;
And I the world, nor wish, nor scorn,
  Its joys and griefs alike resign.

Forlorn my Love, no Comfort near.

Tune—*Let me in this ane Night.*

Forlorn my love, no comfort near.
Far, far from thee, I wander here;
Far, far from thee, the fate severe
  At which I most repine, love.

CHORUS.

Oh wert thou, love, but near me;
But near, near, near me:
How kindly thou wouldst cheer me,
  And mingle sighs with mine, love.

Around me scowls a wintry sky,
That blasts each bud of hope and joy;
And shelter, shade, nor home have I,
  Save in those arms of thine, love.

Cold, alter'd friendship's cruel part,
To poison fortune's ruthless dart—
Let me not break thy faithful heart,
  And say that fate is mine, love,

But dreary tho' the moments fleet,
Oh let me think we yet shall meet!
That only ray of solace sweet
  Can on thy Chloris shine, love.

Hey for a Lass wi' a Tocher.

TUNE—*Balinamona ora.*

AWA wi' your witchcraft o' beauty's alarms,
The slender bit beauty you grasp in your arms.
Oh, gie me the lass that has acres o' charms,
Oh, gie me the lass wi' the weel-stockit farms.

CHORUS.

Then hey for a lass wi' a tocher, then hey for a lass wi' a tocher,
Then hey for a lass wi' a tocher—the nice yellow guineas for me.

Your beauty's a flower, in the morning that blows,
And withers the faster, the faster it grows:
But the rapturous charm o' the bonnie green knowes,
Ilk spring they're new deckit wi bonnie white yowes.

And e'en when this beauty your bosom has blest,
The brightest o' beauty may cloy when possest;
But the sweet yellow darlings wi' Geordie imprest,
The langer ye hae them, the mair they're carest.

Last May a Braw Wooer.

TUNE—*The Lothian Lassie.*

LAST May a braw wooer cam down the lang glen,
And sair wi' his love he did deave me;
I said there was naething I hated like men—
The deuce gae wi'm to believe me, believe me,
The deuce gae wi'm to believe me.

He spak o' the darts o' my bonnie black een,
And vow'd for my love he was dying;
I said he might die when he liked for Jean—
The Lord forgie me for lying, for lying,
The Lord forgie me for lying!

A well-stocked mailen, himsel for the laird,
And marriage aff-hand, were his proffers:
I never loot on that I kenn'd it, or car'd,
But thought I might hae waur offers, waur offers,
But thought I might hae waur offers.

But what wad ye think?—in a fortnight or less,
The deil tak his taste to gae near her!
He up the lang loan to my black cousin Bess (378),
Guess ye how, the jad! I could bear her, could bear her,
Guess ye how, the jad! I could bear her.

But a' the niest week as I fretted wi' care,
I gaed to the tryste o' Dalgarnock,
And wha but my fine fickle lover was there!
I glowr'd as I'd seen a warlock, a warlock,
I glowr'd as I'd seen a warlock.

But owre my left shouther I gae him a blink,
Lest neibors might say I was saucy;
My wooer he caper'd as he'd been in drink,
And vow'd I was his dear lassie, dear lassie,
And vow'd I was his dear lassie.

I spier'd for my cousin fu' couthy and sweet,
Gin she had recovered her hearin',
And how her new shoon fit her auld shachl't feet,
But, heavens! how he fell a-swearin', a-swearin',
But, heavens! how he fell a-swearin'.

He begged, for guidsake, I wad be his wife,
Or else I wad kill him wi, sorrow:
So e'en to preserve the poor body in life,
I think I maun wed him to-morrow, to-morrow,
I think I maun wed him to-morrow.

Fragment.

TUNE—*The Caledonian Hunt's Delight.*

WHY, why tell thy lover,
Bliss he never must enjoy?
Why, why undeceive him,
And give all his hopes the lie?

Oh why, while fancy, raptur'd, slumbers,
Chloris, Chloris all the theme,
Why, why wouldst thou cruel,
Wake thy lover from his dream?

Jessy. (379)

CHORUS.

HERE's a health to ane I loe dear!
Here's a health to ane I loe dear!
Thou art sweet as the smile when fond lover's meet,
And soft as their parting tear—Jessy!

Altho' thou maun never be mine,
Altho' even hope is denied:
'Tis sweeter for thee despairing,
Than aught in the world beside—Jessy!

I mourn thro' the gay, gaudy day,
As hopeless, I muse on thy charms;
But welcome the dream o' sweet slumber,
For then I am lock't in thy arms—Jessy!

I guess by the dear angel smile,
  I guess by the love rolling ee;
But why urge the tender confession,
  'Gainst fortune's fell cruel decree—
    Jessy!

Fairest Maid on Devon Banks.

TUNE—*Rothiemurche.*

CHORUS.

FAIREST maid on Devon banks,
  Crystal Devon, winding Devon,
Wilt thou lay that frown aside,
  And smile as thou were wont to do.

Full well thou know'st I love thee dear,
Could'st thou to malice lend an ear?
Oh, did not love exclaim "Forbear,
  Nor use a faithfu' lover so!"

Then come, thou fairest of the fair,
  Those wonted smiles, oh let me share!
And, by thy beauteous self I swear,
  No love but thine my heart shall know.

Handsome Nell. (380)

OH once I lov'd a bonnie lass,
  Ay, and I love her still;
And whilst that honour warms my breast,
  I'll love my handsome Nell.

As bonnie lasses I hae seen,
  And mony full as braw;
But for a modest gracefu' mien,
  The like I never saw.

A bonnie lass, I will confess,
  Is pleasant to the ee,
But without some better qualities,
  She's no the lass for me.

But Nelly's looks are blythe and sweet,
  And, what is best of a',
Her reputation is complete,
  And fair without a flaw.

She dresses aye sae clean and neat,
  Both decent and genteel:
And then there's something in her gait
  Gars ony dress look weel.

A gaudy dress and gentle air
  May slightly touch the heart;
But it's innocence and modesty
  That polishes the dart.

'Tis this in Nelly pleases me,
  'Tis this enchants my soul;
For absolutely in my breast
  She reigns without control.

My Father was a Farmer. (381)

TUNE—*The Weaver and his Shuttle, O.*

MY father was a farmer upon the Carrick border, O,
And carefully he bred me in decency and order, O;
He bade me act a manly part, though I had ne'er a farthing, O;
For without an honest manly heart, no man was worth regarding, O.

Then out into the world, my course I did determine, O;
Tho' to be rich was not my wish, yet to be great was charming, O:
My talents they were not the worst, nor yet my education, O;
Resolv'd was I, at least to try, to mend my situation, O.

In many a way, and vain essay, I courted fortune's favour, O;
Some cause unseen still stept between, to frustrate each endeavour, O.
Sometimes by foes I was o'erpower'd; sometimes by friends forsaken, O;
And when my hope was at the top, I still was worst mistaken, O.

Then sore harass'd, and tir'd at last, with fortune's vain delusion, O,
I dropt my schemes, like idle dreams, and came to this conclusion, O—
The past was bad, and the future hid; its good or ill untried, O;
But the present hour was in my pow'r, and so I would enjoy it, O.

No help, nor hope, nor view had I, nor person to befriend me, O;
So I must toil, and sweat and broil, and labour to sustain me, O:
To plough and sow, to reap and mow, my father bred me early, O;
For one, he said, to labour bred, was a match for fortune fairly, O.

Thus all obscure, unknown, and poor, thro' life I'm doom'd to wander, O,
Till down my weary bones I lay, in everlasting slumber, O.
No view nor care, but shun whate'er might breed me pain or sorrow, O!
I live to-day as well's I may, regardless of to-morrow, O.

But cheerful still, I am as well, as a monarch in a palace, O,
Tho' fortune's frown still hunts me down, with all her wonted malice, O:
I make indeed my daily bread, but ne'er can make it farther, O;
But, as daily bread is all I need, I do not much regard her, O.

When sometimes by my labour I earn a little mony, O,
Some unforseen misfortune comes gen'rally upon me, O:
Mischance, mistake, or by neglect, or my good-natur'd folly, O;
But come what will, I've sworn it still, I'll ne'er be melancholy, O.

All you who follow wealth and power with unremitting ardour, O,
The more in this you look for bliss, you leave your view the farther, O:
Had you the wealth Potosi boasts, or nations to adore you, O,
A cheerful honest-hearted clown I will prefer before you, O.

Up in the Morning early.

TUNE—*Cold blows the Wind.*

CHORUS.

UP in the morning's no for me,
Up in the morning early:
When a' the hills are cover'd wi' snaw,
I'm sure it's winter fairly.

Cauld blaws the wind frae east to west,
The drift is driving sairly;
Sae loud and shrill I hear the blast,
I'm sure its winter fairly.

The birds sit chittering in the thorn,
A' day they fare but sparely;
And lang's the night frae e'en to morn—
I'm sure it's winter fairly.

Hey, the Dusty Miller.

TUNE—*The Dusty Miller.*

HEY, the dusty miller,
And his dusty coat;
He will win a shilling,
Or he spend a groat.
Dusty was the Coat,
Dusty was the colour,
Dusty was the kiss
That I got frae the miller.

Hey, the dusty miller,
And his dusty sack;
Leeze me on the calling
Fills the dusty peck—
Fills the dusty peck,
Brings the dusty siller;
I wad gie my coatie
For the dusty miller.

Robin. (382)

TUNE—*Dainty Davie.*

THERE was a lad was born in Kyle,
But whatna day o' whatna style
I doubt it's hardly worth the while
To be sae nice wi' Robin.
Robin was a rovin' boy,
Rantin' rovin', rantin' rovin';
Robin was a rovin' boy,
Rantin' rovin' Robin!

Our monarch's hindmost year but ane
Was five-and-twenty days begun,
'Twas then a blast o' Janwar' win'
Blew hansel in on Robin.

The gossip keekit in his loof,
Quo scho, wha lives will see the proof,
This waly boy will be nae coof;
I think we'll ca' him Robin.

He'll hae misfortunes great and sma',
But aye a heart aboon them a';
He'll be a credit till us a'—
We'll a' be proud o' Robin.

But sure as three times three mak nine,
I see by ilka score and line.
This chap will dearly like our kin',
So leeze me on thee, Robin.

The Belles of Mauchline. (383)

IN Mauchline there dwells six proper young belles,
The pride of the place and its neighbourhood a',
Their carriage and dress, a stranger would guess,
In Lon'on or Paris they'd gotten it a'.
Miss Miller is fine, Miss Markland's divine,
Miss Smith she has wit, and Miss Betty is braw,
There's beauty and fortune to get wi' Miss Morton;
But Armour's the jewel for me o' them a'. (384)

Her Flowing Locks. (385)

HER flowing locks, the raven's wing,
Adown her neck and bosom hing;
How sweet unto that breast to cling,
And round that neck entwine her!
Her lips are roses wat wi' dew,
Oh, what a feast her bonnie mou'!
Her cheeks a mair celestial hue,
A crimson still diviner.

The Sons of Old Killie. (386)

TUNE—*Shawnboy.*

YE sons of old Killie, assembled by Willie,
To follow the noble vocation;
Your thrifty old mother has scarce such another
To sit in that honoured station.
I've little to say, but only to pray,
As praying's the ton of your fashion;
A prayer from the muse you well may excuse,
'Tis seldom her favourite passion.

Ye powers who preside o'er the wind and the tide,
Who marked each element's border;
Who formed this frame with beneficent aim,
Whose sovereign statute is order;
Within this dear mansion may wayward contention
Or withered envy ne'er enter;
May secrecy round be the mystical bound,
And brotherly love be the centre.

The Joyful Widower.

TUNE—*Maggy Lauder.*

I MARRIED with a scolding wife,
The fourteenth of November;
She made me weary of my life,
By one unruly member.
Long did I bear the heavy yoke,
And many griefs attended;
But, to my comfort be it spoke,
Now, now her life is ended.

We lived full one-and-twenty years,
A man and wife together;
At length from me her course she steer'd,
And gone I know not whither:
Would I could guess, I do profess,
I speak, and do not flatter,
Of all the women in the world,
I never could come at her.

Her body is bestowed well,
A handsome grave does hide her;
But sure her soul is not in hell,
The deil would ne'er abide her!
I rather think she is aloft,
And imitating thunder;
For why?—methinks I hear her voice
Tearing the clouds asunder!

O, Whare did you Get? (386)

TUNE—*Bonnie Dundee.*

O, WHARE did you get that hauver meal bannock?
Oh silly blind body, oh dinna ye see?
I gat it frae a brisk young sodger laddie,
Between Saint Johnston and bonnie Dundee,
Oh, gin I saw the laddie that gae me't!
Aft has he doudled me upon his knee;
May heaven protect my bonnie Scots laddie,
And send him safe hame to his babie and me!

My blessin's upon thy sweet wee lippie,
My blessin's upon thy bonnie ee-bree!
Thy smiles are sae like my blythe sodger laddie,
Thou's aye the dearer and dearer to me!
But I'll big a bower on yon bonnie banks,
Where Tay rins wimplin' by sae clear;
And I'll cleed thee in the tartan sae fine,
And mak thee a man like thy daddie dear.

There was a Lass.

TUNE—*Duncan Davison.*

THERE was a lass, they ca'd her Meg,
And she held o'er the moors to spin;
There was a lad that follow'd her,
They ca'd him Duncan Davison.
The moor was driegh, and Meg was skeigh,
Her favour Duncan could na win;
For wi' the rock she wad him knock,
And aye she shook the temper-pin.

As o'er the moor they lightly foor,
A burn was clear, a glen was green,
Upon the banks they eas'd their shanks,
And aye she set the wheel between:
But Duncan swore a haly aith
That Meg should be a bride the morn,
Then Meg took up her spinnin' graith,
And flung them a' out o'er the burn.

We'll big a house—a wee, wee house,
And we will live like king and queen,
Sae blythe and merry we will be
When ye set by the wheel at e'en.
A man may drink and no be drunk;
A man may fight and no be slain;
A man may kiss a bonnie lass,
And aye be welcome back again.

Landlady, Count the Lawin!

TUNE—*Hey tuttie, taitie.*

LANDLADY, count the lawin,
The day is near the dawin;
Ye're a' blind drunk, boys,
And I'm but jolly fou.
Hey tuttie, taitie,
How tuttie, taitie—
Wha's fou now?

Cog, an ye were aye fou,
Cog, an ye were aye fou,
I wad sit and sing to you,
If ye were aye fou.

Weel may ye a' be!
Ill may we never see!
God bless the king, boys,
And the companie!

Rattlin' Roarin' Willie.

TUNE—*Rattlin' roarin' Willie.*

OH, rattlin' roarin' Willie,
Oh, he held to the fair,
And for to sell his fiddle,
And buy some other ware;
But parting wi' his fiddle,
The saut tear blin't his ee;
And rattlin' roarin' Willie,
Ye're welcome hame to me!

Oh Willie, come sell your fiddle,
Oh sell your fiddle sae fine;
Oh Willie, come sell your fiddle,
And buy a pint o' wine.
If I should sell my fiddle,
The warl would think I was mad;
For mony a rantin' day
My fiddle and I hae had.

As I cam by Crochallan,
I cannily keekit ben—
Rattlin' roarin' Willie
Was sitting at yon board en'—
Sitting at yon board en',
And amang guid companie;
Rattlin roaring' Willie,
Ye're welcome hame to me!

Simmer's a Pleasant Time.

TUNE—*Aye waukin O.*

SIMMER's a pleasant time,
Flowers of every colour;
The water rins o'er the heugh,
And I long for my true lover.

Aye waukin O,
Waukin still and wearie:
Sleep I can get nane
For thinking on my dearie

When I sleep I dream,
When I wauk I'm eerie:
Sleep I can get nane
For thinking on my dearie.

Lanely night comes on,
A' the lave are sleeping;
I think on my bonnie lad,
And bleer my een wi' greetin'.

My Love she's but a Lassie yet.

TUNE—*Lady Badinscoth's Reel.*

MY love she's but a lassie yet,
My love she's but a lassie yet,
We'll let her stand a year or twa,
She'll no be half sae saucy yet.
I rue the day I sought her, O,
I rue the day I sought her, O;
Wha gets her needs na say she's woo'd,
But he may say he's bought her, O!

Come, draw a drap o' the best o't yet,
Come, draw a drap o' the best o't yet;
Gae seek for pleasure where ye will,
But here I never miss'd it yet.
We're a' dry wi' drinking o't,
We're a' dry wi' drinking o't;
The minister kiss'd the fiddler's wife,
And could na preach for thinking o't.

The Captain's Lady.

TUNE—*O Mount and Go.*

CHORUS.

OH mount and go,
Mount and make you ready;
Oh mount and go,
And be the captain's lady;

When the drums do beat,
And the cannons rattle,
Thou shalt sit in state,
And see thy love in battle.

When the vanquish'd foe
Sues for peace and quiet,
To the shades we'll go,
And in love enjoy it.

First when Maggy was my Care.

TUNE—*Whistle o'er the lave o't.*

FIRST when Maggy was my care,
Heaven I thought was in her air;
Now we're married—spier nae mair—
Whistle o'er the lave o't.
Meg was meek, and Meg was mild,
Bonnie Meg was nature's child;
Wiser men than me's beguil'd—
Whistle o'er the lave o't.

How we live, my Meg and me,
How we love, and how we 'gree,
I care na by how few may see—
Whistle o'er the lave o't.
Wha I wish were maggot's meat
Dish'd up in her winding sheet,
I could write—but Meg maun see't—
Whistle o'er the lave o't.

There's a Youth in this City.

To a Gaelic Air.

THERE's a youth in this city, it were a great pity
That he frae our lasses should wander awa;
For he's bonnie and braw, weel favoured and a',
And his hair has a natural buckle and a'.
His coat is the hue of his bonnet sae blue;
His fecket is white as the new-driven snaw;
His hose they are blae, and his shoon like the slae,
And his clear siller buckles they dazzle us a'.

For beauty and fortune the laddie's been courtin';
Weel-featured, weel-tocher'd, weel-mounted, and braw;
But chiefly the siller, that gars him gang till her,
The penny's the jewel that beautifies a'.
There's Meg wi' the mailen that fain wad a-haen him;
And Susie, whose daddy was laird o' the ha';
There's lang-tocher'd Nancy maist fetters his fancy—
But the laddie's dear sel' he loes dearest of a'.

Oh aye my Wife she Dang me.

TUNE—*My wife she Dang me.*

O AYE my wife she dang me,
And aft my wife did bang me,
If ye gie a woman a' her will,
Guid faith, she'll soon o'ergang ye.
On peace and rest my mind was bent,
And fool I was I married;
But never honest man's intent
As cursedly miscarried.

Some sa'r o' comfort still at last,
When a' my days are done, man;
My pains o' hell on earth are past,
I'm sure o' bliss aboon, man.
Oh aye my wife she dang me,
And aft my wife did bang me,
If ye gie a woman a' her will,
Guid faith, she'll soon o'ergang ye.

Eppie Adair.

TUNE—*My Eppie.*

AND oh! my Eppie,
My jewel, my Eppie!
Wha wadna be happy
Wi' Eppie Adair?
By love, and by beauty,
By law, and by duty,
I swear to be true to
My Eppie Adair!

And oh! my Eppie,
My jewel, my Eppie,
Wha wadna be happy
Wi' Eppie Adair?
A' pleasure exile me,
Dishonour defile me,
If e'er I beguile thee,
My Eppie Adair!

The Battle of Sherriff-Muir.

TUNE—*Cameronian Rant.*

"OH cam ye here the fight to shun,
Or herd the sheep wi' me, man?
Or were ye at the Sherra-muir,
And did the battle see, man?"
"I saw the battle, sair and tough,
And reekin' red ran mony a sheugh,
My heart, for fear, gaed sough for sough,
To hear the thuds, and see the cluds,
O' clans frae woods, in tartan duds,
Wha glaum'd at kingdoms three, man.

The red-coat lads, wi' black cockades,
To meet them were na slaw, man;
They rush'd and push'd, and bluid outgush'd,
And mony a bouk did fa', man:
The great Argyle led on his files,
I wat they glanc'd for twenty miles:
They hack'd and hash'd while broadswords clash'd,
And thro' they dash'd, and hew'd, and smash'd,
Till fey men died awa, man.

But had you seen the philabegs,
And skyrin tartan trews, man;
When in the teeth they dar'd our Whigs,
And covenant true blues, man;

THERE WAS A LASS.

As Robie tauld a tale o'love
Ae e'enin, on the lily lea?

In lines extended lang and large,
When bayonets opposed the targe,
And thousands hasten'd to the charge,
Wi' Highland wrath they frae the sheath
Drew blades o' death, till, out o' breath,
They fled like frighted doos, man."

"Oh how diel, Tam, can that be true?
The chase gaed frae the North, man;
I saw myself, they did pursue
The horseman back to Forth, man;
And at Dunblane, in my ain sight,
They took the brig wi' a' their might,
And straught to Stirling winged their flight;
But, cursed lot! the gates were shut;
And mony a huntit, poor red-coat,
For fear amaist did swarf, man!"

'My sister Kate cam up the gate
Wi' crowdie unto me, man;
She swore she saw some rebels run
Frae Perth unto Dundee, man:
Their left-hand general had nae skill,
The Angus lads had nae good will
That day their neibor's blood to spill;
For fear, by foes, that they should lose
Their cogs o, brose—all crying woes;
And so it goes you see, man.

They've lost some gallant gentlemen
Amang the Highland clans, man:
I fear my Lord Panmure is slain,
Or fallen in Whiggish hands, man:
Now wad ye sing this double fight,
Some fell for wrang, and some for right;
But mony bade the world guid-night;
Then ye may tell, how pell and mell,
By red claymores, and muskets' knell,
Wi' dying yell, the Tories fell,
And Whigs to hell did flee, man."

The Highland Widow's Lament. (388)

Oh! I am come to the low countrie,
Och-on, och-on, och-rie!
Without a penny in my purse,
To buy a meal to me.

It was na sae in the Highland hills,
Och-on, och-on, och-rie!
Nae woman in the country wide
Sae happy was as me.

For then I had a score o' kye,
Och-on, och-on, och-rie!
Feeding on yon hills so high,
And giving milk to me.

And there I had three score o' yowes,
Och-on, och-on, och-rie!
Skipping on yon bonnie knowes,
And casting woo' to me.

I was the happiest of a' the clan,
Sair, sair may I repine;
For Donald was the brawest lad,
And Donald he was mine.

Till Charlie Stewart cam at last,
Sae far to set us free;
My Donald's arm was wanted then,
For Scotland and for me.

Their waefu' fate what need I tell?
Right to the wrang did yield:
My Donald and his country fell
Upon Culloden's field.

Oh! I am come to the low countrie,
Och-on, och-on, och-rie!
Nae woman in the world wide
Sae wretched now as me.

Whare hae ye Been?

TUNE—*Killiecrankie.*

Whare hae ye been sae braw, lad?
Where hae ye been sae brankie, O?
Oh, whare hae ye been sae braw, lad?
Cam ye by Killiecrankie, O?
An ye had been whare I hae been,
Ye wad nae been sae cantie, O;
An ye had seen what I hae seen,
On the braes of Killiecrankie, O.

I fought at land, I fought at sea;
At hame I fought my auntie, O;
But I met the devil and Dundee,
On the braes o' Killiecrankie, O.
The bauld Pitcur fell in a furr,
And Clavers got a clankie, O;
Or I had fed an Athole gled,
On the braes o' Killiecrankie, O,

Theniel Menzie's Bonnie Mary.

TUNE—*The Ruffian's Rant.*

In coming by the brig o' Dye,
At Darlet we a blink did tarry;
As day was dawin in the sky,
We drank a health to bonnie Mary.
Theniel Menzie's bonnie Mary,
Theniel Menzie's bonnie Mary;
Charlie Gregor tint his plaidie,
Kissin' Theniel's bonnie Mary.

Her een sae bright, her brow sae white,
Her haffet locks as brown's a berry;
And aye they dimpl't wi' a smile,
The rosy cheeks o' bonnie Mary.

We lap and danced the lee lang day,
  Till piper lads were wae and weary:
But Charlie gat the spring to pay,
  For kissin' Theniel's bonnie Mary.

Frae the Friends and Land I Love.

AIR—*Carron Side.*

FRAE the friends and land I love
  Driv'n by fortune' felly spite,
Frae my best belov'd I rove,
  Never mair to taste delight;
Never mair maun hope to find
  Ease frae toil, relief frae care:
When remembrance wracks the mind,
  Pleasures but unveil despair.

Brightest climes shall mirk appear,
  Desert ilka blooming shore,
Till the fates nae mair severe,
  Friendship, love, and peace restore;
Till Revenge, wi' laurell'd head,
  Bring our banish'd hame again;
And ilk loyal bonnie lad
  Cross the seas and win his ain.

Gane is the Day.

TUNE—*Guidwife, Count the Lawin.*

GANE is the day, and mirk's the night,
But we'll ne'er stray for fau't o' light,
For ale and brandy's stars and moon,
And bluid-red wine's the rising sun.

  Then guidwife, count the lawin,
    The lawin, the lawin;
  Then guidwife, count the lawin,
    And bring a coggie mair;

There's wealth and ease for gentlemen,
And simple folk maun fight and fen;
But here we're a' in ae accord,
For ilka man that's drunk's a lord.

My coggie is a haly pool,
That heals the wounds o' care and dool;
And pleasure is a wanton trout,
An ye drink but deep ye'll find him out.

The Tither Morn.

TUNE—*To a Highland air.*

THE tither morn, when I forlorn
  Aneath an aik sat moaning,
I did na trow, I'd see my jo,
  Beside me, gain the gloaming.
But he sae trig, lap o'er the rig,
  And dawtingly did cheer me,
When I, what reck, did least expec',
  To see my lad so near me.

His bonnet he, a thought ajee,
  Cock'd sprush when first he clasp'd me;
And I, I wat, wi' fainness grat,
  While in his grips he press'd me.
Deil tak the war! I late and air,
  Hae wish'd since Jock departed;
But now as glad I'm wi my lad,
  As short syne broken-hearted.

Fu' aft at e'en wi' dancing keen,
  When a' were blythe and merry,
I car'd na by, sae sad was I,
  In absence o' my dearie.
But, praise be blest, my mind's at rest,
  I'm happy wi' my Johnny:
At kirk and fair, I'se aye be there,
  And be as canty's ony.

Come Boat me o'er to Charlie.

TUNE—*O'er the Water to Charlie.*

COME boat me o'er, come row me o'er,
  Come boat me o'er to Charlie;
I'll gie John Ross another bawbee,
  To boat me o'er to Charlie.

We'll o'er the water and o'er the sea,
  We'll o'er the water to Charlie;
Come weal, come woe, we'll gather and go
  And live or die wi' Charlie.

I loe weel my Charlie's name
  Tho' some there be abhor him:
But oh, to see auld Nick gaun hame,
  And Charlie's face before him!

I swear and vow by moon and stars,
  And sun that shines so early,
If I had twenty thousand lives,
  I'd die as aft for Charlie.

It is na, Jean, thy Bonnie Face.

TUNE—*The Maid's Complaint.*

IT is na, Jean, thy bonnie face
  Nor shape that I admire,
Altho' thy beauty and thy grace
  Might weel awake desire.
Something, in ilka part o' thee,
  To praise, to love, I find;
But dear as is thy form to me,
  Still dearer is thy mind.

Nae mair ungen'rous wish I hae,
  Nor stronger in my breast,
Than if I canna mak thee sae,
  At least to see thee blest.
Content am I, if Heaven shall give
  But happiness to thee:
And as wi' thee I'd wish to live,
  For thee I'd bear to die.

I hae a Wife o' my Ain. (389)

TUNE—*Naebody.*

I HAE a wife o' my ain—
  I'll partake wi' naebody;
I'll tak cuckold frae nane,
  I'll gie cuckold to naebody.
I hae a penny to spend,
  There—thanks to naebody;
I hae naething to lend,
  I'll borrow frae naebody.

I am naebody's lord—
  I'll be slave to naebody;
I hae a guid braid sword,
  I'll tak dunts frae naebody.
I'll be merry and free,
  I'll be sad for naebody;
If naebody care for me,
  I'll care for naebody.

Withsdale's Welcome Home.

THE noble Maxwells and their powers
  Are coming o'er the border,
And they'll gae bigg Terreagles towers,
  And set them a' in order,
And they declare Terreagles fair,
  For their abode they chuse it;
There's no a heart in a' the land,
  But's lighter at the news o't.

Tho' stars in skies may disappear,
  And angry tempests gather,
The happy hour may soon be near
  That brings us pleasant weather:
The weary night o' care and grief
  May hae a joyful morrow;
So dawning day has brought relief—
  Fareweel our night o' sorrow!

My Collier Laddie.

TUNE—*The Collier Laddie.*

WHERE live ye, my bonnie lass?
  And tell me what they ca' ye;
My name, she says, is Mistress Jean,
  And I follow the Collier Laddie.
My name, she says, is Mistress Jean,
  And I follow the Collier Laddie.

See you not yon hills and dales,
  The sun shines on sae brawlie!
They a' are mine, and they shall be thine,
  Gin ye'll leave your Collier Laddie.
They a' are mine, and they shall be thine,
  Gin ye'll leave your Collier Laddie.

Ye shall gang in gay attire,
  Weel buskit up sae gaudy;
And ane to wait on every hand,
  Gin ye'll leave your Collier Laddie.
And ane to wait on every hand,
  Gin ye'll leave your Collier Laddie.

Tho' ye had a' the sun shines on,
  And the earth conceals sae lowly;
I wad turn my back on you and it a',
  And embrace my Collier Laddie.
I wad turn my back on you and it a',
  And embrace my Collier Laddie.

I can win my five pennies in a day,
  And spen 't at night fu' brawlie;
And make my bed in the Collier's neuk,
  And lie down wi' my Collier Laddie,
And make my bed in the Collier's neuk,
  And lie down wi' my Collier Laddie.

Luve for luve is the bargain for me,
  Tho' the wee cot-house should haud me;
And the world before me to win my bread,
  And fair fa' my Collier Laddie.
And the world before me to win my bread,
  And fair fa' my Collier Laddie.

As I was a-Wandering.

TUNE—*Rinn Meudial mo Mhealladh.*

As I was a-wandering ane midsummer e'enin',
  The pipers and youngsters were making their game;
Amang them I spied my faithless fause lover,
  Which bled a' the wounds o' my dolour again.

  Weel, since he has left me, my pleasure gae wi' him;
    I may be distress'd, but I winna complain.
  I flatter my fancy I may get anither,
    My heart it shall never be broken for ane.

I couldna get sleeping till dawin for greetin',
  The tears trickled down like the hail and the rain;
Had I na got greetin', my heart wad a broken,
  For oh! love forsaken's a tormenting pain.

Although he has left me for greed o' the siller,
I dinna envy him the gains he can win;
I rather wad bear a' the lade o' my sorrow
Than ever hae acted sae faithless to him.

Ye Jacobites by Name.

TUNE—*Ye Jacobites by Name.*

YE Jacobites by name, give an ear, give an ear;
Ye Jacobites by name, give an ear;
Ye Jacobites by name,
Your fautes I will proclaim,
Your doctrines I maun blame—
You shall hear.

What is right and what is wrang, by the law, by the law?
What is right and what is wrang by the law?
What is right and what is wrang?
A short sword and a lang,
A weak arm, and a strang
For to draw.

What makes heroic strife, fam'd afar, fam'd afar?
What makes heroic strife, fam'd afar?
What makes heroic strife?
To whet th' assassin's knife,
Or hunt a parent's life
Wi' bluidie war.

Then let your schemes alone, in the state, in the state;
Then let your schemes alone in the state;
Then let your schemes alone,
Adore the rising sun,
And leave a man undone
To his fate.

Lady Mary Ann.

TUNE—*Craigtown's growing.*

OH, Lady Mary Ann looked o'er the castle wa';
She saw three bonnie boys playing at the ba';
The youngest he was the flower amang them a'—
My bonnie laddie's young, but he's growin' yet.

Oh father! oh father! an ye think it fit,
We'll send him a year to the college yet:
We'll sew a green ribbon round about his hat,
And that will let them ken he's to marry yet.

Lady Mary Ann was a flower i' the dew,
Sweet was its smell, and bonnie was its hue;
And the langer it blossom'd the sweeter it grew:
For the lily in the bud will be bonnier yet.

Young Charlie Cochrane was the sprout of an aik;
Bonnie and bloomin' and straught was it makes,
The sun took delight to shine for its sake,
And it will be the brag o' the forest yet.

The simmer is gane when the leaves they were green,
And the days are awa that we hae seen;
But far better days I trust will come again,
For my bonnie laddie's young, but he's growin' yet.

Out over the Forth.

TUNE—*Charlie Gordon's Welcome Hame.*

OUT over the Forth I look to the north,
But what is the north and its Highlands to me?
The south nor the east gie ease to my breast,
The far foreign land, or the wild-rolling sea.

But I look to the west, when I gae to rest,
That happy my dreams and my slumbers may be;
For far in the west lives he I loe best,
The lad that is dear to my babie and me.

Jockey's taen the Parting Kiss.

TUNE—*Jockey's taen the Parting Kiss.*

JOCKEY'S taen the parting kiss,
O'er the mountains he is gane;
And within him is a' my bliss,
Nought but griefs with me remain.
Spare my luve, ye winds that blaw,
Plashy sleets and beating rain!
Spare my luve, thou feathery snaw,
Drifting o'er the frozen plain

When the shades of evening creep
O'er the day's fair, gladsome ee,
Sound and safely may he sleep,
Sweetly blythe his waukening be!
He will think on her he loves,
Fondly he'll repeat her name;
For where'er he distant roves,
Jockey's heart is still at hame.

The Carles o' Dysart.

TUNE—*Hey ca' thro'*

UP wi' the carles o' Dysart,
And the lads o' Buckhaven,
And the kimmers o' Largo,
And the lasses o' Leven.

Hey, ca' thro', ca' thro',
For we hae mickle ado;
Hey, ca' thro', ca' thro',
For we hae mickle ado.

We hae tales to tell,
And we hae sangs to sing;
We hae pennies to spend,
And we hae pints to bring.

We'll live a' our days,
And them that come behin',
Let them do the like,
And spend the gear they win.

Lady Onlie.

TUNE—*The Ruffian's Rant.*

A' THE lads o' Thornie-bank,
When they gae to the shore o' Bucky,
They'll step in and tak a pint
Wi' Lady Onlie, honest Lucky!
Lady Onlie, honest Lucky,
Brews guid ale at shore o' Bucky!
I wish her sale for her guid ale,
The best on a' the shore o' Bucky.

Her house sae bien, her curch sae clean,
I wat she is a dainty chucky;
And cheerlie blinks the ingle-gleed
Of Lady Onlie, honest Lucky!
Lady Onlie, honest Lucky,
Brews guid ale at shore o' Bucky;
I wish her sale for her guid ale,
The best on a' the shore o' Bucky.

Young Jamie, Pride of a' the Plain.

TUNE—*The Carlin o' the Glen.*

YOUNG Jamie, pride of a' the plain,
Sae gallant and sae gay a swain;
Thro' a' our lasses he did rove,
And reigned resistless king of love:
But now wi' sighs and starting tears,
He strays amang the woods and briers;
Or in the glens and rocky caves
His sad complaining dowie raves.

I wha sae late did range and rove,
And chang'd with every moon my love,
I little thought the time was near,
Repentance I should buy sae dear:
The slighted maids my torment see,
And laugh at a' the pangs I dree;
While she, my cruel, scornfu' fair,
Forbids me e'er to see her mair!

Jenny's a' wat, poor Body.

TUNE—*Coming through the Rye.*

COMING through the rye, poor body,
Coming through the rye,
She draiglet a' her petticoatie,
Coming through the rye.
Jenny's a' wat, poor body,
Jenny's seldom dry;
She draiglet a' her petticoatie,
Coming through the rye.

Gin a body meet a body
Coming through the rye,
Gin a body kiss a body,
Need a body cry?

Gin a body meet a body
Coming through the glen,
Gin a body kiss a body,
Need the world ken?

The Cardin' o't.

TUNE—*Salt-fish and Dumplings.*

I COFT a stane o' haslock woo',
To make a wat to Johnny o't;
For Johnny is my only jo,
I loe him best of ony yet.
The cardin' o't, the spinnin' o't,
The warpin' o't, the winnin' o't;
When ilka ell cost me a groat,
The tailor staw the linn o't.

For though his locks be lyart grey,
And though his brow be beld aboon;
Yet I hae seen him on a day,
The pride of a' the parishen.

To thee, lov'd Nith.

To thee, lov'd Nith, thy gladsome plains,
Where late wi' careless thought I rang'd,
Though prest wi' care and sunk in woe,
To thee I bring a heart unchang'd.

I love thee, Nith, thy banks and braes,
Tho' mem'ry there my bosom tear;
For there he rov'd that brake my heart,
Yet to that heart, ah! still how dear!

Sae far Awa.

TUNE—*Dalkeith Maiden Bridge.*

OH, sad and heavy should I part,
But for her sake sae far awa;
Unknowing what my way may thwart
My native land sae far awa.

Thou that of a' things Maker art,
  That form'd this fair sae far awa,
Gie body strength, then I'll ne'er start
  At this my way sae far awa.

How true is love to pure desert,
  So love to her, sae far awa:
And nocht can heal my bosom's smart,
  While, oh! she is sae far awa.
Nane other love, nane other dart,
  I feel but her's, sae far awa;
But fairer never touch'd a heart
  Than her's, the fair sae far awa.

Wae is my Heart.

TUNE—*Wae is my Heart.*

WAE is my heart, and the tear's in my ee;
Lang, lang, joy's been a stranger to me:
Forsaken and friendless, my burden I bear,
And the sweet voice o' pity ne'er sounds in my ear.

Love, thou hast pleasures, and deep hae I loved:
Love, thou hast sorrows, and sair hae I proved;
But this bruised heart that now bleeds in my breast,
I can feel its throbbings will soon be at rest.

Oh, if I were happy, where happy I hae been,
Down by yon stream, and yon bonnie castle-green;
For there he is wand'ring, and musing on me,
Wha wad soon dry the tear frae Phillis's ee.

Amang the Trees.

TUNE—*The King of France, he rade a Race.*

AMANG the trees where humming bees
  At buds and flowers were hinging, O,
Auld Caledon drew out her drone,
  And to her pipe was singing, O;
'Twas pibroch, sang, strathspey, or reels,
  She dirl'd them aff fu' clearly, O,
When there cam a yell o' foreign squeels,
  That dang her tapsalteerie, O.

Their capon craws, and queer ha, ha's,
  They made our lugs grow eerie, O;
The hungry bike did scrape and pike
  Till we were wae and weary, O.
But a royal ghaist wha ance was cas'd,
  A prisoner aughteen year awa,
He fir'd a fiddler in the North
  That dang them tapsalteerie, O.

The Highland Laddie.

TUNE—*If thou'lt Play me Fair Play.*

THE bonniest lad that e'er I saw,
  Bonnie laddie, Highland laddie,
Wore a plaid, and was fu' braw,
  Bonnie Highland laddie.
On his head a bonnet blue,
  Bonnie laddie, Highland laddie;
His royal heart was firm and true,
  Bonnie Highland laddie.

Trumpets sound, and cannons roar,
  Bonnie lassie, Lowland lassie;
And a' the hills wi' echoes roar,
  Bonnie Lowland lassie.
Glory, honour, now invite,
  Bonnie lassie, Lowland lassie,
For freedom and my king to fight,
  Bonnie Lowland lassie.

The sun a backward course shall take,
  Bonnie laddie, Highland laddie,
Ere aught thy manly courage shake,
  Bonnie Highland laddie.
Go! for yourself procure renown,
  Bonnie laddie, Highland laddie;
And for your lawful king his crown,
  Bonnie Highland laddie.

Bannocks o' Barley.

TUNE—*The Killogie.*

BANNOCKS o' bear meal,
  Bannocks o' barley;
Here's to the Highlandman's
  Bannocks o' barley.
Wha in a brulzie
  Will first cry a parley?
Never the lads wi'
  The bannocks o' barley!

Bannocks o' bear meal,
  Bannocks o' barley;
Here's to the lads wi'
  The bannocks o' barley!
Wha in his wae-days
  Were loyal to Charlie?—
Wha but the lads wi'
  The bannocks o' barley?

Robin Shure in Hairst.

CHORUS.

ROBIN shure in hairst,
  I shure wi' him;
Fient a heuk had I,
    Yet I stack by him.

I gaed up to Dunse,
  To warp a wab o' plaiden;
At his daddie's yett,
  Wha met me but Robin?

Was na Robin bauld,
  Though I was a cotter,
Play'd me sic a trick,
  And me the eller's dochter?

Robin promised me
  A' my winter vittle;
Fient haet he had but three
  Goose feathers and a whittle.

Sweetest May.

SWEETEST May, let love inspire thee;
Take a heart which he desires thee;
As thy constant slave regard it;
For its faith and truth reward it.

Proof o' shot to birth or money,
Not the wealthy but the bonnie;
Not high-born, but noble-minded,
In love's silken band can bind it.

The Lass of Ecclefechan.

TUNE—*Jacky Latin.*

GAT ye me, oh gat ye me,
  Oh gat ye me wi' naething
Rock and reel, and spinnin' wheel,
  A mickle quarter basin.
Bye attour, my gutcher has
  A hich house and a laigh ane,
A' forbye my bonnie sel',
  The lass of Ecclefechan.

Oh haud your tongue now, Luckie Laing,
  Oh haud your tongue and jannier;
I held the gate till you I met,
  Syne I began to wander:
I tint my whistle and my sang,
  I tint my peace and pleasure:
But your green graff, now, Luckie Laing,
  Wad airt me to my treasure.

Here's a Bottle and an Honest Friend.

HERE's a bottle and an honest friend!
  Wha wad ye wish for mair, man?
Wha kens, before his life may end,
  What his share may be o' care, man?
Then catch the moments as they fly,
  And use them as ye ought, man:—
Believe me, happiness is shy,
  And comes na aye when sought, man.

On a Ploughman.

As I was a-wand'ring ane morning in spring,
I heard a young ploughman sae sweetly to sing;
And as he was singing these words, he did say,
There's nae life like the ploughman's in the mouth o' sweet May.

The lav'rock in the morning she'll rise frae her nest,
And mount to the air wi' the dew on her breast,
And wi' the merry ploughman she'll whistle and sing,
And at night she'll return to her nest back again.

The Weary Pund o' Tow.

TUNE—*The Weary Pund o' Tow.*

THE weary pund, the weary pund,
  The weary pund o' tow;
I think my wife will end her life
  Before she spin her tow.

I bought my wife a stane o' lint
  As guid as e'er did grow;
And a' that she has made o' that,
  Is ane poor pund o' tow.

There sat a bottle in a bole,
  Beyont the ingle lowe,
And aye she took the tither souk,
  To drouk the stowrie tow.

Quoth I, for shame, ye dirty dame,
  Gae spin your tap o' tow!
She took the rock, and wi' a knock
  She brak it o'er my pow.

At last her feet—I sang to see't—
  Gaed foremost o'er the knowe;
And ere I wad anither jad,
  I'll wallop in a tow.

The Laddies by the Banks o' Nith. (390)

TUNE—*Up and waur them a'.*

THE laddies by the banks o' Nith,
  Wad trust his Grace wi' a', Jamie,
But he'll sair them as he sair'd the king,
  Turn tail and rin awa, Jamie.

    Up and waur them a', Jamie,
      Up and waur them a';
    The Johnstones hae the guidin' o't,
      Ye turncoat whigs, awa.

The day he stude his country's friend,
 Or gied her faes a claw, Jamie,
Or frae puir man a blessin' wan,
 That day the duke ne'er saw, Jamie.

But wha is he, his country's boast?
 Like him there is na twa, Jamie;
There's no a callant tents the kye,
 But kens o' Westerha', Jamie.

To end the wark, here's Whistlebirck,
 Lang may his whistle blaw, Jamie;
And Maxwell true o' sterling blue,
 And we'll be Johnstones a', Jamie.

Epigrams, &c.

On Captain Grose,

THE CELEBRATED ANTIQUARY. (391)

THE Devil got notice that GROSE was a-dying, [flying;
So whip! at the summons, old Satin came
But when he approach'd where poor FRANCIS lay moaning,
And saw each bed-post with its burden a-groaning (392),
Astonish'd, confounded, cried Satan, "By——
I'll want 'im, ere I take such a damnable load,'

On a Henpecked Country Squire.

OH death, hadst thou but spar'd his life
 Whom we this day lament,
We freely wad exchang'd the wife,
 And a' been weel content.

E'en as he is, cauld in his graff,
 The swap we yet will do't;
Tak thou the carlin's carcase aff,
 Thou'se get the saul to boot.

Another on his Widow.

ONE Queen Artemisia, as old stories tell,
When deprived of her husband she loved so well, [show'd her,
In respect for the love and affection he
She reduc'd him to dust, and she drank off the powder.
But Queen Netherplace, of a different complexion, [tion,
When call'd on to order the fun'ral direc-
Would have ate her dead lord, on a slender pretence, [expense!
Not to show her respect, but—to save the

On Elphinstone's Translations of Martial's Epigrams.

(393)

OH thou, whom poesy abhors,
Whom prose has turned out of doors,
Heard'st thou that groan—proceed no further;
Twas laurelled Martial roaring murther!

On Miss J Scott, of Ayr.

OH! had each SCOT of ancient times,
Been JEANY SCOTT, as thou art;
The bravest heart on English ground,
Had yielded like a coward.

On an Illiterate Gentleman,

WHO HAD A FINE LIBRARY.

FREE through the leaves, ye maggots, make your windings; [bindings!
But for the owner's sake, oh spare the

Written

UNDER THE PICTURE OF MISS BURNS. (394)

CEASE, ye prudes, your envious railings,
 Lovely Burns has charms—confess:
True it is, she had one failing—
 Had a woman ever less?

Written on a Window of the Inn

AT CARRON.

WE cam na here to view your warks
 In hopes to be mair wise,
But only, lest we gang to hell,
 It may be nae surprise:

But whan we tirled at your door,
 Your porter dought na hear us;
Sae may, should we to hell's yetts come,
 Your billy Satan sair us!

Written on a Pane of Glass

IN THE INN AT MOFFAT. (395)

Ask why God made the gem so small,
And why so huge the granite?
Because God meant mankind should set
The higher value on it.

Fragment. (396)

The black-headed eagle
As keen as a beagle,
He hunted owre height and owre howe;
But fell in a trap
On the braes o' Gemappe,
E'en let him come out as he dowe.

On Incivility shown him at Inverary.

(397)

Whoe'er he be that sojourns here,
I pity much his case,
Unless he come to wait upon
The Lord their God, his Grace.

There's naething here but Highland pride,
And Highland scab and hunger;
If providence has sent me here,
'Twas surely in his anger.

Highland Hospitality. (398)

When death's dark stream I ferry o'er,
A time that surely shall come,
In Heaven itself I'll ask no more,
Than just a Highland welcome

Lines on Miss Kemble.

Kemble, thou cur'st my unbelief
Of Moses and his rod;
At Yarico's sweet notes of grief
The rock with tears had flow'd.

On the Kirk at Lamington.

A cauld day December blew,
A cauld kirk, and in't but few,
A caulder minister never spak—
They'll a' be warm ere I come back.

8

The Solemn League and Covenant.

(399)

The Solemn League and Covenant
Cost Scotland blood—cost Scotland tears:
But it seal'd freedom's sacred cause—
If thou'rt a slave, indulge thy sneers.

On a Certain Parson's Looks.

That there is falsehood in his looks
I must and will deny;
They say their master is a knave—
And sure they do not lie.

On Seeing the Beautiful Seat

OF THE EARL OF * * * *

What dost thou in that mansion fair?—
Flit, * * * * and find
Some narrow, dirty, dungeon cave,
The picture of thy mind!

On the Earl of * * * *

No Stewart art thou, * * * *
The Stewarts all were brave;
Besides, the Stewarts were but fools,
Not one of them a knave.

On the Same.

Bright ran thy line, oh * * * *
Thro' many a far-fam'd sire!
So ran the far-fam'd Roman way,
So ended in a mire.

To the Same,

ON THE AUTHOR BEING THREATENED WITH HIS RESENTMENT.

Spare me thy vengeance, * * * *
In quiet let me live:
I ask no kindness at thy hand,
For thou hast none to give.

On an Empty Fellow,

WHO IN COMPANY ENGROSSED THE CONVERSATION WITH AN ACCOUNT OF HIS GREAT CONNEXIONS.

No more of your titled acquaintances boast,
 And what nobles and gentles you've seen;
An insect is still but an insect at most,
 Tho' it crawl on the curl of a Queen!

Written on a Pane of Glass,

ON THE OCCASION OF A NATIONAL THANKSGIVING FOR A NAVAL VICTORY.

YE hypocrites! are these your pranks?—
To murder men, and gie God thanks!
For shame! gie o'er, proceed no further—
God won't accept your thanks for murther!

The True Loyal Natives. (400)

YE true "Loyal Natives," attend to my song
In uproar and riot rejoice the night long:
From envy and hatred your corps is exempt;
But where is your shield from the darts o' contempt?

Inscription on a Goblet.

THERE's death in the cup—sae beware!
 Nay, more—there is danger in touching;
But wha can avoid the fell snare?
 The man and his wine's sae bewitching!

Extempore on Mr. Syme.

No more of your guests, be they titled or not,
 And cookery the first in the nation;
Who is proof to thy personal converse and wit,
 Is proof to all other temptation.

To Mr. Syme,

WITH A PRESENT OF A DOZEN OF PORTER.

OH, had the malt thy strength of mind,
 Or hops the flavour of thy wit,
'Twere drink for first of human kind,
 A gift that e'en for Syme were fit.

The Creed of Poverty. (401)

IN politics if thou would'st mix,
 And mean thy fortunes be,
Bear this in mind:—be deaf and blind,
 Let great folks hear and see.

Written in a Lady's Pocket-Book.

GRANT me, indulgent Heav'n, that I may live, [give,
To see the miscreants feel the pains they
Deal freedom's sacred treasures free as air,
Till slave and despot be but things which were.

To John Taylor. (402)

WITH Pegasus upon a day,
 Apollo weary flying,
Through frosty hills the journey lay,
 On foot the way was plying.

Poor slip-shod giddy Pegasus
 Was but a sorry walker;
To Vulcan then Apollo goes,
 To get a frosty calker.

Obliging Vulcan fell to work,
 Threw by his coat and bonnet,
And did Sol's business in a crack;
 Sol paid him with a sonnet.

YE Vulcan's sons of Wanlockhead,
 Pity my sad disaster;
My Pegasus is poorly shod—
 I'll pay you like my master.

To Miss Fontenelle,

ON SEEING HER IN A FAVOURITE CHARACTER.

SWEET naïveté of feature,
 Simple, wild, enchanting elf,
Not to thee, but thanks to Nature,
 Thou art acting but thyself.

Wert thou awkward, stiff, affected,
 Spurning nature, torturing art;
Loves and graces all rejected,
 Then indeed thou'd'st act a part.

The Toast. (403)

INSTEAD of a song, boys, I'll give you a
toast—
Here's the memory of those on the twelth
that we lost!—
That we lost, did I say? nay, by Heav'n,
that we found;
For their fame it shall last while the world
goes round. [King!
The next in succession, I'll give you—the
Whoe'er would betray him, on high may he
swing; [tution,
And here's the grand fabric, our free Consti-
As built on the base of the great Revolution;
And longer with politics not to be cramm'd,
Be Anarchy curs'd, and be Tyranny damn'd:
And who would to Liberty e'er prove disloyal,
May his son be a hangman, and he his first
trial.

Excisemen Universal,

WRITTEN ON A WINDOW. (404)

YE men of wit and wealth, why all this sneer-
ing [hearing,
'Gainst poor excisemen? give the cause a
What are your landlords' rent-rolls? teazing
ledgers: [mighty gaugers:
What premiers—what? even monarchs'
Nay, what are priests, those seeming godly
wise men?
What are they, pray, but spiritual excisemen?

To Dr. Maxwell,

ON MISS JESSY STAIG'S RECOVERY.

MAXWELL, if merit here you crave,
That merit I deny—
You save fair Jessy from the grave!
An angel could not die.

On Jessy Lewars. (405)

TALK not to me of savages
From Afric's burning sun;
No savage e'er could rend my heart,
As, Jessy, thou hast done.
But Jessy's lovely hand in mine,
A mutual faith to plight,
Not even to view the heavenly choir
Would be so blest a sight.

Toast to the Same. (406)

FILL me with the rosy wine,
Call a toast—a toast divine;
Give the poet's darling flame,
Lovely Jessy be the name;
Then thou mayest freely boast
Thou hast given a peerless toast.

Epitaph on the Same. (407)

SAY, sages, what's the charm on earth
Can turn death's dart aside?
It is not purity and worth,
Else Jessy had not died.

To the Same.

BUT rarely seen since Nature's birth,
The natives of the sky;
Yet still one seraph's left on earth,
For Jessy did not die.

Graces before Meat.

SOME hae meat and canna eat,
And some would eat that want it,
But we hae meat, and we can eat,
Sae let the Lord be thankit.

OH Thou, who kindly dost provide
For every creature's want!
We bless Thee, God of Nature wide,
For all thy goodness lent:

And, if it please Thee, heavenly guide,
May never worse be sent;
But whether granted or denied,
Lord, bless us with content! *Amen!*

OH Thou, in whom we live and move
Who mad'st the sea and shore;
Thy goodness constantly we prove,
And grateful would adore.
And if it please thee, Pow'r above,
Still grant us, with such store,
The friend we trust, the fair we love,
And we desire no more.

Epitaphs.

On the Author's Father.

OH ye whose cheek the tear of pity stains,
Draw near with pious rev'rence and attend!
Here lie the loving husband's dear remains,
The tender father, and the gen'rous friend.
The pitying heart that felt for human woe;
The dauntless heart that fear'd no human pride;
The friend of man, to vice alone a foe;
"For ev'n his failings lean'd to virtue's side." (408)

On a Henpeck'd Country Squire.

As father Adam first was fool'd,
A case that's still too common,
Here lies a man a woman rul'd,
The devil rul'd the woman

On a Celebrated Ruling Elder.

HERE souter Hood in death does sleep—
To hell, if he's gane thither.
Satan, gie him the gear to keep
He'll hand it weel thegither.

On a Noisy Polemic. (409)

BELOW these stanes lie Jamie's banes:
Oh Death, it's my opinion,
Thou ne'er took such a bleth'rin bitch
Into thy dark dominion!

On Wee Johnny. (410)

HIC JACET WEE JOHNNY.

WHOE'ER thou art, oh reader, know,
That death has murder'd Johnny!
And here his body lies fu' low—
For saul he ne'er had ony.

On John Dove.

INNKEEPER, MAUCHLINE.

HERE lies Johnny Pidgeon;
What was his religion?
Wha e'er desires to ken,
To some other warl'
Maun follow the carl,
For here Johnny Pidgeon had nane!

Strong ale was ablution—
Small beer, persecution,
A dram was *memento mori*;
But a full flowing bowl
Was the joy of his soul,
And port was celestial glory.

For Robert Aiken, Esq.

KNOW thou, oh stranger to the fame
Of this much lov'd, much honour'd name!
(For none that knew him need be told)
A warmer heart death ne'er made cold.

On a Friend.

AN honest man here lies at rest
As e'er God with his image blest!
The friend of man, the friend of truth;
The friend of age, and guide of youth;

Few hearts like his, with virtue warm'd,
Few heads with knowledge so inform'd;
If there's another world, he lives in bliss;
If there is none, he made the best of this.

For Gavin Hamilton.

THE poor man weeps—here Gavin sleeps,
Whom canting wretches blam'd:
But with such as he, where'er he be,
May I be sav'd or damn'd!

On Wat.

SIC a reptile was Wat,
Sic a miscreant slave,
That the very worms damn'd him
When laid in his grave.
"In his flesh there's a famine,"
A starv'd reptile cries;
"And his heart is rank poison,"
Another replies.

BANNOCKBURN.

Now's the day and now's the hour;
See the front o' battle lour.

On a Schoolmaster

IN CLEISH PARISH, FIFESHIRE.

HERE lie Willie Michie's banes,
  Oh Satan, when ye tak him,
Gie him the schoolin' of your weans;
  For clever deils he'll mak 'em!

On Mr. W. Cruickshanks.

HONEST Will's to Heaven gane,
  And mony shall lament him;
His faults they a' in Latin lay,
  In English nane e'er kent them.

For William Nicol.

YE maggots, feed on Nicol's brain,
  For few sic feasts you've gotten;
You've got a prize o' Willie's heart,
  For deil a bit o't's rotten.

On W—— ——.

STOP thief! dame Nature cried to Death,
As Willie drew his latest breath;
You have my choicest model taen
How shall I make a fool again?

On the Same.

REST gently, turf, upon his breast,
His chicken heart's so tender;—
But rear huge castles on his head,
His skull will prop them under.

On Gabriel Richardson,

BREWER, DUMFRIES. (409)

HERE Brewer Gabriel's fire's extinct,
  And empty all his barrels;
He's blest—if as he brew'd he drink—
  In upright honest morals.

On John Bushby,

WRITER, DUMFRIES.

HERE lies John Bushby, honest man!
Cheat him, devil, if you can.

On the Poet's Daughter.

HERE lies a rose, a budding rose,
  Blasted before its bloom;
Whose innocence did sweets disclose
  Beyond that flower's perfume.

To those who for her loss are griev'd,
  This consolation's given—
She's from a world of woe reliev'd,
  And blooms a rose in heaven.

On a Picture

REPRESENTING JACOB'S DREAM.

Dear ——, I'll gie you some advice,
  You'll tak it no uncivil:
You shouldna paint at angels mair,
  But try and paint the d—l.

To paint an angel's kittle wark,
  Wi' auld Nick there's less danger;
You'll easy draw a weel-kent face,
  But no sae weel a stranger.

Correspondence of Burns.

Correspondence of Burns.

NO. I.

TO MR JOHN MURDOCH, SCHOOLMASTER,

STAPLES INN BUILDINGS, LONDON.

Lochlea, 15*th January*, 1783.

DEAR SIR.—As I have an opportunity of sending you a letter without putting you to that expense which any production of mine would but ill repay, I embrace it with pleasure, to tell you that I have not forgotten, nor ever will forget, the many obligations I lie under to your kindness and friendship.

I do not doubt, Sir, but you will wish to know what has been the result of all the pains of an indulgent father and a masterly teacher, and I wish I could gratify your curiosity with such a recital as you would be pleased with; but that is what I am afraid will not be the case. I have, indeed, kept pretty clear of vicious habits, and, in this respect, I hope my conduct will not disgrace the education I have gotten; but, as a man of the world, I am most miserably deficient. One would have thought that, bred as I have been, under a father, who has figured pretty well as *un homme des affaires*, I might have been what the world calls a pushing, active fellow; but to tell you the truth, Sir, there is hardly any thing more my reverse. I seem to be one sent into the world to see and observe; and I very easily compound with the knave who tricks me of my money, if there be any thing original about him, which shows me human nature in a different light from any thing I have seen before. In short, the joy of my heart is to "study men, their manners, and their ways;" and for this darling subject, I cheerfully sacrifice every other consideration. I am quite indolent about those great concerns that set the bustling, busy sons of care agog; and if I have to answer for the present hour, I am very easy with regard to any thing further. Even the last, worst shift of the unfortunate and the wretched does nor much terrify me: I know that even then, my talent for what country folks call a "sensible crack," when once it is sanctified by a hoary head, would procure me so much esteem. that, even then, I would learn to be happy. However, I am under no apprehensions about that; for though indolent, yet so far as an extremely delicate constitution permits, I am not lazy, and in many things, especially in tavern matters, I am a strict economist—not, indeed, for the sake of the money, but one of the principal parts in my composition is a kind of pride of stomach; and I scorn to fear the face of any man living—above every thing, I abhor, as hell, the idea of sneaking in a corner to avoid a dun—possibly some pitiful, sordid wretch, who in my heart I despise and detest. 'Tis this, and this alone, that endears economy to me. In the matter of books, indeed, I am very profuse. My favourite authors are of the sentimental kind, such as Shenstone, particularly his "Elegies;" Thomson; "Man of Feeling"—a book I prize next to the Bible;—"Man of the World;" Sterne, especially his "Sentimental Journey;" Macpherson's "Ossian," &c.; these are the glorious models after which I endeavour to form my conduct, and 'tis incongruous, 'tis absurd, to suppose that the man whose mind glows with sentiments lighted up at their sacred flame—the man whose heart distends with benevolence to all the human race—he "who can soar above this little scene of things"—can he descend to mind the paltry concerns about which the terræfilial race fret, and fume, and vex themselves! Oh how the glorious triumph swells my heart! I forget that I am a poor, insignificant devil, unnoticed and unknown, stalking up and down fairs and markets, when I happen to be in them, reading a page or two of mankind. and "catching the manners living as they rise," whilst the men of business jostle me on every side, as an idle incumbrance in their way. But I dare say I have by this time tired your patience; so I shall conclude with begging you to give Mrs Murdoch—not my compliments, for that is a mere common-place story, but my warmest, kindest wishes for her welfare—and accept of the same for vourself, from, dear Sir, yours, R. B.

NO. II.

TO——.

[AN EARLY LOVE LETTER.]

Lochlea, 1783.

I VERILY believe, my dear E., that the pure genuine feelings of love are as rare in the world as the pure genuine principles of virtue and piety. This, I hope, will account for the uncommon style of all my letters to you. By uncommon, I mean their being written in such a hasty manner, which, to tell you the truth, has made me often afraid lest you should take me for some zealous bigot, who conversed with his mistress as he would converse with his minister. I don't know how it is, my dear, for though, except your company, there is nothing on earth gives me so much pleasure as writing to you, yet it never gives me those giddy raptures so much talked of among lovers. I have often thought that if a well-grounded affection be not really a part of virtue, 'tis something extremely akin to it. Whenever the thought of my E. warms my heart, every feeling of humanity; every principle of generosity, kindles in my breast. It extinguishes every dirty spark of malice and envy, which are but too apt to infest me. I grasp every creature in the arms of universal benevolence, and equally participate in the pleasures of the happy, and sympathise with the miseries of the unfortunate. I assure you, my dear, I often look up to the Divine Disposer of events with an eye of gratitude for the blessing which I hope he intends to bestow on me in bestowing you. I sincerely wish that he may bless my endeavours to make your life as comfortable and happy as possible, both in sweetening the rougher parts of my natural temper, and bettering the unkindly circumstances of my fortune. This, my dear, is a passion, at least in my view, worthy of a man, and, I will add, worthy of a Christian. The sordid earthworm may profess love to a woman's person, whilst in reality his affection is centered in her pocket; and the slavish drudge may go a-wooing as he goes to the horse-market, to choose one who is stout and firm, and, as we may say of an old horse, one who will be a good drudge, and draw kindly. I disdain their dirty, puny ideas. I would be heartily out of humour with myself, if I thought I were capable of having so poor a notion of the sex, which were designed to crown the pleasures of society. Poor devils! I don't envy them their happiness who have such notions. For my part, I propose quite other pleasures with my dear partner. R. B.

NO. III.

TO THE SAME.

Lochlea, 1783.

MY DEAR E.—I do not remember, in the course of your acquaintance and mine, ever to have heard your opinion on the ordinary way of falling in love, amongst people of our station in life. I do not mean the persons who proceed in the way of bargain, but those whose affection is really placed on the person.

Though I be, as you know very well, but a very awkward lover myself, yet as I have some opportunities of observing the conduct of others who are much better skilled in the affair of courtship than I am, I often think it is owing to lucky chance, more than to good management, that there are not more unhappy marriages than usually are.

It is natural for a young fellow to like the acquaintance of the females, and customary for him to keep them company when occasion serves: some one of them is more agreeable to him than the rest—there is something, he knows not what, pleases him, he knows not how, in her company. This I take to be what is called love with the greater part of us; and I must own, my dear E., it is a hard game such a one as you have to play when you meet with such a lover. You cannot refuse but he is sincere, and yet though you use him ever so favourably, perhaps in a few months, or at farthest in a year or two, the same unaccountable fancy may make him as distractedly fond of another, whilst you are quite forgot. I am aware, that perhaps the next time I have the pleasure of seeing you, you may bid me take my own lesson home, and tell me that the passion I have professed for you is perhaps one of those transient flashes I have been describing; but I hope, my dear E., you will do me the justice to believe me, when I assure you that the love I have for you is founded on the sacred principles of virtue and honour, and by consequence, so long as you continue possessed of those amiable qualities which first inspired my passion for you, so long must I continue to love you. Believe me, my dear, it is love like this alone which can render the marriage state happy. People may talk of flames and raptures as long as they please—and a warm fancy, with a flow of youthful spirits, may make them feel something like what they describe; but sure I am, the nobler faculties of the mind, with kindred feelings of the heart, can only be the foundation of friendship, and it has always been my opinion that the married life was only friendship in a more exalted degree. If you will be so good as to grant my wishes, and it should please Providence to spare us to the latest period of life, I can look forward and see that even then, though bent down with wrinkled age—even then, when all other worldly circumstances will be indifferent to me, I will regard my E. with the tenderest affection, and for this plain reason, because she is still possessed of those noble qualities improved to a much higher degree, which first inspired my affection for her.

Oh! happy state, when souls each other draw,
When love is liberty, and nature law.

I know were I to speak in such a style to many a girl, who thinks herself possessed of no small share of sense, she would think it ridiculous; but the language of the heart is, my dear E., the only courtship I shall ever use to you.

When I look over what I have written, I am sensible it is vastly different from the ordinary style of courtship, but I shall make no apology—I know your good nature will excuse what your good sense may see amiss. R. B.

NO. IV.

TO THE SAME.

Lochlea, 1783.

I HAVE often thought it a peculiar unlucky circumstance in love, that though, in every other situation in life, telling the truth is not only the safest, but actually by far the easiest way of proceeding, a lover is never under greater difficulty in acting, or more puzzled for expression, than when his passion is sincere, and his intentions are honourable. I do not think that it is very difficult for a person of ordinary capacity to talk of love and fondness which are not felt, and to make vows of constancy and fidelity which are never intended to be performed, if he be villain enough to practice such detestable conduct: but to a man whose heart glows with the principles of integrity and truth, and who sincerely loves a woman of amiable person, uncommon refinement of sentiment and purity of manners—to such a one, in such circumstances, I can assure you, my dear, from my own feelings at this present moment, courtship is a task indeed. There is such a number of foreboding fears and distrustful anxieties crowd into my mind when I am in your company, or when I sit down to write to you, that what to speak, or what to write, I am altogether at a loss.

There is one rule which I have hitherto practised, and which I shall invariably keep with you, and that is, honestly to tell you the plain truth. There is something so mean and unmanly in the arts of dissimulation and falsehood, that I am surprised they can be acted by any one, in so noble, so generous a passion, as virtuous love. No, my dear E., I shall never endeavour to gain your favour by such detestable practices. If you will be so good, and so generous, as to admit me for your partner, your companion, your bosom friend through life, there is nothing on this side of eternity shall give me greater transport; but I shall never think of purchasing your hand by any arts unworthy of a man, and, I will add, of a Christian, There is one thing, my dear, which I earnestly request of you, and it is this, that you would soon either put an end to my hopes by a peremptory refusal, or cure me of my fears by a generous consent.

It would oblige me much if you would send me a line or two when convenient. I shall only add further, that, if a behaviour regulated (though perhaps but very imperfectly) by the rules of honour and virtue, if a heart devoted to love and esteem you, and an earnest endeavour to promote your happiness—if these are qualities you wish in a friend, in a husband, I hope you shall ever find them in your real friend and sincere lover, R. B.

NO. V.

TO THE SAME.

Lochlea, 1783.

I OUGHT, in good manners, to have acknowledged the receipt of your letter before this time, but my heart was so shocked with the contents of it, that I can scarcely yet collect my thoughs so as to write to you on the subject. I will not attempt to describe what I felt on receiving your letter. I read it over and over, again and again, and though it was in the politest language of refusal, still it was peremptory: "you were sorry you could not make me a return, but you wish me"—what, without you, I never can obtain—"you wish me all kind of happiness." It would be weak and unmanly to say that without you I never can be happy; but sure I am, that sharing life with you would have given it a relish, that, wanting you, I can never taste.

Your uncommon personal advantages, and your superior good sense, do not so much strike me: these, possibly, may be met with in a few instances in others; but that amiable goodness, that tender feminine softness, that endearing sweetness of disposition, with all the charming offspring of a warm feeling heart—these I never again expect to meet with, in such a degree, in this world. All these charming qualities, heightened by an education much beyond any thing I have ever met in any woman I ever dared to approach, have made an impression on my heart that I do not think the world can ever efface. My imagination has fondly flattered myself with a wish, I dare not say it ever reached a hope, that possibly I might one day call you mine. I had formed the most delightful images, and my fancy fondly brooded over them; but now I am wretched for the loss of what I really had no right to expect. I must now think no more of you as a mistress; still I presume to ask to be admitted as a friend. As such I wish to be allowed to wait on you; and as I expect to remove in a few days a little further off, and you, I suppose, will soon leave this place, I wish to see or hear from you soon: and if an expression should perhaps escape me, rather too warm for friendship, I hope you will pardon it in, my dear Miss—(pardon me the dear expression for once) * * * R. B.

NO. VI.

TO MR. JAMES BURNESS,

WRITER, MONTROSE. (1)

Lochlea, 21st June, 1783.

DEAR SIR.—My father received your favour of the 10th current, and as he has been for some months very poorly in health, and is in his own opinion (and, indeed, in almost every body's else) in a dying condition, he has only, with great difficulty, written a few farewell lines to each of his brothers-in-law. For this melancholy reason, I now hold the pen for him to thank you for your kind letter, and to assure you, Sir, that it shall not be my fault if my father's correspondence in the north die with him. My brother writes to John Caird, and to him I must refer you for the news of our family.

I shall only trouble you with a few particulars relative to the wretched state of this country. Our markets are exceedingly high —oatmeal, 17d. and 18d. per peck, and not to be got even at that price. We have indeed been pretty well supplied with quantities of white peas from England and elsewhere, but that resource is likely to fail us, and what will become of us then, particularly the very poorest sort, Heaven only knows. This country, till of late, was flourishing incredibly in the manufacture of silk, lawn, and carpet-weaving; and we are still carrying on a good deal in that way, but much reduced from what it was. We had also a fine trade in the shoe way, but now entirely ruined, and hundreds driven to a starving condition on account of it. Farming is also at a very low ebb with us. Our lands, generally speaking, are mountainous and barren; and our landholders, full of ideas of farming gathered from the English and the Lothians, and other rich soils in Scotland, make no allowance for the odds of the quality of land, and consequently stretch us much beyond what in the event we will be found able to pay. We are also much at a loss for want of proper methods in our improvements of farming. Necessity compels us to leave our old schemes, and few of us have opportunities of being well informed in new ones. In short, my dear Sir, since the unfortunate beginning of this American war, and its as unfortunate conclusion, this country has been, and still is, decaying very fast. Even in higher life, a couple of our Ayrshire noblemen, and the major part of our knights and squires, are all insolvent. A miserable job of a Douglas, Heron, and Co.'s bank, which no doubt you have heard of, has undone numbers of them; and imitating English and French, and other foreign luxuries and fopperies, has ruined as many more. There is a great trade of smuggling carried on along our coasts, which, however destructive to the interests of the kingdom at large, certainly enriches this corner of it, but too often at the expense of our morals. However, it enables individuals to make, at least for a time, a splendid appearance; but Fortune, as is usual with her when she is uncommonly lavish of her favours, is generally even with them at the last: and happy were it for numbers of them if she would leave them no worse than when she found them.

My mother sends you a small present of a cheese; 'tis but a very little one, as our last year's stock is sold off; but if you could fix on any correspondent in Edinburgh or Glasgow, we would send you a proper one in the season. Mrs. Black promises to take the cheese under her care so far, and then to send it to you by the Stirling carrier.

I shall conclude this long letter with assuring you that I shall be very happy to hear from you, or any of our friends in your country, when opportunity serves.

My father sends you, probably for the last time in this world, his warmest wishes for your welfare and happiness; and my mother and the rest of the family desire to enclose their kind compliments to you, Mrs. Burness, and the rest of your family, along with those of, dear Sir, your affectionate cousin,

R. B.

NO. VII.

TO MR. JAMES BURNESS, MONTROSE.

Lochlea, 17th February, 1784.

Dear Cousin.—I would have returned you my thanks for your kind favour of the 13th of December sooner, had it not been that I waited to give you an account of that melancholy event, which, for some time past, we have from day to day expected.

On the 13th current I lost the best of fathers. Though, to be sure, we have had long warning of the impending stroke, still the feelings of nature claim their part, and I cannot recollect the tender endearments and parental lessons of the best of friends and ablest of instructors, without feeling what perhaps the calmer dictates of reason would partly condemn.

I hope my father's friends in your country will not let their connexion in this place die with him. For my part I shall ever with pleasure, with pride, acknowledge my connexion with those who were allied by the ties of blood and friendship to a man whose memory I shall ever honour and revere.

I expect, therefore, my dear Sir, you will not neglect any opportunity of letting me hear from you, which will very much oblige, my dear cousin, yours sincerely, R. B.

NO. VIII.

TO MR. JAMES BURNESS, MONTROSE.

Mossgiel, August, 1784.

We have been surprised with one of the most extraordinary phenomena in the moral world, which, I dare say, has happened in the course of this half century. We have had a party of Presbytery relief, as they call themselves, for some time in this country. A pretty thriving society of them has been in the burgh of Irvine for some years past, till about two years ago a Mrs. Buchan from Glasgow came among them, and began to spread some fanatical notions of religion among them, and, in a short time, made many converts; and among others their preacher, Mr White, who, upon that account, has been suspended and formally deposed by his brethren. He continued, however, to preach in private to his party, and was supported, both he and their spiritual mother, as they affect to call old Buchan, by the contributions of the rest, several of whom were in good circumstances; till in spring last, the populace rose and mobbed Mrs. Buchan, and put her out of the town; on which all her followers voluntarily quitted the place likewise, and with such precipitation, that many of them never shut their doors behind them; one left a washing on the green, another a cow bellowing at the crib without food, or any body to mind her, and after several stages, they are fixed at present in the neighbourhood of Dumfries. Their tenets are a strange jumble of enthusiastic jargon; among others, she pretends to give them the Holy Ghost by breathing on them, which she does with postures and practices that are scandalously indecent. They have likewise disposed of all their effects, and hold a community of goods, and live nearly an idle life, carrying on a great farce of pretended devotion in barns and woods, where they lodge and lie all together, and hold likewise a community of women, as it is another of their tenets that they can commit no moral sin. I am personally acquainted with most of them, and I can assure you the above mentioned are facts.

This, my dear Sir, is one of the many instances of the folly of leaving the guidance of sound reason and common sense in matters of religion.

Whenever we neglect or despise these sacred monitors, the whimsical notions of a perturbated brain are taken for the immediate influences of the Deity, and the wildest fanaticism, and the most inconstant absurdities, will meet with abettors and converts. Nay, I have often thought, that the more out-of-the-way and ridiculous the fancies are, if once they are sanctified under the sacred name of religion, the unhappy mistaken votaries are the more firmly glued to them. R. B.

NO. IX.

TO MR. JAMES SMITH, MAUCHLINE.

Mossgiel, Monday Morning, 1786.

My Dear Sir.—I went to Dr. Douglas yesterday, fully resolved to take the opportunity of Captain Smith; but I found the Doctor with a Mr. and Mrs. White, both Jamaicans, and they have deranged my plans altogether. They assure him that to send me from Savannah la Mar to Port Antonio, will cost my master, Charles Douglas, upwards of fifty pounds, besides running the risk of throwing myself into a pleuritic fever, in consequence of hard travelling in the sun. On these accounts, he refuses sending me with Smith; but a vessel sails from Greenock the 1st of September, right for the place of my destination. The captain of her is an intimate friend of Mr. Gavin Hamilton's, and as good a fellow as heart could wish: with him I am destined to go. Where I shall shelter I know not, but I hope to weather the storm. Perish the drop of blood of mine that fears them! I know their worst, and am prepared to meet it:—

I'll laugh, and sing, and shake my leg,
As lang's I dow.

On Thursday morning, if you can muster as much self-denial as to be out of bed about seven o'clock, I shall see you as I ride through to Cumnock. After all, Heaven bless the sex! I feel there is still happiness for me among them:—

Oh woman, lovely woman! Heaven designed you
To temper man!—we had been brutes without you!

R. B.

NO. X.

TO MR. JOHN RICHMOND, EDINBURGH. (2)

Mossgiel, February 17, 1786.

My dear Sir.—I have not time at present to upbraid you for your silence and neglect; I shall only say I received yours with great pleasure. I have enclosed you a piece of rhyming ware for your perusal. I have been very busy with the muses since I saw you, and have composed, among several others:—The Ordination, a poem on Mr. M'Kinlay's being called to Kilmarnock; Scotch Drink, a poem; The Cotter's Saturday Night; An Address to the Devil, &c. I have likewise completed my poem on the Dogs, but have not shown it to the world. My chief patron now is Mr. Aiken in Ayr, who is pleased to express great approbation of my works. Be so good as send me Fergusson, by Connel, and I will remit you the money. I have no news to acquaint you with about Mauchline; they are just going on in the old way. I have some very important news with respect to myself, not the most agreeable—news that I am sure you cannot guess, but I shall give you the particulars another time. I am extremely happy with Smith; he is the only friend I have now in Mauchline. I can scarcely forgive your long neglect of me, and I beg you will let me hear from you regularly by Connel. If you would act your part as a friend, I am sure neither good nor bad fortune should strange or alter me. Excuse haste, as I got your's but yesterday. I am, my dear Sir, your's,

ROBERT BURNS.

NO. XI.

TO MR. JOHN KENNEDY.

Mossgiel, 3rd March, 1786,

SIR.—I have done myself the pleasure of complying with your request in sending you my Cottager. If you have a leisure minute, I should be glad if you would copy it and return me either the original or the transcript, as I have not a copy of it by me, and I have a friend who wishes to see it.

Now, Kennedy, if foot or horse
E'er bring you in by Mauchline Corse (3),
Lord, man, there's lasses there wad force
A hermit's fancy;
And down the gate, in faith, they're worse,
And mair unchancy.

But, as I'm sayin', please step to Dow's,
And taste sic beer as Johnnie brews,
Till some bit callan bring me news
That you are there;
And if we dinna haud a bouze,
I'll ne'er drink mair.

It's no I like to sit and swallow,
Then like a swine to puke and wallow;
But gie me just a true good fallow,
Wi' right engine,
And spunkie ance to make us mellow,
And then we'll shine.

Now, if you're ane o' warld's folk,
Wha rate the wearer by the cloak,
And sklent on poverty their joke,
Wi' bitter sneer,
Wi' you no friendship will I troke,
Nor cheap nor dear.

But if, as I'm informed weel,
Ye hate, as ill's the vera deil,
The flinty heart that canna feel,
Come, Sir, here's tae you!
Hae, there's my haun', I wiss you weel,
And guid be wi' you!

R. B.

NO. XII.

TO MR. ROBERT MUIR, KILMARNOCK.

Mossgiel, 20th March, 1786.

DEAR SIR.—I am heartily sorry I had not the pleasure of seeing you as you returned through Mauchline; but as I was engaged, I could not be in town before the evening.

I here enclose you my "Scotch Drink," and "may the —— follow" with a blessing for your edification. I hope, some time before we hear the gowk, to have the pleasure of seeing you at Kilmarnock, when I intend we shall have a gill between us in a mutchkin-stoup, which will be a great comfort and consolation to, dear Sir, your humble servant,

ROBERT BURNS.

NO. XIII.

TO MR. AIKEN.

Mossgiel, 3rd April, 1786.

DEAR SIR.—I received your kind letter with double pleasure on account of the second flattering instance of Mrs. C.'s notice and approbation. I assure you I

Turn out the burnt side o' my skin,

as the famous Ramsay, of jingling memory, says, at such a patroness. Present her my most grateful acknowledgements, in your very best manner of telling truth. I have inscribed the following stanza on the blank leaf of Miss More's work:—

Thou flattering mark of friendship kind,
Still may thy pages call to mind
The dear, the beauteous donor.
Though sweetly female every part,
Yet such a head, and more the heart,
Does both the sexes honour.
She showed her taste refined and just
When she selected thee,
Yet deviating own I must,
For so approving me;
But kind still, I mind still,
The giver in the gift—
I'll bless her, and wiss her
A friend above the Lift.

My proposals for publishing I am just going to send to press. I expect to hear from you by the first opportunity. I am, ever dear Sir, your's, ROBERT BURNS.

NO. XIV.

TO MR. M'WHINNIE, WRITER, AYR,

Mossgiel, 17th April, 1786.

It is injuring some hearts, those hearts that elegantly bear the impression of the good Creator, to say to them you give them the trouble of obliging a friend; for this reason, I only tell you that I gratify my own feelings in requesting your friendly offices with respect to the enclosed, because I know it will gratify yours to assist me in it to the utmost of your power.

I have sent you four copies, as I have no less than eight dozen, which is a great deal more than I shall ever need.

Be sure to remember a poor poet militant in your prayers. He looks forward with fear and trembling to that, to him, important moment which stamps the die with—with—with, perhaps, the eternal disgrace of, my dear Sir, your humble, afflicted, tormented,

Robert Burns.

NO. XV.

TO MR. JOHN KENNEDY.

Mossgiel, 20th April, 1786.

Sir.—By some neglect in Mr. Hamilton, I did not hear of your kind request for a subscription paper till this day. I will not attempt any acknowledgement for this, nor the manner in which I see your name in Mr. Hamilton's subscription list. Allow me only to say, Sir, I feel the weight of the debt.

I have here, likewise, enclosed a small piece, the very latest of my productions. (4) I am a good deal pleased with some sentiments myself, as they are just the native querulous feelings of a heart, which, as the elegantly melting Gray says, "melancholy has marked out for her own."

Our race comes on apace—that much expected scene of revelry and mirth: but to me it brings no joy equal to that meeting with which you last flattered the expectation of, Sir, your indebted humble servant.

R. B.

NO. XVI.

TO JOHN BALLANTINE, OF AYR.

June, 1786.

Honoured Sir.—My proposals came to hand last night, and, knowing that you would wish to have it in your power to do me a service as early as any body, I enclose you half a sheet of them. I must consult you, first opportunity, on the propriety of sending my quondam friend, Mr. Aiken, a copy. If he is now reconciled to my character as an honest man, I would do it with all my soul; but I would not be beholden to the noblest being ever God created, if he imagined me to be a rascal. Apropos, old Mr. Armour prevailed with him to mutilate that unlucky paper yesterday. Would you believe it?—though I had not a hope, nor even a wish, to make her mine after her conduct, yet, when he told me the names were all out of the paper, my heart died within me, and he cut my veins with the news. Perdition seize her falshood.

R. B.

NO. XVII.

TO MR. DAVID BRICE. (5)

Mossgiel, June 12, 1786.

Dear Brice.—I received your message by G. Paterson, and as I am not very strong at present, I just write to let you know that there is such a worthless, rhyming reprobate, as your humble servant, still in the land of the living, though I can scarcely say in the place of hope. I have no news to tell you that will give me any pleasure to mention, or you to hear.

Poor ill-advised, ungrateful Armour came home on Friday last. (6) You have heard all the particulars of that affair, and a black affair it is. What she thinks of her conduct now I don't know; one thing I do know—she has made me completely miserable. Never man loved, or rather adored, a woman more than I did her; and, to confess a truth between you and me, I do still love her to distraction after all, though I won't tell her so if I were to see her, which I don't want to do. My poor dear unfortunate Jean! how happy have I been in thy arms! It is not the losing her that makes me so unhappy, but for her sake I feel most severely: I foresee she is in the road to, I am afraid, eternal ruin.

May Almighty God forgive her ingratitude and perjury to me, as I from my very soul forgive her; and may his grace be with her and bless her in all her future life! I can have no nearer idea of the place of eternal punishment than what I have felt in my own breast on her account. I have tried often to forget her; I have run into all kinds of dissipation and riots, mason-meetings, drinking-matches, and other mischief, to drive her out of my head, but all in vain. And now for a grand cure: the ship is on her way home that is to take me out to Jamaica; and then, farewell dear old Scotland! and farewell, dear ungrateful Jean, for never, never will I see you more.

You will have heard that I am going to commence poet in print; and to-morrow my works go to the press. I expect it will be a volume of about 200 pages—it is just the last foolish action I intend to do; and then turn a wise man as fast as possible. Believe me to be, dear Brice, your friend and well-wisher, R. B.

NO. XVIII.

TO MRS. DUNLOP,

OF DUNLOP.

Ayrshire, July, 1786.

MADAM.—I am truly sorry I was not at home yesterday, when I was so much honoured with your order for my copies, and incomparably more by the handsome compliments you are pleased to pay my poetic abilities. I am fully persuaded that there is not any class of mankind so feelingly alive to the titillations of applause as the sons of Parnassus: nor is it easy to conceive how the heart of the poor bard dances with rapture, when those whose character in life gives them a right to be polite judges, honour him with their approbation. Had you been thoroughly acquainted with me, Madam, you could not have touched my darling heart-chord more sweetly than by noticing my attempts to celebrate your illustrious ancestor, the saviour of his country.

Great patriot hero! ill- requited chief!

The first book I met with in my early years, which I perused with pleasure, was "The Life of Hannibal;" the next was "The History of Sir William Wallace;" for several of my earlier years I had few other authors; and many a solitary hour have I stole out, after the laborious vocations of the day, to shed a tear over their glorious, but unfortunate stories. In those boyish days I remember, in particular, being struck with that part of Wallace's story where these lines occur:—

Syne to the Leglen wood, when it was late,
To make a silent and a safe retreat.

I chose a fine summer Sunday, the only day my line of life allowed, and walked half-a-dozen of miles to pay my respects to the Leglen wood, with as much devout enthusiasm as ever pilgrim did to Loretto; and as I explored every den and dell where I could suppose my heroic countryman to have lodged, I recollect (for even then I was a rhymer) that my heart glowed with a wish to be able to make a song on him in some measure equal to his merits. R. B.

NO. XIX.

TO JOHN RICHMOND, EDINBURGH.

Mossgiel, July 9th, 1786.

WITH the sincerest grief I read your letter. You are truly a son of misfortune. I shall be extremely anxious to hear from you how your health goes on—if it is any way re-establishing, or if Leith promises well—in short, how you feel in the inner man.

I have waited on Armour since her return home; not from the least view of reconciliation, but merely to ask for her health, and, to you I will confess it, from a foolish hankering fondness, very ill placed indeed. The mother forbade me the house, nor did Jean show that penitence that might have been expected. However, the priest, I am informed, will give me a certificate as a single man, if I comply with the rules of the church, which, for that very reason, I intend to do.

I am going to put on sackcloth and ashes this day. I am indulged so far as to appear in my own seat. *Peccavi, pater; miserere mei.* My book will be ready in a fortnight. If you have any subscribers, return them by Connell. The Lord stand with the righteous—amen, amen. R. B.

NO. XX.

TO MR. DAVID BRICE,

SHOEMAKER, GLASGOW.

Mossgiel, July 17th, 1786.

I HAVE been so throng printing my Poems, that I could scarcely find as much time as to write to you. Poor Armour is come back again to Mauchline, and I went to call for her, and her mother forbade me the house, nor did she herself express much sorrow for what she has done. I have already appeared publicly in church, and was indulged in the liberty of standing in my own seat. I do this to get a certificate as a bachelor, which Mr. Auld has promised me. I am now fixed to go for the West Indies in

October. Jean and her friends insisted much that she should stand along with me in the kirk, but the minister would not allow it, which bred a great trouble, I assure you, and I am blamed as the cause of it, though I am sure I am innocent; but I am very much pleased, for all that, not to have had her company. I have no news to tell you that I remember. I am really happy to hear of your welfare, and that you are so well in Glasgow. I must certainly see you before I leave the country. I shall expect to hear from you soon, and am, dear Brice, yours, R. B.

NO. XXI.

TO MR. JOHN RICHMOND.

Old Rome Forest, July 30th, 1786.

MY DEAR RICHMOND.—My hour is now come—you and I will never meet in Britain more. I have orders within three weeks at farthest, to repair aboard the Nancy, Captain Smith, from Clyde to Jamaica, and to call at Antigua. This, except to our friend Smith, whom God long preserve, is a secret about Mauchline. Would you believe it? Armour has got a warrant to throw me in jail till I find security for an enormous sum. This they keep an entire secret, but I got it by a channel they little dream of; and I am wandering from one friend's house to another, and, like a true son of the gospel, "have nowhere to lay my head." I know you will pour an execration on her head, but spare the poor, ill-advised girl, for my sake; though may all the furies that rend the injured, enraged mother's bosom, await her mother until her latest hour! I write in a moment of rage, reflecting on my miserable situation—exiled, abandoned, forlorn. I can write no more—let me hear from you by the return of coach. I will write you ere I go. I am, dear Sir, yours, here and hereafter,

R. B.

NO. XXII.

TO MR. ROBERT MUIR, KILMARNOCK.

Mossgiel, Friday Morning, [*Aug.* 1786.]

MY FRIEND, MY BROTHER—Warm recollection of an absent friend presses so hard upon my heart, that I send him the prefixed bagatelle (The Calf), pleased with the thought that it will greet the man of my bosom, and be a kind of distant language of friendship.

You will have heard that poor Armour has repaid me double. A very fine boy and a girl have awakened a thought and feelings that thrill, some with tender pressure, and some with foreboding anguish, through my soul.

The poem was nearly an extemporaneous production, on a wager with Mr. Hamilton, that I would not produce a poem on the subject in a given time.

If you think it worth while, read it to Charles and Mr W. Parker, and if they choose a copy of it, it is at their service, as they are men whose friendship I shall be proud to claim, both in this world and that which is to come.

I believe all hopes of staying at home, will be abortive; but more of this when, in the latter part of next week, you shall be troubled with a visit from, my dear Sir, your most devoted, R. B.

NO. XXIII.

TO MR. JOHN KENNEDY.

Kilmarnock, August, 1786.

MY DEAR SIR.—Your truly facetious epistle of the 3rd instant gave me much entertainment. I was only sorry I had not the pleasure of seeing you as I passed your way, but we shall bring up all our lee-way on Wednesday, the 16th current, when I hope to have it in my power to call on you, and take a kind, very probably, a last adieu, before I go to Jamaica; and I expect orders to repair to Greenock every day. I have at last made my public appearance, and am solemnly inaugurated into the numerous class. Could I have got a carrier, you should have had a score of vouchers for my authorship; but, now you have them, let them speak for themselves.

Farewell, dear friend! may guid luck hit you,
And 'mang her favourites admit you,
If e'er Detraction shore to smit you,
May nane believe him,
And ony deil that thinks to get you,
Good Lord, deceive him.

R. B.

NO. XXIV.

TO MR BURNESS, MONTROSE.

Mossgiel, Tuesday noon, Sept. 26, 1786.

MY DEAR SIR.—I this moment receive yours—receive it with the honest hospitable warmth of a friend's welcome. Whatever comes from you wakens always up the better blood about my heart, which your kind little recollections of my parental friends carries as far as it will go. 'Tis there that man is blest!—'Tis there, my friend, man feels a consciousness of something within him above the trodden clod! The grateful reverence to the hoary (earthly) author of his being—the burning glow when he clasps the woman of his soul to his bosom—the tender yearnings of heart for the little angels to whom he has given existence—these nature has poured in milky streams about the human heart; and the man who never rouses them to action, by the inspiring influences of their proper objects, loses by far the most pleasurable part of his existence.

My departure is uncertain, but I do not think it will be till after harvest. I will be on very short allowance of time indeed, if I do not comply with your friendly invitation. When it will be, I don't know, but if I can make my wish good, I will endeavour to drop you a line some time before. My best compliments to Mrs. B.; I should be equally mortified should I drop in when she is abroad; but of that I suppose there is little chance.

What I have wrote Heaven knows; I have not time to review it; so accept of it in the beaten way of friendship. With the ordinary phrase—perhaps rather more than the ordinary sincerity—I am, dear Sir, ever yours, R. B.

NO. XXV.

TO MR ROBERT AIKEN. (7)

Ayrshire, 1786.

SIR.—I was with Wilson my printer t'other day, and settled all our bygone matters between us. After I had paid him all demands, I made him the offer of the second edition, on the hazard of being paid out of the first and readiest, which he declines. By his account, the paper of 1000 copies would cost about twenty-seven pounds, and the printing about fifteen or sixteen; he offers to agree to this for the printing, if I will advance for the paper, but this you know, is out of my power; so farewell hopes of a second edition till I grow richer! an epoch which I think will arrive at the payment of the British national debt.

There is scarcely any thing hurts me so much in being disappointed of my second edition, as not having it in my power to show my gratitude to Mr. Ballantine, by publishing my poem of the Brigs of Ayr. I would detest myself as a wretch, if I thought I were capable, in a very long life of forgetting the honest, warm, and tender delicacy with which he enters into my interests. I am sometimes pleased with myself in my grateful sensations; but I believe, on the whole, I have very little merit in it, as my gratitude is not a virtue, the consequence of reflection, but sheerly the instinctive emotion of my heart, too inattentive to allow worldly maxims and views to settle into selfish habits.

I have been feeling all the various rotations and movements within, respecting the excise. There are many things plead strongly against it; the uncertainty of getting soon into business; the consequences of my follies, which may perhaps make it impracticable for me to stay at home; and besides, I have for some time been pining under secret wretchedness, from causes which you pretty well know:—the pang of disappointment, the sting of pride, with some wandering stabs of remorse, which never fail to settle on my vitals like vultures, when attention is not called away by the calls of society, or the vagaries of the muse. Even in the hour of social mirth, my gaiety is the madness of an intoxicated criminal under the hands of the executioner. All these reasons urge me to go abroad, and to all these reasons I have only one answer—the feelings of a father. This, in the present mood I am in, overbalances every thing that can be laid in the scale against it.

You may perhaps think it an extravagant fancy, but it is a sentiment which strikes home to my very soul; though sceptical in some points of our current belief, yet I think I have every evidence for the reality of a life beyond the stinted bourne of our present existence: if so, then, how should I in the presence of that tremendous Being, the Author of existence, how should I meet the reproaches of those who stand to me in the dear relation of children, whom I deserted in the smiling innocency of helpless infancy? Oh thou great unknown Power!—thou Almighty God! who hast lighted up reason in my breast, and blessed me with immortality! —I have frequently wandered from that order and regularity necessary for the perfection of thy works, yet thou hast never left me nor forsaken me!

Since I wrote the foregoing sheet, I have seen something of the storm of mischief thickening over my folly-devoted head. Should you, my friends, my benefactors, be successful in your applications for me (8), perhaps it may not be in my power in that way, to reap the fruit of your friendly efforts.

What I have written in the preceding pages is the settled tenor of my present resolution; but should inimical circumstances forbid me closing with your kind offer, or enjoying it only threaten to entail further misery * * *

To tell the truth, I have little reason for complaint; as the world, in general, has been kind to me fully up to my deserts. I was, for some time past, fast getting into the pining, distrustful snarl of the misanthrope. I saw myself alone, unfit for the struggle of life, shrinking at every rising cloud in the chance-directed atmosphere of fortune, while, all defenceless, I looked about in vain for a cover. It never occurred to me, at least never with the force it deserved, that this world is a busy scene, and man a creature destined for a progressive struggle; and that, however I might possess a warm heart and inoffensive manners (which last, by the bye, was rather more than I could well boast), still, more than these passive qualities, there was something to be done. When all my school-fellows and youthful compeers (those misguided few excepted, who joined, to use a Gentoo phrase, the "hallachores" of the human race) were striking off with eager hope and earnest intent, in some one or other of the many paths of busy life, I was "standing idle in the market-place," or only left the chase of the butterfly from flower to flower, to hunt fancy from whim to whim.

You see, Sir, that if to know one's errors were a probability of mending them, I stand a fair chance; but according to the reverend Westminster divines, though conviction must precede conversion, it is very far from always implying it. R. B.

NO. XXVI.

TO MRS. STEWART, OF STAIR.

1786.

Madam.—The hurry of my preparations for going abroad has hindered me from performing my promise so soon as I intended. I have here sent you a parcel of songs, &c., which never made their appearance, except to a friend or two at most. Perhaps some of them may be no great entertainment to you, but of that I am far from being an adequate judge. The song to the tune of Ettrick Banks (The Bonnie Lass of Ballochmyle), you will easily see the impropriety of exposing much, even in manuscript. I think, myself, it has some merit, both as a tolerable description of one of nature's sweetest scenes, a July evening, and one of the finest pieces of nature's workmanship, the finest indeed we know anything of, an amiable, beautiful young woman (9); but I have no common friend to procure me that permission, without which I would not dare to spread the copy.

I am quite aware, Madam, what task the world would assign me in this letter. The obscure bard, when any of the great condescend to take notice of him should heap the altar with the incense of flattery. Their high ancestry, their own great and god-like qualities and actions, should be recounted with the most exaggerated description. This, Madam, is a task for which I am altogether unfit. Besides a certain disqualifying pride of heart, I know nothing of your connexions in life, and have no access to where your real character is to be found—the company of your compeers; and more, I am afraid that even the most refined adulation is by no means the road to your good opinion.

One feature of your character I shall ever with grateful pleasure remember—the reception I got when I had the honour of waiting on you at Stair. I am little acquainted with politeness, but I know a good deal of benevolence of temper and goodness of heart. Surely did those in exalted stations know how happy they could make some classes of their inferiors by condescension and affability, they would never stand so high, measuring out with every look the height of their elevation, but condescend as sweetly as did Mrs. Stewart of Stair. R. B.

NO. XXVII.

In the name of the NINE. *Amen.*

We, Robert Burns, by virtue of a warrant from Nature, bearing date the twenty-fifth day of January, anno domini one thousand seven hundred and fifty-nine (10), Poet Laureat, and Bard-in-Chief, in and over the districts and countries of Kyle, Cunningham, and Carrick, of old extent, To our trusty and well-beloved William Chalmers and John M'Adam, students and practitioners in the ancient and mysterious science of confounding wright and wrong.

Right Trusty—Be it known unto you, That whereas in the course of our care and watchings over the order and police of all and sundry the manufacturers, retainers, and venders of poesy; bards, poets, poetasters, rhymers, jinglers, songsters, ballad-singers, &c. &c. &c. &c., male and female—We have discovered a certain nefarious, abominable, and wicked song or ballad, a copy whereof We have here enclosed; Our Will therefore is that ye pitch upon and appoint the most execrable individual of that most execrable species, known by the appellation, phrase, and nickname of The Deil's Yell Nowte (11): and after having caused him to kindle a fire at the Cross of Ayr, ye shall, at noon-tide of the day, put into the said wretch's merciless hands the said copy of the said nefarious and wicked song, to be consumed by fire in presence of all beholders, in abhorrence of, and terror to, all such compositions and composers. And this in nowise leave ye undone, but have it executed in every point as this our mandate bears, before the twenty-fourth current, when in person We hope to applaud your faithfulness and zeal.

Given at Mauchline this twentieth day of November, anno domini one thousand seven hundred and eighty-six.

God save the Bard!

NO. XXVIII.

TO GAVIN HAMILTON, Esq., MAUCHLINE.

Edinburgh, Dec. 7th, 1786.

Honoured Sir.—I have paid every attention to your commands, but can only say, what perhaps you will have heard before this reach you, that Muirkirklands were bought by a John Gordon, W. S., but for whom I know not; Mauchlands, Haugh Miln, &c., by a Frederick Fotheringham, supposed to be for Ballochmyle Laird; And Adam-hill and Shawood were bought for Oswald's folks. This is so imperfect an account, and will be so late ere it reach you, that were it not to discharge my conscience I would not trouble you with it; but after all my diligence I could make it no sooner nor better.

For my own affairs, I am in a fair way of becoming as eminent as Thomas à Kempis or John Bunyan; and you may expect henceforth to see my birth-day inserted among the wonderful events, in the Poor Robin's and Aberdeen Almanacks, along with the black Monday, and the battle of Bothwell-bridge. My Lord Glencairn and the Dean of Faculty, Mr. H. Erskine, have taken me under their wing; and by all probability I shall soon be the tenth worthy, and the eighth wise man of the world. Through my lord's influence, it is inserted in the records of the Caledonian Hunt, that they universally, one and all, subscribe for the second edition. My subscription bills come out to-morrow, and you shall have some of them next post. I have met in Mr. Dalrymyle of Orangefield, what Solomon emphatically calls "a friend that sticketh closer than a brother." The warmth with which he interests himself in my affairs is of the same enthusiastic kind which you, Mr. Aiken, and the few patrons that took notice of my earlier poetic days, showed for the poor unlucky devil of a poet.

I always remember Mrs. Hamilton and Miss Kennedy in my poetic prayers, but you both in prose and verse.

May cauld ne'er catch you but a hap (12),
Nor hunger but in plenty's lap!
Amen! R. B.

NO. XXIX.

TO JOHN BALLANTINE, Esq., BANKER, AYR.

Edinburgh, Dec. 13th, 1786.

My Honoured Friend.—I would not write you till I could have it in my power to give you some account of myself and my matters, which, by the bye, is often no easy task. I arrived here on Tuesday was se'n-night, and have suffered ever since I came to town with a miserable head-ache and stomach complaint, but am now a good deal better. I have found a worthy warm friend in Mr. Dalrymple of Orangefield, who introduced me to Lord Glencairn, a man whose worth and brotherly kindness to me I shall remember when time shall be no more. By his interest it is passed in the "Caledonian Hunt," and entered in their books, that they are to take each a copy of the second edition, for which they are to pay one guinea. I have been introduced to a good many of the *noblesse*, but my avowed patrons and patronesses are, the Duchess of Gordon—the Countess of Glencairn, with my Lord, and Lady Betty (13)—the Dean of Faculty—Sir John Whitefoord. I have likewise warm friends among the literati; Professors Stewart, Blair, and Mr. Mackenzie—the "Man of Feeling." An unknown hand left ten guineas for the Ayrshire bard with Mr. Sibbald, which I got. I since have discovered my generous unknown friend to be Patrick Miller, Esq., brother to the Justice Clerk,—and drank a glass of claret with him by invitation at his own house yesternight. I am nearly agreed with Creech to print my book, and I suppose I will begin on Monday. I will send a subscription bill or two, next post; when I intend writing to my first kind patron,

Mr. Aiken. I saw his son to-day, and he is very well.

Dugald Stewart, and some of my learned friends, put me in the periodical paper called the Lounger (14,) a copy of which I here enclose you. I was, Sir, when I was first honoured with your notice, too obscure; now I tremble lest I should be ruined by being dragged too suddenly into the glare of polite and learned observation.

I shall certainly, my ever-honoured patron, write you an account of my every step; and better health and more spirits may enable me to make it something better than this stupid matter-of-fact epistle. I have the honour to be, good Sir, your ever grateful humble servant, R. B.

If any of my friends write me, my direction is, care of Mr Creech, bookseller,

---

NO. XXX.

TO MR. WILLIAM CHALMERS, WRITER, AYR.

Edinburgh, Dec. 27th, 1786,

My Dear Friend.—I confess I have sinned the sin for which there is hardly any forgiveness—ingratitude to friendship—in not writing you sooner; but of all men living, I had intended to have sent you an entertaining letter; and by all the plodding, stupid powers, that in nodding conceited majesty preside over the dull routine of business—a heavily-solemn oath this!—I am and have been, ever since I came to Edinburgh, as unfit to write a letter of humour as to write a commentary on the Revelation of St. John the Divine, who was banished to the Isle of Patmos by the cruel and bloody Domitian, son to Vespasian and brother to Titus, both emperors of Rome, and who was himself an emperor, and raised the second or third persecution, I forget which, against the Christians, and after throwing the said Apostle John, brother to the Apostle James, commonly called James the Greater, to distinguish him from another James, who was on some account or other known by the name of James the Less—after throwing him into a caldron of boiling oil, from which he was miraculously preserved, he banished the poor son of Zebedee to a desert island in the Archipelago, where he was gifted with the second sight, and saw as many wild beasts as I have seen since I came to Edinburgh; which, a—circumstance not very uncommon in story-telling—brings me back to where I set out.

To make you some amends for what, before you reach this paragraph, you will have suffered, I enclose you two poems I have carded and spun since I passed Glenbuck.

One blank in the Address to Edinburgh —"Fair B——," is heavenly Miss Burnet, daughter to Lord Monboddo, at whose house I have had the honour to be more than once There has not been anything nearly like her in all the combinations of beauty, grace, and goodness, the great Creator has formed, since Milton's Eve on the first day of her existence.

My direction is—care of Andrew Bruce, merchant, Bridge Street. R. B.

NO. XXXI.

TO DR. MACKENZIE, MAUCHLINE;

ENCLOSING HIM VERSES ON DINING WITH LORD DAER.

Wednesday Morning, 1787.

Dear Sir.—I never spent an afternoon among great folks with half that pleasure, as when, in company with you, I had the honour of paying my devoirs to that plain, honest, worthy man, the professor [Dugald Stewart]. I would be delighted to see him perform acts of kindness and friendship, though I were not the object; he does it with such a grace. I think his character, divided into ten parts, stands thus—four parts Socrates—four parts Nathaniel—and two parts Shakspeare's Brutus.

The foregoing verses were really extempore, but a little corrected since. They may entertain you a little, with the help of that partiality with which you are so good as to favour the performances of, dear Sir, your very humble servant, R. B.

NO. XXXII.

TO JOHN BALLANTINE, Esq.

January, 1787.

While here I sit, sad and solitary, by the side of a fire in a little country inn, and drying my wet clothes, in pops a poor fellow of a sodger, and tells me is going to Ayr. By heavens! say I to myself, with a tide of good spirits which the magic of that sound, auld toon o' Ayr, conjured up, I will send my last song to Mr. Ballantine. Here it is—

Ye flowery banks o' bonnie Doon,
How can ye blume sae fair;
How can ye chant, ye little birds,
And I sae fu' of care!—&c. R. B.

NO. XXXIII.

TO THE EARL OF EGLINTON.

Edinburgh, January, 1787.

MY LORD.—As I have but slender pretensions to philosophy, I cannot rise to the exalted ideas of a citizen of the world, but have all those national prejudices which, I believe, glow peculiarly strong in the breast of a Scotchman. There is scarcely anything to which I am so feelingly alive as the honour and welfare of my country; and as a poet, I have no higher enjoyment than singing her sons and daughters. Fate had cast my station in the veriest shades of life; but never did a heart pant more ardently than mine to be distinguished, though till, very lately, I looked in vain on every side for a ray of light. It is easy, then, to guess how much I was gratified with the countenance and approbation of one of my country's most illustrious sons, when Mr. Wauchope called on me yesterday on the part of your lordship. Your munificence, my lord, certainly deserves my very grateful acknowledgments; but your patronage is a bounty peculiarly suited to my feelings. I am not master enough of the etiquette of life to know, whether there be not some impropriety in troubling your lordship with my thanks, but my heart whispered me to do it. From the emotions of my inmost soul I do it. Selfish ingratitude, I hope, I am incapable of; and mercenary servility, I trust, I shall ever have so much honest pride as to detest. R. B.

NO. XXXIV.

TO JOHN BALLANTINE, Esq.

Edinburgh, Jan. 14*th,* 1787.

MY HONOURED FRIEND.—It gives me a secret comfort to observe in myself that I am not yet so far gone as Willie Gaw's Skate, "past redemption;" (15) for I have still this favourable symptom of grace, that when my conscience, as in the case of this letter, tells me I am leaving something undone that I ought to do, it teazes me eternally till I do it.

I am still "dark as was chaos" in respect to futurity. My generous friend, Mr. Patrick Miller, has been talking with me about a lease of some farm or other in an estate called Dalswinton, which he has lately bought near Dumfries. Some life-rented embittering recollections whisper me that I will be happier anywhere than in my old neighbourhood, but Mr. Miller is no judge of land; and though I dare say he means to favour me, yet he may give me, in his opinion, an advantageous bargain that may ruin me. I am to take a tour by Dumfries as I return, and have promised to meet Mr. Miller on his lands some time in May.

I went to a mason-lodge yesternight, where the most Worshipful Grand Master Chartres, and all the Grand Lodge of Scotland, visited. The meeting was numerous and elegant; all the different lodges about town were present, in all their pomp. The Grand Master, who presided with great solemnity and honour to himself as a gentleman and mason, among other general toasts, gave "Caledonia, and Caledonia's Bard, Brother Burns," which rang through the whole assembly with multiplied honours and repeated acclamations. As I had no idea such a thing would happen, I was downright thunderstruck, and, trembling in every nerve, made the best return in my power. Just as I had finished, some of the grand officers said so loud that I could hear, with a most comforting accent, "Very well, indeed!" which set me something to rights again.

I have to-day corrected my 152nd page. My best good wishes to Mr. Aiken. I am ever, dear Sir, your much indebted humble servant, R. B.

NO. XXXV.

TO MRS. DUNLOP.

Edinburgh, January 15*th,* 1787.

MADAM.—Yours of the 9th current, which I am this moment honoured with, is a deep reproach to me for ungrateful neglect. I will tell you the real truth, for I am miserably awkward at a fib, I wished to have written to Dr. Moore before I wrote to you; but, though every day since I received yours of December 30th, the idea, the wish to write to him, has constantly pressed on my thoughts, yet I could not for my soul set about it. I know his fame and character, and I am one of "the sons of little men." To write him a mere matter-of-fact affair, like a merchant's order, would be disgracing the little character I have; and to write the author of "The View of Society and Manners" a letter of sentiment—I declare every artery runs cold at the thought. I shall try, however, to write to him to-morrow or next day. His kind interposition in my behalf I have already experienced, as a gentleman waited on me the other day, on the part of Lord Eglinton, with ten guineas, by way of subscription for two copies of my next edition.

The word you object to in the mention I have made of my glorious countryman and your immortal ancestor, is indeed borrowed from Thomson; but it does not strike me as an improper epithet. I distrusted my own judgment on your finding fault with it, and applied for the opinion of some of the literati here who honour me with their critical strictures, and they all allow it to be proper. The song you ask I cannot recollect, and I have not a copy of it. I have not composed any thing on the great Wallace, except what you have seen in print, and the enclosed, which I will print in this edition. You will see I have mentioned some others of the name. When I composed my Vision long ago, I had attempted a description of Kyle, of which the additional stanzas are a part as it originally stood. My heart glows with a wish to be able to do justice to the merits of the "saviour of his country," which, sooner or later, I shall at least attempt.

You are afraid I shall grow intoxicated with my prosperity as a poet: alas! Madam, I know myself and the world too well. I do not mean any airs of affected modesty; I am willing to believe that my abilities deserve some notice; but in a most enlightened, informed age and nation, when poetry is and has been the study of men of the first natural genius, aided with all the powers of polite learning, polite books, and polite company—to be dragged forth to the full glare of learned and polite observation, with all my imperfections of awkward rusticity and crude unpolished ideas in my head—I assure you, Madam, I do not dissemble when I tell you I tremble for the consequences. The novelty of a poet in my obscure situation, without any of those advantages which are reckoned necessary for that character, at least at this time of day, has raised a partial tide of public notice which has borne me to a height, where I am absolutely, feelingly certain, my abilities are inadequate to support me; and too surely do I see that time when the same tide will leave me, and recede, perhaps, as far below the mark of truth. I do not say this in the ridiculous affectation of self-abasement and modesty. I have studied myself, and know what ground I occupy; and however a friend or the world may differ from me in that particular, I stand for my own opinion, in silent resolve, with all the tenaciousness of propriety. I mention this to you once for all, to disburden my mind, and I do not wish to hear or say more about it. But,

When proud fortune's ebbing tide recedes,

you will bear me witness, that when my bubble of fame was at the highest, I stood unintoxicated, with the inebriating cup in my hand, looking forward with rueful resolve to the hastening time when the blow of calumny should dash it to the ground, with all the eagerness of vengeful triumph.

Your patronising me, and interesting yourself in my fame and character as a poet, I rejoice in—it exalts me in my own idea—and whether you can or cannot aid me in my subscription, is a trifle. Has a paltry subscription-bill any charms to the heart of a bard, compared with the patronage of the descendant of the immortal Wallace?

R. B.

NO. XXXVI.

TO DR. MOORE. (16)

Edinburgh, Jan. 1787.

SIR.—Mrs. Dunlop has been so kind as to send me extracts of letters she has had from you, where you do the rustic bard the honour of noticing him and his works. Those who have felt the anxieties and solicitudes of authorship, can only know what pleasure it gives to be noticed in such a manner, by judges of the first character. Your criticisms, Sir, I receive with reverence; only I am sorry they mostly came too late; a peccant passage or two that I would certainly have altered, were gone to the press.

The hope to be admired for ages, is, in by far the greater part of those even who are authors of repute, an unsubstantial dream. For my part, my first ambition was, and still my strongest wish is, to please my compeers, the rustic inmates of the hamlet, while ever-changing language and manners shall allow me to be relished and understood. I am very willing to admit that I have some poetical abilities; and as few, if any writers, either moral or poetical, are intimately acquainted with the classes of mankind among whom I have chiefly mingled, I may have seen men and manners in a different phasis from what is common, which may assist originality of thought. Still I know very well the novelty of my character has by far the greatest share in the learned and polite notice I have lately had; and in a language where Pope and Churchill have raised the laugh, and Shenstone and Gray drawn the tear; where Thomson and Beattie have painted the landscape, and Lyttleton and Collins described the heart, I am not vain enough to hope for distinguished poetic fame. R. B.

NO. XXXVII.

TO THE REV. G. LAWRIE,

NEWMILLS, NEAR KILMARNOCK.

Edinburgh, Feb. 5th, 1787.

Reverend and Dear Sir.—When I look at the date of your kind letter, my heart reproaches me severely with ingratitude in neglecting so long to answer it. I will not trouble you with any account, by way of apology, of my hurried life and distracted attention; do me the justice to believe that my delay by no means proceeded from want of respect. I feel, and ever shall feel for you, the mingled sentiments for a friend, and reverence for a father.

I thank you, Sir, with all my soul, for your friendly hints, though I do not need them so much as my friends are apt to imagine. You are dazzled with newspaper accounts and distant reports; but, in reality, I have no great temptation to be intoxicated with the cup of prosperity. Novelty may attract the attention of mankind a while; to it I owe my present éclat; but I see the time not far distant when the popular tide, which has borne me to a height of which I am perhaps unworthy, shall recede with silent celerity, and leave me a barren waste of sand, to descend at my leisure to my former station. I do not say this in the affectation of modesty; I see the consequence is unavoidable, and am prepared for it. I had been at a good deal of pains to form a just, impartial estimate of my intellectual powers before I came here; I have not added, since I came to Edinburgh, any thing to the account; and I trust I shall take every atom of it back to my shades, the coverts of my unnoticed early years.

In Dr. Blacklock, whom I see very often, I have found what I would have expected in our friend, a clear head and an excellent heart.

By far the most agreeable hours I spend in Edinburgh, must be placed to the account of Miss Lawrie and her piano-forte. I cannot help repeating to you and Mrs. Lawrie a compliment that Mr. Mackenzie, the celebrated "Man of Feeling," paid to Miss Lawrie, the other night, at the concert. I had come in at the interlude, and sat down by him till I saw Miss Lawrie in a seat not very distant, and went up to pay my respects to her. On my return to Mr. Mackenzie, he asked me who she was; I told him 'twas the daughter of a reverend friend of mine in the west country. He returned, there was something very striking, to his idea, in her appearance. On my desiring to know what it was, he was pleased to say, "She has a great deal of the elegance of a well-bred lady about her, with all the sweet simplicity of a country girl."

My compliments to all the happy inmates of St. Margaret's. I am, my dear Sir, yours most gratefully, Robert Burns.

NO. XXXVIII.

TO JAMES DALRYMPLE, Esq.

ORANGEFIELD.

Edinburgh, 1787.

Dear Sir.—I suppose the devil is so elated with his success with you, that he is determined, by a *coup de main,* to complete his purposes on you all at once, in making you a poet. I broke open the letter you sent me—hummed over the rhymes—and as I saw they were extempore, said to myself, they were very well; but when I saw at the bottom a name that I shall ever value with grateful respect, "I gapit wide, but naething spak." I was nearly as much struck as the friends of Job, of affliction-bearing memory, when they sat down with him seven days and seven nights, and spake not a word.

I am naturally of a superstitious cast, and as soon as my wonder-scared imagination regained its consciousness, and resumed its functions, I cast about what this mania of yours might portend. My foreboding ideas had the wide stretch of possibility; and several events, great in their magnitude, and important in their consequences, occurred to my fancy. The downfall of the conclave, or the crushing of the Cork rumps—a ducal coronet to Lord George Gordon, and the Protestant interest—or St. Peter's keys to * * * * *

You want to know how I come on. I am just in *statu quo*, or, not to insult a gentleman with my Latin, in "auld use and wont." The noble Earl of Glencairn took me by the hand to-day, and interested himself in my concerns, with a goodness like that benevolent being whose image he so richly bears. He is a stronger proof of the immortality of the soul than any that philosophy ever produced. A mind like his can never die. Let the worshipful squire H. L., or the reverend Mast. J. M. go into their primitive nothing. At best, they are but ill-digested lumps of chaos, only one of them strongly tinged with bituminous particles and sulphureous effluvia. But my noble patron, eternal as the heroic swell of magnanimity, and the generous throb of benevolence, shall look on with princely eye at "the war of elements, the wreck of matter, and the crash of worlds." R. B.

NO. XXXIX.

TO DR. MOORE.

Edinburgh, February 15th, 1787.

SIR.—Pardon my seeming neglect in delaying so long to acknowledge the honour you have done me, in your kind notice of me, January 23rd. Not many months ago I knew no other employment than following the plough, nor could boast any thing higher than a distant acquaintance with a country clergyman. Mere greatness never embarasses me; I have nothing to ask from the great, and I do not fear their judgment; but genius, polished by learning, and at its proper point of elevation in the eye of the world, this of late I frequently meet with, and tremble at its approach. I scorn the affectation of seeming modesty to cover self-conceit. That I have some merit, I do not deny; but I see with frequent wringings of heart, that the novelty of my character, and the honest national prejudice of my countrymen: have borne me to a height altogether untenable to my abilities.

For the honour Miss Williams has done me, please, Sir, return her in my name my most grateful thanks. I have more than once thought of paying her in kind, but have hitherto quitted the idea in hopeless despondency. I had never before heard of her; but the other day I got her poems, which, for several reasons, some belonging to the head, and others the offspring of the heart, give me a great deal of pleasure. I have little pretensions to critic lore; there are, I think, two characteristic features in her poetry—the unfettered wild flight of native genius, and the querulous, sombre tenderness of "time-settled sorrow."

I only know what pleases me, often without being able to tell why. R. B. (17)

NO. XL.

TO JOHN BALLANTINE, Esq.

Edinburgh, Feb. 24, 1787.

MY HONOURED FRIEND.—I will soon be with you now, in guid black prent—in a week or ten days at farthest. I am obliged, against my own wish, to print subscribers' names; so if any of my Ayr friends have subscription bills, they must be sent into Creech directly. I am getting my phiz done by an eminent engraver, and if it can be ready in time, I will appear in my book, looking, like all other *fools*, to my title-page.

R. B.

NO. XLI.

TO MR. WILLIAM DUNBAR. (18.)

Lawn Market, Monday Morning, 1787.

DEAR SIR.—In justice to Spenser, I must acknowledge that there is scarcely a poet in the language could have been a more agreeable present to me; and in justice to you, allow me to say, Sir, that I have not met with a man in Edinburgh to whom I would so willingly have been indebted for the gift. The tattered rhymes I herewith present you, and the handsome volumes of Spenser for which I am so much indebted to your goodness, may perhaps be not in proportion to one another; but be that as it may, my gift, though far less valuable, is as sincere a mark of esteem as yours.

The time is approaching when I shall return to my shades; and I am afraid my numerous Edinburgh friendships are of so tender a construction, that they will not bear carriage with me. Yours is one of the few that I could wish of a more robust constitution. It is indeed very probable that when I leave this city, we part never more to meet in this sublunary sphere; but I have a strong fancy that in some future eccentric planet, the comet of happier systems than any with which astronomy is yet acquainted, you and I, among the harum-scarum sons of imagination and whim, with a hearty shake of a hand, a metaphor and a laugh, shall recognise old acquaintance:

Where wit may sparkle all its rays,
  Uncurst with caution's fears;
That pleasure, basking in the blaze,
  Rejoice for endless years.

I have the honour to be, with the warmest sincerity, dear Sir, &c. R. B.

NO. XLII.

TO THE EARL OF GLENCAIRN.

Edinburgh, February, 1787.

MY LORD.—I wanted to purchase a profile of your lordship, which I was told was to be got in town; but I am truly sorry to see that a blundering painter has spoiled a "human face divine." The enclosed stanzas I intended to have written below a picture or profile or your lordship, could I have been so happy as to procure one with any thing of a likeness.

As I will soon return to my shades, I wanted to have something like a material object for my gratitude; I wanted to have it in my power to say to a friend, there is my noble patron, my generous benefactor. Allow me, my lord, to publish these verses. I conjure your lordship, by the honest throe of gratitude, by the generous wish of benevolence, by all the powers and feelings which compose the magnanimous mind, do not deny me this petition. I owe much to your lordship; and, what has not in some other instances always been the case with me, the weight of the obligation is a pleasing load. I trust I have a heart as independent as your lordship's, than which I can say nothing more: and I would not be beholden to favours that would crucify my feelings. Your dignified character in life, and manner of supporting that character, are flattering to my pride; and I would be jealous of the purity of my grateful attachment, where I was under the patronage of one of the much-favoured sons of fortune.

Almost every poet has celebrated his patrons, particularly when they were names dear to fame, and illustrious in their country: allow me, then, my lord, if you think the verses have intrinsic merit, to tell the world how much I have the honour to be, your lordship's highly indebted, and ever grateful humble servant, R. B.

NO. XLIII.

TO MR. JAMES CANDLISH,

STUDENT IN PHYSIC, GLASGOW COLLEGE.

Edinburgh, March 21st, 1787.

MY EVER DEAR OLD ACQUAINTANCE.—I was equally surprised and pleased at your letter, though I dare say you will think, by my delaying so long to write to you, that I am so drowned in the intoxication of good fortune as to be indifferent to old, and once dear connexions. The truth is, I was determined to write a good letter, full of argument, amplification, erudition, and, as Bayes says, *all that.* I thought of it, and thought of it, and by my soul I could not; and, lest you should mistake the cause of my silence, I just sit down to tell you so. Don't give yourself credit, though, that the strength of your logic scares me: the truth is, I never mean to meet you on that ground at all. You have shown me one thing which was to be demonstrated: that strong pride of reasoning, with a little affectation of singularity, may mislead the best of hearts. I likewise, since you and I were first acquainted, in the pride of despising old women's stories, ventured in the "daring path Spinosa trod;" but experience of the weakness, not the strength of human powers, made me glad to grasp at revealed religion.

I am still, in the Apostle Paul's phrase, "The old man with his deeds," as when we were sporting about the "Lady Thorn." I shall be four weeks here yet at least, and so I shall expect to hear from you; welcome sense, welcome nonsense. I am, with the warmest sincerity, yours, &c., R. B.

NO. XLIV.

TO ———,

ON FERGUSSON'S HEADSTONE,

Edinburgh, March, 1787.

MY DEAR SIR.—You may think, and too justly, that I am a selfish, ungrateful fellow, having received so many repeated instances of kindness from you, and yet never putting pen to paper to say "thank you"; but if you knew what a devil of a life my conscience has led me on that account, your good heart would think yourself too much avenged. By the bye, there is nothing in the whole frame of man which seems to be so unaccountable as that thing called conscience. Had the troublesome, yelping cur powers sufficient to prevent a mischief, he might be of use; but at the beginning of the business, his feeble efforts are to the workings of passion as the infant frosts of an autumnal morning to the unclouded fervour of the rising sun: and no sooner are the tumultuous doings of the wicked deed over, than, amidst the bitter native consequences of folly in the very vortex of our horrors, up starts conscience, and harrows us with the feelings of the damned.

I have enclosed you by way of expiation, some verses and prose, that, if they merit a place in your truly entertaining miscellany, you are welcome to. The prose extract is literally as Mr. Sprott sent it me.

The inscription on the stone is as follows:—

"HERE LIES ROBERT FERGUSSON, POET.

Born, September 5th, 1751—Died, 16th October, 1774.

"No sculptured marble here, nor pompous lay,
'No storied urn, nor animated bust;'
This simple stone directs pale Scotia's way
To pour her sorrows o'er her poet's dust.'"

On the other side of the stone is as follows:—

"By special grant of the managers to Robert Burns, who erected this stone, this burial-place is to remain for ever sacred to to the memory of Robert Fergusson."

Session-house within the kirk of Canongate, the twenty-second day of February, one thousand seven hundred eighty-seven years.

Sederunt of the Managers of the Kirk and Kirk-yard funds of Canongate.

Which day, the treasurer to the said funds produced a letter from Mr. Robert Burns, of date the 6th current, which was read and appointed to be engrossed in their sederunt book, and of which letter the tenor follows:—

"To the honourable bailies of Canongate, Edinburgh.—Gentlemen, I am sorry to be told that the remains of Robert Fergusson, the so justly celebrated poet, a man whose talents for ages to come will do honour to our Caledonian name, lie in your church-yard among the ignoble dead, unnoticed and unknown.

Some memorial to direct the steps of the lovers of Scottish song, when they wish to shed a tear over the 'narrow house' of the bard who is no more, is surely a tribute due to Fergusson's memory—a tribute I wish to have the honour of paying.

I petition you then, gentlemen, to permit me to lay a simple stone over his revered ashes, to remain an unalienable property to his deathless fame. I have the honour to be, gentlemen, your very humble servant, *(sic subscribitur)* ROBERT BURNS."

Therefore the said managers, in consideration of the laudable and disinterested motion of Mr Burns, and the propriety of his request, did, and hereby do, unanimously, grant power and liberty to the said Robert Burns to erect a headstone at the grave of the said Robert Fergusson, and to keep up and preserve the same to his memory in all time coming. Extracted forth of the records of the managers, by

WILLIAM SPROTT, Clerk.

NO. XLV.

TO THE EARL OF BUCHAN.

MY LORD.—The honour your lordship has done me, by your notice and advice in yours of the 1st instant, I shall ever gratefully remember:—

Praise from thy lips 'tis mine with joy to boast,
They best can give it who deserve it most.

Your lordship touches the darling chord of my heart, when you advise me to fire my muse at Scottish story and Scottish scenes. I wish for nothing more than to make a leisurely pilgrimage through my native country; to sit and muse on those once hard-contended fields, where Caledonia, rejoicing, saw her bloody lion borne through broken ranks to victory and fame; and catching the inspiration, to pour the deathless names in song. But, my lord, in the midst of these enthusiastic reveries, a long-visaged, dry moral-looking phantom strides across my imagination, and pronounces these emphatic words:—

"I, Wisdom, dwell with Prudence. Friend, I do not come to open the ill-closed wounds of your follies and misfortunes, merely to give you pain: I wish through these wounds to imprint a lasting lesson on your heart. I will not mention how many of my salutary advices you have despised; I have given you line upon line and precept upon precept; and while I was chalking out to you the straight way to wealth and character, with audacious effrontery you have zigzagged across the path, contemning me to my face: you know the consequences. It is not yet three months since home was so hot for you that you were on the wing for the western shore of the Atlantic, not to make a fortune, but to hide your misfortune.

"Now that your dear-loved Scotia puts it in your power to return to the situation of your forefathers, will you follow these will-o'-wisp meteors of fancy and whim, till they bring you once more to the brink of ruin? I grant that the utmost ground you can occupy is but half a step from the veriest poverty; but still it is half a step from it.

If all that I can urge be ineffectual, let her who seldom calls to you in vain, let the call of pride prevail with you. You know how you feel at the iron gripe of ruthless oppression: you know how you bear the galling sneer of contumelious greatness. I hold you out the conveniences, the comforts of life, independence and character, on the one hand; I tender you servility, dependence, and wretchedness, on the other. I will not insult your understanding by bidding you make a choice."

This, my lord, is unanswerable. I must return to my humble station, and woo my rustic muse, in my wonted way, at the plough-tail. Still, my lord, while the drops of life warm my heart, gratitude to that dear-loved country in which I boast my birth, and gratitude to those her distinguished sons who have honoured me so much with their patronage and approbation, shall, while stealing through my humble shades, ever distend my bosom, and at times, as now, draw forth the swelling tear. R. B.

NO. XLVI.

TO MRS. DUNLOP.

Edinburgh, March 22nd, 1787.

MADAM.—I read your letter with watery eyes. A little, very little while ago, I had scarce a friend but the stubborn pride of my own bosom; now I am distinguished, patronised, befriended by you. Your friendly advices, I will not give them the cold name of criticisms, I receive with reverence. I have made some small alterations in what I before had printed. I have the advice of some very judicious friend among the literati here, but with them I sometimes find it necessary to claim the privilege of thinking for myself. The noble Earl of Glencairn, to whom I owe more than to any man, does me the honour of giving me his strictures; his hints, with respect to impropriety or indelicacy, I follow implicitly.

You kindly interest yourself in my future views and prospects; there I can give you no light. It is all

Dark as was chaos ere the infant sun
Was roll'd together, or had tried his beams
Athwart the gloom profound.

The appellation of a Scottish bard is by far my highest pride; to continue to deserve it is my most exalted ambition. Scottish scenes and Scottish story are the themes I could wish to sing. I have no dearer aim than to have it in my power, unplagued with the routine of business, for which, Heaven knows, I am unfit enough, to make leisurely pilgrimages through Caledonia; to sit on the fields of her battles, to wander on the romantic banks of her rivers, and to muse by the stately towers or venerable ruins, once the honoured abodes of her heroes.

But these are all Utopian thoughts; I have dallied long enough with life; 'tis time to be in earnest. I have a fond, an aged mother to care for, and some other bosom ties perhaps equally tender. Where the individual only suffers by the consequences of his own thoughtlessness, indolence, or folly, he may be excusable—nay, shining abilities, and some of the nobler virtues, may half sanctify a heedless character; but where God and nature have intrusted the welfare of others to his care—where the trust is sacred, and the ties are dear—that man must be far gone in selfishness, or strangely lost to reflection, whom these connexions will not rouse to exertion.

I guess that I shall clear between two and three hundred pounds by my authorship; with that sum I intend, so far as I may be said to have any intention, to return to my old acquaintance, the plough, and, if I can meet with a lease by which I can live, to commence farmer. I do not intend to give up poetry; being bred to labour secures me independence, and the muses are my chief, sometimes have been my only enjoyment. If my practice second my resolution, I shall have principally at heart the serious business of life; but while following my plough, or building up my shocks, I shall cast a leisure glance to that dear, that only feature of my character, which gave me the notice of my country, and the patronage of a Wallace.

Thus, honoured Madam, I have given you the bard, his situation, and his views, native as they are in his own bosom. R. B.

NO. XLVII.

TO MRS. DUNLOP.

Edinburgh, April 15th, 1787.

MADAM.—There is an affectation of gratitude which I dislike. The periods of Johnson and the pauses of Sterne may hide a selfish heart. For my part, Madam, I trust I have too much pride for servility, and too little prudence for selfishness. I have this moment broken open your letter, but

Rude am I in speech,
And therefore little can I grace my cause
In speaking for myself—

so I shall not trouble you with any fine speeches and hunted figures. I shall just lay my hand on my heart and say, I hope I shall ever have the truest, the warmest sense of your goodness.

I come abroad, in print, for certain on Wednesday. Your orders I shall punctually attend to; only, by the way, I must tell you that I was paid before for Dr. Moore's and Miss Williams's copies, through the medium of Commissioner Cochrane in this place, but that we can settle when I have the honour of waiting on you.

Dr. Smith (19) was just gone to London the morning before I received your letter to him. R. B.

NO. XLVIII.

TO DR. MOORE.

Edinburgh, April, 23rd 1787.

I RECEIVED the books, and sent the one you mentioned to Mrs. Dunlop. I am ill skilled in beating the coverts of imagination for metaphors of gratitude. I thank you, Sir, for the honour you have done me, and to my latest hour will warmly remember it. To be highly pleased with your book is, what I have in common with the world, but to regard these volumes as a mark of the author's friendly esteem, is a still more supreme gratification.

I leave Edinburgh in the course of ten days or a fortnight, and, after a few pilgrimages over some of the classic ground of Caledonia, Cowden Knowes, Banks of Yarrow, Tweed, &c., I shall return to my rural shades, in all likelihood never more to quit them. I have formed many intimacies and friendships here, but I am afraid they are all of too tender a construction to bear carriage a hundred and fifty miles. To the rich, the great, the fashionable, the polite, I have no equivalent to offer; and I am afraid my meteor appearance will by no means entitle me to a settled correspondence with any of you, who are the permanent lights of genius and literature.

My most respectful compliments to Miss Williams. If once this tangent flight of mine were over, and I were returned to my wonted leisurely motion in my old circle, I may probably endeavour to return her poetic compliment in kind. R. B. (20)

NO. XLIX.

TO MRS. DUNLOP

Edinburgh, April 30th, 1787.

——YOUR criticisms, Madam, I understand very well, and could have wished to have pleased you better. You are right in your guess that I am not very amenable to counsel. Poets, much my superiors, have so flattered those who possessed the adventitious qualities of wealth and power, that I am determined to flatter no created being, either in prose or verse.

I set as little by princes, lords, clergy, critics, &c., as all these respective gentry do by my bardship. I know what I may expect from the world by and bye—illiberal abuse, and perhaps contemptuous neglect.

I am happy, Madam, that some of my own favourite pieces are distinguished by your particular approbation. For my "Dream," which has unfortunately incurred your loyal displeasure, I hope in four weeks, or less, to have the honour of appearing, at Dunlop, in its defence in person. R. B.

NO. L.

TO JAMES JOHNSON,

EDITOR OF THE SCOTS MUSICAL MUSEUM.

Lawnmarket, Friday Noon, May 3rd, 1787.

DEAR SIR.—I have sent you a song never before known for your collection; the air by M'Gibbon, but I know not the author of the words, as I got it from Dr. Blacklock.

Farewell, my dear Sir! I wished to have seen you, but I have been dreadfully throng (21), as I march to-morrow. (22) Had my acquaintance with you been a little older, I would have asked the favour of your correspondence, as I have met with few people whose company and conversation gave me so much pleasure, because I have met with few whose sentiments are so congenial to my own.

When Dunbar and you meet, tell him that I left Edinburgh with the idea of him hanging somewhere about my heart.

Keep the original of this song till we meet again, whenever that may be. R. B.

NO. LI.

TO THE REV. DR. HUGH BLAIR.

Lawnmarket, Edinburgh,
May 3rd, 1787.

Rev. and much-Respected Sir.—I leave Edinburgh to-morrow morning, but could not go without troubling you with half a line, sincerely to thank you for the kindness, patronage and friendship you have shown me. I often felt the embarrassment of my singular situation; drawn forth from the veriest shades of life to the glare of remark, and honoured by the notice of those illustrious names of my country, whose works, while they are applauded to the end of time, will ever instruct and mend the heart. However the meteor-like novelty of my appearance in the world might attract notice, and honour me with the acquaintance of the permanent lights of genius and literature, those who are truly benefactors of the immortal nature of man, I knew very well that my utmost merit was far unequal to the task of preserving that character when once the novelty was over; I have so made up my mind that abuse, or almost even neglect, will not surprise me in my quarters.

I have sent you a proof impression of Beugo's work (23) for me, done on Indian paper, as a trifling but sincere testimony with what heart-warm gratitude I am, &c.

R. B. (24)

NO. LII.

TO WILLIAM CREECH, Esq., EDINBURGH.

Selkirk, May 13th, 1787.

My Honoured Friend.—The enclosed I have just wrote (25), nearly extempore, in a solitary inn in Selkirk, after a miserably wet day's riding. I have been over most of East Lothian, Berwick, Roxburgh, and Selkirk shires, and next week I begin a tour through the north of England. Yesterday I dined with Lady Harriet, sister to my noble patron (26), *Quem Deus conservet!* I would write till I would tire you as much with dull prose, as I daresay by this time you are with wretched verse; but I am jaded to death; so, with a grateful farewell, I have the honour to be, good Sir, yours sincerely,

R. B.

NO. LIII.

TO MR. JAMES CANDLISH.

Edinburgh, 1787.

My Dear Friend.—If once I were gone from this scene of hurry and dissipation, I promise myself the pleasure of that correspondence being renewed which has been so long broken. At present I have time for nothing. Dissipation and business engross every moment. I am engaged in assisting an honest Scotch enthusiast (27), a friend of mine, who is an engraver, and has taken it into his head to publish a collection of all our songs set to music, of which the words and music are done by Scotsmen. This, you will easily guess, is an undertaking exactly to my taste. I have collected, begged, borrowed, and stolen, all the songs I could meet with. Pompey's Ghost, words and music, I beg from you immediately, to go into his second number—the first is already published. I shall show you the first number when I see you in Glasgow, which will be in a fortnight or less. Do be so kind as to send me the song in a day or two—you cannot imagine how much it will oblige me.

Direct to me at Mr. W. Cruikshank's, St. James's Square, New Town, Edinburgh.

R. B.

LIV.

TO MR. PATISON, BOOKSELLER, PAISLEY.

Berry-well, near Dunse,
May 17th, 1787.

Dear Sir.—I am sorry I was out of Edinburgh, making a slight pilgrimage to the classic scenes of this country, when I was favoured with yours of the 11th instant, enclosing an order of the Paisley Banking Company on the Royal Bank, for twenty-two pounds seven shillings sterling, payment in full, after carriage deducted, for ninety copies of my book I sent you. According to your motions, I see you will have left Scotland before this reaches you, otherwise I would send you "Holy Willie" with all my heart. I was so hurried that I absolutely forgot several things I ought to have minded:—among the rest, sending books to Mr. Cowan; but any order of yours will be answered at Creech's shop. You will please remember that non-subscribers pay six shillings, this is Creech's profit; but those who have subscribed, though their names have been neglected in the printed list, which is very incorrect, are supplied at the subscription price. I was not at Glasgow, nor do I intend to go to London; and I think Mrs. Fame is very idle to tell so many lies on a poor poet. When you or Mr. Cowan write for copies, if you should want any, direct to Mr. Hill, at Mr. Creech's shop (28), and I write to Mr. Hill by this post, to answer either of your orders. Hill is Mr. Creech's first clerk, and Creech himself is presently in London. I suppose I shall have the pleasure, against your return to Paisley, of assuring you how much I am, dear Sir, your obliged, humble servant, R. B.

NO. LV.

TO MR. W. NICOL,

MASTER OF THE HIGH SCHOOL, EDINBURGH.

Carlisle, June 1, 1787.

KIND HONEST-HEARTED WILLIE—I'm sitten down here, after seven and forty miles ridin', e'en as forjesket and forniaw'd as a forfoughten cock, to gie you some notion o' my land-lowper-like stravaguin sin' the sorrowfu' hour that I sheuk hands and parted wi' Auld Reekie.

My auld, ga'd gleyde o' a meere has huchyall'd up hill and down brae, in Scotland and England, as teugh and birnie as a very devil wi' me. It's true she's as poor's a sangmaker and as hard's a kirk, and tippertaipers when she taks the gate, first like a lady's gentle-woman in a minuwae, or a hen on a het girdle; but she's a yauld, poutherie girran for a' that, and has a stomach like Willie Stalker's meere, that wad hae digeested tumbler-wheels—for she'll whip me aff her five stimparts o' the best aits at a down-sittin, and ne'er fash her thumb. When ance her ringbanes and spavies, her crucks and cramps, are fairly soupl'd, she beets to, beets to, and aye the hindmost hour the tightest. I could wager her price to a threttie pennies, that for twa or three wooks ridin' at fifty mile a-day, the deil-sticket a five gallopers acqueesh Clyde and Whithorn could cast saut on her tail. (29)

I hae dander'd owre a' the kintra frae Dumbar to Selcraig, and hae forgather'd wi' mony a guid fallow, and mony a weelfar'd hizzie. I met wi' twa dink, quines in particular, ane o' them a sonsie, fine, fodgel lass—baith, braw and bonnie; the tither was a clean-shankit, straught, tight, weel-far'd winch, as blythe's a lintwhite on a flowerie thorn, and as sweet and modest's a new-blawn plum-rose in a hazle shaw. They were baith bred to mainers by the benk, and onie ane o' them had as muckle smeddum and rumblegumption as the half o' some presbytries that you and I baith ken. They play'd me sick a de.l o' a shavie, that I daur say, if my harigals were turn'd out, ye wad see twa nicks i' the heart o' me like the mark o' a kail-whittle in a castock.

I was gaun to write you a lang pystle, but God forgie me, I gat mysel sae noutouriously bitchify'd the day, after kail-time, that I can hardly stoiter bot and ben.

My best respecks to the guidwife and a' our common friens, especially Mr. and Mrs. Cruikshank, and the honest guidman o' Jock's Lodge.

I'll be in Dumfries the morn gif the beast be to the fore, and the branks bide hale. Guid be wi' you, Willie! Amen! R. B.

NO. LVI.

TO WILLIAM NICOL, Esq.

Auchtertyre (30), *June*, 1787.

MY DEAR SIR.—I find myself very comfortable here, neither oppressed by ceremony, nor mortified by neglect. Lady Augusta is a most engaging woman, and very happy in her family, which makes one's outgoings and incomings very agreeable. I called at Mr. Ramsay's of Auchtertyre (31), as I came up the country, and am so delighted with him, that I shall certainly accept of his invitation to spend a day or two with him as I return. I leave this place on Wednesday or Thursday.

Make my kind compliments to Mr. and Mrs. Cruikshank and Mrs. Nicol, if she is returned. I am ever, dear Sir, your deeply indebted R. B.

NO. LVII.

TO MR. W. NICOL,

MASTER OF THE HIGH SCHOOL, EDINBURGH.

Mauchline, June 18, 1787.

MY DEAR FRIEND.—I am now arrived safe in my native country, after a very agreeable jaunt, and have the pleasure to find all my friends well. I breakfasted with your grey-headed, reverend friend, Mr. Smith; and was highly pleased both with the cordial welcome he gave me, and his most excellent appearance and sterling good sense.

I have been with Mr. Miller at Dalswinton, and am to meet him again in August. From my view of the lands, and his reception of my bardship, my hopes in that business are rather mended; but still they are but slender.

I am quite charmed with Dumfries folks:—Mr. Burnside, the clergyman, in particular, is a man whom I shall ever gratefully remember; and his wife—guid forgie me! I had almost broke the tenth commandment on her account. Simplicity, elegance, good sense, sweetness of disposition, good humour, kind hospitality, are the constituents of her manner and heart: in short—but if I say one word more about her, I shall be directly in love with her.

I never, my friend, thought mankind very capable of anything generous; but the stateliness of the patricians in Edinburgh, and the civility of my plebeian brethren (who perhaps formerly eyed me askance) since I returned home, have nearly put me out of conceit altogether with my species. I have bought a pocket Milton, which I carry perpetually about with me, in order to study the sentiments, the dauntless magnanimity, the intrepid, unyielding independence, the desperate daring, and noble defiance of hardship in that great personage, Satan. 'Tis true, I have just now a little cash; but I am afraid the star that hitherto has shed its malignant, purpose-blasting rays full in my zenith,—that noxious planet, so baneful in its influences to the rhyming tribe,—I much dread it is not yet beneath my horizon. Misfortune dodges the path of human life; the poetic mind finds itself miserably deranged in, and unfit for the walks of business; add to all, that thoughtless follies and hair-brained whims, like so many *ignes fatui* eternally diverging from the right line of sober discretion, sparkle with step-bewitching blaze in the idly-gazing eyes of the poor heedless bard, till pop, "he falls like Lucifer, never to hope again." God grant that this may be an unreal picture with respect to me! but should it not, I have very little dependence on mankind. I will close my letter with this tribute my heart bids me pay you—the many ties of acquaintance and friendship which I have, or think I have in life, I have felt along the lines, and damn them, they are almost all of them of such frail contexture, that I am sure they would not stand the breath of the least adverse breeze of fortune; but from you, my ever dear Sir, I look with confidence for the apostolic love that shall wait on me "through good report and bad report"—the love which Solomon emphatically says "is strong as death." My compliments to Mrs. Nicol, and all the circle of our common friends.

P. S. I shall be in Edinburgh about the latter end of July. R. B.

NO. LVIII.

TO WILLIAM CRUIKSHANK. (32)

ST. JAMES'S SQUARE, EDINBURGH.

Auchtertyre, June, 1787.

I HAVE nothing, my dear Sir, to write to you, but that I feel myself exceedingly comfortably situated in this good family—just notice enough to make me easy but not to embarrass me. I was storm-staid two days at the foot of the Ochill Hills, with Mr. Tait of Herveyston and Mr. Johnston of Alva, but was so well pleased that I shall certainly spend a day on the banks of the Devon as I return. I leave this place I suppose on Wednesday, and shall devote a day to Mr. Ramsay, at Auchtertyre, near Stirling—a man to whose worth I cannot do justice. My respectful kind compliments to Mrs. Cruikshank, and my dear little Jeanie, and if you see Mr. Masterton, please remember me to him. I am ever, my dear Sir, &c.

R. B.

NO. LIX.

TO MR. JOHN RICHMOND.

Mossgiel, July 7th, 1787.

MY DEAR RICHMOND.—I am all impatience to hear of your fate since the old confounder of right and wrong has turned you out of place, by his journey to answer his indictment at the bar of the other world. He will find the practice of the court so different from the practice in which he has for so many years been thoroughly hackneyed, that his friends, if he had any connections truly of that kind, which I rather doubt, may well tremble for his sake. His chicane, his left-handed wisdom, which stood so firmly by him, to such good purpose, here, like other accomplices in robbery and plunder, will, now the piratical business is blown, in all probability turn king's evidences, and then the devil's bagpiper will touch him off "Bundle and go."

If he has left you any legacy, I beg your pardon for all this; if not, I know you will swear to every word I said about him.

I have lately been rambling over by Dumbarton and Inverary, and running a drunken race on the side of Loch Lomond with a wild Highlandman; his horse, which had never known the ornaments of iron or leather, zigzagged across before my old spavin'd hunter, whose name is Jenny Geddes, and down came the Highlandman, horse and all, and down came Jenny and my ladyship; so I have got such a skinful of bruises and wounds, that I shall be at least four weeks before I dare venture on my journey to Edinburgh.

Not one new thing under the sun has happened in Mauchline since you left it. I hope this will find you as comfortably situated as formerly, or, if Heaven pleases, more so; but, at all events, I trust you will let me know, of course, how matters stand with you, well or ill. 'Tis but poor consolation to tell the world when matters go wrong, but you know very well your connection and mine stands on a different footing. I am ever, my dear friend, yours,

R. B.

NO. LX.

TO ROBERT AINSLIE, Esq.

Mauchline, July, 1787.

My Dear Sir.—My life, since I saw you last, has been one continued hurry; that savage hospitality which knocks a man down with strong liquors, is the devil. I have a sore warfare in this world; the devil, the world, and the flesh, are three formidable foes. The first I generally try to fly from; the second, alas! generally flies from me; but the third is my plague, worse than the ten plagues of Egypt.

I have been looking over several farms in this country; one in particular, in Nithsdale, pleased me so well, that, if my offer to the proprietor is accepted, I shall commence farmer at Whitsunday. If farming do not appear eligible, I shall have recourse to my other shift; but this to a friend.

I set out for Edinburgh on Monday morning; how long I stay there is uncertain, but you will know so soon as I can inform you myself. However I determine, poesy must be laid aside for some time; my mind has been vitiated with idleness, and it will take a good deal of effort to habituate it to the routine of business. I am, my dear Sir, yours sincerely, R. B.

NO. LXI.

TO ROBERT AINSLIE. (33)

Mauchline, July 23rd, 1787.

My Dear Ainslie.—There is one thing for which I set great store by you as a friend, and it is this, that I have not a friend upon earth, besides yourself, to whom I can talk nonsense without forfeiting some degree of his esteem. Now, to one like me, who never cares for speaking any thing else but nonsense, such a friend as you is an invaluable treasure. I was never a rogue, but have been a fool all my life; and, in spite of all my endeavours, I see now plainly that I shall never be wise. Now it rejoices my heart to have met with such a fellow as you, who, though you are not just such a hopeless fool as I, yet I trust you will never listen so much to the temptations of the devil, as to grow so very wise that you will in the least disrespect an honest fellow because he is a fool. In short, I have set you down as the staff of my old age, when the whole list of my friends will, after a decent share of pity, have forgot me.

Though in the morn comes sturt and strife,
 Yet joy may come at noon;
And I hope to live a merry merry life
 When a' thir days are done.

Write me soon, were it but a few lines just to tell me how that good, sagacious man, your father, is—that kind dainty body your mother—that strapping chiel your brother Douglas—and my friend Rachel, who is as far before Rachel of old, as she was before her blear-eyed sister Leah.

R. B.

NO. LXII.

TO MR. ROBERT MUIR.

Stirling, August 26th, 1787.

My Dear Sir.—I intended to have written you from Edinburgh, and now write you from Stirling to make an excuse. Here am I, on my way to Inverness, with a truly original, but very worthy man, a Mr. Nicol, one of the masters of the High-school in Edinburgh.—I left Auld Reekie yesterday morning, and have passed, besides by-excursions, Linlithgow, Borrowstouness, Falkirk, and here am I undoubtedly. This morning I knelt at the tomb of Sir John the Graham, the gallant friend of the immortal Wallace; and two hours ago I said a fervent prayer for old Caledonia over the hole in a blue whinstone, where Robert de Bruce fixed his royal standard on the banks of Bannockburn; and just now, from Stirling Castle, I have seen by the setting sun the glorious prospect of the windings of Forth through the rich carse of Stirling, and skirting the equally rich carse of Falkirk. The crops are very strong, but so very late that there is no harvest except a ridge or two perhaps in ten miles, all the way I have travelled from Edinburgh.

I left Andrew Bruce (34) and family all well. I will be at least three weeks in making my tour, as I shall return by the coast, and have many people to call for.

My best compliments to Charles, our dear kinsman and fellow-saint; and Messrs. W. and H. Parker. I hope Hughoc (35) is going on and prospering with God and Miss M'Causlin.

If I could think on any thing sprightly, I should let you hear every other post; but a dull, matter-of-fact business like this scrawl, the less and seldomer one writes the better.

Among other matters-of-fact I shall add this, that I am and ever shall be, my dear Sir, your obliged R. B.

NO. LXIII.

TO GAVIN HAMILTON, Esq.

Stirling, August 28th, 1787.

MY DEAR SIR.—Here am I on my way to Inverness. I have rambled over the rich, fertile carses of Falkirk and Stirling, and am delighted with their appearance: richly waving crops of wheat, barley, &c., but no harvest at all yet, except in one or two places an old-wife's ridge. Yesterday morning I rode from this town up the meandering Devon's banks, to pay my respects to some Ayrshire folks at Harvieston. After breakfast, we made a party to go and see the famous Caudron-linn, a remarkable cascade in the Devon, about five miles above Harvieston; and after spending one of the most pleasant days I ever had in my life, I returned to Stirling in the evening. They are a family, Sir, though I had not had any prior tie—though they had not been the brother and sisters of a certain generous friend of mine—I would never forget them. I am told you have not seen them these several years, so you can have very little idea of what these young folks are now. Your brother is as tall as you are, but slender rather than otherwise; and I have the satisfaction to inform you that he is getting the better of those consumptive symptoms which I suppose you know were threatening him. His make, and particularly his manner, resemble you, but he will still have a finer face. (I put in the word *still*, to please Mrs. Hamilton.) Good sense, modesty, and at the same time a just idea of that respect that man owes to man, and has a right in his turn to exact, are striking features in his character; and, what with me is the Alpha and Omega, he has a heart that might adorn the breast of a poet! Grace has a good figure, and the look of health and cheerfulness, but nothing else remarkable in her person. I scarcely ever saw so striking a likeness as is between her and your little Beenie; the mouth and chin particularly. She is reserved at first; but as we grew better acquainted, I was delighted with the native frankness of her manner, and the sterling sense of her observation. Of Charlotte I cannot speak in common terms of admiration: she is not only beautiful but lovely. Her form is elegant; her features not regular, but they have the smile of sweetness and the settled complacency of good nature, in the highest degree; and her complexion, now that she has happily recovered her wonted health, is equal to Miss Burnet's. After the exercise of our riding to the Falls, Charlotte was exactly Dr. Donne's mistress:—

————Her pure and eloquent blood
Spoke in her cheeks, and so distinctly wrought,
That one would almost say her body thought.

Her eyes are fascinating; at once expressive of good sense, tenderness, and a noble mind. (36)

I do not give you all this account, my good Sir, to flatter you. I mean it to reproach you. Such relations the first peer in the realm might own with pride; then why do you not keep up more correspondence with these so amiable young folks? I had a thousand questions to answer about you. I had to describe the little ones with the minuteness of anatomy. They were highly delighted when I told them that John (37) was so good a boy, and so fine a scholar, and that Willie was going on still very pretty: but I have it in commission to tell her from them that beauty is a poor, silly bauble without she be good. Miss Chalmers I had left in Edinburgh, but I had the pleasure of meeting with Mrs. Chalmers; only Lady Mackenzie, being rather a little alarmingly ill of a sore throat, somewhat marred our enjoyment.

I shall not be in Ayrshire for four weeks. My most respectful compliments to Mrs. Hamilton, Miss Kennedy, and Dr. Mackenzie. I shall probably write him from some stage or other. I am ever, Sir, yours most gratefully, R. B.

NO. LXIV.

TO MR. WALKER,

OF BLAIR ATHOLE. (38)

Inverness, September 5th, 1787.

My Dear Sir.—I have just time to write the foregoing (39), and to tell you that it was (at least most part of it) the effusion of a half-hour I spent at Bruar. I do not mean it was extempore, for I have endeavoured to brush it up as well as Mr. Nicol's chat and the jogging of the chaise would allow. It eases my heart a good deal, as rhyme is the coin with which a poet pays his debts of honour or gratitude. What I owe to the noble family of Athole, of the first kind, I shall ever proudly boast—what I owe of the last, so help me God in my hour of need! I shall never forget.

The "little angel-band!" I declare I prayed for them very sincerely to-day at the Fall of Fyers. I shall never forget the fine family-piece I saw at Blair; the amiable, the truly noble duchess (40), with her smiling little seraph in her lap, at the head of the table—the lovely "olive plants," as the Hebrew bard finely says, round the happy mother—the beautiful Mrs. G—, the lovely, sweet Miss C., &c., I wish I had the powers of Guido to do them justice! My Lord Duke's kind hospitality—markedly kind indeed:—Mr. Graham of Fintry's charms of conversation—Sir W. Murray's friendship:—in short, the recollection of all that polite, agreeable company, raises an honest glow in my bosom. R. B.

NO. LXV.

TO MR. GILBERT BURNS.

Edinburgh, 17th September, 1787.

My Dear Brother.—I arrived here safe yesterday evening, after a tour of twenty-two days, and travelling near 600 miles, windings included. My farthest stretch was about ten miles beyond Inverness. I went through the heart of the Highlands by Crief, Taymouth, the famous seat of Lord Breadalbane, down the Tay, among cascades and Druidical circles of stones, to Dunkeld, a seat of the Duke of Athole; thence across Tay, and up one of his tributary streams to Blair of Athole, another of the Duke's seats, where I had the honour of spending nearly two days with his grace and family; thence many miles through a wild country among cliffs, grey with eternal snows and gloomy savage glens, till I crossed Spey and went down the stream through Strathspey,—so famous in Scottish music (41),—Badenoch, &c. till I reached Grant Castle, where I spent half a day with Sir James Grant and family; and then crossed the country for Fort George, but called by the way at Cawdor, the ancient seat of Macbeth; there I saw the identical bed in which tradition says king Duncan was murdered; lastly, from Fort George to Inverness.

I returned by the coast, through Nairn, Forres, and so on, to Aberdeen, thence to Stonehive (42), where James Burness, from Montrose, met me by appointment. I spent two days among our relations, and found our aunts, Jean and Isabel, still alive, and hale old women. John Caird, though born the same year with our father, walks as vigorously as I can;—they have had several letters from his son in New York. William Brand is likewise a stout old fellow; but further particulars I delay till I see you, which will be in two or three weeks. The rest of my stages are not worth rehearsing; warm as I was from Ossian's country, where I had seen his very grave, what cared I for fishing-towns or fertile carses? I slept at the famous Brodie of Brodie's one night, and dined at Gordon Castle next day, with the duke, duchess, and family. I am thinking to cause my old mare to meet me, by means of John Ronald, at Glasgow; but you shall hear farther from me before I leave Edinburgh. My duty and many compliments from the north to my mother; and my brotherly compliments to the rest. I have been trying for a berth for William, but am not likely to be successful. Farewell. R. B.

NO. LXVI.

TO MISS MARGARET CHALMERS. (43)

Sept. 26, 1787.

I send Charlotte the first number of the songs; I would not wait for the second number; I hate delays in little marks of friendship, as I hate dissimulation in the language of the heart. I am determined to pay Charlotte a poetic compliment, if I could hit on some glorious old Scotch air, in number second. (44) You will see a small attempt on a shred of paper in the book; but though Dr. Blacklock commended it very highly, I am not just satisfied with it myself. I intend to make it a description of some kind; the whining cant of love, except in real passion, and by a masterly hand, is to me as insufferable as the preaching cant of old Father Smeaton, whig-minister at Kilmaurs. Darts, flames, Cupids, loves, graces, and all that farrago, are just a Mauchline ———, a senseless rabble.

I got an excellent poetic epistle yesternight from the old venerable author of "Tullochgorum," "John of Badenyon," &c. (45). I suppose you know he is a clergyman. It is by far the finest poetic compliment I ever got. I will send you a copy of it.

I go on Thursday or Friday to Dumfries, to wait on Mr. Miller about his farms. Do tell that to Lady Mackenzie, that she may give me credit for a little wisdom. "I, Wisdom, dwell with Prudence." What a blessed fire-side! How happy should I be to pass a winter evening under their venerable roof; and smoke a pipe of tobacco, or drink water-gruel with them! With solemn, lengthened, laughter-quashing gravity of phiz! What sage remarks on the good-for-nothing sons and daughters of indiscretion and folly! And what frugal lessons, as we straitened the fire-side circle, on the uses of the poker and tongs!

Miss N. is very well, and begs to be remembered in the old way to you. I used all my eloquence, all the persuasive flourishes of the hand, and heart-melting modulation of periods in my power, to urge her out to Harvieston, but all in vain. My rhetoric seems quite to have lost its effect on the lovely half of mankind. I have seen the day —but this is a "tale of other years:"—On my conscience I believe that my heart has been so oft on fire that it is absolutely vitrified. I look on the sex with something like the admiration with which I regard the starry sky in a frosty December night. I admire the beauty of the Creator's workmanship; I am charmed with the wild but graceful eccentricity of their motions, and— wish them good night. I mean this with respect to a certain passion *dont j'ai eu l'honneur d'etre un miserable esclave:* as for friendship, you and Charlotte have given me pleasure, permanent pleasure, "which the world cannot give, nor take away," I hope, and which will outlast the heavens and the earth. R. B.

NO. LXVII.

TO THE REV. JOHN SKINNER.

Edinburgh, October 25, 1787.

REVEREND AND VENERABLE SIR.—Accept, in plain dull prose, my most sincere thanks for the best poetical compliment I ever received. I assure you, Sir, as a poet, you have conjured up an airy demon of vanity in my fancy, which the best abilities in your other capacity would be ill able to lay. I regret, and while I live I shall regret, that when I was in the north, I had not the pleasure of paying a younger brother's dutiful respect to the author of the best Scotch song ever Scotland saw—"Tullochgorum's my Delight!" The world may think slightingly of the craft of song-making, if they please; but, as Job says, "Oh that mine adversary had written a book!"—let them try. There is a certain something in the old Scotch songs, a wild happiness of thought and expression, which peculiarly marks them, not only from English songs, but also from the modern efforts of song-wrights, in our native manner and language. The only remains of this enchantment, these spells of the imagination, rest with you. Our true brother, Ross of Lochlee, was likewise "owre cannie"—"a wild warlock"—but now he sings among the "sons of the morning."

I have often wished, and will certainly endeavour, to form a kind of common acquaintance among all the genuine sons of Caledonian song. The world, busy in low prosaic pursuits, may overlook most of us; but "reverence thyself." The world is not our *peers*, so we challenge the jury. We can lash that world, and find ourselves a very great source of amusement and happiness independent of that world.

There is a work going on in Edinburgh just now, which claims your best assistance. An engraver in this town has set about collecting and publishing all the Scotch songs, with the music, that can be found. Songs, in the English language, if by Scotchmen, are admitted, but the music must all be Scotch. Drs. Beattie and Blacklock are lending a hand, and the first musician in town presides over that department. I have been absolutely crazed about it, collecting old stanzas, and every information remaining respecting their origin, authors, &c., &c. This last is but a very fragment business; but at the end of his second number—the first is already published—a small account will be given of the authors, particularly to preserve those of latter times. Your three songs, "Tullochgorum," "John of Badenyon," and "Ewie wi' the Crookit Horn," go in this second number. I was determined, before I got your letter, to write you, begging that you would let me know where the editions of these pieces may be found, as you would wish them to continue in future times; and if you would be so kind to this undertaking as send any songs, of your own or others, that you would think proper to publish, your name will be inserted among the other authors—"nill ye, will ye." One half of Scotland already give your songs to other authors. Paper is done. I beg to hear from you; the sooner the better, as I leave Edinburgh in a fortnight or three weeks. I am, with the warmest sincerity, Sir, your obliged humble servant, R. B.

NO. LXVIII.

TO JAMES HOY, Esq.

GORDON CASTLE. (46)

Edinburgh, October 30th, 1787.

Sir.—I will defend my conduct in giving you this trouble, on the best of Christian principles—"Whatsoever ye would that men should do unto you, do ye even so unto them." I shall certainly, among my legacies leave my latest curse to that unlucky predicament which hurried—tore me away from Castle Gordon. May that obstinate son of Latin prose [Nicol] be curst to Scotch mile periods, and damned to seven league paragraphs; while Declension and Conjugation, Gender, Number and Tense, under the ragged banners of Dissonance and Disarrangement, eternally rank against him in hostile array.

Allow me, Sir, to strengthen the small claim I have to your acquaintance, by the following request. An engraver, James Johnson, in Edinburgh, has, not from mercenary views, but from an honest Scotch enthusiasm, set about collecting all our native songs, and setting them to music, particularly those that have never been set before. Clarke, the well-known musician, presides over the musical arrangement, and Drs. Beattie and Blacklock, Mr. Tytler of Woodhouselee, and your humble servant to the utmost of his small power, assist in collecting the old poetry, or sometimes, for a fine air, make a stanza when it has no words. The brats, too tedious to mention, claim a parental pang from my bardship. I suppose it will appear in Johnson's second number—the first was published before my acquaintance with him. My request is—"Cauld Kail in Aberdeen" is one intended for this number, and I beg a copy of his Grace of Gordon's words to it, which you were so kind as to repeat to me. (47) You may be sure we won't prefix the author's name, except you like, though I look on it as no small merit to this work that the names of so many of the authors of our old Scotch songs, names almost forgotten, will be inserted. I do not well know where to write to you—I rather write at you; but if you will be so obliging, immediately on receipt of this, as to write me a few lines, I shall perhaps pay you in kind, though not in quality. Johnson's terms are:—each number a handsome pocket volume, to consist of at least a hundred Scotch songs, with basses for the harpsichord, &c. The price to subscribers, 5s.; to non-subscribers, 6s. He will have three numbers, I conjecture.

My direction for two or three weeks will be at Mr. William Cruikshank's, St. James' Square, New Town, Edinburgh. I am, Sir, yours to command, R. B.

NO. LXIX.

TO THE SAME.

GORDON CASTLE.

Edinburgh, November 6th, 1787.

Dear Sir.—I would have wrote you immediately on receipt of your kind letter but a mixed impulse of gratitude and esteem whispered to me that I ought to send you something by way of return. When a poet owes anything, particularly when he is indebted for good offices, the payment that, usually recurs to him—the only coin indeed in which he is probably conversant—is rhyme. Johnson sends the books by the fly, as directed, and begs me to enclose his most grateful thanks; my return I intended should have been one or two poetic bagatelles which the world have not seen, or, perhaps, for obvious reasons, cannot see. These I shall send you before I leave Edinburgh. They may make you laugh a little, which, on the whole, is no bad way of spending one's precious hours and still more precious breath; at any rate, they will be, though a small, yet a very sincere, mark of my respectful esteem for a gentleman whose farther acquaintance I should look upon as a peculiar obligation.

The duke's song, independent totally of his dukeship, charms me. There is I know not what of wild happiness of thought and expression peculiarly beautiful in the old Scottish song style, of which his Grace, old venerable Skinner, the author of "Tullochgorum," &c., and the late Ross, at Lochlee, of true Scottish poetic memory, are the only modern instances that I recollect, since Ramsay, with his contemporaries, and poor Bob Fergusson, went to the world of deathless existence and truly immortal song. The mob of mankind, that many-headed beast, would laugh at so serious a speech about an old song; but as Job says, "Oh that mine adversary had written a book!" Those who think that composing a Scotch song is a trifling business, let them try.

I wish my Lord Duke would pay a proper attention to the Christian admonition—"Hide not your candle under a bushel," but "Let your light shine before men." I could name half a dozen dukes that I guess are a devilish deal worse employed; nay, I question if there are half a dozen better: perhaps there are not half that scanty number whom Heaven has favoured with the tuneful, happy, and I will say, glorious gift. I am, dear Sir, your obliged humble servant,

R. B.

NO. LXX.

TO ROBERT AINSLIE, Esq., EDINBURGH.

Edinburgh, Sunday Morning, Nov. 23, 1787.

I BEG, my dear Sir, you would not make any appointment to take us to Mr. Ainslie's to-night. On looking over my engagements, constitution, present state of my health, some little vexatious soul concerns, &c., I find I can't sup abroad to-night. I shall be in to-day till one o'clock, if you have a leisure hour.

You will think it romantic when I tell you, that I find the idea of your friendship almost necessary to my existence. You assume a proper length of face in my bitter hours of blue-devilism, and you laugh fully up to my highest wishes at my good things. I don't know, upon the whole, if you are one of the first fellows in God's world, but you are so to me. I tell you this just now, in the conviction that some inequalities in my temper and manner may perhaps sometimes make you suspect that I am not so warmly as I ought to be your friend,

R. B.

NO. LXXI.

TO THE EARL OF GLENCAIRN.

Edinburgh, 1787.

MY LORD.—I know your lordship will disapprove of my ideas in a request I am going to make to you; but I have weighed, long and seriously weighed, my situation, my hopes and turn of mind, and am fully fixed to my scheme, if I can possibly effectuate it. I wish to get into the Excise: I am told that your lordship's interest will easily procure me the grant from the commissioners; and your lordship's patronage and goodness, which have already rescued me from obscurity, wretchedness and exile, embolden me to ask that interest. You have likewise put it in my power to save the little tie of home that sheltered an aged mother, two brothers, and three sisters, from destruction. There, my lord, you have bound me over to the highest gratitude.

My brother's farm is but a wretched lease, but I think he will probably weather out the remaining seven years of it; and after the assistance which I have given, and will give him, to keep the family together, I think, by my guess, I shall have rather better than two hundred pounds, and instead of seeking, what is almost impossible at present to find, a farm that I can certainly live by, with so small a stock, I shall lodge this sum in a banking-house, a sacred deposit, excepting only the calls of uncommon distress or necessitous old age.

These, my lord, are my views: I have resolved from the maturest deliberation; and now I am fixed, I shall leave no stone unturned to carry my resolve into execution. Your lordship's patronage is the strength of my hopes; nor have I yet applied to anybody else. Indeed, my heart sinks within me at the idea of applying to any other of the great who have honoured me with their countenance. I am ill qualified to dog the heels of greatness with the impertinence of solicitation, and tremble nearly as much at the thought of the cold promise as the cold denial; but to your lordship I have not only the honour, the comfort, but the pleasure of being your lordship's much obliged and deeply indebted humble servant,

R. B.

NO. LXXII.

TO CHARLES HAY, Esq., ADVOCATE,

(ENCLOSING VERSES ON THE DEATH OF LORD PRESIDENT.) (48)

SIR.—The enclosed poem was written in consequence of your suggestion, last time I had the pleasure of seeing you. It cost me an hour or two of next morning's sleep, but did not please me; so it lay by, an ill-digested effort, till the other day that I gave it a critic brush. These kind of subjects are much hackneyed; and, besides, the wailings of the rhyming tribe over the ashes of the great are cursedly suspicious, and out of all character for sincerity. These ideas damped my muse's fire; however, I have done the best I could, and, at all events, it gives me an opportunity of declaring that I have the honour to be, Sir, your obliged humble servant, R. B.

NO. LXXIII.

TO MISS M——N.

Saturday Noon, No. 2, St. James's Square, New Town, Edinburgh.

HERE have I sat, my dear Madam, in the stony altitude of perplexed study for fifteen vexatious minutes, my head askew, bending over the intended card; my fixed eye insensible to the very light of day poured around; my pendulous goose-feather, loaded with ink, hanging over the future letter, all for the important purpose of writing a complimentary card to accompany your trinket.

Compliment is such a miserable Greenland expression, lies at such chilly polar distance from the torrid zone of my constitution, that I cannot, for the very soul of me, use it to any person for whom I have the twentieth part of the esteem every one must have for you who knows you.

As I leave town in three or four days, I can give myself the pleasure of calling on you only for a minute. Tuesday evening, some time about seven or after, I shall wait on you for your farewell commands.

The hinge of your box I put into the hands of the proper connoisseur. The broken glass, likewise, went under review; but deliberate wisdom thought it would too much endanger the whole fabric. I am, dear Madam, with all sincerity of enthusiasm, your very obedient servant, R. B.

NO. LXXIV.

TO MISS CHALMERS.

Edinburgh, Nov. 21, 1787.

I HAVE one vexatious fault to the kindly welcome well-filled sheet which I owe to your and Charlotte's (49) goodness—it contains too much sense, sentiment and good-spelling. It is impossible that even you two, whom I declare to my God I will give credit for any degree of excellence the sex are capable of attaining—it is impossible you can go on to correspond at that rate; so, like those who, Shenstone says, retire because they have made a good speech, I shall, after a few letters, hear no more of you. I insist that you shall write whatever comes first: what you see, what you read, what you hear, what you admire, what you dislike, trifles, bagatelles, nonsense; or to fill up a corner, e'en put down a laugh at full length. Now, none of your polite hints about flattery; I leave that to your lovers, if you have or shall have any; though, thank Heaven, I have at last two girls who can be luxuriantly happy in their own minds and with one another, without that commonly necessary appendage to female bliss—A LOVER.

Charlotte and you are just two favourite resting-places for my soul in her wanderings through the weary, thorny wilderness of this world. God knows, I am ill-fitted for the struggle: I glory in being a poet, and I want to be thought a wise man—I would fondly be generous, and I wish to be rich. After all, I am afraid I am a lost subject. "Some folk hae a hantle o' fauts, and I'm but a ne'er-do-weel."

Afternoon.—To close the melancholy reflections at the end of the last sheet, I shall just add a piece of devotion, commonly known in Carrick by the title of the "Wabster's grace:"—

Some say we're thieves, and e'en sae are we,
Some say we lie, and e'en sae do we!
Guid forgie us, and I hope sae will he!
——Up and to your looms, lads! R. B.

NO. LXXV.

TO THE SAME.

Edinburgh, Dec. 12, 1787.

I AM here under the care of a surgeon, with a bruised limb extended on a cushion; and the tints of my mind vying with the livid horror preceding a midnight thunder-storm. A drunken coachman was the cause of the first, and incomparably the lightest evil; misfortune, bodily constitution, hell, and myself, have formed a "quadruple alliance" to guarantee the other. I got my fall on Saturday, and am getting slowly better.

I have taken tooth and nail to the Bible, and am got through the five books of Moses, and half way in Joshua. It is really a glorious book. I sent for my book-binder to-day, and ordered him to get me an octavo Bible in sheets, the best paper and print in town, and bind it with all the elegance of his craft.

I would give my best song to my worst enemy—I mean the merit of making it—to have you and Charlotte by me. You are angelic creatures, and would pour oil and wine into my wounded spirit.

I enclose you a proof copy of the "Banks of the Devon," which present with my best wishes to Charlotte. The "Ochil-hills" (50) you shall probably have next week for yourself. None of your fine speeches! R. B.

NO. LXXVI.

TO THE SAME.

Edinburgh, Dec. 19th, 1787.

I BEGIN this letter in answer to your's of the 17th current, which is not yet cold since I read it. The atmosphere of my soul is vastly clearer than when I wrote you last. For the first time, yesterday I crossed the room on crutches. It would do your heart good to see my bardship, not on my poetic, but on my oaken stilts; throwing my best leg with an air! and with as much hilarity in my gait and countenance, as a May frog leaping across the newly harrowed ridge, enjoying the fragrance of the refreshed earth, after the long-expected shower!

I can't say I am altogether at my ease when I see anywhere in my path that meagre, squalid, famine-faced spectre, poverty; attended, as he always is, by iron-fisted oppression and leering contempt; but I have sturdily withstood his buffettings many a hard-laboured day already, and still my motto is—I DARE! My worst enemy is *moi même*. I lie so miserably open to the inroads and incursions of a mischievous, light-armed, well-mounted banditti, under the banners of imagination, whim, caprice and passion; and the heavy-armed veteran regulars of wisdom, prudence and forethought move so very, very slow, that I am almost in a state of perpetual warfare, and, alas! frequent defeat. There are just two creatures I would envy; a horse in his wild state traversing the forests of Asia, or an oyster on some of the desert shores of Europe. The one has not a wish without enjoyment, the other has neither wish nor fear. R. B.

NO. LXXVII.

TO THE SAME.

Edinburgh, Dec., 1787.

MY DEAR MADAM.—I just now have read yours. The poetic compliments I pay cannot be misunderstood. They are neither of them so particular as to point you out to the world at large; and the circle of your acquaintances will allow all I have said. Besides, I have complimented you chiefly, almost solely, on your mental charms. Shall I be plain with you? I will; so look to it. Personal attractions, Madam, you have much above par; wit, understanding and worth, you possess in the first class. This is a cursed flat way of telling you these truths, but let me hear no more of your sheepish timidity. I know the world a little. I know what they will say of my poems—by second sight, I suppose—for I am seldom out in my conjectures; and you may believe me, my dear Madam, I would not run any risk of hurting you by any ill-judged compliment. I wish to show the world the odds between a poet's friends and those of simple prosemen. More for your information, both the pieces go in. One of them, "Where braving angry Winter's Storms," is already set—the tune in Neil Gow's *Lamentation for Abercairny;* the other is to be set to an old Highland air in Daniel Dow's collection of ancient Scots music; the name is "*Ha a Chaillich air mo Dheith.*" My treacherous memory has forgot every circumstance about *Las Incas;* only, I think you mentioned them as being in Creech's possession. I shall ask him about it. I am afraid the song of "Somebody" will come too late—as I shall for certain leave town in a week for Ayrshire, and from that to Dumfries, but there my hopes are slender. I leave my direction in town; so any thing, wherever I am, will reach me.

I saw yours to ———; it is not too severe, nor did he take it amiss. On the contrary, like a whipt spaniel, he talks of being with you in the Christmas days. Mr. ——— has given him the invitation, and he is determined to accept of it. Oh selfishness! he owns, in his sober moments, that from his own volatility of inclination, the circumstances in which he is situated, and his knowledge of his father's disposition, the whole affair is chimerical—yet he *will* gratify an idle *penchant* at the enormous, cruel expense, of perhaps ruining the peace of the very woman for whom he professes the generous passion of love! He is a gentleman in his mind and manners—*tant pis!* He is a volatile school-boy—the heir of a man's fortune who well knows the value of two times two!

Perdition seize them and their fortunes, before they should make the amiable, the lovely ———, the derided object of their purse-proud contempt!

I am doubly happy to hear of Mrs. ———'s recovery, because I really thought all was over with her. There are days of pleasure yet awaiting her:—

> As I cam in by Glenap,
> I met with an aged woman;
> She bade me cheer up my heart,
> For the best o' my days was comin.' (51)

This day will decide my affairs with Creech. Things are, like myself, not what they ought to be; yet better than what they appear to be.

> Heaven's Sovereign saves all but himself—
> That hideous sight—a naked human heart.

Farewell! remember me to Charlotte.

R. B.

NO. LXXVIII.

TO SIR JOHN WHITEFOORD.

Edinburgh, December, 1787.

Sir.—Mr Mackenzie, in Mauchline, my very warm and worthy friend (52), has informed me how much you are pleased to interest yourself in my fate as a man, and (what to me is incomparably dearer) my fame as a poet. I have, Sir, in one or two instances, been patronised by those of your character in life, when I was introduced to their notice by * * * * * friends to them, and honoured acquaintances to me; but you are the first gentleman in the country whose benevolence and goodness of heart has interested himself for me, unsolicited and unknown. I am not master enough of the etiquette of these matters to know, nor did I stay to inquire, whether formal duty bade, or cold propriety disallowed, my thanking you in this manner, as I am convinced, from the light in which you kindly view me, that you will do me the justice to believe this letter is not the manœuvre of the needy, sharping author, fastening on those in upper life who honour him with a little notice of him and his works. Indeed, the situation of poets is generally such, to a proverb, as may, in some measure, palliate that prostitution of heart and talents they have at times been guilty of. I do not think prodigality is, by any means, a necessary concomitant of a poetic turn, but I believe a careless, indolent inattention to economy is almost inseparable from it; then there must be in the heart of every bard of Nature's making a certain modest sensibility, mixed with a kind of pride, that will ever keep him out of the way of those windfalls of fortune which frequently light on hardy impudence and foot-licking servility. It is not easy to imagine a more helpless state than his whose poetic fancy unfits him for the world, and whose character as a scholar gives him some pretensions to the *politessse* of life—yet is as poor as I am.

For my part, I thank Heaven my star has been kinder; learning never elevated my ideas above the peasant's shed, and I have an independent fortune at the plough-tail.

I was surprised to hear that any one who pretended in the least to the manners of the gentleman, should be so foolish, or worse, as to stoop to traduce the morals of such a one as I am, and so unhumanly cruel, too, as to meddle with that late most unfortunate, unhappy part of my story. With a tear of gratitude, I thank you, Sir, for the warmth with which you interposed in behalf of my conduct. I am, I acknowledge, too frequently the sport of whim, caprice and passion; but reverence to God, and integrity to my fellow-creatures, I hope I shall ever preserve. I have no return, Sir, to make you for your goodness but one—a return which, I am persuaded, will not be unacceptable—the honest, warm wishes of a grateful heart for your happiness, and every one of that lovely flock who stand to you in a filial relation. If ever calumny aim the poisoned shaft at them, may friendship be by to ward the blow!

R. B.

NO. LXXIX.

MISS MARGARET CHALMERS.

December, 1787.

I have been at Dumfries, and at one visit more shall be decided about a farm in that county. I am rather hopeless in it; but as my brother is an excellent farmer, and is, besides, an exceedingly prudent sober man (qualities which are only a younger brother's fortune in our family), I am determined, if my Dumfries business fail me, to remove into partnership with him, and at our leisure take another farm in the neighbourhood.

I assure you I look for high compliments from you and Charlotte on this very sage instance of my unfathomable, incomprehensible wisdom.—Talking of Charlotte I must tell her that I have, to the best of my power, paid her a poetic compliment now completed. The air is admirable; true old Highland. It was the tune of a Gaelic song which an Inverness lady sang me when I was there; I was so charmed with it, that I begged her to write me a set of it from her singing, for it had never been set before. I am fixed that it shall go in Johnson's next number; so Charlotte and you need not spend your precious time in contradicting me. I won't say the poetry is first-rate, though I am convinced it is very well; and, what is not always the case with compliments to ladies, it is not only sincere, but just. R. B.

NO. LXXX.

TO MISS WILLIAMS (53),

ON READING THE POEM OF THE SLAVE-TRADE.

Edinburgh, Dec., 1787.

I KNOW very little of scientific criticism, so all I can pretend to in that intricate art is merely to note, as I read along, what passages strike me as being uncommonly beautiful, and where the expression seems to be perplexed or faulty.

The poem opens finely. There are none of those idle prefatory lines which one may skip over before one comes to the subject. Verses 9th and 10th in particular,

Where ocean's unseen bound
Leaves a drear world of waters round,

are truly beautiful. The simile of the hurricane is likewise fine; and, indeed, beautiful as the poem is, almost all the similes rise decidedly above it. From verse 31st to verse 50th is a pretty eulogy on Britain. Verse 36th, "That foul drama deep with wrong," is nobly expressive. Verse 46th, I am afraid, is rather unworthy of the rest; "to dare to feel," is an idea that I do not altogether like. The contrast of valour and mercy, from the 46th verse to the 50th, is admirable.

Either my apprehension is dull, or there is something a little confused in the apostrophe to Mr. Pitt. Verse 55th is the antecedent to verses 57th and 58, but in verse 58th the connection seems ungrammatical:—

Powers * * *
* * * *
With no gradations mark'd their flight,
But rose at once to glory's height.

Ris'n should be the word instead of rose. Try it in prose. "Powers—their flight marked by no gradations, but [the same powers] risen at once to the height of glory." Likewise, verse 53rd, "For this," is evidently meant to lead on the sense of the verses 59th, 60th, 61st and 62nd; but let us try how the thread of connection runs—

For this * * *
* * * *
The deed of mercy, that embrace,
A distant sphere, an alien race,
Shall virtue's lips record, and claim
The fairest honours of thy name.

I beg pardon if I misapprehend the matter, but this appears to me the only imperfect passage in the poem. The comparison of the sun-beam is fine.

The compliment to the Duke of Richmond is, I hope, as just as it is certainly elegant. The thought,

Virtue * * *
* * * *
Sends from her unsullied source,
The gems of thought their purest force,

is exceedingly beautiful. The idea, from verse 81st to the 85th, that the "blest decree" is like the beams of morning ushering in the glorious day of liberty, ought not to pass unnoticed or unapplauded. From verse 85th to verse 108, is an animated contrast between the unfeeling selfishness of the oppressor on the one hand, and the misery of the captive on the other. Verse 88th might perhaps be amended thus:—"Nor ever *quit* her narrow maze." We are said to *pass* a bound, but we *quit* a maze. Verse 100th is exquisitely beautiful:—

They, whom wasted blessings tire.

Verse 110th is, I doubt, a clashing of metaphors; "to load a span" is, I am afraid, an unwarrantable expression. In verse 114th, "Cast the universe in shade," is a fine idea. From the 115th verse to the 142nd is a striking description of the wrongs of the poor African. Verse 120th, "The load of unremitted pain," is a remarkable, strong expression. The address to the advocates for abolishing the slave-trade, from verse 143rd to verse 208th, is animated with the true life of genius. The picture of oppression—

> While she links her impious chain,
> And calculates the price of pain;
> Weighs agony in sordid scales,
> And marks if death or life prevails—

is nobly executed.

What a tender idea is in verse 180th! Indeed, that whole description of home may vie with Thomson's description of home, somewhere in the beginning of his Autumn. I do not remember to have seen a stronger expression of misery than is contained in these verses:—

> Condemned, severe extreme, to live
> When all is fled that life can give.

The comparison of our distant joys to distant objects is equally original and striking.

The character and manners of the dealer in the infernal traffic is a well done, though a horrid picture. I am not sure how far introducing the sailor was right; for though the sailor's common characteristic is generosity, yet, in this case, he is certainly not only an unconcerned witness, but, in some degree, an efficient agent in the business. Verse 224th is nervous and expressive—"The heart convulsive anguish breaks." The description of the captive wretch when he arrives in the West Indies, is carried on with equal spirit. The thought that the oppressor's sorrow, on seeing the slave pine, is like the butcher's regret when his destined lamb dies a natural death, is exceedingly fine.

I am got so much into the cant of criticism, that I begin to be afraid lest I have nothing except the cant of it; and instead of elucidating my author, am only benighting myself. For this reason, I will not pretend to go through the whole poem. Some few remaining beautiful lines, however, I cannot pass over. Verse 280th is the strongest description of selfishness I ever saw. The comparison in verses 285th and 286th is new and fine; and the line, "Your arms to penury you lend," is excellent.

In verse 317th, "like" should certainly be "as" or "so;" for instance:—

> His sway the hardened bosom leads
> To cruelty's remorseless deeds:
> As (or, so) the blue lightning when it springs
> With fury on its livid wings,
> Darts on the goal with rapid force,
> Nor heeds that ruin marks its course.

If you insert the word "like" where I have placed "as," you must alter "darts" to "darting," and "heeds" to "heeding," in order to make it grammar. A tempest is a favourite subject with the poets, but I do not remember any thing, even in Thomson's winter, superior to your verses from the 347th to the 351st. Indeed, the last simile, beginning with "Fancy may dress," &c., and ending with the 350th verse, is, in my opinion, the most beautiful passage in the poem; it would do honour to the greatest names that ever graced our profession.

I will not beg your pardon, Madam, for these strictures, as my conscience tells me, that for once in my life I have acted up to the duties of a Christian, in doing as I would be done by. R. B.

NO. LXXXI.

TO MR. RICHARD BROWN,

IRVINE. (54)

Edinburgh, Dec. 30th, 1787.

My Dear Sir.—I have met with few things in life which have given me more pleasure than Fortune's kindness to you since those days in which we met in the vale of misery; as I can honestly say, that I never knew a man who more truly deserved it, or to whom my heart more truly wished it. I have been much indebted since that time to your story and sentiments for steeling my mind against evils, of which I have had a pretty decent share. My will-o'-wisp fate you know: do you recollect a Sunday we spent together in Eglinton woods? You told me, on my repeating some verses to you, that you wondered I could resist the temptation of sending verses of such merit to a magazine. It was from this remark I derived that idea of my own pieces which encouraged me to endeavour at the character of a poet. I am happy to hear that you will be two or three months at home. As soon as a bruised limb will permit me, I shall return to Ayrshire, and we shall meet; "and faith, I hope we'll not sit dumb, nor yet cast out!"

I have much to tell you "of men, their manners, and their ways," perhaps a little of the other sex. Apropos, I beg to be remembered to Mrs. Brown. There, I doubt not, my dear friend, but you have found substantial happiness. I expect to find you something of an altered, but not a different man; the wild, bold, generous young fellow composed into the steady, affectionate husband, and the fond careful parent. For me, I am just the same will-o'-wisp being I used to be. About the first and fourth quarters of the moon, I generally set in for the trade-wind of wisdom; but about the full and change, I am the luckless victim of mad tornadoes, which blow me into chaos. Almighty love still reigns and revels in my bosom; and I am, at this moment, ready to hang myself for a young Edinburgh widow (55), who has wit and wisdom more murderously fatal than the assassinating stiletto of the Sicilian bandit, or the poisoned arrow of the savage African. My Highland dirk, that used to hang beside my crutches, I have gravely removed into a neighbouring closet, the key of which I cannot command in case of spring-tide paroxysms. You may guess of her wit by the following verses, which she sent me the other day:—

Talk not of love, it gives me pain,
  For love has been my foe;
He bound me with an iron chain,
  And plunged me deep in woe!

But friendship's pure and lasting joys,
  My heart was formed to prove—
There, welcome, win and wear the prize,
  But never talk of love!

Your friendship much can make me blest—
  Oh, why that bliss destroy?
Why urge the odious one request,
  You know I must deny?

My best compliments to our friend Allan. Adieu! R. B.

NO. LXXXII.

TO MR. GAVIN HAMILTON.

Edinburgh, Dec., 1787.

My Dear Sir.—It is indeed with the highest pleasure that I congratulate you on the return of days of ease and nights of pleasure, after the horrid hours of misery in which I saw you suffering existence when last in Ayrshire. I seldom pray for anybody—"I'm baith dead-sweer and wretched ill o't;" but most fervently do I beseech the Power that directs the world, that you may live long and be happy, but live no longer than you are happy. It is needless for me to advise you to have a reverend care of your health. I know you will make it a point never at one time to drink more than a pint of wine (I mean an English pint), and that you will never be witness to more than one bowl of punch at a time, and that cold drams you will never more taste; and, above all things, I am convinced, that after drinking perhaps boiling punch you will never mount your horse and gallop home in a chill late hour. Above all things, as I understand you are in habits of intimacy with that Boanerges of gospel powers, Father Auld, be earnest with him that he will wrestle in prayer for you, that you may see the vanity of vanities in trusting to, or even practising, the casual moral works of charity, humanity, generosity, and forgiveness of things, which you practised so flagrantly, that it was evident you delighted in them, neglecting, or perhaps profanely despising, the wholesome doctrine of faith without works, the only author of salvation. A hymn of thanksgiving would, in my opinion, be highly becoming from you at present, and in my zeal for your well-being, I earnestly press on you to be diligent in chanting over the two enclosed pieces of sacred poesy. My best compliments to Mrs. Hamilton and Miss Kennedy. Yours, &c.

R. B.

NO. LXXXIII.

TO CLARINDA.

Thursday Evening.

Madam, (56)—I had set no small store by my tea-drinking to-night, and have not often been so disappointed. Saturday evening I shall embrace the opportunity with the greatest pleasure. I leave this town this day sen'night, and, probably for a couple of twelvemonths; but must ever regret that I so lately got an acquaintance I shall ever highly esteem, and in whose welfare I shall ever be warmly interested.

Our worthy common friend, in her usual pleasant way, rallied me a good deal on my new acquaintance, and in the humour of her ideas I wrote some lines, which I enclose you, as I think they have a good deal of poetic merit; and Miss—— tells me you are not only a critic, but a poetess. Fiction, you know, is the native region of poetry; and I hope you will pardon my vanity in sending you the bagatelle as a tolerable off-hand *jeu-d'esprit*. I have several poetic trifles, which I shall gladly leave with Miss ——, or you, if they were worth house-room; as there are scarcely two people on earth by whom it would mortify me more to be forgotten, though at the distance of nine-score miles.—I am, Madam, with the highest respect, your very humble servant,

R. B.

NO. LXXXIV.

TO THE SAME. (57)

Saturday Evening.

I CAN say with truth, Madam, that I never met with a person in my life whom I more anxiously wished to meet again than yourself. To-night I was to have had that very great pleasure; I was intoxicated with the idea, but an unlucky fall from a coach has so bruised one of my knees that I can't stir my leg; so if I don't see you again, I shall not rest in my grave for chagrin. I was vexed to the soul I had not seen you sooner; I determined to cultivate your friendship with the enthusiasm of religion; but thus has Fortune ever served me. I cannot bear the idea of leaving Edinburgh without seeing you. I know not how to account for it—I am strangely taken with some people, nor am I often mistaken. You are a stranger to me; but I am an odd being; some yet unnamed feelings, things, not principles, but better than whims, carry me farther than boasted reason ever did a philosopher.—Farewell! every happiness be yours!

NO. LXXXV.

TO THE SAME.

Friday Evening, Dec. 22nd, 1787.

I BEG your pardon, my dear "Clarinda," for the fragment scrawl I sent you yesterday. (58) I really do not know what I wrote. A gentleman, for whose character, abilities, and critical knowledge, I have the highest veneration, called in just as I had begun the second sentence, and I would not make the porter wait. I read to my much respected friend some of my own bagatelles, and, among others, your lines, which I had copied out. He began some criticisms on them as on the other pieces, when I informed him they were the work of a young lady in this town, which, I assure you, made him stare. My learned friend seriously protested that he did not believe any young woman in Edinburgh was capable of such lines: and if you know anything of Professor Gregory, you will neither doubt of his abilities nor his sincerity. I do love you, if possible, still better for having so fine a taste and turn for poesy. I have again gone wrong in my usual unguarded way, but you may erase the word, and put esteem, respect, or any other tame Dutch expression you please in its place. I believe there is no holding converse, nor carrying on correspondence, with an amiable woman, much less a *gloriously amiable, fine woman,* without some mixture of that delicious passion, whose most devoted slave I have more than once had the honour of being.—But why be hurt or offended on that account? Can no honest man have a prepossession for a fine woman, but he must run his head against an intrigue? Take a little of the tender witchcraft of love, and add it to the generous, the honourable sentiments of manly friendship: and I know but *one* more delightful morsel, which few, few in any rank ever taste. Such a composition is like adding cream to strawberries; it not only gives the fruit a more elegant richness, but has a peculiar deliciousness of its own.

I enclose you a few lines I composed on a late melancholy occasion. I will not give above five or six copies of it at all, and I would be hurt if any friend should give any copies without my consent.

You cannot imagine, Clarinda (I like the idea of Arcadian names in a commerce of this kind), how much store I have set by the hopes of your future friendship. I do not know if you have a just idea of my character, but I wish you to see me *as I am.* I am, as most people of my trade are, a strange will-o'-wisp being; the victim, too frequently, of much imprudence and many follies. My great constituent elements are *pride* and *passion.* The first I have endeavoured to humanize into integrity and honour; the last makes me a devotee to the warmest degree of enthusiasm, in love religion, or friendship—either of them, or all together, as I happen to be inspired. 'Tis true, I never saw you but once; but how much acquaintance did I form with you in that once! Do not think I flatter you, or have a design upon you, Clarinda; I have too much pride for the one, and too little cold contrivance for the other; but of all God's creatures I ever could approach in the beaten way of my acquaintance, you struck me with the deepest, the strongest, the most permanent impression. I say, the most permanent, because I know myself well, and how far I can promise either in my prepossessions or powers. Why are you unhappy? And why are so many of our fellow-creatures, unworthy to belong to the same species with you, blest with all they can wish? You have a hand all-benevolent to give; why are you denied the pleasure? You have a heart formed—

gloriously formed—for all the most refined luxuries of love—Why was that heart ever wrung? O Clarinda! shall we not meet in a state, some yet unknown state of being, where the lavish hand of plenty shall minister to the highest wish of benevolence; and where the chill north-wind of prudence shall never blow over the flowery fields of enjoyment? If we do not, man was made in vain! I deserved most of the unhappy hours that have lingered over my head; they were the wages of my labour: but what unprovoked demon, malignant as hell, stole on the confidence of unmistrusting busy Fate, and dashed *your* cup of life with undeserved sorrow?

Let me know how long your stay will be out of town; I shall count the hours till you inform me of your return. Cursed *etiquette* forbids your seeing me just now; and so soon as I can walk I must bid Edinburgh adieu. Lord, why was I born to see misery which I cannot relieve, and to meet with friends whom I cannot enjoy? I look back with the pang of unavailing avarice on my loss in not knowing you sooner: all last winter, these three months past, what luxury of intercourse have I not lost! Perhaps, though, 'twas better for my peace. You see I am either above, or incapable of, dissimulation. I believe it is want of that particular genius. I despise design, because I want either coolness or wisdom to be capable of it. I am interrupted.—Adieu! my dear Clarinda!

SYLVANDER.

NO. LXXXVI. (59)

TO THE SAME

YOU are right, my dear Clarinda; a friendly correspondence goes for nothing, except one writes his or her undisguised sentiments. Yours please me for their intrinsic merit, as well as because they are *yours*, which, I assure you, is to me a high recommendation. Your religious sentiments, Madam, I revere. If you have, on some suspicious evidence, from some lying oracle, learned that I despise or ridicule so sacredly important a matter as real religion, you have, my Clarinda, much misconstrued your friend. "I am not mad, most noble Festus!" Have you ever met a perfect character? Do we not sometimes rather exchange faults than get rid of them? For instance, I am perhaps tired with, and shocked at, a life too much the prey of giddy inconsistencies and thoughtless follies; by degrees I grow sober, prudent, and statedly pious—I say statedly, because the most unaffected devotion is not at all inconsistent with my first character—I join the world in congratulating myself on the happy change. But let me pry more narrowly into this affair. Have I, at bottom, any thing of a secret pride in these endowments and emendations? Have I nothing of a presbyterian sourness, an hypocritical severity, when I survey my less regular neighbours? In a word, have I missed all those nameless and numberless modifications of indistinct selfishness, which are so near our own eyes that we can scarcely bring them within the sphere of our vision, and which the known spotless cambric of our character hides from the ordinary observer?

My definition of worth is short; truth and humanity respecting our fellow-creatures; reverence and humility in the presence of that Being, my Creator and Preserver, and who, I have every reason to believe, will one day be my Judge. The first part of my definition is the creature of unbiassed instinct; the last is the child of after reflection. Where I found these two essentials, I would gently note, and slightly mention, any attendant flaws—flaws, the marks, the consequences, of human nature.

I can easily enter into the sublime pleasures that your strong imagination and keen sensibility must derive from religion, particularly if a little in the shade of misfortune: but I own I cannot, without a marked grudge, see Heaven totally engross so amiable, so charming, a woman as my friend Clarinda; and should be very well pleased at *a circumstance* that would put it in the power of somebody (happy somebody!) to divide her attention, with all the delicacy and tenderness of an earthly attachment.

You will not easily persuade me that you have not a grammatical knowledge of the English language. So far from being inaccurate, you are eloquent beyond any woman of my acquaintance, except one, whom I wish you knew.

Your last verses to me have so delighted me that I have got an excellent old Scots air that suits the measure, and you shall see them in print in the Scots Musical Museum, a work publishing by a friend of mine in this town. I want four stanzas; you gave me but three, and one of them alluded to an expression in my former letter; so I have taken your first two verses, with a slight alteration in the second, and have added a third; but you must help me to a fourth. Here they are: the latter half of the first stanza would have been worthy of Sappho; I am in raptures with it.

Talk not of love, it gives me pain,
For love has been my foe;
He bound me with an iron chain,
And sunk me deep in woe.

But Friendship's pure and lasting joys
My heart was formed to prove;
There, welcome, win, and wear the prize,
But never talk of love.

Your friendship much can make me blest,
O why that bliss destroy!
[only]
Why urge the odious one request,
[will]
You know I must deny.

The alteration in the second stanza is no improvement, but there was a slight inaccuracy in your rhyme. The third I only offer to your choice, and have left two words for your determination. The air is 'The Banks of Spey,' and is most beautiful.

To-morrow evening I intend taking a chair, and paying a visit at Park Place to a much-valued old friend. If I could be sure of finding you at home (and I will send one of the chairmen to call), I would spend from five to six o'clock with you, as I go past. I cannot do more at this time, as I have something on my hand that hurries me much. I propose giving you the first call, my old friend the second, and Miss ——— as I return home. Do not break any engagement for me, as I will spend another evening with you, at any rate, before I leave town.

Do not tell me that you are pleased when your friends inform you of your faults. I am ignorant what they are; but I am sure they must be such evanescent trifles, compared with your personal and mental accomplishments, that I would despise the ungenerous narrow soul who would notice any shadow of imperfections you may seem to have, any other way than in the most delicate, agreeable raillery. Coarse minds are not aware how much they injure the keenly feeling tie of bosom friendship, when, in their foolish officiousness, they mention what nobody cares for recollecting. People of nice sensiability and generous minds have a certain intrinsic dignity that fires at being trifled with, or lowered, or even too nearly approached.

You need make no apology for long letters: I am even with you. Many happy new years to you, charming Clarinda! I can't dissemble, were it to shun perdition. He who sees you as I have done, and does not love you, deserves to be damn'd for his stupidity! He who loves you, and would injure you, deserves to be doubly damn'd for his villany! Adieu. SYLVANDER.

P.S. What would you think of this for a fourth stanza?

Your thought, if love must harbour there,
Conceal it in that thought,
Nor cause me from my bosom tear
The very friend I sought.

NO. LXXXVII.

TO THE SAME.

Monday Evening, 11 *o'clock*,
January 21*st*, 1788.

WHY have I not heard from you, Clarinda? To-day I expected it; and before supper, when a letter to me was announced, my heart danced with rapture; but behold, 'twas some fool who had taken it in his head to turn poet, and made me an offering of the first-fruits of his nonsense. "It is not poetry, but prose run mad." Did I ever repeat to you an epigram I made on a Mr. Elphinstone, who has given a translation of Martial, a famous Latin poet?—The poetry of Elphinstone can only equal his prose notes. I was sitting in the shop of a merchant of my acquaintance, waiting somebody; he put Elphinstone into my hand, and asked my opinion of it; I begged leave to write it on a blank leaf, which I did.

TO MR. ELPHINSTONE, &c.

O thou, whom poesy abhors!
Whom prose has turned out of doors!
Heard'st thou that groan? proceed no further;
'Twas laurel'd Martial roaring Murther.

I am determined to see you, if at all possible, on Saturday evening. Next week I must sing—

The night is my departing night,
The morn's the day I maun awa;
There's neither friend nor foe o' mine,
But wishes that I were awa!
What I hae done, for lack o' wit,
I never, never, can reca';
I hope ye're a' my friends as yet,
Guid night, and joy be wi' you a'!

If I could see you sooner, I would be so much the happier; but I would not purchase the dearest gratification on earth, if it must be at your expense in worldly censure, far less inward peace!

I shall certainly be ashamed of thus

scrawling whole sheets of incoherence. The only *unity* (a sad word with poets and critics!) in my ideas is CLARINDA. There my heart "reigns and revels."

"What art thou, Love? whence are those charms,
That thus thou bear'st an universal rule?
For thee the soldier quits his arms,
The king turns slave, the wise man fool.
In vain we chase thee from the field,
And with cool thoughts resist thy yoke;
Next tide of blood, alas! we yield;
And all those high resolves are broke!"

I like to have quotations for every occasion. They give one's ideas so pat, and save one the trouble of finding expression adequate to one's feelings. I think it is one of the greatest pleasures, attending a poetic genius, that we can give our woes, cares, joys, loves, &c., an embodied form in verse, which to me is ever immediate ease. Goldsmith says finely of his Muse:—

"Thou source of all my bliss and all my woe,
Thou found'st me poor at first, and keep'st me so."

My limb has been so well to-day, that I have gone up and down stairs often without my staff. To-morrow I hope to walk once again on my own legs to dinner. It is only next street—Adieu.

SYLVANDER.

NO. LXXXVIII.

TO THE SAME.

Saturday Noon, January 26th, 1788.

SOME days, some nights, nay, some *hours*, like the "ten righteous persons in Sodom," save the rest of the vapid, tiresome, miserable months and years of life. One of these hours, my dear Clarinda blessed me with yesternight.

———"One well spent hour,
In such a tender circumstance for friends,
Is better than an age of common time!"
THOMSON.

My favourite feature in Milton's Satan is his manly fortitude in supporting what cannot be remedied—in short, the wild broken fragments of a noble exalted mind in ruins. I meant no more by saying he was a favourite hero of mine.

I mentioned to you my letter to Dr. Moore, giving an account of my life: it is truth, every word of it; and will give you the just idea of a man whom you have honoured with your friendship. I am afraid you will hardly be able to make sense of so torn a piece.—Your verses I shall muse on deliciously, as I gaze on your image in my mind's eye, in my heart's core; they will be in time enough for a week to come. I am truly happy your head-ache is better.—O, how can pain or evil be so daringly, unfeelingly, cruelly savage as to wound so noble a mind, so lovely a form!

My little fellow is all my name-sake.—Write me soon. My every, strongest good wishes attend you, Clarinda!

SYLVANDER.

I know not what I have written—I am pestered with people around me.

NO. LXXXIX.

TO THE SAME.

Sunday Night, January 27th, 1788.

THE impertinence of fools has joined with a return of an old indisposition, to make me good for nothing to-day. The paper has lain before me all this evening, to write to my dear Clarinda, but—

"Fools rush'd on fools, as waves succeed to waves."

I cursed them in my soul; they sacrilegiously disturbed my meditations on her who holds my heart. What a creature is man! A little alarm last night and to-day, that I am mortal, has made such a revolution on my spirits! There is no philosophy, no divinity, comes half so home to the mind. I have no idea of courage that braves heaven. 'Tis the wild ravings of an imaginary hero in bedlam.

I can no more, Clarinda; I can scarcely hold up my head; but I am happy you do not know it, you would be so uneasy.

SYLVANDER.

Monday Morning, January 28th, 1788.

I AM, my lovely friend, much better this morning on the whole; but I have a horrid langour on my spirits.

"Sick of the world, and all its joys,
My soul in pining sadness mourns;
Dark scenes of woe my mind employs,
The past and present in their turns."

Have you ever met with a saying of the great, and likewise good Mr. Locke, author of the famous Essay on the Human Understanding? He wrote a letter to a friend, directing it "not to be delivered till after my decease:" it ended thus—"I know you loved me when living, and will preserve my memory now I am dead. All the use to be made of it is, that this life affords no solid satisfaction, but in the consciousness of having done well, and the hopes of another life. Adieu! I leave my best wishes with you.—J. LOCKE."

Clarinda, may I reckon on your friendship for life? I think I may. Thou Almighty Preserver of men! thy friendship, which hitherto I have too much neglected, to secure it, shall all the future days and nights of my life, be my steady care! The idea of my Clarinda follows—

"Hide it my heart, within that close disguise,
Where mix'd with God's, her lov'd idea lies."

But I fear that inconstancy, the consequent imperfection of human weakness. Shall I meet with a friendship that defies years of absence, and the chances and changes of fortune? Perhaps "such things are;" *one honest* man I have great hopes from that way: but who, except a romance writer, would think on a *love* that could promise for life, in spite of distance, absence, chance, and change; and that, too, with slender hopes of fruition? For my own part, I can say to myself in both requisitions, "Thou art the man!" I dare, in cool resolve I dare, declare myself that friend, and that lover. If womankind is capable of such things, Clarinda is. I trust that she is; and feel I shall be miserable if she be not. There is not one virtue which gives worth, nor one sentiment which does honour to the sex, that she does not possess, superiorly to any woman I ever saw: her exalted mind, aided a little, perhaps, by her situation, is, I think, capable of that nobly-romantic love-enthusiasm.

May I see you on Wednesday evening, my dear angel? The next Wednesday again will, I conjecture, be a hated day to us both. I tremble for censorious remark, for your sake; but in extraordinary cases, may not usual and useful precaution be a little dispensed with? Three evenings, three swift-winged evenings, with pinions of down, are all the past; I dare not calculate the future. I shall call at Miss ——'s to morrow evening: 'twill be a farewell call.

I have written out my last sheet of paper, so I am reduced to my last half-sheet. What a strange mysterious faculty is that thing called imagination! We have no ideas almost at all of another world; but I have often amused myself with visionary schemes of what happiness might be enjoyed by small alterations—alterations that we can fully enter into, in this present state of existence. For instance, suppose you and I, just as we are at present; the same reasoning powers, sentiments, and even desires; the same fond curiosity for knowledge and remarking observation in our minds; and imagine our bodies free from pain and the necessary supplies for the wants of nature at all times, and easily within our reach: imagine further, that we were set free from the laws of gravitation, which bind us to this globe, and could at pleasure fly, without inconvenience, through all the yet unconjectured bounds of creation, what a life of bliss would we lead, in our mutual pursuit of virtue and knowledge, and our mutual enjoyment of friendship and love!

I see you laughing at my fairy fancies, and calling me a voluptuous Mahometan; but I am certain I would be a happy creature, beyond any thing we call bliss here below; nay, it would be a paradise congenial to you too. Don't you see us, hand in hand, or rather, my arm about your lovely waist, making our remarks on Sirius, the nearest of the fixed stars; or surveying a comet, flaming innoxious by us, as we just now would mark the passing pomp of a travelling monarch; or in the shady bower of Mercury or Venus, dedicating the hour to love, in mutual converse, relying honour, and revelling endearment, whilst the most exalted strains of poesy and harmony would be the ready, spontaneous language of our souls! Devotion is the favourite employment of your heart; so it is of mine: what incentives then to, and powers for, reverence, gratitude, faith, and hope, in all the fervours of adoration and praise to that Being, whose unsearchable wisdom, power and goodness, so pervaded, so inspired, every sense and feeling!—By this time, I dare say, you will be blessing the neglect of the maid that leaves me destitute of paper!

SYLVANDER.

NO. XC. (C0)

TO THE SAME.

Tuesday Night, 1788.

I AM delighted, charming Clarinda, with your honest enthusiasm for religion. Those of either sex, but particularly the female, who are lukewarm in that most important of all things, "O my soul, come not thou into their secrets!"—I feel myself deeply interested in your good opinion, and will lay before you the outlines of my belief. He who is our Author and Preserver, and will one day be our Judge, must be (not for his sake in the way of duty, but from the native impulse of our hearts,) the object of our reverential awe and grateful adoration: He is Almighty and all-bounteous, we are weak and dependent; hence prayer and every other sort of devotion.——"He is not willing that any should perish, but that all should come to everlasting life;" consequently, it must be in every one's power to embrace his offer of "everlasting life;" otherwise he could not, in justice, condemn those who did not. A mind pervaded, actuated, and governed by purity, truth and charity, though it does not *merit* heaven, yet is an absolutely necessary pre-requisite, without which heaven can neither be obtained nor enjoyed; and, by divine promise, such a mind shall never fail of attaining "everlasting life;" hence the impure, the deceiving, and the uncharitable exclude themselves from eternal bliss, by their unfitness for enjoying it. The Supreme Being has put the immediate administration of all this, for wise and good ends known to himself, into the hands of Jesus Christ, a great personage, whose relation to him we cannot comprehend, but whose relation to us is a guide and Saviour; and who, except for our own obstinacy and misconduct, will bring us all, through various ways, and by various means, to bliss at last.

These are my tenets, my lovely friend; and which, I think, cannot be well disputed. My creed is pretty nearly expressed in the last clause of Jamie Dean's grace, an honest weaver in Ayrshire: "Lord, grant that we may lead a guid life! for a guid life maks a guid end, at least it helps weel!"

I am flattered by the entertainment you tell me you have found in my packet. You see me as I have been, you know me as I am, and may guess at what I am likely to be. I too may say, "Talk not of love," &c., for indeed he has "plunged me deep in woe!" Not that I ever saw a woman who pleased unexceptionably, as my Clarinda elegantly says, "in the companion, the friend, and the mistress." *One* indeed I could except—*One*, before passion threw its mists over my discernment, I knew *the* first of women! Her name is indelibly written in my heart's core—but I dare not look in on it—a degree of agony would be the consequence. Oh! thou perfidous, cruel, mischief-making demon, who presidest over that frantic passion—thou mayest, thou dost poison my peace, but thou shalt not taint my honour—I would not, for a single moment, give an asylum to the most distant imagination that would shadow the faintest outline of a selfish gratification, at the expense of her whose happiness is twisted with the threads of my existence.——May she be as happy as she deserves! And if my tenderest, faithfulest friendship can add to her bliss, I shall, at least, have one solid mine of enjoyment in my bosom! *Don't guess at these ravings!*

I watched at our front window to-day, but was disappointed. It has been a day of disappointments. I am just risen from a two hours' bout after supper, with silly or sordid souls, who could relish nothing in common with me but the port.——*One*—— 'Tis now "witching time of night;" and whatever is out of joint in the foregoing scrawl, impute it to enchantments and spells; for I can't look over it, but will seal it up directly, as I don't care for to-morrow's criticisms on it.

You are by this time fast asleep, Clarinda; may good angels attend and guard you as constantly and faithfully as my good wishes do!

"Beauty, which, whether waking or asleep,
Shot forth peculiar graces."

John Milton, I wish thy soul better rest than I expect on my pillow to-night! O for a little of the cart-horse part of human nature! Good night, my dearest Clarinda!

SYLVANDER.

NO. XCI.

TO THE SAME.

Tuesday Noon, January 17th, 1788.

I AM certain I saw you, Clarinda; but you don't look to the proper story for a poet's lodging—

"Where speculation's roosted near the sky."

I could almost have thrown myself over for very vexation. Why did'nt you look higher? It has spoiled my peace for this day. To be so near my charming Clarinda; to miss her look when it was searching for me—I am sure the soul is capable of disease, for mine has convulsed itself into an inflammatory fever.

You have converted me, Clarinda. I shall love that name while I live: there is heavenly music in it. Booth and Amelia I know well. (61) Your sentiments on that subject, as they are on every subject, are just and noble. "To be feelingly alive to kindness and to unkindness," is a charming female character.

What I said in my last letter, the powers of fuddling sociality only know for me. By yours, I understand my good star has been partly in my horizon, when I got wild in my reveries. Had that evil planet, which has almost all my life shed its baneful rays on my devoted head, been, as usual, in my zenith, I had certainly blabbed something that would have pointed out to you the dear object of my tenderest friendship, and, in spite of me, something more. Had that fatal information escaped me, and it was merely chance, or kind stars, that it did not, I had been undone! You would never have written me, except perhaps *once* more! O, I could curse circumstances, and the coarse tie of human laws, which keep fast what common sense would loose, and which bars that happiness itself cannot give—happiness which otherwise Love and Honour would warrant! But hold—I shall make no more "hair breadth 'scapes."

My friendship, Clarinda, is a life-rent business. My likings are both strong and eternal. I told you I had but one male friend: I have but two female. I should have a third, but she is surrounded by the blandishments of flattery and courtship. * * * I register in my heart's core—* * * *. Miss N—— can tell how divine she is. She is worthy of a place in the same bosom with my Clarinda. That is the highest compliment I can pay her.

Farewell, Clarinda! Remember

SYLVANDER

NO. XCII.

TO THE SAME.

Saturday Morning, January 19th, 1788.

YOUR thoughts on religion, Clarinda, shall be welcome. You may perhaps distrust me, when I say 'tis also my favourite topic; but mine is the religion of the bosom. I hate the very idea of a controversial divinity; as I firmly believe that every honest upright man, of whatever sect, will be accepted of the Deity. If your verses, as you seem to hint, contain censure, except you want an occasion to break with me, don't send them, I have a little infirmity in my disposition, that where I fondly love, or highly esteem, I cannot bear reproach.

"Reverence thyself" is a sacred maxim, and I wish to cherish it. I think I told you Lord Bolingbroke's saying to Swift:—"Adieu, dear Swift, with all thy faults I love thee entirely; make an effort to love me with all mine." A glorious sentiment, and without which there can be no friendship! I do highly, very highly esteem you indeed, Clarinda—you merit it all! Perhaps, too—I scorn dissimulation!—I could fondly love you: judge then, what a maddening sting your reproach would be. "O! I have sins to *Heaven*, but none to *you!*"—With what pleasure would I meet you to-day, but I cannot walk to meet the fly. I hope to be able to see you on *foot* about the middle of next week.

I am interrupted—perhaps you are not sorry for it, you will tell me—but I won't anticipate blame. O, Clarinda! did you know how dear to me is your look of kindness, your smile of approbation! you would not, either in prose or verse, risk a censorious remark.

"Curst be the verse, how well soe'er it flow,
That tends to make one worthy man my foe!"

SYLVANDER.

NO. XCIII.

TO MRS. DUNLOP.

Edinburgh, January 21st, 1788.

AFTER six weeks' confinement I am beginning to walk across the room. They have been six horrible weeks; anguish and low spirits made me unfit to read, write, or think.

I have a hundred times wished that one could resign life as an officer resigns a commission: for I would not take in any poor, ignorant wretch, by selling out. Lately I was a sixpenny private, and, God knows, a miserable soldier enough; now I march to the campaign, a starving cadet—a little more conspicuously wretched.

I am ashamed of all this; for though I do want bravery for the warfare of life, I could wish, like some other soldiers, to have as much fortitude or cunning as to dissemble or conceal my cowardice.

As soon as I can bear the journey, which

will be, I suppose, about the middle of next week, I leave Edinburgh; and soon after I shall pay my grateful duty at Dunlop-House.

R. B.

NO. XCIV.

TO CLARINDA.

Tuesday Morning, January 29th, 1788.

I CANNOT go out to-day, my dearest Clarinda, without sending you half a line, by way of a sin-offering; but, believe me, 'twas the sin of ignorance. Could you think that I *intended* to hurt you by any thing I said yesternight? Nature has been too kind to you for your happiness, your delicacy, your sensibility.—O why should such glorious qualifications be the fruitful source of woe! You have "murdered sleep" to me last night. I went to bed, impressed with an idea that you were unhappy: and every time I closed my eyes, busy Fancy painted you in such scenes of romantic misery that I would almost be persuaded you were not well this morning.

————" If I unwittingly have offended,
Impute it not."
————" But while we live,
But one short hour, perhaps, between us two
Let there be peace."

If Mary is not gone by the time this reaches you, give her my best compliments. She is a charming girl, and highly worthy of the noblest love.

I send you a poem to read, till I call on you this night, which will be about nine. I wish I could procure some potent spell, some fairy charm that would protect injury, or restore to rest that bosom-chord, "tremblingly alive all o'er," on which hangs your peace of mind. I thought, vainly, I fear, thought that the devotion of love—love strong as even you can feel—love guarded, invulnerably guarded, by all the purity of virtue, and all the pride of honour; I thought such a love would make you happy—will I be mistaken? I can no more for hurry * * * *

NO. XCV.

TO THE SAME.

Sunday Morning, February 3rd, 1788.

I HAVE just been before the throne of my God, Clarinda; according to my association of ideas, my sentiments of love and friendship, I next devote myself to you. Yesterday night I was happy—happiness "that the world cannot give."—I kindle at the recollection; but it is a flame where innocence looks smiling on, and honour stands by a sacred guard.—Your heart, your fondest wishes, your dearest thoughts, these are yours to bestow: your person is unapproachable by the laws of your country; and he loves not as I do who would make you miserable.

You are an angel, Clarinda; you are surely no mortal that "the earth owns."—To kiss your hand, to live on your smile, is to me far more exquisite bliss that the dearest favours that the fairest of the sex, yourself excepted, can bestow.

Sunday Evening.

You are the constant companion of my thoughts. How wretched is the condition of one who is haunted with conscious guilt, and trembling under the idea of dreaded vengeance! and what a placid calm, what a charming secret enjoyment it gives, to bosom the kind feelings of friendship, and the fond throes of love! Out upon the tempest of anger, the acrimonious gall of fretful impatience, the sullen frost of louring resentment, or the corroding poison of withered envy! They eat up the immortal part of man! If they spent their fury only on the unfortunate objects of them, it would be something in their favour: but these miserable passions, like traitor Iscariot, betray their lord and master.

Thou Almighty Author of peace, and goodness, and love! do thou give me the social heart that kindly tastes of every man's cup!—Is it a draught of joy?—warm and open my heart to share it with cordial, unenvying rejoicing! Is it the bitter potion of sorrow?—melt my heart with sincerely sympathetic woe! Above all, do thou give me the manly mind that resolutely exemplifies, in life and manners, those sentiments which I would wish to be thought to possess! The friend of my soul—there, may I never deviate from the firmest fidelity and most active kindness! Clarinda, the dear object of my fondest love; there may the most sacred, inviolate honour, the most faithful kindling constancy, ever watch and animate my every thought and imagination!

Did you ever meet with the following lines spoken of Religion, your darling topic?

" '*Tis this*, my friend, that streaks our morning bright!
'*Tis this* that gilds the horrors of our night;

When wealth forsakes us, and when friends are few, [pursue;
When friends are faithless, or when foes
'Tis this that wards the blow, or stills the smart,
Disarms affliction, or repels its dart:
Within the breast bids purest rapture rise,
Bids smiling Conscience spread her cloudless skies."

I met with these verses very early in life, and was so delighted with them that I have them by me, copied at school.

Good night and sound rest, my dearest Clarinda! SYLVANDER.

NO. XCVI.

TO THE SAME.

I WAS on the way, *my Love*, to meet you, (I never do things by halves) when I got your card. M——— goes out of town tomorrow morning to see a brother of his who is newly arrived from ———. I am determined that he and I shall call on you together; so, look you, lest I should never see to-morrow, we will call on you to-night! ——— and you may put off tea till about seven; at which time, in the Galloway phrase, 'an the beast be to the fore, an the branks bide hale,' expect the humblest of your humble servants, and his dearest friend. We propose staying only half an hour, 'for ought we ken.' I could suffer the lash of misery eleven months in the year, were the twelfth to be composed of hours like yesternight. You are the soul of my enjoyment: all else is of the stuff and stocks of stones.

SYLVANDER.

NO. XCVII.

TO THE SAME.

Thursday Morning, February 7th, 1788.

"Unlavish Wisdom never works in vain."

I HAVE been tasking my reason, Clarinda, why a woman who for native genius, poignant wit, strength of mind, generous sincerity of soul, and the sweetest female tenderness, is without a peer, and whose personal charms have few, very, very few parallels among her sex; why, or how she should fall to the blessed lot of a poor harum scarum poet, whom Fortune had kept for her particular use, to wreak her temper on whenever she was in ill-humour. One time I conjectured that, as Fortune is the most capricious jade ever known, she may have taken, not a fit of remorse, but a paroxysm of whim, to raise the poor devil out of the mire, where he had so often and so conveniently served her as a stepping stone, and given him the most glorious boon she ever had in her gift merely for the maggot's sake, to see how this fool head and his fool heart will bear it. At other times I was vain enough to think that Nature, who has a great deal to say with Fortune, had given the coquettish goddess some such hint as, "Here is a paragon of female excellence, whose equal, in all my former compositions, I never was lucky enough to hit on, and despair of ever doing so again; you have cast her rather in the shades of life; there is a certain poet of my making; among your frolics it would not be amiss to attach him to this masterpiece of my hand, to give her that immortality among mankind which no woman of any age ever more deserved, and which few rhymsters of this age are better able to confer."

Evening, 9 *o'clock*.

I AM here, absolutely unfit to finish my letter—pretty hearty after a bowl, which has been constantly plied since dinner till this moment. I have been with Mr. Schetki, the musician, and he has set it (62) finely. ———I have no distinct ideas of anything, but that I have drunk your health twice to-night, and that you are all my soul holds dear in this world.

SYLVANDER.

NO. XCVIII.

TO THE SAME.

Saturday Morning, February 9th, 1788.

THERE is no time, my Clarinda, when the conscious thrilling chords of Love and Friendship give such delight as in the pensive hours of what our favourite, Thomson, calls "Philosophic Melancholy." The sportive insects who bask in the sunshine of prosperity; or the worms that luxuriant crawl amid their ample wealth of earth—they need no Clarinda: they would despise Sylvander —if they durst. The family of Misfortune, a numerous group of brothers and sisters; they need a resting-place to their souls: unnoticed, often condemned by the world;

in some degree, perhaps, condemned by themselves, they feel the full enjoyment of ardent love, delicate tender endearments, mutual esteem, and mutual reliance.

In this light I have often admired religion. In proportion as we are wrung with grief, or distracted with anxiety, the ideas of a compassionate Deity, an Almighty Protector, are doubly dear.

"'*Tis this*, my Friend, that streaks our morning bright;
'*Tis this* that gilds the horrors of our night."

I have been this morning taking a peep through, as Young finely says, "the dark postern of time long elaps'd;" and, you will easily guess, 'twas a rueful prospect. What a tissue of thoughtlessness, weakness, and folly! My life reminded me of a ruined temple; what strength, what proportion in some parts! what unsightly gaps, what prostrate ruins in others! I kneeled down before the Father of mercies, and said, "Father, I have sinned against Heaven, and in thy sight, and am no more worthy to be called thy son!"—— I rose, eased and strengthened. I despise the superstition of a fanatic, but I love the religion of a man. "The future," said I to myself, "is still before me;" there let me

——" On reason build resolve,
That column of true majesty in man!"

"I have difficulties many to encounter," said I; "but they are not absolutely insuperable: and where is firmness of mind shewn but in exertion? mere declamation is bombastic rant." Besides, wherever I am, or in whatever situation I may be—

'——'Tis nought to me:
Since God is ever present, ever felt,
In the void waste as in the city full;
And where He vital breathes, there must be joy!"

Saturday Night—half-after Ten.

What luxury of bliss I was enjoying this time yester-night! My ever-dearest Clarinda, you have stolen away my soul: but you have refined, you have exalted it: you have given it a stronger sense of virtue, and a stronger relish for piety.—Clarinda, first of your sex, if ever I am the veriest wretch on earth to forget you; if ever your lovely image is effaced from my soul,

"May I be lost, no eye to weep my end;
And find no earth that's base enough to bury me!"

What trifling silliness is the childish fondness of the every-day children of the world! 'tis the unmeaning toying of the younglings of the fields and forests: but where Sentiment and Fancy unite their sweets, where Taste and Delicacy refine; where Wit adds the flavour, and Goodness gives strength and spirit to all, what a delicious draught is the hour of tender endearment!—Beauty and Grace, in the arms of Truth and Honour, in all the luxury of mutual love.

Clarinda, have you ever seen the picture realized? Not in all its very richest colouring.

Last night, Clarinda, but for one slight shade, was the glorious picture.

——————Innocence
Look'd gaily smiling on; while rosy Pleasure
Hid young Desire amid her flowery wreath,
And pour'd her cup luxuriant; mantling high,
The sparkling heavenly vintage, Love and Bliss!

Clarinda, when a poet and poetess of Nature's making—two of Nature's noblest productions!—when they drink together of the same cup of Love and Bliss, attempt not, ye coarser stuffs of human nature, profanely to measure enjoyment ye never can know!—Good night, my dear Clarinda!

SYLVANDER.

NO. XCIX.

TO THE SAME.

February, 1788.

MY EVER DEAREST CLARINDA.—I make a numerous dinner party wait me while I read yours, and write this. Do not require that I should cease to love you, to adore you in my soul—'tis to me impossible;—your peace and happiness are to me dearer than my soul; name the terms on which you wish to see me, to correspond with me, and you have them; I must love, pine, mourn, and adore in secret—this you must not deny me; you will ever be to me—

"Dear as the light that visits these sad eyes,
Dear as the ruddy drops that warm my heart!"

I have not patience to read the puritanic scrawl.—Vile sophistry!—Ye heavens! thou God of nature! thou Redeemer of mankind! ye look down with approving eyes on a passion inspired by the purest flame, and guarded by truth, delicacy, and honour; but the half-inch soul of an unfeeling, cold-blooded pitiful, presbyterian bigot cannot forgive any thing above his dungeon bosom and foggy head.

Farewell; I'll be with you to-morrow evening; and be at rest in your mind;—I will be yours in the way you think most to your happiness! I dare not proceed—I love, and will love you, and will with joyous confidence approach the throne of the Almighty Judge of men, with your dear idea, and will despise the scum of sentiment, and the mist of sophistry.

SYLVANDER.

NO. C.

TO THE SAME.

Tuesday Evening, Feb. 12th, 1788.

THAT you have faults, my Clarinda, I never doubted; but I knew not where they existed, and Saturday night made me more in the dark than ever. O Clarinda, why will you wound my soul, by hinting that last night must have lessened my opinion of you? True, I was "behind the scenes with you;" but what did I see? A bosom glowing with honour and benevolence: a mind ennobled by genius, informed and refined by education and reflection, and exalted by native religion, genuine as in the climes of heaven; a heart formed for all the glorious meltings of friendship, love and pity. These I saw.—I saw the noblest immortal soul creation ever showed me.

I looked long, my dear Clarinda, for your letter; and am vexed that you are complaining. I have not caught you so far wrong as in your idea, that the commerce you have with *one* friend hurts you, if you cannot tell every tittle of it to *another*. Why have you so injurious a suspicion of a good God, Clarinda, as to think that Friendship and Love, on the sacred inviolate principles of Truth, Honour, and Religion, can be any thing else than an object of His divine approbation?

I have mentioned, in some of my former scrawls, Saturday evening next. Do allow me to wait on you that evening. Oh, my angel! how soon must we part! and when can we meet again! I looked forward on the horrid interval with tearful eyes! What have I lost by not knowing you sooner! I fear, I fear my acquaintance with you is too short to make that *lasting* impression on your heart I could wish.

SYLVANDER.

NO. CI.

TO THE SAME.

"I AM distressed for thee, my brother Jonathan!" I have suffered, Clarinda, from your letter. My soul was in arms at the sad perusal; I dreaded that I had acted wrong. If I have robbed you of a friend, God forgive me! But, Clarinda, be comforted: let us raise the tone of our feelings a little higher and bolder. A fellow-creature who leaves us, who spurns us without just cause, though once our bosom friend—up with a little honest pride—let him go! How shall I comfort you, who am the cause of the injury? Can I wish that I had never seen you? that we had never met? No! I never will. But have I thrown you friendless?—there is almost distraction in that thought.

Father of mercies! against Thee often have I sinned; through Thy grace I will endeavour to do so no more! She who, Thou knowest, is dearer to me than myself, pour Thou the balm of peace into her past wounds, and hedge her about with Thy peculiar care, all her future days and nights! Strengthen her tender noble mind, firmly to suffer, and magnanimously to bear! Make me worthy of that friendship she honours me with. May my attachment to her be pure as devotion, and lasting as immortal life! O Almighty Goodness, hear me! Be to her at all times, particularly in the hour of distress or trial, a Friend and Comforter, a Guide and Guard.

"How are Thy servants blest, O Lord,
How sure is their defence!
Eternal wisdom is their guide,
Their help, Omnipotence!"

Forgive me, Clarinda, the injury I have done you! To-night I shall be with you; as indeed I shall be ill at ease till I see you.

SYLVANDER.

NO. CII.

TO THE SAME.

Two o'clock.

I JUST now received your first letter of yesterday, by the careless negligence of the penny-post. Clarinda, matters are grown very serious with us; then seriously hear me, and hear me, Heaven:—I met you, my dear * * * *, by far the first of womankind, at least to me; I esteemed, I loved you at first sight, the longer I am acquainted with you, the more innate amiableness and worth I discover in you.—You have suffered a loss, I confess, for my sake: but if the firmest, steadiest, warmest friendship,—if every endeavour to be worthy of your friendship,—if a love, strong as the ties of nature, and holy as the duties of religion—if all these can make anything like a compensation for the evil I have occasioned you, if they be worth your acceptance, or can in the least add to your enjoyments—so help Sylvander, ye Powers above, in his hour of need, as he freely gives these all to Clarinda!

I esteem you, I love you as a friend; I admire you, I love you as a woman, beyond any one in all the circle of creation; I know I shall continue to esteem you, to love you, to pray for you, nay, to pray for myself for your sake.

Expect me at eight.—And believe me to be ever, my dearest Madam, yours most entirely, SYLVANDER.

NO. CIII.

TO MRS. DUNLOP.

Edinburgh, February 12*th*, 1788.

SOME things in your late letters hurt me: not that *you say them*, but that *you mistake me*. Religion, my honoured Madam, has not only been all my life my chief dependence, but my dearest enjoyment. I have, indeed, been the luckless victim of wayward follies; but, alas! I have ever been "more fool than knave." A mathematician without religion is a probable character; an irreligious poet is a monster. R. B.

NO. CIV.

TO CLARINDA.

February 14*th*, 1788.

WHEN matters, my love, are desperate, we must put on a desperate face:—

——"On reason build resolve,
That column of true majesty in man."

Or, as the same author finely says in another place—

——"Let thy soul spring up,
And lay strong hold for help on him that made thee."

I am yours, Clarinda, for life. Never be discouraged at all this. Look forward; in a few weeks I shall be somewhere or other out of the possibility of seeing you: till then, I shall write you often, but visit you seldom. Your fame, your welfare, your happiness, are dearer to me than any gratification whatever. Be comforted, my love! the present moment is the worst: the lenient hand of Time is daily and hourly either lightening the burden, or making us insensible to the weight. None of these friends, I mean Mr. —— and the other gentleman, can hurt your worldly support, and for their friendship, in a little time you will learn to be easy, and, by and bye, to be happy without it. A decent means of livelihood in the world, an approving God, a peaceful conscience, and one firm, trusty friend—can anybody that has these be said to be unhappy? These are yours.

To-morrow evening I shall be with you about eight; probably for the last time till I return to Edinburgh. In the meantime, should any of these two *unlucky* friends question you respecting me, whether I am *the man*, I do not think they are entitled to any information. As to their jealousy and spying, I despise them.—Adieu, my dearest Madam! SYLVANDER.

NO. CV.

TO ROBERT GRAHAM, ESQ.

OF FINTRY.

February, 1788.

SIR.—When I had the honour of being introduced to you at Athole House, I did not think so soon of asking a favour of you. When Lear, in Shakespeare, asked old Kent why he wished to be in his service, he answers:—"Because you have that in your face which I would fain call master." For some such reason, Sir, do I now solicit your patronage. You know, I dare say, of an application I lately made to your Board to be admitted an officer of Excise. I have, according to form, been examined by a super visor, and to-day I gave in his certificate, with a request for an order for instructions. In this affair, if I succeed, I am afraid I shall but too much need a patronising friend, Propriety of conduct as a man, and fidelity and attention as an officer, I dare engage for; but with any thing like business, except manual labour, I am totally unacquainted.

I had intended to have closed my late appearance on the stage of life in the character of a country farmer; but after discharging some filial and fraternal claims, I find I could only fight for existence in that miserable manner, which I have lived to see throw a venerable parent into the jaws of a jail,—whence death, the poor man's last and often best friend, rescued him.

I know, Sir, that to need your goodness, is to have a claim on it; may I, therefore, beg your patronage to forward me in this affair, till I be appointed to a division—where, by the help of rigid economy, I will try to support that independence so dear to my soul, but which has been too often so distant from my situation. R. B.

NO. CVI.

TO THE REV. JOHN SKINNER. (63)

Edinburgh, February, 14th, 1788.

Reverend and Dear Sir—I have been a cripple now near three months, though I am getting vastly better, and have been very much hurried besides, or else I would have wrote you sooner. I must beg your pardon for the epistle you sent me appearing in the Magazine. I had given a copy or two to some of my intimate friends, but did not know of the printing of it till the publication of the Magazine. However, as it does great honour to us both, you will forgive it.

The second volume of the Songs I mentioned to you in my last is published to-day. I send you a copy, which I beg you will accept as a mark of the veneration I have long had, and shall ever have, for your character, and of the claim I make to your continued acquaintance. Your songs appear in the third volume, with your name in the index; as I assure you, Sir, I have heard your "Tullochgorum," particularly among our west-country folks, given to many different names, and most commonly to the immortal author of "The Minstrel," who, indeed, never wrote anything superior to "Gie a sang, Montgomery cried." Your brother has promised me your verses to the Marquis of Huntly's reel, which certainly deserve a place in the collection. My kind host, Mr. Cruikshank, of the high-School here, and said to be one of the best Latins in this age, begs me to make you his grateful acknowledgments for the entertainment he has got in a Latin publication of yours that I borrowed for him from your acquaintance and much respected friend in this place, the Reverend Dr. Webster. (64) Mr. Cruikshank maintains that you write the best Latin since Buchanan. I leave Edinburgh to-morrow, but shall return in three weeks. Your song you mentioned in your last, to the tune of "Dumbarton Drums," and the other, which you say was done by a brother in trade of mine, a ploughman, I shall thank you for a copy of each. I am ever, reverend Sir, with the most respectful esteem and sincere veneration, yours, R. B.

NO. CVII.

TO RICHARD BROWN.

Edinburgh, February 15th, 1788.

My Dear Friend—I received yours with the greatest pleasure. I shall arrive at Glasgow on Monday evening; and beg, if possible, you will meet me on Tuesday. I shall wait you Tuesday all day. I shall be found at Davies's Black Bull inn. I am hurried, as if hunted by fifty devils, else I should go to Greenock; but if you cannot possibly come, write me, if possible, to Glasgow, on Monday; or direct to me at Mossgiel by Mauchline; and name a day and place in Ayrshire, within a fortnight from this date, where I may meet you. I only stay a fortnight in Ayrshire, and return to Edinburgh. I am ever, my dearest friend, yours, R. B.

NO. CVIII.

TO MRS. ROSE, OF KILRAVOCK.

Edinburgh, February 17th, 1788.

Madam—You are much indebted to some indispensable business I have had on my hands, otherwise my gratitude threatened such a return for your obliging favour as would have tired your patience. It but poorly expresses my feelings to say, that I am sensible of your kindness: it may be said of hearts such as yours is, and such, I hope, mine is, much more justly than Addison applies it :—

Some souls by instinct to each other turn.

There was something in my reception at Kilravock so different from the cold, obsequious, dancing-school bow of politeness, that it almost got into my head that friendship had occupied her ground without the intermediate march of acquaintance. I wish I could transcribe, or rather transfuse into language, the glow of my heart when I read your letter. My ready fancy, with colours more mellow than life itself, painted the beautifully wild scenery of Kilravock; the venerable grandeur of the castle; the spreading woods; the winding river, gladly leaving his unsightly, heathy source, and lingering with apparent delight as he passes the fairy walk at the bottom of the garden; your late distressful anxieties; your present enjoyments; your dear little angel, the pride of your hopes; my aged friend, venerable in worth and years, whose loyalty and other virtues will strongly entitle her to the support of the Almighty Spirit here, and his peculiar favour in a happier state of existence. You cannot imagine, Madam, how much such feelings delight me; they are my dearest proofs of my own immortality. Should I never revisit the north, as probably I never will, nor again see your hospitable mansion, were I, some twenty years hence, to see your little fellow's name making a proper figure in a newspaper paragraph, my heart would bound with pleasure.

I am assisting a friend in a collection of Scottish songs, set to their proper tunes; every air worth preserving is to be included; among others I have given "Morag," and some few Highland airs which pleased me most, a dress which will be more generally known, though far, far inferior in real merit. As a small mark of my grateful esteem, I beg leave to present you with a copy of the work, as far as it is printed; the Man of Feeling, that first of men, has promised to transmit it by the first opportunity.

I beg to be remembered most respectfully to my venerable friend, and to your little Highland chieftain. When you see the "two fair spirits of the hill," at Kildrummie (65), tell them that I have done myself the honour of setting myself down as one of their admirers for at least twenty years to come, consequently they must look upon me as an acquaintance for the same period; but, as the Apostle Paul says, "this I ask of grace, not of debt." I have the honour to be, Madam, &c., R. B.

NO. CIX.

TO CLARINDA.

Glasgow, Monday Evening, 9 *o'clock, Feb.* 17*th,* 1788.

THE attraction of love, I find, is in an inverse proportion to the attraction of the Newtonian philosophy. In the system of Sir Isaac, the nearer objects are to one another the stronger is the attractive force; in my system, every mile-stone that marked my progress from Clarinda, awakened a keener pang of attachment to her.

How do you feel, my love? Is your heart ill at ease? I fear it.—God forbid that these persecutors should harass that peace which is more precious to me than my own. Be assured I shall ever think of you, muse on you, and, in my moments of devotion, pray for you. The hour that you are not in all my thoughts—"be that hour darkness! let the shadows of death cover it! let it not be numbered in the hours of the day!"

—"When I forget the darling theme,
Be my tongue mute! my fancy paint no more!
And, dead to joy, forget my heart to beat!"

I have just met with my old friend, the ship captain; guess my pleasure;—to meet you could alone have given me more. My brother William, too, the young saddler, has come to Glasgow to meet me; and here are we three spending the evening.

I arrived here too late to write by post; but I'll wrap half a dozen sheets of blank paper together, and send it by the fly, under the name of a parcel. You shall hear from me next post town. I would write you a long letter, but for the present circumstance of my friend.

Adieu, my Clarinda! I am just going to propose your health by way of grace-drink.

SYLVANDER.

NO. CX.

TO MISS CHALMERS.

Edinburgh, February, 1788.

TO-MORROW, my dear Madam, I leave Edinburgh. I have altered all my plans of future life. A farm that I could live in, I could not find; and, indeed, after the necessary support my brother and the rest of the family required, I could not venture on farming in that style suitable to my feelings. You will condemn me for the next step I have taken. I have entered into the Excise. I stay in the west about three weeks, and then return to Edinburgh for six weeks' instructions; afterwards, for I get employ instantly, I go *où il plait à Dieu —et mon Roi.* I have chosen this, my dear friend, after mature deliberation. The question is not at what door of fortune's palace shall we enter in, but what doors does she open to us? I was not likely to get any thing to do. I wanted *un bût,* which is a dangerous, an unhappy situation. I got this without any hanging on, or mortifying solicitation; it is immediate bread, and though poor in comparison of the last eighteen months of my existence, 'tis luxury in comparison of all my preceding life: besides, the commissioners are some of them my acquaintances, and all of them my firm friends.

R. B.

NO. CXI.

TO RICHARD BROWN.

Mossgiel, February 24th, 1788.

My Dear Sir—I cannot get the proper direction for my friend in Jamaica, but the following will do:—To Mr. Jo. Hutchinson, at Jo. Brownrigg's, Esq., care of Mr. Benjamin Henriquez, merchant, Orange Street, Kingston. I arrived here, at my brother's, only yesterday, after fighting my way through Paisley and Kilmarnock against those old powerful foes of mine, the devil, the world, and the flesh—so terrible in the fields of dissipation. I have met with few incidents in my life which gave me so much pleasure as meeting you in Glasgow. There is a time of life beyond which we cannot form a tie worth the name of friendship. "Oh youth! enchanting stage, profusely blest." Life is a fairy scene: almost all that deserves the name of enjoyment or pleasure is only a charming delusion; and in comes repining age, in all the gravity of hoary wisdom, and wretchedly chases away the bewitching phantom. When I think of life, I resolve to keep a strict look-out in the course of economy, for the sake of worldly convenience and independence of mind; to cultivate intimacy with a few of the companions of youth, that they may be the friends of age; never to refuse my liquorish humour a handful of the sweet-meats of life, when they come not too dear; and, for futurity—

The present moment is our aim,
The next we never saw!

How like you my philosophy? Give my best compliments to Mrs. B., and believe me to be, my dear Sir, yours most truly,

R. B. (66)

NO. CXII.

TO MISS CHALMERS.

March, 1788.

Now for that wayward, unfortunate thing, myself. I have broke measures with Creech, and last week I wrote him a frosty, keen letter. He replied in terms of chastisement, and promised me upon his honour that I should have the account on Monday; but this is Tuesday, and yet I have not heard a word from him. God have mercy on me! a poor damned, incautious, duped, unfortunate fool! The sport, the miserable victim of rebellious pride, hypochondriac imagination, agonising sensibility, and bedlam passions!

"I wish that I were dead, but I'm no like to die!" I had lately "a hair-breadth 'scape in th' imminent deadly breach" of love too Thank my stars, I got off heart-whole, "more fleyd than hurt."—Interruption.

I have this moment got a hint; I fear I am something like—undone—but I hope for the best. Come, stubborn pride and unshrinking resolution; accompany me through this, to me, miserable world! You must not desert me. Your friendship I think I can count on, though I should date my letters from a marching regiment. Early in life, and all my life, I reckoned on a recruiting drum as my forlorn hope. Seriously though, life at this moment presents me with but a melancholy path: but—my limb will soon be sound, and I shall struggle on. R. B.

NO. CXIII.

TO CLARINDA.

Cumnock, March 2nd, 1788.

I hope, and am certain, that my generous Clarinda will not think my silence, for now a long week (67), has been in any degree owing to my forgetfulness. I have been tossed about through the country ever since I wrote you; and am here, returning from Dumfries-shire, at an inn, the post-office of the place, with just so long time as my horse eats his corn, to write you. I have been hurried with business and dissipation almost equal to the insidious decree of the Persian monarch's mandate, when he forbade asking petition of God or man for forty days. Had the venerable prophet been as throng as I, he had not broken the decree, at least not thrice a-day.

I am thinking my farming scheme will yet hold. A worthy intelligent farmer, my father's friend and my own, has been with me on the spot: he thinks the bargain practicable. I am myself, on a more serious review of the lands, much better pleased with them. I won't mention this in writing to any body but you and ———. Don't accuse me of being fickle: I have the two plans of life before me, and I wish to adopt the one most likely to procure me independence. I shall be in Edinburgh next week. I long to see you: your image is omnipresent to me; nay, I am convinced I would soon idolatrize it most seriously; so much do absence and memory improve the medium through which one sees the much-loved object. To-night, at the sacred hour of eight, I expect to meet you—at the Throne of Grace. I hope, as I go home to night, to find a letter from you at the post-office in Mauchline. I have just once seen that dear hand since I left Edinburgh—a letter indeed which much affected me. Tell me, first of womankind! will my warmest attachment, my sincerest friendship, my correspondence, will they be any compensation for the sacrifices you make for my sake! If they will, they are yours. If I settle on the farm I propose, I am just a day and a half's ride from Edinburgh. We will meet—don't you say, "perhaps too often!"

Farewell, my fair, my charming Poetess! May all good things ever attend you! I am ever, my dearest Madam, yours,

SYLVANDER.

NO. CXIV.

TO MR. WILLIAM CRUIKSHANK.

Mauchline, March 3rd, 1788.

MY DEAR SIR — Apologies for not writing are frequently like apologies for not singing—the apology better than the song. I have fought my way severely through the savage hospitality of this country, to send every guest drunk to bed if they can.

I executed your commission in Glasgow. and I hope the cocoa came safe. 'Twas the same price and the very same kind as your former parcel, for the gentleman recollected your buying there perfectly well.

I should return my thanks for your —— hospitality (I leave a blank for the epithet, as I know none can do it justice) to a poor wayfaring bard, who was spent and almost overpowered, fighting with prosaic wickednesses in high places; but I am afraid lest you should burn the letter whenever you come to the passage, so I pass over it in silence. I am just returned from visiting Mr. Miller's farm. The friend whom I told you I would take with me (68) was highly pleased with the farm; and as he is, without exception, the most intelligent farmer in the country, he has staggered me a good deal. I have the two plans of life before me; I I shall balance them to the best of my judgment, and fix on the most eligible. I have written Mr. Miller, and shall wait on him when I come to town, which shall be the beginning or middle of next week: I would be in sooner, but my unlucky knee is rather worse, and I fear for some time will scarcely stand the fatigue of my Excise instructions. I only mention these ideas to you; and, indeed, except Mr. Ainslie, whom I intend writing to to-morrow, I will not write at all to Edinburgh till I return to it. I would send my compliments to Mr. Nicol, but he would be hurt if he knew I wrote to any body and not to him; so I shall only beg my best, kindest, kindest compliments to my worthy hostess, and the sweet little rose-bud.

So soon as I am settled in the routine of life, either as an Excise-officer, or as a farmer, I propose myself great pleasure from a regular correspondence with the only man almost I ever saw who joined the most attentive prudence with the warmest generosity.

I am much interested for that best of men, Mr. Wood; I hope he is in better health and spirits than when I saw him last. I am ever, my dearest friend, your obliged humble servant, R. B.

NO. CXV.

TO ROBERT AINSLIE, ESQ.

Mauchline, March 3rd, 1788.

MY DEAR FRIEND—I am just returned from Mr. Miller's farm. My old friend whom I took with me was highly pleased with the bargain, and advised me to accept of it. He is the most intelligent, sensible farmer in the country, and his advice has staggered me a good deal. I have the two plans before me: I shall endeavour to balance them to the best of my judgment, and fix on the most eligible. On the whole, if I find Mr. Miller in the same favourable disposition as when I saw him last, I shall in all probability turn farmer.

I have been through sore tribulation, and under much buffetting of the wicked one, since I came to this country. Jean I found banished, forlorn, destitute and friendless; I have reconciled her to her fate, and I have reconciled her to her mother.

I shall be in Edinburgh the middle of next week. My farming ideas I shall keep private till I see. I got a letter from Clarinda yesterday, and she tells me she has got no letter of mine but one. Tell her that I wrote to her from Glasgow, from Kilmarnock, from Mauchline, and yesterday from Cumnock as I returned from Dumfries. Indeed, she is the only person in Edinburgh I have written to till this day. How are your soul and body putting up?—a little like man and wife, I suppose. R. B.

NO. CXVI.

TO CLARINDA.

Mossgiel, March 7th, 1788.

CLARINDA, I have been so stung with your reproach for unkindness—a sin so unlike me, a sin I detest more than a breach of the whole Decalogue, fifth, sixth, seventh, and ninth articles excepted—that I believe I shall not rest in my grave about it, if I die before I see you. You have often allowed me the head to judge, and the heart to feel, the influence of female excellence. Was it not blasphemy, then, against your own charms, and against my feelings, to suppose that a short fortnight could abate my passion? You, my Love, may have your cares and anxieties to disturb you, but they are the usual occurrences of life; your future views are fixed, and your mind in a settled routine. Could not you, my ever dearest Madam, make a little allowance for a man, after long absence, paying a short visit to a country full of friends, relations and early intimates? Cannot you guess, my Clarinda, what thoughts, what cares, what anxious forebodings, hopes and fears, must crowd the breast of the man of keen sensibility, when no less is on the tapis than his aim, his employment, his very existence, through future life?

Now that, not my apology, but my defence, is made, I feel my soul respire more easily. I know you will go along with me in my justification—would to Heaven you could in my adoption too! I mean an adoption beneath the stars—an adoption where I might revel in the immediate beams of

"Her, the bright sun of all her sex."

I would not have you, my dear Madam, so much hurt at Miss ——'s coldness. 'Tis placing yourself below her, an honour she by no means deserves. We ought, when we wish to be economists in happiness—we ought, in the first place, to fix the standard of our own character; and when, on full examination, we know where we stand, and how much ground we occupy, let us contend for it as property: and those who seem to doubt, or deny us what is justly ours, let us either pity their prejudices, or despise their judgment. I know, my dear, you will say this is self conceit; but I call it self-knowledge. The one is the overweening opinion of a fool, who fancies himself to be what he wishes himself to be thought; the other is the honest justice that a man of sense, who has thoroughly examined the subject, owes to himself. Without this standard, this column in our own mind, we are perpetually at the mercy of the petulance, the mistakes, the prejudices, nay, the very weakness and wickedness of our fellow-creatures.

I urge this, my dear, both to confirm myself in the doctrine which, I assure you, I sometimes need; and because I know that this causes you often much disquiet.—To return to Miss ——: she is most certainly a worthy soul, and equalled by very, very few, in goodness of heart. But can she boast more goodness of heart than Clarinda? Not even prejudice will dare to say so. For penetration and discernment, Clarinda sees far beyond her: to wit, Miss —— dare make no pretence; to Clarinda's wit, scarcely any of her sex dare make pretence. Personal charms, it would be ridiculous to run the parallel. And for conduct in life, Miss —— was never called out, either much to do or to suffer; Clarinda has been both; and has performed her part where Miss —— would have sunk at the bare idea.

Away, then, with these disquietudes! Let us pray with the honest weaver of Kilbarchan—" Lord, send us a guid conceit o' oursel!" Or, in the words of the auld sang,

"Who does me disdain, I can scorn them again,
And I'll never mind any such foes."

There is an error in the commerce of intimacy with those who are perpetually taking what they, in the way of exchange, have not in equivalent to give us; and, what is still worse, we have no idea of the value of our goods. Happy is our lot, indeed, when we meet with an honest merchant, who is qualified to deal with us on our own terms; but that is a rarity. With almost every body we must pocket our pearls, less or more, and learn, in the old Scotch phrase—"To gie sic like as we get." For this reason, one should try to erect a kind of bank or store-house in one's own mind; or as the Psalmist says, "We should commune with our own hearts, and be still." This is exactly * * * * *

[*rest wanting.*]

NO. CXVII.

TO RICHARD BROWN.

Mauchline, March 7th, 1788.

I HAVE been out of the country, my dear friend, and have not had an opportunity of writing till now, when I am afraid you will be gone out of the country too. I have been looking at farms, and, after all, perhaps I may settle in the character of a farmer. I have got so vicious a bent to idleness, and have ever been so little a man of business, that it will take no ordinary effort to bring my mind properly into the routine; but you will say a "great effort is worthy of you." I say so myself; and butter up my vanity with all the stimulating compliments I can think of. Men of grave, geometrical minds,—the sons of "which was to be demonstrated,"—may cry up reason as much as they please; but I have always found an honest passion, or native instinct, the truest auxiliary in the warfare of this world. Reason almost always comes to me like an unlucky wife to a poor devil of a husband, just in sufficient time to add her reproaches to his other grievances.

I am gratified with your kind inquiries after Jean; as, after all, I may say with Othello—

——————— "Excellent wretch!
Perdition catch my soul, but I do love thee!"

I go for Edinburgh on Monday.

Yours, R. B.

NO. CXVIII.

TO MR MUIR.

Mossgiel, March 7th, 1788.

DEAR SIR—I have particularly changed my ideas, since I saw you. I took old Glenconner with me to Mr. Miller's farm, and he was so pleased with it, that I have wrote an offer to Mr. Miller, which if he accepts, I shall sit down a plain farmer, the happiest of lives when a man can live by it. In this case, I shall not stay in Edinburgh above a week. I set out on Monday, and would have come by Kilmarnock, but there are several small sums owing me for my first edition about Galston and Newmills, and I shall set off so early as to dispatch my business and reach Glasgow by night. When I return, I shall devote a forenoon or two to make some kind of acknowledgment for all the kindness I owe your friendship. Now that I hope to settle with some credit and comfort at home, there was not any friendship or friendly correspondence that promised me more pleasure than yours; I hope I will not be disappointed. I trust the spring will renew your shattered frame, and make your friends happy. You and I have often agreed that life is no great blessing on the whole. The close of life, indeed, to a reasoning age, is

Dark as was chaos, ere the infant sun
Was roll'd together, or had tried his beams
Athwart the gloom profound.

But an honest man has nothing to fear. If we lie down in the grave, the whole man a piece of broken machinery, to moulder with the clods of the valley, be it so; at least there is an end of pain, care, woes and wants: if that part of us called mind does survive the apparent destruction of the man—away with old-wife prejudices and tales! Every age and every nation has had a different set of stories; and as the many are always weak of consequence, they have often, perhaps always, been deceived: a man conscious of having acted an honest part among his fellow-creatures—even granting that he may have been the sport at times of passions and instincts—he goes to a great unknown Being, who could have no other end in giving him existence but to make him happy, who gave him those passions and instincts, and well knows their force.

These, my worthy friend, are my ideas; and I know they are not far different from yours. It becomes a man of sense to think for himself, particularly in a case where all men are equally interested, and where, indeed, all men are equally in the dark.

Adieu, my dear Sir; God send us a cheerful meeting! R. B.

NO. CXIX. (69)

TO CLARINDA.

I OWN myself guilty, Clarinda; I should have written you last week; but when you recollect, my dearest Madam, that your's of this night's post is only the third I have got from you, and that this is the fifth or sixth I have sent to you, you will not reproach me, with a good grace, for unkindness. I have always some kind of idea, not to sit down to write a letter, except I have time and possession of my faculties so as to do some justice to my letter; which at present is rarely my situation. For instance, yesterday I dined at a friend's at some distance; the savage hospitality of this country spent me the most part of the night over the nauseous potion in the bowl: this day—sick—head-ache—low spirited—miserable—fasting, except for a draught of water or small beer: now eight o'clock at night—only able to crawl ten minutes' walk into Mauchline to wait the post, in the pleasureable hope of hearing from the mistress of my soul.

But, a truce to all this! When I sit down to write to you, all is harmony and peace. An hundred times a-day do I figure you, before your taper, your book or work laid aside, as I get within the room. How happy have I been! and how little of that scantling portion of time, called the life of man, is sacred to happiness! I could moralize to-night like a death's head:—

"O what is life, that thoughtless wish of all!
A drop of honey in a draught of gall."

Nothing astonishes me more, when a little sickness clogs the wheels of life, than the thoughtless career we run in the hour of health. "None saith, where is God, my Maker, that giveth songs in the night; who teacheth us more knowledge than the beasts of the field, and more understanding than the fowls of the air."

Give me, my Maker, to remember thee! Give me to act up to the dignity of my nature! Give me to feel "another's woe;" and continue with me that dear-lov'd friend that feels with mine!

The dignified and dignifying consciousness of an honest man, and the well-grounded trust in approving Heaven, are two most substantial sources of happiness.

* * * * * *

SYLVANDER.

NO. CXX.

TO MISS ——.

MY DEAR COUNTRYWOMAN—I am so impatient to show you that I am once more at peace with you, that I send you the book I mentioned directly, rather than wait the uncertain time of my seeing you. I am afraid I have mislaid or lost Collins's Poems, which I promised to Miss Irvin. If I can find them, I will forward them by you; if not, you must apologise for me.

I know you will laugh at it when I tell you that your piano and you together have played the deuce somehow about my heart. My breast has been widowed these many months, and I thought myself proof against the fascinating witchcraft; but I am afraid you will "feelingly convince me what I am." I say, I am afraid, because I am not sure what is the matter with me. I have one miserable bad symptom; when you whisper, or look kindly to another, it gives me a draught of damnation. I have a kind of wayward wish to be with you ten minutes by yourself, though what I would say, Heaven above knows, for I am sure I know not. I have no formed design in all this, but just, in the nakedness of my heart, write you down a mere matter-of-fact story. You may perhaps give yourself airs of distance on this, and that will completely cure me; but I wish you would not—just let us meet, if you please, in the old beaten way of friendship.

I will not subscribe myself your humble servant, for that is a phrase, I think, at least fifty miles off from the heart; but I will conclude with sincerely wishing that the Great Protector of innocence may shield you from the barbed dart of calumny, and hand you by the covert snare of deceit. R. B.

NO. CXXI.

TO MISS CHALMERS.

Edinburgh, March 14th, 1788.

I KNOW, my ever dear friend, that you will be pleased with the news when I tell you, *

* * * I have at last taken a lease of a farm. Yesternight I completed a bargain with Mr. Miller of Dalswinton for the farm of Ellisland, on the banks of the Nith, between five and six miles above Dumfries. I begin at Whitsunday to build a house, drive lime, &c.; and Heaven be my help! for it will take a strong effort to bring my mind into the routine of business. I have discharged all the army of my former pursuits, fancies, and pleasures—a motley host! and have literally and strictly retained only the ideas of a few friends which I have incorporated into a life-guard. I trust in Dr. Johnson's observation, "Where much is attempted, something is done." Firmness, both in suffering and exertion, is a character I would wish to be thought to possess; and have always despised the whining yelp of complaint, and the cowardly, feeble resolve.

Poor Miss K. is ailing a good deal this winter, and begged me to remember her to you the first time I wrote to you. Surely woman, amiable woman, is often made in vain. Too delicately formed for the rougher pursuits of ambition; too noble for the dirt of avarice, and even too gentle for the rage of pleasure; formed indeed for, and highly susceptible of, enjoyment and rapture; but that enjoyment, alas! almost wholly at the mercy of the caprice, malevolence, stupidity, or wickedness of an animal at all times comparatively unfeeling, and often brutal.

R. B.

NO. CXXII.

TO MRS. DUNLOP.

Mossgiel, March 17th, 1788.

MADAM—The last paragraph in yours of the 30th February affected me most, so I shall begin my answer where you ended your letter. That I am often a sinner, with any little wit I have, I do confess: but I have taxed my recollection to no purpose, to find out when it was employed against you. I hate an ungenerous sarcasm a great deal worse than I do the devil, at least as Milton describes him; and though I may be rascally enough to be sometimes guilty of it myself, I cannot endure it in others. You, my honoured friend, who cannot appear in any light but you are sure of being respectable—you can afford to pass by an occasion to display your wit, because you may depend for fame on your sense; or, if you choose to be silent, you know you can rely on the gratitude of many, and the esteem of all; but God help us, who are wits or witlings by profession, if we stand not for fame there, we sink unsupported!

I am highly flattered by the news you tell me of Coila. I may say to the fair painter who does me so much honour, as Dr. Beattie says to Ross, the poet of his muse Scota, from which, by the bye, I took the idea of Coila ('tis a poem of Beattie's in the Scottish dialect, which perhaps you have never seen):—

Ye shak your head, but o' my fegs,
Ye've set auld Scota on her legs:
Lang had she lien wi' beffs and flegs,
Bumbaz'd and dizzie,
Her fiddle wanted strings and pegs,
Wae's me, poor hizzie.

R. B.

NO. CXXIII.

TO RICHARD BROWN.

Glasgow, March 26th, 1788.

I AM monstrously to blame, my dear Sir, in not writing to you, and sending you the Directory. I have been getting my tack extended, as I have taken a farm, and I have been racking shop accounts with Mr. Creech; both of which, together with watching, fatigue, and a load of care almost too heavy for my shoulders, have in some degree actually fevered me. I really forgot the Directory yesterday, which vexed me; but I was convulsed with rage a great part of the day. I have to thank you for the ingenious, friendly and elegant epistle from your friend Mr. Crawford. I shall certainly write to him, but not now. This is merely a card to you, as I am posting to Dumfries-shire, where many perplexing arrangements await me. I am vexed about the Directory; but, my dear Sir, forgive me: these eight days I have been positively crazed. My compliments to Mrs. B. I shall write to you at Grenada. I am ever, my dearest friend, yours, R. B

NO. CXXIV.

TO MR. ROBERT CLEGHORN.

Mauchline, March 31st, 1788.

YESTERDAY, my dear Sir, as I was riding through a tract of melancholy, joyless muirs, between Galloway and Ayrshire, it being

Sunday, I turned my thoughts to psalms, and hymns, and spiritual songs; and your favourite air, "Captain O'Kean," coming at length into my head, I tried these words to it. (70) You will see that the first part of the tune must be repeated.

I am tolerably pleased with these verses, but as I have only a sketch of the tune, I leave it with you to try if they suit the measure of the music.

I am so harassed with care and anxiety, about this farming project of mine, that my muse has degenerated into the veriest prose-wench that ever picked cinders, or followed a tinker. When I am fairly got into the routine of business, I shall trouble you with a longer epistle; perhaps with some queries respecting farming: at present, the world sets such a load on my mind that it has effaced almost every trace of the poet in me.

My very best compliments and good wishes to Mrs. Cleghorn. R. B.

NO. CXXV.

TO MISS CHALMERS.

Mauchline, April 7th, 1788.

I AM indebted to you and Miss Nimmo for letting me know Miss Kennedy. Strange! how apt we are to indulge prejudices in our judgments of one another! Even I, who pique my skill in marking characters—because I am too proud of my character as a man to be dazzled in my judgment for glaring wealth, and too proud of my situation as a poor man to be biassed against squalid poverty—I was unacquainted with Miss K.'s very uncommon worth.

I am going on a good deal progressive in *mon grand bât*, the sober science of life. I have lately made some sacrifices, for which, were I *vivâ voce* with you to paint the situation and recount the circumstances (71), you would applaud me. R. B.

NO. CXXVI.

TO MR. WILLAM DUNBAR,

EDINBURGH.

Mauchline, April 7th, 1788.

I HAVE not delayed so long to write you, my much respected friend, because I thought no farther of my promise. I have long since given up that kind of formal correspondence, where one sits down irksomely to write a letter, because we think we are in duty bound so to do.

I have been roving over the country, as the farm I have taken is forty miles from this place, hiring servants and preparing matters; but most of all, I am earnestly busy to bring about a revolution in my own mind. As, till within these eighteen months, I never was the wealthy master of ten guineas, my knowledge of business is to learn; add to this, my late scenes of idleness and dissipation have enervated my mind to an alarming degree. Skill in the sober science of life is my most serious and hourly study. I have dropped all conversation and all reading (prose reading) but what tends in some way or other to my serious aim. Except one worthy young fellow, I have not one single correspondent in Edinburgh. You have indeed kindly made me an offer of that kind. The world of wits, and *gens comme il faut* which I lately left, and with whom I never again will intimately mix—from that port, Sir, I expect your Gazette: what *les beaux esprits* are saying, what they are doing, and what they are singing. Any sober intelligence from my sequestered walks of life; any droll original; any passing remark, important forsooth, because it is mine; any little poetic effort, however embroyth; these, my dear Sir, are all you have to expect from me. When I talk of poetic efforts, I must have it always understood, that I appeal from your wit and taste to your friendship and good nature. The first would be my favourite tribunal, where I defied censure; but the last, where I declined justice.

I have scarcely made a single distich since I saw you. When I meet with an old Scots air that has any facetious idea in its name, I have a peculiar pleasure in following out that idea for a verse or two.

I trust that this will find you in better health than I did last time I called for you. A few lines from you, directed to me at Mauchline, were it but to let me know how you are, will set my mind a good deal at peace. Now, never shun the idea of writing me, because perhaps you may be out of humour or spirits. I could give you a hundred good consequences attending a dull letter; one, for example, and the remaining ninety-nine some other time—it will always serve to keep in countenance, my much respected Sir, your obliged friend and humble servant,

R. B.

NO. CXXVII.

TO MRS. DUNLOP.

Mauchline, April 28th, 1788.

MADAM—Your powers of reprehension must be great indeed, as I assure you they made my heart ache with penitential pangs, even though I was really not guilty. As I commence farmer at Whitsunday, you will easily guess I must be pretty busy; but that is not all. As I got the offer of the Excise business without solicitation, and as it costs me only six months' attendance for instructions, to entitle me to a commission—which commission lies by me, and at any future period, on my simple petition, can be resumed; I thought five-and thirty pounds a-year was no bad *dernier resort* for a poor poet, if fortune in her jade tricks should kick him down from the little eminence to which she has lately helped him up.

For this reason, I am at present attending these instructions, to have them completed before Whitsunday. Still, Madam, I prepared with the sincerest pleasure to meet you at the Mount, and came to my brother's on Saturday night, to set out on Sunday; but for some nights preceding I had slept in an apartment, where the force of the winds and rains was only mitigated by being sifted through numberless apertures in the windows, walls, &c. In consequence I was on Sunday, Monday, and part of Tuesday, unable to stir out of bed, with all the miserable effects of a violent cold.

You see, Madam, the truth of the French maxim *le vrai n'est pas toujours le vraisemblable*. Your last was so full of expostulation, and was something so like the language of an offended friend, that I began to tremble for a correspondence, which I had with grateful pleasure set down as one of the greatest enjoyments of my future life.

Your books have delighted me, Virgil, Dryden and Tasso, were all equally strangers to me; but of this more at large in my next. R. B.

NO. CXXVIII.

TO MR JAMES SMITH.

AVON PRINTFIELD, LINLITHGOW.

Mauchline, April 28th, 1788.

BEWARE of your Strasburgh, my good Sir! Look on this as the opening of a correspondence, like the opening of a twenty-four gun battery!

There is no understanding a man properly, without knowing something of his previous ideas—that is to say, if the man has any ideas; for I know many who, in the animal-muster, pass for men, that are the scanty masters of only one idea on any given subject, and by far the greatest part of your acquaintances and mine can barely boast of ideas, 1·25—1·5—1·75 (or some such fractional matter); so to let you a little into the secrets of my pericranium, there is, you must know, a certain clean-limbed, handsome, bewitching young huzzy of your acquaintance, to whom I have lately and privately given a matrimonial title to my corpus.

Bode a robe and wear it,
Bode a pock and bear it,

says the wise old Scots adage! I hate to presage ill-luck; and as my girl has been doubly kinder to me than even the best of women usually are to their partners of our sex, in similar circumstances, I reckon on twelve times a brace of children against I celebrate my twelfth wedding day: these twenty-four will give me twenty-four gossippings, twenty-four christenings (I mean one equal to two), and I hope, by the blessing of the God of my fathers, to make them twenty-four dutiful children to their parents, twenty-four useful members of society, and twenty-four approved servants of their God! * * *

"Light's heartsome," quo' the wife when she was stealing sheep. You see what a lamp I have hung up to lighten your paths, when you are idle enough to explore the combinations and relations of my ideas. 'Tis now as plain as a pike-staff why a twenty-four gun battery was a metaphor I could readily employ.

Now for business. I intend to present Mrs. Burns with a printed shawl, an article of which I dare say you have variety: 'tis my first present to her since I have irrevocably called her mine, and I have a kind of whimsical wish to get her the first said present from an old and much valued friend of hers and mine, a trusty Trojan, on whose friendship I count myself possessed of as a life-rent lease.

Look on this letter as a "beginning of sorrows;" I will write you till your eyes ache reading nonsense.

Mrs. Burns ('tis only her private designation) begs her best compliments to you.

R. B.

NO. CXXIX.

TO PROFESSOR DUGALD STEWART.

Mauchline, May 3rd, 1788.

SIR—I enclose you one or two more of my bagatelles. If the fervent wishes of honest gratitude have any influence with that great, unknown Being who frames the chain of causes and events, prosperity and happiness will attend your visit to the continent, and return you safe to your native shore.

Wherever I am, allow me, Sir, to claim it as my privilege to acquaint you with my progress in my trade of rhymes; as I am sure I could say it with truth, that, next to my little fame, and the having it in my power to make life more comfortable to those whom nature has made dear to me, I shall ever regard your countenance, your patronage, your friendly good offices, as the most valued consequence of my late success in life.

R. B.

NO. CXXX.

TO MRS. DUNLOP.

Mauchline, May 4th, 1788.

MADAM—Dryden's Virgil has delighted me. I do not know whether the critics will agree with me, but the Georgics are to me by far the best of Virgil. It is indeed a species of writing entirely new to me, and has filled my head with a thousand fancies of emulation: but, alas! when I read the Georgics, and then survey my own powers, 'tis like the idea of a Shetland pony, drawn up by the side of a thorough-bred hunter, to start for the plate. I own I am disappointed in the Æneid. Faultless correctness may please, and *does* highly please the lettered critic: but to that awful character I have not the most distant pretensions. I do not know whether I do not hazard my pretensions to be a critic of any kind, when I say that I think Virgil, in many instances, a servile copier of Homer. If I had the Odyssey by me, I could parallel many passages where Virgil has evidently copied, but by no means improved, Homer. Nor can I think there is anything of this owing to the translators; for, from everything I have seen of Dryden, I think him, in genius and fluency of language, Pope's master. I have not perused Tasso enough to form an opinion—in some future letter you shall have my ideas of him; though I am conscious my criticisms must be very inaccurate and imperfect, as there I have ever felt and lamented my want of learning most.

R. B.

NO. CXXXI.

TO MR. ROBERT AINSLIE.

Mauchline, May 26th, 1788.

MY DEAR FRIEND—I am two kind letters in your debt; but I have been from home, and horridly busy, buying and preparing for my farming business, over and above the plague of my Excise instructions, which this week will finish.

As I flatter my wishes that I foresee many future years' correspondence between us, 'tis foolish to talk of excusing dull epistles; a dull letter may be a very kind one. I have the pleasure to tell you that I have been extremely fortunate in all my buyings and bargainings hitherto—Mrs. Burns not excepted; which title I now avow to the world. I am truly pleased with this last affair; it has indeed added to my anxieties for futurity, but it has given a stability to my mind and resolutions unknown before; and the poor girl has the most sacred enthusiasm of attachment to me, and has not a wish but to gratify my every idea of her deportment. I am interrupted.—Farewell! my dear Sir,

R. B.

NO. CXXXII.

TO MRS. DUNLOP.

May 27th, 1788.

MADAM—I have been torturing my philosophy to no purpose, to account for that kind partiality of yours, which has followed me, in my return to the shade of life, with assiduous benevolence. Often did I regret, in the fleeting hours of my late will-o'-wisp appearance, that "here I had no continuing city;" and, but for the consolation of a few solid guineas, could almost lament the time that a momentary acquaintance with wealth and splendour put me so much out of conceit with the sworn companions of my road through life—insignificance and poverty.

There are few circumstances relating to the unequal distribution of the good things of this life that give me more vexation (I mean in what I see around me) than the importance the opulent bestow on their trifling family affairs, compared with the very same things on the contracted scale of a cottage. Last afternoon I had the honour to spend an hour or two at a good woman's fire-side, where the planks that composed the floor were decorated with a splendid carpet, and the gay table sparkled with silver and china. 'Tis now about term-day, and there has been a revolution among those creatures, who, though in appearance partakers, and equally noble partakers, of the same nature with Madame, are from time to time—their nerves, their sinews, their health, strength, wisdom, experience, genius, time, nay a good part of their very thoughts—sold for months and years, not only to the necessities, the conveniences, but the caprices, of the important few. We talked of the insignificant creatures; nay, notwithstanding their general stupidity and rascality, did some of the poor devils the honour to commend them. But light be the turf upon his breast who taught, "Reverence thyself." We looked down on the unpolished wretches, their impertinent wives and clouterly brats, as the lordly bull does on the little dirty ant-hill, whose puny inhabitants he crushes in the carelessness of his ramble, or tosses in the air in the wantonness of his pride.

R. B.

NO. CXXXIII.

TO THE SAME.

Ellisland, June 13th, 1788.

Where'er I roam, whatever realms I see,
My heart, untravell'd, fondly turns to thee;
Still to my friend it turns with ceaseless pain,
And drags, at each remove, a lengthen'd chain.

GOLDSMITH.

THIS is the second day, my honoured friend, that I have been on my farm. A solitary inmate of an old, smoky spence; far from every object I love, or by whom I am beloved; not any acquaintance older than yesterday, except Jenny Geddes, the old mare I ride on; while uncouth cares and novel plans hourly insult my awkward ignorance and bashful inexperience. There is a foggy atmosphere native to my soul in the hour of care, consequently the dreary objects seem larger then the life. Extreme sensibility, irritated and prejudiced on the gloomy side by a series of misfortunes and disappointments, at that period of my existence when the soul is laying in her cargo of ideas for the voyage of life, is, I believe, the principal cause of this unhappy frame of mind.

The valiant in himself, what can he suffer?
Or what need he regard his *single* woes?
&c.

Your surmise, Madam, is just; I am indeed a husband.

* * * * * *

To jealousy or infidelity I am an equal stranger My preservative from the first is the most thorough consciousness of her sentiments of honour, and her attachment to me: my antidote against the last is my long and deep-rooted affection for her.

In housewife matters, of aptness to learn and activity to execute, she is eminently mistress: and during my absence in Nithsdale, she is regularly and constantly apprentice to my mother and sisters in their dairy and other rural business.

The muses must not be offended when I tell them, the concerns of my wife and family will, in my mind, always take the *pas;* but I assure them their ladyships will ever come next in place.

You are right that a bachelor state would have insured me more friends; but, from a cause you will easily guess, conscious peace in the enjoyment of my own mind, and unmistrusting confidence in approaching my God, would seldom have been of the number.

I found a once much-loved and still much-loved female, literally and truly cast out to the mercy of the naked elements; but I enabled her to *purchase* a shelter—there is no sporting with a fellow-creature's happiness or misery.

The most placid good-nature and sweetness of disposition; a warm heart, gratefully devoted with all its powers to love me; vigorous health and sprightly cheerfulness, set off to the best advantage by a more than commonly handsome figure; these, I think, in a woman, may make a good wife, though she should never have read a page but the Scriptures of the Old and New Testament, nor have danced in a brighter assembly than a penny pay wedding.

R. B.

NO. CXXXIV.

TO MR. ROBERT AINSLIE.

Ellisland, June 14th, 1788.

THIS is now the third day, my dearest Sir, that I have sojourned in these regions; and during these three days you have occupied more of my thoughts than in three weeks preceding: in Ayrshire I have several variations of friendship's compass, here it points invariably to the pole. My farm gives me a good many uncouth cares and anxieties, but I hate the language of complaint. Job, or some one of his friends, says well—"Why should a living man complain?"

I have lately been much mortified with contemplating an unlucky imperfection in the very framing and construction of my soul; namely, a blundering inaccuracy of her olfactory organs in hitting the scent of craft or design in my fellow-creatures. I do not mean any compliment to my ingenuousness, or to hint that the defect is in consequence of the unsuspicious simplicity of conscious truth and honour: I take it to be, in some way or other, an imperfection in the mental sight; or, metaphor apart, some modification of dullness. In two or three instances lately, I have been most shamefully out.

I have all along, hitherto, in the warfare of life, been bred to arms among the light-horse—the piquet-guards of fancy—a kind of hussars and Highlanders of the brain; but I am firmly resolved to sell out of these giddy battallions, who have no ideas of a battle but fighting the foe, or of a siege but storming the town. Cost what it will, I am determined to buy in among the grave squadrons of heavy-armed thought, or the artillery corps of plodding contrivance.

What books are you reading, or what is the subject of your thoughts, besides the great studies of your profession? You said something about religion in your last. I don't exactly remember what it was, as the letter is in Ayrshire; but I thought it not only prettily said, but nobly thought. You will make a noble fellow if once you were married. I make no reservation of your being well married: you have so much sense and knowledge of human nature, that though you may not realise, perhaps, the ideas of romance, yet you will never be ill married.

Were it not for the terrors of my ticklish situation respecting provision for a family of children, I am decidedly of opinion that the step I have taken is vastly for my happiness. (72) As it is, I look to the Excise scheme as a certainty of maintenance; a maintenance!—luxury to what either Mrs. Burns or I were born to. Adieu!

R. B.

NO. CXXXV.

TO THE SAME.

Mauchline, June 23rd, 1788.

THIS letter, my dear Sir, is only a business scrap. Mr. Miers, profile painter in your town, has executed a profile of Dr. Blacklock for me; do me the favour to call for it, and sit to him yourself for me, which put in the same size as the doctor's. The account of both profiles will be fifteen shillings, which I have given to James Connel, our Mauchline carrier, to pay you when you give him the parcel. You must not, my friend, refuse to sit. The time is short; when I sat to Mr. Miers, I am sure he did not exceed two minutes. I propose hanging Lord Glencairn, the doctor, and you, in trio over my new chimney-piece that is to be. Adieu. R. B.

NO. CXXXVI.

TO THE SAME.

Ellisland, June 30th, 1788.

MY DEAR SIR—I just now received your brief epistle; and, to take vengeance on your laziness, I have, you see, taken a long sheet of writing-paper, and have begun at the top of the page, intending to scribble on to the very last corner.

I am vexed at that affair of the * * *, but dare not enlarge on the subject until you send me your direction, as I suppose that will be altered on your late master and friend's death. (73) I am concerned for the old fellow's exit, only as I fear it may be to your disadvantage in any respect—for an old man's dying, except he have been a very benevolent character, or in some particular situation of life that the welfare of the poor or the helpless depended on him, I think it an event of the most trifling moment to the world. Man is naturally a kind, benevolent animal, but he is dropped into such a needy situation here in this vexatious world, and has such a whore-son, hungry, growling, multiplying pack of necessities, appetites, passions and desires about him, ready to devour him for want of other food, that in fact he must lay aside his cares for others that he may look properly to himself. You have been imposed upon in paying Mr. Miers for the profile of a Mr. H. I did not mention it in my letter to you, nor did I ever give Mr. Miers any such order. I have no objection to lose the money, but I will not have any such profile in my possession.

I desired the carrier to pay you, but as I mentioned only fifteen shillings to him, I will rather enclose you a guinea-note. I have it not, indeed, to spare here, as I am only a sojourner in a strange land in this place; but in a day or two I return to Mauchline, and there I have the bank-notes through the house like salt permits.

There is a great degree of folly in talking unnecessarily of one's private affairs. I have just now been interrupted by one of my new neighbours, who has made himself absolutely contemptible in my eyes by his silly, garrulous pruriency. I know it has been a fault of my own, too; but from this moment I abjure it as I would the service of hell! Your poets, spendthrifts, and other fools of that kidney, pretend, forsooth, to crack their jokes on prudence; but 'tis a squalid vagabond glorying in his rags. Still, imprudence respecting money matters is much more pardonable than imprudence respecting character. I have no objection to prefer prodigality to avarice, in some few instances; but I appeal to your observation if you have not met, with the same disingenuousness, the same hollow-hearted insincerity, and disintegritive depravity of principle, in the hackneyed victims of profusion, as in the unfeeling children of parsimony. I have every possible reverence for the much-talked-of world beyond the grave, and I wish that which piety believes, and virtue deserves, may be all matter-of-fact. But in things belonging to and terminating in this present scene of existence, man has serious and interesting business on hand. Whether a man shall shake hands with welcome in the distinguished elevation of respect, or shrink from contempt in the abject corner of insignificance: whether he shall wanton under the tropic of plenty, at least enjoy himself in the comfortable latitudes of easy convenience, or starve in the arctic circle of dreary poverty; whether he shall rise in the manly consciousness of self-approving mind, or sink beneath a galling load of regret and remorse—these are alternatives of the last moment.

You see how I preach. You used occasionally to sermonise too; I wish you would, in charity, favour me with a sheet full in your own way. I admire the close of a letter Lord Bolingbroke writes to Dean Swift:—"Adieu, dear Swift! with all thy faults I love thee entirely; make an effort to love me with all mine!" Humble servant, and all that trumpery, is now such a prostituted business, that honest friendship, in her sincere way, must have recourse to her primitive, simple, farewell!

R. B.

NO. CXXXVII.

TO MR. PETER HILL.

My Dear Hill—I shall say nothing to your mad present. (74) You have so long and often been of important service to me, and I suppose you mean to go on conferring obligations until I shall not be able to lift up my face before you. In the meantime, as Sir Roger de Coverley, because it happened to be a cold day in which he made his will, ordered his servants great-coats for mourning, so, because I have been this week plagued with an indigestion, I have sent you by the carrier a fine old ewe-milk cheese.

Indigestion is the devil; nay, 'tis the devil and all. It besets a man in every one of his senses. I lose my appetite at the sight of successful knavery, and sicken to loathing at the noise and nonsense of self-important folly. When the hollow-hearted wretch takes me by the hand, the feeling spoils my dinner; the proud man's wine so offends my palate, that it chokes me in the gullet; and the *pulverised*, feathered, pert coxcomb, is so disgustful in my nostril, that my stomach turns.

If ever you have any of these disagreeable sensations, let me prescribe for you patience and a bit of my cheese. I know that you are no niggard of your good things among your friends, and some of them are in much need of a slice. There, in my eye, is our friend Smellie; a man positively of the first abilities and greatest strength of mind, as well as one of the best hearts and keenest wits that I ever met with; when you see him—as, alas! he too is smarting at the pinch of distressful circumstances, aggravated by the sneer of contumelious greatness—a bit of my cheese alone will not cure him, but if you add a tankard of brown stout, and superadd a magnum of right Oporto, you will see his sorrows vanish like the morning mist before the summer sun.

Candlish, the earliest friend, except my only brother, that I have on earth, and one of the worthiest fellows that ever any man called by the name of friend, if a luncheon of my cheese would help to rid him of some of his superabundant modesty, you would do well to give it him.

David (75), with his *Courant*, comes, too, across my recollection, and I beg you will help him largely from the said ewe-milk cheese, to enable him to digest those bedaubing paragraphs with which he is eternally larding the lean characters of certain great men in a certain great town. I grant you the periods are very well turned; so, a fresh egg. is a very good thing, but when thrown at a man in a pillory, it does not at all improve his figure, not to mention the irreparable loss of the egg.

My facetious friend Dunbar I would wish also to be a partaker; not to digest his spleen, for that he laughs off, but to digest his last night's wine at the last field-day of the Crochallan corps. (76)

Among our common friends I must not forget one of the dearest of them—Cunningham. (77) The brutality, insolence and selfishness of a world unworthy of having such a fellow as he is in it, I know sticks in his stomach, and if you can help him to anything that will make him a little easier on that score, it will be very obliging.

As to honest John Somerville, he is such a contented, happy man, that I know not what can annoy him, except, perhaps, he may not have got the better of a parcel of modest anecdotes which a certain poet gave him one night at supper, the last time the said poet was in town.

Though I have mentioned so many men of law, I shall have nothing to do with them professionally;—the faculty are beyond my prescription. As to their clients, that is another thing; God knows, they have much to digest!

The clergy I pass by; their profundity of erudition, and their liberality of sentiment, their total want of pride, and their detestation of hypocrisy, are so proverbially notorious, as to place them far, far above either my praise or censure.

I was going to mention a man of worth, whom I have the honour to call friend, the Laird of Craigdarroch; but I have spoken to the landlord of the King's Arms inn here, to have at the next county meeting a large ewe-milk cheese table, for the benefit of the Dumfries-shire Whigs, to enable them to digest the Duke of Queensberry's late political conduct.

I have just this moment an opportunity of a private hand to Edinburgh, as perhaps you would not digest double postage.

R. B.

NO. CXXXVIII.

TO MR. GEORGE LOCKHART.

MERCHANT, GLASGOW.

Mauchline, July 18th, 1788.

My Dear Sir—I am just going for Nithsdale, else I would certainly have transcribed some of my rhyming things for you. The Miss Baillies I have seen in Edinburgh. "Fair and lovely are thy works, Lord God Almighty! Who would not praise thee for these thy gifts in thy goodness to the sons of men!" It needed not your fine taste to admire them. I declare, one day I had the honour of dining at Mr. Baillie's, I was almost in the predicament of the children of Israel, when they could not look on Moses' face for the glory that shone in it when he descended from Mount Sinaï.

I did once write a poetic address from the Falls of Bruar to his Grace of Athole, when I was in the Highlands. When you return to Scotland, let me know, and I will send such of my pieces as please myself best. I return to Mauchline in about ten days.

My compliments to Mr. Purden. I am in truth, but at present, in haste, yours,

R. B.

NO. CXXXIX.

TO MRS. DUNLOP.

Mauchline, August 2nd, 1788.

Honoured Madam—Your kind letter welcomed me, yesternight, to Ayrshire. I am, indeed, seriously angry with you at the quantum of your luckpenny; but, vexed and hurt as I was, I could not help laughing very heartily at the noble lord's apology for the missed napkin.

I would write you from Nithsdale, and give you my direction there, but I have scarce an opportunity of calling at a post-office once in a fortnight. I am six miles from Dumfries, am scarcely ever in it myself, and, as yet, have little acquaintance in the neighbourhood. Besides, I am now very busy on my farm, building a dwelling-house; as at present I am almost an evangelical man in Nithsdale, for I have scarce "where to lay my head."

There are some passages in your last that brought tears in my eyes. "The heart knoweth its own sorrows, and a stranger intermeddleth not therewith." The repository of these "sorrows of the heart" is a kind of *sanctum sanctorum:* and 'tis only a chosen friend, and that, too, at particular, sacred times, who dares enter into them:—

Heaven oft tears the bosom-chords
That nature finest strung.

You will excuse this quotation for the sake of the author. Instead of entering on this subject farther, I shall transcribe you a few lines I wrote in a hermitage, belonging to a gentleman in my Nithsdale neighbourhood. They are almost the only favours the muses have conferred on me in that country. * * *

Since I am in the way of transcribing, the following were the production of yesterday, as I jogged through the wild hills of New Cumnock. I intend inserting them, or something like them, in an epistle I am going to write to the gentleman on whose friendship my Excise hopes depend, Mr. Graham of Fintry, one of the worthiest and most accomplished gentlemen, not only of this country, but, I will dare to say it, of this age. The following are just the first crude thoughts "unhousel'd, unanointed, unanealed:"—

Pity the tuneful muses' helpless train,—
Weak, timid landsmen on life's stormy main:
The world were blest, did bliss on them depend.—
Ah, that "the friendly e'er should want a friend!"
The little fate bestows they share as soon,
Unlike sage, proverb'd wisdom's hard-wrung boon.
Let Prudence number o'er each sturdy son,
Who life and wisdom at one race begun,
Who feels by reason and who gives by rule.
Instinct's a brute and sentiment a fool!
Who make poor *will do* wait upon *I should;*
We own they're prudent, but who owns they're good?

Ye wise ones, hence! ye hurt the social eye,—
God's image rudely etch'd on base alloy!
But come * * * * * *

Here the muse left me. I am astonished at what you tell me of Anthony's writing me. I never received it. Poor fellow! you vex me much by telling me that he is unfortunate. I shall be in Ayrshire ten days from this date. I have just room for an old Roman farewell. R. B.

NO. CXL.

TO MR. WILLIAM CRUIKSHANKS.

Ellisland, August, 1788.

I HAVE not room, my dear friend, to answer all the particulars of your last kind letter. I shall be in Edinburgh on some business very soon; and as I shall be two days, or perhaps three in town, we shall discuss matters *vivâ voce.* My knee, I believe, will never be entirely well, and an unlucky fall this winter has made it still worse. I well remember the circumstance you allude to, respecting Creech's opinion of Mr. Nicol; but as the first gentleman owes me still about fifty pounds, I dare not meddle in the affair.

It gave me a very heavy heart to read such accounts of the consequence of your quarrel with that puritanic, rotten-hearted, hell-commissioned scoundrel, A———. If, notwithstanding your unprecedented industry in public, and your irreproachable conduct in private life, he still has you so much in his power, what ruin may he not bring on some others I could name?

Many and happy returns of season to you, with your dearest and worthiest friend, and the lovely little pledge of your happy union. May the great Author of life, and of every enjoyment that can render life delightful, make her that comfortable blessing to you both, which you so ardently wish for, and which, allow me to say, you so well deserve! Glance over the foregoing verses, and let me have your blots. Adieu.

R. B.

NO. CLXI.

TO MRS DUNLOP.

Mauchline, August 10th, 1788.

MY MUCH HONOURED FRIEND—Yours of the 24th June is before me. I found it, as well as another valued friend—my wife—waiting to welcome me to Ayrshire: I met both with the sincerest pleasure.

When I write you, Madam, I do not sit

down to answer every paragraph of yours, by echoing every sentiment, like the faithful Commons of Great Britain in Parliament assembled, answering a speech from the best of kings! I express myself in the fulness of my heart, and may, perhaps, be guilty of neglecting some of your kind inquiries; but not from your very odd reason, that I do not read your letters. All your epistles for several months have cost me nothing, except a swelling throb of gratitude, or a deep-felt sentiment of veneration.

When Mrs. Burns, Madam, first found herself "as women wish to be who love their lords," as I loved her nearly to distraction, we took steps for a private marriage. Her parents got the hint; and not only forbade me her company and their house, but, on my rumoured West Indian voyage, got a warrant to put me in jail, till I should find security in my about-to-be paternal relation. You know my lucky reverse of fortune. On my *éclatant* return to Mauchline, I was made very welcome to visit my girl. The usual consequences began to betray her; and as I was at that time laid up a cripple in Edinburgh, she was turned, literally turned, out of doors, and I wrote to a friend to shelter her till my return, when our marriage was declared. Her happiness or misery were in my hands, and who could trifle with such a deposit?

I can easily fancy a more agreeable companion for my journey of life; but, upon my honour, I have never seen the individual instance.

Circumstanced as I am, I could never have got a female partner for life, who could have entered into my favourite studies, relished my favourite authors, &c., without probably entailing on me, at the same time, expensive living, fantastic caprice, perhaps apish affectation, with all the other blessed boarding-school acquirements, which *(pardonnez moi, Madame)* are sometimes to be found among females of the upper ranks, but almost universally pervade the misses of the would-be gentry.

I like your way in your churchyard lucubrations. Thoughts that are the spontaneous result of accidental situations, either respecting health, place or company, have often a strength, and always an originality, that would in vain be looked for in fancied circumstances and studied paragraphs. For me, I have often thought of keeping a letter, in progression by me, to send you when the sheet was written out. Now I talk of sheets, I must tell you, my reason for writing to you on paper of this kind is my pruriency of writing to you at large. A page of post is on such a dis-social, narrow-minded scale, that that I cannot abide it; and double letters, at least in my miscellaneous reverie manner, are a monstrous tax in a close correspondence.

R. B.

NO. CXLII.

TO THE SAME.

Ellisland, August 16th, 1788.

I AM in a fine disposition, my honoured friend, to send you an elegiac epistle, and want only genius to make it quite Shenstonian:—

Why droops my heart with fancied woes forlorn?
Why sinks my soul beneath each wintry sky?

My increasing cares in this, as yet, strange country—gloomy conjectures in the dark vista of futurity—consciousness of my own inability for the struggle of the world—my broadened mark to misfortune in a wife and children;—I could indulge these reflections, till my humour should ferment into the most acid chagrin, that would corrode the very thread of life.

To counterwork these baneful feelings, I have sat down to write to you; as I declare upon my soul I always find that the most sovereign balm for my wounded spirit.

I was yesterday at Mr. Miller's to dinner, for the first time. My reception was quite to my mind: from the lady of the house quite flattering. She sometimes hits on a couplet or two, *impromptu.* She repeated one or two to the admiration of all present. My suffrage as a professional man was expected: it for once went agonising over the belly of my conscience. Pardon me, ye, my adored household gods, independence of spirit, and integrity of soul! In the course of conversation "Johnson's Musical Museum," a collection of Scottish songs with the music, was talked of. We got a song on the harpsichord, beginning,

Raving winds around her blowing.

The air was much admired: the lady of the house asked me whose were the words. "Mine, Madam—they are indeed my very best verses:" she took not the smallest notice of them! The old Scottish proverb says well, "King's caff is better than ither folks' corn." I was going to make a New

Testament quotation about "casting pearls," but that would be too virulent, for the lady is actually a woman of sense and taste.

After all that has been said on the other side of the question, man is by no means a happy creature. I do not speak of the selected few, favoured by partial heaven, whose souls are tuned to gladness amid riches, and honours, and prudence and wisdom. I speak of the neglected many, whose nerves, whose sinews, whose days, are sold to the minions of fortune.

If I thought you had never seen it, I would transcribe for you a stanza of an old Scottish ballad, called "The Life and Age of Man;" beginning thus:—

'Twas in the sixteenth hundredth year
  Of God and fifty-three
Frae Christ was born, that bought us dear,
  As writings testifie.

I had an old grand-uncle, with whom my mother lived a while in her girlish years; the good old man, for such he was, was long blind ere he died, during which time his highest enjoyment was to sit down and cry, while my mother would sing the simple old song of "The Life and Age of Man."

It is this way of thinking; it is these melancholy truths, that make religion so precious to the poor, miserable children of men. If it is a mere phantom, existing only in the heated imagination of enthusiasm,

What truth on earth so precious as the lie?

My idle reasonings sometimes makes me a little sceptical, but the necessities of my heart always give the cold philosophisings the lie. Who looks for the heart weaned from earth; the soul affianced to her God; the correspondence fixed with heaven; the pious supplication and devout thanksgiving, constant as the vicissitudes of even and morn; who thinks to meet with these in the court, the palace, in the glare of public life? No: to find them in their precious importance and divine efficacy, we must search among the obscure recesses of disappointment, affliction, poverty, and distress.

I am sure, dear Madam, you are now more than pleased with the length of my letters. I return to Ayrshire middle of next week: and it quickens my pace to think that there will be a letter from you waiting me there. I must be here again very soon for my harvest. R. B.

NO. CXLIII.

TO MR. BEUGO,

ENGRAVER, EDINBURGH.

Ellisland, Sept. 9th, 1788.

MY DEAR SIR—There is not in Edinburgh above the number of the graces whose letters would have given me so much pleasure as yours of the 3rd instant, which only reached me yesternight.

I am here on my farm, busy with my harvest; but for all that most pleasurable part of life called SOCIAL COMMUNICATION, I am here at the very elbow of existence. The only things that are to be found in this country, in any degree of perfection, are stupidity and canting. Prose, they only know in graces, prayers, &c., and the value of these they estimate, as they do their plaiding webs—by the ell! As for the muses, they have as much an idea of a rhinoceros as of a poet. For my old capricious but good-natured hussy of a muse:—

By banks of Nith I sat and wept
  When Coila I thought on,
In midst thereof I hung my harp
  The willow trees upon.

I am generally about half my time in Ayrshire with my "darling Jean;" and then I, at lucid intervals, throw my horny fist across my be-cobwebbed lyre, much in the same manner as an old wife throws her hand across the spokes of her spinning-wheel.

I will send you the "Fortunate Shepherdess" as soon as I return to Ayrshire, for there I keep it with other precious treasure. I shall send it by a careful hand, as I would not for any thing it should be mislaid or lost. I do not wish to serve you from any benevolence, or other grave Christian virtue; 'tis purely a selfish gratification of my own feelings whenever I think of you.

If your better functions would give you leisure to write me, I should be extremely happy; that is to say, if you neither keep nor look for a regular correspondence. I hate the idea of being obliged to write a letter. I sometimes write a friend twice a-week, at other times once a-quarter.

I am exceedingly pleased with your fancy in making the author you mention place a map of Iceland instead of his portrait before his works: 'twas a glorious idea.

Could you conveniently do me one thing?—whenever you finish any head, I should like to have a proof copy of it. I might tell you a long story about your fine genius; but, as what every body knows cannot have escaped you, I shall not say one syllable about it. R. B.

NO. CXLIV.

TO MISS CHALMERS, EDINBURGH.

Ellisland, near Dumfries, Sept. 16th, 1788.

WHERE are you? and how are you? and is Lady Mackenzie recovering her health? for I have had but one solitary letter from you. I will not think you have forgot me, Madam; and, for my part—

> When thee, Jerusalem, I forget,
> Skill part from my right hand!

"My heart is not of that rock, nor my soul careless as that sea." I do not make my progress among mankind as a bowl does among its fellows—rolling through the crowd without bearing away any mark or impression, except where they hit in hostile collision.

I am here, driven in with my harvest-folks by bad weather; and as you and your sister once did me the honour of interesting yourselves much *à l'egard de moi,* I sit down to beg the continuation of your goodness. I can truly say that, all the exterior of life apart, I never saw two whose esteem flattered the noble feelings of my soul—I will not say more, but so much, as Lady Mackenzie and Miss Chalmers. When I think of you—hearts the best, minds the noblest of human kind—unfortunate even in the shades of life—when I think I have met with you, and have lived more of real life with you in eight days than I can do with almost any body I meet with in eight years—when I think on the improbability of meeting you in this world again—I could sit down and cry like a child! If ever you honoured me with a place in your esteem, I trust I can now plead more desert. I am secure against that crushing grip of iron poverty, which, alas! is less or more fatal to the native worth and purity of, I fear, the noblest souls; and a late important step in my life has kindly taken me out of the way of those ungrateful iniquities, which, however overlooked in fashionable licence, or varnished in fashionable phrase, are indeed but lighter and deeper shades of VILLANY.

Shortly after my last return to Ayrshire, I married "my Jean." This was not in consequence of the attachment of romance, perhaps; but I had a long and much loved fellow-creature's happiness or misery in my determination, and I durst not trifle with so important a deposit. Nor have I any cause to repent it. If I have not got polite tattle, modish manners, and fashionable dress, I am not sickened and disgusted with the multiform curse of boarding-school affectation; and I have got the handsomest figure, the sweetest temper, the soundest constitution, and the kindest heart, in the county. Mrs. Burns believes, as firmly as her creed, that I am *le plus bel espirit, et le plus honnête homme* in the universe; although she scarcely ever in her life, except the Scriptures of the Old and New Testament, and the Psalms of David in metre, spent five minutes together on either prose or verse. I must except also from this last a certain late publication of Scots poems, which she has perused very devoutly; and all the ballads in the country, as she has (oh, the partial lover! you will cry) the finest "wood note wild" I ever heard. I am the more particular in this lady's character, as I know she will henceforth have the honour of a share in your best wishes. She is still at Mauchline, as I am building my house; for this hovel that I shelter in, while occasionally here, is pervious to every blast that blows, and every shower that falls; and I am only preserved from being chilled to death by being suffocated with smoke. I do not find my farm that pennyworth I was taught to expect, but I believe, in time, it may be a saving bargain. You will be pleased to hear that I have laid aside idle *éclat,* and bind every day after my reapers.

To save me from that horrid situation of at any time going down, in a losing bargain of a farm, to misery, I have taken my Excise instructions, and have my commission in my pocket for any emergency of fortune. If I could set all before my view, whatever disrespect you, in common with the world, have for this business, I know you would approve of my idea.

I will make no apology, dear Madam, for this egotistic detail; I know you and your sister will be interested in every circumstance of it. What signify the silly, idle gewgaws of wealth, or the ideal trumpery of greatness! When fellow-partakers of the same nature fear the same God, have the same benevolence of heart, the same nobleness of soul, the same detestation at every thing dishonest, and the same scorn at every thing unworthy—if they are not in the dependence of absolute beggary, in the name of common sense, they are not EQUALS? And if the bias, the instinctive bias of their souls run the same way, why may they not be FRIENDS?

When I have an opportunity of sending you this, Heaven only knows. Shenstone says, "When one is confined idle within doors by bad weather, the best antidote against *ennui* is to read the letters of, or to write to, one's friends;" in that case then, if the weather continues thus, I may scrawl you half a quire.

I very lately—to wit, since harvest began —wrote a poem, not in imitation, but in the manner, of Pope's Moral Epistles. It is only a short essay, just to try the strength of my Muse's pinion in that way. I will send you a copy of it, when once I have heard from you. I have likewise been laying the foundation of some pretty large poetic works: how the superstructure will come on, I leave to that great maker and marrer of projects—TIME. Johnson's collection of Scots songs is going on in the third volume; and, of consequence, finds me a consumption for a great deal of idle metre. One of the most tolerable things I have done in that way, is two stanzas I made to an air a musical gentleman of my acquaintance composed for the aniversary of his wedding-day, which happens on the 7th of November. Take it as follows:—

"The day returns—my bosom burns—
The blissful day we twa did meet," &c.

I shall give over this letter for shame. If I should be seized with a scribbling fit, before this goes away, I shall make it another letter; and then you may allow your patience a week's respite between the two. I have not room for more than the old, kind, hearty farewell!

To make some amends, *mes chères Mesdames*, for dragging you on to this second sheet, and to relieve a little the tiresomeness of my unstudied and uncorrectible prose, I shall transcribe you some of my late poetic bagatelles; though I have, these eight or ten months, done very little that way. One day, in a hermitage on the banks of Nith, belonging to a gentleman in my neighbourhood, who is so good as give me a key at pleasure, I wrote as follows, supposing myself the sequestered, venerable inhabitant of the lonely mansion.

LINES WRITTEN IN FRIARS-CARSE HERMITAGE.

"Thou whom chance may hither lead," &c.
R. B.

NO. CXLV.

TO MR. MORRISON, MAUCHLINE. (78)

Ellisland, September 22nd, 1788.

MY DEAR SIR—Necessity obliges me to go into my new house even before it be plastered. I will inhabit the one end until the other is finished. About three weeks more, I think, will at farthest be my time, beyond which I cannot stay in this present house. If ever you wish to deserve the blessing of him that was ready to perish; if ever you were in a situation that a little kindness would have rescued you from many evils; if ever you hope to find rest in future states of untried being—get these matters of mine ready. My servant will be out in the beginning of next week for the clock. My compliments to Mrs. Morrison. I am, after all my tribulation, dear Sir, yours, R. B.

NO. CLXVI.

TO MRS. DUNLOP, OF DUNLOP.

Mauchline, Sept. 27th, 1788.

I HAVE received twins, dear Madam, more than once; but scarcely ever with more pleasure than when I received yours of the 12th instant. To make myself understood; I had wrote to Mr. Graham, enclosing my poem addressed to him, and the same post which favoured me with yours brought me an answer from him. It was dated the very day he had received mine; and I am quite at a loss to say whether it was most polite or kind.

Your criticisms, my honoured benefactress, are truly the work of a friend. They are not the blasting depredations of a canker-toothed, caterpillar critic; nor are they the fair statement of cold impartiality, balancing with unfeeling exactitude the *pro* and *con* of an author's merits; they are the judicious observations of animated friendship, selecting the beauties of the piece. I am just arrived from Nithsdale, and will be here a fortnight. I was on horseback this morning by three o'clock; for between my wife and my farm is just forty-six miles. As I jogged on in the dark, I was taken with a poetic fit as follows:

"Mrs. Fergusson of Craigdarroch's lamentation for the death of her son—an uncommonly promising youth of eighteen or nineteen years of age.

Fate gave the word—the arrow sped,
And pierced my darling's heart," &c.

You will not send me your poetic rambles, but, you see, I am no niggard of mine. I am sure your impromptus give me double pleasure; what falls from your pen can neither be unentertaining in itself, nor indifferent to me.

The one fault you found is just, but I cannot please myself in an emendation.

What a life of solicitude is the life of a parent! You interested me much in your young couple.

I would not take my folio paper for this epistle, and now I repent it. I am so jaded with my dirty long journey that I was afraid to drawl into the essence of dulness with any thing larger than a quarto, and so I must leave out another rhyme of this morning's manufacture.

I will pay the sapientipotent George most cheerfully to hear from you ere I leave Ayrshire R. B.

NO. CLXVII.

TO MR. PETER HILL.

Mauchline, October 1st, 1788.

I HAVE been here in this country about three days, and all that time my chief reading has been the "Address to Lochlomond" you were so obliging as to send to me. Were I impannelled one of the author's jury, to determine his criminality respecting the sin of poesy, my verdict should be "Guilty! A poet of nature's making!" It is an excellent method for improvement, and what I believe every poet does, to place some favourite classic author in his own walks of study and composition, before him as a model. Though your author had not mentioned the name, I could have, at half a glance, guessed his model to be Thomson. Will my brother-poet forgive me, If I venture to hint that his imitation of that immortal bard is in two or three places rather more servile than such a genius as his required:—*e. g.*

To soothe the maddening passions all to peace. ADDRESS.

To soothe the throbbing passions into peace. THOMSON.

I think the "Address" is in simplicity, harmony, and elegance of versification, fully equal to the "Seasons." Like Thomson, too, he has looked into nature for himself: you meet with no copied description. One particular criticism I made at first reading; in no one instance has he said too much. He never flags in his progress, but, like a true poet of Nature's making, kindles in his course. His beginning is simple and modest, as if distrustful of the strength of his pinion; only I do not altogether like—

—————— Truth,
The soul of every song that's nobly great.

Fiction is the soul of many a song that is nobly great. Perhaps I am wrong: this may be but a prose criticism. Is not the phrase in line 7, page 6, "Great lake," too much vulgarised by every-day language for so sublime a poem?

Great mass of waters, theme for nobler song,

is perhaps no emendation. His enumeration of a comparison with other lakes is at once harmonious and poetic. Every reader's ideas must sweep the

Winding margin of an hundred miles.

The perspective that follows mountains blue—the imprisoned billows beating in vain—the wooded isles—the digression on the yew-tree—"Benlomond's lofty, cloud-envelop'd head," &c. are beautiful. A thunder-storm is a subject which has often been tried, yet our poet in his grand picture has interjected a circumstance, so far as I know, entirely original:—

—————— The gloom
Deep seam'd with frequent streaks of moving fire.

In his preface to the storm, "the glens how dark between," is noble highland landscape! The "rain ploughing the red mould," too, is beautifully fancied. "Benlomond's lofty, pathless, top," is a good expression; and the surrounding view from it is truly great: the

—————— silver mist,
Beneath the beaming sun,

is well described; and here he has contrived to enliven his poem with a little of that passion which bids fair, I think, to usurp the modern muses altogether. I know not how far this episode is a beauty upon the whole, but the swain's wish to carry "some faint idea of the vision bright," to entertain her "partial listening ear," is a pretty thought. But, in my opinion, the most beautiful passages in the whole poem are the fowls crowding, in wintry frosts, to Lochlomond's "hospitable flood;" their wheeling round, their lighting, mixing, diving, &c.: and the glorious description of the sportsman. This last is equal to any thing in the "Seasons." The idea of "the floating tribes distant seen, far glistening to the moon," provoking his eye as he is obliged to leave them, is a noble ray of poetic genius. "The howling winds," the "hideous roar" of "the white cascades," are all in the same style.

I forget that while I am thus holding forth with the heedless warmth of an enthusiast, I am perhaps tiring you with nonsense. I must, however, mention that the last verse of the sixteenth page is one of the most elegant compliments I have ever seen. I must likewise notice that beautiful paragraph beginning "The gleaming lake," &c. I dare not go into the particular beauties of the last two paragraphs, but they are admirably fine, and truly Ossianic.

I must beg your pardon for this lengthened scrawl. I had no idea of it when I began:—I should like to know who the author is; but, whoever he be, please present him with my grateful thanks for the entertainment he has afforded me.

A friend of mine desired me to commission for him two books, "Letters on the Religion essential to Man," a book you sent me before; and "The World Unmasked, or the Philosopher the greatest Cheat." Send me them by the first opportunity. The bible you sent me is truly elegant; I only wish it had been it two volumes. R. B.

NO. CXLVIII.

TO THE EDITOR OF "EDINBURGH EVENING COURANT."

November 8th, 1788.

SIR—Notwithstanding the opprobrious epithets with which some of our philosophers and gloomy sectarians have branded our nature—the principle of universal selfishness, the proneness to all evil, they have given us—still, the detestation in which inhumanity to the distressed, or insolence to the fallen, are held by all mankind, shows that they are not natives of the human heart. Even the unhappy partner of our kind who is undone—the bitter consequence of his follies or his crimes—who but sympathises with the miseries of this ruined profligate brother? We forget the injuries, and feel for the man.

I went, last Wednesday, to my parish church, most cordially to join in grateful acknowledgment to the Author of all Good, for the consequent blessings of the glorious Revolution. To that auspicious event we owe no less than our liberties, civil and religious; to it we are likewise indebted for the present royal family, the ruling features of whose administration have ever been mildness to the subject, and tenderness of his rights.

Bred and educated in revolution principles, the principles of reason and common sense, it could not be any silly political prejudice which made my heart revolt at the harsh, abusive manner in which the reverend gentleman mentioned the House of Stuart, and which, I am afraid, was too much the language of the day. We may rejoice sufficiently in our deliverance from past evils, without cruelly raking up the ashes of those whose misfortune it was, perhaps as much as their crime, to be the authors of those evils; and we may bless God for all his goodness to us as a nation, without at the same time cursing a few ruined, powerless exiles, who only harboured ideas, and made attempts, that most of us would have done, had we been in their situation.

"The bloody and tyrannical House of Stuart" may be said with propriety and justice, when compared with the present royal family, and the sentiments of our days; but is there no allowance to be made for the manners of the times? Were the royal contemporaries of the Stuarts more attentive to their subjects' rights? Might not the epithets of "bloody and tyrannical" be, with at least equal justice, applied to the House of Tudor, of York, or any other of their predecessors?

The simple state of the case, Sir, seems to be this:—At that period, the science of government, the knowledge of the true relation between king and subject, was, like other sciences and other knowledge, just in its infancy, emerging from dark ages of ignorance and barbarity.

The Stuarts only contended for prerogatives which they knew their predecessors enjoyed, and which they saw their contemporaries enjoying; but these prerogatives were inimical to the happiness of a nation and the rights of subjects.

In this contest between prince and people, the consequence of that light of science which had lately dawned over Europe, the monarch of France, for example, was victorious over the struggling liberties of his people: with us, luckily, the monarch failed, and his unwarrantable pretensions fell a sacrifice to our rights and happiness.

Whether it was owing to the wisdom of leading individuals, or to the jostling of parties, I cannot pretend to determine; but, likewise, happily for us, the kingly power was shifted into another branch of the family, who, as they owed the throne solely to the call of a free people, could claim nothing inconsistent with the covenanted terms which placed them there.

The Stuarts have been condemned and laughed at for the folly and impracticability of their attempts in 1715 and 1745. That they failed, I bless God, but cannot join in the ridicule against them. Who does not know that the abilities or defects of leaders and commanders are often hidden until put to the touchstone of exigency; and that there is a caprice of fortune, an omnipotence in particular accidents and conjunctures of circumstances, which exalt us as heroes, or brand us as madmen, just as they are for or against us?

Man, Mr. Publisher, is a strange, weak, inconsistent being: who would believe, Sir, than in this our Augustan age of liberality and refinement, while we seem so justly sensible and jealous of our rights and liberties, and animated with such indignation against the very memory of those who would have subverted them—that a certain people under our national protection should complain, not against our monarch and a few favourite advisers, but against our whole legislative body, for similar oppression, and almost in the very same terms, as our forefathers did of the House of Stuart! I will not, I cannot, enter into the merits of the case, but I dare say the American Congress, in 1776, will be allowed to be as able and as enlightened as the English Convention was in 1668; and that their posterity will celebrate the centenary of their deliverance from us, as duly and sincerely as we do ours from the oppressive measures of the wrong-headed House of Stuart.

To conclude, Sir; let every man who has a tear for the many miseries incident to humanity, feel for a family illustrious as any in Europe, and unfortunate beyond historic precedent; and let every Briton (and particularly every Scotsman), who ever looked with reverential pity on the dotage of a parent, cast a veil over the fatal mistakes of the kings of his forefathers.

R. B.

NO. CXLIX.

TO MRS. DUNLOP,

AT MOREHAM MAINS.

Mauchline, November 13th, 1788.

MADAM—I had the very great pleasure of dining at Dunlop yesterday. Men are said to flatter women because they are weak:—if it be so, poets must be weaker still; for Misses R. and K., and Miss G. M'K., with their flattering attentions and artful compliments, absolutely turned my head. I own they did not lard me over as many a poet does his patron, but they so intoxicated me with their sly insinuations and delicate inuendos of compliment, that if it had not been for a lucky recollection how much additional weight and lustre your good opinion and friendship must give me in that circle, I had certainly looked upon myself as a person of no small consequence. I dare not say one word how much I was charmed with the major's friendly welcome, elegant manner, and acute remark, lest I should be thought to balance my orientalisms of applause over-against the finest quey (79) in Ayrshire which he made me a present of to help and adorn my farm-stock. As it was on hallow-day, I am determined annually as that day returns, to decorate her horns with an ode of gratitude to the family of Dunlop.

So soon as I know of your arrival at Dunlop, I will take the first conveniency to dedicate a day, or perhaps two, to you and friendship, under the guarantee of the major's hospitality. There will soon be threescore and ten miles of permanent distance between us; and now that your friendship and friendly correspondence are entwisted with the heart-strings of my enjoyment of life, I must indulge myself in a happy day of "The feast of reason and the flow of soul."

R. B.

NO. CL.

TO MR. JAMES JOHNSON,

ENGRAVER.

Mauchline, November 15th, 1788.

MY DEAR SIR—I have sent you two more songs. If you have got any tunes, or any thing to correct, please send them by return of the carrier.

I can easily see, my dear friend, that you will probably have four volumes. Perhaps you may not find your account lucratively in this business? but you are a patriot for the music of your country, and I am certain posterity will look on themselves as highly indebted to your public spirit. Be not in a hurry; let us go on correctly, and your name shall be immortal.

I am preparing a flaming preface for your third volume. I see every day new musical publications advertised; but what are they? Gaudy, painted butterflies of a day, and then vanish for ever: but your work will outlive the momentary neglects of idle fashion, and defy the teeth of time.

Have you never a fair goddess that leads you a wild-goose chase of amorous devotion? Let me know a few of her qualities, such as whether she be rather black or fair, plump or thin, short or tall, &c.; and choose your air, and I shall task my muse to celebrate her. R. B.

NO. CLI.

TO DR. BLACKLOCK.

Mauchline, November 15th, 1788.

Reverend and Dear Sir—As I hear nothing of your motions, but that you are, or were, out of town, I do not know where this may find you, or whether it will find you at all. I wrote you a long letter, dated from the land of matrimony, in June; but either it had not found you, or, what I dread more, it found you or Mrs. Blacklock in too precarious a state of health and spirits to take notice of an idle packet.

I have done many little things for Johnson, since I had the pleasure of seeing you; and I have finished one piece in the way of Pope's "Moral Epistles;" but, from your silence, I have everything to fear, so I have only sent you two melancholy things, which I tremble lest they should too well suit the tone of your present feelings.

In a fortnight I move, bag and baggage, to Nithsdale; till then, my direction is at this place; after that period, it will be at Ellisland, near Dumfries. It would extremely oblige me were it but a half a line, to let me know how you are. Can I be indifferent to the fate of a man to whom I owe so much—a man whom I not only esteem, but venerate?

My warmest good wishes and most respectful compliments to Mrs. Blacklock, and Miss Johnston, if she is with you.

I cannot conclude without telling you that I am more and more pleased with the step I took respecting "my Jean." Two things, from my happy experience, I set down as apophthegms in life. A wife's head is immaterial, compared with her heart; and—"Virtue's (for wisdom what poet pretends to it?) ways are ways of pleasantness, and all her paths are peace." Adieu!

R. B.

NO. CLII.

TO MRS. DUNLOP.

Ellisland, December 17th, 1788.

My Dear Honoured Friend—Yours, dated Edinburgh, which I have just read, makes me very unhappy. "Almost blind and wholly deaf," are melancholy news of a much-loved and honoured friend; they carry misery in the sound. Goodness on your part, and gratitude on mine, began a tie which has gradually entwisted itself among the dearest chords of my bosom, and I tremble at the omens of your late and present ailing habit and shattered health. You miscalculate matters widely, when you forbid my waiting on you, lest it should hurt my worldly concerns. My small scale of farming is exceedingly more simple and easy than what you have lately seen at Moreham Mains. But, be that as it may, the heart of the man and the fancy of the poet are the two grand considerations for which I live: if miry ridges and dirty dunghills are to engross the best part of the functions of my soul immortal, I had better been a rook or a magpie at once, and then I should not have been plagued with any ideas superior to breaking of clods and picking up grubs; not to mention barn-door cocks or mallards, creatures with which I could almost exchange lives at any time. If you continue so deaf, I am afraid a visit will be no great pleasure to either of us; but if I hear you are got so well again as to be able to relish conversation, look you to it, Madam, for I will make my threatenings good. I am to be at the New-year-day fair of Ayr: and, by all that is sacred in the world, friend, I will come and see you.

Your meeting, which you so well describe, with your own schoolfellow and friend, was truly interesting. Out upon the ways of the world! They spoil these "social off-springs of the heart." Two veterans of the "men of the world" would have met with little more heart-workings than two old hacks worn out on the road. Apropos, is not the Scotch phrase, "auld lang syne," exceedingly expressive? There is an old song and tune which has often thrilled through my soul. You know I am an enthusiast in old Scotch songs. I shall give you the verses on the other sheet, as I suppose Mr. Ker will save you the postage.

Should auld acquaintance be forgot? &c.

Light be the turf on the breast of the Heaven-inspired poet who composed this glorious fragment! There is more of the fire of native genius in it than in half a dozen of modern English Bacchanalians! Now I am on my hobby-horse, I cannot help inserting two other old stanzas, which please me mightily:

Go fetch to me a pint o' wine, &c.

R. B.

NO. CLIII.

TO MISS DAVIES.

December, 1788.

MADAM—I understand my very worthy neighbour, Mr. Riddel, has informed you that I have made you the subject of some verses. There is something so provoking in the idea of being the burden of a ballad, that I do not think Job or Moses, though such patterns of patience and meekness, could have resisted the curiosity to know what that ballad was; so my worthy friend has done me a mischief, which I dare say he never intended, and reduced me to the unfortunate alternative of leaving your curiosity ungratified, or else disgusting you with foolish verses, the unfinished production of a random moment, and never meant to have met your ear. I have heard or read somewhere of a gentleman who had some genius, much eccentricity, and very considerable dexterity with his pencil. In the accidental group of life into which one is thrown, wherever this gentleman met with a character in a more than ordinary degree congenial to his heart, he used to steal a sketch of the face, merely, he said, as a *nota bene*, to point out the agreeable recollection to his memory. What this gentleman's pencil was to him, my muse is to me: and the verses I do myself the honour to send you are a *memento* exactly of the same kind that he indulged in.

It may be more owing to the fastidiousness of my caprice than the delicacy of my taste, but I am so often tired, disgusted, and hurt, with the insipidity, affectation, and pride of mankind, that when I meet with a person "after my own heart," I positively feel what an orthodox Protestant would call a species of idolatry, which acts on my fancy like inspiration; and I can no more desist rhyming on the impulse, than an Æolian harp can refuse its tones to the streaming air. A distich or two would be the consequence, though the object which hit my fancy were grey-bearded age; but where my theme is youth and beauty, a young lady whose personal charms, wit, and sentiment, are equally striking and unaffected—by Heavens! though I had lived threescore years a married man, and threescore years before I was a married man, my imagination would hallow the very idea: and I am truly sorry that the enclosed stanzas have done such poor justice to such a subject.

R. B.

NO. CLIV.

TO MR. JOHN TENNANT.

December 22nd, 1788.

I YESTERDAY tried my cask of whisky for the first time, and I assure you it does you great credit. It will bear five waters, strong, or six, ordinary toddy. The whisky of this country is a most rascally liquor; and, by consequence, only drunk by the most rascally part of the inhabitants. I am persuaded, if you once get a footing here, you might do a great deal of business, in the way of consumpt; and should you commence distiller again, this is the native barley country. I am ignorant if, in your present way of dealing, you would think it worth your while to extend your business so far as this country side. I write you this on the account of an accident, which I must take the merit of having partly designed to. A neighbour of mine, a John Currie, miller in Carse-mill—a man who is, in a word, a "very" good man, even for a £500 bargain—he and his wife were in my house the time I broke open the cask. They keep a country public-house and sell a great deal of foreign spirits, but all along thought that whisky would have degraded this house. They were perfectly astonished at my whisky, both for its taste and strength; and, by their desire, I write you to know if you could supply them with liquor of an equal quality, and what price. Please write me by first post, and direct to me at Ellisland, near Dumfries. If you could take a jaunt this way yourself, I have a spare spoon, knife and fork, very much at your service. My compliments to Mrs. Tennant, and all the good folks in Glenconner and Barquharrie.

R. B.

NO. CLV.

TO THE REV. P. CARFRAE.

1789.

REV. SIR—I do not recollect that I have ever felt a severer pang of shame, than on looking at the date of your obliging letter which accompanied Mr. Mylne's poem.

I am much to blame: the honour Mr. Mylne has done me, greatly enhanced in its value by the endearing, though melancholy circumstance of its being the last production of his muse, deserved a better return.

I have, as you hint, thought of sending a copy of the poem to some periodical publication; but, on second thoughts, I am afraid that, in the present case, it would be an improper step. My success, perhaps as much accidental as merited, has brought an inundation of nonsense under the name of Scottish poetry. Subscription-bills for Scottish poems have so dunned, and daily do dun the public, that the very name is in danger of contempt. For these reasons, if publishing any of Mr. Mylne's poems in a Magazine, &c., be at all prudent, in my opinion, it certainly should not be a Scottish poem. The profits of the labours of a man of genius are, I hope, as honourable as any profits whatever; and Mr. Mylne's relations are most justly entitled to that honest harvest which fate has denied himself to reap. But let the friends of Mr. Mylne's fame (among whom I crave the honour of ranking myself) always keep in eye his respectability as a man and as a poet, and take no measure that, before the world knows anything about him, would risk his name and character being classed with the fools of the times.

I have, Sir, some experience of publishing; and the way in which I would proceed with Mr. Mylne's poems, is this:—I will publish, in two or three English and Scottish public papers, any one of his English poems which should, by private judges, be thought the most excellent, and mention it, at the same time, as one of the productions of a Lothian farmer of respectable character, lately deceased, whose poems his friends had it in idea to publish soon by subscription, for the sake of his numerous family; not in pity to that family, but in justice to what his friends think the poetic merits of the deceased; and to secure, in the most effectual manner, to those tender connexions, whose right it is, the pecuniary reward of those merits.

R. B. (80)

NO. CLVI.

TO MRS. DUNLOP.

Ellisland, New-year-day Morning, 1789.

THIS, dear Madam, is a morning of wishes, and would to God that I came under the apostle James's description!—*the prayer of a righteous man availeth much.* In that case, Madam, you should welcome in a year full of blessings: every thing that obstructs or disturbs tranquillity and self-enjoyment, should be removed, and every pleasure that frail humanity can taste, should be yours. I own myself so little a Presbyterian, that I approve of set times and seasons of more than ordinary acts of devotion, for breaking in on that habituated routine of life and thought, which is so apt to reduce our existence to a kind of ins inct, or even sometimes, and with some minds, to a state very little superior to mere machinery.

This day; the first Sunday of May; a breezy, blue-skied noon some time about the beginning, and a hoary morning and calm sunny day about the end, of autumn; these, time out of mind, have been with me a kind of holiday.

I believe I owe this to that glorious paper in the Spectator, "The Vision of Mirza," a piece that struck my young fancy before I was capable of fixing an idea to a word of three syllables:—"On the 5th day of the moon, which, according to the custom of my forefathers, I always *keep holy,* after having washed myself and offered up my morning devotions, I ascended the high hill of Bagdad, in order to pass the rest of the day in meditation and prayer."

We know nothing, or next to nothing, of the substance or structure of our souls, so cannot account for those seeming caprices in them, that one should be particularly pleased with this thing, or struck with that, which, on minds of a different cast, makes no extraordinary impression. I have some favourite flowers in spring, among which are the mountain-daisy, the harebell, the foxglove, the wild-briar rose, the budding birch, and the hoary hawthorn, that I view and hang over with particular delight. I never heard the loud, solitary whistle of the curlew in a summer noon, or the wild mixing cadence of a troop of grey plovers, in an autumnal morning, without feeling an elevation of soul like the enthusiasm of devotion or poetry. Tell me, my dear friend, to what can this be owing? Are we a piece of machinery, which, like the Æolian harp, passive, takes the impression of the passing accident? Or do these workings argue something above us above the trodden clod? I own myself partial to such proofs of those awful and important realities—a God that made all things—man's immaterial and immortal nature—and a world of weal or woe beyond death and the grave.

R. B. (81).

NO. CLVII.

TO DR. MOORE.

Ellisland, Jan. 4th, 1789.

Sir—As often as I think of writing to you, which has been three or four times every week these six months, it gives me something so like the idea of an ordinary-sized statue offering at a conversation with the Rhodian colossus, that my mind misgives me, and the affair always miscarries somewhere between purpose and resolve. I have at last got some business with you, and business letters are written by the style-book. I say my business is with you, Sir, for you never had any with me, except the business that benevolence has in the mansion of poverty.

The character and employment of a poet were formerly my pleasure, but are now my pride. I know that a very great deal of my late eclât was owing to the singularity of my situation, and the honest prejudice of Scotsmen; but still, as I said in the preface to my first edition, I do look upon myself as having some pretensions from nature to the poetic character. I have not a doubt but the knack, the aptitude, to learn the muses' trade, is a gift bestowed by Him "who forms the secret bias of the soul;"—but I as firmly believe, that *excellence* in the profession is the fruit of industry, labour, attention, and pains. At least I am resolved to try my doctrine by the test of experience. Another appearance from the press I put off to a very distant day, a day that may never arrive—but poesy I am determined to prosecute with all my vigour. Nature has given very few, if any, of the professions, the talents of shining in every species of composition. I shall try (for until trial it is impossible to know) whether she has qualified me to shine in any one. The worst of it is, by the time one has finished a piece, it has been so often viewed and reviewed before the mental eye, that one loses in a good measure the powers of critical discrimination. Here the best criterion I know is a friend—not only of abilities to judge, but with good-nature enough, like a prudent teacher with a young learner, to praise perhaps a little more than is exactly just, lest the thin-skinned animal fall into that most deplorable of all poetic diseases—heart-breaking despondency of himself. Dare I, Sir, already immensely indebted to your goodness, ask the additional obligation of your being that friend to me? I enclose you an essay of mine, in a walk of poesy to me entirely new; I mean the epistle addressed to R. G., Esq., or Robert Graham, of Fintry, Esq., a gentleman of uncommon worth, to whom I lie under very great obligations. The story of the poem, like most of my poems, is connected with my own story, and to give you the one, I must give you something of the other. I cannot boast of Mr. Creech's ingenuous fair dealing to me. He kept me hanging about Edinburgh from the 7th August, 1787, until the 13th April, 1788, before he would condescend to give me a statement of affairs; nor had I got it even then, but for an angry letter I wrote him, which irritated his pride. "I could" not a "tale," but a detail," unfold;" but, what am I, that should speak against the Lord's anointed Baillie of Edinburgh?

I believe, I shall, in whole, £100 copyright included, clear about £400 some little odds; and even part of this depends upon what the gentleman has yet to settle with me. I give you this information, because you did me the honour to interest yourself much in my welfare. I give you this information, but I give it to yourself only, for I am still much in the gentleman's mercy. Perhaps I injure the man in the idea I am sometimes tempted to have of him—God forbid I should! A little time will try, for in a month I shall go to town to wind up the business if possible.

To give the rest of my story in brief, I have married "my Jean," and taken a farm: with the first step I have every day more and more reason to be satisfied; with the last, it is rather the reverse. I have a younger brother, who supports my aged mother; another still younger brother, and three sisters, in a farm. On my last return from Edinburgh, it cost me about £180 to save them from ruin. Not that I have lost so much—I only interposed between my brother and his impending fate by the loan of so much. I give myself no airs on this, for it was mere selfishness on my part: I was conscious that the wrong scale of the balance was pretty heavily charged, and I thought that throwing a little filial piety and fraternal affection into the scale in my favour, might help to smooth matters at the *grand reckoning*. There is still one thing would make my circumstances quite easy: I have an Excise officer's commission, and I live in the midst of a country division. My request to Mr. Graham, who is one of the Commissioners of Excise, was, if in his power, to procure me that division. If I were very sanguine, I might hope that some of my great patrons might procure me a treasury warrant for supervisor, surveyor-general, &c.

Thus, secure of a livelihood, "to thee, sweet poetry, delightful maid," I would consecrate my future days. R. B.

NO. CLVIII.

TO MR. ROBERT AINSLIE.

Ellisland, January 6th, 1789.

MANY happy returns of the season to you, my dear Sir! May you be comparatively happy up to your comparative worth among the sons of men; which wish would, I am sure, make you one of the most blest of the human race.

I do not know if passing a "writer to the signet" be a trial of scientific merit, or a mere business of friends and interest. However it be, let me quote you my two favourite passages, which, though I have repeated them ten thousand times, still they rouse my manhood and steal my resolutions like inspiration.

——————— On Reason build resolve,
That column of true majesty in man.
YOUNG.

Hear, Alfred, hero of the state
Thy genius heaven's high will declare;
The triumph of the truly great,
Is never, never to despair!
Is never to despair.—*Masque of Alfred.*

I grant you enter the lists of life to struggle for bread, business, notice and distinction, in common with hundreds. But who are they? Men like yourself, and of that aggregate body your compeers, seven-tenths of them come short of your advantages, natural and accidental; while two of those that remain, either neglect their parts, as flowers blooming in a desert, or mis-spend their strength like a bull goring a bramble bush.

R. B.

NO. CLIX.

TO PROFESSOR DUGALD STEWART.

Ellisland, Jan. 20th, 1789.

SIR—The enclosed sealed packet I sent to Edinburgh, a few days after I had the happiness of meeting you in Ayrshire, but you were gone for the continent. I have now added a few more of my productions, those for which I am indebted to the Nithsdale Muses. The piece inscribed to R. G. Esq., is a copy of verses I sent Mr. Graham of Fintry, accompanying a request for his assistance in a matter to me of very great moment. To that gentleman I am already doubly indebted; for deeds of kindness of serious import to my dearest interests, done in a manner grateful to the delicate feelings of sensibility. This poem is a species of composition new to me, but I do not intend it shall be my last essay of the kind, as you will see by the "Poet's Progress." These fragments, if my design succeed, are but a small part of the intended whole. I propose it shall be the work of my utmost exertions, ripened by years; of course I do not wish it much known. The fragment beginning "A little upright, pert, tart," &c., I have not shown to man living, till I now send it you, It forms the postulata, the axioms, the definition of a character, which, if it appear at all, shall be placed in a variety of lights. This particular part I send you merely as a sample of my hand at portrait-sketching; but, lest idle conjecture should pretend to point out the original, please to let it be for your single, sole inspection.

Need I make any apology for this trouble, to a gentleman who has treated me with such marked benevolence and peculiar kindness; who has entered into my interests with so much zeal, and on whose critical decisions I can so fully depend? A poet as I am by trade, these decisions are to me of the last consequence. My late transient acquaintance among some of the mere rank and file of greatness, I resign with ease; but to the distinguished champions of genius and learning, I shall ever be ambitious of being known. The native genius and accurate discernment in Mr. Stewart's critical strictures; the justice (iron justice, for he has no bowels of compassion for a poor poetic sinner) of Dr. Gregory's remarks, and the delicacy of Professor Dalzel's taste, I shall ever revere.

I shall be in Edinburgh some time next month. I have the honour to be, Sir, your highly obliged, and very humble servant,

R. B.

NO. CLX.

TO BISHOP GEDDES. (82)

Ellisland, Feb. 3rd, 1789.

VENERABLE FATHER—As I am conscious that, wherever I am, you do me the honour to interest yourself in my welfare, it gives me pleasure to inform you, that I am here at last, stationary in the serious business of life, and have now not only the retired leisure, but the hearty inclination, to attend to those great and important questions—what I am; where I am; and for what I am destined.

In that first concern, the conduct of the man, there was ever but one side on which I was habitually blameable, and there I have secured myself in the way pointed out by nature and nature's God. I was sensible that, to so helpless a creature as a poor poet, a wife and family were incumbrances, which a species of prudence would bid him shun; but when the alternative was, being at eternal warfare with myself, on account of habitual follies, to give them no worse name, which no general example, no licentious wit, no sophistical infidelity, would, to me, ever justify, I must have been a fool to have hesitated, and a madman to have made another choice. Besides, I had in "my Jean" a long and much-loved fellow-creature's happiness or misery among my hands, and who could trifle with such a deposit?

In the affair of a livelihood, I think myself tolerably secure: I have good hopes of my farm; but should they fail, I have an Excise commission, which, on my simple petition, will at any time procure me bread. There is a certain stigma affixed to the character of an Excise officer, but I do not pretend to borrow honour from my profession; and though the salary be comparatively small, it is luxury to any thing that the first twenty-five years of my life taught me to expect.

Thus, with a rational aim and method in life, you may eaily guess, my reverend and much honoured friend, that my characteristic trade is not forgotten. I am, if possible, more than ever an enthusiast to the muses. I am determined to study man and nature, and in that view incessantly; and to try if the ripening and corrections of years can enable me to produce something worth preserving.

You will see in your book, which I beg your pardon for detaining so long (83), that I have been tuning my lyre on the banks of Nith. Some large poetic plans that are floating in my imagination, or partly put in execution, I shall impart to you when I have the pleasure of meeting with you, which, if you are then in Edinburgh, I shall have about the beginning of March.

That acquaintance, worthy Sir, with which you were pleased to honour me, you must still allow me to challenge; for with whatever unconcern I give up my transient connection with the merely great, I cannot lose the patronising notice of the learned and good without the bitterest regret.

R. B.

NO. CLXI.

TO MR. JAMES BURNESS.

Ellisland, Feb. 9th, 1789.

MY DEAR SIR—Why I did not write to you long ago is what, even on the rack, I could not answer. If you can in your mind form an idea of indolence, dissipation, hurry, cares, change of country, entering on untried scenes of life, all combined, you will save me the trouble of a blushing apology. It could not be want of regard for a man for whom I had a high esteem before I knew him—an esteem which has much increased since I did know him; and this caveat entered, I shall plead guilty to any other indictment with which you shall please to charge me.

After I parted from you, for many months my life was one continued scene of dissipation. Here, at last, I am become stationary, and have taken a farm and—a wife.

The farm is beautifully situated on the Nith, a large river that runs by Dumfries, and falls into the Solway Frith. I have gotten a lease of my farm as long as I pleased; but how it may turn out is just a guess, and it is yet to improve and enclose, &c.: however, I have good hopes of my bargain on the whole.

My wife is my Jean, with whose story you are partly acquainted. I found I had a much-loved fellow-creature's happiness or misery among my hands, and I durst not trifle with so sacred a deposit. Indeed, I have not any reason to repent the step I have taken, as I have attached myself to a very good wife, and have shaken myself loose of every bad failing.

I have found my book a very profitable business, and with the profits of it I have begun life pretty decently. Should fortune not favour me in farming, as I have no great faith in her fickle ladyship, I have provided myself in another resource, which, however some folks may affect to despise it, is still a comfortable shift in the day of misfortune. In the heyday of my fame, a gentleman, whose name, at least, I dare say you know, as his estate lies somewhere near Dundee, Mr. Graham of Fintry, one of the Commissioners of Excise offered me the commission, of an Excise officer. I thought it prudent to accept the offer; and, accordingly, I took my instructions, and have my commission by me. Whether I may ever do duty, or be a penny the better for it, is what I do not know; but I have the comfortable assurance, that, come whatever ill fate will, I can, on my simple petition to the Excise-board, get into employ.

We have lost poor uncle Robert this winter. He has long been very weak, and with very little alteration on him: he expired 3rd January.

His son William has been with me this winter, and goes in May to be an apprentice to a mason. His other son, the eldest, John, comes to me, I expect, in summer. They are both remarkably stout young fellows, and promise to do well. His only daughter, Fanny, has been with me ever since her father's death, and I purpose keeping her in my family till she be quite woman grown, and fit for better service. She is one of the cleverest girls, and has one of the most amiable dispositions, I have ever seen. (84)

All friends in this county and Ayrshire are well. Remember me to all friends in the north. My wife joins me in compliments to Mrs. B. and family. I am ever, my dear cousin, yours sincerely, R. B.

NO. CLXII.

TO MRS. DUNLOP.

Ellisland, March 4th, 1789.

HERE am I, my honoured friend, returned safe from the capital. To a man who has a home, however humble or remote—if that home is like mine, the scene of domestic comfort—the bustle of Edinburgh will soon be a business of sickening disgust.

Vain pomp and glory of this world, I hate you!

When I must skulk into a corner, lest the rattling equipage of some gaping blockhead should mangle me in the mire, I am tempted to exclaim, "What merits has he had, or what demerit have I had, in some state of pre-existence, that he is ushered into this state of being with the sceptre of rule, and the key of riches in his puny fist, and I am kicked into the world, the sport of folly, or the victim of pride?" I have read somewhere of a monarch (in Spain I think it was) who was so out of humour with the Ptolemean system of astronomy, that he said, had he been of the Creator's council, he could have saved him a great deal of labour and absurdity. I will not defend this blasphemous speech; but often, as I have glided with humble stealth through the pomp of Princes' Street, it has suggested itself to me, as an improvement on the present human figure, that a man, in proportion to his own conceit of his consequence in the world, could have pushed out the longitude of his common size, as a snail pushes out his horns, or as we draw out a perspective. This trifling alteration, not to mention the prodigious saving it would be in the tear and wear of the neck and limb-sinews of many of his Majesty's liege-subjects, in the way of tossing the head and tiptoe strutting, would evidently turn out a vast advantage, in enabling us at once to adjust the ceremonials in making a bow, or making way to a great man, and that, too, within a second of the precise spherical angle of reverence, or an inch of the particular point of respectful distance, which the important creature itself requires; as a measuring-glance at its towering altitude would determine the affair like instinct.

You are right, Madam, in your idea of poor Mylne's poem, which he has addressed to me. The piece has a good deal of merit, but it has one great fault—it is by far too long. Besides, my success has encouraged such a shoal of ill-spawned monsters to crawl into public notice, under the title of Scottish poets, that the very term Scottish poetry borders on the burlesque. When I write to Mr. Carfrae, I shall advise him rather to try one of his deceased friend's English pieces. I am prodigiously hurried with my own matters, else I would have requested a perusal of all Mylne's poetic performances, and would have offered his friends my assistance, in either selecting or correcting what would be proper for the press. What it is that occupies me so much, and perhaps a little oppresses my present spirits, shall fill up a paragraph in some future letter. In the meantime, allow me to close this epistle with a few lines done by a friend of mine. * * * * * I give you them, that, as you have seen the original, you may guess whether one or two alterations I have ventured to make in them be any real improvement:—

Like the fair plant that from our touch withdraws,
Shrink, mildly fearful, even from applause,
Be all a mother's fondest hope can dream,
And all you are, my charming * * * * seem.
Straight as the fox-glove, ere her bells disclose,
Mild as the maiden-blushing hawthorn blows,
Fair as the fairest of each lovely kind,
Your form shall be the image of your mind;
Your manners shall so true your soul express,
That all shall long to know the worth they guess;
Congenial hearts shall greet with kindred love,
And even sick'ning Envy must approve.

R. B.

When I received your letter I was transcribing for * * * * my letter to the magistrates of the Canongate, Edinburgh, begging their permission to place a tombstone over poor Fergusson, and their edict in consequence of my petition, but now I shall send them to ———. Poor Fergusson! If there be a life beyond the grave, which I trust there is; and if there be a good God presiding over all nature, which I am sure there is—thou art now enjoying existence in a glorious world, where worth of the heart alone is distinction in the man; where riches, deprived of all their pleasure-purchasing powers, return to their native sordid matter; where titles and honours are the disregarded reveries of an idle dream: and where that heavy virtue, which is the negative consequence of steady dulness, and those thoughtless, though often destructive follies, which are the unavoidable aberrations of frail human nature, will be thrown into equal oblivion as if they had never been!

Adieu, my dear Sir! So soon as your present views and schemes are concentered in an aim, I shall be glad to hear from you; as your welfare and happiness are by no means indifferent to, yours, R. B.

NO. CLXIII.

TO MR. ——— (85)

March, 1789.

My Dear Sir—The hurry of a farmer in this particular season, and the indolence of a poet at all times and seasons, will, I hope, plead my excuse for neglecting so long to answer your obliging letter of the 5th of August.

That you have done well in quitting your laborious concern in * * *, I do not doubt; the weighty reasons you mention, were, I hope, very, and deservedly indeed, weighty ones, and your health is a matter of the last importance; but whether the remaining proprietors of the paper have also done well, is what I much doubt. The * * * *, so far as I was a reader, exhibited such a brilliancy of point, such an elegance of paragraph, and such a variety of intelligence, that I can hardly conceive it possible to continue a daily paper in the same degree of excellence: but if there was a man, who had abilities equal to the task, that man's assistance the proprietors have lost.

NO. CLXIII.

TO DR. MOORE.

Ellisland, March 23rd, 1789

Sir—The gentleman who will deliver this is a Mr. Neilson, a worthy clergyman in my neighbourhood (86), and a very particular acquaintance of mine. As I have troubled him with this packet, I must turn him over to your goodness, to recompense him for it in a way in which he much needs your assistance, and where you can effectually serve him. Mr. Neilson is on his way for France, to wait on his Grace of Queensbury, on some little business of a good deal of importance to him, and he wishes for your instructions respecting the most eligible mode of travelling, &c. for him, when he has crossed the Channel. I should not have dared to take this liberty with you, but that I am told, by those who have the honour of your personal acquaintance, that to be a poor honest Scotchman is a letter of recommendation to you, and that to have it in your power to serve such a character, gives you much pleasure.

The enclosed Ode is a compliment to the memory of the late Mrs. Oswald of Auchencruive. You probably knew her personally, an honour of which I cannot boast; but I spent my early years in her neighbourhood, and among her servants and tenants. I know that she was detested with the most heartfelt cordiality. However, in the particular part of her conduct which roused my poetic wrath, she was much less blameable. In January last, on my road to Ayrshire, I had put up at Bailie Whigham's, in Sanquhar, the only tolerable inn in the place. The frost was keen, and the grim evening and howling wind were ushering in a night of snow and drift. My horse and I were both much fatigued with the labours of the day, and just as my friend the Bailie and I were bidding defiance to the storm, over a smoking bowl, in wheels the funeral pageantry of the late great Mrs. Oswald, and poor I am forced to brave all the horrors of the tempestuous night, and jade my horse, my young favourite horse, whom I had just christened Pegasus, twelve miles farther on, through the wildest moors and hills of Ayrshire, to New Cumnock, the next inn. The powers of poesy and prose sink under me, when I would describe what I felt. Suffice it to say, that when a good fire at New Cumnock had so far recovered my frozen sinews, I sat down and wrote the enclosed Ode.

I was at Edinburgh lately, and settled finally with Mr. Creech; and I must own, that at last he has been amicable and fair with me.

R. B. (87)

NO. CLXV.

TO MR. HILL.

Ellisland, April 2nd, 1789.

I WILL make no excuse, my dear Bibliopolus, (God forgive me for murdering language!) that I have sat down to write you on this vile paper.

It is economy, Sir; it is that cardinal virtue, prudence; so I beg you will sit down, and either compose or borrow a panegyric. If you are going to borrow, apply to * * * * to compose, or rather to compound, something very clever on my remarkable frugality; that I write to one of my most esteemed friends on this wretched paper, which was originally intended for the venal fist of some drunken exciseman, to take dirty notes in a miserable vault of an ale-cellar.

Oh Frugality! thou mother of ten thousand blessings—thou cook of fat beef and dainty greens!—thou manufacturer of warm Shetland hose and comfortable surtouts!—thou old housewife, darning thy decayed stockings with thy ancient spectacles on thy aged nose!—lead me, hand me in thy clutching palsied fist, up those heights, and through those thickets, hitherto inaccessible and impervious to my anxious, weary feet—not those Parnassian crags, bleak and barren, where the hungry worshippers of fame are, breathless, clambering, hanging between heaven and hell, but those glittering cliffs of Potosi, where the all-sufficient, all-powerful deity, wealth, holds his immediate court of joys and pleasures: where the sunny exposure of plenty, and the hot walls of profusion, produce those blissful fruits of luxury, exotics in this world, and natives of paradise! Thou withered sibyl, my sage conductress, usher me into thy refulgent, adored presence! The poet, splendid and potent as he now is, was once the puling nursling of thy faithful care and tender arms! Call me thy son, thy cousin, thy, kinsman, or favourite, and adjure the god by the scenes of his infant years, no longer to repulse me as a stranger, or an alien, but to favour me with his peculiar countenance and protection! He daily bestows his greatest kindness on the undeserving and the worthless—assure him that I bring ample documents of meritorious demerits! Pledge yourself for me, that for the glorious cause of lucre, I will do anything, be anything, but the horse-leach of private oppression, or the vulture of public robbery!

But to descend from heroics.

I want a Shakspeare; I want likewise an English dictionary—Johnson's, I suppose, is best. In these and all my prose commissions, the cheapest is always the best for me. There is a small debt of honour that I owe Mr. Robert Cleghorn, in Saughton Mills, my worthy friend, and your well-wisher. Please give him, and urge him to take it, the first time you see him, ten shillings' worth of any thing you have to sell, and place it to my account.

The library scheme that I mentioned to you is already begun, under the direction of Captain Riddel. There is another in emulation of it going on at Closeburn, under the auspices of Mr. Monteath of Closeburn, which will be on a greater scale than ours. Captain Riddel gave his infant society a great many of his old books, else I had written you on that subject; but, one of these days, I shall trouble you with a commission for "The Monkland Friendly Society." A copy of The Spectator, Mirror, and Lounger, Man of Feeling, Man of the World, Guthrie's Geographical Grammar, with some religious pieces, will likely be our first order.

When I grow richer, I will write to you on gilt-post, to make amends for this sheet. At present every guinea has a five guinea errand with, my dear Sir, your faithful, poor, but honest friend, R. B.

NO. CLXVI.

TO MRS. DUNLOP.

Ellisland, April 4th, 1789.

I NO sooner hit on any poetic plan or fancy, but I wish to send it to you; and if knowing and reading these give half the pleasure to you, that communicating them to you gives to me, I am satisfied.

I have a poetic whim in my head, which I at present dedicate, or rather inscribe, to the Right. Hon. Charles James Fox; but how long that fancy may hold, I cannot say. A few of the first lines I have just rough sketched as follows:—

"SKETCH.

How wisdom and folly meet, mix, and unite;
How virtue and vice blend their black and their white;
How genius, the illustrious father of fiction,
Confounds rule and law, reconciles contradiction—
I sing: if these mortals, the critics, should bustle,
I care not, not I, let the critics go whistle.

But now for a patron, whose name and whose glory,
At once may illustrate and honour my story.

Thou first of our orators, first of our wits,
Yet whose parts and acquirements seem mere lucky hits;
With knowledge so vast, and with judgment so strong,
No man with the half of 'em e'er went far wrong;
With passions so potent, and fancies so bright,
No man with the half of 'em e'er went quite right;
A sorry, poor misbegot son of the muses,
For using thy name offers fifty excuses."

On the 20th current I hope to have the honour of assuring you in person, how sincerely I am, yours, &c. R. B.

NO. CLXVII.

TO MRS. M'MURDO,

DRUMLANRIG. (88)

Ellisland, May 2nd, 1789.

MADAM—I have finished the piece which had the happy fortune to be honoured with your approbation; and never did little Miss with more sparkling pleasure show her applauded sampler to partial Mamma, than I now send my poem to you and Mr. M'Murdo, if he is returned to Drumlanrig. You cannot easily imagine what thin-skinned animals, what sensitive plants, poor poets are. How do we shrink into the embittered corner of self-abasement, when neglected or condemned by those to whom we look up! and how do we, in erect importance, add another cubit to our stature, on being noticed and applauded by those whom we honour and respect! My late visit to Drumlanrig has, I can tell you, Madam, given me a balloon waft up Parnassus, where on my fancied elevation I regard my poetic self with no small degree of complacency. Surely, with all their sins, the rhyming tribe are not ungrateful creatures. I recollect your goodness to your humble guest—I see Mr. M'Murdo adding to the politeness of the gentleman the kindness of a friend, and my heart swells as it would burst, with warm emotions and ardent wishes! It may be it is not gratitude—it may be a mixed sensation. That strange, shifting, doubling animal, MAN, is so generally, at best, but a negative, often a worthless creature, that we cannot see real goodness and native worth, without feeling the bosom glow with sympathetic approbation. With every sentiment of grateful respect, I have the honour to be, Madam, your obliged and grateful humble servant, R. B

NO. CLXVIII.

TO MR. CUNNINGHAM.

Ellisland, May 4th, 1789.

MY DEAR SIR—Your *duty-free* favour of the 26th April I received two days ago; I will not say I perused it with pleasure—that is the cold compliment of ceremony—I perused it, Sir, with delicious satisfaction; in short, it is such a letter, that not you, nor your friend, but the legislature, by express proviso in their postage laws, should frank. A letter informed with the soul of friendship is such an honour to human nature, that they should order it free ingress and egress to and from their bags and mails, as an encouragement and mark of distinction to supereminent virtue.

I have just put the last hand to a little poem, which I think will be something to your taste. One morning lately, as I was out pretty early in the fields, sowing some grass seeds, I heard the burst of a shot from a neighbouring plantation, and presently a poor little wounded hare came crippling by me. You will guess my indignation at the inhuman fellow who could shoot a hare at this season, when all of them have young ones. Indeed, there is something in that business, of destroying for our sport individuals in the animal creation that do not injure us materially, which I could never reconcile to my ideas of virtue.

Inhuman man! curse on thy barb'rous art,
And blasted be thy murder-aiming eye!
May never pity soothe thee with a sigh,
Nor ever pleasure glad thy cruel heart!

Go live, poor wanderer of the wood and field,
The bitter little that of life remains;
No more the thickening brakes or verdant plains,
To thee a home, or food, or pastime yield.

Seek, mangled innocent, some wonted form;
That wonted form, alas! thy dying bed,
The sheltering rushes whistling o'er thy head,
The cold earth with thy blood-stain'd bosom warm.

Perhaps a mother's anguish adds its woe;
The playful pair crowd fondly by thy side;
Ah! helpless nurslings, who will now provide
That life a mother only can bestow?

Oft as by winding Nith, I, musing, wait
The sober eve, or hail the cheerful dawn,
I'll miss thee sporting o'er the dewy lawn,
And curse the ruthless wretch, and mourn thy hapless fate.

Let me know how you like my poem. I am doubtful whether it would not be an improvement to keep out the last stanza but one altogether.

Cruikshank is a glorious production of the author of man. You, he, and the noble Colonel of the Crochallan Fencibles are to me—

Dear as the ruddy drops which warm my heart.

I have got a good mind to make verses on you all, to the tune of "Three guid Fellows ayont the Glen." R. B. (89)

NO. CLXIX.

TO MR. SAMUEL BROWN.

Mossgiel, May 4th, 1789.

Dear Uncle—This, I hope, will find you and your conjugal yoke-fellow in your good old way; I am impatient to know if the Ailsa fowling be commenced for this season yet, as I want three or four stones of feathers, and I hope you will bespeak them for me. It would be a vain attempt for me to enumerate the various transactions I have been engaged in since I saw you last, but this know, I am engaged in a *smuggling trade*, and God knows if ever any poor man experienced better returns, two for one; but as freight and delivery have turned out so dear, I am thinking of taking out a licence and beginning in fair trade. I have taken a farm on the borders of the Nith, and, in imitation of the old patriarchs, get men-servants and maid-servants, and flocks and herds, and beget sons and daughters.

Your obedient nephew, R. B.

NO. CLXX.

TO RICHARD BROWN.

Mauchline, May 1st, 1789.

My Dear Friend—I was in the country by accident, and hearing of your safe arrival, I could not resist the temptation of wishing you joy on your return—wishing you would write to me before you sail again—wishing you would always set me down as your bosom friend—wishing you long life and prosperity, and that every good thing may attend you—wishing Mrs. Brown and your little ones as free of the evils of this world as is consistent with humanity—wishing you and she were to make two at the ensuing lying-in, with which Mrs. B. threatens very soon to favour me—wishing I had longer time to write to you at present; and, finally, wishing that, if there is to be another state of existence, Mr. B., Mrs. B., our little ones, and both families, and you and I, in snug retreat, may make a jovial party to all eternity!

My direction is at Ellisland, near Dumfries. Yours, R. B.

NO. CLXXI.

TO MR. JAMES HAMILTON.

Ellisland, May 26th, 1789.

DEAR SIR—I send you by John Glover, carrier, the above account for Mr. Turnbull, as I suppose you know his address.

I would fain offer, my dear Sir, a word of sympathy with your misfortunes: but it is a tender string, and I know not how to touch it. It is easy to flourish a set of high-flown sentiments on the subjects that would give great satisfaction to—a breast quite at ease; but as ONE observes who was very seldom mistaken in the theory of life, "The heart knoweth its own sorrows, and a stranger intermeddleth not therewith."

Among some distressful emergencies that I have experienced in life, I ever laid this down as my foundation of comfort—*That he who has lived the life of an honest man, has by no means lived in vain!*

With every wish for your welfare and future success, I am, my dear Sir, sincerely yours, R. B.

NO. CLXXII.

TO WILLIAM CREECH, Esq.

Ellisland, May 30th, 1789.

SIR—I had intended to have troubled you with a long letter; but at present the delightful sensation of an omnipotent toothache so engrosses all my inner man, as to put it out of my power even to write nonsense. However, as in duty bound, I approach my bookseller with an offering in my hand —a few poetic clinches, and a song:—to expect any other kind of offering from the rhyming tribe would be to know them much less than you do. I do not pretend that there is much merit in these *morceaux*, but I have two reasons for sending them; *primo*, they are mostly ill-natured, so are in unison with my present feelings, while fifty troops of infernal spirits are driving post from ear to ear along my jaw-bones; and, *secondly*, they are so short, that you cannot leave off in the middle, and so hurt my pride in the idea that you found any work of mine too heavy to get through.

I have a request to beg of you, and I not only beg of you, but conjure you, by all your wishes and by all your hopes, that the muse will spare the satiric wink in the moment of your foibles; that she will warble the song of rapture round your hymeneal couch; and that she will shed on your turf the honest tear of elegiac gratitude! Grant my request as speedily as possible—send me by the very first fly or coach from this place, three copies of the last edition of my poems, which place to my account.

Now may the good things of prose, and the good things of verse, come among thy hands, until they be filled with the *good things of this life*, prayeth R. B.

NO. CLXXIII.

TO MR. M'AULEY, OF DUMBARTON.

Ellisland, June 4th, 1789.

DEAR SIR—Though I am not without my fears respecting my fate, at that grand, universal inquest of right and wrong, commonly called *The Last Day*, yet I trust there is one sin, which that arch-vagabond, Satan, who I understand is to be king's evidence, cannot throw in my teeth,—I mean ingratitude. There is a certain pretty large quantum of kindness for which I remain, and from inability, I fear must still remain, your debtor; but though unable to repay the debt, I assure you, Sir, I shall ever warmly remember the obligation. It gives me the sincerest pleasure to hear by my old acquaintance, Mr. Kennedy, that you are, in immortal Allan's language, "Hale, and weel, and living;" and that your charming family are well, and promising to be an amiable and respectable addition to the company of performers, whom the Great Manager of the Drama of Man is bringing into action for the succeeding age.

With respect to my welfare, a subject in which you once warmly and effectively interested yourself, I am here in my old way, holding my plough, marking the growth of my corn, or the health of my dairy; and at times sauntering by the delightful windings of the Nith, on the margin of which I have built my humble domicile, praying for seasonable weather, or holding an intrigue with the Muses, the only gipsies with whom I have now any intercourse. As I am entered into the holy state of matrimony, I trust my face is turned completely Zion-ward; and as it is a rule with all honest fellows to repeat no grievances, I hope that the little poetic licences of former days will, of course, fall under the oblivious influence of some good-natured statute of celestial prescription. In my family devotion, which, like a good Presbyterian, I occasionally give to my household folks, I am extremely fond of the psalm, "Let not the errors of my youth," &c., and that other, "Lo! children are God's heritage," &c., in which last Mrs. Burns, who, by the bye, has a glorious "wood-note wild" at either old song or psalmody, joins me with the pathos of Handel's Messiah.

R. B.

NO. CLXXIV.

TO MR. ROBERT AINSLIE.

Ellisland, June 8th, 1789.

My dear Friend—I am perfectly ashamed of myself when I look at the date of your last. It is not that I forget the friend of my heart and the companion of my peregrinations; but I have been condemned to drudgery beyond sufferance, though not, thank God, beyond redemption. I have had a collection of poems by a lady put into my hands to prepare them for the press; which horrid task, with sowing corn with my own hand, a parcel of masons, wrights, plasterers, &c., to attend to, roaming on business through Ayrshire—all this was against me, and the very first dreadful article was of itself too much for me.

13th.—I have not had a moment to spare from incessant toil since the 8th. Life, my dear Sir, is a serious matter. You know, by experience, that a man's individual self is a good deal, but believe me, a wife and a family of children, whenever you have the honour to be a husband and a father, will show you that your present and most anxious hours of solitude are spent on trifles. The welfare of those who are very dear to us, whose only support hope and stay we are—this, to a generous mind, is another sort of more important object of care than any concerns whatever which centre merely in the individual. On the other hand, let no young, unmarried, rake-belly dog among you, make a song of his pretended liberty and freedom from care If the relations we stand in to king, country, kindred, and friends, be any thing but the visionary fancies of dreaming metaphysicians; if religion, virtue, magnanimity, generosity, humanity, and justice, be ought but empty sounds; then the man who may be said to live only for others, for the beloved, honourable female, whose tender faithful embraces endears life, and for the helpless little innocents who are to be the men and women, the worshippers of his God, the subjects of his king, and the support, nay the very vital existence, of his COUNTRY, in the ensuing age—compare such a man with any fellow whatever, who, whether he bustle and push in business among labourers, clerks, statesmen; or whether he roar and rant, and drink and sing in taverns—a fellow over whose grave no one will breathe a single heigh-ho, except from the cobweb-tie of what is called good fellowship—who has no view nor aim but what terminates in himself—if there be any grovelling earth-born wretch of our species, a renegade to common sense, who would fain believe that the noble creature man is no better than a sort of fungus, generated out of nothing, nobody knows how, and soon dissipating in nothing nobody knows where; such a stupid beast, such a crawling reptile, might balance the foregoing unexaggerated comparison, but no one else would have the patience.

Forgive me, my dear Sir, for this long silence. *To make you amends*, I shall send you soon, and more encouraging still, without any postage, one or two rhymes of my later manufacture.

R. B

NO. CLXXV.

TO MR. M'MURDO.

Ellisland, June 19th, 1789.

Sir—A poet and a beggar are, in so many points of view, alike, that one might take them for the same individual character under different designations; were it not that though, with a trifling poetic licence, most poets may be styled beggars, yet the converse of the proposition does not hold, that every beggar is a poet. In one particular, however, they remarkably agree; if you help either the one or the other to a mug of ale, or the picking of a bone, they will very willingly repay you with a song. This occurs to me at present, as I have just dispatched a well-lined rib of John Kirkpatrick's Highlander—a bargain for which I am indebted to you, in the style of our ballad printers, "Five excellent new songs." The enclosed is nearly my newest song, and one that has cost me some pains, though that is but an equivocal mark of its excellence. Two or three others, which I have by me, shall do themselves the honour to wait on your after leisure: petitioners for admittance into favour, must not harass the condescension of their benefactor.

You see, Sir, what it is to patronise a poet. 'Tis like being a magistrate in a petty borough; you do them the favour to preside in their council for one year, and your name bears the prefatory stigma of bailie for life.

With, not the compliments, but the best wishes, the sincerest prayers of the season for you, that you may see many and happy years with Mrs. M'Murdo, and your family; wo blessings, by the bye, to which your rank does not, by any means, entitle you—a loving wife and fine family being almost the only good things of this life to which the farm-house and cottage have an exclusive right. I have the honour to be, Sir, your much indebted and very humble servant,

R. B.

NO. CLXXVI.

TO MRS. DUNLOP.

Ellisland, June 21st, 1789.

Dear Madam—Will you take the effusions, the miserable effusions of low spirits, just as they flow from their bitter spring? I know not of any particular cause for this worst of all my foes besetting me; but for some time my soul has been beclouded with a thickening atmosphere of evil imaginations and gloomy presages.

Monday Evening.

I have just heard Mr. Kirkpatrick preach a sermon. He is a man famous for his benevolence, and I revere him; but, from such ideas of my Creator, good Lord, deliver me! Religion, my honoured friend, is surely a simple business, as it equally concerns the ignorant and the learned, the poor and the rich. That there is an incomprehensible Great Being, to whom I owe my existence, and that he must be intimately acquainted with the operations and progress of the internal machinery, and consequent outward deportment of this creature which he has made—these are, I think, self-evident propositions. That there is a real and eternal distinction between virtue and vice, and consequently, that I am an accountable creature; that from the seeming nature of the human mind, as well as from the evident imperfection, nay, positive injustice, in the administration of affairs, both in the natural and moral worlds, there must be a retributive scene of existence beyond the grave—must, I think, be allowed by every one who will give himself a moment's reflection. I will go farther, and affirm, that from the sublimity, excellence, and purity of his doctrine and precepts, unparalleled by all the aggregated wisdom and learning of many preceding ages, though, to *appearance*, he himself was the obscurest and most illiterate of our species—therefore Jesus Christ was from God.

Whatever mitigates the woes, or increases the happiness of others, this is my criterion of goodness; and whatever injures society at large, or any individual in it, this is my measure of iniquity.

What think you, Madam, of my creed? I trust that I have said nothing that will lessen me in the eye of one whose good opinion I value almost next to the approbation of my own mind.

R. B.

NO. CLXXVII.

TO MISS WILLIAMS. (90)

Ellisland, 1789.

Madam—Of the many problems in the nature of that wonderful creature, man, this is one of the most extraordinary:—that he shall go on from day to day, from week to week, from month to month, or perhaps from year to year, suffering a hundred times more in an hour from the impotent consciousness of neglecting what he ought to do, than the very doing of it would cost him. I am deeply indebted to you, first, for a most elegant poetic compliment; then, for a polite, obliging letter; and, lastly, for your excellent poem on the slave-trade; and yet, wretch that I am! though the debts were debts of honour, and the creditor a lady, I have put off and put off even the very acknowledgment of the obligation, until you must indeed be the very angel I take you for, if you can forgive me.

Your poem I have read with the highest

pleasure. I have a way whenever I read a book—I mean a book in our own trade, Madam, a poetic one—and when it is my own property, that I take a pencil and mark at the ends of verses, or note on margins and odd paper, little criticisms of approbation or disapprobation as I peruse along. I will make no apology for presenting you with a few unconnected thoughts that occurred to me in my repeated perusals of your poem. I want to show you that I have honesty enough to tell you what I take to be truths, even when they are not quite on the side of approbation; and I do it in the firm faith that you have equal greatness of mind to hear them with pleasure.

I had lately the honour of a letter from Dr. Moore, where he tells me that he has sent me some books; they are not yet come to hand, but I hear they are on the way.

Wishing you all success in your progress in the path of fame, and that you may equally escape the danger of stumbling through incautious speed, or losing ground through loitering neglect. R. B. (91)

NO. CLXXVIII.

TO MR. JOHN LOGAN. (92)

Ellisland, near Dumfries, Aug. 7th, 1789.

DEAR SIR—I intended to have written you long ere now, and, as I told you, I had gotten three stanzas and a half on my way in a poetic epistle to you; but that old enemy of all *good works*, the devil, threw me into a prosaic mire, and for the soul of me I cannot get out of it. I dare not write you a long letter, as I am going to intrude on your time with a long ballad. I have, as you will shortly see, finished "The Kirk's Alarm;" but now that it is done, and I have laughed once or twice at the conceits in some of the stanzas, I am determined not to let it get into the public; so I send you this copy, the first I have sent to Ayrshire, except some few of the stanzas, which I wrote off in embryo, for Gavin Hamilton, under the express provision and request that you will only read it to a few of us, and do not on any account give, or permit to be taken, any copy of the ballad. If I could be of any service to Dr. M'Gill, I would do it, though it should be at a much greater expense than irritating a few bigoted priests; but I am afraid serving him in his present *embarras* is a task too hard for me. I have enemies enow, God knows, though I do not wantonly add to the number. Still, as I think there is some merit in two or three of the thoughts, I send it to you as a small, but sincere testimony how much, and with what respectful esteem, I am, dear Sir, your obliged humble servant, R. B.

NO. CLXXIX.

TO MRS. DUNLOP.

Ellisland, Sept. 6th, 1789.

DEAR MADAM—I have mentioned in my last, my appointment to the Excise, and the birth of little Frank; who, by the bye, I trust will be no discredit to the honourable name of Wallace, as he has a fine manly countenance, and a figure that might do credit to a little fellow two months older; and likewise an excellent good temper, though when he pleases he has a pipe, only not quite so loud as the horn that his immortal namesake blew, as a signal to take out the pin of Stirling bridge.

I had some time ago an epistle, part poetic and part prosaic, from your poetess, Mrs. J. Little, a very ingenious, but modest composition. I should have written her as she requested, but for the hurry of this new business. I have heard of her and her compositions in this country; and, I am happy to add, always to the honour of her character. The fact is, I know not well how to write to her; I should sit down to a sheet of paper that I knew not how to stain. I am no dab at fine-drawn letter-writing; and, except when prompted by friendship or gratitude, or, which happens extremely rarely, inspired by the muse (I know not her name) that presides over epistolary writing, I sit down, when necessitated to write, as I would sit down to beat hemp.

Some parts of your letter of the 20th August, struck me with the most melancholy concern for the state of your mind at present.

Would I could write you a letter of comfort, I would sit down to it with as much pleasure as I would to write an epic poem of my own composition, that should equal the Iliad. Religion, my dear friend, is the true comfort! A strong persuasion in a future state of existence; a proposition so obviously probable, that, setting revelation aside, every nation and people, so far as investigation has reached, for at least near four thousand years, have, in some mode or other, firmly believed it. In vain would we reason and pretend to doubt. I have myself done so to a very daring pitch; but when I reflected that I was opposing the most ardent wishes, and the most darling hopes of good men, and flying in the face of all human belief, in all ages, I was shocked at my own conduct.

I know not whether I have ever sent you the following lines, or if you have ever seen them; but it is one of my favourite quotations, which I keep constantly by me in my progress through life, in the language of the book of Job:—

Against the day of battle and of war—

spoken of religion:—

"'Tis *this*, my friend, that streaks our morning bright,
'Tis *this* that gilds the horror of our night.
When wealth forsakes us, and when friends are few;
When friends are faithless, or when foes pursue:
'Tis this that wards the blow, or stills the smart,
Disarms affliction, or repels his dart;
Within the breast bids purest raptures rise,
Bids smiling conscience spread her cloudless skies"

I have been busy with Zeluco. The doctor is so obliging as to request my opinion of it; and I have been revolving in my mind some kind of criticisms on novel-writing, but it is a depth beyond my research. I shall, however, digest my thoughts on the subject as well as I can. Zeluco is a most sterling performance.

Farewell! *A Dieu, le bon Dieu, je vous commende!*

NO. CLXXX.

TO CAPTAIN RIDDEL, CARSE.

Ellisland, Oct. 16th, 1789.

SIR—Big with the idea of this important day at Friars Carse, I have watched the elements and skies in the full persuasion that they would announce it to the astonished world by some phenomena of terrific portent. Yesternight until a very late hour did I wait with anxious horror for the appearance of some comet firing half the sky; or aërial armies of sanguinary Scandinavians, darting athwart the startled heavens, rapid as the ragged lightning, and horrid as those convulsions of nature that bury nations.

The elements, however, seem to take the matter very quietly; they did not even usher in this morning with triple suns and a shower of blood, symbolical of the three potent heroes, and the mighty claret-shed of the day. For me, as Thomson in his Winter says of the storm—I shall "Hear astonished, and astonished sing"

The whistle and the man; I sing
The man that won the whistle, &c.

Here are we met, three merry boys,
Three merry boys, I trow, are we;
And mony a night we've merry been,
And mony mae we hope to be.

Wha first shall rise to gang awa,
A cuckold coward loun is he:
Wha *last* beside his chair shall fa',
He is the king amang us three.

To leave the heights of Parnassus, and come to the humble vale of prose. I have some misgivings that I take too much upon me, when I request you to get your guest, Sir Robert Lawrie, to frank the two enclosed covers for me, the one of them to Sir William Cunningham, of Robertland, Bart at Kilmarnock—the other, to Mr. Allan Masterton, Writing-Master, Edinburgh. The first has a kindred claim on Sir Robert, as being a brother baronet, and likewise a keen Foxite: the other is one of the worthiest men in the world, and a man of real genius! so, allow me to say, he has a fraternal claim on you. I want them franked for to-morrow, as I cannot get them to the post to-night. I shall send a servant again for them in the evening. Wishing that your head may be crowned with laurels to-night, and free from aches to-morrow, I have the honour to be, Sir, your deeply indebted humble servant,

R. B.

NO. CLXXXI.

TO CAPTAIN RIDDEL.

Ellisland, 1789.

SIR—I wish from my inmost soul it were in my power to give you a more substantial gratification and return for all the goodness to the poet, than transcribing a few of his idle rhymes. However, "an old song," though to a proverb an instance of insignificance, is generally the only coin a poet has to pay with.

If my poems which I have transcribed, and mean still to transcribe, into your book, were equal to the grateful respect and high esteem

I bear for the gentleman to whom I present them, they would be the finest poems in the language. As they are, they will at least be a testimony with what sincerity I have the honour to be, Sir, your devoted humble servant, R. B.

NO. CLXXXII.

TO MR. ROBERT AINSLIE.

Ellisland, Nov. 1st, 1789.

MY DEAR FRIEND—I had written you long ere now, could I have guessed where to find you, for I am sure you have more good sense than to waste the precious days of vacation time in the dirt of business and Edinburgh. Wherever you are, God bless you, and lead you not into temptation, but deliver you from evil!

I do not know if I have informed you that I am now appointed to an Excise division, in the middle of which my house and farm lie. In this I was extremely lucky. Without ever having been an expectant, as they call their journeymen excisemen, I was directly planted down to all intents and purposes an officer of Excise, there to flourish and bring forth fruits—worthy of repentance.

I know not how the word exciseman, or still more opprobrious, gauger, will sound in your ears. I, too, have seen the day when my auditory nerves would have felt very delicately on this subject; but a wife and children are things which have a wonderful power in blunting these kind of sensations. Fifty pounds a-year for life, and a provision for widows and orphans, you will allow is no bad settlement for a *poet*. For the ignominy of the profession, I have the encouragement which I once heard a recruiting sergeant give to a numerous, if not a respectable audience, in the streets of Kilmarnock:—"Gentlemen, for your further and better encouragement, I can assure you that our regiment is the most blackguard corps under the crown, and consequently with us an honest fellow has the surest chance of preferment."

You need not doubt that I find several very unpleasant and disagreeable circumstances in my business; but I am tired with and disgusted at the language of complaint against the evils of life. Human existence, in the most favourable situations, does not abound with pleasures, and has its inconveniences and ills; capricious foolish man mistakes these inconveniences and ills as if they were the peculiar property of his particular situation; and hence that eternal fickleness, that love of change, which has ruined, and daily does ruin, many a fine fellow, as well as many a blockhead, and is almost without exception a constant source of disappointment and misery.

AA

I long to hear from you how you go on—not so much in business as in life. Are you pretty well satisfied with your own exertions, and tolerably at ease in your internal reflections? 'Tis much to be a great character as a lawyer, but beyond comparison more to be a great character as a man. That you may be both the one and the other is the earnest wish, and that you *will* be both is the firm persuasion of, my dear Sir, &c.

R. B.

NO. CLXXXIII.

TO MR. RICHARD BROWN.

Ellisland, November 4th, 1789.

I HAVE been so hurried, my ever dear friend, that though I got both your letters, I have not been able to command an hour to answer them as I wished; and even now, you are to look on this as merely confessing debt, and craving days. Few things could have given me so much pleasure as the news that you were once more safe and sound on terra firma, and happy in that place where happiness is alone to be found—in the fireside circle. May the benevolent Director of all things peculiarly bless you in all those endearing connections consequent on the tender and venerable names of husband and father! I have indeed been extremely lucky in getting an additional income of £50 a-year, while at the same time, the appointment will not cost me above £10 or £12 per annum of expenses more than I must have inevitably incurred. The worst circumstance is, that the Excise division which I have got is so extensive, no less than ten parishes to ride over; and it abounds besides with so much business, that I can scarcely steal a spare moment. However, labour endears rest, and both together are absolutely necessary for the proper enjoyment of human existence. I cannot meet you anywhere. No less than an order from the board of Excise, at Edinburgh, is necessary before I can have so much time as to meet you in Ayrshire. But do you come, and see me. We must have a social day, and perhaps lengthen it out with half the night, before you go again to sea. You are the earliest friend I now have on earth, my brothers excepted; and is not that an endearing circumstance? When you and I first met, we were at the green period of human life. The twig would easily take a bent, but would as easily return to its former state. You and I not only took a mutual bent, but, by the melancholy, though strong influence of being both of the family of the unfortunate, we were entwined with one another in our growth towards advanced age: and blasted be the sacrilegious hand that should attempt to undo the union! You and I must have one bumper to our favourite toast, "May the companions of our youth be the friends of our old age!" Come and see me one year; I shall see you at Port-Glasgow the next; and if we can contrive to have a gossiping between our two bed-fellows, it will be so much additional pleasure. Mrs. Burns joins me in kind compliments to you and Mrs. Brown. Adieu! I am ever, my dear Sir, yours, R. B.

NO. CLXXXIV.

TO ROBERT GRAHAM, Esq.

OF FINTRY.

December 9th, 1789.

Sir—I have a good while had a wish to trouble you with a letter, and had certainly done it long ere now—but for a humiliating something that throws cold water on the resolution, as if one should say, "You have found Mr. Graham a very powerful and kind friend indeed, and that interest he is so kindly taking in your concerns you ought, by every thing in your power, to keep alive and cherish." Now, though since God has thought proper to make one powerful and another powerless, the connection of obliger and obliged is all fair; and though my being under your patronage is highly honourable, yet, Sir, allow me to flatter myself, that, as a poet and an honest man, you first interested yourself in my welfare, and principally as such, still you permit me to approach you.

I have found the Excise business go on a great deal smoother with me than I expected, owing a good deal to the generous friendship of Mr. Mitchel, my collector, and the kind assistance of Mr. Findlater, my supervisor. I dare to be honest, and I fear no labour. Nor do I find my hurried life greatly inimical to my correspondence with the Muses. Their visits to me, indeed, and I believe to most of their acquaintance, like the visits of good angels, are short and far between; but I meet them now and then as I jog through the hills of Nithsdale, just as I used to do on the banks of Ayr. I take the liberty to enclose you a few bagatelles, all of them the productions of my leisure thoughts in my Excise rides.

If you know or have ever seen Captain Grose, the antiquary, you will enter into any humour that is in the verses on him. Perhaps you have seen them before, as I sent them to a London newspaper. Though I dare say you have none of the solemn-league-and-covenant fire, which shone so conspicuous in Lord George Gordon, and the Kilmarnock weavers, yet I think you must have heard of Dr. M'Gill, one of the clergymen of Ayr, and his heretical book. God help him, poor man! Though he is one of the worthiest, as well as one of the ablest, of the whole priesthood of the Kirk of Scotland, in every sense of that ambiguous term, yet the poor Doctor and his numerous family are in iminent danger of being thrown out to the mercy of the winter-winds. The enclosed ballad on that business is, I confess, too local, but I laughed myself at some conceits in it, though I am convinced in my conscience that there are a good many heavy stanzas in it too.

The election ballad, as you will see, alludes to the present canvass in our string of boroughs. I do not believe there will be such a hard run match in the whole general election.

* * * *

I am too little a man to have any political attachments; I am deeply indebted to, and have the warmest veneration for, individuals of both parties: but a man who has it in his power to be the father of a country, and who * * * * *, (93) is a character that one cannot speak of with patience.

Sir J. J. does "what man can do," but yet I doubt his fate. R. B.

NO. CLXXXV.

TO MRS. DUNLOP.

Ellisland, December 13th, 1789.

Many thanks, my dear Madam, for your sheetful of rhymes. Though at present I am below the veriest prose, yet from you every thing pleases. I am groaning under the miseries of a diseased nervous system—a system, the state of which is most conducive to our happiness, or the most productive of our misery. For now near three weeks I have been so ill with a nervous headache, that I have been obliged for a time to give up my Excise-books, being scarce able to lift my head, much less to ride once a-week over ten muir parishes. What is man? To day, in the luxuriance of health, exulting in the enjoyment of existence; in a few days, perhaps in a few hours, loaded with conscious painful being, counting the tardy pace of the lingering moments by the repercussions of anguish, and refusing or denying a comforter. Day follows night, and night comes after day, only to curse him with life which gives him no pleasure; and yet the awful, dark termination of that life is something at which he recoils.

Tell us, ye dead; will none of you in pity
Disclose the secret——————
What 'tis you are, and we must shortly be?
——————'tis no matter:
A little time will make us learn'd as you are.

Can it be possible, that when I resign this frail, feverish being, I shall still find myself in conscious existence? When the last gasp of agony has announced that I am no more to those that knew me, and the few who loved me; when the cold, stiffened, unconscious, ghastly corse is resigned into the earth, to be the prey of unsightly reptiles, and to become in time a trodden clod, shall I be yet warm in life, seeing and seen, enjoying and enjoyed? Ye venerable sages, and holy flamens, is there probability in your conjectures, truth in your stories, of another world beyond death; or are they all alike baseless visions, and fabricated fables? If there is another life, it must be only for the just, the benevolent, the amiable, and the humane; what a flattering idea then is a world to come! Would to God I as firmly believed it as I ardently wish it! There, I should meet an aged parent, now at rest from the many buffetings of an evil world, against which he so long and so bravely struggled. There should I meet the friend, the disinterested friend of my early life; the man who rejoiced to see me, because he loved me and could serve me. Muir, thy weakness were the aberrations of human nature, but thy heart glowed with every thing generous, manly, and noble; and if emanation from the All-good Being animated a human frame, it was thine! There should I, with speechless agony of rapture, again recognize my lost, my ever dear Mary! whose bosom was fraught with truth, honour, constancy, and love.

My Mary, dear departed shade?
Where is thy place of heavenly rest?
Seest thou thy lover lowly laid?
Hear'st thou the groans that rend his breast?

Jesus Christ, thou amiablest of characters! I trust thou art no impostor, and that thy revelation of blissful scenes of existence beyond death and the grave, is not one of the many impositions which time after time have been palmed on credulous mankind. I trust that in thee "shall all the families of the earth be blessed," by being yet connected together in a better world, where every tie that bound heart to heart, in this state of existence, shall be, far beyond our present conceptions, more endearing.

I am a good deal inclined to think with those who maintain, that what are called nervous affections are in fact diseases of the mind. I cannot reason, I cannot think; and but to you I would not venture to write any thing above an order to a cobbler. You have felt too much of the ills of life not to sympathise with a diseased wretch, who has impaired more than half of any faculties he possessed. Your goodness will excuse this distracted scrawl, which the writer dare scarcely read, and which he would throw into the fire, were he able to write any thing better, or indeed any thing at all.

Rumour told me something of a son of yours, who was returned from the East or West Indies. If you have gotten news from James or Anthony, it was cruel in you not to let me know; as I promised you, on the sincerity of a man, who is weary of one world, and anxious about another, that scarce any thing could give me so much pleasure as to hear of any good thing befalling my honoured friend.

If you have a minute's leisure, take up your pen in pity to *le pauvre miserable*,

R. B.

NO. CLXXXVI.

TO LADY WINIFRED MAXWELL CONSTABLE. (94)

Ellisland, December 16th, 1789.

My Lady—In vain I have, from day to day, expected to hear from Mrs. Young, as she promised me at Dalswinton that she would do me the honour to introduce me at Tinwald; and it was impossible, not from your ladyship's accessibility, but from my own feelings, that I could go alone. Lately, indeed, Mr. Maxwell of Carruchen, in his usual goodness, offered to accompany me, when an unlucky indisposition on my part hindered my embracing the opportunity. To court the notice or the tables of the great, except where I sometimes have had a little matter to ask of them, or, more often, the pleasanter task of witnessing my gratitude to them, is what I never have done, and I trust never shall do. But with your ladyship I have the honour to be connected by one of the strongest and most endearing ties in the whole moral world. Common sufferers, in a cause where even to be unfortunate is glorious, the cause of heroic loyalty! Though my fathers had not illustrious honours and vast properties to hazard in the contest, though they left their humble cottages only to add so many units more to the unnoted crowd that followed their leaders, yet what they could they did, and what they had they lost: with unshaken firmness, and unconcealed political attachments, they shook hands with ruin for what they esteemed the cause of their king and their country. This language and the enclosed verses (95) are for your ladyship's eye alone. Poets are not very famous for their prudence; but as I can do nothing for a cause which is now nearly no more, I do not wish to hurt myself. I have the honour to be, my lady, your ladyship's obliged and obedient humble servant, R. B.

NO. CLXXXVII.

TO PROVOST MAXWELL,

OF LOCHMABEN.

Ellisland, December 20th, 1789.

DEAR PROVOST—As my friend, Mr. Graham, goes for your good town to-morrow, I cannot resist the temptation to send you a few lines, and, as I have nothing to say, I have chosen this sheet of foolscap, and begun, as you see, at the top of the first page, because I have ever observed, that when once people have fairly set out, they know not where to stop. Now that my first sentence is concluded, I have nothing to do but to pray Heaven to help me on to another. Shall I write you on politics or religion, two master subjects for your sayers of nothing? Of the first, I dare say by this time you are nearly surfeited (96); and for the last, whatever they may talk of it, who make it a kind of company concern, I never could endure it beyond a soliloquy. I might write you on farming, on building, on marketing; but my poor distracted mind is so torn, so jaded, so racked and bedeviled with the task of the superlatively damned to make *one guinea do the business of three,* that I detest, abhor, and swoon, at the very word *business,* though no less than four letters of my very short surname are in it.

Well, to make the matter short, I shall betake myself to a subject ever fruitful of themes—a subject the turtle feast of the sons of Satan, and the delicious secret sugar plum of the babes of grace—a subject sparkling with all the jewels that wit can find in the mines of genius, and pregnant with all the stores of learning from Moses and Confucius to Franklin and Priestley—in short, may it please your lordship, I intend to write * * *

[*Here the poet inserted a song.*]

If at any time you expect a field-day in your town, a day when dukes, earls, and knights, pay their court to weavers, tailors, and cobblers, I should like to know of it two or three days before-hand. It is not that I care three skips of a cur dog for the politics, but I should like to see such an exhibition of human nature. If you meet with that worthy old veteran in religion and good fellowship, Mr. Jeffrey, or any of his amiable family (97), I beg you will give them my best compliments. R. B.

NO. CLXXXVIII.

TO MR. SUTHERLAND, PLAYER,

ENCLOSING A PROLOGUE.

Monday Morning.

I WAS much disappointed, my dear Sir, in wanting your most agreeable company yesterday. However, I heartily pray for good weather next Sunday; and whatever aërial Being has the guidance of the elements, may take any other half dozen of Sundays he pleases, and clothe them with

> Vapours, and clouds, and storms,
> Until he terrify himself
> At combustion of his own raising.

I shall see you on Wednesday forenoon. In the greatest hurry, R. B.

NO. CLXXXIX.

TO SIR JOHN SINCLAIR.

1790.

SIR—The following circumstance has, I believe, been omitted in the statistical account, transmitted to you, of the parish of Dunscore, in Nithsdale. I beg leave to send it to you, because it is new, and may be useful. How far it is deserving of a place in your patriotic publication, you are the best judge.

To store the minds of the lower classes with useful knowledge, is certainly of very great importance, both to them as individuals, and to society at large. Giving them a turn for reading and reflection, is giving them a source of innocent and laudable amusement, and, besides, raises them to a more dignified degree in the scale of rationality. Impressed with this idea, a gentleman in this parish, Robert Riddel, Esq., of Glenriddel, set on foot a species of circulating library, on a plan so simple, as to be practicable in any corner of the country; and so useful, as to deserve the notice of every country gentleman, who thinks the improvement of that part of his own species, whom chance has thrown into the humble walks of the peasant and the artizan, a matter worthy of his attention.

Mr. Riddel got a number of his own tenants, and farming neighbours, to form themselves into a society for the purpose of having a library among themselves. They entered into a legal engagement to abide by it for three years; with a saving clause or two, in case of removal to a distance, or of death. Each member, at his entry, paid five shillings; and at each of their meetings, which were held every fourth Saturday, sixpence more. With their entry-money, and the credit which they took on the faith of their future funds, they laid in a tolerable stock of books at the commencement. What authors they were to purchase, was always decided by the majority. At every meeting, all the books, under certain fines and forfeitures, by way of penalty, were to be produced; and the members had their choice of the volumes in rotation. He whose name stood for that night first on the list, had his choice of what volume he pleased in the whole collection; the second had his choice after the first; the third after the second; and so on to the last. At next meeting, he who had been first on the list at the preceding meeting, was last at this; he who had been second was first; and so on through the whole three years. At the expiration of the engagement, the books were sold by auction, but only among the members themselves; and each man had his share of the common stock, in money or in books, as he chose to be a purchaser or not.

At the breaking up of this little society, which was formed under Mr. Riddel's patronage, what with benefactions of books from him, and what with their own purchases, they had collected together upwards of one hundred and fifty volumes. It will easily be guessed that a good deal of trash would be bought. Among the books, however, of this little library, were—Blair's Sermons, Robertson's History of Scotland, Hume's History of the Stuarts, The Spectator, Idler, Adventurer, Mirror, Lounger, Observer, Man of Feeling, Man of the World, Chrysal, Don Quixote, Joseph Andrews, &c. A peasant who can read, and enjoy such books, is certainly a much superior being to his neighbour who, perhaps, stalks beside his team, very little removed, except in shape, from the brutes he drives.

Wishing your patriotic exertions their so much merited success, I am, Sir, your humble servant, A PEASANT (98).

NO. CXC.

TO MR. GILBERT BURNS.

Ellisland, January 11th, 1790.

DEAR BROTHER—I mean to take advantage of the frank, though I have not in my present frame of mind much appetite for exertion in writing. My nerves are in a ——— state. I feel that horrid hypochondria pervading every atom of both body and soul. This farm has undone my enjoyment of myself. It is a ruinous affair on all hands. But let it go to ———! I'll fight it out, and be off with it.

We have gotten a set of very decent players here just now. I have seen them an evening or two. David Campbell, in Ayr, wrote to me by the manager of the company, a Mr. Sutherland, who is a man of apparent worth. On New-year-day evening I gave him the following prologue, which he spouted to his audience with applause:—

"No song nor dance I bring from yon great city," &c.

I can no more. If once I was clear of this damned farm, I should respire more at ease.

NO. CXCI.

TO WILLIAM DUNBAR, W. S.

Ellisland, January 14th, 1790.

SINCE we are here creatures of a day, since "a few summer days, and a few winter nights, and the life of man is at an end," why, my dear much-esteemed Sir, should you and I let negligent indolence—for I know it is nothing worse—step in between us, and bar the enjoyment of a mutual correspondence? We are not shapen out of the common, heavy, methodical clod, the elemental stuff of the plodding selfish race, the sons of Arithmetic and Prudence; our feelings and hearts are not benumbed and poisoned by the cursed influence of riches, which, whatever blessing they may be in other respects, are no friends to the nobler qualities of the heart: in the name of random sensibility, then, let never the moon change on our silence any more. I have had a tract of bad health most part of this winter, else you had heard from me long ere now. Thank Heaven, I am now got so much better as to be able to partake a little in the enjoyments of life.

Our friend, Cunningham, will perhaps have told you of my going into the Excise. The truth is, I found it a very convenient business to have £50 per annum, nor have I yet felt any of these mortifying circumstances in it that I was led to fear.

Feb. 2nd.—I have not, for sheer hurry of business, been able to spare five minutes to finish my letter. Besides my farm business, I ride on my Excise matters at least 200 miles every week. I have not by any means given up the Muses. You will see in the 3rd vol. of Johnson's Scots songs that I have contributed my mite there.

But, my dear Sir, little ones that look up to you for paternal protection are an important charge. I have already two fine healthy stout little fellows, and I wish to throw some light upon them. I have a thousand reveries and schemes about them, and their future destiny. Not that I am a Utopian projector in these things. I am resolved never to breed up a son of mine to any of the learned professions. I know the value of independence; and since I cannot give my sons an independent fortune, I shall give them an independent line of life. What a chaos of hurry, chance, and changes is this world, when one sits soberly down to reflect on it! To a father, who himself knows the world, the thought that he shall have sons to usher into it must fill him with dread; but if he have daughters, the prospect in a thoughtful moment is apt to shock him.

I hope Mrs. Fordyce and the two young ladies are well. Do let me forget that they are nieces of yours, and let me say that I never saw a more interesting, sweeter pair of sisters in my life. I am the fool of my feelings and attachments. I often take up a volume of my Spenser to realise you to my imagination (99), and think over the social scenes we have had together. God grant that there may be another world more congenial to honest fellows beyond this. A world where these rubs and plagues of absence, distance, misfortunes, ill-health, &c., shall no more damp hilarity and divide friendship. This I know is your throng season, but half a page will much oblige, my dear Sir, yours sincerely, R. B.

NO. CXCII.

TO MRS. DUNLOP.

Ellisland, January 25th, 1790.

IT has been owing to unremitting hurry of business that I have not written to you, Madam, long ere now. My health is greatly better, and I now begin once more to share in satisfaction and enjoyment with the rest of my fellow-creatures.

Many thanks, my much-esteemed friend, for your kind letters; but why will you make me run the risk of being contemptible and mercenary in my own eyes? When I pique myself on my independent spirit, I hope it is neither poetic licence, nor poetic rant: and I am so flattered with the honour you have done me, in making me your compeer in friendship and friendly correspondence, that I cannot, without pain, and a degree of mortification, be reminded of the real inequality between our situations.

Most sincerely do I rejoice with you, dear Madam, in the good news of Anthony. Not only your anxiety about his fate, but my own esteem for such a noble, warm-hearted, manly young fellow, in the little I had of his acquaintance, has interested me deeply in his fortunes.

Falconer, the unfortunate author of the "Shipwreck," which you so much admire, is no more. After witnessing the dreadful catastrophe he so feelingly describes in his poem, and after weathering many hard gales of fortune, he went to the bottom with the Aurora frigate!

I forget what part of Scotland had the honour of giving him birth, but he was the son of obscurity and misfortune. He was one of those daring adventurous spirits, which Scotland, beyond any other country, is remarkable for producing. Little does the fond mother think, as she hangs delighted over the sweet little leech at her bosom, where the poor fellow may hereafter wander, and what may be his fate. I remember a stanza in an old Scottish ballad (100), which, notwithstanding its rude simplicity. speaks feelingly to the heart:—

"Little did my mother think,
That day she cradled me,
What land I was to travel in,
Or what death I should die!"

Old Scottish songs are, you know, a favourite study and pursuit of mine; and now I am on that subject, allow me to give you two stanzas of another old simple ballad, which I am sure will please you. The catastrophe of the piece is a poor ruined female, lamenting her fate. She concludes with this pathetic wish:—

"Oh that my father had ne'er on me smil'd;
Oh that my mother had ne'er to me sung;
Oh that my cradle had not e'er been rock'd;
But that I had died when I was young!

Oh that the turf-clad grave it were my bed;
My blankets were my winding-sheet;
The clocks and the worms my bedfellows a';
And oh sae soundly sweet as I should sleep!"

I do not remember in all my reading to have met with anything more truly the language of misery, than the exclamation in the last line. Misery is like love; to speak its language truly, the author must have felt it.

I am every day expecting the doctor to give your little godson (101) the small-pox. It is *rife* in the country, and I tremble for his fate. By the way, I cannot help congratulating you on his looks and spirit. Every person who sees him acknowledges him to be the finest, handsomest child he has ever seen. I am myself delighted with the manly swell of his little chest, and a certain miniature dignity in the carriage of his head, and the glance of his fine black eye, which promise the undaunted gallantry of an independent mind.

I thought to have sent you some rhymes, but time forbids. I promise you poetry until you are tired of it, next time I have the honour of assuring you how truly I am, &c. R. B.

NO. CXCIII.

TO MR. PETER HILL,

BOOKSELLER, EDINBURGH.

Ellisland, Feb. 2nd, 1790.

No! I will not say one word about apologies or excuses for not writing;—I am a poor, rascally gauger, condemned to gallop at least 200 miles every week to inspect dirty ponds and yeasty barrels, and where can I find time to write to, or importance to interest any body? The upbraidings of my conscience, nay the upbraidings of my wife, have persecuted me on your account these two or three months past. I wish to God I was a great man, that my correspondence might throw light upon you, to let the world see what you really are: and then I would make your fortune, without putting my hand in my pocket for you, which, like all other great men, I suppose I would avoid as much as possible. What are you doing, and how are you doing? Have you lately seen any of my few friends? What has become of the BOROUGH REFORM, or how is the fate of my poor namesake, Mademoiselle Burns, decided? Oh man! but for thee and thy selfish appetites, and dishonest artifices, that beauteous form, and that once innocent and still ingenuous mind, might have shone conspicuous and lovely in the faithful wife, and the affectionate mother; and shall the unfortunate sacrifice to thy pleasures have no claim on thy humanity! (102)

I saw lately in a review some extracts from a new poem, called the "Village Curate;" send it me. I want likewise a cheap copy of "The World." Mr. Armstrong, the young poet, who does me the honour to mention me so kindly in his works, please give him my best thanks for the copy of his book. I shall write him, my first leisure hour. I like his poetry much, but I think his style in prose quite astonishing.

Your book came safe, and I am going to trouble you with further commissions. I call it troubling you—because I want only, BOOKS; the cheapest way, the best; so you may have to hunt for them in the evening auctions. I want Smollett's Works, for the sake of his incomparable humour. I have already Roderick Random, and Humphrey Clinker. Perigrine Pickle, Launcelot Greaves, and Ferdinand Count Fathom, I still want; but as I said, the veriest ordinary copies will serve me. I am nice only in the appearance of my poets. I forget the price of Cowper's Poems, but I believe I must have them. I saw, the other day, proposals for a publication, entitled, "Bank's new and complete Christian's Family Bible," printed for C. Cooke, Paternoster Row, London. He promises, at least, to give in the work, I think it is three hundred and odd engravings, to which he has put the names of the first artists in London. (103) You will know the character of the performance, as some numbers of it are published: and if it is really what it pretends to be, set me down as a subscriber, and send me the published numbers.

Let me hear from you, your first leisure minute, and trust me, you shall in future have no reason to complain of my silence. The dazzling perplexity of novelty will dissipate, and leave me to pursue my course in the quiet path of methodical routine.

R. B.

NO. CXCIV.

TO MR. W. NICOL.

Ellisland, Feb. 9th, 1790.

MY DEAR SIR—That —— mare of yours is dead. I would freely have given her price to have saved her; she has vexed me beyond description. Indebted, as I was, to your goodness beyond what I can ever repay, I eagerly grasped at your offer to have the mare with me. That I might at least show my readiness in wishing to be grateful, I took every care of her in my power. She was never crossed for riding above half a score of times by me, or in my keeping. I drew her in the plough, one of three, for one poor week. I refused fifty-five shillings for her, which was the highest bode I could squeeze for her. I fed her up and had her in fine order for Dumfries fair; when four or five days before the fair, she was seized with an unaccountable disorder in the sinews, or somewhere in the bones of the neck; with a weakness or total want of power in her fillets, and, in short, the whole vertebræ of her spine seemed to be diseased and unhinged, and in eight and forty hours, in spite of the two best farriers in the country, she died, and be —— to her! The farriers said that she had been quite strained in the fillets beyond cure before you had bought her; and that the poor devil, though she might keep a little flesh, had been jaded and quite worn out with fatigue and oppression. While she was with me, she was under my own eye, and, I assure you, my much-valued friend, everything was done for her that could be done; and the accident has vexed me to the heart. In fact I could not pluck up spirits to write to you, on account of the unfortunate business.

There is little new in this country. Our theatrical company, of which you must have heard, leave us this week. Their merit and character are, indeed, very great, both on the stage and in private life; not a worthless creature among them; and their encouragement has been accordingly. Their usual run is from eighteen to twenty-five pounds a-night; seldom less than the one, and the house will hold no more than the other. There have been repeated instances of sending away six, and eight, and ten pounds a-night for want of room. A new theatre is to be built by subscription; the first stone is to be laid on Friday first to come. Three hundred guineas have been raised by thirty subscribers, and thirty more might have been got if wanted. The manager, Mr. Sutherland, was introduced to me by a friend from Ayr; and a worthier or cleverer fellow I have rarely met with. Some of our clergy have slipt in by stealth now and then; but they have got up a farce of their own. You must have heard how the Rev. Mr. Lawson of Kirkmahoe, seconded by the Rev. Mr. Kirkpatrick of Dunscore, and the rest of that faction, have accused, in formal process, the unfortunate and Rev. Mr. Heron, of Kirkgunzeon, that, in ordaining Mr. Nielson to the cure of souls in Kirkbean, he, the said Heron, feloniously and treasonably bound the said Nielson to the confession of faith, *so far as it was agreeable to reason and the word of God!*

Mrs. B. begs to be remembered most gratefully to you. Little Bobby and Frank are charmingly well and healthy. I am jaded to death with fatigue. For these two or three months, on an average, I have not ridden less than 200 miles per week. I have done little in the poetic way. I have given Mr. Sutherland two Prologues; one of which was delivered last week. I have likewise strung four or five barbarous stanzas, to the tune of Chevy Chase, by way of Elegy on your poor unfortunate mare, beginning (the name she got here was Peg Nicholson)

Peg Nicholson was a good bay mare,
  As ever trode on airn;
But now she's floating down the Nith,
  And past the mouth o' Cairn.

My best compliments to Mrs. Nicol, and little Neddy, and all the family; I hope Ned

is a good scholar, and will come out to gather nuts and apples with me next harvest.

R. B.

NO. CXCV.

TO MR. CUNNINGHAM. (104)

Ellisland, February 13*th*, 1790.

I BEG your pardon, my dear and much-valued friend, for writing to you on this very unfashionable, unsightly sheet.

My poverty, but not my will, consents.

But to make amends, since of modish post I have none, except one poor widowed half-sheet of gilt, which lies in my drawer, among my plebeian foolscap pages, like the widow of a man of fashion, whom that unpolite scoundrel, Necessity, has driven from Burgundy and Pineapple, to a dish of Bohea with the scandal-bearing help-mate of a village-priest; or a glass of whisky-toddy, with a ruby-nosed yoke-fellow of a foot-padding exciseman—I make a vow to enclose this sheet-full of epistolary fragments in that my only scrap of gilt-paper.

I am, indeed, your worthy debtor for three friendly letters. I ought to have written to you long ere now, but it is a literal fact, I have scarcely a spare moment. It is not that I *will not* write to you: Miss Burnet is not more dear to her guardian angel, nor his grace the Duke of Queensberry to the powers of darkness, than my friend Cunningham to me. It is not that I *cannot* write to you; should you doubt it, take the following fragment, which was intended for you some time ago, and be convinced that I can *anthesize* sentiment, and *circumvolute* periods, as well as any coiner of phrase in the regions of philology.

December, 1789.

MY DEAR CUNNINGHAM — Where are you? And what are you doing? Can you be that son of levity, who takes up a friendship as he takes up a fashion; or, are you, like some other of the worthiest fellows in the world, the victim of indolence, laden with fetters of ever-increasing weight?

What strange beings we are! Since we have a portion of conscious existence, equally capable of enjoying pleasure, happiness, and rapture, or of suffering pain, wretchedness, and misery; it is surely worthy of an inquiry, whether there be not such a thing as a science of life; whether method, economy, and fertility of expedients, be not applicable to enjoyment; and whether there be not a want of dexterity in pleasure, which renders our little scantling of happiness still less; and a profuseness, and intoxication in bliss, which leads to satiety, disgust, and self-abhorrence. There is not a doubt but that health, talents, character, decent competency, respectable friends, are real substantial blessings; and yet, do we not daily see those who enjoy many or all of these good things, contrive, notwithstanding, to be as unhappy as others to whose lot few of them have fallen? I believe one great source of this mistake or misconduct is owing to a certain stimulus, with us called ambition, which goads us up the hill of life; not as we ascend other eminences, for the laudable curiosity of viewing an extended landscape, but, rather, for the dishonest pride of looking down on others of our fellow-creatures, seemingly diminutive in humbler stations, &c &c.

Sunday, February 14*th*, 1790.

GOD help me! I am now obliged to join

Night to day, and Sunday to the week.

If there be any truth in the orthodox faith of these churches, I am ——— past redemption, and, what is worse, ——— to all eternity. I am deeply read in Boston's Four-fold State, Marshall on Sanctification, Guthrie's Trial of a Saving Interest, &c.; but, "there is no balm in Gilead, there is no physician there," for me; so I shall e'en turn Arminian, and trust to "Sincere though imperfect obedience."

Tuesday, 16*th*.

LUCKILY for me, I was prevented from the discussion of the knotty point at which I had just made a full stop. All my fears and cares are of this world: if there is another, an honest man has nothing to fear from it. I hate a man that wishes to be a deist; but I fear, every fair, unprejudiced inquirer must, in some degree, be a sceptic It is not that there are any very staggering arguments against the immortality of man; but, like electricity, phlogiston, &c., the subject is so involved in darkness, that we want data to go upon. One thing frightens me much: that we are to live for ever, seems *too good news to be true*. That we are to enter into a new scene of existence, where, exempt from want and pain, we shall enjoy ourselves and our friends without satiety or separation;—how much should

I be indebted to any one who could fully assure me that this was certain!

My time is once more expired. I will write to Mr. Cleghorn soon. God bless him and all his concerns! And may all the powers that preside over conviviality and friendship be present with all their kindest influence, when the bearer of this, Mr. Syme, and you meet! I wish I could also make one.

Finally, brethren, farewell! Whatsoever things are lovely, whatsoever things are gentle, whatsoever things are charitable, whatsoever things are kind, think on these things, and think on.

R. B.

NO. CXCVI.

TO MR. HILL.

Ellisland, March 2nd, 1790.

AT a late meeting of the Monkland Friendly Society, it was resolved to augment their library by the following books, which you are to send us as soon as possible:—The Mirror, The Lounger, Man of Feeling, Man of the World (these, for my own sake, I wish to have by the first carrier), Knox's History of the Reformation; Rae's History of the Rebellion in 1715; any good History of the Rebellion in 1745; A Display of the Secession Act and Testimony, by Mr. Gib; Hervey's Meditations; Beveridge's Thoughts; and another copy of Watson's Body of Divinity.

I wrote to Mr. A. Masterton three or four months ago, to pay some money he owed me into your hands, and lately, I wrote to you to the same purpose; but I have heard from neither one nor other of you.

In addition to the books I commissioned in my last, I want very much An Index to the Excise Laws, or an Abridgement of all the Statutes now in force relative to the Excise, by Jellinger Symons; I want three copies of this book; if it is now to be had, cheap or dear, get it for me. An honest country neighbour of mine wants, too, a Family Bible, the larger the better, but second-handed, for he does not choose to give above ten shillings for the book. I want likewise for myself, as you can pick them up, second-handed, or cheap, copies of Otway's Dramatic Works, Ben Jonson's, Dryden's, Congreve's, Wycherley's, Vanburgh's, Cibber's, or any Dramatic Works of the more modern Macklin, Garrick, Foote, Colman, or Sheridan. A good copy, too, of Molière, in French, I much want. Any other good dramatic authors in that language I want also; but comic authors chiefly, though I should wish to have Racine, Corneille, and Voltaire too. I am in no hurry for all, or any of these, but if you accidently meet with them very cheap, get them for me. (105)

And now, to quit the dry walk of business, how do you do, my dear friend?—and how is Mrs. Hill? I trust, if now and then not so *elegantly* handsome, at least as amiable, and sings as divinely as ever. My good wife, too, has a charming "wood-note wild;" now could we four ——.

I am out of all patience with this vile world, for one thing. Mankind are by nature benevolent creatures, except in a few scoundrelly instances. I do not think that avarice of the good things we chance to have is born with us: but, we are placed here amid so much nakedness, and hunger, and poverty, and want, that we are under a cursed necessity of studying selfishness, in order that we may EXIST! Still there are, in every age, a few souls, that all the wants and woes of life cannot debase to selfishness, or even to the necessary alloy of caution and prudence. If ever I am in danger of vanity, it is when I contemplate myself on this side of my disposition and character. God knows, I am no saint; I have a whole host of follies and sins to answer for; but if I could, and I believe I do it as far as I can, I would wipe away all tears from all eyes. Adieu! R. B.

NO. CXCVII.

TO MRS. DUNLOP.

Ellisland, April 10th, 1790.

I HAVE just now, my ever-honoured friend, enjoyed a very high luxury, in reading a paper of the Lounger. You know my national prejudices. I had often read and admired the Spectator, Adventurer, Rambler, and World; but still, with a certain regret that they were so thoroughly and entirely English. Alas! have I often said to myself, what are all the boasted advantages which my country reaps from the union, that can counterbalance the annihilation of her independence, and even her very name! I often repeat that couplet of my favourite poet, Goldsmith—

——— States, of native liberty possest,
Though very poor, may yet be very blest.

Nothing can reconcile me to the common terms, English ambassador, English court, &c. And I am out of all patience to see that equivocal character, Hastings, impeached by "the Commons of England." Tell me, my friend, is this weak prejudice? I believe, on my conscience, such ideas as—"my country, her independence, her honour, the illustrious names that mark the history of my native land," &c.—I believe these, among your *men of the world*,—men who, in fact, guide for the most part and govern our world,—are looked on as so many modifications of wrong-headedness. They know the use of bawling out such terms, to rouse or lead THE RABBLE; but for their own private use, with almost all the *able statesmen* that ever existed, or now exist, when they talk of right and wrong, they only mean proper and improper; and their measure of conduct is not what they OUGHT, but what they DARE. For the truth of this, I shall not ransack the history of nations, but appeal to one of the ablest judges of men that ever lived—the celebrated Earl of Chesterfield. In fact, a man who could thoroughly control his vices whenever they interfered with his interests, and who could completely put on the appearance of every virtue as often as it suited his purposes, is, on the Stanhopian plan, the *perfect man;* a man to lead nations. But are great abilities, complete without a flaw, and polished without a blemish, the standard of human excellence? This is certainly the staunch opinion of *men of the world;* but I call on honour, virtue, and worth, to give the Stygian doctrine a loud negative! However, this must be allowed, that, if you abstract from man the idea of an existence beyond the grave, *then* the true measure of human conduct is, *proper and improper;* virtue and vice, as dispositions of the heart, are, in that case, of scarcely the same import and value to the world at large, as harmony and discord in the modifications of sound; and a delicate sense of honour, like a nice ear for music, though it may sometimes give the possessor an ecstacy unknown to the coarser organs of the herd, yet, considering the harsh gratings, and inharmonic jars, in this ill-tuned state of being, it is odds but the individual would be as happy, and certainly would be as much respected, by the true judges of society as it would then stand, without either a good ear or a good heart.

You must know, I have just met with the Mirror and Lounger for the first time, and I am quite in raptures with them; I should be glad to have your opinion of some of the papers. The one I have just read, Lounger, No. 61, has cost me more honest tears than any thing I have read of a long time. (106) Mackenzie has been called the Addison of the Scots, and, in my opinion, Addison would not be hurt at the comparison. If he has not Addison's exquisite humour, he as certainly outdoes him in the tender and the pathetic. His Man of Feeling (but I am not counsel-learned in the laws of criticism) I estimate as the first performance in its kind I ever saw. From what book, moral or even pious, will the susceptible young mind receive impressions more congenial to humanity and kindness, generosity and benevolence—in short, more of all that ennobles the soul to herself, or endears her to others—than from the simple affecting tale of poor Harley?

Still, with all my admiration of Mackenzie's writings, I do not know if they are the fittest reading for a young man who is about to set out, as the phrase is, to make his way into life. Do not you think, Madam, that among the few favoured of Heaven in the structure of their minds (for such there certainly are), there may be a purity, a tenderness, a dignity, an elegance of soul, which are of no use, nay, in some degree, absolutely disqualifying, for the truly important business of making a man's way into life! If I am not much mistaken, my gallant young friend, A******, is very much under these disqualifications; and, for the young females of a family I could mention, well may they excite parental solicitude, for I, a common acquaintance, or as my vanity will have it, a humble friend, have often trembled for a turn of mind which may render them eminently happy, or peculiarly miserable!

I have been manufacturing some verses lately; but as I have got the most hurried season of Excise business over, I hope to have more leisure to transcribe any thing that may show how much I have the honour to be, Madam, yours, &c. R. B.

NO. CXCVIII.

TO COLLECTOR MITCHELL.

Ellisland, 1790.

SIR—I shall not fail to wait on Captain Riddel to-night—I wish and pray that the goddess of justice herself would appear to-morrow among our hon. gentlemen, merely to give them a word in their ear that mercy to the thief is injustice to the honest man. For my part, I have galloped over my ten parishes these four days, until this moment that I am just alighted, or rather, that my poor jackass-skeleton of a horse has let me down; for the miserable devil has been on his knees half a score of times within the last twenty miles, telling me, in his own way, "Behold, am not I thy faithful jade of a horse, on which thou hast ridden these many years!"

In short, Sir, I have broke my horse's wind, and almost broke my own neck, besides some injuries in a part that shall be nameless, owing to a hard-hearted stone of a saddle. I find that every offender has so many great men to espouse his cause, that I shall not be surprised if I am committed to the strong-hold of the law to-morrow for insolence to the dear friends of the gentlemen of the country. I have the honour to be, Sir, your obliged and obedient humble

R. B.

NO. CCXIX.

TO DR. MOORE.

Dumfries, Excise-Office, July 14th, 1790.

SIR—Coming into town this morning to attend my duty in this office, it being collection-day, I met with a gentleman who tells me he is on his way to London; so I take the opportunity of writing to you, as franking is at present under a temporary death. I shall have some snatches of leisure through the day, amid our horrid business and bustle, and I shall improve them as well as I can; but let my letter be as stupid as * * * *, as miscellaneous as a newspaper, as short as a hungry grace-before-meat, or as long as a law-paper in the Douglas cause; as ill-spelt as country John's billet-doux, or as unsightly a scrawl as Betty Byre-Mucker's answer to it; I hope, considering circumstances, you will forgive it; and as it will put you to no expense of postage, I shall have the less reflection about it.

I am sadly ungrateful in not returning you my thanks for your most valuable present, *Zeluco*. In fact, you are in some degree blameable for my neglect. You were pleased to express a wish for my opinion of the work, which so flattered me, that nothing less would serve my overweening fancy, than a formal criticism on the book. In fact, I have gravely planned a comparative view of you, Fielding, Richardson and Smollett, in your different qualities and merits as novel writers. This, I own, betrays my ridiculous vanity, and I may probably never bring the business to bear; but I am fond of the spirit young Elihu shows in the book of Job—"And I said, I will also declare my opinion." I have quite disfigured my copy of the book with my annotations. I never take it up without at the same time taking my pencil, and marking with asterisks, parentheses, &c., wherever I meet with an original thought, a nervous remark on life and manners, a remarkable, well-turned period, or a character sketched with uncommon precision.

Though I should hardly think of fairly writing out my "Comparative View," I shall certainly trouble you with my remarks, such as they are.

I have just received from my gentleman that horrid summons in the book of Revelation—"That time shall be no more!"

The little collection of sonnets have some charming poetry in them. If, *indeed*, I am indebted to the fair author for the book (107), and not, as I rather suspect, to a celebrated author of the other sex, I should certainly have written to the lady, with my grateful acknowledgments, and my own ideas of the comparative excellence of her pieces. I would do this last, not from any vanity of thinking that my remarks could be of much consequence to Mrs. Smith, but merely from my own feelings as an author, doing as I would be done by. R. B.

NO. CC.

TO MR. MURDOCH,

TEACHER OF FRENCH, LONDON.

Ellisland, July 16th, 1790.

MY DEAR SIR—I received a letter from you a long time ago, but, unfortunately, as it was in the time of my peregrinations and journeyings through Scotland, I mislaid or lost it, and, by consequence, your direction along with it. Luckily, my good star brought me acquainted with Mr. Kennedy, who, I understand is an acquaintance of yours: and by his means and mediation, I hope to replace that link which my unfortunate negligence had so unluckily broke in the chain of our correspondence. I was the more vexed at the vile accident, as my brother William, a journeyman saddler, has been for some time in London, and wished above all things for your direction, that he might have paid his respects to his father's friend.

His last address he sent to me was," Wm. Burns, at Mr. Barber's, saddler, No. 181, Strand." I writ him by Mr. Kennedy, but neglected to ask him for your address; so, if you find a spare half minute, please let my brother know by a card where and when he will find you, and the poor fellow will joyfully wait on you, as one of the few surviving friends of the man whose name, and Christian name too, he has the honour to bear.

The next letter I write you shall be a long one. I have much to tell you of "hair-breath 'scapes in th' imminent deadly breach," with all the eventful history of a life, the early years of which owed so much to your kind tutorage; but this at an hour of leisure. My kindest compliments to Mrs. Murdoch, and family. I am ever, my dear Sir, your obliged friend, R. B. (108)

NO. CCI.

TO MR. M'MURDO.

Ellisland, August 2nd, 1790.

Sir—Now, that you are over with the sirens of Flattery, the harpies of Corruption, and the furies of Ambition—these infernal deities, that on all sides, and in all parties, preside over the villainous business of politics—permit a rustic muse of your acquaintance to do her best to soothe you with a song.

You knew Henderson—I have not flattered his memory. I have the honour to be, Sir, your obliged humble servant,

R. B

NO. CCII.

TO MRS. DUNLOP.

August 8th, 1790.

Dear Madam—After a long day's toil, plague and care, I sit down to write to you. Ask me not why I have delayed it so long? It was owing to hurry, indolence, and fifty other things; in short, to anything but forgetfulness of *la plus aimable de son sexe*. By the bye, you are indebted your best courtesy to me for this last compliment, as I pay it from my sincere conviction of its truth—a quality rather rare in compliments of these grinning, bowing, scraping times.

Well, I hope writing to *you* will ease a little my troubled soul. Sorely has it been bruised to-day! A *ci-devant* friend of mine, and an intimate acquaintance of yours, has given my feelings a wound that I perceive will gangrene dangerously ere it cure. He has wounded my pride. R. B.

NO. CCIII.

TO MR. CUNNINGHAM.

Ellisland, August 8th, 1790.

Forgive me, my once dear, and ever dear friend, my seeming negligence. You cannot sit down and fancy the busy life I lead.

I laid down my goose feather to beat my brains for an apt simile, and had some thoughts of a country grannum at a family christening—a bride on the market-day before her marriage, or a tavern-keeper at an election dinner; but the resemblance that hits my fancy best is, that blackguard miscreant, Satan, who roams about like a roaring lion, seeking, *searching* whom he may devour. However, tossed about as I am, if I choose (and who would not choose?) to bind down with the crampets of attention the brazen foundation of integrity, I may rear up the superstructure of indépendence, and from its daring turrets bid defiance to the storms of fate. And is not this a "consummation devoutly to be wished?"

Thy spirit, Independence, let me share;
 Lord of the lion-heart, and eagle-eye!
Thy steps I follow with my bosom bare,
 Nor heed the storm that howls along the sky!

Are not these noble verses? They are the introduction of Smollett's Ode to Independence: if you have not seen the poem, I will send it to you. How wretched is the man that hangs on by the favours of the great! To shrink from every dignity of man, at the approach of a lordly piece of self-consequence, who, amid all his tinsel glitter and stately hauteur, is but a creature formed as thou art — and perhaps not so well formed as thou art—came into the world a puling infant as though didst, and must go out of it, as all men must, a naked corse. R. B. (109)

NO. CCIV.

TO DR. ANDERSON.

Sir—I am much indebted to my worthy friend, Dr. Blacklock, for introducing me to a gentleman of Dr. Anderson's celebrity; but when you do me the honour to ask my assistance in your proposed publication, alas, Sir! you might as well think to cheapen a little honesty at the sign of an advocate's wig, or humility under the Geneva band. I am a miserable hurried devil, worn to the marrow in the friction of holding the noses of the poor publicans to the grindstone of the Excise! and, like Milton's Satan, for private reasons, am forced

To do what yet though damn'd I would abhor.

—and, except a couplet or two of honest execration * * * *

R. B. (110)

NO. CCV.

TO CRAUFORD TAIT, Esq.,

EDINBURGH.

Ellisland, October 15*th*, 1790.

Dear Sir—Allow me to introduce to your acquaintance the bearer, Mr. Wm. Duncan, a friend of mine, whom I have long known and long loved. His father, whose only son he is, has a decent little property in Ayrshire, and has bred the young man to the law, in which department he comes up an adventurer to your good town. I shall give you my friend's character in two words: as to his head, he has talents enough, and more than enough, for common life; as to his heart, when nature had fashioned the kindly clay that composes it, she said, "I can no more."

You, my good Sir, were born under kinder stars; but your fraternal sympathy, I well know, can enter into the feelings of the young man who goes into life with the laudable ambition to *do* something, and to *be* something, among his fellow-creatures, but whom the consciousness of friendless obscurity presses to the earth, and wounds to the soul.

Even the fairest of his virtues are against him. That independent spirit, and that ingenuous modesty, qualities inseparable from a noble mind, are, with the million, circumstances not a little disqualifying. What pleasure is in the power of the fortunate and the happy, by their notice and patronage, to brighten the countenance and glad the heart of such depressed youth! I am not so angry with mankind for their deaf economy of the purse: the goods of this world cannot be divided without being lessened—but why be a niggard of that which bestows bliss on a fellow-creature, yet takes nothing from our own means of enjoyment? We wrap ourselves up in the cloak of our own better fortune, and turn away our eyes, lest the wants and woes of our brother mortals should disturb the selfish apathy of our souls!

I am the worst hand in the world at asking a favour. That indirect address, that insinuating implication, which, without any positive request, plainly expresses your wish, is a talent not to be acquired at a plough-tail. Tell me then, for you can, in what periphrasis of language, in what circumvolution of phrase, I shall envelope, yet not conceal, this plain story—"My dear Mr. Tait, my friend Mr. Duncan, whom I have the pleasure of introducing to you, is a young lad of your own profession, and a gentleman of much modesty and great worth. Perhaps, it may be in your power to assist him in the, to him, important consideration of getting a place, but, at all events, your notice and acquaintance will be a very great acquisition to him; and I dare pledge myself, that he will never disgrace your favour."

You may possibly be surprised, Sir, at such a letter from me; 'tis, I own, in the usual way of calculating these matters, more than our acquaintance entitles me to; but my answer is short:—of all the men at your time of life, whom I knew in Edinburgh, you are the most accessible on the side on which I have assailed you. You are very much altered, indeed, from what you were when I knew you, if generosity point the path you will not tread, or humanity call to you in vain.

As to myself, a being to whose interest I believe you are still a well-wisher, I am here, breathing at all times, thinking sometimes, and rhyming now and then. Every situation has its share of the cares and pains of life, and my situation, I am persuaded, has a full ordinary allowance of its pleasures and enjoyments.

My best compliments to your father and Miss Tait. If you have an opportunity, please remember me in the solemn-league-and-covenant of friendship to Mrs. Lewis Hay. I am a wretch for not writing her; but I am so hackneyed with self-accusation in that way, that my conscience lies in my bosom with scarce the sensibility of an oyster in its shell. Where is Lady M'Kenzie? wherever she is, God bless her! I likewise beg leave to trouble you with compliments to Mr. Wm. Hamilton, Mrs. Hamilton, and family, and Mrs. Chalmers, when you are in that country. Should you meet with Miss Nimmo, please remember me kindly to her.

R. B.

NO. CCVI.

TO DR. BLACKLOCK.

Ellisland, 1790.

DEAR SIR—Whether in the way of my trade, I can be of any service to the Rev. Doctor, is, I fear, very doubtful. Ajax's shield consisted, I think, of seven bull hides, and a plate of brass, which, altogether, set Hector's utmost force at defiance. Alas! I am not a Hector, and the worthy Doctor's foes are as securely armed as Ajax was. Ignorance, superstition, bigotry, stupidity, malevolence, self-conceit, envy—all strongly bound in a massy frame of brazen impudence. Good God, Sir! to such a shield, humour is the peck of a sparrow, and satire the pop-gun of a school-boy. Creation-disgracing scelerats such as they, God only can mend, and the devil only can punish. In the comprehensive way of Caligula, I wish they all had but one neck. I feel impotent as a child to the ardour of my wishes! Oh, for a withering curse to blast the germens of their wicked machinations. Oh, for a poisonous tornado, winged from the torrid zone of Tartarus, to sweep the spreading crop of their villanous contrivances to the lowest hell. R. B.

NO. CCVII.

TO MRS. DUNLOP. (111)

Ellisland, November, 1790.

"As cold waters to a thirsty soul, so is good news from a far country."

Fate has long owed me a letter of good news from you, in return for the many tidings of sorrow which I have received. In this instance, I most cordially obey the apostle—"Rejoice with them that do rejoice."—For me to *sing* for joy, is no new thing; but *to preach* for joy, as I have done in the commencement of this epistle, is a pitch of extravagant rapture to which I never rose before.

I read your letter—I literally jumped for joy. How could such a mercurial creature as a poet lumpishly keep his seat, on the receipt of the best news from his best friend. I seized my gilt-headed Wangee rod, an instrument indispensably necessary, in my left hand, in the moment of inspiration and rapture; and stride, stride—quick and quicker—out skipt I among the broomy banks of Nith to muse over my joy by retail. To keep within the bounds of prose was impossible. Mrs. Little's is a more elegant, but not a more sincere compliment to the sweet little fellow, than I, extempore almost, poured out to him in the following verses:—

Sweet flow'ret, pledge o' meikle love,
  And ward o' mony a prayer,
What heart o' stane wad thou na move,
  Sae helpless, sweet, and fair!

November hirples o'er the lea
  Chill on thy lovely form;
And gane, alas! the shelt'ring tree
  Should shield thee frae the storm.

May He, who gives the rain to pour,
  And wings the blast to blaw,
Protect thee frae the driving show'r,
  The bitter frost and snaw!

May He, the friend of woe and want,
  Who heals life's various stounds,
Protect and guard the mother-plant,
  And heal her cruel wounds!

But late she flourish'd, rooted fast,
  Fair on the summer morn;
Now, feebly bends she in the blast,
  Unshelter'd and forlorn.

Best be thy bloom, thou lovely gem,
  Unscath'd by ruffian hand!
And from thee many a parent stem
  Arise to deck our land!

I am much flattered by your approbation of my "Tam o' Shanter," which you express in your former letter; though, by the bye, you load me in that said letter with accusations heavy and many, to all which I plead *not guilty!* Your book is, I hear, on the road to reach me. As to printing of poetry, when you prepare it for the press, you have only to spell it right, and place the capital letters properly—as to the punctuation, the printers do that themselves.

I have a copy of "Tam o' Shanter" ready to send you by the first opportunity—it is too heavy to send by post.

I heard of Mr. Corbet (112) lately. He, in consequence of your recommendation, is most zealons to serve me. Please favour me soon with an account of your good folks; if Mrs. H. is recovering, and the young gentleman doing well. R. B.

NO. CCVIII.

TO CHARLES SHARPE, Esq.,

OF HODDAM, UNDER A FICTITIOUS SIGNATURE, ENCLOSING A BALLAD.

1791.

It is true, Sir, you are a gentleman of rank and fortune, and I am a poor devil—you are a feather in the cap of Society, and I am a very hobnail in his shoes; yet I have the honour to belong to the same family with you, and on that score I now address you. You will, perhaps, suspect that I am going to claim affinity with the ancient and honourable house of Kirkpatrick. No, no, Sir; I cannot indeed be properly said to belong to any house, or even any province or kingdom; as my mother, who for many years was spouse to a marching regiment, gave me into this bad world, aboard the packet-boat, somewhere between Donaghadee and Portpatrick. By our common family, I mean, Sir, the family of the muses. I am a fiddler and a poet; and you, I am told, play an exquisite violin, and have a standard taste in the *belles lettres*. The other day, a brother catgut gave me a charming Scots air of your composition. If I was pleased with the tune, I was in raptures with the title you have given it; and, taking up the idea, I have spun it into the three stanzas enclosed. Will you allow me, Sir, to present you them, as the dearest offering that a misbegotten son of poverty and rhyme has to give! I have a longing to take you by the hand and unburden my heart by saying,—"Sir, I honour you as a man who supports the dignity of human nature, amid an age when frivolity and avarice have, between them, debased us below the brutes that perish!" But, alas, Sir! to me you are unapproachable. It is true, the muses baptised me in Castalian streams; but the thoughtless gipsies forgot to give me a name. As the sex have served many a good fellow, the Nine have given me a great deal of pleasure; but, bewitching jades! they have beggared me. Would they but spare me a little of their cast-linen! were it only to put it in my power to say that I have a shirt on my back! But the idle wenches, like Solomon's lilies, "they toil not, neither do they spin;" so I must e'en continue to tie my remnant of a cravat, like the hangman's rope, round my naked throat, and coax my galligaskins to keep together their many-coloured fragments. As to the affair of shoes, I have given that up. My pilgrimages in my ballad-trade, from town to town, and on your stony-hearted turnpikes too, are what not even the hide of Job's behemoth could bear. The coat on my back is no more; I shall not speak evil of the dead. It would be equally unhandsome and ungrateful to find fault with my old surtout, which so kindly supplies and conceals the want of that coat. My hat, indeed, is a great favourite; and though I got it literally for an old song, I would not exchange it for the best beaver in Britain. I was, during several years, a kind of factotum servant to a country clergyman, where I picked up a good many scraps of learning, particularly in some branches of the mathematics. Whenever I feel inclined to rest myself on my way, I take my seat under a hedge, laying my poetic wallet on the one side, and my fiddle-case on the other, and, placing my hat between my legs, I can by means of its brim, or rather brims, go through the whole doctrine of the conic sections.

However, Sir, don't let me mislead you, as if I would interest your pity. Fortune has so much forsaken me, that she has taught me to live without her; and, amid all my rags and poverty, I am as independent, and much more happy, than a monarch of the world. According to the hackneyed metaphor, I value the several actors in the great drama of life, simply as they act their parts. I can look on a worthless fellow of a duke with unqualified contempt, and can regard an honest scavenger with sincere respect. As you, Sir, go through your rôle with such distinguished merit, permit me to make one in the chorus of universal applause, and assure you, that, with the highest respect, I have the honour to be, &c. (113) — * — *

NO. CCIX.

TO LADY W. M. CONSTABLE.

Ellisland, 11th January, 1791.

My Lady—Nothing less than the unlucky accident of having lately broken my right arm, could have prevented me, the moment I received your ladyship's elegant present (114) by Mrs. Miller, from returning you my warmest and most grateful acknowledgments. I assure your ladyship, I shall set it apart—the symbols of religion shall only be more sacred. In the moment of poetic composition, the box shall be my inspiring genius. When I would breathe the comprehensive wish of benevolence for the happiness of others, I shall recollect your ladyship; when I would interest my fancy in the distresses incident to humanity, I shall remember the unfortunate Mary

R. B.

NO. CCX.

TO WILLIAM DUNBAR, W. S.

Ellisland January 17th, 1791.

I AM not going to Elysium, most noble colonel (115), but am still here in this sublunary world, serving my God by propagating his image, and honouring my king by begetting him loyal subjects.

Many happy returns of the season await my friend. May the thorns of care never beset his path! May peace be an inmate of his bosom, and rapture a frequent visitor of his soul! May the blood-hounds of misfortune never track his steps, nor the screech-owl of sorrow alarm his dwelling! May enjoyment tell thy hours, and pleasure number thy days, thou friend of the bard! "Blessed be he that blesseth thee, and cursed be he that curseth thee!"

As a further proof that I am still in the land of existence, I send you a poem, the latest I have composed. I have a particular reason for wishing you only to show it to select friends, should you think it worthy a friend's perusal; but if, at your first leisure hour, you will favour me with your opinion of, and strictures on the performance, it will be an additional obligation on, dear Sir, your deeply indebted humble servant,

R. B.

NO. CCXI.

TO MR. PETER HILL.

Ellisland, January 17th, 1791.

TAKE these two guineas, and place them over against that damned account of yours, which has gagged my mouth these five or six months! I can as little write good things as apologies to a man I owe money to. Oh the supreme curse of making three guineas do the business of five! Not all the labours of Hercules; not all the Hebrews' three centuries of Egyptian bondage, were such an insuperable business, such an infernal task!! Poverty, thou half-sister of death, thou cousin-german of hell!—where shall I find force of execration equal to the amplitude of thy demerits? Oppressed by thee, the venerable ancient, grown hoary in the practice of every virtue, laden with years and wretchedness, implores a little, little aid to support his existence, from a stony-hearted son of Mammon, whose sun of prosperity never knew a cloud, and is by him denied and insulted. Oppressed by thee, the man of sentiment, whose heart glows with independence, and melts with sensibility, inwardly pines under the neglect, or writhes, in bitterness of soul, under the contumely of arrogant, unfeeling wealth. Oppressed by thee, the son of genius, whose ill-starred ambition plants him at the tables of the fashionable and polite, must see, in suffering silence, his remark neglected, and his person despised, while shallow greatness, in his idiot attempts at wit, shall meet with countenance and applause. Nor, is it only the family of worth that have reason to complain of thee:—the children of folly and vice, though in common with thee the offspring of evil, smart equally under thy rod. Owing to thee, the man of unfortunate disposition and neglected education, is condemned as a fool for his dissipation, despised and shunned as a needy wretch, when his follies as usual bring him to want; and when his unprincipled necessities drive him to dishonest practices, he is abhorred as a miscreant, and perishes by the justice of his country. But, far otherwise is the lot of the man of family and fortune.—*His* early follies and extravagance are spirit and fire;—*his* consequent wants are the embarrasments of an honest fellow; and when, to remedy the matter, he has gained a legal commission to plunder distant provinces, or massacre peaceful nations, he returns, perhaps, laden with the spoil of rapine and murder; lives wicked and respected, and dies a scoundrel and a lord. Nay, worst of all, alas for helpless woman! —the needy prostitute, who has shivered at the corner of the street, waiting to earn the wages of casual prostitution, is left neglected and insulted, ridden down by the chariot wheels of the coroneted RIP, hurrying on to the guilty assignation—she who, without the same necessities to plead, riots nightly in the same guilty trade.

Well! divines may say of it what they please; but execration is to the mind what phlebotomy is to the body—the vital sluices of both are wonderfully relieved by their respective evacuations. R. B.

NO. CCXII.

TO MR. CUNNINGHAM.

Ellisland Jan. 23d, 1791.

MANY happy returns of the season to you, my dear friend! As many of the good things of this life, as is consistent with the usual mixture of good and evil in the cup of being!

I have just finished a poem ("Tam o' Shanter"), which you will receive enclosed. It is my first essay in the way of tales.

I have these several months been hammering at an elegy on the amiable and accomplished Miss Burnet. I have got, and can get, no farther than the following fragment, on which please give me your strictures. In all kinds of poetic composition, I set great store by your opinion; but in sentimental verses, in the poetry of the heart, no Roman Catholic ever set more value on the infallibility of the Holy Father, than I do on yours. I mean the introductory couplets as text verses.

ELEGY ON THE LATE MISS BURNET OF MONBODDO.

Life ne'er exulted in so rich a prize,
As Burnet lovely from her native skies;
Nor envious death so triumph'd in a blow,
As that which laid th' accomplish'd Burnet low.—&c.

Let me hear from you soon. Adieu!
R. B.

NO. CCXIII.

TO A. F. TYTLER, ESQ. (116)

Ellisland, February 1791.

SIR—Nothing less than the unfortunate accident I have met with could have prevented my grateful acknowledgments for your letter. His own favourite poem, and that an essay in the walk of the muses entirely new to him, where consequently his hopes and fears were on the most anxious alarm for his success in the attempt—to have that poem so much applauded by one of the first judges, was the most delicious vibration that ever thrilled along the heart-strings of a poor poet However, Providence, to keep up the proper proportion of evil with the good, which it seems is necessary in this sublunary state, thought proper to check my exultation by a very serious misfortune. A day or two after I received your letter, my horse came down with me and broke my right arm. As this is the first service my arm has done me since its disaster, I find myself unable to do more than just, in general terms, thank you for this additional instance of your patronage and friendship. As to the faults you detected in the piece, they are truly there; one of them, the hit at the lawyer and priest, I shall cut out; as to the falling off in the catastrophe, for the reason you justly adduce, it cannot easily be remedied. Your approbation, Sir, has given me such additional spirits to persevere in this species of poetic composition, that I am already revolving two or three stories in my fancy. If I can bring these floating ideas to bear any kind of embodied form, it will give me an additional opportunity of assuring you how much I have the honour to be, &c. R. B.

NO. CCXIV.

TO ———.

Ellisland, 1791.

DEAR SIR—I am exceedingly to blame in not writing you long ago; but the truth is, that I am the most indolent of all human beings, and when I matriculate in the Herald's Office, I intend that my supporters shall be two sloths, my crest a slow-worm, and the motto, "Deil take the foremost." So much by way of apology for not thanking you sooner for your kind execution of my commission.

I would have sent you the poem; but somehow or other it found its way into the public papers, where you must have seen it. I am ever, dear Sir, yours sincerely,
R. B.

NO. CCXV.

TO THE REV. G. BAIRD. (117)

Ellisland, 1791.

REVEREND SIR—Why did you, my dear Sir, write to me in such a hesitating style, on the business of poor Bruce? Don't I know, and have I not felt, the many ills, the peculiar ills, that poetic flesh is heir to? You shall have your choice of all the unpublished poems I have; and had your letter had my direction so as to have reached me sooner (it only came to my hand this moment), I should have directly put you out of suspense on the subject. I only ask, that some prefatory advertisement in the book, as well as the subscription bills, may bear, that the publication is solely for the benefit of Bruce's mother. I would not put it in the power of ignorance to surmise, or malice to insinuate, that I clubbed a share in the work from mercenary motives. Nor need you give me credit for any remarkable generosity in my part of the business. I have such a host of peccadilloes, failings, follies, and backslidings (any body but myself might perhaps give some of them a worse appellation), that by way of some balance, however trifling, in the account, I am fain to do any good that occurs in my very limited power to a fellow creature, just for the selfish purpose of clearing a little the vista of retrospection. R. B

NO. CCXVI.

TO MRS. DUNLOP.

Ellisland, Feb. 7th, 1791.

When I tell you, Madam, that by a fall, not from my horse, but with my horse, I have been a cripple some time, and that this is the first day my arm and hand have been able to serve me in writing, you will allow that it is too good an apology for my seemingly ungrateful silence. I am now getting better, and am able to rhyme a little, which implies some tolerable ease, as I cannot think that the most poetic genius is able to compose on the rack.

I do not remember if ever I mentioned to you my having an idea of composing an elegy on the late Miss Burnet of Monboddo. I had the honour of being pretty well acquainted with her, and have seldom felt so much at the loss of an acquaintance, as when I heard that so amiable and accomplished a piece of God's work was no more. I have, as yet, gone no farther than the following fragment, of which please let me have your opinion. You know that elegy is a subject so much exhausted, that any new idea on the business is not to be expected: 'tis well if we can place an old idea in a new light. How far I have succeeded as to this last, you will judge from what follows :— * *

I have proceeded no farther.

Your kind letter, with your kind *remembrance* of your godson, came safe. This last, Madam, is scarcely what my pride can bear. As to the little fellow, he is, partiality apart, the finest boy I have for a long time seen. He is now seventeen months old, has the small-pox and measles over, has cut several teeth, and never had a grain of doctors' drugs in his bowels.

I am truly happy to hear that the "little flow'ret" is blooming so fresh and fair, and that the "mother plant" is rather recovering her drooping head. Soon and well may her "cruel wounds" be healed! I have written thus far with a good deal of difficulty. When I get a little abler, you shall hear farther from, Madam, yours, R. B.

NO. CCXVII.

TO THE REV. ARCH. ALISON.

Ellisland, near Dumfries,
Feb. 14th, 1791.

Sir—You must, by this time, have set me down as one of the most ungrateful of men. You did me the honour to present me with a book, which does honour to science and the intellectual powers of man, and I have not even so much as acknowledged the receipt of it. The fact is, you yourself are to blame for it. Flattered as I was by your telling me that you wished to have my opinion of the work, the old spiritual enemy of mankind, who knows well that vanity is one of the sins that most easily beset me, put it into my head to ponder over the performance with the look-out of a critic, and to draw up, forsooth, a deep learned digest of strictures on a composition, of which, in fact, until I read the book, I did not even know the first principles. I own, Sir, that at first glance several of your propositions startled me as paradoxical. That the martial clangor of a trumpet had something in it vastly more grand, heroic, and sublime, than the twingle twangle of a Jew's harp: that the delicate flexure of a rose-twig, when the half-blown flower is heavy with the tears of the dawn, was infinitely more beautiful and elegant than the upright stub of a burdock; and that from something innate and independent of all associations of ideas—these I had set down as irrefragable, orthodox truths, until perusing your book shook my faith. In short, Sir, except Euclid's Elements of Geometry, which I made a shift to unravel by my father's fireside, in the winter evenings of the first season I held the plough, I never read a book which gave me such a quantum of information, and added so much to my stock of ideas, as your "Essays on the Principles of Taste." One thing, Sir, you must forgive my mentioning as an uncommon merit in the work—I mean the language. To clothe abstract philosophy in elegance of style sounds something like a contradiction in terms; but you have convinced me that they are quite compatible.

I enclose you some poetic bagatelles of my late composition. The one in print is my first essay in the way of telling a tale.

I am, Sir, &c. R. B. (118)

NO. CCXVIII.

TO DR. MOORE.

Ellisland, Feb. 28th, 1791.

I DO not know, Sir, whether you are a subscriber to Grose's Antiquities of Scotland. If you are, the enclosed poem will not be altogether new to you. Captain Grose did me the favour to send me a dozen copies of the proof sheet, of which this is one. Should you have read the piece before, still this will answer the principal end I have in view—it will give me another opportunity of thanking you for all your goodness to the rustic bard; and also of showing you, that the abilities you have been pleased to commend and patronise are still employed in the way you wish.

The *Elegy on Captain Henderson* is a tribute to the memory of a man I loved much. Poets have in this the same advantage as Roman Catholics; they can be of service to their friends after they have passed that bourne where all other kindness ceases to be of avail. Whether, after all, either the one or the other be of any real service to the dead, is, I fear, very problematical, but I am sure they are highly gratifying to the living: and as a very orthodox text, I forget where in Scripture, says, "whatsoever is not of faith is sin;" so say I, whatsoever is not detrimental to society, and is of positive enjoyment, is of God, the giver of all good things, and ought to be received and enjoyed by his creatures with thankful delight. As almost all my religious tenets originate from my heart, I am wonderfully pleased with the idea, that I can still keep up a tender intercourse with the dearly beloved friend, or still more dearly beloved mistress, who is gone to the world of spirits.

The ballad on Queen Mary was begun while I was busy with Percy's Reliques of English Poetry. By the way, how much is every honest heart, which has a tincture of Caledonian prejudice, obliged to you for your glorious story of Buchanan and Targe! 'Twas an unequivocal proof of your loyal gallantry of soul, giving Targe the victory I should have been mortified to the ground if you had not.

I have just read over once more of many times, your Zeluco. I marked with my pencil, as I went along, every passage that pleased me particularly above the rest; and one or two, which, with humble deference, I am disposed to think unequal to the merits of the book. I have sometimes thought to transcribe these marked passages, or at least so much of them as to point where they are, and send them to you. Original strokes that strongly depict the human heart, is your and Fielding's province, beyond any other novelist I have ever perused. Richardson indeed might, perhaps, be excepted; but unhappily, his *dramatis personæ* are beings of another world; and however they may captivate the inexperienced, romantic fancy of a boy or a girl, they will ever, in proportion as we have made human nature our study, dissatisfy our riper years.

As to my private concerns, I am going on, a mighty tax-gatherer before the Lord, and have lately had the interest to get myself ranked on the list of Excise as a supervisor. I am not yet employed as such, but in a few years I shall fall into the file of supervisorship by seniority. I have had an immense loss in the death of the Earl of Glencairn, the patron from whom all my fame and fortune took its rise. Independent of my grateful attachment to him, which was indeed so strong that it pervaded my very soul, and was entwined with the thread of my existence: so soon as the prince's friends had got in (and every dog you know has his day), my getting forward in the Excise would have been an easier business than otherwise it will be. Though this was a consummation devoutly to be wished, yet, thank Heaven, I can live and rhyme as I am; and as to my boys, poor little fellows! if I cannot place them on as high an elevation in life as I could wish, I shall, if I am favoured so much by the Disposer of events as to see that period, fix them on as broad and independent a basis as possible. Among the many wise adages which have been treasured up by our Scottish ancestors, this is one of the best—*Better be the head o' the commonalty, than the tail o' the gentry.*

But I am got on a subject which, however interesting to me, is of no manner of consequence to you; so I shall give you a short poem on the other page, and close this with assuring you how sincerely I have the honour to be, yours, &c. R. B.

NO. CCXIX.

TO MRS. GRAHAM,

OF FINTRY.

Ellisland, 1791.

MADAM—Whether it is that the story of our Mary Queen of Scots has a peculiar effect on the feelings of a poet, or whether I have in the enclosed ballad succeeded beyond my usual poetic success, I know not; but it has pleased me beyond any effort of my muse for a good while past; on that account, I enclose it particularly to you. It is true, the purity of my motives may be suspected. I am already deeply indebted to Mr. Graham's goodness; and what, *in the usual ways of men,* is of infinitely greater importance, Mr. G. can do me service of the utmost importance in time to come. I was born a poor dog; and, however I may occasionally pick a better bone than I used to do, I know I must live and die poor: but I will indulge the flattering faith that my poetry will considerably outlive my poverty; and without any fustian affectation of spirit, I can promise and affirm, that it must be no ordinary craving of the latter shall ever make me do any thing injurious to the honest fame of the former. Whatever may be my failings—for failings are a part of human nature—may they ever be those of a generous heart and an independent mind! It is no fault of mine that I was born to dependence, nor is it Mr. Graham's chiefest praise that he can command influence: but it is his merit to bestow, not only with the kindness of a brother, but with the politeness of a gentleman; and I trust it shall be mine to receive with thankfulness, and remember with undiminished gratitude. R. B.

NO. CCXX.

TO MR. CUNNINGHAM.

Ellisland, March 12th, 1791.

IF the foregoing piece be worth your strictures, let me have them. For my own part, a thing that I have just composed always appears through a double portion of that partial medium in which an author will ever view his own works. I believe, in general, novelty has something in it that inebriates the fancy, and not unfrequently dissipates and fumes away like other intoxication, and leaves the poor patient, as usual, with an aching heart. A striking instance of this might be adduced, in the revolution of many a hymeneal honey-moon. But lest I sink into stupid prose, and so sacrilegiously intrude on the office of my parish priest, I shall fill up the page in my own way, and give you another song of my late composition, which will appear perhaps in Johnson's work, as well as the former.

You must know a beautiful Jacobite air, "There'll never be peace till Jamie comes hame." When political combustion ceases to be the object of princes and patriots, it then, you know, becomes the lawful prey of historians and poets.

"By yon castle wa', at the close of the day,
I heard a man sing, tho' his head it was grey;
And as he was singing, the tears fast down came—
There'll never be peace till Jamie comes hame," &c.

If you like the air, and if the stanzas hit your fancy, you cannot imagine, my dear friend, how much you would oblige me, if, by the charms of your delightful voice, you would give my honest effusion to "the memory of joys that are past," to the few friends whom you indulge in that pleasure. But I have scribbled on till I hear the clock has intimated the near approach of

"That hour, o' night's black arch the key-stane."

So, good night to you! Sound be your sleep, and delectable your dreams! A-propos, how do you like this thought in a ballad I have just now on the tapis?

I look to the west when I gae to rest,
That happy my dreams and my slumbers may be;
Far, far in the west is he I loe best,

The lad that is dear to my babie and
me!
Good night once more, and God bless
you! R. B.

NO. CCXXI.

TO MR. ALEXANDER DALZEL (119), FACTOR, FINDLAYSTON.

Ellisland, March 19th, 1791.

MY DEAR SIR—I have taken the liberty to frank this letter to you, as it encloses an idle poem of mine, which I send you; and, God knows, you may perhaps pay dear enough for it, if you read it through. Not that this is my own opinion: but the author, by the time he has composed and corrected his work, has quite pored away all his powers of critical discrimination.

I can easily guess, from my own heart, what you have felt on a late most melancholy event. God knows what I have suffered at the loss of my best friend, my first and dearest patron and benefactor; the man to whom I owe all that I am and have! I am gone into mourning for him, and with more sincerity of grief than I fear some will, who, by nature's ties, ought to feel on the occasion.

I will be exceedingly obliged to you, indeed, to let me know the news of the noble family, how the poor mother and the two sisters support their loss. I had a packet of poetic bagatelles ready to send to Lady Betty, when I saw the fatal tidings in the newspaper. I see, by the same channel, that the honoured REMAINS of my noble patron are designed to be brought to the family burial-place. Dare I trouble you to let me know privately before the day of interment, that I may cross the country, and steal among the crowd, to pay a tear to the last sight of my ever revered benefactor! It will oblige me beyond expression. R. B.

NO. CCXXII.

TO MRS. DUNLOP.

Ellisland, April 11th, 1791.

I AM once more able, my honoured friend, to return you with my own hand, thanks for the many instances of your friendship, and particularly for your kind anxiety in this last disaster that my evil genius had in store for me. However, life is chequered—joy and sorrow—for on Saturday morning last, Mrs. Burns made me a present of a fine boy; rather stouter, but not so handsome as your godson was at this time of life. Indeed, I look on your little namesake to be my *chef d'œuvre* in that species of manufacture, as I look on "Tam o' Shanter" to be my standard performance in the poetical line. 'Tis true, both the one and the other discover a spice of roguish waggery, that might perhaps be as well spared; but then they also show, in my opinion, a force of genius, and a finishing polish, that I despair of ever excelling. Mrs. Burns is getting stout again, and laid as lustily about her to-day at breakfast, as a reaper from the corn-ridge. That is the peculiar privilege and blessing of our hale, sprightly damsels, that are bred among the *hay and heather.* (120) We cannot hope for that highly polished mind, that charming delicacy of soul, which is found among the female world in the more elevated stations of life, and which is certainly by far the most bewitching charm in the famous cestus of Venus. It is indeed such an inestimable treasure, that where it can be had in its native heavenly purity, unstained by some one or other of the many shades of affectation, and unalloyed by some one or other of the many species of caprice, I declare to Heaven I should think it cheaply purchased at the expense of every other earthly good! But as this angelic creature is, I am afraid, extremely rare in any station and rank of life, and totally denied to such an humble one as mine, we meaner mortals must put up with the next rank of female excellence; as fine a figure and face we can produce as any rank of life whatever; rustic, native grace; unaffected modesty and unsullied purity; nature's mother-wit, and the rudiments of taste; a simplicity of soul, unsuspicious of, because unacquainted with, the crooked ways of a selfish, interested, disingenuous world; and the dearest charm of all the rest, a yielding sweetness of disposition, and a generous warmth of heart, grateful for love on our part, and ardently glowing with a more than equal return; these, with a healthy frame, a sound vigorous constitution, which your higher ranks can scarcely ever hope to enjoy, are the charms of lovely woman in my humble walk of life.

This is the greatest effort my broken arm has yet made. Do let me hear, by first post, how *cher petit Monsieur* (121) comes on with his small-pox. May Almighty goodness preserve and restore him! R. B.

NO. CCXXIII.

TO MR. CUNNINGHAM.

June 11th, 1791.

LET me interest you, my dear Cunningham, in behalf of the gentleman who waits on you with this. He is a Mr. Clarke, of Moffat, principal schoolmaster there, and is at present suffering severely under the persecution of one or two powerful individuals of his employers. He is accused of harshness to boys that were placed under his care. God help the teacher, if a man of sensibility and genius, and such is my friend Clarke, when a booby father presents him with his booby son, and insists on lighting up the rays of science in a fellow's head whose skull is impervious and inaccessible by any other way than a positive fracture with a cudgel—a fellow, whom, in fact, it savours of impiety to attempt making a scholar of, as he has been marked a blockhead in the book of fate, at the Almighty fiat of his Creator.

The patrons of Moffat-school are the ministers, magistrates, and town-council of Edinburgh, and as the business comes now before them, let me beg my dearest friend to do everything in his power to serve the interests of a man of genius and worth, and a man whom I particularly respect and esteem. You know some good fellows among the magistracy and council, but particularly you have much to say with a reverend gentleman, to whom you have the honour of being very nearly related, and whom this country and age have had the honour to produce. I need not name the historian of Charles V. (122) I tell him, through the medium of his nephew's influence, that Mr. Clarke is a gentleman who will not disgrace even his patronage. I know the merits of the cause thoroughly, and say it, that my friend is falling a sacrifice to prejudiced ignorance.

God help the children of dependence! Hated and persecuted by their enemies, and too often, alas! almost unexceptionably, received by their friends with disrespect and reproach, under the thin disguise of cold civility and humiliating advice. Oh! to be a sturdy savage, stalking in the pride of his independence, amid the solitary wilds of his deserts, rather than in civilized life helplessly to tremble for a subsistence, precarious as the caprice of a fellow-creature! Every man has his virtues, and no man is without his failings; and curse on that privileged plain-dealing of friendship, which, in the hour of my calamity, cannot reach forth the helping hand, without, at the same time, pointing out those failings, and apportioning them their share in procuring my present distress. My friends, for such the world calls ye, and such ye think yourselves to be, pass by my virtues if you please, but do, also, spare my follies—the first will witness in my breast for themselves, and the last will give pain enough to the ingenuous mind without you. And since deviating more or less from the paths of propriety and rectitude must be incident to human nature, do thou, Fortune, put it in my power, always from myself, and of myself, to bear the consequence of those errors! I do not want to be independent that I may sin, but I want to be independent in my sinning.

To return in this rambling letter to the subject I set out with, let me recommend my friend, Mr. Clarke, to your acquaintance and good offices; his worth entitles him to the one, and his gratitude will merit the other. I long much to hear from you. Adieu.

NO. CCXXIV.

TO THE EARL OF BUCHAN.

Ellisland, 1791.

MY LORD—Language sinks under the ardour of my feelings, when I would thank your lordship for the honour you have done me in inviting me to make one at the coronation of the bust of Thomson. In my first enthusiasm in reading the card you did me the honour to write me, I overlooked every obstacle, and determined to go; but I fear it will not be in my power. A week or two's absence in the very middle of my harvest, is what I much doubt I dare not venture on. I once already made a pilgrimage *up* the whole course of the Tweed, and fondly would I take the same delightful journey *down* the windings of that delightful stream.

Your lordship hints at an ode for the occasion; but who would write after Collins? I read over his verses to the memory of Thomson, and despaired. I got indeed to the length of three or four stanzas, in the way of address to the shade of the bard, on crowning his bust. I shall trouble your lordship with the subjoined copy of them, which, I am afraid, will be but too convincing a proof how unequal I am to the task. However, it affords me an opportunity of approaching your lordship, and declaring how sincerely and gratefully I have the honour to be, &c. R. B.

NO. CCXXV.

TO LADY E. CUNNINGHAM. (123)

My Lady—I would, as usual, have availed myself of the privilege your goodness has allowed me, of sending you anything I compose in my poetical way; but, as I have resolved, so soon as the shock of my irreparable loss would allow me, to pay a tribute to my late benefactor, I determined to make that the first piece I should do myself the honour of sending you. Had the wing of my fancy been equal to the ardour of my heart, the enclosed had been much more worthy your perusal: as it is, I beg leave to lay it at your ladyship's feet. (124) As all the world knows my obligations to the late Earl of Glencairn; I would wish to show, as openly, that my heart glows, and shall ever glow, with the most grateful sense and remembrance of his lordship's goodness. The sables I did myself the honour to wear to his lordship's memory, were not the "mockery of woe." Nor shall my gratitude perish with me! If, among my children, I shall have a son that has a heart, he shall hand it down to his child as a family honour, and a family debt, that my dearest existence I owe to the noble house of Glencairn!

I was about to say, my lady, that if you think the poem may venture to see the light, I would, in some way or other, give it to the world. R. B.

NO. CCXXVI.

TO MR. THOMAS SLOAN.

Ellisland, Sept. 1st, 1791.

My Dear Sloan—Suspense is worse than disappointment; for that reason, I hurry to tell you that I just now learn that Mr. Ballantine does not chose to interfere more in the business. I am truly sorry for it, but cannot help it.

You blame me for not writing you sooner, but you will please to recollect that you omitted one little necessary piece of information—your address.

However, you know equally well my hurried life, indolent temper, and strength of attachment. It must be a longer period than the longest life "in the world's bald and undegenerate days," that will make me forget so dear a friend as Mr. Sloan. I am prodigal enough at times, but I will not part with such a treasure as that.

I can easily enter into the *embarras* of your present situation. You know my favourite quotation from Young:—

"——— On reason build Resolve!
That column of true majesty in man."

And that other favourite one from Thomson's Alfred:—

"What proves the hero truly GREAT,
Is, never, never to despair."

Or, shall I quote you an author of your acquaintance?

"——Whether DOING, SUFFERING, OR FORBEARING,
You may do miracles—by PERSEVERING."

I have nothing new to tell you. The few friends we have are going on in the old way. I sold my crop on this day se'nnight, and sold it very well. A guinea an acre, on an average, above value. But such a scene of drunkenness was hardly ever seen in this country. After the roup was over, about thirty people engaged in a battle, every man for his own hand, and fought it out for three hours. Nor was the scene much better in the house. No fighting, indeed, but folks lying drunk on the floor, and decanting, until both my dogs got so drunk by attending them, that they could not stand. You will easily guess how I enjoyed the scene, as I was no farther off than you used to see me.

Mrs. B. and family have been in Ayrshire these many weeks.

Farewell! and God bless you, my dear friend! R. B

NO. CCXXVII.

TO COLONEL FULLARTON,

OF FULLARTON. (125)

Ellisland, Oct. 3rd, 1791.

Sir—I have just this minute got the frank, and next minute must send it to post, else I purposed to have sent you two or three other bagatelles that might have amused a vacant hour, about as well as "Six excellent new Songs," or the "Aberdeen prognostications for the year to come." (126) I shall probably trouble you soon with another packet, about the gloomy month of November, when the people of England hang and drown themselves—anything, generally, is better than one's own thoughts.

Fond as I may be of my own productions, it is not for their sake that I am so anxious to send you them. I am ambitious, covetously ambitious, of being known to a gentleman whom I am proud to call my countryman (127); a gentleman, who was a foreign ambassador as soon as he was a man; and a leader of armies as soon as he was a soldier; and that with an *eclât* unknown to the usual minions of a court—men who, with all the adventitious advantages of princely connections, and princely fortunes, must yet, like the caterpillar, labour a whole lifetime before they reach the wished-for height, there to roost a stupid chrysalis, and doze out the remaining glimmering existence of old age.

If the gentleman that accompanied you when you did me the honour of calling on me, is with you, I beg to be respectfully remembered to him. I have the honour to be, your highly obliged and most devoted humble servant, R. B.

NO. CCXXVIII.

TO MISS DAVIES. (128)

It is impossible, Madam, that the generous warmth and angelic purity of your youthful mind can have any idea of that moral disease under which I unhappily must rank as the chief of sinners; I mean a torpitude of the moral powers, that may be called a lethargy of conscience. In vain, Remorse rears her horrent crest, and rouses all her snakes: beneath the deadly fixed eye and leaden hand of Indolence, their wildest ire is charmed into the torpor of the bat, slumbering out the rigours of winter in the chink of a ruined wall. Nothing less, Madam, could have made me so long neglect your obliging commands. Indeed, I had one apology—the bagatelle was not worth presenting. Besides, so strongly am I interested in Miss Davies's fate and welfare in the serious business of life, amid its chances and changes, that to make her the subject of a silly ballad is downright mockery of these ardent feelings; 'tis like an impertinent jest to a dying friend.

Gracious Heaven! why this disparity between our wishes and our powers? Why is the most generous wish to make others blest, impotent and ineffectual, as the idle breeze that crosses the pathless desert? In my walks of life I have met with a few people to whom how gladly would I have said, "Go! be happy! I know that your hearts have been wounded by the scorn of the proud, whom accident has placed above you —or, worse still, in whose hands are perhaps placed many of the comforts of your life. But there! ascend that rock, Independence, and look justly down on their littleness of soul. Make the worthless tremble under your indignation, and the foolish sink before your contempt; and largely impart that happiness to others, which, I am certain, will give yourselves so much pleasure to bestow."

Why, dear Madam, must I wake from this delightful reverie, and find it all a dream? Why, amid my generous enthusiasm, must I find myself poor and powerless, incapable of wiping one tear from the eye of Pity, or of adding one comfort to the friend I love! Out upon the world! say I, that its affairs are administered so ill! They talk of reform; good Heaven! what a reform would I make among the sons, and even the daughters of men! Down, immediately should go fools from the high places where misbegotten chance has perked them up, and through life should they skulk, ever haunted by their native insignificance, as the body marches accompanied by its shadow. As for a much more formidable class, the knaves, I am at a loss what to do with them: had I a world, there should not be a knave in it.

But the hand that could give, I would liberally fill: and I would pour delight on the heart that could kindly forgive, and generously love.

Still, the inequalities of life are, among men, comparatively tolerable; but there is a delicacy, a tenderness, accompanying every view in which we can place lovely woman, that are grated and shocked at the rude, capricious distinctions of Fortune. Woman is the blood-royal of life: let there be slight degrees of precedency among them —but let them be ALL sacred. Whether this last sentiment be right or wrong, I am not accountable; it is an original component feature of my mind. R. B.

NO. CCXXIX.

TO MRS. DUNLOP.

Ellisland, December 17th, 1791

Many thanks to you, Madam, for your good news respecting the little floweret and the mother plant. I hope my poetic prayers have been heard, and will be answered up to the warmest sincerity of their fullest extent; and then Mrs. Henri will find her little darling the representative of his late parent, in every thing but his abridged existence.

I have just finished the following song, which, to a lady, the descendant of Wallace, and many heroes of his truly illustrious line—and herself the mother of several soldiers—needs neither preface nor apology.

[*Here follows the "Song of Death."*]

The circumstance that gave rise to the foregoing verses, was—looking over with a musical friend, M'Donald's collection of Highland airs, I was struck with one, an Isle of Skye tune, entitled "Oran an Aoig," or the "Song of Death," to the measure of which I have adapted my stanzas. I have, of late, composed two or three other little pieces, which, ere yon full-orbed moon, whose broad impudent face now stares at old mother earth all night, shall have shrunk into a modest crescent, just peeping forth at dewy dawn, I shall find an hour to transcribe to you. *A Dieu je vous commende.* R. B.

NO. CCXXX.

TO MR. AINSLIE.

Ellisland, 1791.

My dear Ainslie—Can you minister to a mind diseased?—can you, amid the horrors of penitence, regret, remorse, headache, nausea, and all the rest of the d—— hounds of hell, that beset a poor wretch who has been guilty of the sin of drunkenness—can you speak peace to a troubled soul?

Miserable perdu that I am, I have tried every thing that used to amuse me, but in vain: here must I sit, a monument of the vengeance laid up in store for the wicked, slowly counting every tick of the clock, as it slowly, slowly, numbers over these lazy scoundrels of hours, who, * * * *. are ranked up before me, every one following his neighbour, and every one with a burden of anguish on his back, to pour on my devoted head—and there is none to pity me. My wife scolds me, my business torments me, and my sins come staring me in the face, every one telling a more bitter tale than his fellow. When I tell you even * * * has lost its power to please, you will guess something of my hell within and all around me. I began *Elibanks and Elibraes,* but the stanzas fell unenjoyed and unfinished from my listless tongue: at last I luckily thought of reading over an old letter of yours, that lay by me, in my book-case, and I felt something, for for the first time since I opened my eyes, of pleasurable existence.——Well—I begin to breathe a little since I began to write to you? How are you, and what are you doing. How goes law? A-propos, for connexion's sake, do not address to me supervisor, for that is an honour I cannot pretend to; I am on the list, as we call it, for a supervisor, and will be called out, by and bye, to act as one; but at, present, I am a simple guager, tho' t'other day I got an appointment to an Excise division of £25 per annum better than the rest. My present income, down money, is £70 per annum.

I have one or two good fellows here, whom you would be glad to know.

R. B.

NO. CCXXXI.

TO ——.

Ellisland, 1791.

Thou eunuch of language; thou Englishman, who never was south the Tweed; thou servile echo of fashionable barbarisms; thou quack, vending the nostrums of empirical elocution; thou marriage-maker between vowels and consonants, on the Gretna Green of caprice; thou cobbler, botching the flimsy socks of bombast oratory; thou blacksmith, hammering the rivets of absurdity; thou butcher, embruing thy hands in the bowels of orthography; thou arch-heritic in pronunciation; thou pitch-pipe of affected emphasis; thou carpenter, mortising the awkward joints of jarring sentences; thou squeaking dissonance of cadence; thou pimp of gender; thou Lion Herald to silly etymology; thou antipode of grammar; thou executioner of construction; thou brood of the speech-distracting builders of the Tower of Babel; thou lingual confusion worse confounded; thou scape-gallows from the land of syntax; thou scavenger of mood and tense; thou murderous accoucheur of infant learning; thou *ignis fatuus,* misleading the steps of benighted ignorance; thou pickle-herring in the puppet-show of nonsense; thou faithful recorder of barbarous idiom; thou persecutor of syllabication; thou baleful meteor, foretelling and facilitating the rapid approach of Nox and Erebus. R. B.

NO. CCXXXII.

TO FRANCIS GROSE, Esq. F.S.A. (129)

Dumfries, 1792.

Sir—I believe among all our Scots literati you have not met with Professor Dugald Stewart, who fills the moral philosophy chair in the University of Edinburgh. To say that he is a man of the first parts, and, what is more, a man of the first worth, to a gentleman of your general acquaintance, and who so much enjoys the luxury of unencumbered freedom and undisturbed privacy, is not, perhaps, recommendation enough; but when I inform you that Mr. Stewart's principal characteristic is your favourite feature—*that* sterling independence of mind, which, though every man's right, so few men have the courage to claim, and fewer still the magnanimity to support: when I tell you, that unseduced by splendour, and undisgusted by wretchedness, he appreciates the merits of the various actors in the great drama of life, merely as they perform their parts—in short, he is a man after your own heart, and I comply with his earnest request in letting you know that he wishes above all things to meet with you. His house, Catrine, is within less than a mile of Sorn Castle, which you proposed visiting; or if you could transmit him the enclosed, he would, with the greatest pleasure, meet you any where in the neighbourhood. I write to Ayrshire to inform Mr. Stewart that I have acquitted myself of my promise. Should your time and spirits permit your meeting with Mr. Stewart, 'tis well; if not, I hope you will forgive this liberty, and I have, at least, an opportunity of assuring you with what truth and respect I am, Sir, your great admirer, and very humble servant, R. B.

NO. CCXXXIII.

TO MR. WILLIAM SMELLIE,

PRINTER.

Dumfries, January 22nd, 1792.

I sit down, my dear Sir, to introduce a young lady to you, and a lady in the first ranks of fashion, too. What a task! to you—who care no more for the herd of animals called young ladies, than you do for the herd of animals called young gentlemen. To you—who despise and detest the groupings and combinations of fashion, as an idiot painter that seems industrious to place staring fools and unprincipled knaves in the foreground of his picture, while men of sense and honesty are too often thrown in the dimmest shades. Mrs. Riddel (130), who will take this letter to town with her, and send it to you, is a character that, even in your own way, as a naturalist and a philosopher, would be an acquisition to your acquaintance. The lady, too, is a votary of the muses; and as I think myself somewhat of a judge in my own trade, I assure you that her verses, always correct, and often elegant, are much beyond the common run of the *lady-poetesses* of the day. She is a great admirer of your book (131); and hearing me say that I was acquainted with you, she begged to be known to you, as she is just going to pay her first visit to our Caledonian capital. I told her that her best way was, to desire her near relation, and your intimate friend, Craigdarroch, to have you at his house while she was there; and lest you might think of a lively West Indian girl of eighteen, as girls of eighteen too often deserve to be thought of, I should take care to remove that prejudice. To be impartial, however, in appreciating the lady's merits, she has one unlucky failing—a failing which you will easily discover, as she seems rather pleased with indulging in it—and a failing that you will easily pardon, as it is a sin which very much besets yourself—where she dislikes, or despises, she is apt to make no more a secret of it than where she esteems and respects.

I will not present you with the unmeaning *compliments of the season*, but I will send you my warmest wishes and most ardent prayers, that Fortune may never throw your subsistence to the mercy of a knave, or set your character on the judgment of a fool; but that, upright and erect, you may walk to an honest grave, where men of letters shall say, "Here lies a man who did honour to science," and men of worth shall say, "Here lies a man who did honour to human nature." R. B.

NO. CCXXXIV.

TO MR. WM. NICOL.

February 20th, 1792.

Oh, thou wisest among the wise, meridian blaze of prudence, full moon of discretion, and chief of many counsellors! (132) How infinitely is thy puddle-headed, rattle-headed, wrong-headed, round-headed slave indebted to thy super-eminent goodness, that, from the luminous path of thy own right-lined rectitude, thou lookest benignly down on an erring wretch, of whom the zig-zag wanderings defy all the powers of calculation, from the simple copulation of units, up to the hidden mysteries of fluxions! May one feeble ray of that light of wisdom which darts from thy sensorium, straight as the arrow of Heaven, and bright as the meteor of inspiration, may it be my portion, so that I may be less unworthy of the face and favour of that father of proverbs, and master of maxims, that antipode of folly, and magnet among the sages, the wise and witty Willie Nicol! Amen! Amen! Yea, so be it!

For me! I am a beast, a reptile, and know nothing! From the cave of my ignorance, amid the fogs of my dulness, and pestilential fumes of my political heresies, I look up to thee, as doth a toad through the iron-barred lucerne of a pestiferous dungeon, to the cloudless glory of a summer sun! Sorely sighing in bitterness of soul, I say, when shall my name be the quotation of the wise, and my countenance be the delight of the godly, like the illustrious lord of Laggan's many hills? (133) As for him, his works are perfect—never did the pen of calumny blur the fair page of his reputation, nor the bolt of hatred fly at his dwelling.

Thou mirror of purity, when shall the elfine lamp of my glimmerous understanding, purged from sensual appetites and gross desires, shine like the constellation of thy intellectual powers! As for thee, thy thoughts are pure, and thy lips are holy. Never did the unhallowed breath of the powers of darkness, and the pleasures of darkness, pollute the sacred flame of thy sky-descended and heaven-bound desires; never did the vapours of impurity stain the unclouded serene of thy cerulean imagination. Oh, that like thine were the tenor of my life, like thine the tenor of my conversation!—then should no friend fear for my strength, no enemy rejoice in my weakness! Then, should I lie down and rise up, and none to make me afraid. May thy pity and thy prayer be exercised for, oh thou lamp of wisdom and mirror of morality! thy devoted slave, R. B.

NO. CCXXXV.

TO FRANCIS GROSE, Esq., F.S.A.

Dumfries, 1792.

Among the many witch stories I have heard, relating to Alloway kirk, I distinctly remember only two or three.

Upon a stormy night, amid whistling squalls of wind, and bitter blasts of hail—in short, on such a night as the devil would choose to take the air in—a farmer, or farmer's servant, was plodding and plashing homeward with his plough-irons on his shoulder, having been getting some repairs on them at a neighbouring smithy. His way lay by the kirk of Alloway; and being rather on the anxious look-out in approaching a place so well known to be a favourite haunt of the devil, and the devil's friends and emissaries, he had been struck aghast, by discovering through the horrors of the storm and stormy night, a light, which on his nearer approach plainly showed itself to proceed from the haunted edifice. Whether he had been fortified from above, on his devout supplication, as is customary with people when they suspect the immediate presence of Satan, or whether, according to another custom, he had got courageously drunk at the smithy, I will not pretend to determine; but, so it was, that he ventured to go up to, nay, into the very kirk. As luck would have it, his temerity came off unpunished.

The members of the infernal junto were all out on some midnight business or other, and he saw nothing but a kind of kettle or caldron, depending from the roof, over the fire, simmering some heads of unchristened children, limbs of executed malefactors, &c., for the business of the night. It was, in for a penny, in for a pound, with the honest ploughman: so without ceremony he unhooked the caldron from off the fire, and, pouring out the damnable ingredients, inverted it on his head, and carried it fairly home, where it remained long in the family, a living evidence of the truth of the story.

Another story, which I can prove to be *equally authentic*, was as follows:—

On a market day in the town of Ayr, a farmer from Carrick, and consequently whose way lay by the very gate of Alloway kirk-yard, in order to cross the river Doon at the old bridge, which is about two or three hundred yards further on than the said gate, had been detained by his business, till by the time he reached Alloway it was the wizard hour, between night and morning.

Though he was terrified with a blaze streaming from the kirk, yet, as it is a well-known fact, that to turn back on these occasions is running by far the greatest risk of mischief, he prudently advanced on his road. When he had reached the gate of the kirk-yard, he was surprised and entertained. through the ribs and arches of an old Gothic window, which still faces the highway, to see a dance of witches merrily footing it round their old sooty blackguard master, who was keeping them all alive with the power of his bagpipe. The farmer, stopping his horse to observe them a little, could plainly descry the faces of many old women of his acquaintance and neighbourhood. How the gentleman was dressed, tradition does not say, but that the ladies were all in their smocks: and one, of them happening unluckily to have a smock which was considerably too short to answer all the purpose of that piece of dress, our farmer was so tickled, that he involuntarily burst out, with a loud laugh, "Weel luppen, Maggy wi' the short sark!" and recollecting, himself, instantly spurred his horse to the top of his speed. I need not mention the universally known fact, that no diabolical power can pursue you beyond the middle of a running stream. Lucky it was for the poor farmer that the river Doon was so near, for, notwithstanding the speed of his horse, which was a good one, against he reached the middle of the arch of the bridge, and, consequently, the middle of the stream, the pursuing, vengeful hags, were so close at his heels, that one of them actually sprang to seize him: but it was too late; nothing was on her side of the stream but the horse's tail, which immediately gave way at her infernal grip, as if blasted by a stroke of lightning; but the farmer was beyond her reach. However, the unsightly, tail-less condition of the vigorous steed, was, to the last hour of the noble creature's life, an awful warning to the Carrick farmers not to stay too late in Ayr markets.

The last relation I shall give, *though equally true*, is not so well identified as the two former, with regard to the scene; but as the best authorities give it for Alloway, I shall relate it.

On a summer's evening, about the time nature puts on her sables to mourn the expiry of the cheerful day, a shepherd boy, belonging to a farmer in the immediate neighbourhood of Alloway kirk, had just folded his charge, and was returning home. As he passed the kirk, in the adjoining field, he fell in with a crew of men and women, who were busy pulling stems of the plant Ragwort. He observed that as each person pulled a Ragwort, he or she got astride of it, and called out, "Up horsie!" on which the Ragwort flew off, like Pegasus, through the air with its rider. The foolish boy likewise pulled his Ragwort, and cried with the rest, "Up horsie!" and, strange to tell, away he flew with the company. The first stage at which the cavalcade stopt, was a merchant's wine cellar, in Bourdeaux, where, without saying, by your leave, they quaffed away at the best the cellar could afford, until the morning, foe to the imps and works of darkness, threatened to throw light on the matter, and frightened them from their carousals.

The poor shepherd lad, being equally a stranger to the scene and the liquor, heedlessly got himself drunk; and when the rest took horse, he fell asleep, and was found so next day by some of the people belonging to the merchant. Somebody that understood Scotch, asked him what he was, he said, such-a-one's herd in Alloway, and, by some means or other, getting home again, he lived long to tell the world the wondrous tale. R. B. (134)

NO. CCXXXVI.

TO MR. J. CLARKE,

EDINBURGH.

July 16th, 1792.

MR. BURNS begs leave to present his most respectful compliments to Mr. Clarke. Mr. B. some time ago did himself the honour of writing Mr. C. respecting coming out to the country, to give a little musical instruction in a highly respectable family, where Mr. C. may have his own terms, and may be as happy as indolence, the devil, and the gout, will permit him. Mr. B. knows well how Mr. C. is engaged with another family; but, cannot Mr. C. find two or three weeks to spare to each of them? Mr. B. is deeply impressed with, and awfully conscious of, the high importance of Mr. C.'s time; whether in the winged moments of symphonious exhibition, at the keys of harmony, while listening seraphs cease their own less delightful strains; or, in the drowsy arms of slumb'rous repose, in the arms of his dearly beloved elbow chair, where the frowsy, but potent power of indolence, circumfuses her vapours round, and sheds her dews on the head of her darling son. But half a line, conveying half a meaning from Mr. C., would make Mr. B. the happiest of mortals. R. B.

NO. CCXXXVII.

TO MRS. DUNLOP.

Annan Water-foot, August 22nd, 1792.

Do not blame me for it, Madam—my own conscience, hackneyed and weather-beaten as it is, in watching and reproving my vagaries, follies, indolence, &c., has continued to punish me sufficiently.

Do you think it possible, my dear and honoured friend, that I could be so lost to gratitude for many favours, to esteem for much worth, and to the honest, kind, pleasurable tie of, now old acquaintance,—and I hope, and am sure, of progressive, increasing friendship—as for a single day, not to think of you—to ask the Fates what they are doing, and about to do, with my much-loved friend and her wide scattered connexion, and to beg of them to be as kind to you and yours as they possibly can?

A-propos! (though how it is a-propos, I have not leisure to explain), do you know that I am almost in love with an acquaintance of yours? Almost! said I—I am in love, souce, over head and ears, deep as the most unfathomable abyss of the boundless ocean!—but the word love, owing to the *intermingledoms* of the good and the bad, the pure and the impure, in this world, being rather an equivocal term for expressing one's sentiments and sensations, I must do justice to the sacred purity of my attachment. Know, then, that the heart-struck awe; the distant humble approach; the delight we should have in gazing upon and listening to a messenger of Heaven, appearing in all the unspotted purity of his celestial home, among the coarse, polluted, far inferior sons of men, to deliver to them tidings that make their hearts swim in joy, and their imaginations soar in transport—such, so delighting and so pure, were the emotions of my soul, on meeting the other day with Miss Lesley Baillie, your neighbour, at M——'s. Mr. B., with his two daughters, accompanied by Mr. H. of G., passing through Dumfries a few days ago, on their way to England, did me the honour of calling on me; on which I took my horse (though, God knows, I could ill spare the time), and accompanied them fourteen or fifteen miles, and dined and spent the day with them. 'Twas about nine, I think, when I left them, and, riding home, I composed the following ballad, of which you will probably think you have a dear bargain, as it will cost you another groat of postage. You must know that there is an old ballad beginning with:—

> My bonnie Lizzie Baillie,
> I'll rowe thee in my plaidie, &c.

So I parodied it as follows, which is literally the first copy, "unanointed, unannealed," as Hamlet says:—

> Oh saw ye bonnie Lesley, &c.

So much for ballads. I regret that you are gone to the east country, as I am to be in Ayrshire in about a fortnight. This world of ours, notwithstanding it has many good things in it, yet it has ever had this curse, that two or three people, who would be the happier the oftener they met together, are, almost without exception, always so placed as never to meet but once or twice a-year, which, considering the few years of a man's life, is a very great "evil under the sun," which I do not recollect that Solomon has mentioned in his catalogue of the miseries of man. I hope, and believe, that there is a state of existence beyond the grave, where the worthy of this life will renew their former intimacies, with this endearing addition, that "we meet to part no more!"

> Tell us, ye dead,
> Will none of you in pity disclose the secret
> What 'tis you are, and we must shortly be?

A thousand times have I made this apostrophe to the departed sons of men, but not one of them has ever thought fit to answer the question. "Oh that some courteous ghost would blab it out!" But it cannot be; you and I, my friend, must make the experiment by ourselves, and for ourselves. However, I am so convinced that an unshaken faith in the doctrines of religion is not only necessary, by making us better men, but also by making us happier men, that I should take every care that your little godson, and every little creature that shall call me father, shall be taught them.

So ends this heterogeneous letter, written at this wild place of the world, in the intervals of my labour of discharging a vessel of rum from Antigua. R. B.

NO. CCXXXVIII.

TO MR. CUNNINGHAM.

Dumfries, Sept. 10th, 1792.

No! I will not attempt an apology. Amid all my hurry of business, grinding the faces of the publican and the sinner on the merciless wheels of the Excise; making ballads, and then drinking, and singing them; and, over and above all, the correcting the press-work of two different publications; still, still I might have stolen five minutes to dedicate to one of the first of my friends and fellow-creatures. I might have done, as I do at present, snatched an hour near "witching time of night," and scrawled a page or two. I might have congratulated my friend on his marriage; or I might have thanked the Caledonian archers for the honour they have done me (though, to do myself justice, I intended to have done both in rhyme, else I had done both long ere now.) Well, then, here is to your good health!—for you must know, I have set a nipperkin of toddy by me, just by way of spell, to keep away the meikle horned deil, or any of his subaltern imps, who may be on their nightly rounds.

But what shall I write to you? "The voice said, Cry," and I said, "What shall I cry?" Oh, thou spirit! whatever thou art, or wherever thou makest thyself visible! Be thou a bogle by the eerie side of an auld thorn, in the dreary glen through which the herd-callan maun bicker in his gloamin route frae the fauld! Be thou a brownie, set, at dead of night, to thy task by the blazing ingle, or in the solitary barn, where the repercussions of thy iron flail half affright thyself, as thou performest the work of twenty of the sons of men, ere the cock-crowing summon thee to thy ample cog of substantial brose. Be thou a kelpie, haunting the ford or ferry, in the starless night, mixing thy laughing yell with the howling of the storm and the roaring of the flood, as thou viewest the perils and miseries of man on the foundering horse, or in the tumbling boat! Or, lastly, be thou a ghost, paying thy nocturnal visits to the hoary ruins of decayed grandeur; or performing thy mystic rites in the shadow of the time-worn church, while the moon looks, without a cloud, on the silent, ghastly dwellings of the dead around thee, or, taking thy stand by the bedside of the villain, or the murderer, portraying on his dreaming fancy, pictures, dreadful as the horrors of unveiled hell, and terrible as the wrath of incensed Deity! Come, thou spirit, but not in these horrid forms; come with the milder, gentle, easy inspirations, which thou breathest round the wig of a prating advocate, or the tête of a tea-sipping gossip, while their tongues run at the light-horse gallop of clishmaclaver for ever and ever—come, and assist a poor devil who is quite jaded in the attempt to share half an idea among half a hundred words; to fill up four quarto pages, while he has not got one single sentence of recollection, information, or remark, worth putting pen to paper for.

* * * * * *

A-propos, how do you like—I mean *really* like—the married life? Ah, my friend! matrimony is quite a different thing from what your love-sick youths and sighing girls take it to be! But marriage, we are told, is appointed by God, and I shall never quarrel with any of his institutions. I am a husband of older standing than you, and shall give you *my* ideas of the conjugal state (*en passant;* you know I am no Latinist, is not *conjugal* derived from *jugum*, a yoke!) Well, then, the scale of good wifeship I divide into ten parts. Good-nature, four; Good Sense, two; Wit, one; Personal Charms, viz. a sweet face, eloquent eyes, fine limbs, graceful carriage (I would add a fine waist too, but that is soon spoilt you know), all these, one; as for the other qualities belonging to, or attending on, a wife, such as Fortune, Connections, Education (I mean education extraordinary), Family blood, &c., divide the two remaining degrees among them as you please; only, remember, that all these minor properties must be expressed by *fractions*, for there is not any one of them, in the aforesaid scale, entitled to the dignity of an *integer*.

As for the rest of my fancies and reveries—how I lately met with Miss Lesley Baillie, the most beautiful, elegant woman in the world—how I accompanied her and her father's family fifteen miles on their journey, out of pure devotion, to admire the loveliness of the works of God, in such an unequalled display of them—how, in galloping home at night, I made a ballad on her, of which these two stanzas make a part—

Thou, bonnie Lesley, art a queen,
  Thy subjects we before thee;
Thou, bonnie Lesley, art divine,
  The hearts o' men adore thee.

The very deil he could na scathe
  Whatever wad belang thee!
He'd look into thy bonnie face
  And say, 'I canna wrang thee'—

Behold all these things are written in the chronicles of my imagination, and shall be read by thee, my dear friend, and by thy beloved spouse, my other dear friend, at a more convenient season.

Now, to thee, and to thy before-designed *bosom*-companion, be given the precious things brought forth by the sun, and the precious things brought forth by the moon, and the benignest influences of the stars, and the living streams which flow from the fountains of life, and by the tree of life, for ever and ever! Amen! R. B.

NO. CCXXXIX.

MR. THOMSON (135) TO BURNS.

Edinburgh, September 1792.

Sir—For some years past I have, with a friend or two, employed many leisure hours in selecting and collating the most favourite of our national melodies for publication. We have engaged Pleyel, the most agreeable composer living, to put accompaniments to these, and also to compose an instrumental prelude and conclusion to each air, the better to fit them for concerts, both public and private. To render this work perfect, we are desirous to have the poetry improved, wherever it seems unworthy of the music; and that it is so in many instances, is allowed by every one conversant with our musical collections. The editors of these seem, in general, to have depended on the music proving an excuse for the verses; and hence, some charming melodies are united to mere nonsense and doggrel, while others are accommodated with rhymes so loose and indelicate, as cannot be sung in decent company. To remove this reproach would be an easy task to the author of the "Cotter's Saturday Night;" and, for the honour of Caledonia, I would fain hope he may be induced to take up the pen. If so, we shall be enabled to present the public with a collection, infinitely more interesting than any that has yet appeared, and acceptable to all persons of taste, whether they wish for correct melodies, delicate accompaniments, or characteristic verses. We will esteem your poetical assistance a particular favour, besides, paying any reasonable price you shall please to demand for it. Profit is quite a secondary consideration with us, and we are resolved to spare neither pains nor expense on the publication. Tell me, frankly, then, whether you will devote your leisure to writing twenty or twenty-five songs, suited to the particular melodies which I am prepared to send you. A few songs, exceptionable only in some of their verses, I will likewise submit to your consideration; leaving it to you, either to mend these, or make new songs in their stead. It is superfluous to assure you that I have no intention to displace any of the sterling old songs; those only will be removed which appear quite silly or absolutely indecent. Even these shall be all examined by Mr. Burns, and if he is of opinion that any of them are deserving of the music, in such cases no divorce shall take place. G. Thomson.

NO. CCXL.

BURNS TO MR. THOMSON.

Dumfries, Sept. 16th, 1792.

Sir—I have just this moment got your letter. As the request you make to me will positively add to my enjoyments in complying with it, I shall enter into your undertaking with all the small portion of abilities I have, strained to their utmost exertion by the impulse of enthusiasm. Only, don't hurry me:—"Deil tak the hindmost" is by no means the *cri de guerre* of my muse. Will you, as I am inferior to none of you in enthusiastic attachment to the poetry and music of old Caledonia, and, since you request it, have cheerfully promised my mite of assistance—will you let me have a list of your airs with the first line of the printed verses you intend for them, that I may have an opportunity of suggesting any alteration that may occur to me? You know 'tis in the way of my trade; still leaving you, gentlemen, the undoubted right of publishers to approve or reject, at your pleasure, for your own publication. A-propos, if you are for English verses, there is, on my part, an end of the matter. Whether in the simplicity of the ballad, or the pathos of the song, I can only hope to please myself in being allowed at least a sprinkling of our native tongue. English verses, particularly the works of Scotsmen, that have merit, are certainly very eligible. "Tweedside!" "Ah! the poor shepherd's mournful fate!" "Ah! Chloris, could I now but sit," &c., you cannot mend; but such insipid stuff as "To Fanny fair could I impart," &c., usually set to "The Mill, Mill, O!" is a disgrace to the collections in which it has already appeared, and would doubly disgrace a collection that will have the very superior merit of yours. But more of this in the further prosecution of the business, if I am called on for my strictures and amendments—I say amendments, for I will not alter except where I myself, at least, think that I amend.

As to any remuneration, you may think my songs either above or below price; for they shall absolutely be the one or the other. In the honest enthusiasm with which I embark in your undertaking, to talk of money, wages, fee, hire, &c., would be downright prostitution (136) of soul! A proof of each of the songs that I compose or amend, I shall receive as a favour. In the rustic phrase of the season, "Gude speed the wark!" I am, Sir, your very humble servant, R. BURNS.

NO. CCXLI.

TO MRS. DUNLOP.

Dumfries, Sept. 24th, 1792.

I HAVE this moment, my dear Madam, yours of the 23rd. All your other kind reproaches, your news, &c., are out of my head, when I read and think on Mrs. Henri's situation. Good God! a heart-wounded helpless young woman—in a strange, foreign land, and that land convulsed with every horror that can harrow the human feelings—sick—looking, longing for a comforter, but finding none—a mother's feelings, too—but it is too much: he who wounded (he only can) may He heal!

I wish the farmer great joy of his new acquisition to his family. * * * * * * I cannot say that I give him joy of his life as a farmer. 'Tis, as a farmer, paying a dear, unconscionable rent, a *cursed life!* As to a laird farming his own property; sowing his own corn in hope; and reaping it, in spite of brittle weather, in gladness; knowing that none can say unto him, "What dost thou?"—fattening his herds; shearing his flocks; rejoicing at Christmas; and begetting sons and daughters, until he be the venerated, grey-haired leader of a little tribe—'tis a heavenly life! but devil take the life of reaping the fruits that another must eat.

Well, your kind wishes will be gratified, as to seeing me when I make my Ayrshire visit. I cannot leave Mrs. B. until her nine months' race is run, which may, perhaps, be in three or four weeks. She, too, seems determined to make me the patriarchal leader of a band. However, if Heaven will be so obliging as to let me have them in the proportion of three boys to one girl I shall be so much the more pleased. I hope, if I am spared with them, to show a set of boys that will do honour to my cares and name; but I am not equal to the task of rearing girls. Besides, I am too poor—a girl should always have a fortune. A-propos, your little godson is thriving charmingly, but is a very devil. He, though two years younger, has completely mastered his brother. Robert is indeed the mildest, gentlest, creature I ever saw. He has a most surprising memory, and is quite the pride of his schoolmaster.

You know how readily we get into prattle upon a subject dear to our heart—you can excuse it. God bless you and yours!

R. B.

NO. CCXLII.

TO THE SAME.

I HAD been from home, and did not receive your letter until my return the other day. What shall I say to comfort you, my much-valued, much-afflicted friend! I can but grieve with you; consolation I have none to offer, except that which religion holds out to the children of affliction—(*children of affliction!*—how just the expression!)—and like every other family, they have matters among them which they hear, see, and feel in a serious, all-important manner, of which the world has not, nor cares to have, any idea. The world looks indifferently on, makes the passing remark, and proceeds to the next novel occurrence.

Alas, Madam! who would wish for many years? What is it but to drag existence until our joys gradually expire, and leave us in a night of misery—like the gloom which blots out the stars, one by one, from the face of night, and leaves us, without a ray of comfort, in the howling waste!

I am interrupted, and must leave off. You shall soon hear from me again.

R. B.

NO. CCXLIII.

MR. THOMSON TO BURNS.

Edinburgh, Oct. 13th, 1792.

DEAR SIR—I received with much satisfaction your pleasant and obliging letter and,

I return my warmest acknowledgments for the enthusiasm with which you have entered into our undertaking. We have now no doubt of being able to produce a collection highly deserving of public attention in all respects.

I agree with you in thinking English verses, that have merit, very eligible, where-ever new verses are necessary, because the English becomes every year, more and more, the language of Scotland; but, if you mean that no English verses, except those by Scottish authors, ought to be admitted, I am half inclined to differ from you. I should consider it unpardonable to sacrifice one good song in the Scottish dialect, to make room for English verses; but if we can select a few excellent ones suited to the unprovided or ill-provided airs, would it not be the very bigotry of literary patriotism to reject such, merely because the authors were born south of the Tweed? Our sweet air, "My Nannie, O!" which in the collections is joined to the poorest stuff that Allan Ramsay ever wrote, beginning—"While some for pleasure pawn their health," answers so finely to Dr. Percy's beautiful song, "Oh Nancy, wilt thou go with me?" that one would think he wrote it on purpose for the air. However, it is not at all our wish to confine you to English verses; you shall freely be allowed a sprinkling of your native tongue, as you elegantly express it; and, moreover, we will patiently wait your own time. One thing only I beg, which is, that however gay and sportive the muse may be, she may always be decent. Let her not write what beauty would blush to speak, nor wound that charming delicacy which forms the most precious dowry of our daughters. I do not conceive the song to be the most proper vehicle for witty and brilliant conceits; simplicity, I believe, should be its prominent feature: but, in some of our songs, the writers have confounded simplicity with coarseness and vulgarity; although between the one and the other, as Dr. Beattie well observes, there is as great a difference as between a plain suit of clothes and a bundle of rags. The humorous ballad, or pathetic complaint, is best suited to our artless melodies; and more interesting, indeed, in all songs, than the most pointed wit, dazzling descriptions, and flowery fancies.

With these trite observations, I send you eleven of the songs, for which it is my wish to substitute others of your writing. I shall soon transmit the rest, and, at the same time, a prospectus of the whole collection; and, you may believe, we will receive any hints that you are so kind as to give for improving the work, with the greatest pleasure and thankfulness. I remain, dear Sir, &c.

NO. CCXLIV.

BURNS TO MR. THOMSON,

My Dear Sir—Let me tell you, that you are too fastidious in your ideas of songs and ballads, I own that your criticisms are just; the songs you specify in your list have, all but one, the faults you remark in them; but who shall mend the matter? Who shall rise up and say, "Go to! I will make a better?" For instance, on reading over "The Lea-rig," I immediately set about trying my hand on it, and, after all, I could make nothing more of it than the following, which Heaven knows, is poor enough.

[*Here follow the two first stanzas of "My ain kind dearie O!"*]

Your observation as to the aptitude of Dr. Percy's ballad to the air, "Nannie, O!" is just. It is besides, perhaps, the most beautiful ballad in the English language. But let me remark to you, that in the sentiment and style of our Scottish airs, there is a pastoral simplicity, a something that one may call the Doric style and dialect of vocal music, to which a dash of our native tongue and manners is particularly, nay, peculiarly apposite. For this reason, and, upon my honour, for this reason alone, I am of opinion (but, as I told you before, my opinion is yours, freely yours, to approve or reject, as you please) that my ballad of "Nannie, O!" might perhaps do for one set of verses to the tune. Now don't let it enter into your head, that you are under any necessity of taking my verses. I have long ago made up my mind as to my own reputation in the business of authorship, and have nothing to be pleased or offended at, in your adoption or rejection of my verses. Though you should reject one half of what I give you, I shall be pleased with your adopting the other half, and shall continue to serve you with the same assiduity.

In the printed copy of my "Nannie, O!" the name of the river is horridly prosaic. I will alter it:

"Behind yon hills where Lugar flows."

Girvan is the name of the river that suits

the idea of the stanza best, but Lugar is the most agreeable modulation of syllables.

I will soon give you a great many more remarks on this business; but I have just now an opportunity of conveying you this scrawl, free of postage, an expense that it is ill able to pay; so, with my best compliments to honest Allan, Gude be wi' ye, &c.

Friday Night.

Saturday Morning.

As I find I have still an hour to spare this morning before my conveyance goes away, I will give you "Nannie, O!" at length.

Your remarks on "Ewe-bughts, Marion," are just; still it has obtained a place among our more classical Scottish songs; and what with many beauties in its composition, and more prejudices in its favour, you will not find it easy to supplant it.

In my very early years, when I was thinking of going to the West Indies, I took the following farewell of a dear girl. It is quite trifling, and has nothing of the merits of "Ewe-bughts;" but it will fill up this page. You must know that all my earlier love-songs were the breathings of ardent passion, and though it might have been easy in after-times to have given them a polish, yet that polish, to me, whose they were, and who perhaps alone cared for them, would have defaced the legend of my heart, which was so faithfully inscribed on them. Their uncouth simplicity was, as they say of wines, their race.

[*Here follows the song "Will ye go to the Indies, my Mary?" Mr. Thomson did not adopt the song in his collection.*]

"Gala Water," and "Auld Rob Morris," I think, will most probably be the next subject of my musings. However, even on my verses, speak out your criticisms with equal frankness. My wish is, not to stand aloof, the uncomplying bigot of *opiniâtreté*, but cordially to join issue with you in the furtherance of the work.

NO. CCXLV.

BURNS TO MR. THOMSON.

November 8th, 1792.

If you mean, my dear Sir, that all the songs in your collection shall be poetry of the first merit, I am afraid you will find more difficulty in the undertaking than you are aware of. There is a peculiar rhythmus in many of our airs, and a necessity of adapting syllables to the emphasis, or what I would call the feature-notes of the tune, that cramp the poet, and lay him under almost insuperable difficulties. For instance, in the air, "My wife's a wanton wee thing," if a few lines smooth and pretty can be adapted to it, it is all you can expect. The following were made extempore to it; and though, on further study, I might give you something more profound, yet it might not suit the light-horse gallop of the air so well as this random clink:—

[*Here follows "My Wife's a winsome wee thing."*]

I have just been looking over the "Collier's bonnie dochter;" and if the following rhapsody, which I composed the other day, on a charming Ayrshire girl, Miss Lesley Baillie, as she passed through this place to England, will suit your taste better than the "Collier Lassie," fall on and welcome:—

[*Here follows "Bonnie Lesley."*]

I have hitherto deferred the sublimer, more pathetic airs, until more leisure, as they will take, and deserve, a greater effort. However, they are all put into your hands, as clay into the hands of the potter, to make one vessel to honour, and another to dishonour. Farewell, &c.

NO. CCXLVI.

BURNS TO MR. THOMSON.

November 14th, 1792.

My Dear Sir—I agree with you that the song, "Katharine Ogie," is very poor stuff, and unworthy, altogether unworthy, of so beautiful an air. I tried to mend it; but the awkward sound, Ogie, recurring so often in the rhyme, spoils every attempt at introducing sentiment into the piece. The foregoing song pleases myself; I think it is in my happiest manner: you will see at first glance that it suits the air. The subject of the song is one of the most interesting passages of my youthful days, and I own that I should be much flattered to see the verses set to an air which would ensure celebrity. Perhaps, after all, 'tis the still glowing prejudice of my heart that throws a borrowed lustre over the merits of the composition.

I have partly taken your idea of "Auld Rob Morris." I have adopted the two first verses, and am going on with the song on a new plan, which promises pretty well. I take up one or another, just as the bee of the moment buzzes in my bonnet-lug; and do you, *sans ceremonie*, make what use you choose of the productions. Adieu, &c.

R. B.

[*Here follows a copy of the "Highland Mary."*]

NO. CCXLVII.

MR. THOMSON TO BURNS.

Edinburgh, Nov. 1792.

DEAR SIR—I was just going to write to you, that on meeting with your Nannie, I had fallen violently in love with her. I thank you, therefore, for sending the charming rustic to me, in the dress you wish her to appear before the public. She does you great credit, and will soon be admitted into the best company.

I regret that your song for the "Lea-rig" is so short; the air is easy, soon sung, and very pleasing: so that, if the singer stops at the end of two stanzas, it is a pleasure lost ere it is well possessed.

Although a dash of our native tongue and manners is, doubtless, peculiarly congenial and appropriate to our melodies, yet I shall be able to present a considerable number of the very Flowers of English song, well adapted to those melodies, which, in England, at least, will be the means of recommending them to still greater attention than they have procured there. But, you will observe, my plan is, that every air shall, in the first place, have verses wholly by Scottish poets; and that those of English writers shall follow as additional songs for the choice of the singer.

What you say of the "Ewe-bughts" is just; I admire it, and never meant to supplant it. All I requested was, that you would try your hand on some of the inferior stanzas, which are apparently no part of the original song; but this I do not urge, because the song is of sufficient length, though those inferior stanzas be omitted, as they will be by the singer of taste. You must not think I expect all the songs to be of superlative merit; that were an unreasonable expectation. I am sensible that no poet can sit down doggedly to pen verses, and succeed well at all times.

I am highly pleased with your humorous and amorous rhapsody on "Bonnie Lesley:" it is a thousand times better than the "Collier's Lassie." "The Deil he cou'd na scaith thee," &c., is an eccentric and happy thought. Do you not think, however, that the names of such old heroes as Alexander sound rather queer, unless in pompous or mere burlesque verse? Instead of the line, "And never made anither," I would humbly suggest, "And ne'er made sic anither;" and I would fain have you substitute some other line for "Return to Caledonie," in the last verse, because I think this alteration of the orthography, and of the sound of Caledonia, disfigures the word, and renders it Hudibrastic.

Of the other song, "My wife's a winsome wee thing," I think the first eight lines very good; but I do not admire the other eight, because four of them are a bare repetition of the first verses. I have been trying to spin a stanza, but could make nothing better than the following: do you mend it, or, as Yorick did with the love letter, whip it up in your own way:—

Oh leeze me on my wee thing,
My bonnie blythesome, wee thing;
Sae lang's I hae my wee thing,
I'll think my lot divine.

Tho' warld's care we share o't,
And may see meikle mair o't,
Wi' her I'll blythely bear it,
And ne'er a word repine.

You perceive, my dear Sir, I avail myself of the liberty, which you condescend to allow me, by speaking freely what I think. Be assured, it is not my disposition to pick out the faults of any poem or picture I see: my first and chief object is to discover and be delighted with the beauties of the piece. If I sit down to examine critically, and at leisure, what, perhaps, you have written in haste, I may happen to observe careless lines, the reperusal of which might lead you to improve them. The wren will often see what has been overlooked by the eagle. I remain yours faithfully, &c.

P. S. Your verses upon "Highland Mary" are just come to hand: they breathe the genuine spirit of poetry, and, like the music, will last for ever. Such verses, united to such an air, with the delicate harmony of Pleyel superadded, might form a treat worthy of being presented to Apollo himself. I have heard the sad story of your Mary; you always seem inspired when you write of her.

NO. CCXLVIII

BURNS TO MR. THOMSON.

Dumfries, Dec. 1st, 1792.

YOUR alterations of my "Nannie, O!" are perfectly right. So are those of "My Wife's a winsome wee thing." Your alteration of the second stanza is a positive improvement. Now, my dear Sir, with the freedom which characterises our correspondence, I must not, cannot alter "Bonnie Lesley." You are right; the word "Alexander" makes the line a little uncouth, but I think the thought is pretty. Of Alexander, beyond all other heroes, it may be said, in the sublime language of Scripture, that "he went forth conquering and to conquer."

For nature made her what she is,
And never made anither. (Such a person as
she is)

This is, in my opinion, more poetical than "Ne'er made sic anither." However, it is immaterial: make it either way. "Caledonie," I agree with you, is not so good a word as could be wished, though it is sanctioned in three or four instances by Allan Ramsay; but I cannot help it. In short, that species of stanza is the most difficult that I have ever tried.

The "Lea-rig" is as follows:—

[*Here the poet repeats the first two stanzas, adding a third.*]

I am interrupted. Yours, &c.

NO. CCXLIX.

BURNS TO MR. THOMSON.

December 4th, 1792.

THE foregoing ["Auld Rob Morris" and "Duncan Gray,"] I submit, my dear Sir, to your better judgment. Acquit them, or condemn them, as seemeth good in your sight. "Duncan Gray" is that kind of light-horse gallop of an air, which precludes sentiment. The ludicrous is its ruling feature.

NO. CCL.

TO MRS. DUNLOP.

Dumfries, Dec. 6th, 1792.

I SHALL be in Ayrshire, I think, next week; and, if at all possible, I shall certainly, my much-esteemed friend, have the pleasure of visiting at Dunlop-house.

Alas, Madam! how seldom do we meet in this world, that we have reason to congratulate ourselves on accessions of happiness! I have not passed half the ordinary term of an old man's life, and yet I scarcely look over the obituary of a newspaper, that I do not see some names that I have known, and which I, and other acquaintances, little thought to meet with there so soon. Every other instance of the mortality of our kind, makes us cast an anxious look into the dreadful abyss of uncertainty, and shudder with apprehension for our own fate. But of how different an importance are the lives of different individuals! Nay, of what importance is one period of the same life more than another? A few years ago I could have lain down in the dust, "careless of the voice of the morning;" and now not a few, and these most helpless individuals, would, on losing me and my exertions, lose both their "staff and shield." By the way, these helpless ones have lately got an addition; Mrs. B. having given me a fine girl since I wrote you. There is a charming passage in Thomson's "Edward and Eleanora:"—

"The valiant, *in himself*, what can he suffer?
Or what need he regard his *single* woes?" &c.

As I am got in the way of quotations, I shall give you another from the same piece, peculiarly—alas! too peculiarly—apposite, my dear Madam, to your present frame of mind:—

"Who so unworthy but may proudly deck
him
With his fair-weather virtue, that exults
Glad o'er the summer main? The tempest
comes, [the helm
The rough winds rage aloud; when from
This virtue shrinks, and in a corner lies
Lamenting. Heavens! if privileged from
trial,
How cheap a thing were virtue!"

I do not remember to have heard you mention Thomson's dramas. I pick up favourite quotations, and store them in my mind as ready armour, offensive or defensive, amid the struggle of this turbulent existence. Of these is one, a very favourite one, from his "Alfred:"—

"Attach thee firmly to the virtuous deeds
And offices of life; to life itself,
With all its vain and transient joys, sit loose

Probably I have quoted some of these to you formerly, as indeed, when I write from the heart, I am apt to be guilty of such repetitions. The compass of the heart, in the musical style of expression, is much more bounded than that of the imagination, so the notes of the former are extremely apt to run into one another; but in return for the paucity of its compass, its few notes are much more sweet. I must still give you another quotation, which I am almost sure I have given you before, but I cannot resist the temptation. The subject is religion—speaking of its importance to mankind, the author says:—

'Tis this, my friend, that streaks our morning bright.

I see you are in for double postage, so I shall e'en scribble out t'other sheet. We in this country here, have many alarms of the reforming, or rather the republican spirit, of your part of the kingdom. Indeed, we are a good deal in commotion ourselves. For me, I am a placeman, you know; a very humble one, indeed, Heaven knows, but still so much as to gag me. What my private sentiments are, you will find out without an interpreter.

I have taken up the subject, and the other day, for a pretty actress's benefit night, I wrote an address, which I will give on the other page, called "The Rights of Woman."

I shall have the honour of receiving your criticisms in person at Dunlop. R. B.

NO. CCLI.

TO R. GRAHAM, ESQ., FINTRY.

December, 1792.

Sir—I have been surprised, confounded, and distracted, by Mr. Mitchell, the collector, telling me that he has received an order from your Board (137) to inquire into my political conduct, and blaming me as a person disaffected to government.

Sir, you are a husband, and a father. You know what you would feel, to see the much-loved wife of your bosom, and your helpless, prattling little ones, turned adrift into the world, degraded and disgraced from a situation in which they had been respectable and respected, and left almost without the necessary support of a miserable existence. Alas, Sir! must I think that such soon will be my lot! and from the d——, dark insinuations of hellish groundless envy too! I believe, Sir, I may aver it, and in the sight of Omniscience, that I would not tell a deliberate falsehood, no, not though even worse horrors, if worse can be, than those I have mentioned, hung over my head; and I say, that the allegation, whatever villain has made it, is a lie! To the British Constitution, on revolution principles, next after my God, I am most devoutly attached. You, Sir, have been much and generously my friend; Heaven knows how warmly I have felt the obligation, and how gratefully I have thanked you. Fortune, Sir, has made you powerful, and me impotent—has given you patronage, and me dependence. I would not, for my single self, call on your humanity; were such my insular, unconnected situation, I would despise the tear that now swells in my eye—I could brave misfortune, I could face ruin, for, at the worst, "Death's thousand doors stand open;" but, good God! the tender concerns that I have mentioned, the claims and ties that I see at this moment, and feel around me, how they unnerve courage and wither resolution! To your patronage, as a man of some genius, you have allowed me a claim; and your esteem, as an honest man, I know is my due. To these, Sir, permit me to appeal; by these may I adjure you to save me from that misery which threatens to overwhelm me, and which, with my latest breath I will say it, I have not deserved. R. B.

NO. CCLII.

TO MRS. DUNLOP.

Dumfries, December 31st, 1792.

Dear Madam—A hurry of business, thrown in heaps by my absence, has until now, prevented my returning my grateful acknowledgments to the good family of Dunlop, and you, in particular, for that hospitable kindness which rendered the four days I spent under that genial roof, four of the pleasantest I ever enjoyed. Alas, my dearest friend! how few and fleeting are those things we call pleasures!—on my road to Ayrshire, I spent a night with a friend whom I much valued, a man whose days promised to be many; and on Saturday last we laid him in the dust!

January 2nd, 1792.

I have just received yours of the 30th, and feel much for your situation. However, I heartily rejoice in your prospect of recovery from that vile jaundice. As to myself, I am better, though not quite free of my complaint. You must not think, as you seem to insinuate, that in my way of life I want exercise. Of that I have enough; but occasional hard drinking is the devil to me. Against this I have again and again bent my resolution, and have greatly succeeded. Taverns I have totally abandoned: it is the private parties, in the family way, among the hard-drinking gentlemen of this country, that do me the mischief—but even this, I have more than half given over. (138)

Mr. Corbet can be of little service to me at present; at least I should be shy of applying. I cannot possibly be settled as a supervisor for several years. I must wait the rotation of the list, and there are twenty names before mine. I might, indeed, get a job of officiating, where a settled supervisor was ill, or aged; but that hauls me from my family, as I could not remove them on such an uncertainty. Besides, some envious, malicious devil, has raised a little demur on my political principles, and I wish to let that matter settle before I offer myself too much in the eye of my supervisors. I have set, henceforth, a seal on my lips, as to these unlucky politics; but to you, I must breathe my sentiments. In this, as in everything else, I shall show the undisguised emotions of my soul. War I deprecate: misery and ruin to thousands are in the blast that announces the destructive demon. * *

R. B.

NO. CCLIII.

TO THE SAME. (139)

January 5th, 1793.

YOU see my hurried life, Madam; I can only command starts of time: however, I am glad of one thing; since I finished the other sheet, the political blast that threatened my welfare is overblown. I have corresponded with Commissioner Graham, for the board had made me the subject of their animadversions; and now I have the pleasure of informing you, that all is set to rights in that quarter. Now, as to these informers, may the devil be let loose to —— But, hold! I was praying most fervently in my last sheet, and I must not so soon fall a-swearing in this.

Alas! how little do the wantonly or idly officious think what mischief they do by their malicious insinuations, indirect impertinence, or thoughtless blabbings. What a difference there is in intrinsic worth, candour, benevolence, generosity, kindness—in all the charities and all the virtues—between one class of human beings and another. For instance, the amiable circle I so lately mixed with in the hospitable hall of Dunlop, their generous hearts, their uncontaminated dignified minds, their informed and polished understandings—what a contrast, when compared—if such comparing were not downright sacrilege—with the soul of the miscreant who can deliberately plot the destruction of an honest man that never offended him, and with a grin of satisfaction see the unfortunate being, his faithful wife, and prattling innocents, turned over to beggary and ruin!

Your cup, my dear Madam, arrived safe. I had two worthy fellows dining with me the other day, when I, with great formality, produced my whigmaleerie cup, and told them that it had been a family-piece among the descendants of William Wallace. This roused such an enthusiasm, that they insisted on bumpering the punch round in it; and by and bye, never did your great ancestor lay a *suthron* more completely to rest, than for a time did your cup my two friends. A-propos, this is the season of wishing. May God bless you, my dear friend, and bless me, the humblest and sincerest of your friends, by granting you yet many returns of the season! May all good things attend you and yours, wherever they are scattered over the earth! R. B.

NO. CCLIV.

BURNS TO MR. THOMSON. (140)

January, 1793.

MANY returns of the season to you, my dear Sir. How comes on your publication?—will these two foregoing be of any service to you? I should like to know what songs you print to each tune, besides the verses to which it is set. In short, I would wish to give you my opinion on all the poetry you publish. You know it is my trade, and a man in the way of his trade may suggest useful hints that escape men of much superior parts and endowments in other things.

If you meet with my dear and much-valued Cunningham, greet him, in my name, with the compliments of the season. Yours, &c.

NO. CCLV.

MR. THOMSON TO BURNS.

Edinburgh, January 20th, 1793.

YOU make me happy, my dear Sir, and thousands will be happy, to see the charming songs you have sent me. Many merry returns of the season to you, and may you long continue among the sons and daughters of Caledonia, to delight them and to honour yourself.

The four last songs with which you favoured me, "Auld Rob Morris," "Duncan Gray," "Gala Water," and "Cauld Kail," are admirable. Duncan is indeed a lad of grace, and his humour will endear him to every body.

The distracted lover in "Auld Rob," and the happy shepherdess in "Gala Water," exhibit an excellent contrast: they speak from genuine feeling, and powerfully touch the heart.

The number of songs which I had originally in view was limited, but I now resolve to include every Scotch air and song worth singing; leaving none behind but mere gleanings, to which the publishers of *omnium-gatherum* are welcome. I would rather be the editor of a collection from which nothing could be taken away, than of one to which nothing could be added. We intend presenting the subscribers with two beautiful stroke engravings, the one characteristic of the plaintive, and the other of the lively songs; and I have Dr. Beattie's promise of an essay upon the subject of our national music, if his health will permit him to write it. As a number of our songs have doubtless been called forth by particular events, or by the charms of peerless damsels, there must be many curious anecdotes relating to them.

The late Mr. Tytler of Woodhouselee, I believe, knew more of this than any body; for he joined to the pursuits of an antiquary a taste for poetry, besides being a man of the world, and possessing an enthusiasm for music beyond most of his contemporaries. He was quite pleased with this plan of mine, for I may say it has been solely managed by me, and we had several long conversations about it when it was in embryo. If I could simply mention the name of the heroine of each song, and the incident which occasioned the verses, it would be gratifying. Pray, will you send me any information of this sort, as well with regard to your own songs as the old ones?

To all the favourite songs of the plaintive or pastoral kind, will be joined the delicate accompaniments, &c., of Pleyel. To those of the comic and humorous class, I think accompaniments scarcely necessary; they are chiefly fitted for the conviviality of the festive board, and a tuneful voice, with a proper delivery of the words, renders them perfect. Nevertheless, to these I propose adding bass accompaniments, because then they are fitted either for singing, or for instrumental performance, when there happens to be no singer. I mean to employ our right trusty friend Mr. Clarke, to set the bass to these, which he assures me he will do *con amore*, and with much greater attention than he ever bestowed on any thing of the kind. But for this last class of airs I will not attempt to find more than one set of verses.

That eccentric bard, Peter Pindar, has started I know not how many difficulties about writing for the airs I sent to him, because of the peculiarity of their measure, and the trammels they oppose on his flying Pegasus. I subjoin, for your perusal, the only one I have yet got from him, being for the fine air, "Lord Gregory." The Scots verses printed with that air are taken from the middle of an old ballad, called "The Lass of Lochroyan," which I do not admire. I have set down the air, therefore, as a creditor of yours. Many of the Jacobite songs are replete with wit and humour—might not the best of these be included in our volume of comic songs?

POSTSCRIPT.

FROM THE HON. ANDREW ERSKINE. (141)

MR. THOMSON has been so obliging as to give me a perusal of your songs. "Highland Mary" is most enchantingly pathetic, and "Duncan Gray" possesses native genuine humour—"Spak o' lowpin' o'er a linn," is a line of itself that should make you immortal. I sometimes hear of you from our mutual friend Cunningham, who is a most excellent fellow, and possesses, above all men I know, the charm of a most obliging disposition. You kindly promised me, about a year ago, a collection of your unpublished productions, religious and amorous. I know, from experience, how irksome it is to copy. If you will get any trusty person in Dumfries to write them over fair, I will give Peter Hill whatever money he asks for his trouble, and I certainly shall not betray your confidence. I am your hearty admirer,

ANDREW ERSKINE.

NO. CCLVI.

BURNS TO MR. THOMSON.

January 26th, 1793.

I APPROVE greatly, my dear Sir, of your plans. Dr. Beattie's essay will, of itself, be a treasure. On my part I mean to draw up an appendix to the Doctor's essay, containing my stock of anecdotes, &c., of our Scots songs. All the late Mr. Tytler's anecdotes I have by me, taken down in the course of my acquaintance with him, from his own mouth. I am such an enthusiast, that in the course of my several peregrinations through Scotland, I made a pilgrimage to the individual spot from which every song took its rise, "Lochaber," and the "Braes of Ballenden," excepted. So far as the locality, either from the title of the air, or the tenor of the song, could be ascertained, I have paid my devotions at the particular shrine of every Scots muse.

I do not doubt but you might make a very valuable collection of Jacobite songs; but would it give no offence? In the meantime, do not you think that some of them, particularly "The sow's tail to Geordie," as an air, with other words, might be well worth a place in your collection of lively songs?

If it were possible to procure songs of merit, it would be proper to have one set of Scots words to every air, and that the set of words to which the notes ought to be set. There is a *naïveté*, a pastoral simplicity, in a slight intermixture of Scots words and phraseology, which is more in unison (at least to my taste, and, I will add, to every genuine Caledonian taste) with the simple pathos, or rustic sprightliness of our native music, than any English verses whatever.

The very name of Peter Pindar is an acquisition to your work. (142) His "Gregory" is beautiful. I have tried to give you a set of stanzas in Scotch, on the same subject, which are at your service. Not that I intend to enter the lists with Peter—that would be presumption indeed. My song, though much inferior in poetic merit, has, I think, more of the ballad simplicity in it. (143)

[*Here follows "Lord Gregory."*]

NO. CCLVII.

TO CLARINDA. (144)

1793

BEFORE you ask me why I have not written you, first let me be informed of you *how* I shall write you? "In friendship," you say; and I have many a time taken up my pen to try an epistle of friendship to you; but it will not do: 'tis like Jove grasping a pop-gun, after having wielded his thunder. When I take up the pen, recollection ruins me. Ah! my ever dearest Clarinda! Clarinda!—what a host of memory's tenderest offspring, crowd on my fancy at that sound! But I must not indulge that subject—you have forbid it.

I am extremely happy to learn that your precious health is re-established, and that you are once more fit to enjoy that satisfaction in existence, which health alone can give us. My old friend has indeed been kind to you. Tell him, that I envy him the power of serving you. I had a letter from him a while ago, but it was so dry, so distant, so like a card to one of his clients, that I could scarcely bear to read it, and have not yet answered it. He is a good honest fellow; and *can* write a friendly letter, which would do equal honour to his head, and his heart; as a whole sheaf of his letters I have by me will witness: and though Fame does not blow her trumpet at my approach *now*, as she did *then*, when he first honoured me with his friendship, yet I am as proud as ever; and when I am laid in my grave, I wish to be stretched at my full length, that I may occupy every inch of ground which I have a right to.

You would laugh were you to see me where I am just now!—would to heaven you were here to laugh with me! though I am afraid that crying would be our first employment. Here am I set, a solitary hermit, in the solitary room of a solitary inn, with a solitary bottle of wine by me—as grave and as stupid as an owl, but, like that owl, still faithful to my old song. In confirmation of which, my dear Mrs. Mack, here is your good health! may the hand-waled benisons o' Heaven bless your bonnie face; and the wretch wha skellies at your welfare, may the auld tinkler deil get him to clout his rotten heart! Amen.

You must know, my dearest Madam, that these now many years, wherever I am, in whatever company, when a married lady is called on as a toast, I constantly give you; but as your name has never passed my lips, even to my most intimate friend, I give you by the name of Mrs. Mack. This is so well known among my acquaintances, that when my married lady is called for, the toast-master will say—"O, we need not ask him who it is—here's Mrs. Mack!" I have also, among my convivial friends, set on foot a round of toasts, which I call a round of Arcadian Shepherdesses; that is, a round of favourite ladies, under female names celebrated in ancient songs; and then, you are my Clarinda. So, my lovely Clarinda, I devote this glass of wine to a most ardent wish for your happiness!

In vain would Prudence, with decorous sneer,
Point out a cens'ring world, and bid me fear;
Above that world on wings of love I rise,
I know its worst, and can that worst despise.
"Wrong'd, injur'd, shunn'd, unpitied, unredrest,
The mock'd quotation of the scorner's jest,"
Let Prudence' direst bodements on me fall,
Clarinda, rich reward! o'erpays them all! (145)

I have been rhyming a little of late, but I do not know if they are worth postage.—Tell me. * * * * * * *

SYLVANDER.

NO. CCLVIII.

TO MR. CUNNINGHAM.

March 3rd, 1793.

SINCE I wrote to you the last lugubrious sheet, I have not had time to write you farther. When I say that I had not time, that, as usual, means, that the three demons, indolence, business and ennui, have so completely shared my hours among them, as not to leave me a five minutes' fragment to take up a pen in.

Thank Heaven, I feel my spirits buoying upwards with the renovating year. Now, I shall in good earnest take up Thomson's songs. I dare say he thinks I have used him unkindly; and, I must own, with too much appearance of truth. A-propos, do you know the much-admired old Highland air called "The Sutor's Dochter?" It is a first-rate favourite of mine, and I have written what I reckon one of my best songs to it. I will send it to you as it was sung, with great applause, in some fashionable circles, by Major Robertson, of Lude, who was here with his corps.

There was one commission that I must trouble you with. I lately lost a valuable seal, a present from a departed friend, which vexes me much. I have gotten one of your Highland pebbles, which I fancy would make a very decent one, and I want to cut my armorial bearing on it: will you be so obliging as inquire what will be the expense of such a business? I do not know that my name is matriculated, as the heralds call it, at all, but I have invented arms for myself; so, you know, I shall be chief of the name; and, by courtesy of Scotland, will likewise be entitled to supporters. These, however, I do not intend having on my seal. I am a bit of a herald, and shall give you, *secundum artem*, my arms. On a field, azure, a holy bush, seeded, proper, in base; a shepherd's pipe and crook, saltier-wise, also proper, in chief. On a wreath of the colours, a wood-lark perching on a sprig of bay-tree, proper, for crest. Two mottoes; round the top of the crest, *Wood notes wild;* at the bottom of the shield, in the usual place, *Better a wee bush than nae bield.* (146) By the shepherd's pipe and crook, I do not mean the nonsense of painters of Arcadia, but a *stock and horn*, and a *club*, such as you see at the head of Allan Ramsay, in Allan's quarto edition of the "Gentle Shepherd." By the bye, do you know Allan? (147) He must be a man of very great genius. Why is he not the more known? Has he no patrons?—or do "Poverty's cold wind and crushing rain beat keen and heavy" on him? I once, and but once, got a glance of that noble edition of the noblest pastoral in the world; and dear as it was, I mean dear as to my pocket, I would have bought it but I was told that it was printed and engraved for subscribers only. He is the *only* artist who has hit *genuine* pastoral *costume.* What, my dear Cunningham, is there in riches, that they narrow and harden the heart so? I think, that were I as rich as the sun, I should be as generous as the day; but as I have no reason to imagine my soul a nobler one than any other man's, I must conclude that wealth imparts a bird-lime quality to the possessor, at which the man, in his native poverty, would have revolted. What has led me to this is the idea of such merit as Mr. Allan possesses, and such riches as a nabob or government contractor possesses, and why they do not form a mutual league. Let wealth shelter and cherish unprotected merit, and the gratitude and celebrity of that merit will richly repay it. R. B.

NO. CCLIX.

BURNS TO MR THOMSON.

March 20th, 1793.

MY DEAR SIR—The song prefixed ["Mary Morison"] is one of my juvenile works I leave it in your hands. I do not think it very remarkable, either for its merits or demerits. It is impossible (at least, I feel it so in my stinted powers) to be always original, entertaining, and witty.

What is become of the list, &c., of your songs? I shall be out of all temper with you by and bye. I have always looked on myself as the prince of indolent correspondents, and valued myself accordingly; and I will not, can not, bear rivalship from you, nor any body else. R. B.

NO. CCLX.

TO MISS BENSON,

SINCE MRS. BASIL MONTAGU.

Dumfries, March 21st, 1793.

MADAM—Among many things for which I envy those hale, long-lived old fellows before the flood, is this, in particular—that when they met with anybody after their own heart, they had a charming long prospect of many, many happy meetings with them in after-life.

Now, in this short, stormy, winter-day of our fleeting existence, when you, now and then, in the chapter of accidents, meet an individual whose acquaintance is a real acquisition, there are all the probabilities against you, that you shall never meet with that valued character more. On the other hand, brief as this miserable being is, it is none of the least of the miseries belonging to it, that if there is any miscreant whom you hate, or creature whom you despise, the ill-run of the chances shall be so against you, that in the overtakings, turnings, and jostlings of life, pop, at some unlucky corner, eternally comes the wretch upon you, and will not allow your indignation or contempt a moment's repose. As I am a sturdy believer in the powers of darkness, I take these to be the doings of that old author of mischief, the devil. It is well known that he has some kind of short-hand way of taking down our thoughts; and I make no doubt, that he is perfectly acquainted with my sentiments respecting Miss Benson: how much I admired her abilities and valued her worth, and how very fortunate I thought myself in her acquaintance. For this last reason, my dear Madam, I must entertain no hopes of the very great pleasure of meeting with you again.

Miss Hamilton tells me that she is sending a packet to you, and I beg leave to send you the enclosed sonnet: though to tell you the real truth, the sonnet is a mere pretence, that I may have the opportunity of declaring with how much respectful esteem I have the honour to be, &c. R. B.

NO. CCLXI.

BURNS TO MR. THOMSON.

March, 1793.

WANDERING WILLIE.

HERE awa, there awa, wandering Willie,
  Now tired with wandering, haud awa hame;
Come to my bosom, my ane only dearie,
  And tell me thou brings't me my Willie the same.

Loud blew the cauld winter winds at our parting;
  It was na the blast brought the tear in my ee:
Now welcome the simmer, and Welcome my Willie,
  The simmer to nature, my Willie to me.

Ye hurricanes, rest, in the cave o' your slumbers!
  Oh how your wild horrors a lover alarms!
Awaken, ye breezes! rool gently, ye billows!
  And waft my dear laddie, ance mair to my arms.

But if he's forgotten his faithfullest Nannie,
  Oh still flow between us, thou wide-roaring main;
May I never see it, may I never trow it,
  But, dying, believe that my Willie's my ain!

I leave it to you, my dear Sir, to determine whether the above, or the old "Thro' the lang muir" (148), be the best.

NO. CCLXII.

MR. THOMSON TO BURNS. (149)

Edinburgh, April 2d, 1793.

I WILL not recognise the title you give yourself, "the prince of *indolent* correspondents;" but if the adjective were taken away, I think the title would then fit you exactly. It gives me pleasure to find you can furnish anecdotes with respect to most of the songs: these will be a literary curiosity.

I now send you my list of the songs, which, I believe, will be found nearly complete. I have put down the first lines of all the English songs which I propose giving, in addition to the Scotch verses. If any others occur to you, better adapted to the character of the airs, pray mention them, when you favour me with your strictures upon everything else relating to the work.

Pleyel has lately sent me a number of the songs, with his symphonies and accompaniments added to them. I wish you were here, that I might serve up some of them to you with your own verses, by way of dessert after dinner. There is so much delightful fancy in the symphonies, and such a delicate simplicity in the accompaniments—they are indeed beyond all praise.

I am very much pleased with the several last productions of your muse: your "Lord Gregory," in my estimation, is more interesting than Peter's, beautiful as his is. Your "Here awa, Willie," must undergo some alterations to suit the air. Mr. Erskine and I have been conning it over: he will suggest what is necessary to make them a fit match. (150)

The gentleman I have mentioned, whose fine taste you are no stranger to, is so well pleased, both with the musical and poetical part of our work, that he has volunteered his assistance, and has already written four songs for it, which, by his own desire, I send for your perusal. (151)

NO. CCLXIII.

BURNS TO MR. THOMSON.

April 7th, 1793.

THANK you, my dear Sir, for your packet. You cannot imagine how much this business of composing for your publication has added to my enjoyments. What with my early attachment to ballads, your book, &c., ballad-making is now as completely my hobby-horse as ever fortification was Uncle Toby's; so I'll e'en canter it away till I come to the limit of my race—God grant that I may take the right side of the winning post!—and then cheerfully looking back on the honest folks with whom I have been happy, I shall say or sing, "Sae merry as we a' hae been!" and, raising my last looks to the whole human race, the last words of the voice of "Coila" (152) shall be, "Good night, and joy be wi' you a'!" So much for my last words: now for a few present remarks as they have occurred at random, on looking over your list.

The first lines of "The last time I came o'er the moor," and several other lines in it, are beautiful; but, in my opinion—pardon me, revered shade of Ramsay!—the song is unworthy of the divine air. I shall try to make or mend. "For ever, fortune, wilt thou prove," is a charming song; but "Logan burn and Logan braes" is sweetly susceptible of rural imagery: I'll try that likewise, and, if I succeed, the other song may class among the English ones. I remember the two last lines of a verse in some of the old songs of "Logan Water" (for I know a good many different ones) which I think pretty:—

"Now my dear lad maun face his faes,
Far, far frae me and Logan braes."

"My Patie is a lover gay," is unequal. "His mind is never muddy," is a muddy expression indeed.

"Then I'll resign and marry Pate,
And syne my cockernony—"

This is surely far unworthy of Ramsay, or your book.

"Winter winds blew loud and cauld at our parting,
Fears for my Willie brought tears in my ee;
Welcome now simmer, and welcome my Willie,
The simmer to nature, my Willie to me.

Rest, ye wild storms, in the cave of your slumbers
How your dread howling a lover alarms!
Wauken, ye breezes! roll gently, ye billows!
And waft my dear laddie ance mair to my arms.

But oh, if he's faithless, and minds nae his Nannie,
Flow still between us, thou wide-roaring main!
May I never see it, may I never trow it,
But, dying, believe that my Willie's my ain." (153)

My song, "Rigs of Barley," to the same tune, does not altogether please me; but if I can mend it, and thrash a few loose sentiments out of it, I will submit it to your consideration. "The lass o' Paties mill" is one of Ramsay's best songs; but there is one loose sentiment in it, which my much-valued friend Mr. Erskine will take into his critical consideration. In Sir John Sinclair's statistical volumes, are two claims—one, I think, from Aberdeenshire, and the other from Ayrshire—for the honour of this song. The following anecdote, which I had from the present Sir William Cunningham of Robertland, who had it of the late John Earl of Loudon, I can, on such authorities, believe:—

Allan Ramsay was residing at Loudon-castle with the then Earl, father to Earl John; and one forenoon, riding, or walking, out together, his lordship and Allan passed a sweet romantic spot on Irvine water, still called "Patie's mill," where a bonnie lass was "tedding hay, bareheaded on the green." My lord observed to Allan, that it would be a fine theme for a song. Ramsay took the hint, and, lingering behind, he composed the first sketch of it, which he produced at dinner.

"One day I heard Mary say," is a fine song; but, for consistency's sake, alter the name "Adonis." Were there ever such banns published, as a purpose of marriage between Adonis and Mary! I agree with you that my song, "There's nought but care on every hand," is much superior to "Puirtith cauld." The original song, "The mill, mill, O!" though excellent, is, on account of delicacy, inadmissible; still, I like the title, and think a Scottish song would suit the notes best; and let your chosen song, which is very pretty, follow as an English set. "The banks of the Dee," is, you know, literally "Langolee," to slow time. The song is well enough, but has some false imagery in it; for instance:

And sweetly the nightingale sang from the tree.

In the first place, the nightingale sings in a low bush, but never from a tree; and in the second place, there never was a nightingale seen or heard on the banks of the Dee, or on the banks of any other river in Scotland. Exotic rural imagery is always comparatively flat. If I could hit on another stanza, equal to "The small birds rejoice," &c., I do myself honestly avow, that I think it a superior song. (154) "John Anderson, my jo;"—the song to this tune in Johnson's Museum, is my composition, and I think it not my worst: if it suit you, take it and welcome. Your collection of sentimental and pathetic song, is, in my opinion, very complete; but not so your comic ones. Where are "Tullochgorum," "Lumps o' puddin," "Tibbie Fowler," and several others, which, in my humble judgment, are well worthy of preservation? There is also one sentimental song of mine in the Museum, which never was known out of the immediate neighhourhood, until I got it taken down from a country girl's singing. It is called "Cragieburn wood," and, in the opinion of Mr. Clarke, is one of the sweetest Scottish Songs. He is quite an enthusiast about it; and I would take his taste in Scottish music against the taste of most connoisseurs.

You are quite right in inserting the last five in your list, though they are certainly Irish. "Shepherds, I have lost my love!" is to me a heavenly air—what would you think of a set of Scottish verses to it? I have made one to it, a good while ago, which I think * * *, but in its original state, it is not quite a lady's song. I enclose an altered, not amended copy for you, if you choose to set the tune to it, and let the Irish verses follow. (155)

Mr. Erskine's songs are all pretty, but his "Lone vale" is divine. Yours, &c.

Let me know just how you like these random hints.

NO. CCLXIV.

TO PATRICK MILLER, Esq.,

OF DALSWINTON.

Dumfries, April, 1793.

Sir—My poems having just come out in another edition, will you do me the honour to accept of a copy? A mark of my gratitude to you, as a gentleman to whose goodness I have been much indebted; of my respect for you, as a patriot who, in a venal, sliding age, stands forth the champion of the liberties of my country; and of my veneration for you as a man, whose benevolence of heart does honour to human nature.

There *was* a time, Sir, when I was your dependent: this language *then* would have been like the vile incense of flattery—I could not have used it. Now that that connexion (156) is at an end, do me the honour to accept of this *honest* tribute of respect from, Sir, your much indebted humble servant,

R. B.

NO. CCLXV.

TO JOHN FRANCIS ERSKINE Esq.,

OF MAR. (157)

Dumfries, April 13th, 1793.

Sir—Degenerate as human nature is said to be—and, in many instances, worthless and unprincipled it is—still there are bright examples to the contrary; examples that, even in the eyes of superior beings, must shed a lustre on the name of man.

Such an example have I now before me, when you, Sir, came forward to patronise and befriend a distant obscure stranger, merely because poverty had made him helpless, and his British hardihood of mind had provoked the arbitrary wantonness of power. My much esteemed friend, Mr. Riddel of Glenriddel, has just read me a paragraph of a letter he had from you. Accept, Sir, of the silent throb of gratitude; for words would but mock the emotions of my soul.

You have been misinformed as to my final dismission from the Excise; I am still in the service. Indeed, but for the exertions of a gentleman, who must be known to you, Mr. Graham of Fintry—a gentleman who has ever been my warm and generous friend—I had, without so much as a hearing, or the slightest previous intimation, been turned adrift, with my helpless family, to all the horrors of want. Had I had any other resource, probably I might have saved them the trouble of a dismission; but the little money I gained by publication, is my almost every guinea, embarked to save from ruin an only brother, who, though one of the worthiest, is by no means one of the most fortunate of men.

In my defence to their accusations, I said, that whatever might be my sentiments of republics, ancient or modern, as to Britain I abjured the idea, that a CONSTITUTION, which, in its original principles, experience had proved to be every way fitted for our happiness in society, it would be insanity to sacrifice to an untried visionary theory—that, in consideration of my being situated in a department, however humble, immediately in the hands of people in power, I had forborne taking any active part, either personally or as an author, in the present business of REFORM. But that, where I must declare my sentiments, I would say, there existed a system of corruption between the executive power and the representative part of the legislature, which boded no good to our glorious CONSTITUTION, and which every patriotic Briton must wish to see amended. Some such sentiments as these, I stated in a letter to my generous patron, Mr. Graham, which he laid before the Board at large, where, it seems, my last remark gave great offence; and one of our supervisors general, a Mr. Corbet, was instructed to inquire on the spot, and to document me, "that my business was to act, *not to think;* and that, whatever might be men or measures, it was for me to be ***silent*** and *obedient*."

Mr. Corbet was likewise my steady friend; so between Mr. Graham and him, I have been partly forgiven: only I understand that all hopes of my getting officially forward are blasted.

Now, Sir, to the business in which I would more immediately interest you. The partiality of my COUNTRYMEN has brought me forward as a man of genius, and has given me a character to support. In the POET I have avowed manly and independent sentiments, which I trust will be found in the MAN. Reasons of no less weight than the support of a wife and family, have pointed out as the eligible, and, situated as I was, the only eligible, line of life for me, my present occupation. Still, my honest fame is my dearest concern; and a thousand times have I trembled at the idea of those *degrading* epithets that malice or misrepresentation may affix to my name. I have often, in blasting anticipation, listened to some future hackney scribbler, with the heavy malice of savage stupidity, exulting in his hireling paragraphs—"BURNS, notwithstanding the *fanfaronade* of independence to be found in his works, and after having been held forth to public view, and to public estimation, as a man of some genius, yet, quite destitute of resources within himself to support his borrowed dignity, he dwindled into a paltry exciseman, and slunk out the rest of his insignificant existence in the meanest of pursuits, and among the vilest of mankind."

In your illustrious hands, Sir, permit me to lodge my disavowal and defiance of these slanderous falsehoods. BURNS was a poor man from birth, and an exciseman by necessity; but—*I will* say it!—the sterling of his honest worth no poverty could debase; and his independent British mind, oppression might bend, but could not subdue. Have not I, to me, a more precious stake in my country's welfare, than the richest dukedom in it? I have a large family of children, and the prospect of many more. I have three sons, who, I see already, have brought into the world souls ill qualified to inhabit the bodies of SLAVES. Can I look tamely on, and see any machination to wrest from them the birthright of my boys—the little independent BRITONS, in whose veins runs my own blood? No! I will not, should my heart's blood stream around my attempt to defend it!

Does any man tell me, that my full efforts can be of no service, and that it does not belong to my humble station to meddle with the concern of a nation?

I can tell him, that it is on such individuals as I that a nation has to rest, both for the hand of support and the eye of intelligence. The uninformed MOB may swell a nation's bulk; and the titled, tinsel, courtly throng may be its feathered ornament; but the number of those who are elevated enough in life to reason and to reflect, yet low enough to keep clear of the venal contagion of a court—these are a nation's strength!

I know not how to apologise for the impertinent length of this epistle; but one small request I must ask of you farther:—when you have honoured this letter with a perusal, please to commit it to the flames. BURNS, in whose behalf you have so generously interested yourself, I have here, in his native colours, drawn *as he is;* but should any of the people in whose hands is the very bread he eats, get the least knowledge of the picture, *it would ruin the poor* BARD *for ever!*

My poems having just come out in another edition, I beg leave to present you with a copy, as a small mark of that high esteem and ardent gratitude with which I have the honour to be, Sir, your deeply indebted and ever devoted humble servant, R. B.

NO. CCLXVI.

MR. THOMSON TO BURNS.

Edinburgh, April, 1793.

I REJOICE to find, my dear Sir, that ballad-making continues to be your hobby-horse. Great pity 'twould be were it otherwise. I hope you will amble it away for many a year, and "witch the world with your horsemanship."

I know there are a good many lively songs of merit that I have not put down in the list sent you; but I have them all in my eye. "My Patie is a lover gay," though a little unequal, is a natural and very pleasing song, and I humbly think we ought not to displace or alter it, except the last stanza. (158)

NO. CCLXVII.

BURNS TO MR. THOMSON.

April, 1793.

I HAVE yours, my dear Sir, this moment. I shall answer it and your former letter, in my desultory way, of saying whatever comes uppermost.

The business of many of our tunes wanting, at the beginning, what fiddlers call a starting-note, is often a rub to us poor rhymers.

"There's braw, braw lads on Yarrow braes,
That wander through the blooming heather,"

you may alter to

"Braw, braw lads on Yarrow braes,
Ye wander," &c.

My song, "Here awa, there awa," as amended by Mr. Erskine, I entirely approve of, and return you. (159)

Give me leave to criticise your taste in the only thing in which it is, in my opinion, reprehensible. You know I ought to know something of my own trade. Of pathos, sentiment and point, you are a complete judge; but there is a quality more necessary than either in a song, and which is the very essence of a ballad—I mean simplicity: now, if I mistake not, this last feature you are a little apt to sacrifice to the foregoing.

Ramsay, as every other poet, has not been always equally happy in his pieces; still, I cannot approve of taking such liberties with an author as Mr. W. proposes doing with "The last time I came o'er the moor." Let a poet, if he chooses, take up the idea of another, and work it into a piece of his own; but to mangle the works of the poor bard, whose tuneful tongue is now mute for ever, in the dark and narrow house—by Heaven, 'twould be sacrilege! I grant that Mr. W.'s version is an improvement; but I know Mr. W. well, and esteem him much; let him mend the song, as the Highlander mended his gun—he gave it a new stock, a new lock, and a new barrel.

I do not, by this, object to leaving out improper stanzas, where that can be done without spoiling the whole. One stanza in "The lass o' Patie's mill" must be left out: the song will be nothing worse for it. I am not sure if we can take the same liberty with "Corn rigs are bonnie." Perhaps it might want the last stanza, and be the better for it. "Cauld kail in Aberdeen," you must leave with me yet a while. I have vowed to have a song to that air, on the lady whom I attempted to celebrate in the verses, "Puirtith cauld and restless love." At any rate, my other song, "Green grow the rashes," will never suit. That song is current in Scotland under the old title, and to the merry old tune of that name, which, of course, would mar the progress of your song to celebrity. Your book will be the standard of Scots songs for the future: let this idea ever keep your judgment on the alarm.

I send a song on a celebrated toast in this country, to suit "Bonnie Dundee." I send you also a ballad to the "Mill, Mill, O!" (160)

"The last time I came o'er the moor," I would fain attempt to make a Scots song for, and let Ramsay's be the English set. You shall hear from me soon. When you go to London on this business, can you come by Dumfries? I have still several MS. Scots airs by me, which I have picked up, mostly from the singing of country lasses. They please me vastly; but your learned *lugs* (161) would perhaps be displeased with the very feature for which I like them. I call them simple; you would pronounce them silly. Do you know a fine air called "Jackie Hume's Lament?" I have a song of considerable merit to that air. I'll enclose you both the song and tune, as I had them ready to send to Johnson's Museum. (162) I send you likewise, to me, a beautiful little air, which I had taken down from *vivâ voce.* (163) Adieu.

NO. CCLXVIII.

BURNS TO MR. THOMSON. (164)

[*Here the poet inserts the song, beginning "Farewell, thou Stream that winding flows."*]

April, 1793.

MY DEAR SIR—I had scarcely put my last letter into the post office, when I took up the subject of "The last time I came o'er the moor," and, ere I slept, drew the outlines of the foregoing. How far I have succeeded, I leave on this, as on every other occasion, to you to decide. I own my vanity is flattered, when you give my songs a place in your elegant and superb work; but to be of service to the work is my first wish. As I have often told you, I do not in a single instance wish you, out of compliment to me, to insert any thing of mine. One hint let me give you—whatever Mr. Pleyel does, let him not alter one iota of the original Scottish airs, I mean in the song department, but let our national music preserve its native features. They are, I own, frequently wild and irreducible to the more modern rules; but on that very eccentricity, perhaps, depends a great part of their effect.

NO. CCLXIX.

MR. THOMSON TO BURNS.

Edinburgh, April 26th, 1793.

I HEARTILY thank you, my dear Sir, for your last two letters, and the songs which accompanied them. I am always both instructed and entertained by your observations; and the frankness with which you speak out your mind, is to me highly agreeable. It is very possible I may not have the true idea of simplicity in composition. I confess there are several songs, of Allan Ramsay's for example, that I think silly enough, which another person, more conversant than I have been with country people, would perhaps call simple and natural. But the lowest scenes of simple nature will not please generally, if copied precisely as they are. The poet, like the painter, must select what will form an agreeable, as well as a natural picture. On this subject it were easy to enlarge; but, at present, suffice it to say, that I consider simplicity, rightly understood, as a most essential quality in composition, and the groundwork of beauty in all the arts. I will gladly appropriate your most interesting new ballad, "When wild war's deadly blast," &c., to the "Mill, Mill, O!" as well as the two other songs to their respective airs; but the third and fourth lines of the first verse must undergo some little alteration in order to suit the music. Pleyel does not alter a single note of the songs. That would be absurd indeed! With the airs which he introduces into the sonatas, I allow him to take such liberties as he pleases; but that has nothing to do with the songs.

P.S. I wish you would do as you proposed with your "Rigs of Barley." If the loose sentiments are thrashed out of it, I will find an air for it; but as to this there is no hurry.

NO. CCLXX.

TO MR. ROBERT AINSLIE.

April 26th, 1793.

I AM —— out of humour, my dear Ainslie, and that is the reason why I take up the pen to *you:* 'tis the nearest way (*probatum est*) to recover my spirits again.

I received your last, and was much entertained with it; but I will not at this time, nor at any other time, answer it. Answer a letter!—I never could answer a letter in my life. I have written many a letter in return for letters I have received, but then—they were original matter — spurt-away!—zig, here, zag, there—as if the devil, that my grannie (an old woman, indeed) often told me, rode on will-o'-wisp, or, in her more classic phrase, SPUNKIE, were looking over my elbow. Happy thought that idea has engendered in my head! SPUNKIE, thou shalt henceforth be my symbol, signature, and tutelary genius! Like thee, hop-step-and-loup, here-awa-there-awa, higgledy-piggledy, pell-mell, hither-and-yont, ram-stam, happy-go-lucky, up tails-a'-by-the-light-o'-the-moon—has been, is, and shall be, my progress through the mosses and moors of this vile, bleak, barren wilderness of a life of ours.

Come, then, my guardian spirit! like thee, may I skip away, amusing myself by and at my own light; and if any opaque-souled lubber of mankind complain that my elfin, lambent, glimmerous wanderings have misled his stupid steps over precipices or into bogs, let the thick-headed Blunderbuss recollect that he is not SPUNKIE:—that

SPUNKIE'S wanderings could not copied be:
Amid these perils none durst walk but he.

* * * *

I have no doubt but Scholarcraft may be caught, as a Scotsman catches the itch, by friction. How else can you account for it, that born blockheads, by mere dint of *handling* books, grow so wise that even they themselves are equally convinced of, and surprised at their own parts? I once carried this philosophy to that degree, that in a knot of country folks who had a library amongst them, and who, to the honour of their good sense, made me factotum in the business,—one of our members, a little, wise-looking, squat, upright, jabbering body of a tailor, I advised him, instead of turning over the leaves, *to bind the book on his back.* Johnnie took the hint, and as our meetings were every fourth Saturday, and Pricklouse having a good Scots mile to walk in coming, and, of course, another in returning, Bodkin was sure to lay his hand on some heavy quarto or ponderous folio, with, and under which, wrapt in his grey plaid, he grew wise, as he grew weary, all the way home. He carried this so far, that an old musty Hebrew concordance, which we had in a present from a neighbouring priest, by mere dint of applying it, as doctors do a blistering plaster, between his shoulders, Stitch, in a dozen pilgrimages, acquired as much rational theology as the said priest had done by forty years' perusal of the pages.

Tell me, and tell me truly, what you think of this theory. Yours, SPUNKIE.

NO. CCLXXI.

TO MISS KENNEDY.

MADAM—Permit me to present you with the enclosed song, as a small though grateful tribute for the honour of your acquaintance. I have, in these verses, attempted some faint sketches of your portrait in the unembellished, simple manner of descriptive TRUTH. Flattery I leave to your LOVERS, whose exaggerating fancies may make them imagine you still nearer perfection than you really are.

Poets, Madam, of all mankind, feel most forcibly the powers of BEAUTY; as, if they are really POETS of nature's making, their feelings must be finer, and their taste more delicate, than most of the world. In the cheerful bloom of SPRING, or the pensive mildness of AUTUMN, the grandeur of SUMMER, or the hoary majesty of WINTER, the poet feels a charm unknown to the rest of his species. Even the sight of a fine flower, or the company of a fine woman (by far the finest part of God's works below), have sensations for the poetic heart that the HERD of men are strangers to. On this last account, Madam, I am, as in many other things, indebted to Mr. Hamilton's kindness in introducing me to you. Your lovers may view you with a wish, I look on you with pleasure; their hearts, in your presence may glow with desire, mine rises with admiration.

That the arrows of misfortune, however they should, as incident to humanity, glance a slight wound, may never reach your *heart*—that the snares of villany may never beset you in the road of life—that INNOCENCE may hand you by the path of HONOUR to the dwelling of PEACE—is the sincere wish of him who has the honour to be, &c.

R. B.

NO. CCLXXII.

BURNS TO MR. THOMSON.

June, 1793.

WHEN I tell you, my dear Sir, that a friend of mine, in whom I am much interested, has fallen a sacrifice to these accursed times, you will easily allow that it might unhinge me for doing any good among ballads. My own loss, as to pecuniary matters, is trifling; but the total ruin of a much-loved friend is a loss indeed. Pardon my seeming inattention to your last commands.

I cannot alter the disputed lines in the "Mill, Mill, O!" (165) What you think a defect, I esteem as a positive beauty; so you see how doctors differ. I shall now, with as much alacrity as I can muster, go on with your commands.

You know Frazer, the hautboy-player in Edinburgh—he is here, instructing a band of music for a fencible corps quartered in this county. Among many of his airs that please me, there is one, well known as a reel, by the name of "The Quaker's Wife;" and which, I remember, a grand-aunt of mine used to sing, by the name of "Liggeram Cosh, my bonnie wee lass." Mr. Frazer plays it slow, and with an expression that quite charms me. I became such an enthusiast about it, that I made a song for it, which I here subjoin, and enclose Frazer's set of the tune. If they hit your fancy, they are at your service; if not, return me the tune, and I will put it in Johnson's Museum. I think the song is not in my worst manner.

[*Here Burns inserts the song "Blythe hae I been on yon Hill."*]

I should wish to hear how this pleases you.

NO. CCLXXIII.

BURNS TO MR. THOMSON.

June 25th, 1793.

HAVE you ever, my dear Sir, felt your bosom ready to burst with indignation, on reading of those mighty villains who divide kingdom against kingdom, desolate provinces, and lay nations waste, out of the wantonness of ambition, or often from still more ignoble passions? In a mood of this kind to-day I recollected the air of "Logan Water," and it occurred to me that its querulous melody probably had its origin from the plaintive indignation of some swelling, suffering heart, fired at the tyrannic strides of some public destroyer, and overwhelmed with private distress, the consequence of a country's ruin. If I have done any thing at all like justice to my feelings, the following song, composed in three-quarters of an hour's meditation in my elbow-chair, ought to have some merit:—

[*Here is inserted the song, "Logan Braes."*]

Do you know the following beautiful little fragment, in Witherspoon's collection of Scots songs?

AIR—"*Hughie Graham.*"

"Oh gin my love were yon red rose,
  That grows upon the castle wa';
And I mysel' a drap o' dew,
  Into her bonnie breast to fa'!

Oh there, beyond expression blest,
  I'd feast on beauty a' the night,
Seal'd on her silk-saft faulds to rest,
  Till fley'd awa by Phœbus' light!"

This thought is inexpressibly beautiful; and quite, so far as I know, original. It is too short for a song, else I would forswear you altogether, unless you gave it a place. I have often tried to eke a stanza to it, but in vain. After balancing myself for a musing five minutes, on the hind-legs of my elbow-chair, I produced the following.

The verses are far inferior to the foregoing, I frankly confess; but if worthy of insertion at all, they might be first in place; as every poet who knows any thing of his trade, will husband his best thoughts for a concluding stroke.

Oh were my love yon lilac fair,
  Wi' purple blossoms to the spring;
And I, a bird to shelter there,
  When wearied on my little wing!

How I wad mourn, when it was torn
  By autumn wild, and winter rude!
But I wad sing on wanton wing,
  When youthfu' May its bloom renewed.

NO. CCLXXIV.

MR. THOMSON TO BURNS.

Monday, July 1st, 1793.

I AM extremely sorry, my good Sir, that any thing should happen to unhinge you.

The times are terribly out of tune, and when harmony will be restored, Heaven knows.

The first book of songs, just published, will be dispatched to you along with this. Let me be favoured with your opinion of it, frankly and freely.

I shall certainly give a place to the song you have written for the "Quaker's Wife;" it is quite enchanting. Pray, will you return the list of songs, with such airs added to it as you think ought to be included? The business now rests entirely on myself, the gentlemen who originally agreed to join the speculation having requested to be off. No matter, a loser I cannot be. The superior excellence of the work will create a general demand for it, as soon as it is properly known; and were the sale even slower than it promises to be, I should be somewhat compensated for my labour, by the pleasure I shall receive from the music. I cannot express how much I am obliged to you for the exquisite new songs you are sending me; but thanks, my friend, are a poor return for what you have done—as I shall be benefited by the publication, you must suffer me to enclose a small mark of my gratitude (166), and to repeat it afterwards when I find it convenient. Do not return it, for, by Heaven! if you do, our correspondence is at an end; and though this would be no loss to you, it would mar the publication, which, under your auspices, cannot fail to be respectable and interesting.

Wednesday Morning.

I thank you for your delicate additional verses to the old fragment, and for your excellent song to "Logan Water:"—Thomson's truly elegant one will follow for the English singer. Your apostrophe to statesmen is admirable, but I am not sure if it is quite suitable to the supposed gentle character of the fair mourner who speaks it.

NO. CCLXXV.

BURNS TO MR. THOMSON.

July 2nd, 1793.

My dear Sir—I have just finished the following ballad, and, as I do think it in my best style, I send it you. Mr. Clarke, who wrote down the air from Mrs. Burns's wood-note wild, is very fond of it, and has given it a celebrity by teaching it to some young ladies of the first fashion here. If you do not like the air enough to give it a place in your collection, please return it. The song you may keep, as I remember it.

[*Here follows the song of "Bonnie Jean."*]

I have some thoughts of inserting in your index, or in my notes, the names of the fair ones, the themes of my songs. I do not mean the name at full; but dashes or asterisks, so as ingenuity may find them out.

The heroine of the foregoing is Miss M., daughter to Mr. M., of D., one of your subscribers. I have not painted her in the rank which she holds in life, but in the dress and character of a cottager.

NO. CCLXXVI.

BURNS TO MR. THOMSON.

July, 1793.

I assure you, my dear Sir, that you truly hurt me with your pecuniary parcel. It degrades me in my own eyes. However, to return it would savour of affectation; but, as to any more traffic of that debtor and creditor kind, I swear, by that Honour which crowns the upright statue of Robert Burns's Integrity—on the least motion of it, I will indignantly spurn the bypast transaction, and from that moment commence entire stranger to you! Burns's character for generosity of sentiment and independence of mind, will, I trust, long outlive any of his wants which the cold unfeeling ore can supply:—at least, I will take care that such a character he shall deserve.

Thank you for my copy of your publication. Never did my eyes behold in any musical work such elegance and correctness. Your preface, too, is admirably written, only your partiality to me has made you say too much: however, it will bind me down to double every effort in the future progress of the work. The following are a few remarks on the songs in the list you sent me. I never copy what I write to you, so I may be often tautological, or perhaps contradictory.

"The Flowers o' the Forest," is charming as a poem, and should be, and must be, set to the notes; but, though out of your rule, the three stanzas beginning,

"I have seen the smiling o' fortune beguiling,"

are worthy of a place, were it but to immortalise the author of them, who is an old lady of my acquaintance, and at this moment living in Edinburgh. She is a Mrs. Cockburn, I forget of what place, but from Roxburghshire. (167) What a charming apostrophe is

"Oh fickle fortune, why this cruel sporting,
Why, why torment us, poor sons of a day!"

The old ballad, "I wish I were where Helen lies," is silly, to contemptibility. My alteration of it, in Johnson's, is not much better. Mr. Pinkerton, in his, what he calls, ancient ballads (many of them notorious, though beautiful enough, forgeries), has the best set. It is full of his own interpolations —but no matter.

In my next, I will suggest to your consideration a few songs which may have escaped your hurried notice. In the meantime, allow me to congratulate you now, as a brother of the quill. You have committed your character and fame, which will now be tried, for ages to come, by the illustrious jury of the SONS AND DAUGHTERS OF TASTE—all whom poesy can please, or music charm.

Being a bard of nature, I have some pretensions to second sight; and I am warranted by the spirit to fortell and affirm, that your great-grand-child will hold up your volumes, and say, with honest pride, "This so much admired selection was the work of my ancestor!"

NO. CCLXXVII.

MR. THOMSON TO BURNS.

Edinburgh, August 1st, 1793.

DEAR SIR—I had the pleasure of receiving your last two letters, and am happy to find you are quite pleased with the appearance of the first book. When you come to hear the songs sung and accompanied, you will be charmed with them.

"The bonnie brucket lassie" certainly deserves better verses, and I hope you will match her. "Cauld kail in Aberdeen," "Let me in this ane night," and several of the livelier airs, wait the muse's leisure; these are peculiarly worthy of her choice gifts; besides, you'll notice, that in airs of this sort the singer can always do greater justice to the poet, than in the slower airs of "The bush aboon Traquair," "Lord Gregory," and the like; for, in the manner the latter were frequently sung, you must be contented with the sound, without the sense. Indeed, both the airs and words are disguised by the very slow, languid, psalm-singing style in which they are too often performed; they lose animation and expression altogether, and, instead of speaking to the mind, or touching the heart, they cloy upon the ear, and set us a-yawning!

Your ballad, "There was a Lass, and she was fair," is simple and beautiful, and shall, undoubtedly grace my collection.

NO. CCLXXVIII.

BURNS TO MR. THOMSON.

August, 1793.

MY DEAR THOMSON—I hold the pen for our friend Clarke, who at present is studying the music of the spheres at my elbow. The Georgium Sidus he thinks is rather out of tune; so, until he rectify that matter, he cannot stoop to terrestrial affairs.

He sends you six of the *rondeau* subjects, and if more are wanted, he says you shall have them. R. B.

Confound your long stairs!

S. CLARKE.

NO. CCLXXIX.

BURNS TO MR. THOMSON.

August, 1793.

YOUR objection, my dear Sir, to the passages in my song of "Logan Water," is right in one instance; but it is difficult to mend it: if I can, I will. The other passage you object to does not appear in the same light to me.

I have tried my hand on "Robin Adair," and, you will probably think, with little success; but it is such a cursed, cramp, out-of-the-way measure, that I despair of doing anything better to it.

[*Here follows "Phillis the Fair."*]

So much for namby-pamby. I may, after all, try my hand on it in Scots verse. There I always find myself most at home.

I have just put the last hand to the song I meant for "Cauld kail in Aberdeen." If it suits you to insert it, I shall be pleased, as the heroine is a favourite of mine; if not, I shall also be pleased; because I wish, and will be glad to see you act decidedly in the business. 'Tis a tribute as a man of taste, and as an editor, which you owe yourself.

NO. CCLXXX.

MR. THOMSON TO BURNS.

August, 1793.

MY GOOD SIR—I consider it one of the most agreeable circumstances attending this publication of mine, that it has procured me so many of your much-valued epistles. Pray make my acknowledgements to St. Stephen for the tunes; tell him I admit the justness of his complaint on my staircase, conveyed in his laconic postscript to your *jeu d'esprit*, which I perused more than once, without discovering exactly whether your discussion was music, astronomy, or politics! though a sagacious friend, acquainted with the convivial habits of the poet and the musician, offered me a bet of two to one you were just drowning care together; that an empty bowl was the only thing that would deeply affect you, and the only matter you could then study how to remedy!

I shall be glad to see you give "Robin Adair" a Scottish dress. Peter is furnishing him with an English suit for a change, and you are well matched together. Robin's air is excellent, though he certainly has an out-of-the-way measure as ever poor Parnassian wight was plagued with. I wish you would invoke the muse for a single elegant stanza to be substituted for the concluding objectionable verses of "Down the Burn Davie," so that this most exquisite song may no longer be excluded from good company.

Mr. Allan has made an inimitable drawing from your "John Anderson, my jo," which I am to have engraved as a frontispiece to the humorous class of songs; you will be quite charmed with it, I promise you. The old couple are seated by the fireside. Mrs. Anderson, in great good humour, is clapping John's shoulders, while he smiles and looks at her with such glee, as to show that he fully recollects the pleasant days and nights when they were "first acquent." The drawing would do honour to the pencil of Teniers.

NO. CCLXXXI.

BURNS TO MR. THOMSON.

August, 1793.

THAT crinkum-crankum tune, "Robin Adair," has run so in my head, and I succeeded so ill in my last attempt, that I have ventured, in this morning's walk, one essay more. You, my dear Sir, will remember an unfortunate part of our worthy friend Cunningham's story, which happened about three years ago. That struck my fancy, and I endeavoured to do the idea justice as follows:—

[*Here follows "Had I a Cave."*]

By the way, I have met with a musical Highlander in Breadalbane's Fencibles, which are quartered here, who assures me that he well remembers his mother singing Gaelic songs to both "Robin Adair" and "Gramachree." They certainly have more of the Scotch than Irish taste in them.

This man comes from the vicinity of Inverness: so it could not be any intercourse with Ireland that could bring them; except, what I shrewdly suspect to be the case, the wandering minstrels, harpers and pipers, used to go frequently errant through the wilds both of Scotland and Ireland, and so some favourite airs might be common to both. A case in point—they have lately, in Ireland, published an Irish air, as they say, called "Caun du delis." The fact is, in a publication of Corri's, a great while ago, you will find the same air, called a Highland one, with a Gaelic song set to it. Its name there, I think, is "Oran Gaoil," and a fine air it is. Do ask honest Allan, or the Rev. Gaelic parson, about these matters.

NO. CCLXXXII.

BURNS TO MR. THOMSON.

August, 1793.

MY DEAR SIR—"Let me in this ane night," I will reconsider. I am glad that you are pleased with my song, "Had I a Cave," &c., as I liked it myself.

I walked out yesterday evening with a volume of the Museum in my hand, when, turning up "Allan Water," "What numbers shall the muse repeat," &c., as the words appeared to me rather unworthy of so fine an air, and recollecting that it is on your list, I sat and raved under the shade of an old thorn, till I wrote one to suit the measure. I may be wrong; but I think it is not in my worst style. You must know, that in Ramsay's Tea-table, where the modern song first appeared, the ancient name of the tune, Allan says, is "Allan Water," or "My love Annie's very bonnie." This last has certainly been a line of the original song; so I took up the idea, and, as you will see, have introduced the line in its place, which I presume it formerly occupied; though I likewise give you a choosing line, if it should not hit the cut of your fancy:

[*Here follows "By Allan stream I chanc'd to rove."*]

Bravo! say I; it is a good song. Should you think so too (not else), you can set the music to it, and let the other follow as English verses.

Autumn is my propitious season. I make more verses in it than all the year else. God bless you!

NO. CCLXXXIII.

BURNS TO MR. THOMSON.

August, 1793.

Is "Whistle and I'll come to you, my lad," one of your airs? I admire it much; and yesterday I set the following verses to it. Urbani, whom I have met with here, begged them of me, as he admires the air much; but as I understand that he looks with rather an evil eye on your work, I did not choose to comply. However, if the song does not suit your taste, I may possibly send it him. The set of the air which I had in my eye is in Johnson's Museum.

[*Here follows "Oh whistle, and I'll come to you."*]

Another favourite air of mine is, "The muckin' o' Geordie's byre." When sung slow, with expression, I have wished that it had had better poetry; that I have endeavoured to supply as follows:—

[*Here he gives the song "Adown winding Nith."*]

Mr. Clarke begs you to give Miss Phillis a corner in your book, as she is a particular flame of his. She is a Miss Phillis M'Murdo, sister to "Bonnie Jean." They are both pupils of his. You shall hear from me, the very first grist I get from my rhyming-mill.

NO. CCLXXXIV.

BURNS TO MR. THOMSON.

August, 1793.

THAT tune, "Cauld kail," is such a favorite of yours, that I once more roved out yesterday for gloamin-shot at the muses (168); when the muse that presides o'er the shores of Nith, or rather my old inspiring dearest nymph, Coila, whispered me the following. I have two reasons for thinking that it was my early, sweet, simple inspirer that was by my elbow, "smooth gliding without step," and pouring the song on my glowing fancy;—In the first place, since I left Coila's native haunts, not a fragment of a poet has arisen to cheer her solitary musings, by catching inspiration from her, so I more than suspect that she has followed me hither, or, at least, makes me occasional visits; secondly, the last stanza of this song I send you, is in the very words that Coila taught me many years ago, and which I set to an old Scots reel in Johnson's Museum.

[*Here follows "Come, let me take thee."*]

If you think the above will suit your idea of your favourite air, I shall be highly pleased. "The last time I came o'er the moor" I cannot meddle with, as to mending it; and the musical world have been so long accustomed to Ramsay's words, that a different song, though positively superior, would not be so well received. I am not fond of choruses to songs, so I have not made one for the foregoing.

NO. CCLXXXV.

BURNS TO MR. THOMSON. (169)

August, 1793.

So much for Davie. The chorus, you know, is to the low part of the tune. See Clarke's set of it in the Museum.

N.B. In the Museum they have drawled out the tune to twelve lines of poetry, which is ——— nonsense. Four lines of song, and four of chorus, is the way.

NO. CCLXXXVI.

TO MISS CRAIK. (170)

Dumfries, August, 1793.

MADAM—Some rather unlooked-for accidents have prevented my doing myself the honour of a second visit to Arbigland, as I was so hospitably invited, and so positively meant to have done. However, I still hope to have that pleasure before the busy months of harvest begin.

I enclose you two of my late pieces, as some kind of return for the pleasure I have received in perusing a certain MS. volume of poems in the possession of Captain Riddel. To repay one with an *old song*, is a proverb, whose force, you, Madam, I know, will not allow. What is said of illustrious descent is, I believe, equally true of a talent for poetry—none ever despised it who had pretensions to it. The fates and characters of the rhyming tribe often employ my thoughts when I am disposed to be melancholy. There is not, among all the martyrologies that ever were penned, so rueful a narrative as the lives of the poets. In the comparative view of wretches, the criterion is not what they are doomed to suffer, but how they are formed to bear. Take a being of our kind, give him a stronger imagination and a more delicate sensibility, which between them will ever engender a more ungovernable set of passions than are the usual lot of man; implant in him an irresistible impulse to some idle vagary, such as arranging wild flowers in fantastical nosegays, tracing the grasshopper to his haunt by his chirping song, watching the frisks of the little minnows in the sunny pool, or hunting after the intrigues of butterflies—in short, send him adrift after some pursuit which shall eternally mislead him from the paths of lucre, and yet curse him with a keener relish than any man living for the pleasures that lucre can purchase; lastly, fill up the measure of his woes by bestowing on him a spurning sense of his own dignity—and you have created a wight nearly as miserable as a poet. To you, Madam, I need not recount the fairy pleasures the muse bestows, to counterbalance this catalogue of evils. Bewitching poetry is like bewitching woman: she has, in all ages, been accused of misleading mankind from the councils of wisdom and the paths of prudence, involving them in difficulties, baiting them with poverty, branding them with infamy, and plunging them in the whirling vortex of ruin; yet, where is the man but must own that all our happiness on earth is not worthy the name—that even the holy hermit's solitary prospect of paradisiacal bliss is but the glitter of a northern sun rising over a frozen region, compared with the many pleasures, the nameless raptures, that we owe to the lovely queen of the heart of man! R. B.

NO. CCLXXXVII.

TO LADY GLENCAIRN (171).

My Lady—The honour you have done your poor poet, in writing him so very obliging a letter, and the pleasure the enclosed beautiful verses have given him, came very seasonably to his aid, amid the cheerless gloom and sinking despondency of diseased nerves and December weather. As to forgetting the family of Glencairn, Heaven is my witness with what sincerity I could use those old verses, which please me more in their rude simplicity than the most elegant lines I ever saw.

"If thee, Jerusalem, I forget,
Skill part from my right hand.

My tongue to my mouth's roof let cleave,
If I do thee forget,
Jerusalem, and thee above
My chief joy do not set."

When I am tempted to do anything improper, I dare not, because I look on myself as accountable to your ladyship and family. Now and then, when I have the honour to be called to the tables of the great, if I happen to meet with any mortification from the stately stupidity of self-sufficient squires, or the luxurious insolence of upstart nabobs, I get above the creatures by calling to remembrance that I am patronised by the noble house of Glencairn; and at gala-times, such as New-year's day, a christening, or the kirn-night, when my punch-bowl is brought from its dusty corner, and filled up in honour of the occasion, I begin with—*The Countess of Glencairn!* My good woman, with the enthusiasm of a grateful heart, next cries, *My Lord!* and so the toast goes on until I end with *Lady Harriet's little angel!* (172) whose epithalamium I have pledged myself to write.

When I received your ladyship's letter, I was just in the act of transcribing for you some verses I have lately composed; and meant to have sent them my first leisure hour, and acquainted you with my late change of life. I mentioned to my lord my fears concerning my farm. Those fears were indeed too true; it is a bargain would have ruined me, but for the lucky circumstance of my having an Excise commission.

People may talk as they please of the ignominy of the Excise; £50 a year will support my wife and children, and keep me independent of the world; and I would much rather have it said that my profession borrowed credit from me, than that I borrowed credit from my profession. Another advantage I have in this business, is the knowledge it gives me of the various shades of human character, consequently assisting me vastly in my poetic pursuits. I had the most ardent enthusiasm for the muses when nobody knew me but myself, and that ardour is by no means cooled, now that my Lord Glencairn's goodness has introduced me to all the world. Not that I am in haste for the press. I have no idea of publishing, else I certainly had consulted my noble generous patron; but after acting the part of an honest man, and supporting my family, my whole wishes and views are directed to poetic pursuits. I am aware that, though I were to give performances to the world superior to my former works; still, if they were of the same kind with those, the comparative reception they would meet with, would nortify me. I have turned my thoughts on the drama. I do not mean the stately buskin of the tragic muse.

Does not your ladyship think that an Edinburgh theatre would be more amused with affectation, folly, and whim of true Scottish growth, than manners, which by far the greatest part of the audience can only know at second hand? I have the honour to be, your ladyship's ever devoted and grateful humble servant, R. B.

NO. CCLXXXVIII.

MR. THOMSON TO BURNS.

Edinburgh, Sept. 1*st*, 1793.

My Dear Sir—Since writing you last, I have received half a dozen songs, with which I am delighted beyond expression. The humour and fancy of "Whistle, and I'll come to you, my lad," will render it nearly as great a favourite as "Duncan Gray." "Come, let me take thee to my breast," "Adown winding Nith," and "By Allan stream," &c., are full of imagination and feeling, and sweetly suit the airs for which they are intended. "Had I a cave on some wild distant shore," is a striking and affecting composition. Our friend, to whose story it refers, reads it with a swelling heart, I assure you. The union we are now forming, I think, can never be broken; these songs of yours will descend, with the music, to the latest posterity, and will be fondly cherished so long as genius, taste, and sensibility, exist in our island.

Whilst the muse seems so propitious, I think it right to enclose a list of all the favours I have to ask of her—no fewer than twenty and three! I have burdened the pleasant Peter with as many as it is probable he will attend to; most of the remaining airs would puzzle the English poet not a little—they are of that peculiar measure and rhythm, that they must be familiar to him who writes for them.

NO. CCLXXXIX.

BURNS TO MR. THOMSON.

Sept., 1793.

You may readily trust, my dear Sir, that any exertion in my power is heartily at your service. But one thing I must hint to you; the very name of Peter Pindar is of great service to your publication, so get a verse from him now and then; though I have no objection, as well as I can, to bear the burden of the business.

You know that my pretensions to musical taste are merely a few of nature's instincts, untaught and untutored by art. For this reason, many musical compositions, particularly where much of the merit lies in counterpoint, however they may transport and ravish the ears of you connoisseurs, affect my simple lug no otherwise than merely as melodious din. On the other hand, by way of amends, I am delighted with many little melodies, which the learned musician despises as silly and insipid. I do not know whether the old air, "Hey tuttie taitie," may rank among this number; but well I know that, with Frazer's hautboy, it has often filled my eyes with tears. There is a tradition, which I have met with in many places in Scotland, that it was Robert Bruce's march at the battle of Bannockburn. This thought, in my solitary wanderings, warmed me to a pitch of enthusiasm on the theme of liberty and independence, which I threw into a kind of Scottish ode, fitted to the air, that one might suppose to be the gallant Royal Scot's address to his heroic followers on that eventful morning.

BRUCE TO HIS MEN AT BANNOCKBURN.

Tune—*Hey tuttie taitie.*

Scots, wha hae wi' Wallace bled,
Scots, wham Bruce has aften led,
Welcome to your gory bed,
Or to victory!

Now's the day, and now's the hour:
See the front o' battle lour:
See approach proud Edward's power—
Chains and slavery.

Wha will be a traitor-knave?
Wha can fill a coward's grave?
Wha sae base as be a slave?
Let him turn and flee!

Wha for Scotland's king and law
Freedom's sword will strongly draw,
Freeman stand, or freeman fa',
Let him follow me!

By oppression's woes and pains,
By your sons in servile chains!
We will drain our dearest veins,
But they shall be free!

Lay the proud usurpers low!
Tyrants fall in every foe!
Liberty's in every blow!—
Let us do or die!

So may God ever defend the cause of truth and liberty, as he did that day! Amen.

P.S. I showed the air to Urbani, who was highly pleased with it, and begged me to make soft verses for it; but I had no idea of giving myself any trouble on the subject, till the accidental recollection of that glorious struggle for freedom, associated with the glowing ideas of some other struggles of the same nature, not quite so ancient, roused my rhyming mania. Clarke's set of the tune, with his bass, you will find in the Museum, though I am afraid that the air is not what will entitle it to a place in your elegant selection.

NO. CCXC.

BURNS TO MR. THOMSON.

Sept. 1793.

I DARE say, my dear Sir, that you will begin to think my correspondence is persecution. No matter, I can't help it; a ballad is my hobby-horse, which, though otherwise a simple sort of harmless idiotical beast enough, has yet this blessed headstrong property, that when once it has fairly made off with a hapless wight, it gets so enamoured with the tingle-gingle, tingle-gingle of its own bells, that it is sure to run poor pilgarlick, the bedlam jockey, quite beyond any useful point or post in the common race of men.

The following song I have composed for "Oran-gaoil," the Highland air, that, you tell me in your last, you have resolved to give a place to in your book. I have this moment finished the song, so you have it glowing from the mint. If it suit you, well! —If not, 'tis also well!

[*Here follows "Behold the Hour."*]

NO. CCXCI.

MR. THOMSON TO BURNS.

Edinburgh, Sept. 5th, 1793.

I BELIEVE it is generally allowed that the greatest modesty is the sure attendant of the greatest merit. While you are sending me verses that even Shakspeare might be proud to own, you speak of them as if they were ordinary productions! Your heroic ode is to me the noblest composition of the kind in the Scottish language. I happened to dine yesterday with a party of your friends, to whom I read it. They were all charmed with it; entreated me to find out a suitable air for it, and reprobated the idea of giving it a tune so totally devoid of interest or grandeur as "Hey tuttie taitie." Assuredly your partiality for this tune must arise from the ideas associated in your mind by the tradition concerning it, for I never heard any person,—and I have conversed again and again with the greatest enthusiasts for Scottish airs—I say, I never heard any one speak of it as worthy of notice.

I have been running over the whole hundred airs, of which I lately sent you the list; and I think "Lewie Gordon" is most happily adapted to your ode; at least, with a very slight variation of the fourth line, which I shall presently submit to you. There is in "Lewie Gordon" more of the grand than the plaintive, particularly when it is sung with a degree of spirit, which your words would oblige the singer to give it. I would have no scruple about substituting your ode in the room of "Lewie Gordon," which has neither the interest, the grandeur, nor the poetry, that characterise your verses. Now, the variation I have to suggest upon the last line of each verse, the only line too short for the air is as follows;—

Verse 1st, Or to *glorious* victory.
2nd, *Chains*—chains and slavery.
3rd, Let him, *let him* turn and flee.

4th, Let him *bravely* follow me.
5th, But *they shall*, they shall be free.
6th, Let us, *let us* do or die!

If you connect each line with its own verse, I do not think you will find that either the sentiment or the expression loses any of its energy. The only line which I dislike in the whole song is, "Welcome to your gory bed." Would not another word be preferable to "welcome?" In your next I will expect to be informed whether you agree to what I have proposed. The little alterations I submit with the greatest deference.

The beauty of the verses you have made for "Oran-gaoil" will ensure celebrity to the air.

NO. CCXCII.

BURNS TO MR. THOMSON.

Sept. 1793.

I HAVE received your list, my dear Sir, and here go my observations on it. (173)

"Down the Burn Davie." I have this moment tried an alteration, leaving out the last half of the third stanza, and the first half of the last stanza, thus:—

As down the burn they took their way,
And thro' the flowery dale;
His cheek to hers he aft did lay,
And love was aye the tale.

With "Mary, when shall we return,
Sic pleasure to renew?"
Quoth Mary, "Love I like the burn,
And aye shall follow you." (174)

"Thro' the wood laddie"—I am decidedly of opinion, that, both in this, and "There'll never be peace till Jamie comes hame," the second or high part of the tune being a repetition of the first part an octave higher, is only for instrumental music, and would be much better omitted in singing.

"Cowden-knowes." Remember in your index that the song in pure English to this tune, beginning,

When summer comes, the swains on Tweed,

is the production of Crawford. Robert was his Christian name.

"Laddie, lie near me," must lie by me for some time. I do not know the air; and until I am complete master of a tune, in my own singing (such as it is), I can never compose for it. My way is: I consider the poetic sentiment correspondent to my idea of the musical expression; then choose my theme; begin one stanza: when that is composed, which is generally the most difficult part of the business, I walk out, sit down now and then, look out for objects in nature around me that are in unison and harmony with the cogitations of my fancy, and workings of my bosom; humming every now and then the air with the verses I have framed. When I feel my muse beginning to jade, I retire to the solitary fireside of my study, and there commit my effusions to paper; swinging at intervals on the hind-legs of my elbow chair, by way of calling forth my own critical strictures as my pen goes on. Seriously, this, at home, is almost invariably my way.

What cursed egotism!

"Gill Morice" I am for leaving out. It is a plaguy length; the air itself is never sung; and its place can well be supplied by one or two songs for fine airs that are not in your list—for instance, "Craigieburn wood" and "Roy's wife." The first, beside its intrinsic merit, has novelty; and the last has high merit, as well as great celebrity. I have the original words of a song for the last air, in the handwriting of the lady who composed it; and they are superior to any edition of the song which the public has yet seen.

"Highland-laddie." The old set will please a mere Scotch ear best; and the new an Italianised one. There is a third, and what Oswald calls the old "Highland-laddie," which pleases me more than either of them. It is sometimes called "Ginglin Johnnie;" it being the air of an old humorous tawdry song of that name. You will find it in the Museum, "I hae been at Crookieden," &c. I would advise you, in this musical quandary, to offer up your prayers to the muses for inspiring direction; and, in the meantime, waiting for this direction, bestow a libation to Bacchus; and there is not a doubt but you will hit on a judicious choice. *Probatum est.*

"Auld Sir Simon" I must beg you to leave out, and put in its place "The Quaker's wife."

"Blythe hae I been o'er the hill," is one of the finest songs ever I made in my life, and, besides, is composed on a young lady, positively the most beautiful, lovely woman in the world. As I purpose giving you the names and designations of all my heroines, to appear in some future edition of your work, perhaps half a century hence, you must certainly include "The bonniest lass in a' the warld," in your collection.

"Dainty Davie" I have heard sung nineteen thousand nine hundred and ninety-nine times, and always with the chorus to the low part of the tune; and nothing has surprised me so much as your opinion on this subject. If it will not suit as I proposed, we will lay two of the stanzas together, and then make the chorus follow.

"Fee him, father:" I enclose you Frazer's set of this tune when he plays it slow: in fact, he makes it the language of despair. I shall here give you two stanzas, in that style, merely to try if it will be any improvement. (175) Were it possible, in singing, to give it half the pathos which Frazer gives it in playing, it would make an admirably pathetic song. I do not give these verses for any merit they have. I composed them at the time in which "Patie Allan's mither died—that was, about the back o' midnight;" and by the lee-side of a bowl of punch, which had overset every mortal in company except the hautbois and the muse.

[*Here follows "Thou hast left me ever."*]

"Jockie and Jenny" I would discard, and in its place would put "There's nae luck about the house," which has a very pleasant air, and which is positively the finest love-ballad in that style in the Scottish, or perhaps in any other language. "When she came ben she bobbit," as an air, is more beautiful than either, and in the *andante* way would unite with a charming sentimental ballad.

"Saw ye my father?" is one of my greatest favourites. The evening before last, I wandered out, and began a tender song, in what I think is its native style. I must premise, that the old way, and the way to give most effect, is to have no starting-note, as the fiddlers call it, but to burst at once into the pathos. Every country girl sings "Saw ye my father?" &c.

My song is but just begun; and I should like, before I proceed, to know your opinion of it. I have sprinkled it with the Scottish dialect, but it may be easily turned into correct English. (176)

"Todlin hame." Urbani mentioned an idea of his, which has long been mine, that this air is highly susceptible of pathos: accordingly, you will soon hear him at your concert try it to a song of mine in the Museum, "Ye banks and braes o' bonnie Doon." One song more, and I have done; "Auld lang syne." The air is but mediocre; but the following song, the old song of the olden times, and which has never been in print, nor even in manuscript, until I took it down from an old man's singing, is enough to recommend any air.

[*Here the poet gives "Auld lang syne."*]

Now, I suppose, I have tired your patience fairly. You must, after all is over, have a number of ballads, properly so called. "Gill Morice," "Tranent Muir," "Macpherson's farewell," "Battle of Sheriff-muir," or, "We ran, and they ran" (I know the author of this charming ballad, and his history), "Hardiknute," "Barbara Allan" (I can furnish a finer set of this tune than any that has yet appeared); and besides, do you know that I really have the old tune to which "The cherry and the slae" was sung, and which is mentioned as a well-known air in "Scotland's Complaint," a book published before poor Mary's days? It was then called, "The banks o' Helicon;" an old poem which Pinkerton has brought to light. You will see all this in Tytler's History of Scottish Music. The tune, to a learned ear, may have no great merit; but it is a great curiosity. I have a good many original things of this kind.

NO. CCXCIII.

BURNS TO MR. THOMSON.

September, 1793.

I AM happy, my dear Sir, that my ode pleases you so much. Your idea, "honour's bed," is, though a beautiful, a hackneyed idea; so, if you please, we will let the line stand as it is. I have altered the song as follows:—

BANNOCKBURN.

ROBERT BRUCE'S ADDRESS TO HIS ARMY.

Scots, wha hae wi' Wallace bled,
Scots, wham Bruce has aften led,
Welcome to your gory bed!
Or to glorious victory!

Now's the day, and now's the hour;
See the front o' battle lour;
See approach proud Edward's power!
Edward! chains and slavery.

Wha will be a traitor knave?
Wha can fill a coward's grave?
Wha sae base as be a slave?
Traitor! coward! turn, and flee!

Wha for Scotland's king and law
Freedom's sword will strongly draw,
Freeman stand, or freeman fa',
Sodger! hero! on wi' me!

By oppression's woes and pains!
By your sons in servile chains!
We will drain our dearest veins,
But they shall be—shall be free!

Lay the proud usurpers low!
Tyrants fall in every foe!
Liberty's in every blow!
Forward! let us do or die!

N.B. I have borrowed the last stanza from the common stall edition of Wallace—

A false usurper sinks in every foe,
And liberty returns with every blow.

A couplet worthy of Homer. Yesterday you had enough of my correspondence. The post goes, and my head aches miserably. One comfort! I suffer so much, just now, in this world, for last night's joviality, that I shall escape scot-free for it in the world to come. Amen.

NO. CCXCIV.

MR. THOMSON TO BURNS.

September 12th, 1793.

A THOUSAND thanks to you, my dear Sir, for your observations on the list of my songs. I am happy to find your ideas so much in unison with my own, respecting the generality of the airs, as well as the verses. About some of them we differ, but there is no disputing about hobby-horses. I shall not fail to profit by the remarks you make, and to re-consider the whole with attention.

"Dainty Davie" must be sung, two stanzas together, and then the chorus: 'tis the proper way. I agree with you, that there may be something of pathos, or tenderness at least, in the air of "Fee him, father," when performed with feeling; but a tender cast may be given almost to any lively air, if you sing it very slowly, expressively, and with serious words. I am, however, clearly and invariably for retaining the cheerful tunes joined to their own humorous verses, wherever the verses are passable. But the sweet song for "Fee him, father," which you began about the back of midnight, I will publish as an additional one. Mr. James Balfour, the king of good fellows, and the best singer of the lively Scottish ballads that ever existed, has charmed thousands of companies with "Fee him, father," and with "Todlin hame" also, to the old words, which never should be disunited from either of these airs. Some bacchanals I would wish to discard. "Fy! let's a' to the bridal," for instance, is so coarse and vulgar, that I think it fit only to be sung in a company of drunken colliers; and "Saw ye my father?" appears to me both indelicate and silly.

One word more with regard to your heroic ode. I think, with great deference to the poet, that a prudent general would avoid saying any thing to his soldiers which might tend to make death more frightful than it is. "Gory" presents a disagreeable image to the mind; and to tell them "Welcome to your gory bed," seems rather a discouraging address, notwithstanding the alternative which follows. I have shown the song to three friends of excellent taste, and each of them objected to this line, which emboldens me to use the freedom of bringing it again under your notice. I would suggest,

Now prepare for honour's bed,
Or for glorious victory!

NO. CCXCV.

BURNS TO MR. THOMSON.

September, 1793.

"WHO shall decide when doctors disagree?" My ode pleases me so much that I cannot alter it. Your proposed alterations would, in my opinion, make it tame. I am exceedingly obliged to you for putting me on reconsidering it, as, I think, I have much improved it. Instead of "sodger! hero!" I will have it "Caledonian! on wi' me!"

I have scrutinized it over and over; and to the world, some way or other, it shall go as it is. At the same time, it will not in the least hurt me should you leave it out altogether, and adhere to your first intention of adopting Logan's verses. (177)

I have finished my song to "Saw ye my father?" and in English, as you will see. That there is a syllable too much for the expression of the air, is true; but, allow me to say, that the mere dividing of a dotted crotchet into a crotchet and a quaver, is not a great matter: however, in that I have no pretensions to cope in judgment with you. Of the poetry I speak with confidence; but the music is a business where I hint my ideas with the utmost diffidence.

The old verses have merit, though unequal, and are popular: my advice is to set the air to the old words, and let mine follow as English verses. Here they are :—

[*Here follows the song "Where are the joys."*]

Adieu, my dear Sir! the post goes, so I shall defer some other remarks until more leisure.

NO. CCXCVI.

BURNS TO THOMSON.

September, 1793.

I HAVE been turning over some volumes of songs, to find verses whose measures would suit the airs for which you have allotted me to find English songs.

For "Muirland Willie," you have, in Ramsay's Tea-table an excellent song, beginning, "Ah, why those tears in Nelly's eyes?" As for "The Collier's dochter," take the following old bacchanal :—

[*Here follows "Deluded swain, the pleasure."*]

The faulty line in Logan-Water, I mend thus :—

"How can your flinty hearts enjoy
The widow's tears, the orphan's cry?"

The song otherwise will pass. As to "M'Gregoria Rua-Ruth," you will see a song of mine to it, with a set of the air superior to yours, in the Museum, vol. ii. p. 181. The song begins,

"Raving winds around her blowing."

Your Irish airs are pretty, but they are downright Irish. If they were like the "Banks of Banna," for instance, though really Irish, yet in the Scottish taste, you might adopt them. Since you are so fond of Irish music, what say you to twenty-five of them in an additional number? We could easily find this quantity of charming airs: I will take care that you shall not want songs; and I assure you that you would find it the most saleable of the whole. If you do not approve of "Roy's wife," for the music's sake, we shall not insert it. "Deil tak the wars" is a charming song; so is, "Saw ye my Peggy?" "There's nae luck about the house" well deserves a place. I cannot say that "O'er the hills and far awa" strikes me as equal as your selection. "This is no my ain house" is a great favourite air of mine; and if you will send me your set of it, I will task my muse to her highest effort. What is your opinion of "I hae laid a herrin' in saut?" I like it much. Your Jacobite airs are pretty, and there are many others of the same kind pretty; but you have not room for them. You cannot, I think, insert "Fy! let's a' to the bridal," to any other words than its own.

What pleases me, as simple and *naïf*, disgusts you as ludicrous and low. For this reason, "Fy! gie me my coggie, Sirs," "Fy! let's a' to the bridal," with several others of that cast, are to me highly pleasing; while, "Saw ye my father, or saw ye my mother?" delights me with its descriptive simple pathos. Thus my song, "Ken ye what Meg o' the mill has gotten?" pleases myself so much, that I cannot try my hand at another song to the air, so I shall not attempt it. I know you will laugh at all this; but "ilka man wears his belt his ain gait."

NO. CCXCVII.

BURNS TO MR. THOMSON.

October 1793.

YOUR last letter, my dear Thomson, was indeed laden with heavy news. Alas, poor Erskine! (178) The recollection that he was a coadjutor in your publication, has, till now, scared me from writing to you, or turning my thoughts on composing for you.

I am pleased that you are reconciled to the air of the "Quaker's wife;" though, by the bye, an old Highland gentleman, and a deep antiquarian, tells me it is a Gaelic air, and known by the name of "Leiger m' choss." The following verses, I hope, will please you, as an English song to the air.

[*Here follows "Thine am I, my faithful fair."*]

Your objection to the English song I proposed for "John Anderson, my jo," is certainly just. The following is by an old acquaintance of mine, and I think has merit. The song was never in print, which I think is so much in your favour. The more original good poetry your collection contains, it certainly has so much the more merit.

SONG.—BY GAVIN TURNBULL. (179)

"Oh condescend, dear charming maid,
My wretched state to view;
A tender swain to love betray'd,
And sad despair, by you.

While here, all melancholy,
My passion I deplore,
Yet, urg'd by stern resistless fate,
I love thee more and more.

I heard of love, and with disdain
The urchin's power denied ;
I laugh'd at every lover's pain,
And mock'd them when they sigh'd.

But how my state is alter'd !
Those happy days are o'er ;
For all thy unrelenting hate,
I love thee more and more.

Oh, yield, illustrious beauty, yield !
No longer let me mourn ;
And though victorious in the field,
Thy captive do not scorn.

Let generous pity warm thee,
My wonted peace restore ;
And, grateful, I shall bless thee still,
And love thee more and more."

The following address of Turnbull's to the Nightingale, will suit as an English song to the air, "There was a lass, and she was fair." By the bye, Turnbull has a great many songs in MS., which I can command, if you like his manner. Possibly, as he is an old friend of mine, I may be prejudiced in his favour: but I like some of his pieces very much.

THE NIGHTINGALE.

"Thou sweetest minstrel of the grove,
That ever tried the plaintive strain,
Awake thy tender tale of love,
And soothe a poor forsaken swain.

For though the muses deign to aid,
And teach him smoothly to complain ;
Yet Delia, charming, cruel maid,
Is deaf to her forsaken swain.

All day, with fashion's gaudy sons,
In sport she wanders o'er the plain :
Their tales approves, and still she shuns
The notes of her forsaken swain.

When evening shades obscure the sky,
And bring the solemn hours again,
Begin, sweet bird, thy melody,
And soothe a poor forsaken swain."

I shall just transcribe another of Turnbull's, which would go charmingly to "Lewie Gordon."

LAURA.

"Let me wander where I will,
By shady wood, or winding rill;
Where the sweetest May-born flowers
Paint the meadows, deck the bowers ;
Where the linnet's early song
Echoes sweet the woods among :
Let me wander where I will,
Laura haunts my fancy still.

If at rosy dawn I choose
To indulge the smiling muse ;
If I court some cool retreat,
To avoid the noontide heat ;
If beneath the moon's pale ray,
Thro' unfrequented wilds I stray ;
Let me wander where I will,
Laura haunts my fancy still.

When at night the drowsy god
Waves his sleep-compelling rod,
And to fancy's wakeful eyes
Bids celestial visions rise ;
While with boundless joy I rove
Thro' the fairy land of love :
Let me wander where I will,
Laura haunts my fancy still."

The rest of your letter I shall answer on some other opportunity.

NO. CCXCVIII.

MR. THOMSON TO BURNS.

November 7th, 1793.

My Good Sir—After so long a silence, it gave me peculiar pleasure to recognise your well known-hand, for I had begun to be apprehensive that all was not well with you. I am happy to find, however, that your silence did not proceed from that cause, and that you have got among the ballads once more.

I have to thank you for your English song to "Leiger m' choss," which I think extremely good, although the colouring is warm. Your friend, Mr. Turnbull's songs have doubtless considerable merit; and as you have the command of his manuscripts, I hope you may find out some that will answer as English songs, to the airs yet unprovided. (180)

NO. CCXCIX.

TO JOHN M'MURDO, Esq.

Dumfries, December, 1793.

Sir—It is said that we take the greatest liberties with our greatest friends, and I pay myself a very high compliment in the manner in which I am going to apply the remark. I have owed you money longer than ever I owed it to any man. Here is Ker's account, and here are six guineas; and now, I don't owe a shilling to man—or woman either. But for these d—— dirty, dog-ear'd little pages (181), I had done myself the honour to have waited on you long ago. Independent of the obligations your hospitality has laid me under, the conciousness of your superiority in the rank of man and gentleman, of itself was fully as much as I could ever make head against; but to owe you money too, was more than I could face.

I think I once mentioned something of a collection of Scots songs I have for some years been making—I send you a perusal of what I have got together. I could not conveniently spare them above five or six days, and five or six glances of them will probably more than suffice you. A very few of them are my own. When you are tired of them, please leave them with Mr. Clint, of the King's Arms. There is not another copy of the collection in the world; and I should be sorry that any unfortunate negligence should deprive me of what has cost me a good deal of pains. R. B.

NO. CCC.

TO JOHN M'MURDO, Esq.,

DRUMLANRIG.

Dumfries, 1793.

Will Mr. M'Murdo do me the favour to accept of these volumes (182); a trifling but sincere mark of the very high respect I bear for his worth as a man, his manners as a gentleman, and his kindness as a friend. However inferior now, or afterwards, I may rank as a poet, one honest virtue to which few poets can pretend, I trust I shall ever claim as mine—to no man, whatever his station in life, or his power to serve me, have I ever paid a compliment at the expense of TRUTH. The Author.

NO. CCCI.

TO CAPTAIN ————. (183)

Dumfries, December 5th, 1793.

Sir—Heated as I was with wine yesternight, I was perhaps rather seemingly impertinent in my anxious wish to be honoured with your acquaintance. You will forgive it —it was the impulse of heart-felt respect. "He is the father of the Scottish county reform, and is a man who does honour to the business, at the same time that the business does honour to him," said my worthy friend Glenriddel to somebody by me who was talking of your coming to this country with your corps. "Then," I said, "I have a woman's longing to take him by the hand, and say to him, 'Sir, I honour you as a man to whom the interests of humanity are dear, and as a patriot to whom the rights of your country are sacred.'"

In times like these, Sir, when our commoners are barely able, by the glimmering of their own twilight understandings, to scrawl a frank, and when lords are what gentlemen would be ashamed to be, to whom shall a sinking country call for help? To the independent country gentleman. To him who has too deep a stake in his country not to be in earnest for her welfare; and who, in the honest pride of man, can view, with equal contempt, the insolence of office, and the allurements of corruption.

I mentioned to you a Scots ode or song I had lately composed (184), and which, I think, has some merit. Allow me to enclose it. When I fall in with you at the theatre, I shall be glad to have your opinion of it. Accept of it, Sir, as a very humble, but most sincere tribute of respect for a man who, dear as he prizes poetic fame, yet holds dearer an independent mind. I have the honour to be,

R. B.

NO. CCCII.

TO MRS. RIDDEL,

WHO WAS ABOUT TO BESPEAK A PLAY ONE EVENING AT THE DUMFRIES THEATRE.

I am thinking to send my "Address" to some periodical publication, but it has not got your sanction, so pray look over it.

As to the Tuesday's play, let me beg of you, my dear Madam, to give us "The Wonder, a Woman keeps a Secret!" to which please add, "The Spoilt Child"—you will highly oblige me by so doing.

Ah, what an enviable creature you are! There now, this cursed, gloomy, blue-devil day, you are going to a party of choice spirits—

To play the shapes
Of frolic fancy, and incessant form
Those rapid pictures, assembled train
Of fleet ideas, never join'd before,
Where lively *wit* excites to gay surprise:
Or folly-painting *humour*, grave himself,
Calls laughter forth, deep shaking every nerve.

But, as you rejoice with them that do rejoice, do also remember to weep with them that weep, and pity your melancholy friend,

R. B. (185)

NO. CCCIII.

TO A LADY,

IN FAVOUR OF A PLAYER'S BENEFIT.

Dumfries, 1794.

MADAM—You were so very good as to promise me to honour my friend with your presence on his benefit night. That night is fixed for Friday next: the play a most interesting one—"The Way to Keep Him." I have the pleasure to know Mr. G. well. His merit as an actor is generally acknowledged. He has genius and worth which would do honour to patronage: he is a poor and modest man:—claims which, from their very *silence* have the more forcible power on the generous heart. Alas, for pity! that, from the indolence of those who have the good things of this life in their gift, too often does brazen-fronted importunity snatch that boon, the rightful due of retiring, humble want! Of all the qualities we assign to the author and director of Nature, by far the most enviable is, to be able "to wipe away all tears from all eyes." Oh what insignificant, sordid wretches are they, however chance may have loaded them with wealth, who go to their graves, to their magnificent *mausoleums*, with hardly the consciousness of having made one poor honest heart happy.

But I crave your pardon, Madam; I came to beg not to preach. R. B.

NO. CCCIV.

TO THE EARL OF BUCHAN.

Dumfries, January 12th, 1794.

MY LORD—Will your lordship allow me to present you with the enclosed little composition of mine (186), as a small tribute of gratitude for the acquaintance with which you have been pleased to honour me. Independent of my enthusiasm as a Scotsman, I have rarely met with any thing in history which interests my feelings as a man, equal with the story of Bannockburn. On the one hand, a cruel but able usurper, leading on the finest army in Europe to extinguish the last spark of freedom among a greatly-daring and greatly-injured people; on the other hand, the desperate relics of a gallant nation, devoting themselves to rescue their bleeding country, or perish with her.

Liberty! thou art a prize truly, and indeed invaluable, for never canst thou be too dearly bought!

If my little ode has the honour of your lordship's approbation, it will gratify my highest ambition. I have the honour to be, &c. R. B.

NO. CCCV.

TO CAPTAIN MILLER,

DALSWINTON.

DEAR SIR—The following ode (187) is on a subject which I know you by no means regard with indifference. Oh, Liberty,

Thou mak'st the gloomy face of nature gay,
Giv'st beauty to the sun, and pleasure to the day.

It does me so much good to meet with a man whose honest bosom glows with the generous enthusiasm, the heroic daring of liberty, that I could not forbear sending you a composition of my own on the subject, which I really think is in my best manner. I have the honour to be, dear Sir, &c.

R. B.

NO. CCCVI.

TO MRS. RIDDEL.

DEAR MADAM—I meant to have called on you yesternight; but as I edged up to your box-door, the first object which greeted my view was one of those lobster-coated puppies, sitting like another dragon, guarding the Hesperian fruit. On the conditions and capitulations you so obligingly offer, I shall certainly make my weather-beaten, rustic phiz a part of your box-furniture on Tuesday, when we may arrange the business of the visit.

Among the profusion of idle compliments, which insidious craft, or unmeaning folly, incessantly offer at your shrine—a shrine, how far exalted above such adoration—permit me, were it but for rarity's sake, to pay you the honest tribute of a warm heart and an independent mind,—and to assure you, that I am, thou most amiable, and most accomplished of thy sex, with the most respectful esteem, and fervent regard, thine, &c. R. B.

NO. CCCVII.

TO THE SAME.

I WILL wait on you, my ever-valued friend, but whether in the morning I am not sure. Sunday closes a period of our curst revenue business, and may probably keep me employed with my pen until noon. Fine employment for a poet's pen! There is a species of the human genus that I call *the gin-horse class:* what enviable dogs they are! Round, and round, and round they go. Mundell's ox, that drives his cotton mill, is their exact prototype—without an idea or wish beyond their circle—fat, sleek, stupid, patient, quiet and contented; while here I sit, altogether Novemberish, a d—— melange of fretfulness and melancholy; not enough of the one to rouse me to passion, nor of the other to repose me in torpor; my soul flouncing and fluttering round her tenement, like a wild finch, caught amid the horrors of winter, and newly thrust into a cage. Well, I am persuaded, that it was of me the Hebrew sage prophesied, when he foretold—"And, behold, on whatsoever this man doth set his heart, it shall not prosper!" If my resentment is awaked, it is sure to be where it dare not squeak; and if— * * *

Pray that wisdom and bliss be more frequent visitors of R. B.

NO. CCCVIII.

TO THE SAME.

I HAVE this moment got the song from Syme, and I am sorry to see that he has spoilt it a good deal. It shall be a lesson to me how I lend him anything again.

I have sent you "Werter," truly happy to have any, the smallest, opportunity of obliging you.

'Tis true, Madam, I saw you once since I was at Woodlee; and that once froze the very life-blood of my heart. Your reception of me was such, that a wretch meeting the eye of his judge, about to pronounce sentence of death on him, could only have envied my feelings and situation. But I hate the theme, and never more shall write or speak on it.

One thing I shall proudly say, that I can pay Mrs. R. a higher tribute of esteem, and appreciate her amiable worth more truly, than any man whom I have seen approach her. R. B.

NO. CCCIX.

TO THE SAME.

I HAVE often told you, my dear friend, that you had a spice of caprice in your composition, and you have as often disavowed it; even, perhaps, while your opinions were, at the moment, irrefragably proving it. Could *anything* estrange me from a friend such as you? No! To-morrow I shall have the honour of waiting on you.

Farewell, thou first of friends, and most accomplished of women, even with all thy little caprices! R. B.

NO. CCCX.

TO THE SAME.

MADAM—I return your common-place book. I have perused it with much pleasure, and would have continued my criticisms, but as it seems the critic has forfeited your esteem, his strictures must lose their value.

If it is true that "offences come only from the heart;" before you I am guiltless. To admire, esteem and prize you, as the most accomplished of women, and the first of friends—if these are crimes, I am the most offending thing alive.

In a face where I used to meet the kind complacency of friendly confidence, *now* to find cold neglect, an.. contemptuous scorn—is a wrench that my heart can ill bear. It is, however, some kind of miserable good luck, that while *de haut-en-bas* rigour may depress an unoffending wretch to the ground, it has a tendency to rouse a stubborn something in his bosom, which, though it cannot heal the wounds of his soul, is at least an opiate to blunt their poignancy.

With the profoundest respect for your abilities; the most sincere esteem, and ardent regard for your gentle heart and amiable manners; and the most fervent wish and prayer for your welfare, peace, and bliss—I have the honour to be, Madam, your most devoted humble servant, R. B

NO. CCCXI.

TO JOHN SYME, Esq. (188)

You know that among other high dignities, you have the honour to be my supreme court of critical judicature, from which there is no appeal. I enclose you a song, which I composed since I saw you, and I am going to give you the history of it. (189) Do you know, that among much that I admire in the characters and manners of those great folks whom I have now the honour to call my acquaintances, the Oswald family,—there is nothing charms me more than Mr. Oswald's unconcealable attachment to that incomparable woman. Did you ever, my dear Syme, meet with a man who owed more to the Divine Giver of all good things than Mr. O.? A fine fortune; a pleasing exterior; self-evident amiable dispositions, and an ingenuous, upright mind,—and that informed, too, much beyond the usual run of young fellows of his rank and fortune: and to all this, such a woman!—but of her I shall say nothing at all, in despair of saying anything adequate: in my song, I have endeavoured to do justice to what would be his feelings, on seeing, in the scene I have drawn, the habitation of his Lucy. As I am a good deal pleased with my performance, I, in my first fervour, thought of sending it to Mrs. Oswald, but, on second thoughts, perhaps what I offer as the honest incense of genuine respect, might, from the well-known character of poverty and poetry, be construed into some modification or other of that servility which my soul abhors. R. B.

NO. CCCXII.

TO MISS ———.

Dumfries, 1794

Madam—Nothing short of a kind of absolute necessity could have made me trouble you with this letter. Except my ardent and just esteem for your sense, taste and worth, every sentiment arising in my breast, as I put pen to paper to you, is painful. The scenes I have passed with the friend of my soul, and his amiable connexions! the wrench at my heart to think that he is gone, for ever gone from me, never more to meet in the wanderings of a weary world! and the cutting reflection of all, that I had most unfortunately, though most undeservedly, lost the confidence of that soul of worth, ere it took its flight!

These Madam, are sensations of no ordinary anguish. However, you also may be offended with some *imputed* improprieties of mine; sensibility you know I possess, and sincerity none will deny me.

To oppose those prejudices which have been raised against me, is not the business of this letter. Indeed, it is a warfare I know not how to wage. The powers of positive vice I can in some degree calculate, and against direct malevolence I can be on my guard: but who can estimate the fatuity of giddy caprice, or ward off the unthinking mischief of precipitate folly?

I have a favour to request of you, Madam; and of your sister, Mrs. ———, through your means. You know that, at the wish of my late friend, I made a collection of all my trifles in verse which I had ever written. They are many of them local, some of them puerile and silly, and all of them unfit for the public eye. As I have some little fame at stake—a fame that I trust may live when the hate of those who "watch for my halting," and the contumelious sneer of those whom accident has made my superiors, will, with themselves, be gone to the regions of oblivion—I am uneasy now for the fate of those manuscripts. Will Mrs. ——— have the goodness to destroy them, or return them to me? As a pledge of friendship they were bestowed; and that circumstance, indeed, was all their merit. Most unhappily for me, that merit they no longer possess; and I hope that Mrs. ———'s goodness, which I well know, and ever will revere, will not refuse this favour to a man whom she once held in some degree of estimation.

With the sincerest esteem, I have the honour to be, Madam, &c. R. B.

NO. CCCXIII.

TO MR. CUNNINGHAM.

February 25th, 1794.

CANST thou minister to a mind diseased? Canst thou speak peace and rest to a soul tost on a sea of troubles, without one friendly star to guide her course, and dreading that the next surge may overwhelm her? Canst thou give to a frame, tremblingly alive to the tortures of suspense, the stability and hardihood of the rock that braves the blast! If thou canst not do the least of these, why wouldst thou disturb me in my miseries, with thy inquiries after me?

For these two months I have not been able to lift a pen. My constitution and frame were *ab origine*, blasted with a deep, incurable taint of hypochondria, which poisons my existence. Of late a number of domestic vexations, and some pecuniary share in the ruin of these cursed times—losses which, though trifling, were yet what I could ill bear—have so irritated me, that my feelings at times could only be envied by a reprobate spirit listening to the sentence that dooms it to perdition.

Are you deep in the language of consolation? I have exhausted in reflection every topic of comfort. *A heart at ease* would have been charmed with my sentiments and reasonings; but as to myself, I was like Judas Iscariot preaching the gospel: he might melt and mould the hearts of those around him, but his own kept its native incorrigibilty.

Still, there are two great pillars that bear us up, amid the wreck of misfortune and misery. The ONE is composed of the different modifications of a certain noble, stubborn something in man, known by the names of courage, fortitude, magnanimity. The OTHER is made up of those feelings and sentiments, which, however the sceptic may deny them, or the enthusiast disfigure them, are yet, I am convinced, original and component parts of the human soul; those *senses of the mind*—if I may be allowed the expression—which connect us with, and link us to, those awful obscure realities—an all-powerful, and equally beneficent God, and a world to come, beyond death and the grave. The first gives the nerve of combat, while a ray of hope beams on the field: the last pours the balm of comfort into the wounds which time can never cure.

I do not remember, my dear Cunningham, that you and I ever talked on the subject of religion at all. I know some who laugh at it, as the trick of the crafty FEW to lead the undiscerning MANY; or, at most, as an uncertain obscurity, which mankind can never know anything of, and with which they are fools if they give themselves much to do. Nor would I quarrel with a man for his irreligion, any more than I would for his want of a musical ear. I would regret that he was shut out from what, to me and to others, were such superlative sources of enjoyment. It is in this point of view, and for this reason, that I will deeply imbue the mind of every child of mine with religion. If my son should happen to be a man of feeling, sentiment and taste, I shall thus add largely to his enjoyments. Let me flatter myself, that this sweet little fellow, who is just now running about my desk, will be a man of a melting, ardent, glowing heart,—and an imagination delighted with the painter, and rapt with the poet. Let me figure him wandering out in a sweet evening, to inhale the balmy gales, and enjoy the growing luxuriance of the spring; himself the while in the blooming youth of life. He looks abroad on all nature, and through nature up to nature's God. His soul, by swift, delighting degrees, is rapt above this sublunary sphere, until he can be silent no longer, and bursts out into the glorious enthusiasm of Thomson:—

"These, as they change, Almighty Father these
Are but the varied God. The rolling year
Is full of thee;"—

and so on, in all the spirit and ardour of that charming hymn. These are no ideal pleasures, they are real delights; and I ask, what of the delights among the sons of men are superior, not to say equal, to them? And, they have this precious, vast addition, that conscious virtue stamps them for her own, and lays hold on them to bring herself into the presence of a witnessing, judging, and approving God. R. B..

NO. CCCXIV.

MR. THOMSON TO BURNS.

Edinburgh, April 17th, 1794.

MY DEAR SIR—Owing to the distress of our friend for the loss of his child, at the time of his receiving your admirable but melancholy letter, I had not an opportunity, till lately, of perusing it. How sorry I am to find Burns saying, "Canst thou not minister to a mind diseased?" while he is delighting others from one end of the island to the other. Like the hypochondriac who went to consult a physician upon his case—"Go," says the doctor, "and see the famous Carlini, who keeps all Paris in good humour." "Alas! Sir," replied the patient, "I am that unhappy Carlini!"

Your plan for our meeting together pleases me greatly, and I trust that by some means or other it will soon take place; but your bacchanalian challenge almost frightens me, for I am a miserable weak drinker!

Allan is much gratified by your good opinion of his talents. He has just began a sketch from your "Cotter's Saturday Night," and, if it pleases himself in the design, he will probably etch or engrave it. In subjects of the pastoral and humorous kind, he is, perhaps, unrivalled by any artist living. He fails a little in giving beauty and grace to his females, and his colouring is sombre, otherwise his paintings and drawings would be in greater request.

I like the music of the "Sutor's dochter," and will consider whether it shall be added to the last volume; your verses to it are pretty; but your humorous English song, to suit "Jo Janet," is inimitable. What think you of the air, "Within a mile of Edinburgh?" It has always struck me as a modern English imitation, but it is said to be Oswald's, and is so much liked, that I believe I must include it. The verses are little better than namby-pamby. Do you consider it worth a stanza or two?

NO. CCCXV.

BURNS TO MR. THOMSON.

May, 1794.

My Dear Sir—I return you the plates, with which I am highly pleased; I would humbly propose, instead of the younker knitting stockings, to put a stock and horn into his hands. A friend of mine, who is positively the ablest judge on the subject I have ever met with, and though an unknown, is yet a superior artist with the burin, is quite charmed with Allan's manner. I got him a peep of the "Gentle Shepherd;" and he pronounces Allan a most original artist of great excellence.

For my part, I look on Mr. Allan's choosing my favourite poem for his subject, to be one of the highest compliments I have ever received.

I am quite vexed at Pleyel's being cooped up in France, as it will put an entire stop to our work. Now, and for six or seven months, I shall be quite in song, as you shall see by and bye. I got an air, pretty enough, composed by Lady Elizabeth Heron, of Heron, which she calls "The banks of Cree." Cree is a beautiful romantic stream; and as her ladyship is a particular friend of mine, I have written the following song to it.

[*Here follows the song entitled "The Banks of Cree."*]

NO. CCCXVI.

TO THE EARL OF GLENCAIRN.

May, 1794.

My Lord—When you cast your eye on the name at the bottom of this letter, and on the title-page of the book I do myself the honour to send your lordship, a more pleasurable feeling than my vanity, tells me that it must be a name not entirely unknown to you. The generous patronage of your late illustrious brother found me in the lowest obscurity: he introduced my rustic muse to the partiality of my country; and to him I owe all. My sense of his goodness, and the anguish of my soul at losing my truly noble protector and friend, I have endeavoured to express in a poem to his memory, which I have now published. This edition is just from the press; and in my gratitude to the dead, and my respect for the living (fame belies you, my lord, if you possess not the same dignity of man, which was your noble brother's characteristic feature), I had destined a copy for the Earl of Glencairn. I learnt just now that you are in town: allow me to present it to you.

I know, my lord, such is the vile, venal contagion which pervades the world of letters, that professions of respect from an author, particularly from a poet to a lord, are more than suspicious. I claim, by my past conduct, and my feelings at this moment, an exception to the too just conclusion. Exalted as are the honours of your lordship's name, and unnoted as is the obscurity of mine; with the uprightness of an honest man, I come before your lordship, with an offering—however humble, 'tis all I have to give, of my grateful respect; and to beg of you, my lord, 'tis all I have to ask of you, that you will do me the honour to accept of it. I have the honour to be, R. B.

NO. CCCXVII.

TO DAVID MACCULLOCH, Esq. (190)

Dumfries, June 21st, 1794.

My Dear Sir—My long projected journey through your country is at last fixed; and on Wednesday next, if you have nothing of more importance to do, take a saunter down to Gatehouse about two or three o'clock; I shall be happy to take a draught of M'Kune's best with you. Collector Syme will be at Glens about that time, and will meet us about dish-of-tea hour. Syme goes also to Kerroughtree, and let me remind you of your kind promise to accompany me there; I will need all the friends I can muster, for I am indeed ill at ease whenever I approach your honourables and right-honourables. Yours sincerely, R. B.

NO. CCCXVIII.

TO MRS. DUNLOP.

Castle Douglas, June 25th, 1794.

Here, in a solitary inn, in a solitary village, am I set by myself, to amuse my brooding fancy as I may. Solitary confinement, you know, is Howard's favourite idea of reclaiming sinners; so let me consider by what fatality it happens that I have so long been exceeding sinful as to neglect the correspondence of the most valued friend I have on earth. To tell you that I have been in poor health will not be excuse enough, though it is true. I am afraid that I am about to suffer for the follies of my youth. My medical friends threaten me with a flying gout; but I trust they are mistaken.

I am just going to trouble your critical patience with the first sketch of a stanza I have been framing as I passed along the road. The subject is liberty: you know, my honoured friend, how dear the theme is to me. I design it as an irregular ode for General Washington's birth-day. After having mentioned the degeneracy of other kingdoms, I come to Scotland thus:

Thee, Caledonia, thy wild heaths among,
Thee, famed for martial deed and sacred song,
To thee I turn with swimming eyes;
Where is that soul of freedom fled?
Immingled with the mighty dead,
Beneath the hallowed turf where Wallace lies!
Hear it not, Wallace, in thy bed of death,
Ye babbling winds in silence sweep,
Disturb ye not the hero's sleep.

With the addition of

That arm which nerved with thundering fate,
Braved usurpation's boldest daring!
One quenched in darkness like the sinking star,
And one the palsied arm of tottering, powerless age.

You will probably have another scrawl from me in a stage or two. R. B.

NO. CCCXIX.

TO MR. JAMES JOHNSON.

Dumfries, 1794.

My Dear Friend—You should have heard from me long ago; but over and above some vexatious share in the pecuniary losses of these accursed times, I have all this winter been plagued with low spirits and blue devils, so that *I have almost hung my harp on the willow trees.*

I am just now busy correcting a new edition of my poems, and this with my ordinary business, finds me in full employment.

I send you by my friend, Mr. Wallace, forty-one songs for your fifth volume; if we cannot finish it any other way, what would you think of Scots words to some beautiful Irish airs? In the meantime, at your leisure, give a copy of the "Museum" to my worthy friend, Mr. Peter Hill, bookseller, to bind for me, interleaved with blank leaves, exactly as he did the Laird of Glenriddel's, that I may insert every anecdote I can learn, together with my own criticisms and remarks on the songs. A copy of this kind I shall leave with you, the editor, to publish at some after period, by way of making the "Museum" a book famous to the end of time, and you renowned for ever.

I have got a Highland dirk, for which I have great veneration, as it once was the dirk of Lord Balmerino. It fell into bad hands, who stripped it of the silver mounting, as well as the knife and fork. I have some thoughts of sending it to your care, to get it mounted anew.

Thank you for the copies of my Volunteer Ballad. Our friend Clarke has done *indeed* well!—'tis chaste and beautiful. I have not met with anything that has pleased me so much. You know I am no connoisseur; but that I am an amateur will be allowed me.

R. B.

NO. CCCXX.

BURNS TO MR. THOMSON.

July, 1794.

Is there no news yet of Pleyel? Or is your work to be at a dead stop, until the allies set our modern Orpheus at liberty from the savage thraldom of democrat discords? Alas, the day! And woe is me! That auspicious period, pregnant with the happiness of millions. * * * *

I have presented a copy of your songs to the daughter of a much-valued and much-honoured friend of mine, Mr. Graham of Fintry. I wrote on the blank side of the title-page the following address to the young lady:

"Here, where the Scottish muse immortal lives,
In sacred strains and tuneful numbers join'd,
Accept the gift; tho' humble he who gives,
Rich is the tribute of the grateful mind.

So may no ruffian-feeling (191) in thy breast,
Discordant jar thy bosom-chords among;
But peace attune thy gentle soul to rest,
Or love ecstatic wake his seraph song.

Or pity's notes, in luxury of tears,
As modest want the tale of woe reveals:
While conscious virtue all the strain endears,
And heaven-born piety her sanction seals."

NO. CCCXXI.

TO MR. SAMUEL CLARKE, JUN., DUMFRIES.

Sunday Morning.

DEAR SIR—I was, I know, drunk last night, but I am sober this morning. From the expressions Capt. —— made use of to me, had I had nobody's welfare to care for but my own, we should certainly have come, according to the manners of the world, to the necessity of murdering one another about the business. The words were such as, generally, I believe, end in a brace of pistols; but I am still pleased to think that I did not ruin the peace and welfare of a wife and family of children in a drunken squabble. Farther, you know that the report of certain political opinions being mine, has already once before brought me to the brink of destruction. I dread lest last night's business may be misrepresented in the same way. You, I beg, will take care to prevent it. I tax your wish for Mr. Burns's welfare with the task of waiting, as soon as possible, on every gentleman who was present, and state this to him, and, as you please, show him this letter. What, after all, was the obnoxious toast? "May our success in the present war be equal to the justice of our cause"—a toast that the most outrageous frenzy of loyalty cannot object to. I request and beg, that this morning you will wait on the parties present at the foolish dispute. I shall only add, that I am truly sorry that a man who stood so high in my estimation as Mr. ——, should use me in the manner in which I conceive he has done.

R. B.

NO. CCCXXII.

MR. THOMSON TO BURNS.

Edinburgh, August 10th, 1794.

MY DEAR SIR—I owe you an apology for having so long delayed to acknowledge the favour of your last. I fear it will be, as you say, I shall have no more songs from Pleyel till France and we are friends; but, nevertheless, I am very desirous to be prepared with the poetry; and as the season approaches in which your muse of Coila visits you, I trust I shall, as formerly, be frequently gratified with the result of your amorous and tender interviews!

NO. CCCXXIII.

BURNS TO MR. THOMSON.

August 30th, 1794.

THE last evening, as I was straying out, and thinking of "O'er the hills and far away," I spun the following stanza for it; but whether my spinning will deserve to be laid up in store, like the precious thread of the silk-worm, or brushed to the devil, like the vile manufacture of the spider, I leave my dear Sir, to your usual candid criticism. I was pleased with several lines in it at first, but I own that now it appears rather a flimsy business.

This is just a hasty sketch, until I see whether it be worth a critique. We have many sailor songs, but as far as I at present recollect, they are mostly the effusions of the jovial sailor, not the wailings of his love-lorn mistress. I must here make one sweet exception—"Sweet Annie frae the sea-beach came." Now for the song:—

[*" On the seas and far away."*]

I give you leave to abuse this song, but do it in the spirit of Christian meekness.

NO. CCCXXIV.

MR. THOMSON TO BURNS.

Edinburgh, Sept. 16th, 1794.

My Dear Sir—You have anticipated my opinion of "On the seas and far away;" I do not think it one of your very happy productions, though it certainly contains stanzas that are worthy of all acceptation.

The second is the least to my liking, particularly "Bullets, spare my only joy." Confound the bullets! It might, perhaps, be objected to the third verse, "At the starless midnight hour," that it has too much grandeur of imagery, and that greater simplicity of thought would have better suited the character of a sailor's sweetheart. The tune, it must be remembered, is of the brisk, cheerful kind. Upon the whole, therefore, in my humble opinion, the song would be better adapted to the tune, if it consisted only of the first and last verses, with the choruses.

NO. CCCXXV.

BURNS TO MR. THOMSON.

Sept. 1794.

I shall withdraw my "On the seas and far away" altogether: it is unequal, and unworthy the work. Making a poem is like begetting a son: you cannot know whether you have a wise man or a fool, until you produce him to the world to try him.

For that reason I send you the offspring of my brain, abortions and all; and, as such, pray look over them and forgive them, and burn them. (192) I am flattered at your adopting "Ca' the yowes to the knowes," as it was owing to me that ever it saw the light. About seven years ago I was well acquainted with a worthy little fellow of a clergyman, a Mr. Clunie, who sang it charmingly; and, at my request, Mr. Clarke took it down from his singing. When I gave it to Johnson, I added some stanzas to the song, and mended others, but still it will not do for you. In a solitary stroll which I took to-day, I tried my hand on a few pastoral lines, following up the idea of the chorus, which I would preserve. Here it is, with all its crudities and imperfections on its head.

[*Here follows " Ca' the yowes."*]

I shall give you my opinion of your other newly adopted songs my first scribbling fit.

NO. CCCXXVI.

BURNS TO MR. THOMSON

Sept. 1794.

Do you know a blackguard Irish song called "Onagh's Waterfall?" The air is charming, and I have often regretted the want of decent verses to it. It is too much, at least for my humble rustic muse, to expect that every effort of hers shall have merit; still, I think it is better to have mediocre verses to a favourite air, than none at all. On this principle I have all along proceeded on the Scots Musical Museum; and as that publication is at its last volume, I intend the following song, to the air above mentioned, for that work.

If it does not suit you as an editor, you may be pleased to have verses to it that you can sing in the company of ladies.

[*Here follows "She says she loves me best of a'."*]

Not to compare small things with great, my taste in music is like the mighty Frederick of Prussia's taste in painting; we are told that he frequently admired what the connoisseurs decried, and always without any hypocrisy confessed his admiration. I am sensible that my taste in music must be inelegant and vulgar, because people of undisputed and cultivated taste can find no merit in my favourite tunes. Still, because I am cheaply pleased, is that any reason why I should deny myself that pleasure? Many of our strathspeys, ancient and modern, give me most exquisite enjoyment, where you and other judges would probably be showing disgust. For instance, I am just now making verses for "Rothemurche's rant," an air which puts me in raptures; and, in fact, unless I be pleased with the tune, I never can make verses to it. Here I have Clarke on my side, who is a judge that I will pit against any of you. "Rothemurche," he says, "is an air both original and beautiful;" and, on his recommendation, I have taken the first part of the tune for a chorus, and the fourth or last part for the song. I am but two stanzas deep in the work, and possibly you may think, and justly, that the poetry is as little worth your attention as the music.

[*Here follow two stanzas of the song, beginning "Lassie wi' the lint-white locks."*]

I have begun anew, "Let me in this ane night." Do you think that we ought to retain the old chorus? I think we must retain both the old chorus and the first stanza of the old song. I do not altogether like the third line of the first stanza, but cannot alter it to please myself. I am just three stanzas deep in it. Would you have the *denouëment* to be successful or otherwise?—should she "let him in" or not?

Did you not once propose "The sow's tail to Geordie" as an air for your work? I am quite delighted with it; but I acknowledge that is no mark of its real excellence. I once set about verses for it, which I meant to be in the alternate way of a lover and his mistress chanting together. I have not the pleasure of knowing Mrs. Thomson's Christian name; and yours, I am afraid, is rather burlesque for sentiment, else I had meant to have made you the hero and heroine of the little piece.

How do you like the following epigram which I wrote the other day on a lovely young girl's recovery from a fever? Doctor Maxwell was the physician who seemingly saved her from the grave; and to him I address the following:—

TO DR. MAXWELL,

ON MISS JESSIE STAIG'S RECOVERY.

Maxwell, if merit here you crave,
  That merit I deny:
You save fair Jessie from the grave?
  An angel could not die!

God grant you patience with this stupid epistle!

NO. CCCXXVII.

MR. THOMSON TO BURNS.

I PERCEIVE the sprightly muse is now attendant upon her favourite poet, whose *woodnotes wild* are become as enchanting as ever. "She says she loes me best of a'," is one of the pleasantest table songs I have seen, and henceforth shall be mine when the song is going round. I'll give Cunningham a copy; he can more powerfully proclaim its merit. I am far from undervaluing your taste for the strathspey music; on the contrary, I think it highly animating and agreeable, and that some of the strathspeys, when graced with such verses as yours, will make very pleasing songs, in the same way that rough Christians are tempered and softened by lovely woman, without whom, you know, they had been brutes.

I am clear for having the "Sow's tail," particularly as your proposed verses to it are so extremely promising. Geordie, as you observe, is a name only fit for burlesque composition. Mrs. Thomson's name (Katharine) is not at all poetical. Retain Jeanie, therefore, and make the other Jamie, or any other that sounds agreeably.

Your "Ca' the ewes" is a precious little morceau. Indeed, I am perfectly astonished and charmed with the endless variety of your fancy. Here let me ask you, whether you never seriously turned your thoughts upon dramatic writing? That is a field worthy of your genius, in which it might shine forth in all its splendour. One or two successful pieces upon the London stage would make your fortune. The rage at present is for musical dramas: few or none of those which have appeared since the "Duenna," possess much poetical merit; there is little in the conduct of the fable, or in the dialogue, to interest the audience: they are chiefly vehicles for music and pageantry. I think you might produce a comic opera in three acts, which would live by the poetry, at the same time that it would be proper to take every assistance from her tuneful sister. Part of the songs, of course, would be to our favourite Scottish airs; the rest might be left to the London composer—Storace for Drury-lane, or Shield for Covent-garden, both of them very able and popular musicians. I believe that interest and manœuvring are often necessary to have a drama brought on; so it may be with the namby-pamby tribe of flowery scribblers: but were you to address Mr. Sheridan himself by letter, and send him a dramatic piece, I am persuaded he would, for the honour of genius, give it a fair and candid trial. Excuse me for obtruding these hints upon your consideration. (193)

R. B.

NO. CCCXXVIII.

MR. THOMSON TO BURNS.

Edinburgh, October 14th, 1794.

THE last eight days have been devoted to the re-examination of the Scottish collections. I have read, and sung, and fiddled, and considered, till I am half blind, and wholly stupid. The few airs I have added, are enclosed.

Peter Pindar has at length sent me all the songs I expected from him, which are, in general, elegant and beautiful. Have you heard of a London collection of Scottish airs and songs, just published by Mr. Ritson, an Englishman? I shall send you a copy. His introductory essay on the subject is curious, and evinces great reading and research, but does not decide the question as to the origin of our melodies; though he shows clearly that Mr. Tytler, in his ingenious dissertation, has adduced no sort of proof of the hypothesis he wished to establish, and that his classification of the airs according to the eras when they were composed, is mere fancy and conjecture. On John Pinkerton, Esq., he has no mercy, but consigns him to damnation. He snarls at my publication, on the score of Pindar being engaged to write songs for it; uncandidly and unjustly leaving it to be inferred, that the songs of Scottish writers had been sent a-packing to make room for Peter's! Of you he speaks with some respect, but gives you a passing hit or two, for daring to dress up a little some old foolish songs for the Museum. His sets of the Scottish airs are taken, he says, from the oldest collections and best authorities; many of them, however, have such a strange aspect, and are so unlike the sets which are sung by every person of taste, old or young, in town or country, that we can scarcely recognise the features of our favourites. By going to the oldest collections of our music, it does not follow that we find the melodies in their original state. These melodies had been preserved, we know not how long, by oral communication, before being collected and printed; and, as different persons sing the same air very differently, according to their accurate or confused recollection of it, so, even supposing the first collectors to possess the industry, taste, and discernment, to choose the best they could hear (which is far from certain), still it must evidently be a chance, whether the collections exhibit any of the melodies in the state they were first composed. In selecting the melodies for my own collection, I have been as much guided by the living as by the dead. Where these differed, I preferred the sets that appeared to me the most simple and beautiful, and the most generally approved: and without meaning any compliment to my own capability of choosing, or speaking of the pains I have taken, I flatter myself that my sets will be found equally free from vulgar errors on the one hand, and affected graces on the other.

NO. CCCXXIX.

BURNS TO MR. THOMSON.

October 19th, 1794.

MY DEAR FRIEND—By this morning's post I have your list, and, in general, I highly approve of it. I shall, at more leisure, give you a critique on the whole. Clarke goes to your town by to-day's fly, and I wish you would call on him and take his opinion in general: you know his taste is a standard. He will return here again in a week or two, so please do not miss asking for him. One thing I hope he will do—persuade you to adopt my favourite, "Craigieburn wood," in your selection: it is as great a favourite of his as of mine. The lady on whom it was made is one of the finest women in Scotland; and in fact (*entre nous*) is in a manner to me, what Sterne's Eliza was to him—a mistress, or friend, or what you will, in the guileless simplicity of Platonic love. (Now, don't put any of your squinting constructions on this, or have any clishmaclaver about it among our acquaintances.) I assure you that to my lovely friend you are indebted for many of your best songs of mine. Do you think that the sober, gin-horse routine of existence could inspire a man with life, and love, and joy—could fire him with enthusiasm, or melt him with pathos, equal to the genius of your book? No! no! Whenever I want to be more than ordinary in song—to be in some degree equal to your diviner airs—do you imagine I fast and pray for the celestial emanation? *Tout au contraire!* I have a glorious recipe; the very one that for his own use was invented by the divinity of healing and poetry, when erst he piped to the flocks of Admetus. I put myself in a regimen of admiring a fine woman; and in proportion to the adorability of her charms, in proportion you are delighted with my verses. The lightning of her eye is the godhead of Parnassus, and the witchery of her smile the divinity of Helicon!

To descend to business; if you like my idea of "When she cam ben she bobbit," the following stanzas of mine, altered a little from what they were formerly, when set to another air, may perhaps do instead of worse stanzas:—

[*Here follows " Saw ye my Philly."*]

Now for a few miscellaneous remarks. "The Posie" (in the Museum) is my composition; the air was taken down from Mrs. Burns's voice. (194) It is well known in the west country, but the old words are trash. By the bye, take a look at the tune again, and tell me if you do not think it is the original from which "Roslin Castle" is composed. The second part, in particular, for the first two or three bars, is exactly the old air. "Strathallan's Lament" is mine; the music is by our right trusty and deservedly well-beloved Allan Masterton. "Donocht-Head" (195) is not mine; I would give ten pounds it were. It appeared first in the Edinburgh Herald, and came to the editor of that paper with the Newcastle postmark on it. (196) "Whistle o'er the lave o't" is mine: the music said to be by a John Bruce, a celebrated violin player in Dumfries, about the beginning of this century. This I know, Bruce, who was an honest man, though a red-wud Highlandman, constantly claimed it; and by all the old musical people here, is believed to be the author of it.

"Andrew and his cutty gun." The song to which this is set in the Museum is mine, and was composed on Miss Euphemia Murray, of Lintrose, commonly and deservedly called the Flower of Strathmore.

"How long and dreary is the night!" I met with some such words in a collection of songs somewhere, which I altered and enlarged; and to please you, and to suit your favourite air, I have taken a stride or two across my room and have arranged it anew, as you will find on the other page.

[*Here follows " How long and dreary is the Night."*]

Tell me how you like this. I differ from your idea of the expression of the tune. There is, to me, a great deal of tenderness in it. You cannot, in my opinion, dispense with a bass to your addenda airs. A lady of my acquaintance, a noted performer, plays and sings at the same time so charmingly, that I shall never bear to see any of her songs sent into the world, as naked as Mr. What-d'ye-call-um has done in his London collection. (197)

These English songs gravel me to death. I have not that command of the language that I have of my native tongue. I have been at "Duncan Gray," to dress it in English, but all I can do is deplorably stupid. For instance:—

[*Here follows "Let not Woman e'er complain."*]

Since the above, I have been out in the country taking a dinner with a friend, where I met with the lady whom I mentioned in the second page in this odds-and-ends of a letter. As usual, I got into song; and returning home I composed the following:—

THE LOVER'S MORNING SALUTE TO HIS MISTRESS.

TUNE—*Deil tak the Wars.*

Sleep'st thou, or wak'st thou, fairest creature;
  Rosy morn now lifts his eye,
Numbering ilka bud which nature
  Waters wi' the tears o' joy:
  Now thro' the leafy woods,
  And by the reeking floods,
Wild nature's tenants, freely, gladly stray;
  The lintwhite in his bower
  Chants o'er the breathing flower;
  The lav'rock to the sky
  Ascends wi' sangs o' joy,
While the sun and thou arise to bless the day.

Phœbus gilding the brow o' morning,
  Banishes ilk darksome shade,
Nature gladd'ning and adorning;
  Such to me my lovely maid.
  When absent frae my fair,
  The murky shades o' care

With starless gloom o'ercast my sullen sky;
But when in beauty's light,
She meets my ravished sight,
When through my very heart
Her beaming glories dart;
'Tis then I wake to life, to light, and joy! (198)

If you honour my verses by setting the air to them, I will vamp up the old song, and make it English enough to be understood.

I enclose you a musical curiosity, an East Indian air, which you would swear was a Scottish one. I know the authenticity of it, as the gentleman who brought it over is a particular acquaintance of mine. Do preserve me the copy I send you, as it is the only one I have. Clarke has set a bass to it, and I intend putting it into the Musical Museum. Here follow the verses I intend for it.

[*Here follows "But lately seen in gladsome green."*]

I would be obliged to you if you would procure me a sight of Ritson's collection of English songs, which you mention in your letter. I will thank you for another information, and that as speedily as you please: whether this miserable, drawling, hotchpotch epistle has not completely tired you of my correspondence?

NO. CCCXXX.

MR. THOMSON TO BURNS.

Edinburgh, October 27th, 1794.

I AM sensible, my dear friend, that a genuine poet can no more exist without his mistress than his meat. I wish I knew the adorable she, whose bright eyes and witching smiles have so often enraptured the Scottish bard, that I might drink her sweet health when the toast is going round. "Craigeburn wood" must certainly be adopted into my family, since she is the object of the song; but, in the name of decency, I must beg a new chorus verse from you. "Oh to be lying beyond thee, dearie," is perhaps a consummation to be wished, but will not do for singing in the company of ladies. The songs in your last will do you lasting credit, and suit the respective airs charmingly. I am perfectly of your opinion with respect to the additional airs. The idea of sending them into the world naked as they were born, was ungenerous. They must all be clothed and made decent by our friend Clarke.

I find I am anticipated by the friendly Cunningham in sending you Ritson's Scottish collection. Permit me, therefore, to present you with his English collection, which you will receive by the coach. I do not find his historical essay on Scottish song interesting. Your anecdotes and miscellaneous remarks will, I am sure, be much more so. Allan has just sketched a charming design from "Maggie Lauder." She is dancing with such spirit as to electrify the piper, who seems almost dancing too, while he is playing with the most exquisite glee. I am much inclined to get a small copy, and to have it engraved in the style of Ritson's prints.

P.S. Pray what do your anecdotes say concerning "Maggie Lauder?"—was she a real personage, and of what rank? You would surely "spier for her, if you ca'd at Anstruther town."

NO. CCCXXXI.

BURNS TO MR. THOMSON.

November, 1794.

MANY thanks to you, my dear Sir, for your present; it is a book of the utmost importance to me. I have yesterday begun my anecdotes, &c., for your work. I intend drawing them up in the form of a letter to you, which will save me from the tedious dull business of systematic arrangement. Indeed, as all I have to say consists of ununconnected remarks, anecdotes, scraps of old songs, &c., it would be impossible to give the work a beginning, a middle, and an end, which the critics insist to be abolutely necessary in a work. In my last, I told you my objections to the song you had selected for "My lodging is on the cold ground." On my visit the other day to my fair Chloris (that is the poetic name of the lovely goddess of my inspiration), she suggested an idea, which I, on my return from the visit, wrought into the following song.

"My Chloris, mark how green the groves."

How do you like the simplicity and tenderness of this pastoral? I think it pretty well.

I like you for entering so candidly and so kindly into the story of "*ma chere amie.*" I assure you I was never more earnest in my life, than in the account of that affair which I sent you in my last. Conjugal love is a passion which I deeply feel, and highly venerate; but somehow it does not make such a figure in poesy as that other species of the passion,

Where love is liberty, and nature law.

Musically speaking, the first is an instrument of which the gamut is scanty and confined, but the tones inexpressibly sweet, while the last has powers equal to all the intellectual modulations of the human soul. Still, I am a very poet in my enthusiasm of the passion. The welfare and happiness of the beloved object is the first and inviolate sentiment that pervades my soul; and whatever pleasures I might wish for, or whatever might be the raptures they would give me, yet, if they interfere with that first principle, it is having these pleasures at a dishonest price; and justice forbids, and generosity disdains, the purchase! (199)

Despairing of my own powers to give you variety enough in English songs, I have been turning over old collections, to pick out songs, of which the measure is something similar to what I want; and, with a little alteration, so as to suit the rhythm of the air exactly, to give you them for your work. Where the songs have hitherto been but little noticed, nor have ever been set to music, I think the shift a fair one. A song, which, under the same first verse, you will find in Ramsay's Tea-Table Miscellany, I have cut down for an English dress to your "Dainty Davie," as follows:—

"It was the charming month of May."

You may think meanly of this, but take a look at the bombast original, and you will be surprised that I have made so much of it. I have finished my song to "Rothemurche's rant," and you have Clarke to consult as to the set of the air for singing.

[*Here follows "Lassie wi' the lint-white locks:"*]

This piece has at least the merit of being a regular pastoral: the vernal morn, the summer noon, the autumnal evening, and the winter night, are regularly rounded. If you like it, well; if not, I will insert it in the Museum.

NO. CCCXXXII.

BURNS TO MR. THOMSON.

I AM out of temper that you should set so sweet, so tender an air, as "Deil tak the wars," to the foolish old verses. You talk of the silliness of "Saw ye my father?" (200)—by Heavens! the odds are gold to brass! Besides, the old song, though now pretty well modernised into the Scottish language, is originally, and in the early editions, a bungling low imitation of the Scottish manner, by that genius Tom D'Urfey, so has no pretensions to be a Scottish production. There is a pretty English song by Sheridan, in the "Duenna," to this air, which is out of sight superior to D'Urfey's. It begins,

"When sable night each drooping plant restoring."

The air, if I understand the expression of it properly, is the very native language of simplicity, tenderness, and love. I have again gone over my song to the tune as follows. (201)

Now for my English song to "Nancy's to the greenwoods," &c.

[*Here follows the song "Farewell thou stream."*]

There is an air, "The Caledonian Hunt's delight," to which I wrote a song that you will find in Johnson, "Ye banks and braes o' bonnie Doon:" this air, I think, might find a place among your hundred, as Lear says of his knights. Do you know the history of the air? It is curious enough. A good many years ago, Mr. James Miller, writer in your good town, a gentleman whom possibly you know, was in company with our friend Clarke; and talking of Scottish music, Miller expressed an ardent ambition to be able to compose a Scots air. Mr. Clarke, partly by way of joke, told him to keep to the black keys of the harpsicord, and preserve some kind of rhythm, and he would infallibly compose a Scots air. Certain it is that, in a few days, Mr. Miller produced the rudiments of an air, which Mr. Clarke, with some touches and corrections, fashioned into the tune in question. Ritson, you know, has the same story of the black keys; but this account which I have just given you, Mr. Clarke informed me of several years ago. Now, to show you how difficult it is to trace the origin of our airs, I have heard it repeatedly asserted that this was an Irish air; nay, I met with an Irish gentleman who affirmed he had heard it in Ireland among the old women; while, on the other hand, a countess informed me, that the first person who introduced the air into this country, was a baronet's lady of her acquaintance, who took down the notes from an itinerant piper in the Isle of Man. How difficult, then, to ascertain the truth respecting our poesy and music! I, myself, have lately seen a couple of ballads sung through the streets of Dumfries, with my name at the head of them as the author, though it was the first time I had ever seen them.

I thank you for admitting "Craigieburn wood:" and I shall take care to furnish you with a new chorus. In fact, the chorus was not my work, but a part of some old verses to the air. If I can catch myself in a more than ordinarily propitious moment, I shall write a new "Cragieburn wood" altogether. My heart is much in the theme.

I am ashamed, my dear fellow, to make the request; 'tis dunning your generosity; but in a moment when I had forgotten whether I was rich or poor, I promised Chloris a copy of your songs. It wrings my honest pride to write you this; but an ungracious request is doubly so by a tedious apology. To make you some amends, as soon as I have extracted the necessary information out of them, I will return you Ritson's volumes.

The lady is not a little proud that she is to make so distinguished a figure in your collection, and I am not a little proud that I have it in my power to please her so much. Lucky it is for your patience that my paper is done, for when I am in a scribbling humour, I know not when to give over.

NO. CCCXXXIII.

MR. THOMSON TO BURNS.

November 15*th*, 1794.

My Good Sir—Since receiving your last, I have had another interview with Mr. Clarke, and a long consultation. He thinks the "Caledonian Hunt" is more bacchanalian than amorous in its nature, and recommends it to you to match the air accordingly. Pray, did it ever occur to you how peculiarly well the Scottish airs are adapted for verses in the form of a dialogue? The first part of the air is generally low, and suited for a man's voice; and the second part, in many instances, cannot be sung, at concert pitch, but by a female voice. A song thus performed makes an agreeable variety, but few of ours are written in this form: I wish you would think of it in some of those that remain. The only one of the kind you have sent me is admirable, and will be an universal favourite.

Your verses for "Rothemurche" are so sweetly pastoral, and your serenade to Chloris, for "Deil tak the Wars," so passionately tender, that I have sung myself into raptures with them. Your song for "My lodging is on the cold ground," is likewise a diamond of the first water: I am quite dazzled and delighted by it. Some of your Chlorises, I suppose, have flaxen hair, from your partiality for this colour—else we differ about it; for I should scarcely conceive a woman to be a beauty, on reading that she had lint-white locks!

"Farewell thou stream that winding flows," I think, excellent, but it is much too serious to come after "Nancy;"—at least, it would seem an incongruity to provide the same air with merry Scottish and melancholy English verses! The more that the two sets of verses resemble each other, in their general character, the better. Those you have manufactured for "Dainty Davie" will answer charmingly. I am happy to find you have begun your anecdotes: I care not how long they be, for it is impossible that anything from your pen can be tedious. Let me beseech you not to use ceremony in telling me when you wish to present any of your friends with the songs: the next carrier will bring you three copies, and you are as welcome to twenty as to a pinch of snuff.

NO. CCCXXXIV.

BURNS TO MR. THOMSON.

November 19*th*, 1794.

You see, my dear Sir, what a punctual correspondent I am; though, indeed, you may thank yourself for the *tedium* of my letters, as you have so flattered me on my horsemanship with my favourite hobby, and have praised the grace of his ambling so much, that I am scarcely ever off his back. For instance, this morning, though a keen blowing frost, in my walk before breakfast, I finished my duet, which you were pleased to praise so much. Whether I have uniformly succeeded, I will not say; but here it is for you, though it is not an hour old.

[*Here follows the song "Philly and Willy."*]

Tell me honestly how you like it, and point out whatever you think faulty.

I am much pleased with your idea of singing our songs in alternate stanzas, and regret that you did not hint it to me sooner. In those that remain, I shall have it in my eye. I remember your objections to the name Philly, but it is the common abbreviation of Phillis. Sally, the only other name that suits, has, to my ear, a vulgarity about it, which unfits it for anything except burlesque. The legion of Scottish poetasters of the day, whom your brother editor, Mr. Ritson, ranks with me as my coevals, have always mistaken vulgarity for simplicity; whereas, simplicity is as much *eloignée* from vulgarity on the one hand, as from affected point and puerile conceit on the other.

I agree with you as to the air, "Craigieburn wood," that a chorus would, in some degree, spoil the effect, and shall certainly have none in my projected song to it. It is not, however, a case in point with "Rothemurche;" there, as in "Roy's wife of Aldivalloch," a chorus goes, to my taste, well enough. As to the chorus going first, that is the case with Roy's wife, as well as "Rothemurche." In fact, in the first part of both tunes, the rhythm is so peculiar and irregular, and on that irregularity depends so much of their beauty, that we must e'en take them with all their wildness, and humour the verse accordingly. Leaving out the starting note, in both tunes, has, I think, an effect that no regularity could counterbalance the want of.

Try, { Oh Roy's wife of Aldivalloch.
Oh lassie wi' the lint-white locks.

and

compare with, { Roy's wife of Aldivalloch.
Lassie wi' the lint-white locks.

Does not the tameness of the prefixed syllable strike you? In the last case, with the true furor of genius, you strike at once into the wild originality of the air; whereas, in the first insipid method, it is like the grating screw of the pins before the fiddle is brought into tune. This is my taste; if I am wrong, I beg pardon of the *cognoscenti.*

"The Caledonian Hunt" is so charming, that it would make any subject in a song go down! but pathos is certainly its native tongue. Scottish bacchanalians we certainly want, though the few we have are excellent. For instance, "Todlin hame," is, for wit and humour, an unparalleled composition; and "Andrew and his cutty gun," is the work of a master. By the way, are you not quite vexed to think that those men of genius, for such they certainly were, who composed our fine Scottish lyrics, should be unknown? It has given me many a heart-ache. A-propos to bacchanalian songs in Scotch, I composed one yesterday, for an air I like much —" Lumps o' pudding."

[*Here follows " Contented wi' Little."*]

If you do not relish this air, I will send it to Johnson.

NO. CCCXXXV.

BURNS TO MR. THOMSON.

SINCE yesterday's penmanship, I have framed a couple of English stanzas, by way of an English song to "Roy's Wife." You will allow me, that in this instance my English corresponds in sentiment with the Scottish.

[*Here follows " Canst thou leave me thus, my Katy?"*]

Well! I think this to be done in two or three turns across my room, and with two or three pinches of Irish blackguard, is not so far amiss. You see I am determined to have my quantum of applause from somebody.

Tell my friend Allan (for I am sure that we only want the trifling circumstance of being known to one another, to be the best friends on earth), that I much suspect he has, in his plates, mistaken the figure of the stock and horn. I have, at last, gotten one, but it is a very rude instrument. It is composed of three parts; the stock, which is the hinder thigh-bone of a sheep, such as you see in a mutton ham; the horn, which is a common Highland cow's horn, cut off at the smaller end, until the aperture be large enough to admit the stock to be pushed up through the horn until it be held by the thicker end of the thigh-bone; and lastly, an oaten reed exactly cut and notched like that which you see every shepherd boy have, when the corn-stems are green and full-grown. The reed is not made fast in the bone, but is held by the lips, and plays loose in the smaller end of the stock; while the stock, with the horn hanging on its larger end, is held by the hands in playing.

The stock has six or seven ventiges on the upper side, and one back-ventige, like the common flute. This of mine was made by a man from the braes of Athole, and is exactly what the shepherds are wont to use in that country.

However, either it is not quite properly bored in the holes, or else we have not the art of blowing it rightly; for we can make little of it. If Mr. Allan chooses, I will send him a sight of mine, as I look on myself to be a kind of brother-brush with him. "Pride in poets is nae sin;" and I will say it, that I look on Mr. Allan and Mr. Burns to be the only genuine and real painters of Scottish costume in the world.

NO. CCCXXXVI.

TO PETER MILLER, Jun., Esq. (202), OF DALSWINTON.

Dumfries, November, 1794.

Dear Sir—Your offer is indeed truly generous, and most sincerely do I thank you for it; but in my present situation, I find that I dare not accept it. You well know my political sentiments; and were I an insular individual, unconnected with a wife and a family of children, with the most fervid enthusiasm I would have volunteered my services: I then could and would have despised all consequences that might have ensued.

My prospect in the Excise is something; at least, it is, encumbered as I am with the welfare, the very existence, of near half-a-score of helpless individuals—what I dare not sport with.

In the mean time, they are most welcome to my ode; only, let them insert it as a thing they have met with by accident, and unknown to me. Nay, if Mr. Perry, whose honour, after your character of him, I cannot doubt, if he will give me an address and channel by which any thing will come safe from those spies with which he may be certain that his correspondence is beset, I will now and then send him any bagatelle that I may write. In the present hurry of Europe, nothing but news and politics will be regarded; but against the days of peace, which Heaven send soon, my little assistance may perhaps fill up an idle column of a newspaper. I have long had it in my head to try my hand in the way of little prose essays, which I propose sending into the world through the medium of some newspaper; and should these be worth his while, to these Mr. Perry shall be welcome: and all my reward shall be, his treating me with his paper, which, by the bye, to any body who has the least relish for wit, is a high treat indeed. With the most grateful esteem, I am ever, dear Sir, R. B

NO. CCCXXXVII.

MR. THOMSON TO BURNS.

November 28th, 1794.

I acknowledge, my dear Sir, you are not only the most punctual, but the most delectable correspondent I ever met with. To attempt flattering you never entered into my head; the truth is. I look back with surprise at my impudence, in so frequently nibbling at lines and couplets of your incomparable lyrics, for which, perhaps, if you had served me right, you would have sent me to the devil. On the contrary, however, you have all along condescended to invite my criticism with so much courtesy, that it ceases to be wonderful if I have sometimes given myself the airs of a reviewer. Your last budget demands unqualified praise: all the songs are charming, but the duet is a *chef d'œuvre.* "Lumps o' pudding" shall certainly make one of my family dishes; you have cooked it so capitally, that it will please all palates. Do give us a few more of this cast when you find yourself in good spirits; these convivial songs are more wanted than those of the amorous kind, of which we have great choice. Besides, one does not often meet with a singer capable of giving the proper effect to the latter, while the former are easily sung, and acceptable to every body. I participate in your regret that the authors of some of our best songs are unknown; it is provoking to every admirer of genius.

I mean to have a picture painted from your beautiful ballad "The Soldier's Return," to be engraved for one of my frontispieces. The most interesting point of time appears to me, when she first recognises her ain dear Willy, "She gaz'd, she redden'd like a rose." The three lines immediately following are no doubt more impressive on the reader's feelings; but were the painter to fix on these, then you'll observe the animation and anxiety of her countenance is gone, and he could only represent her fainting in the soldier's arms. But I submit the matter to you, and beg your opinion.

Allan desires me to thank you for your accurate description of the stock and horn, and for the very gratifying compliment you pay him in considering him worthy of standing in a niche by the side of Burns in the Scottish Pantheon. He has seen the rude instrument you describe, so does not want you to send it; but wishes to know whether you believe it to have ever been generally used as a musical pipe by the Scottish shepherds, and when, and in what part of the country chiefly. I doubt much if it was capable of any thing but routing and roaring. A friend of mine says he remembers to have heard one in his younger days, made of wood instead of your bone, and that the sound was abominable.

Do not, I beseech you, return any books.

NO. CCCXXXVIII.

BURNS TO MR. THOMSON.

December, 1794.

It is, I assure you, the pride of my heart to do any thing to forward or add to the value of your book; and as I agree with you that the Jacobite song in the Museum to "There'll never be peace till Jamie comes hame," would not so well consort with Peter Pindar's excellent love-song to that air, I have just framed for you the following:—

"My Nannie's awa," &c.

How does this please you? As to the points of time for the expression, in your proposed print from my "Sodger's Return," It must certainly be at—"She gaz'd." The interesting dubiety and suspense taking possession of her countenance, and the gushing fondness, with a mixture of roguish playfulness in his, strike me as things of which a master will make a great deal. In great haste, but in great truth, yours, R. B.

NO. CCCXXXIX.

BURNS TO MR. THOMSON.

January, 1795.

I fear for my songs; however, a few may please, yet originality is a coy feature in composition, and in a multiplitcity of efforts in the same style, disappears altogether. For these three thousand years, we poetic folks have been describing the spring, for instance; and as the spring continues the same, there must soon be a sameness in the imagery, &c., of these said rhyming folks.

A great critic (Aikin) on songs, says that love and wine are the exclusive themes for song-writing. The following is on neither subject, and consequently is no song; but will be allowed, I think, to be two or three pretty good prose thoughts inverted into rhyme.

"For a' that, and a' that."

I do not give you the foregoing song for your book, but merely by way of *vive la bagatelle;* for the piece is not really poetry. How will the following do for "Craigie-burn wood?"—

[*Here follows "Craigie-burn wood."*

Farewell! God bless you!

NO. CCCXL.

MR. THOMSON TO BURNS.

Edinburgh, January 30, 1795.

My dear Sir—I thank you heartily for "Nannie's awa," as well as for "Craigie-burn," which I think a very comely pair. Your observation on the difficulty of original writing in a number of efforts, in the same style, strikes me very forcibly; and it has, again and again, excited my wonder to find you continually surmounting this difficulty, in the many delightful songs you have sent me. Your *vive la bagatelle* song, "For a' that," shall undoubtedly be included in my list. (203)

NO. CCCXLI.

BURNS TO MR. THOMSON.

Ecclefechan, February 7th, 1795.

My dear Thomson—You cannot have any idea of the predicament in which I write to you. In the course of my duty as supervisor (in which capacity I have acted of late), I came yesternight to this unfortunate, wicked, little village. (204) I have gone forward, but snows, of ten feet deep, have impeded my progress: I have tried to "gae back the gate I cam again," but the same obstacle has shut me up within insuperable bars. To add to my misfortune, since dinner, a scraper has been torturing catgut, in sounds that would have insulted the dying agonies of a sow under the hands of a butcher, and thinks himself, on that very account, exceeding good company. In fact, I have been in a dilemma, either to get drunk, to forget these miseries; or to hang myself, to get rid of them: like a prudent man (a character congenial to my every thought, word, and deed), I, of two evils, have chosen the least, and am very drunk, at your service!

I wrote you yesterday from Dumfries. I had not time then to tell you all I wanted to say; and, Heaven knows, at present I have not capacity.

Do you know an air—I am sure you must know it—"We'll gang no more to yon town?" I think, in slowish time, it would make an excellent song. I am highly delighted with it; and if you should think it worthy of your attention, I have a fair dame in my eye, to whom I would consecrate it.

As I am just going to bed, I wish you a good night.

NO. CCCXLII.

MR. THOMSON TO BURNS.

February 25th, 1795.

I HAVE to thank you, my dear Sir, for two epistles; one containing "Let me in this ane night;" and the other from Ecclefechan, proving that, drunk or sober, your "mind is never muddy." You have displayed great address in the above song. Her answer is excellent, and, at the same time, takes away the indelicacy that otherwise would have attached to his entreaties. I like the song, as it now stands, very much.

I had hopes you would be arrested some days at Ecclefechan, and be obliged to beguile the tedious forenoons by song-making. It will give me pleasure to receive the verses you intend for "Oh wat ye wha's in yon town?"

NO. CCCXLIII.

BURNS TO MR. THOMSON. (205)

May, 1795.

LET me know, your very first leisure, how you like this song.

[*Here follows the song "On Chloris being ill."*]

How do you like the foregoing? The Irish air, "Humours of Glen," is a great favourite of mine, and as, except the silly stuff in the "Poor Soldier," there are not any decent verses for it, I have written for it as follows:—

[*Here follow "Their groves o' sweet myrtle," and "'Twas na her bonnie blue ee was my ruin."*]

Let me hear from you.

[*Burns supposes himself to be writing from the dead to the living.*]

NO. CCCXLIV.

TO MRS. RIDDEL.

MADAM—I dare say that this is the first epistle you ever received from this nether world. I write you from the regions of hell, amid the horrors of the ——. The time and manner of my leaving your earth I do not exactly know, as I took my departure in the heat of a fever of intoxication, contracted at your too hospitable mansion; but, on my arrival here, I was fairly tried, and sentenced to endure the purgatorial tortures of this infernal confine for the space of ninety-nine years, eleven months, and twenty-nine days, and all on account of the impropriety of my conduct yesternight under your roof. Here am I, laid on a bed of pitiless furze, with my aching head reclined on a pillow of ever-piercing thorn, while an infernal tormentor, wrinkled, and old, and cruel, his name, I think, is *Recollection*, with a whip of scorpions, forbids peace or rest to approach me, and keeps anguish eternally awake. Still, Madam, if I could in any measure be reinstated in the good opinion of the fair circle whom my conduct last night so much injured, I think it would be an alleviation to my torments. For this reason, I trouble you with this letter. To the men of the company I will make no apology. Your husband, who insisted on my drinking more than I chose, has no right to blame me; and the other gentlemen were partakers of my guilt. But to you, Madam, I have much to apologise. Your good opinion I valued as one of the greatest acquisitions I had made on earth, and I was truly a beast to forfeit it. There was a Miss I——, too, a woman of fine sense, gentle and unassuming manners—do make, on my part, a miserable ——— wretch's best apology to her. A Mrs. G——, a charming woman, did me the honour to be prejudiced in my favour; this makes me hope that I have not outraged her beyond all forgiveness. To all the other ladies please present my humblest contrition for my conduct, and my petition for their gracious pardon. Oh all ye powers of decency and decorum! whisper to them that my errors, though great, were involuntary—that an intoxicated man is the vilest of beasts—that it was not in my nature to be brutal to any one—that to be rude to a woman, when in my senses, was impossible with me—but ——

* * * * *

Regret! Remorse! Shame! ye three hell-hounds that ever dog my steps and bay at my heels, spare me! spare me!

Forgive the offences, and pity the perdition of Madam, your humble slave, R. B.

NO. CCCXLV.

TO THE SAME.

Dumfries, 1795.

Mr. Burns's compliments to Mrs. Riddel—is much obliged to her for her polite attention in sending him the book. Owing to Mr. B. at present acting as supervisor of Excise, a department that occupies his every hour of the day, he has not that time to spare which is necessary for any belle-lettre pursuit; but as he will in a week or two again return to his wonted leisure, he will then pay that attention to Mrs. R.'s beautiful song, "To thee, loved Nith," which it so well deserves. (206) When "Anacharsis' Travels" come to hand, which Mrs. Riddel mentioned as her gift to the public library, Mr. B. will feel honoured by the indulgence of a perusal of them before presentation: it is a book he has never yet seen, and the regulations of the library allow too little leisure for deliberate reading.

Friday Evening.

P.S. Mr. Burns will be much obliged to Mrs. Riddel if she will favour him with a perusal of any of her poetical pieces which he may not have seen.

NO. CCCXLVI.

TO MR. HERON, OF HERON. (207)

Dumfries, 1795.

Sir—I enclose you some copies of a couple of political ballads, one of which, I believe, you have never seen. (208) Would to Heaven I could make you master of as many votes in the Stewartry—but—

Who does the utmost that he can,
Does well, acts nobly—angels could no more.

In order to bring my humble efforts to bear with more effect on the foe, I have privately printed a good many copies of both ballads, and have sent them among friends all about the country.

To pillory on Parnassus the rank reprobation of character, the utter dereliction of all principle, in a profligate junto, which has not only outraged virtue, but violated common decency; which, spurning even hypocrisy as paltry iniquity below their daring—to unmask their flagitiousness to the broadest day—to deliver such over to their merited fate—is surely not merely innocent, but laudable; is not only propriety, but virtue. You have already as your auxiliary, the sober detestation of mankind on the heads of your opponents; and I swear by the lyre of Thalia to muster on your side all the votaries of honest laughter, and fair, candid ridicule!

I am extremely obliged to you for your kind mention of my interests in a letter which Mr. Syme showed me. At present my situation in life must be in a great measure stationary, at least for two or three years. The statement is this—I am on the supervisors' list, and as we come on there by precedency, in two or three years I shall be at the head of that list, and be appointed *of course*. *Then*, a FRIEND might be of service to me in getting me into a place of the kingdom which I would like. A supervisor's income varies from about a hundred and twenty to two hundred a-year; but the business is an incessant drudgery, and would be nearly a complete bar to every species of literary pursuit. The moment I am appointed supervisor, in the common routine, I may be nominated on the collector's list; and this is always a business purely of political patronage. A collectorship varies much, from better than two hundred a-year to near a thousand. They also come forward by precedency on the list; and have, besides a handsome income, a life of complete leisure. A life of literary leisure, with a decent competency, is the summit of my wishes. It would be the prudish affectation of silly pride in me to say that I do not need, or would not be indebted to, a political friend; at the same time, Sir, I by no means lay my affairs before you thus, to hook my dependent situation on your benevolence. If, in my progress of life, an opening should occur where the good offices of a gentleman of your public character and political consequence might bring me forward, I shall petition your goodness with the same frankness as I now do myself the honour to subscribe myself, R. B.

NO. CCCXLVII.

TO MISS FONTENELLE.

Dumfries, 1795.

MADAM—In such a bad world as ours, those who add to the scanty sum of our pleasures are positively our benefactors. To you, Madam, on our humble Dumfries boards, I have been more indebted for entertainment than ever I was in prouder theatres. Your charms as a woman would ensure applause to the most indifferent actress, and your theatrical talents would ensure admiration to the plainest figure. This, Madam, is not the unmeaning or insidious compliment of the frivolous or interested; I pay it from the same honest impulse that the sublime of nature excites my admiration, or her beauties give me delight.

Will the foregoing lines (209) be of any service to you in your approaching benefit night? If they will, I shall be prouder of my muse than ever. They are nearly extempore: I know they have no great merit; but though they should add but little to the entertainment of the evening, they give me the happiness of an opportunity to declare how much I have the honour to be, &c.

R. B.

NO. CCCXLVIII.

MR. THOMSON TO BURNS.

YOU must not think, my good Sir, that I have any intention to enhance the value of my gift, when I say, in justice to the ingenious and worthy artist, that the design and execution of the "Cotter's Saturday Night" is, in my opinion, one of the happiest productions of Allan's pencil. I shall be grievously disappointed if you are not quite pleased with it.

The figure intended for your portrait, I think strikingly like you, as far as I can remember your phiz. This should make the piece interesting to your family every way. Tell me whether Mrs. Burns finds you out among the figures.

I cannot express the feeling of admiration with which I have read your pathetic "Address to the Woodlark," your elegant panegyric on Caledonia, and your affecting verses on Chloris's illness. Every repeated perusal of these gives new delight. The other song to "Laddie, lie near me," though not equal to these, is very pleasing.

NO. CCCXLIX.

BURNS TO MR. THOMSON. (210)

WELL! this is not amiss. You see how I answer your orders—your tailor could not be more punctual. I am just now in a high fit for poetising, provided that the strait jacket of criticism don't cure me. If you can, in a post or two, administer a little of the intoxicating potion of your applause, it will raise your humble servant's frenzy to any height you want. I am at this moment "holding high converse" with the Muses, and have not a word to throw away on such a prosaic dog as you are.

NO. CCCL.

BURNS TO MR. THOMSON.

May, 1795.

TEN thousand thanks for your elegant present—though I am ashamed of the value of it being bestowed on a man who has not, by any means, merited such an instance of kindness. I have shown it to two or three judges of the first abilities here, and they all agree with me in classing it as a first-rate production. My phiz is sae kenspeckle, that the very joiner's apprentice, whom Mrs. Burns employed to break up the parcel (I was out of town that day), knew it at once. My most grateful compliments to Allan, who has honoured my rustic muse so much with his masterly pencil. One strange coincidence is, that the little one who is making the felonious attempt on the cat's tail, is the most striking likeness of an ill-deedie, d—n'd, wee, rumble-gairie urchin of mine, whom, from that propensity to witty wickedness, and manfu' mischief, which, even at twa days' auld, I foresaw would form the striking features of his disposition, I named Willie Nicol, after a certain friend of mine, who is one of the masters of a grammar-school in a city which shall be nameless.

Give the enclosed epigram to my much-valued friend Cunningham, and tell him, that on Wednesday I go to visit a friend of his, to whom his friendly partiality in speaking of me, in a manner introduced me—I mean a well-known military and literary character, Colonel Dirom.

You do not tell me how you liked my two last songs. Are they condemned?

NO. CCCLI.

MR. THOMSON TO BURNS

May 13th, 1795.

It gives me great pleasure to find that you are all so well satisfied with Mr. Allan's production. The chance resemblance of your little fellow, whose promising disposition appeared so very early, and suggested whom he should be named after, is curious enough. I am acquainted with that person, who is a prodigy of learning and genius, and a pleasant fellow, though no saint.

You really make me blush when you tell me you have not merited the drawing from me. I do not think I can ever repay you, or sufficiently esteem and respect you, for the liberal and kind manner in which you have entered into the spirit of my undertaking, which could not have been perfected without you. So I beg you would not make a fool of me again by speaking of obligation.

I like your two last songs very much, and am happy to find you are in such a high fit of poetising. Long may it last! Clarke has made a fine pathetic air to Mallet's superlative ballad of "William and Margaret," and is to give it to me, to be enrolled among the elect.

NO. CCCLII.

BURNS TO MR. THOMSON.

In "Whistle, and I'll come to ye, my lad," the iteration of that line is tiresome to my ear. Here goes what I think is an improvement :—

"O whistle, and I'll come to ye, my lad;
Oh whistle, and I'll come to ye, my lad;
Tho' father and mother and a' should gae mad,
Thy Jeanie will venture wi' ye, my lad."

In fact, a fair dame, at whose shrine I, the Priest of the Nine, offer up the incense of Parnassus—a dame whom the Graces have attired in witchcraft, and whom the Loves have armed with lightning—a fair one, herself the heroine of the song, insists on the amendment, and dispute her commands if you dare!

[*Here follows "This is no my ain lassie."*]

Do you know that you have roused the torpidity of Clarke at last? He has requested me to write three or four songs for him, which he is to set to music himself. The enclosed sheet contains two songs for him, which please to present to my valued friend Cunningham.

I enclose the sheet open, both for your inspection, and that you may copy the song "Oh bonnie was yon rosy brier." I do not know whether I am right, but that song pleases me; and as it is extremely probable that Clarke's newly-roused celestial spark will be soon smothered in the fogs of indolence, if you like the song, it may go as Scottish verses to the air of "I wish my love was in a mire;" and poor Erskine's English lines may follow.

I enclose you a "For a' that and a' that," which was never in print; it is a much superior song to mine. I have been told that it was composed by a lady.

[*Here follow the songs, "Now spring has clad the grove in green," and "O bonnie was yon rosy briar."*]

Written on the blank leaf of a copy of the last edition of my poems, presented to the lady whom, in so many fictitious reveries of passion, but with the most ardent sentiments of real friendship, I have so often sung under the name of Chloris, is the following:—

["*To Chloris.*"]

COILA.

Une bagatelle de l'amitié.

NO. CCCLIII.

MR. THOMSON TO BURNS.

Edinburgh, August 3rd, 1795.

MY DEAR SIR—This will be delivered to you by a Dr. Brianton, who has read your works, and pants for the honour of your acquaintance. I do not know the gentleman; but his friend, who applied to me for this introduction, being an excellent young man, I have no doubt he is worthy of all acceptation.

My eyes have just been gladdened, and my mind feasted, with your last packet—full of pleasant things indeed. What an imagination is yours!—it is superfluous to tell you that I am delighted with all the three songs, as well as with your elegant and tender verses to Chloris.

I am sorry you should be induced to alter "Oh whistle and I'll come to ye, my lad," to the prosaic line, "Thy Jeanie will venture wi' ye, my lad." I must be permitted to say, that I do not think the latter either reads or sings so well as the former. I wish, therefore, you would in my name petition the charming Jeanie, whoever she be, to let the line remain unaltered.

I should be happy to see Mr. Clarke produce a few airs to be joined to your verses. Everybody regrets his writing so very little, as everybody acknowledges his ability to write well. Pray was the resolution formed coolly before dinner, or was it a midnight vow made over a bowl of punch with the bard?

I shall not fail to give Mr. Cunningham what you have sent him.

P.S.—The lady's "For a' that, and a' that," is sensible enough, but no more to be compared to yours than I to Hercules.

NO. CCCLIV.

BURNS TO MR. THOMSON. (211)

How do you like the foregoing? I have writtten it within this hour: so much for the speed of my Pegasus; but what say you to this bottom.

NO. CCCLV.

BURNS TO MR. THOMSON. (212)

SUCH is the peculiarity of the rhythm of this air, that I find it impossible to make another stanza to suit it.

I am at present quite occupied with the charming sensations of the toothache, so have not a word to spare.

NO. CCCLVI.

MR. THOMSON TO BURNS.

June 3rd, 1795.

MY DEAR SIR—Your English verses to "Let me in this ane night," are tender and beautiful; and your ballad to the "Lothian Lassie" is a master-piece for its humour and *naïveté*. The fragment for the "Caledonian Hunt" is quite suited to the original measure of the air, and, as it plagues you so, the fragment must content it. I would rather, as I said before, have had bacchanalian words, had it so pleased the poet; but, nevertheless, for what we have received, Lord, make us thankful!

NO. CCCLVII.

TO MRS. DUNLOP.

December 15th, 1795.

MY DEAR FRIEND—As I am in a complete Decemberish humour, gloomy, sullen, stupid, as even the Deity of Dulness herself could wish, I shall not drawl out a heavy letter with a number of heavier apologies for my late silence. Only one I shall mention, because I know you will sympathise in it: these four months, a sweet little girl, my youngest child, has been so ill, that every day, a week or less threatened to terminate her existence. There had much need be many pleasures annexed to the states of husband and father, for, God knows, they have many peculiar cares. I cannot describe to you the anxious, sleepless hours these ties frequently give me. I see a train of helpless little folks; myself and my exertions all their stay; and on what a brittle thread does the life of man hang! If I am nipt off at the command of fate, even in all the vigour of manhood, as I am—such things happen every day—Gracious God! what would become of my little flock! 'Tis here that I envy your people of fortune. A father on his death-bed, taking an everlasting leave of his children, has indeed woe enough; but the man of competent fortune leaves his sons and daughters independency and friends; while I—but I shall run distracted if I think any longer on the subject!

To leave talking of the matter so gravely, I shall sing with the old Scots ballad—

"Oh that I had ne'er been married,
I would never had nae care:
Now I've gotten wife and bairns,
They cry crowdie evermair.

Crowdie ance, crowdie twice,
Crowdie three times in a day:
An ye crowdie ony mair,
Ye'll crowdie a' my meal away."

December 24th.

We have had a brilliant theatre here this season; only, as all other business does, it experiences a stagnation of trade from the epidemical complaint of the country, *want of cash*. I mentioned our theatre merely to lug in an occasional Address, which I wrote for the benefit night of one of the actresses, and which is as follows:— * * *

25th, Christmas Morning.

This, my much-loved friend, is a morning of wishes; accept mine—so Heaven hear me as they are sincere!—that blessings may attend your steps, and affliction know you not! In the charming words of my favourite author, The Man of Feeling, "May the Great Spirit bear up the weight of thy grey hairs, and blunt the arrow that brings them rest!"

Now that I talk of authors, how do you like Cowper? Is not the "Task" a glorious poem? The religion of the "Task," bating a few scraps of Calvanistic divinity, is the religion of God and Nature—the religion that exalts, that ennobles man. Were not you to send me your "Zeluco," in return for mine? Tell me how you like my marks and notes through the book. I would not give a farthing for a book, unless I were at liberty to blot it with my criticisms.

I have lately collected, for a friend's perusal, all my letters; I mean those which I first sketched, in a rough draught, and afterwards wrote out fair. On looking over some old musty papers, which from time to time I had parcelled by, as trash that were scarce worth preserving, and which yet, at the same time, I did not care to destroy, I discovered many of these rude sketches, and have written, and am writing them out, in a bound MS. for my friend's library. As I wrote always to you the rhapsody of the moment, I cannot find a single scroll to you, except one, about the commencement of our acquaintance. If there were any possible conveyance, I would send you a perusal of my book. R. B.

NO. CCCLVIII.

TO MR. ALEXANDER FINDLATER (213),

SUPERVISOR OF EXCISE, DUMFRIES.

SIR—Enclosed are the two schemes. I would not have troubled you with the collector's one, but for suspicion lest it be not right. Mr. Erskine promised me to make it right, if you will have the goodness to show him how. As I have no copy of the scheme for myself, and the alterations being very considerable from what it was formerly, I hope that I shall have access to this scheme I send you, when I come to face up my new books. *So much for schemes.* And that no scheme to betray a FRIEND, or mislead a STRANGER; to seduce a YOUNG GIRL, or rob a HEN-ROOST; to subvert LIBERTY, or bribe an EXCISEMAN; to disturb the GENERAL ASSEMBLY, or annoy a GOSSIPPING; to overthrow the credit of ORTHODOXY, or the authority of OLD SONGS; to oppose *your wishes*, or frustrate *my hopes*,—MAY PROSPER—is the sincere wish and prayer of R. B.

NO. CCCLIX.

TO THE EDITOR OF THE MORNING CHRONICLE.

Dumfries, 1795.

SIR—You will see, by your subscribers' list, that I have been about nine months of that number.

I am sorry to inform you that in that time seven or eight of your papers either havé never been sent me, or else have never reached me. To be deprived of any one number of the first newspaper in Great Britain for information, ability, and independence, is what I can ill brook and bear; but to be deprived of that most admirable oration of the Marquis of Lansdowne, when he made the great, though ineffectual attempt (in the language of the poet, I fear too true) "to save a SINKING STATE"—this was a loss that I neither can, nor will forgive you. That paper, Sir, never reached me; but I demand it of you. I am a BRITON, and must be interested in the cause of LIBERTY; I am a MAN, and the RIGHTS OF HUMAN NATURE cannot be indifferent to me. However, do not let me mislead you—I am not a man in that situation of life, which, as your subscriber, can be of any consequence to you, in the eyes of those to whom SITUATION OF LIFE ALONE is the criterion of MAN. I am but a plain tradesman, in this distant, obscure country town; but that humble domicile in which I shelter my wife and children, is the CASTELLUM of a BRITON; and that scanty, hard-earned income which supports them, is as truly my property, as the most magnificent fortune of the most PUISSANT MEMBER of your HOUSE OF NOBLES.

These, Sir, are my sentiments, and to them I subscribe my name; and were I a man of ability and consequence enough to address the PUBLIC, with that name should they appear. I am, &c. (214)

NO. CCCLX.

TO MRS. DUNLOP,

IN LONDON.

Dumfries, 20th December, 1795.

I HAVE been prodigiously disappointed in this London journey of yours. In the first place, when your last to me reached Dumfries, I was in the country, and did not return until too late to answer your letter; in the next place, I thought you would certainly take this route; and now I know not what is become of you, or whether this may reach you at all. God grant that it may find you and yours in prospering health and good spirits! Do let me hear from you the soonest possible.

As I hope to get a frank from my friend Captain Miller, I shall, every leisure hour, take up the pen, and gossip away whatever comes first, prose or poetry, sermon or song. In this last article I have abounded of late. I have often mentioned to you a superb publication of Scottish songs, which is making its appearance in your great metropolis, and where I have the honour to preside over the Scottish verse, as no less a personage than Peter Pindar does over the English.

December 29th.

Since I began this letter, I have been appointed to act in the capacity of supervisor here, and I assure you, what with the load of business, and what with that business being new to me, I could scarcely have commanded ten minutes to have spoken to you, had you been in town, much less to have written you an epistle. This appointment is only temporary, and during the illness of the present incumbent; but I look forward to an early period when I shall be appointed in full form—a consummation devoutly to be wished! My political sins seem to be forgiven me.

This is the season (New-year's-day is now my date) of wishes; and mine are most fervently offered up for you! May life to you be a positive blessing while it lasts, for your own sake; and that it may yet be greatly prolonged, is my wish for my own sake, and for the sake of the rest of your friends! What a transient business is life? Very lately I was a boy; but t'other day I was a young man; and I already begin to feel the rigid fibre and stiffening joints of old age coming fast o'er my frame. With all my follies of youth, and I fear, a few vices of manhood, still I congratulate myself on having had, in early days, religion strongly impressed on my mind. I have nothing to say to any one as to which sect he belongs to, or what creed he believes; but I look on the man who is firmly persuaded of infinite wisdom and goodness superintending and directing every circumstance that can happen in his lot—I felicitate such a man as having a solid foundation for his mental enjoyment—a firm prop and sure stay in the hour of difficulty, trouble, and distress—and a never-failing anchor of hope, when he looks beyond the grave.

January 12th.

You will have seen our worthy and ingenious friend, the doctor, long ere this. I hope he is well, and beg to be remembered to him. I have just been reading over again,

I dare say for the hundred and fiftieth time, his *View of Society and Manners;* and still I read it with delight. His humour is perfectly original—it is neither the humour of Addison, nor Swift, nor Sterne, nor of anybody but Dr. Moore. By the bye, you have deprived me of *Zeluco;* remember that, when you are disposed to rake up the sins of my neglect from among the ashes of my laziness.

He has paid me a pretty compliment, by quoting me in his last publication (215).

R. B.

NO. CCCLXI.

ADDRESS OF THE SCOTCH DISTILLERS

TO THE RIGHT HON. WILLIAM PITT.

Sir—While pursy burgesses crowd your gate, sweating under the weight of heavy addresses, permit us, the quondam distillers in that part of Great Britain called Scotland, to approach you, not with venal approbation, but with fraternal condolence; not as what you are just now, or for some time have been, but as what, in all probability, you will shortly be. We shall have the merit of not deserting our friends in the day of their calamity, and you will have the satisfaction of perusing, at least, one honest address. You are well acquainted with the dissection of human nature; nor do you need the assistance of a fellow-creature's bosom to inform you, that man is always a selfish, often a perfidious being. This assertion, however the hasty conclusions of superficial observation may doubt of it, or the raw inexperience of youth may deny it, those who make the fatal experiment we have done, will feel. You are a statesman, and consequently are not ignorant of the traffic of these corporation compliments. The little great man who drives the borough to market, and the very great man who buys the borough in that market, they two do the whole business; and you well know, they, likewise, have their price. With that sullen disdain which you can so well assume, rise illustrious Sir, and spurn these hireling efforts of venal stupidity. At best they are the compliments of a man's friends on the morning of his execution: they take a decent farewell: resign you to your fate; and hurry away from your approaching hour.

If fame say true, and omens be not very much mistaken, you are about to make your exit from that world where the sun of gladness gilds the paths of prosperous men: permit us, great Sir, with the sympathy of fellow-feeling, to hail your passage to the realms of ruin.

Whether the sentiment proceed from the selfishness or cowardice of mankind, is immaterial; but to point out to a child of misfortune those who are still more unhappy, is to give him some degree of positive enjoyment. In this light, Sir, our downfall may be again useful to you: though not exactly in the same way, it is not, perhaps, the first time it has gratified your feelings. It is true, the triumph of your evil star is exceedingly despiteful. At an age when others are the votaries of pleasure, or underlings in business, you had attained the highest wish of a British statesman; and with the ordinary date of human life, what a prospect was before you! Deeply rooted in *royal favour,* you overshadowed the land. The birds of passage which follow ministerial sunshine through every clime of political faith and manners, flocked to your branches; and the beasts of the field (the lordly possessors of hills and valleys) crowded under your shade. "But behold a watcher, a holy one, came down from heaven, and cried aloud, and said thus: Hew down the tree, and cut off his branches; shake off his leaves, and scatter his fruit; let the beasts get away from under it, and the fowls from his branches!" A blow from an unthought-of quarter, one of those terrible accidents which peculiarly mark the hand of Omnipotence, overset your career, and laid all your fancied honours in the dust. But turn your eyes, Sir, to the tragic scenes of our fate. An ancient nation, that for many ages had gallantly maintained the unequal struggle for independence with her much more powerful neighbour, at last agrees to a union which should ever after make them one people. In consideration of certain circumstances, it was covenanted that the former should enjoy a stipulated alleviation in her share of the public burdens, particularly in that branch of the revenue called the Excise. This just privilege has of late given great umbrage to some interested, powerful individuals of the more potent part of the empire, and they have spared no wicked pains, under insidious pretexts, to subvert what they dared not openly to attack, from the dread which they yet entertained of the spirit of their ancient enemies.

In this conspiracy we fell; nor did we alone suffer—our country was deeply wounded. A number of (we will say) respectable individuals, largely engaged in trade, where we were not only useful, but absolutely necessary, to our country in her dearest interests; we, with all that was near and dear to us, were sacrificed, without remorse, to the infernal deity of political expediency! We fell to gratify the wishes of dark envy, and the views of unprincipled ambition! Your foes, Sir, were avowed; were too brave to take an ungenerous advantage: *you* fell in the face of day. On the contrary, our enemies, to complete our overthrow, contrived to make their guilt appear the villany of a nation. Your downfall only drags with you your private friends and partisans: in our misery are more or less involved the most numerous and most valuable part of the community—all those who immediately depend on the cultivation of the soil, from the landlord of a province down to his lowest hind.

Allow us, Sir, yet further, just to hint at another rich vein of comfort in the dreary regions of adversity—the gratulations of an approving conscience. In a certain great assembly, of which you are a distinguished member, panegyrics on your private virtues have so often wounded your delicacy, that, we shall not distress you with anything on the subject. There is, however, one part of your public conduct which our feelings will not permit us to pass in silence; our gratitude must trespass on your modesty: we mean, worthy Sir, your whole behaviour to the Scots distillers. In evil hours, when obtrusive recollection presses bitterly on the sense, let that, Sir, come, like a healing angel, and speak the peace to your soul which the world can neither give nor take away. We have the honour to be, Sir, your sympathising fellow-sufferers and grateful humble servants,

JOHN BARLEYCORN, Præses.

NO. CCCLXII.

TO THE HON. THE PROVOST, BAILIES, AND TOWN COUNCIL OF DUMFRIES.

GENTLEMEN—The literary taste and liberal spirit of your good town has so ably filled the various departments of your schools, as to make it a very great object for a parent to have his children educated in them. Still, to me, a stranger, with my large family, and very stinted income, to give my young ones that education I wish, at the high-school fees which a stranger pays, will bear hard upon me.

Some years ago your good town did me the honour of making me an honorary burgess. Will you allow me to request that this mark of distinction may extend so far as to put me on a footing of a real freeman of the town, in the schools?

If you are so very kind as to grant my request, it will certainly be a constant incentive to me to strain every nerve where I can officially serve you; and will, if possible, increase that grateful respect with which I have the honour to be, gentlemen, your devoted, humble servant, R. B. (216)

NO. CCCLXIII.

TO MRS. RIDDEL.

Dumfries, January 20th, 1796.

I CANNOT express my gratitude to you for allowing me a longer perusal of "Anacharsis." In fact, I never met with a book that bewitched me so much; and I, as a member of the library, must warmly feel the obligation you have laid us under. Indeed, to me the obligation is stronger than to any other individual of our society; as "Anacharsis" is an indispensable desideratum to a son of the muses.

The health you wished me in your morning's card, is, I think, flown from me for ever. I have not been able to leave my bed to-day till about an hour ago. These wickedly unlucky advertisements I lent (I did wrong) to a friend, and I am ill able to go in quest of him.

The muses have not quite forsaken me. The following detached stanzas I intend to interweave in some disastrous tale of a shepherd. R. B.

NO. CCCLXIV.

TO MRS. DUNLOP.

Dumfries, January 31st, 1796.

THESE many months you have been two packets in my debt—what sin of ignorance I have committed against so highly valued a friend, I am utterly at a loss to guess.

Alas! Madam, ill can I afford, at this time, to be deprived of any of the small remnant of my pleasures. I have lately drunk deep of the cup of affliction. The autumn robbed me of my only daughter and darling child (217), and that at a distance, too, and so rapidly, as to put it out of my power to pay the last duties to her. I had scarcely begun to recover from that shock, when I became myself the victim of a most severe rheumatic fever, and long the die spun doubtful; until, after many weeks of a sick-bed, it seems to have turned up life, and I am beginning to crawl across my room, and once, indeed, have been before my own door in the street.

When pleasure fascinates the mental sight,
  Affliction purifies the visual ray,
Religion hails the drear, the untried night,
  And shuts, for ever shuts! life's doubtful day.

R. B.

NO. CCCLXV.

MR. THOMSON TO BURNS.

February 5th, 1796.

Oh Robby Burns, are ye sleeping yet?
Or are ye wauking, I would wit?

The pause you have made, my dear Sir, is awful! Am I never to hear from you again? I know, and I lament how much you have been afflicted of late; but I trust that returning health and spirits will now enable you to resume the pen, and delight us with your musings. I have still about a dozen Scotch and Irish airs that I wish "married to immortal verse." We have several true-born Irishmen on the Scottish list; but they are now naturalized, and reckoned our own good subjects. Indeed, we have none better. I believe I before told you that I have been much urged by some friends to publish a collection of all our favourite airs and songs in octavo, embellished with a number of etchings by our ingenious friend Allan; what is your opinion of this?

NO. CCCLXVI.

BURNS TO MR. THOMSON.

February, 1796.

Many thanks, my dear Sir, for your handsome, elegant present to Mrs. Burns, and for my remaining volume of P. Pindar, Peter is a delightful fellow, and a first favourite of mine. I am much pleased with your idea of publishing a collection of our songs in octavo with etchings. I am extremely willing to lend every assistance in my power. The Irish airs I shall cheerfully undertake the task of finding verses for.

I have already, you know, equipt three with words, and the other day I strung up a kind of rhapsody to another Hibernian melody, which I admire much.

[*Here follows " Hey for a lass wi' a tocher."*]

If this will do, you have now four of my Irish engagement. In my by-past songs I dislike one thing; the name Chloris—I meant it as the fictitious name of a certain lady: but, on second thoughts, it is a high incongruity to have a Greek appellation to a Scottish pastoral ballad. Of this, and some things else, in my next: I have more amendments to propose. What you once mentioned of "flaxen locks" is just: they cannot enter into an elegant description of beauty. Of this also again—God bless you! (218).

NO. CCCLXVII.

MR. THOMSON TO BURNS.

Your "Hey for a lass wi' a tocher" is a most excellent song, and with you the subject is something new indeed. It is the first time I have seen you debasing the god of soft desire into an amateur of acres and guineas.

I am happy to find you approve of my proposed octavo edition. Allan has designed and etched about twenty plates, and I am to have my choice of them for that work. Independently of the Hogarthian humour with which they abound, they exhibit the character and costume of the Scottish peasantry with inimitable felicity. In this respect, he himself says, they will far exceed the aquatinta plates he did for the Gentle Shepherd, because in the etching he sees clearly what he is doing, but not so with the aquatinta, which he could not manage to his mind.

The Dutch boors of Ostade are scarcely more characteristic and natural than the Scottish figures in those etchings.

NO. CCCLXVIII.

BURNS TO MR. THOMSON.

April, 1796.

Alas! my dear Thomson, I fear it will be some time ere I tune my lyre again! "By Babel streams I have sat and wept" almost ever since I wrote you last; I have only known existence by the pressure of the heavy hand of sickness, and have counted time by the repercussions of pain! Rheumatism, cold and fever, have formed to me a terible combination. I close my eyes in misery, and open them without hope. I look on the vernal day, and say with poor Fergusson,

Say wherefore has an all-indulgent heaven
Light to the comfortless and wretched given?

This will be delivered to you by a Mrs. Hyslop, landlady of the Globe Tavern here, which for these many years has been my house, and where our friend Clarke and I have had many a merry squeeze. I am highly delighted with Mr. Allan's etchings. "Woo'd an' married an' a'," is admirable! The grouping is beyond all praise. The expression of the figures, conformable to the story in the ballad, is absolutely faultless perfection. I next admire "Turnimspike." What I like least is "Jenny said to Jocky," Besides the female being in her appearance * * * * *, if you take her stooping into the account, she is at least two inches taller than her lover. Poor Cleghorn! I sincerely sympathise with him. Happy I am to think that he yet has a well-grounded hope of health and enjoyment in this world. As for me—but that is a sad subject!

NO. CCCLXIX.

MR. THOMSON TO BURNS.

May 4th, 1796.

I need not tell you, my good Sir, what concern the receipt of your last gave me, and how much I sympathise in your sufferings. But do not, I beseech you, give yourself up to despondency, or speak the language of despair. The vigour of your constitution, I trust, will soon set you on your feet again; and then, it is to be hoped, you will see the wisdom and the necessity of taking due care of a life so valuable to your family, to your friends, and to the world.

Trusting that your next will bring agreeable accounts of your convalescence and returning good spirits, I remain, with sincere regard, yours.

P. S. Mrs. Hyslop, I doubt not, delivered the gold seal to you in good condition.

NO. CCCLXX.

BURNS TO MR. THOMSON.

My dear Sir—I once mentioned to you an air which I have long admired—"Here's a health to them that's awa, hiney," but I forget if you took any notice of it. I have just been trying to suit it with verses, and I beg leave to recommend the air to your attention once more. I have only begun it.

[*Here follow the three first stanzas of the song: the fourth was found among his MSS. after his death.*]

NO. CCCLXXI.

BURNS TO MR. THOMSON.

This will be delivered by a Mr. Lewars, a young fellow of uncommon merit. As he will be a day or two in town, you will have leisure, if you choose, to write me by him: and if you have a spare half hour to spend with him, I shall place your kindness to my account. I have no copies of the songs I have sent you, and I have taken a fancy to review them all, and possibly may mend some of them: so, when you have complete leisure, I will thank you for either the originals or copies. (219) I had rather be the author of five well-written songs than of ten otherwise. I have great hopes that the genial influence of the approaching summer will set me to rights, but as yet I cannot boast of returning health. I have now reason to believe that my complaint is a flying gout—a sad business!

Do let me know how Gleghorn is, and remember me to him.

This should have been delivered to you a month ago. I am still very poorly, but should like much to hear from you.

NO. CCCLXXII.

TO MRS. RIDDEL,

WHO HAD DESIRED HIM TO GO TO THE BIRTHDAY ASSEMBLY, ON THAT DAY, TO SHOW HIS LOYALTY.

Dumfries, June 4th, 1796.

I AM in such miserable health as to be utterly incapable of showing my loyalty in any way. Racked as I am with rheumatism, I meet every face with a greeting, like that of Balak—"Come, curse me, Jacob; and come, defy me, Israel!" So say I—Come, curse me that east wind; and come, defy me the north! Would you have me in such circumstances copy you out a love-song!

I may, perhaps, see you on Saturday, but I will not be at the ball. Why should I?—"man delights not me, nor woman either!" Can you supply me with the song, "Let us all be unhappy together"—do if you can, and oblige *le pauvre miserable*, R. B.

NO. CCCLXXIII.

TO MR. CLARKE,

SCHOOLMASTER, FORFAR.

Dumfries, June 26th, 1796.

MY DEAR CLARKE—Still, the victim of affliction! Were you to see the emaciated figure who now holds the pen to you, you would not know your old friend. Whether I shall ever get about again, is only known to Him, the Great Unknown, whose creature I am. Alas, Clarke! I begin to fear the worst. As to my individual self, I am tranquil, and would despise myself if I were not; but Burns's poor widow, and half-a-dozen of his dear little ones—helpless orphans!—there I am weak, as a woman's tear. Enough of this! 'Tis half of my disease.

I duly received your last, enclosing the note. It came extremely in time, and I am much obliged by your punctuality. Again I must request you to do me the same kindness. Be so very good as, by return of post, to enclose me *another* note. I trust you can do it without inconvenience, and it will seriously oblige me. If I must go, I shall leave a few friends behind me, whom I shall regret while consciousness remains. I know I shall live in their remembrance. Adieu, dear Clarke. That I shall ever see you again, is, I am afraid, highly improbable.

R. B.

NO. CCCLXXIV.

TO MR. JAMES JOHNSON,

EDINBURGH.

Dumfries, July 4th, 1796.

How are you, my dear friend, and how comes on your fifth volume! You may probably think that for some time past I have neglected you and your work; but, alas! the hand of pain, and sorrow, and care, has these many months lain heavy on me. Personal and domestic affliction have almost entirely banished that alacrity and life with which I used to woo the rural muse of Scotia.

You are a good, worthy, honest fellow, and have a good right to live in this world—because you deserve it. Many a merry meeting this publication has given us, and possibly it may give us more, though, alas! I fear it. This protracting, slow, consuming illness which hangs over me, will, I doubt much, my ever dear friend, arrest my sun before he has well reached his middle career, and will turn over the poet to far more important concerns than studying the brilliancy of wit, or the pathos of sentiment. However, *hope* is the cordial of the human heart and I endeavour to cherish it as well as I can.

Let me hear from you as soon as convenient. Your work is a great one; and now that it is finished, I see, if we were to begin again, two or three things that might be mended; yet I will venture to prophesy, that to future ages your publication will be the text-book and standard of Scottish song and music.

I am ashamed to ask another favour of you, because you have been so very good already; but my wife has a very particular friend of hers, a young lady who sings well, to whom she wishes to present the "Scots Musical Museum." If you have a spare copy, will you be so obliging as to send it by the very first *fly*, as I am anxious to have it soon. (220) Yours ever,

R. B.

NO. CCCLXXV.

TO MR. CUNNINGHAM.

Brow, Sea-bathing Quarters,
July 7th, 1796.

MY DEAR CUNNINGHAM—I received yours here this morning, and am indeed highly flattered with the approbation of the literary circle you mention—a literary circle inferior to none in the two kingdoms. Alas! my friend, I fear the voice of the bard will soon be heard among you no more. For these eight or ten months I have been ailing, sometimes bedfast, and sometimes not; but these last three months I have been tortured with an excruciating rheumatism, which has reduced me to nearly the last stage. You actually would not know me if you saw me. Pale, emaciated, and so feeble, as occasionally to need help from the chair — my spirits fled! fled!—but I can no more on the subject; only the medical folks tell me that my last and only chance is bathing, and country quarters and riding. The deuce of the matter is this; when an exeiseman is off duty, his salary is reduced to £35 instead of £50. What way, in the name of thrift, shall I maintain myself, and keep a horse in country quarters, with a wife, and five children at home, on £35? I mention this, because I had intended to beg your utmost interest, and that of all the friends you can muster, to move our commissioners of Excise to grant me the full salary; I dare say you know them all personally. If they do not grant it me (221), I must lay my account with an exit truly *en poëte*—if I die not of disease, I must perish with hunger.

I have sent you one of the songs; the other my memory does not serve me with, and I have no copy here; but I shall be at home soon, when I will send it you. A-propos to being at home,—Mrs. Burns threatens in week or or two to add one more to my paternal charge, which, if of the right gender, I intend shall be introduced to the world 'by the respectable designation of *Alexander Cunningham Burns.* My last was *James Glencairn,* so you can have no objection to the company of nobility. Farewell. R. B.

NO. CCCLXXVI.

TO MR. GILBERT BURNS.

July 10*th*, 1796.

DEAR BROTHER—It will be no very pleasing news to you to be told that I am dangerously ill, and not likely to get better. An inveterate rheumatism has reduced me to such a state of debility, and my appetite is so totally gone, that I can scarcely stand on my legs. I have been a week at sea-bathing, and I will continue there, or in a friend's house in the country, all the summer. God keep my wife and children: if I am taken from their head, they will be poor indeed. I have contracted one or two serious debts, partly from my illness these many months, partly from too much thoughtlessness as to expense when I came to town, that will cut in too much on the little I leave them in your hands. Remember me to my mother. Yours, R. B.

NO. CCCLXXVII.

TO MRS. BURNS.

Brow, Thursday.

MY DEAREST LOVE—I delayed writing until I could tell you what effect sea-bathing was likely to produce. It would be injustice to deny that it has eased my pains, and I think has strengthened me; but my appetite is still extremely bad. No flesh nor fish can I swallow: porridge and milk are the only thing I can taste. I am very happy to hear, by Miss Jess Lewars, that you are all well. My very best and kindest compliments to her, and to all the children. I will see you on Sunday. Your affectionate husband, R. B.

NO. CCCLXXVIII.

TO MRS. DUNLOP.

Brow, Saturday, July 12*th*, 1796.

MADAM—I have written you so often, without receiving any answer, that I would not trouble you again, but for the circumstances in which I am. An illness which has long hung about me, in all probability will speedily send me beyond that *bourne whence no traveller returns.* Your friendship, with which for many years you honoured me, was a friendship dearest to my soul. Your conversation, and especially your correspondence, were at once highly entertaining and instructive. With what pleasure did I use to break up the seal! The remembrance yet adds one pulse more to my poor palpitating heart. Farewell!!!

R. B. (222)

NO. CCCLXXIX.

TO MR. JAMES BURNESS.

WRITER, MONTROSE.

Dumfries, July 12th, 1796.

MY DEAR COUSIN—When you offered me money assistance, little did I think I should want it so soon. A rascal of a haberdasher, to whom I owe a considerable bill, taking it into his head that I am dying, has commenced a process against me, and will infallibly put my emaciated body into jail. Will you be so good as to accommodate me, and that by return of post, with ten pounds? Oh, James! did you know the pride of my heart, you would feel doubly for me! Alas! I am not used to beg. The worst of it is, my health was coming about finely, you know; and my physician assured me, that melancholy and low spirits are half my disease:—guess, then, my horrors since this business began. If I had it settled, I would be, I think, quite well in a manner. How shall I use the language to you,—oh do not disappoint me!—but strong necessity's curst command.

I have been thinking over and over my brother's affairs, and I fear I must cut him up; but on this I will correspond at another time, particularly as I shall [require] your advice.

Forgive me for once more mentioning by return of post:—save me from the horrors of a jail! (223)

My compliments to my friend James, and to all the rest. I do not know what I have written. The subject is so horrible, I dare not look it over again. Farewell!

R. B.

NO CCCLXXX.

BURNS TO MR. THOMSON.

Brow, on the Solway-frith,
July 12th, 1796.

AFTER all my boasted independence, curst necessity compels me to implore you for five pounds. A cruel wretch of a haberdasher, to whom I owe an account, taking it into his head that I am dying, has commenced a process, and will infallibly put me into jail. Do, for God's sake, send me that sum, and that by return of post. Forgive me this earnestness, but the horrors of a jail have made me half distracted. I do not ask all this gratuitously; for, upon returning health, I hereby promise and engage to furnish you with five pounds' worth of the neatest song-genius you have seen. I tried my hand on "Rothermurche" this morning. The measure is so difficult that it is impossible to infuse much genius into the lines; they are on the other side. Forgive, forgive me! (224)

NO CCCLXXXI.

MR. THOMSON TO BURNS.

July 14th, 1796.

MY DEAR SIR—Ever since I received your melancholy letters by Mrs. Hyslop, I have been ruminating in what manner I could endeavour to alleviate your sufferings. Again and again I thought of a pecuniary offer, but the recollection of one of your letters on this subject, and the fear of offending your independent spirit, checked my resolution. I thank you heartily, therefore, for the frankness of your letter of the 12th, and, with great pleasure, enclose a draft for the very sum I proposed sending (225). Would I were Chancellor of the Exchequer but for one day, for your sake!

Pray, my good Sir, is it not possible for you to muster a volume of poetry? If too much trouble to you, in the present state of your health, some literary friend might be found here, who would select and arrange from your manuscripts, and take upon him the task of editor. In the meantime, it could be advertised to be published by subscription. Do not shun this mode of obtaining the value of your labour: remember, Pope published the Iliad by subscription. Think of this, my dear Burns, and do not reckon me intrusive with my advice. You are too well convinced of the respect and friendship I bear your to impute anything I say to an unworthy motive. Yours faithfully.

The verses to "Rothermurche" will answer finely. I am happy to see you can still tune your lyre.

NO. CCCLXXXII.

TO JAMES GRACIE, Esq.

Brow, Wednesday morning,
July 16th, 1796.

My Dear Sir—It would be doing high injustice to this place not to acknowledge that my rheumatism has derived great benefits from it already; but, alas! my loss of appetite still continues. I shall not need your kind offer *this week* (226), and I return to town the beginning of next week, it not being a tide week. I am detaining a man in a burning hurry. So, God bless you!

R. B.

NO. CCCLXXXIII.

TO JAMES ARMOUR (227),

MASON, MAUCHLINE.

Dumfries, July, 18th, 1796.

My Dear Sir—Do, for Heaven's sake, send Mrs. Armour here immediately. My wife is hourly expecting to be put to bed, Good God! what a situation for her to be in, poor girl, without a friend! I returned from sea-bathing quarters to-day, and my medical friends would almost persuade me that I am better, but I think and feel that my strength is so gone, that the disorder will prove fatal to me. Your son-in-law,

R. B. (228)

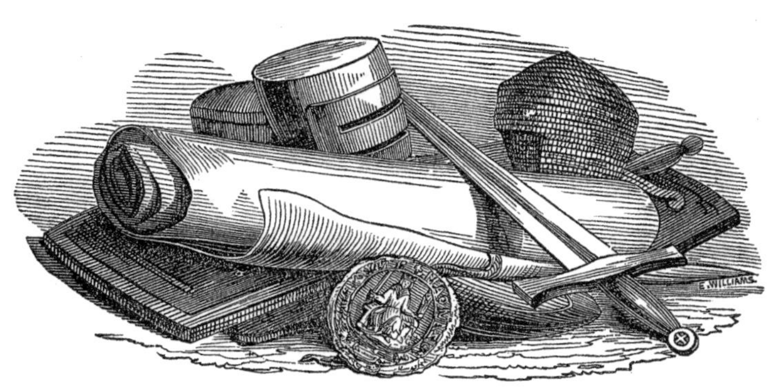

Notes

TO THE LIFE, POEMS, CORRESPONDENCE, &c., &c.
OF BURNS.

Notes to the Life of Burns.

PAGE 4, NOTE 1.—To account for the co-existence of a taste for dancing, music, and song, with the austere religious feelings above described, we must bear in mind that the latter are not of such long standing, having only existed in great force since the time of the civil wars. It is also to be observed, that those tastes and those feelings did not always possess the same minds. Throughout the most rigid times, the young formed a party whom the promptings of nature compelled to favour mirthful recreation and the productions of the muse, all preachings from the old notwithstanding. Then the Episcopalian or Jacobite party, formed a large and important exception from the general spirit of the nation, being declared patrons of not only dancing and song, but of theatricals.

PAGE 4, NOTE 2.—Till a recent period, and previous to the reign of George I., the history of Scottish music was a matter of conjecture only. Even the remark in the text as to the existence of music before the Reformation, had no proper basis. The existence of popular airs at a time little subsequent to the Reformation, including some which still flourish, is at length ascertained, in consequence of the discovery of an MS. collection of airs, which belonged to Sir John Skene of Currie-hill, and must have been written about the year 1620. See an elegant and laborious work by William Dauncy, Esq., Advocate, 4to., 1838.

PAGE 5, NOTE 3.—The North American Indians, among whom the attachment between the sexes is said to be weak, and love, in the purer sense of the word, unknown, seem nearly unacquainted with the charms of poetry and music.—See *Weld's Tour.* We quote this as an explanatory reference. It is, however, very far from the truth in both respects; with due deference to the information whence Dr. Currie drew his authority.

PAGE 5, NOTE 4.—Edward Gibbon.

PAGE 6, NOTE 5.—This practice has ceased to prevail, so that the remarks of Dr. Currie on this subject are no longer applicable.

PAGE 6, NOTE 6.—In this instance, again, the description of Dr. Currie is no longer applicable. And it is rather true, at present, that the tenant farmers of Scotland are superior, than that they are inferior to the same class in England; and there is certainly as much evidence of comfort in their mode of living. There has been a very rapid progress made in agricultural science, especially amongst the Lowland farmers of late years; and even the labouring classes are upon an equal footing in respect of means and comforts in both portions of great Britain, whereas, they are certainly better informed and educated in Scotland. Supposing the remark to be reserved to the holders of land, or the capitalist peasantry, so to call them, the distinction has here even ceased to exist.

PAGE 7, NOTE 7.—The rapid increase in

the consumption of spirituous liquors is truly astonishing. The following figures have been stated by a contemporary: "The amount of the duty on spirits distilled in Scotland is now upwards of £250,000 per annum. In 1777, it did not reach £8000." Allowing for the difference of values, and of the scale of duties levied, there is yet an enormous disparity; and, when it is considered that this is independently of all merely fermented liquors, an idea may be formed of the immense increase in the consumption of intoxicating beverages. Taking again the returns of distillery for 1832, we have a gross of 5,407,097 gallons, and an aggregate duty of nearly a million sterling.

PAGE 11, NOTE 8.—According to some authorities, the fair heroine of this young passion was called Nelly Blair. The lines which immortalized her are those which commence—"Once I loved a bonnie lass."

PAGE 12, NOTE 9.—In October, 1837, the editor conversed at Tarbolton with John Lees, shoemaker, who, when a stripling, used to act as Burns's second in his courting expeditions. The old man spoke with much glee of the aid he had given the poet in the way of *asking out* lasses for him. When he had succeeded in bringing the girl out of doors, he of course became *Monsieur de Trop*, and Burns would say, "Now, Jack, ye may gang hame."

PAGE 12, NOTE 10.—A correspondent of the *Scotsman* newspaper, 1828, communicated the following as recollections of Burns in his early rustic years:—"He was particularly distinguished at that species of merry-making called 'Rockings,' which are frequently alluded to in his writings. This kind of meeting is, or was (for I suppose the change of manners will have suppressed this innocent species of 'play') formed of young people—servants generally, of both sexes, to the neighbouring farmers—who were allowed, during moonlight, to meet alternately at their respective houses, each lass thriftily carrying with her the spinning-wheel, and, while the song and the tale went round, never failing to complete her assigned task of spinning; the lads, in the meanwhile, being as busily employed in knitting the stocking: the entertainment ending with a supper of a particular dish or two of country fare. On these occasions my narrator remembers well the distinguished part Burns used to take in the business of the evening. Often has she met him at the head of a little troop, coming from a distance of three or four miles, with the spinning-wheel of his favourite, for the time being, mounted on his shoulders, and his approach announced by the bursts of merriment which his ready and rough jokes had excited amongst the group. It was always expected that some new effusion of his muse should be produced to promote the enjoyment of the party, and seldom were they disappointed, 'Rob Burns's last night's poem' generally reaching the parlour in the course of the next day. At the kitchen of my friend's father (an extensive land proprietor) Burns's visits were of such frequency and duration as to call down the animadversions of the lady of the house, the alertness of her damsels in the morning being at times impaired by his unreasonable gallantry. This was supposed to be occasioned by a *penchant* he had formed for a certain Nelly Blair, a pretty girl, a servant in the family, and whom he celebrated in more songs and odes than her name appears in; the only one likely to be applied to her now, being one which he himself transcribes, in a letter to Mr. Thomson, as one of his earliest effusions, and of which his 'Handsome Nell,' I think, forms the burden. My friend describes him as being considered at that time as a clever fellow, but a wild scamp."

PAGE 12, NOTE 11.—The songs in question are respectively identified by the first lines of each as follows:—

1. "It was upon a Lammas night."
2. "Now westling winds and slaughterin' guns."
3. "Behind yon hills where Lugar flows."

PAGE 13, NOTE 12.—One Richard Brown, who however lived until within the last few years, and was latterly held in general esteem.

PAGE 13, NOTE 13.—On the birth of an illegitimate child.

PAGE 13, NOTE 14.—"The twa herds."

PAGE 14, NOTE 15.—John Blane, at one time driver of a coach between Glasgow and Cumnock, and now (1838) residing at Kilmarnock, was for four years and a half farm-servant in the Burns family at Lochlee and Mossgiel. With Robert Burns, who was eight years his senior, he slept for a long time in the same bed, *in the stable loft*, at Mossgiel. He reports that Burns had a little deal table with a drawer in it, which he kept constantly beside the bed, with a small desk on the top of it. The best of his poems were here written during the hours of rest; the table-drawer being the depository in which he kept them. To think of the Cotter's Saturday Night, the Lament, and the Vision, being written in the poor garret over a small farmer's stable! He used to employ Blane to read the poems to him, immediately after their composition, that he might be able the more effectually to detect faults in them. When dissatisfied with a particular passage, he would stop the reading, make an alteration, and then desire his companion to proceed. Blane was often awakened by him during the night, that he might serve him in this capacity. It is to be gathered from the old man's conversation, that the bard of Ayr was a most rigid critic of his own compositions, and burned many with which he was displeased.

PAGE 14, NOTE 16.—Miss Helen Maria Williams.

PAGE 14, NOTE 17.—There are various copies of this letter in the author's handwriting; and one of these, evidently corrected, is in the book in which he had copied several of his letters. This has been used for the press, with some omissions, and one slight alteration suggested by Gilbert Burns.

PAGE 14, NOTE 18.—This house is on the right-hand side of the road from Ayr to Maybole, which forms a part of the road from Glasgow to Port-Patrick. When the poet's father afterwards removed to Tarbolton parish, he sold his leasehold right in this house, and a few acres of land adjoining, to the corporation of shoemakers in Ayr. It is now a country ale-house.

PAGE 15, NOTE 19.—Mrs. Burns, the mother of Robert Burns, survived to the advanced age of 88. She died on the 14th of January, 1820.

PAGE 15, NOTE 20.—Quoted from a letter addressed by G. Burns, to Mrs. Dunlop.

PAGE 15, NOTE 21.—The farm alluded to was Mount Oliphant in the parish of Ayr. The passage is quoted from a letter from G. Burns to Mrs. Dunlop.

PAGE 16, NOTE 22.—The reading from Titus Adronicus, was from the revolting passage,—Act ii. Sc. 5.

PAGE 17, NOTE 23.—Mr. Tennant, of Ayr, one of the few surviving early friends of Burns, has the following recollections respecting him:—"He first knew the poet, when attending Mr. Murdoch's school at Ayr, he being then fifteen, and Burns a year and a half older. Burns and he were favourite pupils of Murdoch, who used to take them alternately to live with him, allowing them a share of his bed. Mr. Murdoch was a well-informed and zealous teacher—a particularly good French scholar, insomuch that he at one time taught the language in France. He thought his voice had some peculiar quality or power, adapting it in an uncommon degree for French pronunciation. To this predilection of the teacher, it is probably owing that Burns acquired so much French, and had such a fancy for introducing snatches of it in his letters. Murdoch was so anxious to advance his two favourite pupils, that, while they were lying with him, he was always taking opportunities of communicating knowledge. The intellectual gifts of Burns even at this time greatly impressed his fellow-scholar. Robert and Gilbert Burns were like no other young men. Their style of language was quite above that of their compeers. Robert had borrowed great numbers of books, and acquainted himself with their contents. He read rapidly, but remembered all that was interesting or valuable in what he read. He had the New Testament more at command than any other youth ever known to Mr. Tennant, who was, altogether, more impressed in these his boyish days by the discourse of the youthful poet, than he afterwards was by his published verses. The elocution of Burns resembled that of Edmund Kean—deep, thoughtful, emphatic; and in controversy, no man could stand before him."

PAGE 17, NOTE 24.—Mr. John Murdoch died April 20, 1824, aged seventy-seven. He had published a Radical vocabulary of the French language, 12mo, 1783; Pronunciation and Orthography of the French language, 8vo. 1788; Dictionary of Distinctions, 8vo. 1811; and other works. He was a highly amiable and worthy man. In his latter days, illness had reduced him to the brink of destitution, and an appeal was made to the friends and admirers of his illustrious pupil, in his behalf. Some money was thus raised, and applied to the relief of his necessities. It is stated, in the obituary notice of Mr. Murdoch, published in the London papers, that he had taught English in London to several distinguished foreigners; among the rest, to the celebrated Talleyrand, during his residence as an emigrant in England.

PAGE 19, NOTE 25.—Both Robert and Gilbert speak of the total ruin of their father at the time of his death. "His all," says Robert, "went among the hell-hounds that prowl in the kennel of justice." It appears difficult to reconcile this with the immediately ensuing statement, that Mossgiel was stocked by the property and individual savings of the whole family. But the fact, we understand to be, that at the bankruptcy of William Burns, his children had respectively considerable claims upon his estate, on account of their services to him on the farm, which claims were preferable to those of the other creditors. They thus, with the perfect approbation of the law, and we rather think of justice also, (though some thought otherwise at the time), rescued a portion of his property from the "hell-hounds."

PAGE 19, NOTE 26.—John Blane, already mentioned, reports that, at Lochlee, the whole family, including the daughters, wrought at the various labours of the farm. The second daughter, Annabella by name, had a turn for poetry, but, not having been taught to write, was unable to commit her compositions to paper: few women of the same rank were at that time taught to write. The family was one which regularly went to church, one male and one female being left at home, to take care of the house, and "the beasts." Annabella would contrive to have Blane for her companion, that he might write down her poems during the absence of the rest. She took possession of the manuscripts, but was obliged by the severity of parental discipline, to conceal her love of the divine art.

PAGE 20, NOTE 27.—According to credible authorities, he was in the habit of walking every day to Kilmarnock, for the purpose of superintending the progress of his literary labours, through press; and it is very certain that he was at this time labouring under the utmost privations, and subsisting upon the most scanty fare:—"*dining off a piece of oat cake, and two-pennyworth of ale*," according to one of his biographers.

PAGE 20, NOTE 28.—Burns, himself, in many of his extant letters of this date, declares that he was "skulking from covert to covert, under the terror of a jail," and that he was pursued to persecution by the officers, under proceedings intended to extort a compulsory provision for his twin children, by Miss Armour, which, however, he was bent upon legitimating, by marrying their mother; whilst the relations of Miss A. were driving him from pillar to post, in the hope of effectually separating the lovers.

PAGE 21, NOTE 29.—There is another observation of Gilbert Burns on his brother's narrative, in which some persons will be interested. It refers to where the poet speaks of his youthful friends. "My brother," says Gilbert Burns, "seems to set off his early companions in too consequential a manner. The principal acquaintance we had in Ayr, while boys, were four sons of Mr. Andrew M'Culloch, a distant relation of my mother's, who kept a tea shop, and had made a little money in the contraband trade, very common at that time. He died while the boys were young, and my father was nominated one of the tutors. The two eldest were bred shopkeepers, the third a surgeon, and the youngest, the only surviving one, was bred in a counting-house in Glasgow, where he is now a respectable merchant. I believe all these boys went to the West Indies. Then there were two sons of Dr. Malcolm, whom I have mentioned in my letter to Mrs. Dunlop. The eldest a very worthy young man, went to the East Indies, where he had a commission in the army; he is the person whose heart, my brother says, the *Munny Begum scenes could not corrupt*. The other, by the interest of Lady Wallace, got an ensigncy in a regiment raised by the Duke of Hamilton during the American War. I believe neither of them are now (1797) alive. We also knew the present Dr. Paterson of Ayr, and a younger brother of his, now in Jamaica, who were much younger than us. I had almost forgot to mention Dr. Charles of Ayr, who was a little older than my brother, and with whom we had a longer and closer intimacy than with any of the others, which did not, however, continue in after life."

PAGE 21, NOTE 30.—A Scottish term meaning fire.

PAGE 21, NOTE 31.—The hoary brow.

PAGE 21, NOTE 32.—Wishes or chooses.

PAGE 21, NOTES 33, 34, and 35.—An allusion to some airs known amongst the Scottish Psalmody. Reference is especially made to the three adopted by William Burns.

PAGE 21, NOTE 36.—Supplies, adds fuel to.

PAGE 21, NOTE 37.—The father of the family leading the family devotion.

PAGE 25, NOTE 38.—"This business was first carried on here from the Isle of Man, and afterwards to a considerable extent from France, Ostend, and Gottenburgh. Persons engaged in it found it necessary to go abroad, and enter into business with foreign merchants; and by dealing in tea, spirits, and silks, brought home to their families and friends the means of luxury and finery at the cheapest rate."—*Statistical Account of Kirkoswald*, 1794.

PAGE 28, NOTE 39.—The subjoined anecdote may serve to throw some additional light upon the nature of Burns' connexions at the period referred to. "The poet's Maybole friend, on inspecting the volume, was mortified to find the poetical epistle which had been addressed to him, printed with the name *Andrew* substituted for his own, and the motto from Blair, as was but proper, omitted. He said nothing at the time; but, young, ambitious, and conscious of having done all in his humble power for friendship's cause, he could not forgive so marked a slight. He, therefore, from that time ceased to answer Burns's letters. When the poet was next at Maybole, he asked the cause, and Willie answered by inquiring if he could not himself divine it. He said he thought he could, and adverted to the changed name in the poem. Mr. Robert Aiken, writer in Ayr, had been, he said, a useful friend and patron to him. He had a son commencing a commercial life in Liverpool. I thought, he said, that a few verses addressed to this youth would gratify the father, and be accepted as a mark of my gratitude. But, my muse being lazy, I could not well make them out. After all, this old epistle occurred to me, and by putting his name into it, in place of yours, I made it answer this purpose. Willie told him in reply, that he had just exchanged his friendship for that of Mr. Aiken, and requested that their respective letters might be burnt—a duty which he scrupulously performed on his own part. The two disputants of Kirkoswald never saw or corresponded with each other again."

PAGE 29, NOTE 40.—"Therefore are they before the throne of God, and serve him day and night in his temple: and he that sitteth on the throne shall dwell among them. They shall hunger no more, neither thirst any more; neither shall the sun light on them, nor any heat. For the Lamb which is in the midst of the throne shall feed them, and shall lead them unto the living fountains of waters: and God shall wipe away all tears from their eyes."

PAGE 29, NOTE 41.—We have had several occasions to notice the narrowness of Burns's means, and the straits to which he was often reduced; and the account which we have of the closing scene of his father's life, sufficiently explains how this extremity of distress should have failed to be relieved by his relatives. To those to whom such a circumstance, however, may appear somewhat extraordinary, the subjoined particulars may be interesting:—"It is no uncommon case for a small farmer, or even cotter, in Scotland, to have a son placed at some distant seminary of learning, or serving an apprenticeship to some metropolitan writer or tradesman; in which case, the youth is almost invariably supplied with oatmeal, the staple of the poor Scotsman's life—cheese, perhaps—oaten or barley bread, &c., from the home stores, by the intervention of the weekly or fortnightly carrier. The above passage recals to the Editor an anecdote which is related of a gentleman, now high in consideration at the Scottish bar, whose father, a poor villager in the upper ward of Lanarkshire, having contrived to get him placed at Glasgow University, supported him there chiefly by a weekly bag of oatmeal. On one occasion, the supply was stopped for nearly three weeks by a snow-storm. The young man's meal, like Burns's, was out; but his pride, or his having no intimate acquaintance, prevented him from borrowing. And this remarkable and powerful-minded man had all but perished, before the dissolving snow allowed a new stock of provisions to reach him."

PAGE 29, NOTE 42.—In his letter to Dr. Moore, Burns gives the following account of the consequences of this calamity to himself:—"This was an unlucky affair; as we were giving a welcome carousal to the new year the shop took fire, and burnt to ashes, and *I was left, like a true poet, not worth a sixpence.*" "One who had known Burns at Irvine thus reported his recollection of the poet's appearance and demeanour. He looked older than he was—was of a very dark complexion, and had a strong dark eye; his ordinary look, while in company, was thoughtful, amounting to what might be called a gloomy attentiveness. When not interested in the conversation, he might sometimes be seen, for a considerable space, leaning down on his palm, with his elbow resting on his knee—perhaps the most melancholy of all postures short of the prostration of despair. He was in common silent and reserved; but when he found a man to his mind, he made a point of attaching himself to the company of that person, and endeavouring to bring out his powers. Among women he never failed to exert himself, and always shone. People remarked, even then, that when Robert Burns did speak, he always spoke to the point, and in general with a sententious brevity. From another source we learn that Burns at this time loved to debate theological topics amongst the rustic groups which met in the churchyard after service."

PAGE 30, NOTE 43.—Sillar was a brother rhymster of Burns's, and it was to him that the Epistle to Davie was addressed. Mr. Sillar subsequently became a wealthy magistrate in Irvine, by inheriting, very unexpectedly, a large fortune from a distant relative. He had, however, before this, settled as a teacher in the same place, and lived in competent circumstances. He has only been dead a few years.

PAGE 31, NOTE 44.—At the period at which Dr. Currie wrote his biographical account of Burns, these societies were comparatively scarce, and it was worthy of some remark that works of this particular character were held in preference. The Scotch, besides, being an imaginative people, are, however, essentially a scientific nation, and in these days a great variety of literary material has become popularised amongst them. Indeed, "book societies and village libraries have greatly increased in number, and means, formerly undreamt of, have been taken for furnishing intellectual food to the people. It may, at the same time, be mentioned that no evil result of any kind is known to have arisen from the alleged predilection of the Scottish peasantry for books of elegant literature. We think it likely that this predilection is greatly overstated in the text. One great change has, however, taken place in the tastes of the rural people of Scotland. Their book-shelves or window-soles, which formerly contained only a few books of divinity, with perhaps Blind Harry's Wallace and Ramsay's Gentle Shepherd, or some specimens of secular literature, now exhibit, in many instances, a considerable store of productions in the belles lettres, and of valuable books of information. The individuals who sell books in *numbers*, or small parts, speak strongly of the change which has taken place amongst them, during the last thirty years, from an exclusively theoolgical to a general taste."

PAGE 35, NOTE 45.—In Cobbett's Magazine.

PAGE 35, NOTE 46.—The female infant continued to be nursed by its mother, but unable to provide any better attention for the boy, the family entrusted him to the care of some good people at Mossgiel, where he was reared by hand, being fed upon cow's milk.

PAGE 36, NOTE 47.—Miss Alexander, who had become the purchaser of the estate in the scenery of which Burns delighted to revel. Wilhelmina Alexander was the sister of Mr. Claude Alexander, who has served as paymaster to the troops in India.

PAGE 36, NOTE 48.—This letter is preserved as a great treasure at Ballochmyle. At the close, Burns requests, as a favour, the permission to include the poem which accompanied it in the forthcoming second edition of his works.

PAGE 36, NOTE 49.—This is correct in Scottish phraseology; in strictly grammatical English, we should have used the word *hung* for *hang*.

PAGE 36, NOTE 50.—These lines originally stood thus:—

"The lily's hue and roses' dye
Bespoke the lass o' Ballochmyle."

PAGE 37, NOTE 51.—The individual alluded to was a modest and amiable girl, named Mary Campbell, whose parents resided at Campbelltown in Argyleshire. It can never detract from the pathos of her history, to relate that she was a servant—we believe, the dairy-woman—at Coilsfield House, the seat of Colonel Montgomery, afterwards twelfth earl of Eglinton. Burns partly narrates the tale of his affection for this young woman. "After a pretty long trial," he says, "of the most ardent reciprocal affection, we met, by appointment, on the second Sunday of May, in a sequestered spot by the banks of Ayr, where we spent a day in taking a farewell before she should embark for the West Highlands, to arrange matters among her friends for our projected change of life. At the close of the autumn following, she crossed the sea to meet me at Greenock, where she had scarce landed when she was seized with a malignant fever, which hurried my dear girl to her grave in a few days, before I could even hear of her illness." Mr. Cromek further informs us, that this adieu was performed with all those simple and striking ceremonials, which rustic sentiment has devised to prolong tender emotions and to impose awe. The lovers stood on each side of a small purling brook—they laved their hands in the limpid stream—and, holding a Bible between them, pronounced their vows to be faithful to each other. They parted—never to meet again." It is proper to add," says Mr. Lockhart, "that Mr. Cromek's story has recently been confirmed very strongly by the accidental discovery of a Bible, presented by Burns to Mary Campbell, in the possession of her still surviving sister at Ardrossan. Upon the boards of the first volume is inscribed, in Burns's handwriting—'And ye shall not swear by my name falsely, I am the Lord.'—*Levit.* chap. xix. v. 12.' On the second volume—'Thou shalt not forswear thyself, but shalt perform unto the Lord thine oaths.' —*St. Matth.* chap. v. 33. And, on a blank leaf of either—'Robert Burns, Mossgiel'—with his *mason-mark*." The fine lyrics, Highland Mary, and To Mary in Heaven, with the notes attached to them, tell the remainder of this sorrowful tale.

PAGE 37, NOTE 52.—Gilbert Burns, in a letter addressed to the Editor [Dr. Currie], has given the following account of the friends which Robert's talents procured him before he left Ayrshire, or attracted the notice of the world:—

"The farm of Mossgiel, at the time of our coming to it (Martinmas, 1783), was the property of the Earl of Loudon, but was held in tack by Mr. Gavin Hamilton, writer, in Mauchline, from whom we had our bargain; who had thus an opportunity of knowing, and showing a sincere regard for my brother, before he knew that he was a poet. The poet's estimation of him, and the strong outlines of his character, may be collected from the dedication to this gentleman. When the publication was begun, Mr. Hamilton entered very warmly into its interests, and promoted the subscription very extensively. Mr. Robert Aiken, writer in Ayr, is a man of worth and taste, of warm affections, and connected with a most respectable circle of friends and relations. It is to this gentleman The Cotter's Saturday Night is inscribed. The poems of my brother, which I have formerly mentioned, no sooner came into his hands, than they were quickly known, and well received in the extensive circle of Mr. Aiken's friends, which gave them a sort of currency, necessary in this wise world, even for the good reception of things valuable in themselves. But Mr. Aiken not only admired the poet; as soon as he became acquainted with him, he showed the warmest regard for the man, and did everything in his power to forward his interest and respectability. The Epistle to a Young Friend was addressed to this gentleman's son, Mr. A. H. Aiken, now of Liverpool. He was the oldest of a young family, who were taught to receive my brother with respect, as a man of genius, and their father's friend.

The Brigs of Ayr is inscribed to John Ballantine, Esq., banker, in Ayr; one of those gentlemen to whom my brother was introduced by Mr. Aiken. He interested himself very warmly in my brother's concerns, and constantly showed the greatest friendship and attachment to him. When the Kilmarnock edition was all sold off, and a considerable demand pointed out the propriety of publishing a second edition, Mr. Wilson, who had printed the first, was asked if he would print the second, and take his chance of being paid from the first sale. This he declined, and when this came to Mr. Ballantine's knowledge, he generously offered to accommodate Robert with what money he might need for that purpose; but advised him to go to Edinburgh, as the fittest place for publishing. When he did go to Edinburgh, his friends advised him to publish again by subscription, so that he did not need to accept this offer. Mr. William Parker, merchant in Kilmarnock, was a subscriber for thirty-five copies of the Kilmarnock edition. This may, perhaps, appear not deserving of notice here; but if the comparative obscurity of the poet at this period, be taken into consideration, it appears to me a greater effort of generosity than many things which appear more brilliant in my brother's future history.

"Mr. Robert Muir, merchant in Kilmarnock, was one of those friends Robert's poetry had procured him, and one who was dear to his heart. This gentleman had no very great fortune, or long line of dignified ancestry; but what Robert says of Captain Matthew Henderson, might be said of him with great propriety, *that he held the patent of his honours immediately from Almighty God.* Nature had, indeed, marked him a gentleman in the most legible characters. He died while yet a young man, soon after the publication of my brother's first Edinburgh edition. Sir William Cunningham of Robertland, paid a very flattering attention, and showed a good deal of friendship for the poet. Before his going to Edinburgh, as well as after, Robert seemed peculiarly pleased with Professor Stewart's friendship and conversation.

"But of all the friendships which Robert acquired in Ayrshire and elsewhere, none seemed more agreeable to him than that of Mrs. Dunlop of Dunlop; nor any which has been more uniformly and constantly exerted in behalf of him and his family, of which, were it proper, I could give many instances. Robert was on the point of setting out for Edinburgh before Mrs. Dunlop had heard of him. About the time of my brother's publishing in Kilmarnock, she had been afflicted with a long and severe illness, which had reduced her mind to the most distressing state of depression. In this situation, a copy of the printed poems was laid on her table by a friend; and, happening to open on The Cotter's Saturday Night, she read it over with the greatest pleasure and surprise; the poet's description of the simple cottagers operating on her mind like the charm of a powerful exorcist, expelling the demon *ennui*, and restoring her to her wonted inward harmony and satisfaction. Mrs. Dunlop sent off a person express to Mossgiel, distant fifteen or sixteen miles, with a very obliging letter to my brother, desiring him to send her half a dozen copies of his poems, if he had them to spare, and begging he would do her the pleasure of calling at Dunlop House as soon as convenient. This was the beginning of a correspondence which ended only with the poet's life. The last use he made of his pen, was writing a short letter to this lady a few days before his death.

Colonel Fullarton, who afterwards paid a very particular attention to the poet, was not in the country at the time of his first commencing author. At this distance of time, and in the hurry of a wet day, snatched from laborious occupations, I may have forgot some persons who ought to have been mentioned on this occasion; for which, if it come to my knowledge, I shall be heartily sorry."

The friendship of Mrs. Dunlop was of particular value to Burns. This lady, daughter and sole heiress to Sir Thomas Wallace of Craigie, and lineal descendant of the illustrious Wallace, the first of Scottish warriors, possesses the qualities of mind suited to her high lineage. Preserving, in the decline of life, the generous affections of youth, her admiration of the poet was soon accompanied by a sincere friendship for the man, which pursued him in after-life through good and evil report—in poverty, in sickness, and in sorrow—and which is continued to his infant family, now deprived of their parent. [Mrs. Dunlop was the lineal descendant, not of Sir William Wallace, but of his father's elder brother. This amiable and enlightened person died May 24, 1815, at an advanced age.]

Page 38, Note 53.—"Thomas Blacklock, D.D. (born at Annan, Nov. 10, 1721, died at Edinburgh, July 7, 1791), though blind from the age of six months, acquired the education suitable for the clerical profession, and wrote poetry considerably above mediocrity. It was a fortunate circumstance that the person whom Dr. Laurie applied to, merely because he was the only one of his literary acquaintances with whom he chose to use that freedom, happened also to be the person best qualified to render the application successful. Dr. Blacklock was an enthusiast in his admiration of an art which he had practised himself with applause. He felt the claims of a poet with a paternal sympathy, and he had in his constitution a tenderness and sensibility that would have engaged his beneficence for a youth in the circumstances of Burns, even though he had not been indebted to him, for the delight which he received from his works; for if the young men were enumerated whom he drew from obscurity, and enabled by education to advance themselves in life, the catalogue would naturally excite surprise. * * * He was not of a disposition to discourage with feeble praise, and to shift off the trouble of future patronage, by bidding him relinquish poetry, and mind his plough."—Professor Walker.

The following is the letter of Dr. Blacklock to Dr. Laurie, by which the poet was prevented from going to Jamaica, and had his steps turned towards Edinburgh:—

"I ought to have acknowledged your favour long ago, not only as a testimony of your kind remembrance, but as it gave me an opportunity of sharing one of the finest, and perhaps, one of the most genuine entertainments of which the human mind is susceptible. A number of avocations retarded my progress in reading the poems; at last, however, I have finished that pleasing perusal. Many instances have I seen of Nature's force or beneficence exerted under numerous and formidable disadvantages; but none equal to that with which you have been kind enough to present me. There is a pathos and delicacy in his serious poems, a vein of wit and humour in those of a more festive turn, which cannot be too much admired, nor too warmly approved; and I think I shall never open the book without feeling my astonishment renewed and increased. It was my wish to have expressed my approbation in verse; but whether from declining life, or a temporary depression of spirits, it is at present out of my power to accomplish that intention.

"Mr. Stewart, Professor of Morals in this university, had formerly read me three of the poems, and I had desired him to get my name inserted among the subscribers; but whether this was done or not, I never could learn. I have little intercourse with Dr. Blair, but will take care to have the poems communicated to him by the intervention of some mutual friend. It has been told me by a gentleman, to whom I showed the performances, and who sought a copy with diligence and ardour, that the whole impression is already exhausted. It were, therefore, much to be wished, for the sake of the young man, that a second edition, more numerous than the former, could immediately be printed; as it appears certain that its intrinsic merit, and the exertion of the author's friends, might give it a more universal circulation than anything of the kind which has been published in my memory."

PAGE 38, NOTE 54.—Mr. Dalziel was employed by the Earl of Glencairn, in the capacity of steward to his estates, and was located in Ayrshire, in the estate called Finlayston, belonging to that nobleman.

PAGE 38, NOTE 55.—Mr. Cunningham, in his account of this period, in the poet's career, has given the following portraiture of him:—"After his return to Edinburgh, he seemed for some days, as in earlier life, unfitted with an aim, and wandered about, looking down from Arthur's seat surveying the palace, gazing at the castle, or contemplating the windows of the bookseller's shops, wherein he saw all works save the poems of the ploughman of Ayrshire. He picked his way to the solitary tomb of Fergusson, and kissed the sod as he knelt down; he sought out the house of Allan Ramsay, and on entering it, took off his hat; and when, subsequently, he was introduced to Creech, the bibliopole remembered that he had before heard of his inquiring whether this had been the shop of the author of the *Gentle Shepherd.*

PAGE 38, NOTE 56.—The following are the lines in question:—

This wot ye all whom it concerns,
I, Rhymer Robin, alias Burns,
October twenty-third,
A ne'er-to-be-forgotten day,
Sae far I sprackled up the brae,
I dinner'd wi' a lord.

I've been at drunken writer's feasts,
Nay, been bitch-fou'd 'mang gadly priests,
Wi' rev'rence be it spoken:—
I've even joined the honour'd jorum,
When mighty squireships of the quorum,
Their hydra drouth did sloken.

But wi' a Lord! stand out my shin!
A Lord! a Peer! a true Earl's son!
Up higher yet my bonnet!
And sic a Lord—lang Scotch ells twa,
Our Peerage he o'erlooks them a',
As I look o'er my sonnet.

But, oh! for Hogarth's magic pow'r!
To show Sir Bardy's willyart glow'r,
And how he star'd and stammer'd,
When goavan, as if led wi' branks,
And stumpin' on his ploughman shanks,
He in the parlour hammer'd.

I sliding shelter'd in a nook,
And at his Lordship steal't a look,
Like some portentous omen:
Except good sense and social glee,
And (what surprised me) modesty,
I marked nought uncommon.

I watch'd the symptoms o' the great,
The gentle pride, the lordly state,
The arrogant assuming:
The fient a pride, nae pride had he,
Nor sauce, nor state, that I could see,
Mair than an honest ploughman.

Then from his Lordship I shall learn,
Henceforth to meet with unconcern
One rank as well's another;
Nae *honest worthy* man need care,
To meet with noble youthful DAER,
For he but meets a brother.

The nobleman alluded to in these lines, was, as has been noticed, Basil Lord Daer, the eldest son and heir of Dunbar Earl of Selkirk. Imbued with the equalising notions of the French Revolution, from the seat of which he had but very recently returned, he was free from all the absurd affectation of simplicity and hypocritical pretence of equality, and was as truly simple in his manners and appearance, as genuinely courteous to his inferiors in rank, and as unostentatiously benevolent, as his heart was sound, and his judgment untainted and unbiassed. His early death, on the 5th of November, 1794, was sincerely lamented by the many of the humble, yet meritorious associates whom he had rescued from undeserved obscurity. Lord Daer was only 31 years of age when he died.

PAGE 39, NOTE 57.—Dr. Currie *had* seen and conversed with Burns.

PAGE —, NOTE 58.—Refer to note 59, the number 58 having been omitted in the corrections.

PAGE 41, NOTE 59.—There is some want of preciseness about this date. Gilbert Burns seems to have been under the impression that the real date should have been rendered 1789-90, whilst others amongst the biographers, &c., who furnish us with material relating to the poet, prefer to render the date as 1787-88. I believe, from other documents, that the date is correctly rendered in the text, and from some scraps of memoranda derived originally from Dr. Mackenzie through Mr. Bland, I should say that the matter was beyond a doubt.—[ED.]

PAGE 41, NOTE 60.—The reader is referred from this quotation to the "General Correspondence of Burns" in the foregoing part of this volume, under the date of Feb. 14, 1791. It will be seen that the context furnished by other letters of an approximate date, throw much light on this period in his life.

PAGE 41, NOTE 61.—The recollections of Mr. John Richmond writer in Mauchline, respecting Burns's arrival, and the earlier period of his residence, in Edinburgh, are curious. Mr. Richmond, who had been brought up in the office of a country writer, and was now perfecting his studies in that of a metropolitan practitioner, occupied a room in the house of a Mrs. Carfrae, in Baxter's Close, Lawnmarket, at the rent of three shillings a-week. His circumstances as a youth just entering the world made him willing to share his apartment and bed with any agreeable companion, who might be disposed to take part in the expense. These terms suited his old Mauchline acquaintance, Burns, who accordingly lived with him in Mrs. Carfrae's from his arrival in November till his leaving town in May, on his southern excursions. Mr. Richmond mentions that the poet was so knocked up by his walk from Mauchline to Edinburgh, that he could not leave his room for the next two days. During the whole time of his residence there, his habits were temperate and regular. Much of his time was necessarily occupied in preparing his poems for the press—a task in which, as far as transcription was concerned, Mr. Richmond aided him, when not engaged in his own office duties. Burns, though frequently invited out into company, usually returned at good hours, and went soberly to bed, where he would prevail upon his companion, by little bribes, to read to him till he fell asleep. Mr. Lockhart draws an unfavourable inference from his afterwards removing to the house of his friend Nicol; but for this removal Mr. Richmond supplies a reason which exculpates the bard. During Burns's absence in the south and at Mauchline, Mr. Richmond took in another fellow-lodger; so that, when the poet came back, and applied for re-admission to Mrs. Carfrae's humble menage, he found his place filled up, and was compelled to go elsewhere.

The exterior of Burns for some time after his arrival in Edinburgh, was little superior to that of his rustic compeers. "What a clod-hopper!" was the descriptive exclamation of a lady, to whom he was abruptly pointed out one day in the Lawnmarket. In the course of a few weeks he got into comparatively fashionable attire—a blue coat with metal buttons, a yellow and blue stripped vest (being the livery of Mr. Fox), a pair of buckskins, so tight that he seemed to have grown into them, and top-boots, meeting the buckskins under the knee. His neckcloth of white cambric, was neatly arranged, and his whole appearance was clean and respectable, though the taste in which he was dressed was still obviously a rustic taste.

Though his habits during the winter of 1786-7 were, upon the whole, good, he was not altogether exempt from the bacchanalianism which at this period reigned in Edinburgh. Mr. William Nicol of the High School, and Mr. John Gray, city-clerk, were amongst his most intimate convivial friends. Nicol lived in the top of a house over what is called *Buccleuch Pend*, in the lowest floor of which there was a tavern, kept by a certain Lucky Pringle, having a back entry from the *pend*, through which visitors could be admitted, unwotted of by a censorious world. There Burns was much with Nicol, both before and after his taking up his abode in that gentleman's house. He also attended pretty frequently the meetings of the *Crochallan Fencibles*, at their howff in the Anchor Close; and of Johnnie Dowie's tavern, in Libberton's Wynd, he was a frequent visitor. Mr. Alexander Cunningham, jeweller, and Mr. Robert Cleghorn, farmer at Saughton Mills, may be said to complete the list of Burns's convivial acquaintance in Edinburgh. The intimacy he formed with Mr. Robert Ainslie, then a young writer's apprentice, appears to have been of a different character.

Page 41, Note 62.—Mr. Dalrymple of Orangefield, and the Honourable Henry Erskine, may be mentioned as individuals who exerted themselves in behalf of Burns, immediately after his arrival in Edinburgh. Dr. Adam Fergusson, author of the History of the Roman Republic, may also be added to Dr. Currie's list of his literary and philosophical patrons. At the house of the latter gentleman, Sir Walter Scott met with Burns, of whom he has given his recollections in the following letter to Mr. Lockhart:—

"As for Burns, I may truly say, *Virgilium vidi tantum*. I was a lad of fifteen in 1786-7, when he came first to Edinburgh, but had sense and feeling enough to be much interested in his poetry, and would have given the world to know him; but I had very little acquaintance with any literary people, and still less with the gentry of the west country, the two sets whom he most frequented. Mr. T. Grierson was at that time a clerk of my father's. He knew Burns, and promised to ask him to his lodgings to dinner, but had no opportunity to keep his word; otherwise I might have seen more of this distinguished man. As it was, I saw him one day at the late venerable Professor Fergusson's, where there were several gentlemen of literary reputation, among whom I remember the celebrated Mr. Dugald Stewart. Of course we youngsters sat silent, looked and listened. The only thing I remember which was remarkable in Burns's manner, was the effect produced upon him by a print of Bunbury's, representing a soldier lying dead on the snow, his dog sitting in misery on one side —on the other, his widow, with a child in her arms. These lines were written beneath:—

'Cold on Canadian hills, or Minden's plain,
Perhaps that parent wept her soldier slain—
Bent o'er her babe, her eye dissolved in dew,
The big drops mingling with the milk he drew,
Gave the sad presage of his future years,
The child of misery baptised in tears.'

Burns seemed much affected by the print, or rather the ideas which it suggested to his mind. He actually shed tears. He asked whose the lines were, and it chanced that nobody but myself remembered that they occur in a half-forgotten poem of Langhorne's, called by the unpromising title of 'The Justice of Peace.' I whispered my information to a friend present, who mentioned it to Burns, who rewarded me with a look and a word, which, though in mere civility, I then received, and still recollect, with great pleasure. His person was strong and robust; his manners rustic, not clownish; a sort of dignified plainness and simplicity, which received part of its effect, perhaps, from one's knowledge of his extraordinary talents. His features are represented in Mr. Nasmyth's picture; but to me it conveys the idea that they are diminished, as if seen in perspective I think his countenance was more massive than it looks in any of the portraits. I would have taken the poet, had I not known what he was, for a very sagacious country farmer of the old Scotch school; that is, none of your modern agriculturists, who keep labourers for their drudgery, but the *douce guidman* who held his own plough. There was a strong expression of sense and shrewdness in all his lineaments; the eye alone, I think, indicated the poetical character and temperament. It was large, and of a cast, which glowed (I say literally *glowed*) when he spoke with feeling or interest. I never saw such another eye in a human head, though I have seen the most distinguished men of my time. His conversation expressed perfect self-confidence, without the slightest presumption. Among the men who were the most learned of their time and country, he expressed himself with perfect firmness, but without the least intrusive forwardness; and when he differed in opinion, he did not hesitate to express it firmly, yet, at the same time, with modesty. I do not remember any part of his conversation distinctly enough to quote it; nor did I ever see him again, except in the street, where he did not recognise me, as I could not expect he should. He was much caressed in Edinburgh, but (considering what literary emoluments have been raised since his day) the efforts made for his relief were extremely trifling. I remember, on this occasion I mention, I thought Burns's acquaintance with English poetry was rather limited, and also, that having twenty times the abilities of Allan Ramsay and of Fergusson, he talked of them with too much humility as his models: there was, doubtless, national predilection in his estimate. This is all I can tell you about Burns. I have only to add, that his dress corresponded with his manner. He was like a farmer dressed in his best to dine with the laird. I do not speak *in malam partem*, when I say I never saw a man in company with his superiors in station and information, more perfectly free from either the reality or the affectation of embarrassment. I was told, but did not observe it, that his address to females was extremely deferential, and always with a turn either to the pathetic or humorous, which engaged their attention particularly. I have heard the late Duchess of Gordon remark this. I do not know anything I can add to these recollections of forty years since."

PAGE 41, NOTE 63.—Jane Duchess of Gordon, so remarkable in her time, was one amongst the most striking personages of his acquaintance.

PAGE 42, NOTE 64.—It was by the Earl of Glencairn, or through his instrumentality, that Mr. W. Creech, the bookseller, was introduced to Burns. Mr. Creech had travelled on the continent, in the character of tutor and companion to the young nobleman, and the latter had in view the production of a new edition of Burns's works when he effected the introduction. The Earl did not long survive. He died in the prime of life (at the age of 42 years), on the 30th of January, 1791, at Falmouth.

PAGE 44, NOTE 65.—The second edition of the poems came out in April, 1787—a handsome octavo, price five shillings to subscribers, and one shilling more to others. Above 2,800 copies had been bespoke by rather more than 1,500 subscribers: the

Caledonian Hunt taking 100 copies, Creech 500, the Earl of Eglinton 42, the Duchess of Gordon, 21, the Earl of Glencairn and his Countess 24, while many other individuals subscribed for numbers ranging between two and twelve. The number of names of nobility and gentry is very surprising, the rest being chiefly persons in the middle walks of life, from all districts, however, of Scotland. The list has now some historical value, as a chronicle of the society of the day.

The new edition of his poems was embellished by a portrait of himself, engraved by Beugo, from a painting by Alexander Nasmyth. The engraver, who, to his honour be it said, did his work gratuitously, improved upon the original portrait by a few sittings from the bard; and his production is allowed to be the most faithful likeness of Burns in existence.

PAGE 45, NOTE 66.—After seeing this remark in print, Dr. Somerville never punned more. He was the author of two substantial works on the history of England between the Restoration and the accession of the Brunswick dynasty. He died, May 16, 1830, at the age of ninety years, sixty-four of which had been passed in the clerical profession. A son of Dr. Somerville is husband to a lady distinguished in the scientific world.

PAGE 46, NOTE 67.—"Burns returned to Mauchline on the 8th of June. It is pleasing to imagine the delight with which he must have been received by his family after an absence of six months, in which his fortunes and prospects had undergone so wonderful a change. He left them comparatively unknown, his tenderest feelings torn and wounded by the conduct of the Armours, and in such a wretched state of utter indigence, as to be compelled to lurk about from hiding-place to hiding-place to escape the officers, whose pursuit was unabated, and on account of a very inconsiderable claim against him. He returned; his poetical fame established; the whole country ringing with his praises, from a capital in which he was known to have formed the wonder and delight of the polite and learned; if not rich, yet with more money already than any of his kindred had ever hoped to see him possess, and with prospects of future patronage and permanent elevation in the scale of society, which might have dazzled steadier eyes than those of maternal and fraternal affection. The prophet had at last honour in his own country, but the haughty spirit which had preserved its balance at Edinburgh was not likely to lose it at Mauchline; and we have him writing for "*auld clay biggin,*" on the 18th of July, in terms as strongly expressive as any that ever emanated from his pen; of that jealous pride which formed the groundwork of his character, the dark suspiciousness of fortune which the subsequent course of his history too well justified; that nervous intolerance of condescension, and consummate scorn of meanness, which attended and characterised him through life, and made the study of his species, for which nature had endowed him with such peculiar qualifications, the source of more pain than was ever counterbalanced by the requisite capacity for enjoyment with which he was also endowed. There are few of his letters in which more of the dark abodes and secret lurking places of his spirit are made manifest:—"I never," says he, "my friend, dreamt that mankind were capable of anything very lofty or generous; but the stateliness of the patricians of Edinburgh, and the servility of my own plebeian brethren (who, perhaps, formerly eyed me askance), since I returned home, have almost put me out of conceit altogether of my species. I have bought a pocket-Milton, which I carry continually about me, in order to study the sentiments, the dauntless magnanimity, the intrepid, unyielding independence, the desperate daring, and noble defiance of hardship in that great personage, *Satan.* The many ties of acquaintance or friendship I have, or think I have in life, I have felt along the lines, and, damn them; they are almost all of them of such frail texture, that I am sure they would not stand the breath of the least adverse breeze of fortune."—LOCKHART.

PAGE 46, NOTE 68.—This person was Mr. James Smith, a former resident of Mauchline, but who, at the period in question, had removed to Linlithgow.

PAGE 46, NOTE 69.—All three of these are the titles of popular Scottish songs. They were all collated with the assistance of Burns, and published in the shape of a monthly periodical. Burns used to delight in reverting to the praise of *Tullochgorum*, as a most genuine specimen of Scottish minstrelsy; and this song had been attributed to various authors, but was the work of the Rev. Mr. Skinner.

PAGE 47, NOTE 70.—Here would be sufficient evidence that up to this time Burns was legally, and to all intents and purposes an unmarried man, although much against his own inclination, and his repeated entreaties to the inexorable Armours. The penance to which he had submitted, of itself entitled him to a certificate of single blessedness; which, indeed, was offered by the officiating minister. But here have we in a letter addressed to Mr. Gavin Hamilton, and bearing date from Edinburgh, January 7th, 1787, some additional and conclusive evidence on the subject.

"To tell the truth," says Burns, "amongst friends, I feel a miserable blank in my heart with the want of her (that is Jean Armour), and I don't think I shall ever meet with so delicious an armful again. She has her faults; but so have you and I, and so has everybody else.

'Their tricks and craft have put me daft:—
They've taen me in and a' that;
But clear the decks, and here's the sex,
I loe the jads for a' that!
For a' that and a' that,
And twice as muckle's a' that.'
[*Part wanting.*]

"I have met," he proceeds, with a very pretty lass, a Lothian farmer's daughter, whom I have almost persuaded to accompany me to the west country, should I ever return to settle there. By the bye, a Lothian *farmer* is about an Ayrshire *squire* of the lower kind; and I had a most exquisite ride from Leith to her house yesternight, in a hackney coach, with her brother and two sisters, and brother's wife. We had dined altogether at a common friend's house in Leith, and drank, danced, and sang, till late enough. The night was dark, the claret had been good, and I thirsty ——." Hence, at all events, it is not only evident that Burns considered himself free, but that he did so much against his own inclination. The supposition that the Armours could, according to Scotch law, which recognised a promise as an actual marriage, have enforced the legal observation of all the duties incumbent upon a husband, is completely refuted by the performance of the public penance at their own instance, and by which all contract between the parties was *as legally* annulled, and by the persecution which Jean Armour's friends instituted against Burns, to render the alienation irrevocable. At any rate, at this period there there was a tacit consent of all parties that either or both should be considered free.

PAGE 47, NOTE 71.—Dr. Adair has been dead many years.

PAGE 47, NOTE 72.—A reference to Burns's own account of his wanderings, which may be gathered from the letters of this period, will serve to explain the matter more fully. The Jacobitism of Burns was the offspring of pure national pride and national tradition. The Stuarts were Scots, and Scots who, in the earlier days of their dynasty, had reflected some glory upon the land of their birth, and contributed some *share to her songs*, above all. Their degeneracy was, by the way;—the degradation of more recent Stuarts could not obliterate the charm which the patriotic enthusiasm was apt to fling about their very weaknesses. It is, however, well known that the same sentiment of opposition which fed upon the name of Stuart, in Burns, gradually verged to the greater extreme of republicanism, as this charm faded before his imagination. The following remarks, quoted as they are from the memoranda of a former editor, will serve to furnish some additional elucidation. "It was probably at this time that certain obnoxious stanzas of notoriety were written on a pane of glass in the apartment occupied by the poet and his friend:—

'Here Stuarts once in triumph reigned,
And laws for Scotia's weal ordained;
But now unroofed their palace stands,
Their sceptre's swayed by other hands.
The injured Stuart line is gone,
A race outlandish fills the throne—
An idiot race, to honour lost:
Who know them best, despise them most.'

These lines have usually been attributed to Burns, notwithstanding an obvious want of that peculiar concentration and emphasis which he gave to all his effusions. A writer in the Paisley Magazine, December, 1828, gives the following more satisfactory account of them, involving circumstances which reflect the brightest lustre on the character of the Ayrshire poet:—'They were not,' says this writer, 'the composition of Burns, but of his friend Nicol. This we state,' he continues, 'from the testimony of those who themselves knew the fact as it truly stood, and who were well acquainted with the high-wrought feelings of honour and friendship which induced Burns to remain silent under the obloquy which their affiliation entailed upon him. * * * The individual whose attention they first attracted was a clerk in the employment of the Carron Iron Company, then travelling through the country collecting accounts, or receiving orders, who happened to arrive immediately after the departure of the poet and his friend. * * * On inquiry he learned that the last occupant of the apartment was the far-famed Burns, and on this discovery he immediately transferred a copy of them to his memorandum-book of orders, made every person as wise as himself on the subject, and penned an answer to them, which, with the lines themselves, soon spread over the country, and found a place in every periodical of the day. To this poetic critic of the Carron Works do we owe the first hint of Burns being the author of this tavern effusion. They who saw the writing on the glass know that it was not the handwriting of the poet; but this critic, who knew neither his autograph nor his person, chose to consider it as such, and so announced it to the world. On his return to Stirling, Burns was both irritated and grieved to find that this idle and mischievous tale had been so widely spread and so generally believed. The reason of the cold and constrained reception he met with from some distinguished friends, which at the time he could not occount for, was now explained, and he felt in all its bitterness the misery of being innocently blamed with a thing which he despised as unworthy of his head and heart. To disavow the authorship was to draw down popular indignation on the head of Nicol—a storm which would have anihilated him. Rather than ruin the interests of that friend, he generously and magnanimously, or, as some less fervent mind may think, foolishly, devoted himself to unmerited obloquy, by remaining silent, and suffering the story to circulate uncontradicted. The friend who was with Burns when he indignantly smashed the obnoxious pane with the butt end of his whip, and who was perfectly aware of the whole circumstances as they really stood, long and earnestly pleaded with him to contradict the story that had got wind, and injured him so much in public estimation. * * * It was with a smile of peculiar melancholy that Burns made this noble and characteristic reply. 'I know, ——, I am not the author; but I'll be damned ere I betray the author. It would ruin him—he is my friend.' It is unnecessary to add, that to this resolution he ever after remained firm."

PAGE 47, NOTE 73.—The Mrs. Hamilton here alluded to, was the mother of Mr. Gavin Hamilton, of Mauchline, the constant correspondent of Burns.

PAGE 48, NOTE 74.—Mrs. Bruce was somewhat mistaken about her family dignity; as the common ancestor of all the Bruces of Stirlingshire, Clackmannanshire, and Fife, is only known to have been a *relation* of David II., and has never been supposed to stand higher in genealogy than as a descendant of a younger brother of the father of King Robert. The main line of the Clackmannan family, the head of the name in Scotland, became extinct in the person of Henry Bruce, the husband of this old lady, and is now represented by the Earl of Elgin, in whose house of Broomhall the sword and helmet of the heroic king are yet preserved. Mrs. Katherine Bruce, daughter of Mr. Bruce of Newton, and widow of Henry Bruce of Clackmannan, died November 4, 1791, at the age of ninety-five. There is an interesting portrait of her, taken in 1777, in the possession of Mr. R. Scott Moncrieff, of Edinburgh.

PAGE 48, NOTE 75.—The bard Bruce was no longer living at this period: he died a few years before at an early age.

PAGE 48, NOTE 76.—To Dr. Currie alone we are indebted for this contribution; it is extracted from a letter addressed to himself by Dr. Adair.

PAGE 49, NOTE 77.—This reasoning might be extended, with some modification, to objects of sight of every kind. To have formed beforehand a distinct picture in the mind, of any interesting person or thing, generally lessens the pleasure of the first meeting with them. Though this picture be not superior, or even equal to the reality, still it can never be expected to be an exact resemblance; and the disappointment felt at finding the object something different from what was expected, interrupts and diminishes the emotions that would otherwise be produced. In such cases, the second or third interview gives more pleasure than the first. —See the *Elements of the Philosophy of the Human Mind, by Mr. Stewart*, p. 484. Such publications as The Guide to the Lakes, where every scene is described in the most minute manner, and sometimes with considerable exaggeration of language, are in this point of view objectionable.

PAGE 49, NOTE 78.—This young lady, subsequently married to Dr. Adair, was Miss Katherine Hamilton, sister to the poet's intimate friend, Mr. Gavin Hamilton.

PAGE 49, NOTE 79.—Amongst others, in the lines entitled "Lines on scaring some water-fowl in Loch Turit;" of the date of these, however, there is some doubt, for there is more reason to attribute them to a previous visit to the Highlands. If this conjecture be correct, they were probably written on the occasion of the poet's visit to Ochtertyre, in Perthshire, (as it is in the immediate vicinity of this place that Loch-Turit is situated), in the month of June. Allusions and descriptions of a similar nature are to be found in the "Lines written with a pencil, standing by the Fall of Fyers," and in those "Written at an Inn at Kenmore."

PAGE 50, NOTE 80.—Such an account would have been most applicable, as regards the first introduction of the poet into high society. But in the winter which preceded this period, he had been the lion of the best society of Edinburgh.

PAGE 50, NOTE 81.—The humble petition of Bruar Water.

PAGE 50, NOTE 82.—This account is derived from a letter addressed by Mr. Walker to Mr. Cunningham; and it is to the latter to whom we are indebted for this, as well as for so many other interesting particulars relating to Burns, The letter in question is dated from Perth, October 24th, 1797.

PAGE 50, NOTE 83.—This gentleman, as is well known, held an important office in the administration of William Pitt, and was subsequently raised to the peerage by the title of Lord Melville. At this time he was better known as the Rt. Hon. Henry Dundas.

PAGE 51, NOTE 84.—Such is the purport of a letter addressed to Dr. Currie, by Dr. Couper of Focahbers; and it is to the former that we are immediately indebted for this contribution.

PAGE 51, NOTE 85.—The measure in which these lines are composed, was intended to accomodate them to Burns' very favourite Scotch air of *Morag*.

PAGE 51, NOTE 86.—The subjoined particulars, published by Mr. Lockhart, may be of some interest in respect of this period of our Biography. "At this time the publication called *Johnson's Musical Museum* was conducted at Edinburgh, and the Editor appears to have early prevailed upon Burns to afford him his assistance in the arrangement of his material." [This, indeed, is evident from the letters addressed by Burns himself to his different friends, which will be found amongst his correspondence of this period, and in which he mentions the earnest interest which he was taking in the publication, and the request of its editor that he should do so.] "Though *Green grow the Rashes O!* is the only song which is entirely his (Burns), and which appears in the first volume, published in 1787, many of the old ballads included in that volume bear traces of his hand." [Had Mr. Lockhart examined a little more closely, or, had he possessed the material which has since fallen into our hands, he would have discovered that there are, at least, three more of which no earthly trace could be found, save in the handiwork of the Ayrshire Bard; and that the majority, even the work of his favourite Skinner, had received additions and touches from his hand. At any rate, it was a very pardonable misrepresentation; for, it must be confessed, that the collection is, perhaps, only the more meritorious for his contributions.] "But in the second volume," continues Mr. Lockhart, "which appeared in March 1788, we find no fewer than five songs by Burns:—two that have been already mentioned (*Clarinda*, and *How pleasant the Banks of the clear winding Devon)*, and three far better than them, namely, *Theniel Menzie's Bonny Mary*, that grand lyric which runs as follows:—

Farewell ye dungeons dark and strong,
  The wretch's destiny;—
Macpherson's time will not be long
  On yonder gallows' tree,—

both of which performances bespeak the recent impressions of his highland visit,—and, lastly, *Whistle, and I will come to thee, my lad*. Burns had been, from his youth upwards, an enthusiastic lover of the old minstrelsy and music of his country; but he now studied both subjects with far better opportunities and appliances than he could have commanded previously; and it is from this time that we may date his ambition to transmit *his own* poetry to posterity, in eternal association with those exquisite airs, which had hitherto, in far too many instances, been coupled to verses which did not deserve to be immortal. It is very well known that from this time Burns composed very few pieces but songs; and whether we ought or ought not, to regret that such was the case, must wholly depend upon the estimate which we make of his songs as compared with his other poems:—a point on which critics are to this hour divided, and on which neither they, nor their descendants or successors, are very likely to agree. Mr. Walker, who is one of those who lament Burns's comparative dereliction of the species of composition which he most cultivated in the *early* days of his inspiration, suggests, very sensibly, that if Burns had not taken to song-writing, he would probably have written little or nothing, amidst the various temptations to company and dissipation which now, and from this time forward surrounded him,—to say nothing of the active duties of life in which he was at length about to be engaged"—LOCKHART. To this Mr. Lockhart might have added, or Mr. Walker might have suggested, the peculiarly restless and desultory nature of his disposition, which having been harrassed and rendered more constantly unsettled by a series of successive disappointments, vexations, embarrassments, &c., forbad the lengthened pursuit of any large subject, and which rendered verse a kind of safety valve whereby the ebullition of vexation, sorrow, or excitement of any kind found vent, and in which the brilliancy of a momentary flash of imagery found life and light like a passing meteor. [Ed.]

Page 51, Note 87.—Burns was occupying apartments in the house, or rather chambers of Mr. William Cruikshanks, one of the masters of the high school. The portion in which Burns resided overlooked the enclosure in the rear of the Register House. The house was at that time called No. 2, St. James's Square, (since No. 30,) and it was the top story which was in the occupation of Mr. C. It was in the month of December of this year (1787) that Burns first met and became acquainted with the celebrated Clarinda (Mrs. Mac Lehose) at a tea party in the house of Miss Nimno (of some literary celebrity) in Allison's Square, Potter Row. Mrs. Mac Lehose, whose personal beauty, amiable disposition, and remarkable taste and intelligence made so deep an impression upon the poet, was at this time (and had so been since the desertion of her husband, who had betaken himself to the West Indies in quest of fortune), residing with her young children in Edinburgh upon very limited means, chiefly supplied by the friends or members of her own family. The charms of her person and conversation, added to the peculiar interest of her story, which involved the tender chord of unhappy attachment, at once wrought upon Burns, and one of those peculiar intimacies sprung up between them, which could only be understood by persons of equally refined sensibilities and purity of principle. The correspondence between them was thenceforward almost as ardent as it was constant and innocent, as may be gathered from the letters included in the *correspondence* of the poet. It has been said that the publication of Mrs. Mac Lehose's letters to Burns, and of those of Burns to her, was to be regretted, and was to be attributed to the indiscretion of her friends. It does not at all appear that she was opposed to their publication after her death, nor could any thing serve to reflect higher honour upon her than the contents of this reciprocal correspondence.

Page 52, Note 88.—The commencement of this lyric piece was subsequently introduced into the *Chevallier's Lament*, and the lines so introduced are remarkable for the magnificence of their imagery.

Page 52, Note 89.—Mr. Ramsay was an enthusiastic student of the classics, and had his house and grounds garnished thickly with passages of ancient wisdom. It is necessary to distinguish his house, situated near Stirling, from Ochtertyre near Crieff, the seat of Sir William Murray, where Burns was also entertained. Mr. Ramsay died at his house of Ochtertyre, March 2, 1814.

Page 52, Note 90.—Extract of a letter from Mr. Ramsay to Dr. Currie. This incorrigibility of Burns extended, however, only to his poems printed before he arrived in Edinburgh; for, in regard to his unpublished poems, he was amenable to criticism, of which many proofs might be given.

Page 52, Note 91.—Patrick Miller, Esq., had realised, as a banker in Edinburgh, the means of purchasing the estate of Dalswinton on the Nith. He was a man of enlightened mind, and much mechanical ingenuity, the latter of which qualities he displayed in the invention of a vessel propelled by paddled wheels, to which, at the suggestion of his children's preceptor, Mr. Taylor, the steam engine was afterwards applied, so that he was enabled to make the *first ascertained exemplification of steam navigation* upon a small lake near his house, in October 1788. Some discouraging circumstances, unconnected with the invention, were the sole means of preventing him from bringing it into practical operation—an honour which was reserved for the American Fulton. Mr. Miller died, December 9th, 1815.

Page 52, Note 92.—Mr. Heron states that the poet's appointment to the excise was owing to the kindness of Mr. Alexander Wood, surgeon, (affectionately remembered in Edinburgh by the appellation of *Sandy Wood*), who having, while in attendance on Burns for his bruised limb, heard him express his wishes, waited on Mr. Graham, of Fintry, one of the commissioners, by whom the name of the poet was immediatly put upon the roll.

Page 53, Note 93.—The Edinburgh Magazine for June 1799, contains the following statement, apparently from authority:—"Mr. Miller offered Mr. Burns the choice of several farms on the estate of Dalswinton, which were at that time out of lease. Mr. Burns gave the preference to the farm of Ellisland, most charmingly situated on the banks of the Nith, containing upwards of a hundred acres of most excellent land" (this must be taken with a deduction), "then worth a rent of from eighty to a hundred pounds. Mr. Miller, after showing Mr.

Burns what the farm cost him to a farthing, allowed him to fix the rental himself, and the endurance of the lease. A lease was accordingly given to the poet on his own terms, namely, for fifty-seven years, at the very low rent of fifty pounds. And, in addition to this, when Mr. Burns signed the tack, Mr. Miller presented him with two hundred pounds, to enable him to enclose and improve his farm. It is usual to allow tenants a year's rent for this purpose, but the sum Mr. Miller gave him was at least four years' rent. Mr. Miller has since sold the farm to John M'Morrine, Esq., at nineteen hundred pounds, leaving to himself seven acres on the Dalswinton side of the river." Mr. Lockhart, on the other hand, states that the lease was for four successive terms, of nineteen years each, at fifty pounds for the first three years' crops, and seventy for all the rest; Mr. Miller giving three hundred pounds to renew the farm-house and offices, and agreeing to defray the expense of any plantations which Burns might make on the banks of the river.

PAGE 54, NOTE 94.—In apposite illustration of the feelings roused by this circumstance, we have the following lines which celebrate the moment.

I hae a wife o' my ain,
  I'll partake wi' nae-body;
I'll tak cuckold frae nane,
  I'll gie cuckold to nae-body.

I hae a penny to spend,
  There!—thanks to nae-body;
I hae nae-thing to lend.
  I'll borrow frae nae-body.

I am nae-body's lord,
  I'll be slave to nae-body;
I hae a guid braid sword,
  I'll tak dunts frae nae-body.

I'll be merry and free,
  I'll be sad for nae-body;
If nae-body care for me,
  I'll care for nae-body.

PAGE 54, NOTE 95.—The poem of The Whistle celebrates a bacchanalian contest among three gentlemen of Nithsdale, where Burns appears as umpire. Mr. Riddel died before our bard, who wrote some elegiac verses to his memory, entitled, Sonnet on the Death of Robert Riddel. From him, and from all the members of his family, Burns received not kindness only, but friendship; and the society he met in general at Friar's Carse was calculated to improve his habits as well as his manners. Mr. Ferguson, of Craigdarroch, so well known for his eloquence and social talents, fell a victim to an accidental injury occasioned by a fall from his chaise, according to some, *after* the death of Burns, but more authentically, three months *before* that event, viz., in the month of March, 1796. Sir Robert Laurie, the third person in the drama, has since been engaged in contests of a bloodier nature, and outlived the last century.

PAGE 54, NOTE 96.—Respecting Burns's appointment to the Excise, Mr. W. Nicol wrote in the following terms to Mr. R. Ainslie, from Edinburgh, August 13, 1790: —"As to Burns, poor folks, like you and I, must resign all thoughts of future correspondence with him. To the pride of applauded genius is now superadded the pride of office. He was lately raised to the dignity of an Examiner of Excise, which is a step preparative to attaining that of a *Supervisor*. Therefore, we can expect no less than that his language will become perfectly *Horatian* —'odi profanum vulgus et arceo.' However, I will see him in a fortnight hence, and if I find that Beelzebub has inflated his heart, like a bladder, with pride, and given it the fullest distension that vanity can effect, you and I will burn him in effigy, and write a satire, as bitter as gall and wormwood, against government for employing its *enemies*, like Lord North, to effect its purposes. This will be taking all the revenge in our power."

PAGE 55, NOTE 97.—Some misapprehension, perhaps, exists with respect to Burns's qualifications for ordinary business. The real state of the case we take to have been this: that Burns disliked the drudgery of common worldly affairs, but was by no means deficient in the sagacity, observation, and perseverance required from a man of the world. Colonel Fullerton has paid him a compliment on a farmer-like piece of acumen in a note to his View of Agriculture in Ayrshire, 1793:—"In order," he says, "to prevent the danger arising from horned cattle in studs and straw-yards, the best mode is to cut out the budding knob, or root of the horn, while the calf is very young. This was suggested to me by Mr. Robert Burns, whose general talents are no less conspicuous than the poetic powers which have done so much honour to the county where he was born."

PAGE 55, NOTE 98.—This bowl was made of the stone of which Inverary House is built, the mansion of the family of Argyle. The stone is the *lapis ollaris*. The punch-bowl passed through the hands of Mr

Alexander Cunningham, jeweller, in Edinburgh, to those of Mr. Hastie, present representative of Paisley in parliament, who is said to have refused three hundred guineas for it—a sum that would have set the poet on his legs for ever.

PAGE 56, NOTE 99.—This ballad begins with the following well penned lines :—

The moon had climbed the highest hill
Which rises o'er the source of Dee,
And from the eastern summit shed
Its silver light on tower and tree.

PAGE 56, NOTE 100.—Mr. Gordon has since become Lord Viscount Kenmure.

PAGE 56, NOTE 101.—A very expressive Scotch term, which, as will be seen in the glossary, signifies the brink or margin of flowing water.

PAGE 57, NOTE 102.—The identical Lord Selkirk, of whom Sir Walter Scott has furnished us with a smart and interesting anecdote.

PAGE 58, NOTE 103.—Mr. Chambers's valuable contributions to the anecdotes and traditions relating to Burns, furnish us with the following collectanea :—

"Mr. Ladyman, an English commercial traveller, alighting one afternoon, in the year 1794, at Brownhill, a stage about thirteen miles from Dumfries, was informed by the landlord that Mr. Burns, the celebrated poet, was in the house, and that he had now the best possible opportunity of being introduced to the company of the cleverest man in Scotland. Mr. Ladyman immediately requested the honour of an introduction, and was forthwith shown into the room in which the bard was sitting with two other gentlemen of the road. The landlord, who was a forward sort of a man, and stood upon no ceremony with Burns, presented Mr. Ladyman ; and while the poet rose and received the stranger traveller with that courtesy which always marked his conduct towards strangers, sat down himself along with his guests, and mixed in the conversation.

When Mr. Ladyman entered the inn, it was about two o'clock. The poet had been drinking since mid-day with the two gentlemen, and was slightly elevated with liquor, but not to such a degree as to make any particular alteration upon his voice or manner. He did not speak much, or take any eager share in the conversation. He frequently leant down his head upon the edge of the table, and was silent for a considerable time, as if he had been suffering bodily pain. However, when opportunity occurred, he would start up, and say something shrewd or decisive upon the subject in agitation.

About an hour after Mr. Ladyman arrived, dinner was presented, consisting of beans and bacon, &c., of which the landlord partook, like the rest of the company, evidently to the displeasure of the poet. During the course of the subsequent toddy, Mr. Ladyman ventured to request of Burns to let the company have a small specimen of his poetry upon any subject he liked to think of—'just *anything*, in short—whatever might come uppermost—doggrel or not.' Burns was never offended by any solicitation of this sort, when it was made in a polite manner, and with proper deference to his own good pleasure. In the present case, he granted the request so readily, that, almost immediately after Mr. Ladyman had done speaking, he deliberately uttered the following lines :—

At Brownhill we always get dainty good cheer,
And plenty of Bacon, each day in the year ;
We've all things that's neat, and mostly in season—
But why always BACON ?—come, give me a reason !

It must be understood that Bacon was the name of the landlord, whose habit of intruding into all companies was thus cleverly ridiculed.

As far as Mr. Ladyman can recollect, Burns pronounced the lines without the least hesitation of voice, and apparently without finding any difficulty in embodying the thought in rhyme. No effort seemed necessary. He happened to have the glass in his hand at the time the request was made, and so trifling was the exertion of intellect apparently required, that he did not put it down upon the table, but waited till he concluded the epigram, and then drank off his liquor amidst the roar of applause that ensued. The landlord had retired some little time before, otherwise Burns would not, perhaps, have chosen him as the subject of his satire. There is no doubt, however, that he would see and hear enough of it afterwards : for Burns, at the earnest entreaties of the company, immediately committed it to the breath of Fame, by writing it upon one of the panes in the window behind his chair.—*Extract from an early M.S. note-book.*

The acquaintance which Burns maintained with a considerable number of the gentry of his neighbourhood, was not favourable to him. They frequently sent him game from their estates, and disdained not to come to his house to partake of it. The large quantities of rum which flowed into his stores gratuitously, in consequence of seizures, as was then the custom, were also injurious. Yet, as far as circumstances left him to his own inclinations, he was a man of simple, as well as kindly domestic habits. As he was often detained by company from the dinner provided for him by his wife, she sometimes, on a conjecture of his probable absence, would not prepare that meal for him. When he chanced to come home and find no dinner ready, he was never in the least troubled or irritated, but would address himself with the greatest cheerfulness to any succedaneum that could be readily set before him. They generally had abundance of good Dunlop cheese, sent to them by their Ayrshire friends. The poet would sit down to that wholesome fare, with bread and butter, and his book by his side, and seem, to any casual visitor, such as Miss Lewars, as happy as a courtier at the feast of kings.

He was always anxious that his wife should have a neat and genteel appearance. In consequence, as she alleged, of the duties of nursing and attending to her infants, she could not help being sometimes a little slovenly. Burns disliked this, and not only remonstrated against it in a gentle way, but did the utmost that in him lay to counteract it, by buying for her the best clothes he could afford. Any little novelty in female dress was almost sure to meet with patronage from Burns—all with the aim of keeping up a spirit for neat dressing in his wife. She was, for instance, one of the first persons in Dumfries who appeared in a dress of gingham—a stuff now common to all, but, at its first introduction, rather costly, and almost exclusively used by persons of superior condition."

Page 58, Note 104.—Mr. Lockhart enters into a long discussion of the poet's political sentiments, and the nature of the circumstances here alluded to. He leaves the whole matter in a state of doubt, for which, we think, there is no just occasion. Burns unquestionably felt as a zealous partisan of the French Revolution. A mind so generous and upright as his could have taken no other course. That such was the case, his "Vision" at Lincluden College, his Inscription for an altar of Independence, and his Tree of Liberty, introduced into the present edition of his poems, are sufficient proof: more may be found in some specimens of an unpublished poem given by Mr. Cunningham;—

"Why should we idly waste our prime
Repeating our oppressions?
Come, rouse to arms, 'tis now the time
To punish past transgressions.
'Tis said that kings can do no wrong—
Their murderous deeds deny it;
And, since from us their power is sprung,
We have a right to try it.
Now each true patriot's song shall be,
Welcome death or libertie.

* * *

Proud bishops next we will translate,
Among priest-crafted martyrs;
The guillotine on peers shall wait,
And knights shall hang in garters;
Those despots long have trod us down,
And judges are their engines—
Such wretched minions of a crown
Demand the people's vengeance.

* * *

The golden age we'll then revive,
Each man will be a brother;
In harmony we all shall live,
And share the earth together.
In virtue trained, enlightened youth
Will love each fellow-creature;
And future years shall prove the truth
That man is good by nature.
Then let us toast, with three times three,
The reign of peace and libertie."

A lady with whom a recent editor of Burns's works, once conversed, remembered being present in the theatre of Dumfries, during the heat of the French Revolution, on which occasion, the poet, somewhat heated with liquor, entered the pit. Upon the orchestra, striking up the national anthem, the company, and audience of the theatre rose, with the single exception of Burns, who loudly shouted *ça ira*. An uproar ensued, and the poet was obliged to leave the theatre. The apologists of the government who, say what they will, neglected and slighted the purest genius of his age, make *escapades* of this nature their excuse. They attempt, however, to adduce the testimony of Mr. Alexander Findlater, the officer under whom Burns served in the Excise, to show that the most harmless rebuke only, was levelled at the unruly and independent spirit of the bard. However this may be, his promotion was very much retarded, although it is admitted that ultimately it was not prevented.

Page 59, Note 105.—Mr. Lockhart has favoured us with a most interesting anecdote respecting the effect of the political opinions of Burns upon his social position. To the shame of the Scottish Whiggism be it recorded. "Mr. David Maculloch, a son of the Laird of Ardwell, has told me that he was seldom more grieved, than when riding into Dumfries one fine summer's evening, to attend a county ball, he saw Burns walking alone, on the shady side of the principal street of the town, while the opposite part was gay with successive groups of gentlemen and ladies, all drawn together for the festivities of the night, not one of whom appeared willing to recognise him. The horseman dismounted and joined Burns, who, on his proposing to him to cross the street, said, 'Nay, nay, my young friend—that's all over now;' and quoted, after a pause, some verses of Lady Grizzel Baillie's pathetic ballad:—

'His bonnet stood ance fu' fair on his brow,
His auld ane look'd better than mony ane's new;
But now he lets't wear ony way it will hing,
And casts himsel dowie upon the corn-bing.

Oh were we young, as we ance hae been,
We should hae been galloping doun on yon green,
And linking it ower the lily-white lea—
And werena my heart light I wad die.'

It was little in Burns's character to let his feelings on certain subjects escape in this fashion. He immediately, after citing these verses, assumed the sprightliness of his most pleasing manner; and, taking his young friend home with him, entertained him very agreeably until the hour of the ball arrived, with a bowl of his usual potation, and bonnie Jean's singing of some verses which he had recently composed."—LOCKHART.

PAGE 59, NOTE 106.—See the poem entitled The Dumfries Volunteers.—CURRIE. Previous to one of the public meetings of this body—a regular field-day, which was to terminate in a grand dinner—it was hinted to the bard that something would be expected from him in the shape of a song or speech—some glowing tribute in honour of the patriotic cause that had linked them together, and eke in honour of the martial glory of old Scotland. The poet said nothing, but as silence gives consent, it was generally expected that he would *share* them on the occasion of the approaching festival with another lyric or energetic oration. The day at length arrived; dinner came and passed, and the usual loyal toasts were drunk with all the honours. Now came the poet's turn; every eye was fixed upon him, and, slowly lifting his glass, he stood up and looked around him with an arch, indescribable expression of countenance, 'Gentlemen,' said he, 'may we never see the French, nor the French see us!' The toast fell like a 'wet blanket,' as Moore says, on the hopes of the Volunteers.

'Is that a'?' they muttered one to another, dropping down to their seats—to use the words of my informant, who was present—'like so many old wives at a field-preaching;' 'Is that the grand speech or fine poem that we were to have from him?—but we could hae expected nae better!' Not a few, however, 'raxed their jaws,' as the Ettrick Shepherd says, at the homely truth and humour of the poet's sentiment, heightened by the first rueful aspect of the company; and, long after, in his jovial moments, Burns used to delight in telling how he had cheated the volunteers of Dumfries."—R. CARRUTHERS, *in the Edinburgh Literary Journal.*

PAGE 59, NOTE 107.—These lines were published in the periodical collection of Scottish songs produced under the title of *Johnson's Musical Museum.* They bear date about 1791, and, as the text is given above, they bear the latest corrections of the poet. It is one of the best of Burns's productions, but its merit failed to be strongly or popularly observed until the first few years of the present century, when the martial glory of Great Britain had grown of more general admiration, and had enlisted a more universal enthusiasm, such as to overwhelm all minor political predilections. It is, perhaps, on account of this tardy popularity that Burns was readily dissuaded at the time from reprinting it separately, *in extenso,* with a new and appropriate air.

PAGE 61, NOTE 108.—According to the current story which is generally received at Dumfries, it was in this condition of intoxication that he sat down on the door step of a house on his way homeward, and fell fast asleep. Exposed to the inclemency of the season and night air, and doubly susceptible, owing to the exhausted condition of his nervous system, and to the deleterious effect of liquor, he became so chilled as to induce a fatal disorder.

PAGE 61, NOTE 109.—This was Mrs. Riddel, of Woodlee Park.

PAGE 62, NOTE 110.—According to Mr. Cunningham, Burns expired after a violent and convulsive struggle, "rising at the last moment, and springing to the bottom of the bed." Mr. Cunningham, however, it is admitted, supplies us with this information on hearsay. Another biographer denies the *possibility* of such an effort, stating that Burns was in "*no condition*" (*i. e.* too exhausted), to have made such a movement. Were the question of any importance, and no better refuted than by the *possibility* being called in question, Mr. Cunningham might certainly overthrow the denial of his statement. But there is an account for which we are indebted to Dr. Maxwell, the medical attendant, who was at the bedside of the poet, in which it is averred that poor Burns expired with perfect calmness, and in apparent consciousness, after some hours of low muttering delirium.

PAGE 63, NOTE 111.—Mr. Whyte is the author of a poem entitled *St. Guerdon's Well*, and of the piece entitled a tribute to the memory of Burns.

PAGE 63, NOTE 112.—Dr. Currie mentions that Burns died free of debt. According to another biographer, however, "the strict fact that he owed but £7. 4s. at that period, serves, like the exception with the rule, to confirm the report of the biographer. It is also worthy of notice that he left a collection of books, estimated as worth ninety-two pounds. The terror of a jail, which haunted him a short while before his death, and afterwards recurred in delirium, was excited by a pressing note for payment of his regimentals, which had been sent to him by Mr. David Williamson, a Dumfries shopkeeper—a person, we have been assured, who never could have resorted to any extreme measure with his illustrious debtor. Five pounds, requested from and promptly sent by Mr. Thomson a few days before his death, removed the cause of the terror, but unfortunately did not obliterate the feeling which it had raised."

PAGE 63, NOTE 113.—This Mr. Stobie was in the ordinary service of the Excise as late as 1818, at Pinkie Salt Pans. He is said to have spoken of Burns's musical accomplishments in the following terms:—"He sang like a nightingale; but he had the voice of a boar." The expression appears contradictory; but, by the complimentary part of it, he only understood, in all probability, the readiness with which the poet would attune his voice when requested to do so. [This anecdote has been told by some one else of two different persons, who, although, they affected to *shun Burns* as a *reprobate* whilst living (though God wot, the poet would certainly not have sought their company), were prone to boast of him as an *acquaintance* when his reputation alone remained to hallow and endear popular recollections. I am, therefore, much inclined to exonerate Mr. Stobie from an ill-natured remark, which seems scarcely in accordance with the tenor of his conduct.]

PAGE 63, NOTE 114.—The death of Burns occurred on the 21st of July, and he lost consciousness as early as the 16th, from which time he continued almost continually unconscious and rambling. The letter from Mr. Graham could not, in all probability, as cross country posts went at that time, have been delivered until the 15th, for it was only dated on the 13th.

PAGE 64, NOTE 115.—"During his residence in Glasgow, a characteristic instance occurred of the way in which he would repress petulance and presumption. A young man of some literary pretensions, who had newly commenced business as a bookseller, had been in the practice of writing notices of Burns's Poems in a style so flippant, and withal so patronising, as to excite feelings in the poet towards him very different from what he counted upon. Reckoning, however, upon a very grateful reception from Burns, he was particularly anxious for an early introduction to his company, and, as his friends knew, had been at some pains to prepare himself for making dazzling impressions upon the Ayrshire ploughman—as it was then the fashion, amongst a certain kind of literary folks, to call the poet. At the moment the introduction took place, Burns was engaged in one of his happiest and most playful veins with my friend and another intimate or two; but, upon the gentleman's presentation, who advanced in a manner sufficiently affable, the 'ploughman' assumed an air of such dignified coldness, as froze him into complete silence during the time he remained in his company."—*Correspondent of the Scotsman*, 1828.

PAGE 65, NOTE 116.—Smellie's Philosophy of Natural History.

PAGE 65, NOTE 117.—The subjoined passage quoted from Quintilian, Inst. Orat. ii, 9, is appositely parallel to the sense of this observation:—An vero Isocrates cum de Ephoro atque Theopompo sic judicaret, ut ALTERI FRENIS, ALTERI CALCARIBUS OPUS ESSE diceret; aut in illo lentiore tarditatem, aut in illo pene præcipiti concitationem adjuvandum docendo existimavit, cum alterum alterius natura miscendum arbitraretur? Imbeciliis tamen ingeniis sane sic obsequendum sit, ut tantum in id quo vocat natura, ducantur. Ita enim, quod solum possunt, melius efficient."

PAGE 66, NOTE 118.—The reader must not suppose it is contended, that the same individual could have excelled in all these directions. A certain degree of instruction and practice, is necessary to excellence in every one, and life is too short to admit of one man, however great his talents, acquiring this in all of them. It is only asserted, that the same talents, differently applied, might have succeeded in *any one*, though, perhaps, not equally well in each. And, after all, this position requires certain limitations, which the reader's candour and judgment will supply. In supposing that a great poet might have made a great orator, the physical qualities necessary to oratory are pre-supposed. In supposing that a great orator might have made a great poet, it is a necessary condition, that he should have devoted himself to poetry, and that he should have acquired a proficiency in metrical numbers, which by patience and attention may be acquired, though the want of it has embarrassed and chilled many of the first efforts of true poetical genius. In supposing that Homer might have led armies to victory, more, indeed, is assumed than the physical qualities of a general. To these must be added that hardihood of mind, that coolness in the midst of difficulty and danger, which great poets and orators are found sometimes, but not always, to possess. The nature of the institutions of Greece and Rome produced more instances of single individuals who excelled in various departments of active and speculative life, than occur in modern Europe, where the employments of men are more subdivided. Many of the greatest warriors of antiquity excelled in literature and in oratory. That they had the *minds* of great poets also, will be admitted, when the qualities are justly appreciated which are necessary to excite, combine, and command the active energies of a great body of men; to rouse that enthusiasm which sustains fatigue, hunger, and the inclemencies of the elements, and which triumphs over the fear of death, the most powerful instinct of our nature.

The authority of Cicero may be appealed to, in favour of the close connection between the poet and the orator. "Est enim finitimus oratori poeta, numeris adstrictior paulo, verborum autum licentia liberior," &c.—De Orator. lib. i. c. 16. See also lib. iii. c. 7. It is true, the example of Cicero may be quoted against his opinion. His attempts in verse, which are praised by Plutarch, do not seem to have met the approbation of Juvenal, or of some others. Cicero probably did not take sufficient time to learn the art of the poet; but that he had the *afflatus* necessary to poetical excellence, may be abundantly proved from his compositions in prose. On the other hand, nothing is more clear, than that, in the character of a great poet, all the mental qualities of an orator are included. It is said by Quintilian, of Homer, "Omnibus eloquentiæ partibus exemplum et ortum dedit."—Lib. i. 47. The study of Homer is therefore recommended to the orator, as of the first importance. Of the two sublime poets in our own language, who are hardly inferior to Homer, Shakspeare and Milton, a similar recommendation may be given. It is scarcely necessary to mention how much an acquaintance with them has availed the great orator who is now the pride and ornament of the English bar, a character that may be appealed to with singular propriety, when we are contending for the universality of genius.

The identity, or at least the great similarity, of the talents necessary to *excellence* in poetry, oratory, painting, and war, will be admitted by some who will be inclined to dispute the extension of the position to science or natural knowledge. On this occasion, I may quote the following observations of Sir William Jones, whose own example will, however, far exceed in weight the authority of his precepts:—"Abul Ola had so flourishing a reputation, that several persons of uncommon genius were ambitious of learning the *art of poetry* from so able an instructor. His most illustrious scholars were Feleki and Khakani, who were no less eminent for their Persian compositions than for their skill in every branch of pure and mixed mathematics, and particularly in astronomy—a striking proof that a sublime poet may become master of any kind of learning which he chooses to profess; since a fine imagination, a lively wit, an easy and copious style, cannot possibly obstruct the acquisition of any science whatever, but must necessarily assist him in his studies, and shorten his labour."—*Sir William Jones's Works*, vol. ii. p. 317.

Page 67, Note 119.—These strictures may, however, be very considerably extended. Cobbett is not the only philosopher who has revealed the deleterious properties of other stimulants, or of other productions, which are, to all intents and purposes, employed as such. There are a great number of other substances which may be considered under this point of view—tobacco, tea, and coffee, are of the number. These substances essentially differ from each other in their qualities; and an inquiry into the particular effects of each on the health, morals, and happiness of those who use them, would be curious and useful. The effects of wine and of opium on the temperament of sensibility, the editor intended to have discussed in this place at some length; but he found the subject too extensive and too professional to be introduced with propriety. The difficulty of abandoning any of these narcotics (if we may so term them), when inclination is strengthened by habit, is well known. Johnson, in his distresses, had experienced the cheering but treacherous influence of wine, and, by a powerful effort, abandoned it. He was obliged, however, to use tea as a substitute, and this was the solace to which he constantly had recourse under his habitual melancholy. The praises of wine form many of the most beautiful lyrics of the poets of Greece and Rome, and of modern Europe. Whether opium, which produces visions still more ecstatic, has been the theme of the eastern poets, I do not know.

Wine is drunk in small quantities at a time, in company, where, *for a time*, it promotes harmony and social affection. Opium is swallowed by the Asiatics in full doses at once, and the inebriate retires to the solitary indulgence of his delirious imaginations. Hence, the wine drinker appears in a superior light to the imbiber of opium, a distinction which he owes more to the *form* than to the *quality* of his liquor.

PAGE 68, NOTE 120.—Mrs. Riddel of Woodlee Park.

PAGE 72, NOTE 121.—Take, for instance, the authors or collaters of the *Deliciæ Poetarum Scotorum*, and others.

PAGE 73, NOTE 122.—Lord Kames.

PAGE 74, NOTE 123.—A few Scottish ballads, attributable to the last century, have been got together in the Pepys collection, but without clue to the authorships.

PAGE 74, NOTE 124.—Some strong reasons are assigned by a contributor signing himself J. Runcole, who addresses Mr. Ramsay in the second volume of *The Bee*, for doubting the authenticity of a great number of Scottish Songs of professedly remote antiquity, and of much celebrity. The quotation cited above, is extracted from a letter addressed by Mr. Ramsay, of Ochtertyre, to Dr. Currie, and dated Sept. 11th, 1799.

PAGE 175, NOTE 25.—Allan Ramsay, it is said, was employed in the capacity of a washer of ore, in the lead mines, at Lead Hills, belonging to the Earl of Hopetown. His father was, and had from his youth, also been a workman in the same mines. But it is to be remarked that the limited hours of mine-labour (only six per diem, or, according to some, only four), together with the general good character, sobriety, and intelligence of the people, and the convenience of a good library containing some thousands of volumes, in common amongst them, contributed to afford these men very superior opportunities of intellectual improvement.

PAGE 75, NOTE 126.—Mr. Ramsay of Ochtertyre, writing to one of Burns's Biographers, gives the following account of Allan Ramsay:—"He was coeval with Joseph Mitchell, and his club of small wits, who, about 1719, published a very poor miscellany, to which, Dr. Young, the author of *Night Thoughts*, prefixed a copy of verses."

PAGE 75, NOTE 127.—The first line of this piece runs thus:—

"What beauties does Flora disclose!"

PAGE 75, NOTE 128.—The first line of this piece runs thus:—

"I have heard a lilting at our ewe's milking."

PAGE 76, NOTE 129—This Mrs. Cockburn died before the poet; that is, on the 22nd of November, 1794.

PAGE 76, NOTE 130.—See the *Introduction to the History of Poetry in Scotland*, by T. Campbell, and an article affording a Biographical Sketch of this writer in the *Supplement to the Encyclopædia Britannica*.

PAGE 77, NOTE 131.—Critics and Antiquarians are equally divided on this point. Mr. Tytler has struggled very hard to establish the genuineness of authorship for this piece, whilst Sir D. Dalrymple most unaccountably attributes it to *James V!* Pray, Sir David, where did you discover that the fifth James was either a wit or a poet? That he was an arrant pedant is undoubtedly true. But the first James was certainly one of the best of poets whom Scotland has produced. There is ample evidence of his having fathered verses, and verses of very great merit, and of his peculiar love of music and minstrelsy.

PAGE 78, NOTE 132.—This is the title of the poem selected as an instance; and being rendered into English, would mean *The Farmer's Fireside*.

PAGE 78, NOTE 133.—Why the acute observation, and true portraiture, afforded in this surprising production, should, upon its first appearance, have struck the higher orders of society with astonishment, is readily to be understood. The circumstances and position of the poet, which effectually excluded him from ever having had an opportunity of mingling with any but the society of peasants, seemed to add the charm of inspiration, or of intuitive perception, to the accurate delineation of character, circumstance, &c., in the upper walks of life. But, like all true and *natural* philosophers, Burns saw in *human nature* nothing but *human nature*, and that same nature bearing the indelible stamp of its constitution identical and unerased, notwithstanding the small differences of condition and circumstance. The poem, therefore, is merely a testimony to the natural sagacity of the poet.

PAGE 79, NOTE 134.—The poet's "Earnest Cry and Prayer to the Scottish Representatives in Parliament."

PAGE 79, NOTE 135.—By a "Highland gill," is meant a gill of the native Highland beverage, namely, *whisky*.

PAGE 79, NOTE 136.—In English, we should express these terms by the paraphrase—"the middle of the street, and the footway."

PAGE 79, NOTE 137.—In the piece entitled the "Brigs of Ayr."

PAGE 79, NOTE 138.—As will be seen in the glossary, this term signifies *a messenger*.

PAGE 79, NOTES 139 and 140.—The "Dungeon Clock" (or Tower Clock) and the "Wallace Tower," are the names of the steeples of Ayr.

PAGE 80, NOTE 141.—This festival is still very popularly observed (or rather, was so, until the political and religious agitations had been revived of late years) in some parts of Ireland. In the remote and aboriginal districts of North Wales also, we have many instances of its constant observance.

PAGE 80, NOTE 142.—For truth and exactness of pencilling, for the brightness of colour, and for the delicacy and gentleness of description, this passage is almost unrivalled. In its own melting, soft, impressive monosyllabic diction, it is inimitable. The bold descriptions of Thomson here compared with this passage, have a ruggedness, almost a harshness, which destroys all parallel; and the beautiful lines of Lord Byron, which run on a similar vein of description, are wanting in the *naïf*, inexpressible simplicity of this passage, as for instance:—

"'Tis sweet to hear
At midnight o'er the blue and moonlit deep
The song and oar of Adria's gondolier," &c.

PAGE 81, NOTE 143.—The word *owrie*, used as it is in this instance, may have two interpretations, or may be saddled with both constructions simultaneously. Refer also to the *glossary*. In general, as applied to cattle, or to domestic animals, it signifies such as are *left abroad during the winter* instead of being brought home to the pens, or sheds of the homestead. Added to this, the word *owrie* is also used in the sense of that *pinched, wretched, shivering, drooping, appearance* which cattle sometimes present in wet and cold weather.

PAGE 81, NOTE 144.—The word *silly* is not here to be understood in its offensive sense. It is very commonly used by the Scotch, and occurs very frequently in the poems of Burns, as a term of *affection* and *pity*.

PAGE 82, NOTE 145.—It must be borne in mind, that throughout the portraiture of the Cotter, there is an evident affectionate tracing of the character, situation, &c., of the poet's own father—an acceptation which adds much poignancy to many of its passages.

PAGE 83, NOTE 146.—It is a peculiar feature of the Scottish minstrelsy that it abounds in dialogues between man and wife, To the labours of Mr. Pinkerton, in his earnest and successful pursuit of remote Scottish literary productions, we are indebted for a multiplicity of parallel passages in the songs, as well as amongst the unpolished attempts at comic dramatic writing. The salient point of these pieces, is the invariable triumph of the "*better half*" in the contest, in the course of which as many caustic things have been said, as may conveniently be crammed into a brief conversation.

PAGE 83, NOTE 147.—The subjoined extracts may be cited as illustrations of the question. First let us detail the romance of a Scottish song of the early part of the eighteenth Century. We have a Highland lad wooing a Lowland lass to fly with him to the Highlands, and share his fare and fortune. The scene is on the banks of a most beautiful stream (Ettric banks), in the calm and stillness of a summer's evening, and the exordium of the tale runs as follows:—

"On Ettrick banks, one summer's night
At gloaming when the sheep drove hame,
I met my lassie, braw and tight,
Come wading barefoot a' her lane:
My heart grew light, I ran, I flang
My arms about her lily neck;
And kissed and clasped her here fu' lang;—
My words they were na mony feck."

In another of these pieces we have the heroine lamenting o'er the sweet recollections of the trysting place, and raptured hour. The comparison of the love scene with the present, which quickens the vivid recollection, is most apparent in the contrast between the two subjoined stanzas:—

How blythe, each morn, was I to see
  My swain come o'er the hill;
He skipt the burn, and flew to me:—
  I met him wi' guid will.
* * * *
Oh! the broom,—the bonnie, bonnie broom,
  The Broom of Cowden-Knowes!
I wish I were with my dear Swain,
  With *his* pipe, and *my* ewes.

PAGE 83, NOTE 148.—That the dramatic form of writing characterises the productions of an early, or, what amounts to the same thing, of a rude stage of society, may be illustrated by a reference to the most ancient compositions that we know of, the Hebrew Scriptures, and the writings of Homer. The form of dialogue is adopted in the old Scottish ballads, even in narration, whenever the situations described become interesting. This sometimes produces a very striking effect, of which an instance may be given from the ballad of Edom o' Gordon, a composition, apparently, of the sixteenth century. The story of the ballad is shortly this:—The Castle of Rhodes, in the absence of its lord, is attacked by the robber Edom o' Gordon, The lady stands on her defence, beats off the assailants, and wounds Gordon, who, in his rage, orders the castle to be set on fire. That his orders are carried into effect, we learn from the expostulation of the lady, who is represented as standing on the battlements, and remonstrating on this barbarity. She is interrupted:—

"Oh then bespake her little son,
  Sate on his nourice knee;
Says, 'Mither dear, gi' owre this house,
  For the reek it smithers me.'
'I wad gie a' my gowd, my childe,
  Sae wad I a' my fee,
For ane blast o' the westlin wind,
  To blaw the reek frae thee.'"

The circumstantiality of the Scottish love-songs, and the dramatic form which prevails so generally in them, probably arises from their being the descendants and successors of the ancient ballads. In the beautiful modern song of Mary of Castle-Cary, the dramatic form has a very happy effect. The same may be said of Donald and Flora, and Come under my Pladdie, by the same author, Mr. Macniel.

PAGE 84, NOTE 149.—Mrs. Barbauld has fallen into an error in this respect. In her prefatory address to the works of Collins, speaking of the natural objects that may be employed to give interest to the description of passion, she observes:—"They present an inexhaustible variety, from the Song of Solomon, breathing of cassia, myrrh, and cinnamon, to the Gentle Shepherd of Ramsay, whose damsels carry their milking-pails through the frosts and snows of their less genial, but not less pastoral country." The damsels of Ramsay do not walk in the midst of frost and snow. Almost all the scenes of the Gentle Shepherd are laid in the open air, amidst beautiful natural objects, and at the most genial season of the year. Ramsay introduces all his acts with a prefatory description to assure us of this. The fault of the climate of Britain is not, that it does not afford us the beauties of summer, but that the season of such beauties is comparatively short, and even uncertain. There are days and nights, even in the northern division of the island, which equal, or perhaps surpass, what are to be found in the latitude of Sicily, or of Greece. Buchanan, when he wrote his exquisite Ode to May, felt the charm as well as the transientness of these happy days:—

"Salve fugacis gloria seculi,
Salve secunda digna dies nota,
Salve vetustæ vitæ imago,
Et specimen venientis Ævi!

PAGE 86, NOTE 150.—Those who, primed with the statistics of Sir John Sinclair, attribute the expatriation of the Scotch to a disproportion between the numerical aggregates of the sexes, seem to consider the number stated in round figures above, as inadequate. The latter proposition is easily granted, but the current joke against Sawney, seems to allege some more probable and prevailing cause for the spontaneous expatriation in question. He has enterprise, and requires a broader field, and above all, more ample resources; and those of his own country would be limited but for the adjunct of the sister realm. Whether, or not, the beautiful song of Burns:—

"Their groves of sweet myrtle,"

be addressed to these wandering fellow countrymen, I am fully prepared to admit its excellence, and the probability that it will be read with as much admiration by others.

PAGE 89, NOTE 151.—This was in reply to a report which had come to the ears of Dr. Currie, to the effect that a violent hurricane, which actually levelled a portion of the cottage, occurred simultaneously with the birth of Burns.

PAGE 90, NOTE 152.—This was Mr. Peter Ewart, of Manchester, a friend of Dr. Currie's.

PAGE 95, NOTE 153.—The household effects of Mrs. Burns were sold by public auction on the 10th and 11th of April, and from the anxiety of the public to possess relics of this interesting household, brought uncommonly high sums. According to the *Dumfries Courier*, "the auctioneer commenced with small articles, and when he came to a broken copper coffee-pot, there were so many bidders, that the price paid exceeded twenty-fold the intrinsic value. A tea-kettle of the same metal succeeded, and reached £2 sterling. Of the linens, a table-cloth, marked 1792, which, speaking commercially, may be worth half-a-crown or five shillings, was knocked down at £5. 7s. Many other articles commanded handsome prices, and the older and plainer the furniture, the better it sold. The rusty iron top of a shower-bath, which Mrs. Dunlop, of Dunlop, sent to the poet when afflicted with rheumatism, was bought by a Carlisle gentleman for £1. 8s.; and a low wooden kitchen chair, on which the late Mrs. Burns sat when nursing her children, was run up to £3. 7s. The crystal and china were much coveted, and brought, in most cases, splendid prices. Even an old fender reached a figure which would go far to buy half-a-dozen new ones, and everything towards the close attracted notice, down to grey-beards, bottles, and a half-worn pair of bellows. The poet's eight-day clock, made by a Mauchline artist, attracted great attention, from the circumstance that it had frequently been wound up by his own hand. In a few seconds it was bid up to fifteen pounds or guineas, and was finally disposed of for £35. The purchaser had a hard battle to fight; but his spirit was good, and his purse obviously not a light one, and the story ran that he had instructed Mr. Richardson to secure a preference at any sum under £60."

Additional Note,

RELATING TO THE BACHELOR'S CLUB, AT TARBOLTON.

RULES AND REGULATIONS.

1st. THE club shall meet at Tarbolton every fourth Monday night, when a question on any subject shall be proposed, disputed points of religion only excepted, in the manner hereafter directed; which question is to be debated in the club, each member taking whatever side he thinks proper.

2nd. When the club is met, the president, or, he failing, some one of the members, till he come, shall take his seat; then the other members shall seat themselves; those who are for one side of the question, on the president's right hand; and those who are for the other side, on his left—which of them shall have the right hand, is to be determined by the president. The president and four of the members being present, shall have power to transact any ordinary part of the society's business.

3rd. The club met and seated, the president shall read the question out of the club's book of records (which book is always to be kept by the president); then the two members nearest the president shall cast lots who of them shall speak first, and, according as the lot shall determine, the member nearest the president on that side shall deliver his opinion, and the member nearest on the other side shall reply to him; then the second member of the side that spoke first; then the second member of the side that spoke second—and so on to the end of the company; but if there be fewer members on the one side than on the other, when all the members of the least side have spoken according to their places, any of them, as they please among themselves, may reply to the remaining members of the opposite side; when both sides have spoken, the president shall give his opinion, after which, they may go over it a second or more times, and so continue the question.

4th. The club shall then proceed to the choice of a question for the subject of the next night's meeting. The president shall first propose one, and any other member who chooses may propose more questions, and whatever one of them is most agreeable to the majority of the members, shall be the subject of debate next club-night.

5th. The club shall, lastly, elect a new president for the next meeting; the president shall first name one, then any of the club may name another, and whoever of them has the majority of votes shall be duly elected —allowing the president the first vote, and the casting vote upon a par, but none other. Then, after a general toast to the mistresses of the club, they shall dismiss.

6th. There shall be no private conversation carried on during the time of debate, nor shall any member interrupt another while he is speaking, under the penalty of a reprimand from the president for the first fault, doubling his share of the reckoning for the second, trebling it for the third, and so on in proportion for every other fault; provided always, however, that any member may speak at any time after leave asked and given by the president. All swearing and profane language, and particularly all obscene and indecent conversation, is strictly prohibited, under the same penalty, as aforesaid, in the first clause of this article.

7th. No member, on any pretence whatever, shall mention any of the club's affairs to any other person but a brother member, under the pain of being excluded; and, particularly, if any member shall reveal any of the speeches or affairs of the club, with a view to ridicule or laugh at any of the rest of the members, he shall be for ever excommunicated from the society; and the rest of the members are desired, as much as possible, to avoid and have no communication with him as a friend or comrade.

8th. Every member shall attend at the meetings, without he can give a proper excuse for not attending; and it is desired that every one who cannot attend, will send his excuse with some other member; and he who shall be absent three meetings, without sending such excuse, shall be summoned to the club-night, when, if he fail to appear, or send an excuse, he shall be excluded.

9th. The club shall not consist of more than sixteen members, all bachelors, belonging to the parish of Tarbolton; except a brother-member marry, and in that case he may be continued, if the majority of the club think proper. No person shall be admitted a member of this society, without the unanimous consent of the club; and any member may withdraw from the club altogether, by giving a notice to the president in writing of his departure.

10th. Every man proper for a member of this society, must have a frank, honest, open heart; above any thing dirty or mean; and must be a professed lover of one or more of the female sex. No haughty, self-conceited person, who looks upon himself as superior to the rest of the club, and especially no mean-spirited, worldly mortal, whose only will is to heap up money, shall upon any pretence whatever, be admitted. In short, the proper person for this society is, a cheerful, honest-hearted lad, who, if he has a friend that is true, and a mistress that is kind, and as much wealth as genteelly to make both ends meet, is just as happy as this world can make him.

Notes to the Poems of Burns.

PAGE 101, NOTE 1.—According to Gilbert Burns, this poem may be dated anteriorly to 1784. The subjoined is his account of the circumstance of which these lines are a faithful record:—

"Robert had, partly by way of frolic, bought an ewe and two lambs from a neighbour, and she was tethered in a field adjoining the house at Lochlee. He and I were going out with our teams, and our two younger brothers to drive for us, at midday, when Hugh Wilson (the *Hughoc* of the poem, who was a neighbouring farmer's herd-mate), a curious looking, awkward boy, clad in plaiding, came to us, with much anxiety in his face, with the information that the ewe had entangled herself in the tether, and was lying in the ditch. Robert was much tickled with Hughoc's appearance and postures on the occasion. Poor Mailie was set to rights, and when we returned from the plough, in the evening, he repeated to me her death and dying words, pretty much in the way they now stand."

PAGE 102, NOTE 2.—This Davie was Mr. David Sillar, of whom we have had occasion to speak as a brother rhymester of Burns's. He was one of the intimates of the Batchelour's Club, at Tarbolton, to which he had been introduced in 1781. In his subsequent career he became connected with the borough of Irvine, first as a teacher, and afterwards as a bailie; and he survived to the advanced age of seventy years. He died on the 2nd of May, 1830.

PAGE 102, NOTE 3.—A quotation from Allan Ramsay.

PAGE 102, NOTE 4.—The tolerated beggar was a species of travelling historian, traditionist, bard, or jester, according to the humour of his respective audiences, and he was expected to earn the bounty of his hearers by entertaining them.

PAGE 103, NOTE 5.—Meg (or more properly, Margaret Orr, of whom Burns speaks so familiarly) was nursery maid in the establishment of Mrs Stewart, of Stair. In Sillar's visits to his Meg, he was not unfrequently accompanied by Burns, who would supply verses for the songs of other female servants; some of these accidentally fell, in manuscript, into the hands of Mrs. Stewart, who was so struck with their beauty, that she desired that, upon his next visit, the author should be presented to her. He was accordingly introduced, and Mrs. Stewart is numbered amongst the first friends whom Burns's genius had secured amongst those of superior rank.

PAGE 103, NOTE 6.—This poem may be dated, according to Gilbert Burns, to whom it was first repeated, in the winter of 1784-5.

PAGE 104, NOTE 7.—The original manuscript affords the subjoined version of these lines:—

"Lang syne in Eden's happy scene,
When strapping Adam's days were green,
And Eve was like my bonnie Jean,
My dearest part,
A dancin', sweet, young, handsome quean,
O' guiless heart."

PAGE 106, NOTE 8.—The author's own

notes have been appended to the references throughout this poem, not but that the spells of this characteristic festival are now very generally understood.—"It is thought to be a night when all the superhuman beings who people space, and earth and air, in search of mischief, revel at midnight—and it is also a grand anniversary of the more beneficent tribe of fairies, whose occupation is to baffle each evil genius in his wicked pursuit.—R. B.

PAGE 106, NOTE 9.—Certain little, romantic, rocky, green hills in the neighbourhood of the ancient seat of the Earl of Cassilis.—R. B.

PAGE 106, NOTE 10.—A noted cavern near Colean House, called the Cave of Colean, which, as well as Cassilis Downans, is famed in country story as the haunt of fairies.—R. B.

PAGE 106, NOTE 11.—The heads of the race of Bruce were Earls of Carrick.—R. B.

PAGE 106, NOTE 12—The first ceremony of Halloween is, pulling each a *stock* or plant of kail. They must go out hand in hand with eyes shut, and pull the first they meet with: its being big or little, straight or crooked, is prophetic of the size and shape of the grand object of all their spells—the husband or wife. If any *yird*, or earth, stick to the root, that is *tocher*, or fortune; and the taste of the *custoc*, or heart of the stem, is indicative of the natural temper or disposition. Lastly, the stems, or as they are called, the *runts*, are placed above the cornice of the door; and the Christian names of those whom chance brings into the house, are, according to the order in which the runts were placed, the names in question.—R. B.

PAGE 106, NOTE 13.—They go to the barn yard, and pull each, at three several times, a stalk of oats. If the third stalk wants a *top pickle*, or grain at the top of the stalk, the lady will be wedded, but not a maid.—R. B.

PAGE 106, NOTE 14.—When the corn is in a doubtful state, by being too green or wet, the stackbuilder, by means of old timber, &c., makes a large apartment in his stack, with an opening in the side which is fairest exposed to the wind: this he calls a fause-house.—R. B.

PAGE 106, NOTE 15.—Burning the nuts is a famous charm. They name the lad and lass to each particular nut, as they lay them in the fire, and accordingly as they burn quietly together, or start from beside one another, the course and issue of the courtship will be.—R. B.

PAGE 106, NOTE 16.—Whoever would, with success, try this spell, must strictly observe these directions:—Steal out, all alone, to the kiln, and, darkling, throw into the pot a clue of blue yarn; wind it in a clue off the old one, and, towards the latter end something will hold the thread; demand "wha hauds?" that is, who holds? An answer will be returned from the kiln-pot, by naming the Christian and surname of your future spouse.—R. B.

PAGE 106, NOTE 17.—Take a candle, and go alone to a looking-glass; eat an apple before it, and some traditions say, you should comb your hair all the time; the face of your conjugal companion, to be, will be seen in the glass, as if peeping over your shoulder.

PAGE 107, NOTE 28.—Steal out, unperceived, and sow a handful of hemp-seed, harrowing it with any thing you can conveniently draw after you. Repeat, now and then, "Hemp seed I saw thee; hemp-seed I saw thee; and him (or her) that is to be my true love, come after me and pou thee." Look over your left shoulder, and you will see the appearance of the person invoked, in the attitude of pulling hemp. Some traditions say, "Come after me, and shaw thee," that is, show thyself: in which case it simply appears. Others omit the harrowing, and say, "Come after me, and harrow thee."—R. B.

PAGE 107, NOTE 19.—This charm must likewise be performed unperceived and alone. You go to the barn, and open both doors, taking them off the hinges, if possible; for there is danger that the being about to appear may shut the doors, and do you some mischief. Then take that instrument used in winnowing the corn, which, in our country dialect, we call a wecht; and go through all the attitudes of letting down corn against the wind. Repeat it three times, and the third time, an apparition will pass through the barn, in at the windy door, and out at the other, having both the figure in question, and the appearance or retinue, marking the employment or station in life.—R. B.

PAGE 107, NOTE 20.—Take an opportunity of going, unnoticed, to a bean-stack, and fathom it three times round. The last fathom of the last time, you will catch in your arms the appearance of your future conjugal yoke-fellow.—R. B.

PAGE 107. NOTE 21.—You go out, one or more, for this is a social spell, to a south running spring or rivulet, where "three laird's lands meet," and dip your left shirt-sleeve. Go to bed in sight of a fire, and hang your wet sleeve before it to dry. Lie awake: and some time near midnight, an apparition, having the exact figure of the grand object in question, will come and turn the sleeve, as if to dry the other side of it.—R. B.

PAGE 108, NOTE 22.—Take three dishes: put clean water in one, foul water in another, leave the third empty: blindfold a person, and lead him to the hearth where the dishes are ranged; he (or she) dips the left hand—if by chance in the clean water, the future husband or wife will come to the bar of matrimony a maid; if in the foul, a widow; if in the empty dish, it fortells with equal certainty, no marriage at all. It is repeated three times, and every time the arrangement of the dishes is altered.—R. B.

PAGE 108, NOTE 23.—Sowens, with butter instead of milk to them, is always the Halloween supper.—R. B.

PAGE 108, NOTE 24.—Burns has omitted, amongst the other ceremonies of Halloween, that of ducking for apples in tubs of water, Few of those of which the poet has furnished particulars, are now observed. The lottery of dishes, the pulling kail stalks, and the ducking for apples, comprising the whole, or nearly the whole, of the frolicsome enchantments now in common observance.

PAGE 109, NOTE 25.—The author of a song beginning thus, (John Lapraik, of Dalfram, near Muirkirk):—

"When I upon thy bosom lean,
And fondly ca' thee a' my ain;
I glory in the sacred tie
That made us ane, wha ance were twain."

This song was sung at one of those merry meetings, called *rockings*, from the *rock*, or distaff, which was the invariable accompaniment of the female guests.

PAGE 110, NOTE 26.—A festivity which took place on the road by Burns's farm, at Mossgiel.

PAGE 111, NOTE 27.—William Simpson has accomplished some very passable poetry, amongst which is an elegy on the Emperor Paul. He was first the teacher at Ochiltree, and afterwards engaged in the same capacity at New Cumnock.

PAGE 113, NOTE 28.—Hornbook's career seems to have borne out his claim to some more elevated occupation than the ownership of a shop of all wares, the duties of an obscure dispenser, or those of a wretched parish schoolmaster. Such were his occupations at Tarbolton, where first he was engaged as a teacher. He subsequently stocked a small store of grocery and general wares, to which, after some poring over medical books, he also added the drugs in more ordinary demand This last acquisition was of the more consequence, as there was no medical man in the place; and Hornbook having started up into a medical authority, pompously paraded his knowledge and skill at a Mason meeting at Tarbolton, in the presence of Burns, and thus suggested this poem. Hornbook subsequently settled in Glasgow, and outlived the poet nearly half a century.

PAGE 113, NOTE 29.—Willie's Mill was the name of a mill just out of the village of Tarbolton, on the road to Mossgiel, and on a small stream called the Faile. It was occupied by Mr. William Muir, an intimate friend of the Burns's, and one of the subscribers to the first Edinburgh Edition of Robert's Poems.

PAGE 113, NOTE 30.—Buchan's well-known work on Domestic Medicine.

PAGE 114, NOTE 31.—The Grave-digger.

PAGE 114, NOTE 32.—*(Misprinted 11.)* This poem was probably suggested by Fergusson's *Hallow Fair of Edinburgh*, although it is rather constructed after the model of the same poet's *Leith Races*. The ceremonial of rural communion, as it has been till very recently, or still is observed in some parts of Scotland, furnishes the incidents of the poem.

PAGE 115, NOTE 33.—The popular name of a poor crazy girl, who was in the habit of running for wagers.

PAGE 115, NOTE 34.—This was an exquisite hit at the preaching of Moodie, who was fond of holding forth the terrors of the law. In the first, or Kilmarnock edition, this word was printed *salvation*, which, as applied to Moodie, was comparatively tame. Dr. Blair, of Edinburgh, is said to have suggested the correction. Moodie was the minister of Riccarton.

PAGE 115, NOTE 35.—The minister of Galston, who also figures in the *Kirk's Alarm*, under the name of *Irvine-side*. This person was subsequently better known as a preacher by the name of Dr. George Smith.

PAGE 116, NOTE 36.—Dr. William Peebles, then the Rev. Mr. W. Peebles, who was minister of Newton-upon-Ayr, and who also figures in the *Kirk's Alarm*, as having been prominent in the persecution of Dr. McGill.

PAGE 116, NOTE 37.—Dr. Mackenzie, afterwards minister at Irvine, but at this period of Mauchline, who is thus introduced in allusion to a pamphlet, in exposition of some village controversy which he had promulgated under the title of *Common Sense.*

PAGE 116, NOTE 38.—The name of a street at Mauchline.

PAGE 116, NOTE 39.—This Mr. Miller was subsequently minister at Kilmaur's, and a little portly person he was.

PAGE 116, NOTE 40.—The Rev. John Russell, who also figures in the *Twa Herds.* He subsequently became minister at Stirling, but was at this period attached to the chapel of ease at Kilmarnock.

PAGE 116, NOTE 41.—Expression borrowed from the subjoined passage in *Hamlet.*

"I could a tale unfold—
Would harrow up thy soul; freeze thy young blood;
Make thine eyes like stars start from their spheres;
Thy knotty and combined locks to part;
And each particular hair to stand on end,
Like quills upon the fretful porcupine."

PAGE 117 NOTE 42.—The ultra orthodoxy of the newly-appointed minister of the parochial Kirk of Kilmarnock, on the 6th of April, 1786, and the consequent triumph of the *Auld Lights* over the Moderates, elicited the bitter irony of this poem.

PAGE 117, NOTE 43.—An allusion to the chief occupation of the people of Kilmarnock, in the manufacture of leather and woollen goods, carpets and articles of this nature.

PAGE 117, NOTE 44.—The landlord of a tavern near the parish church.

PAGE 117, NOTE 45.—This passage refers to a satirical ballad, circulated upon the induction of the Rev. Mr. Lindsay, as minister of the parochial church.

PAGE 117, NOTE 46.—See Genesis chap. ix, v. 22.

PAGE 117, NOTE 47.—See Numbers chap. xxv, v. 8.

PAGE 117, NOTE 48.—See Exodus chap. iv, v. 25.

PAGE 117, NOTE 49.—The Rev. Mr. Robertson was the colleague of the new minister; but not of the ultra-orthodox Kirk party.

PAGE 117, NOTE 50.—Netherton was the name of a quarter of the town of Kilmarnock.

PAGE 117, NOTE 51.—The predecessor of the new minister.

PAGE 117, NOTE 52.—The person here alluded to is apparently unknown to all those who have made local researches respecting Burns and his poems. One commentator supposes it to be an allusion to the author of the *Essay on Truth.* This, however, is mere hypothesis.

PAGE 118, NOTE 53.—In the west of Scotland, the term *New Light* is a popular designation of the opinions promulgated by Dr. Taylor and his partisans.

PAGE 118, NOTE 54.—James Smith was formerly a shopkeeper at Mauchline; subsequently, a calico printer, at Avon, near Linlithgow; and lastly, an emigrant to the West Indies, where he died.

PAGE 119, NOTE 55.—The authenticity of this poem has been very erroneously doubted. It was written by Burns in 1785, but was not published in his own editions, probably, because he had retained no copy of it, clearly not that he thought it unworthy of him. In 1801, this piece appeared in a small volume, published at Glasgow, by Messrs. Brash and Reid, under the unpretending title of *Poems ascribed to Robert Burns.* All the more recent authorities have been convinced of its authenticity, which, in fact, appears to be incontestibly established by its style; and Mr. Chambers has furnished some particulars respecting the incident to which it is attributable. The following is the anecdote:—

"It is understood to have been founded on the poet's observation of an actual scene which one night met his eye, when, in company with his friends John Richmond and James Smith, he dropped accidentally, at a late hour, into a very humble hostelry in Mauchline, the landlady of which was a Mrs. Gibson, more familiarly named Poosie Nancy. After witnessing much jollity amongst a company, who, by day, appeared abroad as miserable beggars, the three young men came away, Burns professing to have been greatly delighted with the scene, but, particularly with the gleesome behaviour of an old maimed soldier. In the course of a few days, he recited a part of the poem to Richmond, who has informed the present editor, that, to the best of his recollection, it contained, in its original complete form, songs by a sweep and a sailor, which do not now appear. The landlady of the house was mother to Racer Jess, alluded to in the *Holy Fair,* and her house was at the left hand side of the opening of the *Cowgate,* mentioned in the same poem, and opposite to the church. An account of the house, the characters who frequented it, and the scenes which used to take place in it, is given in *Chambers's Edinburgh Journal,* No 2. A lithographic facsimile of the original manuscript of the *Jolly Beggars* has been published."

Sir Walter Scott, with some taint of a prudery, which accasionally exposed him to the charge of affectation, has, however, been liberal enough in his remarks on this poem, to attach a defence to his own censure. Subjoined is his own criticism *totidem verbis*:—

"In one or two passages of the *Jolly Beggars*, the muse has slightly trespassed on decorum, where, in the language of Scottish song,

'High kilted was she,
As she gaed ower the lea.'

Something, however, is to be allowed to the nature of the subject, and something to the education of the poet: and if from veneration to the names of Swift and Dryden, we tolerate the grossness of the one and the indelicacy of the other, the respect due to that of Burns may surely claim indulgence for a few light strokes of broad humour."

PAGE 119, NOTE 56.—An allusion to the large wooden dish or platter, carried by mendicants in Scotland, to receive any contributions of broken food.

PAGE 120, NOTE 57.—The heights of Abraham, on the land side of Quebec, on which the English army under General Wolfe, succeeded in giving battle to the enemy; and where the general fell, mortally wounded, at the moment of victory, in September, 1759.

PAGE, 120, NOTE 58.—El Morro, the castle which defends the entrance to the harbour of Havannah, in the island of Cuba. In 1762, this castle was stormed and taken by the British, after which, the Havannah was surrendered, with spoil to the value of three millions.

PAGE 120, NOTE 59.—"The destruction of the Spanish floating batteries during the famous siege of Gibraltar, in 1782—on which occasion the gallant Captain Curtis rendered the most signal service—is the heroic exploit here referred to."—MOTHERWELL.

PAGE 120, NOTE 60.—George Augustus Elliot, created Lord Heathfield for his admirable defence of Gibraltar, during a siege of three years. Born 1717, died 1790.

PAGE 122, NOTE 61.—The whisky made at the distillery of that name in Clackmannanshire, and famous throughout the country for its superiority.

PAGE 123, NOTE 62.—Several of the poems were produced for the purpose of bringing forward some favourite sentiment of the author. He used to remark to me, that he could not well conceive a more mortifying picture of human life, than a man seeking work. In casting about in his mind how this sentiment might be brought forward, the elegy, *Man was made to mourn*, was composed.—GILBERT BURNS.

The metre is adopted from an old ballad known by the name of the *Life and Age of Man*, and of which the subjoined are the initiatory lines:—

"Upon the sixteen hunder year,
Of God and fifty-three,
Frae Christ was born, that bought us dear,
As writings testifie;
On January the sixteenth day,
As I did lie alone,
With many a sigh and sob did say,
Ah! Man is made to moan."

That the moral of this ballad had made a deep impression upon the mind of Burns, is evident from the following passage extracted from one of his letters to Mrs. Dunlop:—

"I had an old grand-uncle with whom my mother lived while in her girlish years; the good old man, for such he was, was long blind ere he died; during which time, his happiest moments and his highest enjoyment were, when he sat down and cried, whilst my mother would sit down and sing the simple old ballad, *The Life and Age of Man*.

We are indebted to the compiler of the *Land of Burns*, for the following interesting anecdote in illustration of this poem:—

"Close beside the end of Barskimming old bridge, stands a neat, small house, inhabited, at the time to which this anecdote relates, by an old man named Kemp, and his daughter. The old man, not originally possessed of the best of tempers, was rendered peevish and querulous by disease, and in consequence of slight paralysis, generally supported himself on two sticks. His daughter Kate, however, a trim trig, lass, was one of the leading belles of the district, and, as such, had attracted a share of the attentions of Robert Burns. One evening the poet had come from Mauchline to see Kate; but, on arriving at the house, he found the old man at the door in a more than usually peevish mood, and was informed by him that the cow was lost, and that Kate had gone in quest of her, but she had been so long away he was afraid she was lost too. The poet, leaving the old man, crossed the bridge, and at the further end he met the miller of Barskimming mill, then a young man about his own age, whom he accosted thus: 'Weel, miller, what are you doing here?' 'Na, Robin,' said the miller, 'I should put that question to you, for I am at hame and ye're no.' 'Why,' said Robin, 'I cam doun to see Kate Hemp.' 'I was just gaun the same gate,' said the miller. 'Then ye need gang nae farther,' said Burns, 'for baith she and the cow's lost, and the auld man is perfectly wud at the want o' them. But come, we'll tak a turn or two in the holm till we see if she cast up.' They accordingly went into the holm, and during the first two rounds they made, the poet chatted freely, but subsequently got more and more taciturn, and, during the last two rounds, spoke not a word. On reaching the stile that led from the place, he abruptly bade the miller good night, and walked rapidly towards Mauchline. Next time the miller and he met, he said, 'Miller, I owe you an apology for my silence during our last walk together, and for leaving you so abruptly.' 'Oh, oh!' said he, 'Robin, there is no occasion, for I supposed some subject had occurred to you, and that you were thinking, and perhaps composing something on it.' 'You were quite right, miller,' said Burns, 'and I will now read you what was chiefly the work of that evening.'"

The composition he read was *Man was made to Mourn!*

PAGE 124, NOTE 63.—This exquisite poem was actually composed at the plough-tail, and suggested by an incident which occurred to the poet whilst at work. Burns was handling the plough, and John Blane, one of the farm servants (who many years since remembered the incident), was driving, at the same time holding in his hand the pattle or pettle (a small wooden spud with which the ploughshare was scraped at the commencement of every fresh furrow), when suddenly a mouse started from the furrow, and was running across the field, closely pursued by Blane, pattle in hand, who had started in chase. Burns, however, called his driver back, and very calmly asked him "What hurt the mouse had done him, that he should wish to kill it." From that moment Burns remained moody and silent during the rest of the day, and woke Blane at night (for they were bed-fellows), to repeat to him the lines which the incident of the day had suggested.

PAGE 124, NOTE 64.—*Duan* is the term (analogous to strophe, fytte, &c.) applied by Ossian to the divisions of rambling poems.

PAGE 124, NOTE 65.—*Curling* is a very boisterous game, played upon the ice, when sufficiently strong, and which consists in the trundling of flattened, smoothed round stones. The players are divided into sides.

PAGE 124, NOTE 66.—The parlour of the farm-house of Mossgiel, namely, the only apartment besides the kitchen. This little apartment still exists in the state in which it was when the poet described it as the scene of his vision of Coila. "Though in every respect humble, and partly occupied by fixed beds, it does not appear uncomfortable. Every consideration, however, sinks beneath the one intense feeling, that here, within these four walls, warmed at this little fire-place, and lighted by this little window (it has but one), lived one of the most extraordinary men; here wrote some of the most celebrated poems of modern times."—*Chambers's Journal*, No. 93.

PAGE 125, NOTE 67.—The charter of the borough of Ayr bears date as early as the beginning of the thirteenth century.

PAGE 125, NOTE 68.—The illustrious family of Wallace.

PAGE 125, NOTE 69.—Alluding to the great William Wallace, the hero of Scottish independence.

PAGE 125, NOTE 70.—Adam Wallace, of Richardton, cousin to William Wallace.

PAGE 125, NOTE 71.—The Laird of Craigie, also, of the family of Wallace, who held the second command at the battle fought in 1448, on the banks of Sark, and gained by the Scottish troops, under Douglas, Earl of Ormond, and Wallace, Laird of Craigie; and in which the desperate valour, and masterly skill of the latter, were chiefly instrumental in securing the victory. The Laird of Craigie was mortally wounded in the engagement.

PAGE 125, NOTE 72.—The shade of the supposed Coilus, King of the Picts, who, according to tradition, was buried close to the seat of Montgomeries, of Coilsfield, beneath a small mound crowned with trees. On the 29th of May, 1837, this mound was excavated in search of remains, and two urns were found, which so far corroborated the tradition, that the mound was ascertained to have actually held the remains of some illustrious chiefs.

PAGE 125, NOTE 73.—Alluding to Barskimming, the seat of Sir Thomas Millar, at that time Lord Justice Clerk, and since President of the Court of Session.

PAGE 125, NOTE 74.—This stanza refers to Catrine, the seat of Dugald Stewart (and formerly of his father, the Rev. Dr. Matthew Stewart), and which is situated on the banks of the river Ayr.

PAGE 125, NOTE 75.—Alluding to the two successive possessors of Catrine, Dr. Matthew, and his son, Dugald Stewart; the first eminent for his mathematical attainment, the second for his elegant philosophical writings.

PAGE 125, NOTE 76.—Colonel Fullarton.

PAGE 126, NOTE 77.—Coila (the muse of Burns) had been suggested to the promoter of her fabulous existence, by the equally visionary personage, who figures under the name of *Scota* in Mr. A. Ross's poem, *The Fortunate Shepherdess.*

PAGE 126, NOTE 78.—Mossgiel, which has since become the property of Mr. Alexander, of Ballochmyle, was then amongst the possessions of the Earls of Loudon, that is, of the Loudon branch of the race of *Campbell.*

PAGE 127, NOTE 79.—Towards the close of the year 1785, loud complaints were made by the Scottish distillers respecting the vexatious and oppressive manner in which the Excise laws were enforced at their establishments—such rigour, they said, being exercised at the instigation of the London distillers, who looked with jealousy on the success of their northern brethren. So great was the severity of the Excise, that many distillers were obliged to abandon the trade, and the price of barley was beginning to be affected. Illicit distillation was also found to be alarmingly on the increase. In consequence of the earnest remonstrances of the distillers, backed by the county gentlemen, an Act was passed in the session of 1786, (alluded to by the author), whereby the duties on low wines, spirits, &c., were discontinued, and an annual tax imposed on stills, according to their capacity. This act gave general satisfaction. It seems to have been during the general outcry against fiscal oppression at the end of 1785, or beginning of 1786, that the poem was composed.

PAGE 127, NOTE 80.—William Pitt, who in his twenty-second year was at the head of an administration, and controlling the Exchequer.

PAGE 127, NOTE 81.—Hugh Montgomery, of Coilsfield, afterwards twelfth Earl of Eglinton, at that time M.P. for Ayrshire, and who had served in the army during the American war.

PAGE 127, NOTE 82.—James Boswell, well known to the party politicians of Ayrshire, as one of the orators of their meetings, but better known to the world at large as the *shadow* and biographer of Dr. Johnson.

PAGE 127, NOTE 83.—George Dempster, of Dunnichen, in the county of Forfar, an eminent Scottish Whig representative, of the age of Fox and Pitt. He commenced his parliamentary career in 1762, and closed it in 1790, after having sat in five succeeding parliaments. Every patriotic and liberal scheme had the support of this excellent man, who died in 1818, at the age of eighty-two.

PAGE 127, NOTE 84.—Sir Adam Fergusson, of Kilkerran, Bart. He had several times represented Ayrshire, but at present was member for the city of Edinburgh.

PAGE 127, NOTE 85.—The Marquis of Graham, eldest son of the Duke of Montrose. He afterwards became the third Duke of Montrose, and died in 1836.

PAGE 127, NOTE 86.—The Right Hon. Henry Dundas, Treasurer of the Navy, and M.P. for Edinburghshire, afterwards Viscount Melville.

PAGE 128, NOTE 87.—Probably Thomas Erskine, afterwards Lord Erskine; but he was not then in Parliament.

PAGE 128, NOTE 88.—Lord Frederick Campbell, second brother of the Duke of Argyle, Lord Registrar of Scotland, and M.P. for the county of Argyle in this, and the one preceding, and the two subsequent Parliaments.

PAGE 128, NOTE 89.—Ilay Campbell, Lord Advocate of Scotland, who afterwards became President of the Court of Session, and survived to an advanced age. He was at this period M.P. for the burghs comprehended within the limits of Glasgow. He died in 1823.

PAGE 128, NOTE 90.—This stanza was suppressed in all the editions which Burns himself superintended whilst in press, out of respect for the Montgomery, whose clumsy oratory he could not help ridiculing.

PAGE 128, NOTE 91.—Mr. Pitt's father, the Earl of Chatham, was the second son of Robert Pitt, of Boconnock, in the county of Cornwall.

PAGE 128, NOTE 92.—"Scones made from a mixture of oats, peas, or beans, with wheat or barley, ground fine, and denominated *mashlum*, are in general use, and form a wholesome and palatable food."—*New Statistical Account of Scotland, parish of Dalry, Ayrshire.*

PAGE 128, NOTE 93.—A worthy old hostess of the author's in Mauchline, where he sometimes studies politics over a glass of guid auld Scotch drink. Nanse's story was different. On seeing the poem, she declared that the poet had never been but once or twice in her house.

PAGE 128, NOTE 94.—The young Chancellor of the Exchequer had gained some credit by a measure introduced in 1784 for preventing smuggling of tea by reducing the duty, the revenue being compensated by a tax on windows.

PAGE 129, NOTE 95.—The model which Burns followed in this poem is evidently the *Cauler Water* of Fergusson. The poet's imagination is evidently more concerned in the bacchanalian rant, than his actual predilection; for it does not transpire that he was more especially devoted to Bacchus or his compeers, than the majority of his associates or contemporaries.

PAGE 129, NOTE 96.—The vulgar name of beer being repudiated, and the more refined cognomen of "*ale*" being substituted for such decoctions of malt as grace the tables of the great in silver tankards.

PAGE 129, NOTE 97.—An allusion to the favourite draught of beer after a mess of porridge.

PAGE 129, NOTE 98.—An allusion to the crowding of the congregation round the moveable pulpits out of doors, as was actually the case at a parochial distribution of the sacrament.

PAGE 130, NOTE 99.—The Scottish Parliament passed an Act in the year 1690, empowering Forbes of Culloden to distil whisky free of duty, on his manor of Ferintosh, of Cromartyshire, in consideration of his services, and of the losses which he had sustained in the public service at the period of the Revolution. The immense wealth to which such an immunity opened the way, gradually stimulated the successors of the Forbes to the distillation of so immense a quantity of the spirit, that by degrees *Ferintosh* became a bye-word signifying whisky. This privilege was abolished by the Act of the British parliament, passed in 1785, and which regulated the Scotch distilleries in general. But a provision was reserved in that act to the effect that the Lords of the Treasury should indemnify the present proprietor of the barony for the immense deterioration of his estate, and that if the Lords of the Treasury should fail to settle the matter fairly, it should be submitted to a jury in the Scottish Court of Exchequer. Accordingly, after futile attempts at redress from the Treasury, Mr. Duncan Forbes prosecuted his claim, proving that the right had actually produced £1000 a year to his family, and might have been productive of seven times as much; and the jury awarded him the substantial sum of £21,580 as compensation, on the 29th of November, 1785.

PAGE 130, NOTE 100.—A preacher of very general popularity amongst the poorer classes.

PAGE 130, NOTE 101.—A preacher not much admired by the people generally, but received as an oracle by the select few who were his partisans. Robertson was out of health at the time these lines were written.

PAGE 131, NOTE 102.—Killie, a popular or familiar designation amongst the country people, meaning Kilmarnock.

PAGE 131, NOTE 103.—Thomas Samson, a nurseryman, at Kilmarnock, was one amongst the earliest friends of Burns. He was devoted to sporting. Supposing one of his seasons to be his last in pursuit of game, he had expressed a desire to die, and to be buried in the Muirs, and this suggested to Burns the elegy and epitaph. At his death he was buried in Kilmarnock Churchyard, and at the western extremity of the church is a plain monumental slab, with the inscription:— THOMAS SAMSON,

Died the 12th of December, 1795,
Aged 72 years.
"Tam Samson's weel-worn clay here lies;"
&c., &c.,

in the identical words with which Burns had humorously provided him.

PAGE 132, NOTE 104.—Mr. Aiken was one of the first persons moving in the higher orders of society, who noticed the remarkable talents of Robert Burns, and whose patronage and countenance upheld the poet, and promoted the success of his subsequently brilliant career. He was somewhat distinguished amongst his professional colleagues (being a lawyer), for the superior intellectual qualifications which he possessed, and amongst his friends for the unaffected generosity of his character. He died on the 24th of March, 1807.

PAGE 132, NOTE 105.—"Several of the poems were produced for the purpose of bringing forward some favourite sentiment of the author. He had frequently remarked to me, that he thought there was something peculiarly venerable in the phrase, 'Let us worship God,' used by a decent sober head of a family introducing family worship. To this sentiment of the author, the world is indebted for the *Cotter's Saturday Night*. The hint of the plan, and title of the poem, were taken from Fergusson's *Farmer's Ingle*."—GILBERT BURNS. "The household of the virtuous William Burness was the scene of the poem, and William himself was the saint, and father and husband, of this truly sacred drama."—CUNNINGHAM.

PAGE 134, NOTE 106.—See Pope's Windsor Forest.

PAGE 134, NOTE 107.—This poem is another remarkable instance of the fertility of genius which so strikingly characterised the muse of Burns. Like the lines to a mouse, it is elicited by the simplest and most trivial occurrence, and, nevertheless, is wrought up to a profound degree of thought and sentiment, which the utmost sublimity of scenery could barely have excelled.

PAGE 135, NOTE 108.—The friend to whom this poem is addressed, was Mr. Andrew Aiken, the son of Mr. Aiken, of Ayr, to whom the *Cotter's Saturday Night* is dedicated, and who had been taught by his father to venerate the genius and character of his lowly but illustrious fellow-countryman. Mr. Andrew Aiken survived fifty years after Burns, and died at St. Petersburgh, after a very successful mercantile career into which he had early embarked at Liverpool.

PAGE 136, NOTE 109.—The first person of respectable rank and good education who took any notice of Burns, was Mr. Gavin Hamilton, writer in Mauchline, from whom he took his farm of Mossgiel on a sub-lease. Mr. Hamilton lived in what is still called the Castle of Mauchline, a half-fortified old mansion near the church, forming the only remains of the ancient priory. He was the son of a gentleman who had practised the same profession in the same place, and was in every respect a most estimable member of society—generous, affable, and humane. Unfortunately his religious practice did not square with the notions of the then minister of Mauchline, the *Daddy Auld* of Burns, who, in 1785, is found in the session records to have summoned him for rebuke, on the four following charges:—1. Unnecessary absence from church, for five consecutive Sundays (apparently the result of some dispute about a poor's rate); 2. Setting out on a journey to Carrick on a Sunday; 3. Habitual, if not total neglect of family worship; 4. Writing an abusive letter to the session, in reference to some of their former proceedings respecting him. Strange though this prosecution may seem, it was strictly accordant with the right assumed by the Scottish clergy at that period, to inquire into the private habits of parishioners; and as it is universally allowed that Mr. Auld's designs in the matter were purely religious, it is impossible to speak of it disrespectfully. It was unfortunately, however, mixed up with some personal motives in the members of the session, which were so apparent to the Presbytery, to which Mr. Hamilton appealed, that that reverend body ordered the proceedings to be stopped, and all notice of them expunged from the records. A description of the sufferings of the Mauchline Session, while orator Aiken was exposing them before the Presbytery, is to be found in *Holy Willie's Prayer*. Partly from antipathy to the high orthodox party, but more from friendship for Mr. Hamilton, whom he regarded as a worthy and enlightened man, persecuted by narrow-witted bigots, Burns threw his partisan muse into the quarrel, and produced several poems, that just mentioned amongst the rest, in which it is but too apparent that religion itself suffers in common with those whom he holds up as abusing it.

PAGE 137, NOTE 110.—On reading in the public papers the Laureate's Ode, with the other parade of June 4th, 1786, the author was no sooner dropt asleep, than he imagined himself transported to the birthday levee; and in his dreaming fancy, made the address conveyed in these lines.—R. B. [The Poet Laureate of the time being was Thomas Warton, and the subjoined are the opening lines of the ode of which Burns became the quaint commentator in the dream:—

"When Freedom nursed her native fire
In ancient Greece, and ruled the lyre,
Her bards disdainful, from the tyrant's brow
The tinsel gifts of flattery tore;
But paid to guiltless power their willing vow;
And to the throne of virtuous kings, &c., &c."

Vapid enough, it must be confessed.]

PAGE 138, NOTE 111.—Gait, gett, or gyte, a homely substitute for the word child in Scotland.

PAGE 138, NOTE 112.—When the vote of naval supplies was under discussion in the session of 1786, several modifications of the management of our naval armaments were hotly agitated by a Captain McBride and his adherents. Amongst other projects, the abandonment of 64-gun ships was proposed by him.

PAGE 138, NOTE 113.—Charles James Fox.

PAGE 138, NOTE 114.—In this respect Burns has followed the account of the chronicles, adopted as it had subsequently been by Shakespeare, in speaking of Henry V., as mingling in the wildest frolics of his companions; Prince *Hal* was clearly of such habits in his younger days, if we may trust the anecdotes in which his just punishment, by authority, reflected credit on a worthy and impartial judge. But, according to the memoirist Tyler, these were nothing better than a tissue of ingenious fables. However this may be, Burns only adopted a degree of licence, which the greatest British Poet had considered himself free to use when the traditions were yet more positive on the subject.

PAGE 138, NOTE 115.—A humorous hit at Frederick, Duke of York (the second son of George III.), whose earlier career had been spent in Ecclesiastical vocations, as Bishop of Osnaburg.

PAGE 138, NOTE 116.—William Henry, afterwards Duke of Clarence, and finally King, by the name of William IV., whose profession was the navy.

PAGE 138, NOTE 117.—An allusion to the current tale of some youthful intrigue of the royal sailor.

PAGE 132, NOTE 118.—"The tale of the *Twa Dogs* was composed after the resolution of publishing was nearly taken. Robert had a dog, which he called Luath, that was a great favourite. The dog had been killed by the wanton cruelty of some person, the night before my father's death. Robert said to me that he should like to confer such an immortality as he could bestow on his old Friend Luath, and that he had a great mind to introduce something into the book under the title of Stanzas to the Memory of a Quadruped Friend; but this plan was given up for the poem as it now stands. Cæsar was merely the creature of the poet's imagination, created for the purpose of holding chat with his favourite Luath." —GILBERT BURNS. Allan Cunningham mentions that John Wilson, printer, Kilmarnock, on undertaking the first edition of the poems, suggested the propriety of placing a piece of a grave nature at the beginning, and that Burns, acting on the hint, composed or completed the *Twa Dogs* in walking home to Mossgiel. Its exact date is fixed at February 1786, by a letter of the poet to John Richmond.

PAGE 139, NOTE 119.—Kyle, the native province of the poet, is supposed to derive its name from Coilus, a real or supposed king of the Picts, alluded to in the notes to the *Vision*. Recent antiquaries are disposed to deduce the appellative from quite a different source, from *choillie*, to wit, signifying in the Celtic tongue a woody region. Upon the whole, the popular etymology appears the more rational.

PAGE 139, NOTE 120.—Cuchullin's dog in Ossian's Fingal.

PAGE 141, NOTE 121.—In the early part of 1786, when the friends of his Jean forced her to break the nuptial engagement into which he had clandestinely entered with her, and took legal steps to force him to find security for the maintenance of her expected offspring—in this dismal time, when nothing but ruin seemed before him—our bard poured forth, as in the name of another, the following eloquent effusion of indignation and grief.

PAGE 142, NOTE 122.—Allusion is here made to Miss Eliza Burnet, the *beauty* of her day in Edinburgh—daughter of the eccentric scholar and philosopher, Lord Monboddo. Burns was several times entertained by his lordship at his house in St. John Street, Canongate, where the lady presided. He speaks of her in a letter in the following terms:—"There has not been any thing nearly like her, in all the combinations of beauty, grace, and goodness, the great Creator has formed, since Milton's Eve on the first day of her existence." It may be curious to learn what was thought of this lovely woman by a man of a very different sort from Burns—namely, Hugh Chisholm, one of the seven broken men (usually called robbers) who kept Prince Charles in their cave in Inverness-shire for several weeks, during his hidings, resisting the temptation of thirty thousand pounds to give him up. This man, when far advanced in life, was brought on a visit to Edinburgh, where it was remarked he would never allow any one to shake his right hand, that member having been rendered sacred in his estimation, by the grasp of the Prince. Being taken to sup at Lord Monboddo's, old Hugh sat most of the time gazing abstractedly on Miss Burnet, and being asked afterwards what he thought of her, he exclaimed, in a burst of his eloquent native tongue, which can be but poorly rendered in English, "She is the finest *animal* I ever beheld." Yet an enviously minute inquirer, in the letter-press accompanying the reprint of *Kay's Portraits*, states that she had one blemish, though one not apt to be observed —*bad teeth*. She died, in 1790, of consumption, at the age of twenty-five, and the poet wrote an elegy upon her.—CHAMBERS.

PAGE 143, NOTE 123.—An hostelry of high repute throughout the neighbourhood, situated at the Auld Brig End.

PAGE 143, NOTE 124.—This clock, as well as the tower or steeple in which it stood, has been removed for some years. The steeple was formerly attached to the old gaol of Ayr.

PAGE 143, NOTE 125.—The ancient Wallace Tower, which fell into a dangerous state of repair, was ultimately pulled down, and replaced by a new Tower, which is still known by the same name. The Old Wallace Tower was an incongruous building, partaking of the rude commixture of several styles of architecture, and from it rose a slender spire, which, though, by no means in exact keeping with the basement, certainly contributed to the picturesque aspect of the building. The new tower stands upon the same foundation in the High Street of Ayr.

PAGE 143, NOTE 126.—The falcon, or as it is commonly called, the Gos-hawk. The imagery of this passage is as beautiful as the expression.

PAGE 143, NOTE 127.—A well-known ford in the River, immediately above the Auld Brig.

PAGE 143, NOTE 128.—Generally, as the rapid enlightenment of the Scottish people has dispelled the superstitions which were wont to hang about some localities, even to the charm and poetical imagery with which such superstitions served at times to invest them, the spirits of Garpal Water are yet acknowledged to retain their supremacy, and the spot is as firmly believed to be haunted by many of the peasants, as it was of old.

PAGE 144, NOTE 129.—The source of the river Ayr.

PAGE 144, NOTE 130.—A narrow landing place on the upward side of the chief quay.

PAGE 144, NOTE 131.—Mr. McLachlan was at that time well known, and much admired for his taste in the performance of Scottish airs on the violin.

PAGE 145, NOTE 132.—A complimentary allusion to Captain Hugh Montgomery, otherwise called *Sodger Hugh* by Burns, (who subsequently succeeded to the Earldom of Eglinton), and whose family seat of Coilsfield is situated on the Faile, or Feal, a small stream which falls into the river Ayr, at no great distance.

PAGE 145, NOTE 133.—In the foregoing notes, on the *Epistle to Davie*, the introduction of Burns to Mrs. Stewart, of Stair, has been detailed. The present passage is a complimentary allusion to the same lady.

PAGE 145, NOTE 134.—Catrine was, as we have already had occasion to state, the seat of Dr. Stewart, the father of Professor Dugald Stewart, to whose honour, and in compliment of whom, this allusion is made.

PAGE 145, NOTE 135.—"The Elegy on Captain Henderson is a tribute to the memory of a man I loved much."—BURNS. Captain Henderson was a retired soldier, of agreeable manners, and upright character, who had a lodging in Carrubber's Close, Edinburgh, and mingled with the best society of the city. Mr. Cunningham states, on the authority of Sir Thomas Wallace, who knew him, that he "dined regularly at Fortune's Tavern, and was a member of the Capillaire Club, which was composed of all who inclined to the witty and the joyous." The poem was written in Dumfriesshire, in 1790.

PAGE 145, NOTE 136.—Yearns—Eagles.

PAGE 146, NOTE 137.—"I look on *Tam o' Shanter* as my standard performance in the poetical line."—BURNS.

"When my father fewed his little property near Alloway Kirk, the wall of the church-yard had gone to ruin, and cattle had free liberty of pasture in it. My father and two or three neighbours joined in an application to the town-council of Ayr, who were superiors of the adjoining land, for liberty to rebuild it, and raised by subscription a sum for enclosing this ancient cemetery with a wall: hence, he came to consider it as his burial place, and we learned that reverence for it people generally have for the burial-place of their ancestors. My brother was living in Ellisland, when Captain Grose, on his perigrinations through Scotland, staid some time at Carse-house in the neighbourhood, with Captain Robert Riddel, of Glenriddel, a particular friend of my brother's. The antiquary and the poet were 'unco pack and thick thegither.' Robert requested of Captain Grose, when he should come to Ayrshire, that he would make a drawing of Alloway Kirk, as it was the burial-place of his father, where he himself had a sort of claim to lay down his bones when they should be no longer serviceable to him; and added, by way of encouragement, that it was the scene of many a good story of witches and apparitions, of which he knew the captain was very fond. The captain agreed to the request, provided the poet would furnish a witch story, to be printed along with it. 'Tam o' Shanter' was produced on this occasion, and was first published in 'Grose's Antiquities of Scotland.'"—GILBERT BURNS.

It was while spending his nineteenth summer in the parish of Kirkoswald, in Carrick, that the poet became acquainted with the characters and circumstances afterwards introduced into Tam o' Shanter. The hero was an honest farmer, named Douglas Graham, who lived at Shanter, between Turnberry and Colzean. His wife, Helen M'Taggart, was much addicted to superstitious beliefs. Graham, dealing much in malt, went to Ayr every market day, whither he was frequently accompanied by a shoemaking neighbour, John Davidson, who dealt a little in leather. The two would often linger to a late hour in the taverns at the market town. One night, when riding home more than usually late by himself, in a storm of wind and rain, Graham, in passing over Brown Carrick Hill, near the Bridge of Doon, lost his bonnet, which contained the money he had drawn that day at the market. To avoid the scolding of his wife, he imposed upon her credulity with a story of witches seen at Alloway Kirk, but did not the less return to the Carrick Hill, to seek for his money, which he had the satisfaction to find, with his bonnet, in a plantation near the road. Burns, hearing Graham's story told between jest and earnest among the smugglers of the Carrick shore, retained it in his memory, till, at a comparatively late period of his career, he wove from it one of the most admired of his poems. Douglas Graham and John Davidson, the originals of Tam o' Shanter and Souter Johnnie, have long reposed in the churchyard of Kirkoswald, where the former had a handsome monument, bearing a very pious inscription.—CHAMBERS.

PAGE 146, NOTE 138.—The village where a parish church is situated is usually called the Kirkton in Scotland. A certain Jean Kennedy, who kept a reputable public-house in the village of Kirkoswald, is here alluded to.

PAGE 147, NOTE 139.—"Alloway Kirk, with its little enclosed burial ground, stands beside the road from Ayr to Maybole, about two miles from the former town. The church has long been roofless, but the walls are pretty well preserved, and it still retains its bell at the east end. Upon the whole, the spectator is struck with the idea, that the witches must have had a rather narrow stage for the performance of their revels, as described in the poem. The inner area is now divided by a partition-wall, and one part forms the family burial-place of Mr. Catchcart, of Blairston. The 'winnock bunker in the east,' where sat the awful musician of the party, is a conspicuous feature, being a small window, divided by a thick mullion. Around the buiding are the vestiges of other openings, at any of which the hero of the tale may be supposed to have looked in upon the hellish scene. Within the last few years the old oaken rafters of the kirk were mostly entire, but they have now been entirely taken away, to form, in various shapes, memorials of a place so remarkably signalised by genius. It is necessary for those who survey the ground in reference to the poem, to be informed that the old road from Ayr to this spot, by which Burns supposed his hero to have approached Alloway Kirk, was considerably to the west of the present one, which, nevertheless, has existed since before the time of Burns. Upon a field about a quarter of a mile to the north-west of the kirk, is a single tree enclosed with a paling, the last remnant of a group which covered

'———the cairn
Where hunters faud the murdered bairn;'

and immediately beyond that object is

'———the ford,
Where in the snaw the chapman smoor'd;'

namely, a ford over a small burn (which soon after joins the Doon), being two places which Tam o' Shanter is described as having passed on his solitary way. The road then made a sweep towards the river, and, passing a well which trickles down into the Doon, where formerly stood a thorn, on which an individual, called in the poem 'Mungo's mither,' committed suicide, approached Alloway Kirk upon the west. These circumstances may here appear trivial, but it is surprising with what interest any visitor to the real scene will inquire into, and behold every part of which can be associated, however remotely, with the poem of *Tam o' Shanter*. The churchyard contains several old monuments, of a very humble description, marking the resting-places of undistinguished persons. Among those persons rest William Burness, father of the poet, over whose grave the son had piously raised a small stone, recording his name and the date of his death, together with the short poetical tribute to his memory, which is copied in the works of the bard. But, for this monument, long ago destroyed and carried away piecemeal, there is now substituted one of somewhat finer proportions; and the churchyard of Alloway has now become fashionable with the dead, as well as the living. Its little area is absolutely crowded with modern monuments, referring to persons, many of whom have been brought from considerable distances, to take their rest in this doubly consecrated ground. Among these is one to the memory of a person named Tyrie, who, visiting the spot some years ago, happened to express a wish that he might be laid in Alloway churchyard, and, as fate would have it, was interred in the spot he had pointed out within a fortnight. Nor is this all; for even the neighbouring gentry are now contending for departments in this fold of the departed, and it is probable that the elegant mausolea of rank and wealth will soon be jostling with the stunted obelisks of humble worth and noteless poverty."—*Chambers's Journal.*

PAGE 148, NOTE 140.—It is well known that witches, or any other evil spirits, have no power to follow a poor wight any further than the middle of the nearest running stream. And, at the some time, it may not be superfluous to hint to the benighted traveller, that when he is unfortunate enough to fall in with the wierd sisters, or with bogies on his road,—whatever be the danger of going forward, it is far less than that of retreat.—BURNS.

PAGE 148, NOTE 141.—"In my early years nothing less would serve me than courting the tragic muse. I was, I think, about eighteen or nineteen when I sketched the outlines of a tragedy, forsooth: but the bursting of a cloud of family misfortunes, which had for some time threatened us, prevented my farther progress. In those days I never wrote down any thing; so, except a speech or two, the whole has escaped my memory. These lines, which I most distinctly remember, were the exclamation from a great character—great in occasional instances of generosity, and daring at times in villanies. He is supposed to meet with a child of misery, and to burst out into this rhapsody."—BURNS.

PAGE 148, NOTE 142.—"There is scarcely any earthly object gives me more—I do not know if I should call it pleasure—but something which exalts me—something which enraptures me—than to walk on the sheltered side of a wood or plantation, in a cloudy winter's day, and hear the stormy wind howling amongst the trees, and raving over the plain. It is my best season of devotion; my mind is rapt up in a kind of enthusiasm to Him, who in the pompous language of the Hebrew bard, "Walks on the wings of the wind." In one of these seasons, just after a train of misfortunes, I composed *Winter, a Dirge.*—BURNS. According to Gilbert Burns, this is one of Burns's earliest pieces, and he has assigned 1784 as its date.

PAGE 148, NOTE 143.—A quotation from Young.

PAGE 149, NOTE 144.—"There was a period of my life that my spirit was well nigh broken by repeated losses and disasters, which threatened, and indeed effected, the utter ruin of my fortune. My body, too, was attacked by that most dreadful distemper, a hypochondria, or confirmed melancholy. In this wretched state, the recollection of which makes me yet shudder, I hung my harp on the willow trees, except in some lucid intervals, in one of which I composed these lines."—BURNS.

PAGE 149, NOTE 145.—The "Prayer," and the "Stanzas," were composed when fainting fits, and other alarming symptoms of a pleurisy, or some other dangerous disorder (which indeed still threatens me) first put nature on the alarm."—BURNS.

PAGE 149, NOTE 146.—*Ruisseau,* is the French, as Burn is the Scottish, term for stream. *Ruisseaux* is the plural of *Ruisseau,* as *Burns* is of *Burn;* and hence the humorous translation of his own name in the Elegy of Robert Burns.

PAGE 150, NOTE 147.—The Rev. James Steven, afterwards one of the Scotch clergy in London, and ultimately minister of Kilwinning, in Ayrshire, was the hero of this piece of levity. The tradition in the family of Mr. Gavin Hamilton is, that the poet, in passing to the church at Mauchline, called at Mr. Hamilton's, who, being confined with the gout, could not accompany him, but desired him, as parents do with children, to bring home a note of the text. At the conclusion of the service, Burns called again, and, sitting down for a minute at Mr. Hamilton's business table, scribbled these verses, by way of a compliance with the request. From a memorandum by Burns himself, it would appear that there was a wager with Mr. Hamilton as to his producing a poem in a certain time, and that he gained it by producing *The Calf.*

PAGE 150, NOTE 148.—"At the time when Burns was beginning to exercise his powers as a poet, theological controversy raged amongt the clergy and laity of his native country. The prominent points related to the doctrines of original sin and the Trinity; a scarcely subordinate one referred to the right of patronage. Burns took the moderate and liberal side, and seems to have delighted in doing all he could to torment the zealous party, who were designated as the *Auld Lights.* The first of his poetic offspring that saw the light, was a burlesque lamentation on a quarrel between two reverend Calvinists, which he circulated anonymously, and which, "with a certain description of the clergy, as well as laity, met with roars of applause." This was the *Twa Herds.* The heroes of the piece were the Rev. Alexander Moodie, minister of Riccarton, and the Rev. John Russell, minister of a chapel of ease, at Kilmarnock, both of them eminent as leaders of the Auld Light party. In riding home together they got into a warm dispute regarding some point of doctrine, or of discipline, which led to a rupture that appeared nearly incurable. They appear to have afterwards quarrelled about a question of parish boundaries; and when the point was debated in the Presbytery of Irvine, in presence of a great multitude of the people (including Burns), they lost temper entirely, and "abused each other," says Mr. Lockhart, "with a fiery vehemence of personal invective such as has been long banished from all popular assemblies, wherein the laws of courtesy are enforced by those of a certain unwritten code." Allan Cunningham gives a popular story of this quarrel having ultimately come to blows; but if such had been the case, the poet would certainly have adverted to it:—CHAMBERS.

PAGE 150, NOTE 149.—Russell is described as a "large, robust, dark-complexioned man, imperturbably grave, fierce of temper, and of a stern expression of countenance." He preached with much vehemence, and at the height of a tremendous voice, which, in certain states of the atmosphere, caught the ear at the distance of more than a mile. He subsequently became minister at Stirling, where he died at an advanced age.

PAGE 150, NOTE 150.—Dr. Robert Duncan, minister of Dundonald. Excepting in his limbs, which were short, he bore a strong personal resemblance to Charles James Fox.

PAGE 150, NOTE 151.—Rev. William Peebles, of Newton-upon-Ayr. See notes to *Holy Fair*, and *Kirk's Alarm*.

PAGE 150, NOTE 152.—Rev. William Auld, minister of Mauchline.

PAGE 150, NOTE 153.—Rev. Dr. Dalrymple, one of the ministers of Ayr. He died in 1814, having enjoyed his charge for the uncommon period of sixty-eight years.

PAGE 150, NOTE 154.—Rev. William M'Gill, one of the ministers of Ayr, colleague of Dr. Dalrymple. See note to *Kirk's Alarm*.

PAGE 150, NOTE 155.—Minister of St. Quivox, an enlightened man, and elegant preacher. He has been succeeded in the parish by his son.

PAGE 150, NOTE 156.—Dr. Andrew Shaw, of Craigie, and Dr. David Shaw of Croylton. Dr. Andrew was a man of excellent abilities, but extremely diffident—a fine speaker and an accomplished scholar. Dr. David, in personal respects, was a prodigy. He was ninety-one years of age before he required an assistant. At that period of life he read without the use of glasses, wrote a neat small hand, and had not a furrow in his cheek or a wrinkle on his brow. He was Moderator of the General Assembly in 1775. He had a fine old clergymanly-kind of wit. In the house of a man of rank, where he spent the night, an alarm took place after midnight, which brought all the members of the family from their dormitories. The doctor encountered a countess in her chemise, which occasioned some mutual confusion. At breakfast next morning, a lady asked him what he thought when he met the countess in the lobby. "Oh, my lady," said he, "I was in a *trance*." Trance in Scotland signifies a passage or vestibule, as well as a swoon. This amiable man died, April 26, 1810, in the ninety-second year of his age, and sixty-first of his ministry.

PAGE 150, NOTE 157.—There were three brothers of this name, descended from the church historian, and all ministers—one at Eastwood, their ancestor's charge, the second at Stevenston, and the third, Dr. Peter Woodrow, at Tarbolton. Dr. Peter is the person named in the poem. The assistant and successor, mentioned in the verse, was M'Math, elsewhere alluded to.

PAGE 151, NOTE 158.—The Rev. Mr. (afterwards Dr.) Smith, who figures in the *Holy Fair* as one of the tent preachers.

PAGE 151, NOTE 159.—The hero of this daring exposition of Calvanistic theology, was William Fisher, a farmer in the neighbourhood of Mauchline, and an elder in Mr Auld's session. He had signalised himself in the prosecution of Mr. Hamilton, elsewhere alluded to; and Burns appears to have written these verses in retribution of the rancour he had displayed on that occasion. Fisher was, probably, a poor narrow-witted creature, with just sufficient sense to make a show of sanctity. When removed to another parish, and there acting as an elder, he was found guilty of some peculations in the funds of the poor—to which Burns alludes in the *Kirk's Alarm*. Ultimately, coming home one night from market in a cart, in a state of intoxication, he fell from the vehicle, and was found lifeless in a ditch next morning.

PAGE 151, NOTE 160.—These essays were published in exposition of the doctrines of Dr. Mc Gill, so violently persecuted by the heroes of orthodoxy.

PAGE 152, NOTE 161.—Dr. Taylor of Norwich, whose doctrines were advocated by Goudie and McGill.

PAGE 152, NOTE 162.—A hearty partisan of the heterodox theological school, remarkable amongst his fellow-farmers of the neighbourhood, as a jolly companion and humorous, though somewhat coarse satirist of the orthodox heroes. He occupied a farm called Adam hill, near Tarbolton.

PAGE 152, NOTE 163.—"A certain humorous dream of his was then making some noise in the country-side."—BURNS. Mr. Cunningham gives the following account of the dream—"Lord K., it is said, was in the practice of calling all his familiar acquaintances *brutes*. 'Well, ye brute, how are ye to-day?' was his usual mode of salutation. Once in company, his lordship, having indulged in this rudeness more than his wont, turned to Rankine and exclaimed, 'Brute, are ye dumb? have ye no queer sly story to tell us?' 'I have nae story,' said Rankine; 'but last night I had an odd dream.' 'Out with it, by all means,' said the other. 'Aweel, ye see,' said Rankine, 'I dreamed I was dead, and that for keeping other than gude company on earth, I was sent down stairs. When I knocked at the low door, wha should open it but the deil; he was in a rough humour, and said, 'Wha may ye be, and what's your name?' 'My name,' quoth I, 'is John Rankine, and my dwelling-place was Adam-hill.' 'Gae wa' wi' ye,' quoth Satan, 'ye canna be here; ye're ane o' Lord K.'s brutes—hell's fou o' them already.'" This sharp rebuke, it is said, polished for the future his lordship's speech.

PAGE 152, NOTE 164.—Some occurrence is evidently here alluded to. We have heard the following account of it, but cannot vouch for its correctness:—A noted zealot of the opposite party (the name of Holy Willie has been mentioned, but more probably, from the context, the individual must have been a clergyman), calling on Mr. Rankine on business, the latter invited him to take a glass. With much entreaty, the visitor was prevailed on to make a very small modicum of toddy. The stranger remarking that the liquor proved very strong, Mr. Rankine pointed out, as any other landlord would have done, that a little more hot water might improve it. The kettle was accordingly resorted to, but still the liquor appeared over-potent. Again he filled up. Still no diminution of strength. All this time he was sipping and sipping. By and bye, the liquor began to appear only too weak. To cut short a tale, the reluctant guest ended by tumbling dead-drunk on the floor. The trick played upon him, requires, of course, no explanation.—CHAMBERS.

PAGE 152, NOTE 165.—An allusion to some song which had been promised by John Rankine to Burns.

PAGE 152, NOTE 166.—This epistle was first published by Lapraik himself amongst his own works.

PAGE 153, NOTE 167.—At that time enjoying the appointment of *assistant and successor* to the Rev. Peter Woodrow, minister of Tarbolton. He was an excellent preacher, and a decided moderate. He enjoyed the friendship of the Montgomeries of Coilsfield, and of Burns; but unhappily fell into low spirits, in consequence of his dependent situation, and became dissipated. After being for some time tutor to a family in the Western Isles, it is said that this unfortunate man ultimately enlisted as a common soldier.

PAGE 153, NOTE 168.—Gawn, Gawin, Gavin. Alluding to Gavin Hamilton.

PAGE 154, NOTE 169.—All the allusions contained in this poem are of such a nature and refer to such public events as will be readily understood: and there is something exceedingly humorous in the exposition of the views and remarks of the peasantry respecting the great leaders, or great events, which happen to become matters of notoriety.

PAGE 154, NOTE 170.—An allusion to the unanticipated return of a considerable majority of Scottish members in support of William Pitt, upon the election incidental to the opening of his administration.

PAGE 156, NOTE 171.—An incident which actually occurred, and which was witnessed by Burns, at Mauchline, in December 1785.

PAGE 156, NOTE 172.—Lunardi *Bonnet*. The fashions in those days, as in these, were apt to receive denominations from persons or events which had created general sensation. In our time we have our Kossuth, or Klapka hats and the like. Lunardi had made several balloon ascents during the summer of 1785, in Scotland, and as these excited much interest at the time, Lunardi's name was *suivant les regles*, appended to various articles of dress, and to bonnets amongst others.

PAGE 156, NOTE 173.—In May 1785, Mr. Pitt made a considerable addition to the number of taxed articles, amongst which were female servants, in order to liquidate ten millions of unfunded debt. The poem seems to have been called forth by the receipt of the next annual mandate from Mr. Aiken, of Ayr, surveyor of taxes for the district.

PAGE 156, NOTE 174.—The off fore horse, or leader, in the plough.

PAGE 156, NOTE 175.—The off draught horse in the plough.

PAGE 156, NOTE 176.—The familiar expression for Kilmarnock, amongst the peasantry.

PAGE 156, NOTE 177.—The near wheel horse in the plough.

PAGE 157 NOTE 178.—An allusion to one of the questions (namely "What is effectual calling?") in the Catechism propounded by the Westminster Assembly of Divines, and which continues to preserve its currency throughout Scotland.

PAGE 157, NOTE 179.—A child born to the poet by a servant girl of the name of Elizabeth Paton. She grew up exceedingly like her father, and became the wife of Mr. John Bishop, overseer at Polkemmet in Linlithgowshire, and died there, Dec. 8, 1817.

PAGE 157, NOTE 180.—Tootie lived in Mauchline, and dealt in cows. The age of these animals is marked by rings on their horns, which may of course be cut and polished off, so as to cause the cow to appear younger than it is. This villainy is called *sneck-drawing*, and he who perpetrates it is a sneck-drawer.

PAGE 157. NOTE 181.—The airless—earnest money. (See also Glossary.)

PAGE 157, NOTE 182.—A writer in Ayr, and particular friend of the poet, Mr. Chalmers, asked Burns to write a poetic epistle in his behalf to a young lady whom he admired. Burns, who had seen the lady, but was scarcely acquainted with her, complied by penning the above.—CHAMBERS.

PAGE 185, NOTE 183.—"These verses, in the handwriting of Burns, are copied from a bank note, in the possession of Mr. James F. Gracie, of Dumfries. The note is of the Bank of Scotland, and is dated so far back as 1st March 1780. The lines exhibit the strong marks of the poet's vigorous pen, and are evidently an extempore effusion of his characteristic feelings. They bear internal proof of their having been written at that interesting period of his life, when he was on the point of leaving the country on account of the unfavourable manner in which his proposals for marrying his 'bonny Jean' (his future wife) were at first received by her parents."—MOTHERWELL.

PAGE 138, NOTE 184.—There is some doubt as to the authenticity of these pretty lines. It has been averred upon very good authority that the manuscript in the hand writing of Robert Burns, is yet extant, and in the possession of Mr. A———. At any rate, as the verses are not unworthy of the bard of Ayr, they may be accepted. They were first published at Liverpool, in a periodical called the *Kaleidoscope*.

PAGE 158, NOTE 185.—These verses appear to have been written in the distressing summer of 1786, when the poet's prospects were at the dreariest, and the very wife of his fondest affections had forsaken him. From the time, and other circumstances, we may conjecture that the present alluded to was a copy of the Kilmarnock edition of poems, then newly published. The verses appeared in the *Sun* newspaper, April 1823. — CHAMBERS.

PAGE 158, NOTE 186.—"The first time Robert heard the spinnet played upon, was at the house of Dr. Laurie, minister of Loudon (about October 1786). Dr. L. had several daughters—one of them played; the father and the mother led down the dance; the rest of the sisters, the brother, the poet, and the other guests, mixed in it. It was a delightful family scene for our poet, then lately introduced to the world. His mind was roused to a poetic enthusiasm, and the stanzas were left in the room where he slept."—GILBERT BURNS. Dr. Laurie was the medium through which Dr. Blacklock transmitted the letter, by which Burns was arrested on his flight to the West Indies, and induced to go to Edinburgh. This letter has since been in the possession of the Rev. Mr. Balfour Graham, minister of North Berwick, who is connected with the family by marriage. Dr. Laurie, and his son, who was his successor in the pastoral charge of the parish. are both deceased.

PAGE 159, NOTE 187.—Diogenes.

PAGE 159, NOTE 188.—This meeting took place, October 23, 1786, at Catrine, the seat of Professor Stewart, to which Burns was now taken for the first time by Mr. Mackenzie, surgeon, Mauchline. Lord Daer, who was eldest son to Dunbar, fourth Earl of Selkirk, and had been a pupil of Mr. Stewart, was a young nobleman of the greatest promise. He had just returned from France, where he cultivated the society of some of those men who afterwards figured in the Revolution, and had contracted their sentiments. He was cut off in November, 1794, leaving the succession open to his younger brother, the late Thomas, Earl of Selkirk, distinguished by his exertions in the cause of emigration.—CHAMBERS.

PAGE 159, NOTE 189.—Major Logan, a retired military officer, still remembered in Ayrshire for his wit and humour—of which two specimens may be given. Asked by an Ayr hostess if he would have water to the glass of spirits she was bringing to him on his order, he said, with a grin, "No, I would rather you took the water out o't." Visited on his deathbed by Mr. Cuthill, one of the ministers of Ayr, who remarked that it would take *fortitude* to support such sufferings as he was visited with; "Ay," said the poor wit, "it would take *fiftitude*." At the time when the above letter was addressed to him, Major Logan lived at Parkhouse, in Ayrshire, with his mother and sister, the Miss Logan to whom Burns presented a copy of Beattie's Poems, with verses. The major was a capital violinist.

PAGE 160, NOTE 190.—With the characteristic humour with which he wrote the elegy and epitaph of Thomas Samson and his own elegy, Burns wrote this address to himself, when he anticipated his departure for the West Indies, and before the brilliant career of his reception at Edinburgh had fixed his views as to life.

PAGE 161, NOTE 191.—The haggis is a dish peculiar to Scotland, though supposed to be of French extraction. It is composed of minced offal of mutton, mixed with oatmeal and suet, and boiled in a sheep's stomach. When made in *Elspa's* way, with "a curn o' spice" (see the *Gentle Shepherd*), it is an agreeable, albeit a somewhat heavy dish, always providing that no horror be felt at the idea of its preparation. The *Edinburgh Literary Journal* of November 7, 1829, makes the following statement:—"About sixteen years ago, there resided at Mauchline a Mr. Robert Morrison, cabinet-maker. He was a great crony of Burns, and it was in Mr. Morrison's house that the poet usually spent the 'mids o' the day' on Sunday. It was in this house that he wrote his celebrated *Address to a Haggis*, after partaking liberally of that dish, as prepared by Mrs. Morrison." The Ettrick Shepherd has, on the contrary, averred that the poem was written in the house of Mr. Andrew Bruce, Castle Hill, Edinburgh, after in like manner partaking of the dish. It was first published in the *Scots Magazine* for January 1787.

PAGE 162, NOTE 192.—Miss Logan, sister of Major Logan, to whom also Burns had previously addressed a poetical epistle. (See antea, page 159.)

PAGE 162, NOTE 193.—Mr. Ilay Campbell, of whom we have had several occasions to speak as the subject of complimentary allusions. He was subsequently president of the Court of Cession, and died in 1823.

PAGE 162, NOTE 194.—The Honourable Henry Erskine, whose talents as an advocate had secured him a distinguished reputation. He died in 1817.

PAGE 162, NOTE 195.—Mrs. Scott of Wauchope, in Roxburgshire—a lady of taste and talent, and fitted to use the pencil as well as the pen—had addressed (February 1787) the lines, printed in small type, to Burns, which called forth the ensuing verses, as a reply or acknowledgment.

PAGE 163, NOTE 196.—Mr. Woods had been the friend of Fergusson. He was long a favourite actor in Edinburgh, and was himself a man of some poetical talent. He died, at his house on the Terrace, Edinburgh, December 14, 1802.

PAGE 164, NOTE 197.—The hero of Mackenzie's *Man of Feeling*, of which Burns always spoke in such warm terms of admiration.

PAGE 164, NOTE 198.—Written at Selkirk, May 1787, in the course of the poet's southern tour. Mr. Creech was the poet's Edinburgh publisher, and seems at this time to have been in high favour with him. Burns afterwards found reason considerably to change his feelings towards Creech, who appears to have given him much uneasiness by protracting the settlement of their accounts. The truth is, that Mr. Creech, though a man of literary talent, great pleasantry as a companion, and the first publisher of his day, had a weakness about money matters, and could scarcely draw upon his ample funds for the liquidation of an ordinary debt, without something more than all-common persuasives. He enjoyed high reputation as a teller of quaint stories, and lived on familiar terms with many of the literary men of his day. His house, in one of the elevated floors of a tenement in the High Street, accessible from a wretched alley called Craig's Close, was frequented in the mornings by company of that kind, to such an extent that the meeting used to be called *Creech's Levee*. Burns here enumerates as attending it, Dr. James Gregory, author of the *Conspectus Medicinæ;* Tytler, of Woodhouselee, author of the Defence of of Mary Queen of Scots; Dr. William Greenfield, professor of rhetoric in the Edinburgh University; Henry Mackenzie, author of *The Man of Feeling;* and Dugald Stewart, professor of moral philosophy. Mr. Creech more than once filled the chair of Lord Provost of Edinburgh, and is noted as the only person who ever saved money off the salary then attached to the office. With reference to his penurious bachelorly habits, a native caricaturist once set the town in a roar by depicting, in connection, the respective kitchens of the chief magistrates of London and Edinburgh, the former exhibiting every appearance of plenty that could be expected in a large and munificent establishment, and the latter displaying a poor old pinched housekeeper spinning beside a narrow fire-place, where the cat was perched for warmth upon *a gathering coal.* Mr. Creech died in 1815, aged 70 years.—CHAMBERS.

PAGE 164, NOTE 199.—Edinburgh.

PAGE 164, NOTE 200.—The Chamber of Commerce of Edinburgh, of which Mr. Creech was secretary.

PAGE 165, NOTE 201.—James Hunter Blair was born at Ayr, in 1741. He pursued a successful commercial career, and became a member of the banking firm of Sir William Forbes and Co., and died on the first of July, 1787, universally esteemed.

PAGE 165, NOTE 202.—The Royal Park of Holyrood.

PAGE 165, NOTE 203.—St. Anthony's Well.

PAGE 165, NOTE 204.—St. Anthony's Chapel.

PAGE 166, NOTE 205.—"The first object of interest that occurs upon the public road after leaving Blair, is a chasm in the hill on the right hand, through which the little river Bruar falls in a series of beautiful cascades. Formerly, the falls of the Bruar were unadorned by wood; but the poet Burns, being conducted to see them (September 1787), after visiting the Duke of Athole, recommended that they should be invested with that necessary decoration. Accordingly, trees have been thickly planted along the chasm, and are now far advanced to maturity. Throughout this young forest, a walk has been cut, and a number of fantastic little grottoes erected for the conveniency of those who visit the spot. The river not only makes several distinct falls, but rushes on through a channel, whose roughness and rugged sublimity adds greatly to the merits of the scene, as an object of interest among tourists." —*Picture of Scotland.*

PAGE 167, NOTE 206.—Robert Dundas of Arniston, elder brother of Viscount Melville; born 1713, appointed president in 1760, and died December 13, 1787, after a short illness. Burns sent a copy of the poem to Dundas's son, afterwards Lord Advocate and Lord Chief Baron, but received no answer to it, which he greatly resented.

PAGE 168, NOTE 207.—Printer, Edinburgh—author of the Philosophy of Natural History, and member of the Scottish Antiquarian Society. He died in 1795, in the fifty-fifth year of his age.

PAGE 168, NOTE 208.—A club to which Burns and Smellie belonged, and which met in Douglas's tavern in the Anchor Close, Edinburgh. It took its name of *Crochallan Fencibles* from a beautiful plaintive Highland air, *Cro Chalein*—literally Colin's Cattle—which Douglas occasionally sang with much effect to his guests.

PAGE 168, NOTE 209.—William Tytler, Esq. of Woodhouselee (born 1711, died 1792), a member of the Society of Writers to the Signet, had published in 1759 "An Enquiry, Historical and Critical, into the Evidence against Mary Queen of Scots," in which the favourable side of her case is adopted.

PAGE 169, NOTE 210.—One of a series intended for a projected work, under the title of *The Poet's Progress.* These lines were sent as a specimen, accompanied by a letter, to Professor Dugald Stewart, in which it is thus noticed:—"The fragment beginning, a little, upright, pert, tart, &c., I have not shown to any man living, till I now send it to you. It forms the postulata, the axioms, the definition of a character, which, if it appear at all, shall be placed in a variety of lights. This particular part I send you, merely as a sample of my hand at portrait sketching.

PAGE 169, NOTE 211.—For more explicit particulars in respect of Miss Cruickshank, to whom these lines are addressed, the reader is referred to the notes on the song entitled the *Rosebud.*

PAGE 169, NOTE 212.—It is somewhat remarkable how comparatively few of the pieces written by Burns from this time forward have been addressed directly to "Clarinda," whose influence over him is so powerfully evinced in the letters (already mentioned in that portion of this volume which is devoted to the poet's correspondence), which passed between him and this fair object of admiration. In the foregoing notes to the life we have already had occasion to enter into some particulars respecting the career of Mrs. McLehose (Clarinda), and we shall have further occasion to allude to her hereafter, on which account great detail in this place would be superfluous. It should, however, be remarked that the beautiful song *My Nannie's awa,* and some others of the most exquisite productions of Burns, were dedicated to his passion for Clarinda, although she be not directly invoked.

PAGE 170, NOTE 213.—An early friend of Burns at Kilmarnock. These lines were written in the year 1788, at the period when Burns was commencing his household and farming career at Ellisland.

PAGE 170, NOTE 214.—The first of these sets of verses was written in June, and the second in December, 1788, with reference to a hermitage in the grounds of Friars' Carse, near Ellisland, the seat of the poet's friend, Captain Riddel of Glenriddel.

PAGE 171, NOTE 215.—Captain Riddel had, in the course of poring over a newspaper, fallen upon some critical remarks respecting some production of Burns, and had accordingly despatched the paper to the poet, that he might have an opportunity of observing what was said of him. And it was in returning this paper that Burns accompanied it with the comical note in verse, entitled an "Extempore to Captain Riddel."

PAGE 171, NOTE 216.—"The Mother's Lament was composed partly with a view to Mrs. Fergusson of Craigdarroch, and partly to the worthy patroness of my early unknown muse, Mrs. Stewart of Afton."—BURNS.

PAGE 172, NOTE 217.—"In January last (1789), on my road to Ayrshire, I had to put up at Bailie Wigham's in Sanquhar, the only tolerable inn in the place. The frost was keen, and the grim evening and howling wind were ushering in a night of snow and drift. My horse and I were both much fatigued with the labours of the day; and, just as my friend the bailie and I were bidding defiance to the storm, over a smoking bowl, in wheels the funeral pageantry of the late Mrs. Oswald; and poor I am forced to brave all the terrors of the tempestuous night, and jade my horse—my young favourite horse, whom I had just christened Pegasus—farther on through the wildest hills and moors of Ayrshire to the next inn! The powers of poetry and prose sank under me when I would describe what I felt. Suffice it to say, that when a good fire at New Cumnock had so far recovered my frozen sinews, I sat down and wrote the enclosed ode."—BURNS.

PAGE 172, NOTE 218.—Mr. James Tennant had been an early and constant friend of Robert Burns and his family, and had taken an active part in the selection of the farm of Ellisland for the poet.

PAGE 173, NOTE 219.—Mr. Cunningham mentions that the poor animal whose sufferings excited this burst of indignation on the part of the poet, was shot by a lad named James Thomson, son of a farmer near Ellisland. Burns, who was walking beside the Nith at the moment, execrated the young man, and spoke of throwing him into the water.

PAGE 174, NOTE 220.—At the period at which this biting and well-directed rebuke from the pen of Burns appeared, the neighbourhood, and, in fact, the whole Scottish Kirk was agitated by the most violent controversy, and the Ecclesiastical Courts were engrossed with the persecution vindictively instituted against Dr. William McGill. This was about the month of August, 1789. The original ground of this controversy, in which Dr. McGill was now figuring, was this:—In 1786 he had published a treatise, entitled, *A Practical Essay on the Death of Jesus Christ, in two Parts—1. Containing the History—2. The Doctrine of his Death.* Dr. McGill was at that time one of the ministers of the parochial church of Ayr, and his treatise was alleged to be fraught with Arian and Socinian doctrines, which were deemed injurious to the interests of the clergy. Dr. McGill thus became the butt of many attacks levelled, partly at his person and character, and partly at his work; but he took little or no notice of any of these sallies, until a minister, who had hitherto been a warm and personal friend, became his most bitter assailant. This was Dr. William Peebles, of Newton-upon-Ayr, who in his centenary sermon, preached on the 5th of November, 1788, gratuitously denounced the treatise as heretical, and Dr. McGill as a person "who with one hand received the privileges of the church, while with the other he was endeavouring to plunge the keenest poignard into her heart." McGill published a defence, which led, in April, 1789, to the introduction of the case into the presbyterial court of Ayr, and subsequently into that of the Synod of Glasgow and Ayr. Meanwhile, the public out of doors was agitating the question with the keenest interest, and the strife of the liberal and zealous parties in the church had reached a painful extreme. It was now that Burns took up the pen in behalf of McGill, whom, it is probable, he sincerely looked on as a worthy and enlightened person suffering an unworthy persecution. The war raged, till, in April 1790, the case came on for trial before the Synod, when McGill stopped further procedure, by giving in a document, expressive of his deep regret for the disquiet he had occasioned, explaining the challenged passages of his book, and declaring his adherence to the standards of the church on the points of doctrine in question. Dr. McGill died March 30th, 1807, at the age of seventy-six, and in the forty-sixth year of his ministry.—*Abridged from Murray's Literary History of Galloway.*

PAGE 174, NOTE 221.—Dr. McGill.

PAGE 174, NOTE 222.—Upon the commencement of the proceedings against Dr. McGill before the Synod, the municipal authorities of Ayr published a testimonial in the newspapers, averring their high esteem for the defendant, both as a man and a minister.

PAGE 174, NOTE 223.—Mr. John Ballantine, the Provost of the town of Ayr, who had taken an active part in the demonstration in favour of Dr. McGill.

PAGE 174, NOTE 224.—It was by Mr. Robert Aiken (the lawyer, the friend of Burns, and he to whom the "Cotters' Saturday Night" is dedicated) that Dr. Mc Gill was defended before the Synod. Mr. Aiken, as we have before had occasion to remark, was not a little distinguished for his eloquence as an advocate.

PAGE 174, NOTE 225.—Dr. William Dalrymple, as remarkable for his humble, modest demeanour, as for his superior talents and worth. He was senior minister to the collegiate church of Ayr.

PAGE 174, NOTE 226.—John Russell, the preacher, who also figures in the *Holy Fair.*

PAGE 174, NOTE 227.—The Rev. James McKim, who figures as the hero of the *Ordination.*

PAGE 174, NOTE 228.—Alexander Moodie, the minister of Riccarton, who figures also in the *Twa Herds.*

PAGE 174. NOTE 229.—The Rev. Mr. Auld, of Mauchline.

PAGE 174, NOTE 230.—The clerk was Mr. Gavin Hamilton, whose defence against the charges preferred by Mr. Auld, had occasioned much trouble to this clergyman.

PAGE 174, NOTE 231.—Mr. Grant, of Ochiltree.

PAGE 174, NOTE 232.—Mr. Young, of Cumnock.

PAGE 174, NOTE 233.—The Rev. Dr. Peebles. He had excited some ridicule by a line in a poem on the Centenary of the Revolution:

'And bound in *Liberty's* endearing *chain.*"

The poetry of this gentleman is said to have been indifferent. He translated the *Davidies* of Cowley, which some of his brethren, not exactly understanding what was meant, took the liberty of calling *Dr. Peebles' "Daft Ideas.*"—CHAMBERS.

PAGE 174, NOTE 234.—"Dr. Andrew Mitchell, Monkton. He was so rich as to be able to keep his carriage. Extreme love of money, and a strange confusion of ideas, characterised this presbyter. In his prayer for the royal family, he would express himself thus:—"Bless the King—his Majesty the Queen—her Majesty the Prince of Wales." The word chemistry he pronounced in three different ways—hemistry, shemistry, and tchemistry—but never, by any chance, in the right way. Notwithstanding the antipathy he could scarcely help feeling towards Burns, one of the poets' comic verses would make him laugh heartily, and confess that, "after all, he was a droll fellow."—CHAMBERS.

PAGE 174, NOTE 235.—Rev. Mr. Stephen Young, of Barr.

PAGE 174, NOTE 236.—Rev. Mr. George Smith, of Galston. This gentleman is praised as friendly to common sense in the *Holy Fair.* The offence which was taken at that praise probably embittered the poet against him.

PAGE 174, NOTE 237.—Mr. John Shepherd, of Muirkirk. The statistical account of Muirkirk contributed by this gentleman to Sir John Sinclair's work, is above the average in intelligence, and very agreeably written. He had, however, an unfortunate habit of saying rude things, which he mistook for wit, and thus laid himself open to Burns's satire.

PAGE 174, NOTE 238.—The poor elder, William Fisher, whom Burns has so often scourged.

PAGE 175, NOTE 239.—Robert Heron, who afterwards became a well-known author by profession, and died in misery, in London, in 1807.

PAGE 175, NOTE 240.—Waited for.

PAGE 175, NOTE 241.—This small piece, which was an imitation, was forwarded to the *Star* Newspaper for publication in the month of May, 1789; and it was in recompense for this contribution, that Burns was put on the free list, and supplied with the paper gratuitously, which, however, he received very irregularly. In allusion to the very uncertain manner in which the paper was delivered to him, he addressed the subjoined lines, on one occasion, to the publisher:—

Dear Peter, dear Peter,
We poor sons of metre
Are often negleckit, ye ken;
For instance, your sheet, man,
Though glad I'm to see't man,
I get it no ane day in ten.

PAGE 175, NOTE 242.—"Mrs. Dunlop, daughter and heiress of Sir Thomas Wallace, of Craigie, and at this time widow of John Dunlop, of Dunlop, in Ayrshire, and resident at the last mentioned place, became acquainted with Burns on the publication of his poems at Kilmarnock, and was ever after his steady friend. She was a woman of excellent understanding and heart, with a considerable taste for elegant literature. She died in 1815, at the age of eighty-four.

PAGE 176, NOTE 243.—Subsequently Major General Dunlop, of Dunlop.

PAGE 176, NOTE 244.—Rachel, daughter of Mrs. Dunlop, was engaged upon an imaginative sketch of Burns's Muse, Coila.

PAGE 177, NOTE 245.—A mare, the property of Mr. William Nicol, and lent by that gentleman to Burns, in whose keeping it became ill, and died at his farm, of Ellisland.

PAGE 178, NOTE 246.—This piece was published in a newspaper, and from that time forward remained unnoticed until it was reproduced in Chambers's Edition of Burns's Works.

PAGE 178, NOTE 247.—The parallel between these lines and those of Johnson, as follow, cannot escape the reader:—

In bed we laugh, in bed we cry,
And born in bed, in bed we die;
The near approach a bed may show,
Of human bliss and human woe.

PAGE 179, NOTE 248.—At the general election, 1790, the representation of the five boroughs of Dumfries, Annan, Kirkcudbright, Sanquhar, and Lochmaben, forming one electoral district, was contested by Sir James Johnstone, of Westerhall, in the ministerial or Tory, and Captain Patrick Miller, the younger, of Dalswinton, in the Whig or opposition interest. Burns, who was friendly to the latter party, here allegorises the contest; characterising Dumfries as Maggy on the banks of Nith; Annan, as Bess of Annandale; Kirkcudbright, as Whisky Jean of Galloway; Sanquhar, as Black Joan frae Chrichton Peel; and Lochmaben as Marjory of the many lochs—appellations, all of which have some appropriateness from local circumstances. The contest was decided in favour of Captain Miller.

PAGE 179, NOTE 249.—Sir J. Johnstone.

PAGE 179, NOTE 250.—Captain Miller.

PAGE 179, NOTE 251.—King George the Third.

PAGE 179, NOTE 252.—George, Prince of Wales, afterwards Regent, and King George the Fourth.

PAGE 180, NOTE 253.—This is a description of the contest alluded to in the preceding poem. "Drumlanrig," is the infamous fourth Duke of Queensberry. "Westerha," is Sir James Johnstone, the Tory candidate. M'Murdo, was the Duke of Queensberry's chamberlain at Drumlanrig—a friend of the poet. "Craigdarroch," is Fergusson, of Craigdarroch. "Glenriddel," is Captain Riddel, of Glenriddel, another friend of the poet. "Staig," was the provost of Dumfries; "Welsh," the sheriff of the county.

PAGE 180, NOTE 254.—A piece of ordnance, of extraordinary structure and magnitude, founded in the reign of James IV. of Scotland, about the end of the fifteenth century, and which is still exhibited, though in an infirm state, in Edinburgh castle. The diameter of the mouth is twenty inches.

PAGE 180, NOTE 255.—The "Bullers of Buchan" is an appellation given to a tremendous rocky recess on the Aberdeenshire coast, near Peterhead—having an opening to the sea while the top is open. The sea, constantly raging in it, gives it the appearance of a pot or boiler, and hence the name.

PAGE 181, NOTE 256.—The executioner of Charles I. of England, who, as was the custom, was masked.

PAGE 181, NOTE 257.—John, Earl of Dundee.

PAGE 181, NOTE 258.—The illustrious Graham, Earl, and afterwards Marquis, of Montrose.

PAGE 181, NOTE 259.—Francis Grose, author of the Antiquities of England, Ireland, and Scotland, and of several other publications, some of which display considerable knowledge of mankind, wit, and humour, became acquainted with Burns at Captain Riddel's mansion at Friar's Carse, while making the necessary inquiries for his work on Scottish antiquities. He was a bon-vivant, and had acquired enormous personal bulk. Captain Grose died at Dublin, of an apopletic fit, May 12, 1791, in the fifty-second year of his age.

PAGE 181, NOTE 260.—The extreme parish on the southern frontier of Scotland is called *Kirkmaiden*, of which this word *Maidenkirk* is a mere transposition. Kirkmaiden parish is in Wigtonshire.

PAGE 182, NOTE 261.—One of the old traditional Scottish ballads entitled *Sir John Malcolm*, furnished Burns with the rhythmical model of this piece.

PAGE 182, NOTE 262.—This poem came through the hands of Rankine of Adamhill to those of a gentleman of Ayr, who gave it to the world in the *Edinburgh Magazine* for February 1818, with the following original superscription:—"To the Right Honourable the Earl of Breadalbane, President of the Right Honourable and Honourable the Highland Society, which met on the 23rd of May last, at the Shakspeare, Covent-Garden, to concert ways and means to frustrate the designs of five hundred Highlanders, who, as the society were informed by Mr. M——, of A——s, were so audacious as to attempt an escape from their lawful lords and masters, whose property they were, by emigrating from the lands of Mr. M'Donald, of Glengarry, to the wilds of Canada, in search of that fantastic thing—LIBERTY."

PAGE 183, NOTE 263.—"As the authentic prose history of the *Whistle* is curious, I shall here give it. In the train of Anne of Denmark, when she came to Scotland with our James VI., there came over also a Danish gentleman of gigantic stature and great prowess, and a matchless champion of Bacchus. He had a little ebony whistle, which, at the commencement of the orgies, he laid on the table, and whoever was the last able to blow it, every body else being disabled by the potency of the bottle, was to carry off the whistle as a trophy of victory. The Dane produced credentials of his victories, without a single defeat, at the courts of Copenhagen, Stockholm, Moscow, Warsaw, and several of the petty courts in Germany; and challenged the Scots Bacchanalians to the alternative of trying his prowess, or else of acknowledging their inferiority. After many overthrows on the part of the Scots, the Dane was encountered by Sir Robert Lawrie of Maxwelton, ancestor of the present worthy baronet of that name; who, after three days' and three nights' hard contest, left the Scandinavian under the table,

'And blew on the whistle his requiem shrill.'

Sir Walter, son of Sir Robert before mentioned, afterwards lost the whistle to Walter Riddel, of Glenriddel, who had married a sister of Sir Walter's. On Friday the 16th of October 1790, at Friar's-Carse, the whistle was once more contended for, as related in the ballad, by the present Sir Robert, of Maxwelton: Robert Riddel, Esq., of Glenriddel, lineal descendant, and representative of Walter Riddel, who won the whistle, and in whose family it had continued; and Alexander Fergusson, Esq., of Craigdarroch, likewise descended from the great Sir Robert; which last gentleman carried off the hard-won honours of the field." —BURNS. [The whistle is kept at this day by the Right Honourable R. C. Fergusson, of Craigdarroch, M.P. for the Stewartry of Kirkcudbright—son of the victor.]

The Rhenish Legends supply us with two or three analogous stories, in which certain cups or tankards figure, and of which they commemorate the facts in their preservation.

PAGE 183, NOTE 264.—Vide the Cariothura of Ossian.

PAGE 183, NOTE 265.—Johnson's Tour to the Hebrides.

PAGE 184, NOTE 266.—James, fourteenth Earl of Glencairn, and in whose younger brother this ancient title became extinct in 1796, was a Whig nobleman of great generosity of disposition. He died unmarried at Falmouth, January 30th, 1791, in the forty-second year of his age. Burns, who considered himself greatly indebted to Glencairn, put on mourning for his death, wrote this beautiful poem to his memory, and called a son after him, now Major James Glencairn Burns, of the East India Company's service.

PAGE 186, NOTE 267.—Alexander Monroe, Professor of Anatomy to the University of Edinburgh.

PAGE 186, NOTE 268.—The favour which formed the burthen of the foregoing poetical epistle, was the translation of the poet from the fatiguing Excise division of Ellisland, to the less laborious one of Dumfries, which favour is acknowledged as having been obtained, in these lines.

PAGE 186, NOTE 269.—An allusion to the decline of the fashion which was so prevalent during the last century amongst gentlemen, to drink to excess, swear, and indulge in other equally delicate amusements, and in which the squirearchy so eminently shone. It was this fashion which had been so severely satirized by Fielding in his novels.

PAGE 186, NOTE 270.—The ruins of Lincluden church, near Dumfries.

PAGE 188, NOTE 271.—Though found among the papers of Burns, in his own hand-writing, and printed as his in some former editions, the present editor has scarcely a doubt that this poem is not by the Ayrshire bard. It is much more like the composition of Fergusson, or Beattie.

PAGE 188, NOTE 272.—This piece was first published in the edition of Burns's Works, produced by Messrs Chambers, and was contributed by Mr. James Duncan, of Mosesfield, near Glasgow, in whose possession is the original manuscript.

PAGE 189, NOTE 273.—When General Dumourier, after unparalled victories, left the army of the French Republic, April 1793, and took refuge from the infuriated Convention, with the enemies he had lately beaten, some one expressing joy in the event where Burns was present, he chanted almost extempore the sarcastic stanzas of the text.

PAGE 189, NOTE 274.—Captain Riddel, of Glenriddel, or Mr. Riddel of Woodlee park, which is not very decidly ascertained. In either case, we are informed that the parties were reconciled.

PAGE 189, NOTE 275.—The Maria of this lampoon, and that which follows, was Mrs. Riddel, of Woodlee park, a lady of poetical talent and taste, with whom the poet was generally on the best terms, but who had temporarily repudiated him from her society, in consequence of an act of rudeness committed by him when elevated with liquor. She is the lady alluded to by Dr. Currie, of whom Burns, amongst his last days at Brow, asked if she had any commands for the other world, and who wrote the beautiful paper on his death, which first appeared in the *Dumfries Journal*, and was afterwards transferred entire to Currie's Memoir.

PAGE 190, NOTE 276.—By Æsopus, is meant an actor of the name of Williamson.

PAGE 190, NOTE 277.—Gillespie.

PAGE 190, NOTE 278.—Colonel Mc Dowal, of Logan.

PAGE 191, NOTE 279.—Burns also inscribed the following lines on the windows of a grotto in Captain Riddel's grounds:—

To Riddel, much-lamented man,
This ivied cot was dear;
Reader, dost value matchless worth?
This ivied cot revere.

PAGE 191, NOTE 280.—Mrs. Riddel, of Woodlee.

PAGE 191, NOTE 281.—These lines were written in the fly-leaf of a copy of Thomson's Select Scottish Melodies, presented to Miss Graham, by Robert Burns.

PAGE 192, NOTE 282.—On the night of December the 4th, 1795.

PAGE 193, NOTE 283.—The heroine of several of his songs. Her name was Jean Lorimer, her father being a farmer at Kemeyss-Hall, near Dumfries. Burns seems to have formed an acquaintance with her during his stay at Ellisland, as there is still a pane in the eastern room of that house, bearing her name, and that of her lover John Gillespie, inscribed by her own hand, during a visit she paid there. She afterwards formed an unfortunate alliance with a Mr. Whelpdale, from whom she soon separated. At the time when the following stanzas were addressed to her, she was living in retirement at Dumfries, under depression of spirits, the consequence of her recent domestic unhappiness. Further information respecting this elegant, but unfortunate woman, is given elsewhere.

PAGE 193, NOTE 284.—On the death of General Stewart, representative of the Stewartry of Kirkcudbright, in January 1795, Mr. Heron, of Kerroughtree, a zealous Whig, and a friend of Burns, became candidate for the vacant seat. He was opposed by Gordon of Balmaghie, but gained his election. The third ballad relates to his contest at the general election of 1796, with the Hon. Montgomery Stewart. He was likewise elected on that occasion, but unseated by a committee. It is to be remarked, that the satirical allusions in these ballads, are almost all founded merely in party bitterness, not in truth.

PAGE 194, NOTE 285.—John Busby, of Tinwold Downs.

PAGE 194, NOTE 286.—Alluding to Busby's brother, whose fortune, as it was said, was founded before his emigration to the East Indies, in some transactions in which the Ayr bank was concerned.

PAGE 194, NOTE 287.—Mr. Maxwell, of Cardoness.

PAGE 194, NOTE 288.—Mr. Douglas, of Carlingwark, gave the name of Castle Douglas to a village which rose in his neighbourhood, and which has since become a considerable and thriving town.

PAGE 194, NOTE 289.—Alluding to Mr. John Syme, an intimate friend of Robert Burns.

PAGE 194, NOTE 290.—*Troggin* is a term applied, in Scotland to the various wares carried about by hawkers, who, in the same provincialism, are called *troggers*.

PAGE 194, NOTE 291.—The Earl of Galloway.

PAGE 194, NOTE 292.—Mr. Murray of Broughton.

PAGE 195, NOTE 293.—One of the candidates in this election—Mr. Gordon of Balmaghie.

PAGE 194, NOTE 294.—Alluding somewhat severely, to Busby, of Tinwold.

PAGE 195, NOTE 295.—Burns here alludes to a brother wit, the Rev. Mr. Muirhead, minister of Urr, in Galloway. The hit applied very well, for Muirhead was a wind-dried, unhealthy looking little man, very proud of his genealogy, and ambitious of being acknowledged, on all occasions, as the chief of *the Muirheads!* He was not disposed, however, to sit down with the affront: on the contrary, he replied to it in a virulent diatribe, which may be presented as a remarkable specimen of clerical and poetical irritability; and curious, moreover as perhaps the only contemporary satire upon Burns of which the world has ever heard, except the immortal "trimming letter" from a tailor. Dr. Muirhead's *jeu d'esprit* is in the shape of a translation from Martial's ode, *Ad Vacerram.*

"Vacerras, shabby son of whore,
Why do thy patrons keep thee poor?
Thou art a sycophant and traitor,
A liar, and calumniator,
Who conscience (hadst thou that) wouldst sell,
Nay lave the common sewers of hell
For whisky. Like most precious imp,
Thou art a *gauger*, rhymster, pimp.—
How comes it then, Vacerras, that
Thou still art poor as a church rat?"—
CHAMBERS.

PAGE 195, NOTE 296.—Burns was a private in the volunteer yoeman corps of Dumfries, of which Colonel De Peyster was the commanding officer.

PAGE 195, NOTE 297.—A monument about to be erected by Mr. Heron, of Kerroughtree, in his own grounds.

PAGE 195, NOTE 298.—Alluding to an only daughter, who died in the autumn of 1795, and so far removed from his residence, as to render it impossible for him to visit her at the last. She died, moreover, very suddenly.

PAGE 196, NOTE 299.—The Honourable Henry Erskine was elected Dean of the Faculty of Advocates in 1786, and unanimously re-elected every year till 1796, when it was resolved by some members of the Tory party at the Scottish bar to oppose his re-election, in consideration of his having aided in getting up a petition against the passing of the well-known sedition bills. Mr. Erskine's appearance at the Circus (now the Adelphi Theatre) on that occasion was designated by those gentlemen (among whom were Charles Hope and David Boyle, now respectively Lord President and Lord Justice-Clarke) as "agitating the giddy and ignorant multitude, and cherishing such humours and dispositions as directly tend to overturn the laws." They brought forward Mr. Robert Dundas, of Arniston, Lord Advocate, in opposition to Mr. Erskine; and at the election, January 12th, 1796, the former gained the day by 123 against 38 votes. The following verses by Burns describe the keenness of the contest. The mortification of the displaced dean was so extreme, that he that evening, with a coal-axe, hewed off from his door in Prince's street, a brass-plate on which his designation as Dean of Faculty was inscribed. It is not impossible, that, in characterising Mr. Dundas so opprobriously, and we may add unjustly, Burns might recollect the slight with which his elegiac verses on the father of that gentleman had been treated eight years before.

PAGE 197, NOTE 300.—The Duke of Queensberry stripped his domains of Drumlanrig, in Dumfries-shire, and Neidpath in Peebles-shire, of all the wood fit for being cut, in order to enrich the Countess of Yarmouth, whom he supposed to be his daughter.

PAGE 197, NOTE 301.—Burns was one day being rallied by a friend for wasting his satirical shafts on persons unworthy of his notice, and was reminded that there were such persons (distinguished by rank and circumstance) as the Duke of Queensberry, on whom his biting rhapsodies might more advantageously be expended. He immediately improvised these lines.

PAGE 197, NOTE 302.—Mr. M'Murdo resided at Drumlanrig, as chamberlain to the Duke of Queensberry. He and his wife and daughters are alluded to in the election piece, entitled Second Epistle to Mr. Graham of Fintry. They were kind and hospitable friends of Burns, who celebrated several of the young ladies in his songs.

PAGE 198, NOTE 303.—"Sir Walter Scott possessed a tumbler, on which these lines written by Burns on the arrival of a friend, Mr. W. Stewart, factor to a gentleman of Nithsdale. The landlady being very wrath at what she considered the disfigurement of her glass, a gentleman present appeased her by paying down a shilling, and carried off the relic."—LOCKHART.

PAGE 198, NOTE 304.—According to Burns himself, this song was written when he was about seventeen years old, in honour of a damsel named Isabella Steven, who lived in the neighbourhood of Lochlee.

PAGE 198, NOTE 305.—The old ballad, *McMillan's Peggy*, was the model of this song. The heroine of the piece was a young lady educated in a manner somewhat superior to the peasantry in general, and on whom Burns practised to display his tact in captivating, until, by degrees, he fell in love in earnest, and then discovered that the object of this first sport, then earnest, was previously engaged. "It cost me," says he, "some heartaches to get rid of the affair."

PAGE 198, NOTE 306.—According to Mr. Cunningham, this was the same person as *Montgomery's Peggy*. But more accurate information identifies the heroine of the piece as Margaret Alison, of Lochlee, who was not engaged, and who actually mourned the inconstancy of Burns.

PAGE 199, NOTE 307.—This was the same Peggy Alison mentioned in the foregoing note.

PAGE 199, NOTE 308.—An adaptation of the Old English Ballad, which was rescued from oblivion, obscurity, and black letter (in the Pepys Library, Cambridge), by Mr. Jamieson, who published it in his collection.

PAGE 200, NOTE 309.—Anne Blair, and Anne Ronald, daughters of farmers in Tarbolton parish, and the latter of whom became Mrs. Paterson, of Aikenbrae, have each been spoken of in their native district as the heroine of this song. The poet's family was intimate with Mr. Ronald's, when residing at Lochlee, and even after they had removed to Mossgiel. Mr. Gilbert Burns was at one time considered as a wooer of one of the Miss Ronald's. We learn from Mr. Cunningham that Mr. Ronald liked the conversation of the poet very much, and would sometimes sit late with him; on which one of the girls—probably not Anne—remarked that "she could na see ought about Robert Burns that would tempt her to sit up wi' him till twal o'clock at night."

PAGE 200, NOTE 310.—This song was composed in honour of Margaret Thomson, who lived in a cottage adjoining the Village School of Kirkoswald, where Burns was completing his education, when nineteen years old. Burns himself gives the following account of the matter:—This Miss Thomson afterwards married a Mr. Nielson, and settled with him in the town of Ayr. "A charming fillette," says Burns in speaking of her, "who lived next door to the school, overset my trigonometry, and sent me off at a tangent from the sphere of my studies. I, however, struggled on with my sines and cosines for a few days more; but stepping into the garden one charming noon to take the sun's altitude, there I met my angel,

——— Like Proserpine gathering flowers,
Herself a fairer flower.

It was in vain to think of doing any more good at school. The remaining week I staid, I did nothing but craze the faculties of my soul about her, or steal out to meet her."

PAGE 201, NOTE 311.—"This tune is by Oswald; and the words relate to some part of my private history, which it is of no consequence to the world to know."—BURNS.

PAGE 201, NOTE 312.—In a memoir of Ramsay, in a publication entitled "Lives of Eminent Scotsmen" (3 vols. Boys, London), there is presented a very early song to the tune of *My Nannie, O,* beginning—

"As I came in by Enbro' town,
By the side o' the bonny city, O,
I heard a young man mak his moan,
And O! it was a pity, O.
For aye he cried his Nannie, O!
His handsome, charming Nannie, O!
Nor friend nor foe can tell, O—ho,
How dearly I love Nannie, O!"

An improved song to the same air was written by Ramsay; and finally, Burns wedded the music to the following beautiful effusion of natural sentiment, the heroine of which is believed to have been a certain Agnes Fleming, servant at Calcothill, near Lochlee.

PAGE 202, NOTE 313.—"An improvement upon an ancient homely ditty to the same air. It has been pointed out that the last admirable verse is formed upon a conceit, which was put into print long before the days of Burns, and in a place where it is not at all probable that he could ever have seen it—a comedy entitled *Cupid's Whirligig,* published in 1607. The passage in the comedy is an apostrophe to the female sex, as follows:—"Since we were made before you, should we not admire you as the last, and therefore, perfect work of nature. Man was made when nature was but an apprentice, but woman when she was a skilful mistress of her art."—CHAMBERS.

PAGE 202, NOTE 314.—A quotation from Young's "Night Thoughts."

PAGE 203, NOTE 315.—The "Highland Lassie," celebrated in this song, was the Mary Campbell, to whom Burns was at one time engaged, and devotedly attached, and whose premature death, in fact, prevented her becoming Mrs. Burns.

PAGE 204, NOTE 316.—"Composed on the amiable and excellent family of Whitefoord's leaving Ballochmyle, when Sir John's misfortunes obliged him to sell the estate."—BURNS. Maria was Miss Whitefoord, afterwards Mrs. Cranstone. The purchaser of the property was Claud Alexander, Esq., whose sister Burns has celebrated as the Bonnie Lass of Ballochmyle.

PAGE 205, NOTE 317.—The origin of this beautiful song was the accidental meeting of Miss Wilhelmina Alexander, in the grounds attached to the mansion of Ballochmyle, the property of her brother Mr. Claude Alexander. The song was written in 1786, and immediately forwarded by Burns to Miss Alexander, whose delicacy kept it unknown for the time.

PAGE 205, NOTE 318.—I composed this

song as I conveyed my chest so far on the road to Greenock, where I was to embark in a few days for Jamaica (November, 1786). I meant it as a farewell dirge to my native land."—BURNS.

Professor Walker gives the following account relating to this song. "I requested him (Burns) to communicate some of his unpublished poems, and he recited his farewell song to the Banks of Ayr, introducing it with a description of the circumstances under which it was composed, more striking than the poem itself. He had left Dr. Laurie's family, after a visit which he expected to be the last, and on his way home, had to cross a wide stretch of solitary moor. His mind was strongly affected by parting for ever with a scene where he had tasted so much elegant and social pleasure; and depressed by the contrasted gloom of his prospects, the aspect of nature harmonised with his feelings; it was a lowering and heavy evening in the end of autumn. The wind was up, and whistled through the rushes and long spear grass which bent before it. The clouds were driving across the sky; and cold pelting showers at intervals added discomfort of body to cheerlessness of mind. Under these circumstances, and in this frame, Burns composed this poem.

PAGE 205, NOTE 319.—This song relates to an incident in real life. The unfortunate heroine was a beautiful woman, daughter to a landed gentleman of Carrick, and niece to a baronet. Her lover was a landed gentleman of Wigtonshire. A mother without the sanction of matrimony, and deserted by her lover, she died of a broken heart. On the subsequent death of her brother, her younger sister inherited the family property, but not without opposition from an unexpected quarter. The seducer and deserter of the deceased lady now appeared in a court of law, to endeavour to establish the fact of a secret marriage with her, so as to entitle him to succeed to her brother's estate, as the father and heir of her deceased child, whose claim, of course, would have been preferable to that of the younger sister, if his legitimacy could have been proved. In this attempt, the seducer, it is gratifying to add, was not successful.

The following was the original version of the song, written soon after the poet's departure from Ayrshire, and afterwards altered to suit an air composed by a Mr. Miller, writer in Edinburgh:—

Ye flowery banks o' bonnie Doon,
  How can ye bloom sae fair!
How can ye chant, ye little birds,
  And I sae fu' o' care!

Thou'll break my heart, thou bonnie bird,
  That sings upon the bough;
Thou minds me o' the happy days
  When my fause luve was true.

Thou'll break my heart, thou bonnie bird,
  That sings beside thy mate;
For sae I sat, and sae I sang,
  And wist na o' my fate.

Aft hae I rov'd by bonnie Doon,
  To see the woodbine twine,
And ilka bird sang o' its love;
  And sae did I o' mine.

Wi' lightsome heart I pu'd a rose,
  Frae aff its thorny tree:
And my fause luver staw the rose,
  But left the thorn wi' me.

PAGE 205, NOTE 330.—"I composed these stanzas standing under the falls of Aberfeldy, at or near Moness, in Perthshire."—BURNS. This was in the course of his Highland Excursion, in the month of September, 1787.

PAGE 205, NOTE 321.—James Macpherson was a noted Highland freebooter, of uncommon personal strength, and an excellent performer on the violin. After holding the counties of Aberdeen, Banff, and Moray in fear for some years, he was seized by Duff, of Braco, ancestor of the Earl of Fife, and tried before the sheriff of Banffshire (November 7, 1700), along with certain gipsies who had been taken in his company. In the prison, while he lay under sentence of death, he composed a song, and an appropriate air, the former commencing thus:—

"I've spent my time in rioting,
  Debauched my health and strength;
I squandered fast as pillage came,
  And fell to shame at length.
    But dantonly and wantonly,
      And rantonly I'll gae;
    I'll play a tune, and dance it roun',
      Beneath the gallows tree."

When brought to the place of execution, on the Gallow-hill of Banff (Nov. 16), he played the tune on his violin, and then asked if any friend was present who would accept the instrument as a gift at his hands. No one coming forward, he indignantly broke the violin on his knee, and threw away the fragments; after which he submitted to his fate. The traditionary accounts of Macpherson's immense prowess are justified by his sword, which is still preserved in Duff House, at Banff, and is an implement of great length and weight—as well as by his bones, which were found a few years ago, and were allowed by all who saw them to be much stronger than the bones of ordinary men.

The verses of Burns—justly called by Mr. Lockhart, "a grand lyric,"—were designed as an improvement on those of the freebooter, preserving the same air. In the edition of the poet's works, superintended by Messrs. Hogg and Motherwell (Glasgow, 1834), the reader will find ampler information on the subject of Macpherson and his "Rant."

PAGE 207, NOTE 322.—The individual here meant is William, fourth Viscount of Strathallan, who fell on the insurgent side at the battle of Culloden, April, 1746. Burns, probably ignorant of this his real fate, describes him as having survived the action, and taken refuge from the fury of the government forces in a Highland fastness.

PAGE 207, NOTE 323.—These verses were composed on a charming girl, a Miss Charlotte Hamilton, who was since married to James M'Kitrick Adair, Esq., physician. She is sister of my worthy friend, Gavin Hamilton, of Mauchline, and was born on the banks of Ayr, but was, at the time I wrote these lines, residing at Harvieston, in Clackmannanshire, on the romantic banks of the little river Devon."—BURNS. It was in the course of a short tour in company with Dr. Adair, August 1787, that the poet saw Miss Hamilton, at Harvieston. Introducing his fellow-traveller to the family, he was the means of bringing about an union, from which, says Adair, in 1800, "I have derived, and expect further to derive, much happiness."

PAGE 207, NOTE 324.—"This song," says Burns, "I composed on one of the most accomplished of women, Miss Peggy Chalmers (that was), now Mrs. Lewis Hay, of Forbes and Co.'s bank, Edinburgh."—BURNS. Miss Chalmers was first met by Burns in a trip through Clackmannanshire, in 1787. It was then that he visited Harvieston in the month of August.

PAGE 208, NOTE 325.—"I composed these verses," says Burns, "on Miss Isabella McLeod, of Ramsay, alluding to her feelings on the death of her sister, and the still more melancholy death (1786) of her sister's husband, the late Earl of Loudon, who shot himself out of sheer heartbreak at some mortifications he suffered, owing to the deranged state of his finances."

PAGE 208, NOTE 326.—"The chorus I picked up from an old woman in Dumblane; the rest of the song is mine."—BURNS. It is evident that the poet has understood the chorus in a Jacobite sense, and written his own verses in that strain accordingly. Mr. Peter Buchan, has, nevertheless, ascertained that the original song related to a love attachment between Harry Lumsdale, the second son of a Highland gentleman, and Miss Jeanie Gordon, daughter to the Laird of Knockhespock in Aberdeenshire. The lady was married to her cousin, Habichie Gordon, a son of the laird of Rhymie; and some time after, her former lover having met her, and shaken her hand, her husband drew his sword in anger, and lopped off several of Lumsdale's fingers—which Highland Harry took so much to heart, that he soon after died.—See Hogg and Motherwell's edition of Burns, II., 197.

PAGE 208, NOTE 327.—"I composed these verses," says Burns, "out of compliment to a Mrs. McLachlan, whose husband was an officer in the East Indies."

PAGE 208, NOTE 328.—"I composed these verses while I staid at Ochtertyre with Sir William Murray (father of Sir George Murray, late Secretary for the colonies). The lady, who was also at Ochtertyre at the same time, was the well-known toast, Miss Euphemia Murray, of Lintrose, who was called, and very justly, the *Flower of Strathmore*."—BURNS. This visit to Ochtertyre took place in the month of June, 1787.

PAGE 209, NOTE 329.—"This song," says Burns, "I composed on Miss Jenny Cruickshank, only child of my worthy friend Mr. William Cruickshank, of the High School, Edinburgh." To the same person were also addressed the charming lines which begin :—

"Beauteous rosebud young and gay,"

and which were written by Burns in the fly-leaf of a book presented by him to her. This young lady, who was then only twelve years old, afterwards became the wife of Mr. Henderson, a writer or legal practitioner at Jedburgh. Mr. Cruickshank's house was a floor at the top of a *common stair* now marked, No. 30, in James's Square, Edinburgh; the poet for some time lived with him, his room being one which has a window looking out from the gable of the house upon the green behind the General Register House. Here Burns lay while confined with a bruised limb in the winter of 1787-8. Mr. Cruickshank died, March 8, 1795.

PAGE 209, NOTE 330.—In imitation of a song of which that consummate libertine, Charles II., was the hero.

PAGE 210, NOTE 331.—"I composed this song out of compliment to Miss Ann Masterton, the daughter of my friend Allan Masterton, the author of the air Strathallan's Lament, and two or three others in this work (Johnson's Scots Musical Museum)."—BURNS. Miss Masterton afterwards became Mrs. Derbishire.

PAGE 211, NOTE 332.—"The first half stanza of this song is old; the rest mine."—BURNS. That half stanza was probably the same with the following, which occurs near the close of a homely ballad, printed in Hogg and Motherwell's edition of Burns, as preserved by Mr. Peter Buchan, who further communicates that the ballad was composed in 1636, by Alexander Lesley, of Edinburgh, on Doveran side, grandfather to the celebrated Archbishop Sharpe:—

"Ye'll bring me here a pint of wine,
A salver and a silver tassie,
That I may drink, before I gang,
A health to my ain bonnie lassie."

The fact of Burns pitching upon this one fine stanza of an old ballad, as a foundation for a new song, shows expressively the apt sense he had of all that was beautiful in poetry, and how ready his imagination was to take wing upon the slightest command.

PAGE 211, NOTE 333.—These lines, which were found amongst the papers of Mrs. McLehose, were evidently addressed to her, and allude to the parting scene between the poet and his Clarinda. "These exquisitely affecting stanzas contain the essence of a thousand love tales."—SIR WALTER SCOTT.

PAGE 211, NOTE 334.—The tune of this song was composed by Marshall, who for many years served in the capacity of butler to the Duke of Gordon, and to whose genius we are indebted for some of the most exquisite of Scottish airs. Of the words Burns gives the following brief acconnt. "This song I composed out of compliment to Mrs. Burns. N.B.—It was the honey-moon."

PAGE 212, NOTE 335.—"This air is Oswald's; the song I made out of compliment to Mrs. Burns."—BURNS.

PAGE 212, NOTE 336.—"I composed this song," says Burns, "in the course of a most cheerless ride through the wild muirs which extend between Galloway and Ayrshire."

PAGE 213, NOTE 337.—"This celebrated poem was composed by Burns, in September 1789, on the anniverssry of the day on which he heard of the death of his early love, Mary Campbell. According to Mrs. Burns, he spent that day, though labouring under cold, in the usual work of the harvest, and apparently in excellent spirits. But, as the twilight deepened, he appeared to grow 'very sad about something,' and at length wandered out into the barn-yard, to which his wife, in her anxiety, followed him, entreating him in vain to observe that frost had set in, and to return to the fireside. On being again and again requested to do so, he promised compliance—but still remained where he was, striding up and down slowly, and contemplating the sky, which was singularly clear and starry. At last Mrs. Burns found him stretched on a mass of straw, with his eyes fixed on a beautiful planet, 'that shone like another moon,' and prevailed on him to come in. He immediately, on entering the house, called for his desk, and wrote exactly as they now stand, with all the ease of one copying from memory, these sublime and pathetic verses."

PAGE 213, NOTE 338.—"I composed this song out of compliment to one of the happiest and worthiest married couples in the world, Robert Riddel, Esq., of Glenriddel, and his lady. At their fireside I have enjoyed more pleasant evenings than at all the houses of fashionable people in this country put together."—BURNS. Friars' Carse, closely adjacent to Ellisland, on the bank of the Nith, was the residence of this couple. Mr. Riddel died April, 1794.

PAGE 213, NOTE 339.—"This air is Masterton's; the song mine. The occasion of it was this:—Mr. William Nicol, of the High School, Edinburgh, during the autumn vacation, being at Moffat, honest Allan, who was at that time on a visit to Dalswinton and I, went to pay Nicol a visit. We had such a joyous meeting, that Mr. Masterton and I agreed, each in our own way, that we should celebrate the business."—BURNS. "This meeting," says Currie, writing in 1799, "took place at Laggan, a farm purchased by Mr. Nicol, in Nithsdale, on the recommendation of Burns. These three honest fellows—all men of uncommon talents—are now all *under the turf.*" Masterton has elsewhere been described by Burns as "one of the worthiest men in the world, and a man of real genius." Nicol, who died April 21, 1797, was a man of coarse nature and violent passions.

PAGE 214, NOTE 340.—Composed on Miss Jean Jeffrey, daughter of the minister of Lochmaben. Burns, spending an evening with this gentleman at his manse, was much pleased with the young lady, who did the honours of the table; next morning, at breakfast, he presented her with the song. She is now Mrs. Renwick, and resides in New York.—CHAMBERS.

PAGE 215, NOTE 341.—This is an adaptation of the English ballad of Sir Robert Ayton, who was secretary to the Queen Consort of James I. (of England). The old ballad runs thus:—

"I do confess thou'rt sweet; yet find
Thee such an unthrift of thy sweets,
Thy favours are but like the wind,
That kisseth every thing it meets;
And since thou canst with more than one,
Thou'rt worthy to be kissed by none.

The morning rose that untouched stands,
Arm'd with her briars, how sweetly smells!
But plucked and strained through ruder hands,
Her scent no longer with her dwells,
But scent and beauty both are gone,
And leaves fall from her one by one.

Such fate, ere long, will thee betide,
When thou hast handled been awhile:
Like sun-flowers to be thrown aside,
And I shall sigh while some will smile:
So see thy love for more than one
Has brought thee to be loved by none."

PAGE 217, NOTE 342.—This song is supposed to be one of those which Burns only improved from old versions. William Gordon, sixth Viscount Kenmure, raised a body of troops for the Pretender in 1715, and had the chief command of the insurgent forces, in the south of Scotland. Taken at Preston, he was tried, and condemned to be beheaded, which sentence was executed on the 24th February, 1716. His forfeited estate was bought back by his widow, and transmitted to their son. By the son of that son—now Viscount Kenmure, in consequence of the restoration of the title—Burns was, on one occasion, entertained at his romantic seat of Kenmure Castle, near New Galloway.

PAGE 218, NOTE 343.—"The original title of this song was 'Fair Rabina:' the heroine was a young lady to whom one of the poet's friends was attached, and Burns wrote it in compliment to his passion. Johnson, the proprietor of the Museum, disliked the name, and desiring to have one more suitable for singing, the poet, unwillingly, changed it to Eliza."—CUNNINGHAM.

PAGE 218, NOTE 344.—Mr. Cunningham states that the heroine of this song was the wife of a farmer near Ellisland, and gives the following amusing account of her:—"She was a very singular woman: tea, she said, would be the ruin of the nation; sugar was a sore evil; wheaten bread was only fit for babes; earthenware was a pickpocket; wooden floors were but fit for thrashing upon; slated roofs, cold; feathers, good enough for fowls; in short, she abhorred change; and whenever anything new appeared, such as harrows with iron teeth, 'Ay, ay,' she would exclaim, 'ye'll see the upshot!'

Of all modern things, she disliked china the most; she called it 'burnt clay,' and said it was only fit for 'hauding the broo o' stinking weeds,' as she called tea. On one occasion, a southern dealer in cups and saucers, asked so much for his ware, that he exasperated a peasant, who said, 'I canna purchase, but I ken ane that will: gang there,' said he, pointing to the house of Willie's wife; dinna be blate or burd-mouthed; ask a gude penny—she has the siller.' Away went the poor dealer, spread out his wares before her, and summed up all by asking a double price. A blow from her crummock was his instant reward, which not only fell on his person, but damaged his china. 'I'll learn ye,' quoth she, as she heard the saucers jingle, 'to come with yere brazent English face and yere bits o' burnt clay to me!' She was an unlovely dame—her daughters, however, were beautiful."

PAGE 219, NOTE 345.—"Looking over, with a musical friend, M'Donald's Collection of Highland Airs, I was struck with one, an Isle of Skye tune, entitled *Oran an Aoig*, or the Song of Death, to the measure of which I have adapted my stanzas."—BURNS *to Mrs. Dunlop, December* 17, 1791, at which time the song had just been finished.

PAGE 219, NOTE 346.—Composed in honour of Mrs. Stewart of Stair, whose paternal property was situated on the banks of the Afton, an Ayrshire tributary of the Nith, near New Cumnock. Mrs. Stewart was one of the first persons of rank who knew or extended any friendship to Burns.

PAGE 220, NOTE 347.—In the edition of the Poems of Burns published by Hogg and Motherwell, there is a curious note attached to this song, in which all the parallel songs, ballads, or sketches of other authors are cited, as, in fact, they had, many of them, occurred to Burns.

PAGE 220, NOTE 348.—This song was handed up to the chairman, extemporised on the back of a letter, by Burns, at a meeting of Excise officers, at Dumfries, when the poet was called upon for a song.

PAGE 221, NOTE 349.—According to Mr. Cunningham, the heroine of this song, was Miss Jannette Miller, daughter of Mr. Miller, of Dalswinton, a young lady of very extraordinary beauty, who, subsequently, married (in 1795) Mr. John Thomas Erskine the younger, of Marr (since 13th Earl of Marr).

PAGE 221, NOTE 350.—This song is supposed to express the love and admiration of Mr. Oswald, of Auchincruive, for Miss Lucy Johnstone—afterwards Mrs. Oswald, and who died of decline, at Lisbon, in 1798.

PAGE 222, NOTE 351.—This song, whether absolutely original, or remodelled from some ancient ballad, was contributed by Burns to Johnson's Musical Museum. Mr. Cunningham pronounces it *not* original. I cannot, however, trace any ballad, either amongst the early English, or early Scottish Poesy, which will sustain Mr. Cunningham's judgment; and, moreover, there are sufficient grounds for identifying its absolute originality, the rhythm only being adopted.

PAGE 224, NOTE 352.—"The occasion of this ballad was as follows:—When Mr. Cunninghame, of Enterkin, came to his estate, two mansion-houses on it, Enterkin and Anbank, were both in a ruinous state. Wishing to introduce himself with some *éclat* to the county, he got temporary erections made on the banks of Ayr, tastefully decorated with shrubs and flowers, for a supper and ball, to which, most of the respectable families in the county were invited. It was a novelty, and attracted much notice. A dissolution of parliament was soon expected, and this festivity was thought to be an introduction to a canvass for representing the county. Several other candidates were spoken of, particularly Sir John Whitefoord, then residing at Cloncaird, commonly pronounced Glencaird, and Mr. Boswell, the well-known biographer of Dr. Johnson. The political views of this festive assemblage, which are alluded to in the ballad, if they ever existed, were, however, laid aside, as Mr. Cunninghame did not canvass the county."—GILBERT BURNS.

PAGE 225, NOTE 353.—There is an old superstition, that, out of the slough of adders, are formed the pretty annular pebbles, which have, of late years, become so popular, when polished, for mounting as jewels.

PAGE 225, NOTE 354.—According to the family tradition, this song was composed in honour of Mrs. Riddel of Woodlee Park.

PAGE 226, NOTE 355.—Miss Lesley Baillie was certainly worthy of the delicate and naïf eulogy of this poem. She was the daughter of a landed proprietor in Ayrshire, and, subsequently, married Mr. Cumming, of Logie. The occasion of the meeting, which furnished the impulse to this composition, was that on which, in 1792, Mr. and Miss Baillie were passing through Dumfries in their progress to England:—Burns accompanied them for some distance on their journey, and was thus evidently charmed with the worth as well as the beauty of his fair fellow-traveller,

PAGE 226, NOTE 356.—"In my very early years," says Burns, "when I was thinking of going to the West Indies, I took this farewell of a dear girl (Mary Campbell), whom, although I did *not* leave the country, I never saw again."

PAGE 227, NOTE 357.—The castle here alluded to was that of Coilsfield, near Tarbolton, the seat of Colonel Hugh Montgomery, who was ultimately twelfth Earl of Eglinton. The heroine of the verses was Mary Campbell, who lived in that house as a dairy-woman, but now resides with poetical immortality. Burns, after a long courtship, and having agreed that they should be married, met her on the banks of the Ayr, to live one day of parting love, in anticipation of a visit she was to pay to her relations at Campbeltown in Argyleshire. Mary died at Greenock on her return, and thus left a blank in the poet's affections which nothing thereafter filled up.

PAGE 228, NOTE 358.—This song, which is the version contributed to Thomson's Selection, and which elicited such merited admiration from that elegant compiler, was a rescript of a former song contributed by Burns to Johnson's Musical Museum. The latter, however, was *not* absolutely original, being founded on an old ballad, whereas this version is entirely original. The version furnished to the Musical Museum runs as follows:—

Braw, braw lads of Gala Water;
  Oh, braw lads of Gala Water;
I'll kilt my coats aboon my knee,
  And follow my love thro' the water.

Sae fair her hair, sae brent her brow,
  Sae bonnie blue her een, my dearie;
Sae white her teeth, sae sweet her mou';
  The mair I kiss sh'es aye my dearie.

O'er yon bank, and e'er yon brae,
  O'er yon moss amang the heather;
I'll kilt my coats aboon my knee,
  And follow my love thro' the water.

Down amang the broom, the broom,
  Down amang the broom, my dearie,
The lassie lost her silken snood,
  That cost her mony a blirt and bleary.

PAGE 228, NOTE 359.—"This," says Burns, "was one of my juvenile works." These lines were composed in honour of one of the fair daughters of a neighbour's house at Mauchline. "Of all the productions of Burns, the pathetic and serious love songs which he has left behind him in the manner of old ballads, are perhaps those which take deepest and most lasting hold of the mind. Such are the lines to Mary Morison, &c." —HAZLITT.

PAGE 229, NOTE 360.—"Burns, I have been informed, was one summer evening at the inn at Brownhill with a couple of friends, when a poor wayworn soldier passed the window; of a sudden, it struck the poet to call him in, and get the story of his adventures; after listening to which, he all at once fell into one of those fits of abstraction not unusual with him. He was lifted to the region where he had his 'garland and singing robes about him,' and the result was the admirable song which he sent you for 'the Mill, Mill O.'"—CORRESPONDENCE OF MR. GEORGE THOMSON. Mill-Mannoch, a sweet pastoral scene on the Coyl, near Coylton Kirk, is presumed to have been the spot where the poet imagined the rencontre of the soldier and his mistress to have taken place.

PAGE 230, NOTE 361.—"The air of *Logan Braes* is old, and there are several old songs to it. Immediately before the rise of Burns, Mr. John Mayne, who afterwards became known for a poem entitled the *Siller Gun*, wrote a very agreeable song to the air, beginning,

'By Logan's streams, that rin sae deep.'

It was published in the *Star* newspaper, May 23rd, 1789. Burns, having heard that song, and supposing it to be an old composition, adopted into the above a couplet from it, which he admired:—

'While my dear lad maun face his faes,
Far, far frae me and Logan braes.'

Mr. Mayne lived to a good old age, and died, March 14th, 1836, at Lisson Grove, near London."—THOMSON.

PAGE 230, NOTE 362.—This song was written expressly for Mr. Thomson's Collection, that is, the *two last* stanzas, for the two first were the original words of an old ballad. Burns was struck with the wild beauty of the air, and with the imperfection of the closing part of the verses, and supplied a remodelled version, such as it is in the text.

PAGE 230, NOTE 363.—This song has been erroneously supposed to celebrate Burns's own "Jean." It was really written in honour of the eldest daughter of Mr. John McMurdo, of Drumlanrig—Miss Jean McMurdo, whose exquisite beauty of face and symmetry of figure, were remarkable even in a family uniformly handsome.

PAGE 232, NOTE 364.—"You will remember an unfortunate part of our worthy friend Cunningham's story, which happened about three years ago. That struck my fancy, and I endeavoured to do the idea justice as follows."—BURNS TO G. THOMSON, *August*, 1793. Mr. Alexander Cunningham was a jeweller in Edinburgh, a man of polished and agreeable manners, and admitted into a class of society considerably above his own. The story of his unfaithful mistress, which is here alluded to, made a great noise at the time, and has been kept in remembrance by Burns's song.

PAGE 232, NOTE 365.—Phillis the Fair —Miss Phillis McMurdo, daughter of Mr. John McMurdo, of Drumlanrig, more delicately lovely, though not so commandingly beautiful as her elder sister Jean. She was subsequently married to Mr. Norman Lockhart, of Carnwath. The occasion of this song was the fancied passion of her music master (Burns's friend) Stephen Clarke, who requested the poet to supply him with an adequate copy of verses to celebrate her.

PAGE 232, NOTE 366.—Benleddi is a mountain which rises to an elevation of upwards of 3000 feet, and which is situated to the westward of Strathallan.

PAGE 233, NOTE 367.—An improvement upon an old song, the hero of which is said to have been the Rev. David Williamson, Minister of St. Cuthbert's, Edinburgh, famous for having had seven wives, the first being the Laird of Cherrytree's daughter, with whom he became acquainted in a rather unceremonious manner when skulking during the days of "the Persecution." This remarkable patriarch, though first inducted into his charge in the time of the Commonwealth, was a vigorous preacher down to the days of Queen Anne.

PAGE 233, NOTE 368.—"The old air, 'Hey, tuttie taitie,' with Fraser's hautboy, has often filled my eyes with tears. There is a tradition, which I have met with in many places of Scotland, that it was Robert Bruce's march at the battle of Bannockburn. This thought in my solitary wanderings, warmed me to a pitch of enthusiasm on the theme of liberty and independence, which I threw into a kind of Scottish ode, fitted to the air, that one might suppose to be the gallant Royal Scot's address to his heroic followers on that eventful morning."—BURNS TO G. THOMSON, *September* 1792.

PAGE 233, NOTE 369.—According to some of Burns's commentators, this song was written in 1793, on the occasion of Clarinda's purposed departure to join her husband in the West Indies. This is a mistake. The words might, very possibly, have been *suggested* by such a circumstance; but the song was written in 1794 for Thomson's collection, Burns having previously suggested the air of *Oran Gaoil* to his correspondent, and expressed his admiration of it.

PAGE 236, NOTE 370.—"'How long and dreary is the night!' I met with some such words in a collection of songs somewhere, which I altered and enlarged: and to please you, and to suit your favourite air, I have taken a stride or two across my room, and have arranged it anew, as you will find on the other page."—BURNS TO G. THOMSON, *October*, 1794.

PAGE 237, NOTE 371.—This song was composed in honour of the beautiful Miss Jean Lorimer, afterwards Mrs. Whelpdale. The occasion of the composition was immediately on reaching home, after having met Miss Lorimer at a party · the date 1794.

PAGE 237, NOTE 372.—The title of this song is of remote date in the English version, and even the opening lines have been retained. The air, however, had never before been coupled with it, and the length of the stanzas was cut down, and the song otherwise remodelled by Burns for Thomson's collection, in which it was coupled with Burns's favourite tune of *Dainty Davie*.

PAGE 239, NOTE 273.—The supposition that this song was elicited as a kind of penitential address to Mrs. Riddel, of Woodlee park, in consequence of an affront offered to her by the poet when intoxicated, is by no means well founded. The purport of the song in no way concerned Burns personally, it was written for a friend as an apostrophe to an offended mistress, and the reply was also by the hand of Burns, who was thus employed on both sides in the dispute. The reply runs thus:—

"Stay, my Willie—yet believe me,
Stay, my Willie—yet believe me,
For, ah! thou know'st na' every pang,
Wad wring my bosom shouldst thou leave me.
Tell me that thou yet art true,
And a' my wrongs shall be forgiven,
And when this heart proves fause to thee,
Yon sun shall cease its course in heaven.
But to think I was betrayed,
That falsehood e'er our loves should sunder!
To take the flow'ret to my breast,
And find the guilefu' serpent under.

Could I hope thou'dst ne'er deceive,
Celestial pleasures, might I choose 'em,
I'd slight, nor seek in other spheres
That heaven I'd find within my bosom.
Stay my Willie—yet believe me,
Stay, my Willie—yet believe me,
For, ah! thou knows't na' every pang
Wad wring my bosom shouldst thou leave me."

PAGE 239, NOTE 374.—The following passage, which conveys a very analogous idea, occurs in Wycherley's Comedy of *The Plain Dealer*:—

"I weigh the man, not his title: 'tis not the king's stamp can make the metal better or heavier. Your lord is a leaden shilling, which you bend every way, and who debases the stamp he bears."

PAGE 240, NOTE 375.—"Composed on a passion which a Mr. Gillespie, a particular friend of mine, had for a Miss Lorimer, afterwards Mrs. Whelpdale. The young lady was born at Cragieburn Wood" (near Moffat).—BURNS. Mrs. Whelpdale at a future date became the heroine Chloris, under which appellation she is the subject of many songs by Burns. It is painful to add, that this beautiful woman eventually sank into the lowest state of female degradation, and died in misery at Mauchline a few years ago.—CHAMBERS.

PAGE 240, NOTE 376.—"Craigieburn Wood is situated on the banks of the river Moffat, and about three miles distant from the village of that name, celebrated for its medicinal waters. The woods of Cragieburn and of Dumcrieff, were at one time favourite haunts of our poet. It was there he met the 'Lassie wi' the lint-white locks,' and that he conceived several of his beautiful lyrics."—CURRIE.

PAGE 241, NOTE 377.—This song was composed on the same occasion, and suggested by the same incident, as that to which the song, *Had I a Cave*, is also attributable, namely, a disappointment in love which befel Mr. Alexander Cunningham, the mutual friend of Burns and Thomson. The date of this song is 1795.

PAGE 242, NOTE 378.—In the original manuscript this line runs, "He up the *Gateslack* to my black cousin Bess." Mr. Thomson objected to this word, as well as to the word *Dalgarnock*, in the next verse. Robert Burns replied as follows:—

"Gateslack is the name of a particular place, a kind of passage up among the Lawther hills, on the confines of this county. Dalgarnock is also the name of a romantic spot near the Nith, where are still a ruined church and a burial-ground. However, let the first run *He up the lang loan, &c.*"

"It is always a pity to throw out anything that gives locality to our poet's verses."—CURRIE.

PAGE 243, NOTE 379.—The heroine of this song was Mrs. Burns's endeared young friend, Miss Jessy Lewars, sister to one of Burns's associates in office—since wife of Mr. James Thomson, writer, Dumfries.

PAGE 244, NOTE 380.—This was the first attempt of Burns in verse. It was composed, according to his own account, in his sixteenth year, on a "bonnie sweet sonsie lass," who was his companion on the harvest field. See his letter to Dr. Moore. He says elsewhere—"For my own part, I never had the least inclination of turning poet, till I once got heartily in love, and then rhyme and song were in a manner the spontaneous language of my heart. This composition was the first of my performances, and done at an early period of life, when my heart glowed with honest warm simplicity, unacquainted and uncorrupted with the ways of a wicked world. The performance is, indeed, very puerile and silly; but I am always pleased with it, as it recalls to my mind those happy days when my heart was yet honest, and my tongue was sincere."

PAGE 244, NOTE 381.—This autobiographical song, as it may be called, is understood to have been composed during the most depressed period of the poet's early fortunes, when struggling with family distresses at Lochlee. "It is a wild rhapsody," he says, "miserably deficient in versification; but as the sentiments are the genuine feelings of my heart, I have a particular pleasure in conning it over."—CHAMBERS.

PAGE 245, NOTE 382.—It has been said that there was some foundation in fact for this tale of a gossip—a wayfaring woman, who chanced to be present at the poet's birth, having actually announced some such prophecies respecting the infant placed in her arms. Some similar circumstances attended the birth of Mirabeau.

PAGE 245, NOTE 383.—It may be gratifying to curiosity to know the fates of the six belles of Mauchline. Miss Helen Miller, the first mentioned, became the wife of Burns's friend, Dr. Mackenzie. The divine Miss Markland was married to a Mr. Finlay, an officer of Excise at Greenock. Miss Jean Smith was afterwards Mrs. Candlish. Miss Betty (Miller) became Mrs. Templeton, and Miss Morton married a Mr. Paterson. Of Armour's history immortality has taken charge.

The *Glasgow Herald* of Saturday, September 6th, 1851, has the following notice of the death of the last of the *Mauchline Belles*, "Died on Saturday, the 30th ult. (August 1851), Mrs. Findlay, relict of Robert Findlay, Esq., of the Excise. In ordinary circumstances, the departure from this life of a respectable lady, ripe in years, would not have afforded matter of general interest; but it happens that the deceased was one of the very few persons surviving to our own times, who intimately knew the peasant bard in the first flush of his genius and manhood, and by whom her name and charms have been wedded to immortal verse. She was the "divine" Miss Markland, noticed in the "Belles of Mauchline." Miss Markland became the wife of Mr. Findlay, officer of Excise, of Tarbolton, a gentlemen who was appointed to instruct the bard in the mysteries of gauging. The connection thus formed between Burns and Findlay, led to the introduction of the *latter* to Miss Markland, and his subsequent marriage to her in September of the same year (1788). Mrs. Findlay was in her 23rd year at the time of her marriage, and in her 86th at the time of her death."

PAGE 245, NOTE 384.—Jean Armour, afterwards Mrs. Robert Burns who, as is well known, survived the poet.

PAGE 245, NOTE 385.—This little fragment was composed in consequence of a momentary glimpse which the poet one day obtained of a beautiful young female, who rode up to an inn at Ayr, as the poet was mounting his horse to leave it.

PAGE 246, NOTE 386.—*Killie*, a familiar appellation amongst the country people for *Kilmarnock*. This song was composed in allusion to a meeting of the Kilmarnock Mason Lodge, which took place in 1786, and at which William Parker, one of the poet's oldest friends presided, and which Burns himself attended. The song was an impromptu, and was sung, as it is believed, at this very meeting.

PAGE 246, NOTE 387 (*misprinted* 386).—The air of *Bonnie Dundee* appears in the Skene MS., of date *circa* 1620. The tune seems to have existed at even an earlier period, as there is a song to it amongst those which were written by the English, to disparage the Scottish followers by whom James VI. was attended on his arrival in the south. The first of the following verses is from an old homely ditty, the second only being the composition of Burns.

PAGE 249, NOTE 388.—"This song is said to be a homely version of a Highland lament for the ruin which followed the rebellion of the "forty-five." Burns heard it sung in one of his northern excursions, and begged a transcription."—CUNNINGHAM.

PAGE 251, NOTE 389.—Written at the commencement of his residence at Ellisland, to express the buoyant feelings which animated him on that occasion, when, as he himself informs us, he enjoyed a few days, the most tranquil, if not the happiest, he had ever experienced.

PAGE 255, NOTE 390.—This ballad is, as well as some of those which have preceded it, dedicated to the turmoil of the parliamentary election at Dumfries, in which Burns took as active a part as he well could on the tory side: —to wit, in the election of 1790. In the "Five, Carlines," as well as in the "Second Epistle to Mr. Graham of Fintry;" the poet appeared to reserve a neutral position, merely sketching the events as they occurred; and, in fact, it was obvious, seeing his dependency upon a government situation, that he should observe some measure in his political writings. Burns's genius had moreover acquired for him friends amongst men of all parties, many of whom in the heat of a political contest, might have felt aggrieved at any uncalled for violence on his part. The secret Jacobitish yearnings of Burns naturally impelled him to the side of Sir James Johnstone, the tory and Pittite candidate, whilst being the tenant of Mr. Miller, father of the whig or opposition candidate, to whom he was indebted for much personal kindness, he could not well signalise himself by any very decided exertion against Mr. Miller the younger. In this ballad "the Laddies of the Banks of Nith," he does not retain such very decided neutrality, and pretty clearly allows his tory predilections to oose out. It must be noticed, however, that the toryism of Burns was merely a traditionary love for the native Scotch race of princes, and a detestation for the usurping dynasty (as he thought) of Brunswick; for in abstract political principles, it may easily be gathered from his writings that he had a far greater leaning towards *Jacobinism*, than towards the exploded principle of the *divine right of kings*. Sir Walter Scott, writing to Mr. Lockhart, with an enclosure of a whole parcel of letters of Burns says:—"In one of them to that singular old curmudgeon, Lady Winifred Constable, you will see he plays high Jacobite, and on that account it is curious; though I fancy his Jacobitism, like mine, belonged to the fancy, rather than to the reason. He was, however, a great Pittite down to a certain period, that is, until the influx of *Jacobinism* from the outbreak of 1789, when he certainly became more decidedly *Jacobin* than *Jacobite*. There were some passing stupid verses in the papers, attacking and defending his satire on a certain preacher whom he termed *an unco calf.* In one of them occurred these lines in vituperation of the adversary:—

A whig I guess; but Rab's a tory,
And gies us mony a funny story.

This was in 1787."

In the "Laddies of the banks of Nith," Burns first alludes to the great influence of the Duke of Queensberry, owing to his extensive landed possessions in the neighbourhood.—The Duke of Queensberry figures in no enviable light, either politically or privately.—A life spent in mere selfish gratification and profligacy, and a political career stamped with his protest of December 26th, 1788, on the Regency question, are very concisely lashed.

PAGE 256, NOTE 391.—Captain Grose himself, was the first and most earnest to relish the point of this epigram. It was an impromptu of one of the drinking parties or nightly carousals of these "guid fellows."

PAGE 256, NOTE 392.—An allusion to the excessive corpulency of Captain Grose, which was a common subject of joke with himself.

PAGE 256, NOTE 393.—"Stopping at a merchant's shop, a friend of mine, in Edinburgh, one day put Elphinstone's translation of Martial into my hand, and desired my opinion of it. I asked permission to write my opinion in a blank leaf of the book, which, being granted, I wrote this epigram." —BURNS. A similar idea occurs in a mock-heroic poem, entitled the *Knight*, by William Meston, who, in allusion to Dr. J. Trapp's translation of the Georgics of Virgil, says:—

"Read the commandment, Trapp, proceed no further;
For there 'tis written, thou shalt do no murder."

PAGE 256, NOTE 394.—The Miss Burns who was the subject of these lines, was a young English woman, settled in Edinburgh —as remarkable for the laxity of her demeanour, as for the exquisite beauty of her person. She figured in the less rigid society of some of our wits, and her portrait was engraved and published by Mr. John Kay. It was on one of these engravings that

Burns wrote the lines which it suggested.

PAGE 257, NOTE 395.—These lines were in reply to a question put to the poet: "Wherefore Miss Davies (a particular favourite of Burns's) should have been made so diminutive, and another lady named, so large in proportion?"

PAGE 257, NOTE 396.—The occasion which suggested these lines, was the receipt of intelligence that the Austrians had been totally routed at Gemappes, by General Dumourier (1792.)

PAGE 257, NOTE 397.—Burns, accompanied by a friend, having gone to Inverary at a time when some company were there on a visit to his Grace the Duke of Argyle, finding himself and his companion entirely neglected by the innkeeper, whose whole attention seemed to be occupied with the visitors of his grace, expressed his disapprobation of the incivility with which he was treated, in the above lines.

PAGE 257, NOTE 398.—Composed and repeated by Burns, to the master of the house, on taking leave at a place in the Highlands, where he had been hospitably entertained.

PAGE 257, NOTE 399.—Spoken, in reply to a gentleman, who sneered at the sufferings of Scotland for conscience-sake, and called the Solemn League and Covenant ridiculous and fanatical.

PAGE 258, NOTE 400.—These were a society of friends of the government, who assumed an exclusive loyalty during the fervours of the French Revolution. The above lines were written in consequence of the receipt, at a convivial meeting, of the following senseless quatrain from one of the Loyal Natives:—

"Ye sons of sedition, give ear to my song,
Let Syme, Burns, and Maxwell, pervade every throng,
With Craken the attorney, and Mundell the quack,
Send Willie the monger to hell with a smack."

PAGE 258, NOTE 401.—When the Board of Excise informed Burns that his business was to act, and not to think and speak, he read the order to a friend, turned the paper, and wrote what he called *The Creed of Poverty*—CUNNINGHAM.

PAGE 258, NOTE 402.—"These lines are addressed to John Taylor, blacksmith, at Wanlockhead, on being indebted to him, one winter's day between Dumfries-shire and Ayrshire, for a small cast of his office."—BURNS.

PAGE 259, NOTE 403.—Burns was called upon for a song at a dinner of the Dumfries Volunteers, in honour of Rodney's victory of the 12th of April, 1782. He replied to the call by pronouncing the following.

PAGE 259, NOTE 404.—This was at the King's Arms Inn, Dumfries, and was suggested by hearing some person speak in terms of reproach of the officers of his Majesty's Excise.

PAGE 259, NOTE 405.—This lady, in her early days, was an intimate friend of Mrs. Burns, and also a great favourite with the poet, who esteemed her sprightly and affectionate character. During his last illness, his surgeon, Mr. Brown, brought in a long sheet, containing the particulars of a menagerie of wild beasts which he had just been visiting. As Mr. Brown was handing the sheet to Miss Lewars, Burns seized it, and wrote upon it these verses with red chalk; after which he handed it to Miss Lewars, saying that it was now fit to be presented to a lady. Miss Lewars afterwards married Mr. James Thomson, of Dumfries.

PAGE 259, NOTE 406.—While Miss Lewars was waiting upon him in his sick chamber, the poet took up a crystal goblet containing wine and water, and after writing upon it these verses, in the character of a *Toast*, presented it to her.

PAGE 259, NOTE 407.—At this time of trouble, on Miss Lewars complaining of indisposition, he said, to provide for the worst, he would write her epitaph. He accordingly inscribed these lines on another goblet, saying, "That will be a companion to the *Toast*."

PAGE 260, NOTE 408.—Quotation from Goldsmith.

PAGE 260, NOTE 409.—James Humphry.

PAGE 260, NOTE 410.—Mr. John Wilson, printer, of Kilmarnock, by whom the first edition of Burns's Poems was produced.

PAGE 261, NOTE 411.—(*Misprinted* 409). The father of Dr. Richardson, who accompanied Franklin's expedition.—CHAMBERS.

Notes to the Correspondence of Burns.

PAGE 268, NOTE 1.—Mr. James Burness, of Montrose, stood in the relationship of first cousin to Robert Burns. The father of James was, like his brother William, in humble circumstances, but had pursued a more prosperous career. We have already had occasion to remark that the poet was the first of his family to abbreviate the name of Burness to Burns. The grandson of James Burness, of Montrose, was the Lieutenant Burness of our own time, the author of *Travels in Bokhara.*

PAGE 270, NOTE 2.—Mr. John Richmond was one of the earliest friends of Burns at Mauchline. He had since embarked in the study of the law, and was preparing for that profession at Edinburgh.

PAGE 271, NOTE 3.—Mauchline Corse is the name of the Market Cross, in the centre of the village or town.

PAGE 272, NOTE 4. According to Motherwell, the piece to which Burns alludes in this letter was that entitled the *Mountain Dasiy*, or as it was called in the original manuscript, *The Goavan.*

PAGE 272, NOTE 5.—Mr. David Brice was a shoemaker at Glasgow, and an early associate of the poet.

PAGE 272, NOTE 6.—Alluding to Miss Jean Armour's return from Paisley, to which she had been sent by her parents, to be out of the reach of her too ardent lover. Burns writes in this spirit under the impression that her own feelings towards him had actually been distorted by the influence of her friends. This was, to a certain extent, the case, as we have had occasion to notice

in the foregoing portion of this volume, in the dissertation on the Life of Robert Burns.

PAGE 275, NOTE 7.—The expressions contained in this letter strongly betray the extreme distress from which Burns was suffering, owing to the forced separation between himself and Jean Armour.

PAGE 275, NOTE 8.—An allusion to the efforts which were being made at this time by Mr. Aiken, and the other friends of the poet, to procure for him an appointment to office in the Excise.

PAGE 276, NOTE 9.—Miss Alexander, the sister of Mr. Claude Alexander, who had recently purchased the estate of Ballochmyle.

PAGE 276, NOTE 10.—The 25th of January, 1759, was the day on which Burns was born.

PAGE 277, NOTE 11.—The designation applied to old bachelors.

PAGE 277, NOTE 12.—Without a proper covering or cloak to protect you from its rigour.

PAGE 277, NOTE 13.—Lady Betty Cunningham.

PAGE 278, NOTE 14.—This paper was written by the author of *The Man of Feeling*, Mr. Mackenzie.

PAGE 279, NOTE 15.—One of those traditionary examples with which the lively memory of Burns was so teeming. He appears to have retained and culled these recollections of his early years with peculiar veneration.

PAGE 280, NOTE 16.—Dr. Moore's letter,

to which this letter was a reply, ran as follows :—

"*Clifford Street, January 23rd*, 1787.

"SIR—I have just received your letter, by which I find I have reason to complain of my friend Mrs. Dunlop, for transmitting to you extracts from my letters to her, by much too freely, and too carelessly written for your perusal. I must forgive her, however, in consideration of her good intention, as you will forgive me, I hope, for the freedom I use with certain expressions, in consideration of my admiration of the poems in general. If I may judge of the author's disposition from his works, with all the other good qualities of a poet, he has not the irritable temper ascribed to that race of men by one of their own number, whom you have the happiness to resemble in ease and curious felicity of expression. Indeed, the poetical beauties, however original and brilliant, and lavishly scattered, are not all I admire in your works; the love of your native country, that feeling sensibility to all the objects of humanity, and the independent spirit which breathes through the whole, give me a most favourable impression of the poet, and have made me often regret that I did not see the poems, the certain effect of which would have been my seeing the author, last summer, when I was longer in Scotland than I have been for many years.

"I rejoice very sincerely at the encouragement you receive at Edinburgh, and I think you peculiarly fortunate in the patronage of Dr. Blair, who, I am informed, interests himself very much for you. I beg to be remembered to him; nobody can have a warmer regard for that gentleman than I have, which, independent of the worth of his character, would be kept alive by the memory of our common friend, the late Mr. George B——e.

"Before I received your letter, I sent, enclosed in a letter to ——, a sonnet by Miss Williams, a young poetical lady, which she wrote on reading your *Mountain Daisy*; perhaps it may not displease you :—

'While soon "the garden's flaunting flowers" decay
And scatter'd on the earth neglected lie,
The 'Mountain-Daisy,' cherish'd by the ray
A poet drew from heaven, shall never die.
Ah, like that lonely flower the poet rose!
'Mid penury's bare soil and bitter gale;
He felt each storm that on the mountain blows,
Nor ever knew the shelter of the vale.
By genius in her native vigour nurst,
On nature with impassion'd look he gazed;
Then through the cloud of adverse fortune burst
Indignant, and in light unborrowed blazed.
Scotia! from rude affliction shield thy bard;
His heaven-taught numbers Fame herself will guard.'

"I have been trying to add to the number of your subscribers, but find many of my acquaintance are already among them. I have only to add, that, with every sentiment of esteem, and the most cordial good wishes, I am, your obedient humble servant,

J. MOORE."

PAGE 282, NOTE 17.—Subjoined is Dr. Moore's reply to this letter, which is added to throw additional light on the subject :—

"*Clifford Street, Feb. 28th*, 1787.

"DEAR SIR—Your letter of the 15th gave me a great deal of pleasure. It is not surprising that you improve in correctness and taste, considering where you have been for some time past. And I dare swear there is no danger of your admitting any polish which might weaken the vigour of your native powers.

"I am glad to perceive that you disdain the nauseous affectation of decrying your own merit as as a poet, an affectation which is displayed with most ostentation by those who have the greatest share of self-conceit, and which only adds undeceiving falsehood to disgusting vanity. For you to deny the merit of your poems, would be arraigning the fixed opinion of the public.

"As the new edition of my *View of Society* is not yet ready, I have sent you the former edition, which I beg you will accept as a small mark of my esteem. It is sent by sea to the care of Mr. Creech; and along with these four volumes for yourself, I have also sent my *Medical Sketches* in, one volume, for my friend Mrs. Dunlop, of Dunlop; this you will be so obliging as to transmit, or, if you chance to pass soon by Dunlop, to give to her.

"I am happy to hear that your subscription is so ample, and shall rejoice at every piece of good fortune that befalls you. For you are a very great favourite in my family; and this is a higher compliment than perhaps you are aware of. It includes almost all the professions, and, of course, is a proof that your writings are adapted to various tastes and situations. My youngest son, who is at Winchester school, writes to me, that he is translating some stanzas of your 'Hallowe'en' into Latin verse, for the benefit of his com rades. This unison of taste partly proceeds, no doubt, from the cement of Scottish partiality, with which they are all somewhat tinctured. Even your translator, who left Scotland too early in life for recollection, is not without it. I remain, with great sincerity, your obedient servant, J. MOORE."

PAGE 282, NOTE 18.—Mr. William Dunbar was writer to the Signet, in Edinburgh, and was the person celebrated in the song, *Rattling Roaring Willie*.

PAGE 286, NOTE 19.—Dr. Smith was author of the well-known work, entitled *The Wealth of Nations*, and of some admirable translations of the best Greek authors.

PAGE 286, NOTE 20.—Subjoined is Dr. Moore's reply to this letter:—

"*Clifford Street, May 23rd,* 1787.

"DEAR SIR—I had the pleasure of your letter by Mr. Creech, and soon after he sent me the new edition of your poems. You seem to think it incumbent on you to send to each subscriber a number of copies proportionate to his subscription money, but you may depend upon it, few subscribers expect more than one copy, whatever they subscribed; I must inform you, however, that I took twelve copies for those subscribers, for whose money you were so accurate as to send me a receipt, and Lord Eglinton told me he had sent for six copies for himself, as he wished to give five of them as presents.

"Some of the poems you have added in this last edition are very beautiful, particularly the 'Winter Night,' the 'Address to Edinburgh,' 'Green grow the rashes,' and the two songs immediately following—the latter of which is exquisite. By the way, I imagine you have a peculiar talent for such compositions which you ought to indulge. No kind of poetry demands more delicacy or higher polishing. Horace is more admired on account of his Odes than all his other writings. But nothing now added is equal to your 'Vision' and 'Cotter's Saturday Night.' In these are united fine imagery, natural and pathetic description, with sublimity of language and thought. It is evident that you already possess a great variety of expression and command of the English language; you ought therefore to deal more sparingly for the future in the provincial dialect.—Why should you, by using that, limit the number of your admirers to those who understand the Scottish, when you can extend it to all persons of taste who understand the English language? In my opinion, you should plan some larger work than any you have as yet attempted. I mean, reflect upon some proper subject, and arrange the plan in your mind, without beginning to execute any part of it till you have studied most of the best English poets, and read a little more of history. The Greek and Roman stories you can read in some abridgment, and soon become master of some of the most brilliant facts, which must highly delight a poetical mind. You should also, and very soon may, become master of the heathen mythology, to which there are everlasting allusions in all the poets, and which in itself is charmingly fanciful. What will require to be studied with more attention, is modern history; that is, the history of France and Great Britain, from the beginning of Henry VII.'s reign. I know very well you have a mind capable of attaining knowledge by a shorter process than is commonly used, and I am certain you are capable of making a better use of it, when attained, than is generally done.

"I beg you will not give yourself the trouble of writing to me when it is inconvenient, and make no apology when you do write for having postponed it,—be assured of this, however, that I shall always be happy to hear from you. I think my friend Mr. Creech told me that you had some poems in manuscript by you, of a satirical and humorous nature (in which, by the way, I think you very strong), which your prudent friends prevailed on you to omit, particularly one called 'Somebody's Confession;' if you will entrust me with a sight of any one of these, I will pawn my word to give no copies, and will be obliged to you for a perusal of them.

"I understand you intend to take a farm, and make the useful and respectable business of husbandry your chief occupation: this, I hope, will not prevent your making occasional addresses to the nine ladies who have shown you such favour, one of whom visited you in the 'auld clay biggin.' Virgil, before you, proved to the world that there is nothing in the business of husbandry inimical to poetry; and I sincerely hope that you may afford an example of a good poet being a successful farmer. I fear it will not be in my power to visit Scotland this season; when I do, I'll endeavour to find you out, for I heartily wish to see and converse with you. If ever your occasions call you to this place, I make no doubt of your paying me a visit, and you may depend on a very cordial welcome from this family. I am, dear Sir, your friend and obedient servant, "J. MOORE."

PAGE 286, NOTE 21.—Throng, a very familiar Scottish term for busy—"having one's hands full."

PAGE 286, NOTE 22.—Burns here alludes to his excursion to the south, to visit places of interest, and full of the traditions of the Border contests of early Scottish history.

PAGE 287, NOTE 23.—An engraving executed by Beugo, from Nasmyth's portrait of Robert Burns, and which all persons admitted to be even a more faithful likeness than the picture, although that possessed much merit.

PAGE 287, NOTE 24.—Subjoined is Dr. Blair's reply to this letter:—

"*Argyle Square, Edinburgh, May 4th*, 1787.

"DEAR SIR—I was favoured this forenoon with your very obliging lettter, together with an impression of your portrait, for which I return you my best thanks. The success you have met with I do not think was beyond your merits; and if I have had any small hand in contributing to it, it gives me great pleasure. I know no way in which literary persons who are advanced in years can do more service to the world, than in forwarding the efforts of rising genius, or bringing forth unknown merit from obscurity. I was the first person who brought out to the knowledge of the world the poems of Ossian; first, by the 'Fragments of ancient Poetry,' which I published, and afterwards, by my setting on foot the undertaking for collecting and publishing the 'Works of Ossian;' and I have always considered this as a meritorious action of my life.

"Your situation, as you say, was indeed singular; and in being brought, all at once, from the shades of deepest privacy to so great a share of public notice and observation, you had to stand a severe trial. I am happy that you have stood is so well; and, as far as I have known or heard, though in the midst of many temptations, without reproach to your character and behaviour.

"You are now, I presume, to retire to a more private walk of life; and I trust will conduct yourself there with industry, prudence, and honour. You have laid the foundation for just public esteem. In the midst of those employments which your situation will render proper, you will not, I hope, neglect to promote that esteem, by cultivating your genius, and attending to such productions of it as may raise your character still higher. At the same time, be not in too great a haste to come forward. Take time and leisure to improve and mature your talents; for, on any second production you give the world, your fate, as a poet, will very much depend. There is no doubt a gloss of novelty, which time wears off. As you very properly hint yourself, you are not to be surprised, if in your rural retreat you do not find yourself surrounded with that glare of notice and applause which here shone upon you. No man can be a good poet without being somewhat of a philosopher. He must lay his account, that any one, who exposes him to public observation, will occasionally meet with the attacks of illiberal censure, which it is always best to overlook and despise. He will be inclined sometimes to court retreat, and to disappear from public view. He will not affect to shine always, that he may at proper seasons come forth with more advantage and energy. He will not think himself neglected if he be not always praised. I have taken the liberty, you see, of an old man to give advice and make reflections, which your own good sense will, I dare say, render unnecessary.

"As you mention your being just about to leave town, you are going, I should suppose, to Dumfries-shire, to look at some of Mr. Miller's farms. I heartily wish the offers to be made you there may answer, as I am persuaded you will not easily find a more generous and better-hearted proprietor to live under than Mr. Miller. When you return, if you come this way, I will be happy to see you, and to know concerning your future plans of life. You will find me by the 22nd of this month, not in my house in Argyle square, but at a country house in Restalrig, about a mile east of Edinburgh, near the Musselburg road. Wishing you, with the warmest interest, all success and prosperity, I am, with true regard and esteem, dear Sir, yours sincerely, HUGH BLAIR."

PAGE 287, NOTE 25.—Burns here alludes to an extempore address, which he wrote offhand to Mr. Creech, of which the opening words are *Auld Chuckie Reekie's sair distrest*, and which will be found amongst the poems in the foregoing part of this volume.

PAGE 287, NOTE 26.—This patron was James, Earl of Glencairn, whose countenance had also reared Mr. Creech to eminence:—that celebrated bibliopole having formerly travelled with the earl (then a very young man), in the capacity of tutor and companion to his lordship. It was by Lord Glencairn, as we have already observed, that Burns was introduced to Creech.

PAGE 287, NOTE 27.—Burns here alludes to his friend and correspondent, for whom he penned some of his best songs, namely, Mr. Johnson, the compiler and publisher of the *Scots' Musical Museum.*

PAGE 288, NOTE 28.—Mr. Peter Hill, afterwards in business for himself as a bookseller, and honoured by the poet's correspondence. Reared with Mr. Creech, he was in his turn, master to Mr. Constable. He died at an advanced age in 1836.

PAGE 288, NOTE 29.—This wonderful beast had been named Jenny Geddes by the poet, in honour of the old woman to whom tradition assigns the credit of having cast the first stool at the dean's head in St. Giles's church, July 23, 1637, when the liturgy imposed on Scotland by Charles I. was first read.

PAGE 288, NOTE 30.—Auchtertyre was the seat of Sir William Murray, Bart., situated in a picturesque and romantic district, a few miles from Crieff. The son and successor of the then proprietor, namely, Sir George Murray, was subsequently a member of Pitt's administration, as Secretary for the Colonies.

PAGE 288, NOTE 31.—This was Auchtertyre, near Stirling, on the banks of the Teith. Mr. Ramsay was not only an accomplished scholar, and remarkable for his distinguished classical attainments and refined taste; but was possessed with a warm national enthusiasm, in favour of the simple and truthful imagery and diction of the less polished literature of his own country.

PAGE 289, NOTE 32.—Mr. Cruikshank, of the High School, Edinburgh, and the father of the fair Miss Cruikshank whom Burns has so delicately celebrated in his song of the *Rosebud.*

PAGE 290, NOTE 33.—Mr. Ainslie was educated to the profession of the law, and subsequently became a writer to the Signet, in Edinburgh. He survived the poet nearly half a century, and died at Edinburgh, on the 11th of April 1838, at the advanced age of seventy-two years. At the time in question, he was barely over twenty. He had accompanied Burns on his poetical excursion through the southern or border districts.

PAGE 291, NOTE 34.—Mr. Andrew Bruce, of the North Bridge, Edinburgh.

PAGE 291, NOTE 35.—Hugh, the neighbour's herdsman, who cuts such a quaint figure in the poem of *Poor Mailie,* Burns's pet ewe.

PAGE 291, NOTE 36.—Miss Charlotte Hamilton subsequently married Dr. Adair, a physician, at Harrowgate, and survived the poet nearly forty years. She was celebrated by the poet in the song entitled the *Banks of the Devon.*

PAGE 291, NOTE 37.—Mr. Hamilton's son, who figures in the poem entitled *The Dedication,* by the designation of *Wee curlie Johnnie.*

PAGE 292, NOTE 38.—Mr. Walker was employed by the Duke of Athole, at his seat of Blair Athole, in the capacity of tutor to his grace's children. It was at Blair Athole that Burns had first met him, and become acquainted with him, only a few days before the date of this letter, that is, in the month of September, 1787, in the course of one of his Highland excursions.

PAGE 292, NOTE 39.—The poet here alludes to the lines entitled the *Address of Bruar Water* to the Duke of Athole. It will be remembered that in a previous allusion to this subject, we stated that the spot was originally bare and unadorned by plantations, for which the capabilities of the landscape so especially fitted this beautiful spot. Burns was the first who suggested to the Duke the bestowal of a little art in laying out this portion of his estate in ornamental grounds —a suggestion which the Duke quickly adopted.

PAGE 292, NOTE 40.—The Duchess of Athole of the time being, was the daughter of Charles, Lord Cathcart (the ninth of the title), and the *"little angel band,"* of which Burns speaks with such fervour, were severally, the Lady Charlotte Murray, then only twelve years of age, and subsequently married to Sir John Menzies, of Castle Menzies; Lady Amelia Murray, then seven years of age, and subsequently married to the Lord Viscount Strathallan; and lastly, Lady Elizabeth Murray, then only five months old (an infant in arms), and since married to Macgregor Murray, of Lanrick.

PAGE 292, NOTE 41.—The valley of Strathspey has given its name to the dancing tunes in quick time, so popular in Scotland, and especially in the Highlands, and which derived their origin remotely from this district.

PAGE 292, NOTE 42.—Stonehaven, sometimes also called Stonehive, by the people of the country.

PAGE 292, NOTE 43.—The youngest daughter of the late James Chalmers, Esq., of Fingland. She married, December 9, 1788, Lewis Hay, Esq., of the banking firm of Sir William Forbes, James Hunter, and Company, Edinburgh. Mrs. Hay has since resided at Pau, in the south of France.

PAGE 293, NOTE 44.—The second number of the *Scots Musical Museum,* edited and published by Johnson.

PAGE 293, NOTE 45.—These songs, which Burns enthusiastically admired, were the works of the Rev. John Skinner, the episcopalian officiating minister at Longside, near Peterhead.

PAGE 294, NOTE 46.—Hoy was librarian to the Duke of Gordon for forty-six years antecedent to his death in 1828. He was a simple, pure-hearted man, of the Dominie Sampson genus, and had attracted the regard of Burns during the short stay of the poet at Gordon Castle.

PAGE 294, NOTE 47.—Alexander, fourth Duke of Gordon, who entertained Burns at Gordon Castle, possessed considerable abilities for song writing, though few of his verses have been made public. The song alluded to by Burns seems to have been obtained from Mr. Hoy, as it appears in Johnson's second volume.

PAGE 296, NOTE 48. Mr. Charles Hay, afterwards Lord Newton. He was a man of much wit, and not by any means deficient of learning in the abstruser questions of his profession. That his qualifications as a lawyer were by no means contemptible, his subsequent attainment of a judgeship sufficiently testifies. In his earlier days, and at the period of his correspondence with the poet, however, he was probably more strongly given to the bottle, the song and the repartee, than to very deep questions of jurisprudence.

PAGE 296, NOTE 49.—The Charlotte here meant was Miss Charlotte Hamilton, sister of Mr. Gavin Hamilton, the poet's firm friend.

PAGE 297, NOTE 50.—Alluding to the song dedicated to Miss Chalmers, and of which the initiatory line runs thus :—

"Where braving angry winter's storms."

PAGE 298, NOTE 51—It is not improbable that the locality illustrated in these lines, to wit, *Glenap,* had some considerable share in the deep interest which they excited in the mind of Burns. Glenap is a small place in the southern part of Ayrshire, and the local associations were no doubt powerful to render any song which celebrated them interesting in the eyes of Burns.

PAGE 298, NOTE 52.—After a long and honourable practice as a surgeon at Irvine, Mr. Mackenzie, who had there occupied every honourable post in the township, finally (in 1827) retired to the metropolis, where he continued to reside until his death, on the 11th of January, 1837. In the course of his medical career, he sought and attained a physician's diploma, and it was by him (as Dr. Mackenzie) that Burns was presented to Professor Dugald Stewart, also a warm friend, and great admirer of the genius of the Scottish Bard. Further details on the subject of Burns's intimacy with these two worthy and distinguished contemporaries, may be gathered from the particulars afforded in the memoir which forms the first part of this volume.

PAGE 299, NOTE 53.—Miss Williams had, in the previous month of June, addressed a letter of compliment to Burns, which may be found in the *Edinburgh Magazine* for September, 1817, where the letter in the text also appeared for the first time, along with the following note by the editor, Mr. Thomas Pringle: —"The critique, though not without some traits of his usual sound judgment and discrimination, appears on the whole to be much in the strain of those gallant and flattering responses which men of genius usually find it incumbent to issue, when consulted upon the productions of their female admirers."

PAGE 300, NOTE 54.—This was the person whom Burns, in his autobiographical letter to Dr. Moore, describes as his companion at Irvine—whose mind was fraught with every manly virtue, and who, nevertheless, was the means of making him regard illicit love with levity.

PAGE 301, NOTE 55.—Mrs. McLehose, so well known to those who are conversant with the life and works of Burns, under the fictitious name of *Clarinda.*

PAGE 301, NOTE 56.—This, according to the arrangement of Motherwell, is the first of the letters extant, and addressed by Robert Burns to Mrs. McLehose, although it had previously been published as the *second.* The date, according to the same authority, must have been December 6th, 1787, to which it is added, that the poet "was to have drunk tea with her on that day, but was disappointed by the lady, who afterwards repeated her invitation for Saturday (the next day but one), when he was once more disappointed, in consequence of the accident which confined him to his room for several weeks, and by which his leg was seriously injured.

PAGE 302, NOTE 57.—If our conjecture as to the date of the foregoing letter be correct, as stated in the Note, number 56, it is obvious that this note must have been written and despatched on Saturday, the 8th of December, 1787. We are confirmed as to the date of these letters, by those addressed to others of his correspondents, and to Miss Chalmers in particular, to which Burns had prefixed dates, and which have definitely pointed to Saturday, December the 8th, 1787, as the day upon which the accident occurred, by which his leg was injured. We have already stated that Mrs. McLehose had deferred receiving Burns on the Thursday previous, and had named this day (Saturday) to receive him instead.

PAGE 302, NOTE 58.—The letter of the 21st of December, to which Burns here alludes, has been lost, and we can only infer the contents from the context of the present letter, and from the reply in verse which he received from Mrs. McLehose in the lines beginning—

"Talk not of love, it gives me pain," &c.

This letter was the first of that series which was signed with the Arcadian name of "Clarinda," and which Burns here repeats with marked emphasis.

PAGE 303, NOTE 59.—Judging from the facts communicated, or alluded to, or from the contents of other letters, evidently of the same period, this letter must have been written between the 31st of December 1787, and the 3rd of January 1788. It would almost seem as if we had lost some of the intermediary notes; but it is also evident that there could not have been a very voluminous series of letters intervening between that of December 21st and this one.

PAGE 306, NOTE 60.—The date of this letter was probably before the 20th of January, and it might possibly have been as early as the eighth of the same month; we can only infer ambiguously from the context, and the circumstances which transpire in other letters of the same period. A contemporary of both Burns and Clarinda, has definitely fixed this letter for the 12th of January 1788, but upon what grounds I do not precisely know; possibly, however, from some occurrence of circumstances which might have rendered the date conclusive.

PAGE 308, NOTE 61.—An allusion to the novel of Fielding, entitled *Amelia*, to which Clarinda had drawn his attention especially.

PAGE 310, NOTE 62.—Burns here alludes to the song of which the opening line is

"Clarinda, mistress of my soul."

PAGE 314, NOTE 63.—This letter was a reply to the subjoined letter, received by Burns from Mr. Skinner, in which he alludes to a project for the publication of a complete collection of Scottish songs:—

"*Linsheart*, 14*th November*, 1787.

"SIR—Your kind return without date, but of post-mark October 25th, came to my hand only this day; and, to testify my punctuality to my poetic engagement, I sit down immediately to answer it in kind. Your acknowledgment of my poor but just encomiums on your surprising genius, and your opinion of my rhyming excursions, are both, I think, by far too high. The difference between our two tracks of education and ways of life is entirely in your favour, and gives you the preference in every manner of way. I know a classical education will not create a versifying taste, but it mightily improves and assists it; and though, where both these meet, there may sometimes be ground for approbation, yet where taste appears single, as it were, and neither cramped nor supported by acquisition, I will always sustain the justice of its prior claim to applause. A small portion of taste, this way, I have had almost from childhood, especially in the old Scottish dialect: and it is as old a thing as I remember, my fondness for 'Christ-kirk o' the Green,' which I had by heart ere I was twelve years of age, and which, some years ago, I attempted to turn into Latin verse. While I was young, I dabbled a good deal in these things; but, on getting the black gown, I gave it pretty much over, till my daughters grew up, who, being all good singers, plagued me for words to some of their favourite tunes, and so extorted these effusions, which have made a public appearance beyond my expectations, and contrary to my intentions, at the same time that I hope there is nothing to be found in them uncharacteristic, or unbecoming the cloth, which I would always wish to see respected.

"As to the assistance you propose from me in the undertaking you are engaged in, I am sorry I cannot give it so far as I could wish, and you perhaps expect. My daughters, who were my only intelligencers, are all *foris-familiate*, and the old woman their mother has lost that taste. There are two from my own pen, which I might give you, if worth the while. One to the old Scotch tune of 'Dumbarton's Drums.'

"The other, perhaps, you have met with, as your noble friend, the duchess, has, I am told, heard of it. It was squeezed out of me by a brother parson in her neighbourhourhood, to accommodate a new Highland reel for the Marquis's birth-day to the stanza of

'Tune your fiddles, tune them sweetly,' &c.

"If this last answer your purpose, you

may have it from a brother o. mine, Mr. James Skinner, writer, in Edinburgh, who, I believe, can give the music too.

"There is another humorous thing, I have heard said to be done by the Catholic priest Geddes, and which hit my taste much:—

'There was a wee wifeikie, was coming frae
the fair,
Had gotten a little drapikie, which bred
her meikle care.
It took upo' the wifie's heart, and she
began to spew,
And co' the wee wifeikie, I wish I binna
fou.
I wish,' &c., &c.

"I have heard of another new composition, by a young ploughman of my acquaintance, that I am vastly pleased with, to the tune of 'The humours of Glen,' which I fear won't do, as the music, I am told, is of Irish original. I have mentioned these, such as they are, to show my readiness to oblige you, and to contribute my mite, if I could, to the patriotic work you have in hand, and which I wish all success to. You have only to notify your mind, and what you want of the above, shall be sent you.

"Meantime, while you are thus publicly, I may say, employed, do not sheath your own proper and piercing weapon. From what I have seen of yours already, I am inclined to hope for much good. One lesson of virtue and morality, delivered in your amusing style, and from such as you, will operate more than dozens would do from such as me, who shall be told it is our employment, and be never more minded: whereas, from a pen like yours, as being one of the many, what comes will be admired. Admiration will produce regard, and regard will leave an impression, especially when example goes along with it.

Now binna saying I'm ill bred,
Else, by my troth, I'll no be glad;
For cadgers, ye have heard it said,
And sic like fry,
Maun aye be harland in their trade,
And sae maun I.

"Wishing you, from my poet-pen, all success, and, in my other character, all happiness and heavenly direction, I remain, with esteem, your sincere friend,

"JOHN SKINNER."

PAGE 314, NOTE 64.—Dr. Webster was the officiating minister of the Scottish Episcopalian Church, at Edinburgh.

PAGE 315, NOTE 65.—The "Two fair spirits of the Hill" alluded to, were Miss Sophia Brodie, and Miss Rose, of Kilvarock.

PAGE 316, NOTE 66.—"The letters to Richard Brown, written at a period when the poet was in the full blaze of reputation, showed that he was at no time so dazzled with success, as to forget the friends who had anticipated the public by discovering his merit."—WALKER.

PAGE 316, NOTE 67.—An intervening letter, which probably bore date about the 23rd of February, has not transpired. We are led to the conviction that such a letter, did exist, from the context and the allusions contained in this letter.

PAGE 317, NOTE 68.—Burns here alludes to Mr. James Tennant, of Glenconner, in Ayrshire, to whom he addressed a brief poem (which will be found in its proper place in this volume). It was the same Mr. James Tennant, who had previously inspected other farms which Burns contemplated hiring.

PAGE 320, NOTE 69.—It is probable from the allusions contained in this letter that it was written after the brief visit of the poet to Edinburgh, in which he finally concluded the bargain with Mr. Miller, to take the farm of Ellisland. It was on the 13th of March, that this contract was closed; and judging from circumstances, the date of this letter would have been about the 18th of March, 1788. Burns did not see Mrs. McLehose in this instance, and appears even to have avoided an interview, for private reasons.

PAGE 322, NOTE 70.—The words in question, are those which bear the title of the *Chevallier's Lament.*

PAGE 322, NOTE 71.—The allusion here made is to his marriage with Jean Armour.

PAGE 326, NOTE 72.—Burns, of course, again alludes to his marriage with Jean Armour.

PAGE 326, NOTE 73.—Alluding to the death of Mr. Samuel Mitchelson, writer to the Signet in Edinburgh, who had been the friend and master of Mr. Ainslie, and which occurred on the 21st of June, 1788.

PAGE 327, NOTE 74.—Burns alludes to a parcel of books, which his friend, Mr. Hill, had sent to him as a present.

PAGE 328, NOTE 75.—Mr. David Ramsay, the printer, and publisher, of the *Edinburgh Evening Courant.*

PAGE 328, NOTE 76.—The Crochallan Fencibles, a select club of wits and congenial spirits, to which Burns belonged, and to which he very frequently alludes.

PAGE 328, NOTE 77.—Mr. Alexander Cunningham, jeweller, of Edinburgh, a mutual friend of Robert Burns and George Thomson.

PAGE 333, NOTE 78.—Mr. Morrison was a cabinet maker and upholsterer at Mauchline, who had undertaken to furnish Burns's new house at Ellisland, as soon as it should be completed.

PAGE 336, NOTE 79.—A quey—a heifer.

PAGE 339, NOTE 80.—This letter was a reply to one received by Burns from Mr. Carfrae, of which the subjoined is a copy:—

"*January 2nd*, 1789.

"SIR—If you have lately seen Mrs. Dunlop, of Dunlop, you have certainly heard of the author of the verses which accompany this letter. He was a man highly respected for every accomplishment and virtue which adorns the character of a man or a Christian. To a great degree of literature, of taste and poetic genius, was added an invincible modesty of temper, which prevented, in a great degree, his figuring in life, and confined the perfect knowledge of his character and talents to the small circle of his chosen friends. He was untimely taken from us, a few weeks ago, by an inflammatory fever, in the prime of life; beloved by all who enjoyed his acquaintance, and lamented by all who have any regard for virtue or genius. There is a woe pronounced in Scripture against the person whom all men speak well of; if ever that woe fell upon the head of mortal man, it fell upon him. He has left behind him a considerable number of compositions, chiefly poetical, sufficient, I imagine, to make a large octavo volume. In particular, two complete and regular tragedies, a farce of three acts, and some smaller poems on different subjects. It falls to my share, who have lived in the most intimate and uninterrupted friendship with him from my youth upwards, to submit to you the verses he wrote on the publication of your incomparable poems. It is probable they were his last, as they were found in his escritoire, folded up with the form of a letter addressed to you, and, I imagine, were only prevented from being sent by himself, by that melancholy dispensation which we still bemoan. The verses themselves I will not pretend to criticise, when writing to a gentlemen whom I consider as entirely qualified to judge of their merit. They are the only verses he seems to have attempted in the Scottish style; and I hesitate not to say, in general, that they will bring no dishonour on the Scottish muse; and allow me to add, that if it is your opinion they are not unworthy of the author, and will be no discredit to you, it is the inclination of Mr. Mylnes' friends that they should immediately be published in some periodical work, to give the world a specimen of what may be expected from his performances in the poetic line, which perhaps will afterwards be published for the advantage of his family.

"I must beg the favour of a letter from you acknowledging the receipt of this, and to be allowed to subscribe myself, with great regard, Sir, your most obedient servant. P. CARFRAE."

PAGE 340, NOTE 81.—The piety of this letter receives a harmonious response from the following, addressed on the same day by Gilbert Burns to his poetical brother:—

"*Mossgiel, January 1st*, 1789.

"DEAR BROTHER—I have just finished my new-year's-day breakfast in the usual form; which naturally makes me call to mind the days of former years, and the society in which we used to begin them; and when I look at our family vicissitudes, 'through the dark postern of time long elapsed,' I cannot help remarking to you, my dear brother, how good the GOD of SEASONS is to us, and that, however some clouds may seem to lower over the portion of time before us, we have great reason to hope that all will turn out well.

"Your mother and sisters, with Robert the second, join me in the compliments of the season to you and Mrs. Burns, and beg you will remember us in the same manner to William, the first time you see him. I am, dear brother, yours, GILBERT BURNS."

PAGE 342, NOTE 82.—Alexander Geddes, born at Arradowl, in Banffshire, in 1737, was reared as a Catholic clergyman, and long officiated in that capacity in his native country, and elsewhere. As humbly born as Burns, he possessed much of his strong and eccentric genius, and it is not surprising that he and the Ayrshire bard should have become friends. After 1780, his life was spent in London, chiefly under the fostering patronage of a generous Catholic nobleman, Lord Petre. The heterodox opinions of Dr. Geddes, his extraordinary attempts to translate the Bible, and his numerous fugitive publications on controversial divinity, made much noise at the time; but he is now only remembered for some successful Scotch verses. This singular man died in London, February 20th, 1802, in the sixty-fifth year of his age.

PAGE 342, NOTE 83.—A copy of Burns's Poems, belonging to Dr. Geddes, into which the poet had transferred some of his more recent verses. The volume has since been in the possession of Mrs. Hislop, Finsbury Square, London.

PAGE 343, NOTE 84.—Burns here alludes to his wife's sister-in-law, namely, the wife of Mr. Adam Armour, a mason, at Mauchline (and brother to Mrs. Burns). Mrs. Adam Armour survived the poet nearly half a century.

PAGE 344, NOTE 85.—The following is the letter to which the above was an answer. Dr. Currie has unfortunately suppressed the name of this correspondent of our poet:—

"*London, August* 5*th*, 1789.

"MY DEAR SIR—Excuse me when I say, that the uncommon abilities which you possess must render your correspondence very acceptable to any one. I can assure you I am particularly proud of your partiality, and shall endeavour, by every method in my power, to merit a continuance of your politeness.

* * * * *

"When you can spare a few moments, I should be proud of a letter from you, directed for me, Gerard Street, Soho.

* * * * *

"I cannot express my happiness sufficiently at the instance of your attachment to my late inestimable friend, Bob Fergusson, who was particularly intimate with myself and relations. While I recollect with pleasure his extraordinary talents, and many amiable qualities, it affords me the greatest consolation that I am honoured with the correspondence of his successor in national simplicity and genius. That Mr. Burns has refined in the art of poetry, must readily be admitted; but, notwithstanding many favourable representations, I am yet to learn that he inherits his convivial powers.

"There was such a richness of conversation, such a plentitude of fancy and attraction in him, that when I call the happy period of our intercourse to my memory, I feel myself in a state of delirium. I was then younger than him by eight or ten years, but his manner was so felicitious, that he enraptured every person around him, and infused into the hearts of the young and old, the spirit and animation which operated on his own mind. I am, dear Sir, your's, &c.

PAGE 344, NOTE 86.—Mr. Edward Neilson, officiating Presbyterian Minister of the church of Kirkbean, in the Stewartry of Kirkcudbright.

PAGE 345, NOTE 87.—Subjoined is Dr. Moore's reply to this letter:—

"*Clifford Street, June* 10*th*, 1789.

"DEAR SIR—I thank you for the different communications you have made me of your occasional productions in manuscript, all of which have merit, and some of them merit of a different kind from what appears in the poems you have published. You ought carefully to preserve all your occasional productions, to correct and improve them at your leisure; and when you can select as many of these as will make a volume, publish it either at Edinburgh or London by subscription: on such an occasion, it may be in my power, as it is very much in my inclination, to be of service to you.

"If I were to offer an opinion, it would be, that, in your future productions, you should abandon the Scottish stanza and dialect, and adopt the measure and language of modern English poetry.

"The stanza which you use in imitation of 'Christ's Kirk on the green,' with the tiresome repetition of 'that day,' is fatiguing to English ears, and I should think not very agreeable to Scottish.

"All the fine satire and humour of your 'Holy Fair,' is lost on the English; yet without more trouble to yourself, you could have conveyed the whole to them. The same is true of some of your other poems. In your epistle to J. Smith, the stanzas of that beginning with this line 'This life so far's I understand,' to that which ends with 'short while it grieves,' are easy flowing gaily philosophical and of Horacian elegance:—the language is English, with a few Scottish words, and some of those so harmonious as to add to the beauty: for what poet would not prefer *gloaming* to *twilight?*

"I imagine by carefully keeping, and occasionally polishing and correcting those verses which the muse dictates, you will, within a year or two, have another volume as large as the first ready for the press; and this, without diverting you from every proper attention to the study and practice of husbandry, in which I understand you are very learned, and which I fancy you will choose to adhere to as a wife, whilst poetry amuses you from time to time like a mistress.

"The former, like a prudent wife, must not show ill-humour, although you retain a sneaking kindness to this agreeable gipsy, and pay her occasional visits, which in no manner alienates your heart from your lawful spouse, but tends, on the contrary, to promote her interest.

"I desired Mr. Cadell to write to Mr. Creech to send you a copy of Zeluco. This performance has had great success here; but I shall be glad to have your opinion of it, because I value your opinion, and because I know you are above saying what you do not think.

"I beg you will offer my best wishes to my very good friend Mrs. Hamilton, who, I understand, is your neighbour. If she is as happy as I wish her, she is happy enough. Make my compliments also to Mrs. Burns; and believe me to be, with sincere esteem, dear Sir, your's," &c. &c.

PAGE 346, NOTE 88.—The husband of this lady was chamberlain to the Duke of Queensberry, at whose house of Drumlanrig the family consequently lived. The beautiful daughters of Mr. and Mrs. M'Murdo are the heroines of several of Burns's songs.

PAGE 347, NOTE 89.—Burns had also sent a copy of the lines transcribed in this letter to Dr. Gregory, for his opinion of their merit or demerit, to which Dr. Gregory replied as follows:—

"*Edinburgh, June 2nd,* 1789.

"DEAR SIR—I take the first leisure hour I could command, to thank you for your letter, and the copy of verses enclosed in it. As there is real poetic merit, I mean both fancy and tenderness, and some happy expressions in them, I think they will deserve that you should revise them carefully, and polish them to the utmost. This I am sure you can do if you please, for you have great command both of expression and of rhymes: and you may judge, from the two last pieces of Mrs. Hunter's poetry that I gave you, how much correctness and high polish enhance the value of such compositions. As you desire it, I shall, with great freedom, give you my *most rigorous* criticism on your verses. I wish you would give me another edition of them, much amended, and I will send it to Mrs. Hunter, who, I am sure, will have much pleasure in reading it. Pray give me likewise for myself, and her too, a copy (as much amended as you please) of the 'Water Fowl on Loch Turit.'

"'The Wounded Hare' is a pretty good subject; but the measure or stanza you have chosen for it is not a good one; it does not *flow* well; and the rhyme of the fourth line is almost lost by its distance from the first, and the two interposed close rhymes. If I were you, I would put it into a different stanza yet.

"Stanza 1. The execrations in the first too lines are two strong or coarse; but they may pass. 'Murder-aiming' is a bad compound epithet, and not very intelligible. 'Blood-stained in stanza iii. line 4, has the same fault: *Bleeding* bosom is infinitely better. You have accustomed yourself to such epithets, and have no notion how stiff and quaint they appear to others, and how incongruous with poetic fancy and tender sentiments. Suppose Pope had written, 'Why that blood-stained bosom gored,' how would you have liked it? *Form* is neither a poetic, nor a dignified, nor a plain common word: it is a mere sportsman's word; unsuitable to pathetic or serious poetry.

"'Mangled' is a coarse word. 'Innocent,' in this sense, is a nursery word, but both may pass.

"Stanza 4. 'Who will now provide that life a mother only can bestow?' will not do at all: it is not grammar—it is not intelligible. Do you mean, 'provide for that life which the mother had bestowed and used to provide for?'

"There was a ridiculous slip of the pen, 'Feeling' (I suppose) for 'Fellow,' in the title of your copy of verses; but even fellow would be wrong; it is but a colloquial and vulgar word, unsuitable to your sentiments. 'Shot' is improper too. On seeing a *person* (or a sportsman) wound a hare; it is needless to add with what weapon; but if you think otherwise, you should say, *with a fowling-piece.*

"Let me see you when you come to town, and I will show you some more of Mrs. Hunter's poems."

"It must be admitted, that this criticism is not more distinguished by its good sense, than by its freedom from ceremony. It is impossible not to smile at the manner in which the poet may be supposed to have received it. In fact, it appears, as the sailors say, to have thrown him *quite aback.* In a letter which he wrote soon after, he says, 'Dr. Gregory is a good man, but he crucifies me.' And again, 'I believe in the iron justice of Dr. Gregory; but, like the devils, I believe and tremble.' However, he profited by these criticisms, as the reader will find by comparing this first edition of the poem with that elsewhere published."—CURRIE.

PAGE 350, NOTE 90.—This lady had been introduced to Burns by Dr. Moore. It was Miss Helen Maria Williams.

PAGE 351 NOTE 91.—Subjoined is Miss Williams reply to this letter:—

August 7th, 1789.

"DEAR SIR—I do not lose a moment in

returning you my sincere acknowledgments for your letter, and your criticism on my poem, which is a very flattering proof that you have read it with attention. I think your objections are perfectly just, except in one instance.

"You have indeed been very profuse of panegyric on my little performance. A much less portion of applause from *you* would have been gratifying to me; since I think its value depends entirely upon the source from whence it proceeds—the incense of praise, like other incense, is more grateful from the quality than the quantity of the odour.

"I hope you still cultivate the pleasures of poetry, which are precious, even independent of the rewards of fame. Perhaps the most valuable property of poetry, is its power of disengaging the mind from worldly cares, and leading the imagination to the richest springs of intellectual enjoyment; since, however frequently life may be chequered with gloomy scenes, those who trully love the muse can always find one little path adorned with flowers and cheered by sunshine."

PAGE 351, NOTE 92.—Mr. John Logan, of Knockshinnock, Glen Afton, in the county of Ayr.

PAGE 354, NOTE 93.—Burns had in this place alluded, with extreme acrimony, to the Duke of Queensberry, whom he has elsewhere also dealt with, with exemplary severity. Dr. Currie, however, prudently erased the passage.

PAGE 355, NOTE 94.—Lady Winifred Constable was at this time the lineal representative of the House of Constable, of Nithsdale, and was an uncompromising Jacobite in political opinions. Sir Walter Scott, in alluding to this letter, which he sent to Mr. Lockhart, rallies the opinions of Burns as expressed to that "quaint old curmudgeon, Lady W. Constable."

PAGE 356, NOTE 95.—Burns here alludes to the lines addressed to Mr. William Tytler.

PAGE 356, NOTE 96.—An allusion to the *ex officio* leadership of the provost in the *Marjorie of the Many Locks*, and to the recent political excitement of the district.

PAGE 356, NOTE 97.—In the song "I gaed a waefu' gate yestreen," Burns has celebrated one of the daughters of this gentleman. He was the minister of the church of Lochmaben.

PAGE 357, NOTE 98.—"This letter is extracted from the third volume of Sir John Sinclair's Statistical Account of Scotland, p. 598.—It was enclosed to Sir John by Mr. Riddel himself, in the following letter, also printed there:—

'SIR JOHN—I enclose you a letter, written by Mr. Burns, as an addition to the account of Dunscore parish. It contains an account of a small library which he was so good (at my desire) as to set on foot, in the barony of Monkland, or Friars Carse, in this parish. As its utility has been felt, particularly among the younger class of people, I think that if a similar plan were established in the different parishes of Scotland, it would tend greatly to the speedy improvement of the tenantry, tradespeople, and workpeople. Mr. Burns was so good as to take the whole charge of this small concern. He was treasurer, librarian, and censor, to this little society, who will long have a grateful sense of his public spirit and exertions for their improvement and information. I have the honour to be, Sir John, your's most sincerely, ROBERT RIDDEL."

—CURRIE. Mr. Cunningham adds, that the minister of Dunscore probably omitted to notice the Monkland library scheme, from dislike to the kind of literature patronised by it.

PAGE 358, NOTE 99.—It was Mr. William Dunbar, who had presented a copy of Spenser's Poems to Burns.

PAGE 359, NOTE 100.—An allusion to a ballad, in which one of the ladies in waiting to Mary Queen of Scots, is described as having murdered her illegitimate child, and as having undergone capital punishment in consequence. The stanza here quoted are the supposed last expressions which escaped her at the moment of execution. Mary Queen of Scots had, however, curious enough, four attendants of the same Christian name as her own.

PAGE 359, NOTE 101.—Francis, the second son of the poet, to whom Mrs. Dunlop had stood as godmother.

PAGE 359, NOTE 102.—Burns here alludes to an unfortunate woman, whose laxity had exposed her to some excess of severity from the Magistrates of Edinburgh, in which Creech had been one of the most active persons. The treatment to which she had been subjected had been so severe, indeed, as to awaken general sympathy in her behalf.

PAGE 360, NOTE 103.—Perhaps no set of men more effectually avail themselves of the easy credulity of the public, than a certain description of Paternoster Row booksellers. Three hundred and odd engravings!—and by the first artists in

London, too!—No wonder that Burns was dazzled by the splendour of the promise. It is no unusual thing for this class of impostors to illustrate the Holy Scriptures by plates originally engraved for the History of England, and I have actually seen subjects designed by our celebrated artist Stothard, from Clarissa Harlowe and the Novelist's Magazine, converted, with incredible dexterity, by these bookselling Breslaws, into Scriptural embellishments! One of these venders of 'Family Bibles' lately called on me, to consult me professionally about a folio engraving he brought with him. It represented Mons. Buffon, seated, contemplating various groups of animals that surrounded him: he merely wished, he said, to be informed whether, by unclothing the naturalist, and giving him a rather more resolute look, the plate could not, at a trifling expense, be made to pass for 'Daniel in the Lions' Den!'"—CROMEK.

PAGE 361, NOTE 104.—This letter will be the better understood, when it is added that Burns had a very short time before received the subjoined letter from Mr. Cunningham:—

"*20th January*, 1790.

"In some instances it is reckoned unpardonable to quote any one's own words; but the value I have for your friendship, nothing can more truly or more elegantly express than

'Time but the impression stronger makes,
As streams their channels deeper wear.'

Having written to you twice without having heard from you, I am apt to think my letters have miscarried. My conjecture is only framed upon the chapter of accidents turning up against me, as it too often does, in the trivial, and I may with truth add, the more important affairs of life; but I shall continue occasionally to inform you what is going on among the circle of your friends in these parts. In these days of merriment, I have frequently heard your name *proclaimed* at the jovial board, under the roof of our hospitable friend at Stenhouse-mills; there were no

'Lingering moments number'd with care.'

I saw your 'Address to the New-year,' in the *Dumfries Journal*. Of your productions I shall say nothing; but my acquaintances allege that when your name is mentioned, which every man of celebrity must know often happens, I am the champion, the Mendoza, against all snarling critics and narrow-minded reptiles, of whom *a few* on this planet do *crawl*.

"With best compliments to your wife, and her black-eyed sister, I remain yours, &c."

PAGE 362, NOTE 105.—A letter to Lady Harriet Don, quoted by Mr. Cunningham in his edition of Burns, shows that the poet was now contemplating dramatic composition; and, with that view, was anxious to study the best dramatic authors, English and French being the only languages with which he was acquainted.

PAGE 363, NOTE 106.—The subject of this paper being the existence of peculiar attachments between master and servants, and the anecdote of Albert Blane being aptly introduced at the close, as an illustration of the writer's views.

PAGE 364, NOTE 107.—The sonnets of Charlotte Smith.

PAGE 365, NOTE 108.—This letter was communicated to me, says Cromek, by a gentleman, to whose liberal advice and information I am much indebted, Mr. John Murdoch, the tutor of the poet, accompanied by the following interesting note:—

"*London, Hart-Street, Bloomsbury, December 28th*, 1807.

"DEAR SIR,—The following letter, which I lately found among my papers, I copy for your perusal, partly because it is Burns's, partly because it makes honourable mention of my rational Christian friend, his father; and likewise, because it is rather flattering to myself. I glory in no one thing so much as an intimacy with good men:—the friendship of others reflects no honour. When I recollect the pleasure (and I hope benefit) I received from the conversation of William Burns, especially when on the Lord's day we walked together for about two miles to the house of prayer, there publicly to adore and praise the Giver of all Good, I entertain an ardent hope that together we shall 'renew the glorious theme in distant worlds,' with powers more adequate to the mighty subject—the exuberant beneficence of the great Creator. But to the letter:—

[*Here follows the letter relative to young William Burns.*]

"I promised myself a deal of happiness in the conversation of my dear young friend; but my promises of this nature generally prove fallacious. Two visits were the utmost that I received. At one of them, however, he repeated a lesson which I had given him about twenty years before, when he was a mere child, concerning the pity and tenderness due to animals. To that lesson (which it seems was brought to the level of his capacity), he declared himself indebted for almost all the philanthropy and general sympathy he possessed.

"Let not parents and teachers imagine that it is needless to talk seriously to children. They are sooner fit to be reasoned with than is generally thought. Strong and indelible impressions are to be made before the mind be agitated and ruffled by the numerous train of distracting cares and unruly passions, whereby it is frequently rendered almost unsusceptible of the principles and precepts of rational religion and sound morality.

"But I find myself digressing again. Poor William! then in the bloom and vigour of youth, caught a putrid fever, and in a few days, as real chief mourner, I followed his remains to the land of forgetfulness.

CROMEK. "JOHN MURDOCH."

PAGE 365, NOTE 109.—"The preceding letter to Mrs. Dunlop, explains the feelings under which this was written. The strain of indignant invective goes on some time longer in the style which our bard was too apt to indulge, and of which the reader has already seen so much."—CURRIE.

PAGE 366, NOTE 110.—This fragment, first published by Cromek, is placed by him, and subsequent editors, under 1794, and by Mr. Cunningham is supposed to be addressed to Dr. Robert Anderson, the editor of the British Poets. We have little doubt that the gentleman addressed was Dr. James Anderson, a well-known agricultural and miscellaneous writer, and the editor of a weekly miscellany entitled "The Bee." This publication was commenced in Edinburgh, December, 1790, and concluded in January 1794, when it formed eighteen volumes. The above letter by Burns, from the allusion it makes to his extreme occupation by business, as well as from the bitterness of its tone, seems to have been written in the latter part of 1790, immediately after the poet had commenced Exciseman; it was an answer, probably, to an application for aid in the conduct of "The Bee," then about to be started. For these reasons, the present editor has shifted its place in the poet's correspondence.

PAGE 367, NOTE 111.—Susan, one of Mrs. Dunlop's daughters, had married a French gentleman of rank and fortune, of the name of Henri, and this letter of the poet's was written to Mrs. Dunlop, upon the receipt of intelligence that Madame Henri had given birth to a child some months after the death of the father, who had died in consequence of an inflammatory disease engendered by exposure to wet. M. Henri died on the 22nd of June, 1790, and his Posthumous Child was born on the 4th of November in the same year. Both Mrs. Dunlop's daughter and her son-in-law were residing at Loudon Castle, in Ayrshire. The letter of Burns, enclosed also the lines entitled, "Stanzas on the Birthday of a Posthumus Child." In one of the following letters of Burns to Mrs. Dunlop, he alludes to the perilous situation of Madame Henri, who had been compelled to proceed to France, for the purpose of disposing of some family affairs of her deceased husband, just at the time when the most frightful excesses of the Revolution were being perpetrated. Madame Henri never returned to England, as she died not many months after her arrival in France. To this melancholy occurrence Burns again alludes in another letter to Mrs. Dunlop. Madame Henri had left her orphan child under the care of her deceased husband's father, M. Henri the elder; but he being shortly afterwards compelled to take refuge in Switzerland, had been obliged to leave his grandchild behind him; and no tidings were heard of this child until some years afterwards, when the grandfather was enabled to return to the enjoyment of his property. In the interim of time which had elapsed, the child had been reared by a person of the name of Susette, previously a female servant of the household of M. Henri the elder; and she, though compelled to provide for her orphan charge at the cost of her own toil, had constantly observed all the delicate attentions which could possibly have been enjoyed, had his family been in the full enjoyment of their rank and possessions. This grandson of Mrs. Dunlop subsequently returned to Scotland for a short time, but continued to reside permanently at the chateau which he had inherited from his paternal grandfather; and his faithful preserver long survived to enjoy the grateful recompense of her fidelity.

PAGE 368, NOTE 112.—One of the Supervisors-General of Excise.

PAGE 368, NOTE 113.—Mr. Charles Sharpe, to whom this letter was addressed by Burns, was the father of the Charles Kirkpatrick Sharpe, the intimate friend of Sir Walter Scott, and the contributor of several very beautiful original ballads to the *Border Minstrelsy*.

PAGE 369, NOTE 114.—Burns here alludes to a box or casket presented to him by Lady W. Constable, in the lid of which was a portrait of Mary Queen of Scots, supposed to have been original. Some years ago, according to Chambers, one of the sons of the poet, in leaping on board a vessel in

India, had the misfortune to break this box, and irreparably damage the portrait.

PAGE 369, NOTE 115.—The President of the Convivial Club, called the Crochallan Fencibles, was officially known by the designation of *Colonel.*

PAGE 370, NOTE 116.—This letter was a reply to the subjoined letter from Mr. Tytler :—

"DEAR SIR—Mr. Hill yesterday put into my hands a sheet of 'Grose's Antiquities,' containing a poem of yours, entitled 'Tam o' Shanter, a Tale.' The very high pleasure I have received from the perusal of this admirable piece, I feel, demands the warmest acknowledgments. Hill tells me he is to send off a packet for you this day; I cannot resist, therefore, putting on paper what I must have told you in person, had I met with you after the recent perusal of your tale, which is, that I feel I owe you a debt, which, if undischarged, would reproach me with ingratitude. I have seldom in my life tasted of higher enjoyment from any work of genius, than I have received from this composition; and I am much mistaken, if this poem alone, had you never written another syllable, would not have been sufficient to have transmitted your name down to posterity with high reputation. In the introductory part, where you paint the character of your hero, and exhibit him at the alehouse *ingle*, with his tippling cronies, you have delineated nature with a humour and *naïveté* that would do honour to Matthew Prior; but when you describe the infernal orgies of the witches' Sabbath, and the hellish scenery in which they are exhibited, you display a power of imagination that Shakespeare himself could not have exceeded. I know not that I have ever met with a picture of more horrible fancy than the following:—

'Coffins stood round like open presses,
That shaw'd the dead in their last dresses;
And, by some devilish cantrip sleight,
Each in his cauld hand held a light.'

But when I came to the succeeding lines, my blood ran cold within me :—

'A knife, a father's throat had mangled,
Whom his ain son of life bereft;
The grey hairs yet stack to the heft.'

"And here, after the two following lines, 'Wi' mair o' horrible and awfu',' &c., the descriptive part might, perhaps, have been better closed, than the four lines which succeed, which, though good in themselves, yet, as they derive all their merit from the satire they contain, are here rather misplaced among the circumstances of pure horror.

[The four lines were as follow :—

'Three lawyers' tongues turned inside out,
Wi' lies seemed like a beggar's clout,
And priests' hearts rotten, black as muck,
Lay stinking, vile, in every neuk.'

The poet expunged them, in obedience to the recommendation of Mr. Tytler.]

"The initiation of the young witch is most happily described—the effect of her charms exhibited in the dance of Satan himself—the apostrophe, 'Ah, little thought thy reverend grannie!'—the transport of Tam, who forgets his situation, and enters completely into the spirit of the scene—are all features of high merit in this excellent composition. The only fault it possesses, is, that the winding up, or conclusion of the story, is not commensurate to the interest which is excited by the descriptive and characteristic painting of the preceding parts. The preparation is fine, but the result is not adequate. But for this, perhaps, you have a good apology—you stick to the popular tale.

"And now that I have got out my mind, and feel a little relieved of the weight of that debt I owed you, let me end this desultory scroll by an advice:—You have proved your talent for a species of composition in which but a very few of our own poets have succeeded. Go on—write more tales in the same style—you will eclipse Prior and La Fontaine; for, with equal wit, equal power of numbers, and equal *naïveté* of expression, you have a bolder and more vigorous imagination."

PAGE 370, NOTE 117.—This respectable and benevolent person, since Principal of the University of Edinburgh, had written to Burns, requesting his aid in revising Bruce's poems, and a contribution to swell the volume. It does not appear that the edition which subsequently appeared, contained any poem by Burns.

PAGE 372, NOTE 118.—This is the letter which Mr. Dugald Stewart, in his communication to Dr. Currie respecting Burns (printed in the Memoir written by that gentleman), says he read with surprise, as evincing that the unlettered Ayrshire bard had formed "a distinct conception of the general principles of the doctrine of association." (See the foregoing *résumé* of Dr. Currie's Memoir of Burns. The doctrine here alluded to, is one peculiar, we believe, to the Scotch school of metaphysicians, and mainly consists in an assertion that our ideas of beauty in objects, of all kinds, arise from our associating with them some other ideas of an agreeable kind. For instance, our notion of beauty in the cheek of a pretty maiden arises from our notions of her health, innocence, and so forth; our notion of the beauty of a Highland prospect, such as the Trosachs, from our notions of the romantic kind of life formerly led in it; as if there were no female beauty independent of both health and innocence, or fine scenery where men had not formerly worn tartans and claymores. The whole of the above letter of Burns is, in reality (though, perhaps, unmeant by him), a satire on this doctrine, which, notwithstanding the eloquence of an Alison, a Stewart and a Jeffrey, must now be considered as amongst the dreams of philosophy.

PAGE 374, NOTE 119.—"This gentleman, the factor, or steward of Burns's noble friend, Lord Glencairn, with a view to encourage a second edition of the poems, laid the volume before his lordship, with such an account of the rustic bard's situation and prospects, as from his slender acquaintance with him he could furnish. The result, as communicated to Burns by Mr. Dalzel, is highly creditable to the character of Lord Glencairn. After reading the book, his lordship declared that its merits greatly exceeded his expectation, and he took it with him, as a *literary curiosity*, to Edinburgh. He repeated his wishes to be of service to Burns, and desired Mr. Dalzel to inform him, that in patronising the book, ushering it with effect into the world, or treating with the booksellers, he would most willingly give every aid in his power; adding his request, that Burns would take the earliest opportunity of letting him know in what way or manner he could best further his interests." —CROMEK.

PAGE 374, NOTE 120.—The gist of this passage will be the better understood, when it is explained that Mrs. Burns's accouchement had occurred only two days before the date of this letter, that is, on the 9th of April. It was the birth of William Nicol Burns, to which this letter refers. This child was christened after Mr. W. N., the teacher in the High School, Edinburgh, and the warm friend of Burns.

PAGE 374, NOTE 121.—An allusion to the grandson of Mrs. Dunlop, and son of M. and Madame Henri. For additional particulars the reader is referred to the foregoing Note, number 111.

PAGE 375, NOTE 122.—Dr. Robinson, who stood in the relationship of maternal uncle to Mr. Cunningham.

PAGE 376, NOTE 123.—Lady E. Cunningham was the sister of Burns's best patron, the deceased Earl of Glencairn, as also of the existing nobleman (who had succeeded to his brother). Lady E. C. died in the month of August, 1804, unmarried.

PAGE 376, NOTE 124.—The accompanying poem enclosed in this letter, and to which Burns here alludes, was the "Lament for James, Earl of Glencairn."

PAGE 376, NOTE 125.—Colonel Fullarton is mentioned with praise and respect by Burns, in his poem of *The Vision.* This letter was first published in the year 1828, in the *Paisley Magazine.*

PAGE 376, NOTE 126.—An allusion to eight-page song books, produced in the coarsest manner, and containing equally coarse matter, usually heralded with the title of *Six Excellent Songs for One Halfpenny*, the price at which they were sold; and, secondly, to the Penny Almanacks published at Aberdeen.

PAGE 377, NOTE 127.—Colonel Fullarton was a native of Ayrshire.

PAGE 377, NOTE 128.—Mr. Cunningham, in his edition of Burns, gives a very interesting note respecting the "charming lovely Davies;" from which we learn, that she was the youngest daughter of Dr. Davies, of Tenby, in Pembrokeshire, and a relative of the Riddels of Friars' Carse. She died young, under the distress of mind consequent on the neglect of a lover.

PAGE 379, NOTE 129.—Grose, in the introduction to his "Antiquities of Scotland," acknowledges his obligations to Burns in the following paragraph, some of the terms of which will scarcely fail to amuse the modern reader:—

"To my *ingenious* friend, Mr. Robert Burns, I have been seriously obligated: he was not only at the pains of making out what was most worthy of notice in Ayrshire, the country honoured by his birth, but he also wrote, expressly for this work, the *pretty tale* annexed to Alloway Church:—"

This "pretty tale" being "Tam o' Shanter."

PAGE 379, NOTE 130.—Mrs. Riddel, of Woodlee Park, near Dumfries. Her maiden name was Maria Woodlee, or Woodleigh, of Woodlee. Another Mrs. Riddel (she of Friars' Carse) was also a friend of Burns's.

PAGE 379, NOTE 131.—The Philosophy of Natural History.

PAGE 380, NOTE 132.—An allusion to an

admonitory letter received from W. Nicol, by Burns.

PAGE 380, NOTE 133.—Mr. Nicol had purchased a small piece of ground, called Laggan, on the Nith. There took place the bacchanalian scene which called forth "Willie Brewed a Peck o' Maut."

PAGE 381, NOTE 134.—This letter was communicated by Mr. Gilchrist, of Stamford, to Sir Egerton Brydges, by whom it was published in the *Censura Literaria*, in the year 1796.

PAGE 384, NOTE 135.—The lengthy correspondence which ensued between Mr. G. Thomson and Robert Burns, originated in the circumstances referred to in the first and second letters. Mr. George Thomson, of Edinburgh, having designed a more than usually elegant collection of the national music of Scotland, applied to the poet for his aid in improving the songs, many of which were unworthy of publication. Burns, with that enthusiasm which he entertained on the subject of Scottish music, entered heartily into Mr. Thomson's views, and contributed about sixty songs to the work. The letters which passed between the poet and Mr. Thomson are here given, as prepared for publication by the latter, and presented to the public in the volumes of Dr. Currie, who prefaced them with the following note:—"The undertaking of Mr. Thomson is one on which the public may be congratulated in various points of view, not merely as having collected the finest of the Scottish songs and airs of past times, but as having given occasion to a number of original songs of our bard, which equal or surpass the former efforts of the pastoral muses of Scotland, and which, if we mistake not, may be safely compared with the lyric poetry of any age or country. The letters of Mr. Burns to Mr. Thomson include the songs he presented to him, some of which appear in different stages of their progress; and these letters will be found to exhibit occasionally his notions of song-writing, and his opinions on various subjects of taste and criticism. These opinions, it will be observed, were called forth by the observations of his correspondent, Mr. Thomson; and without the letters of this gentlemen, those of Burns would have been often unintelligible. He has, therefore, yielded to the earnest request of the trustees of the family of the poet, to suffer them to appear in their natural order; and, independently of the illustration they give to the letters of our bard, it is not to be doubted that their intrinsic merit will ensure them a reception from the public, far beyond what Mr. Thomson's modesty would permit him to suppose."

Mr. George Thomson was born at Limekilns, in Fife, about the year 1759, and educated at Banff, his father being a schoolmaster successively at these two places. Through the recommendation of Mr. Home, the author of "Douglas," he was admitted, in 1780, to the office of the Board of Trustees for the Encouragement of Manufactures in Scotland, as their junior clerk: and he is now (1838), after a service of fifty-eight years, principal clerk to the Board. His natural taste for music was cultivated, in his early years, at the meetings of the St. Cecilia Society in Edinburgh—an amateur body, whose performances used to attract no inconsiderable share of notice in those days. Mr. Thomson's Collection of Scottish Airs, first designed about 1792, was not completed for many years: it has been, in fact, the employment of the leisure hours of the better part of his life.

Mr. Thomson's work is entitled, "A Select Collection of Original Scottish Airs for the Voice: to which are added, Introductory and Concluding Symphonies and Accompaniments for the Piano Forte and Violin, by Pleyel and Kozeluch; with Select and characteristic Verses, by the most admired Scottish Poets," &c. London: Printed and sold by Preston, No. 97, Strand. It has been completed in five volumes—one edition being in folio, and another in 8vo.

PAGE 385, NOTE 136.—We have been informed that Burns marked his loathing of remuneration, by the use of even a stronger term than this, which was substituted by the original editor.

PAGE 390, NOTE 137.—The Commissioners of the Scottish Board of Excise were, at this time, George Brown, Thomas Wharton, James Stodart, Robert Graham (of Fintry), and John Grieve, Esqrs.

PAGE 391, NOTE 138.—"The following extract from a letter addressed by Mr. Bloomfield to the Earl of Buchan, contains so interesting an exhibition of the modesty inherent in real worth, and so philosophical, and at the same time, so poetical an estimate of the different characters and destinies of Burns and its author, that I should esteem myself culpable were I to withhold it from the public view.

"'The illustrious soul that has left amongst us the name of Burns, has often been lowered down to a comparison with me; but the comparison exists more in circumstances than in essentials. That man stood up with the stamp of superior intellect on his brow; a visible greatness: and great and patriotic subjects would only have called into action the powers of his mind, which lay inactive while he played calmly and exquisitely the pastoral pipe.

"'The letters to which I have alluded in my Preface to the "Rural Tales," were friendly warnings, pointed with immediate reference to the fate of that extraordinary man. "Remember Burns" has been the watchword of my friends. I do remember Burns; but *I am* not Burns! neither have I his fire to fan or to quench, nor passions to control! Where, then, is my merit, if I make a peaceful voyage on a smooth sea, and with no mutiny on board? To a lady (I have it from herself) who remonstrated with him on his danger from drink, and the pursuits of some of his associates, he replied:—"Madam, they would not thank me for my company, if I did not drink with them. I *must* give them a slice of my constitution." How much is it not to be regretted that he did not give them thinner slices of his constitution, that it might have lasted longer.'"—CROMEK.

PAGE 391, NOTE 139.—This letter is correctly dated, according to Chambers's arrangement, in the year 1793. The allusions to the untoward influence of his political opinions on his Excise promotion, which it contains, sufficiently identify it as having been written in this year. And in that respect I fully agree with Mr. Chambers, in opposition to Dr. Currie, who has attributed it to the year 1792 in his own arrangement.

PAGE 391, NOTE 140.—At the head of this letter was a transcribed copy of the two songs, "Puirtith Cauld" and "Gala Water," which will respectively be found in the foregoing part of this volume, amongst the poems.

PAGE 392, NOTE 141.—Third son of Alexander, fifth Earl of Kellie, by Janet, daughter of the celebrated physician and wit, Dr. Pitcairn. Mr. Erskine was a wit and a poet, and the author, in part of a curious and rare volume, entitled "Letters between the Hon. Andrew Erskine and James Boswell, Esq., London, 1763"—an amusing specimen of youthful frolic and vivacity. Mr. E. died in 1793.

PAGE 393, NOTE 142.—The song of Dr. Walcot (Peter Pindar), on the same subject, is as follows:—

"Ah ope, Lord Gregory, thy door!
  A midnight wanderer sighs;
Hard rush the rains, the tempests roar,
  And lightnings cleave the skies."

"Who comes with woe at this drear night—
  A pilgrim of the gloom?
If she whose love did once delight,
  My cot shall yield her room."

"Alas! thou heard'st a pilgrim mourn,
  That once was prized by thee;
Think of the ring by yonder burn,
  Thou gav'st to love and me."

"But should'st thou not poor Marion know,
  I'll turn my feet and part;
And think the storms that round me blow,
  Far kinder than thy heart."

"It is but doing justice to Dr. Walcot to mention that HIS song is purely original. Mr. Burns saw it, liked it, and immediately wrote the other on the same subject, which is derived from an old Scottish ballad of uncertain origin."—CURRIE.

PAGE 393, NOTE 143.—In closing this letter, Burns here transcribed and appended his own ballad of "Lord Gregory," as it stands in the text, now amongst the poems, and as it was published in Mr. Thomson's collection.

PAGE 393, NOTE 144.—This letter bears date subsequently to the marriage of Robert Burns.

PAGE 394, NOTE 145.—The following recent account of Clarinda, written in Feb. 1837, appears in a note, to the Memoir of Lord Craig, in "Kay's Edinburgh Portraits," and will be read with interest by all admirers of the poet:—"It may, perhaps, be worthy of notice that Lord Craig was cousin-german of Mrs. M'Lehose, the celebrated Clarinda of Burns, who is still living in Edinburgh, and was left an annuity by his lordship. She is now nearly eighty years of age, but enjoys excellent health. We found her sitting in the parlour, with some papers on the table. Her appearance, at first, betrayed a little of that languour and apathy which attend age and solitude; but the moment she comprehended the object of our visit, her countenance, which even yet retains the lineaments of what Clarinda may be supposed to have been, became animated and intelligent. 'That,' said she, rising up and pointing to an engraving over the mantel-piece, 'is a likeness of my relative (Lord Craig), about whom you have been inquiring. He was the best friend I ever had! After a little conversation about his Lordship, she directed our attention to a picture of Burns, by Horsburgh, after Taylor, on the opposite wall of the apartment. 'You well know who that is—it was presented to me by Constable and Co., for having simply declared what I knew to be true, that the likeness was good.' We spoke of the correspondence betwixt the poet and Clarinda, at which she smiled, and pleasantly remarked on the great change which the lapse of so many years had produced on her personal appearance. Indeed, any observation respecting Burns seemed to afford her pleasure; and she laughed at a little anecdote we told of him, which she had never before heard.

"Having prolonged our intrusion to the limits of courtesy, and conversed on various topics, we took leave of the venerable lady, highly gratified by the interview."

PAGE 394, NOTE 146.—A seal with these fanciful bearings was actually cut for the poet, and used by him for the remainder of his life. Its impression is represented under a profile of the poet, in Mr. Cunningham's edition of Burns, vol. viii., p. 168.

PAGE 394, NOTE 147.—The poet here alludes to David Allan, painter, usually called the Scottish Hogarth. He was born at Alloa, in 1744, and educated through the kindness of some generous ladies. His serious paintings are not much admired; but he had a happy knack at hitting off Scottish rustic figures. At his death in 1796, he left a series of drawings illustrative of Burns's works.

PAGE 395, NOTE 148.—An old song, commencing with the two following stanzas:

"Here awa, there awa, here awa Willie,
Here awa, there awa, here awa hame;
Lang have I sought thee, dear have I bought thee,
Now I hae gotten my Willie again.

Through the lang muir I have followed my Willie,
Through the lang muir I have followed him hame,
Whatever betide us, nought shall divide us,
Love now rewards all my sorrow and pain."

PAGE 395, NOTE 149.—In Dr. Currie's edition of Burns's works, there precede two additional letters before this one; but as these consist absolutely and entirely of transcripts of the two songs "Oh open the Door to Me, O!" and "Jessie," respectively, it will suffice simply to refer the reader to those songs, as they will be found amongst the poems; and to add, that they were written for, and first published, in Mr. Thomson's collection.

PAGE 396, NOTE 150.—"Wandering Willie," as altered by Mr. Erskine and Mr. Thomson.

"Here awa, there awa, wandering Willie,
Here awa, there awa, haud awa hame;
Come to my bosom, my ain only dearie,
Tell me thou bring'st my Willie the same.

Winter winds blew loud and caul' at our parting,
Fears for my Willie brought tears in my ee,
Welcome now simmer, and welcome my Willie,
As simmer to nature, so Willie to me.

Rest ye wild storms in the cave o' your slumbers,
How your dread howling a lover alarms!
Blow soft ye breezes! roll gently ye billows!
And waft my dear laddie ance mair to my arms."

PAGE 396, NOTE 151.—The next communication of Burns to Mr. Thomson, (namely, that which intervenes between letters No. 262 and 263,) marked No. XVIII. in Currie's publication of their correspondence, consisted merely of the songs, "The Soldier's Return," and "Meg o' the Mill," respectively, to be found in the accompanying edition of Burns's Poetical Works.

PAGE 396, NOTE 152.—"Burns here calls himself the 'Voice of Coila,' in imitation of Ossian, who denominates himself the 'Voice of Cona.' 'Sae merry as we a' hae been!' and "Good night, and joy be wi' you a'!' are the names of two Scottish tunes."—CURRIE.

PAGE 396, NOTE 153.—"Several of the alterations seem to be of little importance in themselves, and were adopted, it may be presumed, for the sake of suiting the words better to the music. The Homeric epithet for the sea, *dark-heaving*, suggested by Mr. Erskine, is in itself more beautiful, as well, perhaps, as more sublime, than, *wide-roaring*, which he has retained; but, as it is only applicable to a placid state of the sea, or, at most, to the swell left on its surface after the storm is over, it gives a picture of that element not so well adapted to the ideas of eternal separation, which the fair mourner is supposed to deprecate. From the original song of 'Here awa, Willie,' Burns has borrowed nothing but the second line and part of the first. The superior excellence of this beautiful poem will, it is hoped, justify the different editions of it which we have given."—CURRIE.

PAGE 397, NOTE 154.—This was subsequently effected to the mutual satisfaction both of Burns and of Mr. Thomson, and will be gathered from the poems in question, as printed in the foregoing part of this volume.

PAGE 397, NOTE 155.—"Mr. Thomson, it

appears, did not approve of this song, even in its altered state. It does not appear in the correspondence; but it is probably one to be found in his manuscripts, beginning

Yestreen I got a pint of wine
 A place where body saw na,
Yestreen lay on this breast of mine,
 The gowden locks of Anna.

It is highly characteristic of our bard, but the strain of sentiment does not correspond with the air to which he proposes it should be allied."—CURRIE.

PAGE 397, NOTE 156.—Alluding to the time when he held the farm of Ellisland, as tenant to Mr. Miller.

PAGE 397, NOTE 157.—This gentleman most obligingly favoured the editor with a perfect copy of the original letter, and allowed him to lay it before the public. It is partly printed in Dr. Currie's edition.—CHAMBERS.

"It will be necessary to state, that in consequence of the poet's freedom of remark on public measures, maliciously misrepresented to the Board of Excise, he was represented as actually dismissed from his office. This report induced Mr. Erskine to propose a subscription in his favour, which was refused by the poet with that elevation of sentiment that peculiarly characterised his mind, and which is so happily displayed in this letter. See letter to R. Graham of Fintry, December 1792, written by Burns, with even more than his accustomed pathos and eloquence, in further explanation."—CROMEK. Mr. Erskine, of Mar, at all times of his life a noted Whig, became Earl of Mar, in 1824, in consequence of the reversal of his grandfather's attainder. He died August 20, 1825, aged eighty-four.

PAGE 399, NOTE 158.—"The original letter from Mr. Thomson contains many observations on the Scottish songs, and on the manner of adapting the words to the music, which, at his desire, are suppressed. The subsequent letter of Mr. Burns refers to several of these observations."—CURRIE.

PAGE 399, NOTE 159.—"The reader has already seen that Burns did not finally adopt all of Mr. Erskine's alterations."—CURRIE.

PAG 400, NOTE 160.—"The song to the tune of 'Bonnie Dundee' is that named 'Jessie.' The ballad of the 'Mill, Mill O!' is that beginning, 'When wild war's deadly blasts are blawn.'"—CURRIE.

PAGE 400, NOTE 161.—*Lugs*, a Scottish popular term for ears.

PAGE 400, NOTE 162.—The song here mentioned, is that published in Number xviii of the *Scot's Musical Museum* and of which the first line runs thus:—

Oh ken ye what Meg O' the Mill has
 gotten.

"This song," says Mr. Thomson, in an original note, "is surely Mr. Burns's own writing, though he does not generally praise his own songs so much."

PAGE 400, NOTE 163.—The air here mentioned, is that for which he wrote the ballad of *Bonnie Jean*.

PAGE 400, NOTE 164.—The original version of the song enclosed with this letter, differed somewhat materially from the present version in the text.

PAGE 402, NOTE 165.—"The lines were the third and fourth:—

Wi' mony a sweet babe fatherless,
And mony a widow mourning.

As our poet had maintained a long silence, and the first number of Mr. Thomson's musical work was in the press, this gentleman ventured, by Mr. Erskine's advice, to substitute for them in that publication,

'And eyes again with pleasure beam'd
 That had been bleared with mourning.'

Though better suited to the music, these lines are inferior to the original. This is the only alteration adopted by Mr. Thomson, which Burns did not approve, or at least assent to."—CURRIE.

PAGE 403, NOTE 166.—A remittance of five pounds.

PAGE 404, NOTE 167.—Katherine Rutherford, of Fernilee, in the county of Selkirk, who married Mr. Patrick Cockburn.—She died full of years in 1794.

PAGE 406, NOTE 168.—"Gloamin'—twilight, probably from glooming. A beautiful poetic word, which ought to be adopted in England. A gloamin'-shot, a twilight interview."—CURRIE.

PAGE 406, NOTE 169.—The poet inserts the song of "Dainty Davie," which it seems to have been the purpose of this letter to communicate. Burns had previously communicated, for Johnson's Museum, a song nearly the same, the stanzas of which conclude with the awkward expression, "The gardener wi' his paidle," and to which he makes allusion in the brief prose text of this epistle.

PAGE 406, NOTE 170.—This Miss Craik was the daughter of Mr. Craik of Arbigland, in the Stewartry of Kircudbright.

PAGE 407, NOTE 171.—The dowager Lady Glencairn, widow of William, thirteenth Earl of Glencairn, and, consequently, mother of James, the fourteenth Earl, and Burns's best patron.

PAGE 407, NOTE 172.—Lady Harriet Don was the daughter of the Dowager Countess of Glencairn, and sister to James, fourteenth Earl of Glencairn. The *little angel* to whom Burns alludes, was the Dowager Countess's grandson, then a child, and afterwards better known for his urbanity and accomplishments, as Sir Alexander Don, of Newton Don.

PAGE 410, NOTE 173.—"Mr. Thomson's list of songs for his publication. In his remarks the bard proceeds in order, and goes through the whole; but on many of them he merely signifies his approbation. All his remarks of any importance are presented to the reader."—CURRIE.

PAGE 410, NOTE 174—"This alteration Mr. Thomson has adopted (or at least intended to adopt), instead of the last stanza of the original song, which is objectionable in point of delicacy."—CURRIE.

PAGE 411, NOTE 175.—It is very surprising that Burns should have thought it necessary to substitute new verses for the old song to this air, which is one of the most exquisite effusions of genuine natural sentiment in the whole range of Scottish lyrical poetry. Its merit is now fully appreciated, while Burns's substituted song is never sung.

PAGE 411, NOTE 176.—The song to which Burns here alludes, is one of which he afterwards sent a perfected copy, and which was published in Mr. Thomson's collection. The first line runs thus:—

Where are the joys I hae met in the morning?

This song, however, was by no means so successful as the majority of his compositions, and the original words, to the same tune for which he had intended to adapt them, have outlived his newer version, and still continue to retain their former popularity and preference. Indeed, they are actually more spirited, and possess more essentially poetical spirit, than the lines supplied by Burns.

PAGE 412, NOTE 177.—"Mr. Thomson has very properly adopted this song (if it may be so called) as the bard presented it to him. He has attached it to the air of 'Lewie Gordon,' and, perhaps, among the existing airs he could not find a better; but the poetry is suited to a much higher strain of music, and may employ the genius of some Scottish Handel, if any such should in future arise. The reader will have observed, that Burns adopted the alterations proposed by his friend and correspondent in former instances, with great readiness; perhaps, indeed, on all indifferent occasions. In the present instance, however, he rejected them, though repeatedly urged, with determined resolution. With every respect for the judgment of Mr. Thomson and his friends, we may be satisfied that he did so. He, who in preparing for an engagement, attempts to withdraw his imagination from images of death, will probably have but imperfect success, and is not fitted to stand in the ranks of battle, where the liberties of a kingdom are at issue. Of such men the conquerors of Bannockburn were not composed. Bruce's troops were inured to war, and familiar with all its sufferings and dangers. On the eve of that memorable day, their spirits were, without doubt, wound up to a pitch of enthusiasm suited to the occasion: a pitch of enthusiasm, at which danger becomes attractive, and the most terrific forms of death are no longer terrible. Such a strain of sentiment this heroic 'welcome' may be supposed well calculated to elevate—to raise their hearts high above fear, and to nerve their arms to the utmost pitch of mortal exertion. These observations might be illustrated and supported by a reference to the martial poetry of all nations, from the spirit-stirring strains of Tyrtæus, to the war-song of General Wolfe. Mr. Thomson's observation, that 'Welcome to your gory bed,' is a discouraging address, seems not sufficiently considered. Perhaps, indeed, it may be admitted, that the term *gory* is somewhat objectionable, not on account of its presenting a frightful, but a disagreeable image to the mind. But a great poet, uttering his conceptions on an interesting occasion, seeks always to present a picture that is vivid, and is uniformly disposed to sacrifice the delicacies of taste on the altar of the imagination. And it is the privilege of superior genius, by producing a new association, to elevate expressions that were originally low, and thus to triumph over the deficiencies of language. In how many instances might this be exemplified from the works of our immortal Shakespeare:—

'Who would *fardels* bear,
To groan and *sweat* under a weary life—
When he himself might his *quietus* make
With a *bare bodkin?*'

It were easy to enlarge, but to suggest such reflections is probably sufficient."—CURRIE.

PAGE 413, NOTE 178.—Burns here alludes to the melancholy death of the Honourable A. Erskine, respecting which

Thomson had written the poet a most feeling letter. Thomson, from a mistaken sense of delicacy, withheld this letter, when it subsequently fell into his hands.

PAGE 413, NOTE 179.—This Mr. Gavin Turnbull had, in 1788, published a volume of poems, entitled Poetical Essays. The work was published at Glasgow, and enjoyed even very little of its ephemeral admiration. It soon sunk into oblivion. The pieces which Burns himself quotes at full length in this letter, are really very inadequate to the brilliant eulogy with which he accompanies them. And it would seem as if his prejudice in favour of an old acquaintance had blinded his better judgment and taste; for he was very rarely guilty of such misprisions.

PAGE 414, NOTE 180.—In Dr. Currie's edition is inserted a letter from Burns to Thomson immediately following this, and before the next which I have adopted of the letters of Mr. Thomson. As the letter, No. 49, in Dr. Currie's edition, however, consisted merely of transcripts of the songs "Wilt thou be my Dearie, O!" and "Husband, husband, cease your strife," both of which are inserted amongst the poems, I did not think it necessary to re-insert them in the form of a letter. The two songs in question, however, are thus identified as having been written especially for Mr. Thomson's collection.

PAGE 415, NOTE 181.—Burns here alludes to the well-worn Scottish bank notes.

PAGE 415, NOTE 182.—A present, consisting of the edition of his own poems, as published in 1793, which were despatched by Burns with this letter.

PAGE 415, NOTE 183.—It has been supposed that this letter was addressed to Captain Robertson, of Lude.

PAGE 415, NOTE 184.—Bruce's address to his troops before the Battle of Bannockburn:—

Scot's wha hae wi' Wallace bled.

PAGE 416, NOTE 185.—"The lady to whom the bard has so happily and justly applied the quotation in this letter, paid the debt of nature a few months ago. The graces of her person were only equalled by the singular endowments of her mind; and her poetical talents rendered her an interesting friend to Burns, in a part of the world where he was, in a great measure, excluded from the sweet intercourse of literary society."—GILBERT BURNS, 1820.

PAGE 416, NOTE 186.—Bruce's address to his troops before the Battle of Bannockburn:—

Scot's wha hae wi' Wallace bled.

PAGE 416, NOTE 187.—The same as stated in the foregoing Note, number 186.

PAGE 418, NOTE 188.—This gentleman held the office of Distributor of Stamps at Dumfries. Burns, who at first lived in the floor above his office, formed an intimacy with him, which lasted till the death of the poet. Mr. Syme was an agreeable table companion, and possessed considerable wit, the effusions of which were sometimes mistaken for Burns's. He died at his house of Ryedale, near Dumfries, November 24, 1831, in his seventy-seventh year.

PAGE 418, NOTE 189.—Burns here alludes to the song, of which the first line runs thus:—

Oh wat ye what's in yon town,

And which was composed in honour of Mrs. Oswald, of Auchincruive.

PAGE 421, NOTE 190.—Mr. David Macculloch is no longer living. One of his sisters, subsequently to the date of this letter, married Mr. Thomas Scott, brother to Sir Walter Scott.

PAGE 422, NOTE 191.—Dr. Currie objects to the expression "ruffian feeling." He suggests that the word "ruder" would have possessed more euphony, and been more in keeping with the tenderness of the piece. I do not exactly agree in his criticism, nor do I think that the expression in the text is too "rugged an epithet" for the sense which Burns evidently intended to convey. It is one of the essential beauties of the poetry of Burns, that he seems almost invariably to have hit, as if by intuition, upon the most apt, appropriate, and positive expression whereby to convey the particular sentiment which he sought to communicate. He rarely says too much, and as rarely too little: a merit which has not been attributable to many of our most polished poets, and of which Shakepeare is the only pure example in English literature.

PAGE 423, NOTE 192.—"This Virgilian order of the poet should, I think, be disobeyed with respect to the song in question, the second stanza excepted."—NOTE BY MR. THOMSON.

"Doctors differ. The objection to the second stanza does not strike the editor."—CURRIE.

PAGE 425, NOTE 193.—Our bard had before received the same advice, and so far took it into consideration, as to have cast about for a subject.

PAGE 426, NOTE 194.—This, as well as other poems to which he alludes in this letter, had previously been published by Mr. Johnson in the *Scots' Musical Museum*, and Mr. Thomson, suspecting the authorship, had inquired of Burns if they were his composition.

PAGE 426, NOTE 195.—The name of a mountain in the north.

PAGE 426, NOTE 196.—"The reader will be curious to see this poem, so highly praised by Burns. He it is :—

'Keen blaws the wind o'er Donnocht-Head,
The snaw drives snelly through the dale,
The gaberlunzie tirls my sneck,
And, shivering, tells his waefu' tale.
"Cauld is the night, oh, let me in,
And dinna let your minstrel fa',
And dinna let his winding-sheet
Be naething but a wreath o' snaw.

"Full ninety winters hae I seen,
And pip'd where gor-cocks whirring flew,
And mony a day I've danc'd, I ween,
To lilts which from my drone I blew."
My Eppie wak'd, and soon she cried,
"Get up guidman, and let him in;
For weel ye ken the winter night
Was short when he began his din."

My Eppie's voice, oh wow it's sweet,
Even though she bans and scaulds a wee;
But when it's tun'd to sorrow's tale,
Oh, haith, it's doubly dear to me!
"Come in, auld carl, I'll steer my fire,
I'll make it bleeze a bonny flame;
Your bluid is thin, ye've tint the gate,
Ye should na stray sae far frae hame."

"Nae hame have I," the minstrel said,
Sad party-strife o'erturned my ha';
And, weeping at the eve of life,
I wander through a wreath o' snaw." '

"This affecting poem is apparently incomplete. The author need not be ashamed to own himself. It is worthy of Burns, or of Macneill."—CURRIE. [It was written by a gentleman of Newcastle, named Pickering.]

PAGE 426, NOTE 197.—Mr. Ritson, who had published a collection of Scottish songs in London.

PAGE 427, NOTE 198.—"Variation :—

Now to the streaming fountain,
Or up the heathy mountain, [stray;
The hart, hind, and roe, freely, wildly-wanton
In twining hazel bowers
His lay the linnet pours;
The lav'rock to the sky
Ascends wi' sangs o' joy, [day.
While the sun and thou arise to bless the

When frae my Chloris parted,
Sad, cheerless, broken-hearted,
The night's gloomy shades, cloudy, dark, o'ercast my sky.
But when she charms my sight,
In pride of beauty's light;
When through my very heart
Her beaming glories dart;
'Tis then, 'tis then I wake to life and joy!"
—CURRIE.

PAGE 428, NOTE 199.—Burns here alludes to Mrs. Whelpdale, whose maiden name, Jean Lorimer, is more familiar to our readers.

PAGE 428, NOTE 200.—Mr. Thomson must have completely misunderstood the character of this old song. It is a most romantic one, clothed in the most poetical language.

PAGE 428, NOTE 201.—"See the song, in its first and best dress. Our bard remarks upon it :—'I could easily throw this into an English mould; but, to my taste, in the simple and the tender of the pastoral song, a sprinkling of the old Scottish has an inimitable effect.' "—CURRIE.

PAGE 431, NOTE 202.—"In a conversation with his friend Mr. Perry (the proprietor of *The Morning Chronicle*), Mr. Miller represented to that gentleman the insufficiency of Burns's salary to answer the imperious demands of a numerous family. In their sympathy for his misfortunes, and in their regret that his talents were nearly lost to the world of letters, these gentlemen agreed on the plan of settling him in London. To accomplish this most desirable object, Mr. Perry, very spiritedly, made the poet a handsome offer of an annual stipend for the exercise of his talents in his newspaper. Burns's reasons for refusing this offer are stated in the present letter."—CROMEK.

PAGE 432, NOTE 203.—In Burns's next communication to Mr. Thomson, marked No. LXIX, in Currie's series of their correspondence, he merely transcribes the compound song, inserted in his Poetical Works, under the title of "Oh lassie, art thou sleeping yet?" and adds, "I do not know whether it will do."

PAGE 433, NOTE 204.—Dr. Currie was born in the neighbourhood of Ecclefechan, and with the characteristic prejudice in favour of his native village, he states, that Burns *must* have been exceedingly tipsy to have so maligned the place.

PAGE 433, NOTE 205.—At the head of this letter, Burns had inserted a copy of the song, entitled an "Address to the Woodlark," to which he alludes in the first two lines.

PAGE 434, NOTE 206.—Two verses of this song have been given to the public :—

And now your banks and bonnie braes
  But waken sad remembrance smart;
The very shades I held most dear
  Now strike fresh anguish to my heart:
Deserted bower! where are they now—
  Ah! where the garlands that I wove
With faithful care, each morn to deck
  The altars of ungrateful love?

The flowers of spring, how gay they bloomed
  When last with him I wandered here!
The flowers of spring are passed away
  For wintry horrors dark and drear.
Yon osier'd stream, by whose lone banks
  My songs have lulled him oft to rest,
Is now in icy fetters locked—
  Cold as my false love's frozen breast.

PAGE 434, NOTE 207.—Mr. Heron is sometimes, indeed frequently, spoken of as Mr. Heron of *Kerroughtree*. His proper designation, however, was Heron of Heron.

PAGE 434, NOTE 208.—These ballads, which related to Mr. Heron's contest for the representation of the Stewartry of Kirkcudbright, will be found amongst the poems in the former portion of this work.

PAGE 435, NOTE 209.—Burns here alludes to the lines which open as follow:—

Still anxious to secure your partial favour,

And which had been composed especially for Miss Fontenelle. The lines will be found at length amongst the poems.

PAGE 435, NOTE 210.—The pieces to which this letter referred, formed the introduction to the letter itself, Burns having transcribed them at length. They were those which respectively begin "How cruel are the parents," and "Mark yonder pomp of costly fashion."

PAGE 437, NOTE 211.—The song to which Burns here alludes, and a copy of which headed the letter, was that of which the initiatory line runs thus:—

Forlorn my love, no comfort near.

PAGE 437, NOTE 212.—The lines to which Burns here refers, and which he had transcribed at the head of his letter, are those which commence respectively as follows:—

Last May, a braw woer,

And,

Why, why tell thy lover.

PAGE 438, NOTE 213.—This gentleman has since resided at Glasgow in retirement: 1838.

PAGE 439, NOTE 214.—"This letter owes its origin to the following circumstance:—A neighbour of the poet's at Dumfries called on him, and complained that he had been greatly disappointed in the irregular delivery of the paper, of *The Morning Chronicle* Burns asked, 'Why do not you write to the editors of the paper?' 'Good God, Sir, can *I* presume to write to the learned editors of a newspaper?' 'Well, if *you* are afraid of writing to the editors of a newspaper, *I* am not; and, if you think proper, I'll draw up a sketch of a letter which you may copy.'

Burns tore a leaf from his Excise book, and instantly produced the sketch which I have transcribed, and which is here printed. The poor man thanked him, and took the letter home. However, that caution which the watchfulness of his enemies had taught him to exercise, prompted him to the prudence of begging a friend to wait on the person for whom it was written, and request the favour to have it returned. This request was complied with, and the paper never appeared in print."—CROMEK.

PAGE 440, NOTE 215.—The novel entitled "Edward."

PAGE 441, NOTE 216.—The request conveyed in this letter was immediately compiled with.

PAGE 442, NOTE 217.—The child died suddenly at Mauchline, and Burns was unable to see her at the last.

PAGE 442, NOTE 218.—No subsequent explanation was received by Mr. Thomson, of the name which should be substituted for Chloris in these poems, and in the midst of this work which created such general interest, it was arrested by the last and fatal illness of the poet.

PAGE 443, NOTE 219.—His proposed revisal was prevented by the untimely death of the poet.

PAGE 444, NOTE 220.—"In this humble and delicate manner did poor Burns ask for a copy of a work, of which he was principally the founder, and to which he had contributed, *gratuitously*, not less than 184 *original, altered, and collected songs!* The editor has seen 180 transcribed by his own hand for the *Museum*."—CROMEK.

PAGE 445, NOTE 221.—It is truly painful to mention, that the request was *not* granted.—CHAMBERS.

PAGE 445, NOTE 222.—Just before his death, however, Burns had the satisfaction of receiving a most satisfactory explanation of Mrs. Dunlop's silence, and the warmest assurances, that if any thing *untoward should* occur to him, her friendship should unremittingly be extended to his widow and children. The subsequent history of his family sufficiently proves how nobly, generously, and devotedly Mrs. Dunlop kept her promise to the poor dying poet.

PAGE 446, NOTE 223.—Mr. James Burness immediately complied with the request.

PAGE 446, NOTE 224.—The song of which Burns here alludes, is that of which the initiatory line runs thus:—

Fairest maid on Devon's banks.

Dr. Currie adds the following note:—"These verses, and the letter enclosing them, are written in a character that marks the very feeble state of Burns's bodily strength. Mr. Syme is of opinion that he could not have been in any danger of a jail at Dumfries, where certainly he had many firm friends, nor under any such necessity of imploring aid from Edinburgh. But about this time his reason began to be at times unsettled, and the horrors of a jail perpetually haunted his imagination. He died on the 21st of this month."

PAGE 446, NOTE 225.—The pecuniary circumstances attending Mr. Thomson's connection with Burns, appear liable, at the present day, to much misapprehension. This gentleman, whose work has ultimately met with a good sale, seems to be regarded by some, as an enriched man who measured a stinted reward to a poor one, looking for a greater recompense: and several writers have, on this ground, spoken of him in an ungracious manner.

When we go back to the time of the correspondence between the two men, and consider their respective circumstances, and the relation in which they came to stand towards each other, the conduct of Mr. Thomson assumes quite a different aspect. He and Burns were enthusiasts, the one in music, the other in poetry; they were both of them servants of the government, on limited salaries, with rising families. Mr. Thomson, with little prospect of profit, engaged in the preparation of a work which was designed to set forth the music of his native land to every possible advantage, and of which the paper and print alone were likely to exhaust his very moderate resources. For literary aid in this labour of love, he applied to the great Scottish poet, who had already gratuitously assisted Johnson in his Scottish Musical Museum. Mr. Thomson offered reasonable remuneration, but the poet scorned the idea of recompense, and declared he would write only because it gave him pleasure. Nevertheless, Mr. Thomson, in the course of their correspondence, ventured to send a pecuniary present, which, although not forming an adequate recompense for Burns's services, was still one which such men might be apt, at that period, to offer and accept from each other. This Burns, with hesitation, accepted, but sternly forbade any further remittance, protesting, that it would put a period to their correspondence. Yet Mr. Thomson, from time to time, expressed his sense of obligation, by presents of a different nature, and these the poet accepted. Burns ultimately, on an emergency, requested a renewal of the former remittance, using such terms on the occasion, as showed that his former scorn of all pecuniary remuneration was still a predominant feeling in his mind. Mr. Thomson, therefore, sent the very sum asked, believing, if he presumed to send more, that he would run a greater risk of offending than of gratifying the poet, in the then irritable state of his feelings. In all this, we humbly conceive that no unprejudiced person at the time would have seen grounds for any charge against Mr. Thomson.

It may further be remarked, that, at the time of the poet's death, though many songs had been written, only six had been published, namely, those in the first half volume, so that during the life of the poet, the publisher had realised nothing by the songs, and must have still been greatly doubtful if he should ever recover what he had already expended on the work. Before many more of the songs had appeared in connection with his music, the friends of the poet's family had resolved to collect his works for publication; upon which, Mr. Thomson thought it a duty incumbent on him to give up the manuscripts of the whole of the songs, together with the poet's and his own letters, to Dr. Currie, that they might form part of the edition of Burns's works. The full benefit of them, as literary compositions, was thus realised *for the poet's family*, Mr. Thomson only retaining an exclusive right to publish them afterwards in connection with the music. And hence, after all, the debtor side of his account with Burns is not so great as it is apt to appear. No further debate could arise on this subject, if it were to be regarded in the light in which the parties chiefly interested have regarded it. We see that Burns himself manifests no trace of a suspicion that his correspondent was a selfish or niggardly man; and it is equally certain, that his surviving family always looked on that gentleman as one of the poet's and their own kindest friends. Here, we trust, the matter will at length rest.

It is a curious fact, not hitherto known to

the public, nor even to Mr. Thomson himself, that the five pounds sent by him to Burns, as well as the larger sum which the poet borrowed about the same time from his cousin, Mr. Burness of Montrose, was not made use of on the occasion, but that the bank orders for both sums remained in Burns's house at the time of his death. This is proved by the following document, for which we are indebted to Mr. Alexander Macdonald, of the General Register House, Edinburgh:—

"The Testament Dative, and Inventory of the debts and sums of money which were justly owing to umquhile Robert Burns, officer of excise in Dumfries, at the time of his decease, viz. the 21st day of July last, faithfully made out and given up by Jean Armour, widow of the said defunct, and executrix qua relict decerned to him by decreet dative of the Commissary of Dumfries, dated 16th September last."

There was justly owing to the said defunct, at the time of his decease aforesaid, the principal sum of five pounds sterling, contained in a promissory note, dated the 14th July last, granted by Sir William Forbes and Co., bankers in Edinburgh, to George Thomson, payable on demand; which note is by the said George Thomson indorsed, payable to the defunct: Item, the principal sum of ten pounds sterling, contained in a draft dated the 15th July last, drawn by Robert Christie upon the manager for the British Linen Co. in Edinburgh, in favour of James Burness or order; which draft is by the said James Burness indorsed payable to the defunct.

"Sum of the debts owing to the defunct, £15 sterling.

"Thomas Goldie of Craigmuie, commissary of the commissariat of Dumfries, specially constituted for confirmation of te[illegible] within the bounds of the said commissa[illegible] of Dumfries, understanding that, after due summoning and lawful warning, made by public form of edict of the executors, testamentary spouse, bairns, if any were, and intromitters with the goods and gear of the said umquhile Robert Burns, and all others having or pretending to have interest in the matter underwritten, &c. &c., I decerned therein, &c,. and in his Majesty's name, constitute, ordain, and confirm the said Jean Armour, executrix qua relict to the defunct, and in and to the debt and sums of money above written.

"At Dumfries, 6th Oct. 1796."

—CHAMBERS.

PAGE 447, NOTE 226.—Alluding to an offer made by Mr. Gracie, a banker in Dumfries, to have Burns conveyed home in a post-chaise.

PAGE 447, NOTE 227.—Burns's father-in-law (the father of Mrs. Burns).

PAGE 447, NOTE 228.—This letter was written only three days before the death of Robert Burns, and is the last of the written memorials which he has bequeathed to the world.

Glossary.

"The *ch* and *gh* have always the guttural sound. The sound of the English diphthong *oo*, is commonly spelled *ou*. The French *u*, a sound which often occurs in the Scotch language, is marked *oo*, or *ui*. The *a*, in genuine Scottish words, except when forming a diphthong, or followed by an *e* mute after a single consonant, sounds generally like the broad English *a* in *wall*. The Scotch diphthong *ae*, always, and *ea*, very often, sound like the French *e* masculine. The Scottish diphthong *ey* sounds like the Latin *ei*."—R. B.

A.

A'. All.
Aback. Away, aloof.
Abeigh. At a shy distance.
Aboon. Above, up.
Abread. Abroad, in sight.
Abreed. In breadth.
Ae. One.
Aff. Off.
Afore. Before.
Aft. Oft.
Aften. Often.
Agley. Off the right line, wrong.
Aiblins. Perhaps.
Ain. Own.
Airn. Iron.
Aith. An Oath.
Aits. Oats.
Aiver. An old horse.
Aizle. A hot cinder.
Alake. Alas!
Alane. Alone.
Akwart. Awkward.
Amaist. Almost.
Amang. Among.
An'. And, if.
Ance. Once.
Ane. One, and.
Arent. Over against.
Anither. Another.
Ase. Ashes.
Asteer. Abroad, stirring.
Aught. Possession; as, *in a' my aught*, in all my possession.
Auld. Old.
Auldfarran, or **Auld-farrant.** Sagacious, cunning, prudent.
Ava. At all.
Awa'. Away.
Awfu'. Awful.
Awn. The beard of barley, oats, &c.
Awnie. Bearded.
Ayont. Beyond.

B.

Ba'. Ball.
Backets. Ash boards.
Backlins. Comin', coming back, returning.
Bade. Did bid.
Baide. Endured, did stay.
Baggie. The belly.
Bainie. Having large bones, stout.
Bairn. A child.
Bairntime. Time of having a family.
Baith. Both.
Ban. To swear.
Bane. Bone.
Bang. To beat, to strive.
Bannock. A kind of thick cake of bread, a small jaanack or loaf made of oatmeal.
Bardie. Diminutive of bard.
Barefit. Barefooted.
Barmie. Of, or like barm.
Batch. A crew, a gang.
Batts. Botts.
Baudrons. A cat.
Bauld. Bold.
Baws'nt. Having a white stripe down the face.
Be. To let be, to give over, to cease.
Bear. Barley.
Beastie. Diminutive of beast.
Beet. To add fuel to fire.
Belyve. By and bye.
Ben. In, inner room.
Bethankit. Grace after meat.
Beuk. A book.
Bicker. A kind of wooden dish, a short race.
Bie, or **Bield.** Shelter.
Bien. Wealthy, plentiful.
Big. To build.
Biggin. Building, a house.
Biggit. Built.
Bill. A bull.
Billie. A brother, a young fellow.
Bing. A heap of grain, potatoes, &c.
Birk. Birch.
Birkie. A clever fellow.
Birring. The noise of partridges, &c., when they spring.
Bit. Crisis, nick of time.
Bizz. A bustle, to buzz.
Blastie. A shrivell'd dwarf, a term of contempt.
Blastit. Blasted.
Blate. Bashful, sheepish.
Blather. Bladder.
Blaud. A flat piece of anything, to slap.
Blaw. To blow, to boast.
Bleezin'. Blazing.
Blellum. Idle, talking fellow.
Blether. To talk idly, nonsense.
Bleth'rin. Talking idly.
Blink. A little while, a smiling look, to look kindly, to shine by fits.
Blinker. A term of contempt.
Blinkin'. Smirking.
Blue-gown. One of those beggars who get annually on the king's birth-day, a blue cloak or gown, with a badge.
Bluid. Blood.
Blype. A shred, a large piece.
Bock. To vomit, to gush intermittingly.
Bocked. Gushed, vomited.
Bodle. A small old coin.
Bonnie, or **Bonny.** Handsome, beautiful.
Boord. A board.
Bore. A hole in the wall.
Boortree. The shrub elder, planted much of old in hedges of barn-yards, &c.
Bood, or **Buid.** Behoved.
Botch. An angry tumour.
Bousing. Drinking.
Bow-kail. Cabbage.
Bowt. Bended, crooked.
Brae. A declivity, a precipice, the slope of a hill.
Braid. Broad.
Braik. A kind of harrow.
Braingc. To run rashly forward.
Brang't. Reeled forward.
Brak. Broke, made insolvent.
Branks. A kind of wooden curb for horses.
Brash. A sudden illness.
Brats. Coarse clothes, rags, &c.
Brattle. A short race, hurry.
Braw. Fine, handsome.
Brawlyt, or **Brawlie.** Very well, finely, heartily.
Braxie. A diseased sheep.
Breastie. Diminutive of breast.
Breastit. Did spring up or forward.
Breckens. Fern.
Breef. An invulnerable or irresistible spell.
Breeks. Breeches.
Brewin'. Brewing.
Brie. Juice, liquid.
Brig. A bridge.
Brunstane. Brimstone.
Brisket. The breast, the bosom.
Brither. A brother.
Brock. A badger.
Brogue. A hum, a trick.
Broo. Broth, liquid, water.
Broose. A race at country weddings, who shall first reach the bridegroom's house on returning from church.
Brugh. A burgh.
Bruilzie. A broil, a combustion.
Brunt. Did burn, burnt.
Brust. To burst, burst.
Buchan-bullers. The boiling of the sea among the rocks on the coast of Buchan.
Buirdly. Stout made, broad built.
Bum-clock. A humming beetle that flies in the summer evenings.
Bummin'. Humming as bees.
Bummle. To blunder.
Bummler. A blunderer.
Bunker. A window-seat.
Burdies. Diminutive of birds.
Bure. Did bear.
Burn. Water, a rivulet.
Burnewin: i. e. *burn the wind*. A blacksmith.
Burnie. Diminutive of burn.
Buskit. Dressed.
Busle. A bustle, to bustle.
But. Without.
But an' ben. Outer and inner apartment.
By himself. Lunatic distracted.
Byke. A bee-hive.
Byre. A cow-stable, a shippen.

C.

Ca'. To call, to name, to drive.
Ca't or **ca'd.** Called, driven, calved.
Cadger. A carrier.
Cadie or **caudie.** A person, a young fellow, an errand boy.
Caff. Chaff.
Caird. A tinker.
Cairn. A loose heap of stones.
Calf-ward. A small enclosure for calves.
Callan. A boy.
Caller. Fresh, sound.
Cannie. Gentle, mild, dexterous.
Cannilie. Dexterously, gently.
Cantie or **canty.** Cheerful, merry.
Cantrip. A charm, a spell.
Cap-stane. Cope-stone, keystone.
Careerin. Cheerfully.
Carl. An old man.
Carlin. A stout old woman.
Cartes. Cards.
Castock. The stalk of a cabbage.
Caudron. A cauldron.
Cauk and keel. Chalk and red clay.
Cauld. Cold.
Caup. A wooden drinking vessel.
Chanter. A part of a bagpipe.
Chap. A person, a fellow, a blow.
Chaup. A stroke, a blow.
Cheekit. Cheeked.
Cheep. A chirp, to chirp.
Chiel or **Cheel.** A young fellow.
Chimla or **Chimlie.** A fire-grate, fire-place.
Chimla-lug. The fire-side.

Chittering. Shivering, trembling.
Chokin'. Choking.
Chow. To chew; *cheek for chow*, side by side.
Chuffie. Fat-faced.
Clachan. A small village about a church, a hamlet.
Claise, or claes. Clothes.
Claith. Cloth.
Claithing. Clothing.
Claivers. Nonsense, not speaking sense.
Clap. Clapper of a mill.
Clarkit. Wrote.
Clash. An idle tale, the story of the day.
Clatter. To tell little idle stories, an idle story.
Claught. Snatched at, laid hold of.
Claut. To clean, to scrape.
Clauted. Scraped.
Claw. To scratch.
Cleed. To clothe.
Cleekit. Having caught.
Clinkin'. Jerking, clinking.
Clinkumbell. Who rings the church bell.
Clips. Shears.
Clishmaclaver. Idle conversation.
Cloak. To hatch, a beetle.
Cloakin'. Hatching.
Cloot. The hoof of a cow sheep, &c.
Clootie. An old name for the devil.
Clour. A bump or swelling after a blow.
Coaxin'. Wheedling.
Coble. A fishing boat.
Coft. Bought.
Cog. A wooden dish.
Coggie. Diminutive of cog.
COILA. From *Kyle*, a district of Ayrshire, so called saith tradition, from Coil, or Coilus, a Pictish monarch.
Collie. A general and sometimes a particular name for country curs.
Commaun. Command.
Cood. The cud.
Coof. A blockhead, a ninny.
Cookit. Appeared and disappeared by fits.
Coost. Did cast.
Coot, or Kuit. The ancle.
Cootie. A wooden kitchen dish; also those fowls whose legs are clad with feathers are said to be cootie.
Corbies. A species of the crow.
Core. Corps, party, clan.
Corn't. Fed with oats.
Cotter. The inhabitant of a cot-house, or cottage.
Couthie. Kind, loving.
Cowe. To terrify, to keep under, to lop; a fright, a branch of furze, broom, &c.
Cowp, To barter, to tumble over, a gang.
Cowpit. Tumbled.
Cowrin'. Cowering.
Cowte. A colt.
Cozie. Snug.
Cozily. Snugly.
Crabbit. Crabbed, fretful.
Crack. Conversation, to converse.
Crackin'. Conversing.
Craft, or Croft. A field near a house, in old husbandry.
Craiks. Cries or calls incessantly, a bird.
Crambo-clink, or crambo-jingle. Rhymes, doggerel verses.
Crank. The noise of an ungreased wheel.
Crankous. Fretful, captious.
Cranreuch. The hoar frost.
Crap. A crop, to crop.
Craw. A crow of a cock, a rook.
Creel. A basket. To have one's wits in a creel, to be crazed, to be fascinated.
Creeshie. Greasy.
Crood, or croud. To coo as a dove.
Croon. A hollow and continued moan; to make a noise like the continued roar of a bull; to hum a tune.
Crooning. Humming.
Crouchie. Crook-backed.
Crouse. Cheerful, courageous.
Crously. Cheerfully, courageously.
Crowdie. A composition of oatmeal and boiled water, sometimes from the broth of beef, mutton, &c.
Crowdie-time. Breakfast-time.
Crowlin. Crawling.
Crummock. A cow with crooked horns.
Crump. Hard and brittle, spoken of bread.
Crunt. A blow on the head with a cudgel.
Cuif. A blockhead, a ninny.
Cummock. A short staff with a crooked head.
Curchie. A curtsey.
Curler. A player at a game on the ice, practised in Scotland, called curling.
Curlie. Curled, whose hair falls naturally in ringlets.
Curling. A well-known game on ice.
Curmurring. Murmuring, a slight rumbling noise.
Curpin. The crupper.
Cushat. The dove, or wood-pigeon.
Cutty. Short, a spoon broken in the middle, a short pipe.

D.

Daddie. A father.
Daffin. Merriment, foolishness.
Daft. Merry, giddy, foolish.
Daimen. Rare, now and then; daimen icker, an ear of corn now and then.
Dainty. Pleasant, good-humoured, agreeable.
Dales. Plains valleys.
Darklins. Darkling.
Daud. To thrash, to abuse.
Daur. To dare.
Daurt. Dared.
Dawd. A large piece.
Daurg, or Daurk. A day's labour.
Dautit, or Dautet. Fondled, caressed.
Dearies. Diminutive of dears.
Dearthfu'. Dear.
Deave. To deafen.
Deil-ma-care. No matter! for all that!
Deleerit. Delirious.
Descrive. To describe.
Dight. To wipe, to clean corn from chaff.
Dight. Cleaned from chaff.
Dinna. Do not.
Ding. To worst, to push.
Dirl. A slight tremulous stroke or pain.
Disjaskit. Jaded, worn out with fatigue.
Dizzen, or Diz'n. A dozen.
Doited. Stupified, hebetated.
Dolt. Stupified, crazed.
Donsie. Unlucky.
Dool. Sorrow; to sing dool, to lament, to mourn.
Dorty. Saucy, nice.
Douce, or Douse. Sober, wise, prudent.
Doucely. Soberly, prudently.
Dought. Was or were able.
Doure. Stout, durable, stubborn, sullen.
Dow. Am or are able, can.
Dowff. Pithless, wanting force.
Dowie. Worn with grief, fatigue, &c., half asleep.
Downa. Am or are not able, cannot.
Drap. A drop, to drop.
Drapping. Dropping.
Dreep. To ooze, to drop.
Dreigh. Tedious, long about it.
Dribble. Drizzling.
Drift. A drove.
Droddum. The breech.
Droop. Rumped, that droops at the crupper.
Drouth. Thirst, drought.
Drucken. Drunken.
Drumly. Muddy.
Drummock. Meal and water mixed, raw.
Drunt. Pet, sour humour.
Dub. A small pond.
Duds. Rags, clothes.
Duddie. Ragged.
Dung. Worsted, pushed, driven.
Dush. To push as a ram, &c.
Dusht. Pushed by a ram, ox, &c.

E.

Ee. The eye.
Een. The eyes.
E'enin'. Evening.
Eerie. Frighted, dreading spirits.
Eild. Old age.
Elbuck. The elbow.
Eldritch. Ghastly, frightful.
En'. End.
ENBRUGH. EDINBURGH.
Eneugh. Enough.
Especial. Especially.
Ettle. To try, attempt.
Eydent. Diligent.

F.

Fa'. Fall, lot, to fall.
Faddom't. Fathomed.
Fae. A foe.
Faem. Foam.
Faiket. Unknown.
Fairin. A fairing, a present.
Fallow. Fellow.
Fand. Did find.
Farl. A cake of bread.
Fash. Trouble, care, to trouble, to care for.
Fasht. Troubled.
Fasten-e'en. Fasten's Even.
Fauld. A fold, to fold.
Faulding. Folding.
Faut. Fault.
Fawsont. Decent, seemly.
Feal. A field, smooth.
Fearfu'. Frightful.
Fear't. Frighted.
Feat. Neat, spruce.
Fecht. To fight.
Fechtin. Fighting.
Feck. Many, plenty.
Feckfu'. Large, brawny, stout.
Feckless. Puny, weak, silly.
Feg. Fig.
Feid. Feud, enmity.
Fell. Keen, biting; the flesh immediately under the skin, a field pretty level, on the side or top of a hill.
Fend. To live comfortably.
Ferlie, or Ferley. To wonder; a wonder, a term of contempt.
Fetch. To pull by fits.
Fetch't. Pulled intermittently.
Fidge. To fidget.
Fient. Fiend, a pretty oath.
Fier. Sound, healthy; a brother, a friend.
Fit. A foot.
Fisle. To make a rustling noise, to fidget, to bustle.
Fittie-lan. The nearer horse of the hindmost pair in the plough.
Fizz. To make a hissing noise, like fermentation.
Flainen. Flannel.
Fleech. To supplicate in a flattering manner.
Fleechin. Supplicating.
Fleesh. A fleece.
Fleg. A kick, a random blow.
Fletherin. Flattering.
Flether. To decoy by fair words.
Fley. To scare, to frighten.
Flitcher. To flutter, as young nestlings, when their dam approaches.
Flinders. Shreds, broken pieces.
Flingin-tree. A piece of timber hung by way of partition between two horses in a stable, a flail.
Flisk. To fret at the yoke.
Fliskit. Fretted.
Flitter. To vibrate like the wings of small birds.
Flittering. Fluttering, vibrating.
Flunky. A servant in livery.
Foord. A ford.
Forbears. Forefathers.
Forbye. Besides.
Forfairn. Distressed, worn out, jaded.
Forfoughten. Fatigued.
Forgather. To meet, to encounter with.
Forgie. To forgive.
Forjaskit. Jaded, worn out with fatigue.
Fou'. Full, drunk.
Foughten. Troubled, harrassed.
Fouth. Plenty, enough, or more than enough.
Fow. A bushel, &c., also a pitch-fork.
Frae. From.
Fraeth. Froth.
Frien'. Friend.
Fu'. Full.
Fud. The scut, or tail of the hare, coney, &c.

Fuff. To blow intermittently.
Fuff't. Did blow.
Funnie. Full of merriment.
Fur. A furrow.
Furm. A form, a bench.
Fyke. Trifling cares; to piddle, to be in a fuss about trouble.
Fyle. To soil, to dirty.
Fyl't. Soiled, dirtied.

G.

Gab. The mouth, to speak boldly, or pertly.
Gae. To go; gaed, went; gaen or gane, gone; gaun, going.
Gaet, Gait, or Gate. Way, manner, road.
Gang. To go, to walk.
Gar. To make, to force to.
Gar't. Forced to.
Garten. A garter.
Gash. Wise, sagacious, talkative, to converse.
Gashin'. Conversing.
Gaucy. Jolly, large.
Gear. Riches, goods of any kind.
Geck. To toss the head in wantonness or scorn.
Ged. A pike.
Gentles. Great folks.
Geordie. A guinea.
Get. A child, a young one.
Ghaist. A ghost.
Gie. To give; gied, gave; gien, given.
Giftie. Diminutive of gift.
Gillie. Diminutive of gill.
Gilpey. A half-grown, half-informed boy or girl, a romping lad, a hoyden.
Gimmer. An ewe from one to two years old.
Gin. If, against.
Gipsey. A young girl.
Girn. To grin, to twist the features in rage, agony, convulsion, &c.
Girning. Grinning.
Gizz. A periwig.
Glaikit. Inattentive, foolish.
Glaive. A sword.
Gawky. Half-witted, foolish, romping.
Glaizie. Glittering, smooth like a glass.
Gleg. Sharp, ready.
Gley. A squint, to squint; a-gley, off at a side, wrong.
Glib-gabbet. That speaks smoothly and readily.
Glint. To peep.
Glinted. Peeped.
Glintin'. Peeping.
Gloamin'. The twilight.
Glowr. To stare, to look; a stare, a look.
Glowred. Looked, stared.
Goavan. Looking in a stupid manner.
Gowan. The wild daisy.
Gowd. Gold.
Gowff. The game of golf; to strike as the bat does the ball at golf.
Gowff'd. Struck.
Gowk. A cuckoo, a term of contempt.
Gowl. To howl.
Grane, or Grain. A groan, to groan.
Grain'd. Groaned.
Graining. Groaning.
Graip. A pronged instrument for cleaning stables.
Graith. Accoutrements, furniture, dress.
Grannie. Grandmother.
Grape. To grope.
Grapit. Groped.
Great. Intimate, familiar.
Gree. To agree, to bear the gree, to be decidedly victor.
Gree't. Agreed.
Greet. To shed tears, to weep.
Greetin'. Crying, weeping.
Greusome. Loathesomely, grim.
Grippet. Caught, seized.
Groat. To get the whistle of one's groat, to play a losing game.
Grozet. Gooseberry.
Grumph. A grunt, to grunt.
Grumphie. A sow.
Grun'. Ground.
Grunstane. A grindstone.
Gruntle. The phiz, a grunting noise.
Grushie. Thick, of thriving growth.
Gude. The SUPREME BEING; good.
Guid-mornin'. Good-morrow.
Guid-e'en. Good-evening.
Guidman and Guidwife. The master and mistress of the house; young guidman, a man newly married.
Gully, or Gullie. A large knife.
Guidfather, Guidmother. Father-in-law and mother-in-law.
Gusty. Tasteful.

H.

Ha'. Hall.
Ha'-bible. The great bible that lies in the hall.
Hae. To have.
Haen. Had, participle of have.
Haet, fient haet. A petty oath of negation, nothing.
Haffet. The temple, the side of the head.
Haffins. Nearly half, partly.
Hag. A scaur or gulf in mosses and moors.
Haggis. A kind of minced pudding boiled in the stomach of a cow or sheep.
Hain. To spare, to save.
Hain'd. Spared.
Hairst. Harvest.
Haith. A petty oath.
Haivers. Nonsense, speaking without thought.
Hal', or Hald. An abiding place.
Hale. Whole, tight, healthy.
Hame. Home.
Hallan. A partition wall in a cottage near the doorway.
Hallow-e'en. The eve of All Saints Day, or All Hallows.
Hamely. Homely, affable.
Han' or Haun'. Hand.
Hap. An outer garment, mantle, plaid, &c.; to wrap, to cover, to hap.
Happer. Hopper.
Happing. Hopping.
Hap, step, an' loup. Hop, skip, and jump.
Harkit. Hearkened.
Harn. Very coarse linen.
Hash. A fellow that neither knows how to dress nor act with propriety.
Hastit. Hastened.
Haud. To hold.
Haughs. Low-lying rich lands, valleys.
Haurl. To drag, to peel.
Haurlin'. Peeling.
Haverel. A half-witted person, half-witted.
Havins. Good manners, decorum, good sense.
Hawkie. A cow, properly one with a white face.
Heapit. Heaped.
Healsome. Healthful, wholesome.
Hearse. Hoarse.
Hear't. Hear it.
Heather. Heath.
Hech! Oh! strange.
Hecht. Promised to foretell something that is to be got or given; foretold; the thing foretold.
Heeze. To elevate, to raise.
Herd. To tend flocks, one who tends flocks.
Herrin. A herring.
Herry. To plunder, most properly to plunder birds' nests.
Herryment. Plundering, devastation.
Hersel. Herself.
Het. Hot.
Heugh. A crag, a coal-pit.
Hilch. A hobble, to halt.
Hilchin'. Halting.
Himsel'. Himself.
Hing. To hang.
Hirple. To walk lamely, to creep.
Hirsel. A herd of cattle, or flock of sheep.
Histie. Dry, chapt, barren.
Hitcht. A loop, a knot.
Hizzie. Hussy, a young girl.
Hoddin. The motion of a sage countryman, riding on a carthorse.
Hog-score. A kind of distance line, in curling, drawn across the *rink*.
Hog-shouther. A kind of horse-play, by jostling with the shoulder; to jostle.
Hool. Outer-skin or case, a nut-shell, peas swade.
Hoolie. Slowly, leisurely; take leisure, stop.
Hoord. A hoard; to hoard.
Hoordit. Hoarded.
Horn. A spoon made of horn.
Hornie. One of the many names of the devil.
Host, or hoast. To cough.
Hostin'. Coughing.
Hotch'd. Turned topsy-turvy, blended, mixed.
Houghmagandie. Something improper.
Houlet. An owl.
Housie. Diminutive of house.
Hove. To heave, to swell.
Hov'd. Heav'd, swelled.
Howdie. A midwife.
Howe. Hollow, a hollow or dell.
Howebackit. Sunk in the back, spoken of a horse, &c.
Howk. To dig.
Howkit. Digged.
Howkin'. Digging.
Hoy. To urge.
Hoy't. Urged.
Hoyse. To pull upwards.
Hoyte. To amble crazily.
Hughoc. Diminutive of Hugh.
Hurcheon. A hedgehog.
Hurdies. The loins, the crupper.

I.

I'. In.
Icker. An ear of corn.
Ier-oe. A great-grandchild.
Ilk, or Ilka. Each, every.
Ill-willie. Ill-natured, malicious, niggardly.
Ingine. Genius, ingenuity.
Ingle. Fire, fire-place.
I'se. I shall or will.
Ither. Other, one another.

J.

Jad. Jade; also a familiar term among country folks for a giddy young girl.
Jauk. To dally, to trifle.
Jaukin'. Trifling, dallying.
Jaup. A jerk of water; to jerk as agitated water.
Jaupit. Soiled with sparks of mud.
Jaw. Coarse raillery, to pour out, to shut, to jerk as water.
Jillet. A jilt, a giddy girl.
Jimp. To jump, slender in the waist, handsome.
Jink. To dodge, to turn a corner, a sudden turning, a corner.
Jinker. That turns quickly, a gay sprightly girl, a wag.
Jinkin'. Dodging.
Jirk. A jerk.
Jocteleg. A kind of knife.
Jouk. To stoop, to bow the head.
Jow. To jow; a verb which includes both the swinging motion and pealing sound of a large bell.
Jumlie. Muddy.
Jundie. To justle.

K.

Kae. A daw.
Kail. Colewort, a kind of broth.
Kail-runt. The stem of colewort.
Kain. Fowls, &c., paid as rent by a farmer.
Kebbuck. A cheese.
Keek. A peep, to peep.
Kelpies. A sort of mischievous spirits, said to haunt fords and ferries at night, especially in storms.
Ken. To know; kend, or ken't, knew.
Kennin. A small matter.
Ket. Matted, hairy, a fleece of wool.
Kiaugh. Carking, anxiety.
Kilt. To truss up the clothes.
Kin. Kindred.
Kimmer. A young girl, a gossip.
Kin'. Kind.
King's-hood. A certain part of the entrails of an animal.

Kintra. Country.
Kirn. The harvest supper, a churn.
Kirsen. To christen or baptise.
Kist. Chest.
Kitchen. Sauce; anything that eats with bread, to serve for soup, gravy, &c.
Kittle. To tickle, ticklish.
Kittlin'. A young cat.
Knaggie. Like knags, or points of rocks.
Knappin'-hammer'. A hammer for breaking stones.
Knowe. A small round hillock.
Kuittle. To cuddle.
Kuittlin'. Cuddling.
Kye Cows.
Kyle. A district in Ayrshire.
Kyte. The belly.
Kythe. To become evident, to show one's self.

L.

Laddie. Diminutive of lad.
Laggen. The angle between the side and bottom of a wooden dish.
Laigh. Low.
Lairing. Wading, and sinking in snow, mud, &c.
Laith. Loath.
Laithfu'. Bashful, sheepish.
Lallans. Lowland dialect.
Lambie. Diminutive of lamb.
Lampit. A kind of shellfish.
Lan'. Land, estate.
Lane. Lone, my lane, thy lane, &c, myself alone.
Lanely. Lonely.
Lang. Long; to think lang, to long, to weary.
Lap. Did leap.
Lave. The rest, the remainder, the others.
Laverock. The lark.
Lawlan'. Lowland.
Lea'e. To leave.
Leal. Loyal, true, faithful.
Lear. Learning.
Lee-lang. Live-long.
Leeze me. A phrase of congratulatory endearment; I am happy in thee, or proud of thee
Leister. A three-pronged dart for striking fish.
Leugh. Did laugh.
Leuk. A look, to look.
Lift. Sky.
Lightly. Sneeringly, to sneer at.
Lilt. A ballad, a tune, to sing.
Limmer. A kept mistress, a strumpet.
Limp't. Limped, hobbled.
Link. To trip along.
Linkin'. Tripping.
Linn. A waterfall.
Lint. Flax; lint i' the bell, flax in the flower.
Lintwhite, Lintie. A linnet.
Loan. The place of milking.
Loof. The palm of the hand.
Loot. Did let.
Looves. The plural of loof.
Loun. A fellow, a waggish lad.
Lowe. A flame.
Lowin'. Flaming.
Lowrie. Abreviation of Lawrence.
Lowse. To loose.
Lows'd. Loosed.
Lug. The ear, a handle.
Lugget. Having a handle.
Luggie. A small wooden dish with a handle.
Lum. The chimney.
Lunch. A large piece of cheese, flesh, etc.
Lunt. A column of smoke; to smoke.
Luntin'. Smoking.
Lyart. Of a mixed colour, grey.

M.

Mae. More.
Mair. More.
Maist. Most, almost.
Maistly. Mostly.
Mak. To make.
Makin'. Making.
Mallie. Molly.
Mang. Among.
Manse. The parsonage house, where the minister lives.
Manteele. A mantle.
Mark, marks. This, and several other nouns, which in English require an *s* to form the plural, are in Scotch like the words *sheep, deer*, the same in both numbers.
Mar's year. The year 1715, in which the rebellion broke out under the Earl of Mar.
Mashlum, meslin. Mixed corn.
Mask. To mash, to infuse as tea.
Maskin'-pat. A tea-pot.
Maukin. A hare.
Maun. Must.
Mavis. The thrush.
Maw. To mow.
Mawin'. Mowing.
Meere. A mare.
Melder. Corn, or grain of any kind, sent to the mill to be ground.
Mell. To mingle; also a mallet.
Melancholious. Mournful.
Melvie. To soil with meal.
Men'. To mend.
Mense. Good manners, decorum; something that looks respectable.
Menseless. Ill-bred, rude, impudent.
Merle. The blackbird.
Messin. A small dog.
Midden. A dunghill.
Midden-hole. A gutter at the bottom of a dunghill.
Mim. Prim, affectedly meek.
Min'. Mind, remembrance.
Mind't. Mind it, resolved, intending.
Minnie. Mother, dam.
Misca'. To abuse, to call names.
Misca'd. Abused.
Mislear'd. Mischievous, unmannerly.
Misteuk. Mistook.
Mither. Mother.
Mixtie-maxtie. Confusedly mixed.
Moistify. To moisten.
Mony, or **Monie.** Many.
Moop. To nibble as a sheep.
Moop and Mell. To eat and consort together.
Moorlan'. Of or belonging to moors.
Morn. The next day, tomorrow.
Mou. The mouth.
Moudiwort. A mole.
Mousie. Diminutive of mouse.
Muckle, or **Mickle.** Great, big, much.
Musie. Diminutive of muse.
Muslin-kail. Broth composed simply of water, shelled barley and greens.
Mutchkin. An English pint.
Mysel'. Myself.

N.

Na'. No, not, nor.
Nae. No, not any.
Naething, or **Naithing.** Nothing.
Naig. A nag, a horse.
Nane. None.
Nappy. Brisk-ale, to be tipsy.
Negleckit. Neglected.
Neebor. A neighbour.
Neuk. Nook.
Niest. Next.
Nieve. The fist.
Nievefu'. Handful.
Niffer. An exchange; to exchange; to barter.
Nigger. A negro.
Nine-tailed-cat. A hangman's whip.
Nit. A nut.
Norland. Of or belonging to the North.
Notic't. Noticed.
Nowte. Black cattle.

O.

O'. Of.
Ony, or **Onie.** Any.
Or. Is often used for ere, before.
O't. Of it.
Ourie. Shivering, drooping.
Oursel', or **Oursels.** Ourselves.
Outlers. Cattle not housed.
Owre. Ovre, too.
Owre-hip. A way of fetching a blow with the hammer over the arm.

P.

Pack. Intimate, familar.
Painch. Paunch.
Paitrick. A partridge.
Pang. To cram.
Parritch. Oatmeal pudding a well-known Scotch dish.
Pat. Did put, a pot.
Pattle, or **Pettle.** A ploughstaff.
Paughty. Proud, haughty.
Pauky. Cunning, sly
Pay't. Paid, beat.
Pech. To fetch the breath short, as in an asthma.
Pechan. The crop, the stomach.
Peelin'. Peeling.
Pet. A domesticated lamb.
Pettle. To cherish; a ploughstaff.
Phraise. Fair speeches, flattery, to flatter.
Phraisin'. Flattery.
Pickle. A small quantity.
Pine. Pain, uneasiness.
Pit. To put.
Placad. A public proclamation, to publish publicly.
Plackless. Penniless, without money.
Plack. An old Scotch coin, the third part of a Scotch penny, 12 of which make an English penny.
Plaitie. Diminutive of plate.
Plew, or **pleugh.** A plough.
Pliskie. A trick.
Poind. To seize cattle or take goods by legal execution.
Poortith. Poverty.
Pou. To pull.
Pouk. To pluck.
Poussie. A hare, or cat; a demure old woman.
Pout. A poult, a chick.
Pou't. Did pull.
Pouthery. Like powder.
Pow. The head, the skull.
Pownie. A pony, a little horse.
Powther, or **pouther.** Powder.
Preen. A pin.
Prent. Printing.
Prie. To taste.
Prie'd. Tasted.
Prief. Proof.
Prig. To cheapen, to dispute.
Priggin'. Cheapening.
Primsie. Demure, precise.
Propone. To lay down, to propose.
Provoses. Provosts.
Pund. Pound, pounds.
Pyle. A pyle o' caff, a single grain of chaff.

Q.

Quat. To quit.
Quak. To quake.
Quey. A cow from one to two years old; a heifer.

R.

Ragweed. Herb ragwort.
Raible. To rattle nonsense.
Rair. To roar.
Raize. To madden, to inflame.
Ram-feezl'd. Fatigued, overspread.
Ram-stam. Thoughtless, forward.
Raploch. Properly a coarse cloth, but used as an adjective for coarse.
Rarely. Excellently, very well.
Rash. A rush; rash-buss, a bush of rushes.
Ratton. A rat.
Raucle. Rash, stout, fearless.
Raught. Reached.
Raw. A row
Rax. To stretch.
Ream. Cream; to cream.
Reaming'. Brimful, frothing.
Reave. Rove.
Reck. To heed.
Rede. Counsel; to counsel.
Red-wat-shod. Walking in blood over the shoetops.
Red-wud. Stark mad.
Ree. Half tipsy, in high spirits.
Reek. Smoke.
Reekin'. Smoking.
Reekit. Smoked, smoky.
Reisle. A rousing.
Remead. Remedy.
Requite. Requited.
Rest. To stand restive.
Restit. Stood restive, stunted, withered

Restricked. Restricted.
Rief. Reef, plenty.
Rig. A ridge.
Rin. To run, to melt; rinnin', running.
Rink. The course of the stones, a term in curling on ice.
Rip. A handful of unthrashed corn.
Riskit. Made a noise like the tearing of roots.
Rockin'. An evening meeting, one of the objects of which is spinning with the rock or distaff.
Rood. Stands likewise for the plural roods.
Roon. A shred.
Roose. To praise, to commend.
Roopit. Hoarse, as with a cold.
Roun'. Round, in the circle of the neighbourhood.
Row. To roll, to wrap.
Row't. Rolled, wrapped.
Rowte. To low, to bellow.
Rowth. Plenty.
Rowtin. Lowing.
Rozet. Rosin.
Rung. A cudgel.
Runt. The stem of a colewort or cabbage.
Runkled. Wrinkled.

S.

Sae. So.
Saft. Soft.
Sair To serve, a sore.
Sairly, or **Sairlie.** Sorely.
Sair't. Served.
Sark. A shirt.
Sarkit. Provided in shirts.
Saugh. The willow.
Saul. Soul
Saumont. Salmon.
Saunt. A saint.
Saut. Salt.
Saw. To sow.
Sawin'. Sowing.
Sax. Six.
Scar. To scare, a scare.
Scaud. To Scald
Scauld. To scold.
Scaur. Apt to be scared.
Scawl. A scold.
Scone. A thin cake of bread.
Scraich. To scream, as a hen, partridge, &c.
Screed. To tear, a rent.
Scrieve. To glide swiftly along.
Scriven. Gleesomely, swiftly.
Scrimp. To scant.
Scrimpet. Did scant, scanty.
Scunner. A loathing, to loathe.
Seizin'. Seizing.
Sel. Self; a body's self, one's self alone.
Sell't. Did sell.
Sen'. To send.
Servan.' Servant.
Settlin'. Settling; to get a settlin', to be frighted into quietness.
Shaird. A shred, a shaird.
Shangan. A stick cleft at one end for putting the tail of a dog, &c. into, by way of mischief, or to frighten him away.
Shaver. A humorous wag, a barber.
Shaw. To show, a small wood in a hollow place.
Sheen. Bright, shining.
Sheep-shank. To think one's self nae sheep-shank to be conceited.
Sherra-muir. The battle of Sheriff-Moor, fought in the Rebellion of 1715.
Sheugh. A ditch, a trench, a sluice.
Shill. Shrill.
Shog. A shock, a push off at one side.
Shool. A shovel.
Shoon. Shoes.
Shore. To offer, to threaten.
Shor'd. Offered.
Shouther. The shoulder.
Sic. Such.
Sicker. Sure, steady.
Sidelins. Sidelong, slanting
Siller. Silver, money.
Simmer. Summer.
Sin'. Since.
Skaith. To damage, to injure, injury.
Skellum. A worthless fellow.
Skelp. To strike, to slap; to walk with a smart tripping step; a smart stroke.
Skelpi-limmer. A wild girl, a term in female scolding
Skelpin'. Stepping, walking.
Skeigh. Proud, nice, highmettled.
Skirling. Shrieking, crying.
Skirl. To shriek, to cry shrilly.
Skirl't. Shrieked.
Sklent. Slant, to run aslant, to deviate from truth.
Sklented. Ran, or hit, in an oblique direction.
Skriegh. A scream, to scream.
Slae. Sloe.
Slade. Did slide.
Slap. A gate, a breach in a fence.
Slaw. Slow.
Slee. Sly; sleest, slyest.
Sleekit. Sleek, sly.
Sliddery Slippery.
Slype. To fall over, as a wet furrow from the plough.
Slypet. Fell.
Sma'. Small.
Smeddum. Dust, powder, mettle, sense.
Smiddy. A smithy.
Smoor. To smother.
Smoor'd Smothered.
Smytrie. A numerous collection of small individuals.
Snash. Abuse, Billingsgate.
Snaw. Snow, to snow.
Snaw-broo. Melted snow.
Snawie. Snowy.
Sned. To lop, to cut off.
Sneeshin. Snuff.
Sneeshin-mill. A snuff-box.
Snell. Bitter, biting.
Snick-drawing. Trick-contriving.
Snick. The latchet of a door.
Snool. One whose spirit is broken with oppressive slavery; to submit tamely; to sneak.
Snoove. To go smoothly and constantly, to sneak.
Snowk. To scent or snuff, as a dog, horse, &c.
Snowkit. Scented, snuffed.
Sonsie. Having sweet, engaging looks; lucky, jolly.
Soom. To swim.
Sooth. Truth, a pretty oath.
Sowens. A dish made of oatmeal soured, &c., boiled up till they make an agreeable pudding.
Souple. Flexible, swift.
Souter. A shoemaker.
Sowp. A spoonful, a small quantity of any thing liquid.
Sowth. To try over a tune, with a low whistle.
Sowther. Solder, to solder, to cement.
Spae. To prophesy, to divine
Spaul. The loin bone.
Spairge. To dash, to soil, as with mire.
Spaviet. Having the spavin.
Speat. A sweeping torrent, after rain or thaw.
Speel. To climb.
Spence. The parlour in a country house.
Spier. To ask, to inquire.
Spier't. Inquired.
Splatter. A splutter, to splutter.
Spleughan. A tobacco-pouch.
Splore. A frolic, a noise, riot.
Sprattle. To scramble.
Spreckled. Spotted, speckled.
Spring. A quick air in music, a Scottish reel.
Sprit. A tough-rooted plant, something like rushes.
Sprittie. Full of sprits.
Spurtle. The stick used in making oatmeal porridge.
Spunk. Fire, mettle, wit.
Spunkie Mettlesome, fiery, will-o'-wisp, or ignis-fatuus.
Squad. A crew, a party.
Squatter. To flutter in water, as a wild duck, &c.
Squattle. To sprawl.
Squeel. A scream, a screech, to scream.
Stacher. To stagger.
Stack. A rick of corn, hay, &c.
Staggie. Diminutive of stag.
Stan'. To stand; stan't, did stand.
Stane. A stone.
Stank. Did stink; a pool of standing water.
Stap. Stop.
Stark. Stiff, stout.
Startle. To run as cattle, stung by the gadfly.
Staumrel. A blockhead, half-witted.
Staw. Did steal, to surfeit.
Stech. To cram the belly.
Stechin' Cramming.
Steek. To shut, a stitch.
Steer. To molest, to stir.
Steeve. Firm, compacted.
Stell. A still.
Sten. To bound or rise hurriedly.
Sten't. Reared.
Stents. Tribute, dues of any kind.
Stibble. Stubble; stibble-rig, the reaper in harvest who takes the lead.
Stey. Steep; steyest, steepest.
Stick an' stow. Totally, altogether.
Stilt. A crutch; to limp; to halt
Stimpart. The eighth part of a Winchester bushel.
Stirk. A cow or bullock a year old.
Stock. A plant or root of colewort, cabbage, &c.
Stockin'. Stocking; throwing the stockin', when the bride and bridegroom are put into bed, and the candle out, the former throws a stocking at random among the company and the person whom it strikes is the next tha will be married.
Stook. A shock of corn.
Stooked. Made up in shocks.
Stoor. Sounding hollow, strong and hoarse.
Stot. An ox.
Stoup, or **Stowp.** A kind of jug or dish with a handle.
Stoure. Dust, more particularly dust in motion.
Stowlins. By stealth.
Stowen. Stolen.
Strack. Did strike.
Strae. Straw; to die a fair strae death, to die in bed.
Straik. Did strike.
Straikit. Stroked.
Strappan. Tall and handsome.
Straught. Straight.
Streek. Stretched, to stretch.
Striddel. To straddle.
Stroan. To spout.
Studdie. An anvil.
Stumpie. Diminutive of stump.
Strunt. Spirituous liquor of any kind; to walk sturdily.
Stuff. Corn or pulse of any kind.
Sturt. Trouble; to molest.
Sturtin. Frighted.
Sucker. Sugar.
Sud. Should.
Sugh. The continued rushing noise of wind or water.
Suthron. Southron, an old name for the English nation.
Swaird. Sward.
Swall'd. Swelled.
Swank. Stately, jolly.
Swankie, or **Swanker.** A tight, strapping young fellow or girl
Swap. An exchange, to barter.
Swat. Did sweat.
Swatch. A sample.
Swats. Drink, good ale.
Sweatin'. Sweating.
Sweer. Lazy, averse; dead-sweer, extremely averse.
Swoor. Swore, did swear.
Swinge. To beat, to whip.
Swirlie. Knaggy, full of knots.
Swirl. A curve, an eddying blast, or pool; a knot in wood.
Swith. Get away.
Swither. To hesitate in choice, an irresolute wavering in choice.
Syne. Since, ago, then.

T.

Tackets. Hobnails for driving into shoes.
Tae. A toe; three-tae'd, having three prongs.
Tak. To take; takin', taking.
Tangle. A sea-weed.
Tap. The top.
Tapetless. Heedless, foolish.
Tarrow. To murmur at one's allowance.
Tarrow't. Murmured.
Tarry-breeks. A sailor.
Tauld, or Tald. Told.
Taupie. A foolish, thoughtless girl.
Tauted, or Tautie. Matted together, spoken of hair or wool.
Tawie. That allows itself peaceably to be handled, spoken of a horse, cow, &c.
Teat. A small quantity, a handful.
Ten-hours'-bite. A slight feed to the horses while in the yoke in the forenoon.
Tent. A field pulpit, heed, caution; to take heed.
Tentie. Heedful, cautious.
Tentless. Heedless.
Teugh. Tough.
Thack. Thatch; thack an' rape, clothing, necessaries.
Thae. These.
Thairms. Small guts, fiddle-strings.
Thankit. Thanked.
Thegither. Together.
Themsels. Themselves.
Thick. Intimate, familiar.
Thieveless. Cold, dry, spited, spoken of a person's demeanour.
Thir. These.
Thirl. To thrill.
Thirled. Thrilled, vibrated.
Thole. To suffer, to endure.
Thowe. A thaw, to thaw.
Thowless. A want of energy, fingerless.
Thrang. Busy, crowded.
Thrapple. Throat, windpipe.
Thraw. To sprain, to twist, to contradict.
Thrawin'. Twisting, &c.
Thrawn. Sprained, twisted, contradicted, contradiction.
Threap. To maintain by dint of assertion.
Threshin'. Thrashing.
Threteen. Thirteen.
Thristle. Thistle.
Through. To go on with, to make out.
Through-other. Pell-mell, confusedly.
Thud. To make a loud intermittent noise.
Thumpit. Thumped.
Thysel'. Thyself.
Till't. To it.
Timmer. Timber.
Tine. To lose; tint, lost.
Tinkler. A Tinker.
Tip. A ram.
Tippence. Twopence.
Tirl. To make a slight noise, to uncover.
Tirlin'. Uncovering.
Tither. The other.
Tittle. To whisper.
Tittlin'. Whispering.
Tocher. Marriage portion.
Tod. A fox.
Toddle. To totter like the walk of a child.
Toddlin'. Tottering.
Toom. Empty.
Toop. A ram.
Toun. A hamlet, a farm-house.
Tout. The blast of a horn, or trumpet, to blow a horn, &c.
Tow. A rope.
Towmond. A twelvemonth.
Towzie. Rough, shaggy.
Toy. A cap of an old fashion in female head-dress.
Toyte. To totter like old age.
Transmogrify'd. Transmigrated, metamorphosed.
Trashtrie. Trash.
Trickie. Full of tricks.
Trig. Spruce, neat.
Trimly. Excellently.
Trow. To believe.
Trowth. Truth, a petty oath.
Try't. Tried.
Tug. Raw hide, of which, in old times, plough traces were frequently made.
Tulzie. A quarrel; to quarrel, to fight.
Twa. Two.
Twa-three. A few.
'Twad. It would.
Twal. Twelve; twal-penny worth, a small quantity, a pennyworth.
N.B. One penny English is 12d. Scots.
Twin. To part.
Tyke. A dog.

U.

Unco. Strange, uncouth, very, very great, prodigious.
Uncos. News.
Unkenn'd. Unknown.
Unskaith'd. Undamaged, unhurt.
Upo'. Upon.

V.

Vap'rin. Vapouring.
Vera. Very.
Virl. A ferule.

W.

Wa'. Wall; wa's, walls.
Wabster. A weaver.
Wad. Would, to bet, a bet, to pledge.
Wadna. Would not.
Wae. Woe, sorrowful.
Waesucks! or waes me! Alas! Oh, the pity!
Waft. The cross thread that goes from the shuttle through the web.
Waifu'. Wailing.
Wair. To lay out, to expend.
Wale. Choice, to choose.
Wal'd. Chose, chosen.
Walie. Ample, large, jolly; also an interjection of distress.
Wame. The belly.
Wamefou'. A bellyful.
Wanchansie. Unlucky.
Wanrestfu'. Restless.
Wark. Work.
Wark-lume. A tool to work with.
Warle, or Warld. World.
Warlock. A wizard.
Warly. Worldly, eager on amassing wealth.
Warran'. A warrant, to warrant.
Warst. Worst.
Warstl'd, or Warsl'd. Wrestled.
Wastrie. Prodigality.
Wat. Wet; I wat, I wot, I know.
Water-brose. Brose made of meal and water simply, without the addition of milk, butter, &c.
Wattle. A twig, a wand.
Wauble. To swing, to reel.
Waukit. Thickened, as fullers do cloth.
Waukrife. Not apt to sleep.
Waur. Worse, to worst.
Waur't. Worsted.
Wean, or Weanie. A child.
Wearie, or Weary. Many a weary body. Many a different person.
Weason. Weasand.
Wee. Little; wee things, little ones; wee bit, a small matter.
Weel. Well; weelfare, welfare.
Weet. Rain, wetness.
We'se. We shall.
Wha. Who.
Whaizle. To wheeze.
Whalpit. Whelped.
Whang. A leathern string, a piece of cheese, bread, &c; to give the strappado.
Whare. Where; whare'er, wherever.
Wheep. To fly nimbly, to jerk; penny-wheep, small beer.
Whase. Whose.
Whatreck. Nevertheless.
Whid. The motion of a hare, running but not frighted; a lie;
Whiddin'. Running as a hare or coney.
Whigmaleeries. Whims, fancies, crochets.
Whingin'. Crying, complaining, fretting.
Whirligigums. Useless ornaments, trifling appendages.
Whissle. A whistle, to whistle.
Whisht. Silence; to hold one's whisht, to be silent.
Whisk. To sweep, to lash.
Whiskit. Lashed.
Whitter. A hearty draught of liquor.
Whun-stane. A whinstone.
Whyles. Whiles, sometimes.
Wi'. With.
Wick. To strike a stone in an oblique direction, a term in curling.
Wiel. A small whirlpool.
Wifie. A diminutive or endearing term for wife.
Wimple. To meander.
Wimpl't. Meandered.
Wimplin'. Waving, meandering.
Win'. To wind, to winnow.
Win'. Wind; w'n's, winds.
Win't. Winded, as a bobbin of yarn.
Winna. Will not.
Winnock. A window.
Winsome. Hearty, vauntie, gay.
Wintle. A staggering motion; to stagger, to reel.
Winze. An oath.
Wiss. To wish.
Withoutten. Without.
Wizen'd. Hide-bound, dried, shrunk.
Wonner. A wonder, a contemptuous appellation.
Woo'. Wool.
Woo. To court, to make love to.
Woodie. A rope, more properly one made of withs or willows.
Wooer-bab. The garter knotted below the knee with a couple of loops.
Wordy. Worthy.
Worset. Worsted.
Wrack. To teaze, to vex.
Wraith. An apparition exactly like a living person, whose appearance is said to forbode the person's approaching death.
Wrang. Wrong, to wrong.
Wreath. A drifted heap of snow.
Wud. Mad, distracted.
Wumble. A wimble.
Wyliecoat. A flannel vest.
Wyte. Blame, to blame.

Y.

Ye. This pronoun is frequently used for thou.
Yearns. Longs much.
Yearlings. Born in the same year, coevals.
Year. Is used both for singular and plural years.
Yell. Barren, that gives no milk.
Yerk. To lash, to jerk.
Yerkit. Jerked, lashed.
Yestreen. Yesternight.
Yill. Ale.
Yird. Earth.
Yokin. Yokin, about.
Yont. Beyond.
Yoursel'. Yourself.
Yowe. An ewe.
Yowie. Diminutive of yowe.
Yule. Christmas.

Finis.

Appendix.

Letters of Clarinda to Burns.

NO. I.

[*Compare with Letters Nos.* 83 *and* 84, *pp.* 301 *and* 302.]

FOR MR. ROBERT BURNS,

CARE OF MR. CRUIKSHANK.

2, *St. James's Square,*
December 8*th*, 1787.

THIS is truly a great source of vexation and discouragement. It seems really as if some malignant foredoom had determined that we should not meet, and that none of our little arrangements should be consummated. But if I lament the disappointment* which once more prevents us from enjoying that delicate "converse of soul," or "feast of reason," which I have promised myself in your society, how much more keenly do I feel for its cause!

What a profusion of sentiments, and such like, has this accident not marred! perhaps even choked in the earliest incipient development!

When you flatter me with the idea of being a favourite of yours, you little know "how subtle is the unction." I have longed and longed that Miss Nimmo, who was blessed with your acquaintance, would have imparted a small share of that blessing to me, by making us known to each other. But when you were informed that I was a poetess, you were mislead by the pleasant irony of our mutual and gentle friend. That I am passionately fond, nay, even "abandoned" (save the word!) to poetry, is true; that I have, from time to time, done something in the way of rhyme is true enough; but that I have ever written poetry, I fear, is no "true bill."

How exquisite are the lines* which you send me; not only for the delicate nature of the flattery, to which every woman is a little alive, but as *poetry*. Do not think that I am weak enough to be spoiled by such adulation. It is a poet's adulation, and, as you yourself observe, "*Fiction* is the native region of poetry." I doubt even, if ten years earlier in life, I should have suffered myself to be "*befooled*" by even such beautiful, simple, and musical praise as yours.

But now for my own poetical *as*pirations, or for my own claim to poetical *in*spiration. Look over the following; I look to your candour, not your compliments. You will admit that they possess anything in verse except the spirit of poetry.

[*Here follow the "Lines to a Blackbird."*†]

Do not forget to let me hear *of* you or *from* you, or both, as often as convenient;

* As will be noticed in the foregoing Notes to the Correspondence, in respect of the first two letters of Burns to Clarinda, the poet had been engaged to take tea with Mrs. M'Lehose on the 6th (Thursday). She had then deferred the entertainment of the poet until this day, Saturday the 8th, when an accident, causing severe injury to his leg, laid him up.

* Alluding to some verses enclosed in Burns's note, to which this was a reply.

† These lines, modified by Burns, and with the addition of four lines of his own, appeared in the *Scots Musical Museum*.

for you know the rigid forms of the world now keep us apart, otherwise than by this sort of converse. But we must and shall meet, and till then be of good cheer. I console *myself* in my disappointment by the thought of what gratification is in store for me, and with the sensation, that this pleasure is daily accumulating intensity. Adieu.

A. M.

NO. II.

FOR MR. ROBERT BURNS.

2 *St. James Square,*
Dec. 16*th*, 1787.

I HAD no idea till last night that Miss Nimmo was so nearly concerned in your accident. She is now laying to her own charge a share of the cause of it.

You are well attended.—I know of no better surgeon and worthier man than Mr. Wood; and the knowledge that you are under his care, if you will but have patience, and follow his directions, reassures me considerably.

What letters you write! Do you think you are addressing a love-lorn foolish girl of sixteen? Have you any idea your correspondent is a married woman, and a widow only in temporary separation—a widow of the heart rather than of the law?

You are not likely to play Jacob over again, and serve your seven years, and your seven years again, in expectation of this shadow of future happiness, nor do you know yourself; at least, I *think* not. But do let me entreat you not to fatigue yourself with too much writing, or to work yourself up with excitement. I can rely upon daily intelligence of you through Miss Nimmo; and I would not have you do anything to retard your recovery. For heaven's sake, be calm, and patient, and quiet, and we shall soon have the pleasure of your society again.

A. M.

NO. III.

[*Compare with Letter No.* 85, p. 302.]

Dec. 20*th*, 1787.

I KNOW you too well; at least I think so, to suspect you of really transgressing the unvarying boundary of true decorum, much more the limits of honour. I have, if I mistake not, thoroughly read your character in your imperishable poems. I have perceived an impetuous generosity and high-mindedness, which are apt to overlook the ordinary regulations, observed or feigned by sordid souls, and in their own native purity to be heedless of the *interpretations* of the world. But those *interpretations*—those constructions! Do they not require some more guarded consideration? Were I your judge, alas! I do not think even your "handsome troop of follies" would meet with much reproof; for "undisciplined" as they be, they are as much a part of what I am obliged to admire in your character, as is that indomitable independence which distinguishes you itself.

I am much joyed to hear that you are so greatly improving with respect of your wound—but as to calling you a "stupid fellow," I do not think either you or I would have much consciousness of attaching meaning to the expression. I have proposed to myself a more pastoral name for you, although it be not much in keeping with the shrillness of the *Ettrick Pipe*. What say you to *Sylvander?* I feel somewhat less restraint when I subscribe myself

CLARINDA.*

NO. IV.

[*Reply to Letter No.* 85, pp. 302, 303.]

Dec. 21*st*, 1787.

I HAVE just received your long and too pleasing letter, and seize a few moments to write some acknowledgments before I leave town, which will be to-morrow morning. I am at a loss where to begin? Is it to you or to Dr. Gregory, that I should first reply? What will become of the severer discipline to which I must subject my natural foibles and vanities?

I should be devoid of that strong sense of gratitude for good which characterises all innocent hearts, did I acknowledge or *feel* myself *unhappy*. No, no! Sylvander, that is not the word. I am not *unhappy!* The trials and misfortunes which I have undergone, and at which, I fain would shudder,

* This is the first letter which had been signed in the assumed name of *Clarinda*, and it has been omitted and described as *wanting* in all the previous editions of this Correspondence.

even now, in the retrospective glance at them, are of the past. But I have done no wrong; I am conscious of no misdoing; I am *innocent;* and therefore, I am not unhappy. I believe even those misfortunes to which you recal my memory with lamentation, have much contributed to chasten those keen sensibilities of which I am made up, and to make me as capable of the real enjoyments of life as I now am. I have sought Religion, nor have I sought it in vain. And could you but catch a glimpse of her in the benign, seemly garb and aspect in which she has answered to my appeals of sorrow, you would fain see in her the real, ultimate, and only comforter!

On my return here, which I expect will take place towards the middle of next week, that is, after Christmas day, I will reply to your letter more categorically; but do not speak of our correspondence, for innocent as I am, and conscious as I am of that innocence, you know how censorious are those whose vulgar minds are incapable of a similar communion.—Farewell! may God bless you and keep you. CLARINDA.

NO. V.

[*Compare with the last, i.e. No.* 4.]

January 1*st*, 1798.

THIS shall be, at all events, a partial fulfilment of the promise by which I bound myself in my last, to treat of your letter a little more at length, and more categorically. In the first place, however, let me tell you that I have been paying a visit to a country friend of mine, who runs complete riot in her praise and admiration of you, and whose personal endowments and charms would make her a truly worthy *Clarinda* to such a *Sylvander*. You have once met this fair admirer of yours at the house of Mrs. Bruce, and I must take some occasion, sooner or later, of making you personally acquainted, as I am sure the admiration will be reciprocal. Before I proceed to your letter, let me wish you all the kindest, best, and most humane of wishes on this first day of a new year, in which, with the help of heaven, may you number your days by enjoyment, and the accession of a year by wisdom. Now for your epistle, respecting which, let me first thank you for the touching lines which you enclose.*

That Dr. Gregory should have found mine wanting, in many respects, is not to be wondered at. The faults I had observed myself; but they were *part* of the verses, and I, as incapable of amending, as I had been incapable of suppressing the expression of a particular sentiment. All my grammatical knowledge is merely that which is acquired by the habits of conversation, writing, or reading. I was never taught.

I think I may rightly interpret your sentiment that "there is no corresponding with an agreeable woman without a mixture of the tender passion." How little do the majority of the children of the world feel or appreciate the sentiments of love and friendship! How coarsely and constantly do they not misapply the one, and desecrate the other!

That a gentle sentiment should be inevitably commingled in the communion between the sexes, where delicacy of sentiment, extreme, nay exquisite sensibility and lofty consciousness of innocence preside, is natural and intelligible. It is the more essentially entitled, in this case, to the pure appellation of *love*, that it is free from all the gross pursuits of selfish gratification; that it is devoted solely to the elevated purpose of conveying real happiness to its object; in fact, that it is honest and unpolluted. In such a manner, why should not an intercourse of sympathy and intelligence exist between those of different sexes? I would frankly avow that I think it might, and does in perfect innocence; and I do not feel that I should be bound to discard even the term which implies the utmost tenderness.

Nor should we reject the conditions supplied by circumstance. It is from circumstance, really, that the purest philosophy (I mean the wisdom of life) is to be acquired. Had you reflected on this,—had you subjected my career to the test of comparison with circumstance,—had you formed a just estimate of my character, after this moralizing fashion, you would not have deplored that any "malignant demon should have been permitted to dash my cup of life and sorrow." On the contrary, the all-wise Disposer of the world, estimating the peculiar bent of that supremacy of passion (corrigible for good, or capable of running wild for evil), has subjected it to the schooling, tempering, and subduing which were requisite. Thus, by calling religion to our aid in the consideration of ourselves, our lives, our fortune, or our misfortune, may we distinguish in each sorrow a chastening and gentle provision for more enduring happiness than is to be

* Lines *addressed to Clarinda*, as they are now inserted amongst the Poetical Works, in the former part of this volume.

gathered from the sunny field of a perishable prosperity!

Wherefore do I tenderly believe in the "unknown state of being," in which, as you say, we shall one day meet for endless communion of unalloyed affection! Consider: should we attain it, except it were through the trials of which you complain? But to what unlimited extent of gravity am I not tending? Shall I not thus surfeit you of my sentiments? Will you not condemn our correspondence to an untimely and abrupt cessation, on account of the tedium with which I oppress you? But you should not: I feel, and must express all I feel. I know no reserve; and in that true and heartfelt interest for your happiness, I cannot help preaching a doctrine which, I believe, may compass it, though it be tardily. It is your fault to dash at the first impulse of a generous, but tumultuous passion, "into mid stream." You would forestall events, or deprecate the turn of affairs, from which you are to derive all the good which is in store for you.

I am still engaged in reading those poems in which your character is so indelibly writ, and which will inevitably perpetuate the record of your foibles, as well as of your loftier qualities. Do favour me with any scraps you can spare. Perhaps, also, from time to time, you will allow me the freedom of expressing the ideas which they suggest, the merits which I observe, or even the faults which I may distinguish. How much am I not pleased, that Dr. Gregory, whose reputation for virtue, as well as for genius, is so generally acknowledged, should be numbered amongst your trusty friends. If for this alone, I should like to be acquainted with him; for there must be a *je ne sçais quoi* that is kindred in us, for the acceptation and discernment of your character, to have been common to us both.

I look upon him as a warm friend of mine, also, although we are not even acquainted. There is some unseen link between us. But I weary you, and must wish you good bye.

CLARINDA.

NO. VI.

[*Reply to a Letter from Burns, which is wanting.*]

Friday, January 4th, 1788.

MELANCHOLY is really one of the first of incentives to the record of our sentiments in verse, and the universal gaiety of the season recoils upon me with a sense of desotion, and makes me insuparably melancholy. It is the season of household enjoyments of home happiness, and you know I have none. What, wonder, then, if, on receiving your lines, I should venture upon a reply "in kind?" I cannot resist the impulse, however inadequate be my capacity. Look to it. Here are my lines.

[*The lines opening, " Talk not of Love! it gives me Pain," were here inserted.*]

I have not, for some time, heard how your recovery proceeds. Miss Nimmo, even, has not been my companion of late; and, I should, therefore, like to hear an account of progress directly from yourself. Does it not strike you as very quaint and droll, that we two, who have only met once in person, should be carrying on so persistent an intercourse by means of pen and ink? If you could possibly venture as far as this, in some conveyance, I should be happy to receive you to-morrow evening, as I ought to have done nearly a month ago. If you *can* come, do not omit to take every care of yourself.

CLARINDA.

NO. VII.

[*Reply to No.* 86, pp. 303, 304.]

January 6th, 1788.

How was I not delighted, my dear friend, with your letters of last night! I do not know why so lively an interest should be excited in one's heart or recollection, by the description of an early love-scene, if it be not, that all of us have felt the rapture of such meetings once, and *only once,* in our lives. The indelible impression which such an incident makes upon the mind, is, I apprehend, the result of the singularity of the feelings which accompany it, and which never recur. I do not know whether a greater degree of interest is not created in me by the fact, that you instal me as your confidant, and unreservedly lay bare your foibles and follies to me. This complete confidence adds much charm to your letters. I cannot resist the fulness of feeling—of sympathy—which it arouses. I can recal similar recollections of my own. Nor do I believe that, in all the lofty sentiment, refined delicacy, and keener discernment of maturer years, there is anything which can equal the rapture of an early—a first and rural love-interview.

But to reason on other matters:—Why are you so bitter an adversary of Calvinism? Your avowal confirms the dread which had been awakened by some of your satirical poems. Wherefore, my dear Sylvander, will you impugn these doctrines which are so dear to me? You should not charge a creed with the failings, nay, even the knaveries of its professed ministers. Where will you find a sect which numbers no hypocrites? Calvinism is amongst my strongest and dearest convictions, and stands confirmed in my conscience by the best examples—that of an angelic mother, whom I lost when quite young, and that of the only true and devoted friend whom I have since possessed. It was not the creed which I was taught in infancy, and, therefore, does not consist in the attachment of prejudice.

My father was attached to Arminianism; and I myself continued in the profession inculcated by my education, until the friend to whom I allude, forced conviction upon me; and if I may record a more peaceful and confident state of mind and hope, since the period of this conviction (which I certainly can do), may I not infer, that the true mission of religion, that of inspiring fortitude, long suffering, confidence, hope, resignation, and complete peace of mind, has been fulfilled by this means? You little think, Sylvander, how deeply, how seriously our lives, our thoughts, our deeds—everything—is affected by a thorough religious conviction! It is a sad reflection for me, who hold your well-being so dear, to think that the misdoing of men should have so warped that brilliant understanding with which God has gifted you, as to have driven you almost from the capability of patiently entertaining thoughts of this kind. Would to heaven, I could prevail with you in this! Would, that you should seriously try the merits of such objections as occur to you! Yet, may I not flatter myself, that my Sylvander is not without esteem for my ordinary judgment. No event would exercise so much influence for my gratification, as the knowledge, the assurance, that you would entertain the question. Do not be wearied with my reflections; do not allow yourself to give way to the first impulse of ridicule. And when you are seriously inclined, and can reason with me calmly, and leisurely, turn your attention to this letter.

* * * * *

How is it with the aspect of your apartments? Do your windows look out on the square, or on the close? If on the square, I shall have, at least, the small gratification of exchanging glances of recognition with you to-morrow afternoon, or the day after, as I shall be in that neighbourhood.——Beware of wedlock, unless you can meet with a mate equally ardent in love with yourself. You say you fear the improbability of your meeting with such a companion; do not, therefore, be precipitate, lest after "marriage in haste, you repent at leisure." I have many things to say, which I would fain write; but it is an endless affair to write the long stories which might be uttered in a short half-hour of sweet companionship. So, till we meet, let me defer some of these burthens which I would gladly have lifted from me. Adieu. Write soon.

CLARINDA.

NO. VIII.

*January,** 1788.

I HAVE been equally disappointed with yourself. I had, as you know, promised myself "a glance of recognition," which should be mutual from the window of your prison. The weather has been very unfavourable; and I have been obliged to remain in-doors; in addition to which, my youngest child is very ailing. So much so, that for the last three or four nights, I have had little time for rest. The "bottle" has evidently not impaired your intellect, or your feelings, but I should think your companions had not been exactly to your taste; and I take it as a most unpremeditated compliment, that you should turn from those ill assorted beings, to our mutual intercourse, to pour out the fulness of your heart. How often do I not feel, that there are few of fellow-feeling with my own intense sensibility, and that the majority, consequently, misinterpret the warmth and unrestrained overflowings of my heart! My poor child is fretful again, and is evidently suffering, and I really do believe, I cannot be anything else but a good and tender mother. What should you think of a mean-spirited woman who should be surprised at my attachment to children, whom I owe to an unnatural husband? Such was, however, the actual exclamation of an acquaintance yesterday. I could not restrain the bitterness of my reply to a suggestion, which was unfeeling as regards me, as it was

* Probably about the 9th, 10th, or 11th.

unnatural towards the poor helpless innocent children. Do I not feel that I owe them a double share of parental love?

Besides this, their father's misdoing is their misfortune; and this misfortune alone, apart from the tender ties to which it relates, would constitute a bond of attachment. With what a keen relish and sense of gratification do I not read Fielding's *Amelia*. You have, doubtless, read it, and have, like me, admired, nay, felt the domestic tenderness, which could only have been portrayed by one who deeply felt it. Can you not admire a Booth in his ardent, but thoughtless attachment, before a cold, calculating husband, whose artificial virtues are as repulsive as the reckless vices of the other. It is so like you! I could love and forgive him, but should shrink with abhorrence from the other.

Of your religious reflections, anon. I am not in a controversial mood at this moment, and do not like to give away a vantage in a matter of such consequence. I have been rambling away on any subject which came uppermost, for lack of intelligence to convey. Who in the world is *she* of whom you rave with such frenzied passion, and of whom you would not have me "guess?" Can it be your Jean? If so, the indelible nature of an attachment which has so constantly outlived the first gratification of mere desire, is an undeniable evidence of real, pure devotion. It does you honour, as it will contribute, one day or other, to your happiness. I receive your "good wishes," and you well know, that mine as constantly attend you. And if there be a guardianship whereby one spirit is suffered to exercise its never-failing agency in defence of another, Sylvander, my soul is watching over you this night.

CLARINDA.

NO. IX.

*January** 1788.

THE morning opens auspiciously. This is the first bright day which we have seen this week; and it is the first morning also, on which my poor child awakes refreshed by calm and uninterrupted sleep of some hours' duration. I think, at last, I may promise myself the fulfilment of the expectation which both of us have entertained for several days, of a silent interview between your window and the square. This is the third time I announce the intended visit. Bruce did not despair at the seventh. We seem to be peculiarly unlucky in our appointments. The first, second, and third, in which I promised myself the pleasure of your company, were equally frustrated by trivial, or grave circumstances. Perhaps, however, this was a dispensation which should lead to a more unreserved communion of our most secret thoughts and feelings, than would have resulted from the formalities of society. I fancy we have become more thoroughly and mutually acquainted, than we otherwise should have done; and, I trust, we have both of us profited in consequence. Be of good cheer, Sylvander! Clarinda will not ever continue to be one of those will-o'-the-wisps—those visionary beings which are doomed to elude the realization; and, if the strange destiny which presides over our meeting, be at last propitious, this afternoon, at two, I will be revealed, as I am—your own

CLARINDA

* This letter was evidently written on the day following after that in which the foregoing (No. 8) was penned. Both of these letters were probably sent by the same carrier.

NO. X.

HOW was it I could not discover you, even in the loftiest regions of the square? Twice did I return, to make the search in vain, upon some pretext which satisfied me sufficiently to warrant the inquiring gaze. It was not that I did not survey the topmost stories. Can you not give me a more definite idea of the whereabouts to search? Something seemed to say to me, that you did not descry me either. I am grateful for your kind and tender inquiries respecting my boy, No very decided change has taken place, nor can we expect it yet. It will be a long affair, even if he recover. And patience is a virtue, which, in this case, must necessarily be practised.

Of the conversion of which you speak, Sylvander, I should like to hear more. How has it been effected? And how have I participated in its agency? If it be a real conversion, or a conversion from some of those *harum scarum* vagaries which render the unbridled son of fancy the sport of his own whim;—the latter even were something; but if it be conversion on subjects of yet higher consequence, how shall I glory to have effected it!

But why the wild frenzy of passion with which you assail me? It boots little to level imprecations at ties, and laws, and fashions. For what if they were not? Think you 'twould be conducive to the substantial happiness of Clarinda? I am at a loss to understand you. But, perhaps, also, 'twere better that you should preserve the *veil of mystery* which it may not be fit to raise from your rhapsody. Are you not satisfied with the unity, the integrity of a friendship, than which, nothing can be more earnest, pure, devoted, and immutable?

Dissolve the ties of which you complain, and what do either of us gain? Some romantic dream of Utopia; but little or no reality. What have either of us to depend upon?

Why do you not number Miss Nimmo in the same category as Miss Chalmers? How flattered ought I not to be, to be thus associated and to be compared with that incomparably admirable woman! I do not think, however, you have a more firm and true well-wisher on earth than Miss Nimmo, who seems to tremble for every mis-step which your impetuous temperament urges you to take. I wonder now if I could possibly refrain from writing to you, and from laying bare my actual sentiments; for I write some records of feelings, prompted by the thought of you, which never leave my hands. And, even now, I would send you some lines which were suggested by observing you mixed up with society which was not likely to contribute any good impressions, had I but your promise not to be annoyed for my freedom.

I sadly fear our correspondence will dwindle away after you leave town, and when new objects have distracted your attention; and therefore, in somewhat jealous enjoyment of my present gratification, I write on more profusely. Nevertheless, and although I feel that your marriage would be fatal to our intercourse, I really should be happy to see you well matched; for I am well assured that you can never rest satisfied or happy, without some permanent object of attachment. I propose to abandon myself in my next epistle to one of my rambling preachings, and to discuss religion with you again, having much to observe in relation to the sentiments expressed in your recent letter; but I shall try to keep myself from worrying you for some days to come. I am off the day after to-morrow, with my poor boy, to Leith, and should then have been overjoyed of your company, had you been capable of joining us. You are a great glutton in reading; does it happen that Sancho's Letters have fallen in your way? If not, by all means obtain a copy. What a beautiful piece is the epitaph which you enclose me; but it suggests a melancholy train of thoughts, and the fore-dwelling on the loss of those to whom we are best attached, only serves to shed a gloom over our existence, without being productive of an equivalent of good results upon our character. Oh that I had only half your power of expression, and a little of that brilliancy and vividness which you possess! What could I not express! CLARINDA.

NO. XI.

January 12th, 1788.

AH! Sylvander, at last have you seen me divested of those imaginary perfections wrought up in your own fancy, and in my own fulness of failing. Doubtless, have you "weighed, and found me wanting." And I would fain confess that, notwithstanding the very pressing desire which I had to enjoy your society, I had, at the same time, a dread lest it should destroy the spell which attached you to me. As for myself, I do not ever remember to have enjoyed such transcendental gratification. Nor do I believe, Sylvander, that such enjoyment is reserved for many amongst human kind, nor for the few who are capable of it, very frequently. Why is it, then, that I have not slept? I inquire of my conscience, whether I have done wrong, and that conscience acquits me. No limit of propriety or virtue have I transgressed. Still have I some indomitable dread, lest in the eye of the Deity, the fine distinctions of my reasoning be susceptible of revealing something which might lead to displeasure. The idea that a friend, to whom I am much indebted, should not be prepared to concur in the propriety of my conduct, and the dread that you yourself, Sylvander, may have grown to think less well of me—all these things continue to agitate my thoughts.

Enough of myself. Can you tell on the ground of what predestined privilege those of birth and rank, that is of genealogical distinction, who possess no other merit, assume so much? I cannot admit any reverence for rank or lineage in itself. I can even admire personal beauty, to the extent of giving it some degree of precedence; I can yield admiration and superiority to genius or to virtue; but to mere high birth —no! And how is it that, amongst my acquaintance, I only, with the exception of

Mary,* entertain this seemingly heterodox notion. I must relate you an anecdote, to which all this is *a-propos*. On Sunday last, between church hours, I spent my time with an acquaintance, upon whom, also, a sister of my Lord Napier happened to call at the same time. I knew the lady well by sight, but was so disgusted with her obtrusive manner, her impertinent interruptions, and her coarseness, and, at the same time, with the despicable adulation which the lady of the house offered her, that I was even more reserved towards her than I otherwise should have been. At all events, I should not have been inclined to bestow any particular mark of attention upon her; and, as it was, she repelled even the ordinary courtesy with which, *with others*, I should naturally have treated her.

By the way, I was just now mentioning Mary; I think of spending a day with her soon, if I feel a little more fit for society; I daily grow to like her better, and the undisguised admiration which she expresses when your name is mentioned, is an additional link of attachment between us. Wherefore do you vainly trust to pillar your religion in a good life? What you call "*religion of the bosom*," is, in my estimation, also the *only religion*. But pardon me, Sylvander, if I intimate that yours, according to your own showing, is more a religion of the head than a "religion of the bosom." What avails your imagined good life, unless you place your full reliance for its acceptation upon the redemption, effected at a terrible sacrifice, by the Son of God. The best of men commits innumerable sins; the best of lives, in the eyes of a Being all pure, all innocent, must be polluted by countless stains; and do you vainly hope that you, with an excess of passion and sensibility, will be capable of effecting what the sternest philosophers have failed to do? I want to impress upon you the religion of the Gospel, which is the only real "religion of the bosom." On all points of general morality we are, doubtless, agreed. But how can we be otherwise? these will not bear two interpretations. But look to it, search through the philosophy of the ancients, with all its classical beauty, with all its refinement, with all its subtlety, and with as perfect a moral code as any other extant, and tell me, if it be not barren and unsatisfactory at best? Do you really, Sylvander, discern the celestial consolation in the lives and deaths of Socrates or Cato? No, no! some important bond was wanting, and that was only supplied in the revelation of Christianity. But I must leave the subject now! I will take it up again from time to time. But now I am weary, and have wearied you. Farewell.

CLARINDA.

* Miss Peacock, who subsequently married Mr. James Gray, of the High School, Edinburgh.

NO. XII.

[*Reply to Letter No.* 87, pp. 304, 305.]

January 17th, 1788.

I AM not a little surprised at your warm defence of Miss Napier; and I understand she has merits such as you describe. Most persons are pleased with her, and, perhaps, she was to be excused for not attributing as much importance to Clarinda, as her own friends would have done. Yet there is a general evidence of good breeding which she certainly failed to exhibit on this occasion. Her face is not ill-looking, but her figure and carriage are awkward.

As to your Epigram on Elphinstone, it is exquisite and well merited;—a more arrant pedant one seldom meets with. Can I have the pleasure of your company this evening, or, if you like it better, to-morrow evening, either at tea or about eight o'clock. I should much like to see you; but I should prefer your coming on foot, even if you should be obliged to order a chair to take you back, for you well know what a quiet, humble set of people we are about here, and how great a disturbance is likely to be created, by the appearance of equipages in a quarter such as ours.

You have a magical influence over me; you seem to possess every secret clue to my most secret inclinations, thoughts, or impulses; and if it be possible for letters to utter all one's most tender and unspeakable sentiments, they are yours. But whence, then, can be the charm which you attach to mine? Do you really, truly take pleasure in these wretched scrawls, or is it merely a self-deception, of some peculiar partiality, which you do not attempt to control, which deceives you into a belief of gratification? Wherefore do you doubt the "lasting impression" which you have made? You who possess the unreserved access to my innermost thoughts.

Do not forget to write me word when you will come and spend the evening with me; and on that occasion, whenever it be, be careful how you tamper with the lock of secrets which you have at your command, in your CLARINDA.

NO. XIII.

[*Reply to Letters Nos.* 89 *and* 90. pp, 305,* 306.]

Thursday, January, 1788.

I CANNOT help shuddering, when I find myself, for an instant, suffering the least infraction of the strictest rules of propriety. I shrink from myself at the thought of possible transgressions.

For these reasons, I am depressed and uneasy to-day; everything about me appears gloomy, and sad, and reproachful. I feel a sort of dark and ill-defined remorse for what transpired last night, and I would conjure you not to suffer *me* in future—not to expose me to the temptation of doing ought that may not preserve the dignity and delicacy of our intercourse. Otherwise, we shall destroy the most irrefragable bond of union, which should have perpetuated our intercourse. Yet we shall have to part one of these days, and, painful as that parting would be of itself, how much more so, would it not be made, did any intervening follies tend to depreciate the mutual esteem, and thus to damp the more distant colloquy which we should otherwise maintain. How I dread, Sylvander, to be lowered in your estimation! And how my heart recoils from any act or thought which I dare not entertain in the abstraction of my daily devotion!

I have told you how wretched love has made me, and is doomed to make me. Let me then abstain from indulging in the fatal passion to which the ardent temperament which I possess, so peculiarly exposes me.

I can picture to myself the delight of reading your letters, when the bitter parting is once well over, and distance between us has mellowed down the excessive ardour of passion, which now impels me at times to do, or own that which may degrade me in your estimation.

Oh, why do I not hear from you to-day? Why do I receive no more of those spontaneous outpourings of a soul which, in its elevation, seems to waft us nearer to the sublime expanse of eternity and immortality? I dare not trust myself to see you on Saturday, unless the flutter of my feelings be lowered to the compass of my own control; and then, I believe, an interview, maintained with proper reserve, that is, in preserving the strictest rules of conduct which I have from the first prescribed for us, would much conduce to restore my disturbed peace of mind. Farewell. CLARINDA.

* Probably Thursday, January 24th. This date has actually been assigned to a letter written by Clarinda to Burns, of which the purport is very analogous.

NO. XIV.

Tuesday Evening, January 29th, 1788.

MY VERY DEAR SYLVANDER—If my appreciation of your sincerity of interest in the real welfare of your Clarinda had needed any confirmation from you, your noble conduct, in our interview of Saturday night, would have satisfied the most tender scruples. And if we did allow ourselves to infringe some of those stern barriers which retain the correspondence between ardent persons of different sexes within the sphere of arctic frigidity, I do not feel myself conscious of wrong-doing, and the retrospect calls no blush to my cheek, nor disquiet to my heart. But we must assert a redoubled caution and observation on our very thoughts, lest we admit the least ascendancy of temptation over the purest dictates of virtue. Oh, if there be spirits—which we would fain believe in for our consolation—whose kindly office is to preserve us from the first insidious advent of evil, may they guard, watch, and protect each of us!

Sylvander, I have no power to reserve my feelings towards those whose sympathies are so wound up with mine. Must I then confess the love which I have so long struggled to suppress? Yes! and should not this awaken me more keenly to a sense of danger? Yet can you tell me, Sylvander, why this confession should in my heart be associated with an idea of wrong?

Is it not that I feel myself irrevocably bound to another, who has forfeited all claim to the love which is thus left desolate?

I will not complain of my doom. No! nor will I pain my Sylvander, by dwelling upon a condition which neither he nor I can dissolve.

But I have unbosomed myself to my best of advisers and pastors, Mr. Kemp* to

* The Minister of Tolbook Church, Edinburgh.

whom I am in the habit of communicating my perplexities, and I feel as if a load had been lifted from my oppressed and bursting heart.

Ah! Sylvander, if you and Mr. Kemp were known to each other, would not a reciprocal esteem spring up between you. You could not help admiring his sterling piety, his judgment, and his benevolence, as well as his talents; whilst he would be enchanted with that fresh and glowing imagination, that exquisite sensibility, and that intuitive benevolence of character, which distinguish you above all the weaknesses which sometimes betray themselves in your conduct.

I do not know why it is so, but I cannot help feeling some secret satisfaction that your Excise project has not succeeded. I do not mean to intimate that I would rather see you pursuing your present indefinite career, than firmly settled in some desirable, profitable, and competent occupation. But, Sylvander, if you have a weakness above any other, which is likely to lead you to mischief, if not to ruin, it is a love of conviviality, which, in the capital, might seduce you from the direct career of honour and respectability, and I shudder at the thought of your being despised by the worldlings of a town, in which wits and scholars, noblemen, and burgesses, have all bowed down and worshipped you. I should burst with anguish at the triumph of malicious envy over your fall. If I have two things at heart more earnestly than any others in this world, they are to impress you with my own ideas and fervour in religion, and to see you provided with some calling which should occupy your time and talents in such a manner, as to maintain *you honourably in the highest social position which the supremacy of your genius has atchieved.*

I fear that, in being revealed to those to whom you have vaunted the "divinity" of Clarinda," she falls sadly from the misty elevation of her glory. You forget, my dear Sylvander, that all do not see with your eyes, hear with your ears, or feel with your sensibilities; and, therefore, amongst others I dread the judgment of Mr. Ainslie on my account. I really fancy he must have smiled in pity for what he may have looked upon as your hallucination.

I dread the visit of Mr. —— to morrow. He is evidently uneasy for me, and ventures only upon those oblique inuendoes which are intended to elicit an explanation from me. I cannot conceal from you, nevertheless, that your society is all in all to me; but had we not better—or rather had I not better—exercise a little self-denial? Do you think it prudent, now the jealous vigilance of some of these Argus-eyed, and suspicious people of the world is awakened, to attract more marked attention? Will you, under these circumstances come the day after to-morrow, or had we not better meet more rarely? No! I have not resolution to force the separation. Come unless I warn you between this and then, and may the spirits I have invoked preserve the innocence of your CLARINDA.

NO. XV.

February, 1788.

OH! were I free—free to dispose of those fond ties which bind us in mysterious sympathies, how should I not reply to your charming letter! I only dread myself when I think how nearly I may be prompted by feelings, which, I believe, in themselves to be innocent, to do, or even to *think*, that, which the calmer reflections would pronounce as verging on guilt.

What boots it that we have congenial communion? for all which should consecrate that communion is due to another from me, although his claim be founded rather upon conventionality than upon merit. If I bring myself to reflect more impartially on my relations, I cannot conceal from myself the serious consideration that, however *he* may have forfeited, by wrong, all those tender ties by which we are bound, although *his* acts shall not have been in keeping with his most sacred promises, such dereliction on *his* part can never dissolve the bond by which we are united, or exonerate *me*, should I be tempted to return a wrong for wrong. No, no! The most elevated sentiments of regard, sympathy, appreciation, nay, even attachment, as far as they fail to infringe the promises by which I am bound, are mine to bestow, and you have possessed them, and do possess them; but so much as verges into more tender and less qualifiable affection is an unclaimed overflow of feeling—it is true —but unclaimed as it is, it belongs to the Giver of life, and to him it must be devoted as a free-will offering. I give you my best and indelible friendship; but, Sylvander, you must not dare to ask for more, lest by tempting me to entertain a thought which conscience cannot calmly confirm, you sacrifice the substantial happiness of life to the frantic dream of bliss which shall illumine an instant alone.

Why are you not satisfied? Why should not the elicitation of such a declaration from me, be sufficient to gratify your most ardent wishes?

I know, and feel too well, too keenly, that the union which has fettered me, is one which was as unworthy of my heart, as it was incapable of satisfying the redundancy of eager sensibilities of which I am made up; that your heart was capable of having fulfilled the most ample conceptions of mortal happiness for me; that no two souls were ever so matched for the most complete identity of thoughts, feelings, hopes, fears, and affections; and that as we are hopelessly separated by a barrier which neither of us should dare to transgress, I, at least, can never be happy in this world, although by subduing the swelling passions which sometimes threaten to rise in rebellion against my better feelings, I may retain a partial peace of mind, which otherwise I should for ever forfeit.

How strangely have our sensibilities been coincident! I have been pondering over your own account of yourself, that is, of your early years, as you ingenuously revealed it to Dr. Moore. Amongst all your early predilections, whether in art, literature, or the admiration of nature, there is barely one which was not also mine! I have loved the same poems; I have culled the same flowers; and seen the same incomparable symmetry in the landscape or the firmament.

Yet withal, you see, Sylvander, there is an over-ruling doom, an everlasting predestination, which has forbidden more than the recognition of these sympathies of soul—and we must be separated.

You will leave the capital, and retire into the homely retreat of a peasant once more, whence I can only hear of you by letter, whither my heart will follow you, but where, probably, new ties will encircle themselves about you, and engross the little share which I possessed in your recollection. Possibly I shall not hear from you; and the next time we meet—the next time!—it will be for eternal communion, where none can part us, and no sinister power will be present to impede the interchange of sympathies which must draw us together.

How I dread the day of parting which is drawing near! I feel as if it would be the last on earth—as if we should not meet again in this world; and I shudder at it. Could you not creep stealthily away, and spare me that moment of anguish? Yet no! I could not bear to think that you had shunned me. You will *not* forget me. There will surely be something in the daily aspect of everything about you, which will remind you of Clarinda!

Oh God! is to-morrow—to-morrow that last day on which we shall meet.—You will come—you will not desert me without one last meeting. Early in the day I will do as you wish, and will give Miers* a sitting. Remember this shall be the bond of eternal friendship between us—yes, *friendship*:—do not think, breathe, or utter, a more tender attachment. I do not feel that I should be attended in sitting for the portrait. I should have been glad of Mary's company, because she understands me thoroughly; but she is in the country; and the only other person whom I *could* ask to accompany me is Miss Nimmo; and in this matter there is a *je ne sçais quoi* which forbids me.

How could you rend me with that parting song! It is too much. Even you could scarcely have equalled the touching appeal more than once. I burst into tears. Can you doubt that I will be your friend to eternity? Ah! that "*I may reca'*." Would it were not so! And yet why? Should I not have lived without having felt the divinest sympathies of humanity, and would not the deepest spring of feeling have been unsounded.

Oh! Sylvander, how deeply do I regret that I had not known you, before you proclaimed yourself the adversary of our creed in the biting satires with which you have assailed it. If the lines on Religion which you now send me in that dear letter had been of earlier production, I should have been yet doubly happy in you. Would I not have implored eternal silence and forgetfulness for the "Twa Herds," and the "Holy Fair." I had rather admire you for goodness than for wit; and *your* genius might accomplish as much *for* true religion as a thousand preachers, even as it may deal a fatal blow if levelled *against* it.

I wish you would come and hear Mr. Kemp's preaching, on Sunday next; and I am convinced that with all the rhetorical skill and flowery diction of Mr. Gould, whom you so warmly admire, and whom I have heard, you could not fail to admit that Mr. Kemp's elocution, though more simple, is more impressive; that it carries with it a stronger impression of earnest conviction; and that whereas Mr. Gould addresses him-

* Mr. Miers was the miniature painter at Edinburgh, by whom Burns wished to have Mrs. McLehose's portrait executed.

self to the mind, Mr. Kemp speaks to the heart, and in a language too which the heart can readily interpret.

You know how earnestly I have striven for your conversion to more serious thoughts on religion; you know how I have endeavoured to wean you from the indefinite reliance on a vague and unsatisfactory philosophy, which coldly sneers at the more earnest zeal of religious fervour. I have done something; but how feeble a preacher am I! And I feel that you could not hear Mr. Kemp, without gaining in peace what you would inevitably obtain in conviction. Let me entreat you to hear him.

Sylvander, I do not know why it is I can unburden myself to you with a degree of freedom which my heart shrinks from extending to any other living. Let me ask your advice. You well know who it is *alone* who really possesses any community of thought and sympathy with me. You must have discovered that no degree of kindness without this thorough interchange of mysterious sympathy would win me beyond a grateful — very grateful — but reserved respect. Well, some time since, when, as you have heard, I came to Edinburgh friendless and unknown, one warm, faithful, earnest friend attached himself to my cause, aided and defended me. I need not tell you who this was: suffice it that such was the case. I was not slow to observe. guarded and reserved as was his respectful attention, that with him a warmer, closer, and more secret attachment was growing and being nourished within him. I do not think he knew or was willing to know this for some length of time; but I believe he is no longer a stranger to his own feelings. At one time I do not hesitate to own that the tender, delicate attentions which I received at his hands, combined with an overflow of grateful regard for his generous and profitless aid, had, in some degree, conveyed a degree of tenderness to my own regard for him. But withal, there was no deep interchange of sympathies, and *one* (you well know who), meanwhile, had quickly weaned me from this momentary surrender, by enforcing an absolute and irresistable surrender to *his own* mysterious power and control over all my most secret impulses. But with my sturdy friend it was otherwise;—his secret passion continued to grow, and to this day feeds upon prospective hopes, which cannot, alas! ever now be realised.

What can I do? How can I proceed, to spare so generous a friend a pang, which, one day or other, I shall be condemned to inflict upon him? Shall I unreservedly own my preference for Sylvander? Yet there is, perhaps, equal danger to our mutual peace of mind in this. I cannot, nevertheless, bear to practice a tacit deception; I cannot dissemble an attachment which I do not feel, and I shudder at the thought of allowing a secret passion, so strong, so earnest, and so apparently resistless, to be fostered until years shall have indomitably confirmed it.

* * * *
* * * *

The thought of that parting, which is so soon to take place between us; of the distance which is to interpose itself, and of the new associations which will gradually wean away your heart from me—all this *will* return to my mind. I have been endeavouring to chase the reflection from me, but in vain. A few brief hours hence! I cannot bear it! May Heaven pour upon you, as fully as it is implored, the blessing of

CLARINDA.

NO. XVI

Thursday, Feb. 21st, 1788.

MY DEAR SYLVANDER—Like yourself, Clarinda feels with everyone, and for everyone. Is it not a strange, yet glorious, privilege which the heart possesses, to expand beyond the narrow limits of our cell of clay, to participate in the emotions of other beings of kindred texture? It cannot have escaped any one of enlarged capacities for passion or intelligence, much less such capacities as you possess for both, that the vitality comprised within the compass of one body is inadequate to its yearnings. Hence, I imagine, solitude—that is, perfect solitude, is impossible—and society, whether actual or imaginary, must be created.

But there is a higher vocation for this necessity of sympathies; a gospel mission, which is designed to contribute to the wellbeing of mankind. Did not our Saviour preach that doctrine of sympathies?

It is, perhaps, in this sacred acceptation, that sorrow and joy are equally conducive to the perfection of some Divine purpose, and that there is a holy pleasure, which I can barely express, but most intensely feel, "to weep with those who weep, and be glad with those who rejoice." But, wherefore the seeming contradiction which, whilst my greatest desire is to distribute blessings to mankind, seems to withhold the means of contributing, even the smallest share, to such blessings, even if it does not condemn me unwittingly, and without design, to inflict suffering. Why have I not means to place you above the reach of the contemptible malice, which springs from the envy of those who cannot match you, and glories in the affected superiorities of rank and fortune.

If anything could have made me regard the adventitious vantage of circumstances with less esteem than I was naturally inclined to do, it is the comparison which vulgar minds would draw between the splendour of wealth, and the glory of virtuous genius, to the disparagement of the latter. It is this, perhaps, which has more deeply impressed Goldsmith's immortal lines upon my mind of late:—

"In nature's simplest habits clad,
Nor wealth nor power had he;
Genius and worth were all he had,
But these were all to me."

They are ceaselessly ringing in my ears.

I love Miss Chalmers for her attachment to you. But here, again, the sad contradiction, that those who most appreciate your noble character, and incomparable talent, should be least able to place you in a position which should for ever free you from dependence upon the mean-spirited world. I never before sighed for the advantages of circumstance. I do not ever recollect to have wished for wealth or grandeur; but at this moment, what would I not give up for the means of raising Sylvander to that lofty position, to which his matchless worth entitles him.

Yet I could almost quarrel with Mary, for her ardent admiration of him, even whilst I love her the better for it. Her guileless and unreserved expression of almost adoration, have recurred to me an hundred times through a wakeful night; and, although I well know that she herself is not conscious of transgressing the rights which have been asserted by Clarinda, I cannot help dreading such passionate admiration. She has been gratified to-day with the appreciation of Mrs. Cockburn's refined and acknowledged taste, and the praise of her "Henry," by the authoress of "I've seen the smiling of fortune's beguiling," has made her as completely happy as she appeared to have been last night, with the converse of *my* Sylvander —if such may be the assumed claim of *your* own CLARINDA.

The End.

www.ingramcontent.com/pod-product-compliance
Lightning Source LLC
LaVergne TN
LVHW021106110826
845150LV00001B/183